16 FEB, 1990

Phil—

Merry Christmas, partner!

If anyone could make good use of this you could. It's the most helpful & pertinent book I've come across. Repair in good health. And amongst all your car repairs remember "¡VIVA LA VEGA!" The clearest testimony to your resourcefulness & tenacity. God bless.

With love,

J.

AUTOMOTIVE TECHNICIAN'S HANDBOOK

OTHER MCGRAW-HILL AUTOMOTIVE BOOKS OF INTEREST

By William H. Crouse

Automotive Electrical Equipment
Automotive Engine Design
Automotive Service Business: Operation and Management
Automotive Mechanics

By William H. Crouse and Donald L. Anglin

Automotive Air Conditioning
Automotive Chassis and Body
Automotive Emission Control
Automotive Engines
Automotive Fuel, Lubricating, and Cooling Systems
Automotive Transmissions and Power Trains
Automotive Tuneup
Motor Vehicle Inspection
The Auto Book
Automotive Body Repair and Refinishing

AUTOMOTIVE TECHNICIAN'S HANDBOOK

William H. Crouse
and
Donald L. Anglin

THE MCGRAW-HILL BOOK COMPANY

New York St. Louis San Francisco Auckland Bogotá
Düsseldorf Johannesburg London Madrid Mexico
Montreal New Delhi Panama Paris São Paulo
Singapore Sydney Tokyo Toronto

Library of Congress Cataloging in Publication Data

Crouse, William Harry, 1907-
Automotive technician's handbook.

Includes index.
1. Motor vehicles—Maintenance and repair.
I. Anglin, Donald L., joint author. II. Title.

67890 HDHD 8654

The editors for this book were Harold B. Crawford and Lester Strong, the designer was Richard A. Roth, and the production supervisor was Thomas G. Kowalczyk. It was set in Optima by The Clarinda Company.

Printed and bound by Halliday Lithograph.

CONTENTS

PREFACE

The *Automotive Technician's Handbook* (ATH) is the first comprehensive handbook that contains the service information needed today by the general automotive mechanic and technician. The handbook is aimed at practicing automotive mechanics, service technicians, and technical specialists who need to review or update their job skills in automotive service.

ATH will be of special use to anyone preparing to take the series of one or all of the mechanics certification tests offered by the National Institute for Automotive Service-Excellence (NIASE). Also benefitting from use of this book will be anyone in an automotive mechanics apprenticeship program.

This handbook is divided into eight parts. Each one of the parts relates to the test in one of the eight areas of automotive service offered by NIASE. The parts in the book are:

Part 1 Engine Repair
Part 2 Emission Controls and Engine Tuneup
Part 3 Automotive Electrical Equipment
Part 4 Manual Transmissions and Power Trains
Part 5 Automatic Transmissions
Part 6 Steering and Suspension
Part 7 Brakes
Part 8 Heating and Air Conditioning

In addition to the eight parts listed above, at the back of the book is a comprehensive glossary of automotive words and phrases. Included in the glossary are many widely used abbreviations and metric equivalents. Metric conversion and other tables useful to the professional automotive technician also are included at the back of the book.

Each part of the book follows the standards of the automotive service industry, covering all aspects of automotive service work. This includes discussions of the construction and operation of each system and component. Inspection, diagnosis, repair, and recheck and roadtest procedures (where applicable) are then covered. These use standard quick checks, and progress through the use of meters, instruments, and other test and shop equipment. Specific procedures needed for the most frequently performed jobs on the most widely serviced components and systems are discussed. These include the removal and replacement, or the repair and reinstallation, of all serviceable automotive components.

This book should prove useful to men and women who are involved in nearly every level of automotive service, or who need to know about any area of automotive service. This could, for example, include executives and engineers who need a fill-in on some technical point or recent development, or the service station operator who needs to know the how and why of replacing disk-brake pads. Every automotive technician planning to take or retest in any or all of the NIASE certification areas will find the book to be a "must-have" item.

In the preparation of each part of the book, many trouble-diagnosis charts have been included. To simplify key concepts, basic line drawings and block drawings have been used. To illustrate the service procedures, schematics, technical illustrations, and photographs of important steps in the service procedure have been included. The emphasis throughout the book is on presenting the actual shop service procedure for each component. This is done by following the recommendations of the automotive manufacturers, test equipment manufacturers, and accepted trade practice.

The authors are very grateful to the many people, both in industry and in education, whose contributions and comments helped shape this book. They share, with the authors, a hope that this book will help automotive mechanics and technicians to more efficiently perform a greater variety of tasks. By so doing, the customers are better served, and the mechanics can, with pride and respect, take their proper place in the automotive service profession.

WILLIAM H. CROUSE
DONALD L. ANGLIN

PART 1 Engine Repair

SECTION 1-1 Four-Cycle Engine Fundamentals

Figure 1 Piston engine removed from an automobile so it can be seen. *(Cadillac Motor Car Division of General Motors Corporation.)*

There are two basic types of engines, external combustion and internal combustion. The external combustion engine has its fuel burned outside the engine. Steam engines are external combustion engines. The steam engine runs on steam produced by boiling water outside the engine. The internal combustion engine burns fuel inside the engine. The engines in automobiles are all internal combustion engines. One important aim of this and other sections in the Handbook is to describe the operation of those engines and how to disassemble, service, and repair them.

■ **1-1-1 The Engine Cylinder** Figure 1 shows an automotive engine. The engine is the source of power that makes the wheels turn and the car move. It is usually referred to as an "internal combustion engine." This is because the fuel (gasoline) is burned inside the engine—within the engine cylinders, or combustion chambers. The combustion, or burning, of the gasoline creates high pressure. The high pressure thus produced causes a shaft to turn, or rotate. This rotary motion is carried to the car wheels by the power train so that the wheels rotate and the car moves.

Most automotive engines have four, six, or eight cylinders. Since the actions are similar in all cylinders, let us examine one cylinder in detail. Figure 2 shows the construction of a single cylinder of an engine with the cylinder and piston sliced in half. Essentially, the cylinder is nothing more than a cylindrical air pocket that is closed at one end and open at the other. The piston fits snugly into the open end of the cylinder

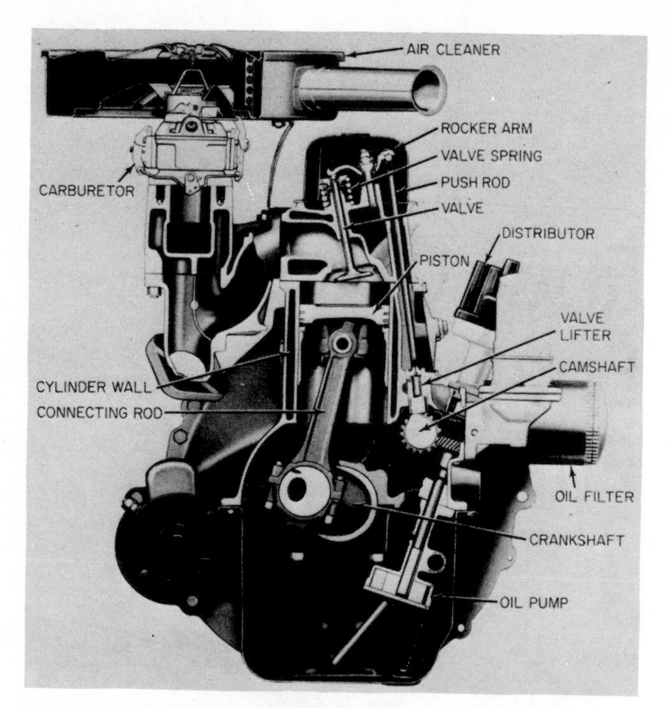

Figure 2 Sectional view of a six-cylinder engine. The piston is near the top of its stroke. The piston and cylinder are shown cut in half. *(Ford Motor Company.)*

Figure 3 Typical piston with piston rings in place and connecting rod attached. When the piston is installed in the engine cylinder, the rings are compressed into the grooves in the piston. *(Chrysler Corporation.)*

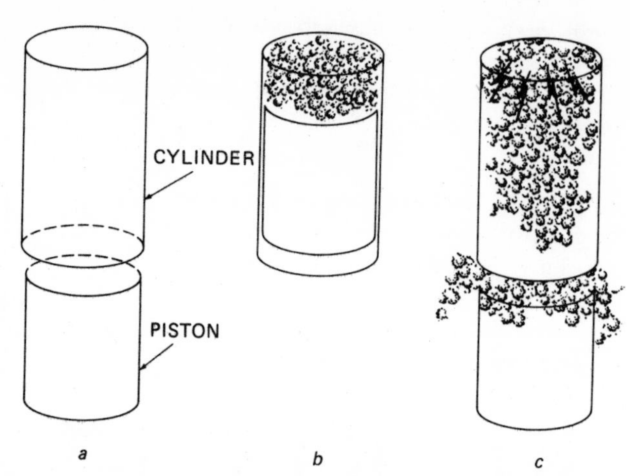

Figure 4 Three views showing the action in an engine cylinder. *(a)* The piston is a second cylinder that fits snugly into the engine cylinder. *(b)* When the piston is pushed up into the engine cylinder, air is trapped and compressed. The cylinder is drawn as though it were transparent so that the piston can be seen. *(c)* The increase of pressure as the air-fuel mixture is ignited pushes the piston out of the cylinder.

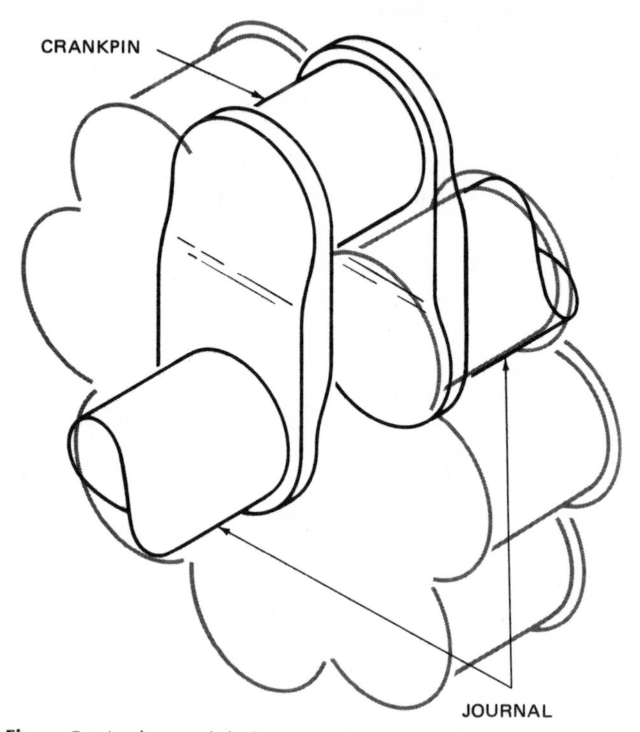

Figure 5 As the crankshaft rotates, the crankpin swings in a circle around the shaft.

but is still loose enough to slide easily up and down inside the cylinder. The piston is made of aluminum or other suitable metal. There are grooves cut in the side of the piston, and piston rings are fitted into these grooves. This is shown in Fig. 3. The rings fit tightly against the cylinder wall and provide such a good seal that very little air can escape between the piston and cylinder wall. Thus, when the piston is pushed up in the cylinder, the air in the cylinder is trapped above the piston and is compressed.

Figure 4 shows this action very simply. In Fig. 4*a*, the piston is shown below the cylinder. The cylinder is drawn as though it were transparent so that the piston can be seen as it moves up into the cylinder. See Fig. 4*b*. The air above the piston is compressed as it is pushed up into the cylinder. (Neither the piston rings nor the means of pushing the piston up into the cylinder are shown.) If we put some gasoline vapor into the compressed air and then applied a lighted match or spark to the air-vapor mixture, the gasoline vapor would burn. High pressure would be created, and the piston would be blown out of the cylinder, as shown in Fig. 4*c*. Actually, in a modified form, this is what happens in the cylinder. A mixture of air and gasoline vapor enters the cylinder, the piston is pushed up in the cylinder, the mixture is ignited, and the piston is pushed down in the cylinder.

■ **1-1-2 Reciprocating to Rotary Motion** The up-and-down movement of the piston is called "reciprocating motion." The piston moves in a straight line. This straight-line motion must be changed to rotary, or turning, motion in order to make the car wheels rotate. Reciprocating motion is changed to rotary motion by a crank on the crankshaft and a connecting rod. This action is shown in Figs. 5 to 8.

The crank is an offset section of the crankshaft. It swings around in a circle as the shaft rotates. This action is shown in Fig. 5. The connecting rod connects the crankpin of the crank and the piston. This is shown in Figs. 6 and 7. The crank end of the connecting rod is attached to the crankpin by fastening the rod-bearing cap to the connecting rod with the rod-cap bolts (Fig. 7). The cap and rod have bearings which permit the crankpin to rotate freely within the rod. The piston end of the rod is attached to the piston by the piston pin, or wrist pin. The piston pin is held in two bearings in the piston. A bearing in the piston-pin end of the connecting rod (or bearings in the piston) permits the rod to swing back and forth on the piston pin.

The crank end of the connecting rod is sometimes called the rod "big end." The piston end is sometimes called the rod "small end."

Figure 8 shows what happens as the piston moves up and down in the cylinder. The crankpin moves in a circle as the crankshaft rotates. As the piston starts moving down, the connecting rod tilts to one side so that the lower end can follow the circular path of the crankpin. Follow the sequence of actions shown in Fig. 8 (or steps numbered 1 to 8). Note that the connecting rod tilts back and forth on the piston pin while the lower end moves in a circle along with the crankpin.

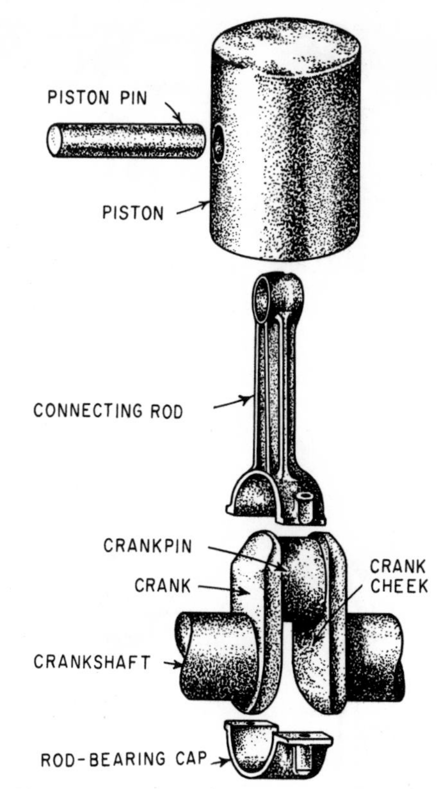

Figure 6 Piston, connecting rod, piston pin, and crank of a crankshaft in disassembled view. The piston rings are not shown.

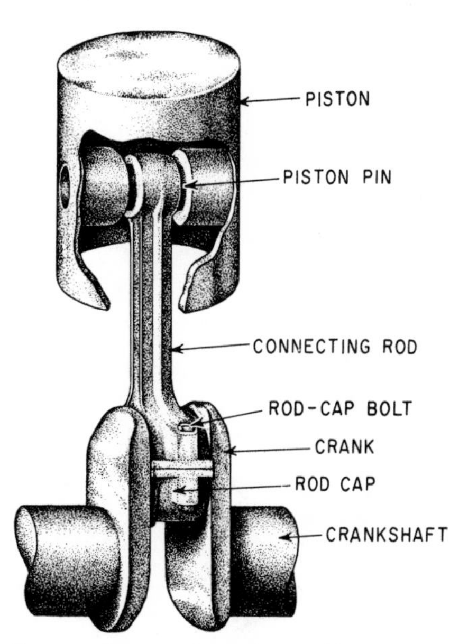

Figure 7 Piston and connecting-rod assembly attached to a crankpin on a crankshaft. The piston rings are not shown. The piston is partly cut away so you can see how it is attached to the connecting rod.

■ **1-1-3 The Valves** There are two openings, or ports, in the enclosed end of the cylinder, one of which is shown in Fig. 2. One of these ports permits the entrance of the mixture of air and gasoline vapor into the cylinder. The other port permits the burned gases to exhaust, or escape, from the cylinder after combustion.

The two ports have valves assembled into them, and these valves close off one or the other port, or both ports, during various stages of the actions taking place in the cylinder. The valves are accurately machined metal plugs that close the openings when the valves are seated, that is, when they have moved up into the openings. Figure 9 shows a valve and a valve seat of the type used in the engine illustrated in Fig. 2. This type is called a "poppet valve." The valve is shown open in Fig. 9, that is, pushed down off its seat. When closed, the valve moves up so that the outer edge of its head rests on the seat. In this position, the valve port is closed so that no air or gas can pass through it.

A spring on the valve stem (Fig. 2) tends to hold the valve on its seat. The lower end of the spring rests against a flat section of the cylinder head. The upper end rests against a flat washer, or spring retainer, which is attached to the valve stem by a retainer lock, or keeper. The spring is under compression, which means it tries to expand and thus tries to keep the valve seated.

The valve-opening mechanism includes a valve lifter and a

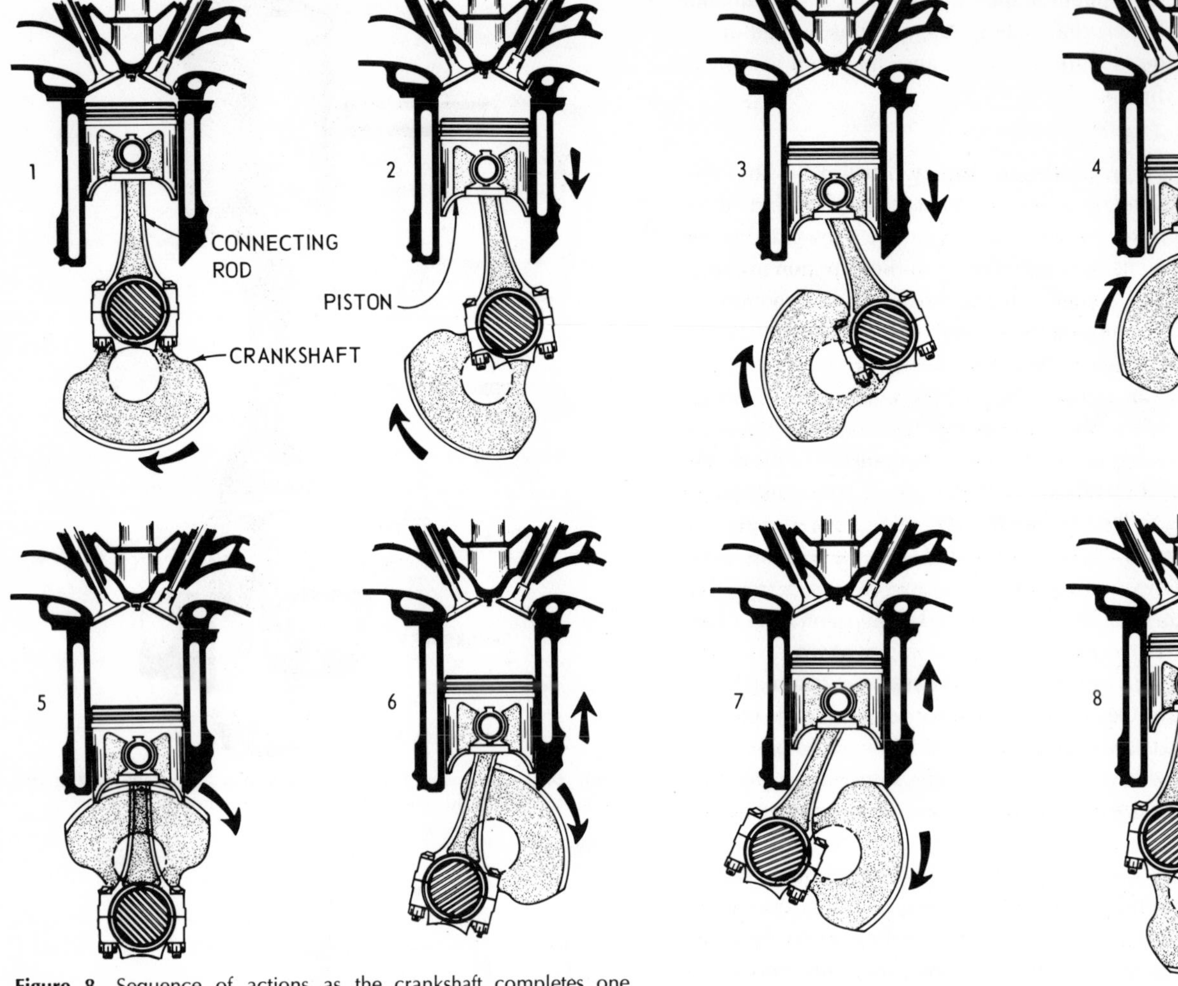

Figure 8 Sequence of actions as the crankshaft completes one revolution and the piston moves from top to bottom to top again.

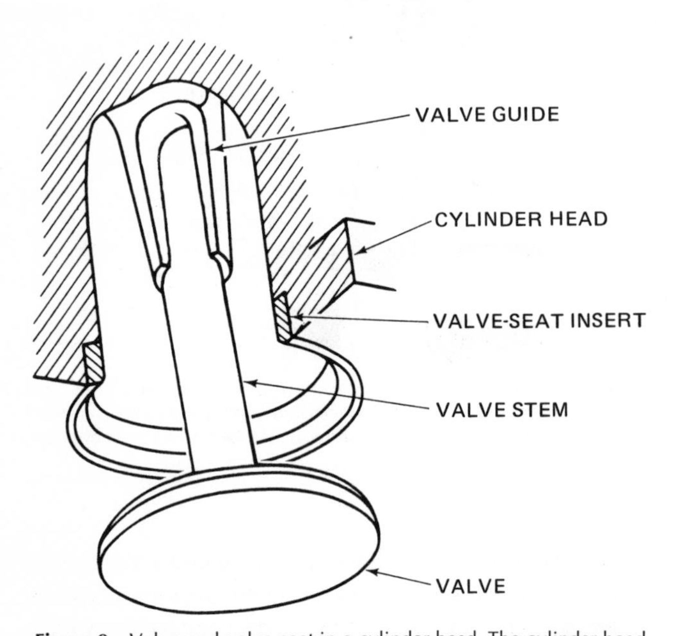

Figure 9 Valve and valve seat in a cylinder head. The cylinder head and valve guide have been cut away so that the valve stem can be seen.

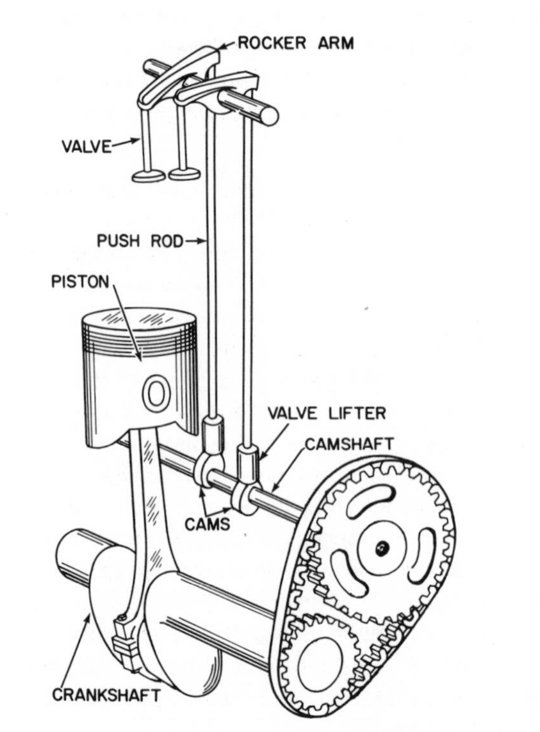

Figure 10 Valve-operating mechanism for an I-head, or overhead-valve, engine. Only the essential moving parts for one cylinder are shown.

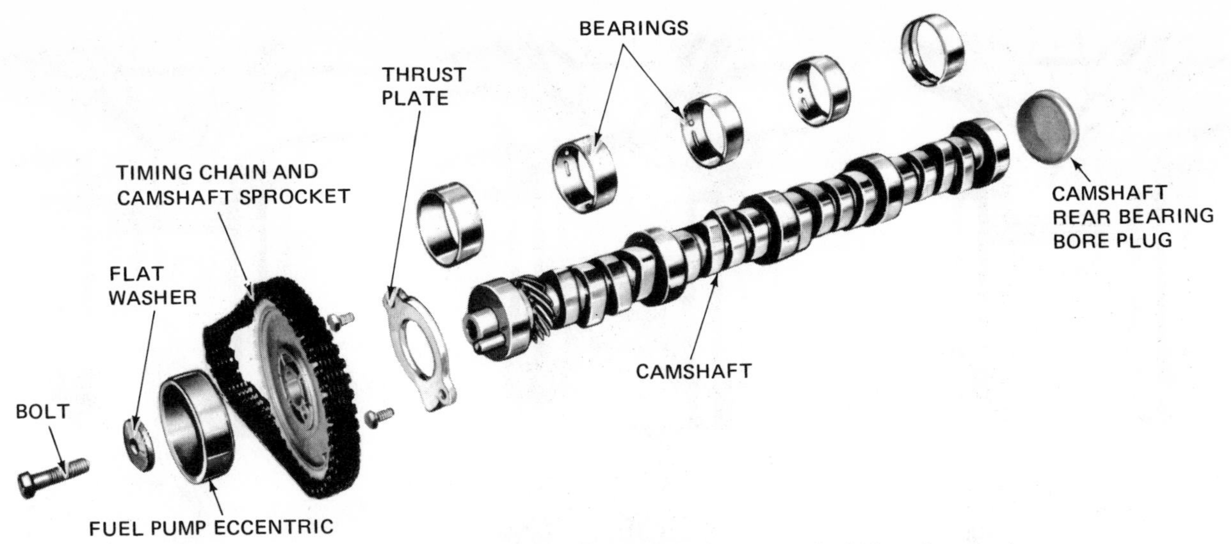

Figure 11 Camshaft and related parts for a six-cylinder engine. *(Ford Motor Company.)*

cam on a camshaft (Fig. 10). As the camshaft turns, the "bump," or lobe, on the cam comes around under the valve lifter, moving it upward. The valve lifter, in turn, pushes up on the pushrod. The pushrod then causes one end of the rocker arm to move up. The rocker arm pivots on its supporting shaft so that the valve end of the rocker arm is forced down, thus opening the valve. After the cam lobe moves out from under the valve lifter, the valve spring forces the valve up on its seat again. Figure 10 shows an overhead-valve mechanism. There are other types which are discussed in ■ 1-1-17.

Figure 11 shows a typical camshaft. It has a cam for each valve in the engine, or two cams per cylinder. The camshaft is driven by gears, a toothed belt, or a chain, from the crankshaft, and it turns at one-half crankshaft speed. The cam lobes are so positioned on the camshaft as to cause the valves to open and close in the cylinders at the proper time with respect to the activities taking place in the cylinders.

NOTE: In all the engines we have discussed so far, the camshaft is located in the cylinder block. (See Figs. 2 and 10, for example.) However, in many engines now being produced, the camshaft is located on top of the cylinder head. This type of engine is called an overhead-camshaft (OHC) engine and is described in detail in ■ 1-1-17.

■ **1-1-4 Engine Operation** The actions taking place in the engine cylinder can be divided into four stages, or strokes. The term "stroke" refers to piston movement. The upper limit of piston movement (position 1 in Fig. 8) is called top dead center (TDC). The lower limit of piston movement is called bottom dead center (BDC). A stroke occurs when the piston moves from TDC to BDC or from BDC to TDC. The piston completes a stroke each time it changes direction of motion.

When the entire cycle of events in the cylinder requires four strokes (or two crankshaft revolutions), the engine is called a four-stroke-cycle engine, or a four-cycle engine. The term "Otto cycle" is also applied to this type of engine (after Friedrich Otto, a German scientist of the nineteenth century). The four piston strokes are intake, compression, power, and exhaust. (Two-stroke-cycle engines are also in use; in these, the entire cycle of events is completed in two strokes, or one crankshaft revolution.)

NOTE: For the sake of simplicity in the following discussion, the valves are considered to open and close at TDC and BDC. Actually, they are not timed to open and close at these points. Also, the illustrations showing the four strokes (Figs. 12 to 15) are greatly simplified. They show the intake and exhaust valves separated and placed on either side of the cylinder so that both valves can be seen. Not all engines have the valves in this position.

1. INTAKE (Fig. 12) On the intake stroke, the intake valve has opened. The piston is moving down, and a mixture of air and vaporized gasoline is being "drawn" into the cylinder through the valve port. The mixture of air and vaporized gasoline is delivered to the cylinder by the fuel system and carburetor.

Actually, the piston does not "draw" the air-fuel mixture into the cylinder. Instead, atmospheric pressure (or pressure of the air) outside the engine pushes air into the cylinder. This air passes through the carburetor, where it picks up a charge of gasoline vapor, and then through the intake manifold and intake-valve port.

2. COMPRESSION (Fig. 13) After the piston reaches BDC, or the lower limit of its travel, it begins to move upward. As this happens, the intake valve closes. The exhaust valve is also closed, and so the cylinder is sealed. As the piston moves upward (pushed now by the revolving crankshaft and connect-

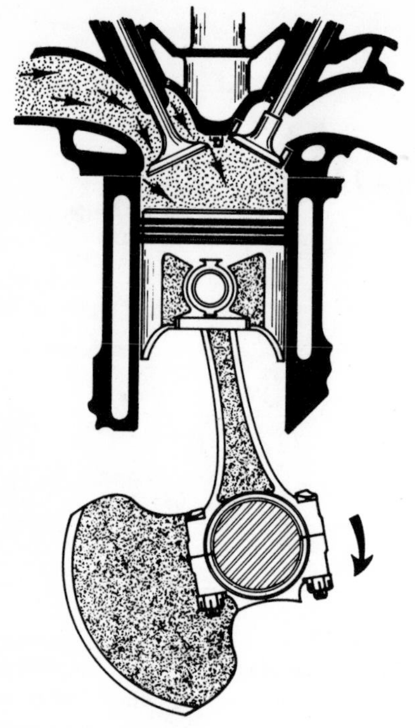

Figure 12 Intake stroke. The intake valve (upper left) has opened. The piston is moving downward, drawing a mixture of air and gasoline vapor into the cylinder.

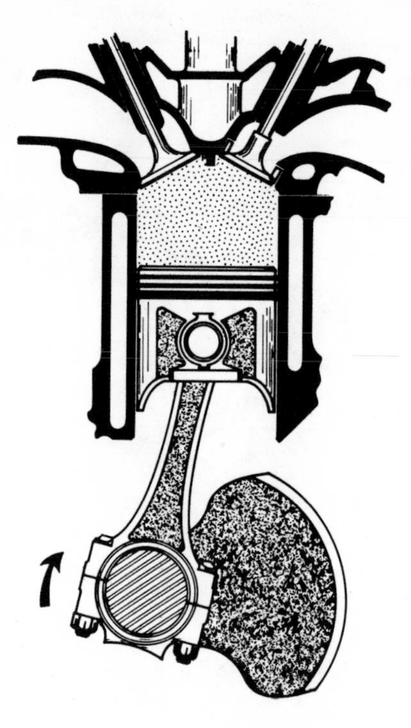

Figure 13 Compression stroke. The intake valve has closed, the piston is moving upward, compressing the mixture.

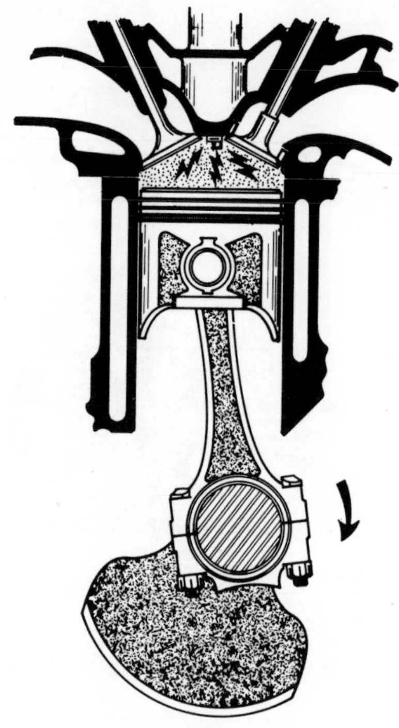

Figure 14 Power stroke. The ignition system has delivered a spark to the spark plug that ignites the compressed mixture. As the mixture burns, high pressure is created which pushes the piston downward.

ing rod), the air-fuel mixture is compressed. By the time the piston reaches TDC, the mixture has been compressed to as little as one-eighth of its original volume or even less. This compression of the air-fuel mixture increases the pressure in the cylinder. When the air-fuel mixture is compressed, not only does the pressure in the cylinder increase, but also the temperature of the mixture increases.

3. *POWER* (Fig. 14) As the piston reaches TDC on the compression stroke, an electric spark is produced at the spark plug. The spark plug consists essentially of two wire electrodes that are electrically insulated from each other. The ignition system delivers a high-voltage surge of electricity to the spark plug to produce the spark. The spark ignites, or sets fire to, the air-fuel mixture. The mixture begins to burn very rapidly, increasing the cylinder pressure to as much as 600 psi (pounds per square inch) (42.18 kg/cm^2) or even more. This means that the hot gases are pushing against every square inch (6.45 cm^2) of the combustion chamber and pistonhead with a pressure of 600 psi (42.18 kg/cm^2) or more. For example, a piston 3 inches (76.2 mm) in diameter with a head area of about 7 square inches (45.16 cm^2) would have a pressure on it of over 4,000 pounds (1,814 kg). This strong push against the piston forces it downward, and a power impulse is transmitted through the connecting rod to the crankpin on the crankshaft. The crankshaft is rotated as the piston is pushed down by the pressure above it.

4. *EXHAUST* (Fig. 15) As the piston reaches BDC again, the exhaust valve opens. Now, as the piston moves up on the exhaust stroke, it forces the burned gases out of the cylinder through the exhaust-valve port. Then, when the piston reaches TDC, the exhaust valve closes and the intake valve opens. Now, a fresh charge of air-fuel mixture will be drawn into the cylinder as the piston moves down again toward BDC. The above four strokes are continuously repeated during the operation of the engine.

■ **1-1-5 Multiple-Cylinder Engines** A single-cylinder of a four-stroke-cycle engine provides only one power impulse every two crankshaft revolutions. It is delivering power only one-fourth of the time. To provide for a more continuous flow of power, automotive engines use four, six, eight, or more cylinders. The power impulses are so arranged as to follow one another or overlap (on six- and eight-cylinder engines). This gives a more nearly even flow of power from the engine.

■ **1-1-6 Flywheel** Even though the power impulses in a multicylinder engine follow each other or overlap to provide a fairly even flow of power, additional leveling off of the power impulses is desirable. This would make the engine run still

Figure 15 Exhaust stroke. The exhaust valve (upper right) has opened. The piston is moving upward, forcing the burned gases from the cylinder.

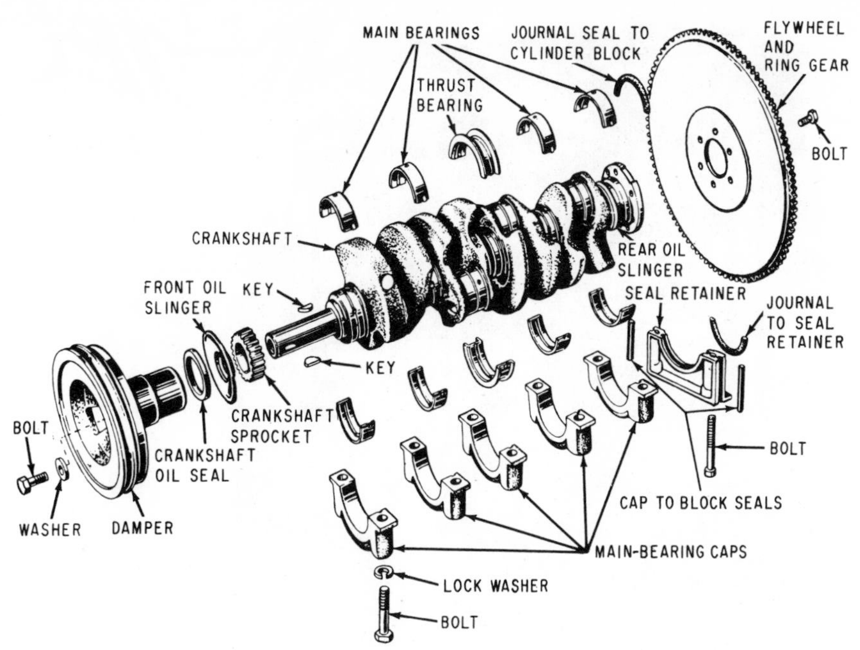

Figure 16 Crankshaft and related parts used in an eight-cylinder V-type engine. *(Ford Motor Company.)*

more smoothly. To achieve this, a flywheel is used (Fig. 16). The flywheel is a fairly heavy steel wheel attached to the rear end of the crankshaft.

To get a better idea of how the flywheel does its job, let us look at a single-cylinder engine. This engine delivers power only one-fourth of the time: during the power stroke. During the other three strokes it is absorbing power—to push out the exhaust gas, to produce a vacuum on the intake stroke, and to compress the air-fuel mixture. Thus, during the power stroke the engine tends to speed up. During the other strokes, it tends to slow down. Any rotating wheel, including the flywheel, resists any effort to change its speed of rotation (owing to inertia). When the engine tends to speed up, the flywheel resists the speedup. When the engine tends to slow down, the flywheel resists the slowdown.

Of course, in the single-cylinder engine, some speedup and slowdown times occur, but the flywheel minimizes them. In effect, the flywheel absorbs power from the engine during the power stroke (or speedup time) and then gives power back to the engine during the other three strokes (or slowdown time).

In the multicylinder engine, the flywheel acts in a similar manner to smooth out further the peaks and valleys of power flow from the engine. In addition, the flywheel forms part of the clutch. The flywheel also has teeth on its outer circumference that mesh with the electric-starting-motor drive pinion when the engine is being cranked to start it.

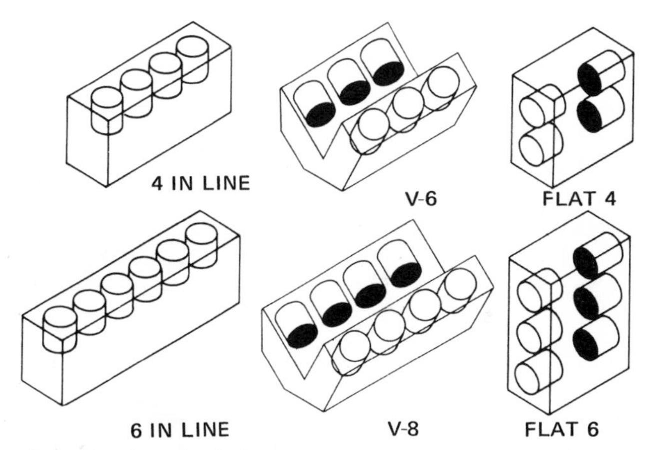

Figure 17 Several cylinder arrangements.

■ 1-1-7 Engine Types

Engines are classified in various ways. All automotive engines are of the internal-combustion type; that is, combustion of the fuel takes place inside the engine (as opposed to engines in which combustion of the fuel takes place outside the engine, for example, steam engines). Engines are classified according to (1) number of cylinders, (2) arrangement of cylinders, (3) arrangement of valves, (4) type of cooling system, (5) number of cycles (two or four), (6) type of fuel, (7) type of cycle (Otto or diesel).

There are also a number of automotive power plants that cannot be classified in the above manner because of their unorthodox design. These include the gas turbine, Wankel engine, and Stirling engine.

Figure 18 Partial cutaway view of a four-cylinder, in-line, overhead-valve engine. *(Chevrolet Motor Division of General Motors Corporation.)*

■ 1-1-8 Number and Arrangement of Cylinders

American passenger-car engines have four, six, or eight cylinders. Imported cars offer a greater variety, using engines of two, three, four, five, six, eight, or twelve cylinders. Engines with four, five, six, and eight cylinders are described and illustrated in following sections. Cylinders can be arranged in several ways: in a row (in-line); in two rows, or banks, set at an angle (V-type); in two rows opposing each other (flat or pancake); or like spokes on a wheel (radial-airplane type). Figure 17 shows various cylinder arrangements.

■ 1-1-9 Four-Cylinder Engines

The cylinders of a four-cylinder engine can be arranged in any of three ways: in-line, V, or opposed. In the V-type engine, the cylinders are arranged in two banks, or rows, of two cylinders each. The rows are set at an angle to each other. In the opposed-type engine, the cylinders are arranged in two banks, or rows, of two cylinders each and the rows are set opposite each other.

1. IN-LINE ENGINES Figure 18 is a cutaway view of a four-cylinder in-line engine. The cylinders are arranged in one row, or line. A very similar engine is the slant-four engine. Its cylinders are slanted to one side to permit a lower hood line. In

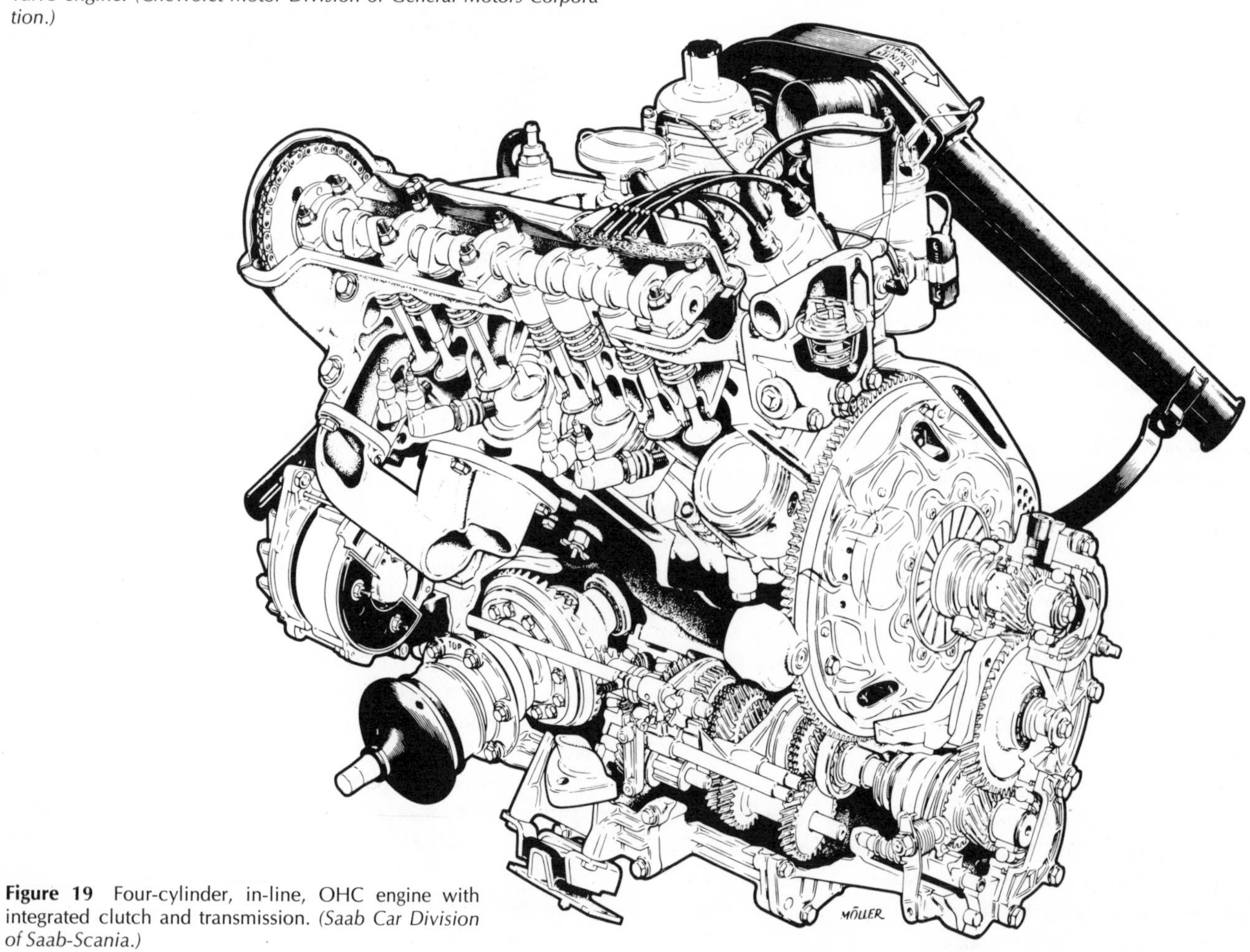

Figure 19 Four-cylinder, in-line, OHC engine with integrated clutch and transmission. *(Saab Car Division of Saab-Scania.)*

a sense, this engine is just one-half of a V-8 engine. There are relatively few slant-four engines produced in the United States.

Another slant-four engine, with an overhead camshaft (OHC) and integrated clutch, transmission, and differential, is shown in Fig. 19. This engine is especially interesting because of its overhead camshaft. Other engines previously described have the camshaft located in the lower part of the engine, the valves being operated by lifters, pushrods, and rocker arms (see Figs. 1, 2, 10, etc.) However, with the camshaft located in the cylinder head, as shown in Fig. 19, there is no need for pushrods, nor, in some engines, for rocker arms or lifters. This design has certain advantages, as explained later.

2. V-4 ENGINES The V-4 engine has two rows, or banks, of two cylinders each, and the rows are set at an angle, or a V, to each other. The crankshaft has only two cranks, with connecting rods from opposing cylinders in the two banks being attached to the same crankpin. Each crankpin has two connecting rods attached to it. Figure 20 is a phantom view of a V-4 engine with the internal moving parts emphasized. This type of engine is rather difficult to balance with counterweights on the crankshaft. In the engine shown in Fig. 20, balance is achieved by using a balance shaft that turns in a direction opposite to the crankshaft. Use of a balance shaft also is shown in Fig. 21.

3. OPPOSED FOUR-CYLINDER ENGINES Figure 22 shows the opposed, or flat, four-cylinder engine used by Volkswagen. The two rows, or banks, of cylinders oppose each other. The flat design, sometimes called a "pancake" engine, requires very little headroom, so that the engine compartment can be very compact. The Volkswagen engine is air-cooled and is mounted at the rear of the car.

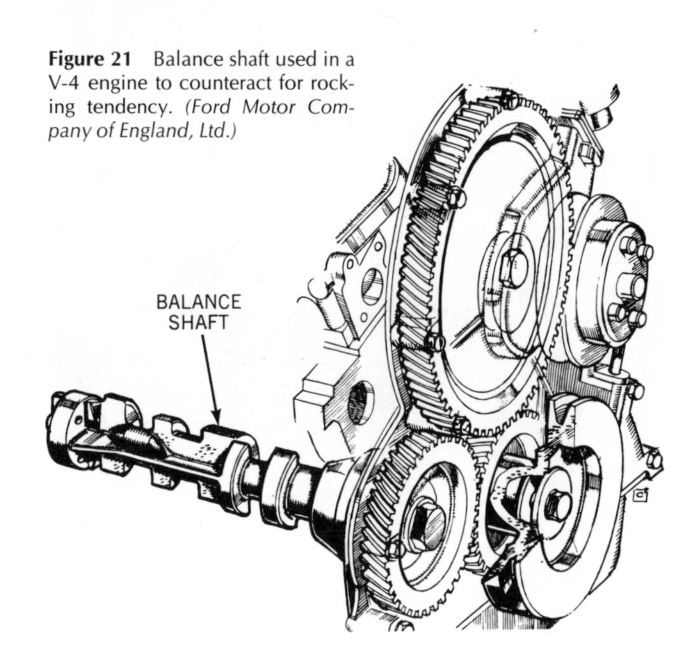

Figure 21 Balance shaft used in a V-4 engine to counteract for rocking tendency. *(Ford Motor Company of England, Ltd.)*

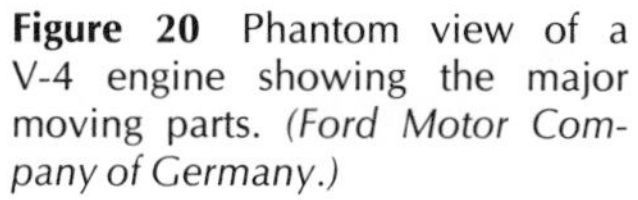

Figure 20 Phantom view of a V-4 engine showing the major moving parts. *(Ford Motor Company of Germany.)*

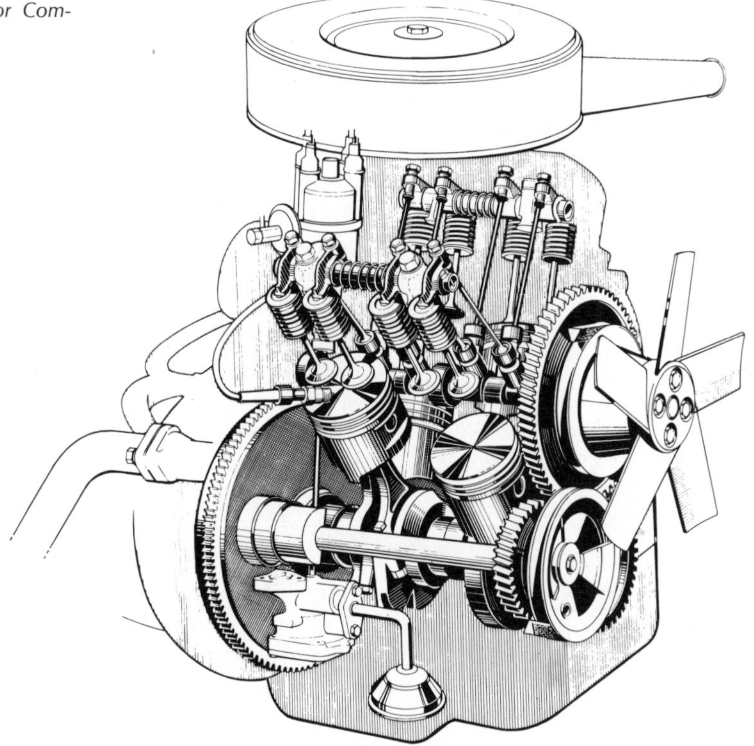

Figure 22 Flat four-cylinder engine with two banks of two cylinders each, opposing each other. This is an air-cooled engine. *(Volkswagen of America, Inc.)*

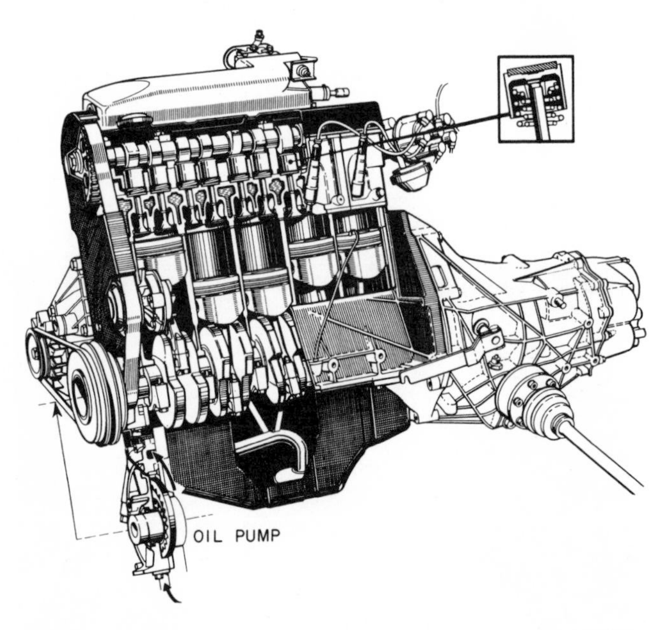

Figure 23 A five-cylinder in-line engine, with overhead camshaft and fuel injection, used in the Audi car. *(Volkswagen of America, Inc.)*

■ **1-1-10 Five-Cylinder Engines** A few-in-line engines are made with five cylinders. These vary little in design from conventional in-line fours and sixes, as shown in Fig. 23. The crankpins are spaced 72 degrees apart (72 × 5 = 360), and the engine has even firing impulses. Hardened bucket tappets, shown in the inset of Fig. 23, are offset to make them rotate from contact with the overhead camshaft.

■ **1-1-11 Six-Cylinder Engines** As with four-cylinder engines, six-cylinder engines may be in-line, V, or opposed. Most six-cylinder engines are in-line, although there are V-6 and flat-six engines.

1. IN-LINE ENGINES Figure 24 shows a six-cylinder, in-line engine that is partly cut away so that the internal construction can be seen. The valves are overhead. This is an I-head or overhead-valve engine. The crankshaft is supported by seven main bearings. Thus, there is a bearing on each side of every crank for additional support and rigidity.

Figure 25 shows a slant-six overhead-valve engine. This engine is similar to other six-cylinder in-line engines. However, the cylinders are slanted to one side, similar to the four-cylinder engine shown in Fig. 19, so that the hood line can be lowered. The engine has been supplied with either a cast-iron or a die-cast aluminum cylinder block.

Figure 26 is a partial cutaway view of a six-cylinder in-line OHC engine, with the camshaft driven by a neoprene belt reinforced with fiberglass cords. The belt has a facing of woven nylon fabric on the tooth side. The teeth on the belt fit teeth molded into the outer diameters of the drive and driven pulleys. This is very similar to the metal chain-and-sprocket arrangement used in chain-driven camshafts. However, the neoprene belt is quieter and does not require lubrication.

Figure 24 Six-cylinder, in-line engine with overhead valves, partly cut away to show the internal construction. *(Ford Motor Company.)*

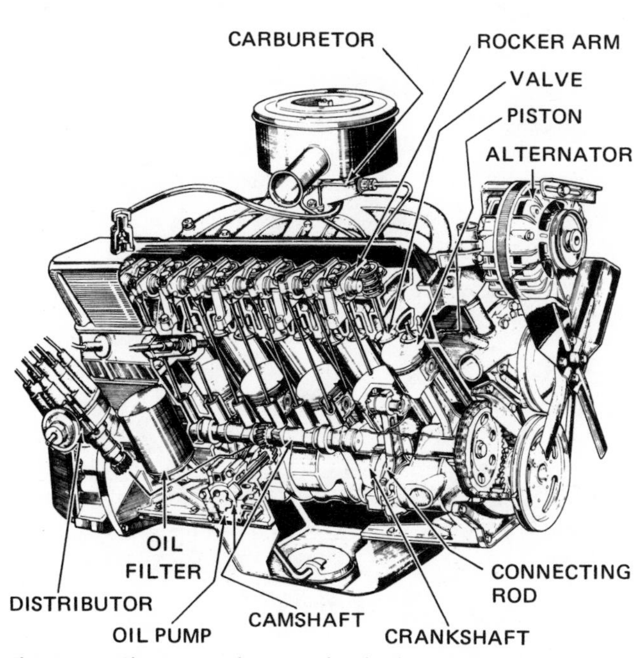

Figure 25 Slant-six, in-line, overhead-valve engine, cut away to show the internal parts. Cylinders are slanted to permit a lower hood line. *(Chrysler Corporation.)*

Figure 26 Partial cutaway view of a six-cylinder engine with the overhead camshaft driven by a toothed neoprene belt. *(Pontiac Motor Division of General Motors Corporation.)*

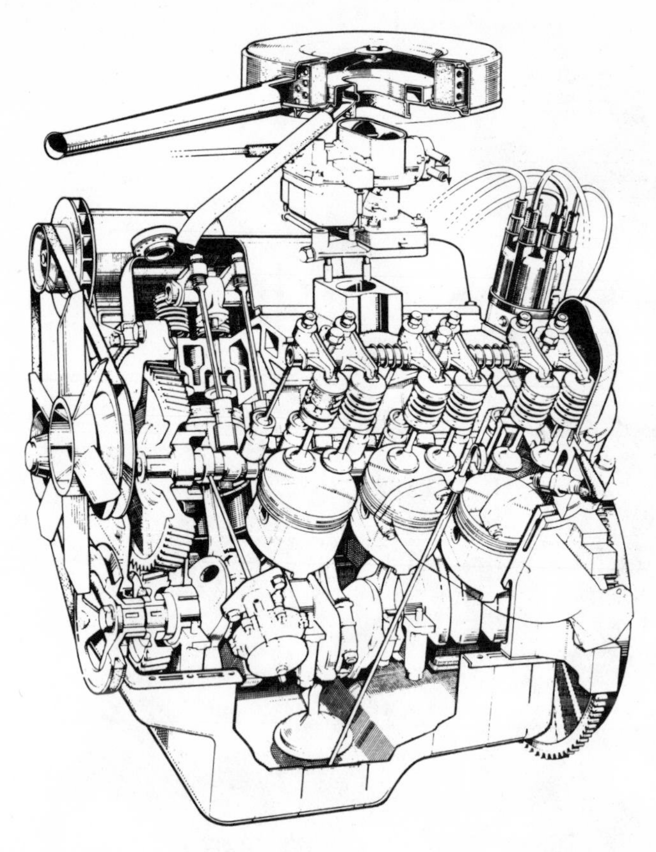

Figure 27 Cutaway view of a V-6, overhead-valve engine. *(Ford Motor Company of Germany.)*

2. V-6 ENGINES Several V-6 engines have been built. This design uses two three-cylinder rows, or banks, that are set at an angle, or V, to each other. In some engines, the crankshaft has only three cranks, with connecting rods from opposing cylinders in the two banks attached to the same crankpin. Each crankpin has two connecting rods attached to it. Figure 27 illustrates one version of this design. Other V-6 engines use a "splayed" crankshaft which provides a separate offset crankpin for each rod.

3. FLAT-SIX ENGINES Figure 28 shows the flat-six engine used in the Chevrolet Corvair. It is air-cooled and mounted at the rear of the vehicle.

■ **1-1-12 Eight-Cylinder Engines** At one time the eight-cylinder in-line engine was widely used, but it was replaced by the V-8 engine. A partial cutaway view of a typical V-8 engine is shown in Fig. 29. In the V-8, the cylinders are arranged in two rows, or banks, of four cylinders each, with the two rows set at an angle to each other. In effect, this engine is much like two four-cylinder in-line engines mounted on the same crankcase and working to a single crankshaft. The crankshaft in the V-8 has four cranks, with connecting rods from opposing cylinders in the two rows being attached to a single crankpin. Thus, two rods are attached to each crankpin, and two pistons work to each crankpin. The crankshaft is usually supported on five bearings.

Figure 28 Sectional view from the top of a flat six-cylinder, overhead-valve, air-cooled engine, sometimes referred to as a pancake engine. *(Chevrolet Motor Division of General Motors Corporation.)*

Figure 29 Cutaway view of a 365-hp V-8 engine. *(Ford Motor Company.)*

The V-8 engine shown in Fig. 29 has overhead valves operated by valve lifters, pushrods, and rocker arms from a single camshaft located between the two cylinder banks. Some high-performance engines have overhead camshafts, with the camshafts located in the cylinder heads. One version of this design has a single overhead camshaft in each cylinder head. Another version has two overhead camshafts in each cylinder head—one for the intake valves, the other for the exhaust valves. So this version has a total of four camshafts in the engine. An engine of this type is shown in Fig. 30.

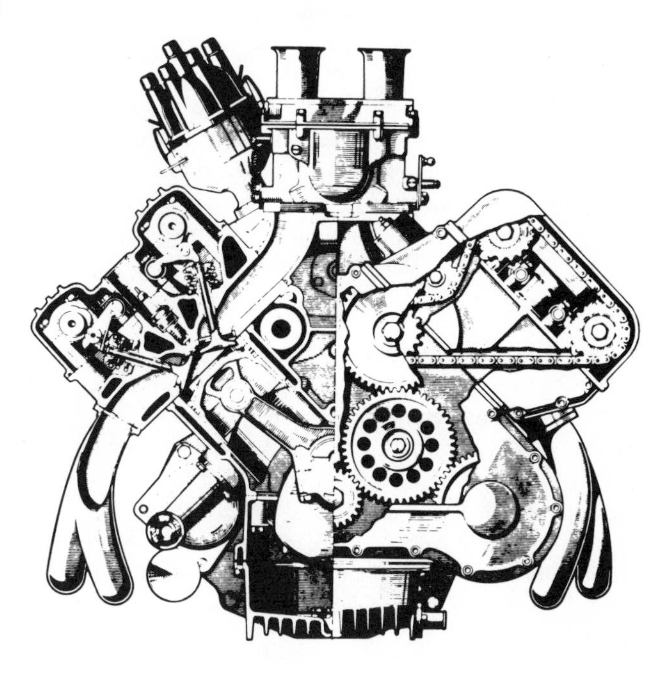

Figure 30 Sectional view from the end of a V-8 engine with four overhead camshafts. Right bank has been cut away to show the camshaft drive arrangement. Left bank has been cut away to show the internal construction of the engine and location of the valves and other components. *(Renault.)*

■ 1-1-13 Twelve- and Sixteen-Cylinder Engines

These engines have been used in automobiles, buses, trucks, and industrial installations. The cylinders are usually arranged in two banks (V-type or pancake type), three banks (W-type), or four banks (X-type). The pancake engine is similar to the V-type except that the two banks are arranged in a plane, but opposing. The cylinders work to the same crankshaft. At present, the only automobiles imported into the United States being made with 12-cylinder engines are the Jaguar and Lamborghini.

■ 1-1-14 Radial Engines

The radial engine has the cylinder radiating from a common center, like the spokes of a wheel. All connecting rods work to the common crankpin; the crankshaft has only one crankpin. The radial engine is air-cooled and is used mainly for aircraft applications, although some have been used in military vehicles. Another design is the multiple-bank radial, which is essentially two or more radial engines, one mounted back of another, using a multiple-crankpin crankshaft.

■ 1-1-15 Eight-Cylinder In-Line Engines Compared with V-8 Engines

Although eight-cylinder in-line engines were once widely used in automobiles, they were superseded by V-8 engines. The V-8 engine is a shorter, lighter, and more rigid engine. The arrangement permits the use of intake manifolding that ensures relatively even distribution of the air-fuel mixture to all cylinders (since all cylinders are relatively close together). This contrasts with the in-line engine, where the end cylinders could be fuel-starved while the center cylinders received adequate fuel, or vice versa. (Some eight-cylinder in-line engines used two carburetors for better fuel distribution.)

The more rigid V-8 engine permits higher running speeds and combustion pressures (higher power outputs) with less difficulty from flexing, or bending, of the cylinder block and crankshaft. Flexing throws the engine out of line, increases frictional losses and wear, and may also set up internal vibrations.

The shorter engine makes possible more passenger space on the same wheelbase or a shorter wheelbase car. In addition, the V-8 engine permits a lower hood line and thus a lower vehicle profile. This is because the carburetor and other parts can be nested between the two rows of cylinders so that they do not take up headroom above the cylinders.

■ 1-1-16 Firing Order

The firing order, or order in which the cylinders deliver their power strokes, is selected as part of the engine design. The best design provides a well-distributed pattern along the crankshaft. A design that permits two cylinders at the same end of the crankshaft to fire one after another is avoided as far as possible.

In-line engine cylinders are numbered from front to rear. Several different cylinder-numbering systems are used for V-6 and V-8 engines. For example, Ford V-8 engine cylinders are numbered:

Front of car

Left bank	*Right bank*
⑤	①
⑥	②
⑦	③
⑧	④

General Motors numbers the cylinders of its V-8 engines (except for some Buicks) in this way:

Front of car

Left bank	*Right bank*
①	②
③	④
⑤	⑥
⑦	⑧

The Chrysler Corporation's V-8 engines are numbered in the same way as the General Motors V-8 engines, above. Some Buick engines have the cylinders numbered:

Front of car

Left bank	*Right bank*
②	①
④	③
⑥	⑤
⑧	⑦

The Volkswagen flat-four engine has the cylinders numbered:

Front of car

Left bank	*Right bank*
③	①
④	②

The Corvair flat-six engine has the cylinders numbered:

Front of car

Left bank	*Right bank*
⑥	⑤
④	③
②	①

The General Motors V-6 engine has the cylinders numbered:

Front of car

Left bank	*Right bank*
①	②
③	④
⑤	⑥

When working on an engine, always check the shop manual to find how the cylinders are numbered.

Firing orders of different engines also vary. The two firing orders used in four-cylinder in-line engines are 1-3-4-2 and 1-2-4-3.

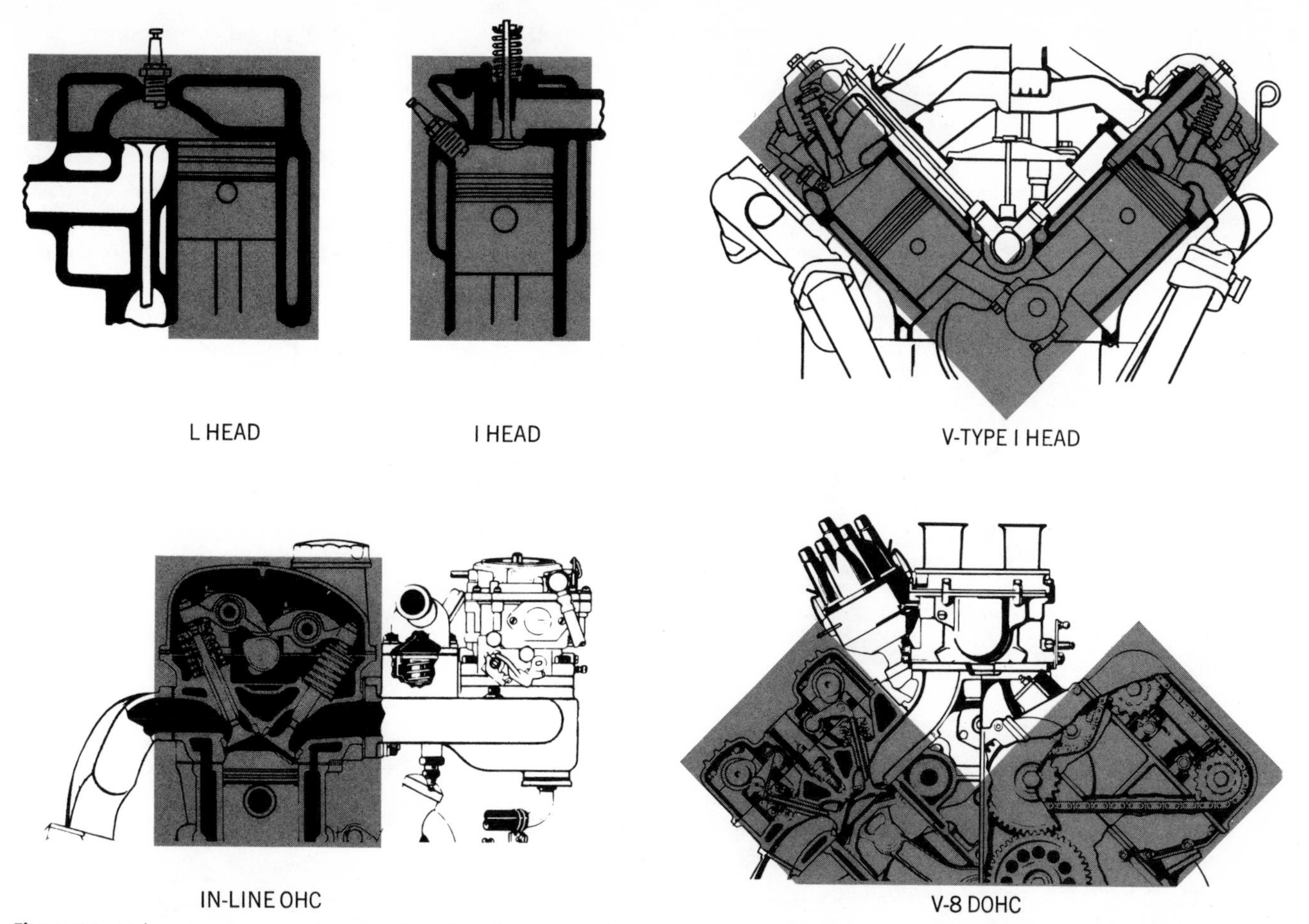

Figure 31 Valve arrangements. Compare these line drawings with the sectional and cutáway views of various engines shown elsewhere in the book.

The firing orders are possible in six-cylinder in-line engines: 1-5-3-6-2-4 or 1-4-2-6-3-5. All modern six-cylinder in-line engines are 1-5-3-6-2-4.

The V-6 engine uses this firing order: 1-6-5-4-3-2. This gives alternate firing between the cylinder banks and scatters the power strokes along the crankshaft.

General Motors V-8 engines use different firing orders. For example, most V-8 engines use this firing order: 1-8-4-3-6-5-7-2. Late-model Cadillac engines use this firing order: 1-5-6-3-4-2-7-8. Chrysler Corporation V-8 engines follow this firing order: 1-8-4-3-6-5-7-2. Ford V-8 engines use two firing orders: 1-5-4-2-6-3-7-8 and 1-3-7-2-6-5-4-8.

When working on an engine, it is essential to know the proper firing order, especially when doing ignition work. The firing order is found in the shop manual and in tuneup charts.

> **NOTE:** On some engines, the cylinder number and the firing order are cast into the intake manifold.

types of valve arrangements. The I-head, or overhead-valve, design is the most common.

1. L-HEAD ENGINE In the L-head engine, the combustion chamber and cylinder form an inverted L (Fig. 31). The intake and exhaust valves are located side by side, and all valves for the engine are arranged in one line (except for V-8 L-head engines, in which they are arranged in two lines). This design permits the use of a single camshaft to operate all valves. Since the valve mechanisms are in the block, removal of the cylinder head for major overhaul of the engine is relatively easy.

However, the L-head engine, though rugged and dependable, cannot be adapted to higher compression ratios. One reason is that the valves require a certain minimum space to move up into when they open. This space plus the minimum clearance required above the top of the piston determines the minimum possible clearance volume, or the volume with the piston at top dead center (TDC). Since the clearance volume cannot be decreased below this minimum, there is a limit as to how much the compression ratio of the engine can be increased.

The compression ratio is the ratio between cylinder volume at bottom dead center (BDC) and clearance volume, or the volume at TDC. The I-head (overhead-valve) engine is better suited to higher compression ratios, as explained below.

2. I-HEAD ENGINE In the I-head, or overhead-valve, engine, the valves are carried in the cylinder head (Fig. 2). In most in-line engines, the valves are arranged in a single row, as shown in Figs. 2 and 18. In V-type engines, the valves can be arranged in a single row in each bank (Fig. 27) or in a double row in each bank (Fig. 30). Regardless of arrangement, in an I-head engine a single camshaft actuates all valves. The valve lifters, pushrods, and rocker arms carrying the motion from the cams to the valves. This is shown in Fig. 10.

The overhead-valve arrangement has come into widespread use since it is more adaptable to the higher-compression-ratio

Figure 32 Sectional view from end of the Cosworth Vega engine. *(Chevrolet Motor Division of General Motors Corporation.)*

Figure 33 Six-cylinder, in-line, overhead-camshaft engine partly cut away to show the engine cooling system. Arrows indicate the direction of water flow in the engine water jackets. Only small parts of the radiator are shown at the lower and upper right. *(Pontiac Motor Division of General Motors Corporation.)*

engines. In an engine with overhead valves, it is practical to reduce the clearance volume a proportionally greater amount than in an L-head engine. If you study the illustrations of the various I-head engines in this Handbook, you will see that the method of grouping the valves directly above the piston permits a small clearance volume. In some I-head engines, there are pockets in the piston heads into which the valves can move when the valves are open with the piston at TDC. In some engines, the clearances between the piston and valves are only a few thousandths of an inch.

3. OVERHEAD-CAMSHAFT ENGINES (Figs. 19, 23, 26 30, and 31) The I-head engine, in its most common version, uses pushrods and rocker arms to operate the valves. This design is often referred to as a "pushrod engine." The pushrods and rocker arms impose some inertia loads that tend to affect valve action. That is, the pushrods and rocker arms flex or bend slightly before they move to open the valve. This slows valve action and also can cause irregular valve action. At low speeds, this does not matter. But as speed increases, the flexing also increases. This causes increasingly irregular valve action, which tends to limit top engine speed. However, in overhead-camshaft (OHC) engines, the cams work directly on the rocker arms or valve stems. This results in quicker valve response so that higher engine speeds are possible. Figure 26 shows an engine with a single overhead camshaft. In this engine, rocker arms work directly on the cams. Figure 23 shows a single-overhead-camshaft engine in which the cams act on the end of the valve stems. No rocker arms are used.

The single-overhead-camshaft engine (one camshaft in each cylinder head) is called an SOHC engine. The double-overhead-camshaft engine (two camshafts in each cylinder head) is called a DOHC engine. Figure 30 shows a DOHC engine. In a DOHC engine, one camshaft operates the intake valves and the other camshaft operates the exhaust valves. Figure 32 shows the camshaft for the intake valves on the left side of the picture, and the camshaft for the exhaust valves on the right.

The overhead camshaft (or camshafts) is driven by sprockets and a metal chain or neoprene belt. Figures 19 and 30 show overhead-camshaft engines using sprockets and chain to drive the camshafts. Typical applications of the neoprene-belt type of camshaft drive are shown in Figs. 23 and 26.

4. V-TYPE AND PANCAKE ENGINES V-type and pancake engines may use either L or I heads. Most engines, however, use the I-head arrangement for the reasons given above. All newer high-output engines have the valves mounted in the cylinder head.

■ 1-1-8 Type of Cooling System

Engines are classified as liquid-cooled or air-cooled. Most automotive engines are liquid-cooled. The Corvair, Volkswagen, and some other automotive engines are air-cooled. Figures 22 and 28 show different air-cooled automobile engines. Almost all motorcycle engines are air-cooled. Also, the small one- and two-cylinder engines used on power lawn mowers and other garden equipment are air-cooled. In air-cooled engines, the cylinder barrels are usually separate and are equipped with metal fins which provide a large surface area. This permits engine heat to be carried away from the cylinders by the passing air. Many air-cooled engines are also equipped with metal shrouds which direct the air flow around the cylinders for improved cooling.

Liquid-cooled engines ordinarily use water with an antifreeze compound added to serve as the cooling medium. The mixture is called the "coolant." The engines have water jackets surrounding the cylinders and the combustion chambers in the cylinder block and head (Fig. 33). The coolant can circulate freely through these jackets. The coolant enters from the bottom of the engine radiator and circulates through the engine, where it absorbs heat and thus becomes hot. It then exits from the engine water jackets and pours into the radiator upper tank. From there, the coolant passes down through the radiator to the lower tank.

The radiator has two sets of passages: coolant passages (from top to bottom) and air passages (from front to back). The air passing through (pulled by the engine fan and the forward motion of the car) picks up the heat from the hot coolant passing down through the radiator. The result is that the coolant entering the lower tank is cool and ready for another trip through the engine. This constant circulation is kept going by the water pump, which is mounted on the front end of the engine and is driven by the fan belt. The fan is usually mounted on the water-pump pulley, and so both turn together.

SECTION 1-2 Valve Train Service

This section covers the servicing procedures on valves and valve trains. Other sections describe servicing of the other engine components.

■ **1-2-1 Cleanliness** The major enemy of good engine-service work is dirt. A trace of dirt or abrasive on a cylinder wall or other working engine part can ruin an otherwise good service job. Before the engine is opened for a major service job, it should be cleaned to remove dirt or grease. All engine parts should be cleaned as they are removed and kept clean until reinstalled. As soon as a part is cleaned, it should be dried and a light coat of oil applied to bright surfaces to prevent rust.

■ **1-2-2 Valve Trouble-Diagnosis Chart** The engine valves can cause engine trouble if they stick, burn, break, or wear excessively. The chart that follows lists these, and other possible valve troubles, along with possible causes, checks, and corrections.

NOTE: The complaints and possible causes are not listed in the chart in the order of frequency of occurrence. That is, item 1 (or item a under "Possible Cause") does not necessarily occur more frequently than item 2 (or item *b*).

VALVE TROUBLE-DIAGNOSIS CHART
(See ■1-2-3 to 1-2-8 for detailed explanations of trouble causes and corrections listed below.)

COMPLAINT	POSSIBLE CAUSE	CHECK OR CORRECTION
1. Valve sticking (■1-2-3)	a. Deposits on valve stem	See item 6
	b. Worn valve guide	Replace
	c. Warped valve stem	Replace valve
	d. Insufficient oil	Service lubricating system; add oil
	e. Cold-engine operation	Valves free up as engine warms up
	f. Overheating valves	See item 2
2. Valve burning (■1-2-4)	a. Valve sticking	See item 1
	b. Distorted valve seat	Check cooling system; tighten cylinder-head bolts

COMPLAINT	POSSIBLE CAUSE	CHECK OR CORRECTION
	c. Valve-tappet clearance too small	Readjust
	d. Spring cocked or weak	Replace
	e. Overheated engine	Check cooling system
	f. Lean air-fuel mixture	Service fuel system
	g. Preignition	Clean carbon from engine; use colder spark plugs
	h. Detonation	Adjust ignition timing; use higher-octane fuel
	i. Valve-seat leakage	Use an interference angle
	j. Overloaded engine	Reduce load or try heavy-duty valves
	k. Valve-stem stretching from strong spring or overheated engine	Use weaker spring; eliminate overheating
3. Valve breakage (■1-2-5)	a. Valve overheating	See item 2
	b. Detonation	Adjust ignition timing; use higher-octane fuel; clean carbon from engine
	c. Excessive tappet clearance	Readjust
	d. Seat eccentric to stem	Service
	e. Cocked spring or retainer	Service
	f. Scratches on stem from improper cleaning	Avoid scratching stem when cleaning valves
4. Valve-face wear (■1-2-6)	a. Excessive tappet clearance	Readjust
	b. Dirt on face	Check air cleaner
	c. See also causes listed under item 2	
5. Valve-seat recession (■1-2-7)	a. Valve face cuts valve seat away	Use coated valves and valve-seat inserts
6. Valve deposits (■1-2-8)	a. Gum in fuel (intake)	Use proper fuel
	b. Carbon from rich mixture (intake)	Service fuel system
	c. Worn valve guides	Replace
	d. Carbon from poor combustion (exhaust)	Service fuel, ignition system, or engine as necessary
	e. Dirty or wrong oil	Service lubricating system; replace oil

■ **1-2-3 Valve Sticking** Valves will stick from gum or carbon deposits on the valve stem (see ■1-2-8). Worn valve guides, which pass excessive amounts of oil, speed up the formation of deposits since the oil carbonizes on the hot valve stem. If the valve stem warps, it will stick in the valve guide. Warpage could result from overheating (■1-2-4), an eccentric seat (which throws pressure on one side of the valve face), or a cocked spring or retainer (which puts bending pressure on the stem). Of course, insufficient oil would also cause valve sticking. Also, sometimes valves will stick when the engine is cold but work themselves free and function normally as the engine warms up.

NOTE: When valves and piston rings have become so clogged with deposits that they no longer operate properly, it is usually necessary to overhaul the engine. However, some authorities suggest the use of special compounds in the oil and fuel which help in freeing valves and rings. One of these compounds comes in a pressurized can and is sprayed into the running engine through the carburetor (air cleaner off). When parts are not too badly worn and the major trouble seems to be from deposits, use of these compounds often postpones engine overhaul, at least for a while.

CAUTION: Before using a chemical additive in an engine equipped with a catalytic converter, make sure that the additive is harmless to the catalyst. To find this information, carefully read the label on the can and the section in the car manufacturer's service manual on the catalytic converter.

■ **1-2-4 Valve Overheating and Burning** Valve overheating and burning is usually an exhaust-valve problem. Any condition that causes the valve to stick so that it does not close tightly will cause valve burning. Not only does the poor seat prevent normal valve cooling through the valve seat, but it also allows hot gases to blow by, further heating the valve. The valve is cooled through both the valve seat and the valve guide, and so poor seating or a worn guide can cause overheating and burning. Also, if the water jackets or distributing tubes in the cooling system are clogged, local hot spots may develop around valve seats. These hot spots may cause seat distortion, which then prevents normal seating and thus permits blow-by and valve burning. Valve seat distortion can also result from improper tightening of the cylinder-head bolts. Other conditions that prevent normal seating include a weak or cocked valve spring and insufficient valve-tappet clearance. If the tappet clearance is too closely adjusted, the valve may be held open.

On engines equipped with valve rotators, check the valve-stem tip of valves that have burned to see whether or not the rotators are working. Figure 1 shows tip patterns indicating

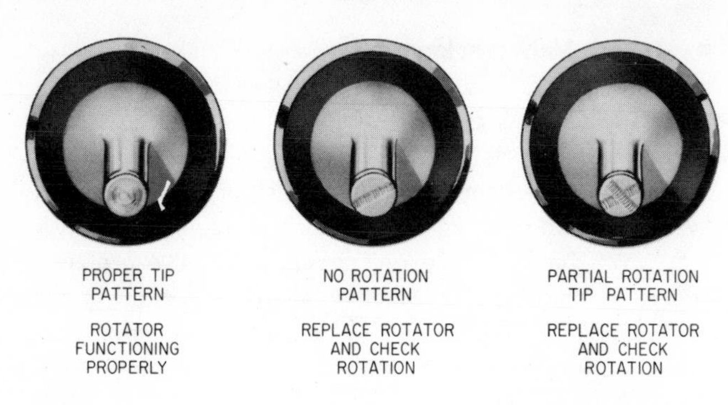

Figure 1 Valve-stem-wear patterns on valves with valve rotators. *(Oldsmobile Division of General Motors Corporation.)*

proper and improper rotator action. If the tip shows no rotation or a partial rotation pattern, the rotator should be replaced.

A lean air-fuel mixture may cause exhaust-valve burning since some combustion may still be going on (the lean mixture burns slowly) when the valve opens. If a lean air-fuel mixture is the cause, the fuel system should be serviced.

Preignition and detonation, both of which produce excessively high combustion pressures and temperatures, have an adverse effect on valves as well as on other engine parts. They can be eliminated by cleaning out carbon, retiming the ignition, or using higher-octane fuel.

In some persistent cases of valve seat leakage (especially where deposits on the valve seat and face prevent adequate sealing), the use of an interference angle has proved helpful. The valve is faced at an angle ½ to 2 degrees flatter than the valve seat angle (Fig. 2). This gives greater pressure at the lower edge of the valve seat, which tends to cut through any deposits that have formed and thereby establish a good seal.

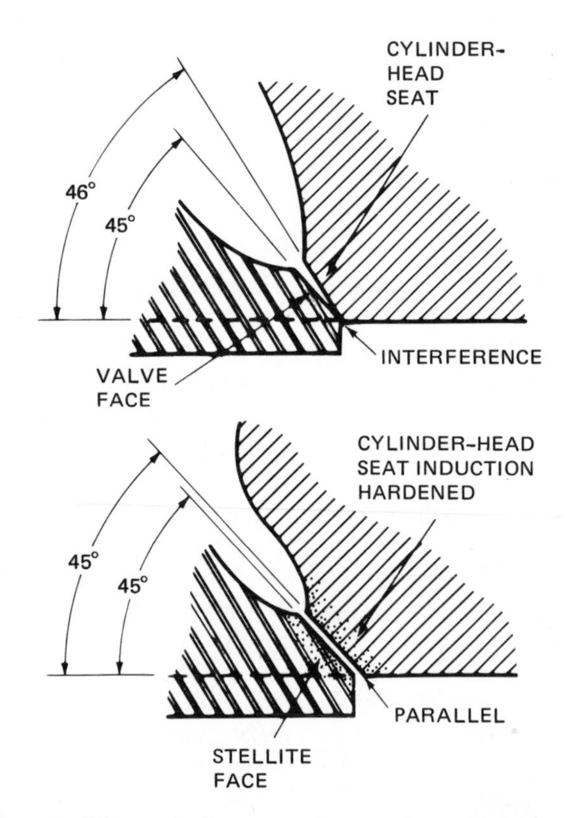

Figure 2 Valve and valve seat angles. Top, the interference angle recommended for many intake and exhaust valves and seats. Bottom, the parallel faces recommended for stellite-faced exhaust valves and induction-hardened exhaust-valve seats. *(Chevrolet Motor Division of General Motors Corporation.)*

Figure 2 illustrates one manufacturer's recommendation for the valve and seat angles to get interference. Note that this manufacturer does not recommend interference on stellite-faced exhaust valves and induction-hardened exhaust-valve seats. These surfaces are so hard that no appreciable improvement in seating would be obtained by interference.

Any condition that causes the engine to labor hard or overheat will also overheat the valves. If the engine must be operated under heavy load and this causes valve trouble, heavy-duty valves should be installed.

In some cases valve stems have been found to stretch because of a combination of heavy springs and overheating. Lighter springs should be used and the overheating eliminated.

■ 1-2-5 Valve Breakage

Any condition that causes the valve to overheat (■ 1-2-4) or to be subjected to heavy pounding, as from excessive detonation or tappet clearance, may cause valves to break. Excessive tappet clearance permits heavy impact seating. If the seat is eccentric to the stem or if the valve spring or retainer is cocked, then the valve will be subjected to side movement or pressure every time it seats. Ultimately, this may cause it to fatigue and break. If the stem has been scratched during cleaning, the scratch may serve as a starting point for a crack and a break in the stem.

■ 1-2-6 Valve Face Wear

In addition to the conditions discussed in ■1-2-4, excessive tappet clearance or dirt on the valve face or seat can cause valve face wear. Excessive tappet clearance causes heavy impact seating that is wearing on the valve and may cause valve breakage (■1-2-5). Dirt may cause valve face wear if the engine operates in dusty conditions or if the carburetor air cleaner is not functioning properly. The dirt enters the engine with the air-fuel mixture, and some of it deposits on the valve seat. The dirt will also cause bearing, cylinder-wall, and piston and ring wear.

■ 1-2-7 Valve Seat Recession

Valve seat recession is caused by the wearing away of the valve seat. This is produced by the action of the valve face which, under certain conditions, can cut the seating surface of the valve seat. Valve seat recession has become more of a problem in recent years because lead has been removed from gasoline. Lead additives in the gasoline form a lubricant between the valve face and the valve seat. This lubricant prevents iron particles that flake off the valve seat from sticking on the valve face. However, without this lead coating on the valve face and seat, particles of iron flake off the valve seat and tend to stick on the valve face. Gradually these particles embed in the valve face and build up into tiny bumps, or warts. This turns the valve face into a cutting surface. The valve seat is gradually cut away. The resulting valve seat recession causes lash loss, or a decrease in valve-tappet clearance. That is, as the valve gradually cuts into the valve seat, clearance in the valve train is reduced. In an engine using mechanical valve lifters, the result can be a complete loss of clearance so that the valve can no longer close completely. The result will be valve and valve seat burning.

To prevent valve seat recession in engines run on lead-free gasoline, the valves are given a very thin coating of aluminum or other metal. This coating, less than 0.002 inch (0.052 mm) in thickness, prevents the iron particles from adhering to the valve face and prevents valve seat recession. The coating gives the valve face a dull, almost rough, appearance. The natural tendency for the automotive mechanic would be to reface the valve. However, this must not be done. Coated valves should not be refaced or lapped. Doing so would remove the coating and deny the valve seat the protection produced by the coating. The result could be very short valve and valve seat life. (Valve servicing is discussed in ■1-2-26.)

■ 1-2-8 Valve Deposits If the fuel has excessive amounts of gum in it, some of this gum may deposit on the intake valve as the air-fuel mixture passes the valve on the way to the engine cylinder. Carbon deposits may form from an excessively rich mixture or from oil passing a worn valve guide (intake valve). Improper combustion, due to a rich mixture, a defective ignition system, loss of compression in the engine, a cold engine, and so on, will result in carbon deposits on the exhaust valves. Dirty or improper oil will cause deposits to form on the valves.

■ 1-2-9 Valve Service In servicing valves, a number of components must be considered. These include valves, valve seats and guides, valve springs and retainers, rocker-arm mechanisms (in overhead-valve engines), valve tappets, camshaft, camshaft drive, and bearings.

The service jobs on valves include adjusting valve-tappet clearances (also called adjusting valve lash), grinding valves and valve seats, installing new seat inserts (on engines so equipped), cleaning or replacing valve guides, removing and checking the camshaft, servicing camshaft bearings, and timing the valves.

■ 1-2-10 Adjusting Valve-Lifter Clearance The procedure for checking and adjusting valve-tappet, or valve-lifter, clearance (or adjusting valve lash) varies with the type and model of engines. Some engines with hydraulic valve lifters normally require no clearance adjustment. Others require checking and adjustment whenever valve service work is performed. The following procedures are typical.

■ 1-2-11 L-Head Engine with Mechanical Valve Lifters Some specifications call for checking the clearance with the engine cold. According to other specifications, the engine should be warmed up and idling. Remove the valve-

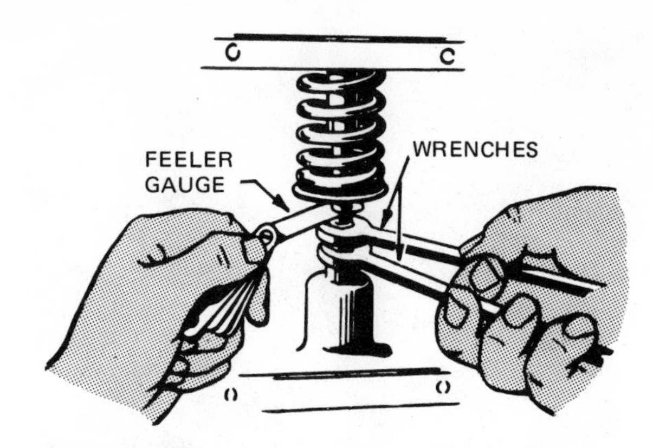

Figure 3 Adjusting valve-tappet clearance on an L-head engine.

cover plates. Use a feeler gauge to check the clearance between the valve stem and the adjusting screw in the valve lifter (Fig. 3). A two-step "go no-go" feeler gauge of the specified thicknesses can be used. Adjustment is correct when the "go" step fits the clearance but the "no-go" step does not.

If the clearance is not correct, the adjusting screw must be turned in or out as necessary to correct it. Some tappet-adjusting screws are self-locking; others have a locking nut. On the latter type, the locking nut must be loosened. This requires two wrenches – one to hold the screw, the other to turn the nut. On both types of tappet-adjusting screws, one wrench must be used to hold the valve lifter while a second wrench is used to turn the adjusting screw. Adjustment is correct when the feeler gauge can be moved between the screw and valve stem with some drag when the valve is closed. When a locking nut is used, it should be tightened after the adjustment is made and the clearance should be checked again. After the adjustment is completed, replace the cover plates, using new gaskets.

■ 1-2-12 I-Head Engine with Mechanical Valve Lifters Most specifications call for making the check with the engine hot and not running. First, remove the valve cover. Measure the clearance between the valve stem and rocker arm, as shown in Fig. 4. The clearance is measured with the valve lifter on the base circle of the cam. Turn the crankshaft by bumping the engine with the starting motor until the base circle of the cam is under the valve lifter.

> **NOTE:** Refer to the engine manufacturer's shop manual for details of the procedure by which one crankshaft position will allow you to check half or a third of the valves. When you use this procedure, you need position the crankshaft and camshaft only two or three times to adjust all valves.

There are two kinds of rocker arms: One is shaft-mounted, and the other is ball-stud-mounted. The shaft-mounted type (Fig. 4) usually has an adjustment screw. This screw is normally self-locking and does not require a locking nut. Use a box-

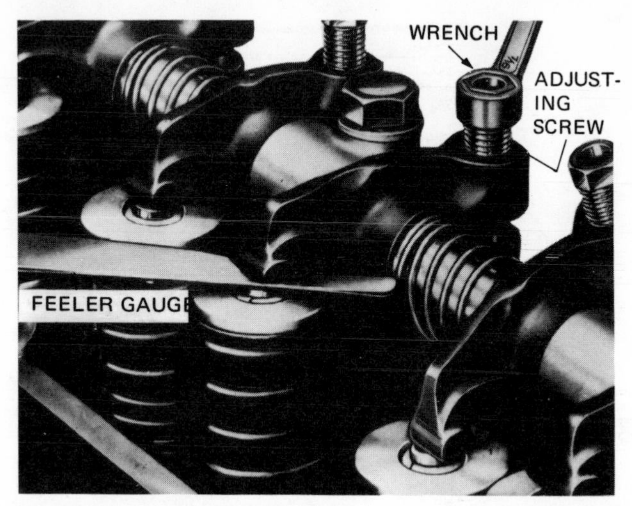

Figure 4 Adjusting valve-tappet clearance on an I-head engine. *(Ford Motor Company.)*

wrench to turn the adjustment screw and adjust the clearance to specifications. Do not use an open-end wrench. This could damage the screw head.

On the ball-stud-mounted rocker arms (Fig. 5), turn the self-locking rocker-arm-stud nut to make the adjustment. Turning the nut down reduces clearance.

■ **1-2-13 Free-Type Valve Rotators** Free-type valve rotators are checked in the same way as the mechanical-lifter type. The clearance is checked between the tip cup on the valve stem and the adjusting screw in the valve lifter.

■ **1-2-14 I-Head Engines with Hydraulic Valve Lifters** On some engines with hydraulic valve lifters, no adjustment is provided in the valve train. In normal service, no adjustment is necessary. The hydraulic valve lifter

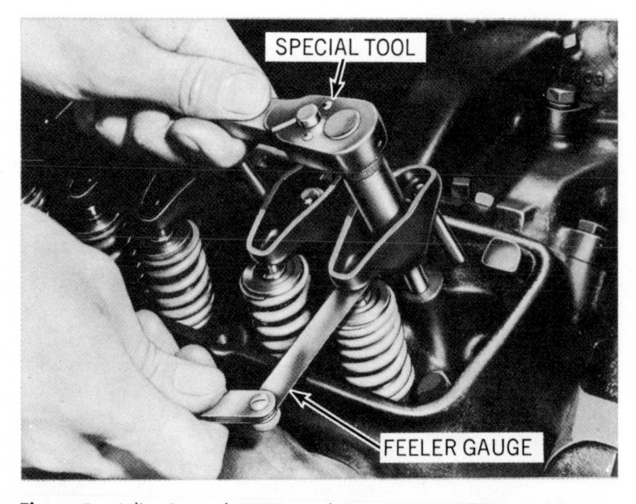

Figure 5 Adjusting valve-tappet clearance on an engine with rocker arms independently mounted on ball studs. Backing the stud nut out increases clearance. *(Chevrolet Motor Division of General Motors Corporation.)*

takes care of any small changes in the valve-train length. However, adjustment may be needed if valves and valve seats are ground. Unusual and severe wear of the pushrod ends, rocker arm, or valve stem may also require adjustment. Then some correction may be required to reestablish the correct valve-train length. Typical checking and correcting procedures follow.

■ **1-2-15 Ford Engines with Hydraulic Valve Lifters** Ford engines use two types of rocker arms: shaft-mounted and ball-stud-mounted. On both types the clearance in the valve train is checked with the valve lifter bled down so that the valve-lifter plunger is bottomed. First, the crankshaft must be turned so that the lifter is on the base circle or low part of the cam (rather than on the lobe). This is done by setting the piston in the No. 1 cylinder at top dead center (TDC) at the end of the compression stroke. Then check both valves in the No. 1 cylinder. The crankshaft can then be rotated as necessary to put other lifters on the base circles of their cams so that they can be checked.

To make a check, a special tool is used to apply slow pressure on the rocker arm. The slow pressure gradually forces oil out of the valve lifter so that the plunger bottoms. Then, the clearance gauge is used to check the clearance between the valve stem and rocker arm. If the clearance is too small, install a shorter pushrod. If the clearance is excessive, install a longer pushrod. The clearance might become too small if valves and seats have been ground. The clearance might become excessive as a result of wear of the valve-train parts. This includes wear of the pushrod ends, valve stem, and rocker arm.

■ **1-2-16 Plymouth Engines with Hydraulic Valve Lifters** The procedure for setting Plymouth valves is typical of the engines manufactured by Chrysler Corporation. It is necessary only when valves and valve seats have been ground. When this happens, the increased height of the valve stem above the cylinder head should be checked. With the valve seated, place the special gauge tool over the valve stem. If the end of the valve stem sticks out too far above the tool, the end of the valve stem must be ground off to reduce the height to within limits. The hydraulic-valve-lifter plunger will then work near its center position rather than near the bottom, as it would with an excessively high valve stem.

■ **1-2-17 Chevrolet Engines with Hydraulic Valve Lifters** The procedure for the Chevrolet engines is typical of General Motors engines using the ball-pivot type of rocker arm (Fig. 5). With the valve lifter on the base circle of the cam, back off the adjustment nut until the pushrod is loose. Then slowly turn the adjustment nut down. At the same time, rotate the pushrod with your fingers until the pushrod is tight. That is, until you cannot easily rotate the pushrod. Then turn the adjustment nut down one additional full turn. This places the plunger of the valve lifter in its center position.

■ 1-2-18 Overhead-Camshaft Engines

Overhead-camshaft (OHC) engines have several arrangements for carrying the cam action to the valve stems. In some engines, cam action is carried directly to the valve stem through a cap, called the "valve tappet." This cap fits over the valve stem and spring. In other engines, cam action is carried through a rocker arm. We shall look at both arrangements. (Checks and adjustments are made with the engine cold.)

1. CHEVROLET VEGA Figure 6 shows the valve-train parts of the Chevrolet Vega engine. Adjustment of valve clearance is made by turning the adjustment screw located in the valve tappet. The adjustment screw has a flat on one side. Therefore, adjustment must be made by turning the screw full turns only.

Turn the camshaft so the valve tappet is on the base circle. Then measure the clearance between the cam and the valve tappet with a feeler gauge. Use a special tool to turn the adjustment screw. The screw must be turned complete revolutions so that the flat on the screw ends up directly above the valve stem. Turning the screw in, or clockwise, decreases clearance. Each full turn of the screw changes the clearance 0.003 inch (0.076 mm).

2. CHEVROLET LUV ENGINE The Chevrolet LUV engine has rocker arms which are held in place by springs. The rocker arms have dome-shaped ends which fit over ball studs in the cylinder head. The valve ends of the rocker arms fit into a depression in the valve-spring retainer and rest on the valve stems. To check the valve clearance, measure the clearance between the cam surface of the rocker arm and the base circle of the cam. Use a flat feeler gauge. Adjust with the Phillips-head screwdriver inserted through the hole in the rocker arm dome, as shown.

3. FORD 2,000-CC FOUR-CYLINDER ENGINE This Ford engine has rocker arms which float between a stationary stud on one side and the valve stem on the other. The center of the rocker arm rests on the cam. (This is similar to the arrangement in the Chevrolet LUV engine.) Figure 7 shows the use of a feeler gauge to check the clearance between the case circle of the cam and the rocker arm. Adjustment is made by loosening the locknut. Use a 15-mm (0.59-inch) open-end wrench to turn the adjustment screw in or out. Turning the screw in increases the clearance. Tighten the locknut securely after the adjustment and recheck the clearance.

■ 1-2-19 The Complete Valve Job

A complete valve job requires the following steps. The details of valve and valve seat service are described in ■1-2-20 to 1-2-30.

1. Drain the cooling system and disconnect the upper radiator hose from engine.

2. Remove the air cleaner and disconnect the throttle linkage, fuel line, and air and vacuum hoses from the carburetor.

3. Remove or set aside the necessary lines and hoses to get at the cylinder head.

4. Disconnect the spark-plug wires and temperature-sending unit.

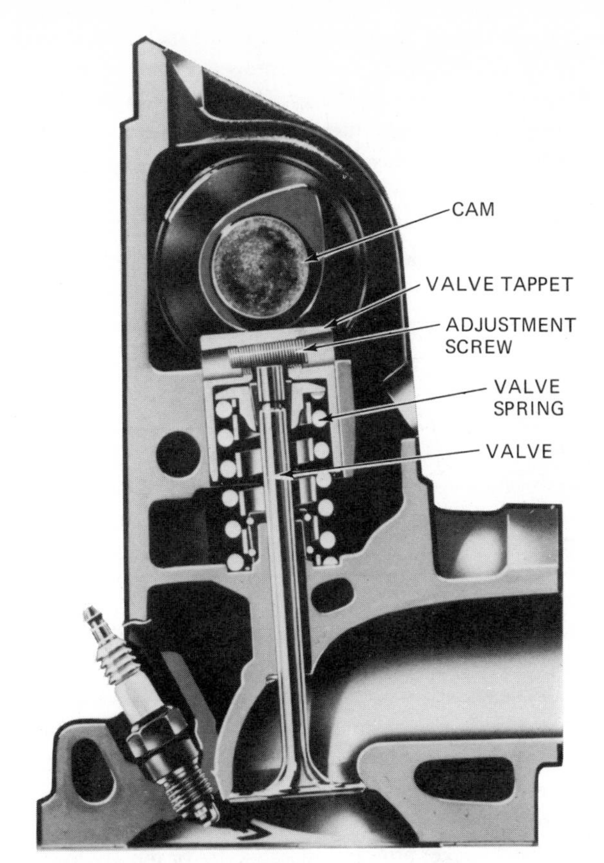

Figure 6 Valve train for the Vega engine. *(Chevrolet Motor Division of General Motors Corporation.)*

5. Remove the crankcase ventilating system and, on air-injection systems, disconnect the air hose at the check valve. Then remove the air-supply-tube assembly.

6. On V-8 engines, remove the carburetor and intake manifold. (On many in-line engines, it is not necessary to remove the manifolds.)

7. Remove the rocker-arm cover or covers.

8. On engines with ball-stud-supported rocker arms, remove the rocker arms and pushrods at this time. If they are left

Figure 7 Checking valve-tappet clearance on the Ford 2,000-cc engine. *(Ford Motor Company.)*

on, the nuts should be loosened so that the rocker arms can be moved aside and the pushrods removed. Pushrods should be placed in a rack in proper order. Then, they can be put back into the same spot from which they were removed.

9. On engines with rocker arms supported on shafts, remove the shaft assembly or assemblies (■1-2-22) and then remove the pushrods in order.

10. Remove the head bolts. Take the head off the engine.

11. Remove the valves and springs from the head (keeping them in proper order so that they can be put back into their proper positions).

NOTE: If a valve-stem end has mushroomed, the valve cannot be pulled out by hand. The mushroom must be removed, as explained in ■1-2-24. Otherwise, if you try to pull the valve, you can damage or break the valve guide.

12. Check valves and valve seats. Clean the valve heads and stems on a wire wheel. Grind the valve seats and reface valves as necessary. Check valve seating. Reface and chamfer valve-stem ends if necessary. If you are installing new valves of the coated type, do not reface them. Refacing or lapping coated valves removes the protective coating and greatly shortens valve and seat life.

13. Check rocker arms for wear. Service or replace them as necessary.

14. Check valve guides for wear. Clean, replace, or knurl and ream for same-size valve stem if necessary. Or ream for a larger-diameter valve stem.

15. Replace valves and springs in head.

16. Install head, pushrods, rocker arms, rocker-arm cover, and other parts removed during head removal.

17. Check and adjust valve-stem clearance as necessary.

■ 1-2-20 Removing, Cleaning, and Replacing Cylinder Heads

On some engines, the manifolds must be removed before the cylinder heads can be taken off (■1-2-33). On other engines, the manifolds may be left in place.

1. REMOVING THE CYLINDER HEAD Follow the general instructions in ■1-2-19, for removing the cylinder head. Slightly loosen all cylinder-head bolts first to ease the tension on the head. Then remove the bolts. If the head sticks, carefully pry it loose. Do not pry hard. Do not insert the pry bar too far between the head and block. This could mar the mating surfaces and lead to leaks. Lift the head off and place it in a head-holding fixture.

NOTE: Never remove a cylinder head from a hot engine. Wait until the engine cools. If the head is removed hot, it can be distorted so that it cannot be used again.

2. CLEANING THE CYLINDER HEAD After the valves and other parts are removed (as explained later), clean and inspect the cylinder head. Clean carbon from the combustion chamber and valve ports. Use a wire brush driven by an air or electric drill motor. Keep the wire brush away from valve seats because it could scratch the seating surfaces. Scratched seats can cause poor valve seating and serious trouble. Blow out all dust with an air hose.

Clean gasket surfaces with a flat scraper. Be very careful not to scratch the gasket surface. All traces of old gasket material and sealer should be removed.

Remove dirt and grease from the cylinder head. Then clean the water jackets and passages by soaking the head in a boil tank. Flush the water jackets as recommended by the manufacturer of the cleaning agent.

3. INSPECTING THE CYLINDER HEAD As you remove the cylinder head, examine the gasket and mating surface for traces of leakage or cracks. A blown gasket or coolant leakage could result from a warped head or improper gasket installation. In the head, cracks usually occur between valve seats. If they are not too bad, they can often be repaired by cold welding. First, drill a small hole in the crack and thread it. Screw in the threaded rod and cut it off. Repeat until the crack is completely treated. Make sure to get to both ends of the crack to relieve the stress that caused the crack. Sometimes it is desirable to install a seat insert when the crack runs into the valve seat. This is done by making an undercut in the head and pressing in the insert (■1-2-29).

Clean and inspect valve guides. Note the condition of valve seats and ball studs (on heads using them). We cover servicing of valve guides, ball studs, and seats later.

Check the cylinder head for cracks, warpage, and rough gasket surfaces. If cracks are suspected, have the head checked with Magna-Flux equipment.

Warpage is detected by laying a straightedge against the gasket surface of the head (Fig. 8). Check crosswise and lengthwise. One specification calls for not more than 0.005 inch (0.137 mm) maximum out of straight. More than this requires either a new head or machining the head so that the gasket surface is back to straight again.

Check the gasket surface of the head for nicks or rough spots. These can be removed with a fine-cut mill file.

NOTE: If one head from a V-8 engine requires machining to remove gasket-surface roughness, then the other head should be machined a like amount. Otherwise, uniform compression and manifold alignment will be lost. Also, removing metal from the gasket surface lowers the head with respect to the intake manifold. Therefore, a compensating amount may have to be machined from the manifold to restore alignment.

4. REPLACING THE CYLINDER HEAD Reassemble the cylinder head so that valve springs, rocker arms, and other parts are in place. Then install the head, as follows. Always use a new gasket.

Before installing the head, check the cylinder block. Make

Figure 8 Checking the cylinder head for warpage with a straightedge and feeler gauge. *(TRW Inc.)*

sure the gasket surface is flat and in good condition. Make sure all traces of gasket material are removed from the block. Bolt holes in the block (where present) should be cleaned out. Cylinder-block studs (where present), should be in good condition. Cylinder-head bolts should be cleaned with a wire brush or wheel. Cylinder-block studs (where present) can be cleaned with a thread chaser if the threads are damaged.

Use care when handling the gasket. If it is of the lacquered type, do not chip the lacquer. If the block has studs, put the gasket into place, right side up. Some are marked "TOP" so that you know which side goes up. Also, some are marked "FRONT" so that you know which end goes to the front. Use gasket cement only if specified by the manufacturer. For example, one manufacturer says to use cement on steel gaskets but not on composition steel-asbestos gaskets.

If the block does not have studs, use two pilot pins set into two bolt holes to ensure gasket alignment. Then lower the head into position. Substitute bolts for pilot pins (if used). Run on the nuts or bolts finger tight.

NOTE: Make sure that all bolt holes in the block have been cleaned. If they are not clean and the bolts bottom on the foreign material, the head will not be tight.

Use a torque wrench to tighten the nuts or bolts. They must be tightened in the proper sequence and to the proper tension. If they are not, head or block distortion, gasket leakage, or bolt failure may occur. Refer to the sequence chart for the engine being serviced and note the torque called for. Each bolt should be tightened in two or more steps. In other words, the complete circuit should be made at least twice, with each bolt or nut being drawn down little by little. After engine assembly is completed, the engine should be run until it is warm. Then the tensions should be checked again. Also, some engines using aluminum heads must be turned off and allowed to cool. Then the tensions should be checked again.

Some torque specifications call for clean, dry threads. Others call for lightly lubricated threads. Antiseize or sealing compounds are often used on bolts in aluminum blocks.

NOTE: If the rocker arms are in place, tighten the bolts slowly. This gives the hydraulic valve lifters time to bleed down to their operating length. If the bolts are tightened too rapidly, excessive pressure will be put on the lifters. They could be damaged, and the pushrods could be bent. On most engines, the head bolts cannot be tightened if the rocker arms are in place.

On overhead-valve cylinder heads with the rocker arms and shaft in place, make sure that the pushrods are in position. That is, make sure the lower ends of the pushrods are in the valve-lifter sockets.

■ **1-2-21 Ball-Stud Service** If a ball stud is loose in the cylinder head, has damaged threads, or has begun to pull out, it should be replaced. The old stud is removed with a special puller. The stud hole is then reamed to a larger size to take the oversize stud. For example, Chevrolet supplies 0.003- and 0.013-inch (0.0763 and 0.330 mm) oversize studs. If the 0.003-inch oversize stud is to be installed, the special 0.003-inch oversize reamer must be used.

NOTE: Always ream the stud hole oversize before installing an oversize stud. Otherwise, you may crack the head.

To install the new stud, use the special tool and drive the stud down into place. When the tool is firmly driven down to the cylinder head, the stud is in the correct position.

NOTE: Some replacement studs are threaded. On these, the stud hole must be tapped to take the stud.

■ **1-2-22 Servicing Rocker-Arm Assemblies** There are two methods of attaching the rocker arms to the cylinder head. In one method, the rocker arms are mounted on a common shaft. In the other, the rocker arms are mounted individually on separate studs. The rocker arms move on ball pivots instead of a shaft.

There are several variations of the shaft-mounted arrangement. Figure 9 shows one of these. With this design, remove the rocker arms by first taking out the shaft-locking plug. Then slide the shaft out from the five supporting shaft struts on the head. In another design, the shaft is removed with the rocker arms on it. First remove the five bolts that hold the five shaft support brackets and shaft on the head. Then slip the rocker arms, brackets, and spacers off the shaft. On a different design

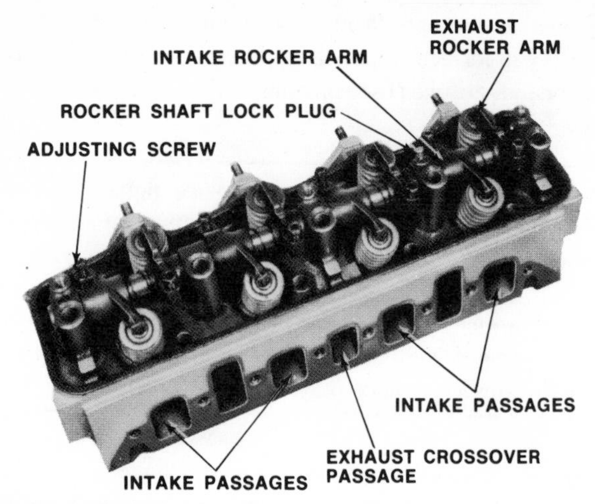

Figure 9 Cylinder-head assembly. *(Chrysler Corporation.)*

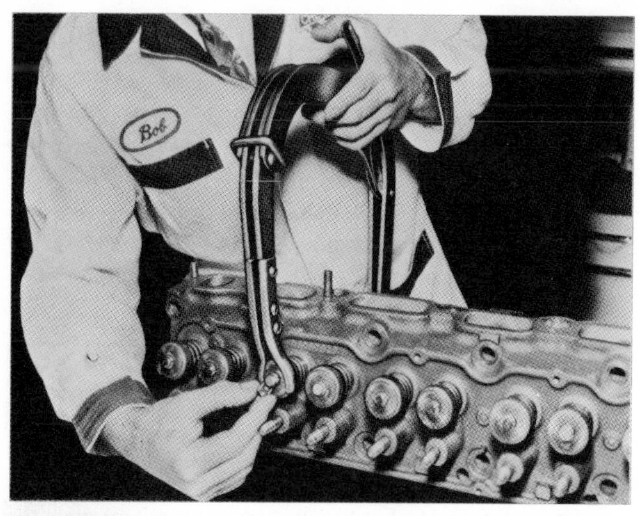

Figure 10 Using a valve-spring compressor on the valve assemblies in a cylinder head. *(Chevrolet Motor Division of General Motors Corporation.)*

there are four shaft supports. Also, the end rocker arms are held in place by washers and cotter pins. Several other variations can be found on different engines.

On engines with independently mounted ball-pivot rocker arms (Fig. 5), remove the rocker arm by taking off the adjusting nuts. The rocker-arm studs in the head can be replaced if they have become loose or if the stud threads are damaged (■1-2-21).

After rocker arms are removed, they should be inspected for wear or damage. Rocker arms with bushings can be rebushed, if the old bushings are worn. On some rocker arms, the valve ends, if worn, can be ground down on the valve-refacing machine. Excessively worn rocker arms should be discarded.

When reinstalling rocker arms and shafts on the cylinder head, make sure that the oilholes (in shafts so equipped) are on the underside. Otherwise, they will not feed oil to the rocker arms. Be sure that all springs and rocker arms are in their original positions when the shafts are reattached to the head.

■ 1-2-23 Servicing Pushrods Pushrods should be inspected for wear at the ends. Roll the rods on a flat surface to check for straightness. Replace defective rods. On certain engines, rods have one tip hardened and are marked with strips of color. The pushrod should be installed so that the hardened end is toward the rocker arm. Always make sure that the lower end of the pushrod is seated in the valve-lifter socket.

Special short-length pushrods are available. These may be used in engines after valves and valve seats have been reground. Regrinding may result in excessive lengthening of the valve train since the valve stem rises higher out of the cylinder head. Therefore, the plunger may almost bottom in the hydraulic valve lifter. Using a shorter pushrod corrects this condition (see ■1-2-15). Instead, some engine manufacturers recommend grinding off the end of the valve stem. This procedure brings the valve-train length back to normal after a valve and valve seat grinding job (■1-2-16).

■ 1-2-24 Removing Valves After the cylinder head is removed and interfacing rocker-arm mechanisms are removed from it, the valves should be taken out. Valves and valve parts must not be interchanged. Each valve, with its own spring, retainer, and lock, should be reassembled in the same valve port from which it was removed. For this reason, a special valve rack is recommended. Likewise, each rocker arm and pushrod should be replaced in its original position.

> **NOTE:** Before removing a valve from the cylinder head, examine the valve stem. Look for burrs at the retainer-lock grooves and for mushrooming on the end. Burrs and mushrooming must be removed with a file or small grinding stone in a drill motor. If they are not removed, the valve guide could be badly damaged or broken when the valve is forced out. This would mean extra work in replacing the valve guide.

1. L-HEAD ENGINES To remove the valves, first remove any manifolds that may be in the way. Then use a valve-spring compressor to compress the valve spring. This releases the retainer lock so that the lock and the retainer can come off. Do not drop the lock down into the crankcase. It could jam in moving parts and ruin the engine. Then remove the spring and take out the valve.

2. OVERHEAD-VALVE ENGINES After everything else is removed from the head, the valves can be removed. This requires a spring compressor, as shown in Fig. 10. As the handle is pressed, the spring is compressed. This allows removal of the retainer lock. Then the spring can be released so that the retainer and spring can be removed.

Valve-stem seals or shields (Fig. 11) should always be carefully inspected and replaced if they are found to be worn or damaged. Many manufacturers recommend installation of new seals or shields whenever valves or valve springs are removed.

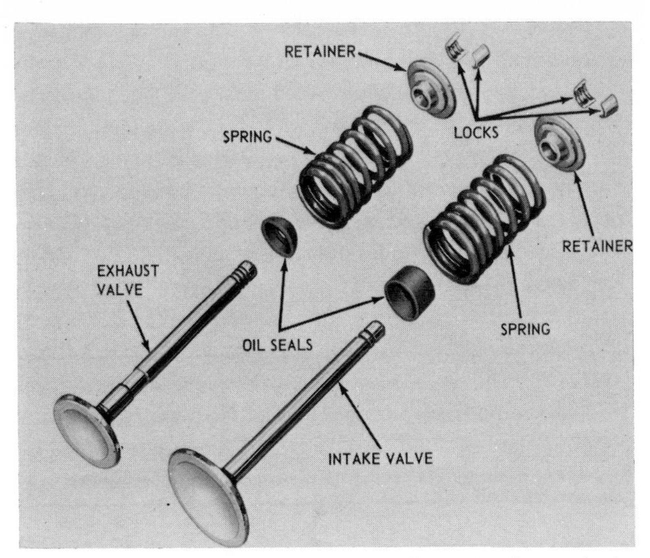

Figure 11 Exhaust and intake valves and associated parts in the proper assembly relationship. *(Chrysler Corporation.)*

NOTE: Some mechanics use a 6-inch (152.4 mm) length of ¾-inch (19.05 mm) water pipe instead of a spring compression to break loose the retainer locks. The pipe is centered on the retainer and hit on the end with a hammer. This forces the retainer down against the spring tension enough to break the retainer locks loose.

On many models, the valve springs, stem seals, or shields can be replaced without removing the cylinder head. For example, on the engine using the ball-pivot-type rocker arm, a special spring compressor is installed in place of the rocker arm to compress the spring. To hold up the valve while the spring is being compressed, compressed air from the shop air supply is introduced into the cylinder through the spark-plug hole (Fig. 12). A special air-hose adaptor, which can be screwed into the spark-plug hole, is required. The air pressure will hold the valve closed while the spring is compressed. If the air pressure does not hold the valve closed, then the valve is stuck or damaged. The cylinder head should be removed for a closer look.

NOTE: Be prepared for the crankshaft to rotate slightly when the air is applied. The air pressure may push the piston to BDC.

On some engines with the rocker arms mounted on a shaft, it is possible to bleed down the hydraulic valve lifter. To do this, you apply pressure with a special tool. Then you can remove the pushrod, and move the rocker arm to one side. With the rocker arm wired out of the way use a valve-spring compressor to compress the spring. Then you can remove the retainer, spring, and seal. Air pressure must be applied to the cylinder to hold the valve on its seat when the spring is compressed.

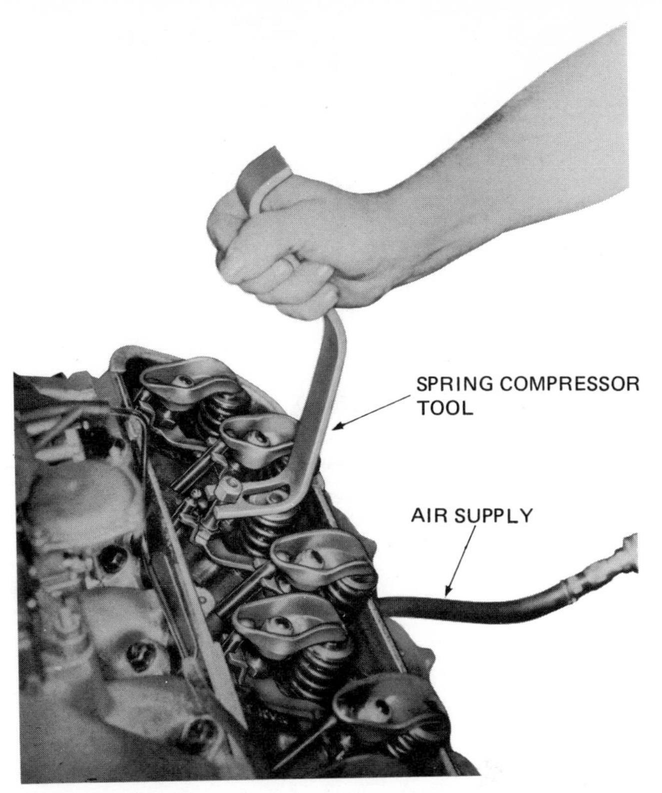

Figure 12 Compressing a valve spring while the valve is held closed with air pressure. *(Chevrolet Motor Division of General Motors Corporation.)*

■ **1-2-25 Inspecting Valves** As you take the valves out of the head, inspect each one. Decide whether it can be serviced and used again. (See ■ 1-2-1 to 1-2-8.) If the valve looks good enough to use again, put it into the proper place in the valve rack. If it looks too bad to be cleaned up for further service, discard it. Put a new valve into the appropriate place in the valve rack.

■ **1-2-26 Servicing Valves** Once all the valves are out of the cylinder head, remove them one by one from the valve rack. Clean the carbon from each valve with a wire wheel. (Wear goggles to protect your eyes from flying particles of metal and dirt.) Polish the stems, if necessary, with a fine emery cloth. Do not take off more than the dirty coating on the surface of the stems.

NOTE: Do not scratch the valve-seating surface or valve stem with the wire brush or emery cloth.

As you clean the valves, reexamine them to make sure all are usable. Small pits or burns in the valve-seating face can be removed by grinding the valve. Larger pits or burns cannot be removed. New valves will be required. Figure 13 shows specific parts of the valve to be examined. Some engine manufacturers recommend the use of a runout gauge to check for a bent valve stem. Eccentricity can also be checked in the valve

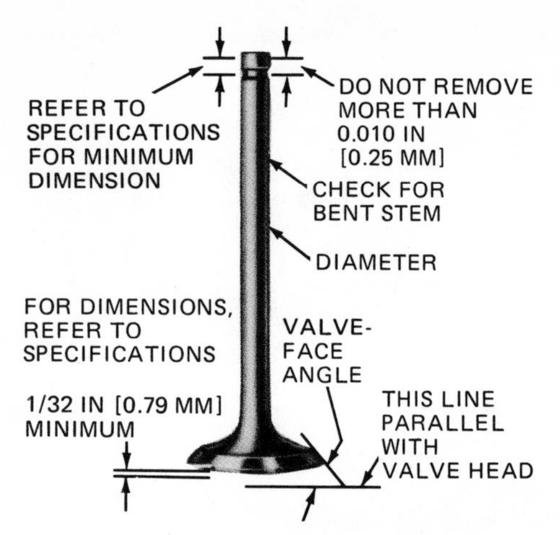

Figure 13 Valve parts to be checked. On the valve shown, the stem is hardened at the end. Therefore, not more than 0.010 inch (0.25 mm) should be removed. *(Ford Motor Company.)*

grinder. If the runout, or eccentricity, is excessive, discard the valve.

After cleaning the valves, replace then temporarily in their valve guides to check for guide wear. This procedure and valve-guide service are covered in ■1-2-28.

1. REFACING OR GRINDING VALVES If the valves are good enough to reuse, the next step is to grind or reface them. This requires a valve-refacing machine. The valve refacer has a grinding wheel, coolant delivery system, and chuck that holds the valve for grinding. Set the chuck to grind the valve face at the specified angle. [This angle must just match the valve-seat angle or be the interference angle recommended by the engine manufacturer (Fig. 2).] Then put the valve into the chuck and tighten it. The valve should be deep in the chuck, so that not too much sticks out. Otherwise, the valve can slip during grinding.

To start the operation, align the coolant feed so that it feeds coolant on the grinding wheel. Then start the machine. Move the lever to carry the valve face across the grinding wheel. The first cut should be a light one. If this cut removes metal from only one-half or one-third of the face, the valve may not be centered in the chuck. Or the valve stem may be bent, in which case the valve should be discarded. Cuts, after the first one, should remove only enough metal to true up the surface and remove pits. Do not take heavy cuts. If so much metal must be removed that the margin is lost, discard the valve. (See Fig. 14.) Loss of the margin causes the valve to run hot, and it will soon fail. If new valves are required, they will not need to be refaced. Seating should be checked, however, as already explained. Never reface or lap coated valves!

> **NOTE:** Follow the operating instructions of the valve refacer manufacturer. Dress the grinding wheel as necessary with the diamond-tipped dressing tool. As the diamond is moved across the rotating face of the grinding wheel, it cleans and aligns the grinding face.

2. REFACING VALVE-STEM TIPS If the tip of a valve stem is rough or worn unevenly, it can be ground lightly. Use the special attachment furnished with the valve-refacing machine. The attachment allows you to swing the valve slightly and rotate it. In this way, the tip can be ground to produce a slightly crowned, or rounded, end. One recommendation is to grind off as much from the stem as you ground off the valve faces. That way, you make up for the amount the valve sinks into the seat owing to face grinding.

> **NOTE:** The ends of some valve stems are hardened. These should have no more than a few thousandths of an inch ground off them (see Fig. 13). Excessive grinding exposes soft metal so that the stem wears rapidly in service.

■ **1-2-27 Replacing Valves** As the valves are refaced and cleaned, they should be returned to the valve rack. They are now ready for installation in the cylinder head. First, however, the valve guides and valve seats must be serviced (■1-2-28 and 1-2-29). Also, the other components of the valve train—pushrods, rocker arms, and valve lifters—must be checked and serviced as necessary.

The valve-assembly sequence for an overhead-valve engine is shown in Fig. 11. New shields or seals should be installed if the old ones are worn or if the manufacturer recommends them. To avoid damage to some types of seals, special plastic caps can be placed over the ends of the valve stems. The seals will then slip on without being damaged by the sharp edges of the stem end or lock grooves.

> **NOTE:** If valves and seats have been ground, the effective length of the valve spring will not be great enough. In order to restore normal spring tension, spring shims may be required.

Using a spring compressor (Fig. 10), install the springs, spring retainers, and locks. Measure the installed spring height.

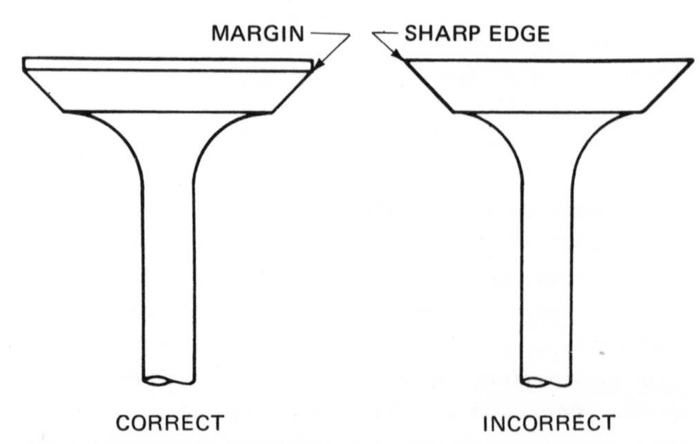

Figure 14 Correct and incorrect valve-face grinding. The valve to the right, having no margin, would soon fail. *(TRW, Inc.)*

If the spring height is excessive, a spring shim is required. It is installed between the spring and cylinder head.

The procedure of installing the spring and then measuring the installed spring height is slow and can ruin stem seals if the spring has to be removed to install shims. Some mechanics do a faster job, as follows. Put the valve in the guide and install the retainer and locks. Pull the stem down until the retainer hits the cylinder head. Tap the end of the stem with a plastic hammer to seat the locks. Then pull the valve up to close it. Measure the distance between the head and retainer. Compare it with the spring height specified. Add shims if necessary to reduce the height to specifications.

NOTE: Do not install a shim that would reduce the spring height below the specified minimum. This results in excessive spring pressure and rapid wear of valve train parts.

Install the valve springs with the proper side against the cylinder head. Generally, the close-spaced coils go next to the head (on springs with differential spacing of coils). Also, a damper spring (when used) must be placed inside the valve spring in an exact relationship with the spring coils. One typical example is that the coil end of the damper spring should be 135 degrees counterclockwise from the coil end of the valve spring.

■ 1-2-28 Servicing Valve Guides

The valve guide must be clean and in good condition for normal valve seating. It must be serviced before the valve seats are ground if grinding is required. As a first step, the valve guide should be cleaned with a wire brush or adjustable-blade cleaner. Then, the guide should be checked for wear. If it is worn, it requires service. The type of service depends on whether the guide is replaceable or integral. If it is replaceable, the old guide should be pressed out. Then a new guide should be installed and reamed to size. If the guide is integral it can be serviced in either of two ways: (1) by reaming it to a larger size and installing a valve with an oversize stem and (2) by knurling and reaming it. All these services are described below.

1. TESTING VALVE GUIDES FOR WEAR One method of testing valve guides uses a dial indicator. With the valve in place, attach the dial indicator so that its contact button just touches the edge of the valve head. A special tool is used sometimes to hold the valve off its seat. Then rotate the valve and move it sideways to determine the amount of guide wear. On some engines, the recommendation is to seat the valve and measure stem end movement with the dial indicator.

Another method of testing the valve guide is to insert a tapered pilot into the guide until the pilot is tight. Then, pencil-mark the pilot at the top of the guide and remove it. Measure the pilot diameter ½ inch (12.7 mm) below the pencil mark. This gives the guide diameter, which can then be compared with the valve-stem diameter.

Neither of these two methods will accurately show valve-guide eccentricity and bellmouthing, however. The valve guide may wear bellmouthed or oval-shaped because the valve tends to wobble as it opens and closes. A small-hole gauge will detect oval or bellmouth wear. It is used as follows: The split ball is adjusted until it is a light drag fit at the point being checked. Then, the split ball is measured with a micrometer. By checking the guide at various points, any eccentricity will be detected.

2. REMOVING VALVE GUIDES (REPLACEABLE TYPE) A valve-guide puller is used for removing an old valve guide. As the nut is turned on the screw, the guide is pulled out. On some L-head engines, the guide can be driven down into the valve-spring compartment. On I-head engines, the valve guide can be pressed out of the head with a press.

3. INSTALLING VALVE GUIDES (REPLACEABLE TYPE) New valve guides can be installed with a special driver, or replacer. (On I-head engines, valve guides can be installed with a press.) Valve guides must be installed to the proper depth in the block or head. Then they must be reamed to size. This is usually done in two steps: a rough ream and then a second, or final, finishing ream.

4. KNURLING THE VALVE GUIDE In the knurling operation, a knurling tool is run down through the valve guide. One type of knurling tool has a small wheel set in a rod, or arbor. It is rotated by a slow-speed electric drill as it is pushed down into the guide. This action causes the wheel to form a spiral groove in the guide. The metal displaced from the groove is pushed inward. Then the guide is reamed. The procedure usually takes several steps: for example, first knurl, first ream, second knurl, final ream. When the job is finished, the valve guide should be the right size to provide a good fit for the valve stem. Also, the grooves that are left are filled with oil. This provides better lubrication of the valve stem.

5. CHECKING CONCENTRICITY WITH THE VALVE SEAT After the valve guide is serviced and checked for size, check its concentricity with the valve seat. Usually, the seat is ground as part of the service job (■1-2-29).

■ 1-2-29 Valve Seat Service

For effective valve seating and sealing, the valve face must be concentric with the valve stem. Also, the valve guide must be concentric with the valve face. In addition, the valve-face angle must match the valve seat angle (or have an interference angle). Thus, as a first step in valve seat service, the valve guides must be cleaned and serviced (■ 1-2-28).

Valve seats are of two types. The integral type is actually the cylinder block or head. The insert type is a ring of special metal set into the block or head. Replacing seat inserts and grinding seats are described below.

1. REPLACING VALVE SEAT INSERTS A valve seat insert may be badly worn. Or it may have been ground down on previous occasions so that there is insufficient metal for another grind. In either case, it must be replaced. The old seat must be removed with a special puller. If a puller is not available, the insert is punch-marked on two opposite sides and an electric drill used to drill holes almost through the insert. Then, a chisel and hammer can be used to break the insert into halves so that it can be removed. Care must be taken that the counterbore is not damaged. If the new insert fits too loosely, the counterbore must be rebored oversize. Then an oversize insert is installed. The new insert should be chilled in dry ice for 15 minutes to shrink it so that it can be driven into place. Then, the valve seat should be ground.

2. GRINDING VALVE SEATS Two types of valve seat grinders are used: concentric and eccentric grinders. The concentric grinder rotates a grinding stone of the proper shape on the valve seat (Fig. 15). The stone is kept concentric with the valve seat by a pilot installed in the valve guide (Fig. 15). This means that the valve guide must be cleaned and serviced (■1-2-28) before the valve seat is ground. In the unit shown in Fig. 15, the stone is automatically lifted about once a revolution. This permits the stone to clear itself of grit and dust by centrifugal force. After the valve seat is ground, it may be too wide. It must be narrowed with upper and lower grinding stones to grind away the upper and lower edges of the seat. A typical valve seat is shown in Fig. 16. A valve seat width gauge or a steel scale can be used to measure valve seat width.

In the eccentric valve seat grinder, the grinding stone is offset from the center of the valve seat. It makes only line contact with the valve seat. As the stone revolves, its center rotates slowly on an eccentric shaft. The slow rotation permits the line contact at which grinding is taking place to progress evenly around the entire valve seat. The eccentric valve seat grinder also pilots in the valve guide.

NOTE: Follow the operating instructions furnished with the valve seat grinder set. The grinding stone must be dressed frequently with the diamond-tipped dressing tool.

3. CHECKING VALVE GUIDES AND SEATS FOR CONCENTRICITY After the valve guides are serviced and valve seats ground, the concentricity of both can be checked with a valve-seat dial gauge. The gauge is mounted in the valve guide and is rotated so that the indicator finger sweeps around the valve seat. Any eccentricity (or runout) of the seat registers on the gauge dial.

4. TESTING VALVE SEATING Contact between the valve face and seat may be tested as follows: Mark lines with a soft pencil about 1/4 inch (6.35 mm) apart around the entire valve face. Then put the valve into place and, with light pressure, rotate it half a turn to the left and then half a turn to the right. If this removes the pencil marks, the seating is good.

The seating can also be checked with prussian blue. Coat the valve face lightly with prussian blue. Put the valve on its seat and turn it with light pressure. If blue appears all the way around the valve seat, the valve seat and guide are concentric with each other. Now, check the concentricity of the valve face with the valve stem by removing the prussian blue from the valve and seat. Lightly coat the seat with prussian blue and then lightly rotate the valve on the seat. If blue transfers all the way around the valve face, the valve face and stem are concentric. This is a check similar to the runout check.

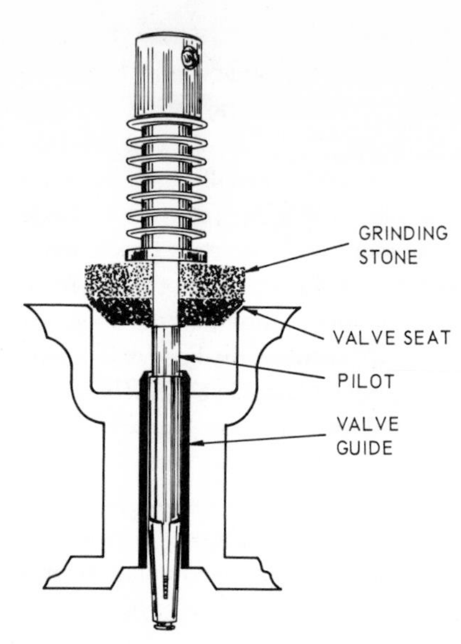

Figure 15 Pilot on which grinding stone rotates. The pilot keeps the stone concentric with the valve seat. *(Black and Decker Manufacturing Company.)*

■ 1-2-30 Valve-Spring Inspection

Valve springs should be checked for proper tension and squareness. A valve spring tester checks tension. To check for squareness, stand the spring, closed-coil end down, on a flat surface. Hold a steel square next to it. Rotate the spring slowly to see if the top coil moves away from the square more than 1/16 inch (1.587 mm) (Ford). If the spring is excessively out of square, or has lost tension, discard it. One manufacturer's recommendation is to replace all valve springs during the complete valve job. Then good spring action is assured.

■ 1-2-31 Camshaft Service

Camshaft removal varies somewhat from engine to engine. It is less complex in overhead-camshaft engines. In an overhead-valve engine the general procedure begins with removal of the radiator. Then take the pulley from the crankshaft and remove the gear or timing-chain cover. Detach the camshaft thrust plate (where present). Take off the camshaft sprocket and chain (where used). Remove the distributor or oil pump (whichever has the driven gear) so that the gear will not interfere with camshaft removal.

Remove the pushrods so that the valve lifters can be raised up out of the way. Now, the camshaft is free and can be pulled forward and out. Be very careful to keep the journals and cams from scratching the camshaft bearings. Support the rear of the camshaft as it is pulled out so that the bearings are not damaged.

> **NOTE:** Supporting the camshaft is easier said than done. One most engines, it is necessary to remove the crankshaft in order to get to the camshaft and support it.

1. CHECKING THE CAMSHAFT Check the camshaft for alignment by rotating the camshaft in V blocks and using a dial indicator. Journal diameters should be checked with a micrometer, and the bearings with a telescope gauge. The two dimensions can be compared to determine whether bearings are worn and require replacement. Pits or wear on the journals or cam lobes require camshaft replacement.

2. CHECKING FOR CAM WEAR Figure 17 shows normal and abnormal cam wear. Normal cam wear is close to the center of the cam, as shown. The reason for this is that the cam is slightly tapered in most engines. Also, the lifter foot is slightly spherical, or crowned, in shape. If wear shows across the full width of the cam, a new camshaft is required. The lifter should also be checked (■1-2-32).

The cam lobe lift can be checked with the camshaft in or out of the engine. A dial indicator is used to check the camshaft in the engine. The setup also can be used to measure the lobe lift with the camshaft out of the engine.

3. REPLACING CAMSHAFT BEARINGS A camshaft bearing installation tool is required to replace the camshaft bearings. On some tools, the puller bar is threaded and a nut is turned to remove the bearings. On others, a hammer is used to drive against the bar and force the bearings out. When a screw-type puller is used to remove center bearings in a V-8 and an in-line engine, you must work from one end of the block and then the other. The two end bearings are removed with a different tool. It is used to drive the end bearings inward so that they can be forced into the block and then taken out. When installing new bearings, the end bearings must be driven in first. These bearings serve as pilots for pulling new bearings into place with the screw-type tool.

Some engine manufacturers recommend a driver-type remover and replacer bar. The bar is put into position, and a hammer is used to drive out the bearings, one at a time. The same tool is used to drive the new bearings into place. Oil holes in the new bearings should align with the oil holes in the block. Also, new bearings should be staked in place if the old bearings are staked.

4. TIMING THE VALVES The timing gears, sprockets and chain, or sprockets and toothed belt, are marked for proper positions and correct valve timing. To get to these markings, however, the front of the engine must be partly disassembled. Some engines have another marking system for checking valve timing. This marking is on the flywheel or vibration damper near the ignition-timing markings. When this marking is visible or registers with a pointer, a designated valve should be just opening or should have opened a specified amount. Valve action is observed by removing the valve cover.

5. TIMING GEAR AND CHAIN Gear runout can be checked by mounting a dial indicator on the block. The indicating finger should rest on the side of the gear. Runout will then be indicated as the gear is rotated. Gear backlash is measured by inserting a narrow feeler gauge between the meshing teeth. Excessive runout or backlash requires gear replacement. Excessive slack in the timing chain indicates a worn chain and possible worn sprockets.

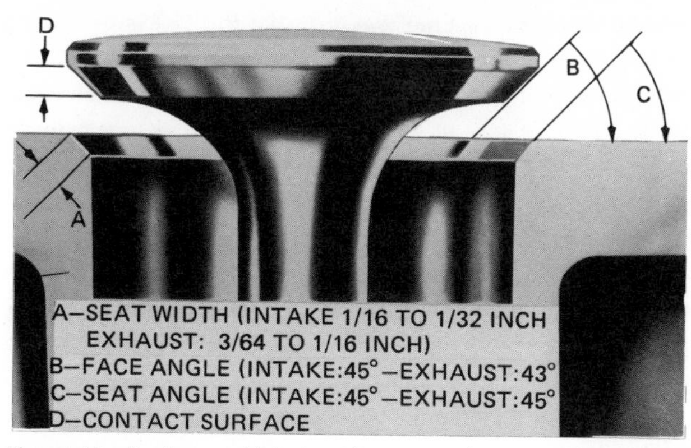

Figure 16 Angles to which the valve seat and upper and lower cuts must be ground on one engine. The dimensions and angles vary with different engines. *(Chrysler Corporation.)*

■ 1-2-32 Valve Lifters

Solid and hydraulic valve lifters require different servicing procedures.

1. SOLID VALVE LIFTERS On some engines, the solid valve lifters are removed from the camshaft side. This procedure requires camshaft removal as a first step. In most engines, solid valve lifters are removed from the valve or pushrod side. As they are removed, the valve lifters should be kept in order so that they can be restored to the bores from which they were removed. On many engines, oversize valve lifters may be installed if the lifter bores have become worn. Before this is done, however, the lifter bores must be reamed oversize.

> **NOTE:** If the lifters have mushroomed on the bottom, they must be removed from the camshaft side.

2. HYDRAULIC VALVE LIFTERS On some engines, a leak-down test is used to determine the condition of the hy-

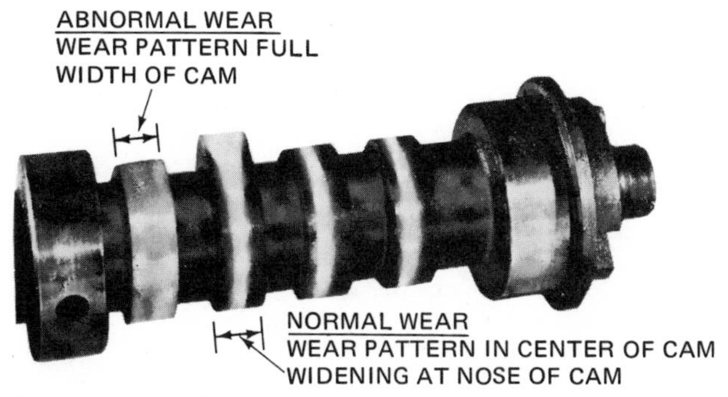

Figure 17 Normal and abnormal cam wear. *(Oldsmobile Division of General Motors Corporation.)*

draulic valve lifters. One way to make this test is to insert a feeler gauge between the rocker arm and valve stem. Then, note the time it takes for the valve lifter to leak enough oil to allow the valve to seat. As the valve seats, the feeler gauge becomes loose. This indicates the end of the test. If the leakdown time is too short, the valve lifter is defective.

A more accurate leak-down test is made with the valve lifter out of the engine and installed in a leak-down tester. With this tester, the time required for a uniform pressure (from the weight on the end of the lever) to force the lifter plunger to bottom is measured. If it is too short, the lifter is defective.

To remove the hydraulic valve lifters from some engines, the pushrod cover and rocker-arm assembly must be removed first. Then the pushrods are taken out. On some engines with shaft-mounted rocker arms, a rocker arm can be moved by compressing the spring so that the pushrod can be removed. Thus, the rocker-arm assembly does not have to be taken off.

Another type of valve-lifter-removing tool is inserted through the pushrod opening in the block and is seated firmly on the end of the valve lifter. The valve lifter is then removed through the pushrod opening.

3. SERVICING HYDRAULIC VALVE LIFTERS If a hydraulic valve lifter is defective, it usually is cheaper to replace it than to disassemble and service it. The labor required would probably cost more than the new lifter. However, if you prefer to spend the time, you can service the valve lifter as follows: Disassemble the lifter and clean all parts in solvent. If any part is defective, replace the lifter. On reassembly, fill the lifter with clean, light engine oil.

Work on only one valve lifter at a time so that you do not mix lifter parts. Also, make sure each lifter goes back into the bore from which it was removed.

NOTE: When servicing and handling hydraulic valve lifters, be extremely careful to keep everything clean. It takes only one tiny particle of dirt to cause a lifter to malfunction.

4. CHECKING THE VALVE LIFTER FOOT The foot or cam-lobe end of the valve lifter should be slightly spherical, or crowned. If it is worn or pitted, it can often be reground and reused. The crown is produced by rocking and rotating the lifter during finish-grind.

■ 1-2-33 Removing and Replacing Manifolds

Take the carburetor off. (Handle it with care to avoid damaging it or spilling gasoline from the float bowl.) Disconnect vacuum lines, exhaust pipes, emission control hoses, and any other pipe or wire connected to the manifolds. Remove the nuts or bolts and take the manifolds off.

When reinstalling manifolds, be sure all old gasket material has been removed from the manifolds and cylinder head. Use new gaskets. Tighten nuts or bolts to the proper tension and in the proper sequence.

NOTE: Some mechanics now are using plastic gasket compound (silicone rubber) that comes in a tube. It is squeezed out of the tube onto the gasket surfaces and it spreads to form the gasket.

SECTION 1-3 Servicing Connecting Rods, Pistons, and Rings

This section covers the servicing procedures on connecting rods, pistons, and piston rings. Other sections describe the servicing of valves, crankshafts, and cylinder blocks.

■ **1-3-1 Cleanliness** The major enemy of good engine-service work is dirt. A trace of dirt or abrasive on a cylinder wall or other working engine part can ruin an otherwise good service job. Before the engine is opened for a major service job, it should be cleaned to remove dirt and grease. All engine parts should be cleaned as they are removed and kept clean until reinstalled. As soon as a part is cleaned, it should be dried and a light coat of oil applied to bright surfaces to prevent rust.

■ **1-3-2 Checking Bearings with the Engine-Bearing Prelubricator** The engine-bearing prelubricator can be used to check for bearing wear before a service job is started. It is used with the oil pan off. Worn bearings pass much more oil than good bearings. This means that more oil gets on the cylinder walls and works up into the combustion chamber where it is burned. A normal bearing will leak between 20 and 150 drops of oil per minute when the prelubricator is used. If the bearing leaks more, it is worn. If it leaks less than 20 drops per minute, then either the bearing clearance is too small or the oil line to the bearing is stopped up.

> **NOTE:** When oilholes in the crankshaft and in the bearing align, considerable oil is forced through the bearing. This will give the appearance of excessive wear. In such a case, the crankshaft should be turned a few degrees to move the oilholes out of register.

■ **1-3-3 Preparing to Remove Rods** Connecting rods and pistons are removed from the engine as assemblies. On most engines, the piston-and-rod assemblies are removed from the top of the engine. The first step is to remove the cylinder head (■ 1-2-20). Cylinders should be examined for wear. If wear has taken place, there will be a ridge at the top of the cylinder. This ridge, called the "ring ridge," marks the upper limit of piston-ring travel. If the ring ridge is not removed, the top ring could jam under it as the piston is moved upward. This could break the rings of the piston-ring-groove lands (Fig. 1). Thus, the ridge, if present, must be removed.

A quick way to check for a ring ridge is to see if your fingernail catches under it. If your fingernail catches on the ring ridge, so will the piston rings. A more accurate check is to use an inside micrometer. Measure the diameter on the ring ridge and then immediately below it. If the difference is more than 0.004 inch (0.102 mm), remove the ring ridge.

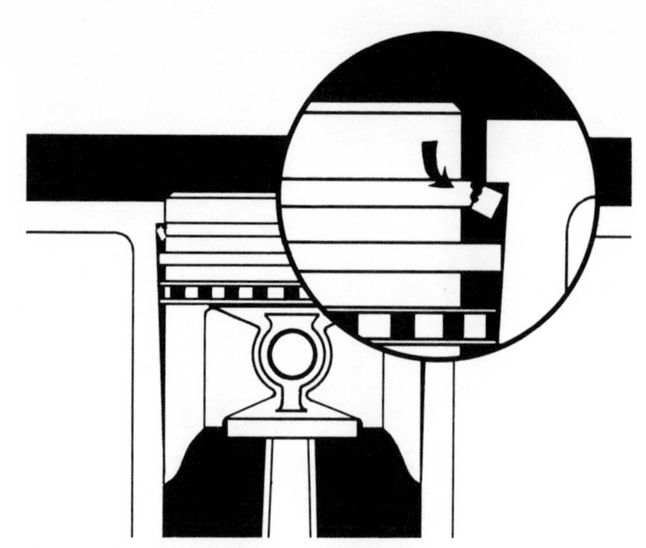

Figure 1 How a ring ridge caused by cylinder wear might break the ring if the piston is withdrawn without removing the ridge. *(Sealed Power Corporation.)*

■ **1-3-4 Removing the Ring Ridge** To remove a ring ridge, use a special ring ridge remover. With the piston near BDC, stuff cloths into the cylinder and install the ridge remover.

> **NOTE:** There are several different kinds of ridge removers. Be sure to read and follow the instructions carefully when you use a ridge remover.

Adjust the cutter blades to take off just enough metal to remove the ridge. Cover the other cylinders to keep cuttings from getting into them. Rotate the tool to cut the ridge away.

> **NOTE:** Turn the ridge remover by hand, not with an impact wrench! Do not remove too much metal. That is, do not undercut the top of the cylinder deeper than the material next to the ring ridge. Do not run the cutting tool above the cylinder. This would taper the edge.

Remove the tool, take the cloth out, and wipe the cylinder clean. Repeat the process for the other cylinders.

■ **1-3-5 Removing the Oil Pan** The oil pan must be removed, so that the connecting rods can be detached from the crankshaft. First, remove the drain plug to drain the engine oil. On many cars, the steering idler or other steering linkage must be removed. In such cases, note how the linkage is attached. Note the number and location of shims (if used). On some cars, the oil pan is easier to remove if the engine mounting bolts are removed and the engine is raised slightly. Other parts may require removal before the oil pan can be taken off. These include exhaust pipe, oil-level tube, brake-return spring, and starting motor.

Next, the nuts or bolts holding the oil pan to the engine cylinder block can be removed. Steady the pan as the last two nuts or bolts are removed so that it does not drop. If the oil pan strikes the crankshaft so that the pan does not come free, turn the crankshaft over a few degrees. If the oil pan does not break loose when the last bolt is out, tap the sides of the oil pan with a rubber mallet. If it still doesn't come loose, carefully force the claw or flat edge of a pry bar or scraper between the edge of the pan and the cylinder block. Try to get the flat edge on the pan side of the gasket to avoid scratching the block. Tap the pry bar with a hammer to help free the oil pan.

> **NOTE:** Many engines have metal reinforcements under the corner bolts of the oil pan. These reinforcements help seal around the rear main bearings and bottom of the timing cover. Do not loose these when you remove the bolts.

Clean the oil pan, oil screen, and oil pump thoroughly before replacing the oil pan. Make sure that the gasket material is scraped off the pan and block gasket surfaces. Then check the flatness of the oil pan gasket surfaces. Make sure that the bolt holes have not been dished in by overtightening of the bolts. The gasket surfaces can be straightened by laying the oil pan on a flat surface and tapping the gasket-surface flanges with a hammer.

Apply new gasket cement, if specified. Lay the gasket (or gaskets) in place on the oil pan. Be sure that the bolt holes in the gasket and oil pan line up. Install the oil pan and tighten the bolts or nuts to the proper tension.

> **NOTE:** Some oil pans are installed with plastic gasket material.

■ **1-3-6 Removing Piston-and-Rod Assemblies** After the preliminaries are out of the way, as noted in previous sections, remove the piston-and-rod assemblies, as follows.

> **NOTE:** Handle pistons and rods with care because they can be easily damaged. Never clamp a rod tightly in a vise. This can bend the rod and ruin it. Never clamp a piston in a vise. This can nick or break the piston. Do not allow the pistons to hit against each other or against other hard objects or bench surfaces. Distortion of the piston or nicks in the soft aluminum piston material may result from careless handling. These conditions will ruin the piston.

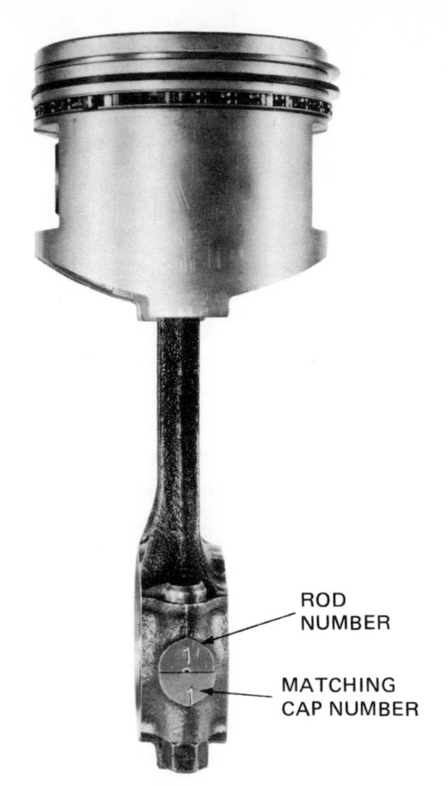

Figure 2 Piston-and-connecting-rod assembly. The numbers on the rod and rod cap indicate that the assembly is to be installed in the No. 1 cylinder. *(American Motors Corporation.)*

With the cylinder head and oil pan removed, crank the engine so that the piston of the No. 1 cylinder is near the bottom. Examine the rod and cap for identifying marks (Fig. 2). If none can be seen, use a small watercolor brush and a little white metal paint to make a "1" on the rod and rod cap. Marks are needed to make sure that the parts go back into the cylinders from which they were removed. Each piston should also be numbered.

NOTE: Do not mark the rods and rod caps with metal numbering dies or a center punch and hammer. This can distort and ruin the rods and caps.

Remove the rod nuts and caps. Slide the rod-and-piston assembly up into the cylinder away from the crankshaft. Use guide sleeves on the rod bolts. These prevent the bolt threads from scratching the crankshaft journals. Also, the long handle permits easy removal and replacement of the piston-and-rod assembly. Short pieces of rubber hose, split and slipped over the rod bolts, will also protect the crankshaft journals.

Turn the crankshaft as you go from rod to rod so that you can reach the rod nuts. When all rods are detached and the assemblies have been moved up to the top of the cylinders, remove the assemblies. Lay the assemblies out in order on a cloth spread out on a bench or set them in a wooden piston box. Make sure all rods, rod caps, and pistons are marked with the number of the cylinder from which they were removed.

■ 1-3-7 Separating Rods and Pistons

There are five basic piston-rod-bushing arrangements, as shown in Fig. 3. The rods and pistons are separated by removing the piston pins. If the pin is free-floating (Fig. 3*A*), remove the retainer ring and slide the pin out. If the pin is locked to the connecting rod or piston with a lock bolt (Fig. 3*B, C, E*), loosen the lock bolt and slide the pin out.

If the pin is a press fit in the connecting rod (Fig. 3*D*), the pin must be pressed out. This requires a special tool. The tool is put together and then a press is used to push the pin out.

NOTE: Be careful to avoid nicking or scratching the pistons or piston rings.

■ 1-3-8 Attaching Connecting Rods and Pistons

After connecting rods and pistons have been cleaned, serviced, and checked, lay them out on a clean bench in their engine order. Make sure parts match as in the original assembly. The pistons should then be attached to the rods with the piston pins, as follows. Make sure the piston is in the correct position on the rod as the two are attached. On many engines, the piston notches face to the front of the engine. Also, the rod oilhole faces toward the inside of the block.

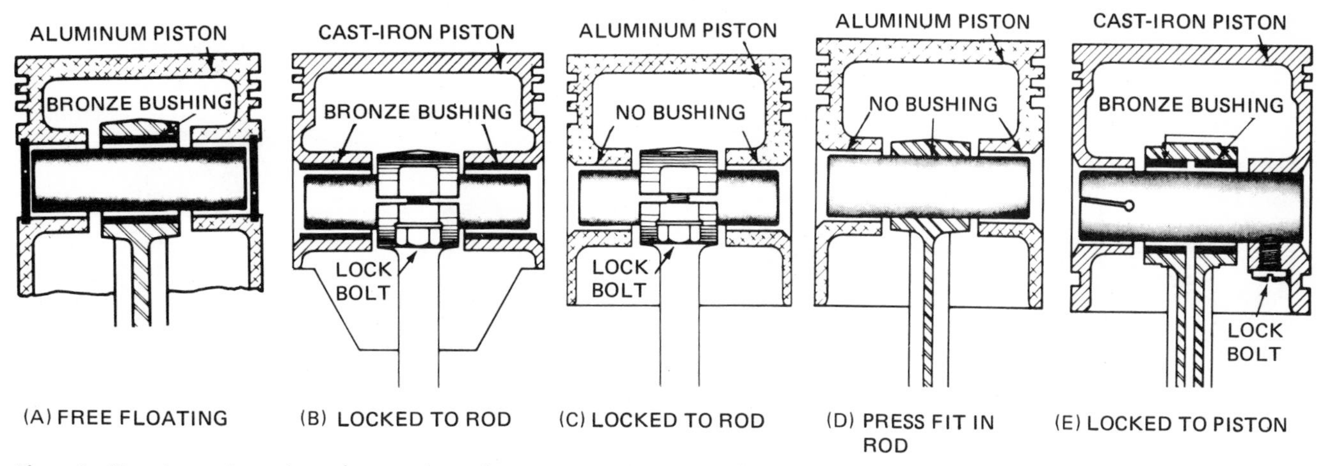

Figure 3 Five-piston, piston-pin, and connecting-rod arrangements. *(Sunnen Products Company.)*

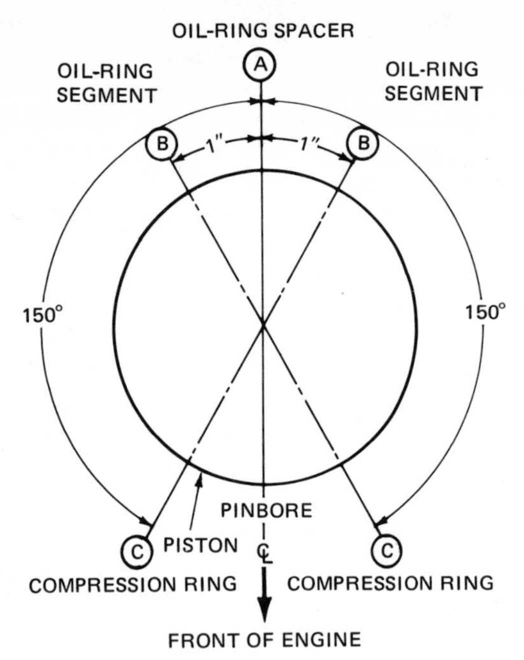

Figure 4 Proper arrangement of ring gaps, as specified by one automotive manufacturer. *(Ford Motor Company.)*

To attach the piston and connecting rod where a lock bolt is used, simply put the pin through the piston and rod. Then tighten the lock bolt to hold the parts together. On the free-floating type (Fig. 3*A*), install the pin and retainer rings.

On the type with a press fit of the pin in the rod (Fig. 3*D*), a special assembly tool is required to press the pin in. The tool is properly assembled with the pin ready for installation. Then a press is used to push the pin into place. Plymouth recommends a fit test after the pin has been installed. This is done by placing the assembly tool in a vise before removing the piston assembly. A torque wrench is used to apply 15 pound-feet (2.07 kg-m) of torque to the nut on the end of the tool. If this amount of torque causes the connecting rod to move down on the piston pin, the press fit is too loose. The connecting rod must be discarded. If the rod does not move, the fit is satisfactory.

■ 1-3-9 Installing Piston-and-Rod Assemblies

After rods are reattached to their pistons and the piston rings are installed (■1-3-26), the assemblies go back into the engine. Rings should be positioned so that the ring gaps are uniformly spaced around the piston or as specified by the manufacturer. For example, Fig. 4 shows a Ford recommendation. Note that the gaps in the compression rings are toward the front, while the gaps in the oil ring parts are toward the back.

Dip the piston assembly to above the piston pin in SAE30 oil. Drain out the excess oil. Use a piston-ring compressor or a loading sleeve to compress the rings into the piston-ring grooves (Fig. 5). Install guide sleeves on the rod bolts, or cover the rod bolts with rubber hose. Then push the piston down into the cylinder. Tapping the head of the piston with the wooden handle of a hammer helps get the piston started. Make sure the assembly is installed with the piston facing in the right direction. Many pistons have a notch or other mark that should face toward the front of the engine (Fig. 4).

> **NOTE:** Section ■1-3-28 explains in detail how to use the loading sleeve that comes with some ring sets.

Attach the rod cap with the nuts turned down lightly. Then tap the cap on its crown lightly to help center it. Tighten the nuts to specifications with a torque wrench.

> **NOTE:** Bearing clearances must be checked (■1-3-15).

■ 1-3-10 Checking Rod Side Clearance

Make sure that the rods are centered on the crankshaft crankpins. If a rod is offset to one side, the rod-and-piston assembly probably has been put in backward. It probably has been turned 180 degrees from its correct position. Also, offset could mean a bent rod (see ■1-3-11). Clearance between connecting rods on V-type engines should also be checked. Incorrect side clearance means a bent rod.

■ 1-3-11 Checking Connecting Rods

After connecting rods are detached from the pistons, the rods and rod caps should be cleaned and inspected. Make sure to clean out the oilholes in the rods. Blow them out with compressed air.

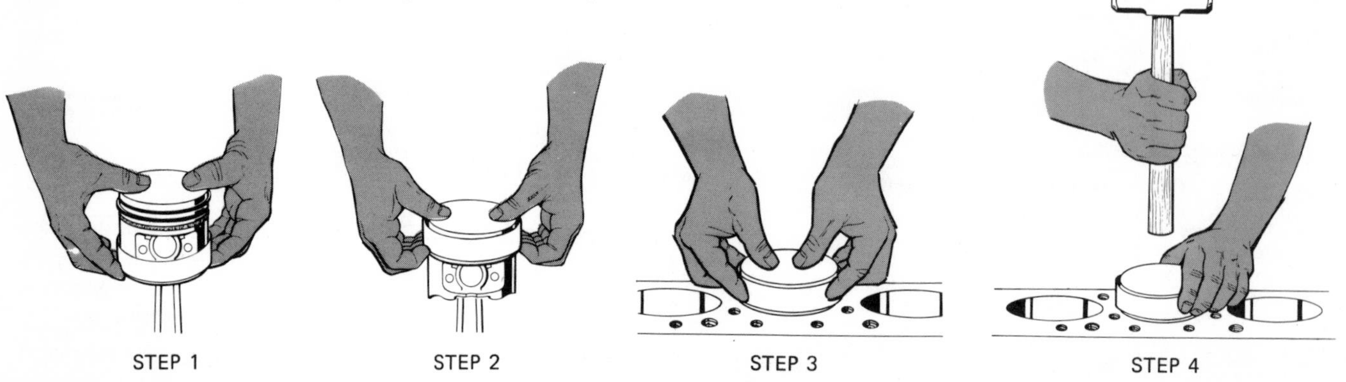

Figure 5 Using the loading sleeve which comes with the new ring set to install the piston-and-ring assembly in the cylinder bore. *(Chrysler Corporation.)*

Inspect the rod big-end bearings (see ■ 1-3-14). If the rod has a bushing in the small end, check its fit with the piston pin. If it is not correct, service is required (see ■ 1-3-12).

Check rod alignment. Figure 6 is an exaggerated view of the effects of a misaligned connecting rod. Heavy loading at points *A* and *B* on the bearing would cause bearing failure at these points. The heavy-pressure spots *C* and *D* on the piston cause heavy wear and possible scoring of the piston and cylinder wall. A basic inspection check recommended by engine manufacturers is to look for uneven wear or shiny spots on the pistons. If any are found, the piston, pin, and rod should all be replaced.

A rough check for rod alignment can be made by detaching the oil pan and watching the rod while the engine is cranked. The rod should stay centered on the pin. If the rod moves back and forth on the piston pin or is not centered, the rod is out of line.

To check rod alignment out of the engine, reinstall the piston pin in the rod. Then mount the rod on the arbor of the rod aligner by attaching the rod cap. Put the V block over the piston pin and move it in against the faceplate. If the V block does not fit squarely against the faceplate, the rod is out of line. (This same fixture can be used to check alignment of the rod-and-piston assembly before the rings are installed.)

If the rod is out of line, check the crankpin for taper (■ 1-3-16). A tapered crankpin causes the rod to be subjected to bending stress.

Bent rods must be straightened or replaced. To straighten a rod, use a straightening bar inserted into the piston-pin hole. Bend the rod a little past straight and then back to straight again. This relieves the stress set up by the bending process.

NOTE: Experience has shown that bent connecting rods tend to take on a permanent set. Even if they are straightened, they may drift back to the bent condition. Most engine manufacturers require that bent connecting rods be replaced.

■ 1-3-12 Piston-Pin Bushings in Rods When the connecting rod has a piston-pin bushing (Fig. 3*A* and *E*), check the fit of the pin. If the fit is correct, the pin will not drop through the bushing of its own weight when held vertical. It will require a slight push to force it through. If the fit is too loose, the bushing should be reamed or honed for an oversize pin or replaced.

NOTE: Aluminum pistons have no bushings. They are supplied with prefitted piston pins as a matched set. If the pin is worn or is too loose a fit in the piston, a new pin-piston set is required. However, some automotive shops hone the piston-pin holes and install oversize pins, provided the piston is otherwise in good condition. This is not a recommended practice, according to most automotive-engine manufacturers.

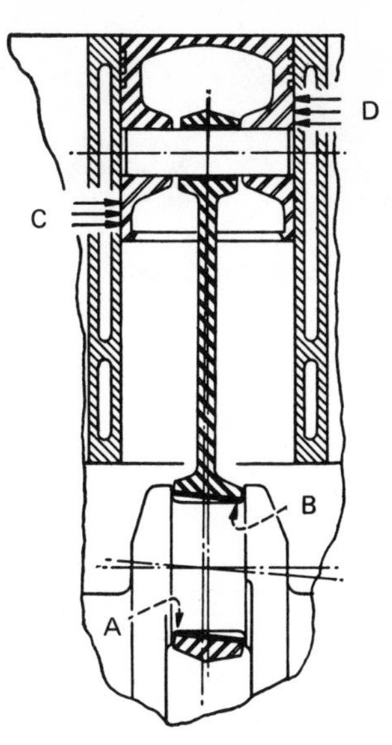

Figure 6 Heavy-pressure areas caused by a bent rod. (The bent condition is exaggerated.) Areas of heavy pressure (A, B, C, and D) wear rapidly so that early failure results. *(Federal-Mogul Corporation.)*

On some rods, the bushing cannot be replaced; if the bushing is so worn that it cannot be reamed or honed for an oversize pin, the complete rod must be replaced. On other rods, worn bushings can be replaced. The new bushings can be reamed or honed to fit the old pins (if they are in good condition) or new standard-size pins. Pins that are worn, pitted, or otherwise defective should be discarded. To replace a bushing, press out the old bushing in an arbor press. Burrs on the edges of the bushing bore in the rod should be removed with a hand scraper or tapered burring reamer. Then, a new bushing can be pressed in with an arbor press. A tapered mandrel should then be used to expand the edges of the bushing. This procedure swages, or expands, them firmly in the rod. Make sure the oilholes in the bushing and rod align. Ream or bore the new bushing to size.

When reaming a set of bushings, proceed slowly on the first rod. Use an expansion reamer. Expand the reamer in easy stages, taking off a little metal each time. Try the pin fit after each reaming operation. This guards against overreaming. Then, after the first rod is reamed, all other rods may be rough-reamed quickly by reducing the reamer diameter about 0.0005 inch (0.0127 mm). Then expand the reamer to take the final cut. At this stage, check the pins with a micrometer, so that any slight variation in size can be taken care of. Suppose you find that one pin is slightly larger than the others. Then the bushing into which the pin will fit can be reamed slightly larger to provide a good fit. This ensures a good matching fit of pins to bushings.

To hone a set of bushings, follow the same two-step procedure. Rough-hone the bushings to within about 0.0005 inch (0.0127 mm) of the proper size. Then change hones, and finish-hone to size. Check pins with a micrometer during finish-honing so that variations in pin size can be taken care of. A special clamp is used to hold the connecting rod during honing. The bushing should be moved from one end of the stone

Figure 7 Types of engine-bearing failures. The appearance of a bearing usually indicates the cause of its failure. *(Ford Motor Company.)*

to the other and should not be held in one spot. However, the bushing should not be moved past the end of the stone. Doing so would wear the edges of the bushing bell-shaped.

■ 1-3-13 Connecting-Rod Bearings

Connecting-rod big-end bearings are of two types: direct-bonded and precision-insert. Some adjustment is possible on the direct-bonded type (■1-3-15), but if this bearing is worn, the complete rod and cap must be replaced. The precision-insert bearing is not adjustable. However, this type of bearing can be replaced without difficulty provided the rod, crankpin, and other engine components are in good condition. Whenever a rod bearing fails, an analysis should be made to determine the cause. Then the cause can be eliminated so that the failure will not be repeated quickly (■ 1-3-14).

■ 1-3-14 Analysis of Bearing Failures

The following are the various types of bearing failure.

1. BEARING FAILURE DUE TO LACK OF OIL (Fig. 7*A*) When insufficient oil flows to a bearing, actual metal-to-metal contact results. The bearing overheats, and the bearing metal melts or is wiped out of the bearing shell. Welds may form between the rotating journal and bearing shell. There is a chance that the engine will "throw a rod." In other words, the rod will "freeze" to the crankpin and break, and parts of the rod will go through the engine block. Oil starvation of a bearing could result from clogged oil lines, a defective oil pump or pressure regulator, or insufficient oil in the crankcase. Also, bearings with excessive clearance may pass all the oil from the pump so that other bearings are starved and thus fail.

2. BEARING FAILURE DUE TO FATIGUE (Fig. 7*B*) Repeated application of loads on a bearing will ultimately fatigue the bearing metal. It starts to crack and flake out. Craters, or pockets, form in the bearing. As more and more of the metal is lost, the remainder is worked harder and fatigues at a faster rate. Ultimately, complete bearing failure occurs.

Fatigue failure seldom occurs under average operation conditions. However, certain special conditions will cause this type of failure. For instance, if a journal is worn out of round, the bearing will be overstressed with every crankshaft revolution. Also, if the engine is idled or operated at low speed much of the time, the center part of the upper rod-bearing half will carry most of the load and will "fatigue out." On the other hand, if the engine is operated at maximum torque with wide-open throttle (that is, if the engine is "lugged"), then most or all of the upper bearing half will fatigue out. High-speed operation tends to cause fatigue failure of the lower bearing half.

3. BEARING SCRATCHED BY DIRT IN THE OIL (Fig. 7*C*) Embeddability enables a bearing to protect itself by allowing dirt particles to embed so that they will not gouge out bearing material or scratch the rotating journal. When a particle embeds, the metal is pushed up around the dirt particle, reducing oil clearance in the area. Usually the metal can flow outward enough to restore adequate oil clearance. However, if the dirt particles are too large, they do not embed completely and are carried with the rotating journal, gouging out scratches in the bearing. Also, if the oil is very dirty, the bearing becomes overloaded with particles. In either case, bearing failure soon occurs.

4. BEARING FAILURE DUE TO TAPERED JOURNAL (Fig. 7*D*) If the journal is tapered, one side of the bearing carries most or all of the load. This side will overheat and lose its bearing metal. Do not confuse this type of failure with the failure that would result from a bent connecting rod. With a tapered journal, both bearing halves will fail on the same side. With a bent rod, failure will be on opposite sides.

5. BEARING FAILURE FROM RADII RIDE (Fig. 7*E*) If the journal-to-crank-cheek radius is not cut away sufficiently, the edge of the bearing rides on this radius. The condition causes cramming of the bearing, possibly poor seating, rapid fatigue, and early failure. This trouble would be most likely to occur after a crankshaft-grind job during which the radii were not sufficiently relieved.

6. *BEARING FAILURE FROM POOR SEATING IN THE BORE* (Fig. 7F) Poor seating of the bearing shell in the bore causes local high spots where oil clearances are too low. When particles of dirt are left between the bearing shell and the counterbore, this reduces oil clearance. Also, an air space exists which prevents proper cooling of the bearing. The combination can lead to quick bearing failure.

7. *BEARING FAILURE FROM RIDGING* Crankpin ridging, or "camming," may cause failure or a partial-oil-groove type of replacement bearing installed without removal of the ridge. The ridge forms on the crankpin because of uneven wear between the part of the crankpin in contact with the partial oil groove and the part that runs on the solid bearing. The original bearing wears to conform to this ridge. However, when a new bearing is installed, the center zone may be overloaded at the ridge and may soon fail. A ridge so slight that it can hardly be detected (except with a carefully used micrometer) may be enough to cause this failure. Failures of this sort have been reported in engines having ridges of less than 0.001 inch (0.025 mm).

■ 1-3-15 Inspecting the Connecting-Rod-Bearing Fit

Precision-insert bearings must be inspected in one way, the direct-bonded bearings in another.

> **NOTE:** Before installing new bearings, the crankpins should always be checked for taper or out-of-roundness (■1-3-16).

1. *PRECISION-INSERT BEARINGS* The fit of these bearings can be inspected with Plastigage, shim stock, or with micrometer and telescope gauge.

a. *Plastigage* Plastigage is a plastic material that comes in strips and flattens when pressure is applied to it. Put a strip of the material into the bearing cap. Install the cap and tighten the rod nuts to the specified tension. Then, remove the cap and measure the amount of flattening. If the Plastigage is flattened only a little, then oil clearances are large. If it is flattened considerably, oil clearances are small. Actual clearance is measured with a special scale supplied with the Plastigage (Fig. 8).

The bearing cap and crankpin should be wiped clean of oil before the Plastigage is used. The crankshaft should be turned so that the crankpin is about 30 degrees back of BDC. Do not move the crankshaft while the cap nuts are tight. This would flatten the Plastigage further and throw off the clearance measurement.

b. *Shim Stock* Lubricate a strip of 0.001-inch (0.0254 mm) shim stock ½-inch (12.7 mm) wide. Lay it lengthwise in the center of the bearing cap. Install the cap, and tighten cap nuts lightly. Note the ease with which the rod can be moved endwise on the crankpin. If the rod moves easily, tighten the nuts a little more and recheck. Repeat the procedure until the nuts have been drawn down to the specified tightness or until the rod tightens up on the crankpin. If the rod tightens up, the clearance is less than the thickness

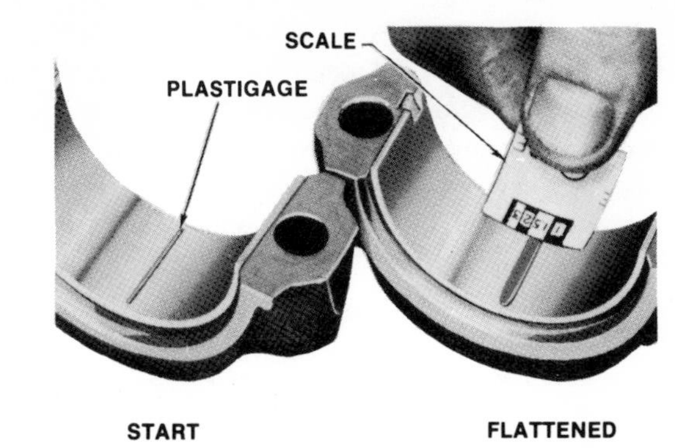

Figure 8 Bearing clearance being checked with Plastigage. Left, Plastigage in place before tightening the cap; right, measuring the amount of flattening (or bearing clearance) with a scale. *(Buick Motor Division of General Motors Corporation.)*

of the shim stock. If the rod does not tighten up, the clearance is greater than the thickness of the shim stock. With the latter condition, lay an additional strip of shim stock on top of the first and repeat the checking procedure. If the rod still does not tighten up, keep adding shim stock until the actual bearing clearance is determined. Then remove the cap, take out the shim stock, replace the cap, and torque the cap nuts to specifications. Excessive clearance requires bearing replacement (■1-3-16).

c. *Micrometer and Telescope Gauge* Inspect the crankpin diameter with a micrometer. Inspect the bearing diameter (cap in place) with a telescope gauge and micrometer (or an inside micrometer). Compare the two diameters to determine the difference, or bearing clearance. At the same time, inspect the crankpin for taper or eccentric wear. Measure the diameter at several places along the crankpin (to check for taper). Also measure around the crankpin (to check for eccentricity, or out-of-roundness).

2. *DIRECT-BONDED CONNECTING-ROD BEARINGS* On these bearings, adjustment is made by installation or removal of shims under the cap. Shims placed between the cap and rod (at the bolt bosses) hold the cap away from the rod when the nuts are tightened. This increases the bearing clearance. Clearance can be checked with a micrometer and telescope gauge, as noted previously. It can also be checked by attempting to snap the rod back and forth on the crankpin with one hand. If the rod moves easily, take off the rod cap. Remove one shim only from each side of the cap. Replace the cap and try to move the rod. If the rod still moves easily, take off another pair of shims. Repeat this procedure until the rod will not move. Then add one shim to each side of the cap, replace and tighten the cap, and retest.

If the bearing is worn, pitted, scored, chipped, or otherwise damaged, replace the rod and cap as a unit. Rebabbitting of this type of rod should not be attempted in the field. Special equipment is required to do this job.

■ 1-3-16 Installing Precision Connecting-Rod Bearings

New precision connecting-rod bearings are required if the old ones are defective (■1-3-14) or have worn so much that clearances are excessive. They are also required if the crankpins have worn out of round or have tapered so much that they must be reground. In this case, new undersize bearings are required. Engine rebuilders usually replace the bearings in an engine when it is torn down whether or not the old bearings are in bad condition. Their reasoning is that when the engine is torn down for rebuilding, it costs only slightly more to put in new bearings. However, if the engine had to be torn down especially for bearing installation, the cost would be high. They believe it is cheap insurance against failure to install new bearings during an engine-rebuilding job.

1. INSPECTING CRANKPINS Crankpins should always be inspected with a micrometer for taper and concentricity. Measurements should be taken at several places along the crankpin to check for taper. Diameter should be checked all the way around for out-of-roundness. If crankpins are out of round or tapered more than 0.0015 inch (0.037 mm), the crankshaft must be replaced or the crankpins reground (■ 1-4-15). Bearings working against taper or out-of-roundness of more than 0.0015 inch (0.037 mm) will not last long. And when bearings go, there is the chance that the engine will be severely damaged.

2. INSTALLING NEW BEARINGS When new bearings are to be installed, make sure your hands, the workbench, tools, and all engine parts are clean. Keep the new bearings wrapped up until you are ready to install them. Then handle them carefully. Wipe each with a fresh piece of cleaning tissue just before installing it. Be very sure that the bores in the cap and rod are clean and not excessively out of round.[1] Then put the bearing shells in place. If they have locking tangs, make sure the tangs enter the notches provided in the rod and cap. Note the following comments about bearing spread and crush. Check clearance after installation (see ■ 1-3-15).

NOTE: Do not attempt to correct clearance by filing the rod cap. This destroys the original relationship between cap and rod and will lead to early bearing failure.

3. BEARING SPREAD Bearing shells are usually manufactured with "spread." That is, the shell diameter is somewhat greater than the diameter of the rod cap or rod bore into which the shell will fit. When the shell is installed into the cap or rod, it snaps into place and holds its seat during later assembling operations.

4. BEARING CRUSH In order to make sure that the bearing shell will "snug down" into its bore in the rod cap or rod when the cap is installed, the bearings have "crush." They are manufactured to have some additional height over a full half. This additional height must be crushed down when the cap is installed. Crushing down the additional height forces the shells into the bores in the cap and rod. It ensures firm seating and snug contact with the bores.

NOTE: Never file off the edges of the bearing shells in an attempt to remove crush. When you select the proper bearings for an engine (as recommended by the engine manufacturer), you will find that they have the correct crush. Precision-insert bearings must not be tampered with in any way to make them "fit better." This usually leads only to rapid bearing failure.

■ 1-3-17 Piston Service

After the piston-and-rod assemblies are removed from the engine, the pistons and rods should be separated (■ 1-3-3 to 1-3-7). Then the rings can be removed from the pistons. (The rings can also be removed from the pistons before the pistons and rods are separated.) A special ring-expander tool can be used for ring removal. The tool has two small claws that catch under the ends of the ring. When pressure is applied to the tool handles, the ring is sprung enough so that it can be lifted out of the ring grooves and off the piston. Discard the old piston rings. As a rule, expert mechanics replace the old rings with new ones during an engine overhaul. Once the ring break-in coating and tool marks are worn off, the ring will not reseat itself if it is reinstalled.

■ 1-3-18 Piston Cleaning

Remove carbon and varnish carefully from piston surfaces. Do not use a caustic cleaning solution or wire brush! These could damage the piston-skirt finish. You may decide to reinstall the pistons in the engine; therefore, you should not damage them. Use the cleaning method provided in your shop to clean the pistons. Clean out ring grooves with a ring-groove cleaning tool. You can also use the end of a broken piston ring filed to a sharp edge. Oil-ring slots, or holes, must be clean so that oil can drain back through them. Use a drill of the proper size. Do not remove metal when cleaning the slots or holes.

■ 1-3-19 Piston Inspection

Examine the pistons carefully for wear, scuffs, scored skirts, worn ring grooves, and cracks. Defects such as excessive wear, scuffs (Fig. 9*A*), scores, or cracks require piston replacement. Pistons that have failed due to preignition (Fig. 9*B*) or detonation (Fig. 9*C*) obviously must be replaced. Look for cracks at the ring lands, skirts, bushing or pin bosses, and heads. Any defects require replacement of the piston, with these exceptions: Worn ring grooves can sometimes be repaired by cutting the grooves larger and using ring-groove spacers (■ 1-3-20). Piston-skirt wear or collapse (reduction in skirt diameter) can sometimes be corrected by knurling the piston skirt (■ 1-3-21).

Inspect the fit of the piston pins to the pistons or piston bushings. One way to do this is to use a small-hole gauge to check the piston bearing bores and a micrometer to measure the pin diameter. On the type of piston without a bushing in which the pin oscillates (Fig. 3), the piston and pin are supplied in

[1]Some manufacturers recommend a check of bore symmetry with the bearing shells removed. The cap should be attached with nuts drawn up to specified tension. Then a telescope gauge and micrometer or special out-of-round gauge can be used to check the bore.

Figure 9 Typical piston failures. *A,* piston that has failed from scuffing. Note the scratch or scuff marks, usually caused by overheating or lack of oil, that run vertically on the piston skirt. *B,* piston that has failed due to preignition. The excessive temperature has melted a hole through the piston head. *C,* piston that has failed due to detonation. Note how the shock waves from detonation have shattered and broken the outer edges of the piston, rings, and ring lands. *(TRW, Inc.)*

matched sets. If the fit is too loose or there are other pin or piston defects, the pin and piston are replaced as a matched set. [Chevrolet specifies a fit no looser than 0.001 inch (0.0254 mm).]

NOTE: Some engine shops hone the piston-pin holes and install oversize piston pins, provided the piston is otherwise in good condition. However, this is not generally recommended by most automotive-engine manufacturers.

Check the piston with a micrometer. Some manufacturers specify taking various measurements. It is important to take the measurement at the sizing point (Fig. 10) because this is the point of maximum wear.

Compare the sizing-point measurement with the cylinder diameter, measured 90 degrees from the piston pin. This measurement may be made with a telescope gauge and micrometer. Measurement may also be made with a cylinder bore gauge and a micrometer.

If the cylinder wall is excessively worn or tapered, it will require refinishing (■ 1-4-20 to 1-4-25). If the cylinder wall is refinished, then a new oversized piston is required.

Piston fit can also be checked another way. Some manufacturers specify using a feeler ribbon and spring scale. The feeler ribbon, with the spring scale attached, and the piston are placed in the cylinder. If only a light pull is required to pull the ribbon out, the fit is the thickness of the ribbon. If the feeler ribbon comes out too easily, the fit is too loose.

■ 1-3-20 Ring-Groove Repair

If a piston is in good condition except for excessive ring-groove wear, it can often be repaired. The top ring groove is the one that wears most because it gets the highest temperatures and pressures. One piston-ring manufacturer states that almost all aluminum pistons checked at the time of overhaul have excessively worn top ring grooves. The ring groove may be checked with a special gauge, as shown in Fig 11. If the ring groove is excessively worn [as much as 0.006 inch (0.152 mm) or more], the groove can be machined to a larger width with a special hand-operated lathe. The lathe squares up the top and bottom sides of the ring groove. Then the ring is installed with a spacer.

■ 1-3-21 Piston Resizing

Resizing of modern pistons is not recommended by automotive manufacturers. The procedure can damage the piston finish. One piston-ring manufacturer has developed a knurling procedure, called "nurlizing." The piston skirt is run between a supporting wheel and a nurlizing tool. The procedure displaces metal and expands the diameter of the piston skirt. Also, the indentations form little pockets that can hold lubricating oil.

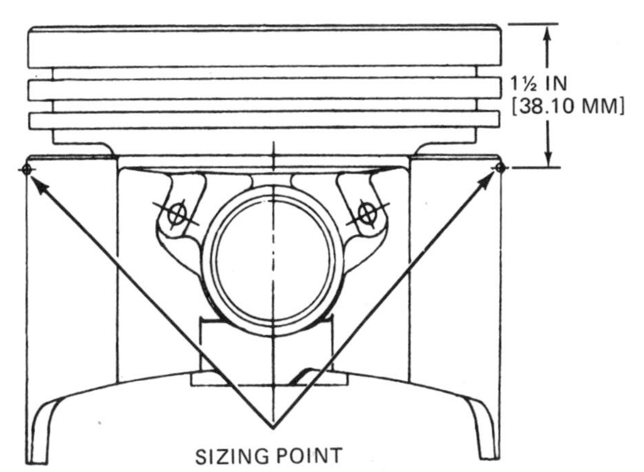

Figure 10 Piston sizing point. *(Pontiac Motor Division of General Motors Corporation.)*

Figure 11 Using a special gauge to check the top ring groove for wear. *(Federal-Mogul Corporation.)*

■ **1-3-22 New Pistons** New pistons are of the finished type, ready for installation. They are available in several oversizes. When these are used, the cylinders are finished to fit the pistons. Engine manufacturers supply oversize pistons of the same weight as the original pistons. Thus it is not necessary to replace all pistons when only some of the cylinders require service. There is no problem of balance if all pistons are of the same weight even if some are oversize.

> **NOTE:** Aluminum pistons are usually supplied with piston pins already fitted. This ensures factory specifications on the pin fit to the piston.

Finished pistons have a special finish. They must not be buffed with a wire wheel or finished to a smaller size. This would remove the finish and cause rapid piston wear after installation.

■ **1-3-23 Fitting Piston Pins in Pistons** On pistons with piston-pin bushings, worn bushings may be replaced. The new bushings are honed to size to fit the piston pins.

> **NOTE:** Aluminum pistons have no bushings. They are supplied with prefitted piston pins as a matched set. If a pin is worn or has too loose a fit in the piston, a new pin-piston set is required. However, some engine shops hone the piston-pin holes and install oversize piston pins, provided the piston is otherwise in good condition. But this is not recommended by most engine manufacturers.

■ **1-3-24 Rod-and-Piston Alignment** After the rod and piston have been reassembled, but before the rings are installed on the piston, alignment should be checked. The rod alignment tool is used for this check. The V block is held against the piston. If the V block does not line up with the faceplate as the piston is moved to various positions, the connecting rod is twisted.

■ **1-3-25 Piston-Ring Service** If an engine is torn down for service, the old piston rings should be discarded. Rings that have been used, even for only short mileage, will not seat properly to provide sealing.

If the engine trouble is due to rings sticking in the piston-ring grooves, a special compound can be introduced into the intake manifold and engine oil before engine disassembly. This will sometimes free the rings (■ 1-2-3).

> **NOTE:** Before adding any chemical to an engine equipped with a catalytic converter, be sure that the chemical will not harm the catalyst.

Proper selection of new piston rings depends on the condition of the cylinder walls and whether they are to be reconditioned. (■ 1-4-21 describes the inspection of cylinder walls for wear and taper.) If the cylinder walls are only slightly tapered or out of round (consult the manufacturer's specifications for maximum allowable deviations), then standard-type rings can be used. Where the cylinder walls have some taper but not enough to warrant the extra expense of a rebore or hone job, special "severe," or "drastic," rings should be used. These rings have greater tension and are more flexible. This enables them to expand and contract as they move up and down in the cylinder. Thus, they follow the changing contours of the cylinder wall and provide adequate sealing (preventing blow-by) and oil control. Figure 12 shows a set of replacement rings for tapered cylinder walls.

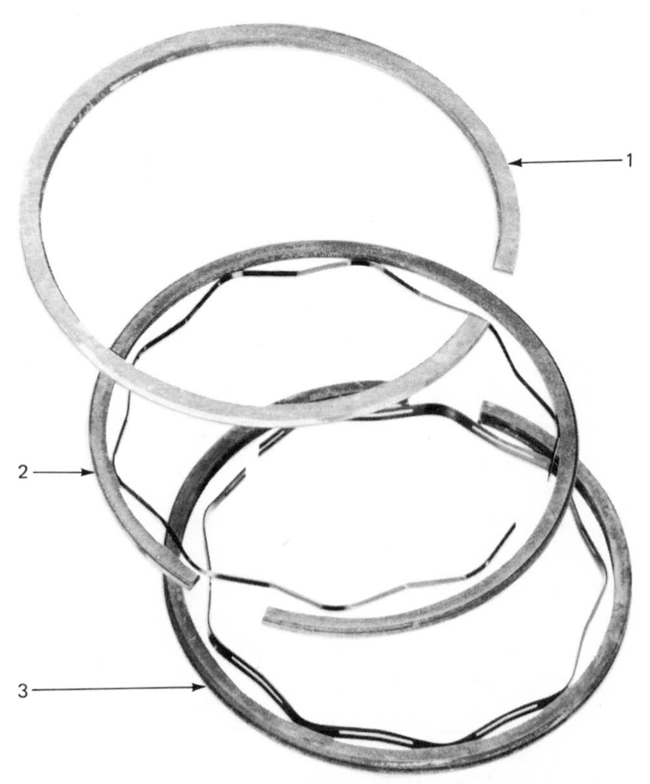

Figure 12 Disassembled view of a set of replacement piston rings: (1) top compression rings; (2) second compression ring, which includes an expander spring; (3) oil-control ring, which includes an expander spring. *(Grant Piston Rings.)*

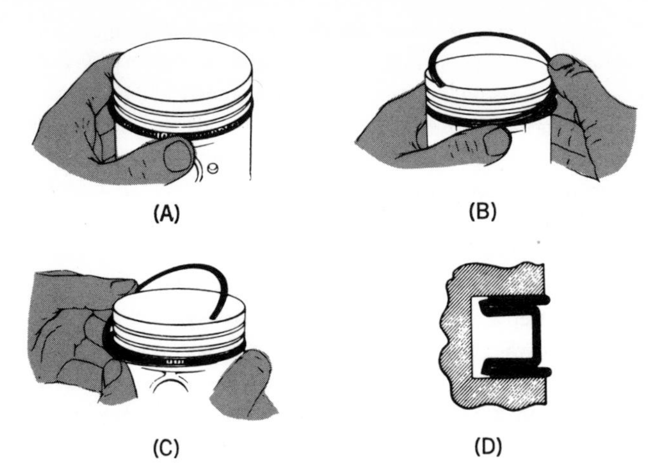

Figure 13 Installation of three piece oil-control ring. *(a)* Place expander-spacer in oil-ring groove with ends of spacer above a solid part of the groove bottom. *(b)* Hold ends of spacer together, and install steel rail above the spacer. *(c)* Install other steel rail on lower side of spacer. Make sure ends of spacer are not overlapping. *(d)* Sectional view of the three parts fitted into groove. *(Federal-Mogul Corporation.)*

Automotive manufacturers generally recommend honing the cylinder walls lightly (■ 1-4-22 to 1-4-23) before the piston-ring installation to "break the glaze." Cylinder walls take on a hard, smooth glaze after the engine has been in use for a while. In some automotive shops it is the practice to knock off this glaze by running a hone or glaze-breaker up and down the cylinder a few times before putting in new rings. However, at least one piston-ring manufacturer says that honing does not have to be done on cast-iron cylinder walls, provided the walls are not wavy or scuffed. The glaze is a good antiscuff material and will not unduly retard the wear-in of new rings. However, the walls should be reasonably concentric and in relatively good condition.

The best honing job leaves a cross-hatch pattern with hone marks intersecting at a 60-degree angle. This leaves the best surface for proper seating of new rings. (See ■ 1-4-22 and 1-4-23 on honing procedures.)

■ 1-3-26 Fitting Piston Rings Piston rings must be fitted to the cylinder and to the ring grooves in the piston. Rings come in packaged sets in graduated sizes to fit various sizes of cylinders. All packages have instruction sheets that describe in detail exactly how to install the rings. These instructions should be carefully followed.

NOTE: Never throw away the instructions until you have finished the ring-installation job.

As a first step in fitting a piston ring, the ring should be pushed down into the cylinder with a piston and the ring gap measured. The ring gap is the space between the ends of the ring. It is measured with a feeler gauge with the ring pushed down to the lower limit of ring travel. If the cylinder is worn, that is where the ring gap will be smallest. If the ring gap is too small, check the package that the ring came in. The ring set may be wrong for the job. (Rings come in sets in different oversizes.) If the ring gap is wrong, then either you have the wrong rings, you have incorrectly measured the cylinder diameter, or the wrong-size rings were inserted in the package.

On older-model engines, the recommendation was to file the ends of the ring with a fine-cut file. The file was first clamped in a vise. Then the ring was worked back and forth on the file (with the ring ends on the two sides of the file). This procedure is no longer recommended. Filing the ring ends can remove some of the ring coating and cause early ring failure.

NOTE: Remember that if the cylinder is tapered, the diameter at the lower limit of ring travel (in the assembled engine) will be smaller than the diameter at the top. This means the ring must be fitted to the diameter at the lower limit of ring travel. If it is fitted to the upper part of the cylinder, the ring gap will not be great enough at the lower limit of ring travel. As a result, the ring ends will butt together. The ring will be broken, and the cylinder wall will be scuffed. Always measure the ring gap with the ring pushed down to the point of minimum diameter at the lower limit of ring travel.

If the ring gap is correct, insert the outside surface of the ring into the proper ring groove in the piston. Then roll the ring around in the groove to make sure the ring has a free fit around the entire piston. An excessively tight fit probably means that the ring groove has been nicked or burred with the blade of the ring-groove cleaning tool. Some manufacturers recommend using the end of a broken ring which has been filed to a sharp edge to clean the ring grooves. This is preferred by many technicians because the piece of ring will not cause nicks or burrs.

Install the rings in the ring grooves, using the ring tool. Then, recheck the fit of the rings in the ring grooves. Insert a feeler gauge of the proper size between the ring and the side of the groove.

■ 1-3-27 Cautions on Installing Rings The three-part oil-control ring is installed one part at a time, as shown in Fig. 13. Various types of compression rings and their proper installation are shown in Fig. 14. Never spiral the compression rings into the grooves. (Spiraling the rails of the oil-control rings is shown in Fig. 13.) This could distort or break the compression ring and cause major loss of compression and blow-by. Instead, always use a ring expander tool. Also, never overexpand the compression rings.

■ 1-3-28 Installing the Piston-and-Rod Assembly We have already covered this procedure in ■ 1-3-9. When installing the piston-and-rod assembly, be sure to use a ring compressor. Install the assembly with the correct side facing forward.

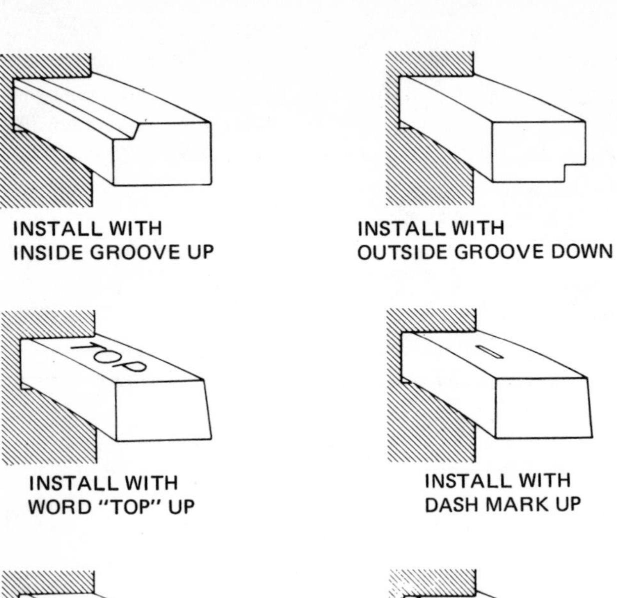

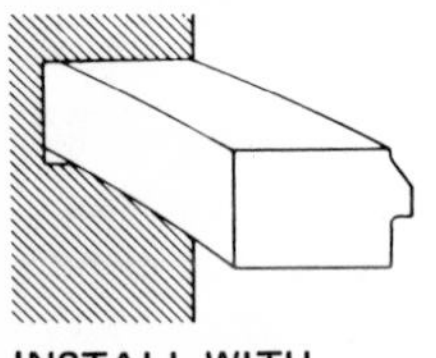

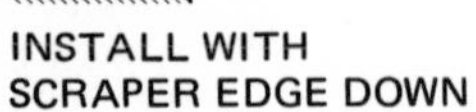

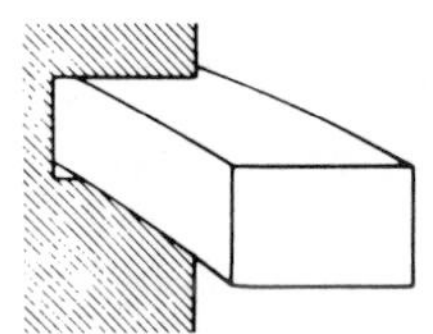

Figure 14 Types of compression rings, and the proper way to install them. *(Federal-Mogul Corporation.)*

Some ring sets are now supplied with a special ring compressor, or loading sleeve, which is used as shown in Fig. 5. The loading sleeve has a larger inside diameter at the top than at the bottom. Therefore when the piston, with rings, slides down through the loading sleeve, it compresses the rings in the piston-ring grooves. Note the four steps. First, make sure the rings are free in the grooves. Lubricate the piston and rings. Insert the assembly through the large end of the loading sleeve. Next center the rings on the piston, and slide the sleeve up as shown in step 2. Put the assembly into the cylinder bore and press downward on the piston until the loading sleeve rests on the cylinder block. (Be sure to use protective guide sleeves, as explained in ■ 1-3-9). Then hold the loading sleeve firmly against the block. With a hammer handle, thrust downward with one fast motion, as shown in step 4. This pushes the piston-and-rod assembly into the cylinder bore.

NOTE: If the piston-and-rod assembly does not enter the bore easily—STOP! Remove the assembly and push the assembly with the rings through the loading sleeve by hand. Examine the rings for damage and if everything looks okay, repeat the procedure. Examine the ring grooves in the piston. If these are not cleaned out properly, they may prevent the rings from compressing enough to enter the cylinder.

SECTION 1-4 Servicing Crankshaft and Cylinder Blocks

This section covers the servicing procedures on crankshafts and cylinder blocks. Other sections cover the servicing of the other engine components.

NOTE: If the cylinder block, crankshaft, and main bearings all need service, it is often cheaper to buy a short block than to invest the time required for the reconditioning services.

■ **1-4-1 Cleanliness** The major enemy of good engine-service work is dirt. A trace of dirt or abrasive on a cylinder wall or other working engine part can ruin an otherwise good service job. Before the engine is opened for a major service job, it should be cleaned to remove dirt and grease. All engine parts should be cleaned as they are removed and kept clean until reinstalled. As soon as a part is cleaned, it should be dried and a light coat of oil applied to bright surfaces to prevent rust.

■ **1-4-2 Removing an Engine** Many engine-service jobs can be performed with the engine in the vehicle. Other jobs, such as boring cylinders or main-bearing bores, require removal of the engine from the vehicle. Specific removal procedures vary, so always check the manufacturer's shop manual for the car you are servicing before starting the job. What follows is a typical procedure.

1. Drain the cooling system and remove the hood.

2. Disconnect the battery ground cable and the alternator ground cable from the cylinder block.

3. Remove the air cleaner.

4. Disconnect the radiator hoses from the head and water pump.

5. Disconnect the automatic transmission oil-cooler lines (where present) from the radiator.

6. Remove the fan shroud (if present) and the radiator.

7. Disconnect the oil-pressure and coolant-sending-unit wires.

8. Disconnect the fuel-pump hoses and plug the hoses to prevent leaks.

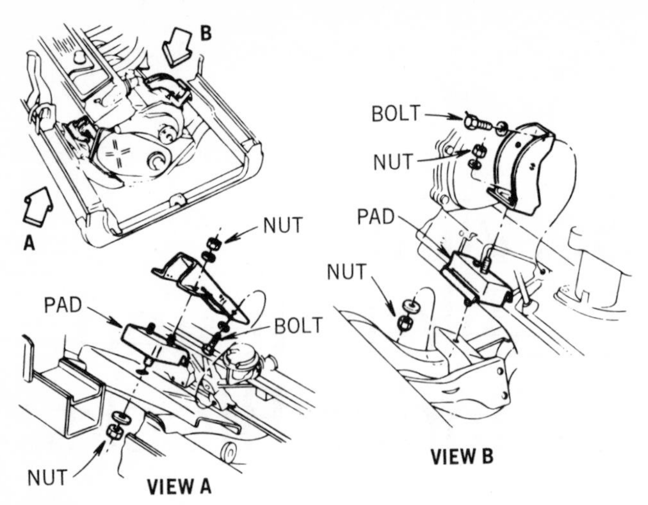

Figure 1 Front flexible engine mounts used to support the engine on the frame. *(Chrysler Corporation.)*

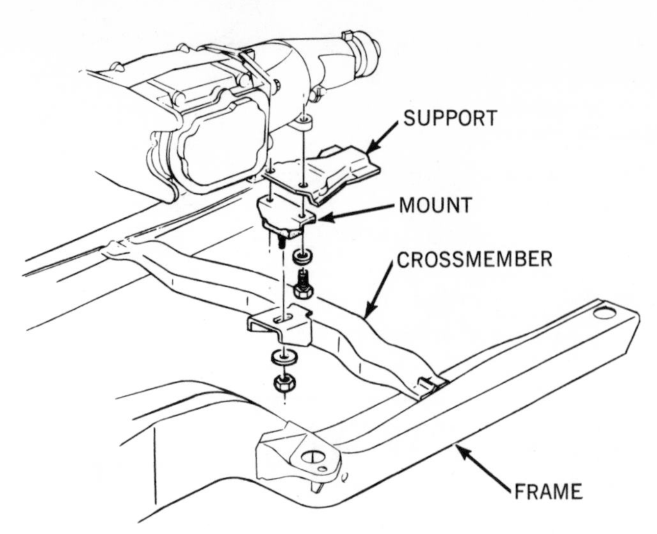

Figure 2 Rear engine mount. *(Chevrolet Motor Division of General Motors Corporation.)*

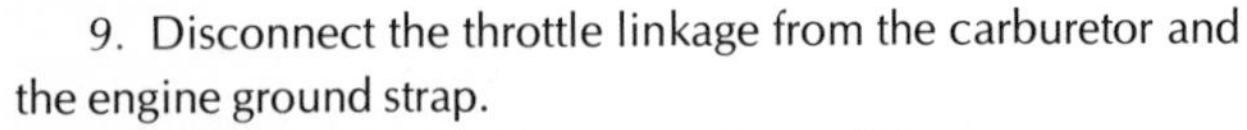

9. Disconnect the throttle linkage from the carburetor and the engine ground strap.

10. Such units as the alternator, air-conditioner compressor, and power-steering pump need not be removed from the engine compartment. Instead, they can be detached from the engine and moved to one side out of the way.

> **CAUTION:** Do not disconnect the air-conditioner pressure hoses unless necessary. These hoses hold Freon-12 under pressure, and disconnecting them would allow Freon-12 to escape. This can be dangerous. In addition, it would then be necessary to purge and recharge the system with Freon-12.

11. Disconnect the heater hoses from the water pump, intake manifold, and choke housing (if present).

12. Disconnect the primary wire from the ignition coil. Remove the wiring harness from the top of the engine.

13. Raise the vehicle. Drain the engine oil.

14. Disconnect the starting motor cable from the starting motor. (The starting motor may also have to be removed.)

15. Disconnect the exhaust pipe (or pipes) from the exhaust manifold (or manifolds). Wire up the exhaust system to support it.

16. Disconnect the engine mounts from the frame brackets.

17. Disconnect the clutch or automatic transmission. Make sure the converter (automatic transmission) is secure in its housing.

> **NOTE:** It is sometimes easier to remove the transmission with the engine because it is simpler and prevents damage to the seal.

18. Lower the vehicle. Support the transmission with a floor jack.

19. Attach the engine-lift cable to the engine. Raise the engine enough to remove the mount bolts. Make a final check to make sure all wiring, hoses, and other parts are free and clear of the engine.

20. Raise the engine enough to clear the mounts. Then alternately raise the transmission jack and engine until the engine separates from the transmission.

21. Carefully pull the engine forward from the transmission. Then lift the engine out of the engine compartment.

> **NOTE:** Engine installation is essentially the reverse of the preceding procedure.

■ 1-4-3 Replacing Engine Mounts

A typical engine mount is shown in Fig. 1. Broken or deteriorated engine mounts put extra strain on other mounts and the drive line. They should be replaced with new mounts. Always check the manufacturer's shop manual before attempting to replace an engine mount. Typical procedures follow.

1. REPLACING A FRONT ENGINE MOUNT Support the engine with a jack and wood block under the engine oil pan. Raise the engine enough to take the weight off the mount. Remove the nut and through bolt. Remove the mount-and-frame-bracket assembly from the cross member, as shown in Fig. 1. Install the new mount on the cross member. Use new self-locking bolts and nuts. Do not tighten the bolts until you have lowered the engine. Then tighten them to the specified tension.

2. REPLACING A REAR ENGINE MOUNT Support the weight with a jack and wood block under the oil pan, or (on a hoist) place transmission jack under the transmission. Remove the cross-member-to-mount bolts, and the mount-to-transmission bolts (Fig. 2). On some engines, you must remove the cross member. Then take off the mount. Install the new mount on the transmission. Then, as you lower the transmission, align and start the cross-member-to-mount bolts. Tighten all bolts to the proper torque specifications.

■ **1-4-4 Crankshaft and Bearing Service** Modern automotive engines have precision-insert main bearings that can be replaced without removing the crankshaft. Many main-bearing difficulties can be taken care of by this method of bearing replacement. However, bearing replacement will not fix stopped-up oil passages, worn crankshaft journals, a damaged crankshaft, or a block in which a bearing has spun. That is, the bearing and crankshaft journal can become so hot, owing to lack of oil, that they weld momentarily. Then the bearing spins with the crankshaft and gouges the bearing bore in the cylinder block. Bearing spin will damage the cylinder block, and block replacement will be required.

If all bearings have worn fairly evenly, then probably only crankshaft-journal inspection and bearing replacement will be required. Usually all bearings do not wear the same amount. Some bearings will wear more than others. This is acceptable provided none of the bearings wear beyond manufacturer's specifications. The lower bearing half wears the most. It takes the weight of the crankshaft and combustion pressures through the rods and cranks. Uneven wear can result from normal aging of the oil pump. As the oil pump wears, oil pressure and volume drop. The main and rod bearings farthest from the oil pump get less oil. Thus they wear the most. Also, a clogged oil passage will starve bearings. When this happens, the bearings fail (they may also spin, as noted previously).

If main bearings have worn very unevenly, the best service procedure is to remove the crankshaft from the engine block. Then the block and crankshaft can be checked separately for damage and clogged oil lines.

■ **1-4-5 Inspecting Crankshaft Journals** Both the crankpins and crankshaft main journals should be inspected whenever the bearing caps are removed. Inspecting crankpins was discussed in ■1-3-16. Main journals can be checked in the block with a special crankshaft gauge or on the bench with an outside micrometer. Measurements should be taken in several places along the journal to check for taper. Also, the crankshaft should be rotated by one-quarter or one-eighth turns to check for out-of-round wear. (See ■ 1-3-14 for discussion of what a tapered, ridged, or out-of-round journal will do to the bearing.) If journals are tapered or out of round by more than 0.003 inch (0.076 mm), they should be reground. Some manufacturers consider 0.0025 inch (0.063 mm) the maximum tolerable limit of wear. They point out that any measurable out-of-round or taper shortens bearing life.

To check journals, remove the oil pan and bearing caps (■ 1-4-6). It is not necessary to detach the connecting rods from the crankshaft. However, the spark plugs should be removed so that the crankshaft can be turned over easily.

■ **1-4-6 Removing Bearing Caps** Sometimes it is difficult to remove all bearing caps with the engine in the car. In some cars, the front cross member is so close to the engine that the engine must be lifted to get enough clearance to remove the cap. Also, the rear main-bearing cap may be hard to remove because of interference with other parts.

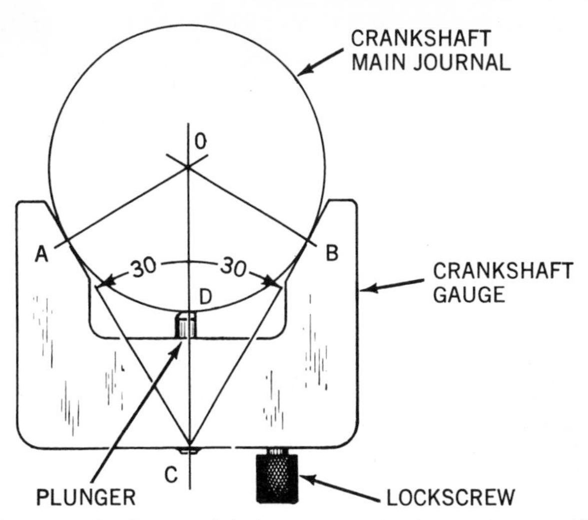

Figure 3 Checking crankshaft main journal with a crankshaft gauge. *(Federal-Mogul Corporation.)*

If you are planning to merely check journals and bearings, then remove bearing caps one at a time to make the checks. If the crankshaft is to come out of the engine, the connecting rods should be detached and all main-bearing caps removed.

Caps should be marked so that they can be replaced on the same journals from which they were removed. (See ■ 1-3-6 on marking rod caps.) To remove a cap, remove the nuts or bolts. Bend back the lock-washer tangs (if used). Disconnect oil lines where necessary. (Use new lock washers on reassembly.)

If a cap sticks, work it loose carefully to avoid nicking or cracking it. In some engines, a screwdriver or pry bar can be used to work the cap loose. Sometimes tapping the cap lightly on one side and then the other with a brass or plastic hammer will loosen it.

NOTE: Heavy hammering or prying can nick or crack the cap, bend the dowel pins, or damage the dowel holes. In such a case, the bearing may not fit when the cap is replaced, and early bearing failure will occur. Also, remember that the bearing caps are made of cast iron and so are brittle. A hard blow can crack or break a cap. A damaged cap will have to be discarded, and a new cap used. A cracked cap can break if it is reinstalled on the engine. Such a break usually means a ruined engine.

When a bearing cap is damaged or lost, a new cap is required. Some new caps are supplied with a shim pack so that the cap can be shimmed into alignment. However, it is difficult to get a good fit this way. So it may become necessary to take the engine out of the car, disassemble it, and install the caps, without bearings, back in the block. Then the block will have to be line-bored to reestablish bearing-bore alignment. (This procedure is discussed in ■ 1-4-19).

■ **1-4-7 Measuring Main Journals with Crankshaft Gauge** The special crankshaft gauge is shown in Fig. 3. The journal and gauge pads and plunger must be clean. Then, the plunger is retracted, and the gauge is held tightly against the journal (Fig. 3). Next, the plunger is released so that it moves out into contact with the journal. The plunger is then locked in this position by tightening the lockscrew. Finally, an outside micrometer is used to measure the distance between *D*, the end of the plunger, and *C*, the button on the bottom of the gauge. This measurement, multiplied by 2, is the diameter of the journal.[1]

NOTE: Take the measurements from one end of the journal to the other. Rotate the crankshaft by one-eighth turn to repeat the checks. This repeated measurement will detect journal taper and out-of-round. Write down the readings as you take them.

■ 1-4-8 Measuring Main Journals with Micrometer

To use the micrometer, the upper bearing half must be removed. This is done with a special roll-out tool, as explained in ■1-4-11. Then the micrometer can be used. Take measurements from one end of the journal to the other. Rotate the crankshaft by one-eighth turns to repeat the check. This procedure will detect journal taper and out-of-round.

■ 1-4-9 Inspecting Main Bearings

Main, or crankshaft, bearings should be replaced if they are worn, burned, scored, pitted, rough, flaked, cracked, or otherwise damaged. (See ■1-3-14 on bearing failures.) It is important to inspect the crankshaft journals (■ 1-4-5 to 1-4-8) before installing new bearings. If the journals are not in good condition, the new bearings may soon fail. Also, bearings may have worn unevenly; that is, some bearings may be worn considerably more than others. If so, or if a bearing is damaged, the possibility of a bent crankshaft or clogged oil passage should be considered. This means the crankshaft should come out so it and the oil galleries in the block can be inspected. The following sections describe checking bearing fit, replacing bearings, and servicing crankshafts.

NOTE: If one main bearing requires replacement, then all main bearings should be replaced even though the others appear to be in good condition. If only one main bearing is replaced, crankshaft alignment might be lost. This would overload some bearings, causing them to fail rapidly.

[1]If you are interested in the geometry of the gauge, note the following, and refer to Fig. 3.

$2AO = OC$ [In a 30° right triangle, the hypotenuse *(OC)* is twice the side opposite the 30° angle.]

$AO = OD$

$2OD = OC = OD + DC$

$OD = DC$

Since *DC* is therefore equal to the radius of the journal, *2DC* equals the diameter of the journal.

■ 1-4-10 Inspecting Main-Bearing Fit

Bearing fit (or oil clearance) should always be inspected after new bearings are installed. The fit should also be inspected whenever the condition of the bearings is being determined. (Crankshaft-journal condition should also be inspected at the same time.)

1. PRECISION-INSERT MAIN BEARINGS Bearing clearance can be checked with shim stock or Plastigage.

a. *With Shim Stock* Put a piece of shim stock of the right size and thickness in the bearing cap after the cap has been removed. Coat the shim stock lightly with oil. Replace the cap. Tighten the cap nuts or bolts to the specified tension. Note the ease with which the crankshaft can be turned.

NOTE: Do not attempt to rotate the crankshaft, as this could damage the bearing. Instead, see whether it will turn about 1 inch (25.4 mm) in one direction or the other.

If the crankshaft is locked or drags noticeably, the bearing clearance is less than the thickness of the shim stock. If it does not drag, an additional thickness of shim stock should be placed on top of the first. The ease of crankshaft movement should again be checked. Clearance normally should be about 0.002 inch (0.05 mm) (see the engine manufacturer's specifications for exact clearance). After clearance is determined, remove the cap, take out the shim stock, replace the cap, and torque the cap nuts according to specifications.

b. *With Plastigage* Wipe the journal and bearing clean of oil. Put a strip of Plastigage lengthwise in the center of the journal. Replace and tighten the cap. Then remove the cap and measure the amount the Plastigage has been flattened. Do not turn the crankshaft with the Plastigage in place. (See ■1-3-15 for more information on Plastigage.)

NOTE: The crankshaft must be supported so that its weight will not cause it to sag. A sagging crankshaft could result in an incorrect measurement. One way to support it is to position a small jack under the crankshaft. Let the jack bear against the counterweight next to the bearing being checked. Another method is to put shims in the bearing caps of the two adjacent main bearings. Then tighten the cap bolts. This lifts and supports the crankshaft. (If the engine is out of the car and inverted, this is not necessary.)

2. SHIM-ADJUSTED MAIN BEARINGS Loosen all bearing caps just enough to permit the crankshaft to turn freely. Take off the rear main-bearing cap. Remove one shim from each side of the cap. Replace and tighten the cap bolts or nuts to the specified tension. Rotate the crankshaft to see whether it now drags. If it does not drag, remove additional shims (in pairs). Check for drag after each pair is removed. When a drag is felt, replace one shim on each side of the cap. If the crankshaft now turns freely when the cap is tightened, the clearance is correct. Loosen the cap bolts or nuts. Go to the next bearing and adjust its clearance in the same way. Finally, when all bearings are adjusted, tighten all cap bolts or nuts to the proper tension. Then recheck for crankshaft drag as it is turned. If it drags, then recheck and readjust the bearings.

3. INSPECTING CRANKSHAFT END PLAY Crankshaft end play will become excessive if the thrust bearings are worn. This condition produces a noticeably sharp, irregular knock. If the wear is considerable, the knock will occur every time the clutch is released and applied. This action causes sudden endwise movements of the crankshaft. Check end play by forcing the crankshaft endwise as far as it will go. Then measure the clearance at the thrust bearing with a feeler gauge (Fig. 4). Consult the engine manufacturer's shop manual for allowable end play.

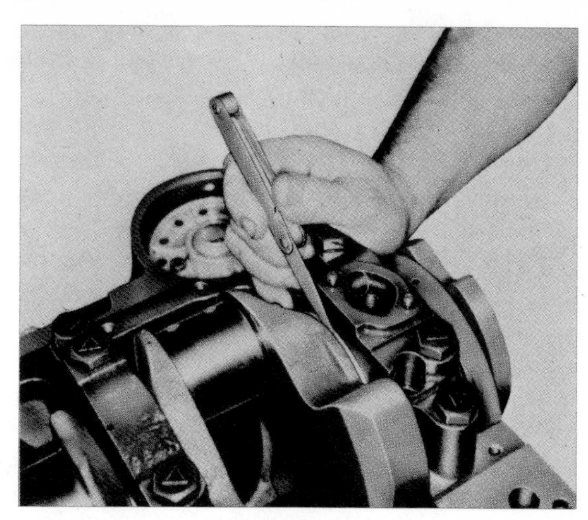

Figure 4 Crankshaft end play being checked at the thrust bearing with a feeler gauge. *(Chevrolet Motor Division of General Motors Corporation.)*

■ 1-4-11 Replacing Precision Main Bearings

Before replacing bearings, crankshaft journals should be checked (■1-4-5). Also, after bearings are installed, bearing fit should be checked (■1-4-10). Precision-insert main bearings can be replaced without removing the crankshaft. However, some technicians do not recommend this. They say that you are working blind. You cannot be sure that the counterbore in the cylinder block is perfectly clean and the shell is seating tightly. Furthermore, neither the crankshaft nor the block can be checked for alignment. With uneven bearing wear, the crankshaft should be removed for further inspection (■1-4-5).

To remove a precision-insert main bearing without removing the crankshaft, use a special roll-out tool. The tool is inserted into the oilhole in the crankshaft journal. Then the crankshaft is rotated. The tool forces the bearing shell to rotate with the crankshaft so that the bearing is turned out of the bore. The crankshaft must be rotated in the proper direction so that the lock, or tang, in the bearing is raised up out of the notch in the cylinder block.

To install a new bearing half, coat the bearing surface with engine oil. Leave the outside of the bearing dry. Make sure that the bore, or bearing seat, in the block is clean. Do not file the edges of the shell (this would remove the crush). Use the tool to slide the bearing shell into place. Make sure that the tang on the bearing shell seats in the notch in the block. Then place a new bearing shell in the cap. Install the cap, and tighten the cap bolts or nuts to the specified tension. Tap the crown of the cap lightly with a plastic hammer while tightening it. This helps to align the bearings properly. After all bearings are in place, check bearing fit.

> **NOTE:** If the crankshaft is removed, it is easier to install main bearings. Also, you can wipe the bearing bores in the cylinder block and make sure they are in good condition. Then, the bearing inserts can be slid into position.

Some bearing sets have annular (or ring) grooves in only one bearing half; others have grooves in both halves. Some do not use grooves. Be sure to check the service manual for the engine you are servicing to determine what kind of bearing half goes where.

Some crankshaft journals have no oilhole. For example, the rear main journals of many in-line engines do not. To remove and replace the upper bearing half on these journals, first start the bearing half with a small pin punch and hammer. Then use a pair of pliers with taped jaws to hold the bearing half against the oil slinger. Rotate the crankshaft. This movement will pull the old bearing out. The new bearing is put into position in the same manner. The last fraction of an inch can be pushed into place by holding only the oil slinger with the pliers while rotating the crankshaft. Or the bearing may be tapped down with a pin punch and hammer. Be careful that you do not damage the bearing.

> **NOTE:** While removing and replacing the upper bearing shell of a rear main bearing, hold the oil seal in position in the cylinder block; otherwise, it may move out of position (see ■ 1-4-12).

Bearing fit should be checked after all bearing caps have been replaced, as explained in ■ 1-4-10. If excessive clearances are found with the new bearings, the journals are worn. This means the crankshaft must be removed for service (■1-4-13) Then, undersize bearings must be installed. (Bearings are available in several undersizes.) The journals should be ground down enough to remove imperfections and then ground an additional amount to fit the next undersize bearings.

On all but a very few engines, precision-insert bearings are installed without shims. Never use shims on these bearings unless the engine manufacturer specified them. Similarly, bearing caps should not be filed in an attempt to improve bearing fit.

■ 1-4-12 Replacing the Main-Bearing Oil Seal

An oil seal is required at the rear main bearing to prevent oil leakage at that point (Fig. 5). When main-bearing service is being performed, or whenever leakage is noted at the rear main bearing, the oil seal must be replaced.

Replacement of the main-bearing oil seal varies with different constructions. On some engines using a split-type oil seal, the crankshaft must be removed. A special oil-seal compressor or installer is then used to insert the new seal in the cylinder-block bearing. The seal should then be trimmed flush with the block. The oil seal in the cap can be replaced by removing the cap, installing the oil seal, and trimming it flush. On other engines it is not necessary to remove the crankshaft since removal of the flywheel will permit access to the upper oil-seal retainer. The retainer cap screws can then be removed along with the retainer for oil-seal replacement.

Some engines use a one-piece rubber-type oil seal. It can be pulled from around the crankshaft with a pair of pliers. Then a new oil seal can be worked into place. The new oil seal should be coated with oil. Then coat the crankshaft contact surfaces of the seal with a suitable grease. Install the seal, using a seal-installing tool if required.

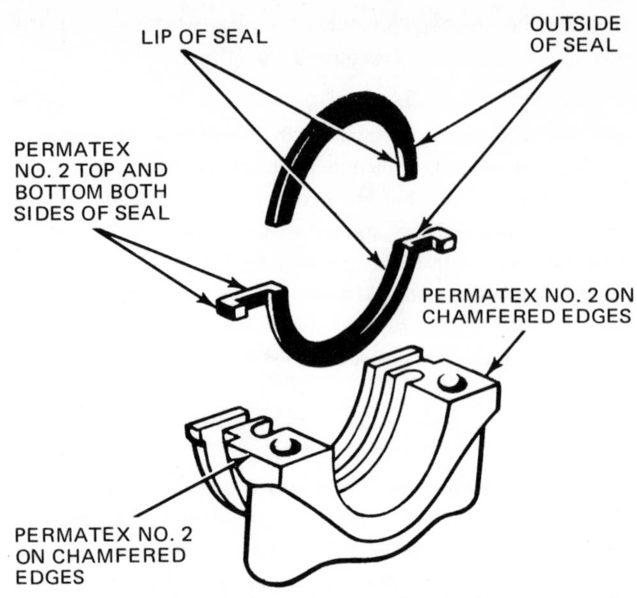

Figure 5 Crankshaft rear main-bearing oil seal. The upper part fits in a groove in the block. *(American Motors Corporation.)*

■ 1-4-13 Removing the Crankshaft

Such parts as the oil pan, timing-gear or timing-chain cover, crankshaft timing gear or sprocket, interfering oil lines, and oil pump must be removed before the crankshaft can be taken off. Also, on some engines, the flywheel must be detached from the crankshaft. With other parts off, the bearing caps are removed to release the crankshaft.

> **CAUTION:** The crankshaft is heavy! Support it adequately as you remove the bearing caps. Do not let it fall on you or on the floor.

> **NOTE:** For a complete engine overhaul, the cylinder head and piston-and-rod assemblies must be removed. However, if only the crankshaft is being removed, the piston-and-rod assemblies need not be removed. Instead, they can be detached from the crankshaft and pushed up out of the way. Be careful not to push them up too far! If you do, the top piston ring may move up beyond the cylinder block. In this case, the ring may jump out and catch on the top of the block. You will then be unable to pull the piston-and-rod assembly back down. You will have to remove the cylinder head and use a ring compressor to get the ring back down into the block again.

■ 1-4-14 Inspecting and Servicing the Crankshaft

Inspect the crankshaft for alignment and for main journal and crankpin wear. Alignment can be checked with V blocks and a dial indicator. As the crankshaft is rotated in the V blocks, the dial indicator will show any misalignment. Make sure the V blocks are clean. Oil them lightly so they do not scratch the crankshaft journals rotated on them.

> **NOTE:** Do not leave the crankshaft supported only in V blocks at the ends. This could cause the crankshaft to sag and go out of alignment from its own weight. To prevent misalignment, set the crankshaft on end or hang it from one end.

If the crankshaft is out of line, a new or reground crankshaft should be installed. It is very difficult to straighten a bent crankshaft.

Inspection of the journals and crankpins for taper or out-of-round is discussed in ■ 1-3-16 and ■ 1-4-5 to 1-4-8. If journals or crankpin taper or out-of-round exceeds allowable limits, or if they are rough, scratched, pitted, or otherwise damaged, they must be ground (■ 1-4-15). Then new undersize bearings must be installed. The crankshaft journals and crankpins must be ground down to fit the next undersize bearings available.

> **NOTE:** It is possible to "metalize" journals and crankpins and then regrind them to their original sizes. This is done by first rough-turning the journals and crankpins in a special crankshaft lathe. Then, a high-temperature flame is used to spray liquid metal onto the prepared surfaces. This metal adheres and can be ground to form a new journal surface. The procedure is useful for crankshafts from large, heavy-duty engines. A second procedure uses an electric arc to add metal to the journal. The cost of these rebuilt crankshafts sometimes makes saving the old crankshaft worthwhile.

■ 1-4-15 Finishing Main and Crank Journals

A special lathe, or crankshaft grinder, is required to service main and crank journals. This machine is found in automotive machine shops specializing in crankshaft service and in some engine-rebuilding shops.

The bearing surface must be finished to extreme smoothness. When installing the crankshaft, some authorities recommend a final polishing with a long strip of oiled crocus cloth (a special cloth used to polish metal). Wrap the strip halfway around the journal and pull it back and forth, being careful to work all the way around the journal.

> **NOTE:** When a crankshaft is reground on a crankshaft grinder, be sure to relieve (grind back) the journal and crankpin radii (where they curve up to the crank cheeks). This procedure will guard against bearing failure from radii ride (see ■1-3-14, item 5). Also, use care in cleaning the flange on the journal that takes the thrust bearing. These faces must be smooth and square with the crankshaft journal.

1. CLEANING THE CRANKSHAFT Any time that a crankshaft is out of the engine or after grinding journals and crankpins, the crankshaft should be thoroughly cleaned. Journals and crankpins can be cleaned with a long strip of oiled crocus cloth. Then the crankshaft should be washed in a suitable solvent. A valve-guide or rifle cleaning brush should be used to clean out oil passages. Any trace of abrasive left in an oil passage can work out onto a bearing surface and cause early bearing failure. Oil the bearing surfaces immediately after they have been cleaned to prevent rusting.

2. GRINDING CRANKPINS ON ENGINE A special crankpin grinder can be used to grind crankpins with the crankshaft still in the engine. The grinder is attached to a crankpin, and the crankshaft is rotated by a driving device at the rear wheel (the transmission in gear). This is not a recommended procedure.

■ 1-4-16 Cylinder Wear

The piston-and-ring movement, the high temperatures and pressures of combustion, the washing action of gasoline entering the cylinder—all these tend to cause cylinder-wall wear. At the start of the power stroke, pressures are the greatest. The compression rings are forced with the greatest pressure against the cylinder wall. Also, at the same time, the temperatures are highest. The oil film is therefore least effective in protecting the cylinder wall. Thus, the most wear will take place at the top of the cylinder. As the piston moves down on the power stroke, the combustion pressure and temperature decrease. Less wear takes place. Therefore, the cylinder wears irregularly, as shown in Fig. 6. This is taper wear, which leaves a large ridge at the top and a smaller ridge at the bottom. These ridges mark the limits of ring travel.

In addition to taper wear, the cylinder tends to wear oval-shaped because the piston tends to push sideways against the cylinder wall as it moves up and down in the cylinder. These side thrusts of the piston are due to the tilting of the connecting rod. For example, on the power stroke the total push on the piston is almost straight down. Most of this push is carried downward through the connecting rod. But a small component of the total push thrusts the piston sideways against the cylinder wall. Although this sideward force does tend to cause wear, it is actually not a major factor in cylinder wear because it is relatively small.

It is easy to be fooled by "oval wear" because cylinders have different shapes at different temperatures. When you

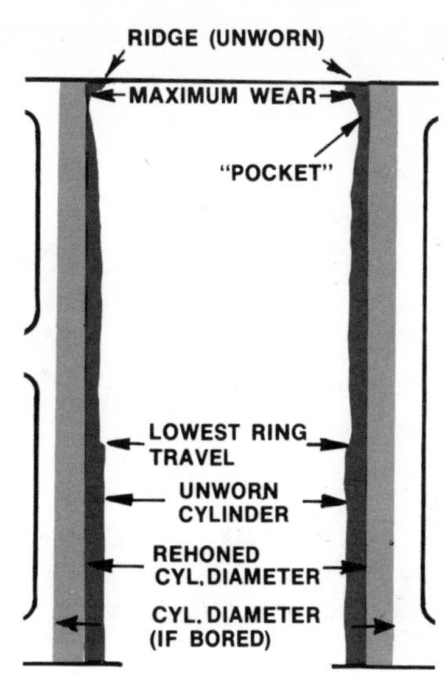

Figure 6 Taper wear of an engine cylinder (shown exaggerated). Maximum wear is at the top, just under the ring ridge. Honing the cylinder usually requires removal of less material than boring, as indicated. Material to be removed by honing is shown solid. Material to be removed by boring is shown both solid and shaded. *(Sunnen Products Company.)*

remove the cylinder head of a cold engine and carefully measure cylinders for eccentricity, you are quite likely to find that they are indeed oval. What happens, however, when you put the head back on and run the engine? First, in replacing the head and drawing the bolts or nuts down right you are introducing certain stresses into the block. These stresses alter the shape of the cylinder. Then, when the engine is started and the block warms up, the expansion of the metal alters the cylinder shape still further. In many cases these changes in cylinder shape reduce the out-of-roundness; that is, replacing the head and warming the block reduce the eccentricity of the cylinders. Here is how this condition comes about. When the block is first manufactured, the bores are all machined to be perfectly round when cold. But installing the head and warming the new block (by running the engine) cause the cylinders to be distorted out of round. However, as the engine operates, the piston-ring action tends to wear the cylinders round. In other words, the cylinders wear round when hot. After that, when the block cools and the heat is removed, the stresses are changed so that the cylinders distort out of round. But replacing the head and warming the block reduce this distortion; the cylinders become more nearly round.

Another type of cylinder wear results from the washing action of entering gasoline. This wear is more likely to occur on the cylinder wall opposite the intake valve. At times the air-fuel mixture is not perfectly blended, and small droplets of gasoline, still unvaporized, enter the cylinder. These droplets of gasoline strike the cylinder wall and tend to wash away the protective film of lubricating oil. With reduced protection, some additional wear takes place. A closed choke, which excessively enriches the air-fuel mixture, hastens this sort of wear. Quantities of unvaporized gasoline are likely to enter the cylinder as long as the closed choke causes the carburetor to supply a rich mixture.

Figure 7 Checking the cylinder block for warpage with a straightedge.

■ 1-4-17 Cleaning and Inspecting the Cylinder Block

As a first step, make a visual inspection of the block. Major damage resulting from a main bearing spinning or a broken connecting rod going through the block means the block must be discarded. If the engine has overheated and there are cracks in the cylinder walls, discard the block.

Inspect the cylinder bores for cracks, grooves, scratches, or discoloration. Inspect for cracks across the top of the block between cylinders, between bolt holes, on the outside of the block, and in the main-bearing-bore webs. (See ■1-4-27 on block repairs.) If everything looks okay, measure the cylinder bores with a micrometer. If the bores are not too badly worn and they can be honed or rebored within specified limits, then clean the block. In other words, if you have decided to reuse the block, you should clean and service it.

To clean the block, first remove the cam bearings and expansion (freeze) plugs (see ■1-4-28). Then use the cleaning method that is available in the shop. One method uses a jet of steam from a steam cleaner directed by a nozzle onto the block to wash away dirt, sludge, and oil. Another method is to boil the block in a hot solution of caustic soda or similar chemical. A good solvent can also be brushed on to clean the block. Be sure that all old gasket material is removed from machined surfaces. All pipe plugs that close off oil passages should be removed so the passages can be blown out with compressed air. Long rods of the proper diameter or valve-guide cleaning brushes can be pushed through the oil passages. This will clear out sludge that does not easily blow out. Clogged oil passages prevent normal bearing lubrication so that the bearings wear rapidly and fail. Make sure the passages are clean.

Threaded holes in the block should be blown out with compressed air. If the threads are not in good condition, use a tap or thread chaser of the correct size to clean them. Then blow out the holes. Dirty or battered threads may give false torque readings that will prevent normal tightening of bolts on reassembly. This could cause failure from loose engine parts. Dirt in the bottom of a bolt hole may prevent normal tightening of the bolt. In addition, it could cause the block to break because of the pressure applied at the bottom of the hole as the bolt is tightened. Repairing damaged threads with thread inserts is described in ■1-4-29.

If there is any suspicion of cracks, the block should be Magna-Fluxed. In this procedure, a strong magnetic field is put on the block. Then, powdered iron is sprinkled on the block. If there is a crack, the powdered iron is attracted to it and the crack is shown plainly.

Machined gasket surfaces should be inspected for burrs, nicks, and scratches. Minor damage can be removed with a fine-cut file. Check the head mating surfaces of the block for warpage by laying a long straightedge against the sealing surfaces (Fig. 7). If there is any clearance between the straightedge and the cylinder block, measure it with a feeler gauge, as shown. The surface of the block should be flat and true within the manufacturer's specifications. A typical specification is that the surface should not be more than 0.003 inch (0.076 mm) out of true for each 6 inches (152.4 mm) of surface. If the surface is out of true more than this, it should be refaced in a surface grinder. This is a job for the automotive machine shop. No more than the minimum amount of metal should be removed as required to true the surface.

Inspect the main-bearing bores for alignment and out-of-roundness (■1-4-18). Bearing shells must be removed, but caps must be in place for this check.

If expansion plugs have not been removed (that is, if the block has not been cleaned), they should be checked for leaks. Any plugs that look as though they have leaked should be replaced (■1-4-28).

■ 1-4-18 Inspecting Bearing Bores

Very uneven bearing wear with some bearings worn much more than others may mean out-of-round bearing bores or a warped block. Inadequate oiling could also be a factor, possibly resulting from a worn oil pump or clogged oil passages (■1-4-4).

To check for out-of-round bores, the crankshaft and main bearings must be removed. The bearing bores must be clean and the caps installed with the bolts torqued to specifications. Then an inside micrometer can be used to check for out-of-round. If the bores are out of round or out of true, they must be line-bored to restore roundness (■1-4-19).

To check bores for alignment, a special alignment bar is installed in place of the crankshaft with the bearings removed. The bar is 0.001 inch (0.03 mm) smaller than the diameter of the bores. When the cap bolts are torqued to specifications, the bar should turn with the help of an extension handle on the bar. If it does not turn, the block is out of line and the bores must be machined (■1-4-19).

NOTE: If a bearing cap is damaged or lost, a new cap is required. It is sometimes hard to get good cap alignment when a new cap is installed. To secure good alignment, the bearing bores may require line boring (■1-4-19).

■ **1-4-19 Line-Boring the Bearing Bores** As a first step, all bearing caps should have about 0.015 inch (0.38 mm) removed from their parting faces. The parting face is the surface that meets the cylinder block when the cap is installed. One method is to gang the caps together in a special fixture. Then use a surface grinder to grind all the caps at once.

Next, the caps are installed and the cap bolts torqued to specifications. Then, the block is clamped in the boring machine. Bores should be measured to determine how much metal has to be removed. Enough metal should be removed to allow the bores to take standard bearings. Then the boring tool is adjusted to cut the bores to their original diameters. The adjustment must allow most of the material to be removed from the caps. If any amount of material is removed from the bore half in the block, the distance between the crankshaft and camshaft centerlines will be shortened. This could cause timing-gear meshing problems.

After the bore job is finished, remove the caps. Scrape off any burrs from the edges of the caps and block bores. Then clean the block and cap, making sure you remove all traces of dirt and metal particles. The block and oil passages must be clean!

■ **1-4-20 Cylinder Service** Up to certain limits, cylinders may wear tapered or out of round and not require refinishing. As discussed in ■1-3-25, special severe replacement rings will control compression and oil in cylinders with some taper and out-of-round wear. But when wear goes beyond a certain point, even the severest rings cannot hold compression and control oil. Loss of compression, high oil consumption, poor performance, and heavy carbon accumulations in the cylinders will result. Then, the only way to get the engine back into good operating condition is to refinish the cylinders. New pistons (or resized pistons) and new rings must be installed at the same time.

■ **1-4-21 Inspecting Cylinder Walls** Wipe walls and examine them for scores and spotty wear (which show up as dark, unpolished spots). Hold a light at the opposite end of the cylinder so that you can see the walls better. Scores or spots mean the walls must be refinished. Even severe rings cannot give satisfactory performance on such walls.

Next, measure the cylinders for wear, taper, and out-of-roundness (Fig. 8). This can be done with an inside micrometer, a telescope gauge, and an outside micrometer, or cylinder bore gauge. The cylinder bore gauge is moved up and down in the cylinder and rotated at various positions to detect wear. To measure taper, start with the dial set to zero and with the dial indicator at the top of ring travel. Then push the dial indicator to the bottom of the cylinder. The movement of the indicator needle will tell you how much the cylinder has worn tapered. To check for out-of-round wear, rotate the dial indicator at various positions in the cylinder. Note the amount of needle movement. Write down the wear measurements for each cylinder. Compare them with the allowable maximum

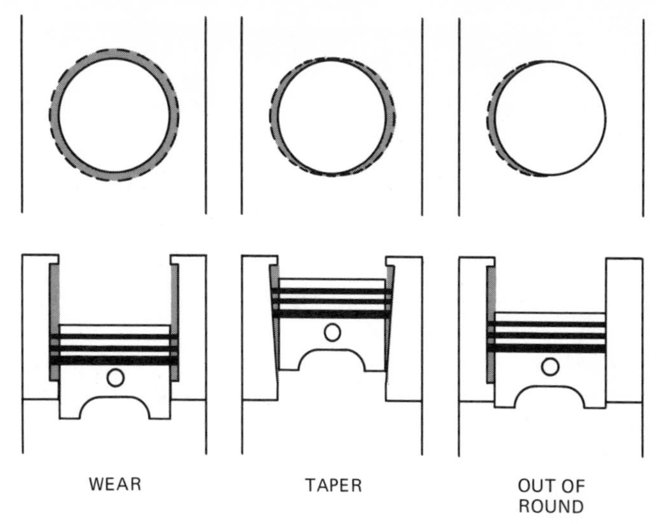

Figure 8 Cylinder wear, taper, and out-of-roundness.

specified by the engine manufacturer to decide what has to be done.

A quick way to measure cylinder taper is to push a compression ring down to the lower limit of ring travel. Measure the ring gap with a feeler gauge. Then pull the ring up to the upper limit of ring travel. Remeasure the ring gap. The top gap minus the bottom gap divided by 3 gives you the approximate cylinder taper.

■ **1-4-22 Refinishing Cylinders** As a first step, the block should be cleaned (■1-4-17). A decision must be made on whether the cylinders are to be honed or bored. This decision depends on the amount of cylinder wear. Figure 6 illustrates the amount of metal removed by the hone and by boring. The hone uses a set of abrasive stones which are turned in the cylinder. The boring machine uses a revolving cutting tool. Where cylinder wear is not too great, only honing is necessary. But if wear has gone so far that a considerable amount of material must be removed, then honing will not do the job and the cylinder must be rebored.

> **NOTE:** If cylinders are within specifications and do not require honing or boring, a glaze breaker should be run through the cylinders. Three or four strokes of the glaze breaker will "break the glaze" on the cylinder wall. This practice produces a slightly roughened surface which will let the new rings wear in properly.

If the crankshaft has not been removed, the main bearings and crankshaft must be protected from grit and cuttings. Stuff clean rags down in the cylinders to catch the cuttings.

■ **1-4-23 Honing Cylinders** If wear, taper, or out-of-round are not too great, only honing will be required. During the honing operation, the cylinder is sprayed with a honing lubricant. When using a hand-held hone, sometimes the stones are frequently dipped in solvent.

NOTE: Dry honing is also done. With dry honing, a vacuum device removes the dust produced by the operation.

If a considerable amount of material must be removed, start with coarse stones. Sufficient material must be left, however, so that all rough hone marks can be removed with fine or finishing stones. (See ■1-3-25 for information about how the cylinder wall should look after final honing.) The proper honing pattern is important in obtaining good wearing-in of new piston rings. This pattern is obtained by moving the hone up and down as it rotates.

Final honed size should be just right to take a standard oversize piston and rings. In other words, the cylinder should be finished so that the piston and rings will fit it. Here is the way it is done. First, the piston is miked. Then the cylinder is honed to take the piston plus the proper clearance. Usually, the clearance is about 0.001 inch (0.03 mm). That is, the cylinder is finished 0.001 inch (0.03 mm) larger than the piston diameter.

During the later stages of honing, the hone should be withdrawn periodically and the cylinder measured. This guards against overhoning.

Cylinders must be cleaned after honing (see■ 1-4-25).

NOTE: Only those cylinders requiring service need be honed. Oversize pistons can be installed in some cylinders of an engine, and standard pistons in other cylinders. Manufacturers supply oversize pistons that weigh the same as the standard pistons. Thus, there is no problem of balance when pistons of different sizes are used in an engine. To service only one or two cylinders, you can leave the pistons in the other cylinders. That way, you would not have to install new rings on all pistons. And you wouldn't have to break the glaze on the cylinders not requiring honing. However, it is best to have all cylinder bores the same size.

■ 1-4-24 Boring Cylinders If cylinder wear is too great to be cleaned up by honing, the cylinder must be bored. The size to which it is rebored depends on the amount of material that must be removed from the cylinder wall. It also depends on the size of oversize pistons available. For example, Chevrolet supplies pistons 0.010, 0.020, and 0.030 inch (0.25, 0.51, and 0.76 mm) oversize.

Modern thin-wall engines are limited as to the amount of material that can be taken from the cylinder walls. If you take more than the maximum specified, the cylinder wall will be so thin that it will not hold up in service.

NOTE: First, refinish the cylinder that has the most wear. If you cannot clean up that cylinder when refinishing it to take the maximum-size piston available, discard the cylinder block. Or, if the block is otherwise in good condition, you could consider installing cylinder sleeves (■ 1-4-26).

One type of boring bar is centered by fingers that can be moved in or out. The centering fingers of the cutting head extended so that the head will be centrally located in the cylinder. The centering should be done with the cutting head at the bottom of the cylinder. Then, when the centering fingers are extended, the cutting head will be centered in the original, unworn, center part of the cylinder. This is one of several types of boring bars.

Several cautions must be observed in the use of the boring bar. First, the top of the cylinder block must be smooth and free of any nicks or burrs. Nicks or burrs upset the alignment of the bar. They cause the cylinder to be bored at an angle to the crankshaft. Nicks and burrs should be removed with a fine-cut file. All main bearing caps should be in place. The cap bolts or nuts should be tightened to the specified tension. If this is not done, the bearing bores may become distorted from the cylinder boring operation.

The boring operation should remove just enough material to clean up the cylinder wall so that all irregularities are removed. One recommended procedure is to bore the cylinder to the same diameter as the oversize piston to be installed. The final honing will remove enough additional material to give the recommended clearance. This is usually 0.001 to 0.002 inch (0.03 to 0.05 mm), depending on the engine model.

NOTE: Only those cylinders requiring it need to be rebored and final honed. However, it is recommended practice to rebore all cylinders in an engine to the same oversize.

The last step in the boring operation is to use a hone or glaze breaker to roughen the cylinder walls. This roughs up the cylinder walls enough to provide a surface suitable for ring wear-in. The boring bar can leave a very smooth surface, particularly if a light final cut has been taken. This surface can be too smooth to properly seat the rings. So it should be roughed with a glaze breaker or hone.

■ 1-4-25 Cleaning Cylinders Cylinders must be cleaned thoroughly after the honing or boring operation. Even slight traces of grit or dust on the cylinder walls may cause rapid ring and wall wear and early engine failure. As a first step, some engine manufacturers recommend wiping down the cylinder walls with very fine crocus cloth. This loosens embedded grit and also knocks off "fuzz" left by the honing stones or cutting tool. Then use a stiff brush and hot soapy water to wash down the walls. It is absolutely essential to clean the walls of all abrasive material. If not removed, such material causes rapid wear of pistons, rings, and bearings.

After washing down the walls, swab them down several times with a cloth dampened with light engine oil. Wipe off the oil each time with a clean, dry cloth. At the end of the cleaning job, the cleaning cloth should come away from the walls showing no trace of dirt.

Clean out all coolant and oil passages in the block, as well as stud and bolt holes, after the walls are cleaned (see ■1-4-17).

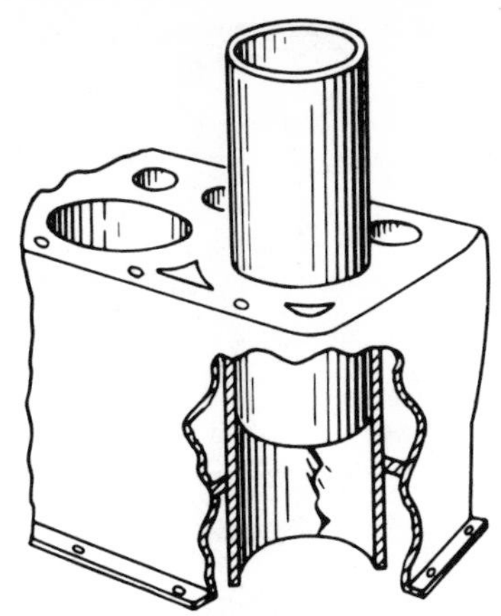

Figure 9 Cracked block and badly scored or worn cylinder bores can sometimes be repaired by installing cylinder sleeves. *(Sealed Power Corporation)*

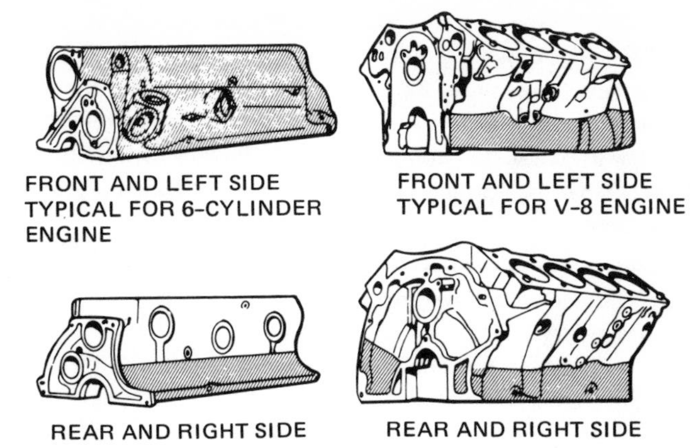

Figure 10 Areas of cylinder blocks that can be repaired with epoxy. *(Ford Motor Company)*

> **NOTE:** Gasoline and kerosene will not remove all the grit from cylinder walls. Their use to clean grit or dust off cylinder walls is not recommended.

■ 1-4-26 Replacing Cylinder Sleeves

There are two types of cylinder sleeves: wet and dry. The wet sleeve is sealed to the block at the top and bottom. It is in direct contact with the coolant. The dry sleeve is pressed into the cylinder. This type is in contact with the cylinder wall from top to bottom.

Cracked blocks, scored cylinders, cylinders worn so badly that they must be rebored to an excessively large oversize—all these can often be repaired by the installation of cylinder sleeves (Fig. 9). As a first step, the cylinders are bored oversize to take the sleeves. Then the sleeves are pressed into place.

Some shops use a pneumatic hammer, which uses compressed air to hammer the sleeves down into place in the cylinder block.

■ 1-4-27 Repairing Cylinder-Block Cracks or Porosity

Sometimes a cylinder block is in good condition except for some cracks or sand holes (left in the block during casting). It may then be worthwhile to repair the block. Areas which are not subjected to temperatures of more than 500°F (260°C) or pressure (from coolant, oil, or cylinders) can be repaired with a metallic plastic or epoxy. Permissible repair areas for one manufacturer's engines are shown in Fig. 10.

The epoxy repair is started by cleaning the porous or cracked area down to bright metal with a grinder. Chamfer or undercut the crack or holes. If a hole is larger than ¼ inch (6.35 mm), drill, tap, and plug it. Smaller holes or cracks can be repaired with epoxy. Mix the two ingredients according to the directions on the package. Apply the mixture with a putty knife or similar tool. Fill cracks and holes and smooth the surface as much as possible. Allow the mixture to cure according to directions on the package. Then sand or grind the surface smooth and paint it.

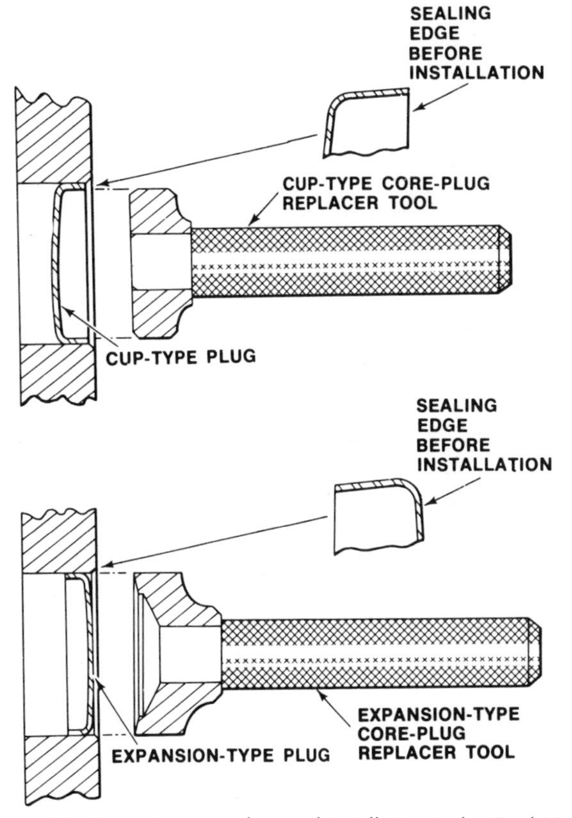

Figure 11 Expansion-core plugs and installation tools. *(Ford Motor Company.)*

A crack in a critical area, as for example between bolt holes or cylinders on the gasket surface, may often require cold welding to repair it. First, drill a small hole in the crack and thread it. Screw in a threaded rod, and cut it off. Then drill a second hole overlapping the first, and thread it. Screw in a threaded rod, and cut it off. Repeat until the whole crack is treated. Make sure to get to both ends of the crack to relieve the stress that caused the crack. Then resurface the block in a surface grinder. [This is the same procedure used to repair cracks in cylinder heads (■ 1-2-20).]

■ 1-4-28 Expansion-Core Plugs

You may have to remove an expansion plug from the block (because of coolant) leakage, for example). To do this, put the pointed end of a pry bar against the center of the plug. Tap the end of the bar with a hammer until the point goes through the plug. Then press the pry bar to one side to pop the plug out. Another method is to drill a small hole in the center of the plug and then pry the plug out.

> **NOTE:** Do not drive the pry bar or drill past the plug. On some engines the plug is only about 3/8 inch (9.52 mm) from a cylinder wall. You could damage the cylinder wall if you drove the pry bar or drill too far. Do not drive the plug into the water jacket. You would have trouble getting it out, and it could block coolant circulation.

Inspect the bore for roughness or damage that would prevent proper sealing of a new plug. If necessary, bore out the bore to take the next-size-larger plug. Before installing the new plug, coat it with the proper sealer (water-resistant for cooling systems and oil-resistant for oil galleries). Use the proper installation tool and proceed as follows, depending on the type of plug (Fig. 11).

1. CUP-TYPE PLUG The cup-type plug is installed with the flanged edge outward. The proper size of tool must be used. It must not contact the flange, but all driving must be against the internal cup. The flange must be brought down below the chamfered edge of the bore.

2. EXPANSION-TYPE PLUG The expansion-type plug is installed with the flanged edge inward, as shown. The proper tool must be used. The crowned center part must not be touched when the plug is driven in. Instead, the tool must drive against the outer part of the plug, as shown. The plug should be driven in until the top of the crown is below the chamfered edge of the bore.

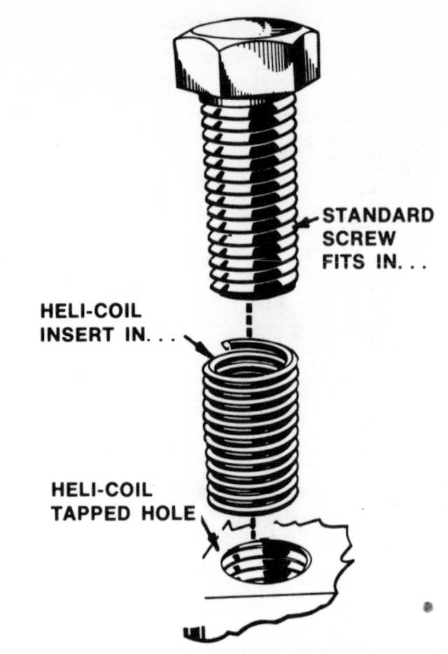

Figure 12 Heli-Coil installation. *(Chrysler Corporation)*

■ 1-4-29 Threaded Inserts

Damaged or worn threads in the block or head can often be repaired with a threaded insert. One such is the Heli-Coil (Fig. 12). First, drill out the worn threads. Tap the hole with the special Heli-Coil tap to make new threads. Then screw a Heli-Coil insert into the new threads, to bring the hole back to its original thread size. The original bolt can then be used in the hole.

SECTION 1-5 | Ignition System Service

This section is divided into three parts, ignition trouble diagnosis and tests, ignition testers and tests, and ignition-distributor service.

IGNITION TROUBLE DIAGNOSIS AND TESTS

■ **1-5-1 Causes of Ignition Failure** Ignition-system failures can be grouped into three categories, as follows:

1. Loss of energy in the primary circuit. This, in turn, may be caused by several conditions.

a. Resistance in the primary circuit due to defective leads, bad connections, burned distributor contact points or switch, or open coil primary circuit
b. Points not properly set
c. Discharged battery or defective alternator
d. Defective condenser (shorted, low insulation resistance, or high series resistance)
e. Grounded primary circuit in coil, wiring, or distributor

f. Defective electronic amplifier unit or pickup-coil circuit

2. Loss of energy in the secondary circuit.
   a. Spark plugs fouled, broken, or out of adjustment
   b. Defective high-voltage wiring which allows high-voltage leaks
   c. High-voltage leakage across coil head, distributor cap, or rotor
   d. Defective connections in high-voltage circuits
3. Out of time.
   a. Timing not set properly
   b. Distributor bearing or shaft worn, or shaft bent
   c. Centrifugal advance defective
   d. Preignition due to plugs of wrong heat range, fouled plugs, etc.

■ 1-5-2 Ignition-System Trouble-Diagnosis Chart

The chart to the right lists (1) various ignition-system troubles and possible engine troubles that might originate in the ignition system, (2) possible causes of these various troubles, and (3) checks or corrections to be made.

■ 1-5-3 Quick Checks to Locate Troubles

There are several quick checks that can be made when certain types of troubles are reported. These quick checks often immediately indicate the cause of trouble. On the other hand, it may be necessary to use special testing instruments (as explained on following pages) to find the cause. Often the first step will be to replace the battery, since the driver may have run it down in a vain attempt to start. Quick checks to be made as well as causes and corrections of various ignition troubles, are described below.

> **NOTE:** If an oscilloscope is available and the engine can be started, the oscilloscope can pinpoint many trouble causes in the ignition system.

■ 1-5-4 Engine Cranks Normally but Will Not Start

If the starting motor cranks the engine at normal cranking speed but the engine will not start, the trouble is probably in the ignition system or the fuel system. First test the ignition system by trying the spark test, as follows: Disconnect the lead from one spark plug and hold the lead clip about 3/16 inch (5 mm) from the engine block while cranking the engine. Or pull the lead from the center terminal of the distributor cap and hold it close to the engine block. If a good spark jumps to the block, the chances are the primary and secondary circuits are in good condition. These circuits must both function normally to produce a good spark. If they do, then failure to start could be due to badly fouled spark plugs or out-of-time ignition. However, it should be remembered that many other conditions—including faulty fuel-system action, malfunctioning valves, loss of engine compression, and so on—could prevent normal starting. Most often failure to start (with normal cranking) is due to trouble in the ignition or fuel system.

IGNITION-SYSTEM TROUBLE-DIAGNOSIS CHART

CONDITION	POSSIBLE CAUSE	CHECK OR CORRECTION
1. Engine cranks normally but will not start (■1-5-4)	a. Open primary circuit	Check connections, coil, contact points, and switch for open
	b. Coil primary grounded	Replace coil
	c. Points not opening	Adjust
	d. Points burned	Clean or replace
	e. Out of time	Check and adjust timing
	f. Condenser defective	Replace
	g. Coil secondary open or grounded	Replace coil
	h. High-voltage leakage	Check coil head, distributor cap and rotor, and leads
	i. Spark plugs fouled	Clean and adjust or replace
	j. Defects in electronic amplifier or pickup-coil circuit	Replace defective part
	k. Fuel system faulty	See Part 1, Sec. 6
	l. Engine faulty	
2. Engine runs but misses—one cylinder (■1-5-5)	a. Defective spark plug	Clean or replace
	b. Distributor cap or lead defective	Replace
	c. Engine defects such as stuck valve, defective rings, piston, gasket	
3. Engine runs but misses—different cylinders (■1-5-6)	a. Points dirty, worn, or out of adjustment	Clean, replace, or adjust as necessary
	b. Condenser defective	Replace
	c. Advance mechanisms defective	Repair or replace distributor
	d. Defective high-voltage wiring	Replace
	e. Defective (weak) coil	Replace
	f. Bad connections	Clean and tighten connections
	g. High-voltage leakage	Check coil head, distributor cap and rotor, and leads
	h. Defective spark plugs	Clean, adjust, or replace
	i. Defective fuel system	See Part 1, Sec. 6
	j. Defects in engine such as loss of	See Part 1, Sec. 2

CONDITION	POSSIBLE CAUSE	CHECK OR CORRECTION
	compression or faulty valve action	
4. Engine lacks power (■1-5-7)	a. Timing off	Retime ignition
	b. Exhaust system clogged	Clean
	c. Excessive rolling resistance	Check tires, brakes, wheel bearings, and alignment
	d. Heavy engine oil	Use correct oil
	e. Wrong fuel	Use correct fuel
	f. Engine overheats	See item 5
	g. Other defects listed under item 3	
5. Engine overheats (■1-5-8)	a. Late ignition timing	Retime ignition
	b. Lack of coolant or other trouble in cooling system	See Part 1, Sec. 7
	c. Late valve timing or other engine conditions	See Part 1, Sec. 2
6. Engine backfires (■1-5-9)	a. Ignition timing off	Retime ignition
	b. Ignition crossfiring	Check high-voltage wiring, cap, and rotor for leakage paths
	c. Spark plugs of wrong heat range	Install correct plugs
	d. Engine overheating	See item 5
	e. Fuel system not supplying proper air-fuel ratio	See Part 1, Sec. 6
	f. Engine defects such as hot valves or carbon	See Part 1, Sec. 2
	g. Malfunctioning antibackfire valve	
7. Engine pings (■1-5-10)	a. Improper timing	Retime engine
	b. Advance mechanisms faulty	Rebuild or replace distributor
	c. Points out of adjustment	Readjust
	d. Distributor bearing worn or shaft bent	Rebuild or replace distributor
	e. Spark plugs of wrong heat range	Replace with correct plugs
	f. Low-octane fuel	Use fuel of proper octane
	g. Conditions listed under item 6	
8. Rapid wear of centrifugal-advance mechanism (■1-5-11)	a. Loose or worn valve-timing gears	See Part 1, Sec. 2
	b. Worn oil pump	See Part 1, Sec. 8
9. Pitted contact points (■1-5-12)	a. Transfer of point material	Buildup on positive point: install new condenser with higher capacity; separate leads or move closer to ground; shorten condenser lead. Buildup on negative point: install new condenser with lower capacity; move leads closer together or away from ground; lengthen condenser lead
10. Burned or oxidized contact points (■1-5-13)	a. Excessive resistance in condenser circuit	Tighten condenser mounting and connections; replace condenser if bad
	b. High voltage	Readjust voltage regulator
	c. Excessive contact angle	Reset contacts
	d. Weak spring tension	Adjust contact-spring tension
	e. Oil or crankcase vapors entering distributor	Clear engine PCV system; avoid overlubricating distributor
11. Spark plugs defective (■1-5-14)	a. Cracked insulator	Careless installation; install new plug
	b. Plug sooty	Install hotter plug; correct condition in fuel system or engine causing oil burning or high fuel consumption
	c. Plug white or gray, with blistered insulator	Install cooler plug

NOTE: Another way to check for a spark is to remove the distributor cap and snap the contact points open and closed. The ignition switch should be on, and the lead from the coil high-voltage terminal should be held close to the engine block. This check does not test the distributor drive or the secondary wiring.

If a spark does not occur when the spark test is made, it means the ignition system is not doing its job of producing high voltage. Check further by watching the instrument-panel ammeter while cranking.

NOTE: If the car does not have an ammeter, connect a test ammeter into the ignition primary circuit to make this test.

1. If there is a small reading which fluctuates slightly during cranking, then the primary circuit is probably okay. The trouble is most likely in the secondary and is due to a defective coil secondary, defective secondary connections or leads, or high-voltage leakage across the coil head, cap, or rotor. Also, an open or "weak" condenser could be preventing high-voltage buildup in the secondary.

2. If the ammeter shows a fairly high and steady discharge reading with no fluctuations during cranking, then the trouble is probably in the primary circuit. Either the points are not opening because they are out of adjustment or the condenser is grounded, or else the primary circuit is grounded in the coil or primary wiring.

3. If there is no ammeter reading, the primary circuit is open. The open could be due to a loose connection, defective wiring or switch, distributor contact points out of adjustment or burned, or an open coil primary. A voltmeter can be used to find the open by checking from various terminals in the primary to ground to see where voltage is available. First, check from the distributor primary-lead terminal on the coil to ground. If there is voltage there, the trouble is inside the distributor. If there is no voltage at the distributor primary-lead terminal on the coil, check from the other ignition-coil primary terminal to ground. If you now get a reading, the trouble is in the coil primary winding. If you get no reading, the trouble is in the wiring or the switch. Disassemble the switch extension if the coil has one, so that the coil and switch may be checked separately.

■ 1-5-5 Engine Runs but Misses—One Cylinder You can locate a missing cylinder by shorting out each cylinder spark plug in turn with the engine running at various speeds. This prevents a spark from occurring in the spark plug and causes the cylinder to miss. On late-model cars, the spark plugs have neoprene boots over the spark-plug terminals. A quick way to check these is to remove the cables from the distributor cap one by one and note any change in engine speed. If the engine rhythm or speed changes when the plug is shorted out or its circuit is opened, then that cylinder was delivering power before being shorted out. However, if no change in the operation of the engine is noted when a spark plug is shorted or its circuit is opened, then the cylinder is not delivering power; it is missing. If you locate a missing cylinder, remove the lead from the spark plug (with other cylinders operating) and hold it close to the engine block to see if a good spark occurs. If it does not, the cause of trouble is in the secondary circuit of the ignition system. It could be due to defective cable insulation or to a cracked or burned distributor cap. Either of these could allow high-voltage leakage to ground. But if a good spark occurs, then it could be that the spark plug is defective. Install a new plug. If the cylinder now performs normally, the trouble was a defective plug. If changing the plug does not help, then the trouble is in the engine cylinder (stuck valve, defective rings, piston, head gasket, and so on).

CAUTION: On the High-Energy Ignition System, use rubber gloves or an insulated pliers to handle spark-plug cables on a running engine. You can get a severe shock from this system because of the high voltage it produces.

NOTE: A quick way to locate the cause of engine-missing trouble is to check the system with an oscilloscope. Most oscilloscopes have a built-in device that can be operated to short any selected spark plug.

■ 1-5-6 Engine Runs but Misses—Different Cylinders If the miss seems to jump around and you cannot pin it down to any particular cylinder, then the trouble could be due to any of several conditions in the ignition system, fuel system, or engine. The distributor contact points could be worn, dirty, or out of adjustment. The condenser or ignition coil could be "weak," so that the spark would not be uniform, and erratic missing would occur. The advance mechanisms might be erratic in action and cause uneven timing and missing. Distributors with the breaker plate supported by balls running in the ball track in the distributor housing may have the following troubles: The ball track wears, or the balls get dirty or worn; this causes the breaker plate to hang up or tilt when the vacuum-advance mechanism operates. This then causes a momentary erratic miss.

Bad ignition-circuit connections or defective wiring can also cause missing. If high-voltage leakage occurs across the coil head, distributor cap, or rotor, or if there is leakage through secondary-wiring insulation, missing may occur. Long-continued leakage across the coil head or the rotor will etch a visible path. If this occurs, the part will require replacement. Otherwise, wiping dirt from the part and keeping it clean and dry will prevent such leakage. If the insulation on the secondary wiring has deteriorated (is cracked or rotting), it may allow high-voltage leakage. This condition requires replacement of the wiring.

Installing a coil with incorrect connections so that the secondary polarity is reversed could increase the voltage requirements so much that missing would result. The reversed connections mean that the electrons must jump from the relatively cool outer electrode to the center electrode. This requires a considerably higher secondary voltage and increases the possibility of engine missing, especially at high speeds. Normally, the coil is connected so as to cause the electrons to jump from the hot center electrode to the outer electrode. With the emitting electrode hot, voltage requirements are considerably lower.

To test for reversed polarity, hold an ordinary pencil tip between the high-voltage-wire clip and the spark-plug terminal. The spark should flare out between the pencil tip and the spark plug. If it flares out between the pencil tip and the wire clip, the polarity is reversed. Another test is to use a neon bulb (NE-2 or similar) between the spark-plug terminal (high-voltage lead connected) and ground. With the engine running, the end of the neon bulb connected to the spark-plug terminal should glow. If the end of the bulb connected to ground glows, the polarity is reversed.

Worn or fouled spark plugs will miss, especially during a hard pull or on acceleration.

Many other conditions in the engine and fuel system could cause missing. If the fuel system fails to deliver an air-fuel mixture of the proper proportions or if the engine has faulty valve action or loss of compression, missing will occur.

■ **1-5-7 Engine Lacks Power** Many conditions can cause lack of power. With the timing off, or with any of the conditions discussed in ■1-5-6, the engine will not deliver normal power. In addition, if the exhaust system is clogged, if heavy engine oil or the wrong fuel is being used, or if there is excessive rolling resistance due to underinflated tires, dragging brakes, and so on, then the engine will seem sluggish and lacking in power.

■ **1-5-8 Engine Overheats** Engine overheating may be caused by many conditions in the engine cooling system or in the engine itself. It can also be caused by late ignition timing. See the sections covering the engine cooling system.

■ **1-5-9 Engine Backfires** Backfiring can be caused by several conditions in the ignition system. If the ignition timing is considerably off or if ignition crossfiring occurs (due to spark jumpover from one terminal or lead to another), ignition may result before the intake valve closes. This causes a backfire.

If a spark plug runs too hot, it may glow enough to ignite the air-fuel mixture before the intake valve closes. Here, the remedy is to use a cooler-running plug.

Preignition, and possibly backfiring, will also occur if valves run red hot or if carbon in the combustion chambers gets so hot it glows. Incorrect air-fuel ratio may also cause backfiring.

■ **1-5-10 Engine Pings** Spark knock or ping is often blamed on the ignition system. But there are many other conditions that will cause pinging. In the ignition system, pinging may result from such conditions as excessively advanced timing, faulty advance mechanisms (which cause excessive advance), out-of-adjustment points, distributor bearing worn or shaft bent (which causes erratic point opening and possible excessive advance to some cylinders), spark plugs of wrong heat range (which glow and cause preignition), and so on. Other causes of pinging include fuel with an octane rating too low for the engine and the type of operation, excessive carbon in the engine combustion chambers, and conditions listed in ■1-5-9. Actually, of all these conditions, the most usual causes of pinging are excessive ignition advance and gasoline with an octane rating too low for the engine and operating conditions.

■ **1-5-11 Rapid Wear of Centrifugal-Advance Mechanism** Rapid wear of the centrifugal-advance mechanism will occur on certain engines as a result of loose or worn valve-timing gears or a worn oil pump. Either of these causes backlash and torsional vibration in the distributor drive. This, in turn, wears the centrifugal-advance mechanism rapidly.

■ **1-5-12 Pitted Contact Points** Some arcing across the contact points will occur in spite of condenser action. Under some conditions, this arcing may cause point pitting. Pitting is due to the transfer of point material from one contact to the other. A pit is left in one contact and there is a matching buildup of material on the other contact. Normally, the system is balanced, so pitting is at a minimum. But under certain unusual conditions, it will occur. To correct point pitting, note the following:

If a negative point loses material, with the buildup on the positive points, then one or more of the following steps should be taken.

1. Install a new condenser with a higher capacity.

2. Separate the low- and high-voltage leads or move these leads closer to ground. This reduces the capacity effect between these leads.

3. Shorten the condenser leads if possible.

If the positive point loses material and the buildup is on the negative point, install a new condenser with a lower capacity, move the leads closer together or away from the ground, or lengthen the condenser lead.

■ **1-5-13 Burned or Oxidized Contact Points** Burning or oxidizing of contact points can be caused by several conditions, as follows:

1. Excessive resistance in the condenser circuit. This is detectable with a high-frequency condenser tester and is corrected by either tightening the condenser mounting and connections or replacing the condenser, according to where the resistance is.

2. High voltage, which causes excessive current draw through the points. This can be detected by making a voltmeter check with the engine operating at medium speed. Correction normally requires readjustment of the voltage-regulator setting or reduction of alternator output.

3. Dwell too long (point opening too small). Points remain closed for too large a part of total operating time, so they burn rapidly. This requires checking of the cam angle or point opening and readjustment as necessary.

4. Weak spring tension, which causes the points to flutter, bounce, and arc at high speeds. Measure the spring tension, readjust, or replace points.

NORMAL

Brown to grayish tan color and slight electrode wear. Correct heat range for engine and operating conditions.

RECOMMENDATION: Properly service and reinstall. Replace if over 10,000 miles of service.

SPLASHED DEPOSITS

Spotted deposits. Occurs shortly after long-delayed tune-up. After a long period of misfiring, deposits may be loosened when normal combustion temperatures are restored by tune-up. During a high-speed run, these materials shed off the piston and head and are thrown against the hot insulator.

RECOMMENDATION: Clean and service the plugs properly and reinstall.

CARBON DEPOSITS

Dry soot.

RECOMMENDATION: Dry deposits indicate rich mixture or weak ignition. Check for clogged air cleaner, high float level, sticky choke or worn breaker contacts. Hotter plugs will temporarily provide additional fouling protection.

HIGH-SPEED GLAZING

Insulator has yellowish, varnish-like color. Indicates combustion chamber temperatures have risen suddenly during hard, fast acceleration. Normal deposits do not get a chance to blow off, instead they melt to form a conductive coating.

RECOMMENDATION: If condition recurs, use plug type one step colder.

OIL DEPOSITS

Oily coating.

RECOMMENDATION: Caused by poor oil control. Oil is leaking past worn valve guides or piston rings into the combustion chamber. Hotter spark plug may temporarily relieve problem, but positive cure is to correct the condition with necessary repairs.

MODIFIER DEPOSITS

Powdery white or yellow deposits that build up on shell, insulator, and electrodes. This is a normal appearance with certain branded fuels. These materials are used to modify the chemical nature of the deposits to lessen misfire tendencies.

RECOMMENDATION: Plugs can be cleaned or, if replaced, use same heat range.

TOO HOT

Blistered, white insulator, eroded electrodes and absence of deposits.

RECOMMENDATION: Check for correct plug heat range, overadvanced ignition timing, cooling system level and/or stoppages, lean air-fuel mixtures, leaking intake manifold, sticking valves, and if car is driven at high speeds most of the time.

PREIGNITION

Melted electrodes. Center electrode generally melts first and ground electrode follows. Normally, insulators are white, but may be dirty due to mis-firing or flying debris in combus-tion chamber

RECOMMENDATION: Check for correct plug heat range, overadvanced ignition timing, lean fuel mixtures, clogged cooling system, leaking intake manifold, and lack of lubrication.

Figure 1 Appearance of spark plugs related to causes. *(Champion Spark Plug Company.)*

5. Oil or crankcase vapors entering the distributor housing and depositing on the point surfaces, causing them to burn rapidly. A glance at the breaker plate usually discloses this condition, since the oil on the point surfaces, in burning, causes a black smudge on the breaker plate under the point. A clogged engine crankcase ventilating system, which forces oil into the distributor, excessive oiling of the distributor, or worn distributor bearings will produce this trouble.

■ **1-5-14 Spark Plugs Defective** Spark plugs may fail for a variety of reasons. They are subjected to high temperature, high pressure, and high voltage. Spark plugs must not only withstand these conditions but they must also operate at the proper temperature. If a plug becomes too hot, it will wear rapidly and may burn. If it does not become hot enough, it may foul, since oil and fuel soot or carbon may deposit on it. If enough of this material is deposited, then the high-voltage current will leak to ground through the deposit instead of jumping the spark gap. Thus the plug will not fire and the engine will miss.

The temperature the plug reaches is governed by the heat range of the plug. The heat range is a function of the shape of the plug and the distance heat must travel from the center electrode of the plug to reach the cylinder head. If the path the heat must travel is long, then the plug will run hot. If it is short, the plug will run cool.

You can tell from its appearance whether a plug is of the correct heat range for the application. Figure 1 illustrates several spark-plug conditions and explains their causes. If a plug is operating too cold, there will be a sooty deposit on the insulator around the center electrode; the plug is not hot enough to keep this deposit burned away. Even with a plug of the heat range specified for the engine, a deposit may form if (1) the air-fuel mixture is excessively rich (from excessive choking, worn carburetor jets, and so on), or (2) excessive amounts of oil enter the combustion chamber (due to worn rings or cylinder wall, excessive intake-valve-stem clearance, and so on). In such cases, a hotter plug would help to prevent formation of excessive deposits on the plug. But it would not cure the basic trouble.

If the plug runs too hot, a white or grayish cast will appear on the insulator, and the insulator may also appear blistered. A plug that runs hot will wear more rapidly; the electrodes will burn away more rapidly. One cause of high plug temperature, aside from improper heat range, is incorrect installation of the plug in the engine. If the plug is not tightened to the correct tension, the plug gasket will not be sufficiently compressed. In such a case, the heat path is somewhat restricted; the plug will therefore run hotter. This may also result if the plug seat in the cylinder head is not cleaned before the plug is installed. Dirt could block off the heat path and cause a hot-running plug. On many late-model cars, the plugs do not use gaskets. On these, the seating faces (on plug and head) must be clean and smooth to form a good seal and heat path.

Cracked insulators usually are caused by careless installation or by improper adjustment of the plug gap.

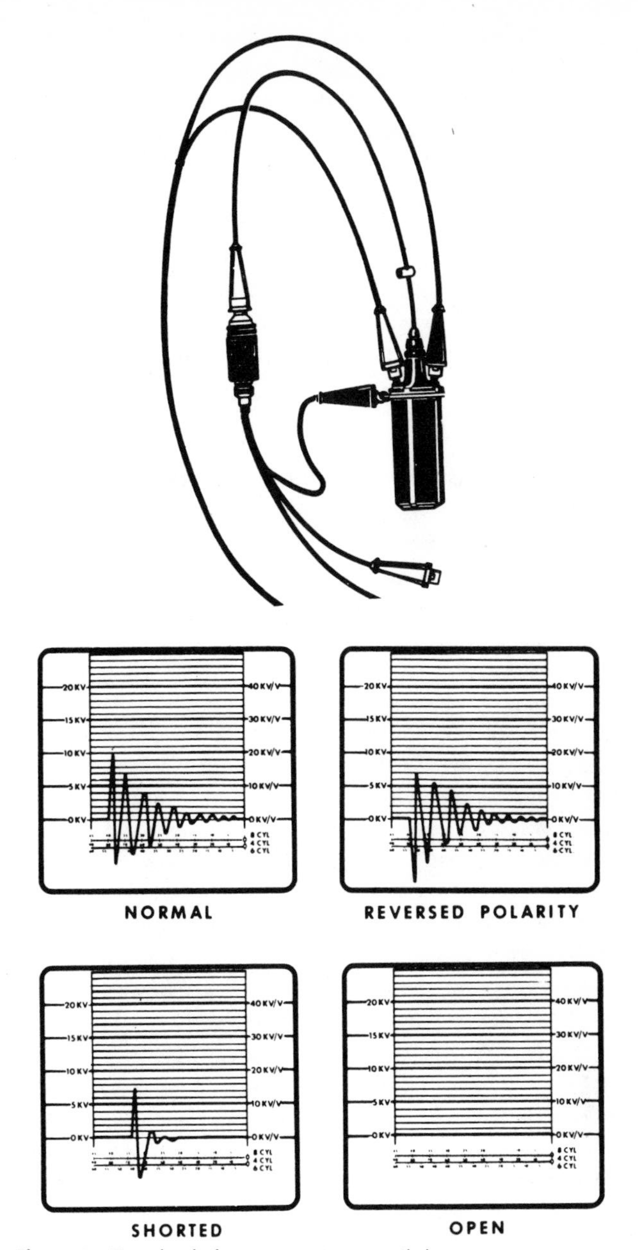

Figure 2 Top, leads from scope to test coil; bottom, scope patterns for various coil conditions. *(Sun Electric Corporation)*

IGNITION TESTERS AND TESTS

■ **1-5-15 Ignition-Coil Testers** Two general types of ignition-coil testers are widely used. One type makes use of a spark gap or neon tube. The coil to be tested is connected to the spark gap, and the spark it can produce is measured. A coil known to be good is then tested, and its performance is compared with that of the coil in question. Variations may creep in and distort the conclusions on this type of test unless great care is taken in making connections: adjusting the gap, selecting the proper coil for comparison (it should have the same number of turns of wire, connected in the same manner), etc. This type of coil tester will not always detect such defects as shorted primary turns in a coil.

Most technicians now recommend the use of a scope-type coil tester (Fig 2). This type of tester measures coil performance and thereby gives an accurate picture of coil condition.

■ **1-5-16 Ignition-Condenser Testers** Ignition condensers (also called "capacitors") are relatively inexpensive, and many technicians often replace the condenser on any ignition job. Yet it is sometimes desirable to test the condenser, particularly where trouble is being traced. Four factors are important in the operation and testing of an ignition condenser. These are:

1. Grounding or shorting of the condenser, caused by a breakdown of the insulation between the two condenser plates. This condition prevents any condenser action. It can be detected with a test light.

2. Low insulation resistance, which prevents the condenser from holding a charge, so that the condenser is said to be "weak." The insulation permits the charge to leak from one plate to the other. The presence of moisture weakens the insulation and is one cause of low insulation resistance.

3. High-series resistance, which results from a defective condenser lead or poor connection within the condenser. No means of testing for this condition is available except by high frequency. Condenser testers usually have a high-frequency test for checking the condenser for high series resistance.

4. Capacity, which determines the amount of charge that the condenser can take. The capacity of any condenser depends on the area of the plates and on insulating and impregnating materials. It will not normally change in service.

Condenser testers of all these conditions are available, and they should be used whenever possible if a check of a condenser is necessary.

■ **1-5-17 Distributor Testers** Distributor testers or synchroscopes are variable-speed devices into which the distributor is clamped for the checking of the centrifugal-advance mechanism. As the distributor speed is increased, the synchroscope indicates the distributor rpm and the amount of centrifugal advance. Many such testers incorporate vacuum-advance testers, wherein a source of vacuum is applied to the vacuum-advance mechanism on the distributor so that the degree of vacuum advance and the amount of vacuum required to secure it can be checked. These testers will also detect shaft eccentricity caused by worn bearings and bent shafts. (■ 1-5-40 and 1-5-41 cover disassembly and repair of distributors.) Usually the tester includes a dwell meter for measuring contact-point settings. If it does not, then a separate meter, a feeler gauge, or a dial indicator should be used to measure point opening.

The distributor tester must include a source of vacuum if the full-vacuum-control distributor is to be tested and adjusted.

NOTE: To test electronic distributors on the tester, a special "distributor pulse amplifier" must be fitted to the tester. This takes the place of the amplifier which is left on the car.

■ **1-5-18 Contact-Point-Opening Checking Devices** Two general types of devices are used to check contact-point opening: wire feeler gauges and dwell meters. Before the contact-point opening is measured, the contacts should be inspected for alignment and general condition. If they are worn or burned, they should be replaced (■ 1-5-33). As a rule, alignment is a possible problem only on new contacts; they will not go out of alignment in service. See ■ 1-5-34 for the alignment procedure. The contact-point-opening checking devices are discussed below.

1. WIRE FEELER GAUGE At the speeds with which the ignition system operates, a small error in point-opening adjustment would cause poor ignition performance. If the point opening were too wide, the points would remain closed too short a time. This would not allow sufficient magnetic energy to be stored in the coil. The result would be that too weak a high-voltage surge would be obtained from the secondary winding. The engine would not perform properly and would

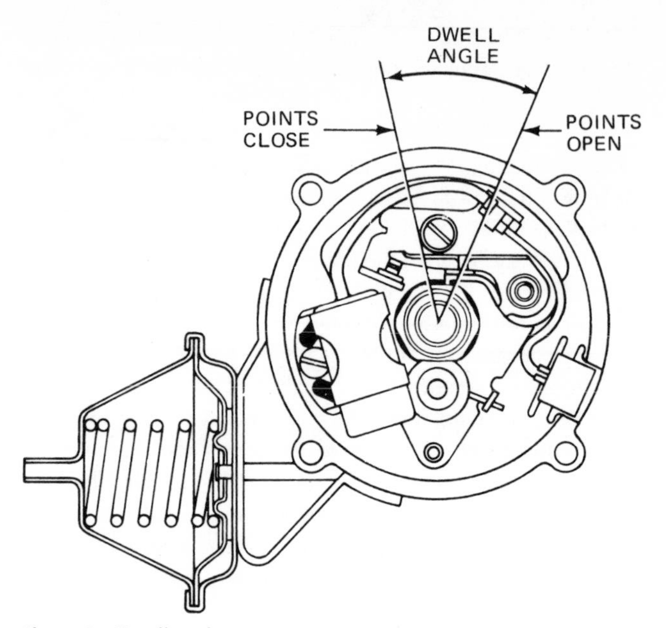

Figure 3 Dwell angle.

develop a miss, particularly at high speed. Adjustment is made as explained in ■ 1-5-34.

A round wire feeler gauge can be used to check contact-point openings, but it is not always accurate, especially if the points are not new. On used points that have become rough, the feeler gauge measures from high point to high point on the contacts, so that the true point opening cannot be obtained. With new points, accurate point-opening settings can be made by a feeler gauge. The feeler gauge can be used when no other means of setting the point opening is available, but some technicians prefer not to use this method.

2. DWELL METER Another method of setting the point opening is by using a dwell meter. The dwell angle is the number of degrees the distributor cam rotates from the instant that the points close until they open again (Fig. 3). As the point opening is increased, dwell is reduced, and vice versa. In other words, to increase gap—decrease dwell. To increase dwell—decrease gap. Since this definite relationship between point opening and dwell angle exists, only one needs to be checked under some conditions. If one is correct, then the other should be correct provided that the points are properly aligned. Point adjustment is covered in ■ 1-5-34.

The dwell meter measures electrically the time in degrees per cam revolution that the points remain closed. It records the dwell on a meter face. Engine analyzers and distributor testers have dwell meters so that the dwell angle may be checked along with the advance mechanism.

■ **1-5-19 Contact-Pressure Gauge** If the contact-point pressure is not correct, trouble may result. A low point pressure will cause point bouncing and chattering at high speed, with a resulting high-speed miss. Excessive pressure will cause rapid cam, contact-point, and breaker-lever rubbing-block wear. The pressure is measured with a spring gauge hooked to the breaker-lever arm. The amount of pull at the point, in a line vertical to the point faces, required to separate the points should be measured. See ■ 1-5-35 for the adjustment procedure.

■ 1-5-20 Oscilloscope Testers

Today, most tune-up and ignition work is performed with the aid of an oscilloscope. It can quickly pinpoint the cause of trouble in the ignition system. The oscilloscope is a high-speed voltmeter that uses a televisionlike picture tube to show ignition voltages. It draws a picture of the ignition voltages on the face of the tube. The picture shows what is happening in the ignition system. If something is wrong, the picture will show where it is.

■ 1-5-21 Electronic-Ignition Testers

Electronic ignition systems require special testing procedures and equipment. Figure 4 shows the special electronic-ignition tester recommended by Chrysler Corporation. It is simple to use. You plug the tester into the wiring harness between the distributor connector and the electronic control-unit connector. Then, with the ignition switch turned on, you check the ignition system with the tester. The green light comes on if everything is okay. The red light comes on to signal trouble. When you use the tester, follow the special instructions that explain the testing procedure.

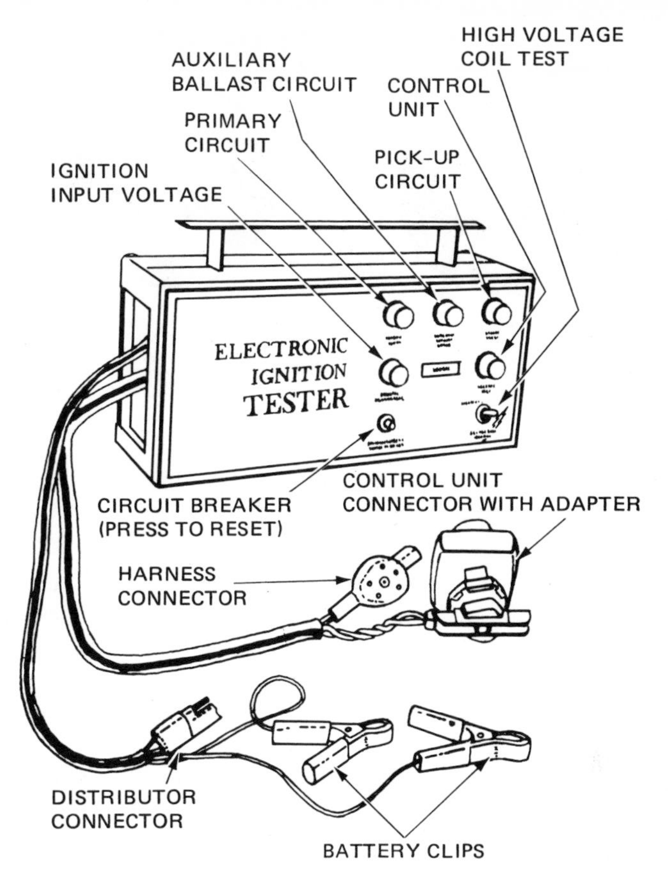

Figure 4 Electronic-ignition tester. *(Chrysler Corporation)*

■ 1-5-22 Ignition Timing

There are various timing devices for timing the engine. The spark must occur at the sparkplug gap as the piston reaches some definite position in the compression stroke. Adjusting the distributor on the engine so the spark occurs at this correct instant is called ignition timing. You adjust the distributor by turning it in its mounting. If you rotate the distributor in the direction opposite to normal distributor shaft rotation, you move the timing ahead. That is, the contact points will open earlier (or the electrical pulse from the pickup coil will occur earlier). This advances the spark so the sparks will appear at the spark plugs earlier. Turning the distributor in the opposite direction, or in the direction of distributor shaft rotation, will retard the sparks. The sparks appear at the plugs later.

1. TIMING WITH A TIMING LIGHT To time the ignition, check the markings on the crankshaft pulley with the engine running. Since the pulley turns rapidly, you cannot see the markings in normal light. But by using a special timing light, you can make the pulley appear to stand still. The timing light is a stroboscopic light. You use it by connecting the timing light lead to the No. 1 spark plug. Every time the plug fires, the timing light gives off a flash of light (Fig. 5). The light lasts only a fraction of a second. The repeated flashes of light make the pulley seem to stand still.

To connect the timing light, an inductive pickup is clamped around the spark-plug cable. Ice picks, pins, or wires should never be forced through the spark-plug nipple in order to connect the timing light.

To set the ignition timing, loosen the clamp screw that holds the distributor in its mounting. Then turn the distributor one way or the other. As you turn the distributor, the marking on the pulley will move ahead or back. When ignition timing is

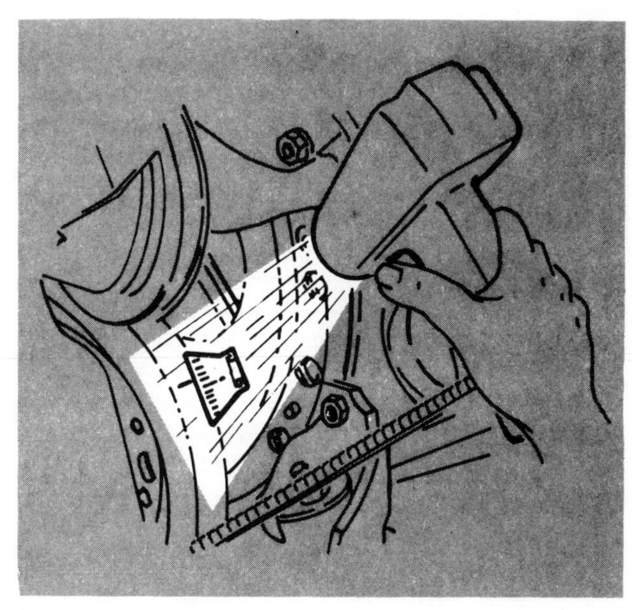

Figure 5 The timing light flashes every time the No. 1 spark plug fires.

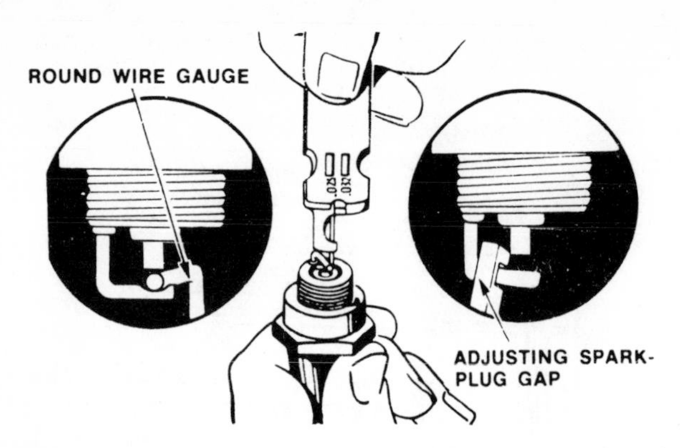

Figure 6 Using a special gauge and adjusting tool to adjust the spark-plug gap.

correct, the markings will align with a timing pointer, or timing mark, as shown in Fig 5. Tighten the distributor clamp.

2. MONOLITHIC TIMING Monolithic timing is a relatively new timing method used by Ford. The method requires a special location indicator machined on the rear end of the crankshaft. Also, a probe receptacle is combined with the timing pointer. As the crankshaft rotates, the indicator produces a magnetic pulse in the monolithic timing equipment installed on the engine. The pulse then triggers the timing light and adjustment is made as already described.

The advantage claimed for monolithic timing is that the timing is done on the crankshaft, not on a pulley that is driven through a rubber ring. Here's how it operates. The crankshaft pulley includes a torsional-vibration damper to reduce crankshaft vibrations. This damper works through a rubber ring that is between the driving flange on the crankshaft and the pulley itself. The rubber ring can reduce the accuracy of the setting because it allows the pulley to shift away from normal alignment with the crankshaft. Since the triggering device in the monolithic timing system is on the crankshaft itself, more accurate timing is claimed for this system.

CAUTION: When connecting a timing light, always connect the leads to the battery first. Then make the connection to the No. 1 spark plug. When disconnecting the timing light, always disconnect the timing light lead from the No. 1 spark plug first. Then disconnect the battery leads. If you disconnect the battery leads first, you may get a high-voltage shock when you touch the battery connections.

NOTE: There are other timing methods. Late-model Cadillacs can be timed without a timing light. A special probe-type advance meter is used. Another method, seldom used today, employs a test light connected across the points. With the engine not running but the timing marks aligned, the distributor is turned so that the points just open. This is shown by the test light which comes on. Then the distributor clamp is tightened. Another method uses a piston position gauge. It is inserted into the spark-plug hole to determine the exact position of the piston in the No. 1 cylinder.

■ **1-5-23 Spark-Plug Service** Spark plugs will foul or the electrodes will wear rapidly if their heat range is wrong for the engine. Figure 1 relates spark-plug appearance to various conditions in the engine. To clean a spark-plug, the plug is put into a spark-plug cleaner. The cleaner uses compressed air to send a blast of grit against the electrodes and insulator to clean them. After cleaning, the spark-plug electrodes should be filed flat with an ignition file. Then a round wire gauge is used to adjust the electrode gap (Fig. 6).

NOTE: The cost of labor is high, and the cost of spark plugs is relatively low. Many technicians insist that is it cheaper and more efficient to install new plugs than to clean and regap the old ones. One manufacturer (of small engines) strongly opposes the use of cleaned and regapped plugs in the engines it makes. It says that if the plug is not perfectly cleaned, particles of grit will be introduced into the engine. This can severely damage pistons, rings, and cylinder.

CAUTION: The Delco-Remy High-Energy Ignition System requires special wide-gap spark plugs. The gap specified for some applications is 0.080 inch (2.03 mm). A standard plug cannot be satisfactorily adjusted to this wide a gap because it would bend the outer electrode at a sharp angle. Always use the special plugs specified for the High-Energy Ignition System.

■ **1-5-24 Removing Spark Plugs from the Engine** Spark-plug manufacturers recommend installing new spark plugs at intervals of 10,000 miles (16,093 km). This avoids loss of engine operating economy and atmospheric pollution, which are caused by worn plugs. Before the plugs are removed, the area surrounding them should be cleaned thoroughly so that dirt will not fall into the cylinders. One method of doing this is to blow the dirt away with a compressed air hose. Another is to loosen the plugs a little and then start the engine. Running the engine for a few seconds will allow the leakage of compression to blow dirt away from around the plugs.

NOTE: See 1-5-25 on the proper way to disconnect the high-voltage cables from the spark plugs. This must be done properly to avoid damaging the cables.

Some engines, such as the Chrysler hemi (hemispheric) engine, have the spark plugs mounted in wells. On these, the spark-plug covers must first be pulled out, with the cables. Then, a special thin-walled spark-plug socket must be used to reach down into the wells to loosen and remove the plugs.

■ **1-5-25 Ignition Wiring** An important part of ignition service is to inspect the wiring to make sure it is in good condition. Cracks or punctures in the secondary-wiring insulation can allow high voltage leakage and engine miss, particularly under heavy load.

Visually inspect the secondary wiring for cracks, burned spots caused by being too close to the exhaust manifold, and brittleness. Feel the wiring to see if it is hard or crumbly. You can make a secondary-insulation check with the oscilloscope. If you do not have an oscilloscope, you can check secondary-wiring insulation as follows: With the engine not running, connect one end of a test probe to a good ground such as the engine block. The other end is left with the test point free to probe. Disconnect the cable from a spark plug, and insulate the clip end from ground. Now start the engine, and move the test probe along the entire length of the wire. If there are punctures or cracks, a spark will jump through the insulation to the end of the test point.

Here is one recommended way to install new spark-plug cables. Grasp the nipple and clip end of the cable. Gently push the cable clip into the cap tower. Pinch the larger diameter of the nipple to release trapped air. Then push the cable and nipple until the cable clip is fully entered into the cap terminal. The nipple should be all the way down around the terminal. Special insulated pliers are available to remove the wires from spark plugs on a running engine. If the connectors on the wires become loose on the coil terminals, the fit can be improved by lightly squeezing together with pliers.

NOTE: If you are replacing a set of ignition cables, replace one cable at a time. This avoids getting mixed up and connecting a cable from the distributor cap to the wrong spark plug. If all cables have been removed, first determine which direction the rotor turns and the firing order. From these, you will be able to figure out how the cables are to be connected.

Never remove cable and nipple assemblies from the distributor or coil towers unless (1) the nipples are damaged or (2) cable testing shows that the cables are bad and that they must be replaced. You can ruin a cable by careless removal and installation.

Do not puncture cables or nipples with test probes. Puncturing cable insulation or a nipple can ruin a cable. The probe can separate the conductor and cause high resistance. Also, breaking the insulation can result in high-voltage leakage to ground. Either of these can cause engine miss.

■ **1-5-26 Location of Secondary Wiring** The high-voltage cables, or secondary wiring, must be connected correctly between the distributor cap and the spark plugs. Also, the secondary wiring must be positioned correctly and held apart by the plastic looms provided. Cables are positioned and separated.

Improper placement or the bundling of cables together can cause crossfiring. That is, the high-voltage surge leaks from one cable to another, causing the wrong spark plug to fire. This can cause engine missing or backfire (see ■1-5-9).

IGNITION DISTRIBUTOR SERVICE

■ **1-5-27 Distributor Service** Other sections cover testing of the battery, cables, ignition coil, condenser, and the complete ignition system. Now, we shall look at the various checks and services required for distributors, both the contact-point type and the electronic type. The contact-point distributor is a little more complicated to service because it requires installation and adjustment of the contact points. Both distributors require checking of the centrifugal and vacuum advance mechanisms and of the cap and rotor. The distributors for the electronic ignition systems and HEI distributors require different testing procedures, which we shall cover later.

■ **1-5-28 Checking Cap and Rotor** The cap with the spring-loaded screw clamps is removed by pressing down on the screw and then turning the screw either way. The cap with spring clamps is removed by prying it with a screwdriver. Do not apply pressure to this cap, as it might break. Check the cap and rotor as shown in Fig. 7. Wipe the cap out with a cloth dampened with solvent. Discard the cap if it is cracked or broken, or has carbonized paths inside or out that could permit high-voltage leakage. You should also replace the cap if the rotor button is worn or broken. To replace a defective cap, hold the old and new caps side by side (Fig. 7, upper right) and change the leads one by one from the old cap to the new cap. In this way, you will not get the leads mixed up. When removing a lead, grasp it through the rubber boot, as close to the tower as possible. Twist slightly to break the seal of the boot on the tower and then pull straight out. When inserting the lead, be sure to push it all the way down into the high-voltage towers. On the type which enters the towers vertically (Fig. 7), push the lead down first and then slip the rubber boot down snugly over the tower. On the type which has a right-angle bend, push the terminal clip down into place through the rubber boot. Before pushing the boot all the way down into place, pinch the larger part of the boot to squeeze out the trapped air. Then push the boot all the way down into place.

NOTE: See also ■1-5-25 on ignition wiring inspection and replacement.

Various types of rotors are used in distributors. Most of these rotors will slip off the breaker cam. However, in the widely used Delco distributor, the rotor is attached to the advance mechanism with screws. Examine the rotor for wear or erosion of the metal segment and for cracks or carbonized paths that could permit high-voltage leakage. Discard rotors in doubtful condition. If the rotor has a carbon resistor, discard the rotor if the resistor is damaged.

■ **1-5-29 Checking the Advance Mechanisms** On some distributors, the centrifugal- and vacuum-advance

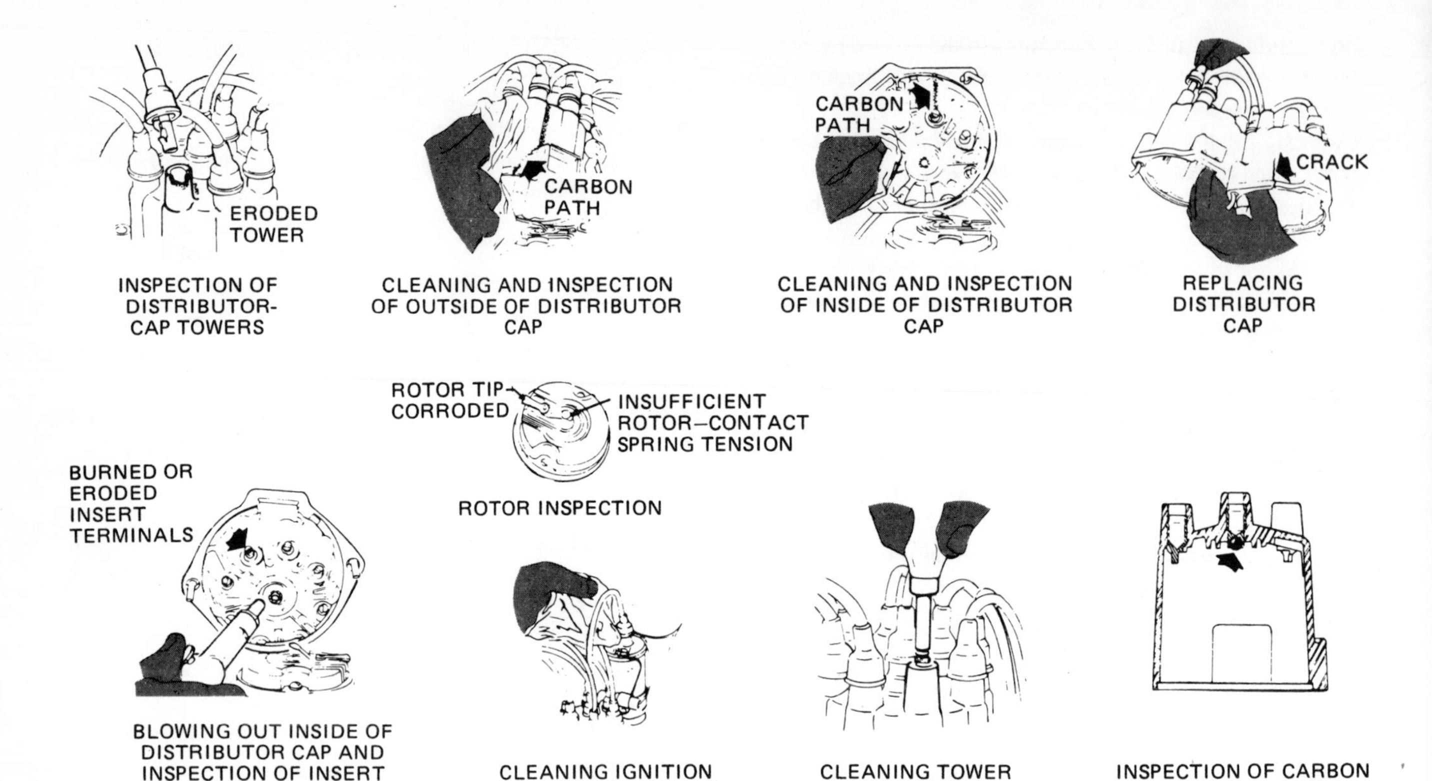

Figure 7 Checking and servicing a distributor cap and rotor. *(Chevrolet Motor Division of General Motors Corporation)*

mechanisms can be checked for freeness of action. The centrifugal-advance mechanisms advance the breaker cam or reluctor according to the speed of the engine. The vacuum-advance mechanism advances the breaker plate or pickup-coil assembly according to intake manifold vacuum, or the load on the engine. Thus if the advance springs are not too strong, it is possible to turn the cam or reluctor to see if the centrifugal advance is free. Likewise, on some distributors, it is possible to turn the breaker plate or pickup coil assembly to check the freeness of the vacuum advance.

NOTE: Do not put too much pressure on the parts to turn them! You can damage the reluctor or pickup-coil assembly. Also, do not try to turn the breaker cam or reluctor by putting pressure on the rotor. You can break it.

The most accurate way to check the advance mechanism is to remove the distributor from the engine (see ■1-5-42) and put it in a distributor tester. You can then drive the distributor in the direction of its rotation and check out the advance curve. That is, you start out at low speed and gradually increase speed, noting when the advance starts and how the advance increases with speed. On some distributors, the centrifugal advance can be adjusted (■ 1-5-30). On others, if the advance is not within specifications, the distributor must be disassembled for replacement of the advance springs and other parts.

Vacuum advance is checked with the distributor being driven at a specified speed. Vacuum is then applied to the vacuum-advance mechanism and the amount of advance obtained is noted. Some distributors have provision for adjusting vacuum advance (■ 1-5-31). On others, failure to provide the proper advance requires replacement of the advance unit.

■ 1-5-30 Adjusting Centrifugal Advance Some distributors have provision for adjusting centrifugal advance. To adjust the centrifugal advance on Ford six- and eight-cylinder distributors, bend the adjustment bracket out to increase the spring tension. This decreases centrifugal advance. Bend the adjustment bracket in to decrease the spring tension and increase centrifugal advance.

Other distributors have different adjustment procedures. Refer to the manufacturer's shop manual for the specifications and procedures.

■ 1-5-31 Adjusting Vacuum Advance Some distributors have provision for adjusting vacuum advance. On some late-model Ford distributors, use an allen wrench to turn the hollow allen-head screw in the vacuum connection to the vacuum-advance mechanism. Turn it clockwise to increase the vacuum advance, or counterclockwise to decrease it. On some earlier models, adjustment was made by installing or removing spacing washers under the vacuum-connection plug in the vacuum-advance unit.

■ **1-5-32 Inspecting Contact Points** Use a screwdriver to carefully separate the contact points. Note their color and roughness. Points should be uniform and gray in color. If they are blue or burned, it may mean excessive current in the primary, possibly due to a high voltage-regulator setting. Points get rather rough in service. Actually, rough points may have a greater contact area than new contacts. However, if the contacts are burned or if roughness has progressed too far, they should be replaced. For example, if the contact-material transfer has produced a buildup on one point of 0.020 inch (0.508 mm) (see Fig. 8), the contact set should be replaced. See ■ 1-5-12 and 1-5-13 for causes of contact-point pitting and burning.

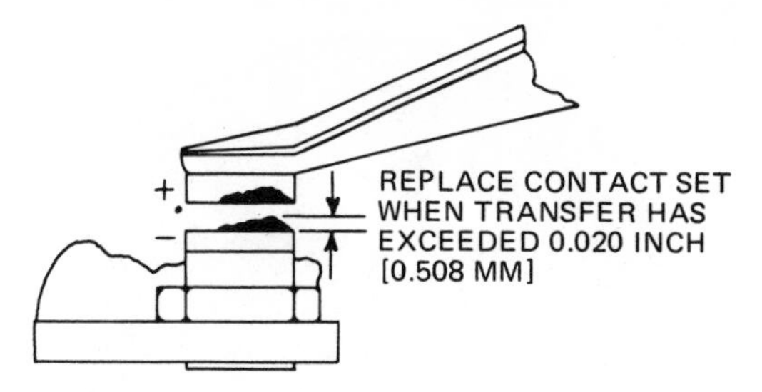

Figure 8 If contact-material transfer exceeds 0.020 inch (0.508 mm), the contact points should be replaced. *(Delco-Remy Division of General Motors Corporation)*

■ **1-5-33 Replacing Contact Points** Some contact points are supplied as assembled sets. On these, the stationary contact and the movable contact are replaced as a unit. On others, the breaker arm and then the stationary-contact base are removed. After the lead screw is loosened and the leads are detached, the two screws holding the contact set to the breaker plate are loosened. The contact set will then slip out from under the screws.

To replace the set, first wipe the breaker plate clean. If the distributor does not have a cam lubricator, apply a trace of high-temperature grease to the cam. Install the new contact set, attach leads, and adjust the contacts as explained in ■ 1-5-34.

> **NOTE:** Many contact sets are now supplied with the condenser as part of the assembly. These are called Uniset by the manufacturer, Delco-Remy. The installation procedure is the same as for other sets except that it is not necessary to bother with a separately installed condenser. Many automotive technicians normally replace the condenser when new points are installed.

The separately mounted contact lever and stationary contact are removed by loosening the lever-spring attaching nut. Then the screw that holds the stationary contact to the breaker plate is removed. The lever and stationary point can then be lifted off separately. Adjust the new contacts after they have been installed (1-5-34).

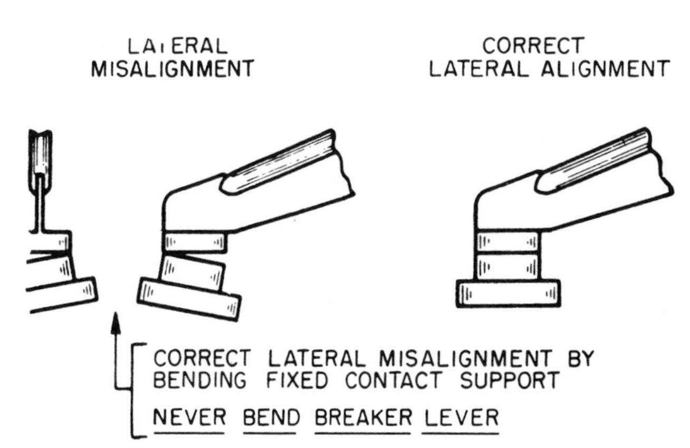

Figure 9 Correct and incorrect lateral alignment of flat contact points.

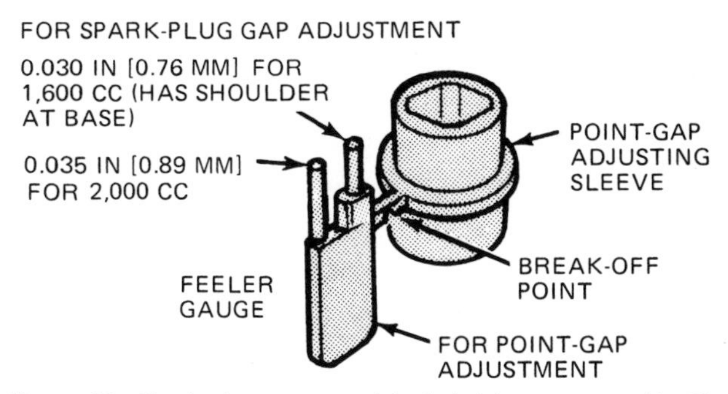

Figure 10 Plastic throwaway tool included in a tune-up kit. The tool is used to adjust the contact-point opening and also spark-plug gap. *(Ford Motor Company)*

■ **1-5-34 Adjusting Contact-Point Opening** Before adjusting the point opening or dwell angle, align the points. Figure 9 shows right and wrong ways of aligning points. Never bend the level arm! This can break it. After the points are aligned, adjust the point opening or dwell angle.

New contact points can be adjusted with a feeler gauge. Turn the distributor shaft until the peak of the cam lobe is under the center of the lever rubbing block. If the distributor is on the engine, rotate the distributor in its mounting. Measure the gap between the lever contact and the stationary contact. Adjust the contact-point opening. The stationary-contact support is moved to make the adjustment. Then, the lock screw is tightened.

Some tuneup kits come with special disposable ignition tools. For example, Fig. 10 shows a special plastic tool for contact point and spark-plug gap adjustment. This tool comes in the Ford tuneup kit with the contact-point set. To use the tools, first break off the feeler gauge (see the break-off point in Fig. 10). Then, slip the sleeve over the cam. Note that the position of the cam lobes makes no difference. The sleeve and the special feeler gauge used together will provide the proper spacing for the contact points. Insert the feeler gauge and adjust the points. The round feeler gauges also are used to check spark-plug gaps. (See ■ 1-5-23.)

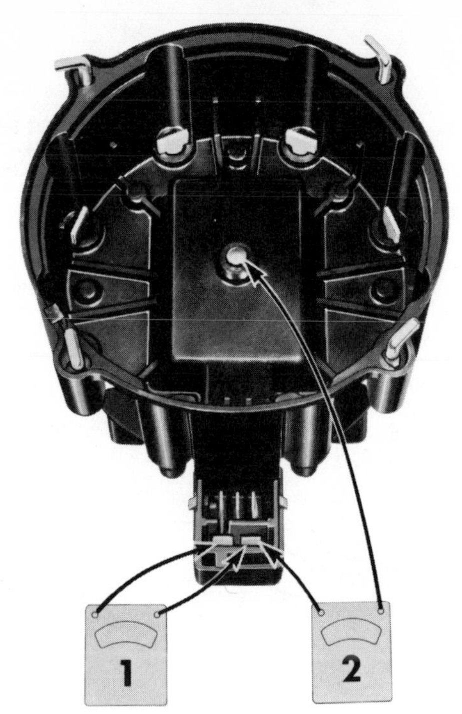

Figure 11 Checking the ignition coil in the High-Energy Ignition System. *(Cadillac Motor Car Division of General Motors Corporation)*

You should not attempt to adjust used contacts with a feeler gauge. The roughness of the contact surfaces makes it impossible to get an accurate setting. A dwell meter can be used on both new and used contacts to get an accurate setting (■ 1-5-18). The dwell meter permits you to make adjustments of the contact points in the Delco window-type distributor without removing the cap.

■ 1-5-35 Adjusting Contact-Point Spring Tension The preassembled contact set has the spring tension checked at the factory and does not require adjustment. On other contact sets, the spring tension should be measured. To make the adjustment, disconnect the primary lead wire and the condenser lead. Loosen the nut holding the spring in position. Move the spring toward the breaker-arm pivot to decrease tension. Move it in the opposite direction to increase tension. Tighten the locknut and recheck the tension. Repeat the procedure until the tension is right. Then reconnect the primary lead wire and condenser lead.

■ 1-5-36 Synchronizing Dual-Contact Distributors On dual-contact distributors, first adjust the point opening of each set separately. Then, with the distributor mounted in a distributor tester, check the dwell angle of each contact set. Adjust to get the proper dwell by moving the adjustable plate. Tighten the locking screws after the adjustment is completed. Then check the total dwell.

■ 1-5-37 Distributor Lubrication Most distributors now have built-in oil reservoirs to lubricate the shaft bushings. Also, they have a cam lubricator. These distributors may require no lubrication except during overhaul. However, the cam lubricator requires turning or replacement at periodic intervals. Rotate the cam lubricator 180 degrees every 12,000 miles (19,312 km) and replace it every 24,000 miles (38,624 km). Also, some distributors should have the cam lightly lubricated periodically or during overhaul. See the manufacturer's shop manual for specific recommendations.

■ 1-5-38 Testing Electronic Distributor and Control Unit We mentioned in ■ 1-5-21 and illustrated in Fig. 4 the electronic-ignition tester recommended by Chrysler to test its electronic ignition systems. The tester is connected into the ignition system at the wiring harness by unplugging the connector between the distributor and control unit. Then, the tester connectors are plugged into the male and female halves of the wiring-harness-circuit connector.

The Ford testing procedure uses a voltmeter and an ohmmeter. If the voltage or ohms resistance does not measure correctly, replace the unit or wire that does not test properly. Refer to the Ford shop manual for procedures and specifications.

■ 1-5-39 Testing the HEI Distributor A quick check of the electronic module can be made using a dwell meter. At idle, the HEI distributor will show about 12 degrees dwell. At about 2,500 rpm, dwell should extend to about 30 degrees. If the dwell does not extend as the engine is accelerated, the module is defective and should be replaced.

The High-Energy Ignition System distributor is shown in Fig. 12. To test the ignition coil, remove the cap by disconnecting the wiring harness and turning the four latches so the cap can be taken off. Connect an ohmmeter as at 1 in Fig. 11. This connection is to the BAT (battery) and TACH (tachometer) terminals. Reading should be zero or nearly zero. If it is not, replace the coil. Then connect the ohmmeter as at 2 in Fig. 11. Reading should not be infinite. If it is, the coil is open and should be replaced.

Next, disconnect the two leads from the electronic module (Fig. 12). Connect the ohmmeter from one of these leads to ground, as shown at 1. Apply vacuum to the vacuum advance gradually so that the pickup-coil assembly is moved. The reading should be infinite at all times. If it is not, replace the pickup-coil assembly. Check the other pickup-coil lead the same way. It should give an infinite reading. Now connect the ohmmeter as shown at 2 in Fig. 12. Apply vacuum and note the ohmmeter reading. It should be between 650 and 850 ohms. If it is outside these limits, replace the pickup-coil assembly.

If everything else checks okay but the engine still will not run or misses, replace the electronic module.

■ 1-5-40 Distributor Disassembly The procedure of disassembling a distributor varies somewhat because different distributors are constructed differently. On the typical ignition distributor, after the cap, rotor, and dust seal or radio-frequency-interference shield are off, the terminal (where present) is disassembled and the breaker plate taken out. Then the coupling or gear is removed by grinding or filing off the peened-over head of the pin and driving out the pin. Next, the shaft and advance-mechanism assembly can be lifted out of the distributor housing.

NOTE: Before attempting to take out the shaft, be sure that there are no burrs around the pinhole. Burrs might damage the distributor bearing when the shaft is removed from the housing. File down any burrs before removing the shaft.

The advance mechanism can be disassembled by taking off the nuts or screws holding the weight hold-down plate in place. Note the condition of the bearing in the distributor housing, and replace it if it is excessively worn (see ■ 1-5-41).

NOTE: Some distributors have a flexible-drive-gear arrangement which incorporates rubber cushions to absorb engine vibration and prevent it from getting back into the distributor. On such units, the old driving blocks, cushions, retainers, and pin should be discarded and new ones installed. If the old ones are used again, they will probably fit too loosely to provide proper vibration absorption.

On some of the heavy-duty and special-application distributors, special features are incorporated. These include two-piece housings, ball bearings, dual contacts, engine-governor drives or tachometer drives, and others. On such units, disassembly is more complex than on the simple distributor discussed above. However, these units should be easily serviced provided that you make careful note of the locations and relationships of the parts before you begin to disassemble them. If you have any doubts about the reassembly procedure, always refer to the manufacturer's service manual.

■ 1-5-41 Distributor Reassembly

During reassembly, several checks should be made.

1. CHECKING FOR BEARING WEAR Note condition of the bearing in the distributor housing, and replace the bearing if it is worn. A worn bearing will cause variations in contact-point opening, sometimes to such an extent that engine missing will occur. The bearing can be checked for wear by placing the shaft in its normal position in the bearing and then attempting to move the shaft sideways. A dial indicator can be attached to the housing so that the actual side movement of the shaft in thousandths of an inch can be checked. One manufacturer recommends that if the side play is more than 0.006 inch (0.152 mm) with 5 pounds (2.268 kg) of side pull applied with a spring gauge, the bearing is sufficiently worn to require replacement. An arbor press should be used to press out the old bearing and to press in a new one. To install the new bearing, a special arbor is required. The extension on the special arbor is of the right length and diameter to maintain the proper bearing inside diameter when the bearing is pressed into the housing. However, some bearings may require reaming to size after they are installed. On some distributors, the bushings are not replaceable. If bushings are worn, the distributor housing and the bushing should be replaced as a unit.

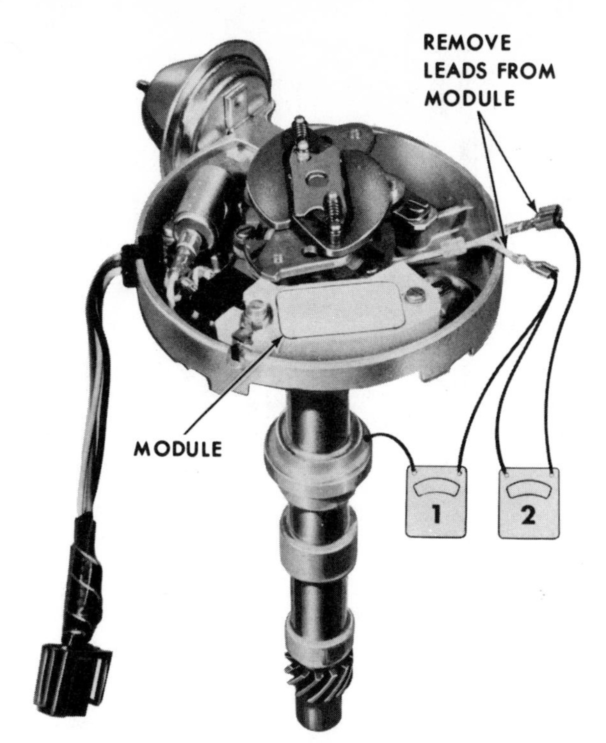

Figure 12 Checking the pickup coil in the High-Energy Ignition system. *(Cadillac Motor Car Division of General Motors Corporation)*

2. INSTALLING THE SHAFT When installing the gear or the coupling, be sure that the shaft end play is correct, since it varies with different distributors. (See the manufacturer's specifications.) On some distributors, end play is adjusted by adding or removing shims on the lower end of the shaft between the coupling, or gear, and the distributor housing. On other distributors, the end play is established by drilling a new hole through the shaft if necessary. During reassembly, the shaft is put into position in the distributor housing or base and pushed down as far as it will go. Then the gear or coupling is slipped onto the shaft and up against a feeler gauge held between the gear and housing (or washer if used). Finally a hole is drilled through the gear and shaft and the pin is installed. A check of the end play can be made after the gear, or coupling, pin has been put into place but before it has been peened over. The end play should be rechecked after peening to make sure that it is still within specifications.

3. BALL-SUPPORTED BREAKER-PLATE INSTALLATION On distributors in which the breaker plate is supported by three balls, place a small amount of petroleum jelly in the ball seats in the breaker plate. Then put the balls in the seats. The

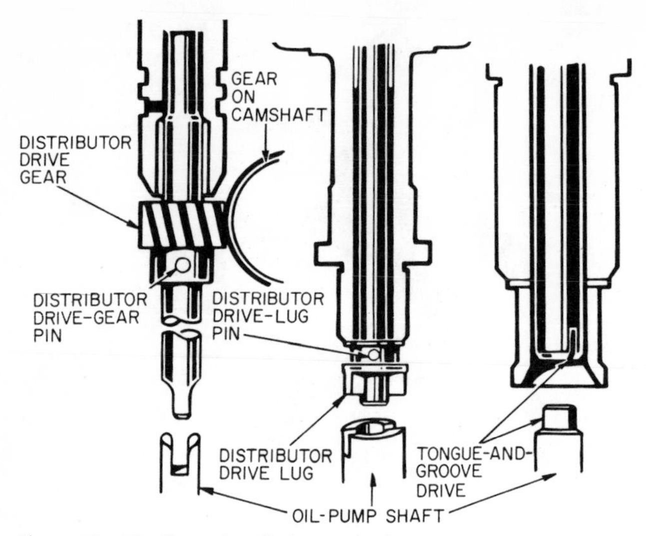

Figure 13 Distributor installation methods.

jelly will keep the balls in place while the plate is being installed. Then align the balls with the vertical grooves in the housing. The spring seat should be on the plate next to the vacuum-control-link slot in the housing. Finally, push the plate down and turn it slightly to bring it into position.

4. BEARING-SUPPORTED BREAKER-PLATE INSTALLATION In Delco-Remy window-type distributors, the breaker plate fits on a bearing in the distributor housing. After the plate is in place, it is secured with a retainer spring.

5. CONTACT-POINT ADJUSTMENT Installation and adjustment of the contact points has already been described (■1-5-33 to 1-5-35).

6. ADJUSTMENT OF ADVANCES In some distributors, adjustment of the advance mechanisms is possible, as already explained (■1-5-30 and 1-5-31).

7. LUBRICATION During reassembly, lubricate the distributor by the means provided. Refill oil reservoirs with oil of the specified type. (See also ■1-5-37.)

■ 1-5-42 Distributor Removal and Installation

Distributor removal and installation is simple if the engine is left undisturbed while the distributor is out. However, if the engine is cranked so that the crankshaft and camshaft are turned with the distributor out, installation is a little more complicated.

1. DISTRIBUTOR REMOVAL Remove the air cleaner and disconnect the vacuum hose or hoses from the distributor. Disconnect the primary lead running from the ignition coil to the distributor. Remove the distributor cap, and push the cap-and-wire assembly aside.

Scratch a mark on the distributor housing. Scratch another mark on the engine block, lining it up with the first mark. These marks locate the position of the distributor housing in the block. Scratch a third mark on the distributor housing exactly under the rotor tip. This mark locates the position of the rotor in the housing.

Remove the distributor hold-down bolt and clamp. Lift the distributor out of the block.

> **NOTE:** If the engine is not cranked while the distributor is out, the distributor can easily be installed in the correct position. Simply align the marks on the distributor housing and cylinder block.

2. DISTRIBUTOR INSTALLATION If the engine has been cranked with the distributor out, timing has been lost. The engine must be retimed. This is necessary to establish the proper relationship between the distributor rotor and the No. 1 piston.

Remove No. 1 spark plug from the cylinder head. Place a shop towel over your finger and cover the spark-plug hole. Crank the engine until you feel compression pressure on your finger.

Bump the engine with the starting motor until the timing marks on the crankshaft pulley and timing cover are aligned. This means that No. 1 piston is in firing position.

Now, the distributor can be installed in the cylinder block. Make sure to align the marks you made on the distributor housing and cylinder block. Check to make sure that the distributor gasket or rubber O ring is in place when you install the distributor.

> **NOTE:** Three different distributor drives are shown in Fig. 13. You may have to turn the rotor slightly to engage the drive. Also, when the distributor goes down into place on the spiral-gear drive, the rotor will turn. So you must start with the rotor back of the proper position. Then it will turn into the correct position as the distributor goes down into place.

Make sure the distributor housing is fully seated against the cylinder block. If it is not, the oil-pump shaft is not engaging. Hold the distributor down firmly and bump the engine a few times until the distributor housing drops into place.

Install, but do not tighten, the distributor clamp and bolt. Rotate the distributor until the contact points just start to open to fire No. 1 cylinder. Hold the distributor cap in place above the distributor. Make sure that the rotor tip lines up with the No. 1 terminal on the cap. Install the cap, with wires. Connect the primary wire from the ignition coil to the distributor.

Start the engine. Set the ignition timing (■1-5-22). Connect the vacuum hose or hoses to the distributor. Replace the air cleaner.

SECTION 1-6 Fuel System Troubleshooting and Service

This section describes the testing instruments used in fuel-system service, how to find fuel system troubles, and how to service the fuel system and its component parts.

■ **1-6-1 Testing Instruments** A variety of instruments are used to test the fuel system and engine performance. These include fuel-mileage testers (■ 1-6-2), which measure fuel consumption per mile of car travel; exhaust-gas analyzers (■ 1-6-3), which check the amount of pollutants in the exhaust gas; fuel-pump testers (■ 1-6-4 to 1-6-6); vacuum gauges for measuring intake-manifold vacuum, engine-cylinder compression tester; cylinder linkage leakage testers; rpm indicators, or tachometers, for checking engine speed; and dynamometers for measuring engine power output.

■ **1-6-2 Fuel-Mileage Testers** A complaint that is sometimes difficult to analyze is poor fuel economy. Many conditions can cause excessive fuel consumption. Sometimes it is necessary to make an accurate measurement of the fuel consumed if the cause of the trouble is hard to find. Fuel-mileage testers vary from a fuel meter that computes fuel consumption electronically to a small container of gasoline that

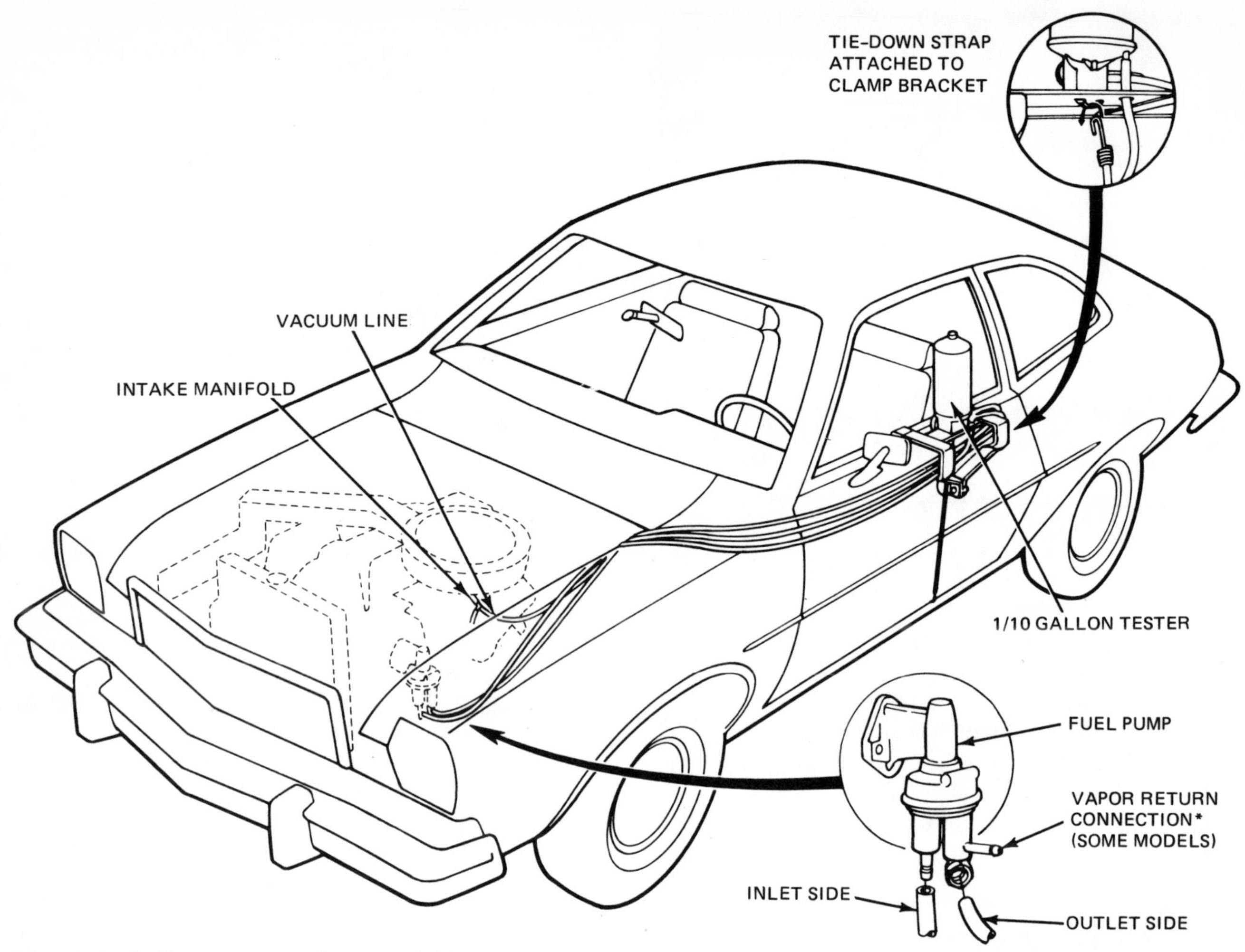

Figure 1 Fuel-mileage tester. A small container holding exactly 1/10 gal (0.45 1) is mounted on the driver's door. *(Ford Motor Company.)*

is connected into the fuel line. Figure 1 shows this type of fuel-mileage tester. The test is performed by connecting the fuel-mileage tester as shown in Fig. 1, and then writing down the mileage shown on the odometer. Then the container is filled with gasoline. Operate the car until the gasoline in the container is consumed. Then, take the mileage reading again from the odometer and figure the miles per gallon.

■ **1-6-3 Exhaust-Gas Analyzer** Several emission-control systems have been added to the automobile engine to reduce the amounts of HC, CO, and NO_x emitted. The amounts of these pollutants in the exhaust gases are measured with an exhaust-gas analyzer. This tests the operation of the emission controls and the adjustments of the ignition system and carburetor.

At one time, the major use of the exhaust-gas analyzer was to adjust the carburetor. Changing the carburetor adjustment changes the amount of HC and CO in the exhaust gas. Adjusting the idle-mixture screw, for example, can increase the richness of the idle mixture. This increases the amount of HC and CO in the exhaust gas. One of the anti-emission steps taken in the modern automobile is to get the idle mixture as lean as possible with a satisfactory idle. This reduces the amount of HC and CO in the exhaust.

Today, the exhaust-gas analyzer is used to check how well the emission controls on the car are working, as well as the idle adjustment. To use an exhaust-gas analyzer, you insert a probe into the tail pipe of the car. The probe draws out some of the exhaust gas and carries it through the analyzer. Two dials on the face of the analyzer (Fig. 2) report how much HC and CO are in the exhaust gas. Federal and state laws set maximum legal limits on the amounts of HC and CO permitted in the exhaust.

To use the exhaust-gas analyzer, check the vehicle exhaust system to be sure it is free of leaks. A quick check is to block the tail pipe and listen for exhaust leaks anywhere in the system. If no leaks are heard, insert the exhaust-gas pickup probe at least 18 inches (457.2 mm) into the tail pipe. Be sure the probe is securely in place.

Note that the engine to be tested should be at normal operating temperature. If the vehicle is equipped with a dual exhaust, insert the probe into the side opposite the exhaust-manifold heat valve.

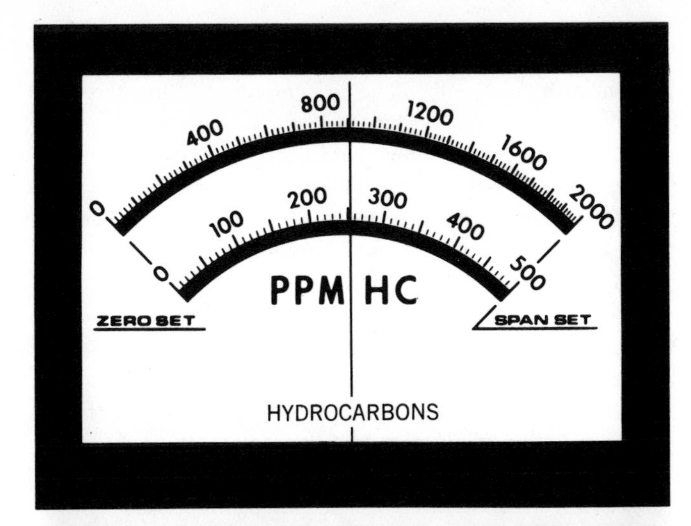

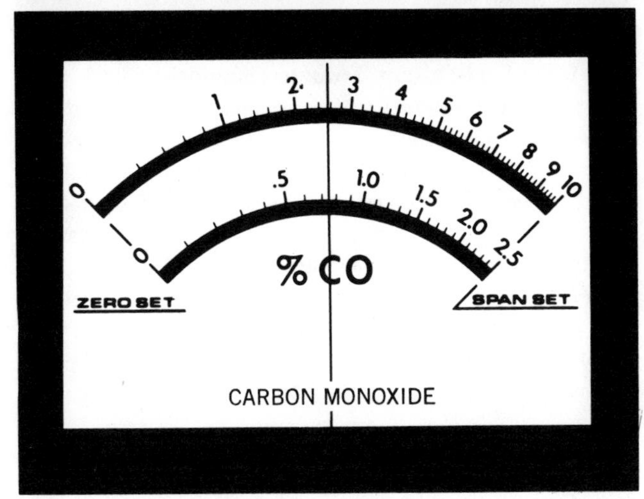

Figure 2 HC and CO meter faces. *(Sun Electric Corporation.)*

To measure CO, run the engine at fast idle (1,500 to 2,000 rpm) for about 30 seconds. This will clear any excess fuel out of the engine. Then run the engine at the specified idle speed. Use the idle-speed adjustment screw as necessary to obtain the specified speed. Allow 10 seconds for the meter to stabilize after each adjustment, before reading the meter.

Read CO at idle on the CO meter. Be sure you are reading the correct scale on the meter. Write down the reading, so you will have a record of it. Then run the engine at 2,500 rpm. Read the CO meter again, and write the reading in the proper space.

A good CO reading is within specifications at idle, and the same or lower at 2,500 rpm. A CO reading that is higher than specified at idle or that increases at 2,500 rpm is bad. In general, the higher the CO reading, the richer the air-fuel mixture. For tuneup testing, most vehicles with exhaust-emission controls should have less than 2.5 percent CO at idle. Vehicles without exhaust-emission controls should have less than 5 percent CO at idle.

To measure HC, run the engine at fast idle (1,500 to 2,000 rpm) for about 30 seconds. This will clear any excess fuel out of the engine. Then run the engine at the specified idle speed.

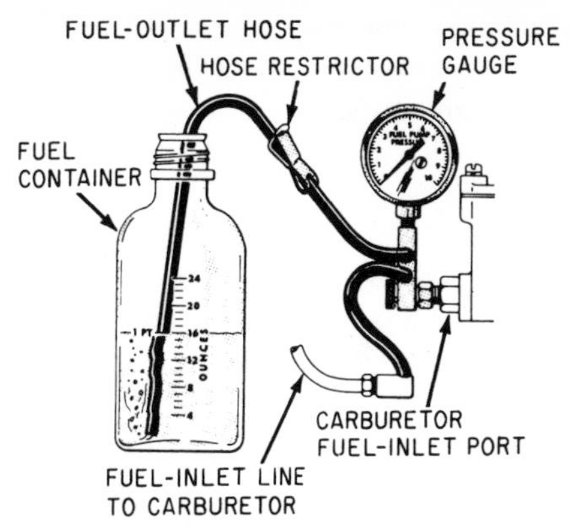

Figure 3 Fuel-pump pressure and capacity tests.

Read HC at idle on the HC meter. Be sure you are reading the correct scale on the meter. Write the reading in the proper space. Then run the engine at 2,500 rpm. Read the HC meter again, and write the reading in the proper space.

A good HC reading is within specifications at idle, and the same or less at 2,500 rpm. An HC reading that is higher than specified at idle or that increases at 2,500 rpm is bad. In general, the higher the HC reading, the more unburned air-fuel mixture is passing out the tail pipe. For tuneup testing, most vehicles with exhaust-emission controls should have fewer than 300 ppm (parts per million) HC at idle. Vehicles without exhaust-emission controls should have fewer than 500 ppm HC at idle.

■ **1-6-4 Fuel-Pump Pressure Test** The pressure at which the fuel pump delivers fuel to the carburetor must be within definite limits. If it is too low, insufficient fuel will be delivered, and faulty engine performance will result. The air-fuel mixture will tend to lean out excessively at high speeds or on acceleration. If the pressure is too high, flooding may result. The mixture will be too rich, causing the engine to be sluggish. An overrich mixture will also cause engine trouble from carbon deposits in the combustion chambers and on valves and rings. Also, crankcase-oil dilution and rapid wear of engine parts may result.

Fuel-pump pressure is tested with a pressure gauge connected to the outlet of the fuel pump. The engine is run at approximately 2,500 rpm on the fuel in the carburetor while the static fuel pressure is checked. In the flow-pressure test the gauge is connected into the fuel line between the pump and the carburetor with a T fitting (Fig. 3). The engine is idled with the pump delivering fuel to the carburetor in the normal manner. Specifications vary considerably from one type of pump to another. In general, they will specify from 4 to 8 psi (0.281 to 0.563 kg/cm²) static pressure and about 25 percent less flow pressure.

■ **1-6-5 Fuel-Pump Capacity Test** The fuel-pump capacity tester is a container that you fill to measure the amount of fuel the pump can deliver in a given time. Figure 3 shows the fuel container. Install a T fitting into the fuel line at the carburetor and bleed off a portion of the fuel passing in the line. The amount that can be bled off with the engine running determines the capacity and operating condition of the pump.

A setup to test both the pressure and the capacity of a fuel pump is shown in Fig. 3. To make the pressure test (■ 1-6-4), start the engine, and let it idle. Open the hose restrictor momentarily, to vent any air trapped in the fuel system. Then close the hose restrictor. As soon as the pressure-gauge needle is steady, read the fuel-pump pressure. Some fuel pumps have a vapor-return line from the fuel pump to the fuel tank. The vapor-return line must be squeezed closed to check fuel-pump capacity.

Check the fuel-pump specifications in the shop manual. If fuel pump pressure is not within specifications, the pump is defective. If fuel pump pressure is within specifications, perform the fuel-pump capacity test.

With the engine running at idle, open the hose restrictor (Fig. 3). Allow the fuel to discharge into the graduated container for 30 seconds. On most engines in full-size, American-built cars, the fuel-pump should deliver at least 1 pint (0.47 liter) of fuel in 30 seconds or less.

■ 1-6-6 Fuel-Pump Vacuum Test

To make a fuel-pump vacuum test, attach the fuel-pump tester to the vacuum side of the fuel pump. Disconnect the fuel-pump tester to the vacuum side of the fuel pump. Disconnect the fuel line at the carburetor. Idle the engine for a few seconds, while it runs on the gasoline in the float bowl. Read the fuel-pump vacuum on the gauge of the fuel-pump tester. A typical fuel pump should have at least 10 inches (254 mm) Hg (mercury) of vacuum while the engine is idling.

■ 1-6-7 Troubleshooting the Fuel System

The tracing of trouble in the fuel system usually is a logical procedure. Fuel-system troubles fall into several classifications that require specific corrections. However, there is sometimes a question as to whether the cause of complaint lies in the fuel system or in some other engine component. Thus, the real problem is often to isolate the trouble in the improperly operating component. The trouble sometimes may be made more puzzling because it could result in not one condition but several. For example, suppose the power valve in the carburetor were to be held open. This would produce an excessively rich mixture for all running conditions except full-power, open-throttle operation. This, in turn, would not only cause excessive fuel consumption but might ultimately foul the spark plugs, causing poor ignition and missing; also, the carbon deposits might cause defective piston-ring and valve action.

The chart that follows in ■ 1-6-8 lists the various troubles that might be blamed on the fuel system, together with their possible causes, checks to be made, and corrections needed.

■ 1-6-8 Fuel-System Trouble-Diagnosis Chart

Most fuel-system troubles can be listed under a few headings: excessive fuel consumption, poor acceleration, lack of power and high-speed performance, poor idle, engine not starting except when primed, hard starting, slow warmup, stalling, smoky exhaust, and backfiring. The chart that follows lists possible causes of each of these troubles. Included in the chart are references to later sections which contain fuller explanations of the way to locate and eliminate the troubles. When trouble has been traced to some component outside the fuel system, reference is made to the section in the Handbook.

NOTE: The troubles and possible causes are not listed in the chart in the order of frequency of occurrence. That is, item 1 (or item *a* under "Possible Cause") does not necessarily occur more frequently than item 2 (item *b*). Generally, fuel-system troubles and possible causes are listed first in the chart. However, in many cases, other automotive components are more apt to have caused the troubles listed.

FUEL-SYSTEM TROUBLE-DIAGNOSIS CHART

(See ■ 1-6-9 to 1-6-21 for detailed explanation of trouble causes and corrections listed below.)

COMPLAINT	POSSIBLE CAUSE	CHECK OR CORRECTION
1. Excessive fuel consumption (■ 1-6-9)	a. "Hard" driving	Drive more reasonably
	b. High speed	Drive more slowly
	c. Short-run and "start-and-stop" operation	Make longer runs
	d. Excessive fuel-pump pressure or pump leakage	Reduce pressure; repair pump
	e. Choke not opened properly	Open; repair or replace automatic choke
	f. Clogged air cleaner	Clean
	g. High carburetor float level or float leaking	Adjust or replace float
	h. Stuck or dirty float needle valve	Free and clean or replace

COMPLAINT	POSSIBLE CAUSE	CHECK OR CORRECTION
	i. Worn carburetor jets	Replace
	j. Stuck metering rod or power piston	Free
	k. Too-rich or too-fast idle	Readjust
	l. Stuck accelerator-pump check valve	Free
	m. Carburetor leaks	Replace damaged parts; tighten loose couplings, jets, etc.
	n. Faulty ignition	Check coil, condenser, plugs, contact points, wiring (Part 1, Sec. 5)
	o. Loss of engine compression	Check compression; repair engine (Part 1, Secs. 2 to 4)
	p. Defective valve action	Check compression; repair engine (Part 1, Secs. 2 to 4)
	q. Excessive rolling resistance from low tires, dragging brakes, wheel misalignment, etc.	Correct cause of rolling resistance (Part 6, Sec. 11)
	r. Clutch slipping	Adjust or repair clutch (Part 4, Sec. 2)
	s. Transmission slipping or not upshifting	Adjust or repair
2. Engine lacks power, acceleration, or high-speed performance (■1-6-10)	a. Accelerator pump malfunctioning	Adjust; free; repair
	b. Power stepup on metering rod not clearing jet	Free or adjust
	c. Power piston or valve stuck	Free
	d. Low float level	Adjust
	e. Dirt in filters or in line or clogged fuel-tank-cap vent	Clean; install correct cap
	f. Choke stuck or not operating	Adjust or repair
	g. Air leaks around carburetor	Replace gaskets; tighten nuts or bolts
	h. Antipercolator valve stuck	Free; adjust
	i. Manifold heat-control valve stuck	Free
	j. Throttle valves or secondary valves not fully opening	Adjust linkage
	k. Rich mixture due to worn jets, high float level, stuck choke, clogged air cleaner	Adjust; repair; clean; replace worn jets
	l. Vapor lock	Use different fuel or shield fuel line or pump
	m. Fuel pump defective	Service or replace
	n. Clogged exhaust	Clean
	o. Ignition defective	Check timing, coil, plugs, distributor, condenser, wiring (Part 1, Sec. 5)
	p. Loss of compression	Check engine compression; repair engine (Part 1, Secs. 2 to 4)
	q. Excessive carbon in engine	Clean out (Part 1, Secs. 2 to 4)
	r. Defective valve action	Check compression; repair engine (Part 1, Secs. 2 to 4)
	s. Heavy engine oil	Use lighter oil
	t. Cooling system not operating properly	Check system, flush system (Part 1, Sec. 7)
	u. Engine overheats	Check cooling system (Part 1, Sec. 7)
	v. Excessive rolling resistance from low tires, dragging brakes, wheel misalignment, etc.	Correct the defect causing rolling resistance
	w. Clutch slippage or excessive friction in power train	Adjust or repair (Part 4, Sec. 2)
	x. Transmission not downshifting or torque converter defective	Check transmission (Part 5, Sec. 2)
3. Poor idle (■1-6-11)	a. Idle mixture or speed not adjusted	Readjust
	b. Automatic-level-control compressor operating	Check vacuum-regulator valve
	c. PCV valve stuck	Replace
	d. Other causes listed under item 2	

COMPLAINT	POSSIBLE CAUSE	CHECK OR CORRECTION
4. Engine will not start (■1-6-12)	a. Ignition defective	Check (Part 1, Sec. 5)
	b. Line clogged	Clear
	c. Fuel pump defective	Repair or replace
	d. Carburetor jets or lines clogged	Clean
	e. Filter clogged	Clean
	f. Air leaks into intake manifold or carburetor	Replace gaskets; tighten nuts or bolts
5. Hard starting with engine warm (■1-6-13)	a. Choke valve closed	Open; adjust or repair
	b. Manifold heat control stuck closed	Open; free valve
	c. Throttle-cracker linkage out of adjustment	Adjust
	d. Vapor lock	Use correct fuel or shield fuel line or pump
	e. Engine parts binding	Repair engine (Part 1, Secs. 2 to 4)
6. Slow engine warmup (■1-6-14)	a. Choke valve open	Adjust or repair
	b. Manifold heat-control valve stuck open	Close; free valve
	c. Cooling-system thermostat stuck open	Free; replace if necessary
7. Smoky exhaust (■1-6-15)		
a. Blue smoke	a. Excessive oil consumption	Oil burning in combustion chamber due to engine trouble (Part 1, Secs. 2 to 4)
b. Black smoke	b. Excessively rich mixture	See item 1 and ■1-6-9
c. White smoke	c. Steam in exhaust	Check cooling-system cylinder-head bolts, to eliminate coolant leakage (Part 1, Sec. 7)
8. Engine stalls cold or as it warms up (■1-6-16)	a. Choke valve closed	Open choke valve; free or repair automatic choke
	b. Fuel not getting to or through carburetor	Check fuel pump; lines, filter, float-and-idle systems
	c. Manifold heat-control valve stuck	Free valve
	d. Engine overheats	Check cooling system (Part 1, Sec. 7), ignition timing (Part 1, Sec. 5)
	e. Engine idling speed set too low	Increase idling speed to specified value
	f. Malfunctioning PCV valve	Replace
9. Engine stalls after idling or slow-speed drive (■1-6-16)	a. Defective fuel pump	Repair or replace fuel pump
	b. Overheating	Check cooling system (Part 1, Sec. 7), ignition timing (Part 1, Sec. 5)
	c. High float level	Adjust
	d. Idling adjustment incorrect	Adjust
	e. Malfunctioning PCV valve	Replace
10. Engine stalls after high-speed drive (■1-6-16)	a. Vapor lock	Use different fuel or shield fuel line (Part 1, Secs. 2 to 4)
	b. Carburetor antipercolator defective	Check and repair
	c. Engine overheats	Check cooling system (Part 1, Sec. 7)
	d. Malfunctioning PCV valve	Replace
11. Engine backfires (■1-6-17)	a. Excessively rich or lean mixture	Replace fuel pump; repair or readjust carburetor
	b. Overheating of engine	Check cooling system (Part 1, Sec. 7), ignition timing (Part 1, Sec. 5)
	c. Engine conditions such as excessive carbon, hot valves, overheating	Repair engine (Part 1, Secs. 2 to 4)
	d. Ignition timing incorrect	Retime (Part 1, Sec. 5)
	e. Spark plugs of wrong heat range	Install correct plugs (Part 1, Sec. 5)
12. Engine runs but misses (■1-6-18)	a. Fuel pump erratic in operation	Repair or replace
	b. Carburetor jets or lines clogged or worn	Clean or replace
	c. Fuel level not correct in float bowl	Adjust float; clean needle valve
	d. Ignition-system defects, such as incorrect timing or defective plugs, coil, points, cap, condenser, wiring	Check ignition system (Part 1, Sec. 5)

COMPLAINT	POSSIBLE CAUSE	CHECK OR CORRECTION
	e. Clogged exhaust	Check tail pipe, muffler; eliminate clogging
	f. Engine overheating	Check cooling system (Part 1, Sec. 7), ignition timing (Part 1, Sec. 5)
	g. Engine conditions such as valves sticking, loss of compression, defective rings, etc.	Check engine (Part 1, Secs. 2 to 4)
13. Engine run-on, or dieseling (■1-6-19)	a. Idle-stop solenoid adjustment incorrect	Adjust; fix solenoid
	b. Engine overheating	Check cooling system (Part 1, Sec. 7)
	c. Hotspots in cylinders	Check engine (Part 1, Secs. 2 to 4)
14. Too much HC and CO in exhaust (■1-6-20)	a. Carburetor troubles	Check choke, float level, idle-mixture screw
	b. Ignition troubles	Check for miss, timing (Part 1, Sec. 5)
	c. Faulty air injection	Check air-injection system
	d. Defective TCS or catalytic system	Check

■ **1-6-9 Excessive Fuel Consumption** The first step in analyzing a complaint of excessive fuel consumption is to make sure that the car is really having this trouble. Usually, this means taking the word of the car owner that the car is using too much fuel. A fuel-mileage tester (■1-6-2) can be used to determine accurately how much fuel the car is using. After it has been determined that the car is using too much fuel, the cause of trouble must be found. It could be in the fuel system, ignition system, engine, or elsewhere in the car.

The compression tester and the intake-manifold-vacuum gauge will determine the location of the trouble and whether it is in the fuel system, ignition system, engine, or elsewhere.[1]

If the trouble appears to be in the fuel system, the following points should be considered.

[1]A rough test of mixture richness that does not require any testing instruments is to install a set of new or cleaned spark plugs of the correct heat range for the engine. Then take the car out on the highway for 15 to 20 minutes. Stop the car; remove and examine the plugs. If they are coated with a black carbon deposit, the indication is that the mixture is too rich.

1. Nervous drivers or drivers who pump the accelerator pedal when idling and jump away when the stoplight changes use an excessive amount of fuel. Each downward movement of the accelerator pedal causes the accelerator pump to discharge a flow of gasoline into the carburetor air horn. This extra fuel is wasted, since it contributes nothing to the movement of the car.

2. High-speed operation requires more fuel per mile. A car that will give 20 miles per gallon at 30 miles per hour may give less than 15 miles per gallon at 60 miles per hour. At 70 to 80 miles per hour the mileage may drop to well below 10 miles per gallon. Thus, a car operated consistently at high speed will show poorer fuel economy than a car driven consistently at intermediate speed.

3. Short-run, "stop-and-start" operation uses more fuel. In short-run operation, when the engine is allowed to cool off between runs, the engine is operating mostly cold or on warm-up. This means that fuel consumption is high. When the car is operated in heavy city traffic, or under conditions requiring frequent stops and starts, the engine is idling a considerable part of the time. Also, the car is accelerated to traffic speed after each stop. All this uses up a great deal of fuel, and fuel economy will be poor.

4. If the fuel pump has excessive pressure, it will maintain an excessively high fuel level in the carburetor float bowl. This will cause a heavier discharge at the fuel nozzle or jet, thereby producing high fuel consumption. Excessive pump pressure is not a common cause of excessive fuel consumption, however. It could result only from installation of the wrong pump or diaphragm spring or from incorrect reinstallation of the pump diaphragm during repair. Fuel pumps can develop leaks that will permit loss of gasoline to the outside or into the crankcase. This requires replacement of the diaphragm, tightening of the assembling screws, or replacement of the pump.

5. If a manually operated choke is left partly closed, the carburetor will deliver too much fuel for a warm engine, and fuel consumption will be high. On manually operated chokes, it is possible for the choke-valve linkage to get out of adjustment so that the valve will not open fully. This requires readjustment to prevent high fuel consumption. With an automatic choke, the choke valve should move from the closed to the open position during engine warmup, reaching the full-open position when the engine reaches operating temperature. This action can be observed by removing the air cleaner and noting the changing position of the choke valve during warmup. If the automatic choke does not open the choke valve normally, excessive fuel will be used. The choke must be serviced.

6. Clogged air cleaner (on an unbalanced carburetor) acts much like a closed choke valve, since it chokes off the free flow of air through it. The element should be cleaned or replaced, and fresh oil added (on the oil-bath type of air cleaner). This is not a problem with a balanced carburetor.

7. In the carburetor itself, the following conditions could cause delivery of an excessively rich air-fuel mixture.

a. A high float level or a leaking float will permit delivery of too much fuel to the float bowl and consequently through the fuel nozzle or jet. The float level must be readjusted and a leaky float replaced.

b. A stuck or dirty float needle valve will not shut off the flow of fuel from the fuel pump. Too much fuel will be delivered through the carburetor fuel nozzle or jet. The needle valve should be freed and cleaned or replaced.

c. Worn carburetor jets pass too much fuel, causing the air-fuel mixture to be too rich. Worn jets must be replaced.

d. If the power system operates during part-throttle operation, too much fuel will be delivered through the main fuel nozzle. This could be due to a stuck metering rod or power piston, which must be freed.

e. An idle mixture that is set too rich or too fast wastes fuel. Resetting of the idle mixture and idle speed is required.

f. If the accelerator-pump check valve sticks open, it may permit discharge of fuel through the pump system into the carburetor air horn, causing excessive fuel consumption. This requires freeing and servicing of the check valve.

g. Carburetor leaks, either internal or external, cause loss of fuel. The correction is to replace gaskets or damaged parts and tighten loose couplings on fuel lines, loose jets or nozzles, and loose mounting nuts or screws.

8. Faulty ignition can also cause excessive fuel consumption. The ignition system could cause engine miss and thus failure of the engine to utilize all the fuel. Faulty ignition would also be associated with the loss of power, acceleration, or high-speed performance (see Part 1, Sec. 5). Conditions in the ignition system that might cause trouble include a "weak" coil or condenser, incorrect timing, faulty advance-mechanism action, dirty or worn spark plugs or contact points, defective pickup coil or electronic control unit (electronic ignition system), and defective wiring.

9. Several conditions in the engine can also produce excessive fuel consumption. Loss of engine compression from worn or stuck rings, worn or stuck valves, or a loose or burned cylinder-head gasket causes loss of power. This means that more fuel must be burned to achieve the same speed or power.

10. Any condition that increases rolling resistance and makes it harder for the car to move along the road increases fuel consumption. For example, low tires, dragging brakes, and misalignment of wheels increase fuel consumption. Similarly, losses in the power train, for example, from a slipping clutch, increase fuel consumption.

■ 1-6-10 Engine Lacks Power, Acceleration, or High-Speed Performance

This type of complaint may be difficult to analyze. Almost any component of the engine or car, from the driver to the tires, could cause the problem. As a first step in solving this sort of complaint, some technicians road test the car to verify the complaint. The car should be driven so as to duplicate the conditions that cover the problem. Also, the engine can be checked on the chassis dynamometer or given a complete tuneup as detailed in Part 2 of the Handbook.

Here are some conditions that might cause the complaint. Fuel-system conditions are discussed first.

1. Many conditions in the carburetor could prevent delivery of proper amounts of fuel for good acceleration and full power. Possibilities to be considered follow.

a. Incorrect functioning of the accelerator pump can be checked on many engines by removing the air cleaner and observing the accelerator-pump discharge jet when the throttle is opened. If the pump is functioning correctly, a steady stream of fuel will be discharged from the jet as the throttle is opened. The stream should continue for a few seconds after the throttle has reached the full-open position. If the pump does not operate correctly, disassembly and servicing of the carburetor are required. Some pumps can be adjusted to change the amount of fuel delivered during acceleration.

b. If the power-stepup diameter on the metering rod does not clear the metering-rod jet during wide-open throttle, insufficient fuel will be delivered for full-power performance. This requires readjustment of metering-rod linkage.

c. If the power piston or valve sticks so that the valve cannot open for full power, insufficient fuel will be delivered. The piston or valve must be freed and cleaned.

d. A low float-level adjustment will starve the main nozzle or jet, preventing delivery of normal amounts of fuel and causing a loss of engine power. The float level should be readjusted.

e. Dirt in filters of fuel line will starve the carburetor main nozzle or jet and the engine. The dirt restricts fuel flow. Also, on older cars not equipped with a fuel-vapor-recovery system, some fuel-tank caps have a vent to permit air to enter as fuel is withdrawn. If this vent is clogged, no air can enter. A vacuum will develop in the fuel tank. The vacuum prevents delivery of fuel through the fuel pump to the carburetor. On later-model cars with a fuel-vapor-recovery system, installing an old-style cap could prevent fuel delivery. The fuel tanks of cars with fuel-vapor-recovery systems are sealed. The special tank cap required has a vacuum valve that opens when fuel is withdrawn so that air can enter. This prevents a vacuum from forming. If the wong cap, without a vent or vacuum valve, is installed, a vacuum may form that will prevent fuel from being delivered to the carburetor.

f. A stuck or inoperative choke will cause loss of power when the engine is cold. It may also cause loss of power when the engine is hot if it is stuck in a partly closed position. This produces an excessively rich mixture. The choke should be serviced.

g. If air leaks into the intake manifold around the carburetor or manifold mounting, or past worn throttle-shaft bearing, the air-fuel mixture may become too lean for good operation. Gaskets should be replaced and mounting nuts or screws tightened as necessary. Excessively worn throttle-shaft bearings require carburetor-body replacement.

h. A stuck antipercolator valve may also cause an excessively lean mixture. The valve requires freeing or adjustment.

i. A stuck manifold heat-control valve, if stuck in the closed position, overheats the air-fuel mixture in the intake manifold with the engine hot, so that the mixture expands excessively. This starves the engine, causing inferior performance. If the valve sticks open, warmup will be slowed. The valve should be freed.

j. If the throttle-valve linkage is out of adjustment, the throttle may not open fully, preventing delivery of full power. Throttle linkage should be correctly adjusted.

k. Most of these conditions produce an excessively lean mixture. However, conditions that produce an excessively rich mixture (see ■ 1-6-9) also cause poor engine performance.

2. Vapor lock also causes fuel starvation in the engine. Vaporization or boiling of the fuel in the fuel pump or fuel line prevents delivery of normal amounts of fuel to the carburetor and carburetor nozzles and jets. One way to check for this condition is by inserting a section of clear plastic tubing in the fuel line. Then watch for bubbles in the fuel to pass through the tube with the engine hot and running. To prevent vapor lock, use a fuel with lower volatility or shield the fuel line and fuel pump from engine heat.

3. A defective fuel pump also can starve the engine by not delivering sufficient amounts of fuel to the carburetor. This requires servicing or replacement of the fuel pump (■ 1-6-33 to 1-6-35).

4. A clogged exhaust system due to rust, dirt, or mud in the muffler or tail pipe or a pinched or damaged muffler or tail pipe could create sufficient back pressure to prevent normal exhaust-gas flow from the engine. This would result in reduced engine performance, particularly on acceleration or at high speed. Some exhaust systems include exhaust pipes that are laminated. A laminated exhaust pipe consists of a single ordinary exhaust pipe placed tightly inside a slightly larger pipe. This combination reduces exhaust noise because the laminated exhaust pipe deadens the "ringing" noise from some engines that gets through the standard muffler. There have been cases where the inner layer of steel separated from the outer layer and sagged or collapsed, partly blocking the exhaust. This is another point to check carefully, since collapse of the inner pipe cannot be seen by visual inspection.

5. Defective ignition can reduce engine performance, just as it can increase fuel consumption (■ 1-6-9). Conditions in the ignition system that might cause the trouble include a "weak" coil or condenser, incorrect timing, faulty advance-mechanism action, dirty or worn contact points or spark plugs, defective pickup coil or electronic control unit (electronic ignition system), and defective wiring.

6. A sluggish engine will result from loss of compression, excessive carbon in the engine cylinder, defective valve action, or heavy engine oil.

7. Failure of the cooling system to operate properly could cause the engine to overheat, with a resulting loss of power (Part 1, Sec 7). Also if the cooling-system thermostat fails to close as the engine cools, it will prolong engine warmup the next time the engine is started. This reduces engine performance during warmup.

8. Any condition that increases rolling resistance reduces acceleration and top speed. These conditions include low tires, dragging brakes, and misaligned wheels.

9. Clutch slippage or excessive friction in the power train will reduce acceleration and top speed.

10. An automatic transmission that does not downshift, or a defective torque converter, can reduce performance and acceleration.

■ **1-6-11 Poor Idle** If the engine idles roughly, too slowly, or too fast, the probability is that the idle mixture and idle speed require adjustment, as explained in ■ 1-6-38. In addition, other conditions such as malfunctioning choke, a high or low float level, vapor lock, clogged idle system, air leaking into the intake manifold, loss of engine compression, improper valve action, overheating engine, or an improperly operating ignition system, would cause poor idle. These conditions, discussed in ■ 1-6-10, would also cause poor engine performance at speeds above idle. Improper idle-mixture or idle-speed adjustment can be checked only with the engine idling. Another possible cause is the PCV valve being stuck in the open or high-speed position. This could allow too much air flow from the crankcase which would lean out the idle mixture excessively. This would cause a poor idle.

■ **1-6-12 Engine Will Not Start** When the engine turns over at normal cranking speed but will not start, the trouble is probably in the ignition or fuel system. The ignition system can be quickly checked by disconnecting the lead from one spark plug. Hold the lead clip about 3/16 inch (5 mm) from the engine block and crank the engine. If a good spark occurs, the ignition system is probably operating normally, although it could be out of time. See Part 1 Sec. 5.

If the ignition system operates normally, remove the carburetor air cleaner to check the accelerator-pump system. Open the throttle quickly and see whether or not the accelerator-pump system is delivering fuel to the carburetor air horn. If it is not, the carburetor probably is not getting fuel from the fuel pump, due to a defective fuel pump, a clogged fuel filter or fuel line, or an empty fuel tank. Also, if the car is equipped with a fuel-vapor-recovery system, installing the wrong fuel-tank cap could prevent fuel delivery. The tanks of cars equipped with fuel-vapor-recovery systems have special vacuum-pressure tank caps. The tanks are sealed. When fuel is withdrawn, the vacuum valve on the cap opens to admit air to the tank. If this cap is replaced with a different cap which does not have the valves, no air can enter to replace fuel withdrawn. The result is that a vacuum develops in the tank which can prevent delivery of fuel through the fuel pump to the carburetor.

If the accelerator-pump system does deliver fuel to the carburetor air horn, try starting again. If the engine starts when primed by the pump operation, but then stalls, the carburetor idle or main metering systems probably are clogged and not functioning normally. If the engine still does not start when primed, there is probably some problem in the engine which prevents starting.

CAUTION: Put the air cleaner back on after priming the engine with the accelerator pump before you attempt to start. If you fail to do this, the engine could backfire through the carburetor. This could burn you and also cause a fire. Any fuel in or around the carburetor could be ignited by a backfire.

■ 1-6-13 Hard Starting with Engine Warm

If the engine starts hard when warm, it could be due to the choke sticking closed, improper throttle-cracker linkage, vapor lock (■ 1-6-10), or engine binding due to overheating. Choke action can be watched with the air cleaner removed. If the choke does not open wide with the engine hot, it should be serviced (■ 1-6-26).

■ 1-6-14 Slow Engine Warmup If the engine warms up slowly, the trouble could be due to an open choke (it should be partly closed with the engine cold). This can be seen with the air cleaner off. Also, the manifold heat-control valve or the cooling-system thermostat could be stuck open.

■ 1-6-15 Smoky Exhaust The color of the smoky exhaust is a clue to what is causing it. For example, if the exhaust is blue, that means the engine is burning oil. This is normally an engine problem and is caused by oil entering the combustion chambers. Oil can enter through the PCV system, through clearances between the valve stems and valve guides, and past piston rings.

If the exhaust is black or sooty, it means the air-fuel mixture is too rich so that it is not burning completely. Refer to ■ 1-6-9 for causes of excessive fuel consumption.

If the smoke is white, coolant from the engine cooling system probably is leaking into the combustion chambers. The water turns into steam in the heat of combustion and gives the exhaust gas the white color. The remedy here is to tighten cylinder-head bolts or replace the cylinder-head gasket. This is a likely place for coolant to leak into the combustion chambers. The condition also could be caused by a cracked cylinder head or cylinder block.

NOTE: A quick check for coolant leakage is to put a drop of oil from the crankcase on a sheet of aluminum foil. Then apply heat to the foil under the drop of oil. If the oil begins to crackle and pop, there is water in it. If coolant is leaking into the combustion chambers, it will also probably be found in the engine oil.

■ 1-6-16 Engine Stalls If the engine starts and then stalls, note whether the stalling takes place before or after the engine warms up, after idling or slow-speed driving, or after high-speed or full-load driving. Check the PCV valve. If this valve becomes clogged or sticks, it can cause poor idling and stalling. A malfunctioning PCV valve should be replaced.

1. ENGINE STALLS BEFORE IT WARMS UP This could be due to an improperly set fast or slow idle, or to improper adjustment of the idle-mixture screw in the carburetor. Also, it could be due to a low carburetor float setting or to insufficient fuel entering the carburetor. This condition could result from a faulty float needle valve, dirt or water in the fuel lines or filter, a defective fuel pump, or a plugged fuel-tank vent. Also, the carburetor could be icing. In some cases, certain ignition troubles could cause stalling after starting. Generally, if ignition troubles are bad enough to cause stalling, they also would prevent starting. Burned contact points or defective spark plugs might permit starting but could fail to keep the engine running. The other condition might be an open primary resistance. When the engine is cranked, this resistance is bypassed. Then, when the engine starts and cranking stops, the resistance is inserted into the ignition primary circuit. If the resistor or resistance wire is open, the engine will stall when the key is released.

2. ENGINE STALLS AS IT WARMS UP This condition might result if the choke valve is stuck closed (■ 1-6-25 and 1-6-26). The mixture becomes too rich for a hot engine and the engine stalls. Also, if the manifold heat-control valve is stuck, the ingoing air-fuel mixture might become overheated and too lean, causing the engine to stall. If the hot-idle speed setting is too low, the engine may stall when it warms up because its idling speed will drop too low. It is also possible that the engine is overheating, which could cause vapor lock.

3. ENGINE STALLS AFTER IDLING OR SLOW-SPEED DRIVING This may occur if the fuel pump is defective and has a cracked diaphragm, weak spring, or defective valve. The pump cannot deliver enough gasoline at low speed to replace that used by the engine. Therefore, the carburetor float bowl runs dry and the engine stops. If the float level is set too high or the idle adjustment is too rich, the engine may load up with an overrich mixture and stall. A lean idle adjustment also will cause stalling when the engine is hot. Overheating can cause vapor lock and engine stalling. The engine may overheat during sustained idling or slow-speed driving. Under these conditions, the air movement through the radiator may not be great enough to keep the engine temperature down. If overheating is excessive or abnormal, consider the conditions listed in ■ 1-7-2.

4. ENGINE STALLS AFTER HIGH-SPEED DRIVING This may occur if sufficient heat accumulates to cause the fuel to boil in the line and produce a vapor lock. Shielding the fuel line or using a less volatile fuel reduces the tendency for vapor lock to occur. Another condition that might cause stalling after high-speed driving is failure of the antipercolator valve in the carburetor. This causes the mixture to become too rich and the engine to stall. Stalling might also result from engine overheating (see ■ 1-7-2).

■ **1-6-17 Engine Backfires** It is not uncommon for backfiring to occur in a cold engine because of a temporarily improper air-fuel-mixture ratio or sluggish intake valves. However, after the engine has started and is warming up, backfiring becomes a more serious matter. It may be due to an excessively rich or lean mixture which will not ignite properly, causing backfiring through the carburetor. Backfiring may also be due to preignition caused by such engine conditions as hot valves or excessive carbon, and by such ignition-system conditions as incorrect timing or plugs of the wrong heat range.

■ **1-6-18 Engine Runs but Misses** If the engine runs but misses, the fuel system may be erratic in its action so that fuel delivery is not uniform. This could result from clogged fuel lines, clogged nozzles or passages in the carburetor, incorrectly adjusted or malfunctioning float level or needle valve, or a defective fuel pump. Other conditions that might cause missing include ignition defects, such as incorrect timing or defective plugs, coil, points, cap, condenser, or wiring. The exhaust system might be clogged, causing back pressure that prevents normal air-fuel-mixture delivery to the cylinders. Also, the engine might be overheating, or it might have sticky valves, loss of compression, defective piston rings, etc.

■ **1-6-19 Engine Run-On, or Dieseling** Modern engines with emission control devices require a fairly high hot-idle speed for best operation. This makes run-on, or dieseling, possible. If there is any source of ignition, the engine will continue to run even after the ignition switch is turned off. Hot spots in the combustion chamber can take the place of the spark plugs. If the throttle is slightly open, enough air-fuel mixture can be getting past it to keep the engine running. Many engines have an idle-stop solenoid to close the throttle completely when the ignition switch is turned off.

If an engine diesels, check the idle-stop solenoid. It may need adjustment so that it will allow the throttle to close completely when the ignition is turned off. Also, make sure the engine is not overheating. This can contribute to the problem of run-on. (See ■ 1-7-2.)

■ **1-6-20 Too Much HC and CO in Exhaust** If the exhaust-gas analyzer (■ 1-6-3) indicates that there is too much HC and CO in the exhaust gases, several conditions could be the cause. In the fuel system, a choke sticking closed, worn jets, high float level, and other conditions listed in ■ 1-6-9 could be the cause. In the ignition system, missing or incorrect timing could be responsible. Also, emission controls such as the air-injection system, transmission-controlled spark system, or defective catalytic converters could be causing the problem.

■ **1-6-21 Quick Carburetor Checks** Several quick carburetor checks can be made to give an indication of whether the various carburetor systems are functioning. The results of these checks must not be considered final. They give only a preliminary indication of possible trouble. Accurate diagnosis requires an exhaust-gas analyzer and an intake-manifold vacuum gauge.

1. FLOAT-LEVEL ADJUSTMENT With the engine running at idle speed, remove the air cleaner. Look for fuel dribbling from the main metering nozzle. If it is, the float level is high.

> **CAUTION:** A backfire can occur with the air cleaner off. Removing the air cleaner can lean the air-fuel mixture enough to cause backfiring. A malfunctioning carburetor can also cause backfiring.

2. LOW-SPEED (OFF-IDLE) AND IDLE SYSTEM If the engine does not idle smoothly, the idle system may be malfunctioning. Other possible causes of poor idling are noted in ■ 1-6-10 and ■ 1-6-13. Open the throttle slowly to increase engine speed to about 2,500 rpm. If engine speed does not increase evenly and the engine runs roughly through this speed range, the low-speed system probably is malfunctioning.

3. ACCELERATOR-PUMP SYSTEM With the engine off and the air cleaner removed, look down the carburetor. Open the throttle suddenly and note whether the accelerator-pump jet discharges a flow of fuel. If no fuel discharges, and you are sure the float bowl is full, the accelerator-pump system is malfunctioning.

4. MAIN METERING SYSTEM With the engine warmed up and running at approximately 2,500 rpm, slowly cover part of the air-cleaner air intake with a piece of stiff cardboard. Do not use your hand! The engine should speed up slightly since this should cause the main metering system to discharge more fuel.

■ **1-6-22 Cleanliness** The major enemy of good service work is dirt. A trace of dirt in the wrong place in a carburetor or fuel pump may cause serious difficulty. For example, dirt in the needle-valve seat in the carburetor float bowl may prevent closing of the needle valve. The float bowl will overfill and cause an excessively rich mixture and high fuel consumption. Similarly, dirt in the idle system or accelerator-pump system may produce malfunctioning of the carburetor and poor engine operation. When you are servicing a fuel pump or a carburetor, be sure that your hands, the bench, and your tools are clean.

> **CAUTION 1:** An air hose often is used to air-dry carburetor parts after they have been soaked in carburetor cleaner and also to blow out carburetor passages. When using an air hose, always wear eye protection. The compressed air drives dirt particles at high velocity. Such particles could get into your eyes and injure them. Be very careful where you point the hose to avoid injuring anyone else.

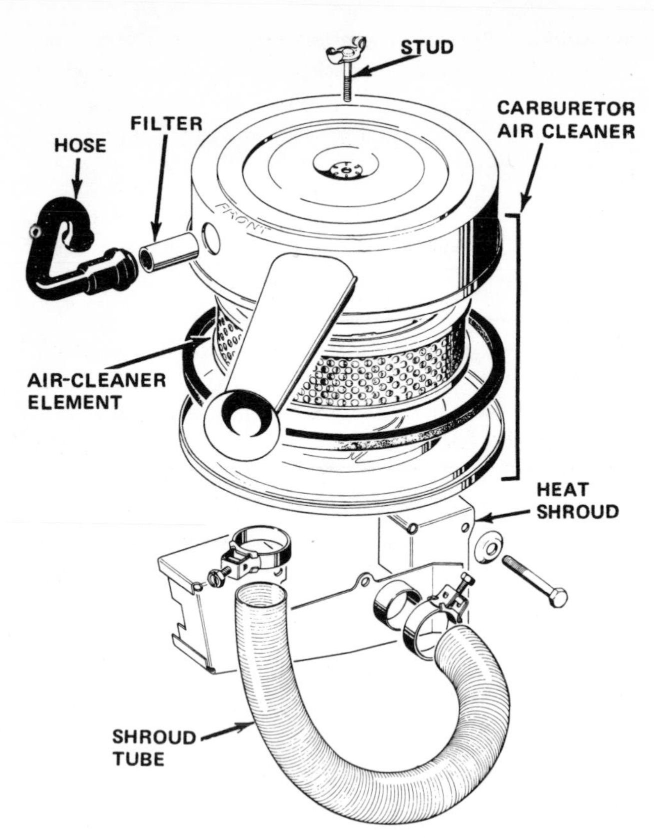

Figure 4 Disassembled view of a carburetor air cleaner and associated parts for a six-cylinder engine. *(American Motors Corporation.)*

CAUTION 2: Gasoline vapor is highly explosive. Use extreme care in handling fuel-system parts that are covered or filled with gasoline. When removing a carburetor, fuel pump, filter, or fuel tank, drain it into a safety container. Then wipe up all spilled gasoline with cloths. Put the cloths outside to dry. NEVER BRING AN OPEN FLAME NEAR GASOLINE! This could result in an explosion and fire.

CAUTION 3: Never remove a carburetor from a hot engine. Any spilled gasoline could ignite from hot engine parts and cause an explosion and fire.

CAUTION 4: Never prime an engine with the air cleaner off by pouring or squirting fuel into the carburetor as the engine is cranked. The engine could backfire and cause an explosion or fire.

CAUTION 5: Be very careful if you must run the engine with the air cleaner off. Removing the air cleaner can lean out the air-fuel mixture enough to cause backfiring. Also, a malfunctioning carburetor or other engine conditions can cause backfire, and a fire in the carburetor may result.

■ **1-6-23 Air-Cleaner Service** The air cleaner passes a large amount of air through its filter element. The filter element removes dirt and dust from the air. This dirt gradually accumulates in the element and partially clogs it. On the oil-bath cleaner, much of this dirt is washed down into the oil, and so the oil gradually gets dirty. At one time, car manufacturers recommended that the air cleaner be removed periodically so that the filter element could be cleaned. Now, only Chrysler recommends a cleaning method. The carburetor on the modern car is balanced. That is, it is internally vented to the air cleaner. With this arrangement, a partial clogging of the filter element will not produce a richer mixture.

Because of this, and because of improved filter elements, most manufacturers now recommend that the filter element should be replaced periodically. They do not give cleaning instructions.

Figure 4 shows an air cleaner with related parts. The filter element is removed in some models simply by taking off the wing nut and air-cleaner cap. Then the element can be lifted out. On other models, as shown in Fig. 4, the cap is part of the air-cleaner cover. The assembly includes the snorkel, the connections to the positive crankcase ventilating system, and the heat stove for the heated-air-intake system. On these, the air cleaner cover can usually be lifted up enough to remove the element. If it cannot, the hoses will have to be disconnected.

With the element out, the bottom of the air cleaner, gasket surfaces, and cover should be cleaned. Check the cover seal for tears or cracks, and replace it if it is damaged.

NOTE: Chrysler recommends that if the air cleaner must be loosened from the carburetor for any purpose, remove the air cleaner from under the hood. If the air cleaner rests on or hooks into linkage parts, the parts can be damaged. Cap all carburetor air fittings which could leak air if the engine is to be run without the air cleaner.

1. CLEANING PAPER ELEMENT Here is the procedure recommended by Chrysler for cleaning the paper element. Examine the element, and if it is saturated with oil over more than half its circumference, discard it. Check the crankcase ventilating system since it has delivered the oil to the air cleaner. Use compressed air to blow from inside the element out. Hold the nozzle at least 2 inches (51 mm) away from the inside screen of the element. Do not blow from the outside in! This will embed dust in the paper.

After cleaning the element, examine it for punctures. If you can see any pinholes when you hold the element up to the light, discard it. Make sure the plastic sealing rings on both sides of the element are smooth and uniform. If these are in good condition, install the element. Be sure it seals both top and bottom when the cover is replaced.

2. CLEANING POLYURETHANE ELEMENT On some Chevrolet models, a polyurethane element is used outside the paper element. After the polyurethane element is removed, inspect it carefully for rips or other damage. Discard it if it is not in good condition. Wash the element in kerosene. Then, squeeze it gently to remove excess kerosene.

NOTE: Do not use solvents containing acetone or similar compounds, since they could ruin the element. Also, never wring out, shake, or swing the element. This could tear it. Instead, fold over the element and gently squeeze it.

Clean the cover and bottom parts of the cleaner. Then, dip the cleaned element in engine oil, and squeeze out the excess. Reinstall the element and its support in the cleaner bottom. Make sure that the element is not folded or creased and that it seals all the way around the bottom. Install the cover, making sure the element seals all the way around on it. Use a new gasket when installing the air cleaner on the carburetor.

3. *OIL-BATH CLEANER* After removing the filter element, clean it by sloshing it up and down in cleaning solvent. Dry it with compressed air. Dump old oil from the cleaner body, wash it out with solvent and dry it. Refill the body to the FULL mark with clean engine oil. Reinstall the filter element and cleaner body on the engine.

NOTE: Air filters which are not installed directly on the carburetor are connected to the carburetor by a flexible hose. This hose must have an airtight connection to both the filter and the carburetor. Also, the hose must have no tears or punctures, as they would admit unfiltered air.

■ 1-6-24 Thermostatically Controlled Air Cleaner

The thermostatically controlled air cleaner can be checked for proper operation with a temperature gauge or thermometer. Remove the air-cleaner cover and install the gauge as closely as possible to the sensor. Allow the engine to cool to below 85°F (29.4°C) if it is hot. Install the air-cleaner cover without the wing nut.

Start and idle the engine. When the damper begins to open, remove the air-cleaner cover and note the temperature reading. It should be between 85 and 115°F (29.4 and 46.1°C). If it is difficult to see the damper, use a mirror.

If the damper does not open at the correct temperature, check the vacuum motor and sensor.

With the engine off, the control damper should be in the compartment or cold-air delivery-mode position. To determine whether the vacuum motor is operating, apply at least 9 inches (228.6 mm) of vacuum to the fitting on the vacuum motor. The vacuum can be from the engine or from a vacuum source in the shop. With vacuum applied, the damper should move to the hot-air delivery-mode position.

If the vacuum motor does not work satisfactorily, it should be replaced. This can be done by drilling out the spot welds and unhooking the linkage. The new motor can be installed with a retaining strap and sheet-metal screws.

If the vacuum motor does work okay, the sensor should be replaced. This is done by prying up the tabs on the retaining

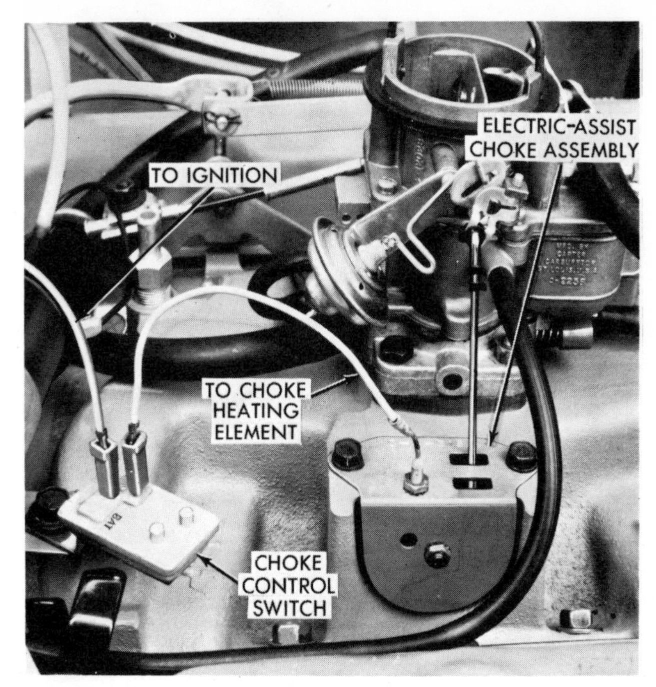

Figure 5 Electric-assist choke assembly showing the location of the thermostatic choke control switch. *(Chrysler Corporation.)*

clip. The new sensor is then installed and the tabs bent down again.

■ 1-6-25 Manual-Choke Adjustment

On manual chokes, a choke button on the dash is linked through a control wire in a conduit to the choke valve in the carburetor. If the wire slips in the screw clamp or if the wire kinks, the choke valve may not open and close properly as the choke control is moved in and out. Loosen the screw clamp and slide the wire one way or the other to get proper adjustment. With the choke button in, the choke valve should be open. With the choke button pulled out, the choke valve should be closed. Kinks can be straightened by bending the wire. Sometimes the conduit supports are bent out of line, causing the wire to bind inside the conduit. The supports should be straightened. If the wire still binds, put a few drops of penetrating oil along the conduit. The oil will penetrate to the wire and lubricate it.

■ 1-6-26 Automatic-Choke Adjustment

Automatic chokes are of several types, some that can be adjusted, others that require no adjustment. In normal operation, a properly adjusted choke does not usually get out of adjustment. It is possible for a choke to become stuck because of accumulation of dirt or gum. Adjustments would not help this. The choke would require cleaning and freeing up and then readjustment. If hard starting is a problem, other causes should be eliminated before the choke is adjusted. If some other condition is causing the trouble (faulty spark plugs, for example), readjusting the choke could make the condition worse (by further fouling the plugs from an overrich mixture).

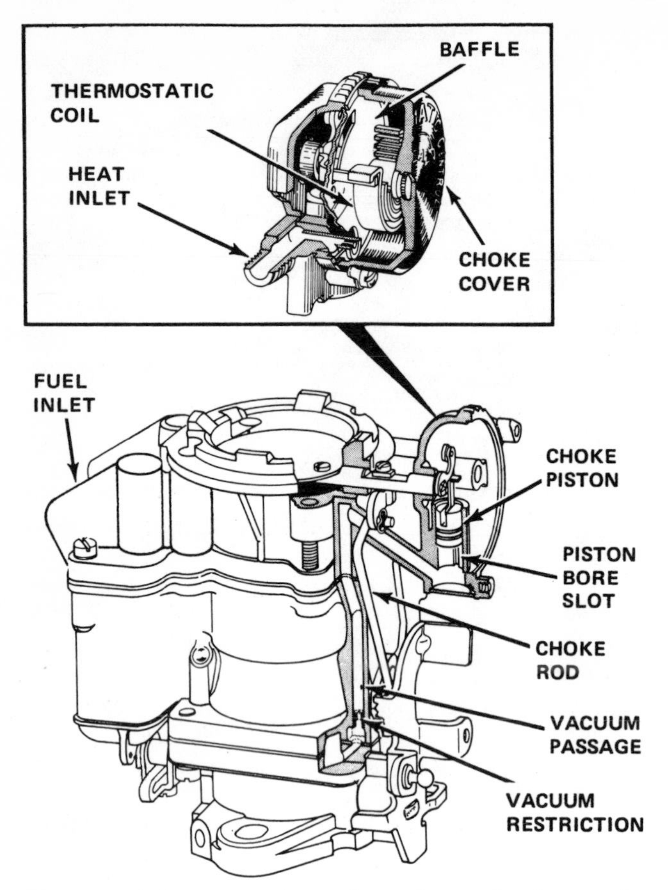

Figure 6 Choke system using a choke piston and a thermostatic spring (coil) mounted on the carburetor. *(American Motors Corporation.)*

The two types of chokes are those mounted on the carburetor and those with the thermostatic coil in a well in the intake or exhaust manifold. Some chokes have an electric-assist coil to speed up the choke action. Other chokes are water-heated. That is, hot coolant from the engine cooling system flows through them to hasten choke action.

One electric-assist choke installation is shown in Fig. 5. This choke is not adjustable. The choke control switch is thermostatic. It is connected to the battery and to the choke heater. Below 58°F (14.4°C) it connects the choke heater to the battery through a resistance, thus allowing some current to flow. Above 58°F (14.4°C), the control switch connects the choke heater to the battery directly for fast heating and quick defrosting. At approximately 110°F (43.3°C), it disconnects the choke heater.

The carburetor-mounted choke shown in Fig. 6 can be adjusted by loosening the two or three cover clamp screws and turning the cover one way or the other to lean out or enrich the mixture. Some chokes that have the thermostatic coil in the exhaust manifold can be adjusted by bending the rod connecting the coil to the choke. Others cannot be adjusted. Details of adjustment are covered in the latter part of this section (■ 1-6-36 to 1-6-42), which discusses the servicing of carburetors.

■ **1-6-27 Fuel-Filter Service** Fuel filters require no service except periodic checks to make sure they are not clogged, and replacement of the filter element or cleaning of the filter, according to type. On some earlier models, the filter is part of the fuel pump and can be removed so that the element can be replaced. Another type is in the in-line filter. In this type, the filter is replaced by unclamping and detaching the fuel hose from the filter. The filter can then be unscrewed from the carburetor and replaced. On other carburetors, the fuel line is detached. Then the nut is removed so that the old filter can be slipped out and a new filter installed.

■ **1-6-28 Fuel Tank** Seldom does a fuel tank require service. If it is damaged, it will require repair or possibly replacement. Some car manufacturers recommend that the fuel tank be drained once a year to remove accumulated dirt and water. Some tanks have a drain plug. Fuel tanks usually are supported by straps bolted to the frame. Removal of these straps permits removal of the tank. Before the tank is removed, the fuel-gauge wire and fuel line must be detached. Fuel should be drained from the tank into a safety container.

CAUTION: If a tank is to be repaired, great care must be used to make sure that it is completely free of gasoline vapors. A spark from a hammer blow or from a torch might set off vapor remaining in the tank and cause an explosion.

The fuel filter in the tank (where present) can be cleaned, if the tank is removed, by blowing air through it from an air hose. Air should be directed through the filter from the fuel outlet.

When installing a tank, make sure that the support straps are firmly fastened. Also, if the fuel-gauge terminal is dirty, clean it so that good contact will be made when the wire is connected.

■ **1-6-29 Fuel Lines** Fuel lines (or pipes, or tubes, as they are also called) are attached to each other and to the carburetor, fuel pump, and tank by means of different types of coupling. When loosening a coupling of the type having two nuts, use two wrenches. This prevents twisting the line and possibly damaging it.

When installing a new line of the flared type, double-flare the tube. Double flaring assures a safer and tighter connection.

Fuel lines should be adequately supported at various points along the frame. If a line is rubbing against a sharp corner, it should be moved slightly to avoid wear and a possible leak. Fuel lines must not be kinked or bent unnecessarily, since this treatment is likely to cause a crack and a leak.

If the fuel line between the pump and tank is thought to be clogged, it can be tested by disconnecting the line at the pump and applying an air hose to it. Remove the tank filler cap. Do not apply too much air, since this might blow gasoline out of the tank. If the line will not pass air freely, it could be clogged with dirt; or perhaps it has become badly kinked or pinched at a bend or support. Also, on tanks with an internal filter, the filter may have become clogged. Kinked or pinched lines should be replaced, since the kinked or pinched place, even if straightened, may ultimately crack open and leak.

■ **1-6-30 Fuel Gauges** There is very little in the way of service that fuel gauges require. Defects in either the dash unit or the tank unit usually require replacement of the defective unit. However, on the type of gauge that makes use of vibrating thermostatic blades, dirty contact points may cause fluctuations of the needle. The points can be cleaned by pulling a strip of clean bond paper between them. Be sure that no particles of paper are left between the points. Never use emery cloth to clean the points. Particles of emery will embed in the points and cause very erratic gauge action.

If a fuel gauge is defective, or if a malfunctioning gauge is suspected, substitute a new tank unit for the old one. This can be done without removing the old tank unit. Disconnect the tank-unit terminal lead from the old unit and connect it to the terminal of the substitute unit. Then connect a jumper wire from the frame of the substitute unit to a good ground on the car. Turn on the ignition switch and operate the float arm of the substitute unit. If the dash unit now works and indicates as the float arm is moved up and down, then the old tank unit is defective. If the dash unit still does not work, then either it is at fault or the wiring is defective.

NOTE: On the thermostatic type of fuel gauge, it takes a minute or so for the thermostat to heat up and start the instrument-panel (dash) unit indicating. Therefore, on these, wait a minute or so after turning on the ignition switch.

■ **1-6-31 Fuel-Pump Inspection** The fuel pump can be checked for pressure, capacity, and vacuum with the fuel-pump tester (see ■1-6-4 to 1-6-6). The vacuum pump of the combination pump can also be tested with the vacuum gauge. Readings obtained should be compared with the specifications. A quick check of fuel-pump operation can be made by disconnecting the fuel line from the carburetor and sticking the fuel line in a suitable container. Then crank the engine. Ignition should be off and the distributor primary lead should be disconnected from the coil so that the engine does not start. During cranking, the fuel pump should deliver a spurt of gasoline with each rotation of the engine camshaft. Wipe up any spilled gasoline with cloths and put the cloths outside to dry.

In addition to checks of the operating action, the fuel pump should be checked for leaks. Leaks might occur at fuel-line connections or around sealing gaskets. For example, leaks may occur at the joint between the sediment bowl and the fuel-pump cover or at the joint between the cover and the fuel-pump body.

If the fuel-pump pressure is too high or too low, if the pump does not deliver fuel normally to the carburetor, if leaks show up, if the pump has a cracked diaphragm or other defect, or if the pump is noisy, then the pump should be replaced. The following section describes various pump troubles and their causes.

■ **1-6-32 Fuel-Pump Troubles** The Trouble-Diagnosis Chart in ■1-6-8 lists various fuel-system troubles and their causes. Some of these causes may be in the fuel pump. Many troubles are in the other fuel-system or engine components. Following is a discussion of fuel-system troubles that might be caused by the fuel pump.

1. INSUFFICIENT FUEL DELIVERY Insufficient fuel delivery could result from low pump pressure, which in turn could be due to any of the following:

a. Broken, worn-out, or cracked diaphragm
b. Improperly operating fuel-pump valves.
c. Broken diaphragm spring
d. Broken or damaged rocker arm
e. Clogged pump-filter screen
f. Air leaks into sediment bowl due to loose bowl or worn gasket.

In addition to these causes of insufficient fuel delivery due to conditions within the pump, many other conditions outside the pump could prevent delivery of normal amounts of fuel. These are listed and described elsewhere. They include such causes as a clogged fuel-tank cap vent, a clogged fuel line or filter, air leaks into the fuel line, and vapor lock. In the carburetor, an incorrect float level, a clogged inlet screen, or a malfunctioning inlet needle valve would prevent delivery of adequate amounts of fuel to the carburetor.

2. EXCESSIVE PUMP PRESSURE High-fuel pump pressure will cause delivery of too much fuel to the carburetor. The excessive pressure will tend to lift the needle valve off its seat so that the fuel level in the float bowl will be too high. This results in an overrich mixture and excessive fuel consumption. Usually, high pump pressure would result only after a fuel pump has been removed, repaired, and replaced. If a fuel pump has been operating satisfactorily, it is hardly likely that its pressure would increase enough to cause trouble. High pressure could come from installation of an excessively strong diaphragm spring or from incorrect reinstallation of the diaphragm. If the diaphragm is not flexed properly when the cover and housing are reattached, it will have too much tension and produce too much pressure.

3. FUEL-PUMP LEAKS The fuel pump will leak fuel from any point where screws have not been properly tightened and also where the gasket is damaged or incorrectly installed. If tightening the screws does not stop the leak, the pump must be serviced or replaced. Leaks may occur at fuel-line connections which are loose or improperly coupled.

4. FUEL-PUMP NOISES A noisy pump is usually the result of worn or broken parts inside the pump. These include a weak or broken rocker-arm spring, a worn or broken rocker-arm pin or rocker arm, or a broken diaphragm spring. In addition, a loose fuel pump or a scored rocker arm or cam on the camshaft may cause noise. Fuel-pump noises may sound something like engine valve-tappet noise, since its frequency is the same as camshaft speed. If the noise is bad enough, it can actually be felt by gripping the fuel pump firmly in the hand. Also, careful listening will usually disclose that the noise is originating in the vicinity of the fuel pump. Tappet noise is usually distributed along the engine or is located distinctly in the valve compartment of the engine.

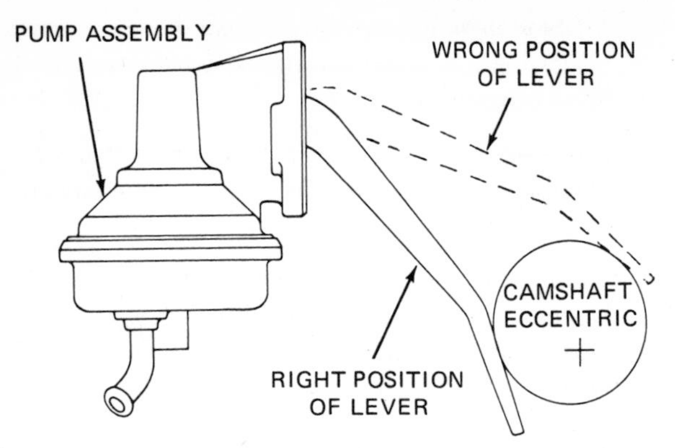

Figure 7 Correct positioning of the fuel-pump lever on the camshaft eccentric. *(Chevrolet Motor Division of General Motors Corporation.)*

■ **1-6-33 Fuel-Pump Removal** As a first step in removing the fuel pump, wipe off any dirt or accumulated grease so that dirt will not get into the engine. Then take off the heat shield (where present) and disconnect the fuel lines. Remove attaching nuts or bolts, and lift off the pump. If it sticks, work it gently from side to side, or pry lightly under the mounting flange with a screwdriver to loosen it. Do not damage the flange or attaching studs. On engines using a pushrod to operate the fuel pump, remove the rod so that it can be examined for wear or sticking.

■ **1-6-34 Fuel-Pump Service** Today, most fuel pumps cannot be disassembled for any service. They are put together by crimping and are only serviced by complete replacement. Earlier fuel pumps could be disassembled. On these, you purchased a repair kit which had all the necessary parts to rebuild the fuel pump. Now the cost of labor is high and the cost of a new pump is relatively low. Thus, it is generally cheaper to buy a new pump than it is to repair an old, defective pump.

■ **1-6-35 Fuel-Pump Installation** Make sure that the fuel-line connections are clean and in good condition. All gasket material must be off the mounting pad on the engine and on the pump flange. Connect the fuel lines to the pump before attaching the pump to the engine. Then place a new gasket on the studs of the fuel-pump mounting or over the opening in the crankcase. Many automotive manufacturers recommend coating both sides of the new gasket with oil-resistant sealer before installation. The mounting surface of the engine should be clean. Insert the rocker arm of the fuel pump into the opening, making sure that the arm goes on the proper side of the camshaft (Fig. 7), or that it is centered over the pushrod. If it is hard to get the holes in the fuel-pump flange to align with the holes in the crankcase, turn the engine over until the low side of the camshaft eccentric is under the fuel-pump rocker arm. On V-8 engines that have a pushrod, use a mechanical fingers tool to hold the pushrod up while installing the pump. Attach the pump with bolts or nuts. Check the pump operation as explained in ■1-6-31.

■ **1-6-36 Cleanliness** Keep carburetor parts and passages as clean as possible. Bits of dirt or dust that are allowed to get into the carburetor will probably cause carburetor and engine trouble sooner or later. The jets or nozzles and passages through which gasoline flows are carefully calibrated. Dirt or gum that changes this calibration will have a bad effect on carburetor and engine performance. Careless cleaning of the nozzles or jets may enlarge them slightly. This will cause an overrich mixture, fuel waste, and excessive carbon deposits in the combustion chambers. The Cautions listed in ■1-6-22 also apply to carburetor service.

■ **1-6-37 Carburetor Troubles** Various carburetor troubles are outlined in detail in ■1-6-8 to 1-6-20. The Trouble-Diagnosis Chart in ■1-6-8 lists the various causes of fuel-system complaints. In the carburetor, such conditions are incorrect fuel level in the float bowl, incorrect idle-speed and idle-mixture adjustments, clogged idle or main metering systems, or malfunctioning accelerator-pump system. Quick checks of these systems are outlined in ■1-6-21.

Various engine troubles that can be caused by the carburetor are listed below. Many other conditions outside the carburetor can also cause these troubles. See the Trouble-Diagnosis Chart in ■1-6-8 for more complete information.

1. Excessive fuel consumption can result from:

a. A high float level or a leaky float
b. Sticking or dirty float needle valve
c. Worn jets or nozzles
d. A stuck metering rod or power piston
e. A too-rich idle mixture or too-fast idle speed
f. A stuck accelerator-pump check valve
g. A leaky carburetor
h. Excessive fuel-pump pressure

2. Lack of engine power, acceleration, or high-speed performance can result from:

a. The power step-up on the metering rod not clearing the jet
b. Dirt or gum clogging the fuel nozzle or jets
c. A stuck power piston or valve
d. A low float level
e. A dirty air filter
f. The choke stuck or not operating
g. Air leakage into the manifold
h. The throttle valve not fully opening
i. A rich mixture, due to causes listed under item 1, above
j. A heat-control valve stuck closed

3. Poor idle can result from a leaky vacuum hose, stuck PCV valve, or retarded timing. Also, it could be due to an incorrectly adjusted idle mixture or speed, a clogged idle system, or any of the causes listed under item 2, above.

4. Failure of the engine to start unless primed (by the accelerator pump) could be due to: no gasoline in the fuel tank or carburetor, the wrong tank cap (1970 cars and later), or clogged tank or cap vent. The latter causes a vacuum to develop in the tank, which prevents delivery of fuel to the carburetor. Holes in the fuel-pump flex line will allow air leakage which prevents fuel delivery. Other possible causes are clogged carburetor jets or lines, a defective choke, a clogged fuel filter, or air leakage into the manifold.

5. Hard starting with the engine warm could be due to a defective choke, a closed choke valve, or improperly adjusted throttle-cracker linkage.

6. Slow engine warm-up could be due to a defectively operating choke or manifold heat-control valve.

7. A smoky, black exhaust is due to a very rich mixture. Carburetor conditions that could cause this are listed under item 1.

8. If the engine stalls as it warms up, this could be due to a defective choke or a closed choke valve.

9. If the engine stalls after a period of high-speed driving, this could be due to a malfunctioning antipercolator.

10. If the engine backfires, this could be due to an excessively rich or lean mixture. If the backfire is in the exhaust system, it is usually caused by an excessively rich mixture in the exhaust. This often results from a defective air-injection-system antibackfire valve. Lean mixtures usually cause a pop-back in the carburetor.

11. If the engine runs but misses, a likely cause is that a vacuum hose has come off an intake-manifold fitting, causing the nearest cylinders to miss. Missing might also be caused by a leaky intake-manifold gasket. In addition, the proper amount and ratio of air-fuel mixture may not be reaching the engine, possibly due to clogged or worn carburetor jets or to an incorrect fuel level in the float bowl.

Some of the conditions noted above can be corrected by carburetor adjustment. Others require removal of the carburetor from the engine so that it can be disassembled, repaired, and reassembled. Following sections discuss carburetor adjustments and servicing procedures.

■ **1-6-38 Typical Carburetor Adjustments** At one time, there were several adjustments that could be made on carburetors. In recent years, however, automotive emission-control laws have been passed which limit the adjustments that can be made. The only adjustment now recommended for late-model cars during tuneup is to adjust the idle speed. The idle mixture is preset at the factory, and a limiter cap is installed to prevent tampering. The adjustment procedure is spelled out in a special tune-up decal in the engine compartment. This decal lists the specific procedure that must be followed. If some carburetor trouble has occurred which requires disassembling the carburetor, the locking cap or caps may be removed. The idle mixture must then be readjusted and new limiter caps installed. Procedures follow.

1. SETTING IDLE SPEED Here is a typical procedure.

a. Disconnect the fuel-tank hose from the vapor canister.

b. Disconnect the vacuum hose to the distributor. Plug the hose leading to the carburetor.

c. Make sure distributor contact-point dwell and ignition timing are correct (as described in Part 1, Sec. 5).

d. Adjust idle speed by the means provided. In earlier models, this was a screw in the throttle linkage at the carburetor. In later models equpped with idle-speed solenoids, the adjustment screw is in the solenoid. Regardless of the location of the adjustment screw, use a tachometer to measure engine speed. Make the adjustment to get the specified idle speed.

e. Reconnect the distributor vacuum hose and the fuel-tank hose.

2. SETTING IDLE MIXTURE This adjustment is permissible only if the carburetor has required major service. A typical procedure is:

a. With limiter caps off, turn the mixture screws in until they lightly touch the seats. Then back them off two full turns.

b. Adjust the idle speed as already noted.

c. Connect a CO meter to the exhaust system. Adjust the idle-mixture screws to get a satisfactory idle at the specified rpm and a CO reading at or below the specified allowable maximum. The engine should be running at normal idle with automatic transmission in D (drive) or manual transmission in neutral.

d. After setting the idle mixture, recheck the idle speed as previously. If everything checks, install new limiter caps on the idle-mixture screws.

NOTE: Refer to the manufacturer's service manual covering the model being serviced for specific instructions and specifications for carburetor adjustments.

■ **1-6-39 Carburetor Removal** To remove a carburetor, first disconnect the air and vacuum lines and take off the air cleaner. Next, disconnect the throttle and choke linkages. Disconnect the hot-air tube to the choke (if present). Disconnect the fuel line and the distributor vacuum-advance line from the carburetor. Use two wrenches, as necessary to avoid damage to the lines or couplings. Disconnect wires from switches and other electric controls (where present). Take off the carburetor attaching nuts or bolts, and lift off the carburetor. Try to avoid jarring the carburetor. It may have accumulations of dirt in the float bowl. Rough treatment may stir up this dirt and cause it to get into carburetor jets or circuits.

After the carburetor is off, it should be put in a clean place where dirt and dust cannot get into openings.

CAUTION: Do not remove a carburetor from a hot engine. Fuel could splash on hot engine parts and ignite, causing a fire. Wait for the engine to cool off before removing the carburetor or fuel pump.

If the carburetor is to be off the engine for any length of time, cover the exposed manifold holes with masking tape. Protecting the manifold holes in this way will prevent engine damage from loose parts dropped into the manifold. Parts dropped in the manifold could end up in the engine combustion chambers where they could cause serious damage.

■ 1-6-40 Carburetor Overhaul Procedures

Disassembly and reassembly procedures on carburetors vary according to design. The manufacturer's recommendations should be followed carefully. The time required to overhaul a carburetor varies from approximately 3/4 to 2 hours, according to type. A few special carburetor tools may be required. Gauges needed to gauge float clearance, float centering, float height, choke clearance, and so on, are usually included in the carburetor overhaul kit.

Complete carburetor overhaul kits are supplied for many carburetors. These kits contain instructions and all necessary parts (jets, gaskets, washers, and so forth) required to overhaul the carburetor and restore it to its original performing condition. Following are some general comments about carburetor service.

CAUTION: When removing and handling a carburetor, be extremely careful to avoid spilling any gasoline. Remember that the carburetor float bowl will have gasoline in it, and so keep the carburetor upright. Gasoline is extremely flammable. Any gasoline that is spilled should be wiped up immediately. Put the gasoline-soaked towels outside the building in a safe area to dry.

Disassembly and assembly procedures on carburetors vary greatly according to their design. What follows are general service procedures used on all carburetors.

1. Disassemble the carburetor. Note carefully the position of each part as it is removed. Place the parts in a small pan. When overhauling a carburetor, disassemble the carburetor only as far as necessary for proper cleaning and replacing of defective parts.

2. Thoroughly clean the carburetor castings and metal parts in carburetor cleaner. Be sure that both the inside and outside of the castings are clean.

CAUTION: Do not splash cleaner in your eyes. It can seriously harm them. Wear goggles to protect your eyes.

Never soak the pump plunger or any fiber or rubber parts in carburetor cleaner. Wipe these parts clean with a clean, dry shop towel.

3. Wash off the parts carefully in hot water or kerosene, as recommended by the cleaner manufacturer. Blow off all parts until they are dry. Blow out all passages in the castings with compressed air. Make sure all jets and passages are clean.

CAUTION: Use the air hose with care. Goggles should be worn while blowing out the carburetor.

Do not use drills or wires for cleaning out fuel passages or air bleeds. (This may enlarge the openings.) Instead, clean out the openings with a chemical cleaner.

4. Check all parts for damage and wear. If damage or wear is noted, the part or assembly must be replaced. Check the float needle and seat for wear. Check the float-hinge pin for wear and the floats for dents or distortion. Shake metal floats to see if they have water or fuel in them. Power pistons that are scored or burned should be replaced. Check the throttle and choke-shaft bores for wear and out-of-round.

5. Inspect the idle-mixture adjusting screws for burrs or grooves. These conditions require replacement of the screws. Inspect the accelerator-pump plunger cup. If the cup is damaged, worn, or hard, it must be replaced. Inspect the pump well in the fuel bowl for wear or scoring.

6. Check the fuel filter and fuel screen (if used) for dirt or lint. Check the automatic-choke housing for exhaust deposits or corrosion. Check the choke piston for free movement. Deposits or corrosion in the choke housing indicate a defective choke heat tube.

7. Carefully inspect the cluster assembly. If any parts are loose or damaged, replace the cluster assembly. Inspect all gasket mating surfaces for nicks or burrs. Repair any damage to the gasket mating surfaces. Inspect any remaining carburetor parts for damage or excess looseness. Replace any parts that are worn, damaged, or excessively loose.

8. Assemble the carburetor in the proper order. Install all the gaskets and parts contained in the overhaul kit.

NOTE: Be sure your hands, workbench, and tools are clean.

■ 1-6-41 Carburetor Installation

Fill the carburetor float bowl before installing the carburetor. This reduces the strain on the starting motor and battery and also reduces the possibility of backfiring when starting.

Use a new gasket to assure a good seal between the carburetor and the mounting pad. Put the carburetor into position on the intake manifold, and attach it with nuts or bolts. Connect the fuel line and the distributor vacuum-advance line to the carburetor. Use two wrenches if necessary, to avoid damage to the lines or couplings. Connect wires to switches and other electric controls (where present). Make idle-speed, idle-mixture, and other adjustments. Install the air cleaner.

■ 1-6-42 Carburetor Servicing Instructions

The technician can get servicing instructions on specific carburetor models in two ways. First, the automobile manufacturer issues such instructions. They are found in the shop manuals that the manufacturers prepare on their automobiles. Second, there is an instruction sheet in every tuneup kit. For general servicing and adjustments that do not require new parts, the service technician should consult the automobile shop manual that contains information on the specific model being adjusted. When new parts are required, an overhaul kit should be used and the instructions therein followed. Also, all the new parts in the kit should be used to restore the carburetor to standard operating condition.

SECTION 1-7 Engine Cooling-System Service

This section describes trouble diagnosis, testing, care, and servicing of the automotive-engine cooling system and its component parts.

■ **1-7-1 Cooling-System Trouble Diagnosis** Two common complaints related to the engine cooling system are engine overheating and cooling-system leaks. If the engine is slow to warm up, this could also be a fault of the cooling system. Possible causes of these complaints are discussed in following sections.

■ **1-7-2 Overheating** The driver may notice that the red light stays on or the temperature gauge registers in the overheating zone. Also, the driver may complain that the engine boiled over. Possible causes of engine overheating include:

1. Low coolant level due to leakage of coolant from the system, as described in ■1-7-3.

2. Accumulation of rust and scale in the system which prevents normal circulation of coolant. This is less common today, because modern antifreeze compounds contain agents that fight rust.

3. Collapsed hoses which prevent normal coolant circulation.

4. Defective thermostat which does not open normally and thus blocks circulation of coolant. If the engine overheats without the radiator becoming normally warm, and if the fan belt is properly tightened, then the thermostat is probably at fault. Sometimes, on new cars, sand from the engine block or head core will lodge in the thermostat, preventing it from opening.

5. Defective water pump which does not circulate enough coolant through the engine. Water-pump operation can be tested by installing a section of clear plastic hose in place of the upper radiator hose and then running the engine. You can then see how much coolant is circulating and if air is leaking into the system. One of the more common causes of water-pump bearing failure is an overtight fan belt. Fan belts should always be tightened to specifications with a belt-tension gauge.

A bearing that has failed usually is noisy. With the engine off, a quick check of the bearing can be made by grasping the tips of the fan blades and attempting to move the fan toward and away from the radiator. Any movement indicates a worn bearing.

6. Loose or worn fan belt will slip. It should be tightened or replaced. Where a pair of belts is used, both should be replaced at the same time, not just the one that appears more worn. If you replace any one belt, you put all the work on the new belt, and it will wear rapidly. If both are replaced with a new matched pair, then each belt will handle half the job.

7. The trouble may be due to afterboil. That is, the coolant starts to boil after the engine has been turned off. This could happen, for example, after a long, hard drive.

8. Boiling can occur if the coolant (or water) in the radiator is frozen. This hinders or stops the circulation of coolant. Then the coolant in the engine becomes so hot that it boils. Freezing of the coolant in the radiator, engine block, or head may crack the block or head and can open up seams in the radiator. A frozen engine may be damaged seriously.

There are other causes of engine overheating that have nothing to do with conditions in the cooling system. High-altitude operation, insufficient oil, overloading of the engine, hot-climate operation, improperly timed ignition, long periods of slow-speed or idling operation—any of these can cause overheating of the engine.

■ 1-7-3 Loss of Coolant

Leakage of coolant from the cooling system is somewhat more common now than it used to be. This is because modern engines have pressurized cooling systems. Leaks are usually obvious, for two reasons. First, the system requires frequent refilling with water or coolant. Second, the point of the leak is usually indicated by telltale scale or water marks below the leak. A leaky gasket (at the cylinder head or water pump) may require replacement. The attaching bolts should be tightened to the correct tension.

If the leak is in the radiator, the radiator should be removed and either repaired (■1-7-17) or replaced.

If the leak is at a hose connection, the hose connection should be tightened. If a hose is leaking, the hose should be replaced.

■1-7-12 describes pressure-testing the cooling system to locate leaks.

■ 1-7-4 Slow Warmup

The probable cause of slow engine warmup is a thermostat that is stuck open. This open position allows the coolant to circulate between the engine and the radiator even though the engine is cold. The engine therefore has to run longer to reach operating temperature. As a result, engine wear will be greater because the engine operates cold for a longer time. The driver's complaint here would be that it takes a long time for the car heater to start putting out heat. If you get this complaint, suspect a defective thermostat that is stuck in the open position (see ■1-7-8).

■ 1-7-5 Cooling-System Tests

Cooling-system tests include:

1. Checking coolant level
2. Checking coolant antifreeze strength
3. Testing the thermostat
4. Checking the hose and hose connections
5. Testing the water pump
6. Checking for exhaust-gas leakage into the system
7. Pressure testing the system and cap
8. Checking the fan belt or belts for wear and tension
9. Checking the system for accumulation of rust and scale

These are covered in detail in following sections.

■ 1-7-6 Checking Coolant Level

On cooling systems using expansion tanks, it is not necessary to remove the radiator cap to check the coolant level. In fact, car manufacturers warn against removing the radiator cap except for major service. The coolant level can be checked by looking at the expansion tank, which is plastic so that you can see the level of the coolant.

On cooling systems without an expansion tank, you remove the radiator cap to check the coolant level.

CAUTION: Use care when removing a pressure-type radiator cap, especially when the engine is hot. Cover the cap with a cloth to protect your hand, and turn the cap only to the first stop. Any pressure in the system will be released through the overflow tube. Then turn the cap further to remove it. Some manufacturers warn against taking the cap off when the system is hot and there is pressure in the cooling system. They state that if the cap is turned slightly and you hear a hissing sound, you should retighten the cap at once. The cap should be left tight until the engine has cooled and the pressure has dropped. They also say that it should never be necessary to check the coolant level in the system, unless the engine has been overheating.

■ 1-7-7 Testing Antifreeze Strength

The strength of the antifreeze solution must be strong enough to protect against freezing at the lowest expected temperatures. The strength of the antifreeze can be checked with any of three testers. One is the hydrometer. The higher the float rises in the coolant, the higher the percentage of antifreeze in the coolant. To use the hydrometer, put the rubber tube into the coolant, and then squeeze and release the rubber bulb. Note how high the float rises in the coolant. Check the scale which shows how low the temperature must go before the coolant will freeze.

A second tester has several balls in a glass tube. Coolant is drawn into the tube by squeezing and releasing a rubber bulb. The stronger the solution, the more balls will float.

A third tester, called a refractometer (Fig. 1) uses the principle of light refraction (bending of light rays) as light passes through a drop of the coolant. To use the refractometer, open the plastic cover at the slanted end of the tester. Wipe the measuring window and the bottom of the plastic cover with a tissue or a clean cloth.

Close the plastic cover. Release the tip of the pump from the tester housing. Insert the tip of the tube into the radiator-filler neck. Be sure the end of the tube is well below the level of the coolant. Now press and release the bulb, so that a sample of the coolant is drawn up. Bend the tube around so that the tip can be inserted into the cover-plate opening. Squeeze the bulb to put a few drops of coolant into the measuring surface.

Now point the tester toward the light, and look into the eyepiece (Fig. 1). The antifreeze-protection reading is where the dividing line between light and dark (the edge of the shadow) crosses the scale. Readings on the lower half of the scale indicate solutions without sufficient antifreeze protection.

> **CAUTION:** Coolant is poisonous! It can cause serious illness and even death if it is swallowed!

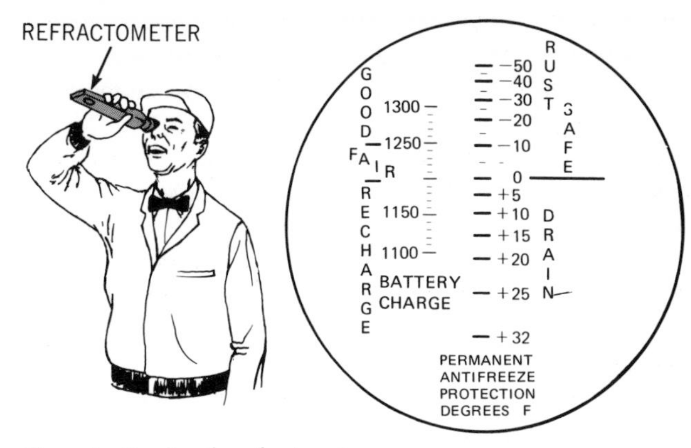

Figure 1 Reading the refractometer.

■ 1-7-8 Testing the Thermostat

Different car manufacturers have different thermostat testing procedures. Chevrolet, for example, recommends suspending the thermostat in a solution of one-third antifreeze and two-thirds water. The solution should be heated to 25°F (13.9°C) above the temperature stamped on the thermostat. The thermostat should open. Then submerge the thermostat in a solution of one-third antifreeze and two-thirds water. This solution should be 10°F (5.5°C) below the temperature stamped on the thermostat. The thermostat should close. If it does not open and close during the test, it is defective.

Plymouth recommends testing the thermostat in the engine. With the cooling system filled to the proper level, warm the engine by driving the car for about 10 minutes. Remove the radiator cap, observing the cautions in ■1-7-6. Insert a thermometer into the coolant. Idle the engine with the hood raised. The coolant temperature should remain steady at no lower than 8°F (4.4°C) below the thermostat opening temperature.

Ford recommends immersing the thermostat in boiling water. If it does not open, it is defective. If the problem is slow warmup, the thermostat may be leaking. Hold the thermostat up to the light to see if the valve is closing completely. If there is a gap between the valve and the valve seat, replace the thermostat.

■ 1-7-9 Checking the Hose and Hose Connections

The appearance of the hose and hose connections usually indicates their condition. If the hose is rotten and soft and collapses easily when squeezed, it should be replaced. The hose must be in good condition and connections should be properly tightened to avoid leaks.

■ 1-7-10 Testing the Water Pump

The test for water pump operation is described in ■1-7-2.

■ 1-7-11 Checking for Exhaust-Gas Leakage into Cooling System

A defective cylinder-head gasket may allow exhaust gas to leak into the cooling system. This is very damaging. Strong acids can form as the gas unites with the water in the coolant. These acids corrode the radiator and other cooling-system parts. A test for exhaust-gas leakage can be made with a Bloc-Chek tester which is installed in the radiator-filler neck, as shown in Fig. 2.

The test is made by putting the tester in the radiator opening with the engine running and then squeezing and releasing the bulb. This draws an air sample from the cooling system up through the special test fluid, which is sensitive to combustion gases. The test fluid is ordinarily blue. If, however, combustion gas is leaking into the cooling system, the test fluid will change to yellow. If a leak is indicated, the exact location can be found by removing one spark-plug wire at a time and retesting. When a leaking cylinder is firing, the liquid will change to yellow. When nonleaking cylinders only are firing, the liquid will remain blue in color.

Undetected combustion leaks in the valve area can cause cracked valve seats and cylinder heads. The coolant is forced away from the cracked area during heavy acceleration by the combustion gases seeping through the leak. This causes excessive heat buildup. When acceleration stops, the diverted coolant rushes back to the overheated area. The sudden cooling of the area can crack the cylinder head and valve seat.

■ 1-7-12 Pressure-Testing the System

To pressure-test the system, apply pressure with a cooling system pressure tester. The tester quickly shows a leaky cooling system. To

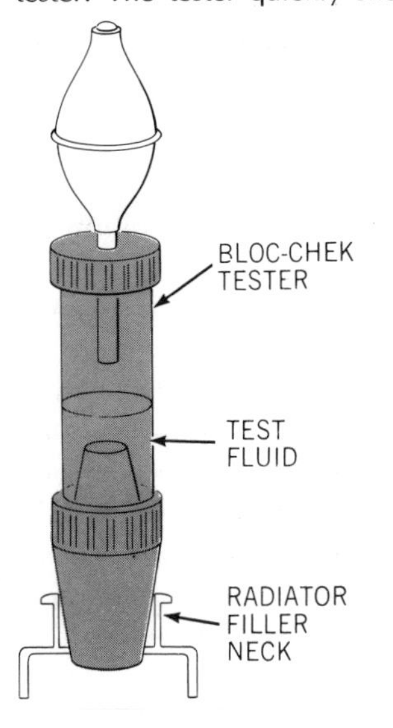

Figure 2 Checking for exhaust-gas leakage into the system with a Bloc-Chek.

use the tester, remove the radiator cap, fill the radiator within ½ inch (12.7 mm) of the filler neck. Wipe the neck sealing surface clean and attach the tester. Then operate the tester pump to apply a pressure that does not exceed 3 psi (0.210 kg/cm^2) above the manufacturer's specifications for the cooling system being checked. If the pressure holds steady, the system is not leaking. If the pressure drops, there are leaks. Look for external leaks at hose connections, hose, engine expansion plugs, water-pump and cylinder-head gaskets, water-pump drive shaft, and radiator. Often you will see the coolant shooting out of even a small hole.

If no external leaks are visible, remove the tester and start the engine. Run the engine until operating temperature is reached. Reattach the tester, apply a pressure of 15 psi (0.055 kg/cm^2), and increase engine speed to about half throttle. If the needle of the pressure gauge fluctuates, it indicates an exhaust-gas leak, probably through a cylinder-head gasket. On a V-type engine, you can determine which bank is at fault by grounding the spark plugs in one bank.

If the needle does not fluctuate, sharply accelerate the engine several times and check for abnormal discharge of water through the tail pipe. This would indicate a cracked block or head or a defective head gasket.

■ **1-7-13 Pressure-Testing the Radiator Cap** The cooling system pressure tester can be used to check the radiator pressure cap. If the cap will not hold its rated pressure, it should be discarded.

■ **1-7-14 Testing the Fan Belt** Fan belts should be checked for wear and tension. If worn, fan belts should be replaced. On cars with two fan belts running in parallel, if one is worn and requires replacement, then both should be replaced. They come in matched sets. If only one is replaced, the new belt will take most of the wear because it is not stretched like the old belt. This means the new belt will wear rapidly while the old belt may slip, overheat, and also wear rapidly.

Use a belt-tension gauge to check and adjust fan-belt tension.

The fan belt should be checked periodically to make sure it is still in good condition. A fan belt that has become worn or frayed, or has separated plies, should be discarded. A faulty belt may slip and cause engine overheating and a run-down battery.

■ **1-7-15 Testing the System for Accumulation of Rust and Scale** At one time, it was common practice to use only water in the cooling system during the summer months. However, with pressurized systems and the use of antifreeze all year around, less rust collects in the cooling system. Some scale may accumulate from minerals in the water. This is the reason why many manufacturers recommend periodic cleaning of the cooling system. In modern high-temperature engines, the cooling system is sensitive to excessive accumulation of scale and rust. There is no accurate way to determine the actual amount of scale and rust. However, if you know the original capacity of the cooling system, you can drain the system and refill it. Measure the amount of water you added. Then compare the amount of water added with the capacity of the system. The difference is an indication of the amount of rust and scale that has accumulated.

■ **1-7-16 Cleaning the Cooling System** The cooling system should be cleaned periodically to remove collected rust and scale. Recommendations vary. Chevrolet, for example, recommends that the system be drained and flushed every 2 years. Coolant with new antifreeze should be put in at that time. Here is the procedure that Chevrolet recommends:

1. Drain the cooling system. Remove the thermostat. Reinstall the thermostat housing. Close drain cocks, and add the liquid part of the cooling-system cleaner. Fill the system with water to about 3 inches (76.2 mm) below the top of the overflow pipe.

2. Cover the radiator. Run the engine at moderate speed until the water reaches 180°F (82.2°C). Remove the cover from the radiator, and run the engine for another 20 minutes. Stop the engine if the water begins to boil.

CAUTION: Do not scald your hands.

3. With the engine running, add the powder part of the cooling-system cleaner. Run the engine for another 10 minutes.

4. Stop the engine, and wait for it to cool. Then open the drain cocks again to drain the system. Remove the lower hose connection from the radiator.

5. Blow dirt and bugs from the radiator fins with compressed air, blowing from the engine side. Do not bend the radiator fins because this will decrease cooling-system efficiency.

6. Reverse-flush the radiator and engine block. In reverse-flushing, water is forced through the system in the direction opposite to normal flow. This gets behind the scale and rust to loosen it so it will be flushed away.

7. To reverse-flush the radiator, remove the radiator upper and lower hoses. Then install the radiator cap.

8. Connect a leadaway hose to the inlet at the top of the radiator. Connect a new hose to the radiator outlet at the bottom of the radiator. Connect the water hose of the flushing gun to a water outlet, and the air hose to an air line. Connect the flushing gun to the new hose at the bottom of the radiator.

9. Turn on the water. When the radiator is full, turn on the air in short blasts. Allow the radiator to fill with water between blasts of air.

Apply the air gradually because the radiator will stand only about 20 psi (1.406 kg/cm^2).

10. Continue until the water from the leadaway hose runs clear.

11. To reverse-flush the cylinder block and head, first disconnect the heater hose. Cap the connections at the engine. With radiator hose removed, attach a leadaway hose to the water-pump inlet. Connect a length of new hose to the coolant outlet at the top of the engine. Connect the flushing gun to the new hose at the top of the engine.

12. Turn on the water. When the engine water jacket is full, turn on the air in short blasts.

> **NOTE:** Excessive pressure can blow out the cylinder-block freeze plugs (also called expansion-core plugs and water-jacket plugs). Servicing these plugs is covered in ■1-7-19.

13. Continue flushing until the water from the leadaway hose runs clear.

14. The heater radiator core should also be reverse-flushed. Take care to avoid too much air pressure. The core can be damaged by excessive air pressure.

15. Install the thermostat and the radiator upper and lower hoses. Use new hoses if the old hoses are worn or damaged in any way. Make sure the hoses are fully engaged on the tubes and that the clamps are properly tightened.

16. Add enough antifreeze to give full protection against freezing in the lowest temperatures expected. Fill the system with water. Since the water is put in cold, the thermostat will close and prevent quick filling. With the thermostat closed, air is trapped in back of the closed thermostat. The thermostat has a small hole that will permit air to leak out, but this takes some time. You may have to wait and refill the radiator a couple of times. The engine can be started and run for a few moments until the thermostat heats up and opens. Then completely fill the radiator with water.

17. Check the system for leaks after running the engine for a few minutes.

■ 1-7-17 Locating and Repairing Radiator Leaks Leaks in a radiator are usually obvious. Telltale scale marks or water-marks form on the outside of the core below the leaks. An accurate way to locate radiator leaks is to remove the radiator from the car and drain out all water. Then close the openings at top and bottom, and immerse the radiator in water. Air bubbles will escape from the radiator through any leaks. Small leaks can sometimes be repaired without removing the radiator from the car. Certain liquid compounds, when poured into the radiator, seep through the leaks. The compounds harden on contact with the air, sealing off the openings. A more effective way of repairing leaks is to solder them. If there are several leaks at various places in the radiator, it may not be worthwhile to attempt repair. The radiator is probably corroded to a point where other leaks will soon develop.

> **NOTE:** Radiator repair is usually done in a radiator shop that specializes in radiator service.

Removing a radiator is a simple job, although it takes a considerable amount of work. The procedure varies somewhat from car to car but, in general is as follows:

1. Drain the engine and radiator by opening the drain cocks in the radiator and engine block.

2. Detach the upper and lower radiator hoses.

3. Remove any support bolts, horns, wiring harnesses, and so forth, that might interfere with radiator removal.

4. With these parts out of the way and the radiator loose, lift it straight up and off the car.

■ 1-7-18 Water-Pump Service The water pump requires little service in normal operation. Some pumps require periodic lubrication. Others have sealed ball bearings and require no lubrication. If the pump develops noise or leaks or becomes otherwise defective, it must be removed for repair. The procedures of removal and replacement vary for different cars. Typical procedures follow.

To remove the water pump, drain the cooling system and remove the water-inlet hose and the heater hose from the pump. Remove the fan belt and attaching bolts and take off the pump.

On six-cylinder engines, pull the pump straight out to avoid damaging the impeller and shaft.

When reinstalling the pump on the engine, adjust the fan belt to the proper tension (■1-7-14).

■ 1-7-19 Expansion-Core Plugs You might have to remove an expansion plug from an engine block (because of coolant leakage, for example). To do this, put the pointed end of a pry bar against the center of the plug. Tap the end of the bar with a hammer until the point goes through the plug. Then press the pry bar to one side to pop the plug out. Another method is to drill a small hole in the center of the plug and then pry the plug out.

Do not drive the pry bar or drill past the plug. On some engines, the plug is only about 3/8 inch (9.52 mm) from a cylinder wall. You could damage the cylinder wall if you drove the pry bar or drill too far in. Do not drive the plug into the water jacket. You would have trouble getting it out and it could block coolant circulation.

Inspect the bore for roughness or damage that would prevent proper sealing of a new plug. If necessary, bore out the bore to take the next larger-size plug. Before installing the new plug, coat it with proper sealer (water resistant for cooling systems, oil-resistant for oil galleries). Use the proper installation tool and proceed as follows, depending on the type of plug.

1. CUP TYPE The cup-type plug is installed with the flanged edge outward. The proper size tool must be used. It must not contact the flange, but all driving must be against the internal cup. The flange must be brought down below the chamfered edge of the bore.

2. EXPANSION TYPE The expansion-type plug is installed with the flanged edge inward. The proper tool must be used. The crowned center part must not be touched when the plug is driven in. Instead, the tool must drive against the outer part of the plug. The plug should be driven until the top of the crown is below the chamfered edge of the bore.

SECTION 1-8 Lubricating-System Service

The three lubricating-system services most frequently performed are changing the oil, changing the oil filter, and servicing the oil pump. Oil-pump service is seldom required. The pump is designed to run for many miles without trouble, and often lasts the life of the engine.

■ 1-8-1 Testing Instruments

The lubricating system is an integral part of the engine. Consequently, any test of the oiling system involves testing the engine. Two testing devices used in troubleshooting the lubricating system are the pressure gauge and the bearing prelubricator. On cars that have an oil-pressure indicator light, it is necessary to connect a pressure gauge to determine the oil pressure in the lubricating system. This is also required on cars with an oil-pressure gauge in the dash when there is any question about the accuracy of the dash unit. To connect a separate oil-pressure gauge, remove the sending unit from the block and screw in the hose for the pressure gauge. On some engines, this is not required, as an oil gallery plug can be removed and the pressure-gauge hose screwed in.

The bearing prelubricator detects oil leaks in the lubricating system. It also detects excessively worn bearings, since worn bearings have excessive clearances that allow oil leakage. Various lubricating-system checks, the troubles encountered in the lubricating system, and the problems with lubricating oils are discussed below.

The bearing prelubricator consists of a pressure tank, partly filled with SAE30 oil, with fittings and hose for attaching the tank to a source of compressed air and to the engine lubricating system. The prelubricator is connected to the outlet line of the oil pump or to any point in the system where oil pressure can be applied. With the oil pan removed so that the main and connecting-rod bearings can be seen, air pressure is applied to the prelubricator tank. This forces oil under pressure into the engine oil lines. Any oil leak, as well as tight bearings or oil-passage obstructions, can thus be readily detected. In addition, a worn bearing will be disclosed, since it will permit the escape of a steady stream of oil around the ends of the bearing. One manufacturer of a prelubricator specifies that with SAE30 oil and 25 psi (1.758 kg/cm^2) of air pressure, 20 to 150 drops of oil per minute escaping from a bearing indicates that the bearing condition is satisfactory. Less than 20 drops of oil per minute indicates a tight bearing or an obstruction in the oil passage. More than 150 drops per minute indicates worn bearings.

When an oil-passage hole in the crankshaft indexes with an oil-passage hole in a bearing, considerable oil will be fed to the bearings. Oil will stream out as though the bearing were worn. The crankshaft must be rotated slightly to move the holes out of index before the test can be made. Bearings that have annular grooves into which oil is constantly fed cannot be tested by this method.

■ 1-8-2 Lubricating-System Checks

As an oil-level gauge, most engines use a dipstick that can be withdrawn from the crankcase to determine its oil level. The dipstick should be withdrawn, wiped clean, reinserted, and again withdrawn so that the oil level on the gauge can be seen. The dipstick is marked to indicate the proper oil level. If the oil level is low, oil should be added to the crankcase.

■ 1-8-3 Troubles in the Lubricating System

Relatively few troubles occur in the lubricating system that are not directly related to engine troubles. The lubricating-system troubles most commonly experienced are discussed below.

1. EXCESSIVE OIL CONSUMPTION Most lubricating-system troubles produce excessive oil consumption. However, its cause is not always easy to determine. Oil is lost from the engine in three ways: by burning in the combustion chamber, by leaking in liquid form, and by passing out of the crankcase through the crankcase ventilating system in the form of vapor, or mist. Excessive oil consumption is not difficult to detect. It is the need to add oil more frequently than the accumulated mileage should require, to maintain the proper crankcase oil level. Oil consumption can be accurately checked. Fill the crankcase to the correct level with oil. Operate the car until the dipstick indicates the oil level is 1 quart (0.946 liter) low. Then figure the distance driven.

External leaks can often be detected by inspecting the seals around the oil pan, valve-cover plate, and timing-gear housing, and at oil-line and oil-filter connections. Presence of an excessive amount of oil indicates leakage.

The burning of oil in the combustion chamber usually produces a bluish tinge in the exhaust gas. Engine oil can enter the combustion chamber through the clearance between intake-valve guides and stems, and around the piston rings.

a. *Intake-Valve Guides* Oil can enter the combustion chamber through clearance cause by wear between the valve guides and the stems. When clearance is excessive, oil is drawn into the combustion chamber on each intake stroke. The appearance of the underside of a valve provides a clue to the condition of its stem and the guide. If the underside of the valve has an excessive amount of carbon, the valve guide and possibly the valve stem are excessively worn. Some of the oil that passes around the valve remains on the underside, forming carbon. When this condition is found, it is usually necessary to install valve seals or a new valve guide. A new valve also may be required.
b. *Rings and Cylinder Walls* Another common cause of excessive oil consumption is passage of oil to the combustion chamber between the piston rings and the cylinder walls (sometimes known as oil pumping). This results from worn, tapered, or out-of-round cylinder walls or from worn or carboned piston rings. In addition, when the bearings are worn, excessive amounts of oil are thrown onto the cylinder walls. The piston rings, unable to control all of it, allow too much oil to work up into the combustion chamber.
c. *Speed* Another factor that must be considered in any analysis of oil consumption is engine speed. High speed produces high oil temperatures and thin oil. This combination causes more oil to be thrown onto the cylinder walls. Piston rings, moving at high speed, cannot function effectively, and so more oil works up into the combustion chamber past the rings. In addition, the churning effect on the oil in the crankcase creates more oil vapor, or mist, at high speed, and so more oil is lost through the crankcase ventilation system. Tests have shown that an engine uses several times as much oil at 60 mph (96.56 km/h) as it does at 30 mph (48.28 km/h).

There is one misleading aspect of this matter of high-speed operation and oil consumption. For example, take the case of a car that is driven around town in start-and-stop driving where the engine never really gets warmed up. With this condition, some oil will be used, but the remaining oil may be diluted with water and unburned gasoline. Then, even though some of the oil is gone, the crankcase will still measure full, due to the addition of the dilutes. However, suppose the car is now taken out on the highway and driven at high speed. The dilution elements will boil off rapidly and the engine will appear to have consumed one quart of oil in 100 miles (161 km) or less.

2. *LOW OIL PRESSURE* Low oil pressure can result from a weak relief-valve spring, a worn oil pump, a broken or cracked oil line, obstructions in the oil lines, insufficient or excessively thin oil, or bearings so badly worn that they can pass more oil than the oil pump is capable of delivering. A defective oil-pressure indicator may record low oil pressure.

3. *EXCESSIVE OIL PRESSURE* Excessive oil pressure may result from a stuck relief valve, from an excessively strong valve spring, from a clogged oil line, or from excessively heavy oil. A defective oil-pressure indicator may record high oil pressure.

4. *OIL DILUTION* When the car is used for short runs with sufficient time between runs to allow the engine to cool, the engine is operating most of the time on warm-up. Under this condition, the oil is subject to dilution by unburned gasoline seeping down into the crankcase past the piston rings. In addition, water collects in the crankcase, since the engine does not operate long enough at temperatures high enough to evaporate the water. These two substances, water and gasoline, change the lubricating properties of the oil by forming sludge, and engine parts wear more rapidly. When this type of operation is experienced, the oil should be changed at frequent intervals to remove the sludge and diluted oil.

■ **1-8-4 Lubricating-System Service** There are certain lubricating-system service jobs that are done more or less automatically when an engine is repaired. For example, the oil pan is removed and cleaned during such engine-overhaul jobs as replacing bearings or rings. When the crankshaft is removed, it is the usual procedure to clean out the oil passages in the crankshaft. Also, the oil passages in the cylinder block should be cleaned out as part of the block-servicing job. Other sections in the Handbook describe the engine-servicing jobs. See Part 1, Secs. 2 to 4. In following articles, we describe lubricating-system service jobs such as changing the oil, cleaning the oil pan, servicing the relief valve, changing or cleaning the oil filter, and servicing the oil pump and the oil-pressure indicator.

■ **1-8-5 Changing Oil** It is the using up of the oil additives, and the accumulation of contaminants, that makes oil changes necessary. To change engine oil, raise the car on a lift, place a container under the oilpan drain hole, and remove the drain plug. Let the old oil drain out. Install the plug, lower the car, and add the correct amount of engine oil to the engine. Replace the old oil-change sticker with a new one marked with the date and mileage at which the oil change was made.

CAUTION: Be careful if the engine is hot. The oil can be hot enough to give you a severe burn.

NOTE: Every time a vehicle is raised on a hoist, make a quick check of the "under-the-car" components. This includes the steering linkage, suspension parts, exhaust system, and tires. This is a quick safety inspection, since it is often possible to detect trouble before failure occurs.

■ 1-8-6 Changing Oil Filter

According to the manufacturers' recommendations, the oil filter should be changed the first time the oil is changed in a new engine. After that, the filter should be changed every other time the oil is changed. To check if the filter on the engine is working, feel the filter after the engine has been running for a while. If the filter is hot to the touch, it has been passing hot engine oil.

On most engines, the filter element and container are replaced as a unit. The old filter can be unscrewed and a new filter screwed on by hand. A drip pan should be placed under the old filter as it is removed to catch any oil that runs out. With the old filter off, the recess and sealing face of the filter bracket should be wiped with a clean shop towel. Then the sealing gasket of the new filter should be coated with clean oil. Finally, the new filter should be hand-tightened until the gasket comes up against the bracket face. It should then be hand-tightened another half turn.

After installation, the engine should be operated at fast idle to check for leaks. Check the oil level in the crankcase and add oil if necessary. A new filter can take as much as 1 pint (0.473 liter) of oil, and so the addition of oil may be required.

NOTE: Engine oil should be changed before the new filter is installed. A new filter should always start out with new oil.

On other filters, oil lines must be disconnected and reconnected when the filter is changed. Some filters have replaceable elements. On these, the procedure is as follows: Remove the drain plug (if present) from the bottom of the housing. Take the cover off by loosening the center bolt or clamp. Lift out the element. If the filter housing has no drain plug, remove the oil or sediment with a special pump. Wipe the inside of the housing with a clean cloth. Be sure that no trace of lint or dirt remains. Install the new filter element. Replace the plug and cover, using a new gasket. Start the engine, and check for leaks around the cover. Note whether the oil pressure has changed. (With a new element, which passes oil more easily, oil pressure may be lower.) Check the level of the oil in the crankcase, and add oil if necessary.

■ 1-8-7 Oil-Pan Service

Whenever the oil pan is removed from engine service, it should be cleaned out thoroughly to remove accumulated sludge and grime. At the same time, the oil strainer, if present, should be cleaned.

1. REMOVING OIL PAN Oil-pan removal varies somewhat on different cars because of the interference of various other parts. On many cars, the steering idler or other steering linkage must be detached. In such cases, carefully note how the linkage is attached and also the number of shims (when used) so that the linkage can be correctly reattached. In addition, certain other parts may require removal. For example, on some engines the exhaust crossover pipe, starting motor, and flywheel-housing cover must be removed. On other cars it is necessary to remove engine mounting bolts and to raise the front end of the engine. On Plymouth engines the clutch-housing dustcover should be removed to prevent damage to the oil-pan gaskets.

Remove the drain plug and drain out the oil. Then, attaching bolts or nuts should be taken off so that the oil pan can be removed. To prevent the pan from dropping, steady it while the last two bolts are being taken out. If the pan sticks, pry it loose, but proceed carefully to avoid distorting the pan. If the pan strikes the crankshaft and will not come free, turn the engine crankshaft a few degrees so that the counterweights move out of the way.

2. CLEANING OIL PAN After removal, the oil pan should be scraped and cleaned with solvent or with a steam cleaner. All traces of gasket material and cement should be removed from the pan and engine block. The oil screen should also be cleaned so that all trace of sludge or dirt is removed.

Before installing the oil pan, all solvent must be removed from the pan. It must be clean and dry. Even small amounts of solvent retained in the oil pan may cause engine trouble later. Some types of solvent have a damaging effect on engine parts in a running engine.

3. INSTALLING OIL PAN To install the pan, apply gasket cement to the gasket surfaces of the oil pan. Be sure that the gasket and pan bolt holes align, and put the gasket (or gaskets) into position. Lift the oil pan into place and temporarily attach it with two bolts, one on each side. Then examine the gaskets to make sure that they are still in position. On some oil pans, the end gaskets appear to be somewhat too long. Their ends project slightly beyond the mounting flange of the oil pan. These ends should not be cut off, since they will crush down against the block to provide a better seal. If the gaskets are all still in position, install the rest of the attaching bolts, and tighten them to the proper tension. Install the oil plug, and add the correct amount and grade of oil. Install other parts that have been removed or loosened. Check the oil-pan gaskets for leakage after the engine has been run for a while and allowed to warm up.

■ 1-8-8 Relief Valves

Most relief valves are not adjustable, but a change in oil pressure can be obtained by installing springs of different tension. This is not usually recommended, however, since a spring of the proper tension is originally installed on the engine. Any change of oil pressure is usually brought about by some defect which requires correction. For example, badly worn bearings may pass so much oil that the oil pump cannot deliver sufficient oil to maintain normal pressure in the lines. Installing a stronger spring in the relief valve does not increase oil pressure. Under such conditions the relief valve is not operating anyway.

■ 1-8-9 Oil Pumps

The oil pump is a relatively simple mechanism and requires little service in normal operation. If the pump is badly worn, it will not maintain oil pressure and should be removed for repair or replacement. The procedure of removal, repair, and replacement varies on different cars. Typical procedures follow.

1. CHEVROLET (GEAR TYPE) The pump shown in Fig. 1 is used on a six-cylinder engine. It is serviced as follows:

a. Drain the oil, remove the front engine-mounting through bolts, raise the engine, and put a 2-inch (50 mm) block between the mount and the support. Remove the cranking motor. Remove the oil-pan screws and lower the pan to the frame. Tilt the pan to the left side of the engine so that you can get at the oil pump. Remove the two flange-mounting bolts and the pickup-pipe attaching bolt. Take out the pump and its screen as an assembly.

b. To disassemble the oil pump (Fig. 1), remove the four cover bolts, cover, gasket, idler gear, and drive gear and shaft. Remove the pressure-regulator valve and its parts. Pull the pipe from the body if necessary. Do not separate the screen from the pipe. Wash all parts in cleaning solvent.

c. Inspect all parts. Replace worn gears. Replace the housing if it is damaged or if the shaft bearing surface is worn. Check the cover for wear that would allow oil leakage past the ends of the gears.

d. On reassembly, install the idler gear so that the smooth side is toward the cover. Use a new cover gasket.

e. In reinstallation, align the oil-pump drive-shaft slot with the distributor-shaft tang. Then put the pump into position and attach it with two mounting bolts. The pump should go into place easily. If it does not, recheck the relationship of the slot in the shaft and the distributor-shaft tang.

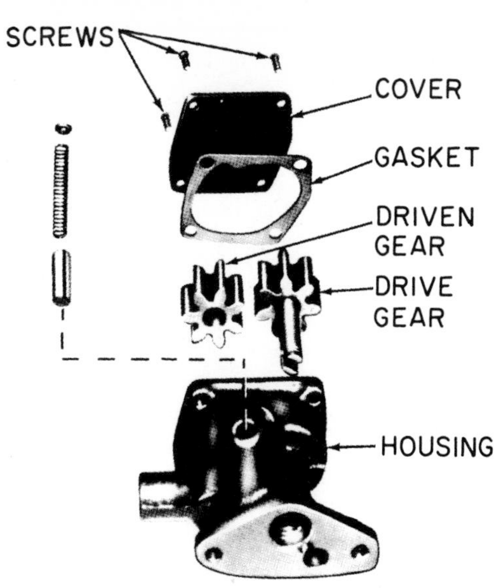

Figure 1 Disassembled view of a gear-type oil pump. *(Chevrolet Motor Division of General Motors Corporation.)*

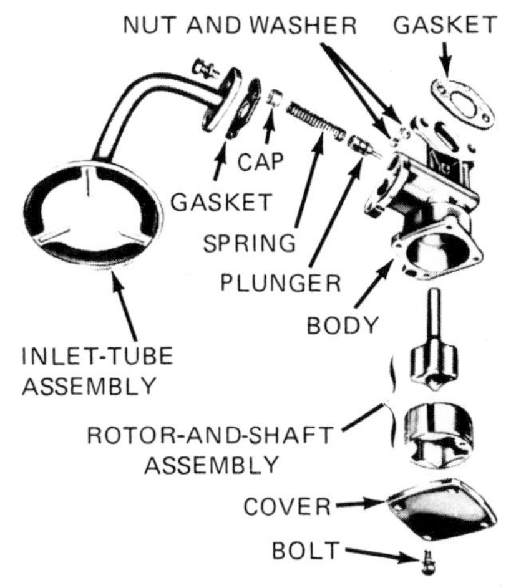

Figure 2 Disassembled view of a rotor-type oil pump. *(Ford Motor Company.)*

2. FORD (ROTOR TYPE) Figure 2 is a disassembled view of a rotor-type oil pump used in a six-cylinder engine. It is serviced as follows:

a. To remove the oil pump, drain the oil and remove the oil pan. Some models require removal of the stabilizer-bar lower control arm before the oil pan can come off. Then the oil pump can be removed by taking off its attaching bolts.

b. Refer to Fig. 2 for disassembly. Removing the cover permits removal of the rotor-shaft assembly from the pump body.

c. Inspect all parts after washing them in solvent. Check the mating surfaces of the pump cover and rotor for wear. Measure the clearance between the outer race and the housing. Measure the clearance between a straightedge resting on the housing and rotor and outer race. Excessive clearance requires replacement of the worn parts.

The outer race and rotor are replaced as an assembly. If one is worn or otherwise defective, then both must be replaced. Also, make sure that the relief valve is free to work in the body and that the spring tension is within specifications.

d. Follow Fig. 2 to obtain the proper relationship of parts during reassembly.

■ 1-8-10 Oil-Pressure Indicators

Oil-pressure indicators require very little service. Defects in either the dash unit or the engine unit usually require replacement of the defective unit. On the type of unit that makes use of vibrating thermostatic blades, dirty contact points, which may cause incorrect readings, can usually be cleaned by pulling a strip of bond paper between them. Be sure that no particles of paper are left between the points. Never use emery cloth to clean the points, since particles of emery might embed and prevent normal indicator action. If the indicator is not functioning in a normal manner, a new engine indicating unit can be temporarily substituted for the old one to determine whether the fault is in the engine unit or the dash unit.

PART 2

Emission Controls and Engine Tuneup

SECTION 2-1 Sources of Automotive Pollution

In this section, we describe the sources of air pollution from the automobile. If piston rings sealed perfectly, there would not be any crankcase blow-by gases to escape into the atmosphere. If combustion were absolutely complete, there would not be any atmospheric pollution from the exhaust system. Water and carbon dioxide are the products of perfect, complete combustion. However, these ideal conditions cannot be achieved by internal-combustion piston engines. Therefore, automotive engineers must continue to make design and specification changes. On most cars, they must add mechanical devices to control the known sources of automotive pollution.

■ **2-1-1 Controlling Automobile Pollution Sources** In the modern automobile, each pollution source is controlled by a separate emission-control system. For example, crankcase pollution is controlled by the crankcase emission control system.

Exhaust emissions are controlled by a variety of techniques and devices. The air-injection reactor (AIR), or air pump, was one of the first devices widely used to control hydrocarbons and carbon monoxide in the engine exhaust gas. Another approach to controlling exhaust emissions is the engine modification, or controlled-combustion system (CCS). It is a combination of several engine modifications and calibrations. This system does not use an air pump.

To control the amounts of nitrogen oxides that form in the engine during the combustion process, most late-model engines are equipped with an exhaust-gas recirculation (EGR) system. A small amount of exhaust gas is returned to the intake manifold, so that air-fuel mixture burns at a lower temperature. This reduces the formation of nitrogen oxides (NO_x). Another exhaust-emission-control device is the catalytic converter. Fuel evaporation from the carburetor and fuel tank is controlled by the evaporative control system.

■ **2-1-2 Photochemical Smog** The most common type of air pollution in southern California is called "photochemical smog." It is the result of sunlight reacting with hydrocarbons and nitrogen oxides in the atmosphere.

Nitrogen oxides (NO_x) are formed as a result of high combustion temperatures in the engine. However, other factors affect the engine's formation of NO_x. These include the air-fuel ratio, spark timing, intake-manifold vacuum, coolant temperature, combustion-chamber deposits, and distribution of the air-fuel charge to each cylinder.

Carbon monoxide (CO) is a tasteless, odorless, colorless, poisonous gas. The percentage of CO in the exhaust gas varies with the air-fuel ratio. The richer the mixture, the higher the percentage of CO.

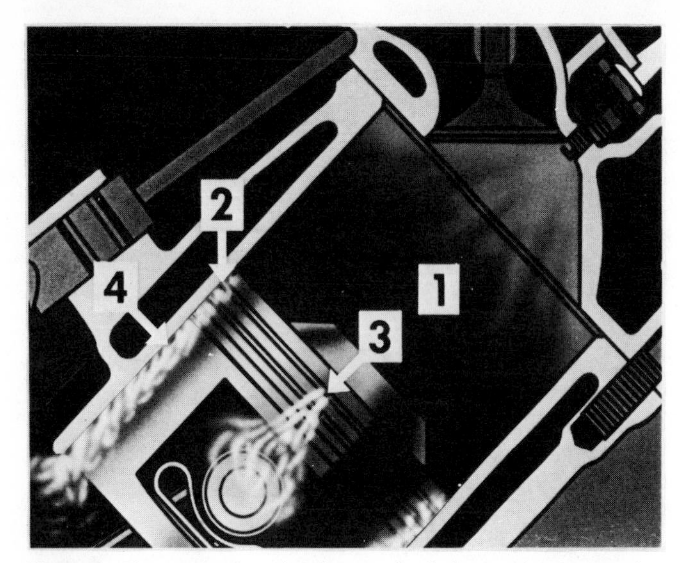

Figure 1 The combustion-chamber gas that leaks past the piston and rings into the crankcase during the compression and power strokes is called "blow-by." Blow-by is the result of (1) high combustion-chamber pressures; (2) necessary working clearances of piston rings in their grooves; (3) normal ring shifting that sometimes lines up the clearance gaps of two or more rings; (4) reduction in ring sealing-contact wear with changes in the direction of piston travel. *(Chevrolet Motor Division of General Motors Corporation.)*

Carbon monoxide is not involved in smog or smog formation, either as a smogmaker or as a catalyst. We are concerned about CO because it is a dangerously poisonous gas that is emitted into the air in relatively large quantities by the automobile engine.

■ 2-1-3 The Crankcase and Its Contaminants

The crankcase supports and encloses the revolving crankshaft in an oiltight area. This is the area between the lower ends of the pistons and the cylinder block above, and the oil pan below.

During engine operation, blow-by enters the crankcase (Fig. 1). Blow-by is the leakage of compressed air-fuel mixture and burned gases past the piston rings into the crankcase.

In addition to blow-by, small amounts of gasoline, in the form of liquid droplets, may leak down into the crankcase. This effect is more pronounced when the engine is cold. It results from the condensation of fuel vapor on the cold metal surfaces of the cylinder and combustion chamber. These surfaces are cold, for example, when the engine is first cranked and started in the morning. Then, some of the fuel vapor condenses into drops of liquid. These small drops run down the cylinder walls, past the pistons and rings, and into the crankcase.

Water (H_2O) collects in the crankcase of a running engine in two ways. First, water is formed as a product of combustion. Gasoline is a hydrocarbon (HC), made up of hydrogen and carbon. During combustion, the hydrogen unites with oxygen in the air to form hydrogen oxide, which has the chemical formula H_2O and the common name "water." Some of this water is contained in the blow-by gas that escapes into the crankcase. Second, the crankcase ventilation system carries fresh air through the crankcase. Fresh air has moisture in it. If the crankcase or other engine parts are cold, the water vapor from both sources condenses to a liquid and drops down into the crankcase.

■ 2-1-4 Crankcase Ventilation

The unburned and partly burned gasoline, and the combustion gases and water, must be cleared out of the crankcase. Otherwise, serious engine trouble can occur. The churning action of the rotating crankshaft can whip the water and engine oil into a thick, black, gooey substance called "sludge." The combustion gases can form acids in this sludge and oil that will corrode the metal parts of the engine. To prolong engine life, these trouble-causing substances must be removed from the crankcase. On older engines, the crankcase was ventilated by an opening at the front and another opening at the back (Fig. 2). The forward motion of the car created a road draft under the car. In addition, the rotating crankshaft acted like a fan. Together, they kept fresh air passing through the crankcase. The air swept out the potentially damaging substances before they had a chance to do any harm.

However, this crankcase ventilation system, using a road-draft tube, vented the fumes and gases into the atmosphere. This polluted the air. Today, crankcase emission controls are installed to prevent or control this air pollution.

■ 2-1-5 Crankcase Emission Control Systems

All automobile engines built today are equipped with a positive crankcase ventilation (PCV) system of crankcase emission control. In this system (Fig. 3) fresh air flows through the crankcase and mixes with the crankcase fumes. From the crankcase, the fumes and air travel to the intake manifold and are mixed with the fresh incoming air-fuel charge. The mixture then enters the engine cylinders. This gives the previously unburned gasoline contained in the blow-by another chance

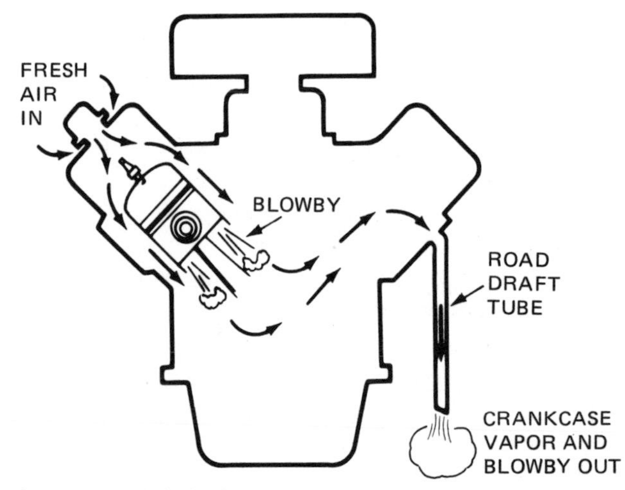

Figure 2 Road-draft-tube system of crankcase ventilation. *(Chrysler Corporation.)*

Figure 3 Positive crankcase ventilation (PCV) system on a six-cylinder engine. The arrows indicate the path taken by the fresh air. *(Ford Motor Company.)*

to burn, instead of being wasted by escaping into the atmosphere.

■ 2-1-6 Crankcase Emission Controls Required

In 1961, auto manufacturers began installing crankcase emission control systems on cars built for registration in California. The early systems were known as "open" systems, because the oil-filter cap was open, or vented to the atmosphere. Two years later, beginning with 1963-model vehicles, crankcase emission controls were required on all new cars manufactured for sale anywhere in the United States. All California cars built in 1964 and later, and all cars built in this country in 1968 or later, used the closed PCV system.

■ 2-1-7 The Exhaust System The exhaust system is the source of the pollutants that are most harmful to human life and most difficult to control. There are three exhaust pollutants for which state and federal emission levels are set. These pollutants are unburned hydrocarbons (HC), partly burned HC or carbon monoxide (CO), and nitrogen oxides (NO_x).

■ 2-1-8 Incomplete Combustion Why does the gasoline fail to burn completely at the time of combustion? After all, it is this failure that results in unburned gasoline (HC), and partly burned HC or carbon monoxide (CO), in the exhaust gas. If we could get perfect combustion, then only carbon dioxide (CO_2) and water vapor would come out the tail pipe, along with any air that was not needed for combustion. Why this failure to obtain perfect combustion? There are several reasons.

The combustion chamber is enclosed by relatively cool metal surfaces (Fig. 4). The bottom of the combustion chamber is sealed by the head of the piston. Above is the cylinder head with its intake and exhaust valves. The combustion starts at the spark plug when it produces a high-temperature electric spark. The flame spreads outward from the spark-plug electrodes in a rapidly expanding wall of fire. But not all of the air-fuel mixture burns completely.

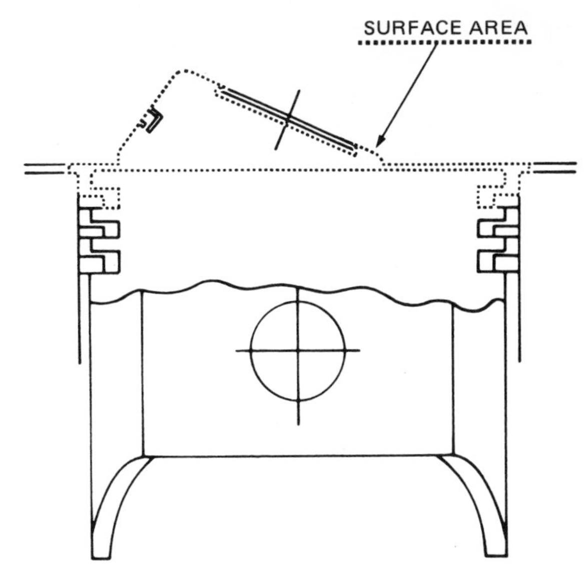

Figure 4 Combustion surface area in combustion chamber. The surface area is shown in dotted lines.

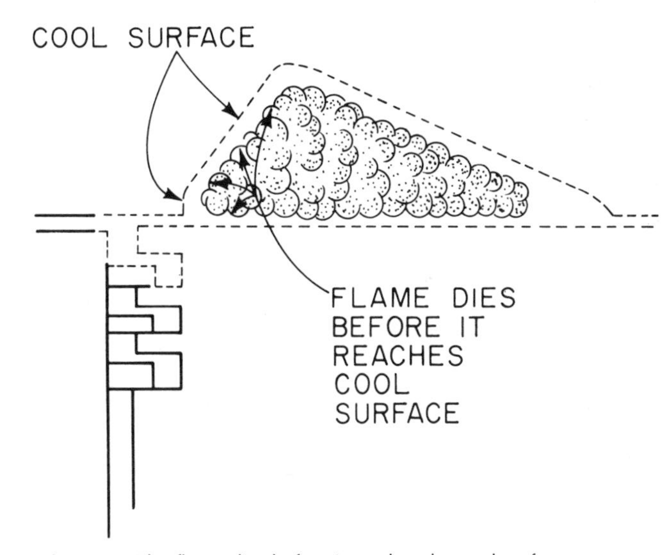

Figure 5 The flame dies before it reaches the cool surface, preventing complete combustion of the fuel.

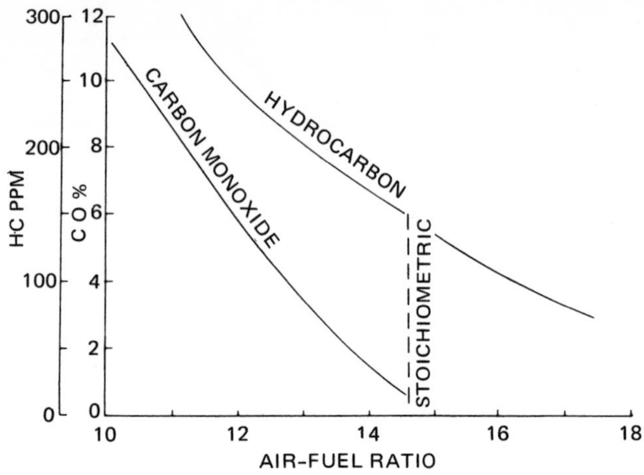

Figure 6 Chart showing the relationship between the air-fuel-mixture ratio and exhaust emissions. *(California Motor Vehicle Pollution Control Board.)*

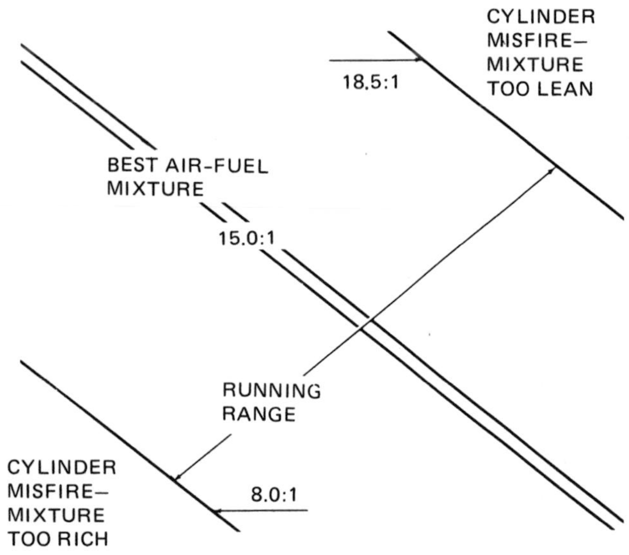

Figure 7 Chart showing the mixture limits for a combustible air-fuel mixture. *(Chevrolet Motor Division of General Motors Corporation.)*

■ **2-1-9 Flame Quench** As the wall of flame approaches the cool metal surfaces, something happens that prevents the flame from actually getting to these surfaces. The layers of air-fuel mixture next to the metal surfaces are chilled by the cooler metal. These layers become too cool to burn (Fig. 5). The cooler metal surfaces take heat away from the layers of air-fuel mixture faster than the combustion process can add it. The result is that these layers of air-fuel mixture do not burn. This process is known as "quench." Quench puts out the flame close to the combustion-chamber surfaces by the continual removal of heat. When the exhaust stroke starts, the cylinder is swept out by the upmoving piston. The unburned fuel, including that in the quench area, leaves along with the other exhaust gases. The result is that unburned gasoline vapor (HC) and partly burned gasoline or carbon monoxide (CO) come out the tail pipe.

■ **2-1-10 Combustion Temperature** You might think that an easy way to lower HC and CO in the exhaust would be to raise the engine operating temperature. Then the unburned and partly burned gasoline vapor in the quench area would burn. Raising the engine operating temperature does lower the amount of unburned hydrocarbons in the exhaust gas. However, any increase in engine temperature increases the combustion temperature. That creates another problem. Nitrogen oxides form more readily at higher temperature. Therefore, combustion temperatures must be kept down to prevent the formation of an excessive amount of NO_x.

■ **2-1-11 Air-Fuel Mixtures** Another reason for incomplete combustion is that a perfect air-fuel-mixture ratio cannot be achieved in every cylinder of a multicylinder engine each time a cylinder fires. With a perfect mixture, the cylinder contains just enough oxygen to completely burn all the gasoline in the air-fuel charge. This is called a "stoichiometric" mixture; it is the same as the familiar ideal air-fuel ratio of 14.7:1 (Fig. 6). This means that it takes 14.7 pounds (6.67 kg) of air to burn completely 1 pound (0.45 kg) of gasoline.

A mixture that is too rich has more gasoline vapor than can be burned completely by the available oxygen. When such a mixture is ignited, some of the excess gasoline will not burn. A high percentage of carbon monoxide will be formed during combustion (Fig. 6). There will be excess amounts of both HC and CO in the exhaust gas. A mixture that is too lean (that is, has insufficient gasoline vapor) will not burn completely.

As shown in Fig. 7, to fire the cylinder charge every time a spark occurs, the air-fuel ratio must lie in a fairly narrow range. A combustible mixture must not be richer than about 9.0:1, and not leaner than about 18.5:1 (Fig. 7). Mixtures outside these limits will misfire. In either case, the result is the same—unburned gasoline vapors (HC) coming out the tail pipe.

Fuel and air are always discussed in terms of weight (pounds or kilograms), instead of the more usual gallons or liters. One reason is that we would introduce some awkward numbers if we compared volumes (gallons or liters) of fuel and air. For instance, a 15:1 air-fuel ratio (by weight) is about 9,000 gallons (34,069 liters) of air to 1 gallon (3.78 liters) of gasoline. If we used volume ratios, we would have to refer to the air-fuel ratio as 9,000:1. The weight ratio (15:1, for example) gives numbers that are much easier to handle.

■ **2-1-12 Mixture Distribution** In a typical six-cylinder in-line engine, the carburetor sits in the middle of the row of cylinders, between the No. 3 and No. 4 cylinders. The air-fuel mixture passes from the carburetor through the intake manifold to the intake-valve ports in the cylinder head. The ideal arrangement would be for exactly the same amount of air-fuel mixture, with all fuel vaporized, to be delivered to each cylinder. Also, the mixture should be identical in richness as it enters each cylinder. As discussed in ■2-1-11, "richness" refers to the proportion of vaporized fuel in the mixture.

The intake manifold can affect the proportions of air and fuel in the mixture reaching the different cylinders. As mentioned, the ideal would be for all fuel to vaporize, and for all cylinders to receive the same amount of mixture of the same richness. However, the intake manifold sometimes acts as a sorting device, supplying some cylinders with a richer mixture than others. Figure 8 shows how this can happen. If the fuel does not completely vaporize, there will be droplets (liquid particles) in the mixture. These particles, being relatively heavy, cannot turn the corner as easily as the vaporized fuel. Therefore, they continue moving in a fairly straight line until they hit the walls of the manifold.

In Fig. 8, the intake valve in cylinder No. 5 is open, and the air-fuel mixture is flowing toward and into this cylinder. (The vaporized fuel and air can turn the corner and enter cylinder No. 5.) However the fuel droplets continue until they strike the the wall of the manifold. Now, when the intake valve for cylinder No. 6 opens, the mixture flows into cylinder No. 6. As it enters, it picks up some of the fuel on the manifold walls. This enriches the mixture.

The result is that the center cylinders, closest to the carburetor, may receive a relatively lean mixture. At the same time, the mixture entering the end cylinders may be relatively rich. This results from the failure of all the fuel to vaporize and from the sorting effect of the intake manifold. If sufficient heat is supplied to the intake manifold during engine warmup, and the carburetor vaporizes the fuel sufficiently, the mixture will be reasonably uniform.

In addition, air-fuel ratios change with (1) different engine speeds; (2) different manifold-passage shapes; and (3) varying air speeds through these passages, in response to changing engine speed and throttle opening. In a typical engine, one cylinder can be receiving a relatively rich mixture at low speeds and a relatively lean mixture at higher speeds. Meanwhile, another cylinder in the same engine may get just the opposite—a relatively lean mixture at low speeds and a relatively rich mixture at higher speeds.

Even distribution of the air-fuel charge is very important if engines are to operate without polluting excessively.

■ 2-1-13 Exhaust-Emission Controls Required

Exhaust-emission control systems control HC and CO in the exhaust gases. They were required on all 1966 and later-model American-manufactured vehicles first sold and registered in California. Federal regulation required auto manufacturers to add an exhaust-emission control system to all 1968 and later-model American-manufactured vehicles.

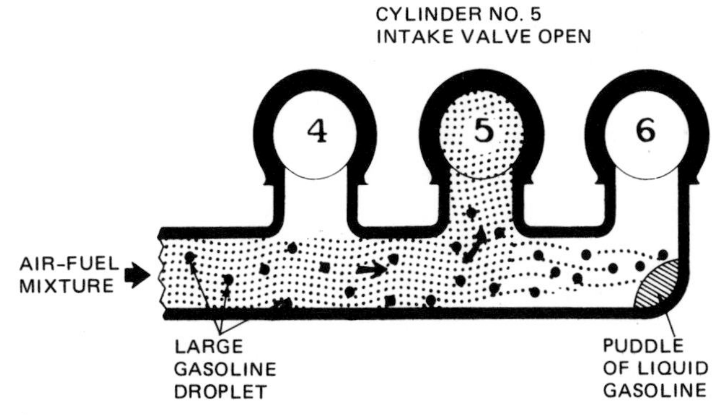

Figure 8 Distribution pattern in an intake manifold. The gasoline particles tend to continue to the end of the manifold, enriching the mixture going to the end cylinders. *(Chevrolet Motor Division of General Motors Corporation.)*

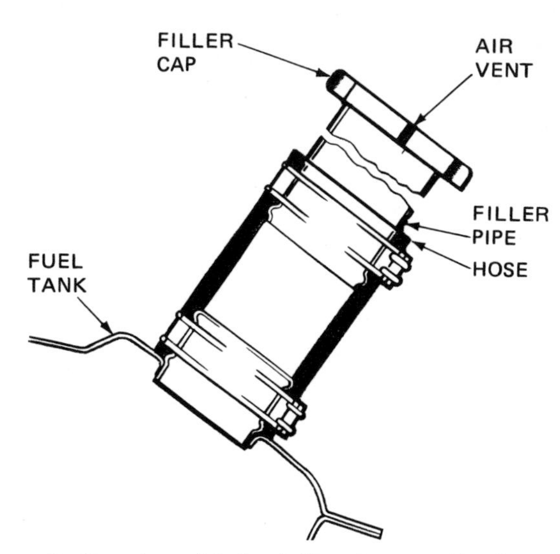

Figure 9 Open type of fuel-tank filler pipe assembly, showing the air-vent hole through the filler cap. *(Ford Motor Company.)*

Then later, in 1971, California law required that new automotive vehicles sold and registered in California must not exceed the state's nitrogen-oxides standards. To meet these standards, some vehicle manufacturers redesigned engines and added new features to the exhaust-emission control systems. Other manufacturers introduced the exhaust-gas recirculation (EGR) system to reduce NO_x. Federal regulations imposed NO_x exhaust-emission standards on all 1973-model passenger vehicles, and the EGR system came into wide use. The EGR system is described in Sec. 3 of this part.

■ 2-1-14 Fuel Evaporation

Two other major sources of air pollution are the carburetor and the fuel tank. Gasoline is a highly volatile liquid. It evaporates easily. On older cars, gasoline vapors could escape from the fuel tank through its atmospheric vent (Fig. 9). When this vent became plugged, the engine would stop (see ■ 2-1-15).

■ 2-1-15 The Fuel Tank

When the fuel tank is full and the engine is operating, gasoline is transferred to the carburetor by the fuel pump. There is atmospheric pressure of approximately 14.7 psi (1.03 kg/cm^2) above the fuel in the tank, because the tank is vented to the atmosphere. The fuel pump creates a much lower pressure at its vacuum, or inlet, side. This difference in pressure pushes fuel from the tank to the pump.

If the fuel-tank vent is not open, a vacuum is created inside the tank as liquid fuel is pumped out of the tank. Without a vent, air cannot get into the tank to replace the gasoline. When the vacuum in the tank equals the vacuum produced by the fuel pump, no additional gasoline can reach the engine. It starves for fuel and stops. A high vacuum in the fuel tank can cause atmospheric pressure to collapse the tank. To prevent this vacuum from forming, older automobiles used fuel tanks that were open to the atmosphere (Fig. 9). That is, the filler cap had a small hole that let air in or out. Some tanks had an open vent tube in the filler pipe that served the same purpose.

The air vent in the cap, or the vent tube, also relieves the pressure buildup inside the tank. A pressure buildup can occur, for example, while the can is parked in the hot sun. The heat causes the gasoline to expand and to vaporize more readily. However, if the tank is too full and does not have room for the fuel to expand, gasoline runs out the filler-cap vent hole (Fig. 9). The gasoline then dribbles down the side of the vehicle to the ground.

The spilled gasoline quickly evaporates. When you add these vapors to the fuel vapor coming from the fuel-tank vent of an uncontrolled car, you can see that fuel vaporization is a big source of air pollution (HC).

■ **2-1-16 Fuel-Tank Breathing** There is another way in which fuel vapors escape into the atmosphere from the fuel tank. When air is heated, it expands. When air is cooled, it contracts. This is what happens to the air inside the fuel tank. When the temperature goes up, the air inside the tank expands. Some of it is forced out of the tank through the air vent (Fig. 9). When the temperature goes down, the air in the tank contracts. Fresh outside air enters the fuel tank. In this way, the fuel tank "breathes."

The air that the fuel tank breathes out contains "moisture" in the form of gasoline vapor. The tank takes in fresh air when the temperature drops. It breathes out air loaded with gasoline vapor when the temperature goes up. If the car is parked in a hot location, the gasoline in the fuel tank evaporates more readily. Then the loss of gasoline vapor is even greater.

■ **2-1-17 Carburetor Vapor Losses** The carburetor can lose gasoline in a somewhat similar way. During normal operation of the engine, gasoline is pumped from the fuel tank to the carburetor by the fuel pump. The carburetor has a float bowl, which holds a small amount of liquid gasoline. In this way, the float bowl serves as a constant-level reservoir of fuel for the carburetor metering jets and nozzles.

Fuel vapors can escape from the float bowl through external vents, internal vents, and carburetor fuel passages and air bleeds. External vents have been the most common cause of carburetor fuel-vapor loss. Modern carburetors no longer have external float-bowl vents.

Internal vents are usually tubes that carry the gasoline vapor from above the fuel in the float bowl to the carburetor air horn. When the engine is running, any vapor that forms is discharged into the stream of air passing through the carburetor.

The situation is different when the engine is stopped after a run. When the engine is hot, it gives off heat. This heat acts on the gasoline in the float bowl. The gasoline begins to vaporize. The vapor passes from the float bowl, through the internal vent, to the air cleaner where most of the vapor is trapped. However, some vapor can still escape into the atmosphere through the air cleaner.

■ **2-1-18 Evaporative Controls** The loss of gasoline vapor (HC) from the fuel tank and carburetor produces air pollution. To prevent this, new cars are equipped with an evaporative control system. This system traps the gasoline vapor escaping from the fuel tank and carburetor and burns the vapor in the engine.

Evaporative emission control systems were required on all 1970-model cars first registered in California. Beginning with the 1971-model year, an evaporative emission control system was required on every new car sold in the United States.

SECTION 2-2 Servicing PCV and Evaporative Control Systems

This section discusses service procedures for the PCV system and the evaporative control system. These systems require little service. They are relatively troublefree in operation.

■ **2-2-1 Positive Crankcase Ventilation** The PCV system carries filtered air from the carburetor air filter through the crankcase. This air picks up blow-by and gasoline vapors and carries them to the intake manifold. The air then flows through the engine, where the blow-by and gasoline vapors are burned.

The PCV valve is spring-loaded. At low speeds and idle, when intake-manifold vacuum is high, the vacuum holds the valve nearly closed. In this position, the valve passes only a small amount of air. This prevents the idle air-fuel mixture from being upset and producing poor idling. Then, when the throttle is opened wider and engine speed increases, the intake-manifold vacuum drops. With less vacuum, the PCV valve opens, allowing more air to flow through the crankcase.

■ **2-2-2 PCV-System Trouble-Diagnosis Chart**

The chart that follows lists the various PCV-system complaints, their possible causes, and checks or corrections to be made. The information in the chart will shorten the time you need to correct a trouble. If you follow a logical procedure, you can locate the cause of the trouble quickly.

NOTE: The troubles and possible causes are not listed according to how often they occur. That is, item 1 (or item *a* under "Possible Cause") does not necessarily occur more often than item 2 (or item *b*).

PCV-SYSTEM TROUBLE-DIAGNOSIS CHART

(See ■ 2-2-3 to 2-2-6 for detailed explanations of the causes and corrections listed below.)

COMPLAINT	POSSIBLE CAUSE	CHECK OR CORRECTION
1. Rough idle, frequent stalling (■2-2-3)	a. PCV valve plugged	Replace PCV valve
	b. PCV valve stuck open	Replace PCV valve
	c. Restricted PCV air filter	Replace filter; clean system
2. Vapor flow from air cleaner (■2-2-4)	a. PCV valve plugged or stuck in backfire position	Replace PCV valve
	b. PCV valve stuck in idle position	Replace PCV valve
3. Oil in air cleaner (■2-2-5)	a. PCV valve plugged	Replace PCV valve
	b. Leak in crankcase ventilation system	Clean PCV system; inspect and correct leaks to atmosphere
	c. Cylinder-head oil-return holes clogged	Remove valve cover; inspect and clean holes
	d. Valve-cover oil baffle restricted	Remove valve cover; inspect and repair baffle
4. Excessive oil sludging or dilution (■2-2-6)	a. Clogged hoses or fittings	Clean hoses and fittings
	b. Clogged or stuck PCV valve	Replace PCV valve

■ **2-2-3 Rough Idle, Frequent Stalling** Probably the most common problem with the PCV system is sticking of the PCV valve. The driver's complaint depends on the position in which the valve is stuck, but the correction is always the same: Replace the PCV valve.

As oil vapor and blow-by gases pass through the PCV valve, some carbon and sludge remain in the valve. At an average speed of 25 mph (40 km/h), in a car that has traveled 12,000 mi (19,312 km), about 115,200 ft^3 (3,262 m^3) of gases from the crankcase could pass through a PCV valve. This gas contains blow-by, sludge, acids, oil, and other contaminants.

When the valve plugs completely, the engine develops rough idle and often stalls. This results from the blow-by and crankcase vapors discharging irregularly into the air cleaner through the tube, or hose, which connects the crankcase (usually through the valve cover) with the air cleaner. This backflow into the air cleaner increases at wide-open throttle. If the engine operates normally and blow-by is found to discharge from the air cleaner, the PCV valve is stuck in the idle or minimum-flow position.

When the PCV valve sticks in the intermediate position, the engine idles rough and stalls frequently. But when it runs, it runs at about the speed of fast idle. When the valve sticks in the open, or maximum-flow, position, too much air is drawn through the crankcase into the intake manifold. This causes excessive leanout of the air-fuel mixture. Idle is rough, and high-speed miss and power loss may result.

Many problems may be caused by the PCV filter, even though it is usually located inside the air cleaner. Often the PCV air filter does not receive regular maintenance. Remove the filter from the air cleaner, or from the separate housing, and check the filter for damage, dirt, and clogging. If the filter is clean, then clean the tube and fittings leading to the filter.

■ **2-2-4 Vapor Flow from Air Cleaner** A plugged PCV valve, or one that is stuck in the engine-off or backfire position, can cause crankcase vapors to flow from the tube at the air cleaner. When the PCV valve is shut completely, crankcase vapors cannot get to the intake manifold. So after the engine fills with vapors and blow-by, the excess flows to the air cleaner through the fresh-air tube. If the engine runs normally and blow-by vapors discharge from the air cleaner under heavy throttle, the PCV valve is stuck in the idle or minimum-flow position. To correct a sticking PCV valve, replace it.

■ **2-2-5 Oil in Air Cleaner** An accumulation of oil in the air cleaner, or on the air-cleaner element, indicates that a large column of crankcase vapors is flowing into the air cleaner. The large vapor flow carries oil mist from the crankcase. This condition often is found on worn engines having a high blow-by rate. The problem gets worse when the PCV valve becomes plugged.

Oil to lubricate the valve train drains down to the crankcase through holes in the cylinder head. Sludge may clog the holes. Then oil is drawn easily through the tube that, on many engines, connects the valve cover and the oil cleaner. Some engines have a valve-cover oil baffle to prevent oil from passing to the air cleaner.

■ **2-2-6 Excessive Oil Sludging or Dilution** A fairly large quantity of water and liquid gasoline appears in the crankcase of a cold engine. One of the jobs of the PCV system is to remove these crankcase contaminants before the rotating crankshaft mixes them with the oil. If they are not removed, they form sludge and dilute the oil. If any part of the line to the intake manifold clogs, or the PCV valve clogs or sticks, these contaminants remain in the engine. To correct the problem, there must be free flow through the PCV system. This usually means cleaning the hoses and fittings or replacing the PCV valve (■ 2-2-8).

■ **2-2-7 Testing the PCV System** Here is a simple way to check the PCV system and the PCV valve. Remove the valve or valve connection with the engine running. Feel for a slight vacuum pull against your thumb when you place it over the opening. If there is no vacuum action, or if you can feel a positive pressure, then something is wrong. The PCV valve should be checked. Toyota recommends checking the PCV valve by blowing through it from each end. Air should pass freely in the direction of the intake manifold and should be restricted (but not blocked) in the opposite direction. All hoses and connections should be checked for free flow.

Special testers are available which can be used to check the operation of the PCV valve. If the valve becomes clogged, it will cause engine loping (speeding up and slowing down) and rough idle. The PCV valve cannot be cleaned. A clogged or sticking PCV valve must be replaced. For engine loping and rough idle, install a new PCV valve. If the idling improves, leave the new PCV valve in. If the loping or rough idle persists, check for restrictions in the lines. A test can be made to pinpoint the trouble with one type of PCV tester, as follows:

1. With the engine at operating temperature, remove the oil-filler cap and dipstick. Plug the dipstick tube with the hole plug.

2. With the tester body and proper tester adaptor attached to the hose, insert the adaptor into the oil-filler opening. Turn the selector knob to the correct setting for the engine under test.

3. Start the engine, and let it idle. Hold the tester body upright, and note the color displayed in the tester windows.

A second type of tester is shown in Fig. 1. It is used as follows:

1. With the engine at normal operating temperature, remove the oil-filler cap. Hold the tester over the opening in the valve cover. Make sure that there is a tight seal between the cover and the tester. An air leak here will prevent tester operation.

2. Start the engine, and operate it at idle. Note the position of the ball. If the ball settles in the GOOD (green) area, the system is functioning properly. If it settles in the REPAIR (red) area, check the system components as previously noted.

Chrysler's recommended test does not require a tester. Instead, remove the PCV valve from the rocker-arm cover with the engine idling. The valve should hiss, and you should be able to feel a strong vacuum when you place a finger over the valve inlet. Then reinstall the PCV valve, and remove the crankcase-inlet air cleaner. Hold a piece of stiff paper over the opening of the rocker-arm cover. After a few moments, the paper should be sucked against the opening. Then stop the engine. Remove the PCV valve from the rocker-arm cover, and shake it. It should click or rattle, showing that the valve is free. If the system does not meet these tests, replace the PCV valve and try the test again. If the system still does not pass the test, the hose may be clogged. It should be cleaned out or replaced. Or it may be necessary to remove the carburetor and clean the vacuum passage with a ¼-inch (6.35 mm) drill. Also, clean the inlet vent, on the crankcase-inlet air cleaner, that is connected by the hose to the carburetor air cleaner.

Chevrolet offers still another method. With the engine running at idle, remove the PCV valve from the valve cover grommet, with hose attached. Block the opening of the valve, and note the change in engine speed. A decrease of less than 50 rpm indicates a plugged PCV valve. You should use a tachometer when making this test, to get an accurate reading of the change in engine rpm.

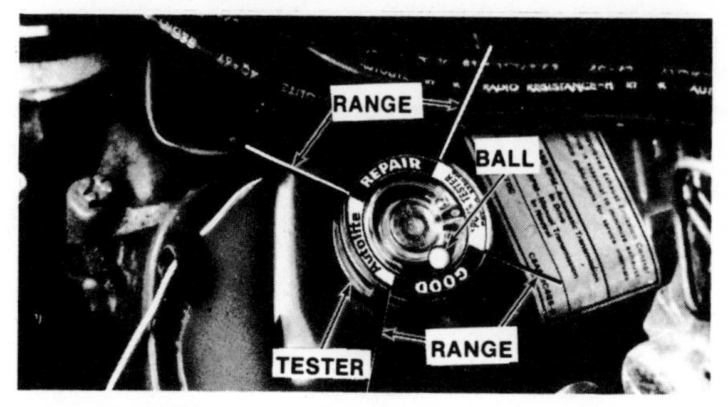

Figure 1 The PCV tester on the valve cover, ready for a test. *(Ford Motor Company.)*

American Motors recommends checking the flow rate of the PCV valve. To do this, a special tester is required. With the engine idling, the PCV valve is removed from the intake manifold or valve cover and connected to the tester. The airflow through the valve (flow rate) can be observed on the special tester and compared with specifications. A PCV valve which allows too much or too little airflow must be replaced.

■ 2-2-8 Servicing the PCV System

The PCV valve must be replaced at regular intervals and whenever it clogs or sticks. When you install a new PCV valve, inspect and clean the system thoroughly. This includes all hoses, grommets, and connectors. To clean the hoses, soak them in mineral spirits. Then clean the insides with a brush, and wash the outsides. Thoroughly clean all connectors, especially the elbow connection. Wash the oil-filler cap in mineral spirits, and shake it dry. Some types of oil-filler caps must not be dried with compressed air.

After all parts of the PCV system are clean, inspect them carefully. Replace any component that shows signs of damage, wear, or deterioration. Be sure the grommet that the PCV valve fits into is not damaged or torn. Replace any cracked or brittle hose with hose of a similar type. Replace any component, hose, or fitting that does not allow a free flow of air after cleaning.

■ 2-2-9 Servicing the PCV Filter

Fresh ventilation air must be filtered before it enters the crankcase. There are two different methods in use. In one method, the carburetor air-cleaner filter does the cleaning. In this system, the hose for the crankcase ventilation air is connected to the downstream, or clean-air, side of the carburetor air filter. No special service is required. The second method of cleaning the crankcase ventilation air is to use a separate filter, called a PCV filter. This filter mounts on the inside of the air-cleaner housing. Ventilation air comes into the air cleaner through the inlet or snorkel. It then passes through the PCV filter and into the crankcase.

Whenever the PCV system is serviced, the PCV filter must also be checked. To check the filter, remove the retainer clip. Then remove the air-cleaner cover, and take out the PCV filter. Check it for damage, dirt buildup, and clogging. If the filter is clean, reinstall it in the air cleaner. A dirty or damaged PCV filter must be replaced.

■ 2-2-10 Evaporative Control Systems

The evaporative control system limits fuel-vapor (HC) losses from the fuel tank and carburetor float bowl into the atmosphere. This is done by catching and storing the fuel vapors in a charcoal canister (or in the engine crankcase) while the engine is off. When the engine is started, the stored fuel vapor passes to the carburetor air cleaner. From there, the vapor is drawn into the engine and burned.

■ 2-2-11 Evaporative-Control-System Trouble-Diagnosis Chart

The chart to the right lists the various complaints that can be caused by the evaporative control system, their possible causes, and checks or corrections to be made. The information in the chart will shorten the time you need to correct a trouble. If you follow a logical procedure, you can locate the cause of the trouble quickly.

NOTE: The troubles and possible causes are not listed according to how often they occur. That is, item 1 (or item a under "Possible Cause") does not necessary occur more often than item 2 (or item *b*).

■ 2-2-12 Fuel Odor, Loss of Fuel

Any noticeable fuel odor usually means that liquid gasoline or fuel vapor is escaping. This may occur when some fuel is spilled in filling the tank with gasoline. But after the cap is installed on the tank of a car, no fuel vapor should escape, and no odor should be noticeable. Overfilling of the fuel tank can cause a loss of liquid gasoline and vapor. Filling the tank, waiting several seconds, and then topping off the filler neck is an improper fueling procedure. It causes leakage. Evaporative control systems have many pipes and hoses through which ventilation air, fuel vapor, and liquid gasoline must flow. Pinched, plugged, disconnected, and leaky lines cause fuel odor.

When you buy gasoline, you have no control of the volatility of the fuel you select. However, fuel volatility is adjusted seasonally by the refiner. Winter grades of gasoline are more volatile than summer grades. In unseasonably hot weather, the service station may be pumping a fuel that is too volatile for the temperature. As a result, part of the gasoline evaporates too quickly, overloading the evaporative control system. This allows some gasoline vapor to escape into the atmosphere, where you can smell it.

■ 2-2-13 Collapsed Fuel Tank

Deformation or "caving in" of the fuel tank may result from either of two causes. The wrong fuel-tank cap may have been installed on the tank filler neck, or the tank vacuum-relief valve may stick closed.

Different fuel tanks can have the same size filler-neck opening. On some cars without evaporative controls, vacuum venting was provided by a small hole through the cap. On other precontrolled cars the cap was sealed, but there was a separate vent line to the atmosphere.

Evaporative controls first began to appear on California cars in 1970 (1971, nationwide). The filler-neck size did not change, but the cap did. Cars began using caps that incorporated two valves. One valve is the pressure-relief valve, which prevents pressure in the tank from rising too high. The second

EVAPORATIVE-CONTROL-SYSTEM TROUBLE-DIAGNOSIS CHART

(See ■ 2-2-12 to 2-2-15 for detailed explanations of the causes and corrections listed below.)

COMPLAINT	POSSIBLE CAUSE	CHECK OR CORRECTION
1. Fuel odor, or loss of fuel (■2-2-12)	a. Overfilled fuel tank	Drain excess fuel; fill tank to proper level
	b. Leaks in fuel, vapor, or vent line	Repair or replace defective line
	c. Wrong or faulty fuel cap	Install correct cap
	d. Faulty liquid-vapor separator	Replace
	e. Fuel volatility too high	Use proper fuel
	f. Vapor-line restrictor missing	Replace
	g. Canister drain cap or hose missing	Replace
2. Collapsed fuel tank (■2-2-13)	Wrong fuel-tank cap, stuck relief valve	Replace cap; repair relief valve; repair or replace fuel tank
3. Excess pressure in fuel tank (■2-2-14)	a. Plugged or pinched vent lines	Repair
	b. Plugged liquid-vapor-separator outlet	Replace liquid-valve separator
	c. Plugged charcoal canister	Replace canister
4. Improper engine idling (■2-2-15)	a. Improper purge-hose routing	Correct hose routing
	b. Disconnected purge hose	Connect
	c. Plugged canister filter	Replace
	d. High-volatility fuel	Use proper fuel
	e. Vapor-line restrictor missing	Replace

valve is the vacuum-relief valve. It opens to allow enough air to enter the tank to replace the gasoline pumped from the tank by the fuel pump. Other cars use a sealed cap and have separate vacuum- and pressure-relief valves.

If a sealed cap is placed on a late-model car that requires a cap with pressure and vacuum valves, a collapsed fuel tank can result. As the gasoline is pumped from the tank, a vacuum develops in it. Then, the atmospheric pressure of about 15 pounds (6.8 kg) on every square inch (6.45 cm^2) of tank surface becomes too great for the tank to support. The tank collapses or caves in at the sides. Depending on how badly the tank deforms, it may or may not have to be replaced.

■ 2-2-14 Excess Pressure in Fuel Tank

Some pressure can be expected in the fuel tank of a car with evaporative controls. The pressure may be most noticeable as the sound of rushing air, or the feel of air moving past your hand, while you remove the fuel-tank cap. This condition may be even more noticeable when the weather turns unseasonably hot and the tank contains a high-volatility or winter-blend fuel.

Excessive pressure may develop in the tank because of plugged or pinched lines, or from a plugged liquid-vapor separator or charcoal canister. (Internal plugging of the charcoal canister may occur.) Pressure can also develop in the fuel tank if the pressure-relief valve in the tank cap sticks closed. In this case, the problem is solved by installing a new cap of the proper type.

■ 2-2-15 Improper Engine Idling

Many different engine-idling problems can result from faulty or improper connection of a hose in the evaporative control system. The correction is to repair or reroute the hose. Another cause of improper engine idling can be a dirty or plugged air filter for the charcoal canister. Most manufacturers recommend inspection and, if necessary, replacement of the filter every 12 months or 12,000 miles (19,312 km), or every 24 months or 24,000 miles (38,624 km). A plugged filter (often caused by excessive driving under dusty conditions, or oil or water getting into it) must be replaced.

A fuel too volatile for the outside temperature, or a missing restrictor in the vapor line, will also cause improper engine idling.

■ 2-2-16 Servicing Evaporative Control Systems

No testers are needed to check evaporative control systems. Almost all problems can be found by visual inspection. Problems are also indicated by a strong odor of fuel. Some technicians suggest that an infrared exhaust analyzer can be used to quickly detect small vapor losses from around the fuel tank, canister, air cleaner, lines, or hose. Any loss will register on the HC meter of the exhaust analyzer.

Figure 2 is a schematic view of the two types of evaporative control systems. The top view shows the commonly used canister storage system, and the bottom view shows the crankcase storage system. Note that the crankcase storage system requires an air-tight crankcase to prevent the escape of HC vapor while it is stored there. Crankcase leaks also can be detected with an infrared exhaust analyzer.

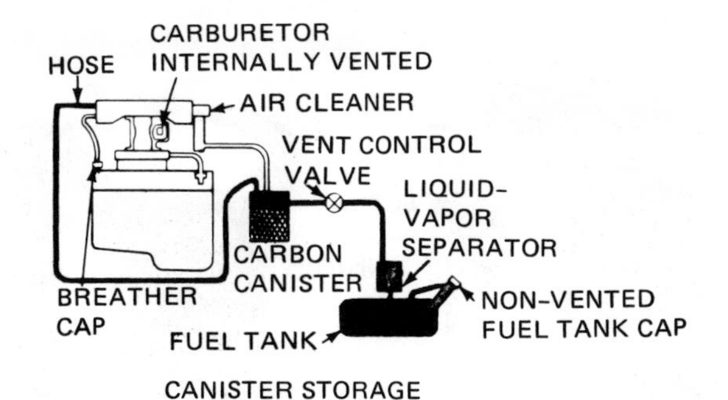

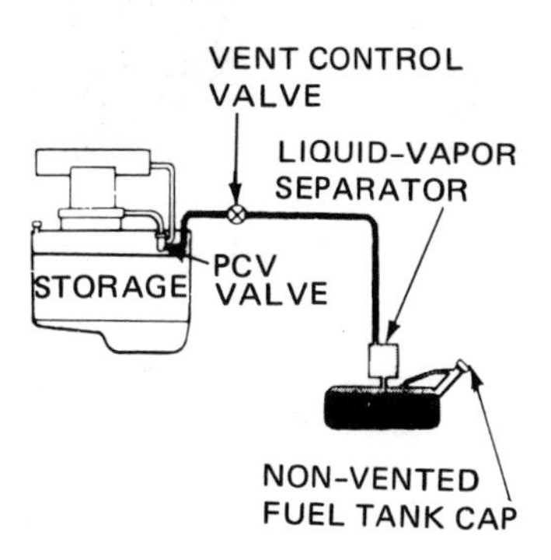

Figure 2 Canister and crankcase types of fuel-vapor storage systems. *(Ford Motor Company.)*

Most problems with evaporative control systems are obvious and can be noticed during an inspection. Typical defects are damaged lines, liquid-fuel and vapor leaks, and missing parts. The filler cap can be damaged or corroded so that its valves fail to work properly. A problem with the fuel-tank cap could result in deforming of the tank. This could also occur when the wrong cap is installed on the tank. Be sure that the fuel-tank filler cap is of a type specified by the manufacturer for the vehicle and that the cap seals the fuel tank.

To service the evaporative control system, inspect the fuel-tank cap. Check the condition of the sealing gasket around the cap. If the gasket is damaged, replace the cap. Check the filler neck and tank for stains resulting from fuel leakage. Usually, you can trace a stain back to its origin. Then fix the cause of the leak. This may require replacing a gasket, clamp, or hose, or replacing the tank.

Inspect all lines and connections in the fuel and evaporative control systems for damage and leakage. Perform any necessary repairs. Check all clamps and connections for tightness.

> **NOTE:** The hoses used in evaporative control systems are specially made to resist deterioration from contact with gasoline and gasoline vapor. When you replace a hose, make sure that the new hose is specified by the manufacturer for use in evaporative control systems. Sometimes this type of hose is marked EVAP.

Figure 3 Replacing the air filter in the charcoal canister.

Check the charcoal-canister lines for liquid gasoline. If any is present, replace the liquid-vapor separator or the liquid check valve.

■ 2-2-17 Servicing the Canister Filter

At scheduled intervals, inspect and replace the filter in the canister (Fig. 3) Servicing evaporative control systems is very simple, and no special tools are required. To replace the canister filter, remove the canister, turn it upside down (Fig. 3), and remove the bottom cover. Pull out the old filter with your fingers, and put the new filter inside. If the canister itself is cracked or internally plugged, a new canister assembly should be installed.

■ 2-2-18 Ford Auxiliary Fuel Tanks

Some 1975 and later models of Ford-built cars are equipped with a separate auxiliary fuel tank. On these cars, the fuel-tank filler tube feeds into the auxiliary fuel tank. When you fuel the car, gasoline enters the auxiliary tank and then flows into the main tank, until both tanks are filled. Fuel for driving comes from the main tank. Fuel drains from the auxiliary tank into the main tank as the car is driven. Each tank has its own vapor separator and a line which connects it to the charcoal canister. The vapor separators are identical and of the single-orifice type (Fig. 4).

The vapor separator has a float valve in it (Fig. 4). If liquid gasoline reaches the valve opening inside the vapor separator, the float rises, closing off the opening. Shown on the right in Fig. 4 is a vapor separator introduced by Ford in 1976. It incorporates an internal spring inside the float, to seal the opening any time the car rolls 90°. For example, if the car rolls over on its side or top in a collision, the float valve shuts so no gasoline can escape through the separator or the line connected to it. All the vapor separators shown in Fig. 4 are installed by pushing the separator into a rubber grommet mounted in the top of the tank, in much the same way as a PCV valve is installed. Never insert a sharp object between the tank seal and the push-in type of separator during removal or installation. It could damage the grommet, and liquid-fuel and vapor leakage could occur.

The auxiliary fuel tank is made of polyethylene. It can be cleaned with a solution of detergent and water.

> **NOTE:** Ford auxiliary fuel tanks must not be steam-cleaned or exposed to extreme heat from any source. The tanks are made of plastic and can be destroyed by heating or steam-cleaning.

Cars equipped with auxiliary fuel tanks are required to comply with state and federal laws prohibiting excessive evapora-

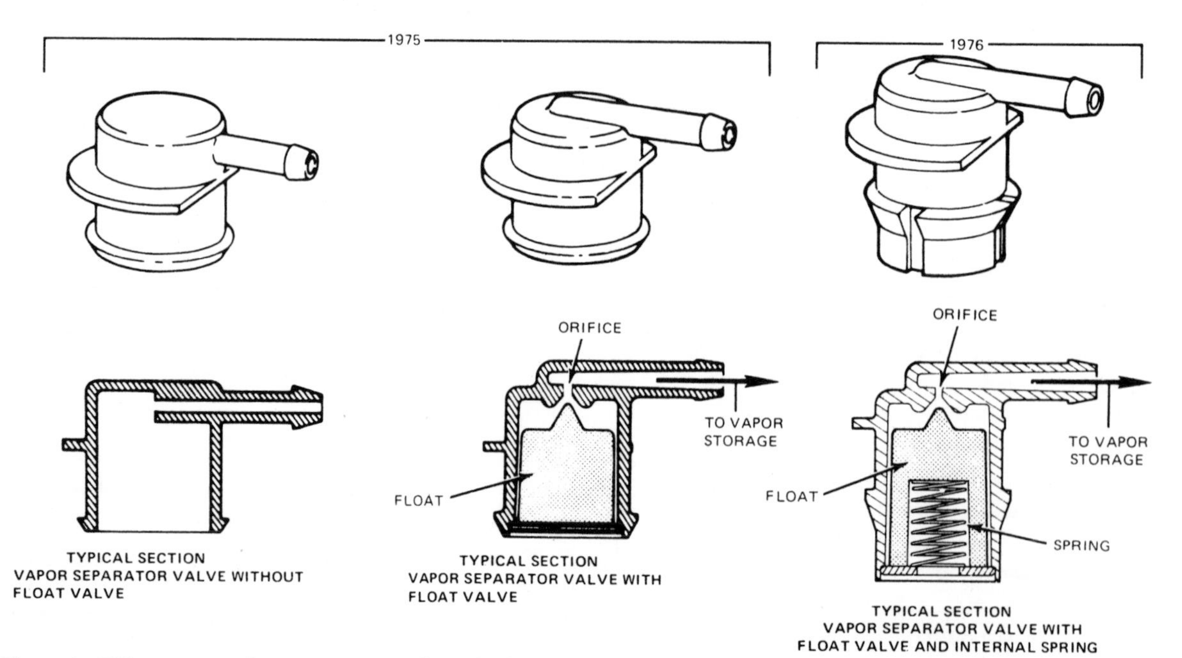

Figure 4 Different types of vapor-separator valves which mount in a grommet in the top of the fuel tank. *(Ford Motor Company.)*

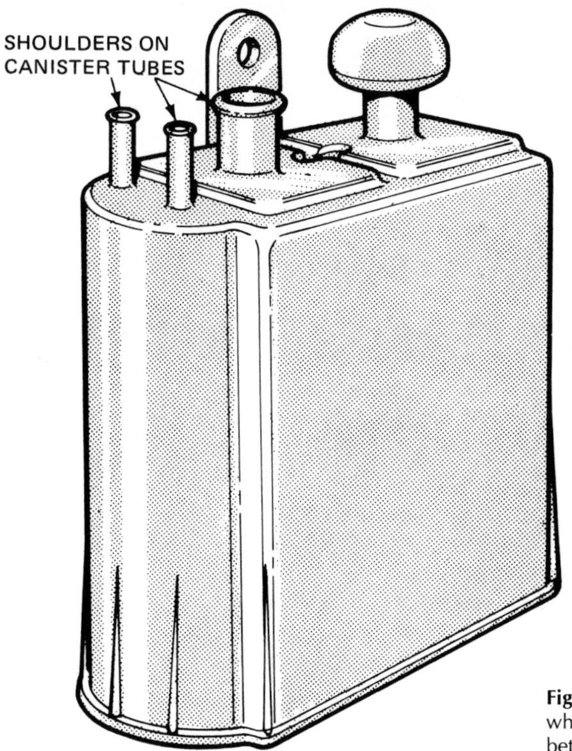

tive emissions, just like other late-model cars. Service procedures on the Ford auxiliary fuel tank, and cars equipped with them, are routine. A plugged, damaged, or defective vapor separator must be replaced. An auxiliary tank must be replaced if damaged, although it can be cleaned with a solution of detergent and water if dirty or contaminated. Each tank is connected through a vapor separator to the carbon canister. Many of these cars are equipped with a nylon carbon canister which has shoulders on the tube nipples (Fig. 5). The shoulders cause the hoses connecting to the canister-tube system to hold better. This canister (Fig. 5) has a different shape from other canisters shown elsewhere. However, it has the same connections to the fuel-vapor sources, and it works in the same way.

Service procedures for cars with auxiliary fuel tanks are the same as for other cars equipped with evaporative control systems.

Figure 5 Late-model nylon-type carbon canister which has shoulders on the nipples to secure the hoses better. *(Ford Motor Company.)*

SECTION 2-3 Servicing Exhaust Control Systems

In this section we discuss service procedures for the most widely used exhaust-emission control systems. Service procedures for other exhaust-emission controls may be found in the manufacturers' service manuals. In general, exhaust-emission controls require little in the way of service. However, many different types of driver complaints may be traced to malfunctions of these devices.

■ **2-3-1 Air Injection** To review the operation of the air-injection system (Fig. 1), an air pump pushes air through the air lines and the air manifold into a series of air-injection tubes. These tubes are located opposite the exhaust valves. In the exhaust manifold, the oxygen in the air helps to burn any HC and CO in the exhaust gas. The check valve (Fig. 1) prevents any backflow of exhaust gases to the air pump in case of

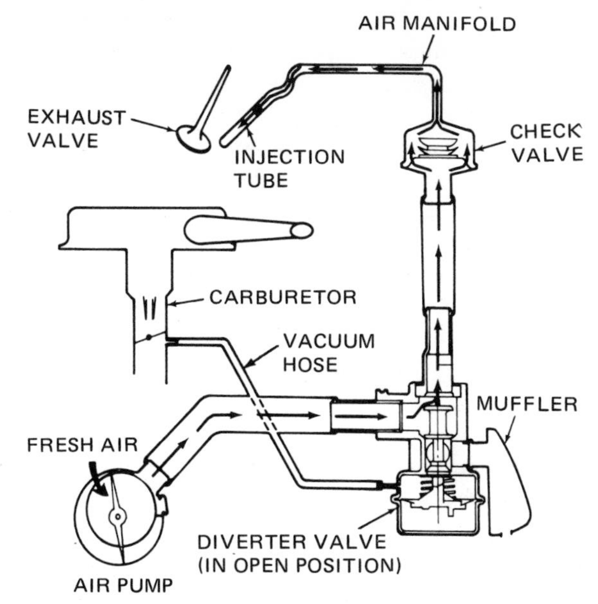

Figure 1 Schematic view of the air-injection system. *(Chevrolet Motor Division of General Motors Corporation.)*

backfire. The air-bypass valve operates during engine deceleration, when intake-manifold is high. The bypass valve momentarily diverts air from the air pump to the air cleaner, instead of to the exhaust manifold. This tends to prevent backfiring in the exhaust system.

■ 2-3-2 An Air-Injection-System Trouble-Diagnosis Chart

The chart to the right lists the various air-injection-system complaints, their possible causes, and checks or corrections to be made. The information in the chart will shorten the time you need to correct a trouble. If you follow a logical procedure, you can locate the cause of the trouble quickly.

> **NOTE:** The troubles and possible causes are not listed according to how often they occur. That is, item 1 (or item *a* under "Possible Cause") does not necessarily occur more often than item 2 (or item *b*).

■ 2-3-3 Excessive Belt Noise

For proper operation of the air pump, the air-pump drive belt must be in good condition and adjusted to the specified tension. The belt should be checked and tightened to the specified tension at least every 12 months or 12,000 miles (19,312 km).

If the air pump seizes, the belt may slide in the pump pulley, making noise. If the pump is not repairable, replace the pump. Check the condition of the belt before tightening it.

■ 2-3-4 Excessive Pump Noise

During normal operation, the air-injection system is not completely noiseless. The normal noise from the pump rises in pitch as engine speed increases. A quick check to determine if the air pump is the source of excessive engine-compartment noise is to remove the pump drive belt and operate the engine. If the noise cannot be heard, the problem is in the air-injection system. When the belt is removed and the pump is turned by hand, the pump frequently squeaks. This is normal and does not indicate a defective pump. Do not oil or lubricate the pump in any way. The only serviceable part of the pump is the centrifugal filter fan. Until properly "broken in," a new pump may make some chirping noises. A continuous knocking noise indicates rear-

AIR-INJECTION-SYSTEM TROUBLE-DIAGNOSIS CHART

(See ■2-3-3 to 2-3-7 for detailed explanations of the causes and corrections listed below.)

COMPLAINT	POSSIBLE CAUSE	CHECK OR CORRECTION
1. Excessive belt noise (■2-3-3)	a. Loose belt	Tighten belt
	b. Seized air pump	Replace air pump
2. Excessive air-pump noise (■2-3-4)	a. Leaking, loose, or disconnected hose	Replace or properly connect hose
	b. Hose touching other engine parts	Adjust hose position
	c. Diverter-valve failure	Replace diverter valve
	d. Check-valve failure	Replace check valve
	e. Pump mounting bolts loose	Retorque all mounting bolts
	f. Centrifugal fan damaged	Replace centrifugal fan
	g. Air pump seized or binding	Replace air pump
	h. Cup plug missing from cover	Replace plug
	i. Bent or misaligned pulley	Replace or align pulley
3. No air supply (■2-3-5)	a. Loose or broken belt	Tighten or replace belt
	b. Leak in hose	Locate source of leak and correct
	c. Leak at hose fitting	Replace or tighten hose clamps
	d. Diverter-valve failure	Replace diverter valve
	e. Check-valve failure	Replace check valve
	f. Air-pump failure	Replace air pump
4. Backfire in exhaust system (■2-3-6)	a. Diverter valve defective	Replace diverter valve
	b. Wrong hose on diverter valve	Correct hose routing
	c. No vacuum to diverter hose	Locate and repair cause of no vacuum
5. High HC and CO levels (■2-3-6)	a. Air supply leaks	Locate and repair
	b. Low air-pump output	Replace air pump
	c. Plugged air-injection tubes	Clean or replace injection tubes

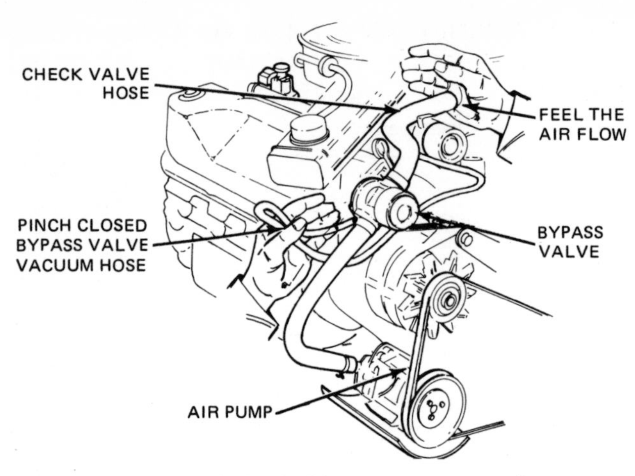

Figure 2 Make a quick check of the air-injection pump by removing the hose from the check valve and feeling for airflow from the hose. *(Ford Motor Company.)*

bearing failure. This may result from excessive drive-belt tension. Any abnormal noise from the pump requires that it be replaced.

■ **2-3-5 No Air Supply** This problem often is the result of the pump not turning. If the drive belt breaks or works loose, the pump cannot turn. Another possible reason for no air supply is seizure, or failure, of the pump. Servicing of the air pump sometimes is limited to replacement of the centrifugal-fan filter. When servicing the pump filter, do not clamp the pump in a vise or hammer on the pump. Be careful, when adjusting the drive belt, not to pry on the pump housing. If a pry bar must be used to properly tension the belt, pry as close to the rear of the pump cover as possible.

> **NOTE:** See ■2-3-9, which describes this procedure.

■ **2-3-6 Backfire in Exhaust System** A backfire in the exhaust system, especially on deceleration, may be caused by failure of the diverter valve. In order for a backfire to occur, an excessively rich mixture must get into the exhaust system. This happens on deceleration. Then, when the fresh air being pumped into the exhaust manifold by the air-injection system hits the hot, rich mixture in the exhaust gas, backfire occurs. Under normal conditions, the diverter valve acts during deceleration to divert the air supply from the air pump into the atmosphere or the air cleaner. Without the fresh air from the air pump, the fuel-rich exhaust gas does not explode, and so no backfire takes place. Failure of the diverter valve to operate may be caused by a disconnected, plugged, or leaking vacuum hose.

■ **2-3-7 High HC and CO Levels** An engine equipped with an air-injection system has a higher than allowable amount of HC and CO leaving the combustion chamber. It is the job of the air-injection system to provide additional air to the exhaust gases, so that the excess amounts of HC and CO become harmless water and carbon dioxide. When an engine with an air-injection system has high levels of HC and CO in the exhaust, the air-pump air may not be getting into the exhaust manifold. If any air hose or the air manifold leaks, air from the pump cannot reach the injection tubes (Fig. 1). High levels of HC and CO result. The same thing happens when the injection tubes become clogged with carbon. This problem may be corrected by removing and cleaning the tubes. A small drill, turned back and forth between the fingers, can be used to remove the carbon and open the tube.

There are many reasons why an engine could have high levels of HC and CO. To determine if the cause is the air-injection system, make the quick test of the air-injection system outlined in ■2-3-8. If the air-injection system is not working, continue testing the system as outlined in ■2-3-2 and 2-3-8.

> **NOTE:** A defective air pump cannot cause poor idle, stalling, or driveability complaints. Check the air-injection system following the procedure outlined in this and previous sections.

■ **2-3-8 Testing the Air-Injection System** Figure 1 shows the air-injection system. A quick check of air-pump operation can be made by temporarily disconnecting the hose from the pump outlet, air manifold, or check valve (Fig. 2). Then run the engine at about 1,500 rpm. When you hold your hand to the disconnected hose, you should feel airflow. If you do not, test the air pump and the diverter valve further.

> **NOTE:** As you can see in Fig. 2, Ford uses a bypass valve instead of a diverter valve. Each valve is a type of antibackfire valve.

If you feel air flowing from the hose, accelerate the engine. If the pump is operating satisfactorily, the airflow should increase as engine speed increases. If the airflow does not increase, either the air-pump belt tension is too low, or there is trouble in the pump. Also, the pressure-relief valve may be stuck open. In this case, you will hear the air leaking out. The remedy is to replace the pump.

Ford recommends checking the bypass valve when the pump checks okay and there is trouble in the air-injection system. For the bypass-valve check, the engine must be at normal temperature, the transmission in neutral, and the engine speed at 1,500 rpm. Pinch the bypass-valve vacuum hose shut for 8 seconds. Then release the hose. Air should flow momentarily from the bypass-valve vent instead of from the check-valve hose.

A similar quick check of the diverter valve can be performed by pinching the diverter-valve vacuum hose shut (Fig. 1) for at least 1 second. Then release the hose. Air should exhaust from the lower portion of the diverter valve for about 4 seconds if the diverter valve is functioning properly.

If the diverter valve fails the test, check the condition and routing of all lines, especially the diverter-valve vacuum line. All lines must be fastened securely, without any crimps or leaks. If the diverter valve does not operate, disconnect the vacuum line from the valve. With the engine running, place your finger over the end of the vacuum line. You should feel a vacuum. If not, the wrong line may be connected to the diverter valve, or the line is plugged between the disconnected end and the intake manifold.

A quick check of the diverter valve can be made with the engine at normal temperature and running at idle speed. No air should be escaping through the muffler, or silencer, on the diverter valve. Quickly open and close the throttle. A short blast of air should discharge through the diverter-valve muffler for at least 1 second. This short discharge of air can be felt and heard. It makes a buzzing noise. If no air discharge occurs, the diverter valve is defective and must be replaced.

A brittle, burned, or charred hose connecting the diverter valve to the check valve (Fig. 1) indicates that the check valve is defective and must be replaced. If check-valve leakage is suspected, remove the hose from the check valve with the engine running at 1,500 rpm. No exhaust noise should be heard. Using a shop towel or rag to protect your hand from the heat, hold your hand over the check-valve opening for about 15 seconds. No exhaust pressure should be felt. If there is any exhaust leakage back through the valve, replace it.

■ 2-3-9 Servicing the Air-Injection System

In general, no routine service is required on the air-injection system. Hoses should be inspected and replaced, if required, whenever a tuneup is performed. Some systems use a separate filter to clean the air entering the pump. On these systems, the filter should be checked every year or every 12,000 miles (19,312 km) of operation. It should be cleaned or replaced as necessary. All late-model air pumps use a centrifugal filter. It is replaced only in case of mechanical damage. The procedure is covered in ■2-3-10.

The air-pump drive belt should be checked periodically to make sure it is in good condition and at the proper tension (Fig. 3). The engine should be hot when the check is made. Inspect the belt for adjustment, wear, cracks, and brittleness. Install a new belt if necessary. Proper belt tension is important. A loose belt does not turn the air pump. This causes high exhaust-emission levels and may result in noise. A tight belt overloads the rear bearing in the air pump. If the bearing becomes noisy or fails, replacement of the air pump is necessary. When tightening the belt, do not pry against the pump housing. It is aluminum and will deform and break easily. Ford recommends the use of a special pump belt-tension adjuster (Fig. 3) to hold the proper belt tension while the air-pump mounting bolts and adjusting-arm bolts are tightened.

■ 2-3-10 Replacing Air-Pump Centrifugal Filter Fan

Should the centrifugal filter fan on the air pump become damaged, the fan must be replaced. Remove the drive belt from the air pump. Then remove the pulley-attaching screws, and pull

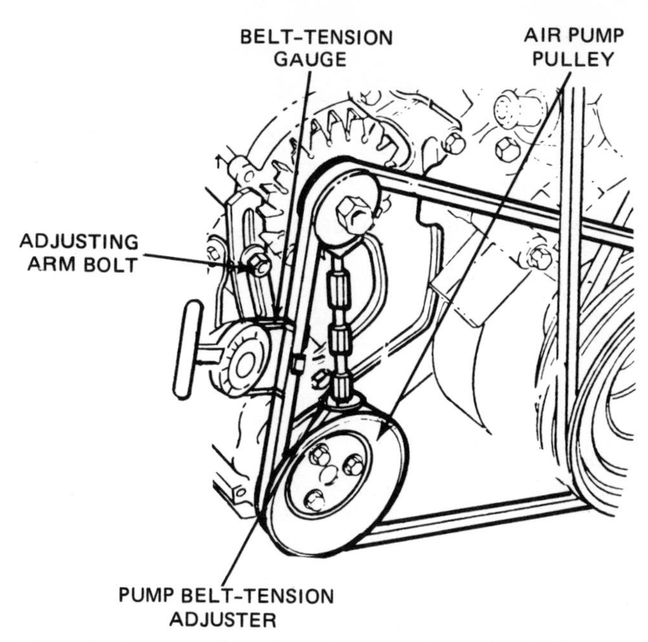

Figure 3 A pump belt-tension adjuster can be used to hold the air pump in place while the adjusting bolts are tightened. *(Ford Motor Company.)*

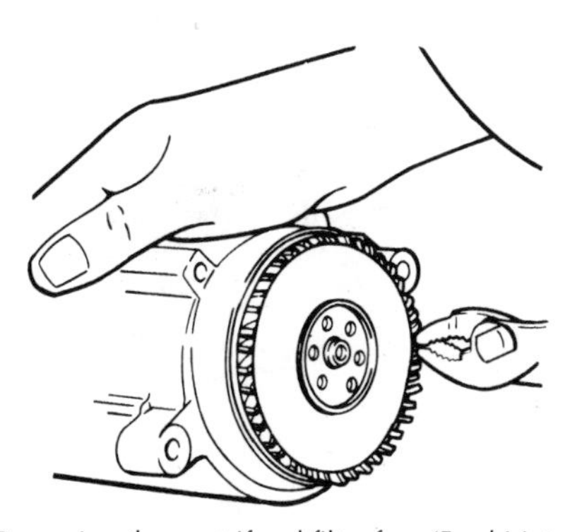

Figure 4 Removing the centrifugal filter fan. *(Ford Motor Company.)*

the pulley off the rotor shaft. Pry the outer disk loose, and remove it. The fan blades are exposed after the outer disk is removed. Grasp the blades of the fan with pliers, and pull the fan from around the drive hub (Fig. 4). Position the new fan, and draw it into place using the pulley and pulley-attaching bolts as an installing tool. Tighten the bolts alternately, to install the fan evenly. In its proper position, the outer edge of the fan slips into the pump housing. A slight interference with the pump-housing bore is normal. When a new fan is installed, it may squeal for the first 20 to 30 miles (32 to 48 km), until its outer-diameter sealing lip has seated.

■ 2-3-11 Transmission-Controlled Spark System

The transmission-controlled spark (TCS) system is an exhaust-emission control system that allows vacuum to the distributor vacuum-advance mechanism only when the transmission is in high gear (Fig. 5).

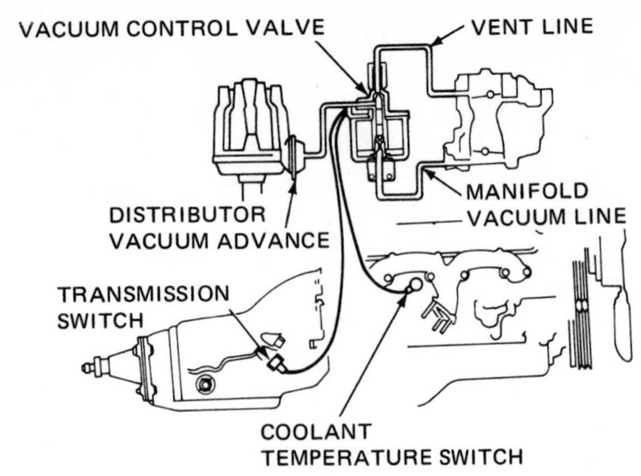

Figure 5 Layout of the transmission-controlled spark (TCS) system on the engine and transmission. *(Chevrolet Motor Division of General Motors Corporation.)*

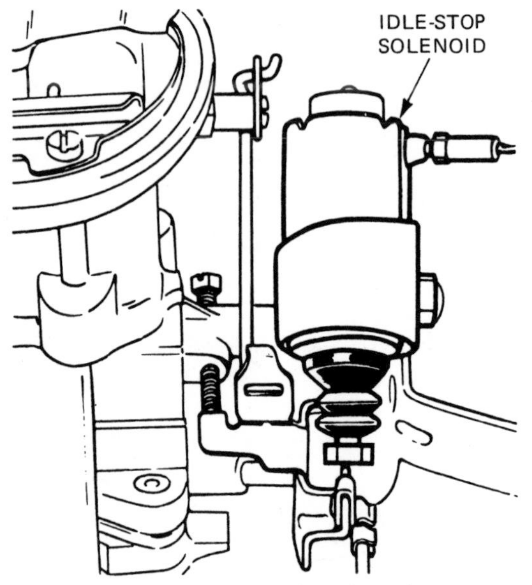

Figure 6 Idle-stop solenoid mounted on the carburetor to prevent engine dieseling when the ignition is turned off. *(Echlin Manufacturing Company.)*

Using the TCS system to control distributor vacuum advance reduces the emission of unburned HC and reduces the formation of NO_x. This is done by retarding the spark, thereby reducing the peak combustion temperature during the power stroke. There are several variations of the basic TCS system. Some systems include a time-delay relay to provide vacuum advance during cold starts and a temperature-override switch to restore full vacuum advance should the engine begin to overheat. This could occur, for example, during long periods of engine idling.

■ 2-3-12 TCS-System Trouble-Diagnosis Chart

The chart that follows lists the various TCS-system complaints, their possible causes, and checks or corrections to be made. The information in the chart will shorten the time you need to correct a trouble. If you follow a logical procedure, you can locate the cause of the trouble quickly.

NOTE: The troubles and possible causes are not listed according to how often they occur. That is, item 1 (or item *a* under "Possible Cause") does not necessarily occur more often than item 2 (or item *b*).

TCS-SYSTEM TROUBLE-DIAGNOSIS CHART

(See ■2-3-13 to 2-3-15 for detailed explanations of the causes and corrections listed below.)

COMPLAINT	POSSIBLE CAUSE	CHECK OR CORRECTION
1. Engine stalls at idle, car creeps excessively at idle, high idle speed, engine diesels (■2-3-13)	Defective or improperly adjusted idle-stop solenoid	Adjust or replace idle-stop solenoid
2. Poor high-gear performance stumble or stall on cold start, excessive fuel consumption, backfire during deceleration (■2-3-14)	a. Inoperative vacuum-advance solenoid	Check vacuum source; replace solenoid
	b. Time relay does not energize	Check wiring; replace relay
	c. Temperature switch defective	Replace temperature switch
	d. Transmission switch inoperative	Replace transmission switch
3. High HC and NO_x emissions, distributor vacuum advance at all times (■2-3-15)	a. Transmission switch defective	Replace transmission switch
	b. Vacuum-advance solenoid defective	Replace vacuum-advance solenoid
	c. Time relay defective	Replace time relay
	d. Temperature switch defective	Replace temperature switch

■ 2-3-13 Engine Stalls at Idle

General Motors includes the idle-stop solenoid as part of the TCS system. On engines equipped with this device (Fig. 6), when there is a problem with high or low idle speed, or dieseling when the ignition is turned off, the operation and adjustment of the idle-stop solenoid should be checked.

■ 2-3-14 Poor High-Gear Performance

As listed in item 2 of the Trouble-Diagnosis Chart, there are several problems related to engine performance that can be caused by troubles in the TCS system. Before testing the components of the system, check for a blown fuse, loose connection, broken wire, broken or disconnected hose, proper electrical ground, and proper routing and connection of hoses. Note in the chart that failure of any electrical device in the TCS system can

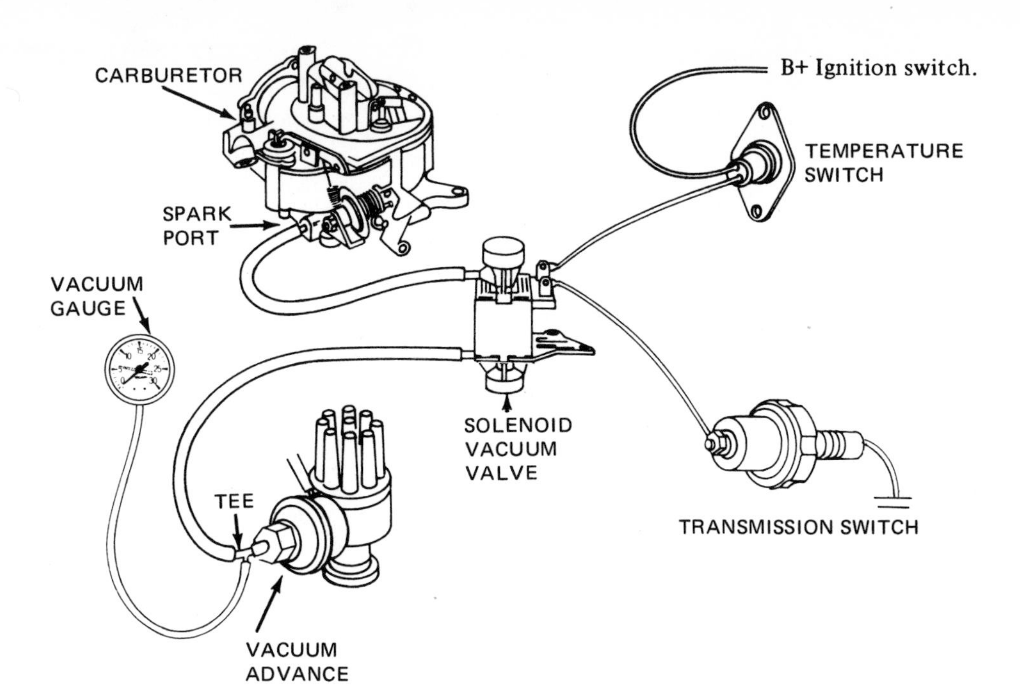

Figure 7 Transmission-regulated spark (TRS) system components. *(Ford Motor Company.)*

cause a complaint of this type. To determine if a problem does exist, test the system as outlined in ■ 2-3-16.

■ 2-3-15 High HC and NO_x Emissions

At idle and in lower gears, high HC and NO_x emissions may be caused by distributor vacuum advance. If there is distributor vacuum advance at all times, follow the procedure in ■ 2-3-16 to determine if the TCS system has failed. On manual-transmission cars, the transmission switch is opened or closed by gear position, or the position of the shifter shaft. Some automatic transmissions are equipped with a switch which opens or closes in relation to car speed. The switch opens or closes at about 36 mph (58 km/h). The switch is operated by governor oil pressure. A governor oil pressure of 1 psi (0.07 kg/cm²) is approximately equal to a car speed in direct drive of 1 mph (1.6 km/h).

■ 2-3-16 Testing the TCS System

A typical TCS system is shown in Fig. 5.

A complaint of engine stall at idle, excessive creep at idle, high idle speed, or dieseling indicates a problem with the idle-stop solenoid (Fig. 6). Check for free movement of the plunger in the idle-stop solenoid. Then check for an incorrectly adjusted plunger. Check that the solenoid energizes when the ignition is turned on and de-energizes when the ignition is turned off. Replace or adjust the idle-stop solenoid as necessary.

Distributor vacuum advance at all times is probably caused by a defective transmission switch. Jack up the drive wheels, and place stands under the vehicle. With the engine warm and running, put the transmission in low forward gear. The advance solenoid should de-energize. If the solenoid energizes, disconnect the wire from the transmission switch (Fig. 6). If the solenoid de-energizes when the wire is disconnected, replace the transmission switch.

Poor high-gear performance, stumble or stall on cold start, excessive fuel consumption, or popping in the exhaust during deceleration may be caused by a malfunction in a TCS-system component. First check for a blown fuse, loose connection, broken wire, broken or disconnected hose, proper ground at all components, and proper routing of hoses.

The problem could be caused by an inoperative vacuum-advance solenoid. Check the intake-manifold vacuum hose at the solenoid for vacuum. If it is okay, then connect a vacuum gauge to the distributor vacuum-advance port on the solenoid valve. With 12 volts applied to the solenoid, the solenoid should be energized. The vacuum gauge should show vacuum at the distributor port.

Check for an inoperative time relay. Remove the temperature-switch connector (Fig. 5). Check the relay to make sure it is cool. Then turn the ignition on. The solenoid should energize for 20 seconds and then de-energize. If the solenoid does not de-energize, remove the blue lead from the time relay. The solenoid will not de-energize if the relay is defective.

Check for an inoperative temperature switch (Fig. 5). On a cold engine, the vacuum-advance solenoid should be energized. If it is not, disconnect and ground the wire from the cold terminal of the temperature switch. If the solenoid energizes, the temperature switch is bad and should be replaced. If the temperature switch is okay, proceed to the next step.

Check for an inoperative transmission switch (Fig. 5). Jack up the drive wheels, and place stands under the vehicle. With the engine warm and running, put the transmission in high gear. The solenoid should be energized. If it is not, remove and ground the connector at the switch. Replace the switch if the solenoid energizes.

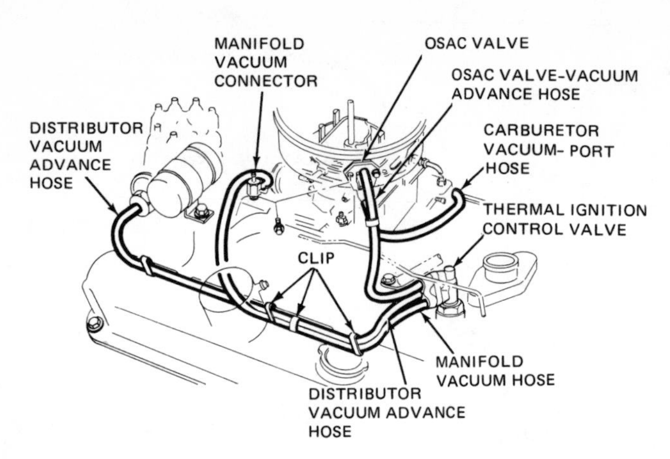

Figure 8 Vacuum-hose routing on an engine equipped with an orifice spark-advance control (OSAC) valve. *(Chrysler Corporation.)*

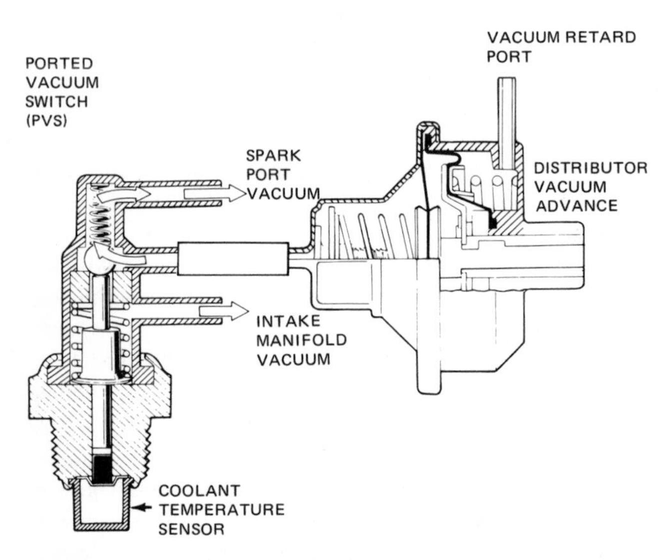

Figure 9 Actions of the ported vacuum switch (PVS) in turning the distributor vacuum advance on and off. *(Ford Motor Company.)*

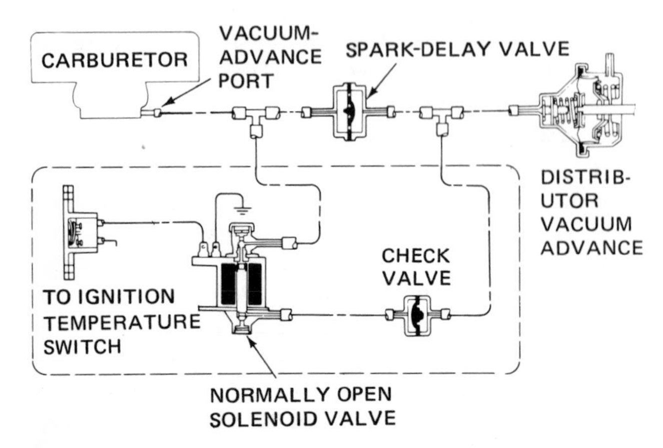

Figure 10 Delayed-vacuum bypass (DVB), used on some engines. *(Ford Motor Company.)*

■ **2-3-17 Servicing the TCS System** The TCS system does not require regular service. However, every 12 months or 12,000 miles (19,312 km), or whenever a tuneup is performed, the operation of the system should be checked, and the idle-stop solenoid adjusted.

■ **2-3-18 Ford Transmission-Regulated Spark (TRS) System** A Ford transmission-regulated spark (TRS) system is shown in Fig. 7. The TRS system is similar in operation to the General Motors TCS system. Both systems prevent vacuum advance when the car is operating in lower gears. However, the TRS system allows vacuum advance when the outside air temperature is below about 60°F (15.6°C). Ford mounts the temperature switch in the door pillar.

A quick check of the TRS system can be made as shown in Fig. 7, by connecting a vacuum gauge into the vacuum-advance line. With the air temperature at about 65°F (18.3°C) or higher, run the engine at 1,500 rpm. In NEUTRAL or PARK, the gauge should show no vacuum to the distributor. With the manual transmission in high gear (clutch disengaged) at 1,500 rpm, the vacuum gauge should show 6 inches Hg (152.4 mm Hg) of vacuum or more. At idle, in reverse gear (with foot brake applied), the vacuum gauge should show 6 inches Hg (152.4 mm Hg) of vacuum or more. If the tests show no vacuum when there should be vacuum, check for vacuum in the hose to the carburetor. Then test the solenoid vacuum valve.

■ **2-3-19 Chrysler Orifice Spark-Advance Control (OSAC) System** In addition to the TCS and TRS systems, there are other vacuum-advance control systems. Most are especially tailored for the engines and vehicles with which they are used. Some cars built by Chrysler use an orifice spark-advance control (OSAC) system (Fig. 8). The OSAC valve includes a very small hole, or orifice. This delays any change in the application of vacuum to the distributor by about 17 seconds (27 seconds on some engines), between idle and part throttle. Therefore, there is a delay in vacuum advance until acceleration is well under way. Acceleration is a critical time during which vacuum advance could produce high NO_x.

A thermal ignition control (TIC) valve (Fig. 8) or thermostatic vacuum switch (also called by Ford a ported vacuum switch or PVS) is used on some engines to reduce the possibility of engine overheating. When the engine-coolant temperature at idle reaches 225°F (107.2°C), the valve opens and allows manifold vacuum to the distributor. This action bypasses the OSAC system. Advancing the spark increases the idle speed, which provides additional cooling. When the engine has cooled to normal temperature, the TIC valve closes, restoring normal operation of the OSAC system. Figure 9 shows a similar system used by Ford to restore vacuum advance when the engine coolant overheats.

Little service is required on the OSAC system. Every 15,000 miles (24,140 km), Chrysler recommends inspecting the hose connections between the valve, carburetor, and distributor. Any cracked or brittle hoses should be replaced. Then inspect the OSAC valve for airtight fittings and hoses, and free operation.

To test the OSAC valve, use a T fitting to connect a vacuum gauge into the distributor vacuum-advance hose. Set the parking brake, and run the engine at 2,000 rpm in neutral. If the vacuum gauge immediately shows manifold vacuum or shows no vacuum, the OSAC valve is not operating and must be replaced. Normal operation of the OSAC valve will show a gradual increase in the gauge vacuum reading, from zero to a normal level in about 20 seconds.

To test the thermal ignition control valve (Fig. 8), adjust the engine idle speed to 600 rpm. Disconnect the hose from the No. 2 valve port, and plug the open end of the hose. Check the idle speed. No change in idle speed indicates the valve is not leaking. If the idle speed drops 100 rpm or more, replace the valve. Next, reconnect the vacuum hose to the No. 2 valve port. Cover the radiator to increase the engine temperature. Be careful not to overheat the engine. When the coolant temperature reaches about 225°F (107.2°C)—about the time the gauge indicator reaches the top of its normal range—the engine speed should increase 100 rpm or more. If no increase occurs, the valve is defective and must be replaced. Then uncover the radiator, and idle the engine until the engine temperature returns to normal. Readjust the idle rpm.

■ **2-3-20 Ford Spark-Delay Valve** Ford uses a system similar to the Chrysler OSAC system. The Ford system is called the spark-delay valve system. Operation of the valve delays vacuum advance during some vehicle acceleration conditions. The spark-delay valve is connected in series with the vacuum hose from the vacuum-advance port on the carburetor and the distributor vacuum-advance mechanism. During mild acceleration, the vacuum to the distributor can increase only gradually. This is because the spark-delay valve only allows the vacuum to pass through slowly. Depending on the valve, vacuum spark advance is delayed between 1 and 28 seconds. During deceleration or heavy acceleration, the difference in pressure across the spark-delay valve is great enough to open it. The opening of the valve instantly cuts off the vacuum spark advance.

Along with the spark-delay valve on some engines, Ford uses a delayed-vacuum-bypass (DVB) system (Fig. 10). It works to bypass the spark-delay valve, and restore vacuum advance, when outside temperature is below about 65°F (18.3°C).

If an engine equipped with a spark-delay valve develops poor acceleration or surge, check that the spark-delay valve is the right one for the engine. Then check the operation of the valve with the vacuum pump on the distributor tester. Connect the black side of the valve to the vacuum hose from the distributor tester. Connect a vacuum gauge to the color side of the valve. Apply 10 inches Hg (254 mm Hg) of vacuum to the valve. Measure the time it takes for the gauge reading to go from 0 to 8 inches Hg (203.2 mm Hg) of vacuum. If the spark-delay valve does not test within specifications, replace it with the proper valve.

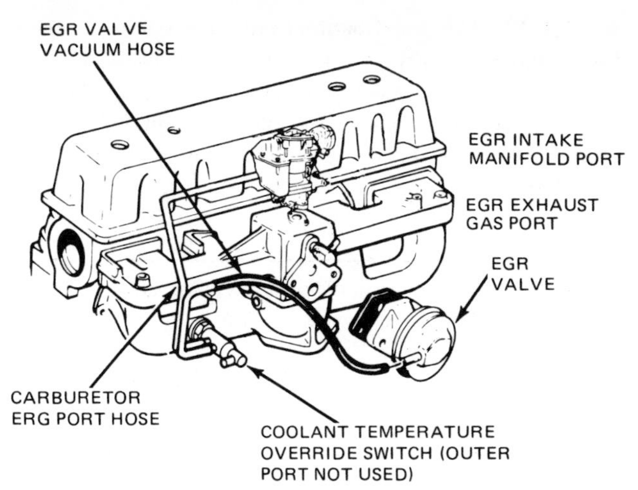

Figure 11 Exhaust-gas recirculation (EGR) system on a six-cylinder engine. *(American Motors Corporation.)*

The delayed-vacuum-bypass system may cause problems such as poor throttle response and poor cold-engine performance. To check out a complaint of poor throttle response, test the check valve for free flow and no flow. Replace the check valve if it fails either test. Poor cold-engine performance may be caused by a check valve that was installed backward or a temperature switch that is stuck closed. To test the temperature switch, remove it from the car and hold it in your hand to warm it. Connect an ohmmeter to the temperature switch. The ohmmeter should read zero, since in warm weather the switch contacts close. Then place the switch in a cup of ice water. The switch contacts should open, and the ohmmeter should show infinity (an open circuit). The temperature switch can also be tested in a car. Warm the switch with a sponge soaked in hot water. Cool the switch by spraying it with a can of aerosol spray. If the temperature switch fails either test, replace it. The solenoid valve may be tested by procedures given in the Ford shop manual.

■ **2-3-21 Exhaust-Gas Recirculation (EGR)** Exhaust-gas recirculation (EGR) is used on many cars to reduce nitrogen oxides (NO_x) emissions from the engine exhaust (Fig. 11). Air is about 80 percent nitrogen. During the combustion process, at temperatures above 2,500°F (1,371°C), some of the nitrogen and oxygen unite to form NO_x. In the engine cylinders, combustion temperatures may go above 4,000°F (2,204°C). Formation of NO_x can be decreased by reducing peak flame, or combustion, temperatures. Exhaust gases are almost totally inactive, or inert. This means they neither burn nor support combustion. When some exhaust gas is mixed with the fresh air-fuel-charge going into the cylinders, the inert exhaust gas absorbs some of the heat of combustion. This lowers the combustion temperature and, in so doing, reduces the amount of NO_x formed in the engine.

■ **2-3-22 Exhaust-Gas-Recirculation-System Trouble-Diagnosis Chart** The chart to the right lists the various EGR-system complaints, their possible causes, and checks and corrections to be made. The information in the chart will shorten the time you need to correct a trouble. If you follow a logical procedure, you can locate the cause of the trouble quickly.

> **NOTE:** The troubles and possible causes are not listed according to how often they occur. That is, item 1 (or item a under "Possible Cause") does not necessarily occur more often than item 2 (or item *b*).

EXHAUST-GAS-RECIRCULATION-SYSTEM TROUBLE-DIAGNOSIS CHART

(See ■ 2-3-23 to 2-3-26 for detailed explanations of the causes and corrections listed below.)

COMPLAINT	POSSIBLE CAUSE	CHECK OR CORRECTION
1. Engine idles rough and stalls (■2-3-23)	a. Exhaust-gas recirculation (EGR) valve vacuum hose misrouted	Correct EGR-valve hose routing
	b. Leaking EGR valve	Clean or replace EGR valve
	c. Incorrect idle speed	Set idle speed; check EGR valve
	d. Wrong vacuum to EGR valve	Check vacuum at carburetor EGR port
	e. Failed thermal vacuum switch	Check vacuum to and from switch
	f. Leaking EGR-valve gasket	Tighten attaching bolts; if not loose, replace gasket
2. Poor part-throttle performance, poor fuel economy, engine runs rough on light acceleration (■2-3-24)	a. EGR-valve vacuum hose misrouted	Correct EGR-valve hose routing
	b. Defective thermal vacuum switch	Check vacuum to and from switch
	c. Deposits in EGR passages	Clean passages
	d. Sticking or binding EGR valve	Clean or replace EGR valve
3. Engine stalls on deceleration (■2-3-25)	EGR vacuum line restricted	Remove restriction; check EGR valve for deposits
4. Detonation at part throttle (■2-3-26)	Insufficient exhaust-gas recirculation	Check hoses, EGR valve, and thermal vacuum switch

■ **2-3-23 Engine Idles Rough and Stalls** This condition may be caused by incorrect hose connections or a leaking EGR valve. The EGR valve is operated by "ported vacuum." That is, the vacuum source for the EGR valve is a port in the carburetor, located above the throttle valve. Unless the throttle is open to a position equivalent to about 20 mph (32 km/h) under light acceleration, practically no vacuum appears at the carburetor port. Without vacuum, a spring in the valve holds it closed. Therefore, at idle or closed throttle, no exhaust gas should recirculate into the engine. A misrouted vacuum hose connected to the EGR valve from a source of intake-manifold vacuum would open the valve, allowing exhaust-gas flow. This would excessively dilute the air-fuel mixture and result in rough idle and stalling.

There are other ways in which exhaust gas can leak into the intake manifold. If the EGR-valve bolts work loose, the exhaust gas can flow between the EGR valve and its gasket. To correct this problem, tighten the bolts. If the bolts are not loose, but a leak is suspected, remove the valve and inspect the gasket. It may be damaged and require replacement. While the EGR valve is removed, check it for leakage. The problem could be caused by deposits on the valve which prevent it from seating.

■ **2-3-24 Poor Part-Throttle Performance** Basically, the EGR system is controlled by carburetor port vacuum and engine-coolant temperature. A problem with any part of these controls may cause the complaints listed in item 2, and others. A defective thermal vacuum switch may stick in the open position, allowing exhaust gas to recirculate when the engine is cold. This may cause poor part-throttle performance, as well as rough engine operation. Deposits in the EGR passages, and a sticking or binding EGR valve, may cause mileage complaints. With some exhaust-gas recirculation during the wrong modes of engine operation, the driver must open the throttle wider to obtain the power needed. As a result, more fuel is used and fuel economy is poor.

■ **2-3-25 Engine Stalls on Deceleration** Engine stalling on decleration can be caused by failure of the EGR valve to close promptly. Vacuum for controlling the EGR valve comes from a carburetor vacuum port above the throttle valve. When the throttle is released, the EGR valve should close almost immediately. This cuts off exhaust-gas recirculation. However, if the EGR vacuum line is restricted, the vacuum in it will decrease slowly. This will keep the EGR valve open with exhaust gas flowing into the intake manifold long enough to stall the engine. Likewise, if there are deposits on the EGR valve so it does not close completely and some exhaust gas continues to flow, the engine may stall.

■ **2-3-26 Detonation at Part Throttle** Detonation, or pinging, in an engine at part throttle may be caused by insufficient exhaust-gas recirculation. Detonation occurs when the air-fuel mixture in the combustion chamber overheats and explodes spontaneously before the flame from the spark plug reaches it. In an engine designed to work with exhaust-gas recirculation, some of the heat of combustion is absorbed by the recirculated exhaust gases. Should a vacuum hose crack or become disconnected, or the thermal vacuum switch stick closed, no exhaust-gas recirculation will occur. The engine will ping, or detonate, during the modes of engine operation when there should be exhaust-gas recirculation.

■ 2-3-27 Testing the EGR System

Some EGR valves have the valve stem visible under the diaphragm, or vacuum actuator. A quick check of this type valve can be made with the engine warmed up and idling. With the transmission in neutral, abruptly open the throttle until the engine accelerates to about 2,000 rpm. If the EGR valve is operating, you will see the stem (and the groove in it) move up as the valve opens. If the stem does not move, check the EGR valve further, as explained below.

Recommended by Ford for a quick check of the EGR valve on the car is to check all hose connections in the EGR system. Then, with the engine warmed up and idling, connect the vacuum tester to the EGR valve. Apply 8 inches Hg (203.2 mm Hg) of vacuum to the valve. If there is no change in idle condition or rpm, the EGR valve is restricted and should be cleaned. If the valve is not dirty, it is defective and must be replaced. However, if the engine idle gets rough when the vacuum is applied, and the rpm drops or the engine stalls, the EGR valve is okay.

General Motors recommends checking the EGR valve in a similar manner, by connecting a hose from the intake manifold to the EGR valve. The engine must be warmed up and running at fast idle. If the valve is good, the engine speed should drop at least 100 rpm on a car with manual transmission, and at least 250 rpm on a car with automatic transmission. Otherwise, clean or replace the valve.

To check the thermal vacuum switch, which Ford calls a ported vacuum switch (PVS) valve, remove both hoses from the valve. Connect a vacuum tester to the lower port and a vacuum gauge to the upper port. When the engine is cold, with the coolant temperature 50°F (10°C) or less, apply vacuum to the valve. If the valve is working properly, no reading should appear on the vacuum gauge. (This closed position of the PVS valve prevents exhaust-gas recirculation on a cold engine.) If the gauge shows a vacuum reading, the PVS valve is defective and must be replaced.

Next, operate the engine until it warms up. Then apply vacuum to the valve. The vacuum gauge should register. If the gauge does not register a vacuum, replace the PVS valve.

> **NOTE:** Chevrolet points out that leakage of up to 2 inches (50.8 mm) of vacuum in 2 minutes through a thermal vacuum switch is okay. This does not indicate that the switch is defective.

■ 2-3-28 EGR-System Service Intervals

There are differences in manufacturers' recommended service intervals for EGR systems. When the engine is operated with leaded gasoline, the EGR system should be checked for proper operation every 12 months or 12,000 miles (19,312 km). For engines operated on unleaded gasoline, the EGR system is checked every 24 months or 24,000 miles (38,624 km). Some cars manufactured by Chrysler have an EGR-maintenance reminder light on the instrument panel. The light comes on automatically at 15,000 miles (24,140 km) to remind the driver to have the EGR system checked. Many late-model cars do not require regular EGR-system service. Instead, if a trouble develops in the EGR system, a diagnosis is performed (■ 2-3-22), along with the needed test or service.

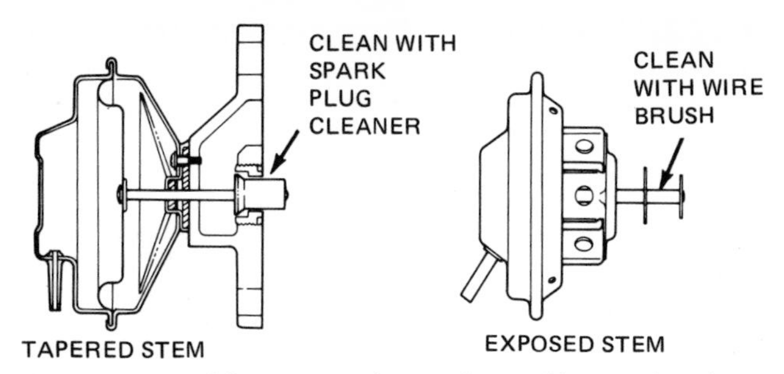

Figure 12 Two different types of EGR valves and how to clean them. *(Ford Motor Company.)*

■ 2-3-29 Servicing the EGR System

A sticking EGR valve should be inspected for deposits. If there is more than a thin film of deposits, clean the EGR valve. Remove any deposits from the mounting surface and from around the valve and seat. The method of cleaning depends on the type of valve (Fig. 12). General Motors recommends cleaning an EGR valve from a V-8 engine by holding the valve assembly in your hand and tapping the protruding stem lightly with a plastic hammer. Then lightly tap the sides of the valve. Shake out the loose particles. If you are not certain of the type of valve or how to clean it, refer to the manufacturer's shop manual.

> **NOTE:** Do not clamp the EGR valve in a vise, or wash the EGR valve in solvent. Either may damage the valve and diaphragm.

Figure 13 shows an exploded view of the spacer-entry EGR system. Figure 14 shows sectional views of the intake-manifold floor-entry EGR system. Whenever an inspection shows a buildup of deposits in any of the passages, they should be cleaned. Deposits can be loosened with a round wire brush, such as a valve-guide cleaning brush. Passages such as the exhaust-gas entry port (Fig. 13), when completely blocked by hard deposits, can be opened by holding a small drill between your fingers and turning it into the deposits to cut them out. When cleaning passages in the manifold, cover the bores with rags or masking tape. This will keep dirt from falling into the manifold.

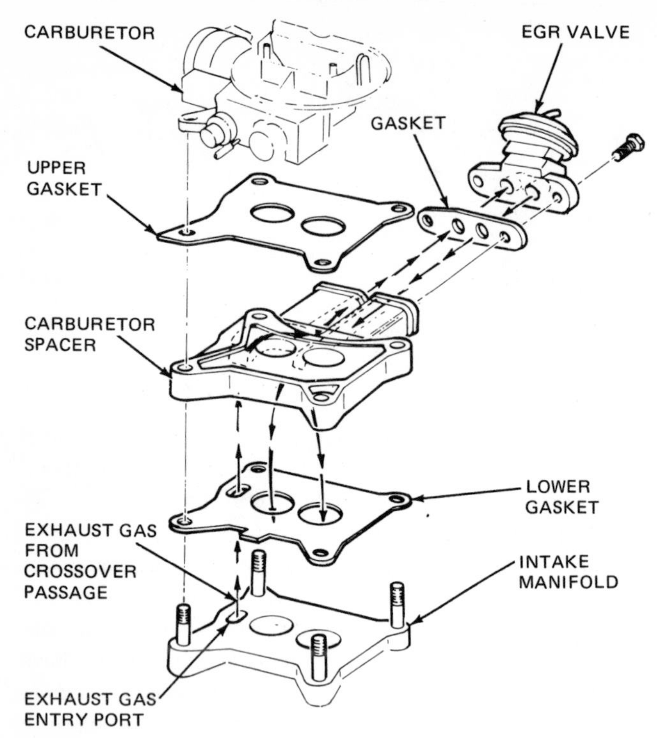

Figure 13 EGR system using a spacer below the carburetor to recycle the exhaust gas. *(Ford Motor Company.)*

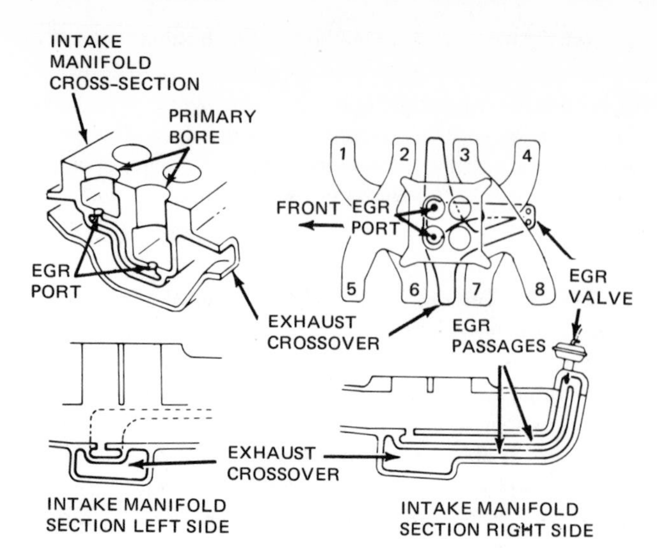

Figure 14 EGR system using ports in the intake-manifold floor to recycle the exhaust gas. *(Ford Motor Company.)*

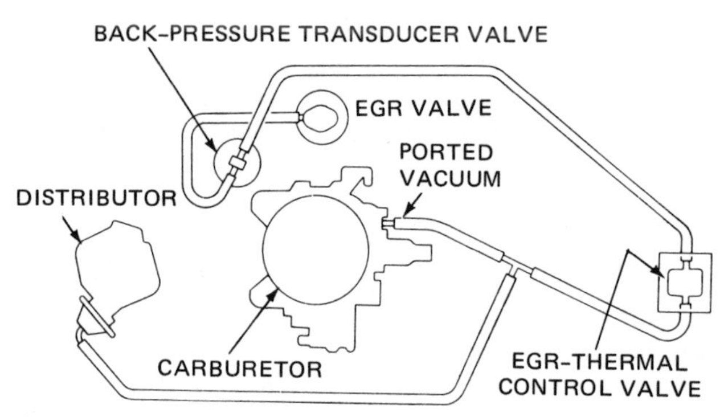

Figure 15 Vacuum-hose routing for the EGR system on a late-model car. *(Oldsmobile Division of General Motors Corporation.)*

For the EGR system to operate properly, the entire system must be free of vacuum leaks. Any cracked, brittle, or broken hoses may leak and must be replaced. Sometimes you will find hoses that are too short. These will not stay connected and will often pull off the connector. Hoses that are too long may interfere with the throttle linkage. Also, long hoses may bend or kink, preventing the vacuum signal from passing through. Short hoses must be replaced. Long hoses must be cut to the correct length.

Figure 15 shows the engine vacuum-hose routing diagram for one car model. Vacuum diagrams, like schematic diagrams of electric circuits, are very important. For any vacuum-sensitive or vacuum-operated device to work, it must have the proper vacuum line connected to it. Many complaints about engine operation and about the EGR system can be caused by a misrouted vacuum hose (■ 2-3-22). There are many vacuum hoses connecting various devices on and around the engine in a late-model car. Always check any questionable connection or hose routing. Refer to the vacuum-hose routing diagram for the engine you are servicing, in the manufacturer's shop manual.

■ 2-3-30 EGR Back-Pressure Transducer Valve

In Fig. 16 a back-pressure transducer valve (BPV) is connected into the vacuum line ahead of the EGR valve. The BPV is used in many late-model cars to help the EGR systems meet lower NO_x exhaust-emission standards. Its purpose is to modulate, or vary, the amount of exhaust-gas recirculation according to the load on the engine. This also improves driveability and fuel economy.

Briefly, here is how the BPV works. Vacuum to the EGR valve passes through an air bleed in the BPV. Under normal conditions of part throttle and light load, the spring above the diaphragm in the BPV forces the diaphragm down (left in Fig. 16). This opens the air bleed and allows a small amount of air to enter. This reduces the vacuum to the EGR valve, which in turn reduces the amount of exhaust-gas recirculation. But when the engine operates with a high load, exhaust back pressure increases in the manifold and in the exhaust-pressure tube. This pressure overcomes the spring in the BPV, raising the diaphragm and closing the air bleed (right in Fig. 16). Now full vacuum is applied to the EGR valve, and the exhaust-gas recirculation system operates normally. As in the EGR system without a BPV, there is no exhaust-gas recirculation at idle or when the throttle is wide open.

The action of converting an exhaust-pressure signal into a vacuum signal is one type of transducer action used on the automobile. A transducer is any device which converts an input signal of one form into an output signal of a different form. A familiar example of a transducer is the car horn. It converts an electric signal into a noise, or audio, signal.

To test the back-pressure transducer valve, remove the air

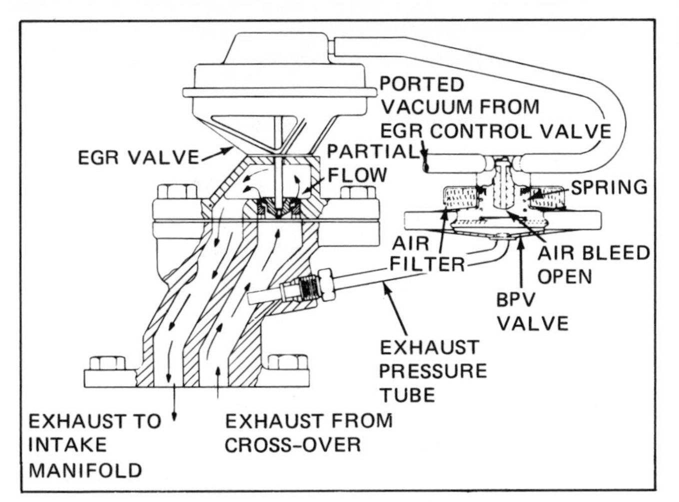

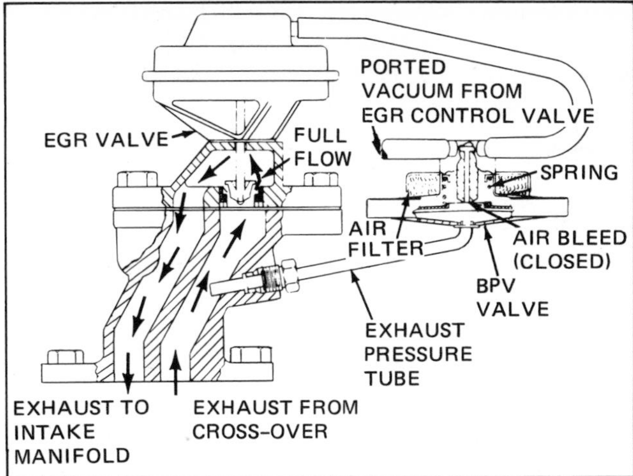

Figure 16 Operation of the EGR-system back-pressure transducer valve (BPV). *(Oldsmobile Division of General Motors Corporation.)*

cleaner and plug the manifold-vacuum fitting. Set the fast-idle cam on the high step. Start the engine, and let it warm up. With a vacuum gauge, check the vacuum to the BPV. Next, use a T fitting to connect the vacuum gauge into the hose connecting the BPV to the EGR valve. Note the reading on the vacuum gauge. The vacuum should be between 1.7 and 2.7 inches Hg (43.2 and 68.6 mm Hg). If the reading is not within specifications, replace the BPV. Remove the hose from the EGR valve, and plug the hose. Now read the vacuum gauge. The vacuum should be the same as the BPV vacuum measured earlier. If the vacuum across the BPV varies by more than 2 inches (50.8 mm) in this test, replace the BPV. If no vacuum is indicated, remove the BPV. Inspect the spacer port (used on some engines) and pressure tube for deposits and restrictions.

The BPV requires no regular service. However, in order for the BPV to work, the holes in the exhaust-manifold end of the pressure tube must be open and clear. Clean this area every time the EGR valve is cleaned.

■ **2-3-31 Catalytic Converters** Another method of treating the exhaust gas to remove excess amounts of unburned hydrocarbons (HC) and carbon monoxide (CO) is to use a catalytic converter. Some cars with V-type engines have two catalytic converters. However, installation and service are the same as for cars with a single converter. Let us briefly review how this exhaust-emission control device works.

A catalyst is a substance that makes a chemical reaction take place faster. Although the catalyst may take part in the chemical reaction, at the end of the reaction the catalyst is unchanged. For example, without a catalyst, a temperature of 1,800°F (982°C) is required to change an amount of carbon monoxide (a harmful gas) to carbon dioxide (a harmless gas). That same amount can be converted at only 1,100°F (593°C) when a catalyst is used.

A catalytic converter is a small mufflerlike device mounted in the exhaust line, close to the exhaust manifold. The catalytic converters used on late-model cars are designed to convert unburned HC and CO to harmless water vapor and carbon dioxide. This chemical reaction takes place when the exhaust gases from the engine come in contact with the catalyst in the presence of heat.

■ **2-3-32 Catalytic-Converter Trouble-Diagnosis Chart** The chart that follows lists the various catalytic-converter complaints, their possible causes, and check or corrections to be made. The information in the chart will shorten the time you need to correct a trouble. If you follow a logical procedure, you can locate the cause of the trouble quickly.

NOTE: The troubles and possible causes are not listed according to how often they occur. That is, item 1 (or item *a* under "Possible Cause") does not necessarily occur more often than item 2 (or item *b*).

CATALYTIC-CONVERTER TROUBLE-DIAGNOSIS CHART

(See ■ 2-3-33 to 2-3-37 for detailed explanations of the causes and corrections listed below.)

COMPLAINT	POSSIBLE CAUSE	CHECK OR CORRECTION
1. Exhaust system noisy (■2-3-33)	a. Exhaust-pipe joints loose	Tighten clamps
	b. Catalytic converter ruptured	Replace catalytic converter
	c. Loose or missing catalyst-replacement plug	Tighten or replace plug; recharge catalyst
2. Poor car performance (■2-3-34)	Failed catalytic converter	Replace catalytic converter; check ignition and air-injection systems

(Continued)

CATALYTIC-CONVERTER TROUBLE-DIAGNOSIS CHART *(Continued)*

(See ■2-3-33 to 2-3-37 for detailed explanations of the causes and corrections listed below.)

COMPLAINT	POSSIBLE CAUSE	CHECK OR CORRECTION
3. BB-size particles coming out of tailpipe (■2-3-35)	Failed catalytic converter	Replace catalytic converter; check ignition and air-fuel systems
4. Rotten-egg smell from exhaust (■2-3-36)	Improper carburetor adjustment	Adjust carburetor
5. High HC and CO levels (■2-3-37)	Failed catalytic converter	Replace catalytic converter; check ignition and air-injection systems; check for use of leaded gasoline

■ 2-3-33 Exhaust System Noisy Any leak of exhaust gas from the exhaust system will cause noise. If no other exhaust-system leak can be located, check the catalytic-converter pipe joints for tightness. If the catalytic converter is bulged, distorted, or punctured, replace it. The converter used by General Motors and American Motors Corporation has a catalyst-replacement plug in the bottom. If this plug works loose or falls out, excessive exhaust noise will be heard. To correct this problem, install the plug.

■ 2-3-34 Poor Car Performance Normally, the catalytic converter does not affect the performance or operation of the car in any way. In fact, engineers like the catalytic converter because engines using it can be tuned for better fuel economy and driveability and still have low exhaust emissions. When a converter no longer provides catalytic action, it fails safe. That is, the only result of an inoperative catalytic converter is that the level of HC and CO in the exhaust gas goes up.

However, excessive engine oil consumption could partially plug the converter with carbon. This would restrict exhaust-gas flow, causing poor car performance. A leaking automatic-transmission vacuum modulator may allow so much automatic-transmission fluid to enter the combustion chambers that spark plugs foul. Should this occur, raw gasoline may pass through the engine into the catalytic converter and start burning inside it. Combustion inside the converter destroys it. Operation of the engine with fouled spark plugs, ignition malfunction, or improper air-fuel mixture will raise the temperature in the catalytic converter. At a high temperature, the converter cover may bulge or distort. Inside the converter, the high temperature may melt the substrate, which is the material that the thin coating of platinum-and-palladium catalyst is applied to. Two different types of substrate construction are used. General Motors and American Motors Corporation use a pelletized substrate which is made of thousands of small, porous, alumina beads about the size of BB shot. Chrysler and Ford use a monolithic substrate which is a single-piece ceramic honeycomb.

If the substrate melts, even partially, normal exhaust-gas flow is blocked and catalytic action is lost. The converter must be replaced. Catalytic converters are installed like mufflers. No special tools are needed. However, when the catalytic converter fails, you must determine why before installing a new one. Damage due to heat is not the fault of the catalytic converter. Melted substrate is caused by high temperature inside the converter. The high temperatures, in turn, may be caused by any malfunction allowing an extremely rich air-fuel mixture to reach the converter, or by failure of the air-injection system. The catalytic converter requires a continuous supply of additional oxygen for catalytic action. For this reason, the air-injection system (■2-3-2 to 2-3-10) is used on engines equipped with catalytic converters.

■ 2-3-35 BB-Size Particles Coming Out of Tail Pipe
General Motors and American Motors use a catalytic converter filled with thousands of small beads. Any time beads are found to be falling out of the tail pipe, the catalytic converter has failed. Inside the converter, the beads are held in place in a stainless-steel catalyst support. High temperatures may cause the catalyst support to distort, opening holes through which the exhaust gas may blow the beads. Although the pellet type of catalytic converter may be recharged with new beads, there is no way to open up a catalytic converter and repair a damaged catalyst support. If beads fall out of the tail pipe, replace the catalytic converter.

Before installing the new catalytic converter, find the cause of the high temperature in the converter. Locate and correct the problem in the ignition or air-injection system, to avoid the same damage to the new catalytic converter. Follow the trouble-diagnosis procedures outlined in this chapter.

■ 2-3-36 Rotten-Egg Smell from Exhaust Occasionally a catalytic converter may produce small amounts of hydrogen sulfide (H_2S) gas. As the catalytic converter ages, there is less tendency to produce this gas. Hydrogen sulfide gas smells like rotten eggs. It may be produced by a momentary rich air-fuel mixture entering a hot catalytic converter. The sulfur is in the gasoline. Since some gasolines contain more sulfur than others, the odor may be more noticeable with certain tankfulls of gasoline. When the rotten-egg smell is noticed, check the carburetor adjustments.

■ 2-3-37 High HC and CO Levels A car equipped with a catalytic converter may fail to pass an inspection-station or other exhaust-emission test owing to contaminated catalyst or a damaged converter. However, high emission levels are generally the result of improper engine adjustments or malfunction of other exhaust-emission-system components. The catalytic converter may not be at fault when a car has high HC and CO levels in the exhaust gas. Check all other exhaust-emission systems and related equipment, including all engine tuneup specifications, before condemning the catalytic converter.

Prolonged use of leaded gasoline decreases the effectiveness of the catalyst. General Motors points out that, in an emergency, a small amount of leaded gasoline may be used.

NOTE: There are serious legal penalties for service stations that fuel catalyst-equipped cars with leaded gasoline.

The pellets recover most of their effectiveness when unleaded gasoline is again used. But each time leaded gasoline is used, the pellets lose some more of their effectiveness, until they are contaminated with lead beyond recovery. In such a case, the exhaust-emission levels of HC and CO rise. The pelletized-type catalytic converter can be recharged with new catalyst pellets. The monolithic-type catalytic converter cannot be recharged and must be replaced.

■ 2-3-38 Checking the Catalytic Converter

If an engine is maintained properly and unleaded gasoline is used, the catalytic converter should last the life of the vehicle. The converter itself does not require maintenance. It requires replacement only when abused (as when it is run on leaded gasoline) or when physically damaged in a collision.

An exhaust-gas analyzer can be used to test the converter for proper operation. A quick check is to insert the probe of the analyzer in the tail pipe, with the engine idling and the transmission in neutral. Note the readings. If the readings are normal, that is, within the specifications for the engine you are testing, the catalyst is working. If one or both of the readings (HC and CO) are high, the catalyst may be damaged.

Some cars have a connection in the exhaust system, ahead of the catalytic converter, into which the exhaust-analyzer probe may be inserted. This enables you to compare readings taken before and after the exhaust gas passes through the converter. If the readings taken ahead of the converter and the readings at the tail pipe are the same, the catalyst is inoperative and possibly destroyed. Locate the cause of the catalyst failure. Then recharge or replace the converter as required. Possible causes of abnormal HC and CO readings are given in the chart in Fig. 17. Exhaust-emission specifications for the engine you are testing can be found in the manufacturer's service manual and in federal and state regulations.

Normal operation of the catalytic converter is indicated by high HC and CO readings ahead of the converter, and lower readings (within specifications) at the tail pipe. If the tail-pipe readings are not within specifications, check all other exhaust-emission systems and related equipment, including all engine tuneup specifications, before blaming the catalytic converter. Because of some engine, ignition, or carburetor malfunction, the engine exhaust gas may be too "dirty" for a properly operating catalytic converter to clean. Locate, in the chart in Fig. 17, the abnormal readings that you recorded. Then check out the causes listed until the problem is located.

READING		SYMPTOMS	CAUSES
CO	HC		
Normal	High	Rough idle	1. Faculty Ignition: a. Condenser defective (point-type ignition) b. Poor point ground (point-type ignition) c. Shortened or fouled spark plugs d. Spark plug wires crossed. e. Distributor cap cracked. f. Timing advanced or retarded. 2. Leaky valves.
Low	High	Rough idle	3. Leaky cylinders.
Low	High	Rough idle	Vacuum leak.
High	High	Rough idle. Black smoke from tailpipe.	1. Restricted air filter. 2. PCV system restricted. 3. Improper carburetion. a. Idle air-fuel mixture too rich. b. Leaking needle and seat. c. Leaky power valve. d. Wrong float setting. e. Faulty choke action.

Figure 17 Idle-speed exhaust-emissions trouble-diagnosis chart. *(Ford Motor Company.)*

On vehicles with an exhaust pipe welded to the catalytic converter, the analyzer probe cannot be inserted into the exhaust system ahead of the converter. Some technicians suggest that approximate engine-emission levels can be obtained for comparison as follows: Remove the EGR valve without disconnecting its vacuum hose. Plug the EGR intake-manifold port (see Fig. 11). Insert the analyzer probe into the EGR exhaust-gas port (Fig. 11). Start the engine, and let it idle while quickly taking HC and CO readings. The EGR-port readings indicate the emission levels of the exhaust gas coming directly from the engine.

NOTE: HC and CO checks at the EGR port are only indicators of engine exhaust-emission levels. The probe does not always enter far enough to provide very accurate readings.

■ 2-3-39 Servicing Precautions for Catalyst-Equipped Cars

Manufacturers recommend that the following servicing and operating precautions be observed for vehicles equipped with catalytic converters:

1. Avoid prolonged idling, especially at fast idle after a cold start.

2. Do not attempt to start a car equipped with a catalytic converter by pushing or towing. Use another battery and jumper cables.

3. Avoid excessively prolonged cranking with an intermittently firing or flooded engine.

4. Avoid operating an engine under load if it is missing.

5. The use of liquid engine or carburetor cleaners, which are injected directly into the carburetor, is not recommended.

6. Do not turn off the ignition with the vehicle in motion.

7. Use only unleaded gasoline. Never use low-lead or leaded gasoline.

8. Avoid running out of gasoline while the engine is operating or while driving on the highway, especially at high speed. This may damage the converter.

9. Do not use engine or ignition replacement parts which

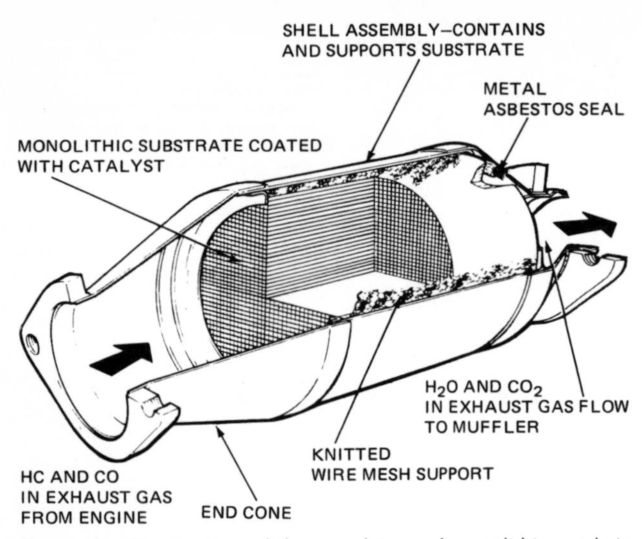

Figure 18 Construction of the round type of monolithic catalytic converter used by Ford. *(Ford Motor Company.)*

are not certified, recommended, or approved as being equivalent to original equipment. The installation of non-original-equipment parts may be a violation of the antitampering provision of the Clean Air Act.

10. Do not pump the accelerator to start a hot engine that has stalled.

11. When raising or lowering the car on a hoist, be sure all hoist arms and other equipment are properly positioned to avoid damaging the converter and other undercar components. If the hoist makes contact with any part of the car other than the proper lift points, check all underbody components for physical damage and clearance before operating the vehicle.

12. A vehicle with a catalytic converter does not require extra time to cool down, but the converter does. With its heavier mass and insulation, the converter cools more slowly than the muffler.

13. When operating an engine equipped with a catalytic converter in a shop, use normal procedures to vent the engine exhaust gas to the outside with shop exhaust fans.

14. Cylinder balance tests and starting-motor tests can be performed in the same way as on cars without converters.

15. Do not run an engine more than 30 seconds with more than one spark-plug wire removed. The resulting overrich mixture may damage the converter. If possible, use an oscilloscope for ignition-system checks.

■ 2-3-40 Servicing the Catalytic Converter

The catalytic converter requires no service or maintenance in normal operation. By law, new-car manufacturers warranty catalytic converters to last for 5 years or 50,000 miles (80,467 km), whichever comes first, in normal usage. The converters used by American Motors Corporation and General Motors have a drain hole in the front bottom of the converter, for removing and replacing the pellets. The procedure is covered in ■ 2-3-42. Defective catalytic converters on Chrysler and Ford cars require installation of a new converter. A cutaway view of the round type of monolithic catalytic converter used by Ford is shown in Fig. 18. The catalyst in it cannot be replaced. Figure 19 shows an exploded view of the monolithic converter used by Chrysler. Like the Ford converter, the Chrysler converter must be replaced if it becomes defective or damaged.

No special tools are needed to replace a catalytic converter. Many converters can be removed by raising the vehicle on a hoist and disconnecting the converter at the front and rear. When installing the new converter, use new nuts and bolts. Other converters have the exhaust pipe attached to the converter inlet. To replace the converter, cut the pipe.

If the bottom cover of a catalytic converter on a General Motors car is bulged, distorted, torn, or damaged, the cover can be replaced with the converter on the car. A repair kit is available from General Motors dealers. However, if the inner shell of the converter is damaged, the converter must be replaced. When heat damage to the converter is indicated (bulging and distortion), inspect the remainder of the exhaust system for damage also. Unless the catalytic converter has a hole in it, or the converter pipe clamps are loose, exhaust-system noise is not the fault of the catalytic converter. Catalytic converters provide virtually no sound deadening. Cars equipped with catalytic converters use conventional mufflers to control exhaust noise.

The use of fuel additives is not recommended on cars equipped with catalytic converters. The additive may harm the catalyst. Before using any fuel additive, either in the fuel tank or in the carburetor, check that the additive is approved for use in cars with catalytic converters. Reasonable use of starting fluid will not harm the catalyst, according to General Motors.

■ 2-3-41 Servicing the Converter Heat Shields

Notice the upper and lower heat shields in Fig 19. During the chemical reaction in the catalytic converter, when the exhaust gas passes over the catalyst, the exhaust-gas temperature may rise to 1,600°F (871°C). Therefore, cars equipped with catalytic converters have heat shields and insulation pads to protect chassis components and the passenger-compartment floor from heat damage.

On some Chrysler cars, aluminized-steel heat shields are installed so that air passing rearward under the car (the road draft) carries away the heat. Interior insulating pads are placed under the carpet in the passenger compartment. They prevent the floor from becoming uncomfortably hot and heating the passenger compartment. General Motors requires a minimum floor-pan-to-exhaust-system clearance of ⅝ inch (16 mm) at all points. Any floor covering and insulation pads that are removed during service must be reinstalled. If any components located in the vicinity of the exhaust system are moved during service, or as a result of a collision, they must be replaced in their original position. This is especially important with regard to wiring harnesses and fuel and brake lines.

The lower heat shield (Fig. 19) provides added protection against road hazards and helps prevent such objects from puncturing the converter.

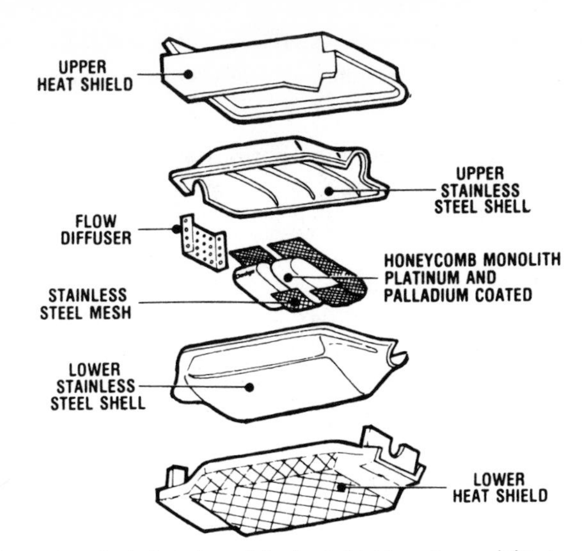

Figure 19 Exploded view of the heat shields and monolithic type of catalytic converter used by Chrysler. *(Chrysler Corporation.)*

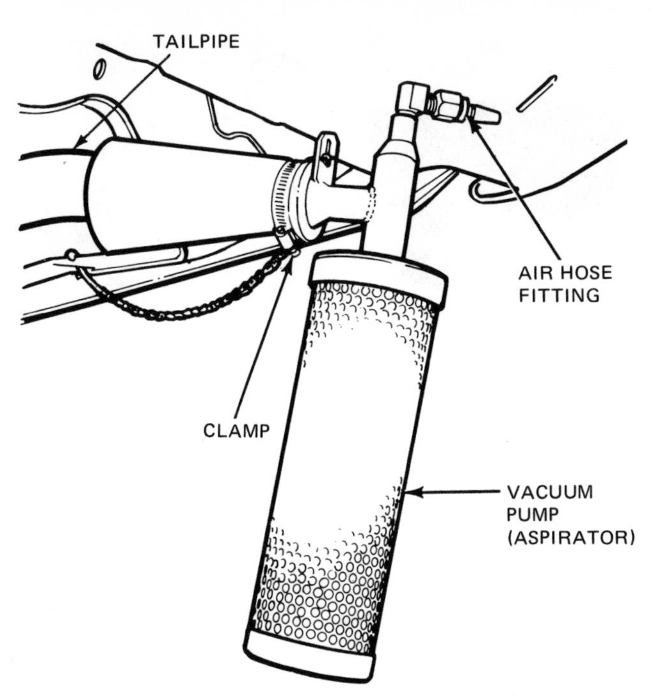

Figure 20 Vacuum pump, or aspirator, mounted on the tail pipe of a car in readiness to change the beads in a pellet-type catalytic converter. *(American Motors Corporation.)*

NOTE: Rustproofing and undercoating must be kept off the heat shields. These coatings reduce the efficiency of the shields in carrying away heat, and cause strong, objectionable odors.

While the catalytic converter requires no periodic maintenance, Ford recommends an inspection of the exhaust-system heat shields every 15 months or 15,000 miles (24,140 km), whichever comes first. The exhaust system should be checked for broken welds, damage, and deterioration. All debris should be removed. If a shield is missing, torn, or ripped, it must be replaced. Remove the damaged shield by carefully chiseling the shield loose at its welds. Whenever the vehicle has been operated on gravel roads, in off-road use, or under severe road-load conditions, Ford recommends a shield inspection at 5,000-mile (8,047) intervals.

■ **2-3-42 Replacing Catalyst Beads** The catalyst beads in the pellet-type catalytic converter can be changed. However, there is no scheduled maintenance for the converter. It is designed to last for the life of the car, in normal operation. If a car has high HC and CO levels, and the engine emission controls are operating to specifications, the catalyst beads may be spoiled and need replacement. The beads can be replaced with the converter in place on the car. For this, a special vibrator and vacuum pump (called an "aspirator" by General Motors) are used (Figs. 20 and 21).

To remove the catalyst beads, raise the car on a hoist. Separate hoses should be available to attach to the vacuum pump and vibrator. Minimum shop air pressure should be at least 80 psi (5.62 km/cm^2). Install the vacuum pump tightly to the tail pipe of the car. If the car has two tail pipes, attach the vacuum pump to one tail pipe (Fig. 20) and place a plug in the other tail pipe. Connect the shop air line to the vacuum pump. The

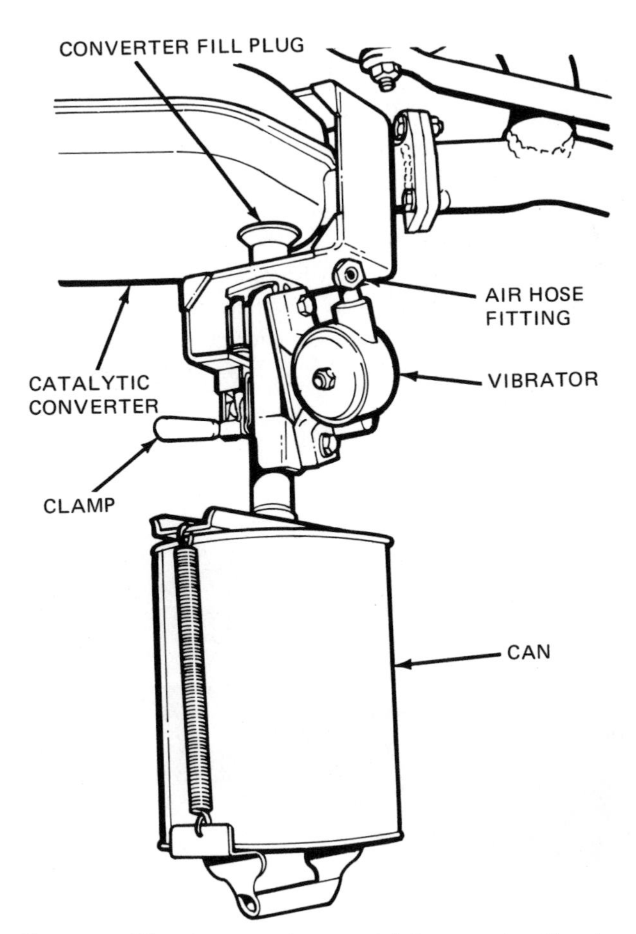

Figure 21 Vibrator mounted on a catalytic converter. *(American Motors Corporation.)*

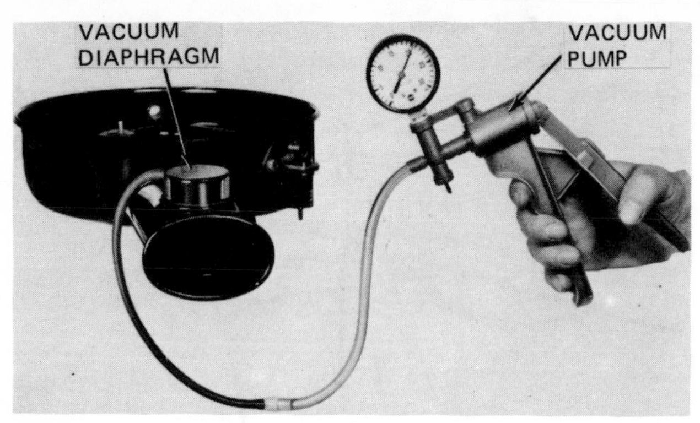

Figure 22 Testing the vacuum motor on a thermostatically controlled air cleaner. *(Chrysler Corporation.)*

vacuum pump creates a vacuum in the converter that holds the beads in place when the converter fill plug is removed. Use a ¾-inch (19-mm) hex wrench to remove the fill plug.

Clamp the vibrator in place on the converter, with the upper tube inside the fill-plug opening (Fig. 21). Remove the fill-tube extension, and install the empty can on the vibrator. Disconnect the air supply to the vacuum pump. Connect the air supply to the vibrator. Now, as the vibrator shakes the converter, catalyst beads will drain from the converter into the can attached to the vibrator. It takes about 10 minutes for the converter to empty. Then discard the used catalyst beads.

To install new catalyst beads, first fill the can on the vibrator with new approved replacement beads. Install the fill-tube extension on the vibrator. Connect the shop air hoses to the vacuum pump and to the vibrator. Attach the can of catalyst to the vibrator. Beads will start flowing into the converter. After the beads stop flowing, disconnect the air hose to the vibrator. Remove the upper tube of the vibrator from the fill-plug opening, and check that the beads have filled the converter flush with the fill-plug hole. Add more catalyst, if required. Apply antiseize compound to the fill plug, and install it. Tighten the fill plug to a torque of 50 pound-feet (6.91 kg-m). Disconnect the air supply to the aspirator, remove it, and lower the car.

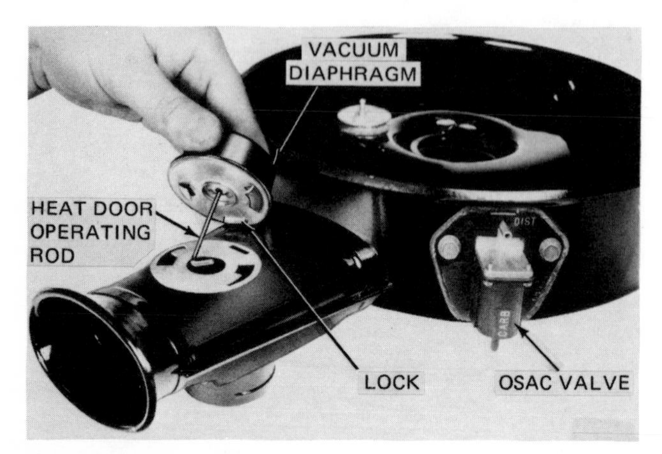

Figure 23 Replacing the vacuum motor on a thermostatically controlled air cleaner. *(Chrysler Corporation.)*

■ **2-3-43 Servicing the Thermostatically Controlled Air Cleaner** To check the system, first make sure the hoses and heat pipe are tightly connected. See that there are no leaks in the system. The system can be checked with a thermometer. Failure of the thermostatic system usually results in the damper door staying open. This means that the driver will probably not notice anything wrong in warm weather. But, in cold weather, the driver will notice hesitation, surge, and stalling. A typical checking procedure follows.

Remove the air-cleaner cover. Install the thermometer as close to the sensor as possible. Allow the engine to cool below 85°F (29.4°C) if it is hot. Replace the air-cleaner cover without the wing nut.

Start and idle the engine. When the damper begins to open, remove the air-cleaner cover, and note the temperature reading. It should be between 85 and 115°F (29.4 and 46.1°C). If it is difficult to see the damper, use a mirror.

If the damper does not open at the correct temperature, check the vacuum motor and sensor.

With the engine off, the control damper should be in the compartment or cold-air-delivery position. To determine if the vacuum motor is operating, apply at least 9 inches Hg (228.6 mm Hg) of vacuum to the fitting on the vacuum motor (Fig. 22). The vacuum can be from the engine, from a distributor tester, or from a hand vacuum pump (Fig. 22). With vacuum applied, the damper should move to the hot-air-delivery position.

If the vacuum motor does not work satisfactorily, it should be replaced (Fig. 23). This can be done by drilling out the spot welds and unhooking the linkage. The new motor can be installed with a retaining strap and sheet-metal screws. Other types of vacuum motors have locking tabs which disengage and engage when the vacuum motor is rotated (Fig. 23).

If the vacuum motor does work well, the sensor should be replaced (Fig. 24) This is done by prying up the tabs on the retaining clip. The new sensor is then installed, and the tabs are bent down again.

■ **2-3-44 Servicing the Early-Fuel-Evaporation (EFE) System** The EFE system is a vacuum-operated manifold heat-control valve. By using vacuum control of the manifold heat valve, the EFE system provides heat quickly to warm the intake manifold when the car is driven cold. Rapid heating is needed for early fuel evaporation and even distribution of the air-fuel mixture. This improves cold-engine driveability.

Ford recommends lubricating and checking the heat-control valve every 30 months or 30,000 miles (48,280 km), whichever comes first. The exposed ends of the valve shaft are lubricated with graphite lube, or approved heat-valve lubricant—never with grease or oil. General Motors recommends checking the EFE valve 6 months or 7,500 miles (12,070 km) after sale of the car, and every 18 months or 22,500 miles (36,210 km) thereafter.

Figure 24 Replacing the temperature sensor in a thermostatically controlled air cleaner. *(Chrysler Corporation.)*

You can make a quick test of the EFE valve with the engine cold. Have someone start the engine while you watch the actuator arm. The arm should move and the valve should close. If the valve does not close, remove the hose from the EFE valve. Check it for vacuum by placing your finger over the open end. If vacuum is felt, check the EFE valve. Apply a vacuum of more than 8 inches Hg (203.2 mm Hg), using a hand pump or other vacuum source. The valve should close. If it does, the EFE valve is okay. If it does not close, be sure the valve shaft is free of deposits and lubricated. Then test the valve again. If the valve does not close now, replace it.

If you do not feel a vacuum when you place your finger over the end of the EFE-valve vacuum hose, be sure the engine is cold. Check the hoses and the vacuum switch to locate the cause of no vacuum to the EFE valve when the engine is cold.

SECTION 2-4 Used-Car Smog Devices

Many kits and devices, now available, enable you to reduce the emissions from older cars. These devices are called "retrofit" devices, or used-car smog devices. California requires the installation of certain of these devices to control crankcase emissions, and of other devices to control exhaust emissions. Under California law, any 1955 or later-model car must have a PCV system. Also, any 1955 through 1965 model must have a device to control exhaust emissions of HC and CO. In addition, California requires 1966 through 1970 cars to have a device that controls NO_x exhaust emissions.

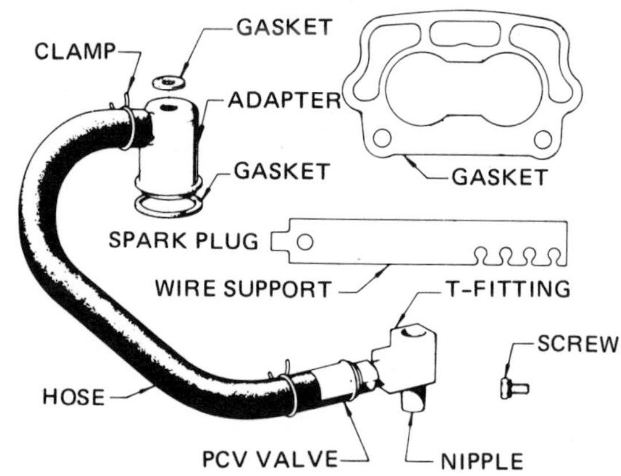

Figure 1 Kit for installing a positive crankcase ventilation system on an engine. *(AC-Delco Division of General Motors Corporation.)*

■ **2-4-1 Crankcase Devices for Used Cars** The road-draft tube was generally used to ventilate the crankcases of passenger-car engines built through 1960. In 1961, automobile manufacturers installed the open PCV system on cars made for sale in California; beginning in 1963, all cars used this system. This system became standard on 1968 and all later cars produced in the United States.

To install a PCV system on a car with a road-draft tube, purchase, at your local auto-parts store, a PCV kit that fits the year, make, and model of engine in the car. Each kit contains the proper gaskets, hose, hardware, and PCV valve, along with detailed installation instructions for that particular engine. Most PCV kits simply bolt in.

To install the kit shown in Fig. 1, remove the road-draft tube from the engine. In its place, bolt in the adapter shown in the upper left of Fig. 1. Use the bolt and washer from the road-draft tube. On some engines, you must reroute the spark-plug wires. In this case, install the new spark-plug-wire support from the kit, and discard the old one from the engine. Remove the carburetor from the engine, and discard the gasket. Clean the gasket surfaces on the carburetor and intake manifold.

At the rear of the carburetor throttle body, there is a vacuum fitting. Remove it. Install the new nipple in the new T fitting from the kit (Fig. 1). Screw the nipple into the carburetor throttle body. Now install the old vacuum fitting (which was removed from the throttle body) into the opening in the T fitting. Assemble the PCV valve from the kit into the side opening of the T (Fig. 1), and tighten the valve.

Place the new gasket on the intake manifold. Install the carburetor and all lines and linkages that were removed. Then connect and clamp the hose from the adapter to the PCV valve. Operation of this system may be checked with the PCV-system testers discussed in Sec. 2 of this part.

PCV installation kits are not all exactly alike. On engines without an accessible source of intake-manifold vacuum, a hole must be drilled into the manifold and a fitting installed.

Other kits use a spacer with a vacuum port that you install between the carburetor and the manifold to obtain a vacuum source.

An open PCV system can be made into a closed system by installing a closed breather cap and adding a tube from the cap to the air cleaner. If you have to add a tube to the air cleaner, purchase, at your local auto-parts store, a closed-crankcase ventilation kit, or an air-cleaner kit, for the year, make, and model of engine in the car. The kit will contain a new closed breather cap that is not vented to the outside air. The cap has a nipple on it, which allows the crankcase vapors to pass through. By connecting a hose from the nipple on the new cap to a suitable connector on the air cleaner, you close the PCV system. Figure 2 shows a typical air-cleaner kit installed on an engine.

Also in the kit are the connector for installation on the air cleaner and a paper template to show you where to drill the holes. Some connectors mount on the clean-air side, or inside, of the air filter. Others mount on the outside, or dirty-air side, of the filter. Follow the instructions in the kit. You must remove any supplementary or external rocker-arm oil system from the engine. This is necessary to prevent excess oil consumption once the kit is installed.

When installing the kit, be careful not to obstruct the airflow through the hose with sharp bends. Make sure that the hose does not interfere with the carburetor linkage. To install the air-cleaner kit, replace the old breather cap with the new cap. Locate the connector on the air cleaner, and mark the best position to avoid interference with any other linkage or hose on the engine. Then remove the air cleaner, and drill the holes for the connector. Install the connector, using the gasket and screws from the kit. Service the air cleaner as recommended by the car manufacturer, and then reinstall it on the engine. Install the hose from the kit between the nipple on the new breather cap and the connector you installed on the air cleaner. If the hose is too long, shorten it to keep water from collecting in low spots.

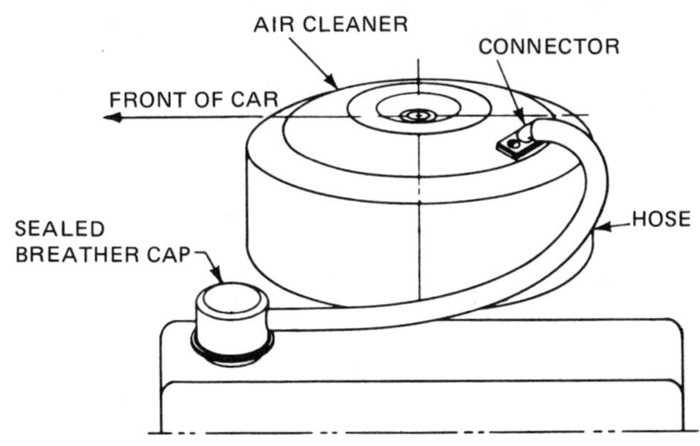

Figure 2 Hose routing and connections after installing a tube-to-air-cleaner kit. *(AC-Delco Division of General Motors Corporation.)*

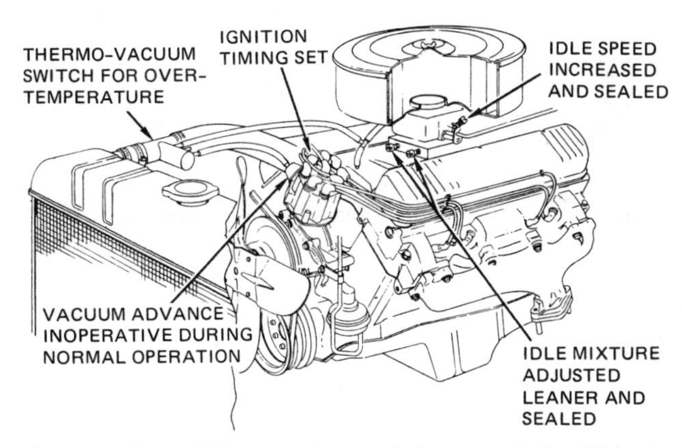

Figure 3 General Motors exhaust-emission control kit which can be installed on 1955 to 1965 model used cars. *(General Motors Corporation.)*

■ 2-4-2 Exhaust-Emission Control Devices for 1955 to 1965 Vehicles

New cars built during the years 1955 through 1965 had no exhaust-emission controls. In 1972, Los Angeles and other municipalities in California began to require installation of exhaust-emission control devices on these cars. Hydrocarbons and nitrogen oxides combine in the presence of sunlight to form photochemical smog. Reducing the amount of HC and NO_x emitted by 1955 to 1965 model cars reduces smog and improves air quality. We shall discuss two different types of devices used to control exhaust emissions on 1955 to 1965 cars. They are the General Motors device and the device manufactured by Air Quality Products.

Installation of the General Motors device requires leaning out of the idle mixture and elimination of the distributor vacuum advance under normal operating conditions. Figure 3 shows the features of this device. It calls for increased idle speed, a leaner idle mixture, and setting of the ignition timing. The thermovacuum switch is connected into the hose at the top of the radiator tank. It has one purpose—to permit vacuum advance in case the engine begins to overheat. During normal operation, the thermovacuum switch blocks off the vacuum line between the intake manifold and the ignition distributor. However, as the engine approaches an overheating condition, a wax pellet inside the switch begins to expand. As it does, it moves a plunger to open the line between the intake manifold and the ignition distributor. Now, vacuum advance increases engine speed so engine temperature falls. This, in turn, shrinks the wax pellet and moves the plunger to close the line to the distributor. Now, vacuum advance is eliminated.

The General Motors exhaust-emission control device is designed to reduce exhaust emissions from an engine under normal operating conditions. The device does not improve engine performance or economy. Do not install the kit on an engine with major problems, such as dead cylinders or misfiring spark plugs, unless the owner is willing to have the engine problems corrected. The General Motors kit can be used on vehicles with gross vehicle weight (GVW) of 6,001 pounds (2,722 kg) or less, and engines with over 140 cubic inches (2,294 cc) of displacement. General Motors does not recommend installing this kit on 1966 and 1967 California model

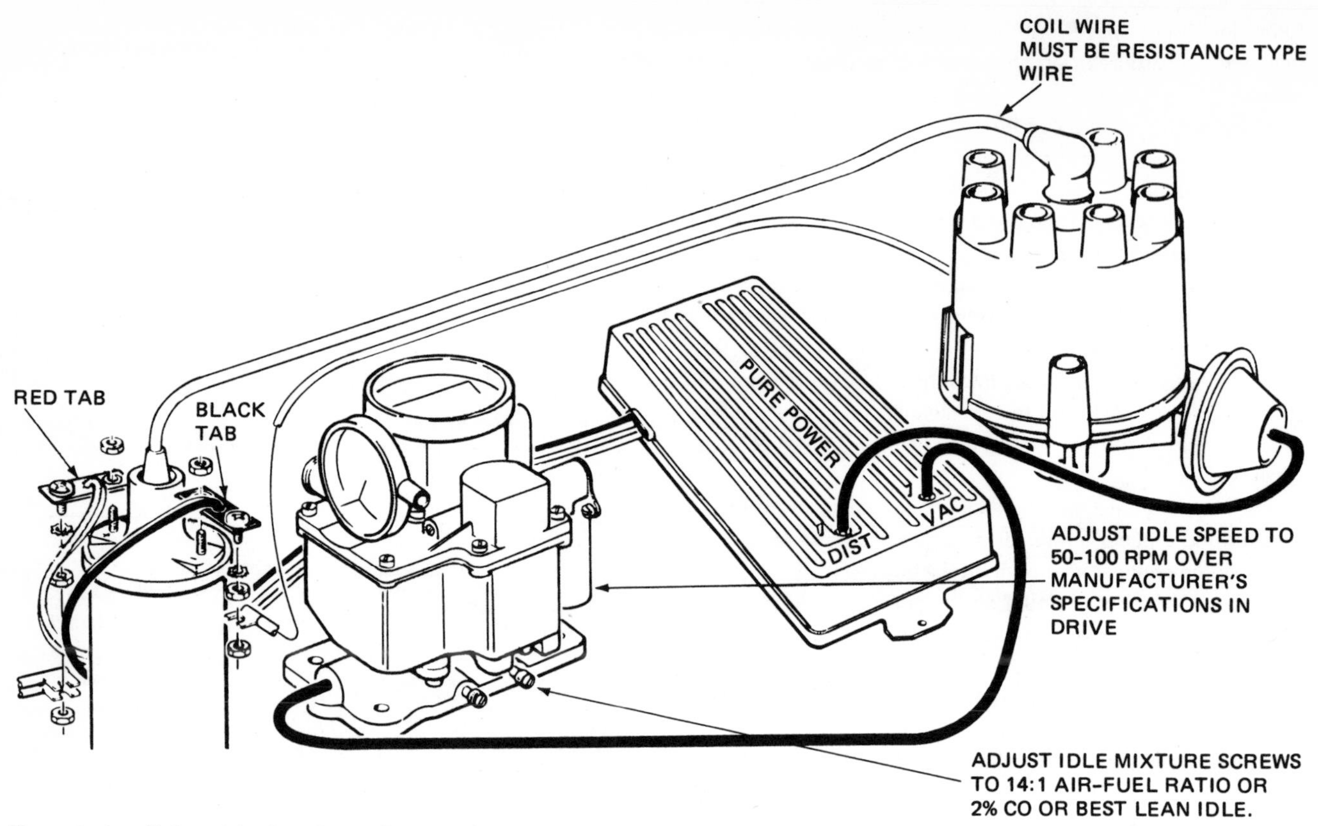

Figure 4 Installation of the Pure Power device on the engine. *(Air Quality Products, Inc.)*

cars, or on any 1968 or later models with factory-installed exhaust-emissions control systems. The kit is not to be installed on engines that use a distributor without a centrifugal-advance mechanism.

Air Quality Products, Inc., manufactures an exhaust-emission control device for 1955 to 1965 cars equipped with six-cylinder or eight-cylinder engines (Fig. 4). This device combines a capacitive-discharge electronic ignition system with a cutoff of the distributor vacuum advance between about 900 and 1,800 rpm. Normal vacuum spark advance is restored at higher speeds, and there is some additional retarding of the spark timing at low speeds. In addition, a lean idle mixture and a fast idle-speed adjustment are used with the device (Fig. 4).

The device mounts under the hood, usually on the fender well near the distributor. The engine is first set to specifications. Then the two vacuum hoses are connected as shown in Fig. 4. All wires are removed from the battery terminal of the coil and attached to the small red tab of the device. All wires are removed from the distributor terminal of the coil and attached to the black tab of the device. Then the red tab is installed on the coil battery terminal, and the black tab on the coil distributor terminal. This completes the installation.

■ 2-4-3 NO_x Exhaust-Emission Control Devices

The exhaust-emission control devices that were factory-installed on most 1966 to 1970 model cars controlled HC and CO. However, these early devices caused an increase of NO_x from the engine. In 1973, to roll back the NO_x emissions to the level of 1965 and earlier cars, California began to require installation of an NO_x exhaust-emission control device on 1966 to 1970 model cars. Several different types of devices are available. Some reduce NO_x emissions by disconnecting the distributor vacuum advance. Other devices provide for exhaust-gas recirculation to control NO_x formation. The Air Quality Products device discussed in ■ 2-4-2 can also be used on 1966 to 1970 cars.

■ 2-4-4 Evaporative Controls for Auxiliary Fuel Tanks

The owners of light trucks—trucks with a gross vehicle weight (GVW) of 6,001 pounds (2,722 kg) or less—often have auxiliary fuel tanks installed. In past years, these auxiliary fuel tanks were vented to the atmosphere. However, beginning in 1974, California required that only approved auxiliary fuel tanks with evaporative control systems be installed on vehicles having factory-installed evaporative control systems as original equipment.

Two different types of auxiliary fuel-tank installations are possible. One type connects the auxiliary fuel tank to the charcoal canister for the evaporative control system on the vehicle. This system can be used when the combined capacity of the standard fuel tank and the auxiliary fuel tank does not exceed 50 gallons (189 liters). The other system requires installation of a second charcoal canister to store vapors from the auxiliary fuel tank. The second canister should be used when the total capacity of both tanks exceeds 50 gallons (189 liters), but does not exceed 100 gallons (378 liters). For each additional 50 gallons (189 liters) of fuel-tank capacity, the fuel vapors must be vented to a 500- or 625-grams-capacity charcoal canister.

SECTION 2-5 Engine Tuneup

This section describes the procedure known as engine tuneup. Tuneup includes testing the various components and accessory systems involved in engine operation. It also includes readjusting or replacing parts as required to restore engine performance. Sometimes, a tuneup will uncover serious problems that require major repair work. Other parts in this Handbook describe many of the service jobs that are performed during an engine tuneup.

■ **2-5-1 What Is Tuneup?** Engine tuneup means different things to different people. To some, it means a quick onceover check of the obvious trouble spots in an engine. To others, it means use of the proper test instruments to do a careful, complete analysis of all engine components. In addition, it means adjusting everything to specifications and repairing or replacing all worn parts. The latter is the proper meaning of engine tuneup. It is the basis for the procedure outlined in this section.

NOTE: In this section, we combine two separate programs: engine tuneup and complete car-care inspection. Engine tuneup includes checking and servicing the engine and its systems. Car-care inspection includes checking all other components on the car, such as brakes, steering, and tires. Together, engine tuneup and car-care inspection cover most things in and on the car that could cause trouble.

See the other parts in this Handbook for the details of servicing automotive components other than the engine.

■ **2-5-2 Tuneup Procedures** An engine tuneup follows a procedure. Many mechanics use a printed form supplied by automotive or test-equipment manufacturers. The mechanic follows the form and checks off the listed items, one by one. This ensures that every part of the procedure is performed. However, not all tuneup forms are the same. Different companies have different ideas about what should be done, and the order in which it should be done. In addition, the tuneup procedure depends on the equipment available. If the shop has an oscilloscope or a dynamometer, it is used as part of the tuneup procedure. If these test instruments are not available, then the tuneup is performed differently.

The procedure that follows includes car-care inspection. It lists essential checks and adjustments in logical sequence.

■ **2-5-3 Tuneup and Car Care** The tuneup procedure restores driveability, power, and performance that have been lost through wear, corrosion, and deterioration of engine parts. Such changes take place gradually in many parts, during normal car operation. Because of federal and state laws limiting automotive emissions, the tuneup procedure must include checks of all emission controls. Here is the procedure.

1. If the engine is cold, operate it for at least 20 minutes at 1,500 rpm, or until it reaches operating temperature.

2. Connect the oscilloscope, if available, and perform an electronic diagnosis. Check for any abnormal ignition-system conditions that appear on the pattern. Make a note of any abnormality and the cylinder(s) in which it appears.

3. Remove all spark plugs. Fully open the throttle and choke valves. Disconnect the distributor lead from the coil primary terminal to prevent engine starting.

4. Check the compression of each cylinder. Record the readings. If one or more cylinders read low, squirt about a tablespoon of engine oil into the spark-plug hole. Recheck the compression. Record the new readings.

NOTE: If the compression is low, indicating either bad rings or valves, tell the owner the engine is not tunable without overhaul or repair.

5. Clean, inspect, file, gap, and test the spark plugs. Discard worn or defective plugs. (Many shops install new plugs instead of servicing the old ones.) Gap all plugs, old and new. Install the plugs.

6. Inspect and clean the battery case, terminals, cables, and hold-down brackets. Test the battery. Add water, if necessary. If severe corrosion is present, clean the battery and cables with brushes and a solution of baking soda and water.

7. Test the starting voltage. If the battery is in good condition but cranking speed is low, test the starting system.

8. If the battery is low or the customer complains that the battery keeps running down, check the charging system (alternator and regulator). If the battery is old, it may have worn out. A new battery is required.

9. Check the drive belts, and replace any that are in poor condition. If you have to replace one belt of a two-belt drive, replace both belts. Tighten the belts to the correct tension, using a belt-tension gauge.

10. Inspect the distributor rotor and cap, and the primary and high-voltage (spark-plug) wires.

11. Clean or replace the distributor contact points. Adjust the points (by setting the point gap). Lubricate the distributor breaker cam if specifications call for this. On distributors with round cam lubricator, turn the cam lubricator 180° every 12, 000 miles (19,312 km). Replace the cam lubricator every 24, 000 miles (38,624 km).

12. Check the distributor cap and rotor. Check the centrifugal and vacuum advances. Set the contact dwell, and then adjust the ignition timing. Make sure the idle speed is not excessive. This could produce centrifugal advance during timing adjustment.

13. Use the oscilloscope to recheck the ignition system. Any abnormal conditions that appeared in step 2 should now have been eliminated.

14. Check the manifold heat-control valve. Lubricate it with heat-valve lubricant. Free up or replace the valve if necessary.

15. Check the fuel-pump operation with a fuel-pump tester. Replace the fuel filter. Check the fuel-tank cap, fuel lines, and connections for leakage and damage.

16. Clean or replace the air-cleaner filter. If the engine is equipped with a thermostatically controlled air cleaner, check the operation of the control damper.

17. Check the operation of the choke and the fast-idle cam. Check the throttle valve for full opening, and the throttle linkage for free movement.

18. Inspect all engine vacuum fittings, hoses, and connections. Replace any brittle or cracked hose.

19. Clean the engine oil-filler cap if a filter-type oil-filler cap is used.

20. Check the cooling system. Inspect all hoses and connections and the radiator, water pump, and fan clutch (if used). Check the strength of the coolant, and record the reading. Pressure-check the cooling system and radiator cap. Squeeze the hoses to check them. Replace any defective hose (collapsed, soft, cracked, etc.).

21. Check and replace the PCV valve if necessary. Clean or replace the PCV filter, if required. Inspect the PCV hoses and connections. Replace any cracked or brittle hose.

22. If the engine is equipped with an air-pump type of exhaust-emission control, replace the pump inlet air filter (if used). Inspect the system hoses and connections. Replace any brittle or cracked hose.

23. If the vehicle is equipped with a fuel-vapor recovery system, replace the charcoal-canister filter.

24. Check the transmission-controlled vacuum spark-advance system, if the vehicle is so equipped.

25. On engines equipped with an EGR system, inspect and clean the EGR valve. Inspect and clean the EGR discharge port.

26. Tighten the intake-manifold and exhaust-manifold bolts to the proper tension in the proper sequence.

27. Adjust the engine valves, if necessary.

28. Adjust the carburetor idle speed. Use an exhaust-gas analyzer to adjust the idle-mixture screw. Check the amounts of CO and HC in the exhaust gas. (Many mechanics check the CO and HC both before and after the tuneup to show how much the tuneup has reduced these pollutants.)

29. Road-test the car on a dynamometer or on the road. Check for driveability, power, and idling. Note any abnormal condition on the repair order before you return the car to the customer.

30. Check the door-jamb sticker to determine if oil and oil-filter changes are due. Also note the schedule for chassis lubrication. Recommend an oil change and a chassis lubrication if they are due. Car manufacturers recommend changing the oil filter every other time the oil is changed.

31. Whenever the car is on the lift, check the exhaust system for leaks which could admit CO into the car. Also check for loose bolts, rust spots, and other under-the-car damage.

NOTE: Items 32 to 37 that follow are not actually part of the tuneup job. They are included here so you will have the complete car-care program all in one place.

32. Check the brakes for even braking and adequate braking power.

33. Check the steering system for ease and smoothness of operation. Check for excessive play in the system. Record any abnormal conditions.

34. Check the tires for inflation and for abnormal wear. Abnormal wear can mean suspension trouble; for this, a front-end alignment job should be recommended.

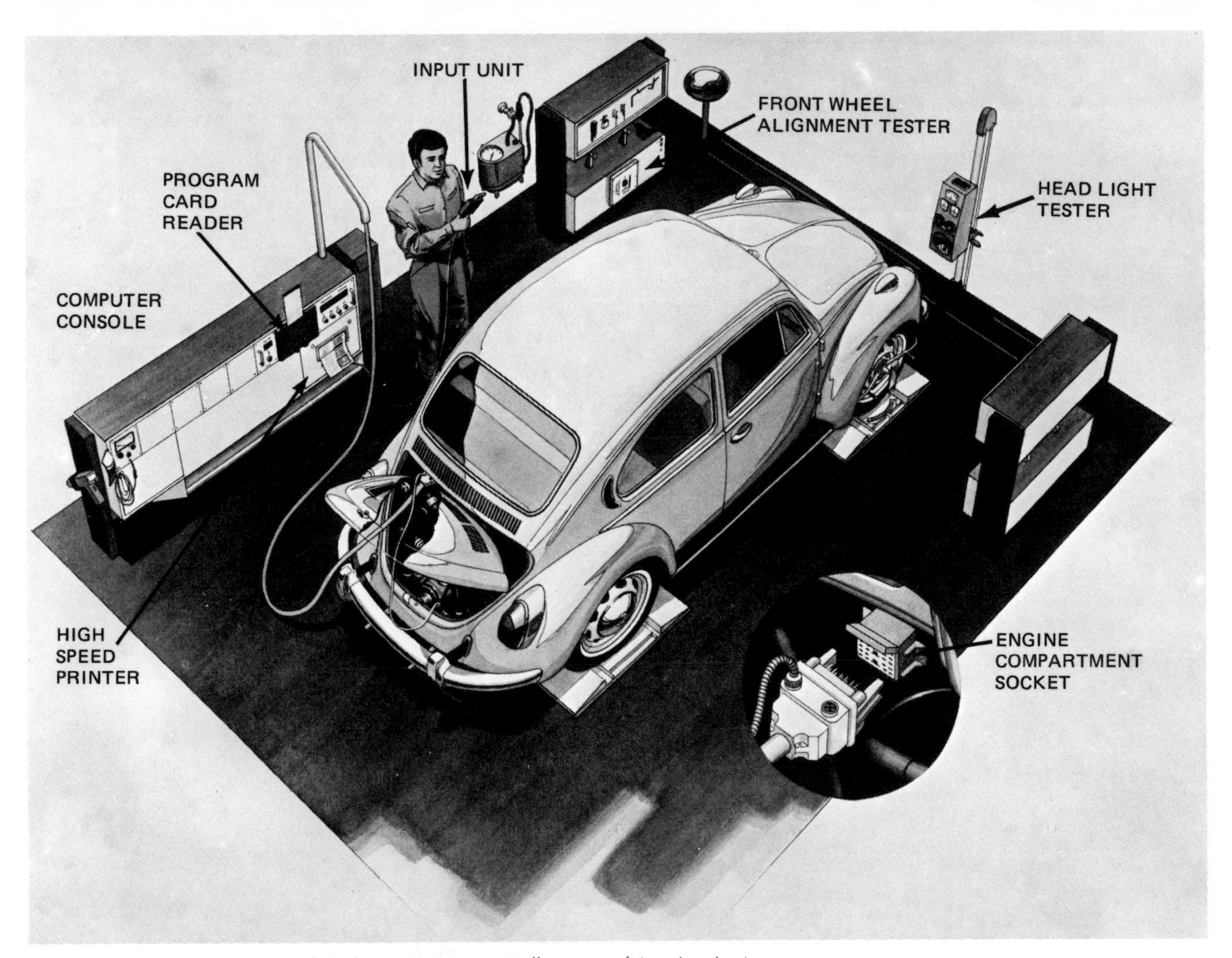

Figure 1 A computerized automobile diagnostic system. *(Volkswagen of America, Inc.)*

35. Check the suspension system for looseness, excessive play, and wear.

36. Check the front wheels and ball joints for excessive wear and loose bearings. Adjust the bearings, if necessary.

37. Check the headlights and horns to make sure they are in good working order. Check all other lights. Replace any burned-out lights. Check headlight alignment, if possible.

> **NOTE:** The preceding tuneup and car-care procedure covers about everything on the vehicle that could cause trouble. The complete procedure will uncover most problems that might affect driveability and performance. If all necessary corrections are made, good performance will be restored to the vehicle.

■ 2-5-4 Engine Analyzers and Computer Testers

An oscilloscope and other instruments are used for making comprehensive tests of all engine components. Once you learn how to use this equipment, you can perform a complete engine analysis in a very short time.

In addition, there are testers that run many of the tests almost

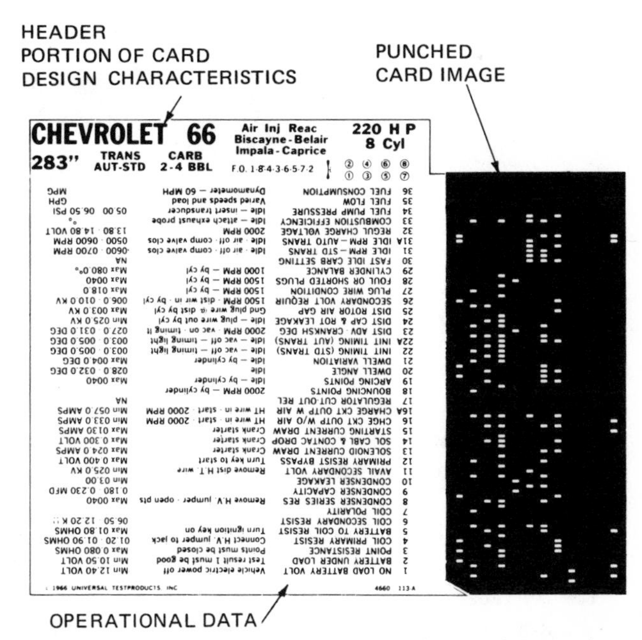

Figure 2 Computer program card listing the specifications for a certain car. *(Universal Test-products, Incorporated.)*

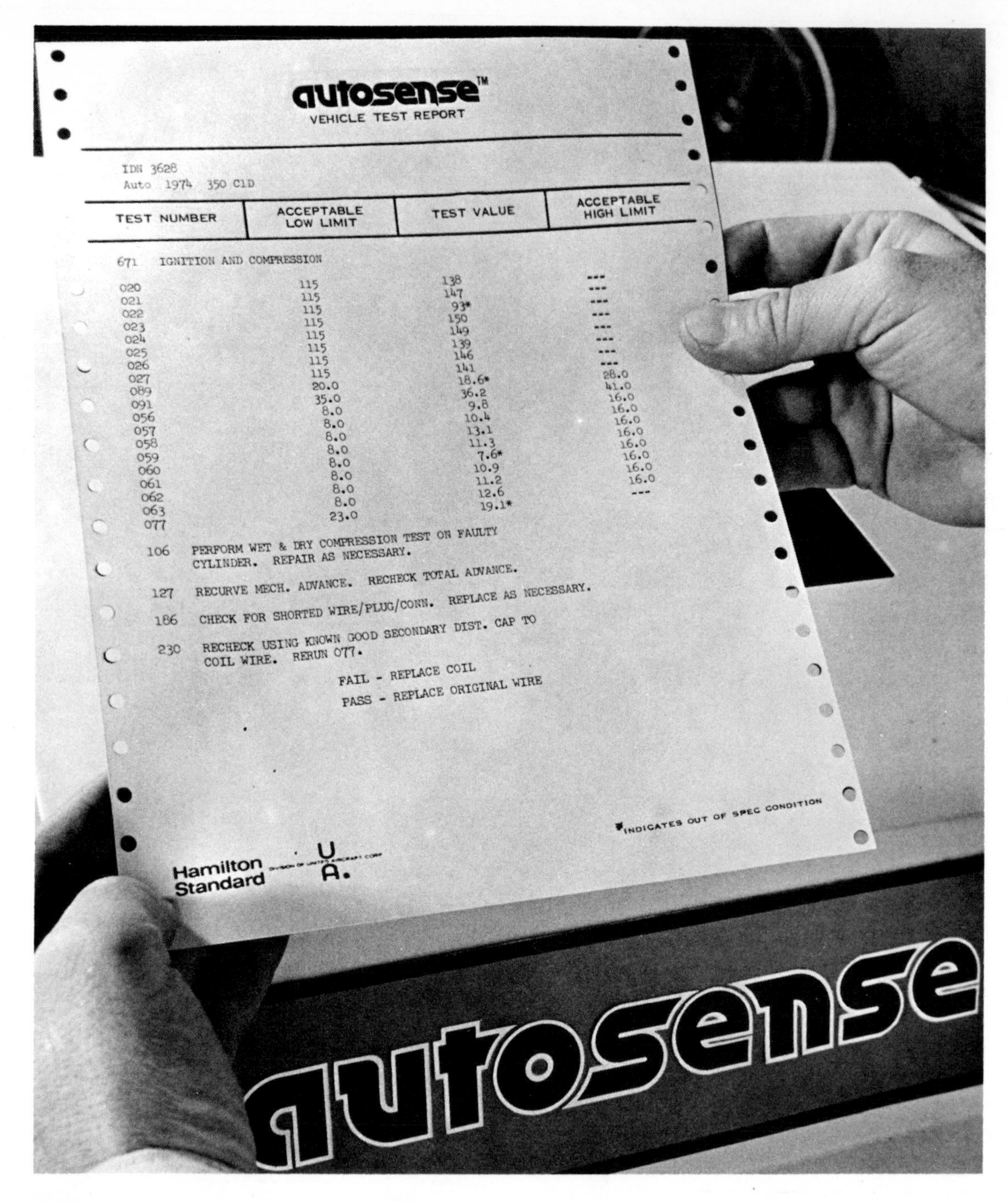

Figure 3 The computer printout tells the mechanic and the customer what work is needed. *(Hamilton Standard Division of United Aircraft Corporation.)*

automatically. They produce a printed record of the tests and the test results.

Figure 1 shows a computerized diagnostic system introduced by Volkswagen. Wiring and sensors built into the car are connected to the computer through a socket in the engine compartment. The system checks more than 70 items. A special program card contains the specifications for the year and model of car being checked. One type of card is shown in Fig. 2. The computer compares the operation of components on the car with values it reads from the program card. The electrical system and engine compression are among the items checked. The results of the tests are recorded by a high-speed printer.

Figure 3 shows the printout from another type of engine diagnostic computer. This printed record tells the mechanic and the customer what work is needed to bring the car up to specifications.

One further refinement has been suggested. This is to put into the computer information on the costs of parts and repair operations. Then the computer could print out, along with the test information, the cost of correcting any troubles. That is, it would print out the cost of parts and labor. The computer

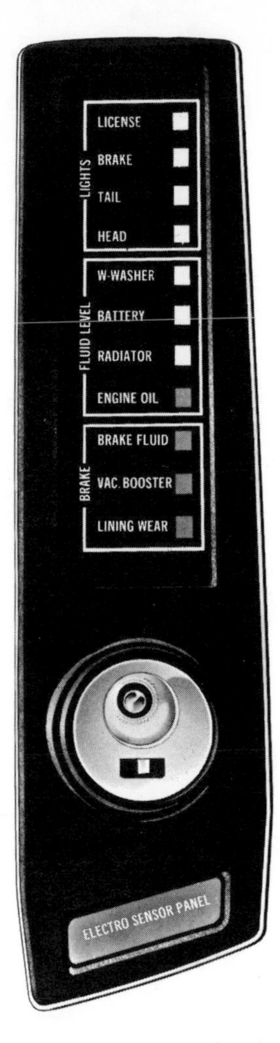

Figure 4 Sensor panel (called the Electro Sensor Panel, or ESP, by the manufacturer). *(Toyota Motor Sales, Limited.)*

Figure 5 Location of the sensor panel in the car. *(Toyota Motor Sales, Limited.)*

Figure 6 Connections from the sensor panel to the 11 service areas. *(Toyota Motor Sales, Limited.)*

might also be programmed to schedule the work, depending on the availability of technicians and space in the shop.

Some car manufacturers are beginning to use on-the-car diagnostic or trouble-indicating devices. One such device is the sensor panel used by Toyota (Fig. 4). This panel is installed on the roof of the car, above the driver (Fig. 5). It is connected to sensors in the light circuits, brakes, windshield washer, battery, cooling-system radiator, and engine crankcase (see Fig. 4). The sensor panel has 11 warning lights to indicate when something needs attention. For example, if any of the four lights at the top of the panel (LICENSE, BRAKE, TAIL, HEAD) come on, it indicates trouble in that light circuit. If one headlight burns out, HEAD comes on to warn the driver of the trouble. The four FLUID LEVEL lights (W-WASHER, BATTERY, RADIATOR, ENGINE OIL) indicate low fluid levels in these four areas. That is, if the car needs engine oil, the ENGINE OIL light comes on. The BRAKE section of the panel warns of low brake fluid, loss of vacuum in the power-brake unit, or excessive brake-lining wear. Figure 6 shows how the 11 warning lights are connected to sensors in the areas they serve.

According to some automotive engineers, the day is coming when a general tuneup procedure, as discussed in this section, will not be used. They see preventive maintenance, as part of a complete vehicle maintenance schedule, evolving to predictive maintenance. That is, on-the-car indicating devices will automatically tell the driver when a part or system is due to fail and needs service.

PART 3 Automotive Electrical Equipment

SECTION 3-1 Electrical Equipment and Systems

This part of the Handbook covers all electrical equipment on the automotive vehicle except the ignition system, which is covered in Part 1, Engine Repair.

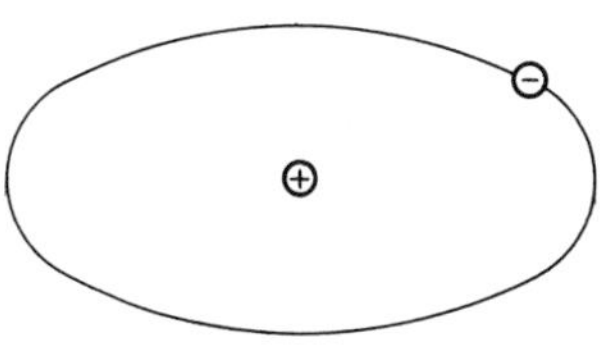

+ MEANS PLUS OR POSITIVE
– MEANS MINUS OR NEGATIVE

Figure 1 The hydrogen atom consists of two particles: a proton with a positive electric charge and an electron with a negative electric charge.

■ **3-1-1 What Electricity Is** What we normally think of as a flow of electricity, or an electric current, is actually a flow of electrons. Electrons are parts of atoms. There are more than 100 varieties of atoms. Each has a special structure and name such as iron, copper, tin, oxygen, nitrogen, and so on. Any substance made up of vast quantities of one of these varieties of atoms is called an element.

Everything in the world is composed of atoms. But they are far too small to be seen, even with the most powerful microscope. Even though atoms cannot be seen, scientists have studied their actions and have been able to work out some clear ideas of how they are constructed. For example, an atom of the gas hydrogen consists of two particles. These are a tiny particle in the center, or nucleus, of the atom and a still smaller particle whirling about the first at terrific speed (Fig. 1). The center, or nucleus, particle is called a "proton." It has a charge of positive electricity. The outer particle is called an "electron." It has a charge of negative electricity.

■ **3-1-2 Electricity and Electrons** The electron in the hydrogen atom is kept whirling in its circular path (or orbit) around the proton by a combination of forces. One force is the attraction that the two oppositely charged particles have for each other. Opposing electric charges always attract. Thus, the negatively charged electron is pulled toward the positively charged proton. This attraction is opposed by the

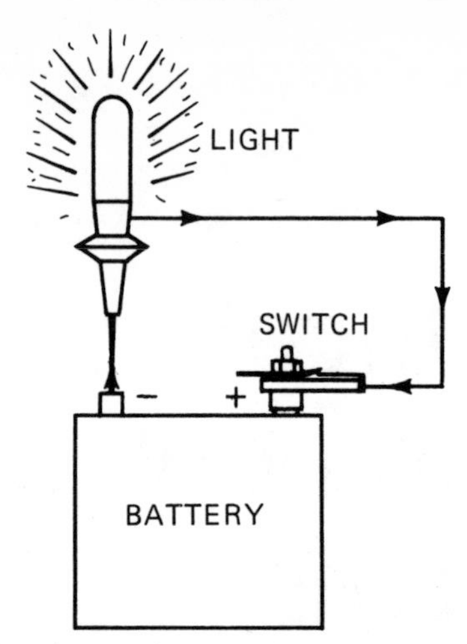

Figure 2 When the switch is closed, electrons (or electric current) move from one battery terminal to the other through the circuit.

tendency of the electron to fly away from the proton. This tendency results from its movement in a circular path around the proton. The attractive force balances the tendency of the electron to fly away, and the electron is held in its orbit.

It is not uncommon for atoms to lose electrons. When such free electrons gather in the same place, we call the effect a "charge" of electricity. When the free electrons begin to move together—for example, along a wire—we call the effect a "current" of electricity. Thus, electricity is made up of electrons.

■ 3-1-3 Strength of Attraction and Repulsion

Even though electrons are extremely tiny, they can exert relatively great force in attracting protons (positive) or in repelling other electrons. The repulsive force between two electrons 3/8 inch (9.525 mm) apart (in a vacuum) is about 2/1,000,000,000,000,000,000,000,000 pound. This seems like a very small force until we realize how many electrons there are in an ounce of a substance. In an ounce of iron, for example, there are about 22 million billion billion electrons.

■ 3-1-4 Electricity in Motion

Since free electrons exert a powerful repulsive force against each other, then tend to move away from each other. If we arrange a path along which free electrons can move, they will always move away from the areas in which there are many electrons into areas where there are few electrons.

Basically, an alternator or a battery is a device that concentrates large numbers of electrons at one place, or terminal, and removes electrons from another place, or terminal. When these two terminals are connected by an electron path, or electric circuit, the electrons can move from one terminal to the other (Fig. 2). This movement of electrons through a circuit is called an "electron flow," or more familiarly, a current of electricity.

The terminal that has a large number of electrons massed in it is called the "negative" terminal (electrons being negative), as shown in Fig 3. The terminal from which the electrons have been removed is called the "positive" terminal. Removing electrons leaves atoms that are positively charged (from the protons).

> **NOTE:** The negative terminal is also called the "minus" terminal and is indicated by a minus (−) sign. The positive terminal is also called the "plus" terminal and is indicated by a plus (+) sign.

■ 3-1-5 Conductors and Semiconductors

Electrons require a path or a circuit in which they can move. Electrons can move through some substances more easily than through others. Some substances—such as copper, iron, aluminum, and other metals—form good paths through which electrons can move. Since such substances conduct the electrons through easily, they are called "conductors." Other substances, such as rubber and glass, strongly oppose movement of electrons through them. These substances are called "nonconductors," or "insulators." In a third category are substances, such as germanium, which are neither good conductors nor good insulators. These are called "semiconductors." Whether a substance is a conductor, a nonconductor, or a semiconductor depends on its atomic structure.

One of the best conductors is copper, and therefore the wires between the electrical components of the automobile are usually made of copper. The copper atom has 29 electrons circling the nucleus in four separate orbits. The inner orbit has 2 electrons, the next larger orbit 8, the third 18, and the outer orbit 1. This outer electron is not very closely tied to the atom. Therefore a copper atom can lose its outer electron.

■ 3-1-6 Atomic Structure and Conductivity

For a substance to be an electric conductor, it must have free electrons. It must furnish these electrons from the outermost or-

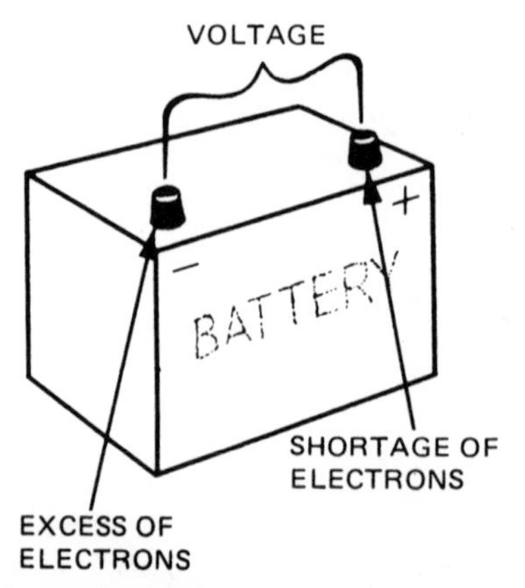

Figure 3 A battery has an excess of electrons at the negative (−) terminal and a shortage of electrons at the positive (+) terminal.

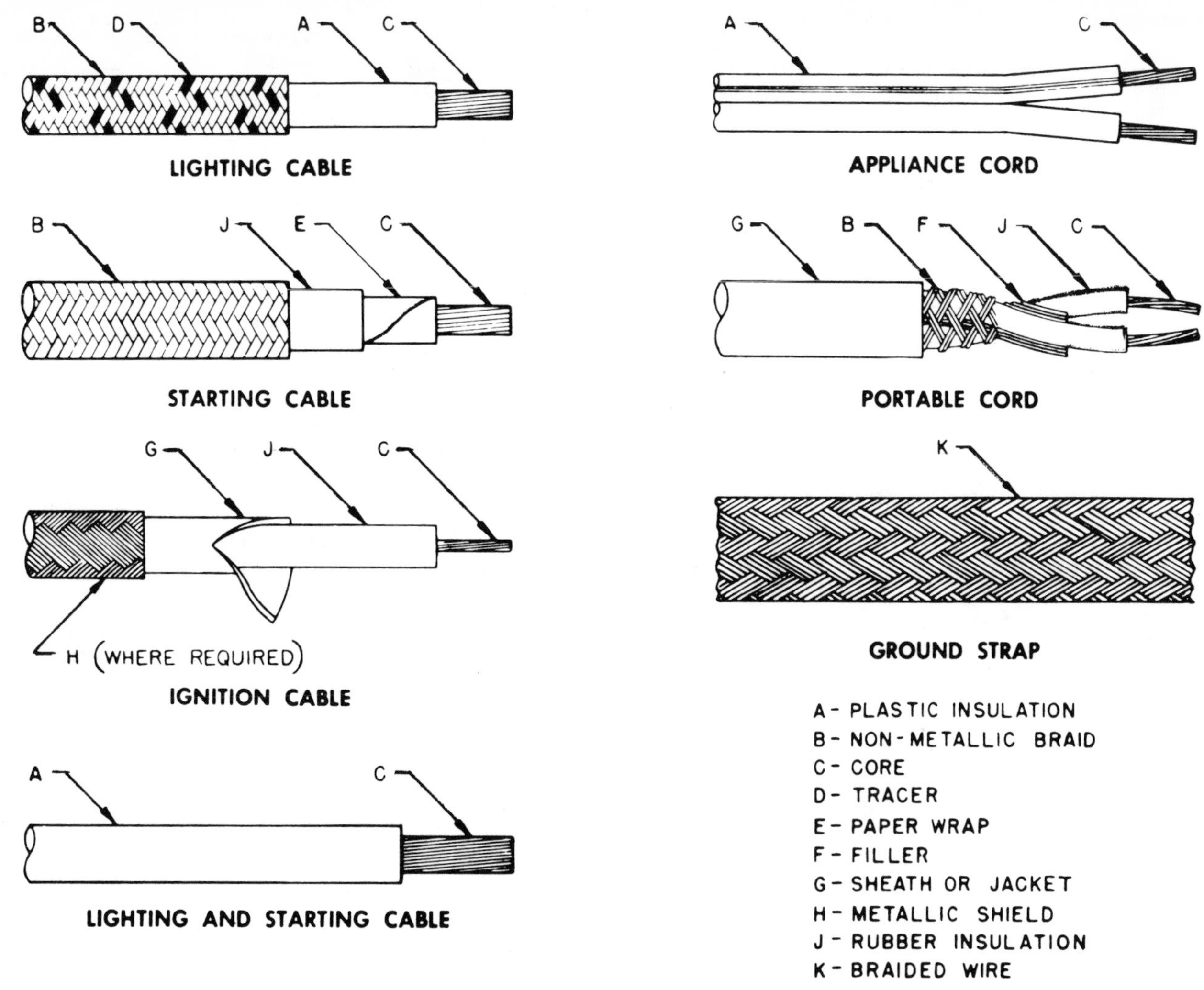

Figure 4 Various types of insulation used on wire cable and cord. *(General Motors Corporation.)*

bits of its atoms. Inner-orbit electrons are bound much more closely to the atom and do not normally take part in the electron flow that we know as electric current.

If the outermost orbit of an atom is nearly empty (with only one, two, or three electrons, for example), the outer-orbit electrons can get away from the atom fairly easily. Therefore the substance is a good conductor. However, if the outermost orbit is filled with all the electrons the orbit can hold, then these electrons are tightly bound to the atom. This type of atom is a good insulator.

There are a few substances, such as germanium, with half-filled outer orbits. These are halfway between conductors and insulators. The substances are called "semiconductors." They are used in transistors.

■ **3-1-7 Insulators** Insulators are composed of atoms or combinations of atoms which do not lose electrons easily. When an insulating material is placed around an alternator negative terminal, few if any electrons can flow into the insulating material. This is because, despite the powerful repulsion between them, the electrons on the terminal cannot push other electrons free from the insulator atoms. Likewise, the insulation around the positive terminal will not give up electrons to the terminal. The attractive force of the positively charged atoms in the terminal cannot pull electrons loose from the atoms of insulating material.

Insulators are essential to the operation of any electrical device. The wires and other parts through which electrons flow are usually covered with insulation. Several types of insulation used on wire cable and cord are shown in Fig 4. Insulation prevents electrons from flowing away from the circuit and prevents electrical loss. Current-carrying (or electron-carrying) parts are covered or supported by mica, rubber, Bakelite, plastic compounds, or fiber insulating material. Also, they are often covered with insulating varnish,a liquid that dries to form a glasslike insulating coating.

NOTE: Air is a good insulating substance, particularly when it is dry. The atoms of the different gases in air are normally neutral electrically and do not take on or give up electrons.

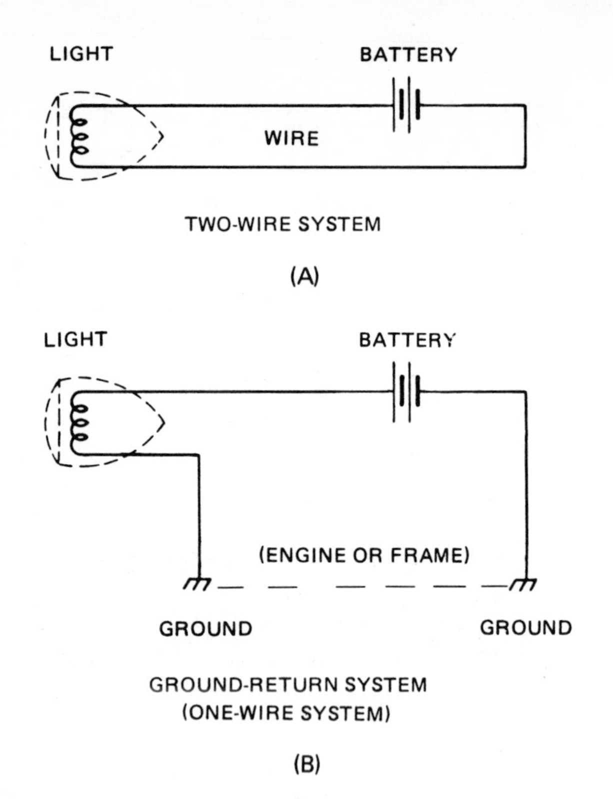

Figure 5 Circuit showing two different wiring systems. *(A)* Two-wire system, and *(B)* ground-return or one-wire system. *(General Motors Corporation.)*

Insulation will fail for a number of reasons. If the insulation becomes water-soaked, for example, the water will fill all the tiny pores or openings in the insulation and form an electron- or current-carrying path. Also, heat may char or burn the insulation, so that its chemical properties are changed. It becomes a conductor instead of an insulator. In addition, if the electrons continue to mass more and more heavily at the alternator terminal (as voltage goes up), the electrons will push harder and harder against each other. If this push increases too much, it may push electrons entirely through the insulation. Such a condition is called a "short," or "short circuit." The electrons take a short circuit instead of taking the longer circuit through the outside wires.

There are two different systems of wiring, the two-wire system and the ground-return or one-wire system. Figure 5 shows the two systems. Automobiles use the ground-return system of wiring. This system utilizes the car frame, body, and engine to form half the electric circuit. Since it is necessary to run only one wire to many of the electrical components (the ground return forming the other part of the circuit), considerable wire is saved and the system is simplified. Short circuits between the insulated and grounded parts of the circuit are often called "grounds."

> **NOTE:** In automobiles, such shorts, or grounds, most often develop because of (1) mechanical damage; (2) accumulation of dirt, oil, or moisture; or (3) ultimate deterioration of the insulation due to all these.

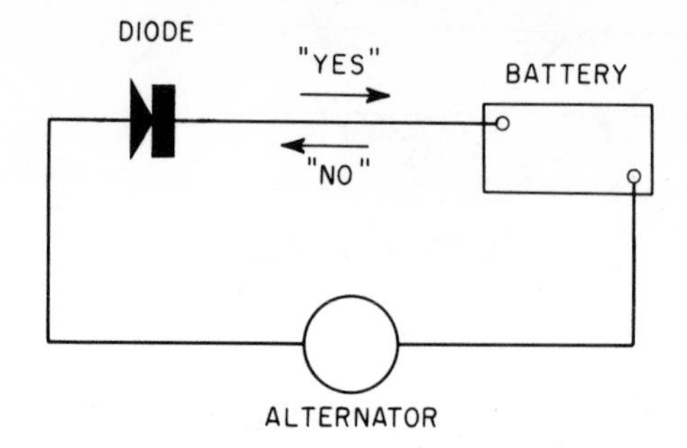

Figure 6 Alternating current from an alternator can be rectified, or changed to direct current, by a diode for charging a battery.

■ 3-1-8 Semiconductors, Diodes, and Transistors

In a sense, the semiconductor is halfway between a conductor and a nonconductor. Transistors, prepared from semiconductor materials, have revolutionized electronics. Transistors now are widely used in automobiles, particularly in charging and ignition circuits.

Germanium is a semiconductor material. It has four electrons in its outermost orbit. Germanium atoms combine with themselves or with atoms of other elements to form either insulators or, under proper condition, conductors.

1. DIODES The diode is a device that permits electric current to flow through in one direction but not in the other. Figure 6 shows the symbol for a diode. Diodes are used in charging systems and other units in which alternating current must be rectified (changed to direct current). The rectifier-type battery charger changes ordinary household alternating current to the direct current needed to charge batteries. Automobiles have alternators which are equipped with diodes to rectify the alternating current.

Figure 6 illustrates the use of a diode and an alternator to charge a battery. When the current flows from the alternator in the charging direction, the diode allows it to pass through so that the battery is charged. But when the current reverses directions, then the diode prevents it from flowing, protecting the battery from current flowing in the discharging direction.

2. TRANSISTORS The transistor acts as an electric switch in which a small current flowing into one part can allow a large current to pass through a different part. To make a transistor, one or more sections of a semiconductor material must be added to the diode. Figure 7 shows a transistor in external and sectional views. Figure 8 is the wiring circuit of one type of transistor used in transistorized alternator regulators. As an example, suppose that with the switch closed as shown, 4.5 amps (amperes) flow. Note that most of the current (4.15 amps) is shown as flowing to the collector. Only 0.35 amp is shown flowing to the base. With the switch open, no current flows. Thus, a small amount of current can control the flow of a much larger amount of current. This amplifying characteristic of transistors makes them valuable for amplifiers in ignition systems and other electronic equipment. They can also be used for many other purposes, as in the automotive alternator regulator. Here a small amount of current through the switch can control a large alternator-field current, as explained in Sec. 6 of this part.

This is how the transistor operates. When the switch is open, no current can flow across the junctions of the transistor. However, when the switch is closed, as in Fig. 8, electrons are fed into the base. These electrons applied to the base permit a relatively heavy current from the emitter to the collector. In effect, the electrons applied to the base open the gates so that the heavy current can get through.

Figure 7 shows an actual transistor. Transistors of many types and shapes now are used.

Diodes and transistors are called "solid-state devices" because they are solid and have no mechanically moving parts. They do their jobs electrically, that is, by the movement of electrons through solid materials.

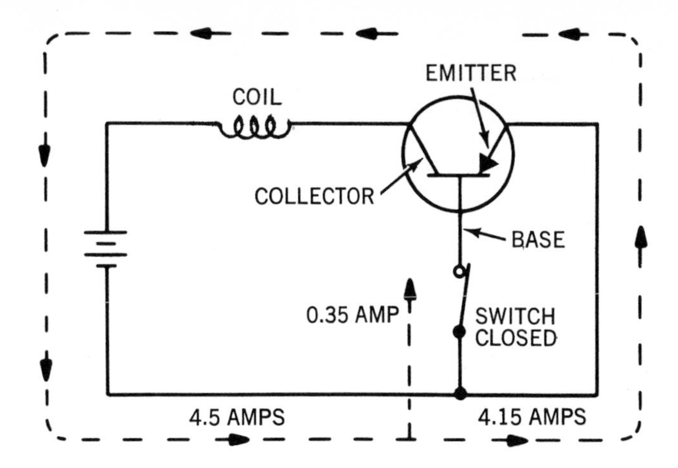

Figure 8 When the switch is closed, current flows.

■ 3-1-9 Voltage

Electric current is a flow of electrons. The more electrons there are in motion, the stronger the current. Also, the greater the concentration of electrons at a generator terminal, the higher the repulsive force, or pressure, between electrons. The higher the pressure goes, the more electrons will flow. Stated another way, the higher the voltage goes, the more current will flow. Figure 9 shows this effect. When the resistance in a circuit remains constant, doubling the voltage also doubles the current flow. A high voltage means a high electric pressure, or a massing of many electrons. Voltage is measured in units of electric pressure called "volts."

■ 3-1-10 Amperage

Electric current, or electron flow, is measured in amperes of electric current or amps. When relatively few electrons flow in an electric circuit, the amperage is low. When many electrons flow, the amperage is high.

NOTE: The actual number of electrons flowing is enormous. For example, a 1-amp generator (a small unit capable of lighting a small light bulb) will supply more than 6 billion billion (6.28×10^{18}) electrons a second.

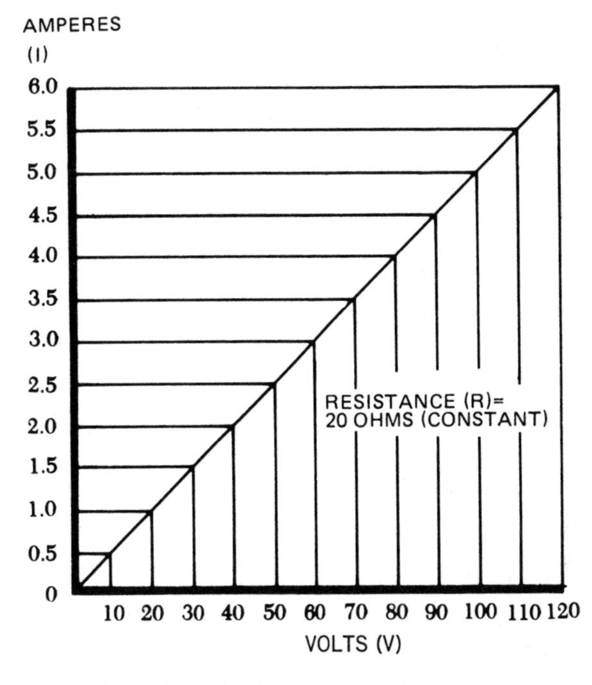

Figure 9 Comparison of voltage vs. current in a constant-resistance circuit. When the voltage doubles, current flow also doubles.

■ 3-1-11 Direct and Alternating Current

A battery furnishes direct current. That is, this current (or electrons) always flows out from the negative terminal through the circuit connected to the battery and back into the positive terminal.

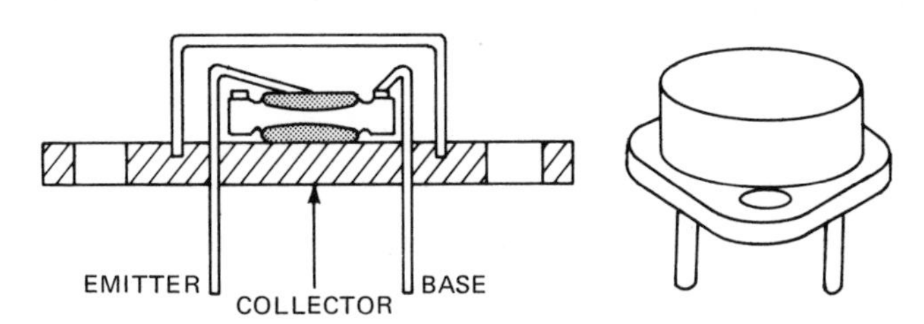

Figure 7 External and sectional views of a transistor.

The current always flows in the same direction when the battery is furnishing current. With alternating current, the current flows first in one direction and then in the other. Alternating current is generated in the generator windings. The direct current (dc) generators have commutators which change this alternating current to direct current. Alternators use diodes to rectify, or change, the alternating current to direct current. Since the battery and other automotive electric units are direct-current devices, they can operate only on direct current. Direct current is usually referred to as "dc" and alternating current as "ac."

■ 3-1-12 Resistance

An insulator is highly resistant to the passage of electrons through it. Conductors offer a rela-

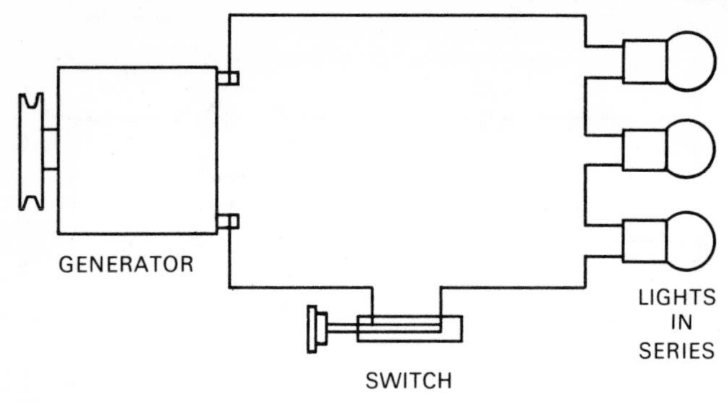

Figure 10 When light bulbs are connected in series, the same current flows through all.

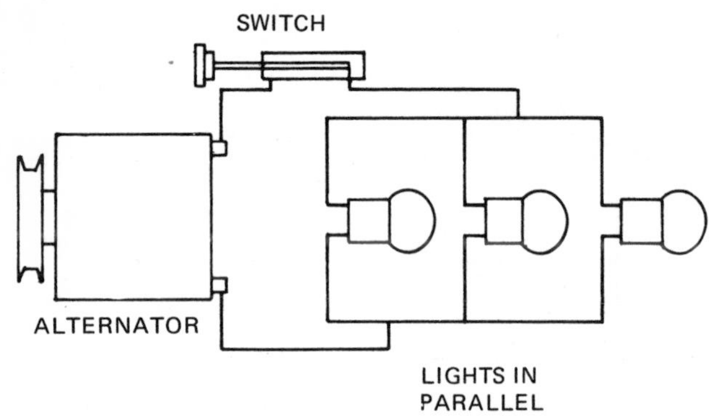

Figure 11 When light bulbs are connected in parallel to the current source, the current divides, part of it flowing through each light bulb.

tively small resistance. Even so, the best of conductors, such as copper wire, resists somewhat the movement of electrons in it. This is because a continuing "push" or pressure is necessary to keep the electrons moving in the same direction along the wire. Without this continuing pressure (or voltage), the electrons would resume their random movements in all directions in the wire.

Resistance of any wire is measured in ohms. A 1,000-foot (304.8 m) length of No. 10 wire (which is about 0.1 inch (3.0 mm) in diameter) has a resistance of 1 ohm. A 2,000-foot (609.6 m) length has a resistance of 2 ohms. If the wire size is increased to No. 4 [which is about 0.2 inch (6.1 mm) in diameter, or four times the cross-sectional area], 1,000 feet (304.8 m) has only 1/4-ohm resistance. It requires 4,000 feet (1219.2 m) of this wire to have a resistance of 1 ohm.

Resistance varies with four factors:

1. Material. (Some materials have more resistance than others.)

2. Cross section. (The larger the cross section, the lower the resistance.)

3. Length. (The longer the wire, the more resistance it has.)

4. Temperature. (With many materials, the higher the temperature, the greater the resistance.)

■ 3-1-13 Ohm's Law

The relationship among resistance, electron flow (or current), and pressure (or voltage) can be summed up by a statement known as Ohm's law, which is:

Voltage is equal to amperage times ohms

This law can be stated as the mathematical formula:

$$V = I \times R$$

Other forms of the formula are:

$$R = \frac{V}{I} \quad \text{and} \quad I = \frac{V}{R}$$

In each of these formulas, V is the voltage in volts, I is the current in amperes, and R is the resistance in ohms.

■ 3-1-14 Series Circuits

In series circuits, each electrical device is connected to other electrical devices in such a way that the same current flows through all (Fig. 10). That is, the whole series of electrical devices is connected together into a single circuit, as between the generator terminals, for example. If any one device is turned off, the circuit is broken. No current flows in any part of the circuit.

■ 3-1-15 Parallel Circuits

In parallel circuits, the various devices are connected by parallel wires (Fig. 11). The current divides, part of it flowing into one device, part into another, and so on. Practically the same voltage is applied to each device, and each device can be turned on or off independently of the others.

NOTE: Many automotive circuits are series-parallel circuits. For example, the headlights are connected to the battery in parallel, but both are connected in series to the battery through a light switch (Fig. 13).

■ 3-1-16 Resistance in Parallel and Series Circuits

To figure the resistance of a series circuit, find the sum of the resistances of the various components of the circuit. In Fig. 12, the total resistance, ignoring the wires between the resistors, is 4 plus 2 plus 5 plus 1, or 12 ohms. Using Ohm's law, 1.0 amp will flow from the 12-volt battery through the 12-ohm circuit.

The resistances of parallel circuits are more difficult to calculate. Paralleling devices reduce the resistance, so that more current flows. For example, the headlights of an automobile are in parallel (Fig. 13). To calculate the resistance of a number or circuits in parallel, use the formula

$$R = \frac{1}{\frac{1}{r_1} + \frac{1}{r_2} + \frac{1}{r_3} + \frac{1}{r_4} \cdots} \quad \text{ohm}$$

in which R is the total resistance of the group in ohms, and r_1, r_2, r_3, r_4, and so on, are the resistances of the individual circuits.

■ 3-1-17 Voltage Drop

If the voltage across each of the resistors in the circuit shown in Fig. 12 were checked with a voltmeter, the voltages would add up to 12 volts. For example, the voltage between A and B, or across the 4-ohm resistor, would be 4 volts. From B to C, it would be 2 volts. From C to D, it would be 5 volts. From D to E, it would be 1 volt. If we did not know the resistance of any of the resistors, we could find it by measuring the voltage and amperage and then using Ohm's law ($R = V/I$). For example, resistance of resistor AB would be 4 volts divided by 1 amp, or 4 ohms.

The voltage is gradually "used up" from one end of the circuit to the other. The voltage drops 4 volts across the 4-ohm resistor so that a voltage measurement between points B and E would be 8 volts. From C to E it would be 6 volts, and from D to E it would be 1 volt. Any resistance in a circuit causes a voltage loss, or voltage drop. The voltage drop is also called the *IR* drop. This comes from the formula $V = IR$.

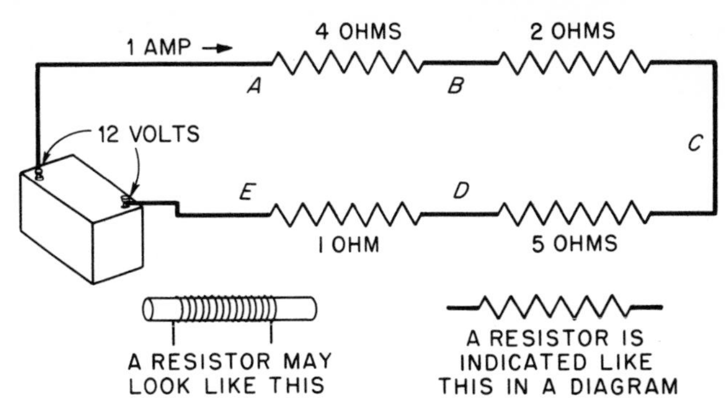

Figure 12 A series circuit made of four resistors of varying resistances.

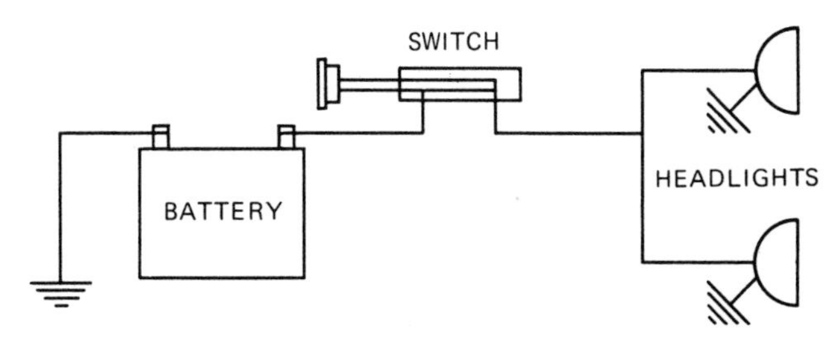

Figure 13 The headlight circuit in an automobile is a series-parallel circuit. The two headlights are in parallel with each other but are connected in series with the light switch to the battery.

■ 3-1-18 Importance of Voltage Drop

The automotive technician must understand voltage drop. Excessive voltage drop in the headlight circuit, for example, means low voltage at the headlights and therefore dim headlights. Excessive voltage drop in the charging circuit between the alternator and the battery might produce an excessively low charging voltage at the battery. The battery would very likely become discharged.

Excessive voltage drop can be caused by too small wires, broken strands in a multistrand wire or cable, bad connections, defective contact points (for example, in the ignition distributor), and so on. These conditions set up added resistance within the circuit. This resistance "uses up" part of the voltage. Then there is not enough voltage left to operate the headlights, radio, ignition coil, and other electrical devices.

There is another way of looking at excessive resistance caused by a bad connection. Such a bad connection cuts down the size of the electron path, so that fewer electrons can get through. Too few electrons then reach the headlight, for example, and it becomes dim.

■ 3-1-19 Resistance Heating

As electric current flows through a conductor, a heating effect results. Normally, the heating effect is very slight and does no harm. But if the wire is too small, there will be considerable heating. Likewise, a bad connection will become hot. Any connection that becomes abnormally hot when current flows through it is not in good condition.

> **NOTE:** An electric light bulb is simply a tungsten conductor, called the "filament," in an airtight glass envelope. When the light bulb is connected to the electric circuit, electrons bombard the tungsten atoms so hard that the filament becomes very hot. It gets so hot that it glows brilliantly and gives off light.

■ 3-1-20 Temperature Effect on Resistance

As current passes through a wire, its resistance—and its temperature—may also increase. Most metals show this effect. A simple explanation might be this: With increased temperatures, the atoms of metal that make up the wire are moving faster. The electrons, therefore, have a harder time jumping between the faster-moving atoms.

Not all substances show this increase of resistance with increases of temperature. The oxides of some metals, such as manganese, nickel, cobalt, copper, iron, and so on, show the reverse effect. That is, as their temperature goes up, their resistance goes down. This effect is made use of in electrical devices called "thermistors." Thermistors have many uses from temperature measurement to control of many types of mechanisms. The temperature-sensing unit in many automobile engines uses a thermistor.

■ 3-1-21 Using Ammeters and Voltmeters

Ammeters are used to measure the current flowing through a circuit. Voltmeters are used to measure the voltage between two points in an electrical circuit. For example, to measure the amperes of current flowing in the circuit shown in Fig. 12, connect an ammeter into the circuit, in series with the resistances. The current flowing through the circuit would also flow through the ammeter.

To measure the voltage across any resistance, use the voltmeter. Connect it to the two sides of the resistance.

The ammeter is connected *into* the circuit, that is, in series. The voltmeter is connected *across* the circuit, in parallel, with the component whose voltage is to be measured.

SECTION 3-2 Battery Service

This section describes battery service as well as the causes of battery failure. Some battery failures are normal—batteries do wear out—but other failures can be prevented by proper battery maintenance. In this section, you will find discussions of battery testing and maintenance procedures, types of battery failure, how to determine whether a battery failure is normal or not, and what to do to prevent early battery failure and short battery life.

■ **3-2-1 Battery Service** Battery service can be divided into two parts: servicing batteries in vehicles and servicing batteries after they have been removed from vehicles. Servicing batteries in vehicles includes inspecting and testing the battery, adding water, cleaning the battery, cleaning and tightening cable clamps or replacing cables if necessary, and keeping the battery hold-down clamps properly tightened. Out-of-the-car battery service includes adding water, testing the battery, recharging the battery if necessary, and cleaning the battery case, terminals, and the battery carrier. All these services and checks are discussed in following sections.

■ **3-2-2 Battery Maintenance** Most drivers tend to forget about their car battery. That is, they forget it until one cold morning, when they try to start their car, the battery won't do its job and the engine won't start. Battery failure is one of the more common car troubles.

If people would check the battery periodically, much of this battery trouble could be avoided. Here are the things that should be done:

1. Visually inspect the battery.
2. Check electrolyte level in all cells.
3. Add water if the level is low.
4. Clean off corrosion around battery terminals and top.
5. Check battery condition with a battery tester.(Battery test instruments are described later.)
6. Recharge the battery if it is low.

CAUTION: Sulfuric acid, the active ingredient in battery electrolyte, is very corrosive. It can destroy most things it touches. It will cause painful and serious burns if it gets on the skin. It can cause blindness if it gets into eyes. If you get battery acid (electrolyte) on your skin, flush it off at once with water. *Continue to flush for at least 5 minutes.* Put baking soda (if available) on the skin. This will neutralize the acid. If you get acid in your eyes, flush your eyes out with water OVER AND OVER AGAIN. GET TO A DOCTOR AT ONCE! Do not wait!

CAUTION: The gases that form in the tops of the battery cells during charging are very explosive. Never light a match or a cigarette near a recently charged battery. Never blow off a battery with an air hose. The compressed air could draw electrolyte from the cell and splash the acid on you or any other person nearby.

■ **3-2-3 Visual Inspection of Battery** Examine the battery for signs of leakage, cracked case or top, corrosion, missing vent plugs, and loose or missing hold-down clamps. Leakage signs, which could indicate a cracked battery case, include white corrosion on the battery carrier, fender inner panel, or the car frame. If the top of the battery is covered with corrosion and the owner complains that the battery needs water frequently, the battery probably is being overcharged. Check the charging system.

The most common cause of a cracked top is improper installation. If the wrong wrench is used to remove or tighten the cable clamps, the battery top may be broken. See ■3-2-19 on how to remove and replace cable clamps.

The most common cause of a cracked case is excessive tightening of the battery hold-down clamps. Also, a front-end crash, even if so minor that little damage is done to the sheet metal, may crack the battery case.

■ **3-2-4 Checking Electrolyte Level and Adding Water** To check the battery, remove the vent caps and look down into the cells. If water is needed, add it. Distilled water is recommended, but any water that is fit to drink may be used. Many batteries have rings in the cell covers which show whether the battery needs water.

NOTE: You cannot check battery cells on sealed batteries. However, make sure the connections are tight at the terminals.

Many batteries have a Delco Eye, which is a special vent cap or plug used in one of the six cells in the battery. It has a transparent rod extending down into the cell. When the end of the rod is immersed, the exposed top of the rod shows black. When the level of the electrolyte falls below the tip, the top of the rod glows. This means water should be added. Vent caps do not need to be removed to check electrolyte level.

NOTE: Do not overfill the battery. Too much water will make the electrolyte leak out. This will corrode or eat away the battery carrier and any other metal around.

■ **3-2-5 Cleaning Corrosion off the Battery** Battery terminals and cables, especially those on top of the battery, tend to corrode. This corrosion builds up around the battery and the cable clamps and, unseen, between the terminal posts and clamps. To get rid of it, and to clean the battery top, mix some common baking soda in a can of warm water. Brush on the solution, wait until the foaming stops, and then flush off the battery top with water. If the buildup of corrosion around the terminals is heavy, detach the cables from the terminals (as explained in■ 3-2-19) and use the wire battery brushes, shown in Fig. 1, to clean the terminal posts and cable clamps. Then coat the terminals with an anti-corrosion compound to retard additional corrosion.

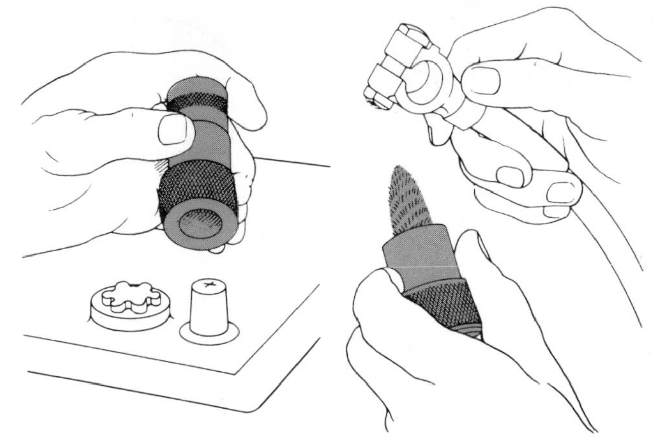

Figure 1 Using special wire brushes to clean battery terminal posts and cable clamps. *(Buick Motor Division of General Motors Corporation.)*

■ **3-2-6 Testing Battery Condition** There are several ways to test battery condition. The most common way is with a battery hydrometer. Other methods use testing meters.

■ **3-2-7 Hydrometer Test** The hydrometer tests the specific gravity of the battery electrolyte. It has a rubber bulb at the top, a glass tube, a float, and a rubber tube at the bottom. You use it by squeezing the bulb, putting the end of the tube into the battery cell, and then releasing the bulb. This draws electrolyte up into the glass tube. The float will rise in the electrolyte. The amount the stem of the float sticks out of the electrolyte tells you the battery state-of-charge. Take a reading at eye level, as shown in Fig. 2.

CAUTION: Do not drop electrolyte on the car or on yourself! It will damage the paint on the car and eat holes in your clothes! See "Caution," ■ 3-2-2

If the float sticks out so the reading on the stem is between 1.260 and 1.290, the battery is fully charged. If the reading at the electrolyte level is between 1.200 and 1.230, the battery is only half charged. If the reading is around 1.140, the battery is run down and needs a recharge. The following list of specific-gravity readings gives you a general idea of battery conditions.

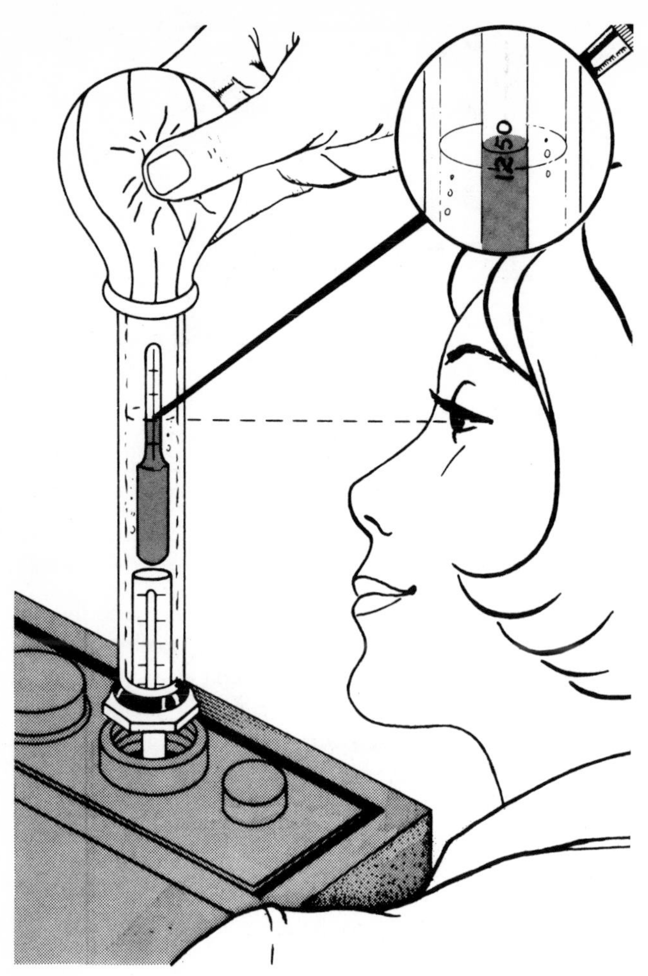

Figure 2 Using a battery hydrometer to check the specific gravity of a battery cell. The reading should be taken at eye level.

1.265 to 1.299	Fully charged battery
1.235 to 1.265	Three-fourths charged
1.205 to 1.235	One-half charged
1.170 to 1.205	One-fourth charged
1.140 to 1.170	Barely operative
1.110 to 1.140	Completely discharged

If a cell tests much lower than others, there is something wrong with that cell. A cracked case has allowed electrolyte leakage, or perhaps there is internal damage to the plates or separators. If the variation is only a few specific-gravity points, then there is probably no cause for concern. But if the cell measures 25 to 50 points lower, it is defective. The battery should be replaced. You could find two or three defective cells in a battery.

> **NOTE:** Some late-model 12-volt batteries for passenger-car service have a somewhat lower specific gravity when charged. For example, one type is fully charged with a specific gravity of 1.270. Other batteries—for example, those used in hot climates—have a specific gravity of 1.225 when fully charged.

The decimal point is not normally referred to in a discussion of specific gravity. For example, "twelve twenty-five" means 1.225, and "eleven fifty" means 1.150. Also, the word "specific" is often dropped, so that the term becomes just "gravity."

■ **3-2-8 Variation of Specific Gravity with Temperature** Varying states of charge affect the specific gravity of the electrolyte. Temperature also changes the specific gravity. This is because a liquid becomes thicker and gains specific gravity as it cools. As a liquid warms, it becomes thinner and loses gravity. Thus, the temperature must be considered when a gravity reading is taken. A correction must be made if the temperature varies from standard. This correction involves the addition or subtraction of gravity points, according to whether the electrolyte temperature is above or below the 80° F (26.7° C) standard. The gravity of electrolyte changes about four points, or four thousandths (0.004), for every 10° F (6.5° C) change in temperature. To make a temperature correction, four points must be subtracted for every 10° F below 80° F (26.7° C). Four points must be added for every 10° F above 80° F.

EXAMPLE: 1.250 at 120° F (48.9° C): Add 0.016 (4 × 0.004) Corrected reading is 1.266. 1.230 at 20° F (−6.7° C): Subtract 0.024 (6 × 0.004). Corrected reading is 1.206.

> **NOTE:** Some types of battery hydrometer, especially those that use floating plastic balls to indicate the state of charge, are compensated for temperature. No temperature corrections have to be made when this type of hydrometer is used.

■ **3-2-9 Loss of Gravity from Age** As the battery ages, the electrolyte gradually loses gravity. This is because active material is lost from the plates (as it sheds and drops into the bottom of the cells) and because gassing causes the loss of acid. Over a period of 2 years, for example, battery electrolyte may drop to a top gravity, when fully charged, of not more than 1.250 from the original top gravity of 1.290. Little can be done to restore gravity, since the losses are an indication of an aging battery.

■ **3-2-10 Loss of Gravity from Self-Discharge** There is always some chemical activity in a battery even though the battery is not connected to a circuit and delivering current. Such chemical action, which does not produce current, is termed "self-discharge." Self-discharge varies with temperature and strength of electrolyte. As might be expected, the higher the temperature, the faster the self-discharge, since the chemical actions are stimulated by the higher temperatures (Fig. 3). Note that the battery kept at 100°F (37.8°C) loses half its charge in 30 days, while the battery kept at 0°F (−17.8°C) suffers almost no loss of charge.

A strong electrolyte, with its higher percentage of sulfuric acid, also causes more rapid self-discharge. This was shown by the more rapid dropping off of the curves during the first few days of the test (Fig. 3) when the electrolyte was the strongest.

The lead sulfate produced by self-discharge is harder to break down during recharging of the battery. If batteries are not recharged periodically to compensate for self-discharge, they may be severely damaged or even completely ruined.

Older batteries and batteries that have impurities in them (often introduced in the water) tend to self-discharge more rapidly.

■ 3-2-11 Battery Gravities for Hot Climates

Batteries operating in hot climates are often readjusted so that their gravity is reduced. Instead of a 1.290 gravity, for example, the electrolyte may be reduced to as low as 1.230 (31 percent acid) for a fully charged battery. This is done by fully charging the battery, dumping the electrolyte, and replacing it with 1.230 specific gravity electrolyte. Or part of the electrolyte may be removed and water added until the gravity is reduced to the desired value. The reduction of the gravity in this manner prolongs the life of the battery and reduces the amount of self-discharge. On discharge, the gravity may drop as low as 1.075 before the battery ceases to deliver current. Where there is no danger of freezing, these lower gravities may be used with safety.

■ 3-2-12 Freezing Point

The higher the gravity, the lower the temperature required to freeze the electrolyte. Freezing must be avoided, since it will usually ruin the battery.

A run-down battery must never be left out in the cold (Fig. 4). Sometimes in winter, a driver may try to start a car and do nothing more than run the battery down. If the car remains out in the cold, the battery may freeze. Then a new battery will have to be installed and the original trouble corrected.

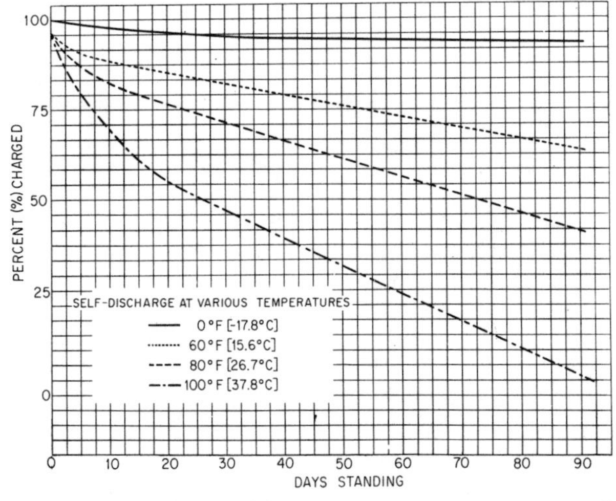

Figure 3 Self-discharge of batteries at various temperatures. The four curves indicate the self-discharge of four batteries kept for 90 days at 0, 68, 80, and 100°F (−17.8, 15.6, 26.7, and 37.8°C). *(Delco-Remy Division of General Motors Corporation.)*

SPECIFIC GRAVITY	FREEZING TEMPERATURE, DEGREES FAHRENHEIT [°C]
1.100	18 [−8]
1.160	1 [−17]
1.200	−17 [−27]
1.220	−31 [−35]
1.260	−75 [−59]
1.300	−95 [−71]

Figure 4 Table showing freezing temperatures of electrolyte at various specific gravities.

Some of the newer 12-volt passenger-car-type batteries have sufficient capacity, even with a low gravity reading, to crank the engine. Although these batteries are still able to crank the engine, the specific gravity of the electrolyte can be so low that the electrolyte will freeze at comparatively mild temperatures. Therefore, with these batteries the ability to crank cannot be related to resistance to freezing.

■ 3-2-13 Refractometer Test

The refractometer test uses the principle of light refraction (bending of light rays) as light passes through a drop of battery electrolyte. To use the refractometer, open the plastic cover at the slanted end of the tester. Wipe the measuring window and the bottom of the plastic cover with a tissue or clean cloth.

Close the plastic cover. Release the black dipstick. Remove a vent plug from a battery cell. Dip the black dipstick into the cell to pick up a couple of drops of electrolyte. Then put the end of the black dipstick into the cover-plate opening. This action deposits the drops of electrolyte in the measuring window.

Now point the tester toward the light and look into the eyepiece (Fig. 5). Note where the dividing line between light and dark (the edge of the shadow) crosses the scale. This indicates the electrolyte strength and determines the battery state of charge. Test all cells in this manner. After each test, wipe the black dipstick, the measuring window, and the plastic cover of the refractometer.

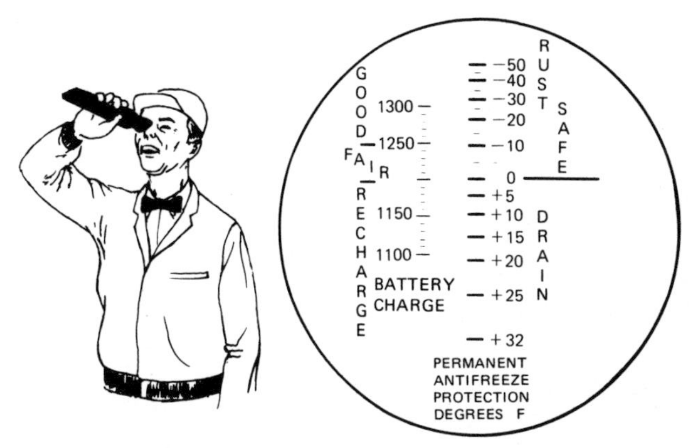

Figure 5 Reading the refractometer.

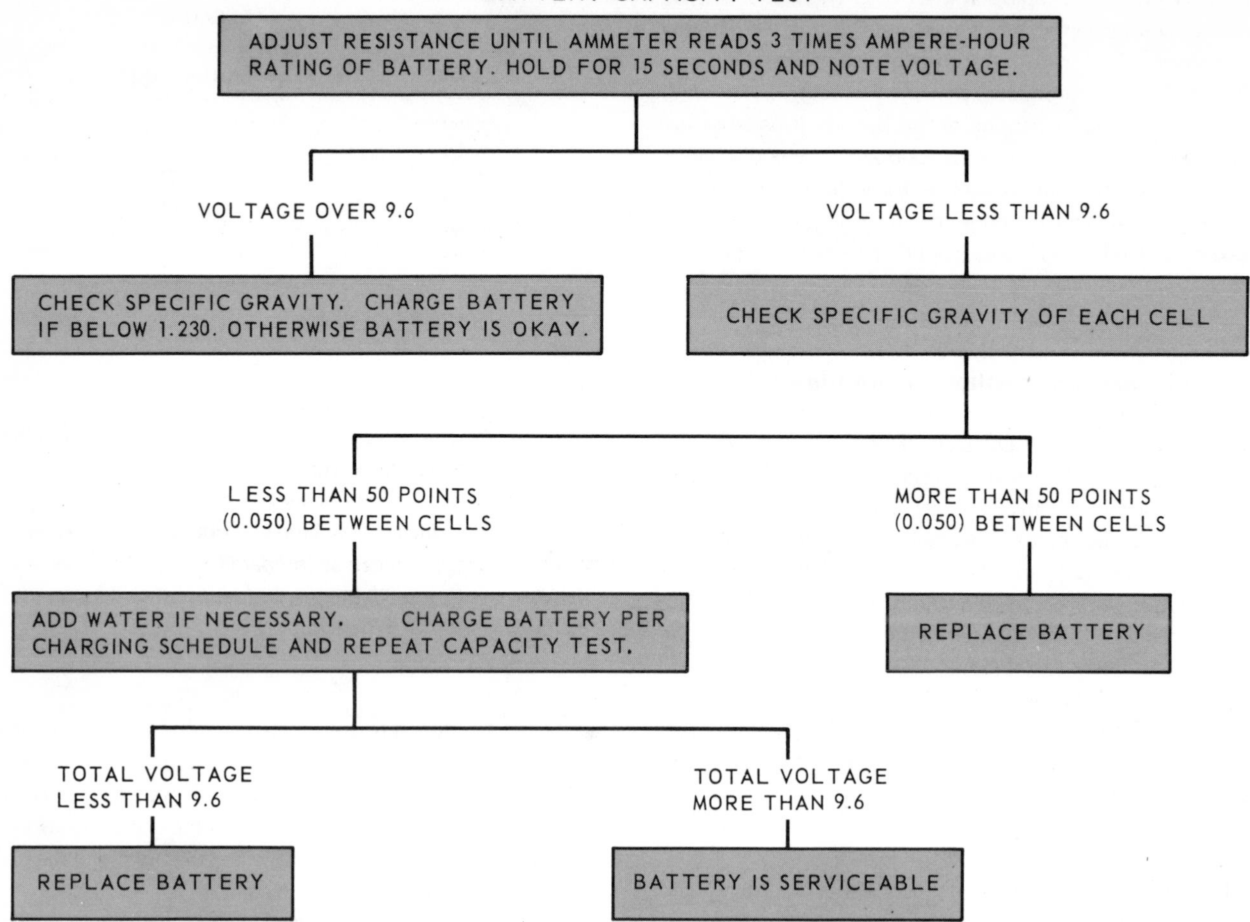

Figure 6 Typical battery capacity test. *(Ford Motor Company.)*

> **CAUTION:** Be careful not to drop electrolyte on yourself or on the car. Remember that electrolyte contains sulfuric acid, and this acid is very corrosive. It will damage the paint on the car, and if you get it on yourself, it will burn your skin. (See "Caution," ■3-2-2.)

■ **3-2-14 Light-Load Test** The light-load test can be used on all batteries except those with one-piece covers. Individual cell voltages cannot be checked on batteries with one-piece covers by the light-load test.

The light-load test is made by first stabilizing the battery with a momentary heavy load and then measuring the cell voltages with a light load applied to the battery, as follows:

1. Add water to the cells if the electrolyte is low (see ■3-2-4).

2. Place a load on the battery by using the starting motor for 3 seconds or until the engine starts. It makes no difference whether or not the engine starts. If it does, turn off the ignition at once and continue with the test.

3. Turn on headlights (low beam) and after 1 minute, and with lights still on, read individual cell voltages with an expanded-scale voltmeter that can read in 0.01-volt divisions accurately.

The light-load test will show up any of four conditions: (1) a good battery in charged condition, (2) a good battery requiring charge, (3) a discharged battery too low to test, or (4) a defective battery.

1. GOOD BATTERY IN CHARGED CONDITION If all cells read 1.95 volts or more and the difference between the highest and lowest cell voltages is less than 0.05 volt, the battery is in good condition and sufficiently charged.

2. GOOD BATTERY REQUIRING CHARGE If cells read both above and below 1.95 volts and the differences between the highest and lowest cell voltages are less than 0.05 volt, the battery is in good condition but requires charging.

3. DISCHARGED BATTERY If all cells read less than 1.95 volts, the battery is too low to test accurately. Quick-charge it (■3-2-26) and repeat the test.

4. DEFECTIVE BATTERY Even if a cell reads 1.95 volts or more but there is a difference of 0.05 volt or more between the highest and lowest cell voltages, the battery is defective and should be replaced.

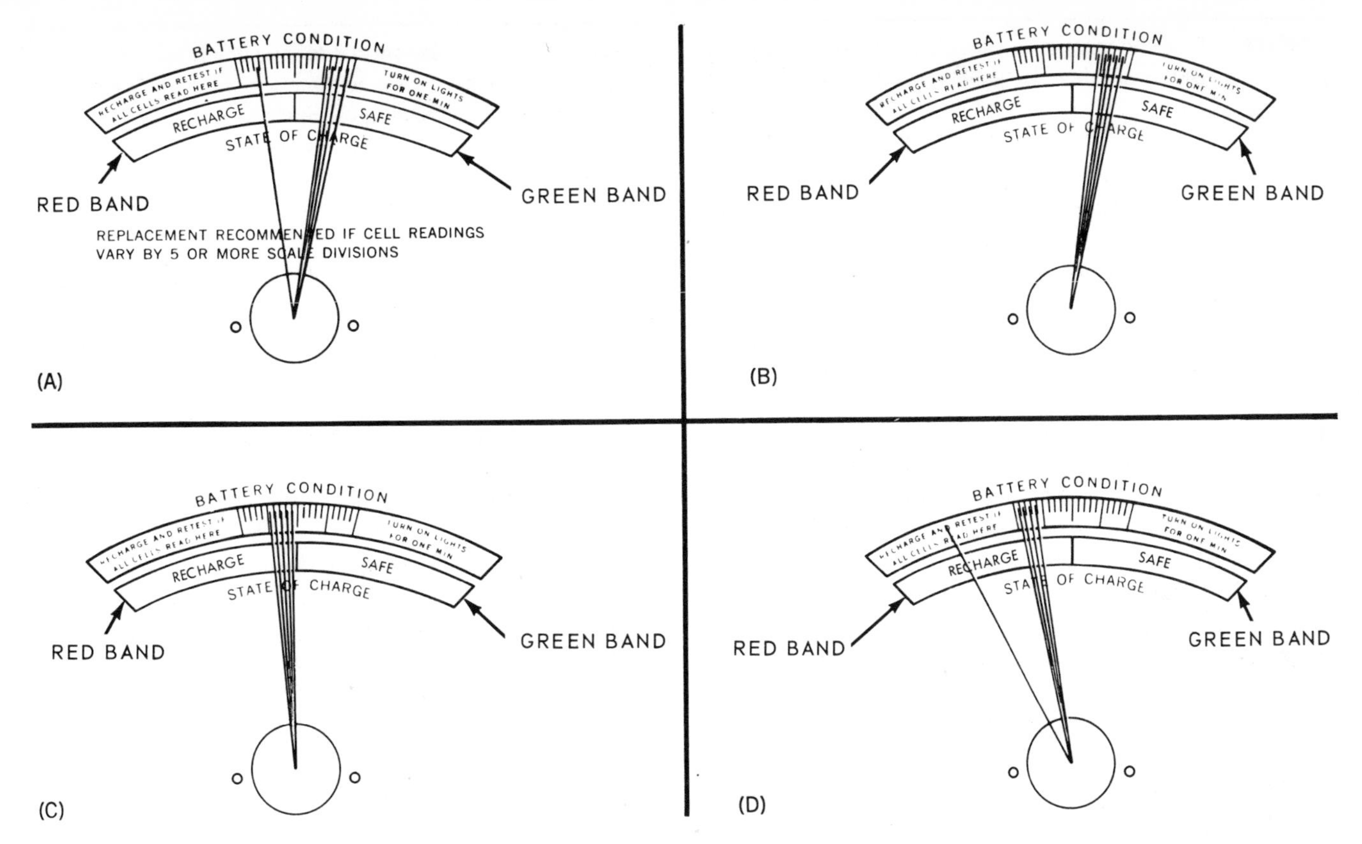

Figure 7 Interpretation of meter readings for the cadmium-tip test. *(Chrysler Corporation.)*

> **NOTE:** Occasionally, a battery may be found which tests "good" on the light-load test but does not perform satisfactorily. Three possibilities exist for this condition: (1) the battery is worn out, (2) it was improperly serviced, or (3) it was improperly activated when it was first placed into service (see ■3-2-30 on activation of dry-charged batteries).

■ 3-2-15 High-Discharge or Capacity Test For the high-discharge, or capacity, test the battery voltage is measured during a high discharge. The battery should be in good condition with no obvious defects, such as a broken cover or case. A special tester is required that can give the battery a high discharge while the voltage is measured. Specifications for the amount of current flow vary. You should always check the manufacturer's manual. Figure 6 outlines the procedure recommended by Ford.

■ 3-2-16 The 421 Test The 421 test was originally designed to test batteries with the one-piece cover, because the light-load test cannot be used on these batteries. However, the test can be used on any battery. The test requires a special 421 tester which applies a discharge load and then a charge, each for a specific number of seconds. The open-circuit voltage readings of the battery are taken immediately after the discharge cycle and after the charge cycle. The difference in the voltage indicates the condition of the battery. Most 421 testers have automatic timers to control the discharge and charge cycles and a medium-rate battery charger as well. The procedure for a typical test follows.

> **NOTE:** Do not charge the battery just before the test. Battery defects can be disguised by a charge, and so the 421 test will not show them up.

1. Inspect the battery for damage, corrosion, and other faulty conditions, as noted in ■3-2-3. Battery, cables, and connections must appear to be in good condition before proceeding with the test.

2. Connect tester leads to the battery. If the battery is still in the car, make sure that all car electric loads are turned off.

> **NOTE:** Connect the 421 tester leads correctly with respect to polarity. Connecting the leads backward could ruin the alternator.

3. Start the tester. It will discharge the battery for 15 seconds at a 50-amp rate. When it turns off, wait 5 seconds and note the open-circuit voltage as registered on the tester dial. Some testers have an indicator light that comes on to signal the end of the 5-second waiting period. Note the voltage immediately.

4. Charge the battery for 45 seconds, or until the indicator light comes on. Note the voltage.

> **NOTE:** Take the voltage readings immediately after the indicator light comes on even though the meter needle may still be slowly moving.

5. A comparison of the two voltage readings will indicate the battery condition. Batteries indicated as "bad" by the tester should be discarded. Batteries indicated as "good" can remain in service. However, if trouble is suspected because of a customer complaint or battery age, make a further test with a hydrometer.

■ 3-2-17 Cadmium-Tip Test

The cadmium-tip test requires a special tester with cadmium tips that are inserted into the electrolyte of adjacent cells after the filler plugs have been removed. Electrolyte must be up to the proper level. If the car has been operated or the battery charged within 8 hours, turn on the headlights for 1 minute. Then turn the headlights off. Start the test by putting the red probe into the end cell that has the positive terminal and the black probe into the adjacent cell. Note the meter reading. Move probes to cells 2 and 3 and so on along the battery, noting meter readings between all cells. Compare readings. Figure 7 shows various readings and the conditions they indicate.

1. If any two cells vary five scale divisions or more (on top scale), the battery is at the point of failure and should be replaced.

2. If all cells vary less than five scale divisions and all read in the green section, the battery is charged and in good condition.

3. If all cells vary less than five scale divisions but if any falls into the red section, the battery is in good condition but needs charging.

4. If any reading falls into the recharge-and-retest area, the battery is too low to make a good test. Recharge and retest it.

■ 3-2-18 Installing a Battery

When a battery is being removed from or installed in a vehicle, certain precautions should be taken to avoid future trouble or damage to the battery. If a new battery is being installed, it should be of a capacity at least as large as the original. A battery of a higher capacity should be installed if the vehicle has extra electrical equipment that may be operating when the engine is not running. The new battery should be in a charged condition. If it is only partly charged, it might not provide satisfactory initial performance. Sometimes it is possible to "get by" with installing a partly charged new battery. The alternator in the car should bring the battery up to charge after the car has been operated for a few days. (See Sec. ■3-2-30 on activating dry-charged batteries.)

After the new battery is in, the charging system should be checked to make sure it is operating normally. If the alternator does not charge the battery in a normal manner, the new battery will soon run down. The driver might conclude that a defective battery was installed. Procedure for removing and installing batteries is detailed below.

> **NOTE:** The discussion that follows refers mainly to the type of battery having the terminals in the battery top and not on the side. On batteries with the terminals on the side, the terminals are more protected and less likely to gather corrosion.

1. REMOVING BATTERY To remove the battery, first disconnect the grounded terminal cable from the battery terminal post. This makes it less likely that the insulated terminal will be grounded while it is being disconnected. If the grounded terminal is not disconnected first, the wrench might be accidentally touched to ground as the clamp nut on the insulated terminal is loosened. In this case, there would be a direct short of the battery through the wrench, producing a shower of sparks.

Note carefully the locations of the positive and negative terminals so the new battery can be put in with the terminals in the correct locations. The negative terminal post is smaller.

When removing the cable clamps, do not use regular pliers or an open-end wrench to loosen the clamp nuts. This may damage the clamp nuts and cause breakage of the cell cover. (See ■3-2-19 on detaching and replacing battery cable clamps.) Never pry the clamp loose from the terminal if it is stuck. Prying will put a great strain on the battery terminal and might cause it to break loose from the battery plates. Use a battery clamp puller. This puller exerts a pulling action between the clamp and the terminal and does not put stress on the terminal itself.

With the terminal cable clamps disconnected, remove the hold-down bracket or clamps. Use a case-type battery carrier to lift the battery from its holder. The type of carrier strap that fastens on the battery posts could break the seals around the posts. Inspect the holder for corrosion. If it is badly corroded, it may require replacement. Otherwise it may be cleaned and repainted.

Inspect and clean the battery cables and terminals as necessary ■3-2-19).

2. INSTALLING BATTERY Install the battery and connect the insulated terminal first, followed by the grounded terminal. Be sure the positive and negative terminals are connected properly. On most cars with a 12-volt electrical system, the negative terminal is grounded.

Be extremely careful not to install the battery backward. The reversed polarity could burn out the diodes in the alternator. It would also work the ignition system harder, possibly causing high-speed miss. Alternator regulators using transistors and a transistorized ignition system may fail to work at all.

> **NOTE:** Always be sure that any new battery installed is fully charged or properly activated. Many customers have complained about the installation of half-charged new batteries. If the customer has purchased a new battery because the old one was run down, check the charging system to make sure it is operating properly. If the alternator is not charging the battery normally, the new battery will soon run down.

■ 3-2-19 Cleaning Terminals and Cable Clamps

Corrosion tends to accumulate around the cable clamps and terminals. This is a normal condition. When electrolyte escapes from the battery cells, through overfilling or overcharging and a resulting spray of electrolyte, the corrosion speeds up. Periodic cleaning of the battery top and of the terminals and cable clamps will prevent the corrosion from progressing so far as to cause a bad connection. A bad connection can cause poor starting or a run-down battery. (Checking the electrical circuit between the battery and starting motor, including the connections at the battery, is covered in Sec. 3 of this part.) To remove the corrosion and reestablish good connections, first detach the clamps from the battery terminal posts. Remove the battery ground cable first so that you will not accidentally ground the insulated terminal with a tool. If this should happen with the ground cable still connected, a heavy current that might cause considerable damage would flow.

To remove a nut-and-bolt type of cable, loosen the clamp nut about 3/8 inch (9.5 mm). Use a box wrench or special battery-nut pliers. Do not use regular pliers or an open-end wrench. The jaw of the pliers or wrench could swing around and break the cell cover. If the clamp sticks to the battery terminal, use a battery-clamp puller to remove the clamp. Do not use a bar or a screwdriver to pry the clamp loose. Prying the clamp off puts a strain on the terminal post and the plates attached to it. The plates might break loose, and other internal damage that would ruin the battery might occur. Prying could also break the cell cover or case.

To detach the spring-ring type of cable clamp, squeeze the ends of the ring apart with Vise-grip or Channellock pliers. This expands the clamp so that it can be lifted off the terminal post.

With the cable clamps off, use the wire battery terminal brush or steel wool to clean the clamps and the terminal posts to bright metal (Fig. 1). Then install the cable clamps. Tighten the nuts (on the nut-and-bolt type) with battery-nut pliers or a box wrench. If necessary, use a clamp spreader to spread the cable clamp to ensure full seating of the clamp on the terminal post. Figure 8 shows the wrong and the right way to seat the clamp on the post. Never hammer or force the clamp down on the post. This may break the cell cover or cause internal damage that could ruin the battery. Do not overtighten the nut since this could damage the clamp.

Make sure the cable clamps are making good connections with the terminal posts (Fig. 9). If the jaws of the clamp come together as shown to the left, the clamp is probably not tight on the post. This could mean starting trouble. Correct the condition by disconnecting the clamp from the post. Shave the clamp jaws so you get a gap, as shown to the right in Fig. 9, when the clamp is installed.

A coating of Permatex, petroleum jelly, or anticorrosion paste spread on the clamps and posts will retard corrosion. Also, keeping the vent plugs tight will help prevent the escape of electrolyte and consequent corrosion on the clamps, posts, and other metal parts around the battery.

If battery cables are badly corroded, if insulation is damaged, or if strands are broken or loose, replace the cables. When replacing cables, always use a size at least as large as the original. Using a cable that is too small may introduce excessive resistance in the circuit, which could cause starting trouble.

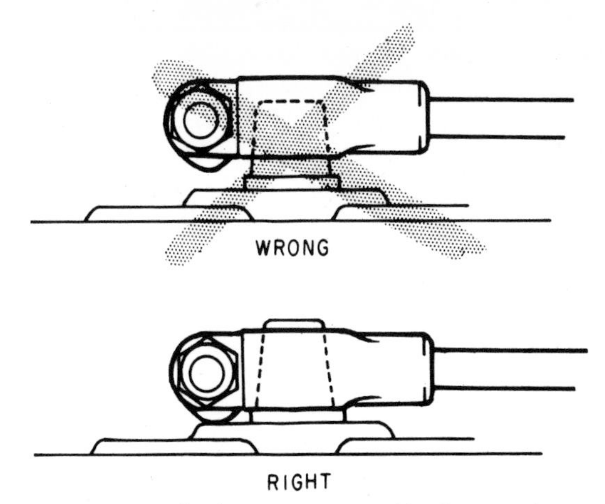

Figure 8 Wrong and right ways to put a cable clamp on the terminal post. *(United Delco Division of General Motors Corporation.)*

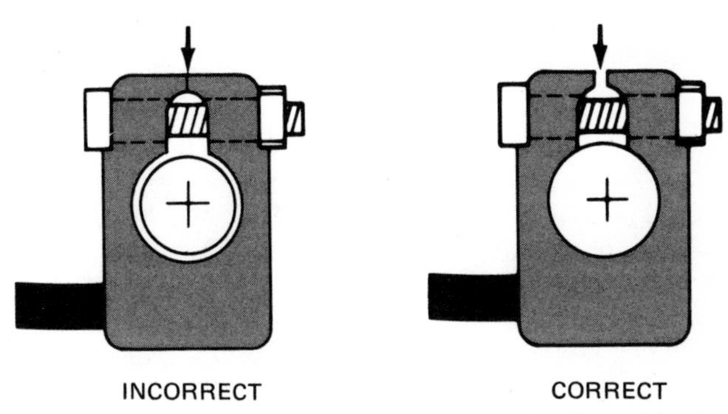

Figure 9 If there is no gap between the jaws of the clamp (left), the clamp is probably loose on the terminal post.

If the battery holder is corroded, the battery should be removed. Then the holder can be cleaned, and painted if necessary.

■ 3-2-20 Tightening Battery Hold-Down Clamps

The hold-down clamps should be kept tight so that the battery will not bounce around or move in its carrier. However, avoid tightening the clamps too much since this will cause the battery case to warp, bulge, or break.

■ 3-2-21 Battery Trouble Diagnosis

When battery trouble is found, the cause should be determined and eliminated. That way, the same problem will not occur again. Following are various battery troubles and their possible causes.

1. OVERCHARGING If the battery requires a considerable amount of water, it is probably being overcharged. That is, too much current is being supplied to the battery. This is a damaging condition that overworks the active materials in the battery and shortens battery life. In addition, overcharging speeds up the loss of water from the battery electrolyte. Unless this water is replaced frequently, electrolyte level is likely to fall below the tops of the plates. This exposes the plates and separators to air and could ruin them. Also, battery overcharge may make battery plates buckle and crumble. A battery subjected to severe overcharging may soon be ruined. Where overcharging occurs or is suspected, check the charging system. Adjust it if necessary to prevent overcharging. See Sec. 5 of this part for the procedures.

2. UNDERCHARGING If the battery is discharged, recharge it as outlined in ■ 3-2-23 to ■ 3-2-26. In addition, try to find out why the battery is discharged. This condition can be caused by:

a. Charging-system malfunction
b. Defective connections in the charging circuit between the alternator and the battery
c. Excessive load demands on the battery
d. A defective battery
e. Permitting the battery to stand idle for long periods so that it self-discharges excessively

In addition, an old battery may have a low specific-gravity reading because it is approaching failure.

CAUTION: If you connect a booster battery to start the engine, observe the procedure in ■ 3-2-22.

3. SULFATION The active materials in the plates are converted into lead sulfate during discharge. This lead sulfate is reconverted into active materials during recharge. However, if the battery stands for long periods in a discharged condition, the lead sulfate is converted into a hard, crystalline substance. This substance is difficult to reconvert into active materials by normal charging processes. Such a battery should be charged at half the normal rate for 60 to 100 hours. Even though this long charging period may reconvert the sulfate to active materials, the battery may still remain damaged. As it forms, the crystalline sulfate tends to break the plate grids.

4. CRACKED CASES Cracked cases may result from excessively loose or tight hold-down clamps, battery freezing, or flying stones.

5. BULGED CASES Bulged cases result from tight hold-down clamps or high temperatures.

6. CORRODED TERMINALS AND CABLE CLAMPS Corrosion occurs naturally on batteries. You should be prepared to remove excessive corrosion from terminals and clamps periodically. Cable clamps should be disconnected from the terminal and the terminal posts and cables cleaned, as covered in ■ 3-2-19.

7. CORRODED BATTERY HOLDER As the battery is being charged, some of the electrolyte commonly sprays from it. This lost electrolyte may cause the battery holder to become corroded. With the battery removed, such corrosion may be cleaned off with a wire brush and a baking-soda-and-water solution.

8. DIRTY BATTERY TOP Dirt and grime mixed with electrolyte sprayed from the battery may accumulate on the battery top. This should be cleaned off periodically, as covered in ■ 3-2-19.

9. DISCHARGE TO METALLIC HOLD-DOWN If the hold-down clamps are of the uncovered metallic type, a slow discharge may occur from the insulated terminal to the hold-down clamp. Discharge is more likely to happen with a dirty battery top, because current can leak across the top. The remedy is to keep the battery top clean and dry.

■ 3-2-22 Starting a Car with a Booster Battery

If the battery in the car is too low to start the engine, another battery can be connected with jumper cables. This other battery, called a "booster" battery, will furnish the current the starting motor needs to start the engine. You should observe certain precautions when using a booster battery. Otherwise, you can damage the electrical equipment. In fact, if you connect the booster battery backward, one of the batteries could explode from the high discharge current taken from it. Here is the procedure that Ford recommends. This procedure is for a negative-ground battery. You need two jumper cables (Fig. 10).

1. Remove the vent caps from both batteries. Cover the holes with cloths to prevent splashing of the electrolyte in case of explosion.

2. Shield your eyes.

3. Do not allow the two cars to touch each other.

4. Make sure all electrical equipment except the ignition is turned off on the car you are trying to start.

5. Connect the end of one jumper cable to the positive (+) terminal of the booster battery. Connect the other end of this cable to the positive (+) terminal of the dead battery.

6. Connect one end of the second cable to the negative (−) terminal of the booster battery.

7. Connect the other end of the second cable to the engine block of the car you are trying to start. Do not connect it to the negative (−) terminal of the car battery! This could damage electrical equipment or cause a battery to explode. Do not lean over the battery while making this connection!

8. Now start the car containing the booster battery. Then start the car containing the low battery. After the disabled car is started, disconnect the booster cables by first disconnecting the cable from the engine block. Then disconnect the other end of this (the negative) cable. Finally, disconnect the positive cable.

NOTE: Never operate the starting motor for more than 30 seconds at a time. Pause for a few minutes to allow it to cool off. Then try again. It takes a very high current to crank the engine. You can overheat and ruin a starting motor if it is used for too long.

■ 3-2-23 Battery-Charging Methods

Two fundamental methods of charging the battery are now in widespread use: slow charging and fast or quick charging. Since most

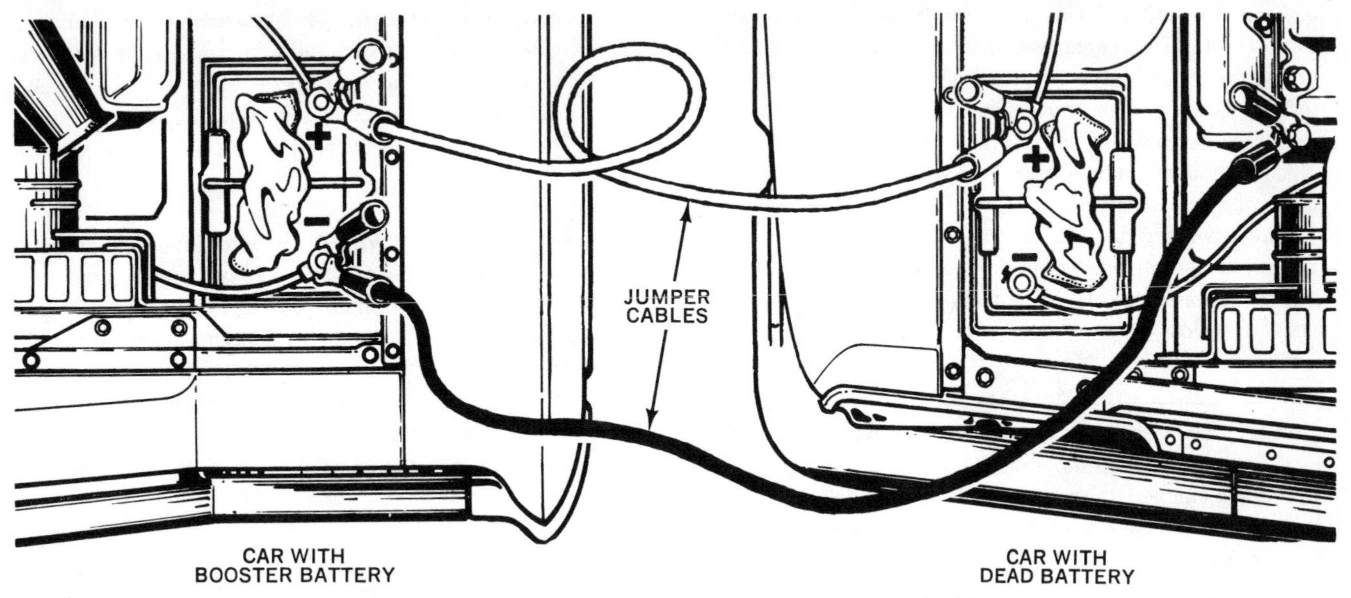

Figure 10 Connections between the booster battery and the dead battery for starting a car with a dead battery.

localities have alternating current only, the battery-charging devices must convert this alternating current (ac) to direct current (dc) and supply it to the battery at a constant current or voltage.

Many battery chargers are designed to charge batteries in automobiles. This is a convenience because the battery does not have to be removed from the car for charging. However, be sure that the ignition switch and all electrical accessories are turned off during charging. The high charging voltage could ruin anything that is turned on. Many manufacturers recommend that the battery ground cable be removed from the battery before charging a battery in the car.

CAUTION: The gasses released by a battery while it is being charged are highly explosive. Therefore, the area around a charging battery should be well ventilated.

NOTE: Side-terminal batteries require adapters in the terminals whenever it is necessary to connect a battery tester or charger.

■ **3-2-24 Slow Charging** The constant-current charger, or slow charger, usually employs a rectifier, which may be a gas-filled bulb or a series of copper-oxide or other chemical disks. In alternating current, the current (or electron flow) moves first one way and then the other. The rectifier permits the current to flow one way only. Current enters the rectifier as alternating current and leaves as direct current. Some form of rheostat is usually incorporated in the charging system, so the amount of current can be adjusted to the value recommended by the battery manufacturer.

If several batteries of different ratings are being charged in series, the charging rate should be determined by the battery with the lowest rating. If the rating cannot be determined, charge the battery at 5-amp rate. The charge should be continued until all cells in the battery are gassing freely and there is no further rise in specific gravity of the electrolyte for 2 hours. You can then be sure that substantially all the lead sulfate in the plates has been reconverted into active material and sulfuric acid.

■ **3-2-25 Constant-Voltage Charging** The constant-voltage charger depends on the fact that as a battery approaches full charge, the terminal voltage increases (current input remaining constant). The charger consists of a motor-generator set or its electronic equivalent. The motor operates on alternating current and drives the generator, which usually has a 7.5-volt rating for 6-volt batteries or a 15-volt rating for 12-volt batteries. When a discharged battery is connected to the charger, a high charging current will flow into the battery. As the battery approaches full charge, its terminal voltage increases and its opposition to the charging current increases. By the time the battery has reached a fully charged state, only a small current will enter it. In other words, the charging current tapers off as the battery approaches a charged condition.

This action is based on the assumption that the battery temperature does not increase excessively. Another characteristic of batteries is that the terminal voltage of a battery being charged will decrease as temperature increases. Thus, if the battery temperature is high, the terminal voltage, or opposition to the charging current, will not increase very much as the battery comes up to charge. The result will be that the current input to the battery will continue high.The battery will be overcharged unless technicians disconnect the battery from the charger.

■ **3-2-26 Quick Charging** Quick or fast chargers charge the battery at a high rate (as much as 100 amperes) for a short time—30 to 34 minutes. The battery is thus brought to a fair state of charge before the battery temperature increases excessively. The quick-charger method does not seem to harm batteries that are not subjected to excessive temperatures. However high charging rates combined with battery-electrolyte temperatures above 125° F (51.7° C) are very damaging to a battery.

Quick chargers usually cannot bring a battery up to full charge in a short time. Suppose a battery has been quick-charged for a short time. If the charging operation is then finished by a slow-charging method, the battery will come up to full charge.

NOTE: A battery with discolored electrolyte or with specific gravity readings more than 25 points apart should not be quick-charged. Likewise, a badly sulfated battery should not be quick-charged. Such batteries may be near failure, but they may give additional service if slow-charged. However, quick-charging them might damage them further. During quick charging, check the color of the electrolyte. Stop charging if the electrolyte becomes discolored as a result of the stirring up of washed-out active material. Likewise, cell voltages should be checked every few minutes. Charging should be stopped if cell voltages vary more than 0.2 volt.

NOTE: When quick-charging a battery in a car, disconnect the battery ground strap to protect the electrical system from damage due to high voltage.

A very low battery may not accept a quick charge. The electrolyte in a very low or "dead" battery does not have much sulfuric acid in it. Therefore, the conductivity of the electrolyte is too low to allow a high current to flow through the battery. You might assume that if a battery refuses to take a quick charge, it is worn out. This may not be true. You may be able to restore such a battery to a charged condition in the following way: First, slow-charge it for a few minutes to see if it starts coming up to charge. If it does, it can then be put on quick charge. Some quick chargers have a special circuit which will slow-charge a dead battery for a short time and then switch to quick charging.

■ 3-2-27 Charging Sulfated Batteries When a battery has been allowed to stand for some time without attention, its plates may have become sulfated to such an extent that it will not take a charge in a normal manner. In fact, the battery may be completely ruined. However, an attempt to save such a battery may be worthwhile, especially if it is not too old. Put the battery on charge at half the normal charging rate for 60 to 100 hours to see whether the sulfation can be broken down so that the battery will take a charge. The "water cure" is sometimes suggested (dumping electrolyte, filling with distilled water, and charging), but there is little advantage in this method over the slow-charge method.

Usually, in a badly sulfated battery, the plate grids and separators are damaged. The sulfate takes more room than the active materials in the plates, and the consequent swelling cracks or breaks the grid structure. A badly sulfated battery may be returned to usable condition, but it can never come back all the way. Part of its life has been lost.

■ 3-2-28 Battery "Dopes" Sometimes electrolyte may be added to a battery if some acid has been lost through spraying or spilling. But other chemicals or "dopes" should never be added. Some of these chemicals may give a battery a temporary boost, but this condition will not last long. Shortly afterward, the battery will probably fail completely, having been ruined by the added chemicals. Furthermore, use of such chemicals voids the manufacturer's guarantee. All battery manufacturers condemn the use of such substances.

■ 3-2-29 Care of Batteries in Stock Batteries are supplied in two ways: wet or dry. The wet batteries have the electrolyte already in them. The dry batteries are in a charged condition but contain no electrolyte. They are ready for use once the electrolyte has been added. (The procedure of activation is explained in ■ 3-2-30.) Dry-charged batteries require little attention in stock. They should be stored in a clean, dry place and put in suitable racks. They should not be stacked one on top of another. Wet batteries require somewhat more attention in stock because they are active and subject to self-discharge.

1. INSPECTION ON ARRIVAL When wet batteries are delivered to the dealer, they should be inspected for damage. The specific gravity should be checked. If the gravity is low, recharge batteries immediately before putting them in stock.

2. STORING WET BATTERIES To store wet batteries, a wood rack should be used. Batteries should never be stacked on top of one another since the weight on the bottom batteries might collapse the plate assemblies and ruin them. Wet batteries should be recharged every 30 days. If a battery is allowed to stand for long periods without attention, it will run down from self-discharge. In addition, the sulfate formed may become so dense that it can never be reconverted, and the battery can never be fully charged. Before charging, the electrolyte level should be checked and brought up to the proper height if necessary.

At low temperature, self-discharge proceeds slowly. Therefore, wet batteries should be stored at a temperature that is low as it can be without posing the risk of freezing the batteries. High temperatures accelerate self-discharge. If batteries are stored in a warm place, they may have to be recharged more often than once a month.

Be sure always to sell the oldest battery in stock. Otherwise, you might eventually find yourself with some very old batteries on hand.

■ 3-2-30 Activating Dry-Charged Batteries Dry-charged batteries have no electrolyte in them and are sealed.

They are chemically inert and can be stored for long periods without attention or deterioration. However, since the plates may oxidize slowly if moisture is present, dry-charged batteries should be kept dry in a clean place and protected from moisture.

Dry-charged batteries are usually packed in shipping cartons. These cartons should be inspected whenever a shipment arrives. If the cartons are damaged or damp, they should be opened so that the batteries themselves can be checked.

The electrolyte for dry-charged batteries is shipped separately in single-application cartons or in 5-gallon (18.93-liter) containers.

CAUTION: Handle electrolyte containers with great care, since electrolyte is highly corrosive (see "Caution," ■3-2-2). Handle electrolyte in an area where plenty of water is available for flushing it away if it should come in contact with the skin or clothes. Wear goggles or eye shields. Refer to the side of the container for the antidotes to use if you should get any electrolyte on your body.

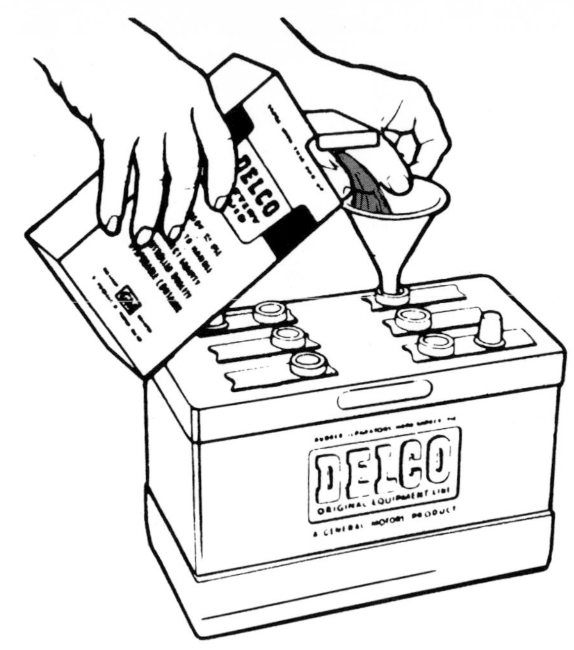

Figure 11 Pouring electrolyte into a battery. *(Delco-Remy Division of General Motors Corporation.)*

To prepare a dry-charged battery for use, or to activate it, proceed as follows:

1. Remove the battery from the carton.

2. Remove the vent plugs. Some batteries which are vacuum-sealed have hard-rubber seals in the vent-plug openings. These seals must be broken by pushing the rod of the Delco Eye down into the vent well. The seal will drop down into the cell, where it will remain without harm.

3. When using the single-application electrolyte cartons, open the carton according to the instructions on the carton. Do not attempt to take the plastic bag from the carton. It is sealed to the carton and could break if an attempt is made to pull it out.

4. Cut a small opening in the corner of the bag, making the opening no larger than necessary. A small hole reduces the chances of splashing the electrolyte when you pour it.

5. Using a glass or acidproof plastic funnel, fill each cell (Fig. 11) to the proper level. Never use a metal funnel, because the metal would contaminate the electrolyte and seriously shorten battery life. Wait a few minutes to allow plates and separators to absorb electrolyte. Then, if necessary, add more electrolyte to bring it up to the proper level. If the container does not have enough electrolyte in it to fill all the cells, open another carton to get whatever additional electrolyte you need. Never complete the filling with water.

6. Wash out the container thoroughly with water before discarding it. Otherwise, someone who does not know how corrosive sulfuric acid is might be seriously hurt by handling the carton.

7. Date-code the battery to indicate the day it was activated.

8. Although the battery can be put into immediate operation, good battery operation can be ensured by checking open-circuit voltage and by charging the battery if it is found to be low. For example, one battery manufacturer states that if a 12-volt battery tests 12.0 volts (6.0 for a 6-volt battery) or more on open circuit, the battery is good and can be put into immediate operation. From 10 to 12 volts (5 to 6 volts for a 6-volt battery) on open circuit indicates some battery-plate oxidation. Such a battery should be charged. Less than 10 volts (5 volts for a 6-volt battery) indicates a defective or reversed cell. This requires battery replacement.

Another check is specific gravity. If, after electrolyte is added, gravity readings drop below 1.235 (new electrolyte is 1.265) or if cells gas violently, the battery should be charged. In this test, the specific gravity readings should be corrected for temperature.

In cold weather a newly activated battery should be given a short charge with a quick charger.

SECTION 3-3 Starting-Motor Troubles and Service

This section explains how to analyze various starting-motor troubles, and it outlines a simple trouble-diagnosis procedure you can use on any car that develops starting trouble. This procedure usually pinpoints the unit in which the trouble lies. If the trouble is in the starting motor, then the testing procedure will show whether the trouble is due to a defective armature, field windings, bearings, brushes, and so on.

■ **3-3-1 Need for Logical Trouble-Shooting Procedure** When starting trouble develops and the starting motor cranks the engine slowly or not at all, a logical checking procedure should be followed. For example, suppose the starting motor does not operate at all. The logical procedure is to use a voltmeter and trace the circuit to find where there is voltage. For example, you would check from the solenoid BAT (battery) terminal to ground for battery voltage. You should get 12 volts here. If you do not, there is an open in the battery-to-starting-motor circuit. Then check from the S (switch) terminal of the solenoid to ground with the voltmeter while an assistant turns the ignition switch to START. If you do not get voltage, the circuit, ignition switch, or neutral starting switch is at fault. Also, on 1974 and later cars with the seat-belt starter interlock system, it may be this system which is at fault.

Thus, the procedure tells you where there is voltage. If you get no voltage at some point, this tells you where the open circuit or other trouble is.

A quick and simple check you can perform is to turn on the lights and try to start the car. You can make this quick check in the darkened garage where the lights will shine on a nearby wall or object, or you can ask an assistant to tell you whether the lights dim. At any rate, the procedure is to turn on the lights and operate (or attempt to operate) the starting motor.

Any one of five conditions will result: (1) lights stay bright, (2) lights dim considerably, (3) lights dim only slightly, (4) lights go out, (5) lights burn dimly or not at all when first turned on, before any attempt to start is made. The causes of trouble with these and other abnormal situations are outlined in the chart that follows, along with checks or corrections to be made. Following the chart are detailed explanations of the checking procedures to be used for each situation. Later we describe tests of the starting motor and starting-motor repair and overhaul procedures.

■ 3-3-2 Starting-Motor Trouble-Diagnosis Chart

About the only starting-motor complaints you will hear are those of slow cranking or no cranking at all. Occasionally there might be a case of the solenoid plunger chattering (overrunning-clutch pinion going into and out of mesh repeatedly) or of slow pinion disengagement. The chart that follows lists possible causes of various conditions and the checks or corrections to be made.

> **NOTE:** The trouble and possible causes are not listed in the chart in the order of frequency of occurrence. That is, item 1 under "Condition" does not necessarily occur more frequently than item 2, nor does item *a* under "Possible Cause" necessarily occur more often than item *b*.

STARTING MOTOR TROUBLE-DIAGNOSIS CHART

(See ■3-3-3 to 3-3-8 for detailed explanations of trouble causes and corrections listed below.)

Condition	Possible Cause	Check or Correction
1. No cranking, lights stay bright (■3-3-3)	a. Open circuit in switch	Check switch contacts and connections
	b. Open circuit in starting motor	Check commutator, brushes, and connections
	c. Open in control circuit	Check solenoid, relay (if used), switch, and connections
2. No cranking, lights dim heavily (■3-3-4)	a. Trouble in engine	Check engine to find trouble (Part 1, Sec. 2)
	b. Battery low	Check, recharge, or replace battery
	c. Very low temperature	Battery must be fully charged, with engine, wiring circuit, and starting motor in good condition
	d. Pinion (Bendix) jammed	Free pinion
	e. Frozen shaft bearings, direct short in starting motor	Repair starting motor
3. No cranking, lights dim slightly (■3-3-4)	a. Pinion (Bendix) not engaging	Clear pinion and sleeve; replace damaged parts
	b. Excessive resistance or open circuit in starting motor	Clean commutator; replace brushes; repair poor connections
4. No cranking, lights go out (■3-3-5)	Poor connection, probably at battery	Clean cable clamp and terminal; tighten clamp
5. No cranking, no lights (■3-3-5)	a. Battery dead	Recharge or replace battery
	b. Open circuit	Clean and tighten connections; replace wiring
6. Engine cranks slowly but does not start (■3-3-6)	a. Battery run down	Check, recharge, or replace battery
	b. Very low temperature	Battery must be fully charged; engine wiring and starting motor in good condition
	c. Starting motor defective	Test starting motor
	d. Undersized battery cables	Install cables of adequate size
	e. Mechanical trouble in engine	Check engine for cause of dragging
	f. Driver may have run battery down trying to start (see item 7)	
7. Engine cranks at normal speed but does not start	a. Ignition system defective	Try spark test; check timing and ignition system
	b. Fuel system defective	Check fuel pump, line, choke, and carburetor (See Part 1, Sec. 6)
	c. Air leaks in intake manifold or carburetor	Tighten mounting; replace gasket as needed
	d. Engine defective	Check compression, valve timing, etc. (See Part 1, Sec. 2)
8. Solenoid plunger chatters (■3-3-7)	a. Hold-in winding of solenoid open	Replace solenoid
	b. Low battery	Charge battery
9. Pinion disengages slowly after starting (■3-3-8)	a. Sticky solenoid plunger	Clean and free plunger
	b. Overrunning clutch sticks on armature shaft	Clean armature shaft and clutch sleeve

■ 3-3-3 Lights Stay Bright

If the lights stay bright as the starting-motor circuit is closed and if no cranking action takes place, no current is flowing from the battery to the starting motor. The tests to locate the open circuit that produces this condition differ according to the type of system.

> **NOTE:** On many cars equipped with an automatic transmission, there is a neutral safety switch that prevents starting unless the selector lever is in park or neutral. On such cars, be sure that the selector lever is in park or neutral and the safety switch and circuit are in normal condition before proceeding with the checks outlined below.

> **NOTE:** On 1974 and later cars equipped with a seatbelt starter interlock system, the car will not start unless the proper starting sequence is followed. Malfunction of this system will also prevent starting.

With the starting-motor system using a solenoid and overrunning-clutch drive or a magnetic switch with Bendix drive, first find out if the control system is doing its job. Try to start the engine. One of two things will happen:

(1) The magnetic switch or solenoid will not operate or (2) the magnetic switch or solenoid will operate but the starting motor will not. Check further, as follows.

1. MAGNETIC SWITCH OR SOLENOID DOES NOT OPERATE This means that current is not getting to or through the magnetic switch or solenoid. One of the various control devices is not doing its job. Before proceeding any further, make sure that the starting motor will operate. Momentarily connect a heavy jumper cable across the two main terminals of the solenoid or magnetic switch (on the nuts, not on the screws, to avoid burning the threads). On some magnetic switches and solenoids, this same test may be made by operating the magnetic switch, or solenoid, by hand. If the starting motor operates, check the control system as follows:

On the magnetic switch, put a jumper lead from the heavy switch terminal connected to the battery to the small magnetic-switch S terminal. This connects the magnetic switch directly to the battery, eliminating the rest of the control circuit. If the magnetic switch does not operate, its winding is open. If it and the starting motor operate, check the other control devices in the system. By using a jumper lead and connecting around each device in turn, you can find the one that is not operating properly.

On some solenoid-operated starting motors on older-model cars, a relay will be found. Remove the relay cover and close the relay points by hand. If the solenoid and starting motor now operate, they are okay. The relay and other control devices should be checked. Disconnect the leads from the relay, ground the relay terminal with a jumper lead, and connect the other terminal to the battery. If the relay does not work, it is out of adjustment or has an open winding. If the relay works, check the other devices in the control circuit by connecting a jumper lead around them.

2. MAGNETIC SWITCH OR SOLENOID OPERATES BUT STARTING MOTOR DOES NOT This indicates that there is an open circuit in the switch or the motor. Usually, the trouble will be in the starting motor. Take the starting-motor cover band off on motors so equipped, and check the brushes and commutator. Starting motors without cover bands must be partly disassembled for inspection of the brushes and the commutator.

The above procedure is quite simple in actual practice. By using it, the service technician can readily solve most cases of starting-motor trouble. If you want to be more specific, you can use a voltmeter, instead of a jumper lead, to locate the open circuit in the system. Connecting the voltmeter across any of the control devices (from one terminal to the other) will tell you whether or not they are operating. If they are closing the circuit, there will be only a small voltage reading. If they are not, the voltage reading will be high. (This does not apply to the solenoid relay.) Another way of making this test is to check from each terminal to ground with the voltmeter. A voltage reading of nearly battery voltage means that current is available up to that point in the circuit. No reading means that there is an open circuit between that point in the circuit and the battery.

■ 3-3-4 Lights Dim

If the lights dim when the starting-motor circuit is closed, it may help to try to find out whether the lights dim only a little or whether they dim a lot. If the lights dim only slightly with no cranking action, there may be too much resistance or a partial open in the starting motor.This condition would prevent all but a small amount of current from flowing. No cranking and only slight dimming of the lights would result. If there is slight dimming along with the sound of a running electric motor, it may be that the pinion (on the Bendix-type drive only) is not engaging. Thus, the motor would run free without cranking the engine. The Bendix pinion might fail to engage because it is stuck on the sleeve. This could be due to dirt or gum or possibly to battered threads that prevent movement on the sleeve. If there is slight dimming along with the sound of pinion engagement without cranking action, the starting-motor solenoid (on overrunning-clutch unit) is producing pinion engagement but there is an open in the starting motor that is preventing cranking action. A slight dimming of the lights with a scraping noise indicates that the overrunning clutch is slipping and must be replaced.

If the lights dim considerably without cranking action, there could be mechanical trouble in the engine, the battery could be run down, temperatures might be very low, or there could be trouble in the starting motor itself. The battery should be checked and recharged or replaced as necessary. At very low temperatures, when engine oil is stiff and cranking is hard, the battery is much less able to maintain voltage under heavy load. As a result, battery voltage will drop considerably and lights will become very dim during cranking at very low temperature. The cold can be so severe that the starting motor cannot turn the engine over at all.

NOTE: Keep in mind that a driver may run the battery down in attempting to start the car. Then there is no cranking action when you test the car, even though the battery may still be in good enough condition to light the lights. The cause of this failure is not in the battery or starting motor but possibly in the ignition system, fuel system, or engine.

■ 3-3-5 No Lights, or Lights Go Out

If the lights burn very dimly or not at all when the light switch is turned on, then either the battery is completely discharged or there is an open in the circuit. Test the battery and check the wiring, connections, and switch.

If the lights come on when the light switch is turned on but go off when the starting-motor circuit is closed, there probably is a bad connection between the starting motor and battery. The bad connection is probably at one of the battery terminals. The poor connection allows little current to flow through it. There will be enough current for the lights, but when the starting-motor circuit is closed, most of the current that does get through then flows through the starting motor. This is because the starting-motor resistance is much lower than the resistance of the lights. However, there will not be enough current to operate the starting motor.

You can often tell whether or not there is a bad connection at a battery terminal by keeping the starting-motor circuit closed for a few seconds while watching the battery-terminal connections. If there is a bad connection, heat will develop. You can feel this heat by touching the cable clamp. Sometimes, there is so much heat that the connection starts to smoke. Moving the cable clamp around on the terminal a little may improve the connection enough to get started. The remedy is to remove the cable clamp, clean the clamp and terminal, and install the clamp tightly. See Sec. 2 of this part.

You can find almost any bad connection in a circuit through which current is flowing by putting a voltmeter across the connection (Fig. 1). If there is resistance in the connection (which means a poor connection), there will be a voltage reading, or a voltage drop, across the connection. Resistance causes a voltage drop, since it takes voltage to push current through a resistance. The higher the resistance, the more voltage required.

■ 3-3-6 Engine Cranks Slowly but Does Not Start

If the engine turns over slowly but does not start when the starting-motor switch is closed, there are several causes to consider. The battery may be run down, the temperature may be so low as to cause cranking difficulty, the starting motor may be defective, undersize cables may have been installed, or there may be mechanical trouble in the engine. It is also possible that the driver has run the battery down trying to start. In this case, the starting motor may crank normally with a fully charged battery but the engine will not start because of trouble

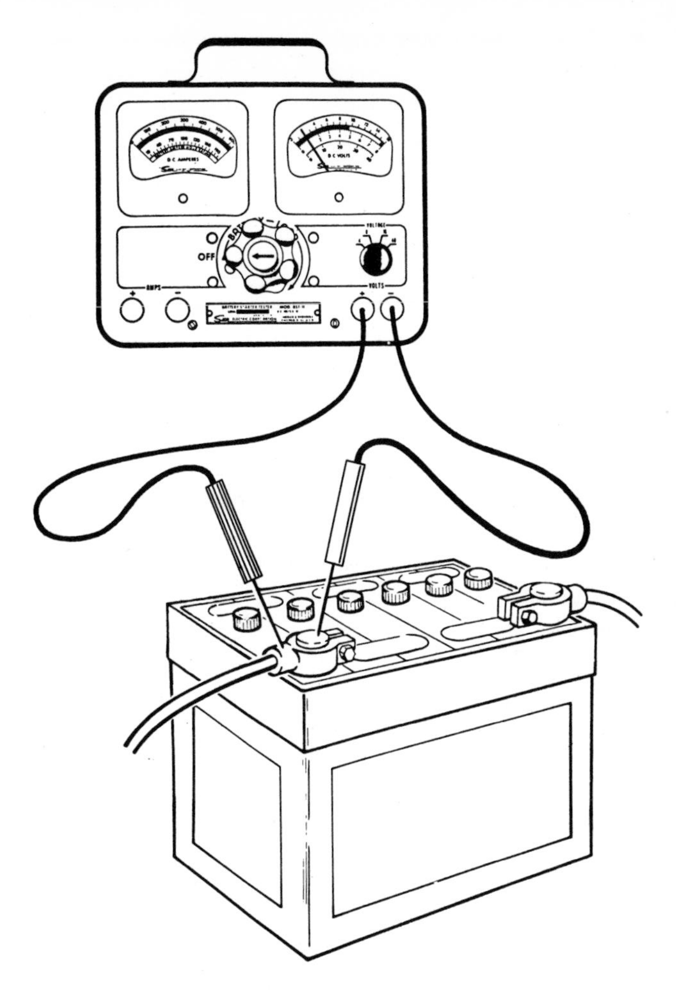

Figure 1 Testing a connection for resistance with a voltmeter. With current flowing through the connection, place prods of the voltmeter on the terminal and the clip, or clamp, as shown. A voltage reading indicates resistance at the connection.

in the ignition or fuel system or because of abnormal conditions in the engine.

■ 3-3-7 Solenoid Plunger Chatters

An open-circuit hold-in winding in the solenoid or magnetic switch will cause the plunger to pull in and release repeatedly when the control circuit is closed. With this defect, the pull-in winding pulls the plunger in and closes the circuit between the battery and starting motor. But as this happens, the switch contacts short out the pull-in winding. Since the hold-in winding is not operative, there is nothing to keep the plunger in, and the plunger is released. The pull-in winding is again energized and pulls the plunger in once more. As a result, the plunger moves in and out of the solenoid or magnetic switch quite rapidly and no cranking takes place.

Another cause of this condition is a low battery. As soon as the circuit between the starting motor and battery is completed, the voltage of the battery drops (the lower the state of battery charge, the lower the voltage). Now the voltage of the discharged battery may drop too low to hold the solenoid plunger in. The plunger, therefore, is pulled back by overrunning-clutch return spring. With the starting-motor disconnected, the battery voltage goes up and the plunger is pulled in again. The action is rapidly repeated.

■ 3-3-8 Pinion Disengages Slowly after Starting

Sometimes, the pinion will not release readily after the engine starts (overrunning-clutch starting motor). Then, after engine speed increases, it may release with a loud "zooming" sound. This results from the overspeeding of the starting-motor armature. Such overspeeding may result in thrown armature windings and complete ruin of the starting motor.

Possible causes are a sticky solenoid plunger, overrunning clutch sticking on the armature shaft, a defective clutch that will not allow the pinion to overrun normally, or a weak shift-lever return spring. If there is slow disengagement, prompt steps to eliminate the trouble should be taken before the armature is ruined by thrown windings. Remove the starting motor, if necessary, to check freeness of the clutch on the armature shaft and clutch operations.

STARTING-MOTOR SERVICE

■ 3-3-9 Periodic Maintenance

Most starting motors require no maintenance between engine overhauls. That is, they have sufficient lubrication and large enough brushes, and none of their parts need attention until the the engine requires overhauling. Other starting motors do need lubrication, and this should be done periodically. Wiring circuits, mounting, and general condition of the starting motor should be checked periodically on all types.

1. LUBRICATION Most starting motors do not require lubrication except during overhaul. On units with lubrication fittings, the recommendation is to lubricate every 5,000 miles (8,047 km) as follows:

a. Hinge-cap oilers should have 8 to 10 drops of medium-grade engine oil.
b. On oil tubes fitted with a pipe plug, the plug should be removed and 8 to 10 drops of medium-grade engine oil added.
c. Grease cups should be turned down one turn, and refilled if necessary. The commutator must never be oiled.

2. LUBRICATION DURING OVERHAUL When a starting motor has been disassembled, oil wicks and oil reservoirs should be saturated, or filled, with light engine oil. Bendix drives should not be lubricated. They should be washed with kerosene and allowed to dry. If, under extreme temperature conditions, some lubricant is necessary, a little graphite can be used. The roller-type overrunning clutch requires no lubrication since it is filled with lubricant during manufacture. It should not be washed or cleaned in a solvent tank as this would wash out the lubricant and cause clutch failure. After partial disassembly, sprag-type clutches should be lubricated with 5W20 oil. (A heavier grade of oil must not be used.) At the same time, the felt washer should be saturated with the same grade of oil. If there is a spiral spline on the shell assembly, it should be lubricated with 10W oil.

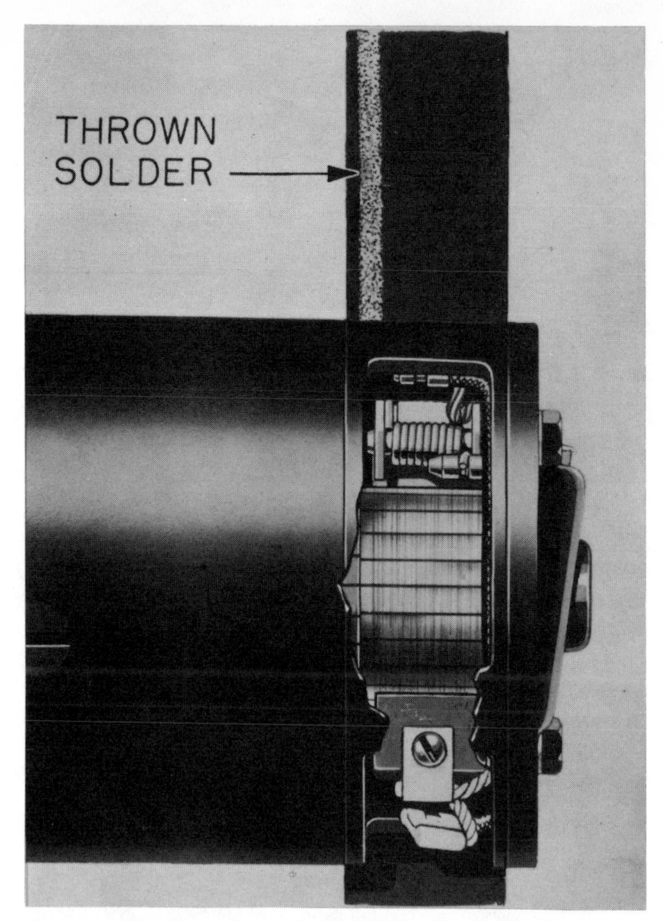

Figure 2 Thrown solder on the starting-motor cover band indicates that the starting motor has been overloaded, probably by excessively long cranking cycles.

3. PERIODIC INSPECTION During an engine tuneup or when checking under the hood for trouble, inspect the starting motor and the circuits. Many starting motors require no lubrication between engine overhauls. For this type, the only check is for tight mounting, electric connections, and general condition of the unit as indicated by its operation.

Starting motors with cover bands can also be inspected for brush and commutator wear after the band has been removed. If there are worn brushes or a badly worn or out-of-round commutator, the starting motor must be removed so that it can be disassembled and serviced. A dirty commutator can be cleaned with a brush-seating stone or with No.00 sandpaper held against the commutator with a piece of wood while the starting motor is operated. Brush-seating paste can also be used. Do not operate the starting motor for more than 30 seconds!

Thrown solder on the cover band (Fig. 2) indicates that the starting motor has overheated as a result of excessively long cranking periods. If you find thrown solder, the starting motor should be rebuilt and the armature replaced.

4. PERIODIC MAINTENANCE FOR SPECIAL CONDITIONS For unusual operating conditions, special maintenance schedules should be set up. For example, on equipment operated door-to-door with many stops and starts daily, the starting motor and the battery should be inspected often. The same holds true for equipment operated in very dusty, wet, hot, or cold conditions. Heavy-duty equipment, especially in severe operating conditions, must have periodic checks and maintenance. Manufacturers' recommendations should be followed.

5. THROTTLE LINKAGE Some applications use a linkage between the starting-motor shift mechanism and the throttle. This linkage partially opens the throttle during cranking. To ensure easy starting, the linkage should be checked and adjusted if necessary to make sure that the throttle is being opened to the correct amount.

6. NEUTRAL SAFETY SWITCH The neutral safety switch is used on cars with automatic transmissions which do not have the steering-column ignition switch. If the neutral safety switch is not correctly adjusted, it will not close when the automatic transmission selector lever is in neutral or park. Thus, cranking would not be possible. The switch is adjusted by shifting its position on the steering column. Refer to the applicable car shop manual for details.

■ **3-3-10 Starting Motor Tests** Different manufacturers have different testing procedures for checking starting motors and circuits on cars. Here, we outline the tests for Chevrolet, Ford, and Plymouth Cars.

■ **3-3-11 Chevrolet Tests** Chevrolet tests include voltage tests of the starting system and an amperage test of the solenoid windings.

1. VOLTAGE TEST OF STARTING SYSTEM First, make sure the battery is in good condition and charged. The engine must be at operating temperature. Then proceed as follows:

a. Disconnect the ignition primary lead from the ignition distributor to the coil so the engine will not start. Connect a voltmeter to the motor terminal of the solenoid and to an engine mounting bracket.
b. Turn ignition switch to START to crank the engine. Quickly take the voltmeter reading. Do not crank over 30 seconds!
c. If the starting motor turns at normal cranking speed and the voltmeter reads 9 volts or more, the motor and switch are satisfactory.
d. If the cranking speed is below normal and the voltmeter reading is above 9 volts, the starting motor is defective.
e. If the cranking speed is below normal, and the voltmeter reading is less than 9 volts, either the battery is low, there is trouble in the starting motor or engine, or the solenoid contacts are burned. Slow cranking could mean that there is too much friction in the engine (perhaps due to the wrong engine oil), the starting-motor armature is dragging, or there is an internal ground (see ■3-3-19).

2. VOLTAGE TEST OF SOLENOID CONTACTS If the solenoid contacts are burned, they could offer a high resistance. This would result in low cranking speed and low voltage at the solenoid terminals. The voltage drop across the contacts can be checked with the voltmeter. With the ignition primary lead from the distributor to the coil disconnected so the engine will not start, turn the ignition switch to START. Immediately note the voltage. If it is more than 0.2 volt, the solenoid should be repaired or replaced.

NOTE: You will have to switch the voltmeter to the low scale during cranking only in order to get an accurate reading. At other times, the voltmeter should be on the high scale.

3. AMPERAGE TEST OF SOLENOID WINDINGS Remove the nut from the motor terminal of the solenoid. Bend the connector strap away from the screw so the motor is disconnected.

a. Ground the solenoid motor terminal with a heavy jumper wire.
b. Connect a 12-volt battery, voltmeter, ammeter, variable resistance, and jumper wire from the starting motor to the battery ground terminal.
c. Adjust variable resistance until the voltmeter reads 10 volts. Ammeter now shows current draw of the two windings in parallel.
d. Remove jumper wire from solenoid motor terminal and readjust resistance to get 10 volts. Ammeter reading shows current draw of hold-in winding alone.

■ **3-3-12 Ford Tests** Late-model Fords use two types of starting motors, the sliding pole-shoe type and the solenoid type. The tests for the two are different.

■ **3-3-13 Ford Sliding Pole-Shoe Starting-Motor Tests** There are three on-the-car starting-motor tests.

1. WITH ENGINE FLOODED Flood the engine by pumping the accelerator pedal about 10 times. Turn the ignition key to START. The engine may fire but not run because it is flooded. If the starting motor continues to crank at normal speed, it should be considered okay.

2. WITH PRIMARY COIL LEAD DISCONNECTED Pull the push-on connector from the ignition coil primary terminal. Put the connector loosely on the coil terminal.

Connect a remote starter switch to the magnetic switch (starter relay). Turn the ignition switch to ON and close the starter switch. As soon as the engine begins to run, pull the push-on connector from the coil terminal. The engine will now stop running, but cranking will continue. If cranking is normal, the starting motor is okay.

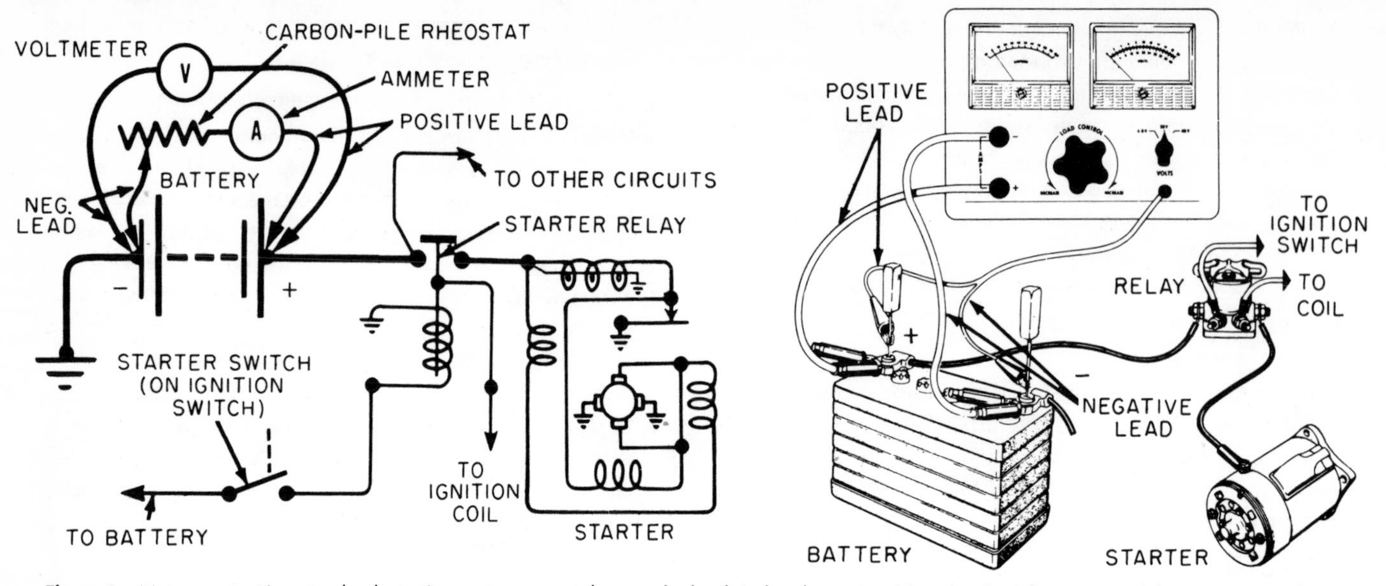

Figure 3 Meter connections to check starting-motor current draw under load. Left, schematic wiring circuit; right, meter and rheostat connections. *(Ford Motor Company.)*

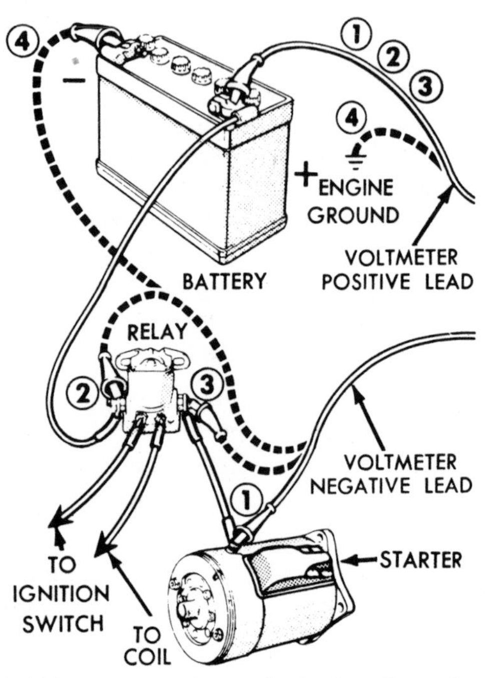

Figure 4 Voltmeter connections to check voltage drop in the starting-motor circuit. Voltage is measured at four places, as shown, during cranking. *(Ford Motor Company.)*

3. STARTING-MOTOR LOAD TEST This test measures the ampere draw of the starting motor under load. Make connections as shown in Fig. 3. Disconnect the distributor primary lead from the ignition coil. Connect a jumper lead from the insulated battery terminal to the S terminal of the relay. Crank the engine with the engine off to determine the cranking voltage. Then stop cranking. Reduce the resistance until the voltmeter indicates the same voltage. Note the current draw, which is the same as the current drawn by the starting motor during cranking.

4. STARTING-MOTOR CIRCUIT TEST Make the test connections as shown in Fig. 4. Crank with the ignition off so the engine will not run (disconnect the distributor primary lead from the coil). Make voltmeter lead connections 1 to 4, as shown, to measure voltage drop in the various parts of the circuit. Check the Ford shop manual for allowable maximum voltage drop. If resistance is excessive, clean and tighten connections or replace wiring as necessary.

■ 3-3-14 Ford Solenoid-Starting-Motor Tests

Ford recommends three on-the-vehicle tests of the starting motor and circuit.

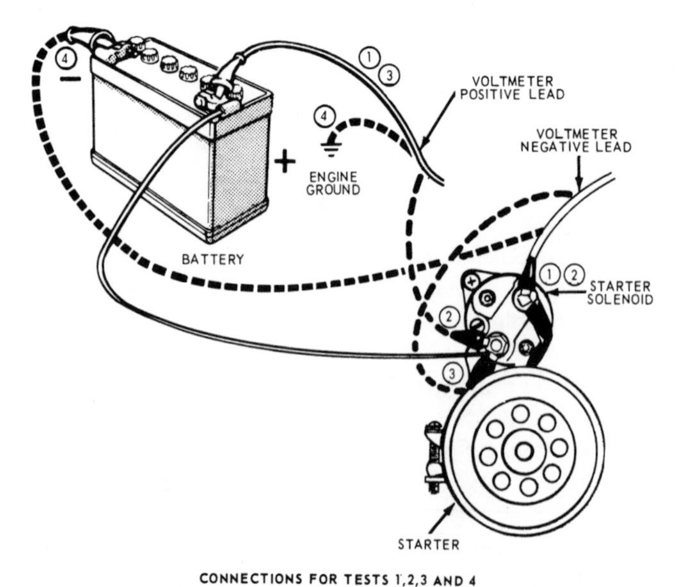

Figure 5 Voltmeter connections to check voltage drop in the starting-motor circuit. Voltage is measured in four places, as shown, during cranking. *(Ford Motor Company.)*

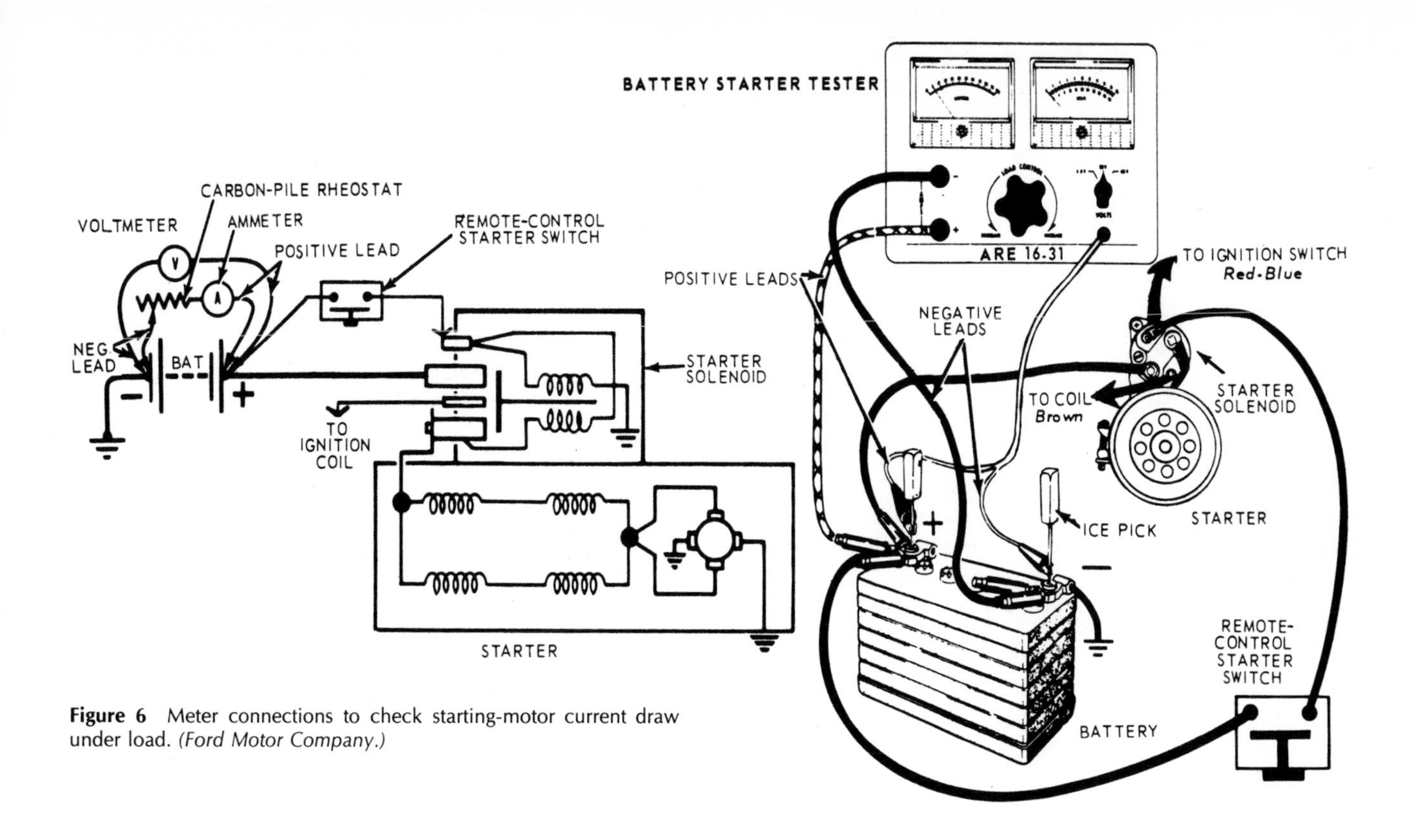

Figure 6 Meter connections to check starting-motor current draw under load. *(Ford Motor Company.)*

> **NOTE:** On some factory production lines, magnetic switches (starter relays) are installed on all vehicles, regardless of whether they take the sliding pole-shoe or the solenoid type. This is to simplify manufacturing procedures. The solenoid type does not need the magnetic switch. To provide normal operation with the magnetic switch, the solenoid has a connector link. If this link were not used, the engine would not start. If the connector link is used on a car without a magnetic switch, the starting motor will operate as soon as the battery is connected.

1. STARTING-MOTOR CIRCUIT TEST Make the four sets of voltmeter lead connections as noted in Fig. 5. Disconnect the distributor lead from the coil to prevent starting. Use a remote starter switch to operate the starting motor. Measure the voltage drop at the four points shown.

2. LOAD TEST Connect the equipment as shown in Fig. 6. The rheostat should be off (at maximum resistance). Crank the engine with the ignition off (distributor lead disconnected from coil). Note the voltage. Then stop cranking. Reduce the resistance until the voltmeter reads the same. Note the ampere draw, which is the same as the current the starting motor drew.

3. SOLENOID-DRAW TEST If the solenoid does not pull in, measure the voltage between the solenoid switch terminal and ground with the ignition switch turned to ON. If the reading is 10 volts or more, the solenoid is defective.

CIRCUIT RESISTANCE CHART

	VOLTMETER LEAD CONNECTION		
CONNECTION	POSITIVE	NEGATIVE	VOLTMETER READING
Positive post on battery to cable clamp	To post	To clamp	0
Negative post on battery to cable clamp	To post	To clamp	0
Battery ground cable to engine block	To bolt	To cable connector	Not to exceed 0.2 volt
Battery cable to starter	To battery positive post	To battery terminal on starter	Not to exceed 0.2 volt
Starter housing to ground	To starter housing	To negative post on battery	Not to exceed 0.2 volt

Figure 7 Table of permissible voltage drops in various parts of the starting-motor circuit during cranking. *(Chrysler Corporation.)*

■ **3-3-15 Plymouth Starting-Motor Tests** Plymouth recommends a current-draw test and a circuit-resistance test. The current-draw test is made in the same way as the Ford solenoid test (■3-3-14). That is, the voltage is measured during cranking. Then the current draw is measured at the same voltage. The circuit-resistance test is made by connecting the voltmeter leads at various points (see Fig. 7) while the engine is being cranked.

The control units in the control circuit may include the interlock system, starting-motor solenoid, starter relay, safety neutral switch (automatic transmissions), and clutch start switch (manual transmission).

1. INTERLOCK-SYSTEM TEST Have a helper sit in the driver's seat, fasten the seat belt, and turn the ignition switch to START. At the same time, use a low-voltage (14 volt) test light connected to ground and the ignition terminal of the starter relay. If the light does not go on, there is trouble in the interlock system.

2. SOLENOID TEST Connect a heavy jumper lead across the starter-relay main terminals. If the starting motor works, the solenoid is okay. If the starting motor does not work, the trouble is in the wiring, connections, solenoid, or starting motor.

3. AUTOMATIC-TRANSMISSION SAFETY NEUTRAL SWITCH With the selector lever in neutral or park, connect a jumper lead between the starter-relay battery and ignition terminals. If the engine cranks, the starter relay is good. If the engine does not crank, connect a second jumper lead between the ground terminal and a good ground. If the starting motor now works, the transmission linkage is out of adjustment or the safety neutral switch is defective. If the engine does not crank, the starter relay is defective.

4. MANUAL-TRANSMISSION CLUTCH START SWITCH Have a helper depress the clutch pedal. Connect a jumper lead between the battery and ignition terminals on the starter relay. If the engine cranks, the starter relay is okay. If the engine does not crank, connect a second jumper wire on the starter relay between the ground terminal and ground. If the engine cranks, the relay is good but the clutch start switch is defective or out of adjustment.

■ **3-3-16 Off-the-Car Starting-Motor Tests** These include a no-load test and a stall test.

■ **3-3-17 No-Load Test** Figure 8 shows a typical setup to no-load-test the starting motor. Refer to the specifications issued by the starting-motor manufacturer. Adjust the variable resistance to get the specified voltage. Then read the current draw and armature rpm (revolutions per minute).

■ **3-3-18 Stall Test** The stall test is made with the starting motor off the car. The drive must be locked so the armature cannot turn, and then a specified voltage is applied to see what current the stalled motor will draw. A high-reading ammeter is required for this test, as well as a high-capacity carbon-pile rheostat.

The starting-motor resistance can be determined at the same time that the stall test is made. With the rheostat adjusted to apply the specified voltage, the current is measured. Then the resistance is calculated by using Ohm's law. See ■3-1-13.

■ **3-3-19 Interpreting Results of Tests** Even without the special equipment for making the no-load and stall tests, an experienced technician can get a good idea of the condition of the starting motor by operating it in the car. However, for an accurate analysis, the unit should be tested as described. Interpreting the results of these tests and further analysis with a test light to pinpoint causes of trouble are discussed below. Note the procedures to follow under the six conditions described.

1. Rated current draw and no-load speed indicate normal condition of the starting motor.

2. Low free speed and a high current draw may result from:

a. Tight, dirty, or worn bearings; bent armature shaft; or loose field-pole screws, which allow the armature to drag on the pole shoes.

b. Grounded armature or fields. Raise the grounded brushes from the commutator and insulate them with cardboard. Then check with a low-voltage test light between the insulated terminal of the starting motor and the frame. If the test light goes on, indicating a ground, raise the other brushes from the commutator and check fields and commutator separately to determine which is grounded. On some units, one end of the field circuit is normally grounded, and the ground screw or screws must be removed before the field can be tested for ground.

c. Shorted armature. Check the armature further on a growler (see ■3-3-28).

3. Failure to operate at all, accompanied by a high current draw, may result from:

a. Direct ground in the switch, terminal, or fields. This may be found with a test light by raising the grounded brushes as in 2*a*, above.

b. Frozen shaft bearings, which prevent the armature from turning.

c. Direct ground of armature windings—for example, due to thrown armature windings (■3-3-29).

4. Failure to operate with no current draw may result from:

a. Open field circuit. Inspect internal connections and trace the circuit with a test light, checking the brushes, armature, and fields.

b. Open armature coils. This condition causes badly burned commutator bars. There is a discussion of this condition in ■3-3-29.

c. Broken or weak brush springs, worn brushes, high mica on the commutator, glazed or dirty commutator, or any other condition that would prevent good contact between the commutator and the brushes will prevent operation of the starting motor.

5. Low no-load speed with a low current draw indicates:
   a. An open field winding. Raise and insulate the ungrounded brushes from the commutator and check the fields with a test light. The light should go on as prods are connected across each field.
   b. High internal resistance due to poor connections, defective leads, dirty commutator, or any other condition listed under 4*c* above.

6. High free speed with a high current draw indicates shorted fields. Since the fields already have a very low resistance, there is no practical way to test for this condition. If shorted fields are suspected, replace the fields and check for improvement in performance. But before going to this trouble, check the other components of the starting motor.

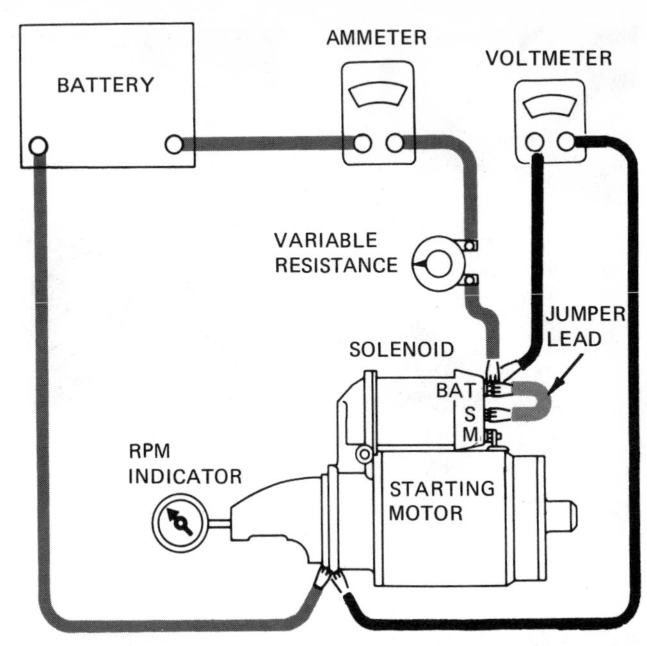

Figure 8 No-load test of a starting motor. A jumper lead must be used, as shown, to energize the solenoid so that it operates to connect the starting motor to the battery. *(Delco-Remy Division of General Motors Corporation.)*

■ 3-3-20 Removal, Servicing, and Replacement of Starting Motors

Many starting motors have a mounting flange on the drive housing and are mounted on the flywheel housing by bolts through holes in the flange. Others have mounting pads. A typical removal procedure follows:

1. Disconnect the battery ground cable from the battery terminal post.
2. Remove heat shield if present.
3. Disconnect all wires at the solenoid terminals. Reinstall nuts on terminals to avoid mixing or losing them.
4. Loosen the starting-motor front-bracket nut or bolt (where present) and remove the starting-motor mounting bolts.
5. Remove the front-bracket nut or bolt and push the bracket out of the way (on installations having a bracket).
6. Pull the starting motor forward and out. On some models, the front end must be lowered first so that the drive end can be brought forward on a slant.

■ 3-3-21 Disassembly

The disassembly procedure varies with different starting motors. The following sections describe methods of disassembling and reassembling various starting motors. Usually, the disassembly should go only as far as is necessary to find and eliminate the defect or condition causing trouble. Inspection and repair of armatures are covered in ■3-3-28. Inspection and replacement of bearings are outlined in ■3-3-31. Removal, repair, and installation of field coils are detailed in ■3-3-33. Usually, it is not necessary to disassemble the field frame and remove the field coils unless the insulation is charred or damaged or the coils are grounded to the frame.

■ 3-3-22 Brushes and Brush-Spring Tension

When a starting motor is being reassembled, the brush-spring tension should be checked with a spring scale. To make the check, put together the armature and commutator end frame so that the brushes are resting on the commutator. Then, use a spring scale to measure the tension required to raise the brush or brush arm from the commutator. Brushes should have full contact on the commutator and be free in their holders. New brushes should be installed if the old ones are worn down to half their original length. Improper spring tension requires replacement of the springs.

> **NOTE:** Do not allow the brush or brush arm to snap down. This might cause the brush to crack or chip.

■ 3-3-23 Disassembly and Assembly of Bendix-Drive Starting Motors

Some starting motors of this type have a magnetic switch. Some may have a center bearing mounted between the field frame and the drive housing. To disassemble the starting motor, remove the magnetic switch (where present) take off the cover band, and disconnect the brush leads if they are fastened to the field leads by screws. If the leads are soldered, remove the brushes from the brush holders, leaving them attached to the field leads. Unscrew the through bolts and separate the commutator end frame, field frame assembly, and drive housing. If there is a center bearing, detach it. Now, remove the armature with Bendix drive from the drive housing. Detach the Bendix drive by bending down the washer tang and unscrewing the head-spring screw. To disassemble the Bendix drive further, unscrew the shaft-spring screw.

Armature service is covered in ■3-3-28, and field-coil service is covered in ■3-3-33.

The Bendix drive can be cleaned by washing it in solvent. It should never be lubricated with grease or oil, as this may prevent normal drive action. In some situations (high-temperature operation, for example) lubrication may be needed. If so, use a small amount of graphite. When reassembling the Bendix, always use new tang lock washers. If old ones are reused, the tangs may break off.

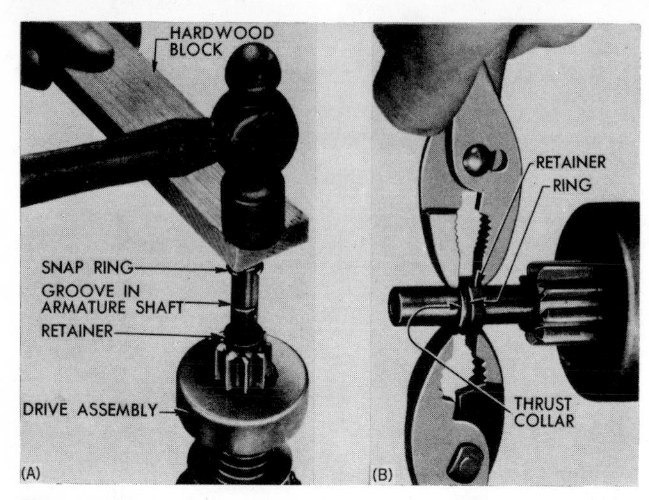

Figure 9 Installing the snap ring and retainer on the armature shaft after drive-assembly installation. *(Buick Motor Division of General Motors Corporation.)*

■ 3-3-24 Overrunning-Clutch Starting Motors

To disassemble a solenoid-operated overrunning-clutch starting motor, remove the solenoid assembly and take off the cover band. Detach the brush leads from the field leads if they are attached by screws. If the leads are soldered, remove the brushes from the brush holders. Then take out the through bolts so the commutator end frame, field frame, and drive housing can be separated. Take the armature with the drive assembly from the drive housing.

On some later models, the drive assembly is held on the armature shaft by a thrust collar, retainer, and snap ring. First remove the thrust collar. Then put a metal cylinder [such as a ½-inch (12.7 mm) pipe coupling] over the end of lightly with a hammer to force the retainer down off the snap ring. Remove the snap ring and slide the retainer and drive assembly from the armature shaft.

Armature service is covered in ■ 3-3-28, while field-coil service is detailed in ■ 3-3-33.

1. OVERRUNNING CLUTCH The overrunning clutch should be wiped clean. Never clean it in solvent. This would remove the lubricant originally packed in the clutch, and the clutch would fail. It is very difficult to relubricate the overrunning clutch mechanism. If the pinion turns roughly or slips in the cranking direction, replace the drive assembly.

To replace the overrunning clutch on the armature shaft (type using retainer and snap ring), first lubricate the end of the shaft with SAE20W oil. Install the drive assembly, pinion out. Slide the stop retainer down over the shaft, recessed side out. Put a new snap ring on the end of the armature shaft and slide it down into the groove in the shaft, tap it down with a plastic hammer, or rest a hardwood block on the ring and strike the block with a hammer (Fig. 9). Install the thrust collar on the shaft. Use two pairs of pliers to squeeze the thrust collar and retainer on opposite sides so that the retainer is forced up over the snap ring (Fig. 9).

2. SPRAG-TYPE CLUTCH There are different types of sprag overrunning clutches. Some are of the heavy-duty type. An intermediate-duty type is also used. You may need to disassemble these units. The intermediate-duty type is disassembled by removing the lockwire, the collar, the jump spring, and stop washer, and the second lockwire. Reassemble by restoring parts in the order in which they were removed. To disassemble the heavy-duty unit, remove the cupped pinion stop and split washer and slide other parts off the shaft as shown. Lubricate the sprags and the felt washer with 5W20 oil and reassemble. You'll probably need a new pinion stop since the old stop will have been damaged during removal. Lubricate spiral splines with SAE10W oil.

NOTE: Some earlier-model sprag clutches could be disassembled so the sprags could be lubricated. However, later models have lifetime lubrication built in and cannot be disassembled.

3. CHECKING PINION CLEARANCE Be sure that the clearance between the pinion and the thrust washer, retainer, or housing is correct. The clearance should be checked with the pinion in the cranking position. On solenoid-operated units, the solenoid should be connected to a battery and in operation, with the pinion in the drive position, when the check is made. However, since the clearance could not be checked if the pinion were rotating, the starting motor should be prevented from operating. One method of doing this is to disconnect the cable between the solenoid and the starting motor. You can not do this on units using a short connector strap between the solenoid motor terminal and the starting motor terminal. On these units the connector must be disconnected from the terminal and carefully insulated. Then, a battery of the same voltage as the solenoid should be connected from the solenoid switch terminal to the solenoid frame (Fig. 10). Mo-

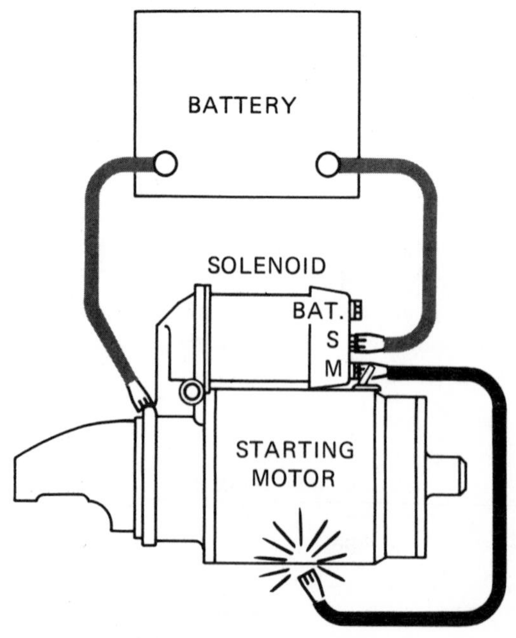

Figure 10 Connections for checking pinion clearance. *(Delco-Remy Division of General Motors Corporation.)*

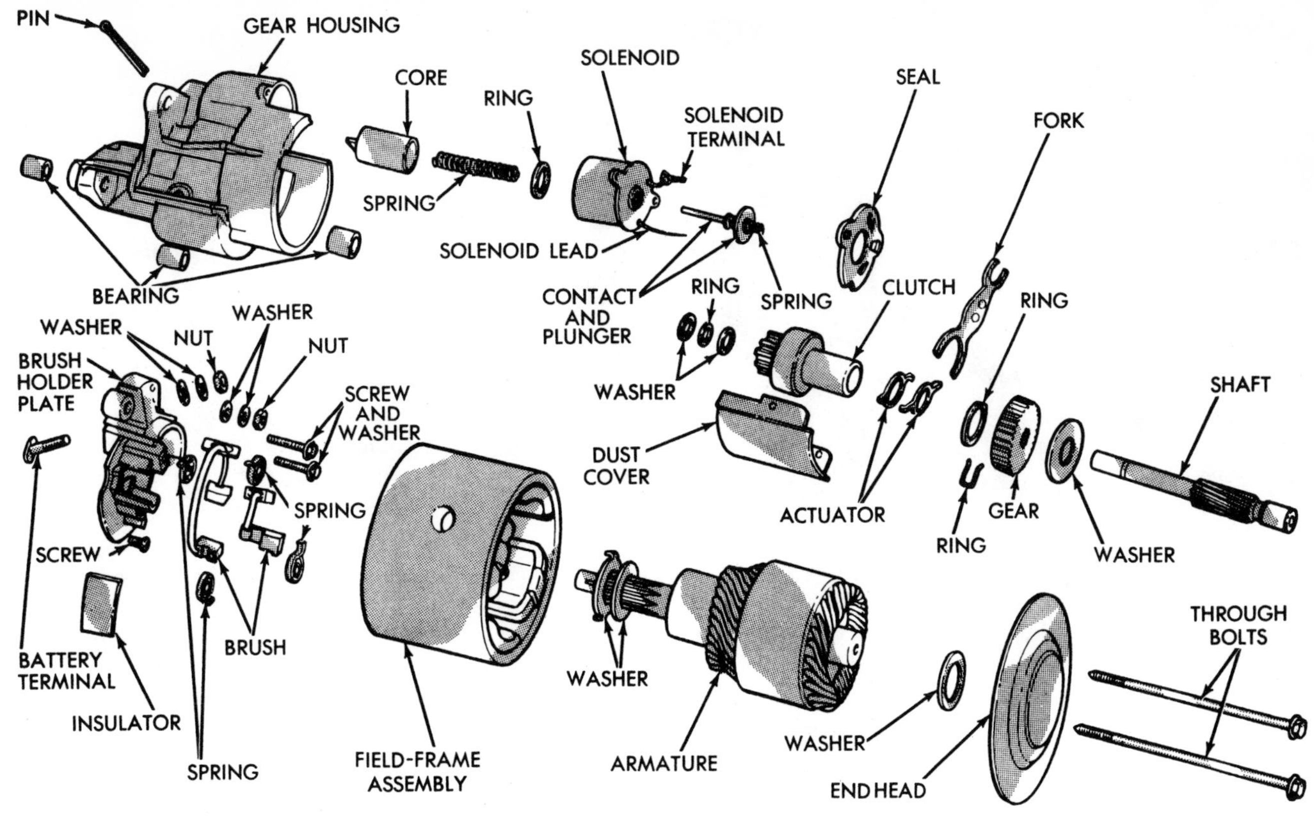

Figure 11 Disassembled view of a gear-reduction overrunning-clutch starting motor. *(Chrysler Corporation.)*

mentarily flash a jumper lead from the solenoid motor terminal to the solenoid frame or to the solenoid ground terminal. This will shift the pinion into cranking position. Push the pinion back and measure clearance.

Another method of checking the pinion clearance is to connect a 6-volt source between the solenoid terminal and ground. This voltage should be enough to make the solenoid work, but it probably will not operate the starting motor. As a further precaution, temporarily connect a jumper lead between the solenoid motor terminal and ground. Push the pinion back and check pinion clearance.

On Delco-Remy units without the retainer and snap ring on the armature shaft, the clearance between the pinion and housing should be 3/16 inch (4.76 mm). On Delco-Remy units using a retainer and snap ring on the armature shaft, clearance between the pinion and retainer—with the pinion pushed away from the retainer as far as possible—should be 0.010 to 0.140 inch (0.254 to 3.56 mm).

On the late-model enclosed-shift-lever type of starting motor, there is no provision for adjustment. Incorrect clearance means that the motor has been incorrectly reassembled or that there are worn or damaged parts. On some earlier models, however, adjustment is possible. For example, the adjustment on some manual types is made by turning the switch button in or out. The adjustment on some solenoid types is made by turning the solenoid-plunger stud in or out. On other solenoid types, the stud is not adjustable. This means that the solenoid itself must be moved back or forth on the field frame. This is done by first loosening the four mounting screws and then moving the solenoid to get the proper clearance. A third arrangement has a serrated shift-lever linkage. On this arrangement, the adjustment is made by loosening the linkage screw. The enclosed shift-lever types are not adjustable.

NOTE: If the old rubber boot (where used) is breaking apart, it should be replaced. Otherwise, dirt or moisture will get into the solenoid and cause the plunger to work hard or jam.

■ 3-3-25 Gear-Reduction Starting Motor

The gear-reduction overrunning-clutch starting motor is shown in Fig. 11, in disassembled view. The disassembly-reassembly procedure for this unit is as follows:

Support the gear housing in the soft jaws of a vise but do not clamp it. Remove two through bolts, end head, armature, and fiber thrust washers. Lift the field and frame assembly up just enough to expose the brush-terminal screw. Support the assembly on blocks and remove the screw. Unsolder the shunt field-coil lead from the brush terminal and lift off the frame assembly. Remove the brush-insulator-plate screw. Lift off the plate with brushes and solenoid as a unit. The overrunning clutch may be removed from the gear housing by removing the dust cover, releasing the snap ring that positions the driven gear on the pinion shaft, releasing the retainer ring at the

Figure 12 Removing the pinion-shaft retaining ring. *(Chrysler Corporation.)*

clutch pinion (Fig. 12), and then pushing the shaft out through the rear of the housing. When releasing the snap ring, be sure to cover the area with a cloth to keep the snap ring from jumping out.

NOTE: There are several other special steps and measurements to be taken in disassembling and reassembling this unit. Refer to the manufacturer's shop manual for details.

■ **3-3-26 Sliding Pole-Shoe Starting Motor** Figure 13 shows a sliding pole-shoe starting motor in disassembled view. To disassemble this unit, remove the cover band, drive-yoke cover, gasket, and brushes. Then remove the through bolts, drive end housing, and yoke return spring. Next, remove the pivot pin and drive yoke. Then take out the armature and drive assembly and remove the brush and plate.

Reassembly is the reverse of disassembly. Figure 14 shows the assembly sequence of the contact assembly.

■ **3-3-27 Checking an Overrunning Clutch** The pinion of an overrunning clutch in good condition should turn freely in the overrunning direction. It should not slip in the opposite direction even under a load of 25 to 50 pound-feet (3.455 to 6.910 kg-m) of torque. To torque-test the clutch, put it on an old armature that has been clamped in a vise.

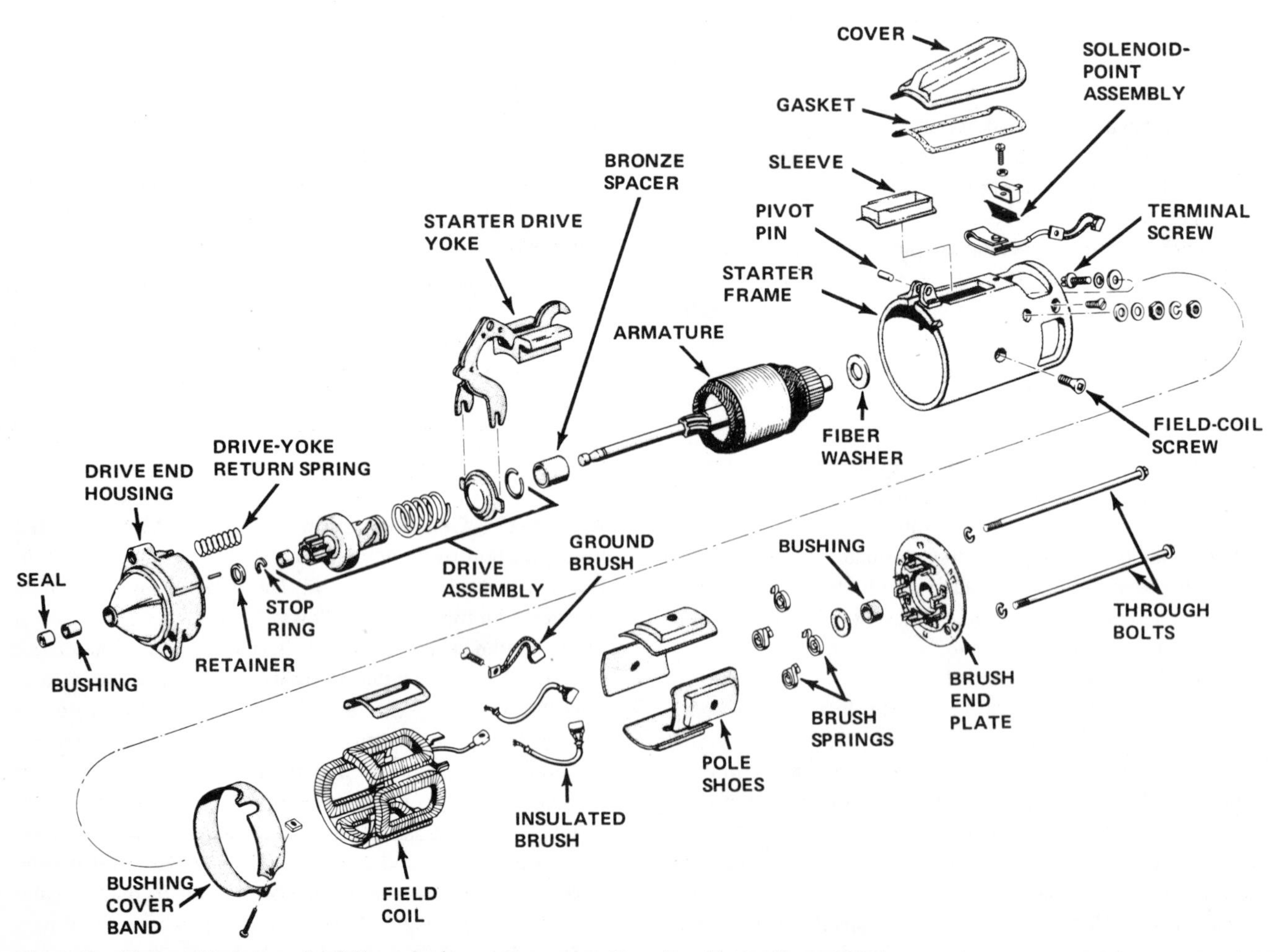

Figure 13 Disassembled view of a sliding pole-shoe starting motor. *(American Motors Corporation.)*

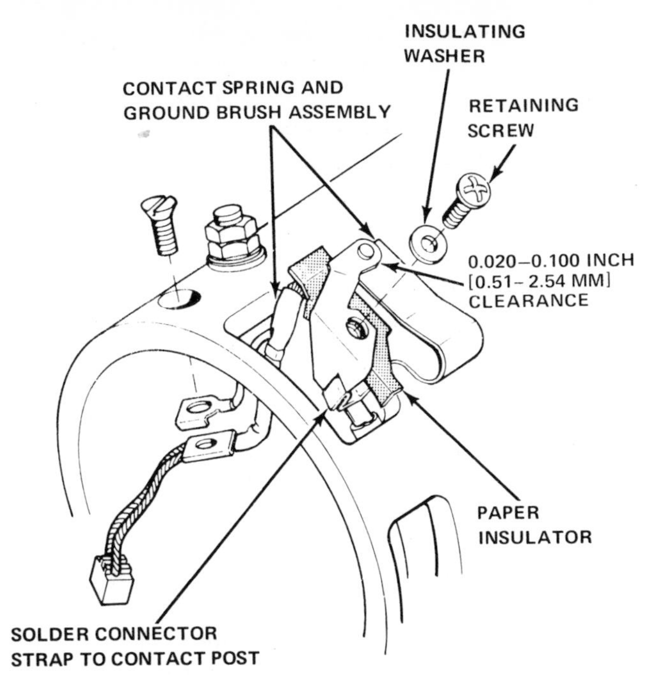

Figure 14 Assembly of the starting-motor contacts. These are the contacts that open when the pole shoe moves into the cranking position. *(American Motors Corporation.)*

Attach an adjustable wrench[1] that has a handle at least 1 foot (0.305 m) long to the drive pinion. Hook a spring scale on the handle 1 foot (0.305 m) from the center of the armature shaft. Exert a pull on the spring scale. The scale reading will be in pound-feet (kg-m) of torque. If the pinion slips when the specified torque is applied (see manufacturer's manual), discard the clutch.

If the pinion turns roughly in the overrunning direction, the rollers probably are chipped or worn and the clutch should be replaced. If the pinion slips in the cranking direction or if the pinion teeth are rough or broken, discard the clutch. Do not try to repair or relubricate an overrunning clutch.

■ 3-3-28 Armature Inspection and Repair Do not clean the armature in solvent, since this might damage the insulation and cause armature failure. Check the armature both mechanically and electrically. As a first step, note the condition of the shaft, commutator, windings, and laminations. Look for such conditions as a bent or worn shaft, thrown windings, burned commutator bars, high commutator mica, worn commutator, and scores or rub marks on the core laminations. If the laminations have scores on them, the armature has been rubbing on the pole shoes. This could be due to worn bearings, a bent armature shaft, or loose pole shoes.

The armature shaft and the commutator may be checked for an out-of-round condition with V blocks and a dial indicator. Rotate the armature and note the "run-out" or out-of-roundness. An out-of-round, worn, or burned commutator should be turned down in a lathe as explained in ■3-3-30. A bent armature can often be straightened, but if the shaft is worn, a new armature is required.

Thrown armature windings result from excessive armature speed, as explained in ■3-3-29. Burned commutator bars are normally caused by open-circuited armature windings, as explained in ■3-3-29.

1. ELECTRICAL TESTS The armature should be tested for grounds, shorts, and opens. It can be tested for grounds with a low-voltage test light. Place one test point on the core and another on the commutator (Fig. 15). Avoid touching the shaft bearing surface or brush-seating area on the commutator, since any arc would cause burning the roughening of the metal. If the light goes on, the armature has a ground and should be replaced. The armature may be tested on a growler for short circuits, as explained below.

Open circuits in a starting-motor armature most often occur at the commutator riser bars where the coils are soldered to the bars. A poor connection or an open produces overheating and thus burning of the bars (see ■ 3-3-29). The motor will overheat if it is cranked too long. Then the solder will melt and be thrown out on the cover band. The armatures of some starting motors have the armature-coil leads welded to the commutator bars instead of soldered. This construction guards against damage due to opens at the connections.

Where starting motors are subjected to heavy moisture, the armature may be treated with one of the special insulating varnishes designed to protect it against moisture. The varnish should be applied to the windings and core so that they are sealed against moisture. Varnish that gets on the shaft or commutator should be wiped off carefully. In particular, no varnish should remain on the commutator. This might cause poor

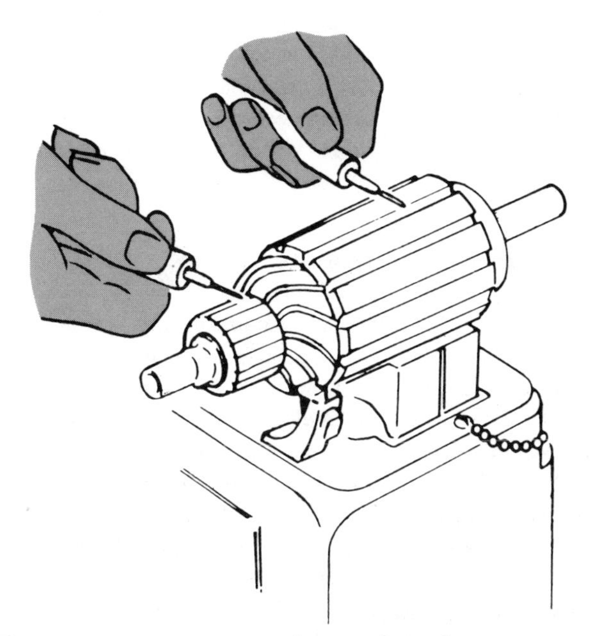

Figure 15 Testing an armature for grounds. *(Delco-Remy Division of General Motors Corporation.)*

[1] A torque wrench can be used if an adapter is made to fit over the pinion.

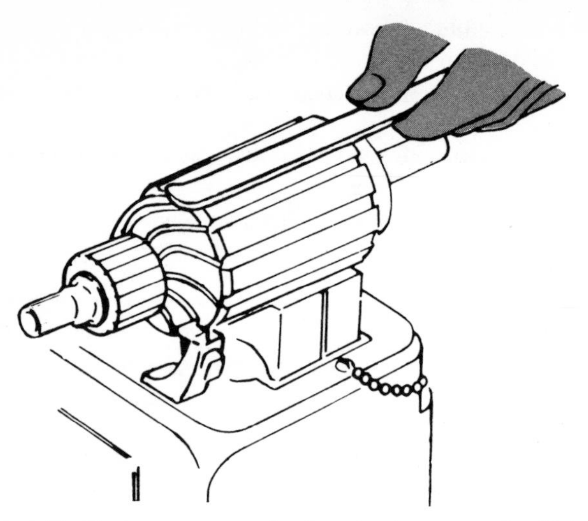

Figure 16 Testing an armature for short circuits on a growler. *(Delco-Remy Division of General Motors Corporation.)*

brush contact and therefore arcing and burning of the commutator.

2. TESTING ARMATURE ON GROWLER The growler (Fig. 16) is an electromagnet that operates on alternating current. If the alternating current is 60-cycle, the current is reversing in direction 120 times a second. This means that the magnetic field in the electromagnet is changing directions 120 times a second. If an armature is placed in the growler, as shown in Fig. 16, the changing magnetism will exert a changing magnetic force on the armature, causing an actual growling noise.

To test the armature for short circuits, hold a hacksaw blade above each armature slot while the armature is slowly revolved by hand. If any winding is shorted, the blade will be alternately attracted to and repelled from the slot in which that winding is assembled. This is because the coil, being shorted, has a closed circuit, which permits current to flow (induced by the changing magnetic field). The flow of current in the shorted winding, alternating with the main magnetic field, sets up an alternating magnetic field of its own. This acts on the blade like a buzzer, causing the blade to vibrate against the core when it is held above the slot containing the shorted winding.

■ 3-3-29 Burned Bars and Thrown Windings

Burned commutator bars usually indicate an open-circuited armature coil. The open circuit is normally at the commutator riser bar. It is caused by overheating due to excessively long periods of cranking. Often, the first sign of this condition is thrown solder on the inside of the cover band. Enough heat will develop to melt the solder at the riser bars. This solder will be thrown, and poor connections will occur. Because of these poor connections, arcing will take place every time the bar passes under the brushes. In a short time, the bar will be so badly burned that the starting motor will stop working. If the bars are not too badly burned, the leads may be resoldered in the riser bars with rosin-core solder. The commutator can then be turned down in a lathe (■ 3-3-30).

Thrown armature windings indicate that the armature has been spun at excessive speeds. This usually happens only to starting motors using the overrunning clutch. Several conditions can cause overspeeding of the armature. For example, if the solenoid plunger is sticky and releases slowly, if the overrunning clutch sticks on the armature shaft, or if the shift-lever return spring is weak, the pinion will disengage slowly after starting. Also if the driver is slow to release the ignition key from the START position, the clutch overruns excessively.

Other evidence of excessive overrunning includes a blued or bronzed armature shaft where the pinion overruns and a polished collar where rollers on the shift-lever yoke ride. Where you find thrown windings, you will usually find evidence that the clutch has been excessively overrun. When replacing the armature, consider replacing the clutch also since it may have been damaged. A defective overrunning clutch could soon ruin the new armature.

■ 3-3-30 Turning the Commutator

Turning the commutator in a lathe is a simple job provided that you have the proper tools and follow the proper procedure (Fig. 17). The cut should be smooth and as light as possible. Remove no more material than is necessary to eliminate the out-of-round, high-mica, rough, or worn condition.

NOTE: Some starting motors use a molded armature commutator. The mica must not be undercut on these. This can damage the commutator. Undercutting can weaken the bonding between the molding material and commutator bars. The molding material is softer than the copper, so it will wear away at the same rate as the copper.Generally, automotive manufacturers' service procedures do not require undercutting of mica on starting-motor armatures.

■ 3-3-31 Bearing Inspection and Replacement

Most starting motors use sleeve bearings or bushings. Some starting motors use ball bearings. On the bushing, check for

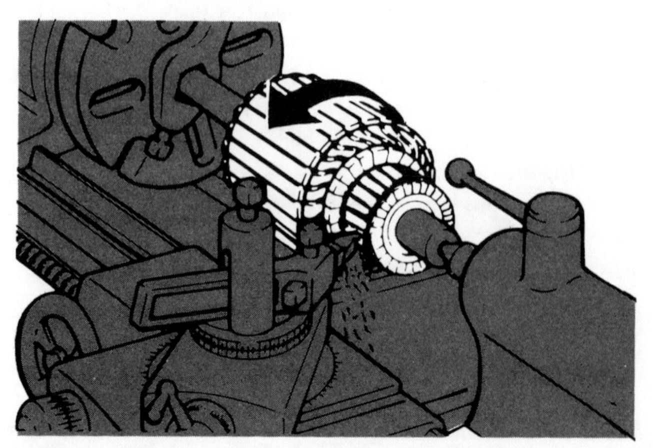

Figure 17 Turning an armature commutator on a lathe.

wear by noting the amount of side play the armature shaft has when inserted into the bearing. If it is excessive, replace the bearing. Usually, the wear will not be uniform but will be greatest on the side that sustains the thrust when cranking takes place. Another sign of bearing wear is rubbing of the armature core on the pole shoes. (This can also be caused by loose pole shoes or a bent armature shaft.)

To replace a bearing, press out the old one and press in a new one. Special drivers are also available. The bushing must have the proper inside dimension after it is installed. If the bushing is lubricated by a wick, drill an oil hole in the side of the bearing after it is in place. Then remove cuttings and install the wick.

NOTE: Some new bushings must be reamed to size after installation.

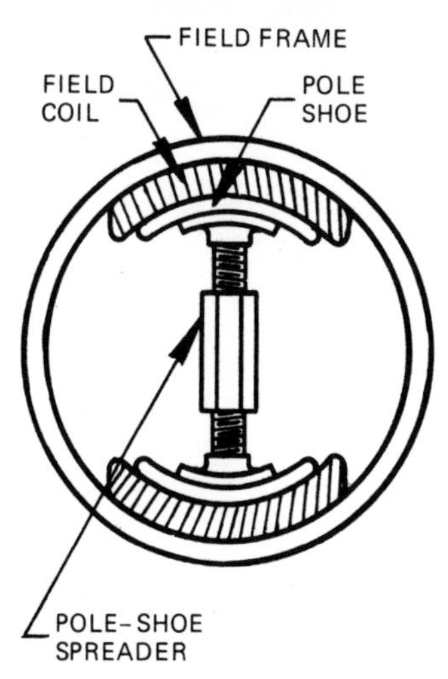

Figure 18 Pole-shoe spreader.

■ **3-3-32 Field-Frame Inspection** Unless the field coils are removed, the field frame should not be cleaned in solvent. This might damage the insulation and cause failure. Inspect the field windings and leads for poor insulation. Check the tightness of the pole shoes. The windings can be checked for grounds with a low-voltage test light. Connect the light to the terminal stud or connector strap and a clean spot on the frame. If the light goes on, the fields are grounded either at the terminal or in the windings. To find out which is at fault, remove the terminal stud from the field frame and let it hang free. Then try the test again. Grounded field windings may sometimes be repaired by removing and reinsulating them with electrical tape. However, avoid too much bulkiness. Thick wrapping might cause the pole shoes to cut through the new insulation and produce another ground when the pole-shoe screws are tightened.

■ 3-3-33 Removing and Replacing Field Coils

Use a poleshoe screwdriver or a 3/8-inch socket wrench to remove and install pole shoes. A useful tool for reassembly is the pole-shoe spreader (Fig. 18). When this device is in place, it forces the pole shoes against the frame, prevents distortion of the frame as the screws are tightened, and makes the tightening job easier. While tightening the screws, strike the frame sharp blows with a plastic or rubber hammer. This helps to align the pole shoes. Coating the screws with Loctite before installation seals them and prevents them from coming loose.

When installing the field windings, be sure to replace the insulating strips (where used) in their original positions. These strips are important. They guard against grounding of the leads or windings.

NOTE: Install the pole shoes in their original positions in the field frame. Also, be sure the pole shoes are not turned around 180°. Some pole shoes have one long and one short lip. Turning this type of pole shoe around will reduce cranking performance.

■ 3-3-34 Installation of Starting Motor Wiring

When inspecting or installing starting-motor wiring, take care to guard against short circuits or grounds. All wires should be of sufficient size to carry the electric load without excessive voltage drop. Stranded wire or cable should be used since it is less apt to break from vibration. All joints and connections should be clean and tight. Terminal clips should be soldered to leads with rosin flux solder.

All leads and cables should be supported at enough points to prevent them from moving and thereby wearing the insulation. On 12- and 24-volt systems, special precautions should be taken to avoid grounds or shorts. Rubber boots, tape, or shellac should be used to protect exposed terminals.

SECTION 3-4 Charging System Trouble Diagnosis

■ **3-4-1 Need for Systematic Procedure** If trouble is suspected or reported, the cause is most easily found through a systematic approach. This will save time and effort. For example, a low battery might be caused by a low voltage setting, or a loose drive belt, or a number of other specific causes. These causes are listed, with the appropriate checks and corrections, in the Alternator-Regulator Trouble-Diagnosis Chart.

You should pinpoint the cause of any problem before attempting to make a correction. The following sections describe various troubles, their causes, and their corrections.

> **NOTE:** The checks to be made on alternators and ac regulators are much different from those to be made on dc equipment. Making dc checks on ac equipment can ruin the equipment.

■ **3-4-2 Service Precautions for AC Charging Systems** There are a number of things to remember when servicing ac charging systems.

1. Belt tension is more critical on alternators than on dc generators, because of the greater inertia of the heavier rotor in the alternator. Check belt tension periodically.

2. Never install a battery backward. The reversed polarity can ruin the alternator because a heavy current will flow through the diodes as soon as the battery is connected. This will burn out the diodes if the fusible link in the line does not burn out first.

3. When applying a booster charge to the battery, be sure to disconnect the battery ground strap from the grounded battery terminal. This will protect the alternator diodes and the transistors (in transistor-type regulators) from the high charging voltage. The transistors in transistorized ignition systems could also be damaged by the high charging voltage. This is another reason for disconnecting the battery ground strap during a booster charge.

4. Be sure to connect the booster charger with the correct polarity to the battery. It is actually possible to reverse battery polarity by charging it backward. If this happens, when the battery ground strap is reconnected, the reversed polarity will ruin the alternator and alternator diodes, as mentioned in item 2 above.

5. If you have to attach a booster battery to jumpstart the engine, be sure to connect the correct terminals together (plus to plus, minus to minus) for the same reason as noted in items 2 and 3 above. (See ■3-2-22.)

6. Never operate the alternator on open circuit. This will allow a damaging high voltage to build up in the alternator.

Make sure all connections in the system are tight before starting the engine.

7. Never short between or ground any of the terminals in the charging system. This could ruin diodes or transistors.

8. Never attempt to polarize the alternator. It does not need it.

9. Never disconnect leads from the alternator or regulator without first disconnecting the ground strap from the battery ground terminal. This guards against accidental grounds or shorts which could permit a high current to flow. This would damage the alternator or other parts.

■ 3-4-3 Checking Out Troubles in AC Charging Systems The basic complaints include:

1. Low battery—usually shows up as slow cranking.

2. Overcharged battery—usually shows up as frequent need of water. Also, since this condition can result from high charging voltage, frequent light replacement could be an added complaint.

3. Faulty indicator light or ammeter operation.

4. Noisy alternator.

> **NOTE:** Always confirm the complaint. That is, check the battery, and note operation of the indicator light or alternator, before making further checks.

■ 3-4-4 Trouble Diagnosis of the AC Charging System The chart to the right lists the various trouble conditions that might be found in the system, together with their possible causes and corrections. The troubles are not listed in order of frequency.

■ 3-4-5 Charged Battery and Low Charging Rate This is normal operation. Routine checks of the voltage setting and alternator output can be made, along with a check of the drive-belt condition and tension.

■ 3-4-6 Charged Battery and High Charging Rate A charged battery with a high charging rate will show up as frequent need for adding water to the battery and also frequent light-bulb replacement. The cause is a high voltage setting, a defective regulator, loose connections, or a poorly grounded regulator base (separate regulator). In the vibrating-point regulator, such troubles as stuck contacts or an open voltage winding could prevent normal regulator operation, so the voltage would go too high. This could also result if the regulator base were poorly grounded. The excessive resistance introduced would prevent a good grounding of the field winding when the upper contacts were closed. Alternator voltage could, therefore, stay high. Checking and adjusting regulator voltage is detailed in Sec. 5 of this part.

ALTERNATOR-REGULATOR TROUBLE-DIAGNOSIS CHART

(See ■3-4-5 to 3-4-11 for detailed explanations of trouble causes and corrections listed in the chart.)

Condition	Possible Cause	Check or Correction
1. Charged battery and low charging rate (■ 3-4-5)	This is normal operation	Check belt tension and voltage setting if desired
2. Charged battery and high charging rate (■3-4-6)	a. High voltage setting	Reduce setting
	b. Regulator defective	Replace regulator
	c. Loose connections	Correct
	d. Regulator base poorly grounded	Correct
3. Discharged battery and low or no charging rate (■3-4-7)	a. Loose drive belt	Tighten, replace belt if necessary
	b. Bad connections in charging circuit	Clean, tighten
	c. Voltage setting low	Readjust
	d. Regulator defective	Replace or repair
	e. Alternator defective	Repair
	f. Field relay defective	Repair or replace
4. Faulty indicator light or ammeter operation (■3-4-8 and 3-4-9)	a. Indicator bulb burned out	Replace
	b. Defective wiring or connections	Repair
	c. Defective regulator	Replace
5. Noisy alternator (■3-4-10)	a. Mounting loose	Tighten
	b. Bad drive belt	Replace
	c. Internal defects	Remove alternator for further checks
6. Discharged battery and high charging rate (■3-4-11)	This is normal operation	Check for cause of low battery. Could be fuel system or engine trouble

■ 3-4-7 Discharged Battery and Low or No Charging Rate A discharged battery with low or no charging rate can be caused by frequent stops and starts, accessories or lights left on, loose drive belt, an old battery that will not accept a charge normally, or defects in the wiring or connections. Checking the belt tension is illustrated in Fig 1. If everything else checks out okay, check the alternator output. Here is the procedure recommended by Chevrolet for an alternator with built-in voltage regulator.

1. Disconnect the battery ground cable. Connect an ammeter into the circuit at the BAT (battery) terminal of the alternator. Reconnect the ground cable.

2. Turn on accessories to load the battery. These include the radio, high-beam headlights, windshield wipers, and heater

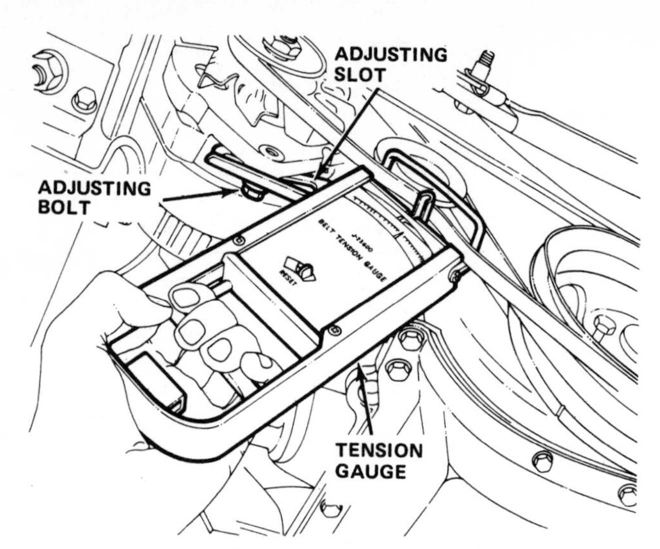

Figure 1 Using a belt-tension gauge to check the tension of the alternator drive belt. *(American Motors Corporation.)*

motor at high speed. Add a carbon pile (a heavy variable resistance) across the battery.

3. Operate the engine at moderate speed. Adjust the carbon pile to get the maximum alternator output.

4. If the output is within 10 percent of the rated output stamped on the alternator, the alternator is okay. The trouble must be in the circuit connections, wiring, or drive belt.

5. If the output is not within 10 percent of rated value, ground the field winding by carefully inserting a screwdriver into the test hole of the alternator (Fig. 2). If the output now increases, the trouble is in the regulator. It must be replaced. If the output does not increase, the trouble is in the diodes, field winding, or stator. The alternator must be removed from the engine and disassembled in order to find the trouble.

NOTE: Other makes of alternators require different testing procedures. Also, alternators that use a separately mounted vibrating-contact type of regulator require a testing procedure that checks the regulator itself. See the manufacturer's shop manual when you work on a specific make and model of regulator and alternator. See also Sec. 5, on regulator checks, and Sec. 6, on alternator service, both in this part.

■ 3-4-8 Faulty Indicator Light or Ammeter Operation If, before the engine starts, the indicator light does not come on when the ignition switch is turned on, it could be due to a burned-out bulb or fuse or to an open in the wiring, regulator, or field. It could also be due to a shorted diode in the alternator (this may also allow the light to burn even with the ignition switch off). Checks for these conditions are outlined in the following sections.

On systems equipped with an ammeter, or charge indicator, faulty ammeter action can be checked out by first turning the ignition switch to ACC (accessories) and then turning on an accessory. The ammeter should read "discharge." If it does not, check the ammeter circuit for an open or poor connection. If the ammeter reads "discharge," check further by starting the engine and watching the ammeter. If it fails to read "charge," the trouble could be that the alternator is not producing output (see ■ 3-4-7) or the ammeter or ammeter circuit is faulty.

If the indicator light (on systems so equipped) fails to go off as the engine is started, the trouble could be low or no alternator output (■3-4-7), a defective field relay, or a shorted diode in the alternator. Checking the relay is outlined in Sec. 5 of this part. Following is a checking procedure recommended by Chevrolet for testing the indicator-light circuit in the circuit using the alternator with the built-in voltage regulator.

■ 3-4-9 Indicator-Light Circuit Check In normal operation, the light should come on when the engine is being cranked. It should go off when the ignition switch is off. There are three troubles that require checking.

1. SWITCH OFF, LIGHT ON Disconnect the two leads from alternator terminals 1 and 2. If the light stays on, there is a short between these two leads. If the light goes off, the short is

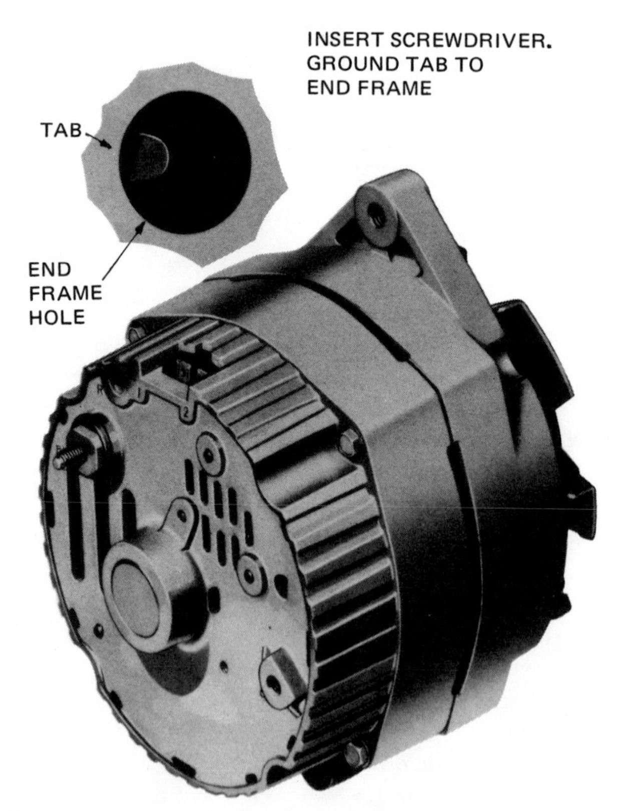

Figure 2 Alternator, showing the test hole. A screwdriver is inserted in the test hole to ground the field circuit. The screwdriver should be pushed in only far enough to touch the tab. If pushed in too far, it could damage the alternator. *(Chevrolet Motor Division of General Motors Corporation.)*

inside the alternator, in the diodes. Replace the rectifier bridge which carries the diodes. This requires disassembly of the alternator.

2. SWITCH ON, LIGHT OFF, ENGINE STOPPED This can be caused by diode defects, by a short between the leads to terminals 1 and 2, by reversal of the two leads to the terminals, or by an open in the circuit. An open can cause a rundown battery. To find the trouble if an open is suspected, proceed as follows:

a. Connect a voltmeter from terminal 2 to ground. If the reading is zero, there is an open between the terminal and the battery. If a reading is obtained, go to step *b*.
b. With ignition switch on and terminal 1 and 2 leads disconnected, momentarily ground the terminal 1 lead.

> **NOTE:** Do not ground the terminal 2 lead! This directly grounds the positive terminal of the battery. It is a direct short across the battery terminals!

c. If the light does not go on with terminal 1 lead grounded, check for a blown fuse or fusible link, a burned-out bulb, or an open in the terminal 1 lead.
d. If the light comes on, unground the terminal 1 lead. Reconnect the two leads to terminals 1 and 2. Carefully insert a screwdriver into the test hole shown in Fig. 2. This grounds the field winding, and the light should come on.
e. If the light does not go on, check the connection between the wiring harness and terminal 1 of the alternator. Other possible troubles could be with the brushes, slip rings, and field winding in the rotor. Checking these requires removal and disassembly of the alternator.
f. If the light comes on and a voltmeter reading was obtained on step *a*, replace the regulator in the alternator.

3. SWITCH ON, LIGHT ON, ENGINE RUNNING There is a problem in the alternator. Check it out as outlined in Sec. 6 of this part.

■ **3-4-10 Noisy Alternator** A noisy alternator could be due to a loose or worn drive belt or loose alternator mounting; internal defects in the alternator such as worn bearings, open or shorted diodes, open or shorts in the stator; or mechanical interference, for example, between the fan and frame.

■ **3-4-11 Discharged Battery and High Charging Rate** This is normal operation. When a battery is discharged, the alternator sends to it a high charging current. When you find a discharged battery, you should always try to determine the cause. It could be that the driver ran the battery down trying to start and that a faulty fuel system or engine trouble is preventing normal starting.

SECTION 3-5 Alternator-Regulator Service

This section describes the procedures for checking and adjusting the adjustable ac regulators. In recent years, solid-state voltage regulators have been adopted by automotive manufacturers. Chrysler Corporation cars (Plymouth, Dodge, Chrysler, etc.) and General Motors cars now have alternators with nonadjustable voltage regulators. If these do not test satisfactorily, new voltage regulators are required. On Chrysler Corporation cars, the regulators are separate units. On General Motors cars, they are built into the alternator. Ford cars use either a vibrating-contact regulator or a transistorized unit, which consists of a field relay and a solid-state, adjustable voltage regulator.

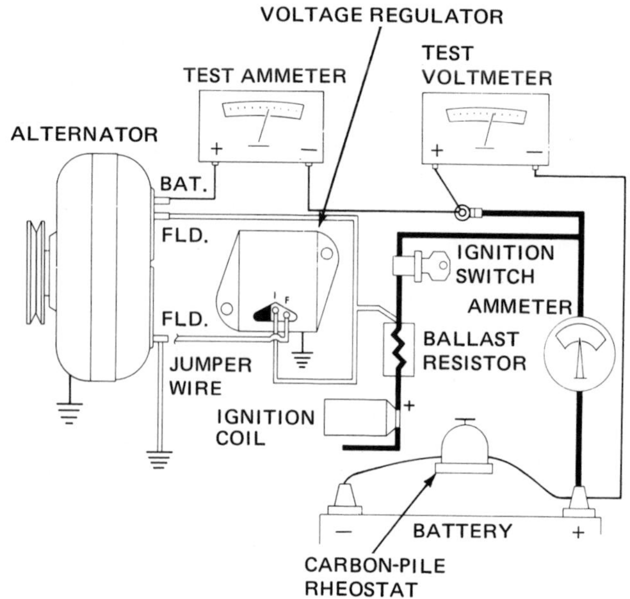

Figure 1 Test meters and carbon-pile rheostat connected for a resistance test of the charging circuit. Note that the lead has been disconnected from the alternator field (FLD) terminal. The terminal has been grounded with a jumper wire. *(Chrysler Corporation.)*

NOTE: Always disconnect the ground cable from the battery ground terminal before disconnecting or connecting leads in the charging system. Then, after all the connections are restored, reconnect the ground strap. This avoids accidental shorting of the battery through the regulator or alternator. Also, always follow the service precautions for ac charging systems, as stated in ■3-4-2.

■ 3-5-1 Chrysler-Plymouth Charging-System Tests

The three Chrysler Corporation tests that follow are for the alternator and the nonadjustable electronic control unit (regulator). They test the charging-circuit resistance, alternator current output, and voltage-regulator setting.

1. CHARGING-CIRCUIT RESISTANCE TEST A voltmeter, an ammeter, and a carbon-pile resistor are connected as in Fig. 1. Then the engine speed and carbon pile are adjusted to maintain a 20-amp flow in the circuit. The voltmeter reading should not exceed 0.7 volt. If it is higher, there is excessive resistance in the circuit due to bad connections or wiring.

2. CURRENT OUTPUT TEST Connect a voltmeter, an ammeter, and a carbon-pile resistor as shown in Fig. 1. Start the engine and operate it at idle. Increase the engine speed and adjust the carbon pile a little at a time. Continue until a speed

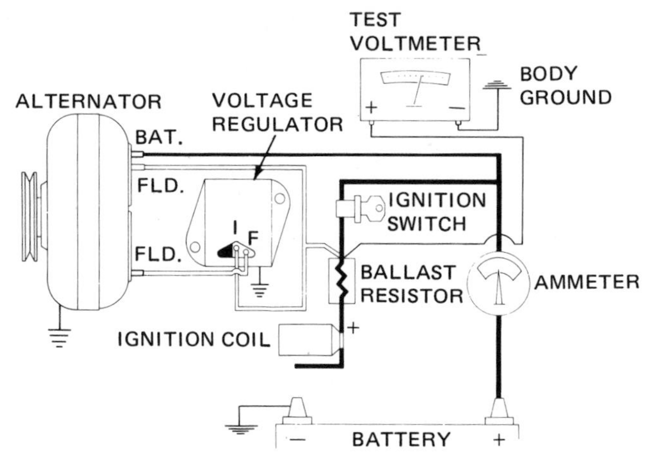

Figure 2 Voltmeter connected for a test of the voltage regulator. *(Chrysler Corporation.)*

of 1,250 rpm (revolutions per minute) and a voltmeter reading of 15 volts are obtained. Use a tachometer to measure engine rpm.

> **NOTE:** Do not allow the voltage to go above 16 volts!

If the ammeter reads within the specified limits for the alternator being checked, the alternator is satisfactory. If the reading is low, remove the alternator from the engine for further checking.

3. VOLTAGE-REGULATOR TEST Connect a voltmeter as shown in Fig. 2. Make sure the battery is in good condition and charged. Start and run the engine at 1,250 rpm (using a tachometer) with all lights and accessories turned off. Compare the voltmeter reading with the specifications for the alternator being checked.

If the voltage is low or fluctuates, check the regulator ground to make sure it is good. Then turn off the ignition switch, and disconnect the voltage-regulator connectors. Check battery voltage at the wiring-harness terminal. If it tests okay, the trouble is in the regulator. It should be replaced.

If the voltage is high, turn off the ignition switch, then disconnect the voltage-regulator connector. Check battery voltage with a voltmeter at the wiring-harness terminal. If the voltage reads okay, replace the regulator.

Plymouth has a special electronic voltage-regulator tester (Tester Tool C-4133) that simplifies the testing procedure.

■ 3-5-2 Ford AC Regulator Service (1968 and Later)

Ford recommends using the Rotunda ARE 20-22 tester shown in Fig. 3 or the Rotunda ARE 27-38 Volt-Amp-Alternator tester shown in Fig. 4. Both procedures are discussed below.

1. ARE 20-22 TESTER The procedure with the ARE 20-22 tester is to connect it, start the engine, make two tests, and then compare the patterns of lights that appear on the tester with the charts accompanying the tester.

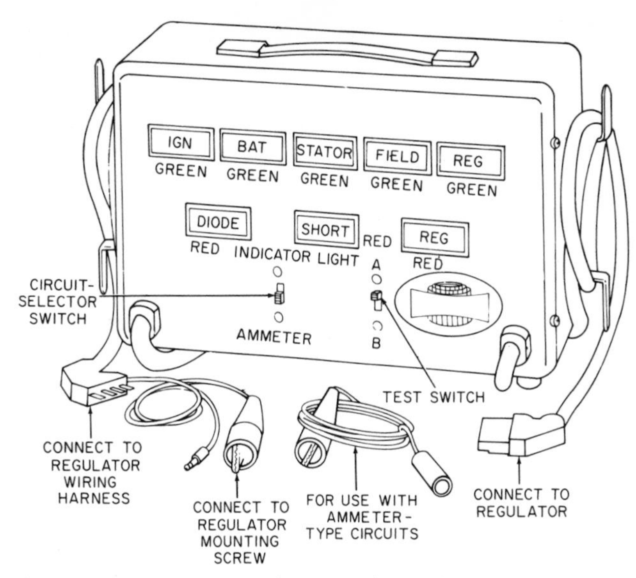

Figure 3 ARE 20-22 tester for testing for ac charging circuit. *(Ford Motor Company.)*

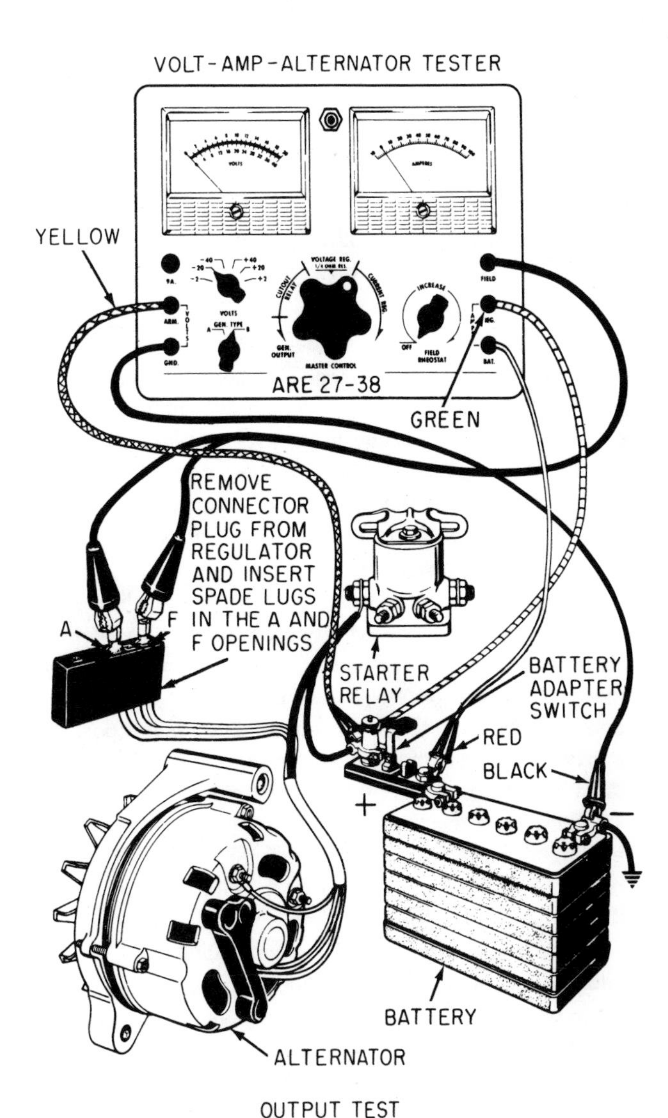

Figure 4 ARE 27-38 tester connected to measure alternator output. *(Ford Motor Company.)*

The battery must be in good condition and of at least 1.230 specific gravity. Disconnect the wiring harness plug from the regulator. Plug the tester's male plug to the wiring harness and the tester's female plug to the alternator. Connect the tester's ground clip to the regulator mounting screw. Set the tester-circuit selector switch (Fig. 3) to the indicator-light position if the system has an indicator light. Set it to the ammeter position if the system has an ammeter.

Start the engine and operate it at 1,000 to 1,500 rpm (using a tachometer). With the test switch in position A, observe the pattern of lights on the tester.

Move the switch to B and hold it in this position for 10 seconds. Then note the pattern of lights on the tester.

Compare the patterns observed with those shown in the charts. The malfunctions and indicated corrections are described in the Ford shop manuals.

2. *ARE 27-38 VOLT-AMP-ALTERNATOR TESTER* Three tests performed with the ARE 27-38 tester are described below. They are tests of alternator output, voltage-regulator setting, and field-relay setting.

NOTE: Starting in 1974, the Ford Car Shop Manuals have carried the warning that the ARE 27-38 tester and similar volt-ampere-alternator testers must not be used to check 1974-type voltage regulators. Instead, use the ARE 20-22 tester. The ARE 27-38 type of tester can damage the electronic ignition system and other electronic devices on the car. The procedure that follows, therefore, is okay only for 1973 and earlier Ford cars.

a. *Alternator Output* To check alternator output make the connections shown in Fig. 4. Note that a battery adapter switch has been connected to the insulated terminal of the battery to provide a quick means of temporarily disconnecting the battery for the tests. Note also the positions of the tester knobs on the tester in Fig. 4. Close the battery adapter switch and start the engine. Open the switch.

Increase engine speed to 2,000 rpm (using a tachometer). Turn off all lights and electrical accessories. Turn the field rheostat knob clockwise until you get 15 volts. Turn the master control knob clockwise until you get between 11 and 12 volts. Hold the master control knob in this position and turn the field rheostat clockwise as far as it will go. Then turn the master control knob counterclockwise to get 15 volts. Note the ammeter reading. Add 2 amps to this reading to get the alternator output. If rated output cannot be attained, increase engine speed to 2,900 rpm and repeat the test.

An output of 2 to 5 amps below specifications usually indicates an open alternator diode. An output of about 10 amps below specifications usually indicates a shorted alternator diode. A shorted diode usually causes alternator whine. Low or no output usually indicates shorts, opens, or grounds in the alternator. If the alternator fails to reach specific output, remove it for service.

b. *Voltage-Regulator Setting* Checking the regulator setting must be done with battery and ignition loads only. The battery must be in good condition and above 1.230 specific gravity. Make the test connections shown in Fig. 5. Close the battery adapter switch, start the engine, and open the switch. Operate the engine at approximately 2,000 rpm for 5 minutes (using a tachometer). The ammeter should indicate less than 10 amps with the master control set at the $\frac{1}{4}$-ohm position.

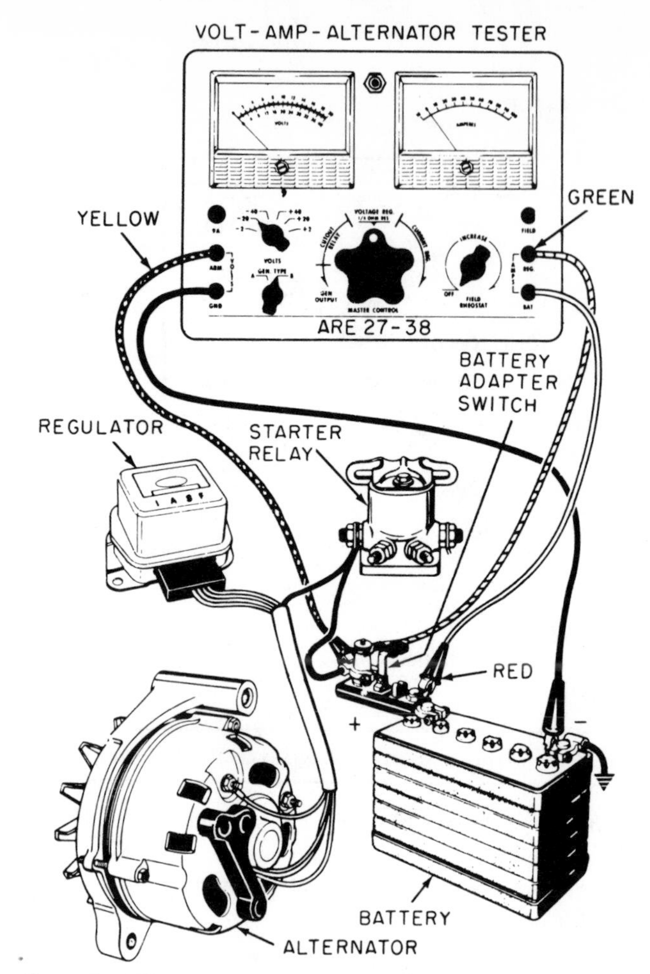

Figure 5 ARE 27-38 tester connected to measure voltage-regulator setting. *(Ford Motor Company.)*

Cycle the regulator by turning the ignition off to stop the engine, closing the battery adapter switch to start the engine, and again opening the adapter switch. Increase engine speed to 2,000 rpm. Allow the battery to charge for 1 minute and then read the voltage on the upper scale. If the voltage is not within specifications, replace the regulator. This unit is sealed, and there is no provision for adjusting it.

c. *Field-Relay Check* If malfunctioning of the field relay is suspected, remove the regulator from the car and make the connections shown in Fig. 6 on the test bench. Slowly rotate the field rheostat clockwise from the maximum counterclockwise position until the test light comes on. Note the voltmeter reading at this instant. This is the relay closing voltage. If it is not within specifications, replace the regulator.

■ 3-5-3 General Motors (Delco-Remy) AC Regulator Service

Delco-Remy has supplied a variety of ac regulators from a three-unit regulator that looks much like the standard dc regulator to completely transistorized regulators with no moving parts. This section on ac regulator checks and adjustments covers regulators without transistors. ■ 3-5-4 covers ac regulators with transistors.

All Delco-Remy regulators without transistors have vibrating voltage regulators. Some have a field relay, and some have an indicator-light relay. The most widely used is the two-unit regulator with a field relay. Checking and adjusting of this regulator are described below

> **NOTE:** Observe the following four service precautions in working on this regulator. Otherwise, serious damage might occur (see also ■ 3-4-2):
>
> *1.* Do not attempt to polarize the alternator.
>
> *2.* Do not short across or ground any terminal on the regulator or alternator.
>
> *3.* Never operate the alternator on open circuit. Make sure all connections are tight.
>
> *4.* Make sure the regulator and alternator are both designed for the same polarity ground. Using a positive ground regulator with a negative ground alternator can ruin both.

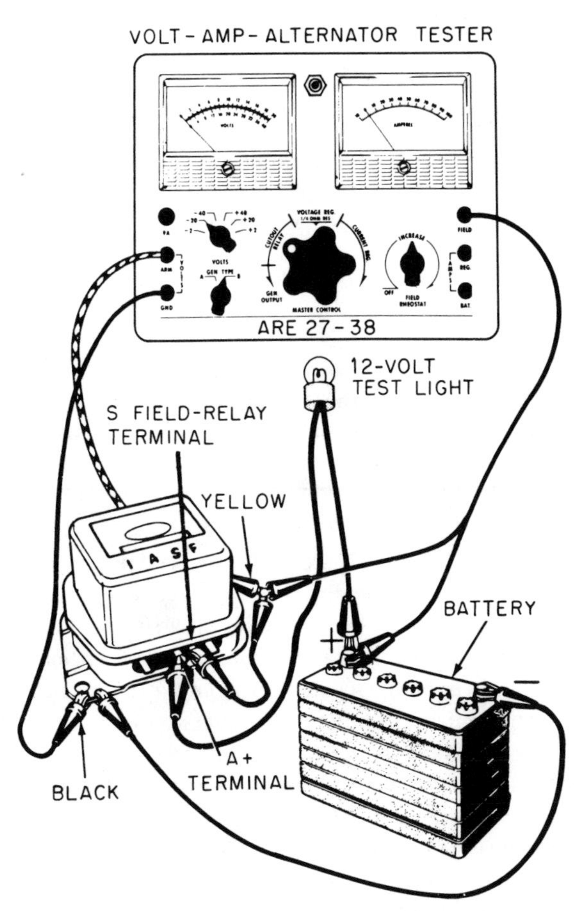

Figure 6 ARE 27-38 tester connected to check field relay. *(Ford Motor Company.)*

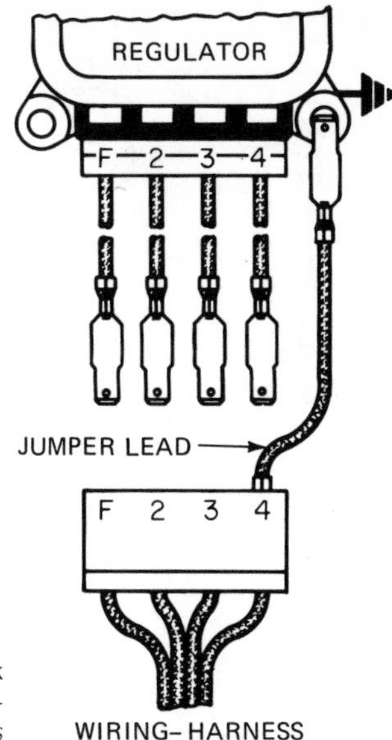

Figure 7 Connections to check indicator-light circuit. *(Delco-Remy Division of General Motors Corporation.)*

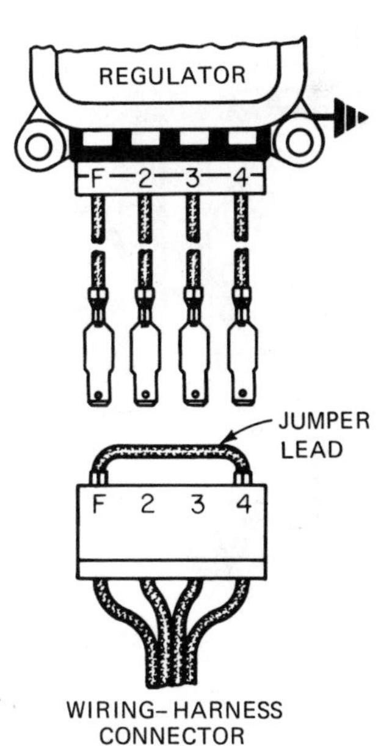

Figure 8 Checking indicator-light circuit. *(Delco-Remy Division of General Motors Corporation.)*

1. CHECKING CIRCUITS A special adapter or jumper wire must be used to fit the slip-on connectors at the regulator terminals. Checking of the various units and circuits is described below.

a. *Indicator-Light Circuit* If the indicator light fails to go on and it is known to be in good condition, check the circuit as follows. Turn the ignition switch on but do not start the engine. Momentarily connect a jumper lead as shown in Fig. 7. If the light does not come on, there is an open in the circuit to the light. If the light comes on, reconnect the jumper lead as shown in Fig. 8. If the light now comes on again, the open is in the regulator. If it does not come on, there is an open either in the field lead between the regulator and the alternator or in the alternator field winding.

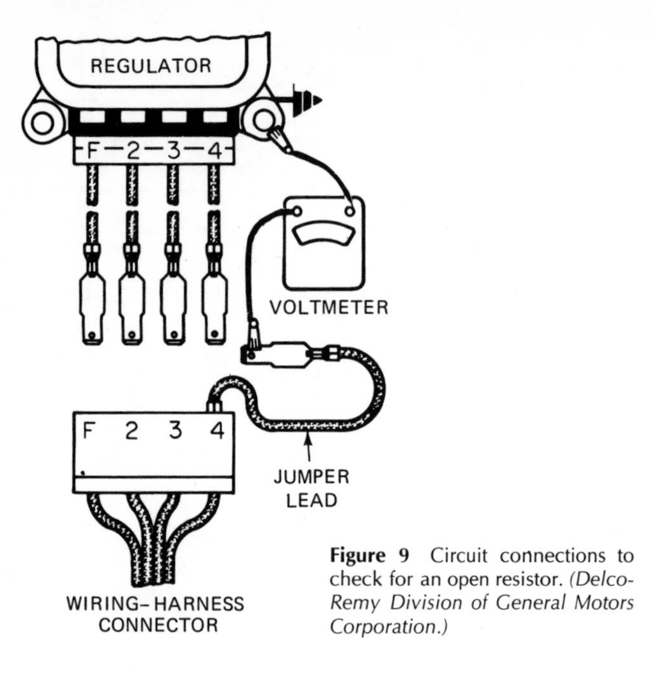

Figure 9 Circuit connections to check for an open resistor. *(Delco-Remy Division of General Motors Corporation.)*

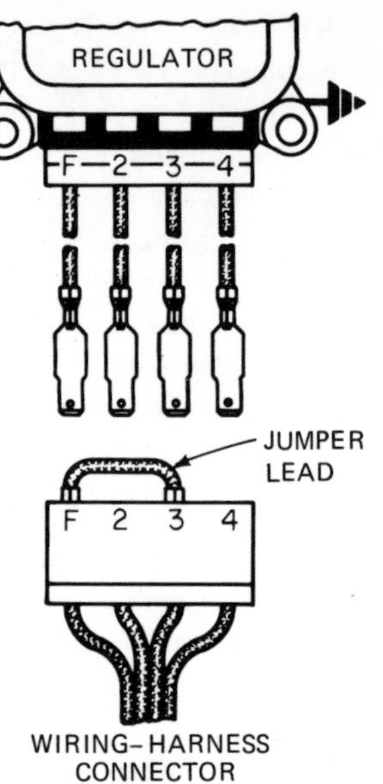

Figure 11 Connections at the adapter to check alternator output. *(Delco-Remy Division of General Motors Corporation.)*

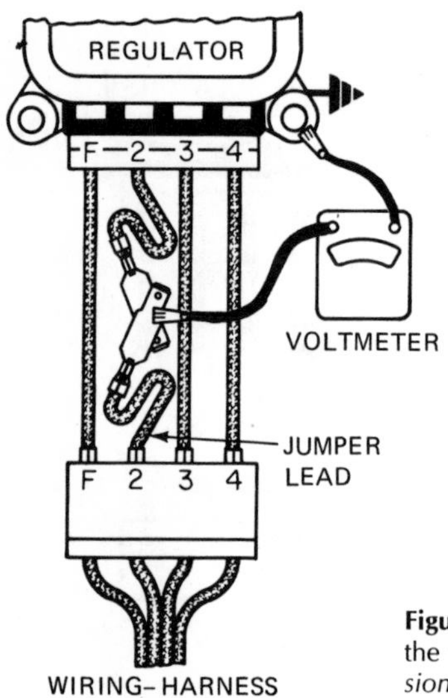

Figure 10 Connections to check the field relay. *(Delco-Remy Division of General Motors Corporation.)*

NOTE: If the indicator light fails to go out when the alternator is operating, the field relay is stuck or the resistor that parallels the light is burned out (see checks below). If the light does not go out when the ignition switch is turned off, the alternator probably has a shorted diode. This is a serious condition because it will allow the battery to discharge through the shorted diode and run down in a few hours.

b. *Checking Resistor* To check for an open resistor (the one that parallels the indicator light), connect a voltmeter as shown in Fig. 9. Turn the ignition switch to the ACC position. If the voltmeter reads zero, the resistor is open. The resistor may be a separate unit, or it may be in the form of resistance wire in the wiring harness.

c. *Checking Field Relay* Make connections to the adapter as shown in Fig. 10. Operate the alternator at moderate speed and note the voltage reading. If the voltage is 5 volts or more and the indicator light does not go out, the field relay is defective and requires checking as explained below. If the voltmeter reading is below 5 volts, the trouble is in the alternator. It should be checked as covered in Sec. 6 of this part.

2. CHECKING ALTERNATOR Connect an ammeter into the charging circuit of the battery terminal of the alternator and a voltmeter from the same battery terminal to ground. Make connections at the adapter as shown in Fig. 11. Operate the alternator at specified speed and check the output. Refer to the manufacturer's service bulletins for specifications. If the output is low, the alternator should be checked (Sec. 6 of this part). If it is normal, the voltage regulator should be checked, as described below.

NOTE: To prevent high voltage during the test, apply a load to the battery with a carbon-pile rheostat or car accessories. Do not allow voltage to exceed the recommended setting!

3. VOLTAGE SETTING (UPPER CONTACTS) To check the voltage setting of the regulator, make the connections shown in Fig. 12. The variable resistor should be a 25-ohm 25-watt unit. It should be turned to the NO RESISTANCE position. Operate the alternator for 15 minutes at 1,500 engine rpm. Leave the cover on the regulator. Then cycle the regulator by turning the variable resistor to the FULL RESISTANCE position and disconnecting the leads at terminals 2 and 4 on the wiring harness connector. Reconnect these leads and turn the resistor to the NO RESISTANCE position.

Bring engine speed up to about 2,500 rpm and note the voltage setting. The regulator should be operating on the upper or shorting contact points. To adjust, turn the adjusting screw (Fig. 13).

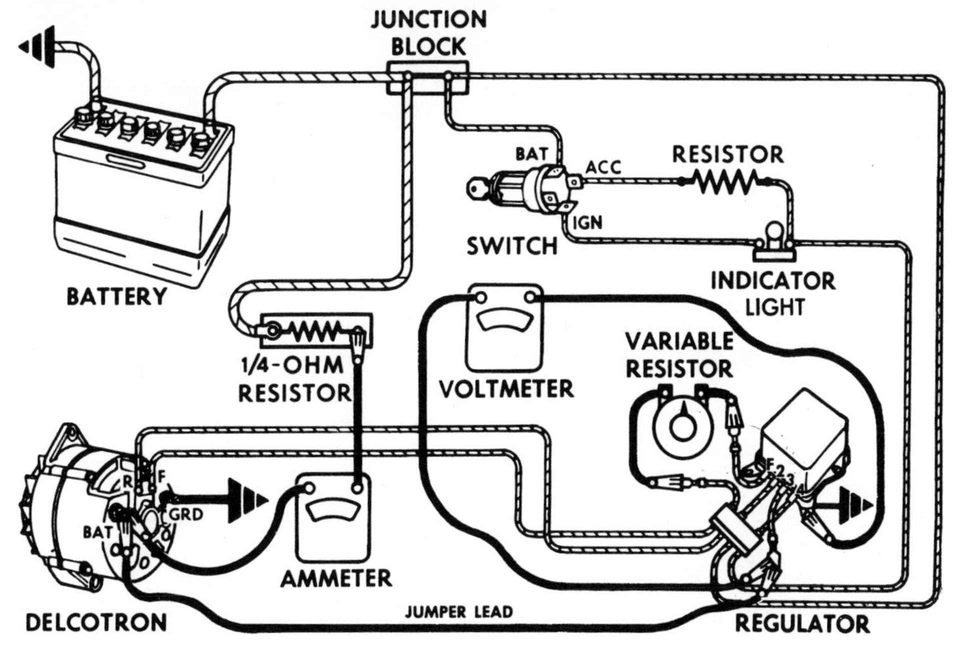

Figure 12 Connections for checking the voltage setting of a regulator. *(Delco-Remy Division of General Motors Corporation.)*

> **NOTE:** When removing or replacing the regulator cover, first disconnect the adapter lead at terminal 4 of the wiring-harness connector and the jumper lead from the battery terminal of the alternator. Failure to do this would cause serious damage if the cover accidentally touched any internal part while it was being removed or replaced. Always turn the screw clockwise when making the final adjustment to make sure the head of the screw is against the spring holder. Cycle the regulator as explained above and, with cover on, note the voltage reading. Readjust as necessary.

4. VOLTAGE SETTING (LOWER CONTACTS) Slowly increase the resistance of the variable resistor with the engine operating at 2,500 rpm until the regulator operates on the lower contacts. If the regulator does not operate on the lower contacts, turn on the car headlights to load the battery. If the lower-contact voltage is not correct, it can be reduced by increasing the air gap.

5. VOLTAGE REGULATOR POINT OPENING AND AIR GAP With the regulator disconnected, check the point opening of the upper contacts with the lower contacts touching. Adjust by bending the upper-contact arm as shown. Check the air gap with the lower contacts touching, and turn the nylon nut to adjust the air gap.

> **NOTE:** Final air-gap adjustment must be made to obtain the correct voltage differential (between operation on upper and lower contacts).

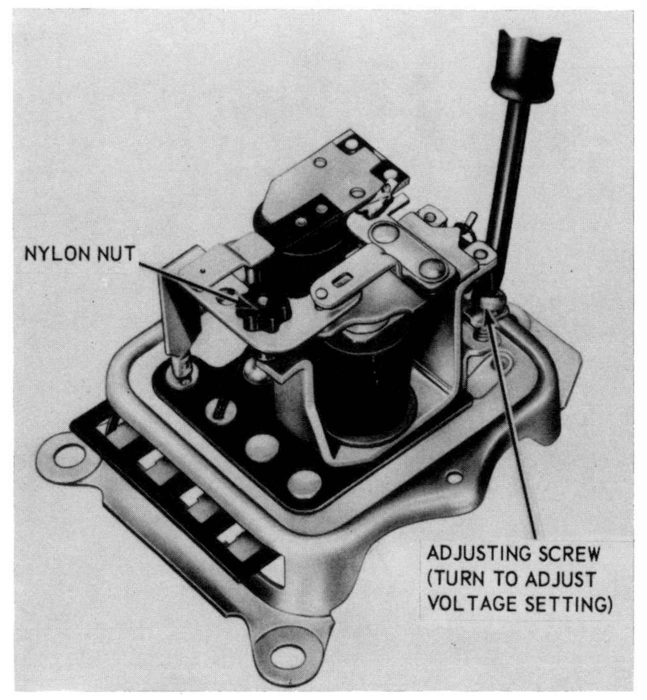

Figure 13 Adjusting the voltage setting of a regulator. *(Delco-Remy Division of General Motors Corporation.)*

6. FIELD-RELAY AIR GAP With the regulator disconnected, check the air gap with the contacts just touching. Adjust by bending the flat contact support spring.

7. FIELD-RELAY POINT OPENING Check the point opening, and adjust by bending the armature stop. (If the relay has no armature stop, this check is not necessary.)

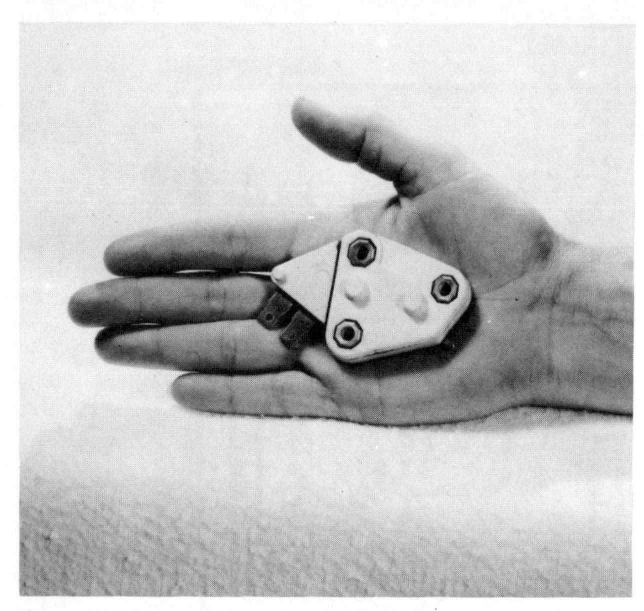

Figure 14 An integral transistorized regulator removed from an alternator. *(Delco-Remy Division of General Motors Corporation.)*

8. FIELD-RELAY VOLTAGE SETTING Check the field-relay closing voltage by connecting a 100-ohm variable resistor, a 60-ohm fixed resistor, and a voltmeter to the adapter. Leave the ignition switch off. Turn the resistor to the FULL RESISTANCE position. Slowly decrease the resistance and note the closing voltage of the relay. Adjust by bending with a heel iron.

■ 3-5-4 Delco-Remy Alternator with Integral Voltage Regulator The procedure for checking this system to locate the cause of trouble if there is a low or no charging rate with a discharged battery is described in ■3-4-7. The procedure for checking the indicator-light circuit if it malfunctions is described in ■3-4-9.

Figure 14 shows an integral regulator that has been removed from a Delco-Remy alternator. Note the size of the regulator. Inside this unit there are four resistors, a capacitor, three diodes, and two transistors. The regulator has no adjustments. The only service ever required is replacement if tests show the regulator is faulty.

SECTION 3-6 Alternator Service

This section discusses the checking and servicing of alternators. Section 4 in this part described the best ways to track down causes of ac charging-system troubles. The service precautions are listed in ■ 3-4-2.

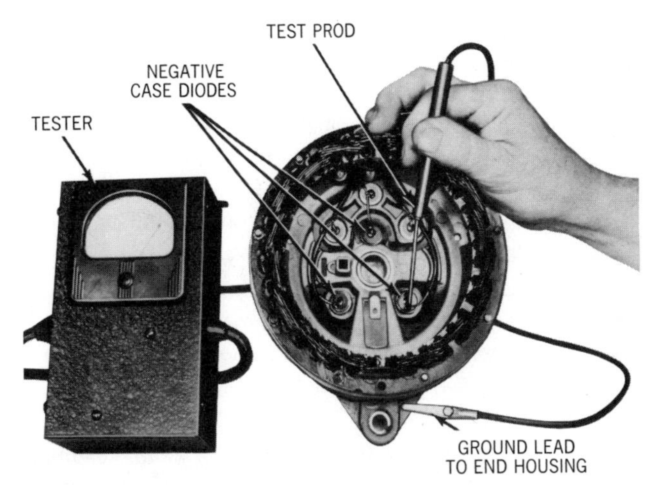

Figure 1 Testing negative diodes with a special tester. *(Chrysler Corporation.)*

■ 3-6-1 Alternator Checks

There are only three parts to check if an alternator fails to produce any output: the stator, the rotor windings and circuits, and the diodes and circuit. Checking alternator output was described in Sec. 5 of this part. Checking of alternator components and servicing procedures are detailed in following sections for the three different alternators.

■ 3-6-2 Chrysler-Plymouth Alternator Service

If the checks outlined in Sec. 4 and 5 of this part point to alternator trouble, the alternator should be removed from the car for further checks and service.

> **NOTE:** Always disconnect the battery ground strap from the battery terminal before disconnecting the leads from the alternator

1. BENCH TESTS Rotor field-coil current draw, field-circuit-ground check, and diode checks are three tests to be made with the alternator on the bench.

a. *Field-Coil Draw* Connect the test-ammeter positive lead to the positive terminal of a fully charged battery. Connect the negative lead of the ammeter to the field terminal of the alternator. Connect a jumper lead to the negative terminal of the battery and to the end shield of the alternator. On alternators with two field terminals, connect the second field terminal to the negative (grounded) terminal of the battery. Slowly turn the rotor by hand. Current flow through the field coil should be 2.3 to 2.7 amps at 12 volts. Low current draw indicates high resistance in the field circuit. This may be due to brushes not seating on slip rings, dirty or worn slip rings, or poor connections in the field coils. Excessive current draw indicates a possible shorted field coil or grounded field circuit.

b. *Testing Field Circuit for Grounds* Remove the ground brush on earlier models (on later models, both brushes are insulated). Use a test light and check from the insulated-brush terminal to the end shield. If the light goes on, there is a ground. Check further by removing the insulated-brush assembly. Then separate the end shields by taking out the three through bolts and prying between the stator and drive-end shield with a screwdriver. Check with a test light between one slip ring and the end shield. If the light goes on, the rotor has an internal ground. If the light does not go on, the ground is in the insulated-brush assembly.

> **NOTE:** The later model (since 1970) of the Chrysler Plymouth alternator has an isolated field. That is, it has two field terminals. Neither of the brushes is grounded in the alternator. This alternator is used with a transistorized voltage regulator which is not adjustable. To test the field circuit for grounds, it is not necessary to remove either brush because both are insulated.

c. *Testing Diodes with Tester* If the special Chrysler testing tool is available (Fig. 1), the diodes may be tested without disconnecting the leads. The rectifier end shield, which contains the diodes, must be removed to check the diodes. First, the ground and insulated brushes must be removed. Then, the three through bolts must be taken out and the end shields separated. Next, plug the tester into a 110-volt source and place the end shield on an insulated surface. Clip the test lead to the alternator battery terminal. Touch the exposed bare metal connections of each of the positive case diodes with the test prod.

> **NOTE:** Do not break the sealing around the diode lead wires. This sealing protects against corrosion. Touch the prod to the exposed metal connection nearest the diode.

Meter readings should be 1-3/4 amps or more. Readings should be about the same for all three diodes. With two good diodes and one shorted diode, the readings at the good ones will be low, and the shorted diode will read zero. If one diode is open, it will read about 1 amp, with the other two readings okay.

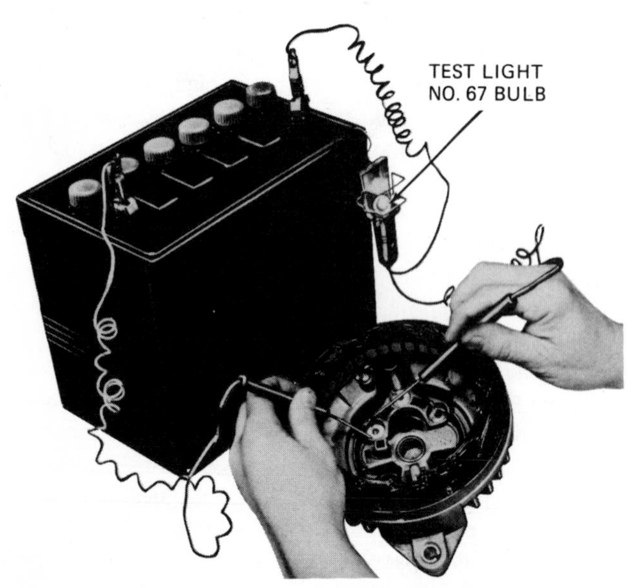

Figure 2 Testing diodes with a low-voltage test light and battery. *(Chrysler Corporation.)*

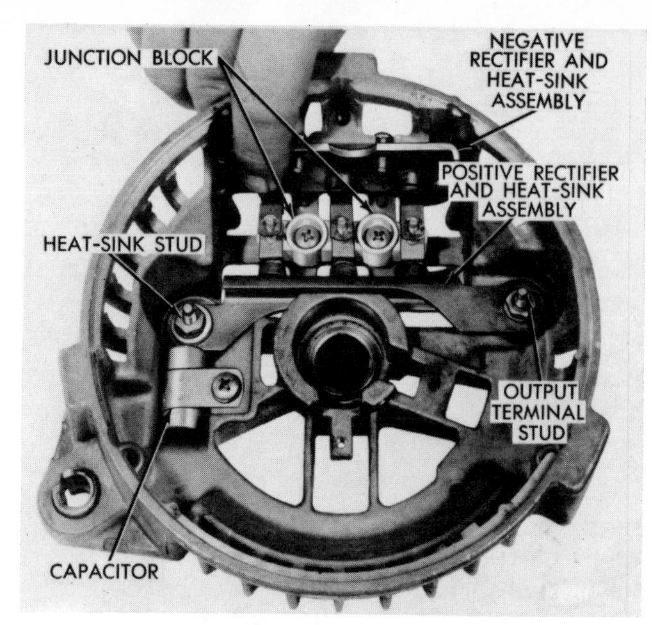

Figure 3 Removing the negative rectifiers and heat-sink assembly. *(Chrysler Corporation.)*

Figure 1 shows the tester being used to check the negative diodes. The same procedure is used, but the meter will read on the opposite side of the scale from its reading when checking the positive diodes.

> **NOTE:** Locations of the diodes are different in different models.

d. *Testing Diodes with Test Light* If the special tester is not available, the stator leads at the Y connections must be cut as close to the Y as possible. Then each diode should be checked with a 12-volt battery and a No. 67 bulb (4 candlepower), as shown in Fig. 2. Touch one probe to the outer case of the diode and the other to the wire in the center of the diode, as shown. Then reverse the probes. The light should go on in one direction but not in the other. If it lights in both directions, the diode is shorted. If it does not light in either direction, the diode is open. Replacement of diodes is explained later.

e. *Testing Stator* To test the stator with a test light, unsolder the diode leads. Do not blow off melted solder with air. Particles could get into the diodes and short them out.

Use a low-voltage test light touching one lead to the stator pole frame and checking with a test prod to each of the three stator leads. If the light goes on, the stator is grounded and must be replaced.

Test stator windings for continuity, or complete circuit, by connecting one test prod to all three stator leads at the Y connection. Touch each of the other stator leads with the test prod. If the light fails to go on, the circuit is open and the stator will require replacement.

f. *Replacing Diodes* A special diode service fixture with a removing adapter must be used to remove the diodes on the earlier alternator models. Clamp the fixture in a vise. Sup-

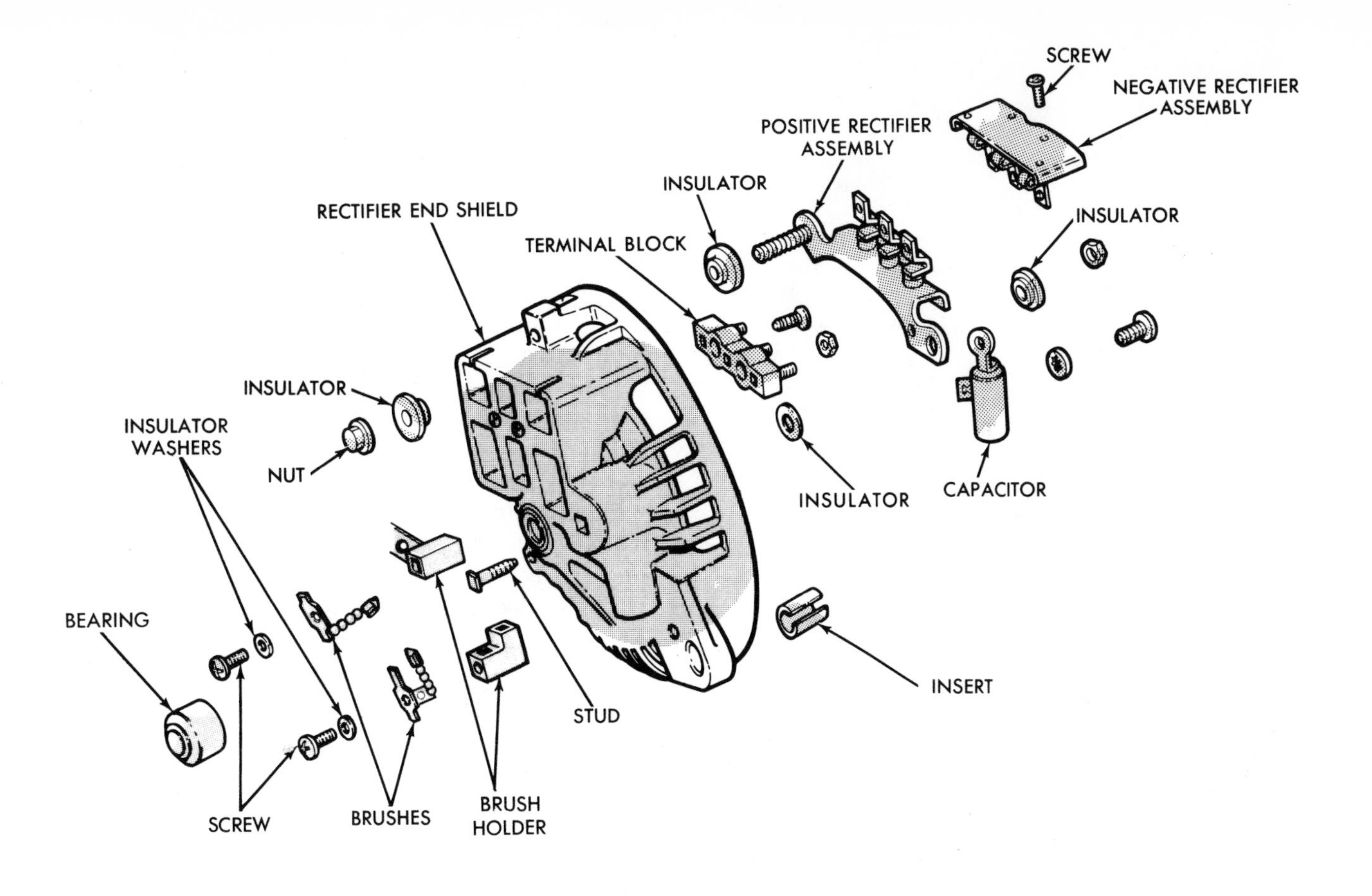

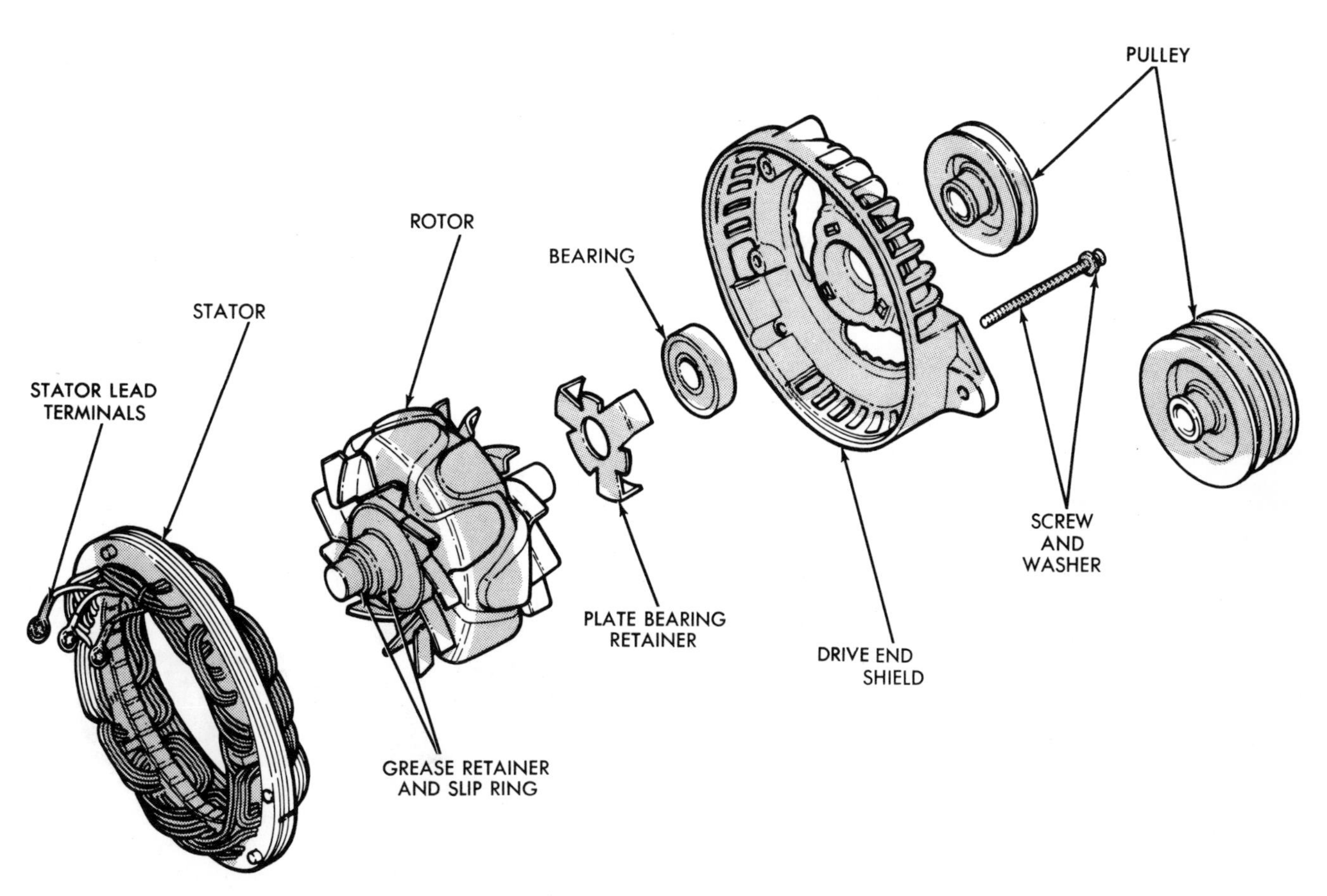

Figure 4 Disassembled view of a late-model alternator. *(Chrysler Corporation.)*

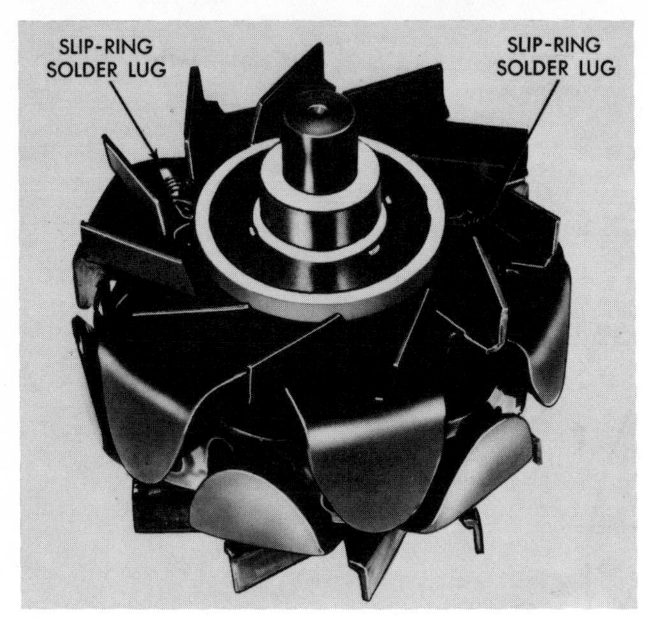

Figure 5 Solder points on the slip rings. *(Chrysler Corporation.)*

port the end shield on the fixture anvil under the diode to be removed. Make sure the bore of the removing adapter completely surrounds the diode. Turn the screw to force the diode out. To install a new diode, make sure it is squarely in the mounting hole. Use a special installing support (in place of the removing adapter) with the same fixture. Apply pressure with the screw to force the diode in until the collar of the diode bottoms against the casting.

> **NOTE:** Never drive the diode in with a hammer. Any sort of mechanical shock—even dropping the diode—could ruin it.

Resolder the connections with rosin-core solder. Avoid overheating the diode, as this could ruin it. Quickly cool the soldered connection with a cloth dampened with water.

On later alternator models with two insulated field terminals, the two heat sinks, holding three diodes each, are removed as assemblies. [Figure 3 shows the removal of the negative rectifier (with three diodes) and heat-sink assembly from the end shield.] This means that four hex-head screws must be removed. Then two nuts and washers are removed to take off the positive rectifier (with three diodes) and the heat-sink assembly.

2. ALTERNATOR DISASSEMBLY AND REASSEMBLY

We have already described most of the steps required to disassemble the alternator. Additional steps include removing the pulley and bearings and replacing the old rotor slip rings with new ones.

a. *Disassembly* (Fig. 4) Further disassembly steps, after the rectifier end shield has been removed, follow:

- Remove the pulley with a puller.
- Pry the drive-end-bearing spring retainer from the end shield with a screwdriver.
- Support the end shield and tap the rotor shaft with a plastic hammer to remove the rotor. The drive-end bearing must be removed, if it is to be replaced, with a puller.
- The output terminal, capacitor, heat-sink insulator, and heat sink are held in place by the terminal nuts and washers. Remove these nuts to separate the parts.
- If the needle bearing in the rectifier end shield requires replacement, support the shield and press the bearing out with special tools.

b. *Inspecting Parts* Electrical checking of the various parts has already been covered. Inspect the various parts for damage and wear. Worn or pitted slip rings should be replaced. This is described later. Worn bearings should be replaced. Check for burned insulation, poor soldering at connections, and cracked or damaged housings. Replace all damaged parts.

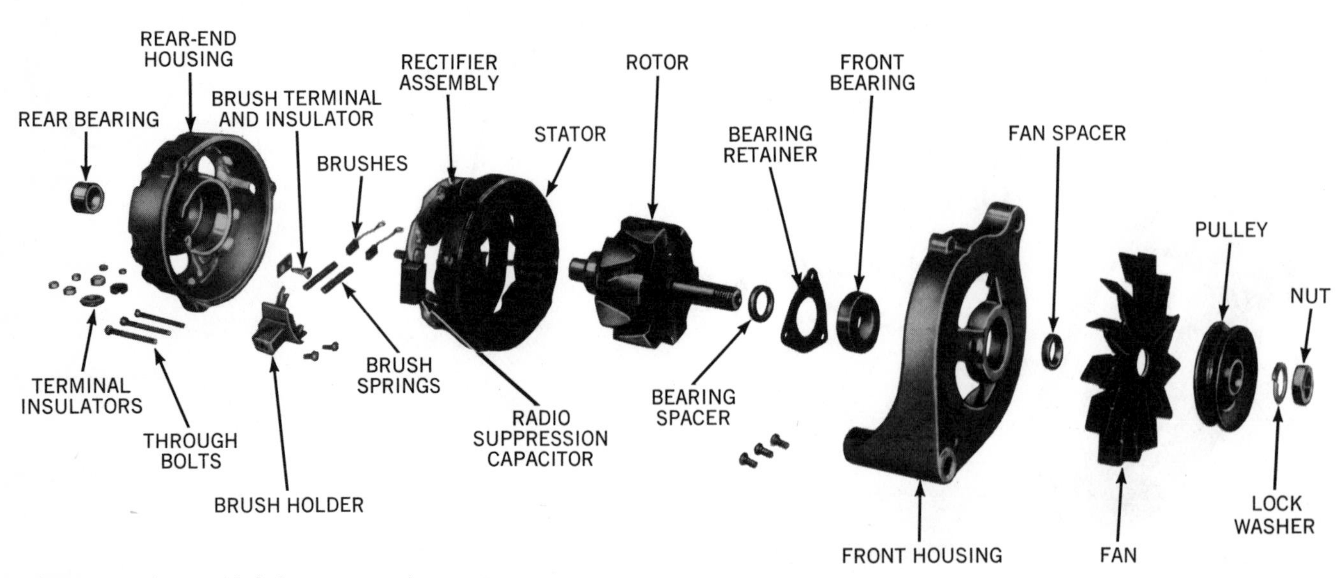

Figure 6 A disassembled alternator. *(Ford Motor Company.)*

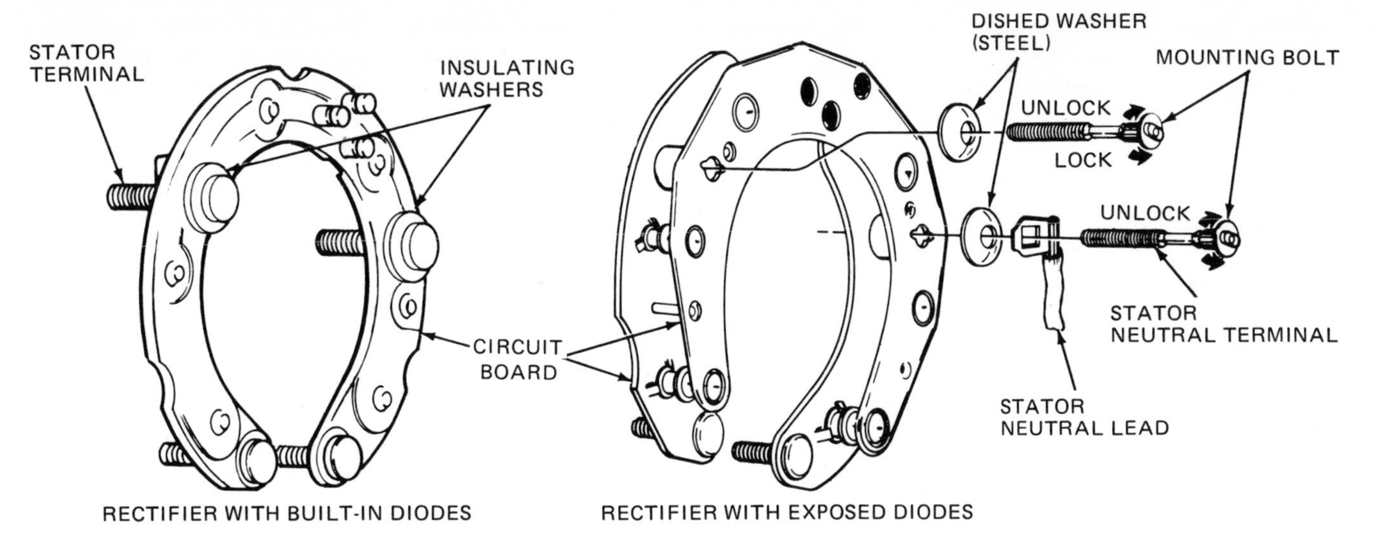

Figure 7 Rectifier assemblies. *(Ford Motor Company.)*

NOTE: Never clean the rotor, stator, bearings, or rectifier parts with solvent. This would probably ruin them. Instead, wipe them with a clean cloth.

c. *Replacing Slip Rings* If the slip rings require replacement, remove the plastic grease retainer from the rotor. Unsolder and unwind the field-coil leads from the slip-ring lugs (Fig. 5). Do not break the leads. Use a chisel to cut the slip rings at opposite points (180° apart). Break the plastic insulator and remove the old rings. Clean the rotor of all old ring parts. Move the leads out of the way and position new slip rings in proper alignment with the leads. Use a special tool to press the rings down into place. The field lead to the insulated slip ring should be clear at the access hole through the fan and pole piece. Tin the leads and wrap them around the slip-ring lugs, starting from the lug shoulders and winding outward. Solder with rosin-core solder.

Test for ground with a low-voltage test light, placing one prod against a ring and the other against the rotor pole piece. If the light goes on, the slip rings are grounded and must be replaced. Test the rotor for complete circuit by putting prods on the two rings. The light should go on. If it does not, the circuit is open. Check for broken leads. If the open is not evident and repairable, replace the rotor assembly.

d. *Reassembly* On reassembly, use special bearing tools to install new bearings if required. After the drive-end shield—with bearing-spring retainer and bearing—has been installed on the rotor, press the pulley onto the rotor shaft. Support the lower end of the rotor shaft on the press table so pressure is applied to the shaft through the pulley and not through the end shield.

Install the heat-sink insulator, capacitor, and terminal screw with insulating washer, lock washers, and nuts. Put the stator and rectifier-end shield into place on the rotor and drive-end shield, pushing the rotor shaft through the rectifier-end-shield bearing. Put the through bolts, washers, and nuts into place and tighten them evenly to 20 to 30 pound-feet (2.764 to 4.146 kg-m).

Install the insulated brush in the end shield, and put the bronze terminal on the plastic holder with the tab of the terminal in the holder recess. Put the nylon washer on the terminal and install the lock washer and attaching screw. Install the ground brush and the attaching screw.

Rotate the pulley slowly by hand to make sure the rotor fan blades do not hit the diodes, capacitor leads, or stator connections.

Install the alternator on the car, and connect the leads and ground wire. Reconnect the battery ground cable, start the engine, and check the alternator output as already described in Sec. 3-5 of this part.

■ **3-6-3 Ford Alternator Service** If the checks described in Sec. 3-5 of this part indicate alternator trouble, the alternator should be removed for further checking.

NOTE: Always disconnect the battery ground strap from the battery before disconnecting the leads from the alternator.

1. ALTERNATOR DISASSEMBLY Figure 6 is a view of a disassembled alternator discussed herein. Ford also supplies high-output alternators. The alternator shown in Fig. 6 is disassembled as follows:

a. Mark both end housings with scribe marks so they can be properly realigned on reassembly. Remove the three through bolts. Separate the front-end housing and rotor from the stator and rear-end housing.
b. Remove nuts and washers from the rear-end housing and separate the housing from the stator and rectifier assembly.
c. Remove brush-holder mounting screws and take off the holder, brushes, springs, insulator, and terminal.

d. If the bearing requires replacement, support the housing on the inner boss to press it out.

e. If the rectifier assembly is being replaced or the stator is being tested, unsolder the stator leads, using a small (100-watt) soldering iron. Avoid excessive heat.

f. If the rectifier has a molded circuit board, remove the screws from the rectifier by rotating the bolt beads one-quarter turn clockwise to unlock them and then removing the screws (Fig. 7). On the type with a fiber circuit board, push the screws out.

g. Remove the drive pulley nut, lock washer, pulley, fan, spacer, rotor, and rotor stop.

h. If the old front bearing is defective, remove the three screws that hold the retainer and remove the retainer. Then support the housing near the boss and press the bearing out.

2. CLEANING AND INSPECTING PARTS Never use solvent to clean the rotor, stator, bearings, or rectifier assembly. This could ruin them. Instead wipe the parts with a clean cloth. Check bearings for wear or loss of lubricant, either of which would require bearing replacement.

Check rear of rotor shaft for roughness or chatter marks. These indicate slippage in the bearing, which would call for rotor replacement.

Replace the pulley if it is out of round or bent.

If the slip rings are rough or pitted, they can be turned down. But do not turn them down below 1.220 inches (31 mm). These slip rings are not replaceable. If they are damaged, the rotor must be replaced.

Check for stripped threads, poor soldered connections, burned insulation, and cracked housing. Replace defective parts. Resolder poor connections. Avoid excessive heat on diodes.

3. ELECTRICAL CHECKS Both before and after the alternator is disassembled, the various components—diodes, rotor, and stator—should be electrically checked, as follows:

a. Rectifier-Short or Ground and Stator-Ground Test Use an ohmmeter. Set the MULTIPLY BY knob at 10, and calibrate the ohmmeter. Touch the probes at the BAT (battery) and STA (stator) terminals. Then reverse the probes and repeat the test. The ohmmeter should read about 60 ohms in one direction and infinity (no needle movement) in the other. A reading in both directions indicates a bad positive diode, a grounded diode plate, or a grounded BAT terminal.

Perform the same test of the STA (stator) and GND (ground) terminals of the alternator. A reading in both directions indicates a bad negative diode, a grounded stator winding, a grounded positive diode plate, or a grounded BAT terminal.

Infinite readings on all four tests indicate an open STA terminal lead inside the alternator.

b. Field-Open or Short-Circuit Test Use the ohmmeter with MULTIPLY BY knob set at 1. Calibrate the meter. Place the probes on the alternator field terminal and ground terminal. Now, spin the alternator pulley. The ohmmeter reading should be between 3.5 and 250 ohms and should fluctuate while the pulley is turning. No needle movement indicates an open brush lead, worn or stuck brushes, or a bad rotor assembly. A reading of less than 3.5 ohms indicates a grounded brush assembly or field terminal or a bad rotor.

c. Diode Test on Bench Disassemble the alternator and remove the rectifier assembly, as explained above. Set the ohmmeter MULTIPLY BY knob at 10 and calibrate the meter. Check each diode first in one direction and then in the other. Diodes should show about 60 ohms in one direction and infinity in the other. If any diode does not, replace the rectifier assembly.

d. Stator-Coil-Open or Ground Test on Bench Disassemble the alternator to separate the stator assembly. Set the ohmmeter MULTIPLY BY knob at 1,000. Probe from one of the stator leads to the stator laminated core. Repeat for each of the stator leads. Reading should be infinite for each (no needle movement). Do not touch the metal probes or the stator leads with your hands. This will cause an incorrect reading.

e. Open-Rotor or Short-Circuit Test on Bench Disassemble the alternator to separate the rotor. Set the ohmmeter MULTIPLY BY knob at 1. Touch the probes to the two rotor slip rings. The meter should read 3.5 to 4.5 ohms. A higher reading indicates a bad connection at the slip ring or a broken wire. A low reading indicates a shorted winding. If the defect is not obvious or not easily repairable, discard the rotor.

Touch one probe to the rotor shaft and the other to one ring and then the other. There should be no reading. If there is, the rotor winding is grounded to the shaft. Unless the ground can be easily fixed, replace the rotor.

4. REASSEMBLY

a. Press in new bearings if the old bearings have been removed. Support the housing at the boss.

b. If the stop ring on the rotor drive shaft is damaged, remove it. Install a new ring by pushing it onto the shaft and into the groove. Do not use snap-ring pliers. They will damage the ring.

c. The rotor stop goes on the shaft with the recessed side against the stop ring. Put the front-end housing, fan spacer, fan, pulley, and lock washer on the shaft. Install the retaining nut, tightening it to specifications.

d. Use a toothpick, as shown in Fig. 8, to hold the brushes in position after placing the brushes, the springs, the terminal, and the insulator in the brush holder.

e. Install the brush-holder assembly in the rear-end housing (Fig. 8). Install the mounting screws.

f. Wrap the three stator-winding leads around the printed-circuit-board terminals. Solder them, using a 100-watt soldering iron and rosin-core solder. Avoid excessive heat on diodes. Position the stator neutral-lead eyelet on the stator terminal insulators. Put the diode assembly in place.

g. The molded-circuit-board rectifier is attached with the mounting bolts (Fig. 7). Note the position of dished washers and stator neutral lead.

h. If the alternator uses a fiber circuit board, push the screws straight through into the holes.

NOTE: Do not use the metal dished washers on the fiber circuit board. This will cause a short circuit.

i. Install the STA and BAT terminal insulators. Put the stator and diode-plate assembly into the rear-end housing. Put insulators on the terminal bolts (black on STA, red on BAT, and white on FLD), and install retaining nuts.

j. Position the rear-end housing and stator assembly over the rotor and align the scribe marks. Bring the housings together, seating the stator core in the steps in the housings. Install the through bolts. Remove the toothpick holding the brushes. Put water-proof cement over the hole to seal it.

k. Test the alternator for output.

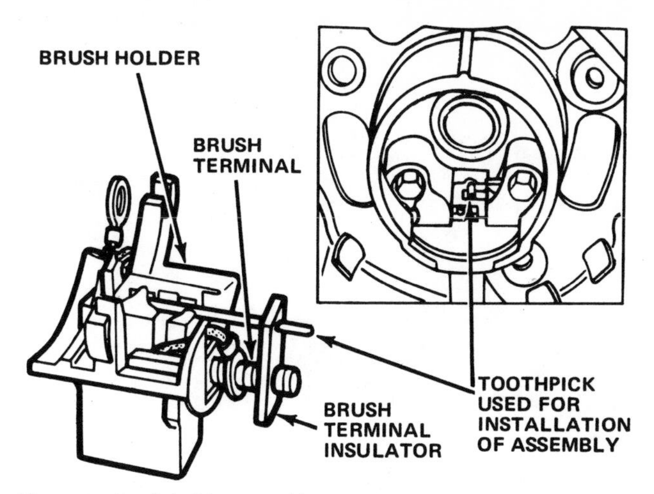

Figure 8 Brush-holder assembly. *(American Motors Corporation.)*

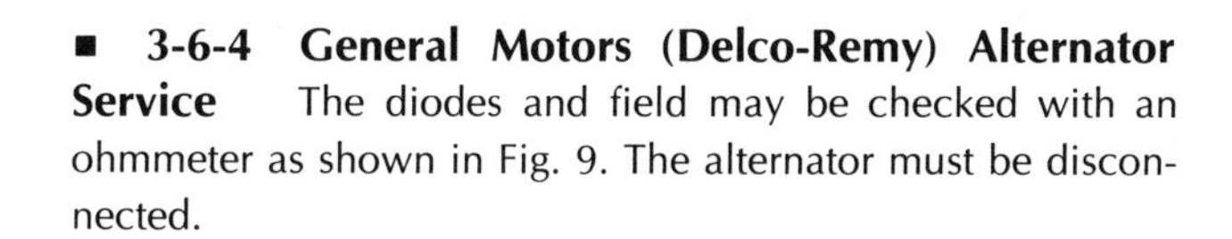

■ 3-6-4 General Motors (Delco-Remy) Alternator Service

The diodes and field may be checked with an ohmmeter as shown in Fig. 9. The alternator must be disconnected.

NOTE: Always disconnect the ground strap from the battery before disconnecting alternator or regulator leads.

Tests A and B are diode tests shown in Fig. 9. Prods should be tried one way and then the other in each test. The meter should read high one way and low the other. If the meter reads the same in either direction (high or low), a diode is defective.

Test C is a field test for open. The meter should be connected between the field terminal and ground and should read within specifications. If it does not, the field is open or grounded.

1. ALTERNATOR DISASSEMBLY If the tests in Sec. 5 of this part or the checks above show the alternator to be defective, it must be disassembled as follows:

a. Clamp the alternator in a vise by the mounting flange. Use box and allen wrenches to remove the pulley retaining nut.

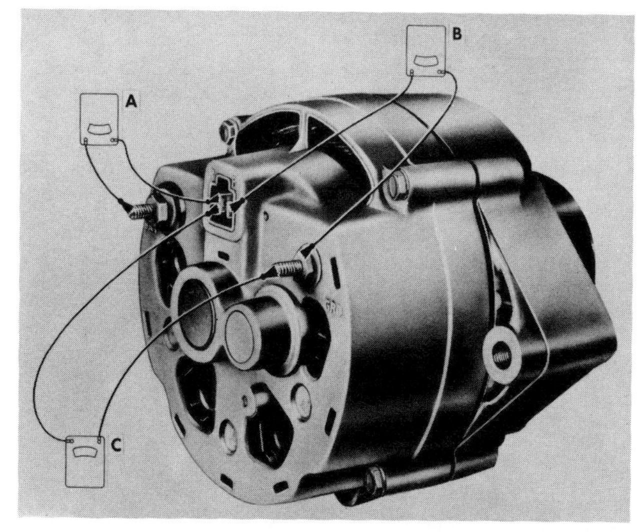

Figure 9 Using an ohmmeter to check the diodes and field (rotor) in an alternator. *(Delco-Remy Division of General Motors Corporation.)*

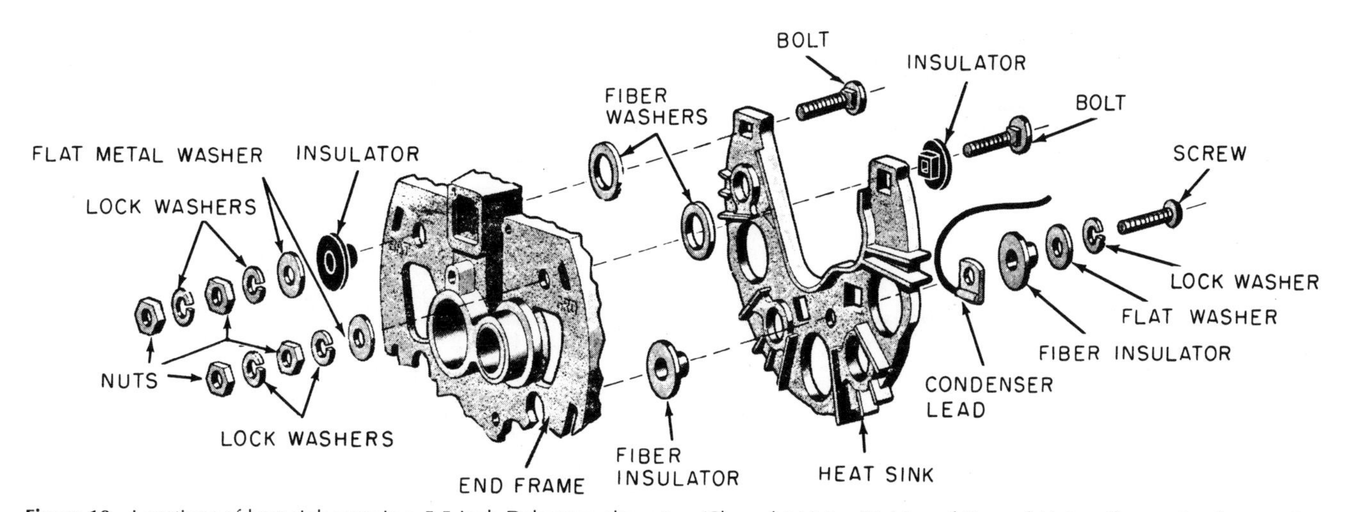

Figure 10 Locations of heat-sink parts in a 5.5-inch Delcotron alternator. *(Chevrolet Motor Division of General Motors Corporation.)*

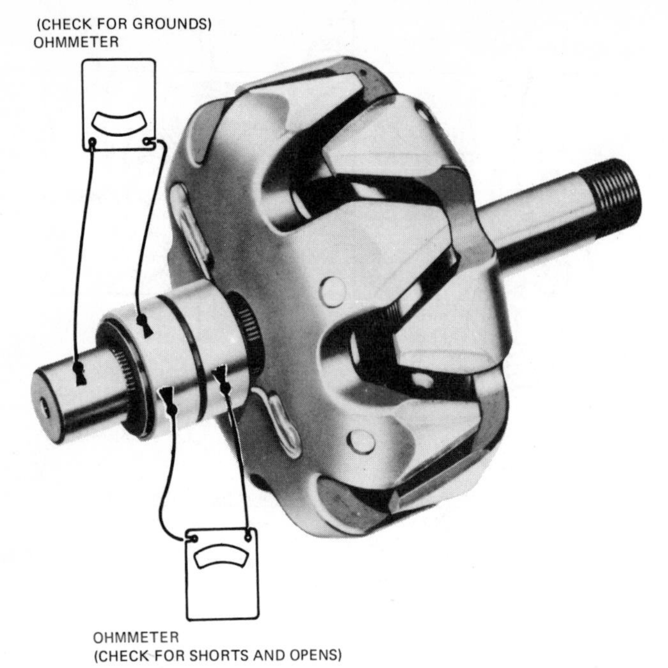

Figure 11 Using an ohmmeter to check a rotor for grounds or opens. *(Chevrolet Motor Division of General Motors Corporation.)*

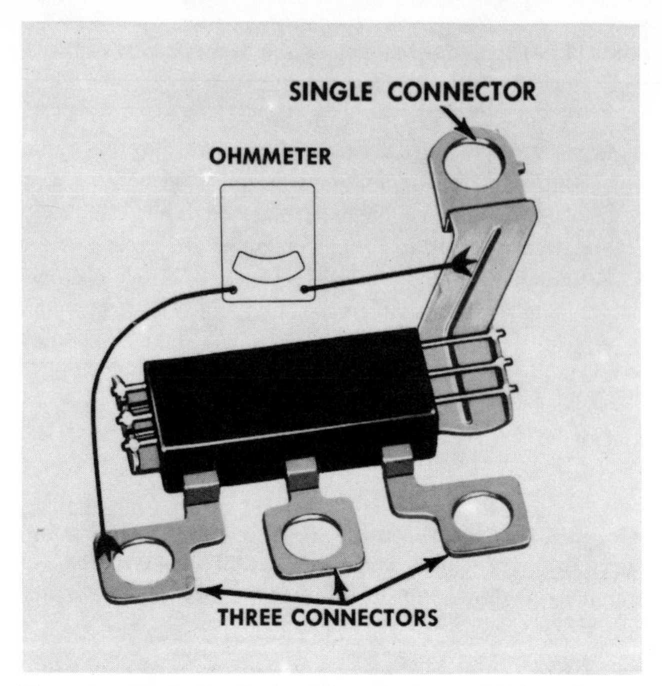

Figure 13 Diode-trio checks. *(Chevrolet Motor Division of General Motors Corporation.)*

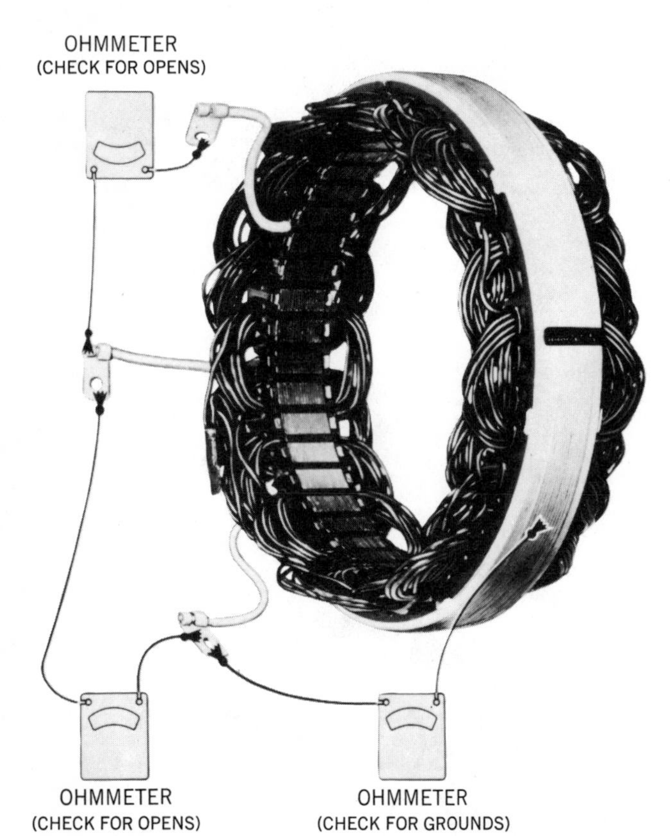

Figure 12 Using an ohmmeter to check a stator for opens or grounds. *(Chevrolet Motor Division of General Motors Corporation.)*

Then remove the washer, pulley, fan, and spacer from the shaft.

b. Remove four through bolts and loosen the end frames by prying at the bolt locations.

c. Remove the slip-ring end frame and stator, as an assembly, from the drive end and rotor assembly. Put a piece of tape (pressure-sensitive and not friction, which would leave a gummy deposit) over the slip-ring end-frame bearing to prevent dirt from entering.

NOTE: If the brushes drop onto the rotor shaft and become contaminated with bearing lubricant, they should be cleaned prior to installation.

d. Remove the three stator-lead attaching nuts and separate the stator from the end frame.

e. Remove screws, brushes, and holder assembly.

f. Remove the heat sink from the end frame by removing BAT and GRD terminals and one attaching screw (Fig. 10).

g. Remove the slip-ring end bearing, if necessary, by removing the inner seal.

h. Take the rotor from the drive-end frame and take out the bearing, if necessary, by removing the retainer plate.

2. CLEANING AND INSPECTING PARTS Clean all parts with a cloth. Do not wash the rotor, stator, diodes, or bearings in solvent. This could ruin them. If bearings are worn or rough, discard them.

Slip rings are not replaceable. If slightly worn, they may be cleaned up with a 400-grain polishing cloth. If they are out of round, they may be turned down in a lathe. They should be true to 0.001 inch (0.0254 mm). If excessive material must be removed or if rings are damaged, discard the rotor assembly.

If brushes are worn down halfway, replace them. Make sure the brush springs have the proper tension and are not distorted. Brushes must move freely in the holders.

a. *Rotor Tests* With an ohmmeter, check from either slip ring to the shaft and from one slip ring to the other to check for grounds or opens (Fig. 11). The rotor is checked for shorts by connecting a 12-volt battery and ammeter in series with the two slip rings. Excessive current draw indicates a short. A grounded, open, or shorted rotor must be discarded.

b. *Stator Tests* Connect an ohmmeter as shown in Fig. 12 to check for opens or grounds in the stator. Shorts are hard to find in the stator because of the low resistance of the winding. Usually, if all other tests are okay but the alternator does not supply rated output, the trouble is due to a shorted stator.

c. *Diode Checks* The stator must be disconnected for a diode check. The diodes may be checked with an ohmmeter connected first in one direction and then in the other across each diode. If both readings are the same (high or low), the diode is defective and should be discarded.

   On later models of this alternator, the diodes are permanently assembled into diode trios (Fig. 13). Two trios are used, one for the positive and one for the negative diodes. On these, remove the diode trios from the slip-ring end frame and check each diode as shown.

> **NOTE:** A 12-volt test light can also be used to check diodes. As the test prods are put across each diode, first in one direction and then in the other, the light should go on one way but not the other.

d. *Rectifier-Bridge Check* Later models require a rectifier-bridge check (Fig. 14). Connect the ohmmeter, as shown. Then reverse connections. If both readings are the same, replace the rectifier bridge. Repeat at each of the three terminals.

e. *Voltage-Regulator and Brush-Lead-Clip Check* Connect an ohmmeter from the brush-lead clip to the end frame as shown in Fig. 15. Reverse the connections. If both readings are zero, either the brush-lead clip is grounded or the voltage regulator is defective. The brush-lead clip will be grounded if, on reassembly, the insulating sleeve or washer is omitted.

3. *ALTERNATOR REASSEMBLY*

a. *Diode Replacement* If a diode requires replacement on the older-model alternator, support the heat sink with a special tool and press out the diode. Press in the new diode with the same tool.

> **NOTE:** Do not strike the diode, as any shock could ruin it. Also, do not bend the diode stem, as this could cause internal damage.

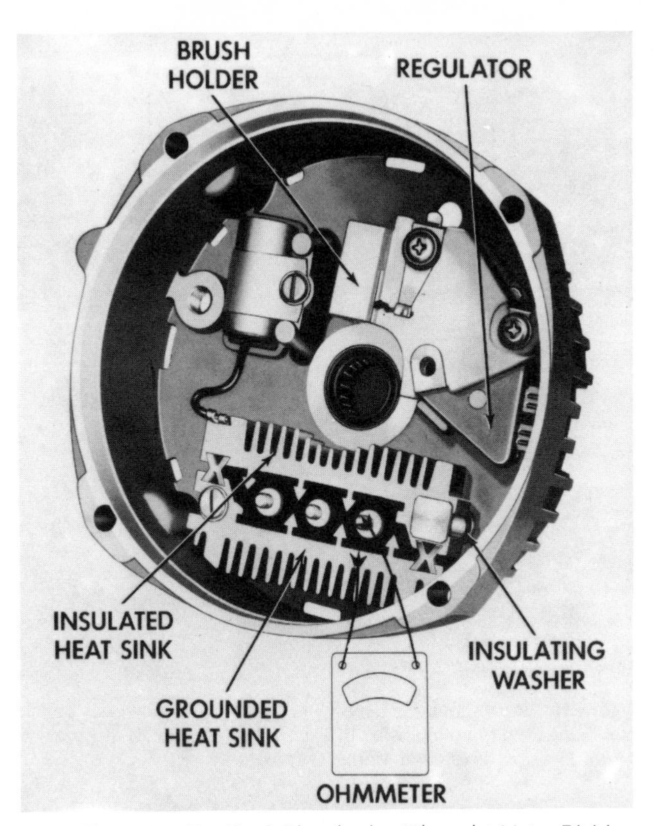

Figure 14 Rectifier-bridge checks. *(Chevrolet Motor Division of General Motors Corporation.)*

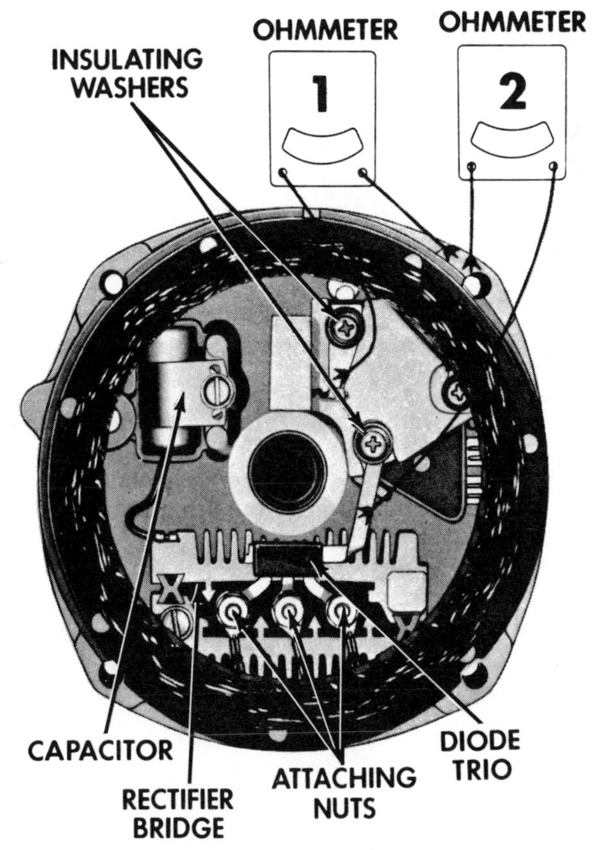

Figure 15 Brush-lead-clip checks. *(Chevrolet Motor Division of General Motors Corporation.)*

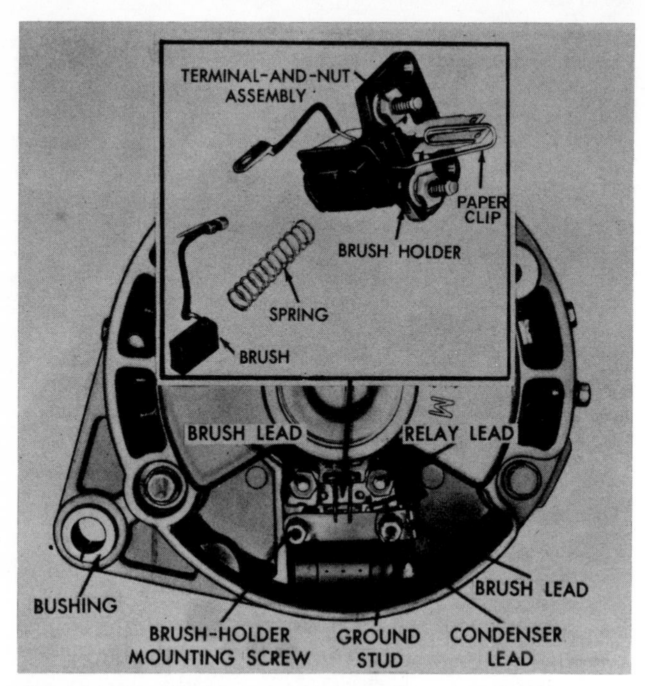

Figure 16 Brush-holder assembly in an alternator, showing a paper clip being used to hold brushes in place during reassembly. *(Chevrolet Motor Division of General Motors Corporation.)*

On the later-model alternator which uses diode trios (Fig. 13), if one diode tests bad, discard the trio.

b. Replace the heat sink, noting proper relationship of parts as shown in Fig. 10. Before putting the heat sink in place, install the brush holder and brushes in the end frame. Use a bent paper clip or stiff wire to hold the brushes down in place in the holder (Fig. 16). Then attach the holder to the end frame. (The paper clip or wire is removed after the alternator assembly is completed.) Finally, install the heat sink.

c. If a new bearing is installed in the drive-end frame, pack it about one-fourth full with the proper grease. Then press the bearing into the end frame and install a new retainer plate. Stake retainer-plate bolts to the plate so they will not loosen.

d. If the slip-ring end bearing requires replacement, press the old one out. Press a new one in with a flat plate over the bearing so it is pressed down flush with the outside of the end frame. Support the end frame from the inside around the bearing boss to avoid damage to the end frame. Saturate the felt seal with SAE20 oil. Install the seal and the retainer at the inner end of the bearing.

e. To finish the reassembly, install the stator assembly in the slip-ring end frame and locate the diode connectors over the relay, diode, and stator leads, and tighten terminal nuts. Then install the rotor, fan, spacer, pulley, washer, and nut. Tighten with a torque wrench.

f. Assemble the slip-ring end frame and stator assembly to the drive-end frame and rotor assembly. Secure with four through bolts. Remove the brush-holding wire to allow brushes to seat on the slip rings.

g. Check alternator output after assembly.

SECTION 3-7 Electric Circuits and Lights

This section describes automotive electric circuits and lighting, including headlights, headlight covers, automatic headlight controls, turn signals, emergency flashers, and stoplights.

■ **3-7-1 Wiring Circuits** With the increasing number of electrically operated devices in the modern automobile, the wiring circuits have become rather complex. The wires among components are bound together into harnesses. Each wire is marked by special colors in the insulation, for example, light green, dark green, blue, red, black with a white tracer, and so on. These markings permit identification of the various wires in the harnesses.

The circuits through the bulkhead, which is between the engine-compartment components and the instrument panel, are completed by connector plugs and receptacles. As many as a dozen separate wires are gathered together and connected to a receptacle. Then the matching wires are connected to the matching plug. It becomes a simple matter, then, to push the plug into the receptacle to complete many connections at one time. Matching tangs and holes complete the connections between the wires. The plugs and receptacles have locking devices that prevent their coming loose in operation.

■ **3-7-2 Printed Circuits** The instrument panel carries a number of indicating devices, switches, and controls (Fig. 1). These must be interconnected electrically, either with separate wires or with a printed-circuit board. Because there must be a dozen or more connections in a small space, and this would make separate wires hard to connect, car manufacturers use printed circuits to make the connections. The location of one printed circuit is in back of the instrument-cluster assembly. The printed circuit is a flat board of insulating material such as plastic on which a series of metallic conducting strips are printed or otherwise applied. Figure 2 shows part of a printed circuit. When it is installed, the conducting strips complete the circuits. The contacts on the indicator lights rest on the conducting strips at the light sockets when the lights are installed. This completes the circuits to the lights.

■ **3-7-3 Fuses and Circuit Breakers** Most electric circuits have fuses or circuit breakers that protect the electrical components from damage due to a short circuit or ground.

The typical fuse is the cartridge type (Fig. 3). It consists of a glass envelope, contact caps on each end, and a strip of soft metal connecting the two contact caps. The fuse is connected

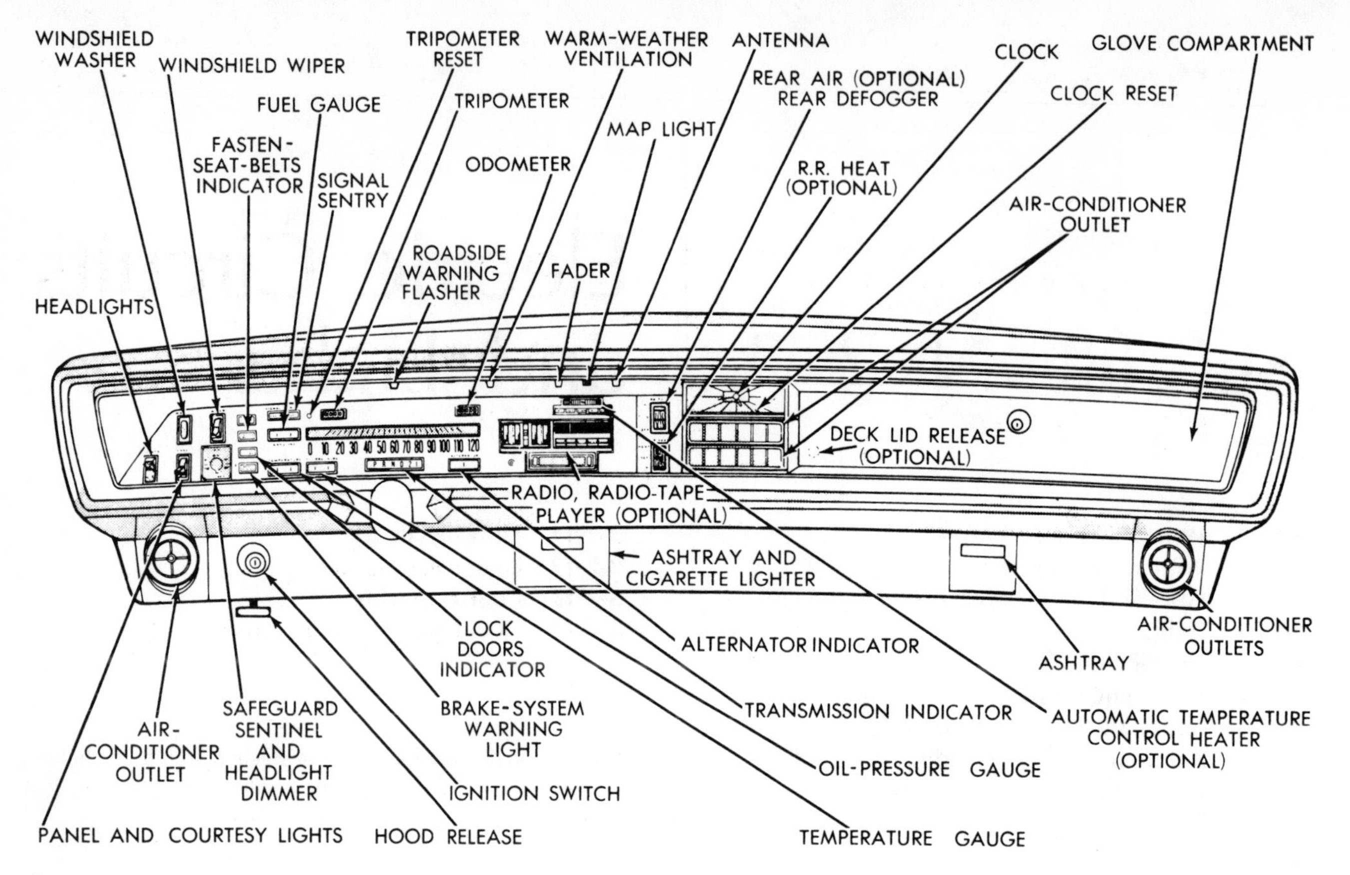

Figure 1 Instrument panel on one model of a fully equipped automobile. *(Chrysler Corporation.)*

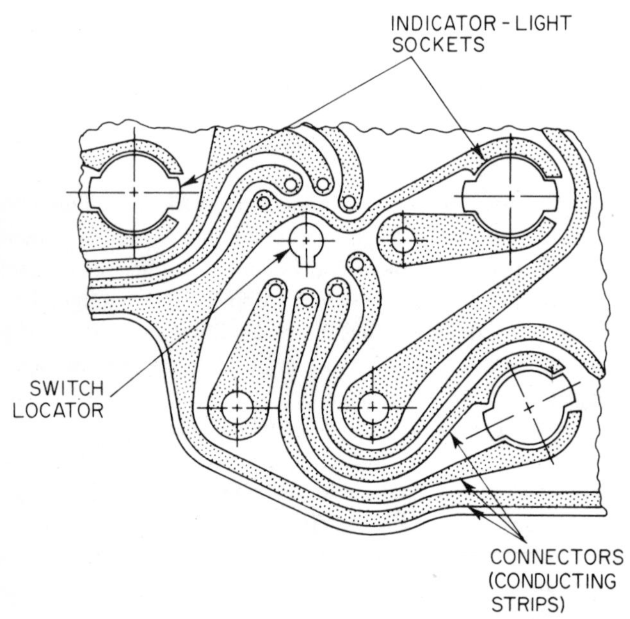

Figure 2 Part of a printed circuit. The connectors are metallic conducting strips printed on the insulating base.

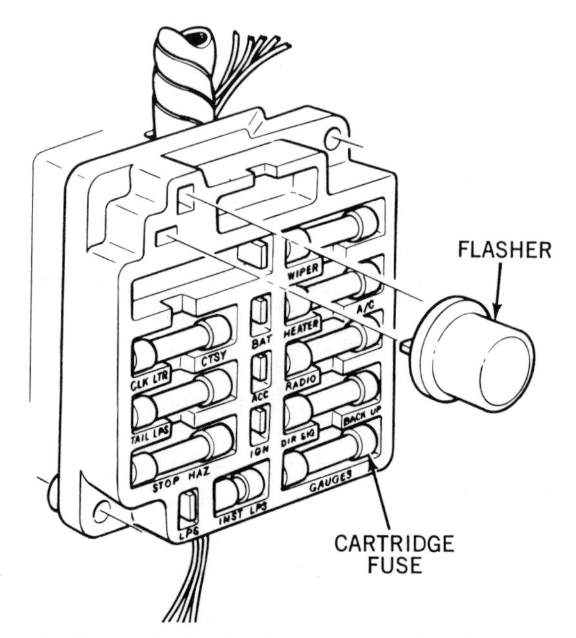

Figure 3 Fuse block, showing fuses in place. *(Chevrolet Motor Division of General Motors Corporation.)*

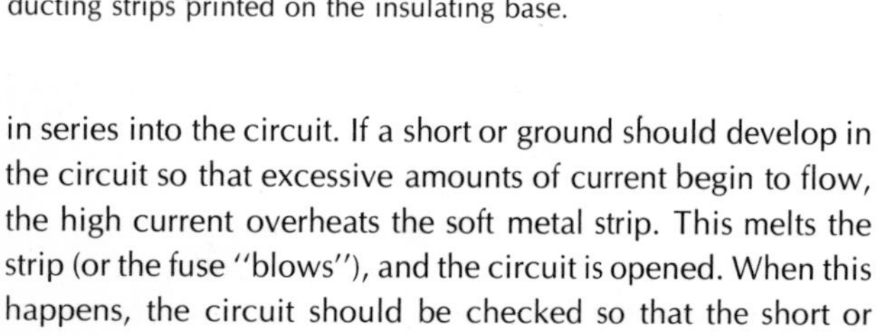
in series into the circuit. If a short or ground should develop in the circuit so that excessive amounts of current begin to flow, the high current overheats the soft metal strip. This melts the strip (or the fuse "blows"), and the circuit is opened. When this happens, the circuit should be checked so that the short or ground can be eliminated. Then, a new fuse should be installed.

Figure 3 is a closeup of a fuse block, showing the fuses in place. Circuit breakers and the horn relay may also be mounted on the fuse block. Circuit breakers perform the same func-

Figure 4 Plug-in type of "minifuse" used on late-model cars. *(Oldsmobile Division of General Motors Corporation.)*

tion as fuses except that they do not "blow" (and thus do not require replacement) when an overload occurs. Instead, they cause contact points to open, interrupting the circuit. When the overload condition is eliminated, the contact points close to complete the circuit again.

Figure 4 shows a new type of fuse first installed in 1977 model cars. It works the same way as the cartridge fuse. However, the new fuse, called the "minifuse," can be plugged in and removed much more easily.

For added protection, many cars have fusible links in the insulated battery cable and in the larger high-current-carrying wires. Figure 5 shows how a fusible link is installed. It is simply a wire several gauges smaller than the wire it is protecting. If a short or ground occurs, the fusible link burns apart before the larger wire does. This protects the rest of the circuit from damage.

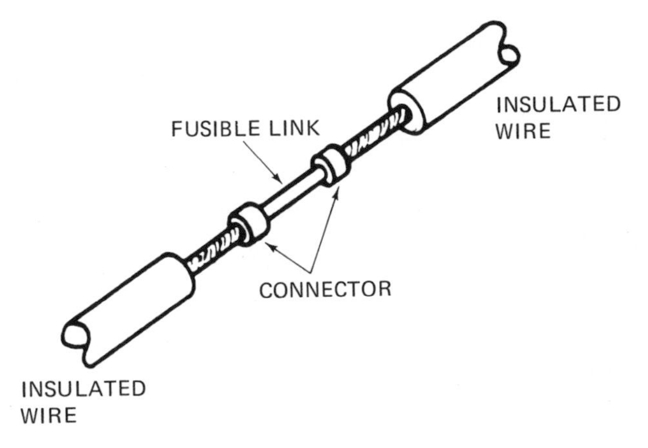

Figure 5 Fusible link connected into an insulated wire circuit.

■ 3-7-4 Lights

The lighting system in a typical automobile includes the headlights, parking lights, turn signals (■3-7-11), side marker lights, stoplights, backup lights, taillights, and interior lights. The interior lights include instrument-panel lights, various warning and indicator lights, and courtesy lights which turn on when a car door is opened. Many cars are equipped with a special emergency flasher or warning-blinker system. When the driver operates the flasher switch, it causes all four turn signals to flash on and off every few seconds. The switch is usually located on the side of the steering column.

> **NOTE:** The correct name for any light on an automotive vehicle is "lamp." For example, we should say "headlamp" instead of "headlight" and "lamp bulb" instead of "light bulb." However, since so many people use the term "light," we shall use it and "lamp" in this book. In either case, what it means is the unit that produces the light.

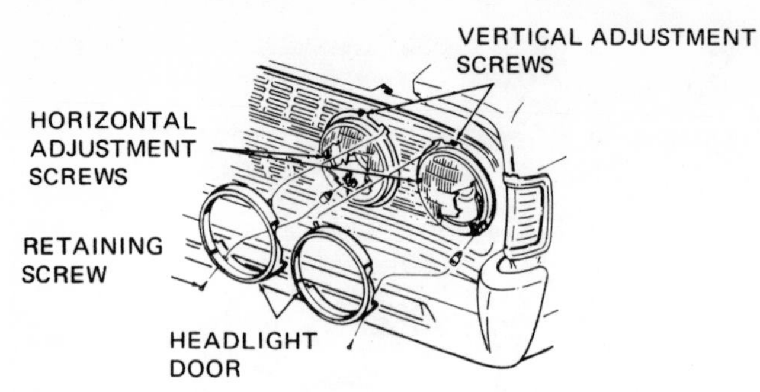

Figure 6 Left front headlights with bezels (doors) removed so the adjustment screws can be seen. *(Ford Motor Company.)*

When the light switch is pulled out, the circuit from the battery to the headlights is completed. This circuit goes through the beam selector switch. This switch has two positions: passing beam (called "low" beam) and driving beam (called "high" beam).

Headlights are made in two types and four sizes (two round and two rectangular). The round sizes are 5¾ inches (146 mm) in diameter and 7 inches (178 mm) in diameter. The rectangular headlights are 6½ by 4 inches (165 by 100 mm) and 7.9 by 5.6 inches (200 by 142 mm). All are identified by the number 1 or 2 molded into the glass at the top of the lens. Type 1 has only one filament. Type 2 has two filaments, one for the high beam and the other for the low beam. The high beam is for driving on the highway when there is no car approaching from the other direction. The low beam is for city driving and for passing a car coming in the opposite direction. The use of the low beam for passing prevents the oncoming driver from being temporarily blinded by the high beam.

Some cars have only one pair of headlights. These are type 2. Other cars have two pairs of headlights: one pair of type 1 and one pair of type 2. Figure 6 shows the method of mounting and adjusting the headlights in one model of car.

When the headlight switch is turned on and the beam selector switch is in the passing or low-beam position, one of the filaments in the type 2 lights is on. When the beam selector switch is operated to switch to high beam, the other filament of the type 2 lights comes on along with the single filament of the type 1 lights. On cars with a single pair of headlights, type 2 headlights are used. The beam-selector switch will then select either the upper beam filament or the lower-beam filament.

The backup lights come on when the driver shifts into reverse. This closes a switch linked to the selector lever which connects the backup lights to the battery.

■ 3-7-5 Headlight Cover

Some cars have vacuum-operated headlight covers that move upward to expose the headlights when they are turned on. The system lowers the covers when the headlights are turned off. At each headlight, there is a separate vacuum motor or actuator linked to a cover (Fig. 7). In operation, the light switch is pulled out all the way to turn on the headlights. This action operates a distribution valve that is mounted on the back end of the light switch. This valve then directs vacuum to the two vacuum motors. Vacuum applied to the diaphragm in the motors causes them to move and lift the headlight covers. The distribution valve also has an opening through which the atmosphere side of the motor diaphragms is vented. Thus atmospheric pressure is always applied to this side of the diaphragm.

When the headlights are turned off, the distribution valve allows atmospheric pressure to enter the vacuum side of the vacuum motors. Now, springs on the headlight covers cause them to drop down to cover the headlights.

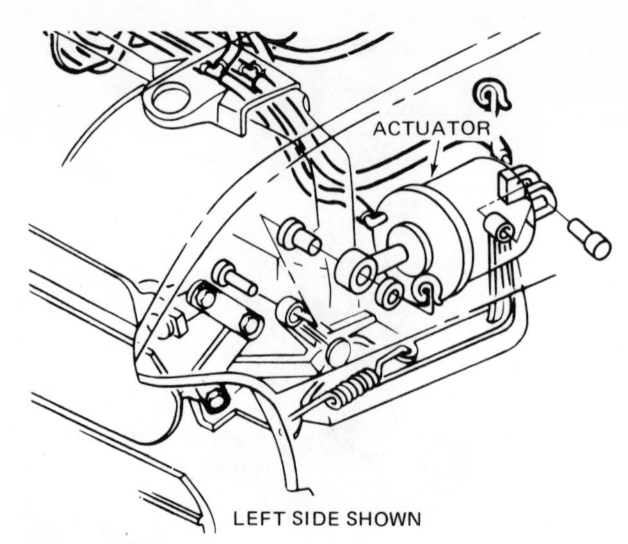

Figure 7 Headlight cover-actuator (vacuum motor) on a late-model Chevrolet. *(Chevrolet Motor Division of General Motors Corporation.)*

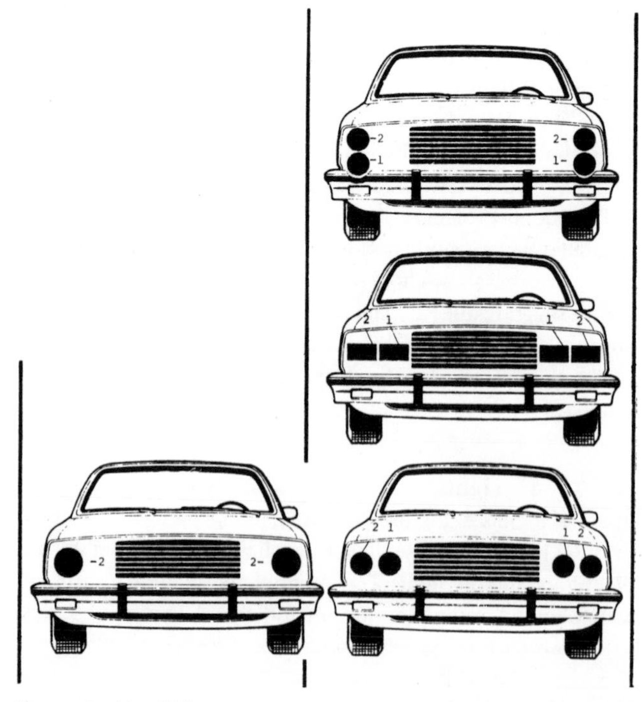

Figure 8 Headlight arrangements. *(Motor Vehicle Manufacturers Association.)*

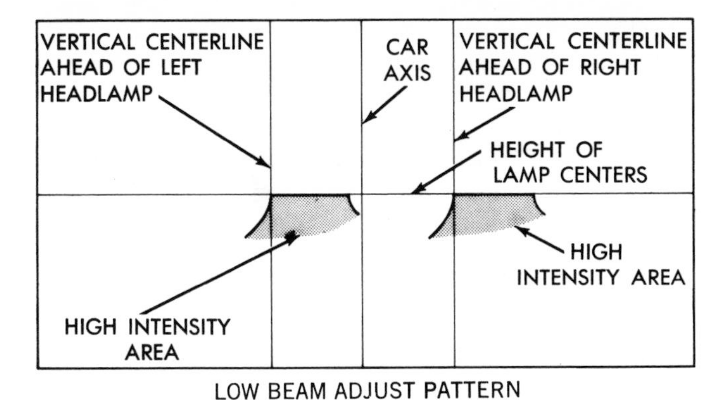

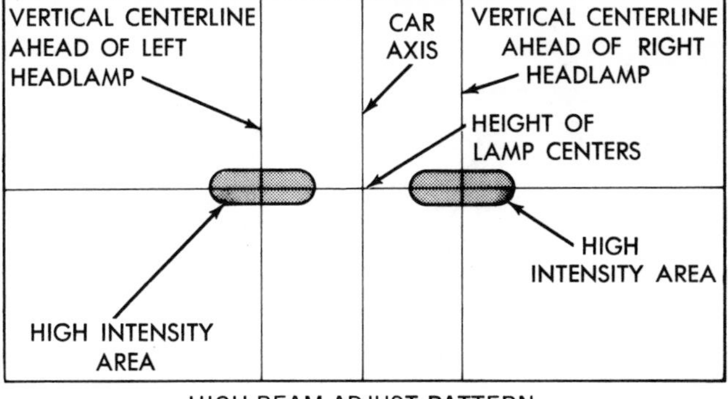

Figure 9 Headlight patterns for low beam (left) and high beam (right). *(Chrysler Corporation.)*

There is a vacuum reservoir which holds sufficient vacuum for several cover operations if the headlights are turned on and off when the engine is not running. Also, the headlight covers can be operated manually in case the vacuum system fails. This is done by turning on the headlights and then lifting the covers by hand.

In some cars, the entire headlight module rotates to swing the headlights up into position when the light switch is turned on.

■ 3-7-6 Headlight Aiming

Before we discuss headlight aiming, let us examine a typical one-filament headlight to find out how it focuses the light beam into a pattern. The headlight is made up of three basic parts: the reflector, the filament, and the lens, or front glass. The headlight is called a sealed-beam because the unit is sealed just like a standard light bulb. In the headlight, the reflector is at the back. Light striking the reflector is thrown forward into a strong light beam. The lens at the front has a series of modified prisms or ridges that bend the light rays into a pattern. When the filament is connected to the battery through the light switch, current flows through the filament. It glows while hot. The light is concentrated by the reflector into a forward beam and is focused by the lens. The low-beam filament, used in the city and in passing, throws most of the light downward and to the right so it does not blind the driver in the oncoming car.

It is important for the headlights to be aimed correctly. If they are aimed too high or to the left, they might blind an oncoming driver and cause an accident. Incorrect aiming can also reduce the driver's ability to see the road properly, and this could also lead to an accident.

Most American cars have four headlights. Figure 6 shows the two headlights on the left side of a car. The four headlights are either in a row (two on the left and two on the right) or they are stacked (an upper and lower headlight on each side). Commonly, there are two distinct types of headlight, the one-filament (type 1) and the two-filament (type 2). The two-filament type is always placed outside or above the one-filament light (Fig. 8). Headlights have aiming pads on the front lens. Headlight adjustments are made by turning spring-loaded screws. There is one spring-loaded screw at the top for up-and-down adjustment and one at the top for left-to-right adjustment (Fig. 6).

There are several methods of checking the aiming of the headlights. The simplest uses a screen set 25 feet (7.62 m) in front of the vehicle and a perfectly level floor. With the car aligned perpendicular to the screen, the low beam and high beam are checked separately (Fig. 9).

Some manufacturers, in their aiming instructions, call for a full fuel tank and an empty car. Others call for a partly full tank and two people in the front seat. Tires must be inflated to the specified pressure. Just before checking the aim, after the car has been positioned, bounce each corner of the car a couple of times to equalize the suspension system.

Several headlight aimers are available. One of the latest, especially good for adjusting the rectangular headlights, is shown in Fig. 10. Two of these devices (one right-hand and one left-hand) are required. Here is the checking and adjusting procedure.

1. Remove large amounts of mud or ice from under the fenders. Drive the vehicle onto a flat surface. It does not have to be exactly level.

2. Tire pressure should be checked and corrected and the vehicle should be loaded with an average weight. This should include the driver and a normal amount of weight in the rear. Vehicle should be rocked from side to side to equalize the springs. Make sure that springs are not broken or sagging. Make sure the automatic level control (where present) is working.

3. Clean headlamp lenses and aiming pads.

4. Attach the floor compensation and calibration adapters

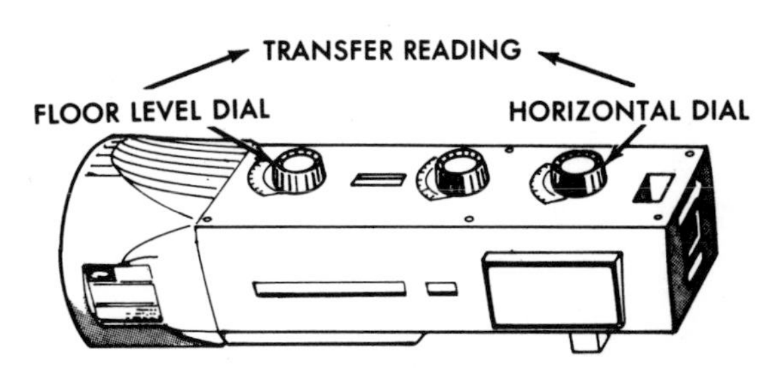

Figure 10 A mechanical headlight aimer. One is required for each headlight. *(Chrysler Corporation.)*

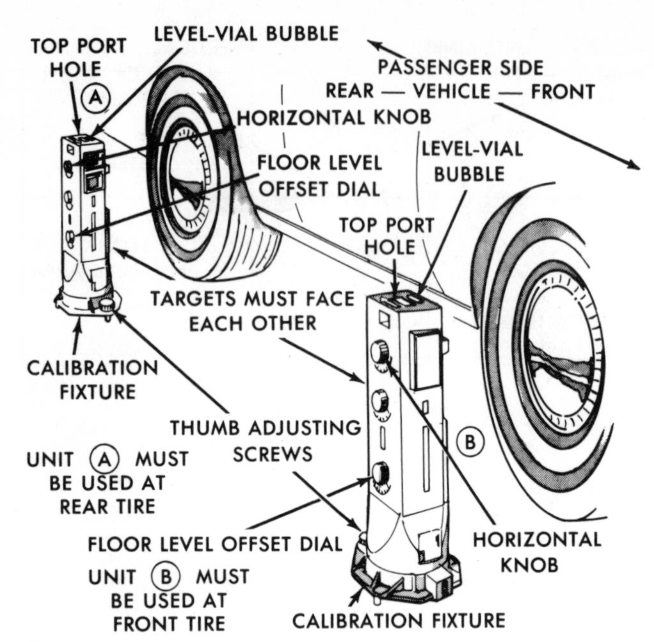

Figure 11 Calibrating the headlight aimers to compensate for floor slope. *(Chrysler Corporation.)*

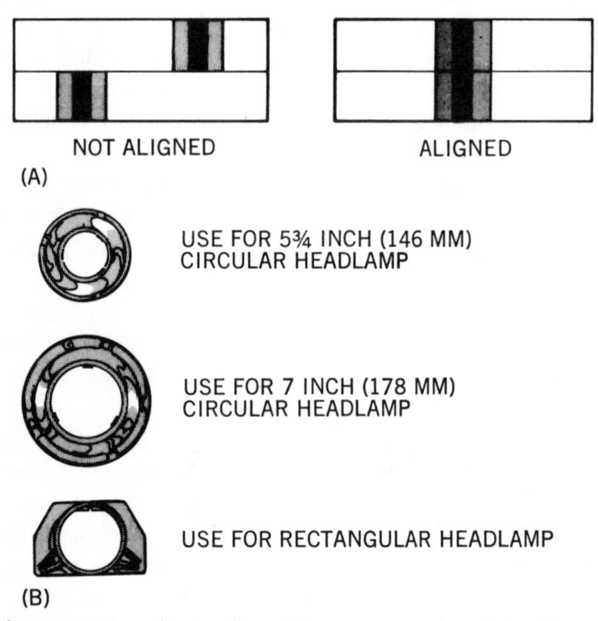

Figure 12 Top, aligning the split image. Bottom, headlight adapters. *(Chrysler Corporation.)*

to the aimers. Put the aimers at the center lines of each wheel on one side of the vehicle as shown in Fig. 11. Unit A of the pair must be at the rear wheel and unit B at the front wheel. The targets must face each other. Now level each unit. Adjust the compensation knob on each adaptor by turning it one way or the other until the level bubble is centered.

5. Now look into the top portholes of unit A (at rear wheel). Turn the horizontal knob to align the split image (Fig. 12A).

6. Transfer the plus or minus reading on the horizontal dial to zero.

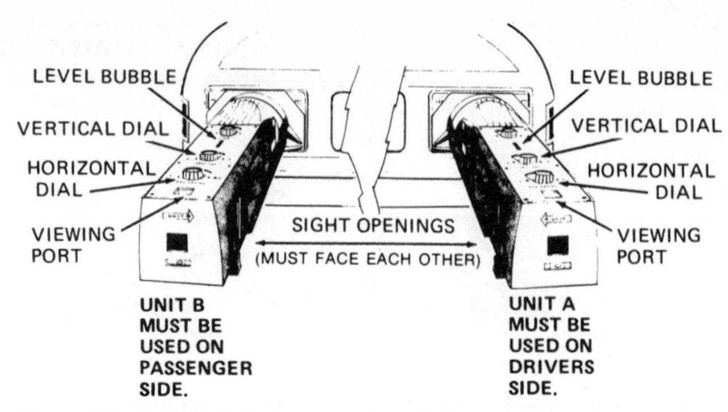

Figure 13 Position of aimers on headlights. *(Buick Motor Division of General Motors Corporation.)*

7. Repeat the procedure at the other aimer. Remove adaptors from the two aimers. If you use the same floor area for aiming all vehicles, you will not need to go through the adjustment-for-floor-slope procedure outlined above for each aiming operation. Instead, use paint or tape to mark off the centerline for the rear wheels of all vehicles. Then check the floor level for several vehicles with varying wheelbase measurements. Indicate on the floor a front-wheel centerline for each wheelbase along with the plus or minus reading for that position.

NOTE: If your floor is abnormally sloped, you may have to check each side of the vehicle for floor slope. Then you will have to split the difference when you set the floor-slope offset dials on the two aimers.

8. You are now ready to check the headlight aiming. Remove the headlight trim, where required. Vehicles made prior to 1970 usually require removal of the trim. Later vehicles usually allow the headlights to be adjusted without removal of the trim.

9. Attach the correct adaptor for the headlights being checked. See Fig 12*B*. Install the aimers on the headlamps so that the three aiming pads on the lamp are in contact with the three steel inserts inside the adaptor. Aimers are secured by pushing the piston handle forward and engaging the rubber suction cups. Then pull the piston handle back to lock the aimer in position. See Fig. 13.

10. Adjust horizontal aim by setting the horizontal dial to zero. Make sure the split-image target lines are visible in the viewing port. Rotate the aimer if necessary to locate the target. Now turn the horizontal adjusting screw on the headlight until a split image of the target line appears in the mirrors as one solid line. To remove backlash, make the final adjustment by turning the screws in a clockwise direction. Repeat these steps with the other aimer and headlamp.

11. Adjust the vertical aiming by setting the vertical dial of one aimer to zero.

NOTE: Special settings may be required for some vehicles. Check the state law in your state.

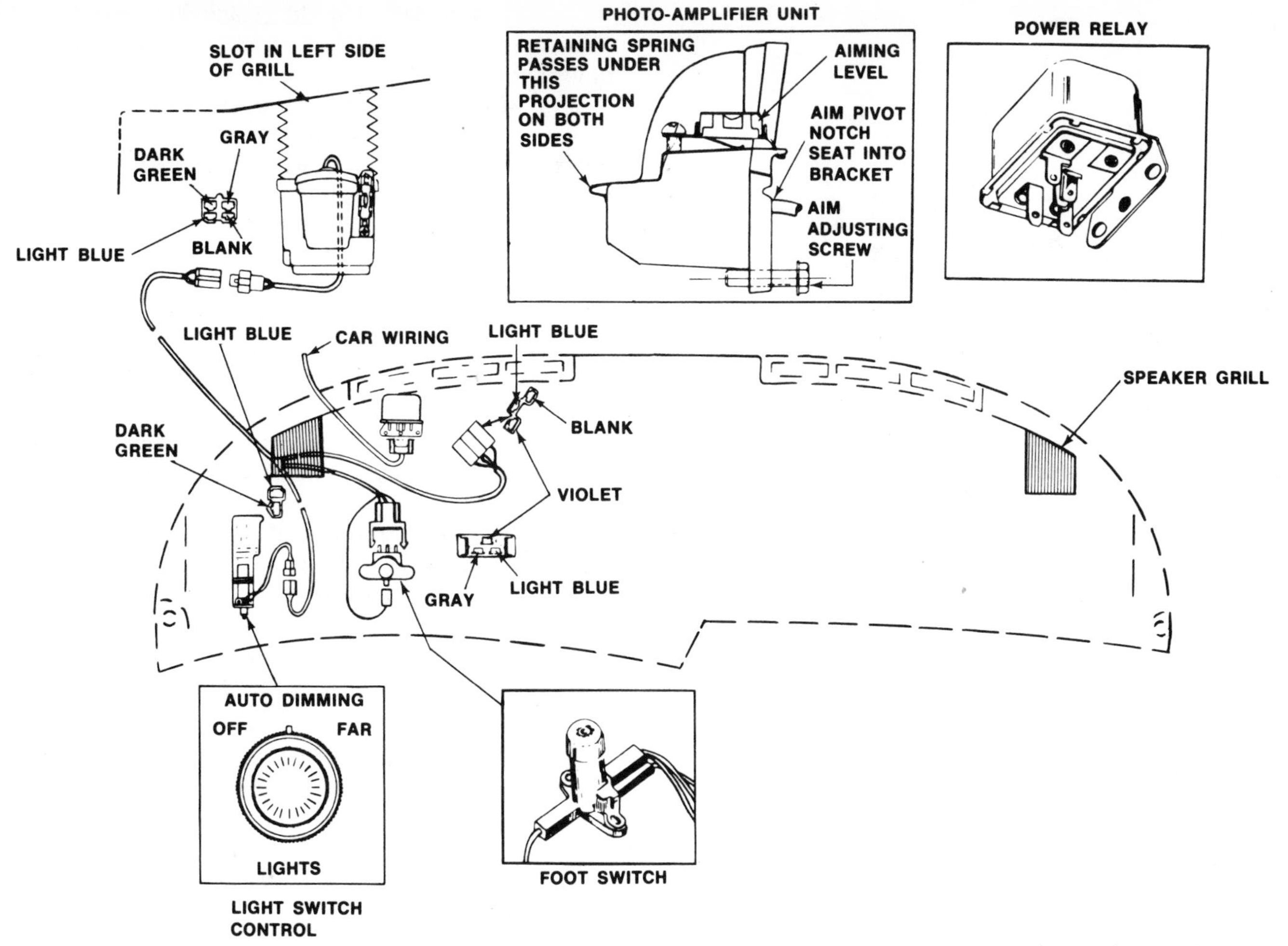

Figure 14 Locations of the components of the automatic headlight control system. *(Cadillac Motor Car Division of General Motors Corporation.)*

12. Turn the vertical adjusting screw at the top of the headlamp until the level bubble is centered between the lines.

13. Adjust the other headlight in the same way.

14. Recheck the horizontal alignments and readjust them as necessary.

15. For a four-headlight system, repeat the aiming procedure for the second set of headlights.

16. Remove the aimers by holding the aimer securely and pressing the VACUUM RELEASE button.

> **NOTE:** Aimers should be checked for calibration periodically as outlined in the manufacturer's service manual. This is important. For example, California law requires checking and recalibration of the aimers every 60 days.

■ 3-7-7 Automatic Headlight Control

The automatic headlight control is an electronic switch that selects the proper headlight beam in response to light from approaching vehicle headlights. It holds the lights on upper or high beam until a car approaches from the other direction. Then, the headlights of the approaching car trigger the photoamplifier so that it shifts the headlights from the upper to lower beam. When the other car has passed, it automatically shifts the headlights back to the upper beam. The device has several names: Autronic Eve, Guide-Matic, Automatic Headlight Dimmer, etc.

The automatic headlight control consists of four units: A photoamplifier, a power relay, a foot switch, and a sensitivity control switch. Figure 14 shows the components and their locations on a late-model car. Operation of each of the components is described below.

1. PHOTOAMPLIFIER The photoamplifier is mounted on the top left side of the instrument panel, or back of the radiator grille (Fig. 14), where it will be in line with the light from a car coming in the opposite direction. The photoamplifier combines a light-sensing photocell and a transistorized ac amplifier into one unit. The photocell releases an electric current when light strikes a light-sensitive plate in it. When light is strong enough (which means the oncoming car is nearing), this current is strong enough to set the amplifier into operation. The amplifier section of the photoamplifier contains an electronic circuit which will amplify current entering it (Fig. 14). Thus,

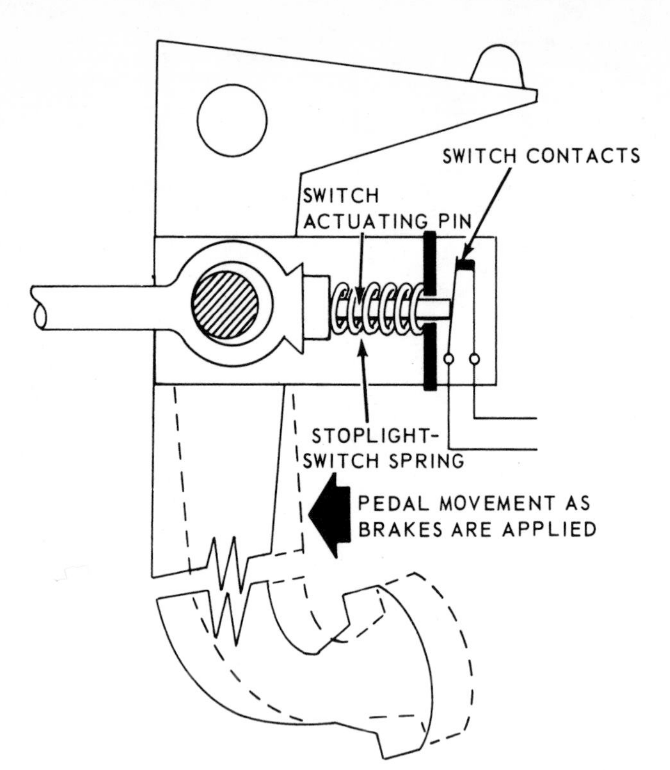

Figure 15 Mechanical spotlight switch shown closed, with brakes applied. *(Ford Motor Company.)*

the current produced by the photoamplifier is strong enough to operate the power relay. The photoamplifier is adjusted and sealed at the factory. If a malfunction occurs, the photoamplifier must be replaced.

2. POWER RELAY The power relay has two sets of contact points. When the upper contacts are closed, they connect the high-beam filaments of the headlights to the battery. When the lower contacts are closed, they connect the low-beam filaments to the battery. Thus, when the photoamplifier supplies enough current to operate the power relay, the relay armature is pulled down so the lower contacts close, the lower beam comes on, and the high beam goes off. Then, when the other car has passed and the light hitting the photocell is reduced, it produces less current. This means the photoamplifier produces less current, and consequently the relay armature is moved up by the armature spring. The upper contacts close to light the high filaments, and the high beam comes on.

3. FOOT SWITCH The foot switch is the same as the regular foot dimmer switch. It gives the driver a means of selecting automatic control, or low-beam only. A slight pressure on top of the switch provides an overriding high beam. This would be used, for example, when signaling another driver, or to determine the "automatic" position.

4. SENSITIVITY CONTROL This driver control is located directly behind the headlight switch knob, as shown to the lower left in Fig. 14. Rotating the ring pointer between OFF and FAR provides a range of sensitivity for the automatic controls. This is the only way that sensitivity can be adjusted in the field.

■ 3-7-8 Automatic On-Off Headlight Control

This is a device that electronically controls the on-off operation of the headlights and taillights. It has various names such as Twilight Sentinel and Safeguard Sentinel. The photocell is similar to the photocell used in the automatic headlight control (■3-7-7). It is mounted under the instrument-panel grille, facing upward so it is exposed to direct outside light through the windshield. The internal resistance of the photocell varies according to the amount of light striking it. As the amount of light is reduced, the internal resistance of the photocell increases until it finally causes the amplifier to turn the lights on. It turns the lights off if the amount of external light increases enough.

The amplifier contains a transistorized amplifier unit, a sensitive relay, a power relay, and a transistorized time-delay unit. The time-delay unit delays the turning on or off of the lights. For example, it delays the turning on of the lights anywhere from 10 to 60 seconds. This keeps the lights from coming on in the daytime when the car is passing under a viaduct or trees. The time delay for turning off the lights is adjustable. There is a control lever on the light switch which can be swung in one direction or the other to change the delay period from a few seconds to 3 minutes. This permits the driver to drive into the garage, leave the lights on, get out of the car, lock the garage, enter the house, and lock the house door, all in the light from the car headlights before they are turned off automatically.

■ 3-7-9 Headlights "On" Warning Buzzer

This system is usually combined with the open-door warning-buzzer system. When the headlights are on and the driver's door is opened, a warning buzzer sounds. This warns the driver to turn off the headlights before leaving the car.

■ 3-7-10 Stoplight Switch

Until the introduction of the dual-brake system, stoplight switches were hydraulic. They contained a small diaphragm that was moved by hydraulic pressure when the brakes were applied. This action closed a switch which connected the stoplights to the battery.

When the dual-brake system come on the scene, however, the hydraulic switch could no longer be used. With this system, there are two separate hydraulic systems, one for the front wheels and one for the rear wheels. If the hydraulic switch were connected into one system and it failed, then the car would have no stoplights even though the other system was still working and stopping the car.

Thus, the mechanical switch came into use. Figure 15 illustrates one design. When the pedal is pushed for braking, it carries the switch contacts with it (to left in Fig. 15). This brings the switch contacts together so the stoplights come on.

■ 3-7-11 Turn Signals

Turn signals permit the driver to signal an intention to turn right or left (Fig. 16). They are operated by a switch on the steering column. When the switch

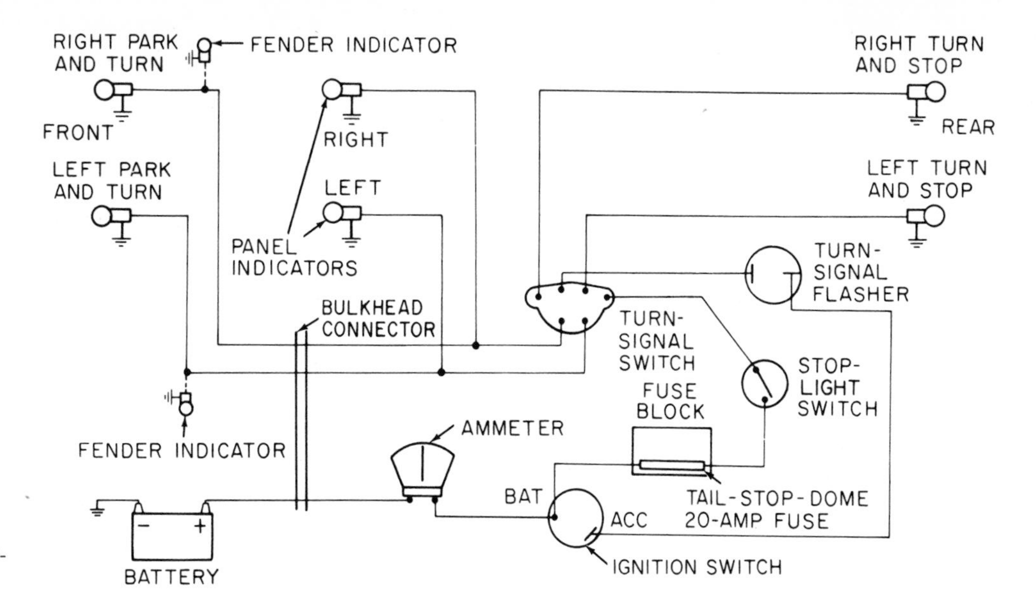

Figure 16 Turn-signal wiring circuit. *(Chrysler Corporation.)*

lever is moved (up for a right turn, down for a left turn), circuits are completed between the battery and the appropriate lights. There is a flasher in the circuit which intermittently closes and opens contacts so as to cause the turn-indicator lights to flash on and off. This intermittent flashing makes the lights more noticeable.

The flasher contains a thermostatic blade and a heater. The heater carries the circuit current and heats up. This heating causes the blade to bend, opening the contacts. Now, current stops flowing, and the blade cools, straightens, and closes the circuit. The cycle is repeated as long as the turn-signal switch is closed. If the stoplight switch is closed by operation of the brakes, it overrides the turn-signal system so that both rear signal lights stay on steadily to signal that the driver is braking the car.

■ 3-7-12 Emergency Flasher

The emergency-flasher, or warning-blinker, system, is designed to signal following cars that a car has stopped or stalled or has pulled to the side of the road. When the driver operates the flasher switch, it causes all four turn signal lights to flash on and off every few seconds. The system includes a flasher similar to the one used for turn signals. The system is operated by a switch usually located on the side of the steering column.

■ 3-7-13 Courtesy Lights

Courtesy lights come on when the car doors are opened so passengers or the driver can see to get in or out of the car. The courtesy lights are operated by switches in the doors. When a door is opened, the switch closes to connect the internal lights in the dome or side to the battery.

■ 3-7-14 Fiber Optic Monitor Systems

In many cars, the instrument panel requires lights at many places—to illuminate the speedometer, the indicating gauges, and the various controls. Because of the small spaces available, it becomes a problem to locate light bulbs at all these places. To eliminate this problem, some cars use fiber optic conductors. These conductors are made up of a very large number of very fine and flexible threads or fibers of glass, which are bound together into a bundle, or cord. Each fiber has the property of being able to conduct light, even around bends or corners. Here is the way it works: As light starts down the fiber, it is reflected off the outer surfaces of the fiber. If the fiber is curved, the light keeps bouncing off the outer surfaces without appreciable loss. By the time it comes out the other end of the fiber, it is almost as strong as when it entered.

To utilize this effect, fiber bundles (each with many fibers) are run from a central light source to the various outlets on the instrument panel where light is needed. Thus only one light bulb is needed to provide light at many places. Installation and servicing problems are made easier to solve by the use of the fiber bundles. Only one light bulb needs to be replaced if a burnout occurs. The fiber bundles can be bent almost any way without being damaged.

PART 4 Manual Transmissions and Power Trains

SECTION 4-1 | Clutch Trouble Diagnosis

■ **4-1-1 Clutch Trouble-Diagnosis Chart** Several types of clutch troubles may be experienced. Usually, the trouble itself is fairly obvious and falls into one of the following categories: slipping, chattering, or grabbing when engaging, spinning or dragging when disengaged, clutch noises, clutch-pedal pulsations, and rapid friction-disk-facing wear. The chart that follows lists possible causes of each of these troubles and gives the numbers of the sections that explain more fully the ways to locate and eliminate the troubles.

> **NOTE:** The complaints and possible causes are not listed in the chart in the order of frequency of occurrence. That is, item 1 (or item *a*) does not necessarily occur more often than item 2 (or item *b*).

CLUTCH TROUBLE-DIAGNOSIS CHART

(See ■4-1-2 to 4-1-9 for detailed explanations of the trouble causes and corrections listed below.)

COMPLAINT	POSSIBLE CAUSE	CHECK OR CORRECTION
1. Clutch slips while engaged (■4-1-2)	a. Incorrect pedal-linkage adjustment	Readjust
	b. Broken or weak pressure springs	Replace
	c. Binding in clutch-release linkage	Free, adjust
	d. Broken engine mount	Replace
	e. Worn friction-disk facings	Replace facings or disk
	f. Grease or oil on disk facings	Replace facings or disk
	g. Incorrectly adjusted release levers	Readjust
2. Clutch chatters or grabs when engaged (■4-1-3)	a. Binding in clutch-release linkage	Free; adjust
	b. Broken engine mount	Replace

(Continued)

CLUTCH TROUBLE-DIAGNOSIS CHART *(Continued)*

(See ■4-1-2 to 4-1-9 for detailed explanations of the trouble causes and corrections listed below.)

COMPLAINT	POSSIBLE CAUSE	CHECK OR CORRECTION
	c. Oil or grease on disk facings or glazed or loose facings	Replace facings or disk
	d. Binding of friction-disk hub on clutch shaft	Clean and lubricate splines; replace defective parts
	e. Broken disk facings, springs, or pressure plate	Replace broken parts
3. Clutch spins or drags when disengaged (■4-1-4)	a. Incorrect pedal-linkage adjustment	Readjust
	b. Warped friction disk or pressure plate	Replace defective part
	c. Loose friction-disk facing	Replace defective part
	d. Improper release-lever adjustment	Readjust
	e. Friction-disk hub binding on clutch shaft	Clean and lubricate splines; replace defective parts
	f. Broken engine mount	Replace
4. Clutch noises with clutch engaged (■4-1-5)	a. Friction-disk hub loose on clutch shaft	Replace worn parts
	b. Friction-disk dampener springs broken or weak	Replace disk
	c. Misalignment of engine and transmission	Realign
5. Clutch noises with clutch disengaged (■4-1-5)	a. Clutch throw-out bearing worn, binding, or out of lubricant	Lubricate or replace
	b. Release levers not properly adjusted	Readjust; replace assembly
	c. Pilot bearing in crankshaft worn or out of lubricant	Lubricate or replace
	d. Retracting spring (diaphragm-spring clutch) worn	Replace
6. Clutch-pedal pulsations (■4-1-6)	a. Engine and transmission not aligned	Realign
	b. Flywheel not seated on crankshaft flange or flange or flywheel bent (also causes engine vibration)	Seat properly, straighten, replace flywheel
	c. Clutch housing distorted	Realign or replace
	d. Release levers not evenly adjusted	Readjust or replace assembly
	e. Warped pressure plate or friction disk	Replace defective part
	f. Pressure-plate assembly misaligned	Realign
7. Rapid friction-disk-facing wear (■4-1-7)	a. Driver "rides" clutch	Keep foot off clutch except when necessary
	b. Excessive and incorrect use of clutch	Reduce use
	c. Cracks in fly-wheel or pressure-plate face	Replace
	d. Weak or broken pressure springs	Replace
	e. Warped pressure plate or friction disk	Replace defective part
	f. Improper pedal-linkage adjustment	Readjust
	g. Clutch-release linkage binding	Free; adjust
8. Clutch pedal stiff (■4-1-8)	a. Clutch linkage lacks lubricant	Lubricate
	b. Clutch-pedal shaft binds in floor mat	Free
	c. Misaligned linkage parts	Realign
	d. Overcenter spring out of adjustment	Readjust
9. Hydraulic-clutch troubles (■4-1-9)	a. Hydraulic clutches can have any of the troubles listed elsewhere in this chart	Inspect the hydraulic system; check for leakage
	b. Gear clashing and difficulty in shifting into or or out of gear	Inspect the hydraulic system; check for leakage

■ 4-1-2 Clutch Slips While Engaged

Clutch slippage is extremely hard on the clutch facings and mating surfaces of the flywheel and pressure plate. The slipping clutch generates considerable heat. The clutch facings wear rapidly and may char and burn. The flywheel face and pressure plate wear. They may groove, crack, and score. The heat in the pressure plate can cause the springs to lose their tension, which makes the situation worse.

Clutch slippage is very noticeable during acceleration, especially from a standing start or in low gear. A rough test for clutch slippage can be made by starting the engine, setting the hand brake, and shifting into high gear. Then slowly release the clutch while accelerating the engine slowly. If the clutch is in good condition, it should hold so that the engine stalls immediately after clutch engagement is completed. The dynamometer can also be used to detect a slipping clutch. Connect a tachometer to read engine rpm. Run the vehicle at intermediate speed at part throttle. Note the engine rpm and speedometer reading. Then push the accelerator all the way down, using the dynamometer to load the engine while opening the throttle. Any increase in engine rpm at the same vehicle speed is clutch slippage.

Several conditions can cause clutch slippage. The pedal linkage may be incorrectly adjusted. If the incorrect adjustment reduces pedal lash too much, the throw-out bearing may be up against the release fingers even with a fully released pedal. This condition can take up part of the spring pressure, so the pressure plate is not locking the friction disk to the flywheel. The remedy for this problem is to readjust the linkage.

Binding linkage or a broken return spring may prevent full return on the linkage to the engaged position. Replace the spring if it is broken. Lubricate the linkage. Much of the clutch linkage is pivoted in nylon or neoprene bushings. These should be lubricated with silicone spray, SAE10 oil, or multipurpose grease, depending on the manufacturer's recommendation.

> **NOTE:** If the linkage is not at fault, the slippage could be caused by a broken engine mount. This could allow the engine to shift enough to prevent good clutch engagement. The remedy here is to replace the mount.

If none of the above is causing slipping, then the clutch should be removed for service. Conditions in the clutch that could cause slipping include worn friction-disk facings, broken or weak pressure-plate or diaphragm springs, grease or oil on the disk facings, or incorrectly adjusted release levers.

The recommendation of most manufacturers is to replace the disk and pressure-plate assembly if there is internal wear or damage or weak springs. Pressure-plate assemblies can be rebuilt, but this is a job for the clutch-rebuilding shop.

> **NOTE:** One clue to a slipping clutch is metal and facing material in the clutch housing. This condition can be detected by removing the inspection cover from under the clutch and flywheel.

If the clutch disk and pressure-plate assembly are replaced, the flywheel should be inspected carefully for damage—wear, cracks, grooves, and checks. Any of these conditions, if well advanced, will require replacement of the flywheel. Putting a new disk facing against a damaged flywheel will lead to rapid facing wear.

■ 4-1-3 Clutch Chatters or Grabs When Engaged

The cause of clutch chattering is most likely inside the clutch. The clutch should be removed for service or replacement. Before this is done, however, check the clutch linkage to make sure it is not binding. If it binds, it could release suddenly to throw the clutch into quick engagement, with a resulting heavy jerk.

A broken engine mount can also cause the problem. The engine is free to move excessively, and this can cause the clutch to grab or chatter when engaged. The remedy is to replace the mount.

Inside the clutch, the trouble could be due to oil or grease on the disk facings or to glazed or loose facings. If this is the case, the facings or disk should be replaced. The trouble could also be due to binding of the friction-disk hub on the clutch shaft. This condition requires cleaning and lubrication of the splines in the hub and on the shaft.

> **NOTE:** Clutch chatter after removal and installation of an engine may be caused by a misaligned clutch housing. Some clutch housings have small shims that can be lost during engine or clutch-housing removal. These shims must be replaced in the same positions to ensure housing alignment. It is also possible for dirt to get between the clutch housing and cylinder block, or either could be nicked or burred. Any of these conditions can throw off the housing alignment.

Other clutch problems—glazed or loose facings, oil or grease on the facings—require disk and pressure-plate replacement.

■ 4-1-4 Clutch Spins or Drags When Disengaged

The clutch friction disk spins briefly after disengagement when the transmission is in neutral. This normal spinning should not be confused with a dragging clutch. When the clutch drags, the friction disk is not releasing fully from the flywheel or pressure plate as the clutch pedal is depressed. Therefore, the friction disk continues to rotate with or rub against the flywheel or pressure plate. The common complaint of drivers is that they have trouble shifting into gear without clashing; the dragging disk keeps the transmission rotating.

The first thing to check with this condition is the pedal-linkage adjustment. If there is excessive pedal lash, or free travel, even full movement of the pedal will not release the clutch fully. If linkage adjustment does not correct the problem, the trouble is in the clutch.

Internal clutch troubles could be due to a warped friction

disk or pressure plate or loose friction-disk facing. One cause of loose friction-disk facings is abuse of the clutch. This abuse includes "popping" the clutch for a quick getaway (letting the clutch out suddenly with the engine turning at high rpm), slipping the clutch for drag-strip starts, and increasing engine power output ("souping up" the engine).

The release levers may be incorrectly adjusted, and so they do not fully disengage the clutch. Also, the friction-disk hub may be binding on the clutch shaft. This condition may be corrected by cleaning and lubricating the splines.

NOTE: A broken engine mount can also cause clutch spinning or dragging. The engine is free to move excessively, which can cause the clutch to spin or drag when disengaged. The remedy is to replace the mount.

■ 4-1-5 Clutch Noises

Clutch noises are usually most noticeable when the engine is idling. To determine the cause, note whether the noise is heard when the clutch is engaged, when it is disengaged, or during pedal movement to engage or disengage the clutch.

Noises heard while the pedal is in motion are probably due to dry or dirty linkage pivot points. Clean and lubricate them as noted in ■4-1-2.

Noises heard in neutral that disappear when the pedal is depressed are transmission noises. (These noises could also be due to a dry or worn pilot bushing in the crankshaft.) They are usually rough-bearing sounds. The cause is worn transmission bearings, sometimes caused by clutch-popping and shifting gears too fast. These conditions throw an extra load on the transmission bearings, and on the gears.

Noises heard while the clutch is engaged could be due to a friction-disk hub that is loose on the clutch shaft. This condition requires replacement of the disk or clutch shaft, or perhaps both if both are excessively worn. Friction-disk dampener springs that are broken or weak will cause noise. This condition requires replacement of the complete disk. Misalignment of the engine and transmission will cause a backward-and-forward movement of the friction disk on the clutch shaft. The alignment must be corrected.

Noises heard while the clutch is disengaged could be due to a clutch throw-out bearing that is worn, binding, or has lost its lubricant. Such a bearing squeals when the clutch pedal is depressed and the bearing comes into operation. The bearing should be lubricated or replaced. If the release levers are not properly adjusted, they will rub against the friction-disk hub when the clutch pedal is depressed. The release levers should be readjusted. If the pilot bearing in the crankshaft is worn or lacks lubricant, it will produce a high-pitched whine when the transmission is in gear, the clutch is disengaged, and the car is stationary. Under these conditions, the clutch shaft (which is piloted in the bearing in the crankshaft) is stationary, but the crankshaft and bearing are turning. The bearing should be lubricated or replaced.

In the diaphragm-spring clutch, worn or weak retracting springs will cause a rattling noise when the clutch is disengaged and the engine is idling. Eliminate the noise by replacing the springs without removing the clutch from the engine.

■ 4-1-6 Clutch-Pedal Pulsations

Clutch-pedal pulsations are noticeable when a slight pressure is applied to the clutch pedal with the engine running. The pulsations can be felt by the foot as a series of slight pedal movements. As pedal pressure is increased, the pulsations cease. This condition often indicates trouble that must be corrected before serious damage to the clutch results.

One possible cause is misalignment of the engine and transmission. If the two are not in line, the friction disk or other clutch parts will move back and forth with every revolution. The result will be rapid wear of clutch parts. Correction is to detach the transmission, remove the clutch, and then check the housing alignment with the engine and crankshaft. At the same time, the flywheel can be checked for wobble. A flywheel that is not seated on the crankshaft flange will also produce clutch-pedal pulsations. The flywheel should be removed and remounted to make sure that it seats evenly.

If the clutch housing is distorted or shifted so that alignment between the engine and transmission has been lost, it is sometimes possible to restore alignment. This is done by installing shims between the housing and engine block and between the housing and transmission case. Otherwise, a new clutch housing will be required.

NOTE: These causes of clutch-pedal pulsation—bent flywheel, flywheel not seated on the crankshaft flange, and housing misalignment—are conditions that usually would not arise during normal operation. Most likely they would result from faulty reassembly after a service job.

Another cause of clutch-pedal pulsations is uneven release-lever adjustment (so that release levers do not meet the throw-out bearing and pressure plate together). Release levers of the adjustable type should be readjusted. Still another cause is a warped friction disk or pressure plate. A warped friction disk must be replaced. If the pressure plate is out of line because of a distorted clutch cover, the cover sometimes can be straightened to restore alignment.

In the diaphragm-spring clutch, a broken diaphragm will cause clutch-pedal pulsations. The clue here is that the pulsations develop suddenly, just as the diaphragm breaks.

■ 4-1-7 Rapid Friction-Disk Facing Wear

Rapid wear of the friction-disk facings is caused by slippage between the facings and the flywheel or pressure plate. Thus, if the driver has the habit of "riding" the clutch (that is, keeping the foot resting on the clutch), part of the pressure-plate-spring pressure will be taken up so that slippage may take place. Likewise, frequent use of the clutch, incorrect clutching and declutching, overloading the clutch, and slow clutch release increase clutch-facing wear. Speed or "snap" gear shifting, increasing engine output ("souping up"), and drag-strip starts shorten clutch life. Also, the installation of wide oversize tires increases the clutch load. (Some manufacturers will not warranty the clutch if oversize tires are installed.)

Rapid facing wear after installation of a new friction disk can be caused by heat checks and cracks in the flywheel and pressure-plate faces. The sharp edges act like tiny knives. They shave off a little of the facing during each engagement. This is the reason why we mentioned, in ■4-1-2, that when a friction disk is replaced, the pressure-plate assembly should also be replaced. In addition, the flywheel face should be inspected, and if it is damaged, the flywheel should be replaced.

Several conditions in the clutch itself can cause rapid friction-disk-facing wear. For example, weak or broken pressure springs will cause slippage and facing wear. In this case, the springs must be replaced. If the pressure plate or friction disk is warped or out of line, it must be replaced or realigned. In addition, an improper pedal-linkage adjustment or binding of the linkage may prevent full spring pressure from being applied to the friction disk. With less than full spring pressure, slippage and wear may take place. The linkage must be readjusted and lubricated at all points of friction.

■ **4-1-8 Clutch Pedal Stiff** A clutch pedal that is stiff or hard to depress is likely to result from lack of lubricant in the clutch linkage, from binding of the clutch-pedal shaft in the floor mat, or from misaligned linkage parts that are binding. In addition, the overcenter spring (on cars so equipped) may be out of adjustment or broken. Also, if the clutch pedal has been bent so that it rubs on the floorboard, it may not operate easily. The remedy for each of these troubles is obvious. Parts must be realigned, lubricated, or readjusted as necessary.

■ **4-1-9 Hydraulic-Clutch Troubles** The hydraulic clutch can have any of the troubles described previously plus several in the hydraulic system. These special troubles include gear clashing and difficulty in shifting into or out of gear. The cause is usually loss of fluid from the hydraulic system. Such loss prevents the system from completely declutching for gear shifting. The hydraulic system should be checked and serviced in the same way as the hydraulic system in hydraulic brakes. Leaks may be in the master or servo cylinder or in the line or connections between the two. Hydraulic brakes and their possible troubles are discussed in Part 7 of this Handbook.

SECTION 4-2 Clutch Service

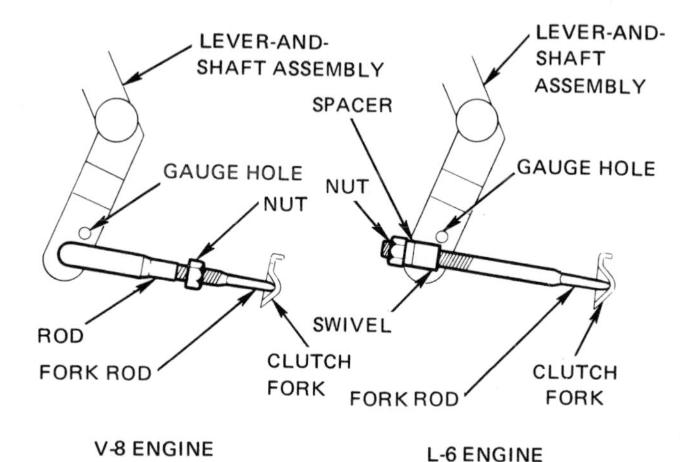

Figure 1 Clutch-pedal free-travel (clutch-linkage) adjustment on Chevrolet cars. *(Chevrolet Motor Division of General Motors Corporation.)*

■ **4-2-1 Clutch Service** The major clutch services include clutch-linkage adjustment, clutch removal and replacement, and clutch disassembly, inspection, adjustment, and reassembly. It is important to remember that if a clutch defect develops, you must do more than just replace a worn part. You must determine what caused the worn part and fix the trouble so that the new part will not wear rapidly. For example, if you install a new friction disk between a cracked or worn flywheel and pressure plate, the new friction disk will not last long. In ■4-1-7, we explained what would happen to the new friction disk.

One of the most common causes of rapid disk-lining wear and clutch failure is improper pedal lash, or free play. If pedal lash is not sufficient, the clutch will not apply completely. It will slip and wear rapidly. In addition, the throw-out bearing will be operating continuously and will soon wear out.

■ **4-2-2 Clutch-linkage Adjustment** Clutch-linkage adjustment may be required from time to time to compensate for friction-disk-facing wear. In addition, certain points in the linkage or pedal support may require lubrication. The adjustment of the linkage changes the amount of clutch-pedal "free" travel (or "pedal lash," as it is also called). The free travel of the pedal is the amount of travel that the pedal has before the throw-out bearing comes up against the release levers in the clutch. After this happens, there is a definite increase in the amount of pressure required for further pedal movement; pedal movement from this point on causes release-lever movement and contraction of the clutch-pressure-plate springs. In normal operation, free travel is lost; it is never gained. The test of pedal free travel should be made with a finger rather than a foot or hand. The finger can detect the increase of pressure more accurately than the hand or foot.

Clutch-linkage adjustments vary somewhat with different cars and models. Basically, what it amounts to is that an adjusting nut is turned on the swivel or fork rod to get the proper amount of free play. Figure 1 shows typical adjustments for some Chevrolet models. Refer to the applicable car shop manual for specifications and procedures.

Some manufacturers call for lubricating the clutch linkage at bushings or connections. These should be lubricated with silicone spray, SAE10 oil, or multipurpose grease, depending on the manufacturer's recommendations.

■ **4-2-3 Clutch Removal and Installation** Variations in construction and design make it necessary to use different procedures and tools when removing and replacing clutches on different cars. As a first step in clutch removal, the transmission must be removed. Transmission removal and replacement are covered in Part 4, Sec. 3. One general caution to observe when the transmission is being removed is to pull it straight back from the clutch housing until the clutch shaft is clear of the friction-disk hub. Then the transmission can be lowered from the car. This procedure prevents distortion of and damage to the friction disk. Recommendations usually call for using special long pilot pins installed in place of two of the transmission bolts so that the transmission will maintain alignment as it is moved back.

1. CLUTCH REMOVAL On some cars, the engine must be supported by a special support bracket during transmission and clutch removal. With the transmission off, the clutch-housing pan or flywheel lower cover must be removed and the clutch-fork or -yoke linkage disconnected. On some cars, the brake-arm linkage also must be detached. Next, the throw-out bearing (where separate and detached) is taken out.

NOTE: The cover must be reattached to the flywheel in exactly the same position as on the original assembly. If it is not, balance may be lost, and so vibration and damage will occur. To ensure correct realignment on reinstallation, both the flywheel and the cover are stamped with an X or some similar marking. These markings should align when the clutch is reinstalled on the engine. If you cannot locate the markings, you should carefully mark the clutch cover and flywheel with a hammer and punch (Fig. 2) before taking the clutch off so that you can restore the clutch to its original position.

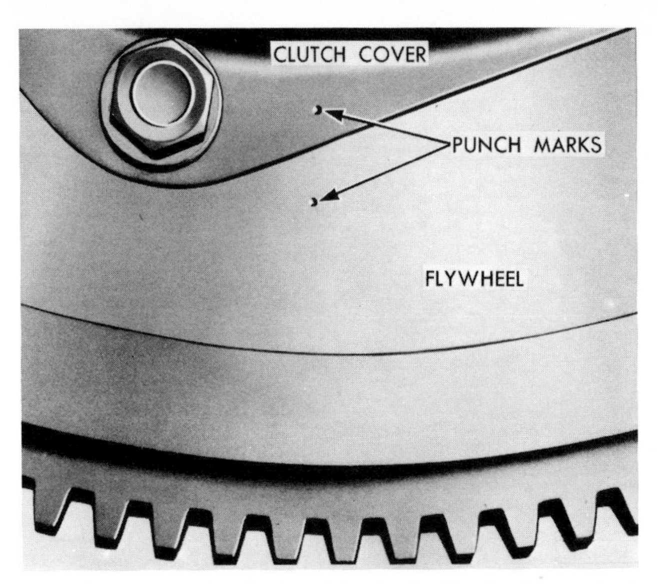

Figure 2 Marking the clutch and flywheel. *(Chrysler Corporation.)*

On some cross-shaft-type clutches, the release fork and shaft must be pulled partly out of the clutch housing in order to provide room for the clutch assembly to pass the cross shaft. This can be done after the clutch-release-fork bracket is disconnected at the clutch housing and the release-fork-flange-cap screws are taken out. On other cross-shaft clutches, it is necessary only to detach the cross shaft so that the fork can be swung up out of the way. On the diaphragm-spring clutch or the clutch using a ball stud on which the fork pivots, snap the fork off the ball stud with a screwdriver after removing the locknut from the adjustment link.

Loosen the clutch-attachment bolts one turn at a time so that the clutch cover will be evenly loosened and distortion will not occur. Loosen the bolts evenly until the spring pressure is relieved; then take the bolts out. A tool such as the one shown in Fig. 3 is very handy for turning the flywheel to get at the upper bolts. When the spring pressure is relieved and the bolts are out, the clutch can be lowered from the car.

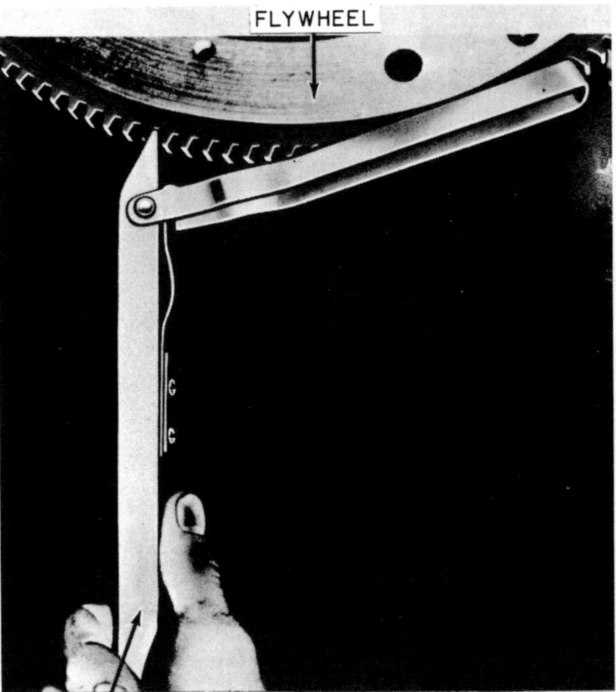

Figure 3 Using a special tool for turning a flywheel so that the upper-clutch attaching bolts can be reached.

2. CLUTCH INSTALLATION In general, installation of the clutch is the reverse of removal. Before the clutch is installed, the condition of the pilot bearing in the end of the crankshaft should be noted and replacement made if necessary (■4-2-4). In addition, the condition of the throw-out bearing and other clutch parts should be checked and defective parts should be discarded (■4-2-4). Figure 4 shows a view of a disassembled clutch and housing, together with instructions for reassembly.

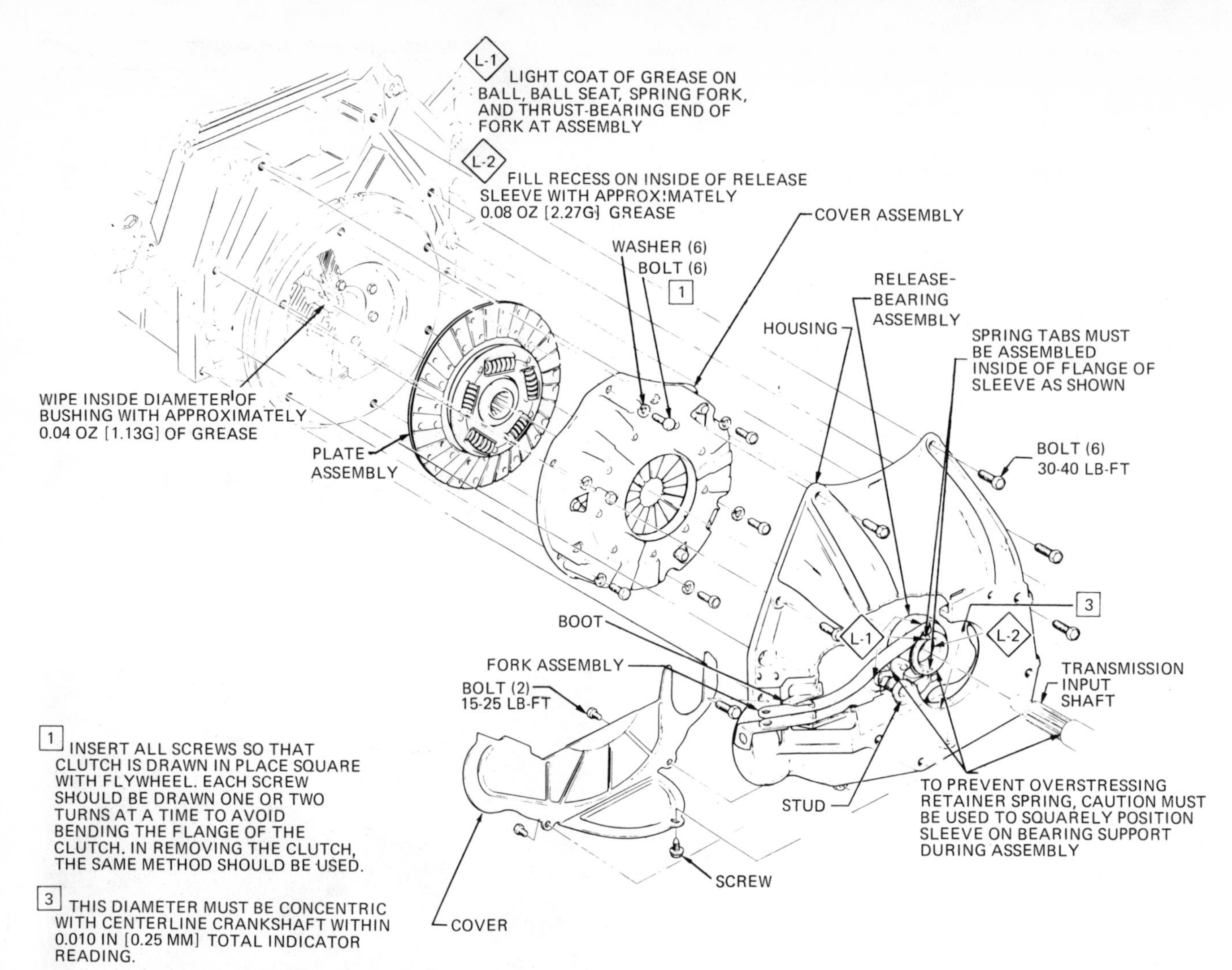

Figure 4 View of a disassembled clutch with assembling instructions. *(Buick Motor Division of General Motors Corporation.)*

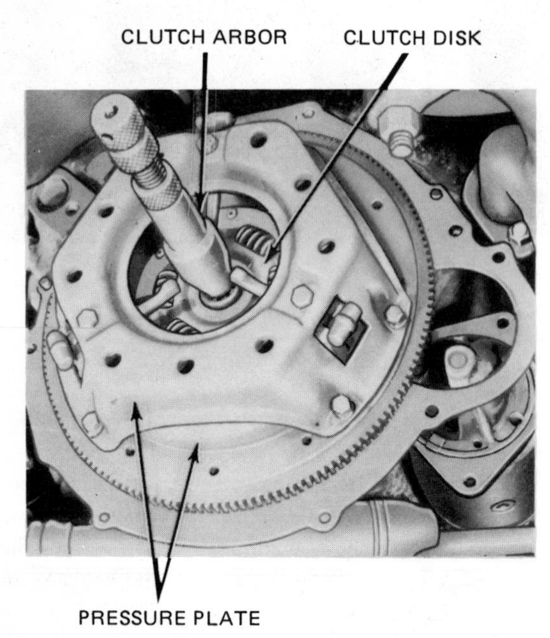

Figure 5 Using a special tool (clutch arbor) to align the clutch during installation. *(Ford Motor Company.)*

NOTE: The clutch-housing alignment must be checked whenever the clutch is removed for service. A misaligned housing can cause improper clutch release, friction-disk failure, front-transmission-bearing failure, uneven wear of the pilot bushing in the crankshaft, clutch noise, and, in extreme cases, clutch vibration and jumping out of gear on deceleration. See ■4-2-6, which describes checking and adjusting clutch-housing alignment.

Turn the flywheel until the X or other marking is at the bottom. Then use the special clutch arbor (friction-disk-aligning tool), as shown in Fig. 5, to maintain alignment of the friction disk and pilot bearing in the crankshaft. Or you can use a spare transmission drive pinion. Put the friction disk and clutch cover in place. Turn the cover until the X or other marking on it aligns with the similar marking on the flywheel. Install attachment bolts, turning them down a turn at a time to take up the spring tension gradually and evenly. Use a flywheel turning tool (Fig. 5) to make it easier to turn the flywheel and get at the upper bolts.

As a final step in the procedure, after the transmission has been reinstalled and the clutch linkages reattached, check the clutch-pedal free travel and make whatever adjustments are necessary (■4-2-2).

■ 4-2-4 Clutch Service

Automotive manufacturers supply the various parts that go into the clutch assembly as service items. Thus, if the pressure springs lose tension because of overheating, or if the release-lever bearings wear enough to cause trouble, then the pressure-plate-and-cover assembly can be torn down so that these parts may be replaced. However, since about 1965, the instructions given in the manufacturers' shop manuals are to replace the old assembly with a complete new one. The shop manuals no longer give disassembly-assembly instructions. In today's shop manuals, the maximum disassembly covered is shown in Fig. 6.

There is one adjustment that manufacturers' shop manuals describe for coil-spring-type clutches: adjustment of the release levers. This adjustment requires a clutch-gauge plate and a clutch-lever-height gauge (Fig. 7). First, place the clutch-gauge plate on a flywheel as shown in Fig. 7. Then put the cover assembly on top with the release levers over the machined lands on the gauge. Next, attach the cover assembly to the flywheel. Draw the screws down a turn at a time in rotation to avoid distorting the cover. Depress the release levers several times to seat them. Measure their height with the height gauge as shown in Fig. 7. Note that the height gauge has four settings that can be used for measuring above and below the hub. Figure 8 shows details of the adjustment.

On the indirect-spring pressure-type clutch, remove the release clip, loosen the locknut, and turn the adjustment screw until the lever is at the specified height. Tighten the locknut and recheck. If okay, install the release clip.

On the direct-spring pressure-type clutch, turn the adjusting nuts until the lever is at the correct height. Work the lever several times. Recheck. If okay, stake the nut with a dull punch.

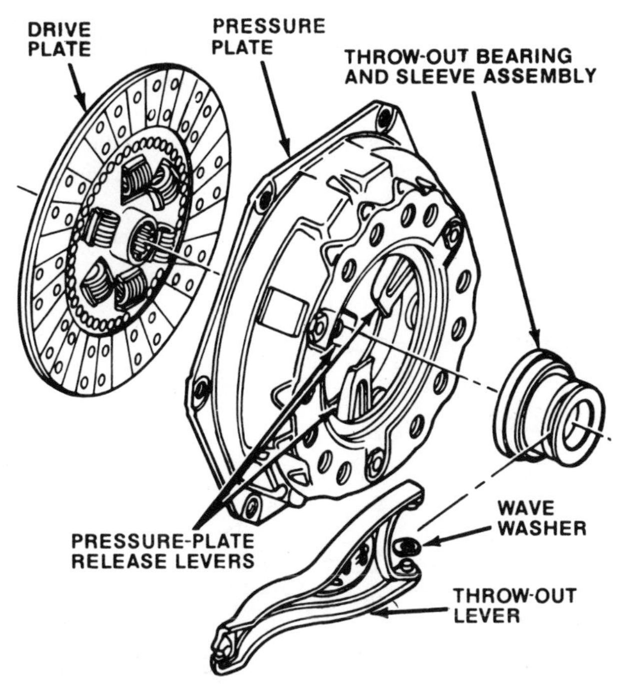

Figure 6 Clutch assembly and related parts. *(American Motors Corporation.)*

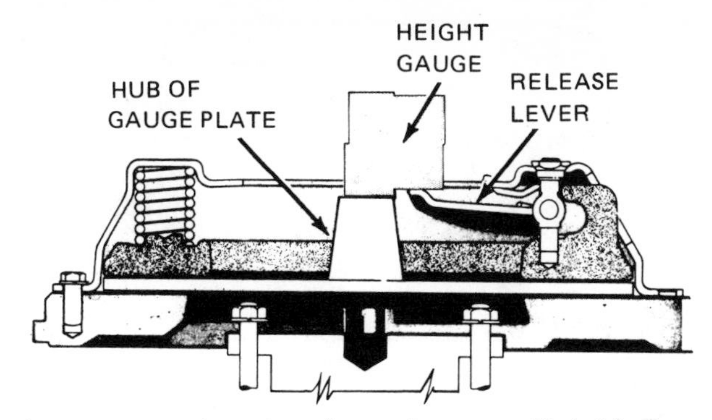

Figure 7 Measuring release-lever adjustment with height gauge. *(American Motors Corporation.)*

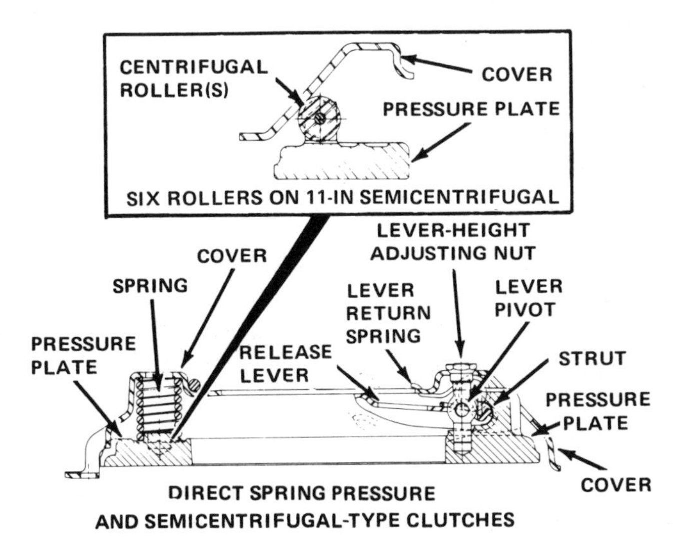

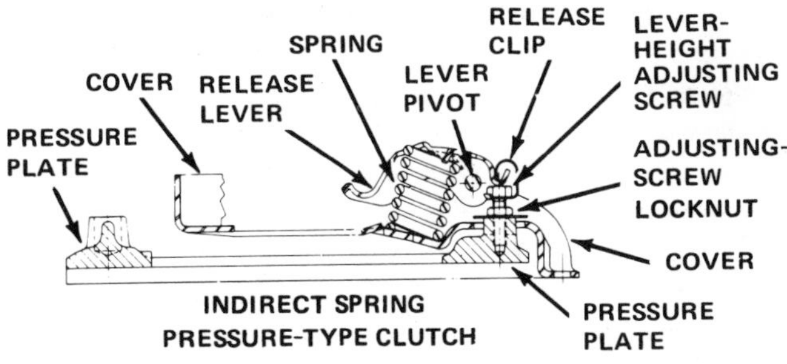

Figure 8 Sectional views of clutches, showing adjustment of release levers. *(American Motors Corporation.)*

■ 4-2-5 Inspecting and Servicing Clutch Parts

The various clutch parts can be checked as follows after the clutch is removed from the vehicle.

1. Carefully clean the dust out of the clutch housing. Check for oil leakage through the engine rear-main-bearing oil seal and transmission drive-pinion seal. If leakage is noted, replace the seal.

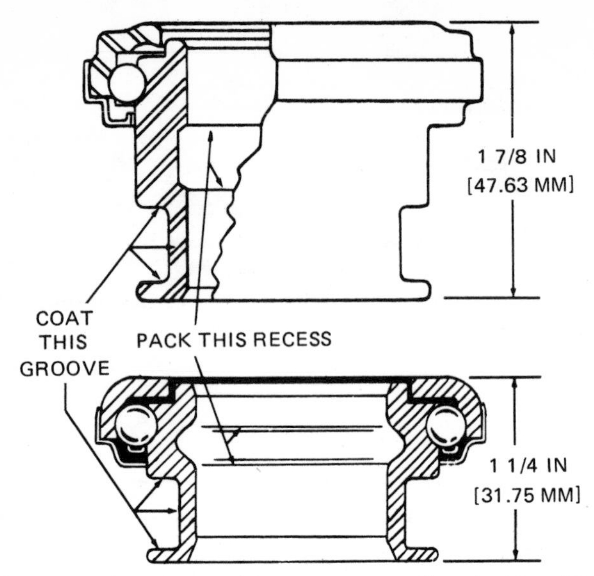

Figure 9 Release-bearing lubrication points. *(Chevrolet Motor Division of General Motors Corporation.)*

Figure 11 Measuring clutch-housing face for squareness with a dial indicator. *(Chrysler Corporation.)*

2. Check the friction face of the flywheel for uniform appearance and for cracks, grooves, and uneven wear. If there is uneven wear, check the flywheel runout with a dial indicator. A warped or otherwise damaged flywheel should be replaced. See ■4-1-7 for the effect of heat checks and cracks on friction-disk-facing wear.

3. Check the pilot bushing in the end of the crankshaft. Replace it if it is worn. To remove it, fill the crankshaft cavity and bushing bore with heavy grease. Insert a clutch-aligning tool or spare transmission drive pinion (see Fig. 5) into the pilot bushing. Tap the end of the tool or drive pinion with a lead hammer. Pressure will force the bushing out. Install a new bushing with the aligning tool.

4. Check the journal on the end of the transmission input (clutch) shaft for wear. Replace it if it is worn.

5. Handle the disk with care. Do not touch the facings. Any trace of oil or grease will cause clutch slippage and rapid facing wear. Replace the disk if the facings show evidence of oil or grease, are worn to within 0.015 inch (0.381 mm) (Plymouth) of the rivet heads, or are loose. The disk should also be replaced if there is other damage, such as worn splines, loose rivets, or evidence of heat.

6: Wipe the pressure-plate face with solvent. Check the face for flatness with a straightedge. Check the face for burns, cracks, grooves, and ridges. See ■4-1-7 for the effect of heat checks and cracks on friction-disk facing wear.

NOTE: If the friction disk is replaced, then the pressure-plate assembly should also be replaced.

7. Check the condition of the release levers. The inner ends should have a uniform wear pattern.

8. Test the cover for flatness on a surface plate.

9. If any of the pressure-plate parts are not up to specifications, replace the assembly. Also replace the friction disk.

10. Examine the throw-out bearing. The bearing should turn freely when held in the hand under a light thrust load. There should be no noise. The bearing should turn smoothly without roughness. Note the condition of the face where the release levers touch. Replace the bearing if it is not in good condition.

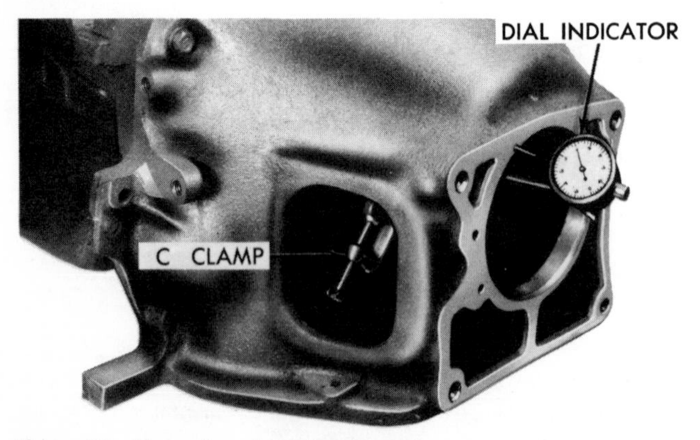

Figure 10 Measuring clutch-housing-bore runout with a dial indicator. *(Chrysler Corporation.)*

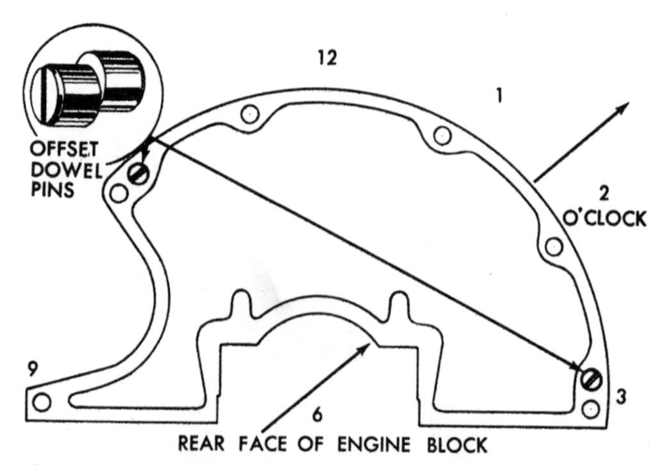

Figure 12 Offset dowel diagram. *(Chrysler Corporation.)*

Figure 9 shows lubrication points of release bearings. Light graphite grease is recommended.

NOTE: Never clean the bearing in solvent or degreasing compound. It is prelubricated and sealed, and such cleaning would remove the lubricant and ruin the bearing.

11. Check the fork for wear on throw-out-bearing attachments or other damage. On reassembly, be sure that the dust seal or cover is in good condition to prevent dirt from entering.

NOTE: Steam cleaning can cause clutch trouble. Steam may enter and condense on the facings of the friction disk, pressure plate, and flywheel. The disk facings will absorb moisture. If the car is allowed to stand for awhile with the facings wet, they may adhere to either the flywheel or the pressure plate. This means that the clutch would not disengage. To prevent this from happening, start the engine immediately after steam cleaning. Slip the clutch in order to heat and dry the facings.

12. Check the alignment of the clutch housing as explained in ■4-2-6.

■ 4-2-6 Checking the Clutch-Housing Alignment

Whenever a clutch has been serviced, the clutch housing should be checked for alignment. This procedure includes checking the housing-bore runout and housing-face squareness (Figs. 10 and 11).

To check bore runout (Fig. 10), substitute a 3-inch (76.2-mm) bolt for one of the crankshaft bolts. Mount a dial indicator on this bolt with a C-clamp. Center the dial indicator in the bore, as shown. Rotate the engine slowly clockwise to check runout. If the runout is excessive, it can be corrected by installing offset dowels (Fig. 12). Dowels come in various sizes, that is, with varying amounts of offset. To install the dowels, remove the clutch housing and the old dowels. Your dial-indicator check has told you how much the bore is out of alignment and in which direction. These facts determine which pair of dowels you should select (the pair with the correct amount of offset). The slots in the dowels should align in the direction of maximum bore runout to correct the alignment.

To check housing-face squareness, reposition the dial indicator as shown in Fig. 11. Rotate the engine clockwise slowly to note how much the housing face is out of line. To correct alignment, place shim stock of the correct thickness in the proper positions between the clutch housing and engine block.

SECTION 4-3 Standard-Transmission and Overdrive Service

This section details the trouble-diagnosis, removal, overhaul, and reassembly procedures on various standard transmissions and overdrives.

■ **4-3-1 Standard-Transmission and Overdrive Trouble Diagnosis** As a first step in any transmission or overdrive service, diagnosis of the trouble should be made in an attempt to pinpoint the trouble in the malfunctioning unit. Sometimes it is not possible to determine the exact location of a trouble, and the unit must be removed from the car so that it can be disassembled and examined. At other times diagnosis will lead to the point of trouble so that it can be eliminated without major disassembly. It is also true that diagnosis may indicate that the transmission or overdrive must be removed. Nevertheless, it is a saving in time and effort in the long run always to check the operation of the assembly on the car to find the source of trouble. It may be that what was thought to be a case of transmission trouble is actually a trouble located in some other component of the car.

■ **4-3-2 Transmission and Overdrive Trouble-Diagnosis Chart** The chart that follows lists the various troubles that might be blamed on the transmission or overdrive, together with their possible causes, checks to be made, and corrections needed. The chart is divided into two parts: Transmission Troubles and Overdrive Troubles. Most transmission troubles can be listed under a few headings, such as "hard shifting," "slips out of gear," "noises," and so on. In the chart, the section numbers are given where fuller explanations are found of how to locate and eliminate the troubles.

NOTE: The troubles and possible causes are not listed in the chart in the order of frequency of occurrence; that is, item 1 (or item *a*) does not necessarily occur more often than item 2 (or item *b*).

TRANSMISSION AND OVERDRIVE TROUBLE-DIAGNOSIS CHART

(See ■4-3-3 to 4-3-10 for detailed explanations of the trouble causes and corrections listed below.)

COMPLAINT	POSSIBLE CAUSE	CHECK OR CORRECTION
Transmission Troubles		
1. Hard shifting into gear (■4-3-3)	a. Gearshift linkage out of adjustment	Adjust
	b. Gearshift linkage needs lubrication	Lubricate
	c. Clutch not releasing	Adjust (■4-2-2)
	d. Excessive clutch-pedal free play	Adjust (■4-2-2)
	e. Shifter fork bent	Replace or straighten
	f. Sliding gears or synchronizer tight on shaft splines	Replace defective parts
	g. Gear teeth battered	Replace defective gears
	h. Synchronizing unit damaged or springs improperly installed (after a service job)	Replace unit or defective parts; install spring properly
	i. Shifter tube binding in steering column	Correct tube alignment
	j. End of transmission input shaft binding in crankshaft pilot bushing	Lubricate; replace bushings
2. Transmission sticks in gear (■4-3-4)	a. Gearshift linkage out of adjustment or disconnected	Adjust; reconnect
	b. Linkage needs lubrication	Lubricate
	c. Clutch not releasing	Adjust (■4-2-2)
	d. Detent balls (lockouts) stuck	Free
	e. Synchronizing unit stuck	Free; replace damaged parts
	f. Incorrect or insufficient lubricant in transmission	Replace with correct lubricant and correct amount
3. Transmission slips out of gear (■4-3-5)	a. Gearshift linkage out of adjustment	Adjust
	b. Insufficient lockout-spring pressure	Replace
	c. Bearings worn	Replace
	d. Excessive end play of shaft or gears	Replace worn or loose parts
	e. Synchronizer worn or defective	Repair; replace
	f. Transmission loose on clutch housing or misaligned	Tighten mounting bolts; correct alignment
	g. Clutch housing misaligned	Correct alignment
	h. Pilot bushing in crankshaft loose or broken	Replace
	i. Input-shaft retainer loose or broken	Replace
4. No power through transmission (■4-3-6)	a. Clutch slipping	Adjust (■4-2-2)
	b. Gear teeth stripped	Replace gears
	c. Shifter fork or other linkage part broken	Replace
	d. Gear or shaft broken	Replace
	e. Drive key or spline sheared off	Replace
5. Transmission noisy in neutral (■4-3-7)	a. Gears worn or tooth broken or chipped	Replace gears
	b. Bearings worn or dry	Replace; lubricate
	c. Defective input-shaft bearing	Replace
	d. Pilot bushing worn or loose in crankshaft	Replace
	e. Transmission misaligned with engine	Realign
	f. Countershaft worn or bent, or damaged thrust plate or washers	Replace worn or damaged parts
6. Transmission noisy in gear (■4-3-7)	a. Defective clutch friction disk	Replace
	b. Incorrect or insufficient lubricant	Replace with correct lubricant and correct amount
	c. Rear main bearing worn or dry	Replace or lubricate
	d. Gears loose on main shaft	Replace worn parts
	e. Worn or damaged synchronizers	Replace worn or damaged parts
	f. Speedometer gears worn	Replace
	g. Any condition noted in item 5	See item 5

(Continued)

TRANSMISSION AND OVERDRIVE TROUBLE-DIAGNOSIS CHART *(Continued)*

(See ■4-3-3 to 4-3-10 for detailed explanations of the trouble causes and corrections listed below.)

COMPLAINT	POSSIBLE CAUSE	CHECK OR CORRECTION
7. Gears clash in shifting (■4-3-8)	a. Synchronizer defective	Repair or replace
	b. Clutch not releasing, incorrect pedal lash	Adjust
	c. Hydraulic system (hydraulic clutch) defective	Check cylinder; and fluid, etc.
	d. Excessive idle speed	Readjust
	e. Pilot bushing binding	Replace
	f. Incorrect gear-shift-linkage adjustment	Adjust
	g. Incorrect lubricant	Replace with correct lubricant
8. Oil leaks (■4-3-9)	a. Foaming due to incorrect lubricant	Replace with correct lubricant
	b. Oil level too high	Use proper amount, no more
	c. Gaskets broken or missing	Replace
	d. Oil seals damaged or missing	Replace
	e. Oil slingers damaged, improperly installed, or missing	Replace correctly
	f. Drain plug loose	Tighten
	g. Transmission retainer bolts loose	Tighten
	h. Transmission or extension case cracked	Replace
	i. Speedometer-gear retainer loose	Tighten
	j. Side cover loose	Tighten
	k. Extension-housing seal worn or drive-line yoke worn	Replace

■ **4-3-3 Hard Shifting into Gear** Hard shifting into gear might be caused by improper linkage adjustment between the gearshift lever and the transmission. Improper adjustment might greatly increase the pressure necessary for gear shifting. The same trouble could result when the linkage is badly in need of lubrication and is rusted or jammed at any of the pivot points. Adjustment and lubrication of linkages are discussed in ■4-4-8 and 4-4-9.

Another cause of this trouble could be failure of the clutch to release completely. If the clutch linkage is out of adjustment or if other conditions, as outlined in ■4-2-2, prevent full clutch disengagement, then it will be difficult to shift gears into or out of mesh. Gear clashing will probably result since the engine will still be delivering at least some power through the clutch to the transmission. See ■4-2-2 for corrections of this sort of clutch trouble.

Inside the transmission, hard gear shifting could be caused by a bent shifter fork, sliding gear or synchronizer tight on the shaft splines, battered gear teeth, or a damaged synchronizi unit. A bent shifter fork, which might make it necessary to exert great pressure in order to shift gears, should be replaced. The splines in the gears or on the shaft may become gummed up or battered from excessive wear so that the gear will not move easily along the shaft splines. If this happens, the shaft and gears should be cleaned or, if worn, replaced. If the gear teeth are battered, they will not slip into mesh easily. Nothing can be done to repair gears with battered teeth; new gears will be required. The synchronizing unit could be tight on the shaft, or it could have loose parts or worn or scored cones. Any of these conditions would increase the difficulty of meshing. To clear up troubles in the transmission, the transmission must be removed and disassembled. Sections later in this part describe these operations.

Another condition that can cause hard shifting is binding of the shifter tube in the steering column. The steering column must be partly disassembled so that the binding can be relieved.

■ **4-3-4 Transmission Sticks in Gear** A number of the conditions that cause hard shifting into gear can also cause the transmission to stick in gear. For example, improper linkage adjustment between the gearshift lever and the transmission, as well as lack of lubrication in the linkage, could make it hard to shift out of mesh. Adjustment and lubrication of linkages are discussed in ■4-4-8 and 4-4-9.

Another cause could be failure of the clutch to release completely. Improper clutch-linkage adjustment, as well as other conditions outlined in ■4-2-2 that prevent full release of the clutch, could make it hard to shift out of mesh. See ■4-2-2 for correction of this type of clutch trouble.

If the detent balls (or the lockout mechanism in the transmis-

Overdrive Troubles

The overdrive may have any of the following troubles. In analyzing trouble on a car equipped with overdrive, be careful not to blame the overdrive for troubles in the transmission, or vice versa. For example, a certain overdrive trouble may prevent shifting the transmission into reverse. It would be easy to blame this on the transmission, whereas the fault would actually lie in the overdrive.

COMPLAINT	POSSIBLE CAUSE	CHECK OR CORRECTION
1. Will not go into overdrive (■4-3-10)	a. Wiring defective	Tighten connections; install new wiring
	b. Governor defective	Install new governor
	c. Kickdown switch defective	Install new switch
	d. Relay defective	Install new relay
	e. Solenoid defective	Install new solenoid
	f. Linkage to control knob on instrument panel out of adjustment	Adjust
	g. Defect in overdrive, including gear jammed or broken, over-running clutch defective, excessive shaft end play	Disassemble overdrive to eliminate defective part; tighten flange nut
2. Will not come out of overdrive (■4-3-10)	a. Wiring defective	Tighten connections; install new wiring
	b. Kickdown switch defective	Install new switch
	c. Solenoid defective	Install new solenoid
	d. Pawl jammed	Free pawl
	e. Sun gear jammed	Disassemble over-drive to eliminate jam and replace defective parts
3. Does not kick down from over-drive (■4-3-10)	a. Pawl jammed in sun-gear control plate	Replace solenoid
	b. Solenoid defective	Replace solenoid
	c. Relay defective	Replace relay
	d. Governor grounded	Replace governor
	e. Reverse-lockout switch grounded	Replace switch
	f. Kickdown switch defective	Replace switch
	g. Wiring defective	Tighten connections; replace wiring
	h. Sun gear jammed	Disassemble over-drive to eliminate jam
	i. Linkage to instrument-panel knob out of adjustment	Adjust
4. No power through overdrive (■4-3-10)	a. Planetary parts broken	Replace defective parts
	b. Overrunning clutch slipping	Replace defective parts in overdrive
5. Noises in overdrive (■4-3-10)	a. Gears worn or chipped	Replace defective gears
	b. Main-shaft bearing worn or scored	Replace
	c. Overrunning-clutch parts worn or scored	Replace
6. Oil leaks (■4-3-10)	a. Excessive lubricant	Put in only specified amount, no more
	b. Loose mounting	Tighten mounting bolts
	c. Defective or broken gaskets or oil seals	Replace

sion) stick and do not unlock readily when shifting is attempted, it will be hard to shift out of gear. They should be freed and lubricated.

If the synchronizers do not slide freely on the shaft splines, then it will be hard to come out of mesh. The shaft and synchronizers should be cleaned or, if worn, replaced. Lack of lubricant in the transmission can cause gears to stick in mesh.

■ 4-3-5 Transmission Slips out of Gear Improperly adjusted linkage between the gearshift lever and the transmission might produce pressure on the linkage in such a way that gears would work out of mesh. Linkage adjustment is outlined in ■4-4-8 and 4-4-9.

Worn gears or gear teeth may also increase the chances of gears coming out of mesh. Likewise, if the detent balls (or lockout mechanism in the transmission) lack sufficient spring pressure, there will be little to hold the gears in mesh and they may slip out. Worn bearings or synchronizers loose on the shaft tend to cause excessive end play or free motion that allows the gears to demesh.

In addition, if the transmission slips out of high gear, it could be due to misalignment between the transmission and the engine. This condition is serious and can soon damage the clutch as well as transmission parts. Misalignment can often be detected by the action of the clutch pedal; it causes clutch-pedal pulsations, as explained in ■4-1-6. The procedure of checking clutch-housing alignment is described in ■4-2-6. If the clutch housing is out of line, then the transmission will also be out of line.

■ 4-3-6 No Power through Transmission

If the transmission is in mesh and the clutch is engaged and yet no power passes through the transmission, then the clutch could be slipping. ■4-1-2 describes the various causes of clutch slippage. If the clutch is not slipping, then the trouble is in the transmission. The indication is that something serious has taken place which will require complete transmission overhaul. Conditions inside the transmission that would prevent power from passing through include gear teeth stripped from gear, a shifter fork or some other linkage part broken, a gear or shaft broken, and a drive key or spline sheared off. The transmission must be taken off and disassembled so that the damaged or broken parts can be replaced.

■ 4-3-7 Transmission Noisy

Several types of noise may be encountered in transmissions. Whining or growling, either steady or intermittent, may be due to worn, chipped, rough, or cracked gears. As the gears continue to wear, the noise may take on a grinding characteristic, particularly in the gear position that throws the greatest load on the worn gears. Bearing trouble often produces a hissing noise that will develop into a bumping or thudding sound as bearings wear badly. Metallic rattles could be due to worn or loose shifting parts in the linkage or to gears loose on shaft splines. Sometimes, if the clutch friction-disk-cushion springs or the engine torsional-vibration dampener are defective, the torsional vibration of the engine will carry back into the transmission. This noise would be apparent only at certain engine speeds.

In analyzing noise in the transmission, first note whether the noise is obtained in neutral with the car stationary or in certain gear positions. If the noise is evident with the transmission in neutral with the car stationary, disengage the clutch. If this does not stop the noise, then the chances are the trouble is not in the transmission at all (provided the clutch actually disengages and does not have troubles such as outlined in ■4-1-4). In this case, the noise is probably in the engine or clutch. But if the noise stops when the clutch is disengaged, then the trouble is probably in the transmission.

A squeal when the clutch is disengaged usually means that the clutch throw-out bearing needs lubrication or is defective. Also, a worn or dry pilot bushing in the crankshaft can become noisy. Noise can occur because the crankshaft continues to turn with the clutch disengaged but the clutch shaft itself (which pilots in the crankshaft bushing) stops turning.

Noise in neutral with the clutch engaged could come from transmission misalignment with the engine, worn or dry bearings, worn gears, a worn or bent countershaft, or excessive end play of the countershaft. Notice that these are the parts which are in motion when the clutch is engaged and the transmission is in neutral.

Noise obtained in gear could result from any of the conditions noted in the previous paragraph. Also, it could be due to a defective friction disk in the clutch or a defective engine torsional-vibration dampener. In addition, the rear main bearing of the transmission could be worn or dry, gears could be loose on the main shaft, or gear teeth could be worn. Another cause of noise could be worn speedometer gears. Careful listening to notice the particular gear position in which the most noise is obtained is often helpful in pinpointing the worn parts that are producing the noise. Worn transmission parts should be replaced after transmission removal and disassembly.

■ 4-3-8 Gears Clash in Shifting

Gear clashing that accompanies shifting may be due to failure of the synchronizing mechanism to operate properly. This condition might be caused by a broken synchronizer spring, incorrect synchronizer end play, or defective synchronizer cone surfaces. It could also be due to gears sticking on the main shaft or failure of the clutch to release fully. Gear clash can be obtained in low or reverse on many cars if a sudden shift is made while the car is in motion. In some transmissions, these two gear positions do not have synchromesh devices. In these transmissions, to prevent gear clash when shifting into either of these positions, it is necessary to pause long enough to allow the gears to come to rest. If the clutch is not releasing fully, then the gears will still be driven and may clash when the shift is made. Conditions that may prevent the clutch from releasing fully are discussed in ■4-1-4.

A worn or dry pilot bushing can keep the clutch shaft spinning even when the clutch is disengaged. This condition can cause gear clash when shifting. So can incorrect lubricant in the transmission.

Later sections describe transmission removal and disassembly to replace defective synchromesh parts.

■ 4-3-9 Oil Leaks

If the lubricant in the transmission is not the correct type or if different brands of lubricant are put into the transmission, the lubricant may foam excessively. As it foams, it will completely fill the case and begin to leak out. The same thing might happen if the oil level is too high. In addition, if gaskets are broken or missing or if oil seals or oil slingers are damaged or missing, oil will work past the shafts at the two ends of the transmission. Also, if the drain plug is loose or if the transmission bearing retainer is not tightly bolted to the case, then oil will be lost. A cracked transmission or extension case will also leak oil. The right amount of the recommended oil should be used in the transmission to prevent excessive oil leakage due to foaming. Later sections explain how to remove and disassemble the transmission so that defective gaskets, oil seals, and slingers can be replaced.

■ 4-3-10 Overdrive Troubles

Certain conditions in the overdrive will cause such troubles as failure to go into overdrive, failure to come out of overdrive, inability to shift into reverse or to pull the instrument-panel control knob out from the overdrive position, power not passing through the overdrive, noises, and oil leaks. Troubleshooting these various conditions is detailed in following paragraphs. Refer to Fig. 1 to locate the various terminals and check points mentioned.

1. WILL NO GO INTO OVERDRIVE

a. With the ignition switch on, ground the KD terminal of the solenoid relay with a jumper lead. If the solenoid clicks, the relay and solenoid circuits are in operating condition. If no click is heard in the relay, check the fuse and replace if defective.

b. If the fuse is good, use a second jumper lead to connect the SOL and BAT terminals of the relay. If a click is now heard in the solenoid, the relay is probably at fault and should be repaired or replaced.

c. If the solenoid does not click in step *b*, check the wiring to terminal 4 of the solenoid and replace if necessary. If the wiring is not defective, the trouble is probably in the solenoid. Remove the solenoid cover, examine the solenoid contacts in series with the pull-in winding, and clean if necessary. Test again for clicks, as in step *b*, after replacing the solenoid cover and lead wires. Replace the solenoid if the trouble has not been corrected.

d. If the relay and solenoid circuits are in good condition, as determined in step *a*, leave the ignition switch on and make sure the manual control knob is in the overdrive position. Ground one and then the other of the two terminals next to the stem of the kickdown switch (identified as SW and REL). If the solenoid clicks when one terminal is grounded but not the other, replace the switch. If the solenoid does not click when either of the terminals is grounded, check the wiring between the relay and the kickdown switch and replace if defective.

e. If the solenoid clicks as each terminal is grounded in step *d*, ground the governor-switch terminal. If the solenoid clicks, the governor switch may be defective. If the solenoid does not click, check the wiring between the kickdown and governor switches and replace if necessary.

2. WILL NOT COME OUT OF OVERDRIVE

a. Remove the connection to the KD terminal of the relay. If this releases the overdrive, look for a grounded control circuit between the relay and governor switch.

b. If the overdrive is not released in step *a*, disconnect the lead to the SOL terminal of the relay. If this releases the overdrive, replace the relay.

3. DOES NOT KICK DOWN FROM OVERDRIVE

a. With the engine running, connect a jumper lead between terminal 6 of the solenoid and the ground. Operate the kickdown switch by hand. This should stop the engine. If it does, the solenoid is probably defective. It should be checked for dirty ground-out contacts or other defects within the ground-out circuit of the solenoid (Fig. 1). Clean the contacts or replace the contact plate, as required.

b. If the engine does not stop in step *a*, ground one and then the other of the two terminals (identified as IGN and SOL) farthest from the stem of the kickdown switch. The engine should stop when one of the two terminals (IGN) is grounded. If the engine does not stop when either of the terminals

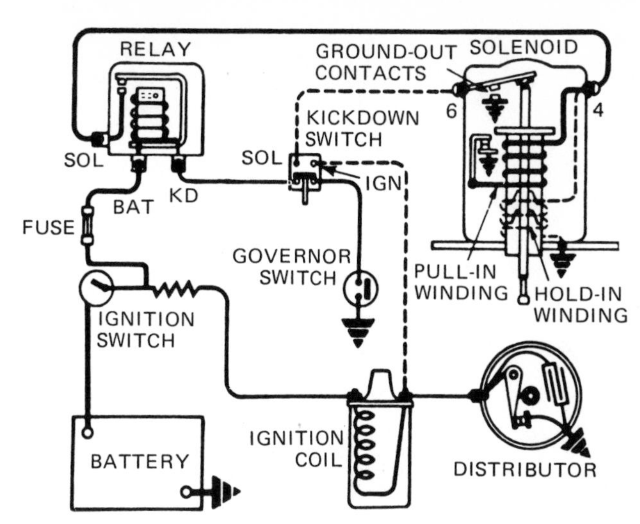

Figure 1 Electric control circuit of the overdrive. *(Chevrolet Motor Division of General Motors Corporation.)*

is grounded, the wiring or connections to the switch between the switch and coil are defective. When the other terminal (SOL) is grounded, the engine should stop when the kickdown switch is operated. If the engine does not stop when the kickdown switch is operated with the second terminal grounded, the kickdown switch is defective. If the trouble is in the kickdown switch, adjust the linkage to give more travel of the switch rod. If this does not correct the trouble, replace the kickdown switch.

If the kickdown switch operates as it should, check for an open circuit in the wiring between the kickdown switch and terminal 6 of the solenoid.

c. If the trouble is not located by the above checks, the upper contacts of the kickdown switch may not be opening. To check for this condition, ground the overdrive control circuit at the governor switch. This should cause the solenoid to click. Operate the kickdown switch by hand. This should cause a second click as the solenoid releases. If there is not a second click, adjust the linkage to give more travel of the switch rod. If this does not correct the trouble, replace the kickdown switch.

4. NO POWER THROUGH OVERDRIVE This condition could result from broken planetary parts or worn or broken overrunning-clutch components which permit the clutch to slip in the driving position. Either of these conditions requires disassembly of the overdrive so that defective parts can be replaced.

5. NOISES IN OVERDRIVE Noises in the overdrive can arise from conditions similar to those in the transmission which produce noise. Thus, worn or chipped gears, worn bearings, or worn or scored overrunning-clutch parts will cause noise. Damaged parts must be replaced after the unit is disassembled.

6. OIL LEAKS Oil will leak from the overdrive if there is excessive lubricant, if the mounting is loose, or if there are defective gaskets or oil seals. Defective gaskets or oil seals must be replaced.

SECTION 4-4 Manual Transmission Service

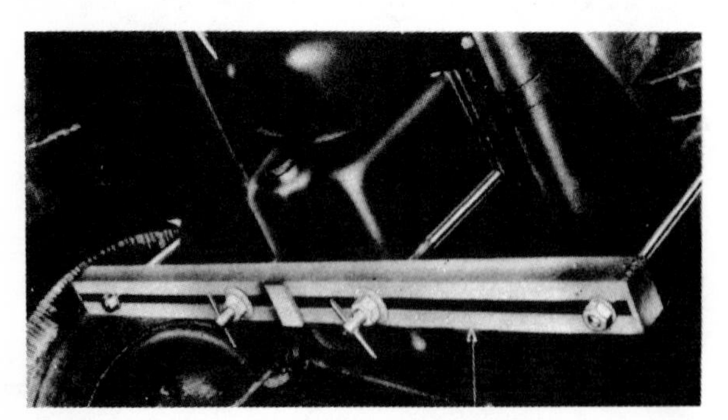

Figure 1 Installing engine support prior to removal of the transmission.

■ 4-4-1 Transmission Removal and Installation

Because of the variations in construction of transmissions on different types of automobiles, different procedures must be followed in the removal, disassembly, repair, assembly, and installation of their transmissions. These operations require about 5 to 7 hours, the difference in time being due to variations in the procedures. Basically, however, the procedures are similar, although it may be helpful to refer to the manufacturer's shop manual before attempting such work. In general, the following steps are required:

1. Drain lubricant from the transmission.

2. Disconnect the rear axle, the front end of the drive shaft, or the universal joint, according to type. Where needle bearings are used, tape the bearing retainers to the shaft to avoid losing the needles.

3. Disconnect the shifting linkages or spring, and speedometer cable. On some floor models, you must remove the shift controls before you can remove the transmissions.

4. Install an engine support where specified (see Fig. 1). On some cars, it is necessary to loosen the engine mounts and raise the rear end of the engine enough to permit removal of a supporting frame member.

5. Remove the attaching bolts or stud nuts. Where recommended, two pilot or guide pins should be used (Fig. 2). These pins are substituted for transmission bolts and prevent damage to the clutch friction disk as the transmission is moved back. Move the transmission toward the rear until the main gear shaft clears the clutch disk. Then lower the transmission to the floor.

NOTE: The transmission is heavy. Always use a transmission jack if one is available. If not, get another person to help you lower the transmission from the car. Do not support the transmission on the hub of the clutch friction disk. Doing so will damage the friction disk. That is the purpose of the guide pins—to carry the weight of the transmission until the shaft splines have slipped out of the disk hub.

6. With the transmission out, inspect the clutch, flywheel, and flywheel bolts for tightness. Check the transmission input-shaft pilot bushing in the crankshaft.

7. In general, installation is the reverse of removal. Just before installation, shift the transmission into each gear and turn the input shaft to see that the transmission works as it should. Be sure the matching faces of the transmission and flywheel housing are clean. Put a small amount of lubricant on the splines of the input shaft. Prealign the splines on the input shaft and the friction-disk hub by turning the input shaft so that the splines line up. Install guide pins, and lift the transmission. Slide the transmission forward into position. Turn the shaft, if necessary, to secure alignment of the shaft and friction-disk-hub splines. Put the bolts into place, and tighten them to the correct tension. Replace the guide pins with bolts, and tighten them.

NOTE: If the transmission does not fit snugly against the flywheel housing, or if you cannot move it easily into place, do not force it. It may be that the splines on the shaft and hub are not aligned. Or perhaps roughness, dirt, or a loose retainer ring in the transmission may be blocking the transmission. If the bolts are tightened under such conditions, the transmission case may break. And there will not be alignment. Instead, move the transmission back and try to determine the cause of the trouble.

8. As a final step in the installation procedure, fill the transmission with the proper kind and amount of lubricant. Then attach and adjust the gearshift linkage.

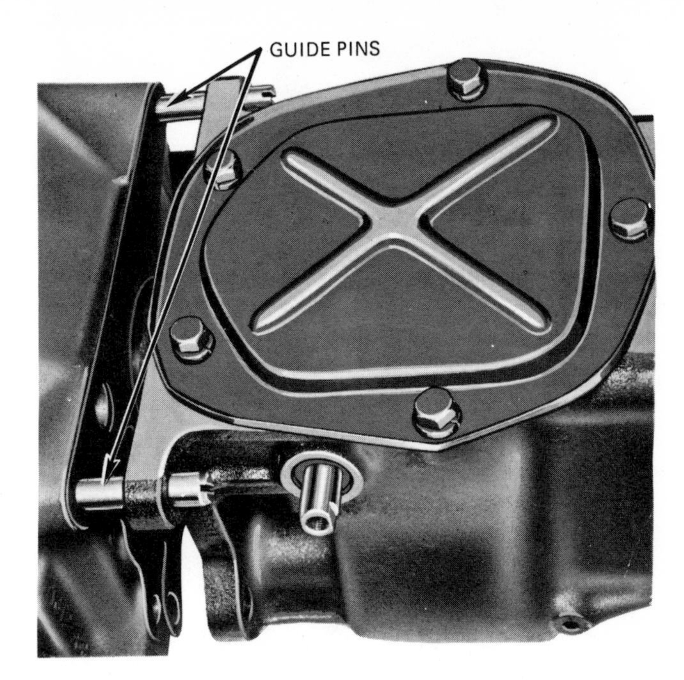

Figure 2 Using guide, or pilot, pins in transmission removal or replacement. The pins maintain transmission alignment with the clutch as the transmission is moved backward or forward so that the clutch will not be damaged. *(Buick Motor Division of General Motors Corporation.)*

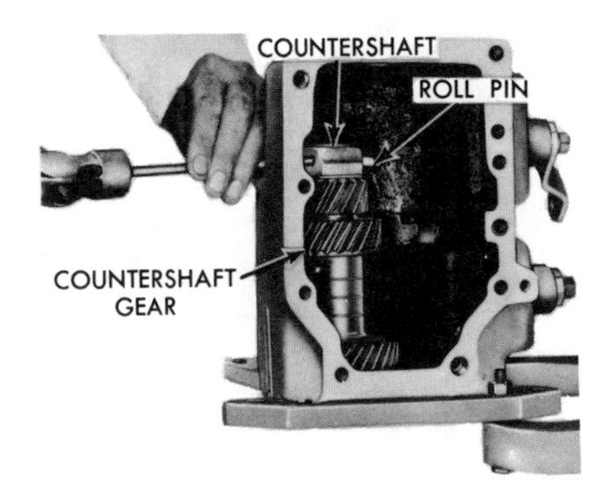

Figure 3 Driving out the countershaft roll pin. *(Ford Motor Company.)*

■ **4-4-2 Transmission Disassembly** Transmission service requires a number of special tools, and transmission disassembly should not be attempted without them. The following pages describe and illustrate these tools in use. Because transmission construction varies with different cars, it is suggested that the manufacturer's shop manual be referred to before disassembly is attempted. Typical disassembly and overhaul procedures follow.

■ **4-4-3 Disassembly of a Three-Speed Fully Synchronized Transmission** With the transmission in a holding fixture, remove the capscrews, cover gasket, extension housing, and gasket from the transmission case.

From the front of the case, remove the front-bearing retainer and gasket after removing the attaching screws. Remove the lubricant filler plug from the side of the case and, working through the plug opening, drive the roll pin out of the countershaft and case with a 1/4 inch (6.35-mm) punch (Fig. 3). Hold the countershaft gear with a hook and use a dummy shaft to push the countershaft out the rear of the case. Lower the countershaft gear with thrust washers on the dummy shaft to the bottom of the case.

Pull the input (clutch) gear forward until it contacts the case and then remove the large snap ring. On some models, the gear can now be removed from the front of the case. On others, it must be removed from the top of the case after the output-shaft assembly has been removed. Remove the snap ring, speedometer drive gear, and drive-gear lock ball from the output shaft.

Remove the output-shaft rear-bearing snap ring and then use the special tool to remove the bearing (Fig. 4). Put both shift levers in neutral (center) and remove the setscrew, detent spring, and plug (Fig. 5).

Remove the first-and-reverse shift-fork setscrew and slide the first-and-reverse shift rail out the rear of the case (Fig. 5). Slide the first-and-reverse synchronizer forward as far as possible and then rotate the shift fork up and take it out of the case.

Move the second-and-third shift fork to the second-speed position and remove the setscrew from the fork. Rotate the shift rail 90°, as shown in Fig. 6, and lift the interlock plug (Fig. 5) from the case with a magnet. Tap on the end of the second-and-third shift rail to knock out the expansion plug and remove the shift rail. Rotate the shift fork upward and lift it from the case.

Now the output-shaft assembly is free. It can be removed through the top of the case. If the clutch gear has not been removed, take it out from the top of the case.

Lift the reverse idler gear and thrust washers from the case. Lift the countershaft gear, thrust washers, and dummy shaft from the case.

Disassemble the output shaft by removing the snap rings. Follow Fig. 7.

Figures 8 and 9 will serve as guides to the disassembly and reassembly of the synchronizers. Do not mix the inserts and insert springs between the two synchronizers. If the tip of the rear insert spring (Fig. 8) of the first-and-reverse synchronizer is less than 0.120 inch (3.048 mm), replace the spring. When assembling this spring, make sure the inserts are properly located (Fig. 10).

If the input- (clutch-) shaft bearing requires replacement, it can be pressed off the shaft and a new one pressed on. The

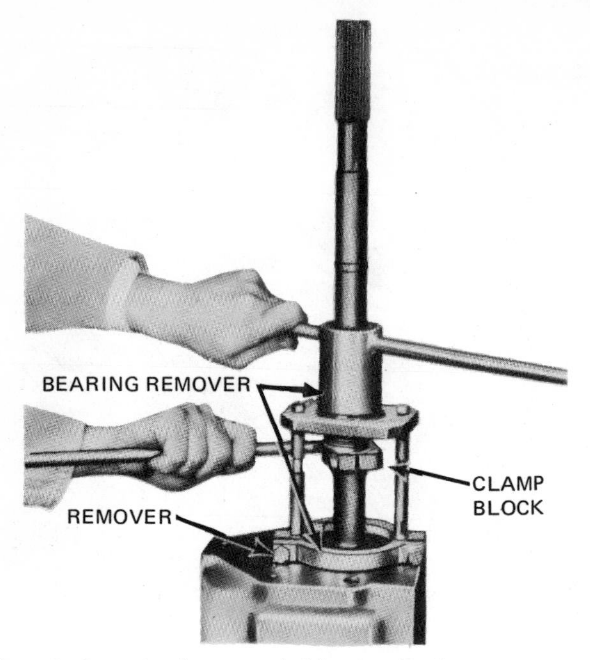

Figure 4 Removing the output-shaft bearing. *(Ford Motor Company.)*

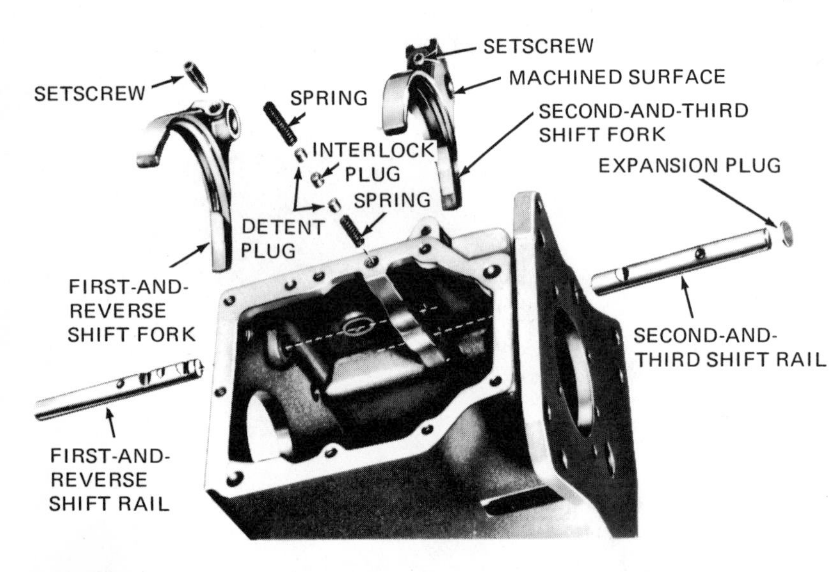

Figure 5 Shift rails, forks, and interlock arrangement. *(Ford Motor Company.)*

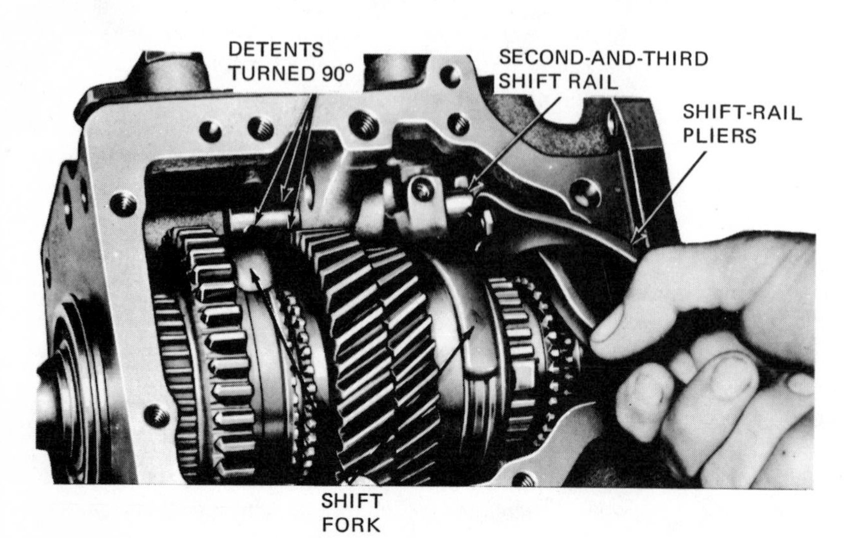

Figure 6 Rotating the second-and-third-speed shift rail. *(Ford Motor Company.)*

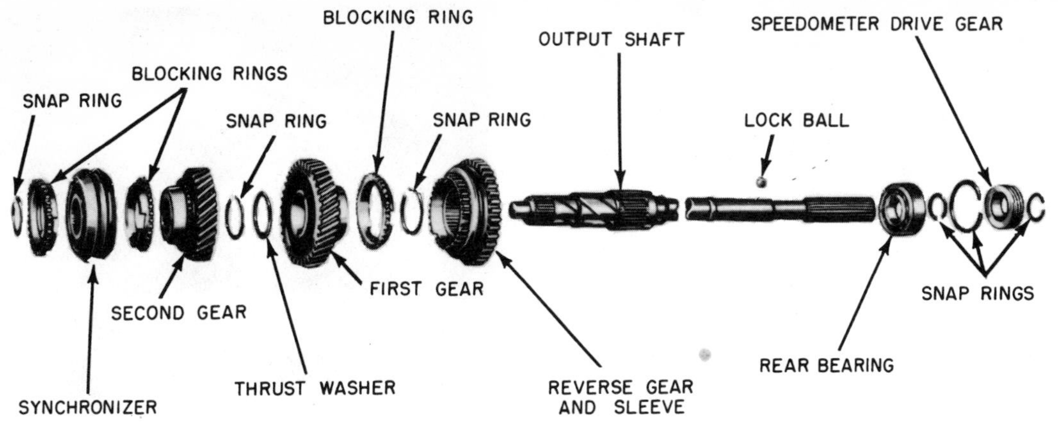

Figure 7 Relationship of parts on the output shaft. *(Ford Motor Company.)*

countershaft roller bearings can be examined by removing the dummy shaft. Then, to replace the rollers, coat the bore in each end of the countergear with grease, insert the dummy shaft, and install the rollers (25) and retainers in each end of the countergear.

■ 4-4-4 Inspection of Transmission Parts

As a first step in inspecting transmission parts, wash them, except for the ball or roller bearings and seals, in a suitable solvent. Brush or scrape all dirt from the parts. Do not damage any part with the scraper. Dry parts with compressed air.

> **NOTE:** Do not clean, wash, or soak transmission seals in cleaning solvents.

To clean the bearings, rotate them slowly in cleaning solvent to remove all lubricant. Hold the bearing assembly stationary so it will not rotate and dry it with compressed air. Immediately lubricate bearings with approved transmission lubricant and wrap them in clean, lintfree cloth or paper.

Clean the magnet at the bottom of the case with solvent.

1. PARTS INSPECTION Check the transmission case for cracks and worn or damaged bearings, bores, or threads. Check the front of the case for nicks or burrs that could cause misalignment of the case with the flywheel housing. Remove all nicks with a fine stone.

If any cover is bent, replace it. Make sure the vent hole is

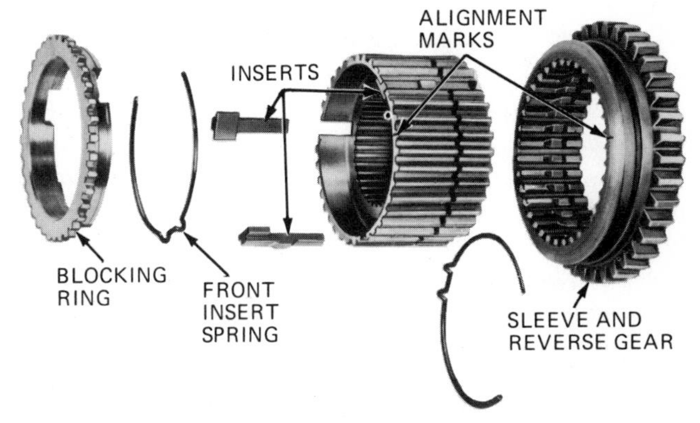

Figure 8 Disassembled first-and-reverse synchronizer. *(Ford Motor Company.)*

open. Check the condition of the shift levers, forks, shift rails, and the lever and shafts.

Check the ball bearings as explained in item 2 below. Replace roller bearings that are broken, worn, or rough.

Replace the countershaft-gear assembly if gear teeth are broken, chipped, or worn. Replace the shaft if it is bent, worn, or scored. Replace the reverse-idler gear or sliding gear if teeth are damaged. Replace the reverse-idler shaft if it is bent, worn, or scored.

Replace the input shaft and gear if the splines are damaged or if the teeth are chipped, worn, or broken. If the roller-bearing surface in the bore of the gear is worn or rough, or if the cone surface is damaged, replace the gear and the gear rollers.

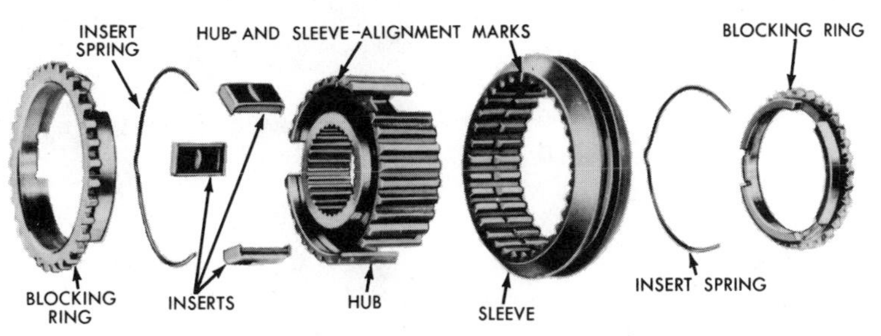

Figure 9 Disassembled second-and-third synchronizer. *(Ford Motor Company.)*

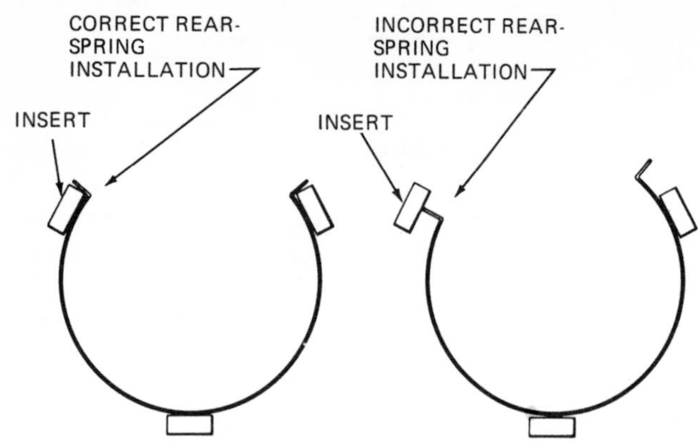

Figure 10 Correct and incorrect installation of the first-and-reverse synchronizer insert spring. *(Ford Motor Company.)*

Check the synchronizer sleeves for free movement on their hubs. Make sure that the alignment marks (if present) are properly indexed. Check the synchronizer blocking rings for widened index slots, rounded clutch teeth, and internal surfaces that are too smooth (they must have machined grooves). Put the blocker ring on the cone and measure the distance between the face of the blocker ring and the clutch teeth on the gear. The distance must be not less than 0.020 inch (0.508 mm).

Replace the speedometer-drive gear if the teeth are stripped or damaged. Be sure you install a replacement gear of the correct size. Otherwise, the speedometer and odometer will not register correctly.

Replace the output shaft if there is any evidence of wear or spline damage. Inspect the bushing and seal in the extension housing, and replace them if they are worn or damaged.

> **NOTE:** The bushing and seal must be replaced after the extension housing has been installed on the transmission.

Replace the seals in the input-shaft-bearing retainer and on the cam and shafts.

2. *BALL-BEARING INSPECTION* There are four checks:

a. *Inner-Ring Raceway* Hold the outer ring stationary and rotate the inner ring three times. Examine the raceway of the inner ring for pits or spalling (Fig. 11). Note the types of damage and those that require a bearing replacement.

b. *Outer-Ring Raceway* Hold the inner ring stationary and rotate the outer ring three times. Examine the outer ring raceway for damage (Fig. 11). Note the types of damage and those that require bearing replacement.

c. *External Surfaces* Replace the bearing if there are radial cracks on the front or rear faces of the outer or inner rings. Replace the bearing if there are cracks on the outside diameter or outer ring (check carefully around the snap-ring groove). Also replace the bearing if the ball cage is cracked or deformed.

d. *Spin Test* Lubricate the bearing raceways with a little clean oil. Turn the bearing back and forth slowly to coat the raceways and balls. Hold the bearing by the inner ring in a

Figure 11 Inspection of ball bearings. *(Ford Motor Company.)*

vertical position. Some vertical movement between the inner and outer rings is okay. Spin the outer ring several times by hand. Do not use an air hose! If you notice roughness or vibration, or if the outer ring stops abruptly, reclean the bearing, relubricate it, and spin it again. Roughness is usually caused by particles of dirt in the bearing. If the bearing is still rough after cleaning and lubricating it three times, discard it.

Now hold the bearing by the inner ring in a *horizontal* position with the snap-ring groove up. Spin the outer bearing several times by hand, as described previously. If the bearing is still rough after cleaning and relubricating it three times, discard it.

■ **4-4-5 Assembly of a Three-Speed Fully Synchronized Transmission** After all parts have been inspected, as noted (■4-4-4), the transmission is reassembled as follows.

Lay the countershaft assembly with the dummy shaft in place in the bottom of the case. Reassemble the output shaft (except for the rear bearing and the speedometer-drive gear) as shown in Fig. 7. Make sure that all parts are restored in their original relationship and as shown in Fig. 7. All machined surfaces and splines should be lubricated with transmission lubricant on assembly.

Coat the bore of the clutch-gear shaft with a thin film of grease (a thick film will plug lubricant holes) and install 15 bearing rollers. On some models the clutch-gear assembly may now be installed through the top of the case. On others, it must be installed through the front of the case after the output shaft is installed. When installed, secure the clutch-gear assembly with the snap ring in the bearing groove.

Position the output-shaft assembly in the case, and position the second-and-third shifter fork on its synchronizer. Put a detent spring and plug in the case (Fig. 5). Move the second-and-third-speed synchronizer to the second-speed position, align the fork, and install the second-and-third speed shift rail. The detent plug must be pushed down to allow the rail to move into place. Move the rail forward until the plug engages the notch in the rail. Attach the fork to the shaft with the setscrew. Move the synchronizer to the neutral position.

Install the interlock plug in the case. With the second-and-third shift rail in neutral position, the interlock plug should be slightly below the surface of the first-and-reverse shift-rail bore. Move the first-and-reverse synchronizer forward to the first-speed position. Put the first-and-reverse shift fork into position and install the shift rail. Move the rail in until the center (neutral) notch is aligned with the detent bore. Attach the fork with a setscrew. Install the other detent plug and spring and secure with a setscrew turned down flush with the case.

Put a new expansion plug in the front of the case.

Hold the clutch (input) shaft and blocking ring in position and move the output shaft forward to seat the pilot in the clutch roller bearings. Tap the clutch-gear bearing into place while holding the output shaft to prevent rollers from dropping. Install the front-bearing retainer with a new gasket, making sure the oil-return slot is at the bottom.

Install the large snap ring on the rear bearing as in Fig. 4 (except that the replacer, not the remover, is used at the bearing). Secure the bearing on the shaft with a snap ring. Hold the speedometer-drive-gear lock ball in the shaft detent and slide the gear into place. Secure with a snap ring.

Turn the transmission to a vertical position and, working through the drain hole in the bottom of the case, align the bore of the countershaft gear and the thrust washers with the bore of the case, using a screwdriver. Working from the rear of the case, push the countershaft into position, pushing the dummy shaft out ahead of it. Before the countershaft is completely in position, make sure the roll-pin holes in the case and shaft will align. Then push the countershaft into place and install the roll pin.

Coat the new extension-housing gasket with sealer, put it into place, and attach the extension. Coat the screw threads with sealer before installing screws.

Install the filler and drain plugs in the case. Put the transmission in gear and turn it to a horizontal position. Pour transmission lubricant over all moving parts while turning one of the shafts. Coat the cover gasket with sealer and install the cover and gasket, coating screws threads with sealer before installing screws.

Check the transmission in all gear positions before installing it on the car.

■ **4-4-6 Disassembly of a Four-Speed Fully Synchronized Transmission** Figure 12 is a view of a disassembled four-speed fully synchronized transmission, the disassembly procedures of which are outlined below.

First, remove the transmission side cover, as follows: Shift the transmission into second speed by moving the 1-2 shifter lever into forward position. Then remove the cover assembly and allow oil to drain.

Remove four bolts and two bolt lock strips from the front-bearing retainer (1 in Fig. 12) and gasket. Use a special tool to remove the main-drive-gear retaining nut. To do this you must lock up the transmission by shifting into two gears.

Put the transmission gears in neutral and drive the lockpin from the reverse-shifter-lever boss. Pull the shifter shaft out about 1/8 inch (3.18 mm) to disengage the shift fork from reverse gear.

Remove the six bolts attaching the case extension to the case. Tap the extension with a soft hammer away from the transmission case. When the reverse-idler shaft is out as far as it will go, move the extension to the left so that the reverse fork clears the reverse gear. Now, the extension and gasket can be removed.

Remove the reverse-idle gear, flat thrust washer, shaft, roll spring pin, speedometer gear, and reverse gear.

Slide the 3-4 synchronizer clutch sleeve to fourth-speed position (forward). Now, carefully remove the rear-bearing retainer and entire main-shaft assembly from the case by tapping the bearing retainer with a soft hammer.

Unload the 17 bearing rollers from the main drive gear and then remove the fourth-speed synchronizer blocker ring. Lift

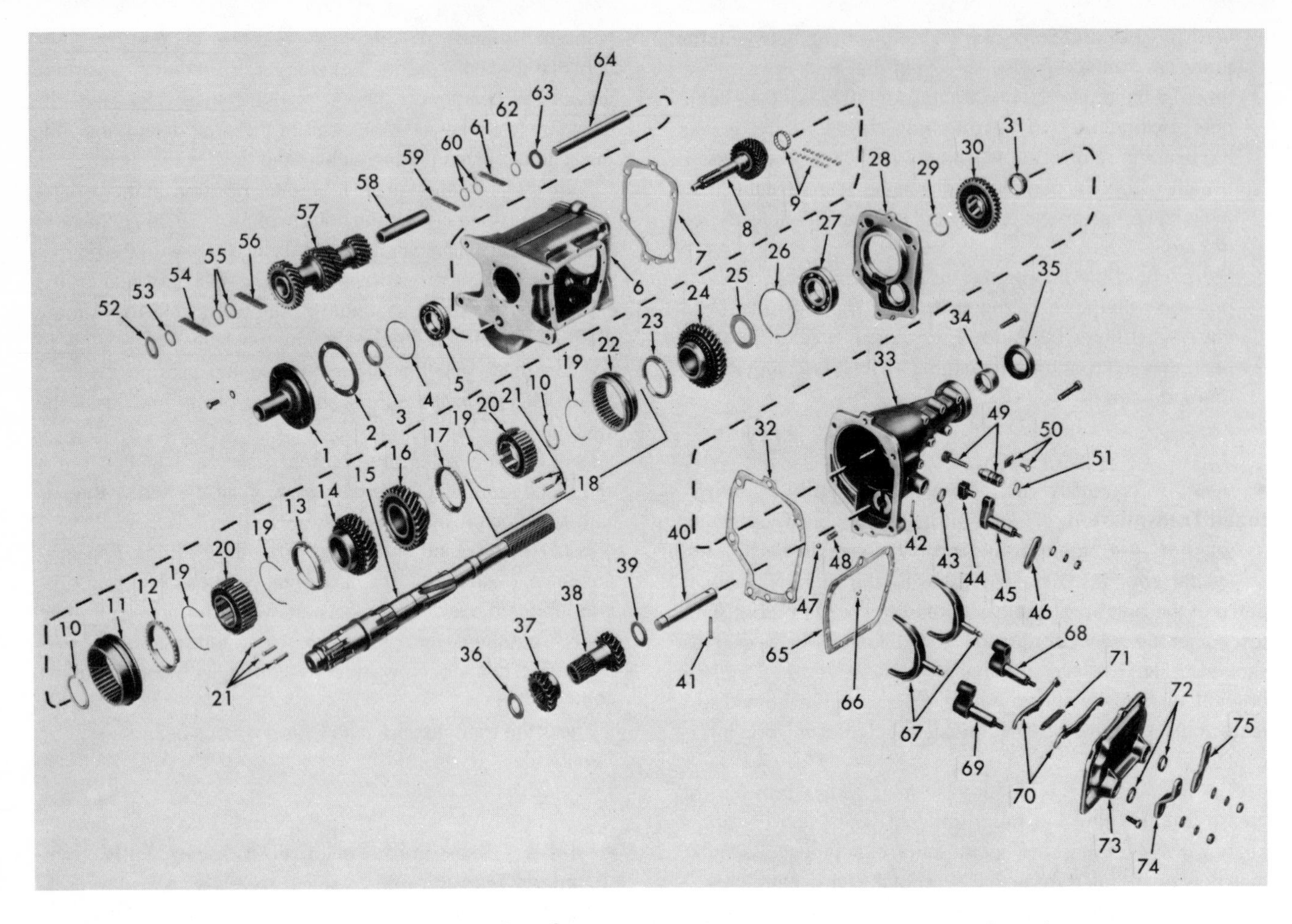

1. Bearing retainer
2. Gasket
3. Bearing retaining nut
4. Bearing snap ring
5. Main-drive-gear bearing
6. Transmission case
7. Rear-bearing-retainer gasket
8. Main drive gear
9. Bearing rollers (17), cage
10. Snap ring
11. Third-and-fourth-speed-clutch sliding sleeve
12. Fourth-speed-gear synchronizing ring
13. Third-speed synchronizing ring
14. Third-speed gear
15. Main shaft
16. Second-speed gear
17. Second-speed-gear synchronizing ring
18. First-and-second-speed-clutch assembly
19. Clutch key spring
20. Clutch hub
21. Clutch keys
22. First-and-second-speed-clutch sliding sleeve
23. First-speed-gear synchronizing ring
24. First-speed gear
25. First-speed-gear sleeve
26. Rear-bearing snap ring
27. Rear bearing
28. Rear-bearing retainer
29. Selective-fit snap ring
30. Reverse gear
31. Speedometer drive, clip
32. Rear-bearing-retainer-to-case extension gasket
33. Case extension
34. Extension bushing
35. Rear oil seal
36. Reverse idler front thrust washer (tanged)
37. Reverse idler gear (front)
38. Reverse idler gear (rear)
39. Flat thrust washer
40. Reverse idler shaft
41. Reverse-idler-shaft roll pin
42. Reverse-shifter-shaft lockpin
43. Reverse-shifter-shaft lip seal
44. Reverse shift fork
45. Reverse shifter shaft and detent plate
46. Reverse shifter lever
47. Reverse-shifter-shaft detent ball
48. Reverse-shifter-shaft ball detent spring
49. Speedometer driven gear and fitting
50. Retainer and bolt
51. O-ring seal
52. Tanged washer
53. Spacer
54. Bearing rollers (28)
55. Spacer
56. Bearing rollers (28)
57. Countergear
58. Countergear roller spacer (seam type)
59. Bearing rollers (28)
60. Spacer
61. Bearing rollers (28)
62. Spacer
63. Tanged washer
64. Countershaft
65. Gasket
66. Detent-cam retainer ring
67. Forward-speed shift forks
68. First-and-second-speed-gear shifter shaft and detent plate
69. Third-and-fourth-speed-gear shifter shaft and detent plate
70. Detent cams
71. Detent-cam spring
72. Lip seals
73. Transmission side cover
74. Third-and-fourth-speed shifter lever
75. First-and-second-speed shifter lever

Figure 12 Disassembled four-speed transmission. *(Chevrolet Motor Division of General Motors Corporation.)*

the front half of the reverse-idler gear, and remove the tanged thrust washer from the case.

Use an arbor press to press the main drive gear down from the front bearing. From inside the case, tap out the front bearing and snap ring. Also from the front of the case, press out the countershaft with a special tool. Then remove the countergear and both tanged washers.

Remove 112 rollers, six 0.070-inch (1.778-mm) spacers, and the roller spacer from the countergear. Remove the main-shaft front snap ring and slide the third-and-fourth-speed clutch assembly, third-speed gear, and synchronizing ring from the front of the main shaft.

Spread the rear-bearing-retainer snap ring and press the main shaft out of the retainer. Remove the main-shaft rear snap ring. Support the second-speed gear and press on the rear of the main shaft to remove the rear bearing, first-speed gear and sleeve, first-speed synchronizing ring, 1-2 speed synchronizing ring, and second-speed gear.

Inspect the transmission parts, as explained in ■4-4-13.

■ 4-4-7 Reassembly of a Four-Speed Fully Synchronized Transmission

1. ASSEMBLE THE MAIN SHAFT Install the second-speed gear with the hub toward the rear of the shaft. Install the 1-2 synchronizer clutch assembly (taper to rear, hub to front), with a synchronizer ring on either side of the clutch assembly so that their keyways line up with the clutch keys. Use a pipe of the correct diameter to press the first-gear sleeve onto the main shaft.

Install the first-speed gear (hub to front) and use a pipe of the correct diameter to press the rear bearing on. Install the snap ring of the correct thickness to get maximum distance of 0 to 0.005 inch (0.127 mm) between the ring and rear face of the bearing.

Install the third-speed gear (hub to front) and synchronizer ring (notches to front). Install the third-and-fourth-speed-gear clutch assembly (hub and sliding sleeve) with both sleeve taper and hub toward the front. Make sure the keys in the hub correspond with the notches in the synchronizer ring.

Install the snap ring in the groove in the main shaft in front of the third-and-fourth-speed clutch assembly, with ends of the snap ring seated behind the spline teeth. Install the rear-bearing retainer. Spread the snap ring in the plate to allow the snap ring to drop around the rear bearing. Press on the end of the main shaft until the snap ring engages the groove in the rear bearing.

Install the reverse gear, shift collar to rear, and the two anti-rattle springs. Install the retaining clip and speedometer gear.

2. ASSEMBLE THE COUNTERGEAR Install the roller spacer in the countergear, then install the rollers, as follows: Use heavy grease to retain the rollers and install a spacer, 28 rollers, a spacer, 28 more rollers, and then another spacer. Then at the other end, install a spacer, 28 rollers, a spacer, 28 more rollers, and another spacer. Insert a special tool into the countergear.

Figure 13 Checking countergear end play. *(Chevrolet Motor Division of General Motors Corporation.)*

3. ASSEMBLE THE TRANSMISSION Lay the transmission case on its side, with the side cover opening toward you. Put the countergear tanged washers in place, retaining them with grease. Make sure the tangs are in the case notches.

Put the countergear in the bottom of the case. Turn the case on end, front end down. Lubricate the countershaft and start it into the case. The flat on the end of the shaft should face the bottom of the case. Align the countergear and press the countershaft into the case until the flat on the shaft is flush with the rear of the case. Make sure the thrust washers remain in place.

Check the end play of the countergear by attaching a dial indicator to the case (Fig. 13). If the end play is greater than 0.025 inch (0.63 mm), install new thrust washers.

Into the main drive gear, install the pinion carrier and 17 roller bearings, using grease to hold them in place. Install the main drive gear and pilot the bearings through the side cover opening and into position in front of the case.

Put the gasket in position on the front face of the rear-bearing retainer. Install the fourth-speed synchronizing ring on the main drive gear with the notches toward the rear of the case.

Slide the 3-4 synchronizing clutch sleeve forward into the fourth-speed detent position. Lower the main-shaft assembly into the case. Make sure the notches on the fourth-speed synchronizing ring correspond to the keys in the clutch assembly (Fig. 14). Also, make sure the main drive gear engages both the countergear and the antilash plate (on standard-ratio models).

With the guide pin in the rear-bearing retainer aligned with the hole in the rear of the case, tap the rear-bearing retainer into position with a soft hammer.

From the rear of the case, insert the rear reverse-idler gear, engaging the splines with the front gear inside the case. Stick a gasket on the rear face of the rear-bearing retainer with grease.

Install the remaining flat thrust washer on the reverse-idler shaft, and install the shaft, roll pin, and thrust washer into the gears and front boss of the case. Make sure the front tanged washer stays in place. The roll pin should be in a vertical position.

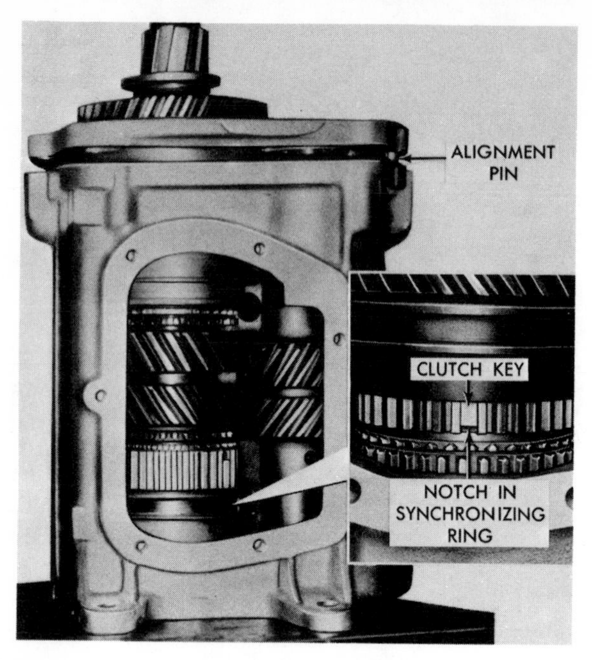

Figure 14 Installing the main-shaft assembly. *(Chevrolet Motor Division of General Motors Corporation.)*

Pull the reverse-shifter shaft to the left side of the extension and rotate the shaft to bring the reverse-shift fork forward (to reverse detent position). Start the extension onto the transmission shaft while pushing in on the shifter shaft to engage the shift fork with the reverse gearshift collar. Then pilot the reverse idler shaft into the extension housing to permit the extension to slide onto the case. Install the six extension-and-retainer-to-case bolts and torque to specifications.

Push or pull the reverse-shifter shaft to line up the groove in the shaft and holes in the boss, and drive in the lockpin. Install the shifter lever.

Press the bearing onto the main drive gear (snap-ring groove to front) and into the case until several main-drive-gear threads are exposed. Lock the transmission by shifting into two gears. Install the main-drive-gear retaining nut and torque to specifications. Stake the nut into place at the gear-shaft hole. Do not damage threads on the shaft.

Install the main-drive-gear bearing retainer, gasket, four retaining bolts, and two strip-bolt-lock retainers. Use a sealer on the bolts and torque to specifications.

Shift the main-shaft 3-4 sliding clutch sleeve into neutral and the 1-2 sliding clutch sleeve into second. Install the side-cover

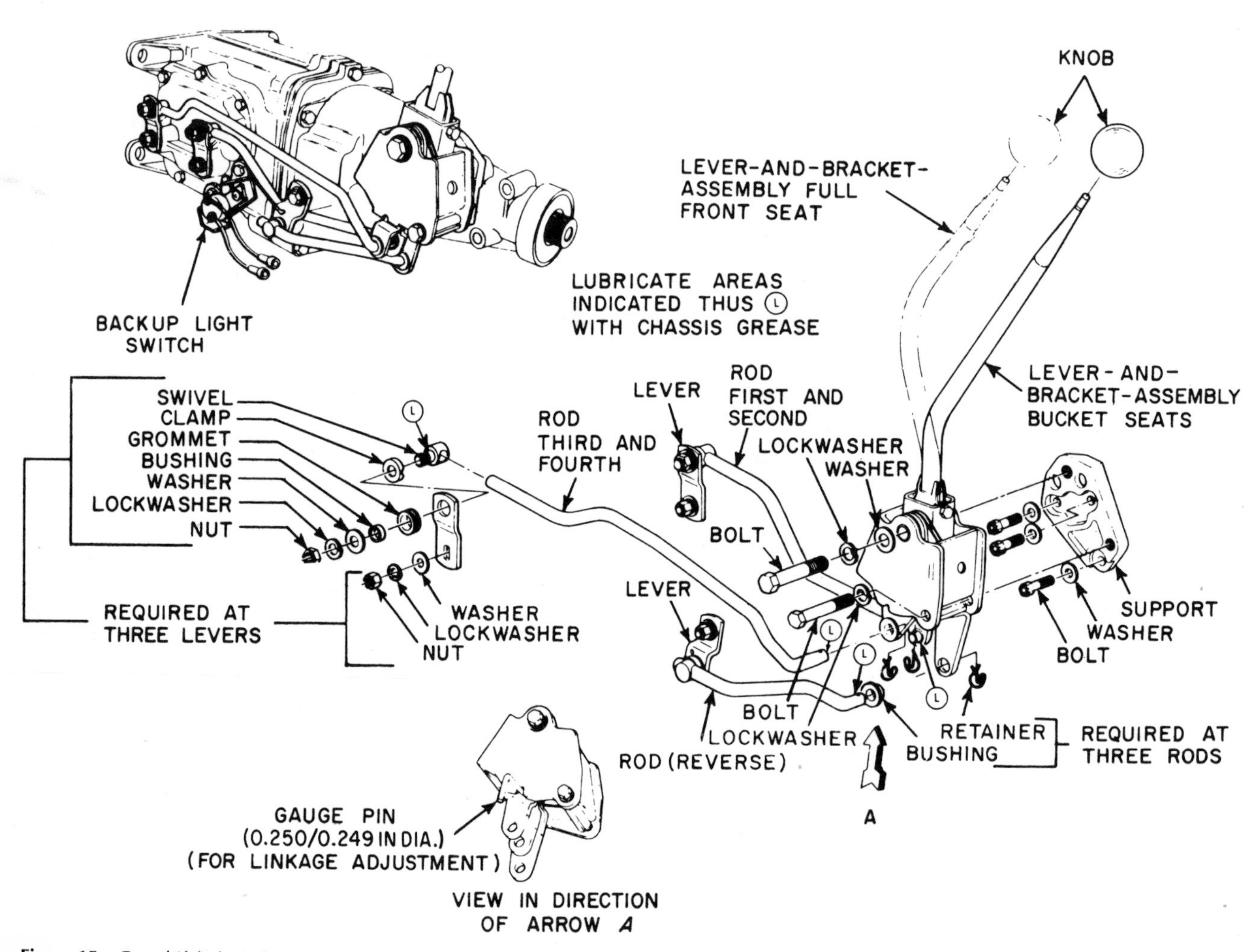

Figure 15 Gearshift linkage for a four-speed transmission. *(Pontiac Motor Division of General Motors Corporation.)*

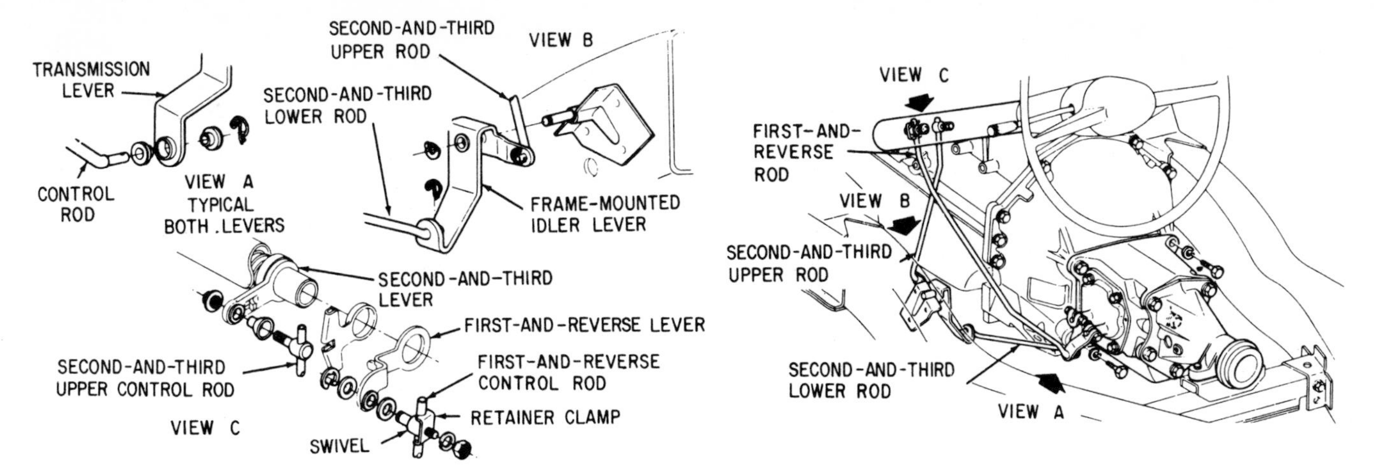

Figure 16 Steering-column shift-lever linkage for a three-speed transmission. *(Chevrolet Motor Division of General Motors Corporation.)*

gasket and put the side cover in place. Be sure the dowel pin aligns. Install attaching bolts and torque to specifications.

■ 4-4-8 Floor-Shift-Lever Adjustments

Whenever linkage of a floor-shift lever for a four-speed transmission is disconnected, the linkage joints should be lubricated with a little chassis grease. Linkage adjustment for the model shown in Fig. 15 follows.

Position the selector lever in neutral and loosen the three swivel-nut assemblies. Insert a 1/4-inch-(6.35-mm) diameter gauge pin into the bracket and holes in the control levers, as shown at the bottom of Fig. 15, to align them in the neutral position. Tighten the swivel-nut assemblies on the linkage rods and remove the gauge pin. Check the complete shift pattern with the engine off. Try it again with the engine on.

■ 4-4-9 Steering-Column Shift-Lever Adjustments

Figure 16 shows a typical steering-column shift lever with its linkage to the transmission. Linkage adjustments are made at the swivels on the ends of the two shifter-tube levers at the bottom of the shifter tube.

Whenever gearshift linkage has been disconnected, adjust it by moving the two transmission shift levers until the transmission is in neutral. Both neutral detents must be engaged. To check, start the engine with the clutch disengaged and engage the clutch slowly. If the transmission is in neutral, stop the engine and proceed as follows.

Move the selector lever at the wheel to neutral. Align the first-and-reverse-shifter-tube lever with the second-and-third shifter-tube lever on the mast jacket (view *C* in Fig. 16). Install both control rods on the transmission shifter levers and secure them with retaining clips (view *A*).

Put the swivel on the end of the first-and-reverse shifter control rod and adjust until the swivel is in position to enter the mast-jacket shifter-lever hole. Put the retaining clamp on the swivel, install the swivel in the lever hole, and secure with a swivel nut (view *C*).

Install the lower second-and-third shifter control rod between the idler lever (view *B*) and the transmission lever. Then install the upper second-and-third shifter control rod between the idler lever and the swivel in the second-and-third shifter-tube lever. Be sure the shifter-tube levers remain aligned in the neutral position. Check the adjustments by shifting into all gear positions.

SECTION 4-5 | Drive-Line Service

■ 4-5-1 Universal-Joint and Drive-Line Service

Most universal joints require no maintenance. They are lubricated for life and cannot be lubricated on the car. If a universal joint becomes noisy or worn, it must be replaced. Manufacturers supply service kits that include all necessary parts to make the replacement.

The drive shaft is a balanced unit. On some cars, if the shaft is unbalanced enough to cause undesirable vibrations, it can be rebalanced with the addition of hose clamps, as noted later. On other cars, the recommendation is to replace the drive shaft. Typical service procedures follow.

> **NOTE:** The propeller shaft and universal joints are carefully balanced during original assembly. To ensure correct relationship so that balance can be maintained, mark all parts before disassembly (if they are not already marked). Then, you can put everything back together in the original positions.

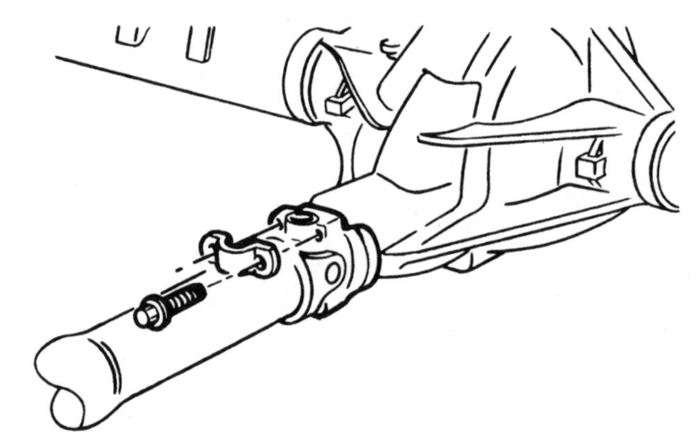

Figure 1 Strap attachment of the rear end of the drive shaft. *(Chevrolet Motor Division of General Motors Corporation.)*

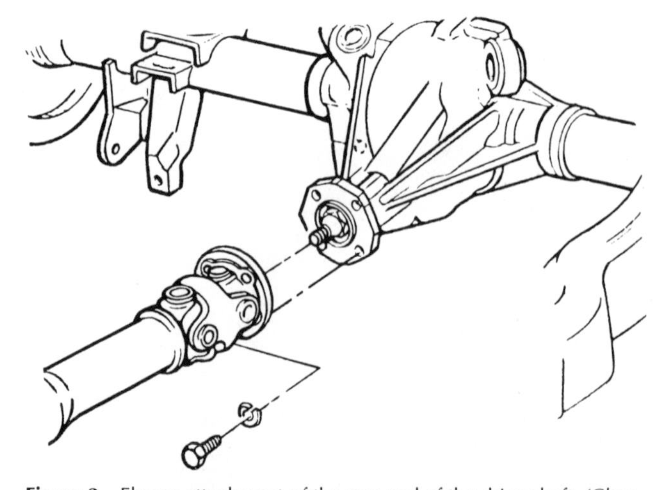

Figure 2 Flange attachment of the rear end of the drive shaft. *(Chevrolet Motor Division of General Motors Corporation.)*

■ 4-5-2 Chevrolet Drive-Line Service

To remove the drive-shaft assembly, mark the relationship of the shaft to the companion flange at the differential. Then disconnect the rear universal joint by removing trunnion bearing straps or flange attaching bolts (Figs. 1 and 2). On the strap-attachment type, tape the bearing cups to the trunnion to keep bearing rollers from falling out.

Then withdraw the propeller-shaft front yoke from the transmission by moving the shaft to the rear. Pass it under the axle housing. Watch for leakage from the transmission extension housing.

1. UNIVERSAL-JOINT SERVICE Three universal joint designs are used on Chevrolet: The Cleveland, Saginaw, and double-Cardan constant-velocity types. Special service kits are supplied for all these designs (see Figs. 3 and 4). As examples of service procedure, we shall discuss the Cleveland and constant-velocity universal joints.

a. *Cleveland Universal-Joint Disassembly* Remove bearing lock rings from the trunnion yoke. Support the trunnion yoke on a piece of 1¼-inch (31.75-mm) inside-diameter pipe in an arbor bed.

Apply pressure to the trunnion until the bearing cup is almost out. It cannot be pressed all the way out. Grasp the cup in a vise or pliers and work it out of the yoke. Reverse the position of the trunnion and remove the other bearing cup.

Clean and inspect dust seals, bearing rollers, and trunnion. If everything is in order, repack the bearings and lubricate the reservoirs at the ends of trunnions with high-melting-point wheel-bearing lubricant. Use new seals. Then reassemble as explained in *b*. If any part is defective, replace everything with new parts included in the repair kit (Fig. 3).

b. *Cleveland Universal-Joint Reassembly* When packing lubricant into the lubricant reservoirs at the ends of the trunnions, make sure that they are completely filled from the bottom. The use of a squeeze bottle is recommended to prevent air pockets at the bottom.

Use a trunnion seal installer, as shown in Fig. 5, to install the seals. Then position trunnion in yoke. Partly install one bearing cup, as shown in Fig. 6. Then partly install the other bearing cup. Align the trunnion into the cups and press the cups into the yoke.

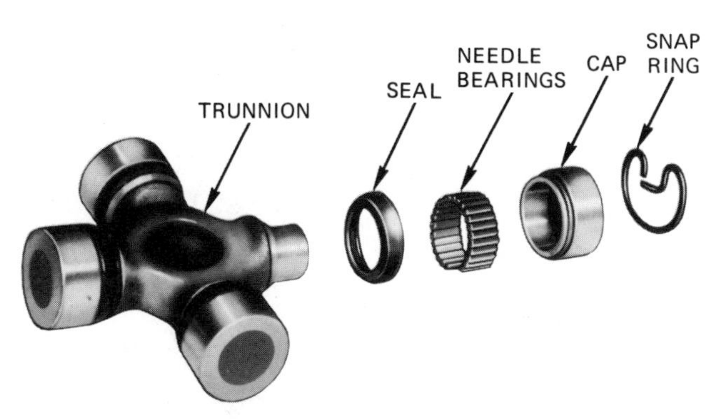

Figure 3 Cleveland-type universal-joint repair kit. *(Chevrolet Motor Division of General Motors Corporation.)*

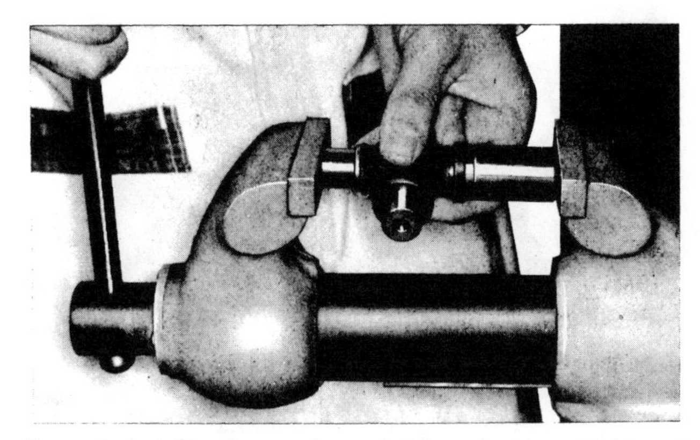

Figure 5 Installing the trunnion seal. *(Chevrolet Motor Division of General Motors Corporation.)*

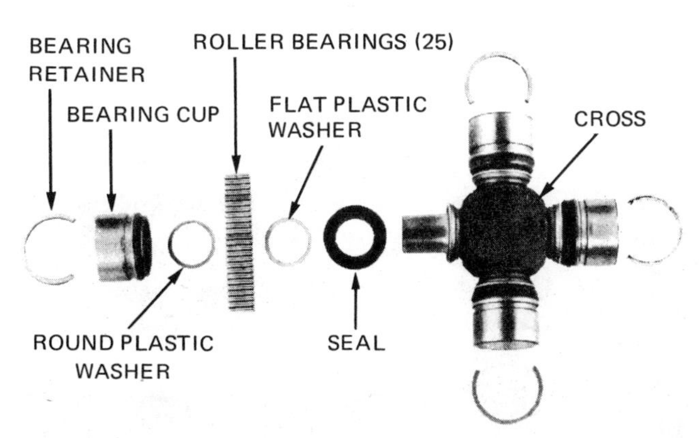

Figure 4 Saginaw-type universal-joint repair kit. *(Chevrolet Motor Division of General Motors Corporation.)*

Figure 6 Installing the bearing cup and trunnion. *(Chevrolet Motor Division of General Motors Corporation.)*

> **NOTE:** A bench vise can also be used to exert the pressure necessary to press the bearing cup loose.

c. *Constant-Velocity Universal-Joint Service* In Fig. 7, the constant-velocity universal joint is shown with the bearing cups numbered in the order in which they should be re-

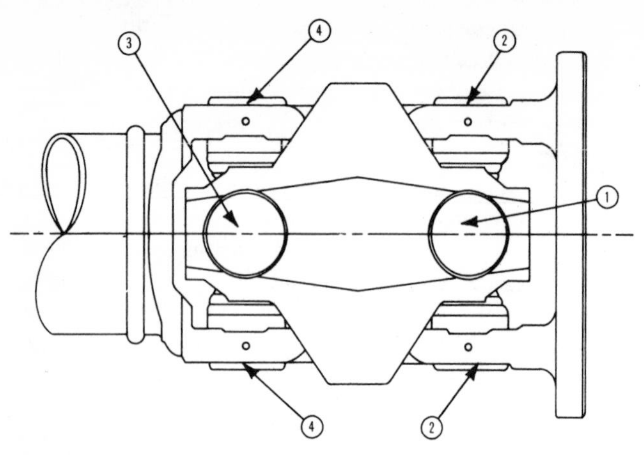

Figure 7 Sequence in which bearing cups should be removed from a constant-velocity universal joint. *(Chevrolet Motor Division of General Motors Corporation.)*

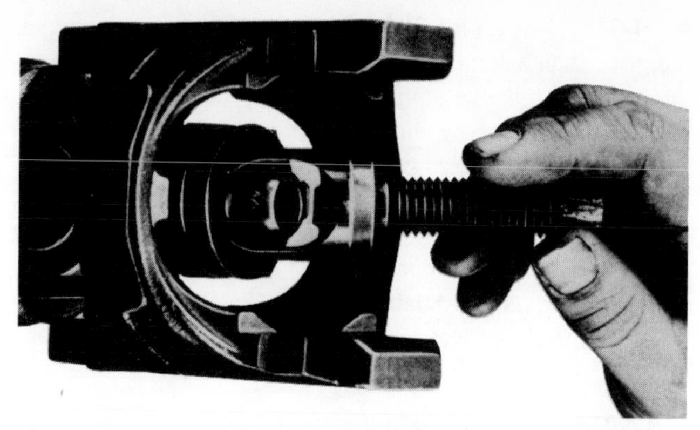

Figure 10 Special tool for removing the ball from the stud. When a collar is placed over the tool and a nut is tightened on the screw threads, the ball is pulled off the stud. *(Chevrolet Motor Division of General Motors Corporation.)*

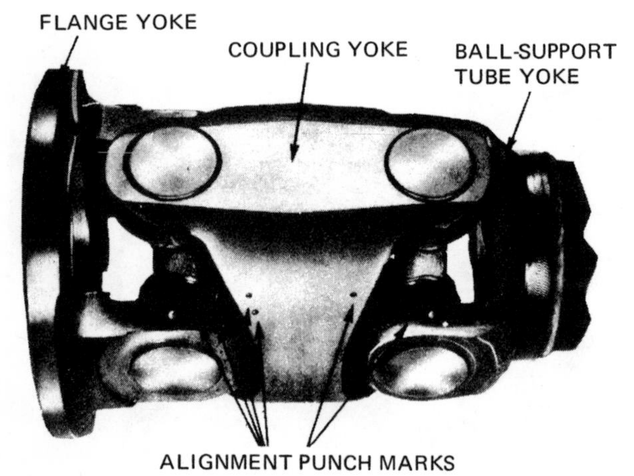

Figure 8 Alignment punch marks on a constant-velocity universal joint which aid in proper reassembly of the joint. *(Chevrolet Motor Division of General Motors Corporation.)*

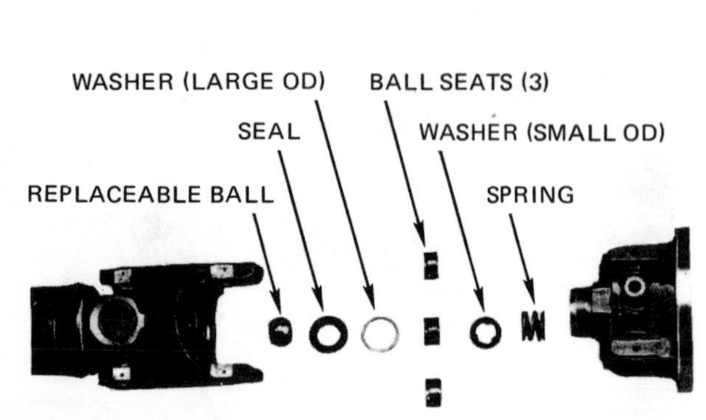

Figure 9 Disassembled view of the centering-ball mechanism in a constant-velocity universal joint. *(Chevrolet Motor Division of General Motors Corporation.)*

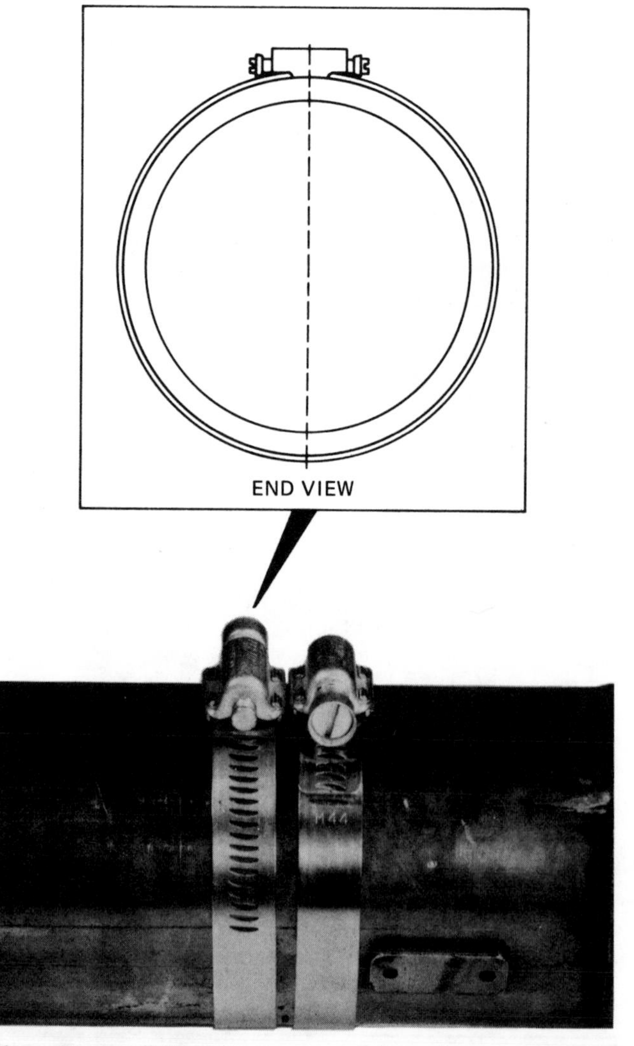

Figure 11 Installation of two worm-type hose clamps on the drive shaft. *(American Motors Corporation.)*

moved. Figure 8 shows the universal joint with alignment punch marks which serve as a guide for reassembly. See also Fig. 14 for a disassembled view of this type of joint.

Remove the bearing cups in the same manner as for the Cleveland unit. Then disengage the flange yoke and trunnion from the centering ball. Note, in Fig. 9, that the ball socket is part of the flange-yoke assembly. The centering ball is pressed onto a stud and is part of the ball-stud yoke. Pry the seal from the ball socket and remove the washers, spring, and ball seats. Replace everything with a service kit.

Remove all plastic from the groove of the coupling yoke. To replace the centering ball, use the special puller tool, shown in Fig. 10. The fingers of the tool are placed under the ball. Then a collar is put on the tool and a nut tightened on the tool screw threads. This pulls the ball off the ball stud. A new ball can then be driven on the stud.

NOTE: The ball must seat firmly against the shoulder at the base of the stud.

Use the grease furnished with the service kit to lubricate all parts. Install parts into the clean ball seat cavity in this order: spring, washer (small), three ball seats (largest opening outward to receive the ball), large washer, and seal. Press the seal flush with the special tool. Fill the cavity with grease provided in the kit. Install the flange yoke to the centering ball, making sure that the alignment marks line up. Install the trunnion and bearing cups in the same manner as for the Cleveland unit.

d. Propeller-Shaft Installation Inspect the yoke seal at the transmission extension. Replace it if necessary. Apply a light coating of transmission oil to the transmission-shaft splines. Insert the front-shaft yoke into the transmission extension, making sure that the output-shaft splines mate with the shaft splines. Align the propeller shaft with companion flange using the reference marks established during removal. Remove the tapes used to retain the bearing cups. Connect the exposed bearing cups to the companion flange by installing the retainer strap and screws or bolts (Figs. 1 and 2).

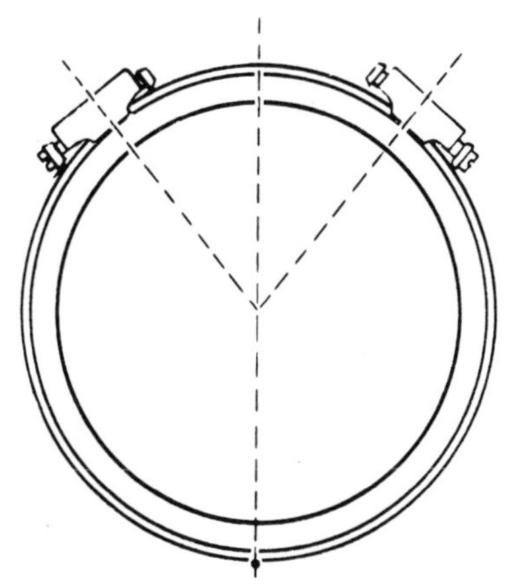

Figure 12 Heads of hose clamps moved equal distance toward the heavy spot to achieve shaft balance. *(American Motors Corporation.)*

e. Correcting Propeller-Shaft Imbalance To check for imbalance, put the car up on a hoist so that the rear wheels are free to rotate. Remove both rear-tire-and-wheel assemblies and brake drums.

NOTE: Do not apply brakes with the drums removed!

With the transmission in gear and the engine running at the speed at which disturbance was noted, observe the intensity of the vibration. Stop the engine and check for mud or undercoating on the drive shaft. Remove any found. Check again. If the vibration is still there, stop the engine and disconnect the drive shaft from the companion shaft. Rotate the shaft 180° and reconnect it. Try again. If the problem is not corrected, install a new drive shaft.

NOTE: American Motors Corporation suggests using an electronic wheel balancer to check for unbalance. With rear axles free to spin and rear wheels removed, put the electronic pickup under the axle housing as close to the pinion yoke as possible. Use crayon or chalk and mark four equally spaced horizontal lines on the propeller shaft. Make the lines of different lengths so that you can identify each one. Operate the car and use the wheel balancer to locate the heavy spot as identified by the length of line.

American Motors Corporation further suggests the use of two hose clamps (worm type) as near the rear of the shaft as possible (Fig. 11). The heads of the clamps should be 180° from the heavy spot on the shaft. Then start the engine and make the test again. If vibration still exists, move the clamp heads equal distances away from their original spots (Fig. 12). Move them only a few degrees and try again. If the problem is not quite solved, move the clamp heads some more. You will find spots at which good balance at the rear can be achieved. Then repeat the procedure at the front of the drive shaft. If the transmission has an aluminum extension, install a steel hose clamp around the transmission so that the magnet will stay put.

■ 4-5-3 Ford Drive-Line Service

Ford Motor Company vehicles use two types of universal joints: the single spider and double-Cardan constant-velocity universal joints (Figs. 13 and 14). The drive shaft is removed and installed in the same manner as for the Chevrolet units, described in the previous section. Disassembly and reassembly are also similar, but Ford recommends the use of a special C-clamp type of tool (Figs. 15 and 16).

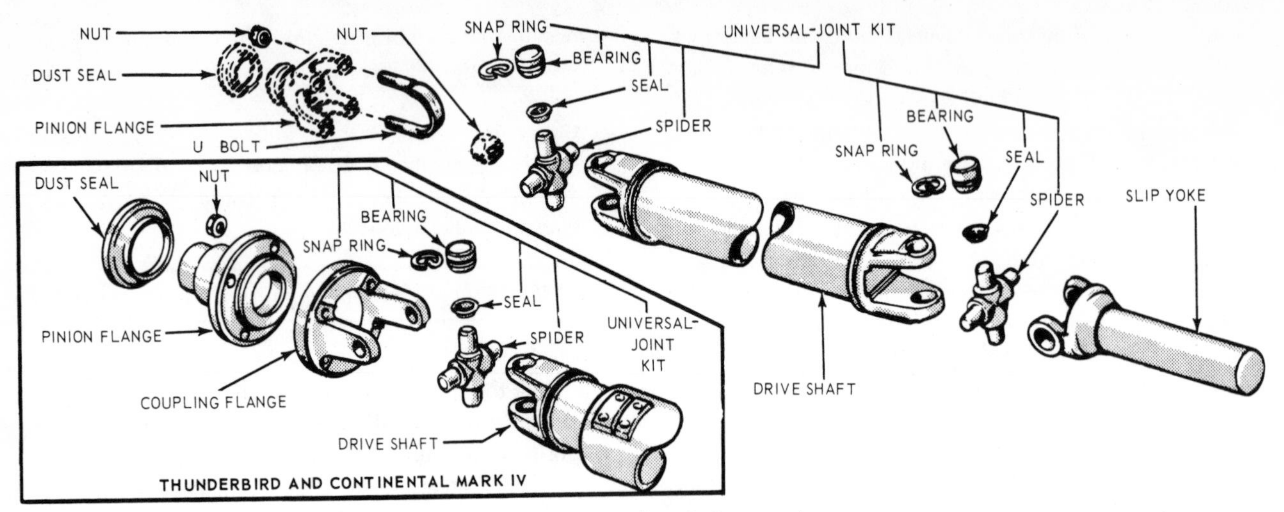

Figure 13 Disassembled view of the drive shaft and universal joints. *(Ford Motor Company.)*

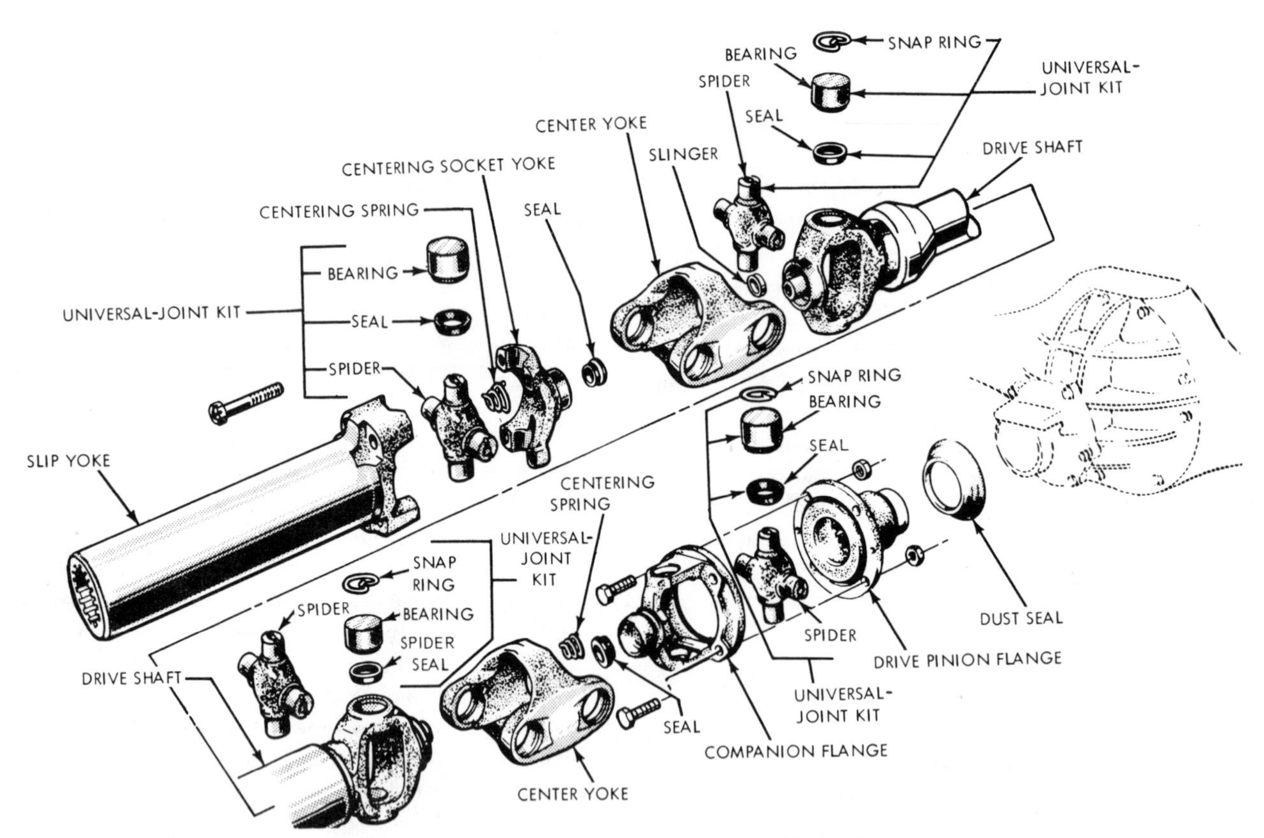

Figure 14 Disassembled view of the drive shaft and constant-velocity universal joint. *(Ford Motor Company.)*

1. SHAFT-BALANCE CHECK To check drive-shaft balance, bring a crayon or colored pencil up to the rear end of the rotating drive shaft (Fig. 17). The car must be on a hoist so that the wheels can spin, and the speedometer should read 40 to 45 mph (64 to 72 km/h). If the shaft is unbalanced, the mark on the shaft will be light on one side and heavy on the other.

CAUTION: Keep away from the balance weights on the shaft so that you don't hurt yourself!

Ford recommends the use of two worm-type hose clamps, as already described and recommended by American Motors Corporation. See Figs. 18 and 19.

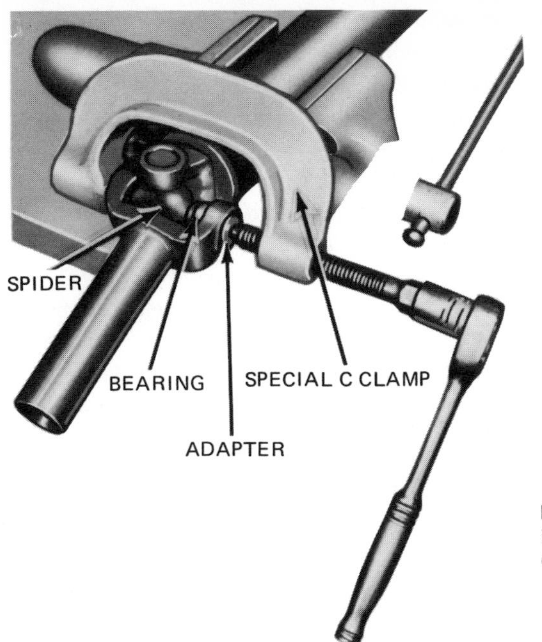

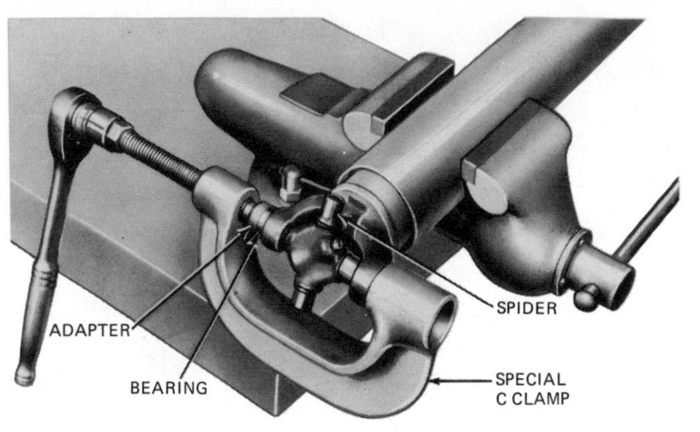

Figure 16 Installing a universal-joint bearing with a special C-clamp. *(Ford Motor Company.)*

Figure 15 Removing a universal-joint bearing with a special C-clamp. *(Ford Motor Company.)*

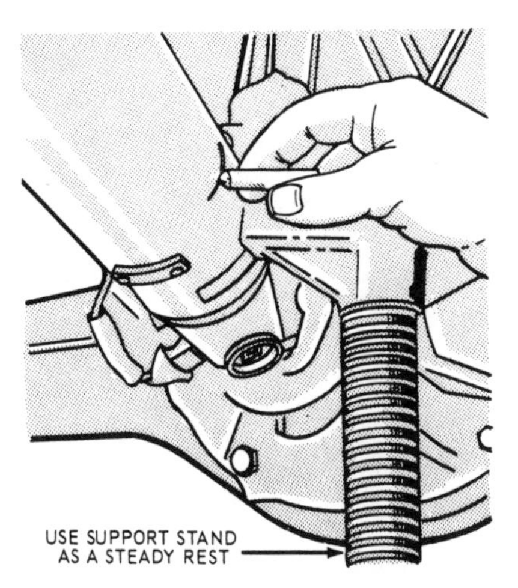

Figure 17 Marking a drive shaft. *(Ford Motor Company.)*

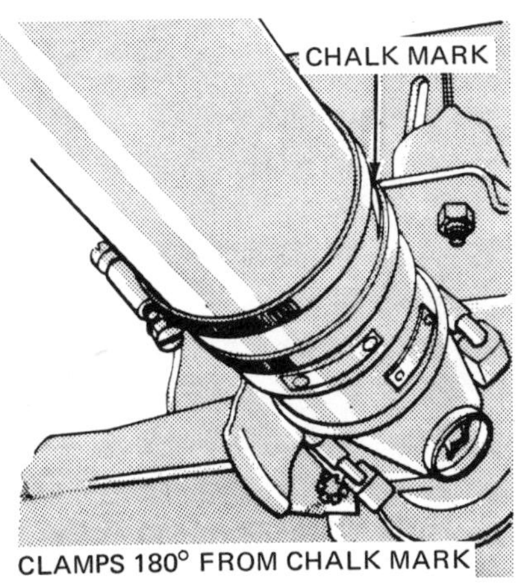

Figure 18 Installation of worm-type hose clamps on a drive shaft. *(Ford Motor Company.)*

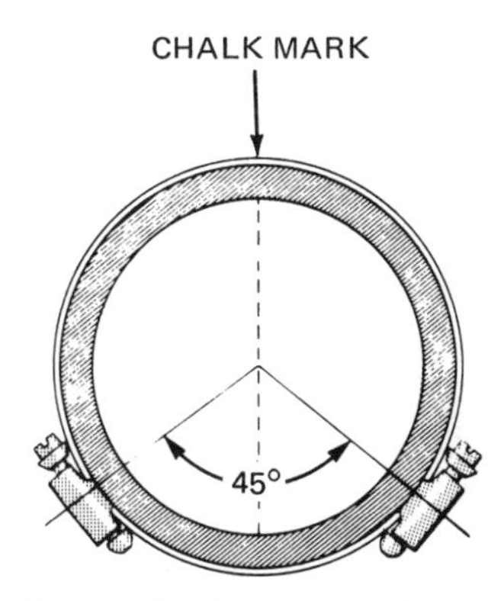

Figure 19 Separating clamps away from light spot to achieve shaft balance. *(Ford Motor Company.)*

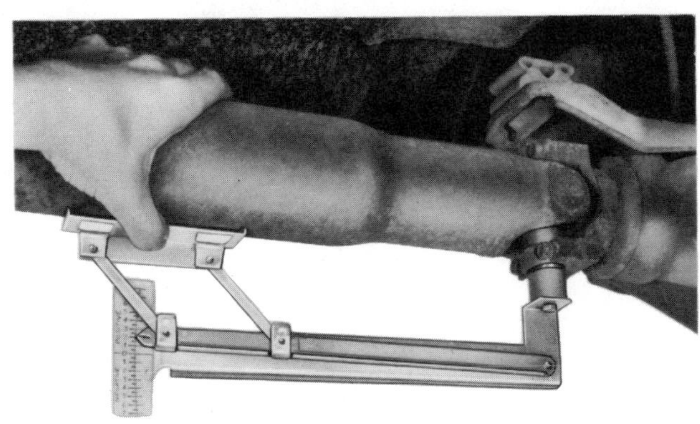

Figure 20 Using a special measuring instrument to check the universal-joint angle at the rear of the drive shaft. *(Chrysler Corporation.)*

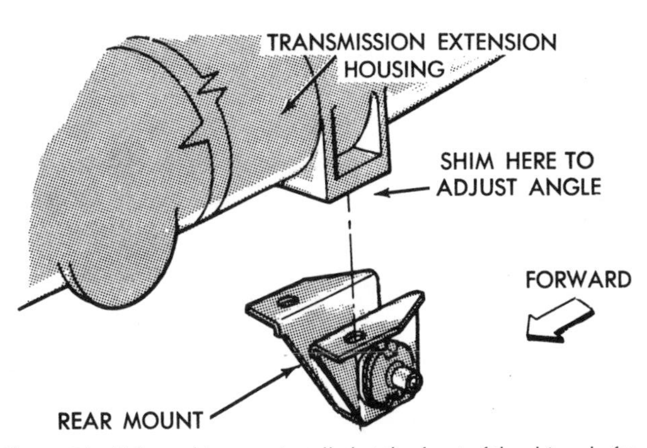

Figure 21 Where shims are installed at the front of the drive shaft to correct universal-joint angle. *(Chrysler Corporation.)*

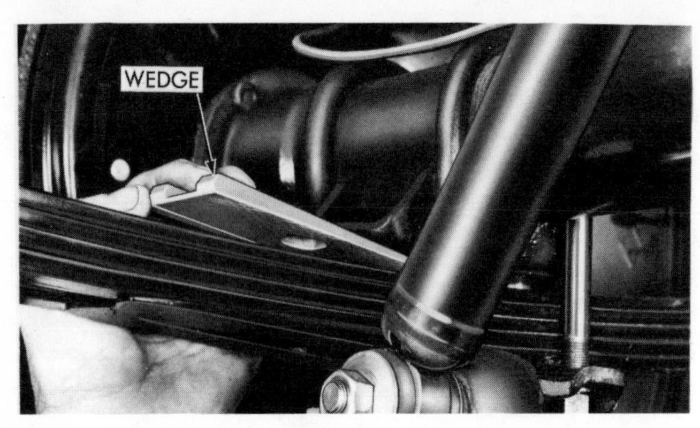

Figure 22 Installing a tapered wedge above the spring to correct the rear universal-joint angle. *(Chrysler Corporation.)*

■ **4-5-4 Plymouth Drive-Line Service** The drive-line service recommended for Chrysler Corporation cars is very similar to that already described for Chevrolet and Ford. However, one additional service is recommended by Chrysler: checking the universal-joint angles. These angles are very important. The greater the angles, the greater the fluctuation of speed through the universal joint (except for the constant-velocity type). A wide difference in speed will cause drive-line vibration.

Figure 20 shows the use of a special angle-measuring instrument at the rear and front of the drive line. If the front angle requires correction, install shims as shown in Fig. 21. To correct the angle at the rear, install tapered shims between the springs and spring seats (Fig. 22).

SECTION 4-6 Rear-Axle and Differential Service

■ **4-6-1 Rear-Axle and Differential Trouble Diagnosis** Most often, it is noise that draws attention to trouble existing in the rear axles or differential. It is not always easy, however, to diagnose the trouble by determining the sort of noise and the operating conditions under which noise is obtained. Such conditions as defective universal joints, rear-wheel bearings, and muffler or tire noises may be improperly diagnosed as differential or rear-axle trouble. Some clue to the cause of trouble may be gained by noting whether the noise is a hum, growl, or knock; whether it is obtained when the car is operating on a straight road or on turns only; and whether the noise is most noticeable when the engine is driving the car or when the car is coasting.

A humming noise in the differential is often caused by improper drive-pinion or ring-gear adjustment, which prevents normal tooth contact between the gears. This condition produces rapid gear-tooth wear, and so the noise will gradually take on a growling characteristic. Correction should be made before the trouble progresses this far since such wear will require pinion and gear replacement.

If the noise is most prominent when the car accelerates, the probability is that there is heavy heel contact on the gear teeth. The ring gear must be moved nearer the drive pinion. If the noise is most prominent when the car coasts in gear with the throttle closed, it is probable that there is heavy toe contact on the gear teeth. The ring gear must be moved away from the drive pinion. Following subsections describe how gear-tooth contact is tested and ring-gear or pinion-drive adjustment is made.

NOTE: The noise is sometimes mistaken for differential noise. Tire noise varies considerably according to the type of pavement, while differential noise does not. The car should be driven over various types of pavement to determine whether the noise is resulting from tires or from the differential.

If the noise is present only when the car is rounding a curve, the trouble is due to some condition in the differential-case assembly. Differential pinion gears tight on the pinion shaft, differential side gears tight in the differential case, damaged gears or thrust washers, or excessive backlash between gears could produce noise when the car turns. A knocking noise will result if bearings or gears are damaged or badly worn.

■ 4-6-2 Rear-Axle and Differential Repair

A considerable variety of differentials will be found on late-model cars. Plymouth describes five different types in recent shop manuals. Ford describes 12, including those used in its heavy-duty trucks; and Chevrolet describes 10, also including those used in its heavy-duty trucks. The repair procedures on these differentials vary, even though the differentials are much alike in basic construction and operation. As examples of service procedures, we include here the procedures for two standard differentials and three nonslip differentials.

> **NOTE:** Always refer to the applicable shop manual before attempting to service a specific make and model of differential.

■ 4-6-3 Rear-Axle In-Car Repairs (Standard)

The rear-axle shafts, wheel bearings, and oil seals can be replaced without removing the differential assembly, as follows:

1. SHAFT, WHEEL BEARING (BALL-BEARING TYPE), AND OIL SEAL Remove the wheel. Detach the brake drum from the axle flange. Work through the hole in the axle-shaft flange to remove the nuts that attach the wheel-bearing-retainer plate. Pull the axle assembly with a slide hammer. Do not dislodge the brake-carrier plate. Install one nut to hold it in place after the axle is removed.

To replace the wheel bearing, first loosen the inner retaining ring by nicking it deeply in several places with a cold chisel. This action loosens the ring so that is slides off. Then use the tool shown in Fig. 1 to press off the wheel bearing.

Whenever a rear axle is removed, the oil seal must be replaced. The old oil seal is removed with a special tool and slide hammer. The new oil seal must be soaked in SAE10 oil for 30 minutes before installation. It is installed with a special tool. Coat the outer edge of the oil seal with oil-resistant sealer before installation. Do not get sealer on the sealing lip!

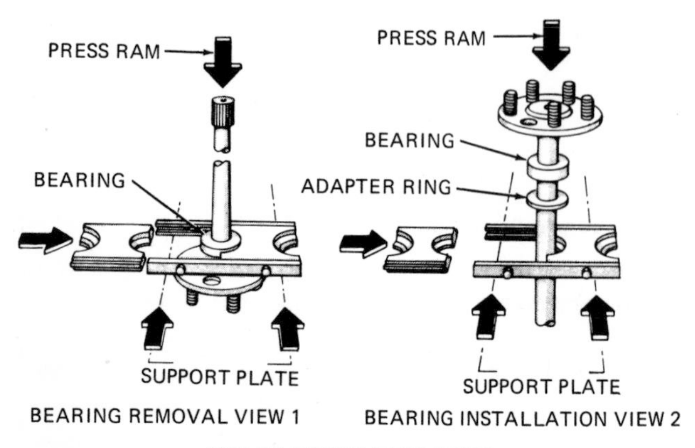

Figure 1 Wheel-bearing removal and replacement. *(Ford Motor Company.)*

> **NOTE:** Do not attempt to press the wheel bearing and the bearing-retainer ring on at the same time. Press each on separately (Fig. 1).

Put a new gasket on each side of the brake-carrier plate and then slide the axle shaft into the housing, working carefully so that the rough edges on the shaft will not damage the oil seal. Align the axle splines with the side-gear splines, and push the shaft in until the bearing bottoms. Install the bearing-retainer plate and nuts, brake drum and nuts, and wheel.

2. SHAFT, WHEEL BEARING (TAPERED ROLLER TYPE), AND OIL SEAL Remove the axle-shaft-retainer nuts and bolts from the housing. The tapered bearing cup will normally stay in the axle housing. A standard slide-hammer puller can be used to remove it. On reinstallation, put the bearing cup on the shaft and install the complete bearing as a unit with the shaft.

To remove the tapered bearing and seal, drill a 1/4-inch (6.35-mm) hole in the outside diameter of the inner retainer (Fig. 2). Make the hole about three-fourths the thickness of the retainer. Do not drill all the way through because this could damage the axle shaft. Then use a chisel to break the ring. Use a puller to pull the bearing cone. Do not allow the puller jaws to get behind the outer retainer.

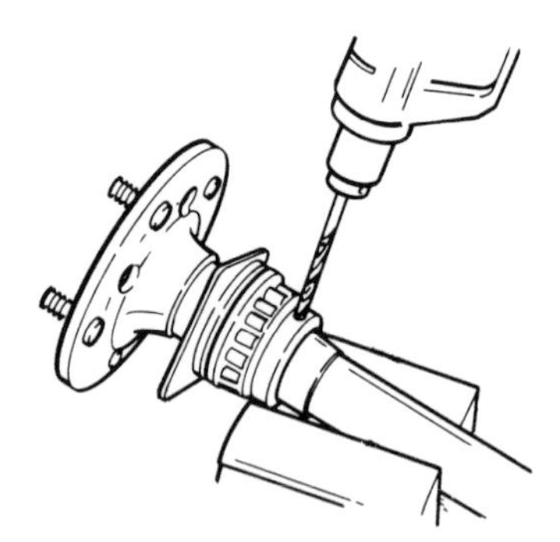

Figure 2 Drilling the retainer ring. *(Ford Motor Company.)*

> **NOTE:** If the oil seal requires replacement, the entire bearing assembly must also be replaced.

Figure 3 shows the installation of a seal and bearing. It is pressed down into place with pressure on the inside race only. The inner cone must seat squarely on the shaft shoulder. Press a new retainer onto the axle shaft so that it seats firmly against the bearing.

3. DRIVE-PINION OIL SEAL The new oil seal should be

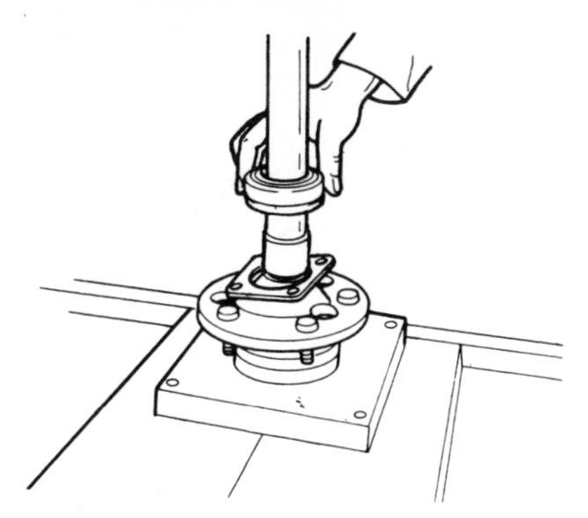

Figure 3 Installing the bearing and seal. *(Ford Motor Company.)*

soaked for 30 minutes in SAE10 oil before installation. Mark scribe lines on the drive-shaft end yoke and the U-joint flange to ensure proper reassembly. Disconnect the drive shaft, being careful not to drop the loose universal-joint-bearing cups. (See also ■4-5-2 on drive-shaft removal.) Detach the drive shaft at the transmission. Install an oil-seal replacer tool in the transmission extension housing to prevent leakage of oil from the transmission.

> **NOTE:** Figures 4 and 5 show the servicing of a detached differential. However, the special tool shown can also be used on a differential in the car.

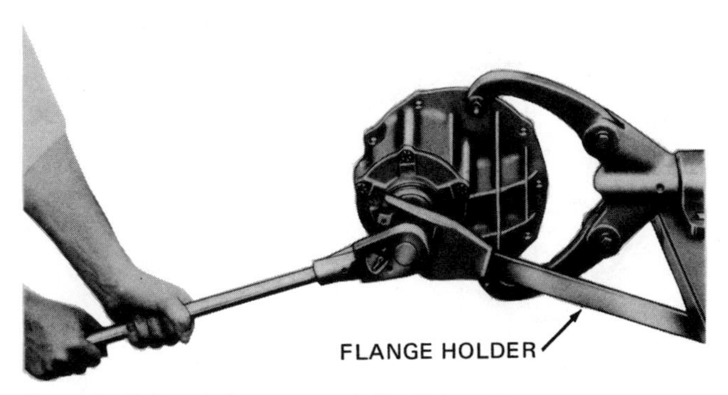

Figure 4 Pinion-shaft-nut removal. *(Ford Motor Company.)*

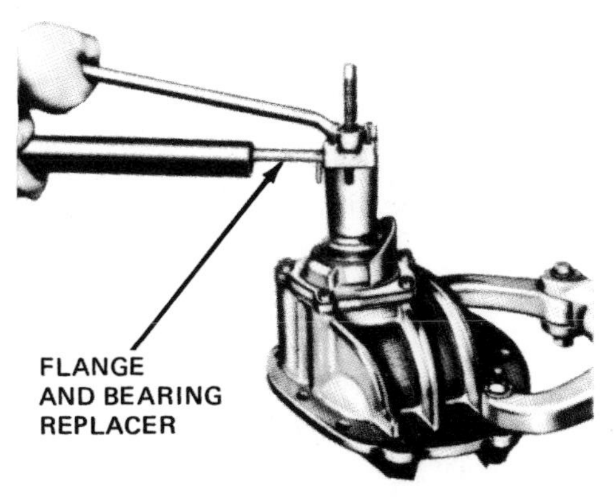

Figure 5 U-joint flange installation. *(Ford Motor Company.)*

Mark punch marks on the end of the pinion shaft, shaft nut, and U-joint flange inner surface so that parts can be properly aligned on reassembly. Use a special tool to hold the flange and remove the pinion nut and washer (Fig. 4).

Clean the pinion bearing retainer around the oil seal. Put a drain pan under the seal or raise the front of the car so that the differential oil will not run out. Remove the U-joint flange with a special puller. Then use a slide hammer to remove the pinion seal. Clean the oil-seal seat.

Coat the outer edge of the new seal with oil-resistant sealer. Do not get sealer on the sealing lip. Install the seal with a special driver. Then install the U-joint flange with the tool shown in Fig. 5. Install the integral retaining nut and washer on the pinion shaft, tightening it until the punch mark on the nut aligns with those on the pinion shaft and inner surface of the U-joint flange.

Tighten the nut an additional 1/4 turn. Hold the flange with a special tool, as shown in Fig. 4. Reinstall the drive shaft, aligning the scribe marks made on the drive yoke and U-joint flange. Check the lubricant level in the differential and add lubricant if necessary.

■ 4-6-4 Differential Removal and Installation

1. REMOVAL Raise the rear of the car on a hoist and remove the two rear wheels and axle shafts, as described in ■4-5-2. Disconnect the drive shaft, as described in ■4-5-2.

Place a drain pan under the differential carrier. Remove the carrier retaining nuts and drain the axle. Remove the carrier assembly.

2. INSTALLATION Clean the axle housing and shafts with a shop towel rinsed in solvent. Do not allow any solvent to run onto the wheel bearings. It could dissolve the lubricant and damage the bearings. Clean the mating surfaces of the axle housing and carrier.

Position the differential carrier on the studs in the axle housing, using a new gasket between the carrier and housing. Install retaining nuts. Then reattach the drive shaft (both ends) and reinstall the axle shafts, brake drums, and rear wheels as described in the previous section. Fill the differential to the proper level with differential lubricant.

■ 4-6-5 Axle-Housing Removal and Installation

These procedures vary somewhat with different makes and models of automobile. A typical procedure follows for a car with leaf springs in the rear suspension (Fig. 6).

1. REMOVAL Remove the carrier assembly, as described in the previous section. Support rear frame members with safety stands. Disconnect the brake line from the clips on the axle housing. Disconnect the vent tube from the housing. After removing the brake-carrier plates from the housing, support them with wire so that the brake lines will not need to be disconnected. Disconnect the shock absorbers and move them out of the way. Lower the rear axle to reduce spring tension and then remove the spring U-bolt nuts, U bolts, and plates.

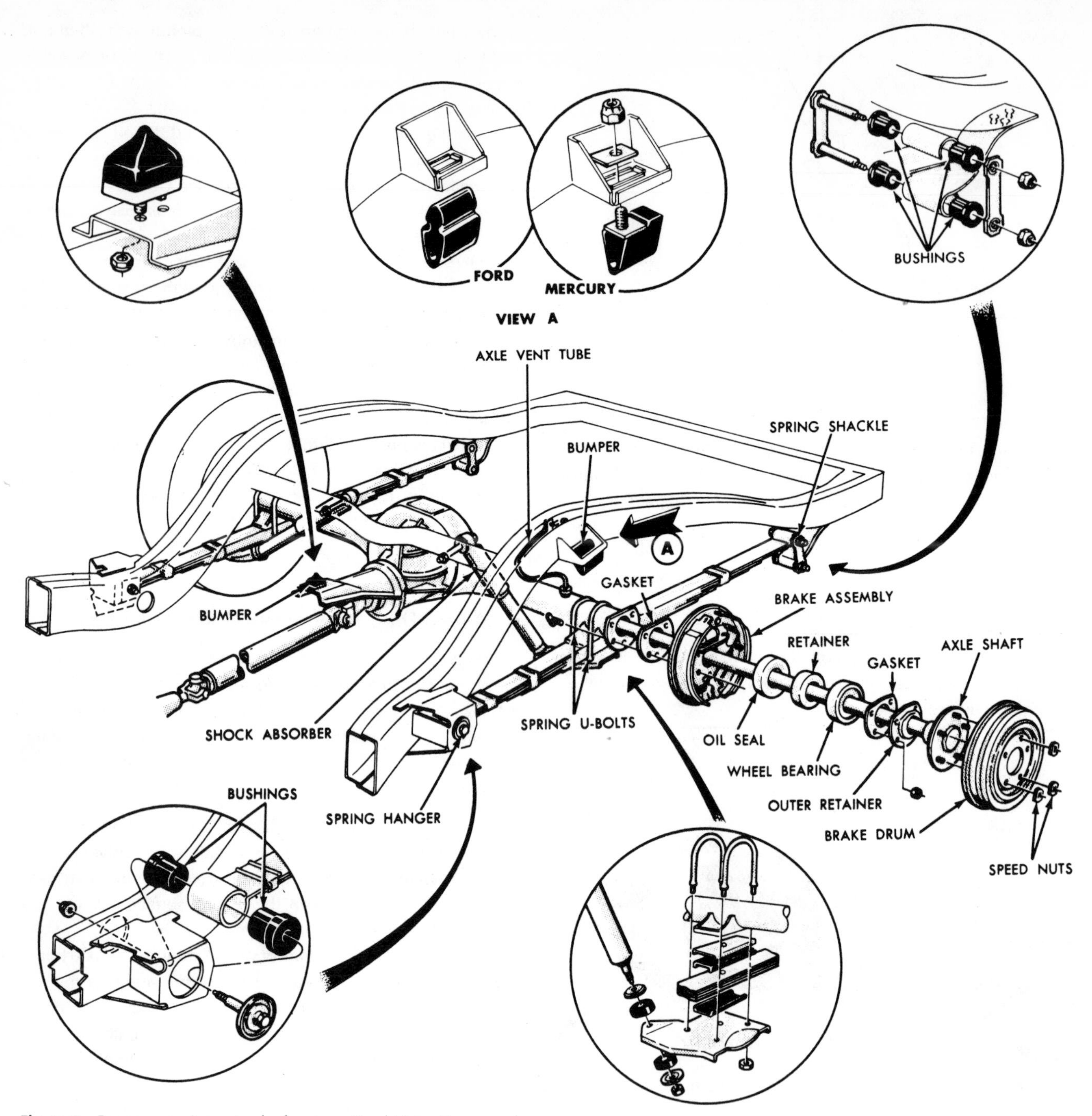

Figure 6 Rear-suspension using leaf-springs. *(Ford Motor Company.)*

Remove the spring lower insulator and retainer, and remove the axle housing.

2. INSTALLATION Install new rear-wheel-bearing oil seals in the ends of the rear-axle housing, as described in ■4-6-3. Position the rear axle on the rear springs with spring upper insulators and retainers between the axle housing and spring with the retainer flange forward (see Fig. 6). Install the lower insulators and retainers (flange to rear) and secure with spring U bolts, plates, and nuts. Torque the spring U-bolt nuts evenly, making sure the lower insulator retainer contacts the upper retainer. Connect the vent tube, brake line (with clips), and shock absorbers. Install the carrier assembly and two axle assemblies as already described.

■ 4-6-6 Gear-Tooth-Contact Patterns

Before disassembly, the differential should be inspected and the gear-tooth contact pattern checked. Install the differential in a bench fixture. Wipe lubricant from the gears and check for wear or damage. Rotate the gears to see if there is roughness or

Figure 7 Checking backlash with a dial indicator. *(Ford Motor Company.)*

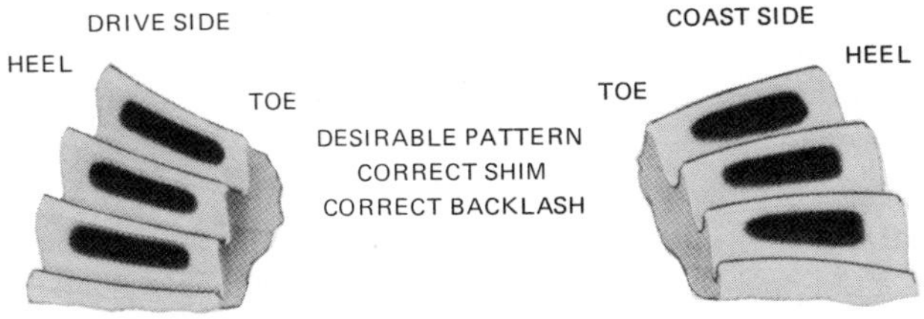

DRIVE SIDE
HEEL
TOE
DESIRABLE PATTERN
CORRECT SHIM
CORRECT BACKLASH
COAST SIDE
HEEL
TOE

Figure 8 Ideal gear-tooth-contact pattern. *(Ford Motor Company.)*

Figure 9 Acceptable pattern for nonhunting gearset showing center-to-toe-to-center eccentricity. *(Ford Motor Company.)*

signs of scoring or abnormal wear. Set up a dial indicator, as shown in Fig. 7, and check for gear backlash at several points around the ring gear.

1. CHECKING GEAR-TOOTH CONTACT Paint the gear teeth with a suitable gear-marking compound such as prussian blue. Hold the drive-pinion flange with a cloth as a brake and rotate the drive gear back and forth with a box wrench on the drive-gear attachment bolts.

In the nonhunting gearset, only a few rotations are required to obtain the full pattern of gear-tooth contact. In the hunting gearset, quite a few rotations are required. The ideal pattern is shown in Fig. 8. However, the pattern can vary somewhat from this ideal and still be satisfactory. Generally speaking, the drive pattern should be fairly well centered on the tooth. The coast pattern should also be fairly well centered, but it can be slightly toward the toe. There should be some clearance between the pattern and the top of the tooth, and there should be no hard lines indicating high pressure.

In general, the nonhunting gearset can have a more eccentric pattern than the hunting gearset and still function satisfactorily. For example, Figs. 9 and 10 show two acceptable patterns for nonhunting gearsets.

If the gear-tooth-contact pattern is not correct, it could be due to drive-gear runout. Check by using a dial indicator, as

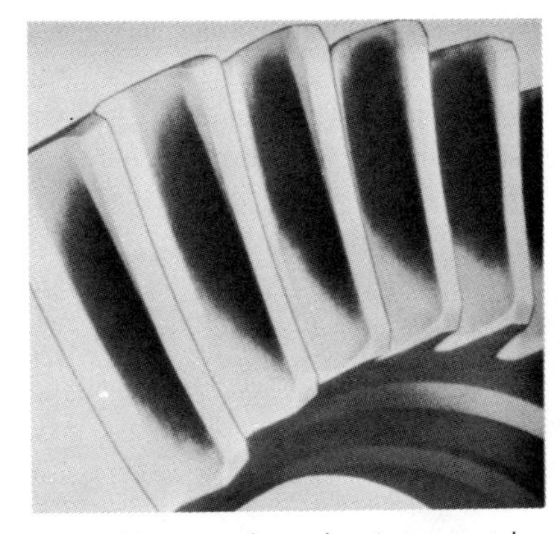

Figure 10 Acceptable pattern for nonhunting gearset showing center-to-heel-to-center eccentricity. *(Ford Motor Company.)*

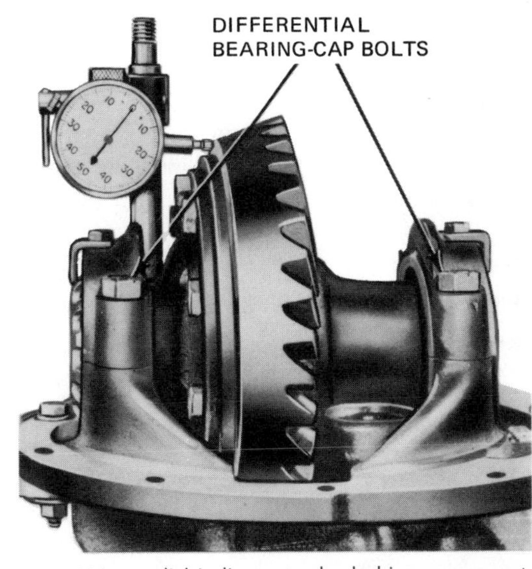

Figure 11 Using a dial indicator to check drive-gear runout. *(Ford Motor Company.)*

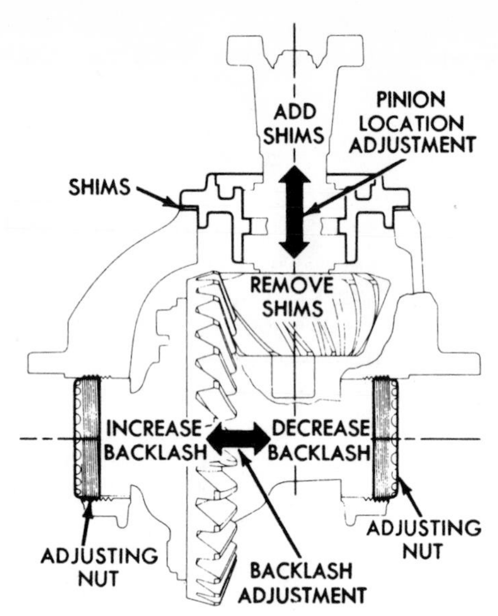

Figure 12 Drive-pinion and drive-gear adjustments to improve gear-tooth-contact patterns requiring correction. *(Ford Motor Company.)*

shown in Fig. 11. If drive-gear runout is excessive, the differential must be disassembled so that defective parts can be replaced.

Gear-tooth contact can often be improved if no parts are excessively worn or defective by turning the adjustment nuts or adding or removing shims (Fig. 12). For example, see Fig. 13, which shows four conditions and the steps required to correct them. In 1, the backlash is correct, as shown by the pattern being about halfway between the base and the top of the teeth. However, because the pattern is not centered between the heel and toe, a thicker shim is required.

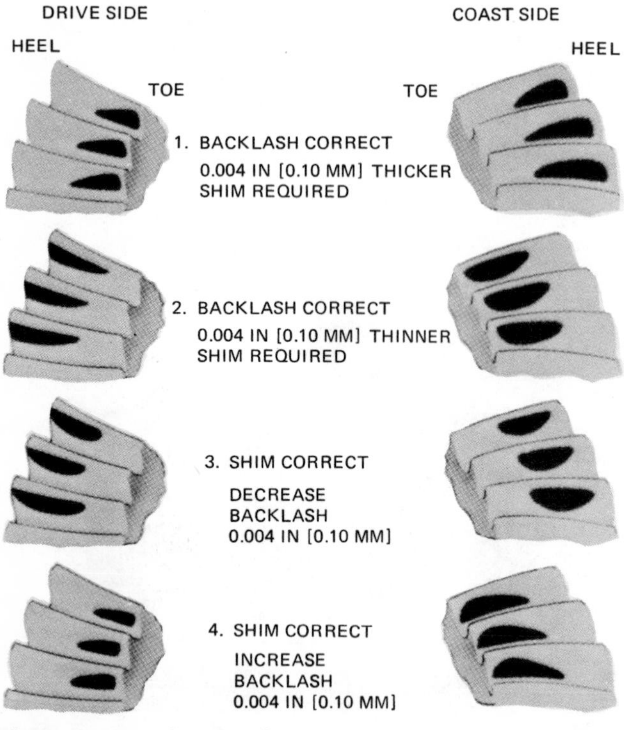

Figure 14 illustrates various drive-gear-tooth impressions and corrective adjustments to be made, as recommended by Plymouth for one model of its standard differential. Note that the adjustment procedures are very similar to those shown in Fig. 14. Plymouth refers to the drive gear as the "ring gear."

2. ADJUSTING BACKLASH To adjust the backlash between the drive pinion and the drive gear, one adjustment nut is tightened while the other is loosened (Fig. 12). To make an adjustment, first remove the adjustment-nut locks, loosen the differential bearing-cup bolts, and then torque the bolts to 25 pound-feet (3.455 kg-m).

The left-hand adjustment nut is on the drive-gear side of the carrier, and the right-hand nut is on the pinion side (as shown in Fig. 12). As a first step, loosen the right-hand nut until it is away from the cup. Tighten the left-hand nut until the drive gear is just forced into the pinion with no backlash. Recheck the right-hand nut to make sure it is still loose. Now, tighten the right-hand nut two notches beyond the position where it first contacts the bearing cup. Rotate the drive gear several revolutions in each direction while the bearings are being loaded so that the bearings will seat.

Again loosen the right-hand nut to release the preload. If there is any backlash between the gears, tighten the left-hand nut just enough to remove the backlash. Carefully tighten the right-hand nut until it just contacts the bearing cup. Then tighten it further 2½ to 3 notches to apply correct preload. This should force the drive gear away from the drive pinion, giving the proper backlash.

Tighten the differential cup bolts to the correct specifications and check the backlash (Fig. 7). If the backlash is uneven, the drive gear is running out (see Fig. 11 for the setup to check runout). If backlash is even but incorrect, readjust the adjustment nuts.

> **NOTE:** Always make the final adjustment in a tightening direction to make sure that the nut is in contact with the bearing cup.

3. ADJUSTING THE DRIVE-PINION LOCATION Adjustment of the drive-pinion location is made by detaching the bearing retainer from the carrier and adding or removing shims (Fig. 15). Refer to Figs. 12 and 13 to determine whether shims must be removed or added.

Be careful not to pinch the O ring during reinstallation. Coat it with axle lubricant, and snap it into the groove; do not roll it. Before installing the bearing retainer on the carrier, determine whether the gearset is of the hunting or the nonhunting type. If of the nonhunting or partial-hunting type, it will be identified by painted timing marks on the gear teeth (Fig. 16). Be sure to align these timing marks on reassembly, as shown.

DRIVE SIDE
COAST SIDE
HEEL
HEEL
TOE
TOE
1. BACKLASH CORRECT
0.004 IN [0.10 MM] THICKER SHIM REQUIRED
2. BACKLASH CORRECT
0.004 IN [0.10 MM] THINNER SHIM REQUIRED
3. SHIM CORRECT
DECREASE BACKLASH 0.004 IN [0.10 MM]
4. SHIM CORRECT
INCREASE BACKLASH 0.004 IN [0.10 MM]

Figure 13 Typical gear-tooth-contact patterns requiring correction. *(Ford Motor Company.)*

PATTERN CLOSE TO CENTER

TOE END

HEEL END—DRIVE SIDE (CONVEX)

HEEL END—COAST SIDE (CONCAVE)

DESIRED TOOTH-CONTACT PATTERN UNDER LIGHT LOAD

THICKER SPACER NEEDED

TOE END

HEEL END—DRIVE SIDE (CONVEX)

HEEL END—COAST SIDE (CONCAVE)

INCORRECT TOOTH-CONTACT PATTERN (INCREASE SPACER THICKNESS)

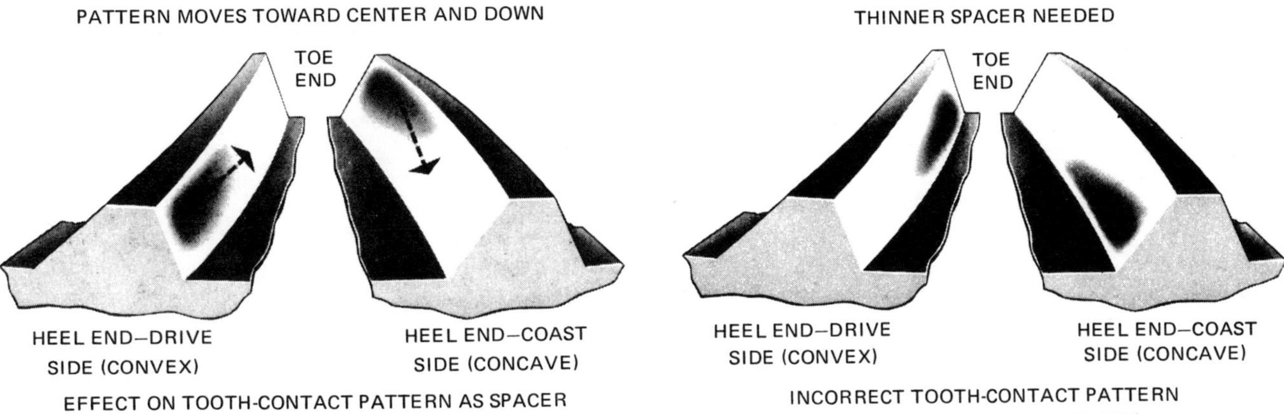

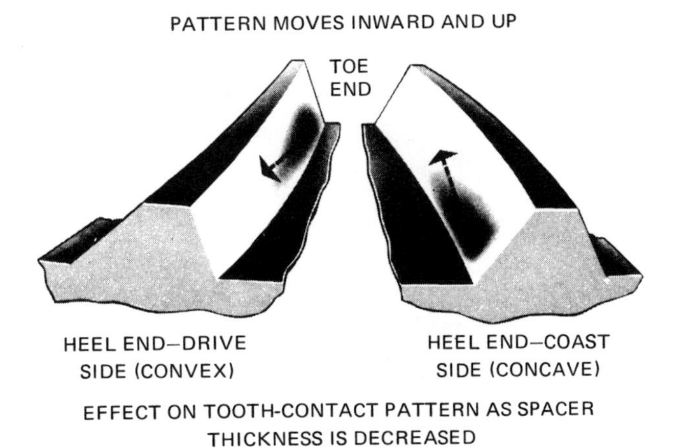

Figure 14 Correct and incorrect gear-tooth-contact patterns and adjustments to correct them. *(Chrysler Corporation.)*

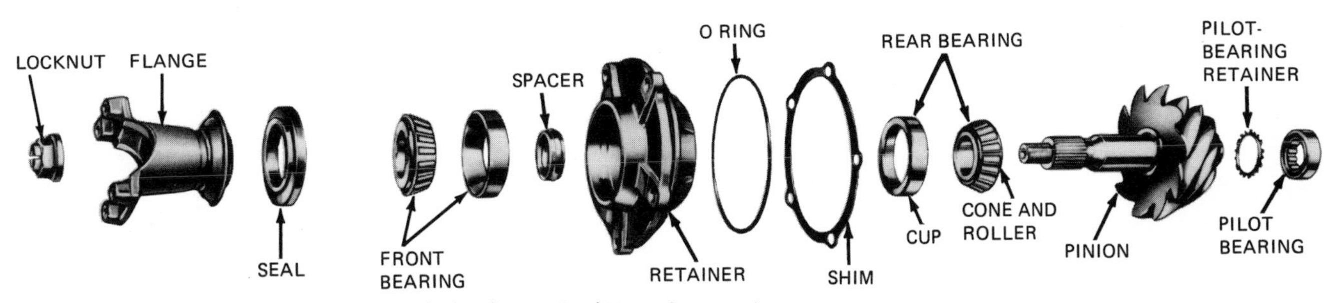

Figure 15 Pinion, bearing retainer, shim, and related parts. *(Ford Motor Company.)*

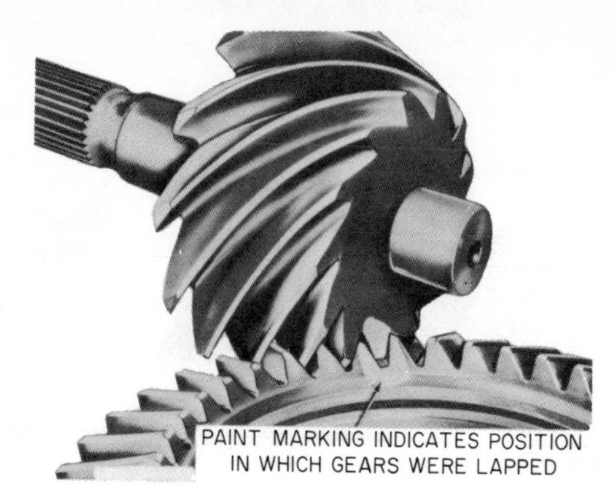

Figure 16 Gear-timing marks on a nonhunting gearset. *(Ford Motor Company.)*

> **NOTE:** Noise and probability of early failure will be greatly increased if the gears are not properly aligned on nonhunting or partial-hunting gearsets.

On hunting-type gearsets, the drive pinion and drive gear can be reassembled without regard to any special tooth relationship.

Install the retainer-to-carrier mounting bolts and torque to specifications. Adjust the backlash between the drive pinion and the drive gears, as already explained, and recheck the tooth pattern. If the tooth pattern is still not correct, additional changing of the shims will be required.

■ 4-6-7 Standard-Differential Disassembly and Reassembly

Figure 17 is a disassembled view of the differential discussed in this section.

1. DISASSEMBLY Use a punch to mark one bearing cap and mating bearing support. Make scribe marks on one of the bearing adjustment nuts and carrier so that the parts can be reassembled in the proper relationship.

Remove the adjustment-nut locks, bearing cups, and adjustment nuts. Lift the differential assembly from the carrier. Pull the differential bearings with a special bearing remover. Detach the drive gear from the differential case, using a soft-face hammer or an arbor press to loosen it. Use a drift to drive out the differential-pinion-shaft lockpin. Separate the two-piece differential case. Drive out the pinion shaft with a brass drift and remove the gears and thrust washers.

The drive pinion and bearing retainer (Fig. 15) can be disassembled by removing the U-joint flange and pinion seal. Then, special tools are required to press out the bearings. Use a protective sleeve (rubber hose) on the drive-pinion pilot-bearing surface and a fiber block on the end of the shaft to protect finished surfaces.

2. INSPECTION All parts should be carefully inspected. Worn or otherwise defective bearings, gears, or other parts should be discarded.

If the ring-gear runout is excessive, the cause may be a warped gear or case or worn differential bearings. To determine the cause, assemble the two halves of the differential case without the drive gear, and press the two differential side

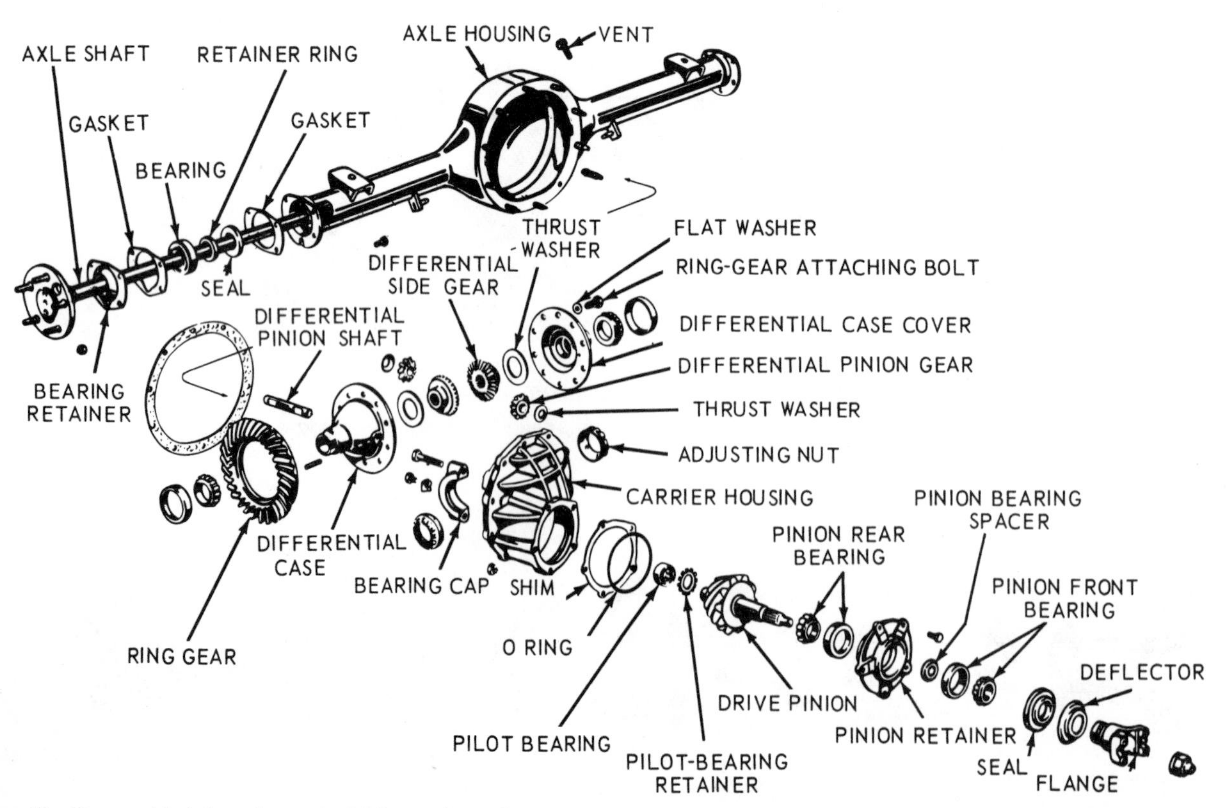

Figure 17 Disassembled view of a standard differential. *(Ford Motor Company.)*

bearings on the case hubs. Put the cups on the bearings, and set the differential case in the carrier. Install the bearing caps and adjusting nuts (see item 3 below) and adjust the bearings, as described in the previous subsection.

Check the runout of the differential-case flange. If the runout exceeds specifications, the case is defective or the bearings are worn. However, if the runout is within specifications, the trouble is with the drive gear, and a new drive gear is required.

3. REASSEMBLY First reassemble the drive pinion and bearing retainer (Fig. 15), using special tools to install the bearings. Install a new oil seal and the U-joint flange (Fig. 15), as previously described.

Refer to Fig. 18 for assembly of the differential case. Lubricate all parts liberally during assembly. Drive the pinion shaft into the case only far enough to retain a pinion thrust washer and pinion gear. Put the second pinion gear and thrust washer into position, and drive the pinion shaft into place. Be sure to line up the pinion-shaft lockpin holes.

Put the second side gear and thrust washer into position, and install the cover on the differential case. Insert an axle-shaft spline into a side gear to check for free rotation of the gears.

Insert two 7/16 N.F. bolts 2 inches (50.8 mm) long through the case flange. Thread them several turns into the drive gear as an aid to aligning the drive gear to the case. Press or tap the gear into place. Install and tighten the gear attachment bolts, using washers. Torque them alternately across the gear to ensure alignment. If the differential bearings have been removed, press them on. Install the bearing-retainer-and-drive-pinion assembly, as described in the previous subsection, making sure that the gearset timing marks are properly aligned, as shown in Fig. 16 (nonhunting type).

Adjust backlash and drive-pinion location, as described in the previous subsection. Then make a final tooth-pattern check before installing the carrier assembly in the axle housing.

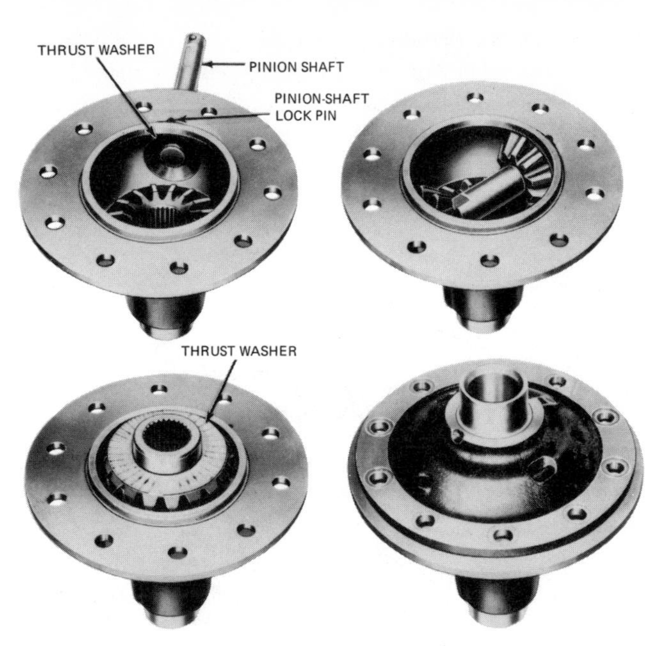

Figure 18 Assembling a differential case. *(Ford Motor Company.)*

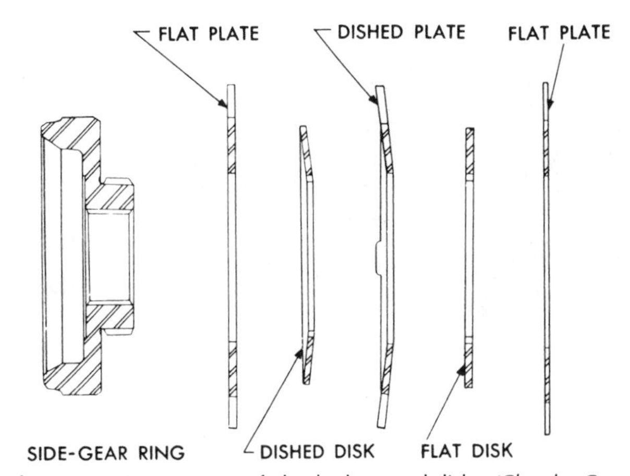

Figure 19 Arrangement of clutch plates and disks. *(Chrysler Corporation.)*

■ 4-6-8 Nonslip-Differential Disassembly and Reassembly

The nonslip differential discussed here is the earlier type, with two sets of clutch plates. The later types, with spring-loaded clutch plates or spring-loaded cones, are discussed in the following subsection.

1. DISASSEMBLY Remove the axle drive gear (ring gear) and measure the runout of the gear mounting flange on the case. Replace both halves of the case if the runout is excessive. Put scribe marks on the case halves before disassembly. Remove the case-cap attachment bolts, cap, and clutch plates. Then lift off side-gear retainer, side gear, and pinion shafts with pinion gears. Take out the other side gear, side-gear retainer, and remaining clutch plates.

2. INSPECTION After cleaning all parts, check them for wear, nicks, burrs, and similar defects. Replace worn or distorted clutch plates. If the case is defective, replace both halves.

3. REASSEMBLY Position the clutch plates and disks in their proper locations in each half of the case (Fig. 19). Put the

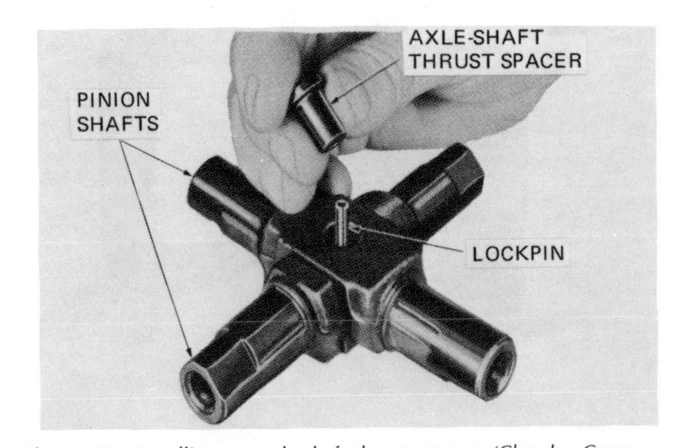

Figure 20 Installing an axle-shaft thrust spacer. *(Chrysler Corporation.)*

side gears in their retainers. Insert the splines of the retainers through the splines of the clutch disks. Put the aligning pin through one axle-shaft thrust spacer. Assemble the pinion shafts on the aligning pin. Put the pinion gears on the shafts, and install the assembly on the drive-gear half of the case. Insert the thrust spacer into the pinion shaft (Fig. 20).

Slide the cap half of the case over the edge of the bench just far enough to insert one finger up through the assembly to hold it together. Put the assembly on the drive-gear half, matching the scribe marks. Install the differential-case bolts, and turn them in a few threads.

Insert the axle shafts from the vehicle to align the splines. Make sure the axle shafts engage the side-gear splines as well as the clutch-disk splines.

With the shafts installed, center the cross shafts between the two ramp surfaces in the differential case. Tighten the differential-case bolts evenly by alternately turning the opposite bolts until all are tightened to the specified tension. After reassembly, any slight misalignment of the splines can be corrected by moving the axle shafts back and forth until free. Remove the axle shafts.

With the differential resting on one hub, insert two feeler blades, one over each end of the pinion shaft having ramps above it (Fig. 21). Invert the differential and check the opposite pinion shaft in a like manner. Excessive clearance means that the clutch disks are worn and should be replaced. With new disks and plates, the clearance may be as little as 0.002 inch (0.051 mm).

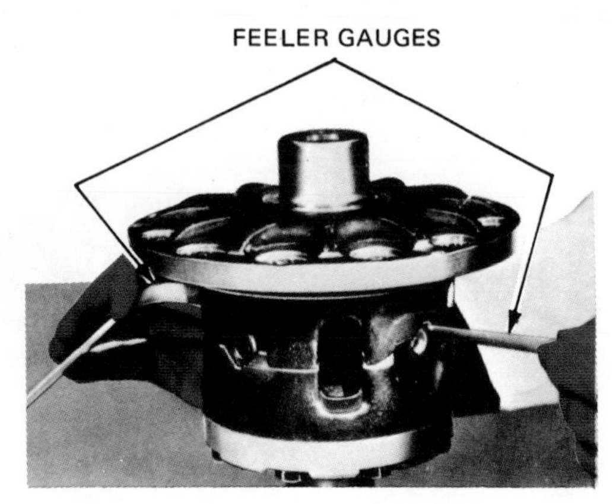

Figure 21 Checking clearance between the pinion shaft and case. *(Chrysler Corporation.)*

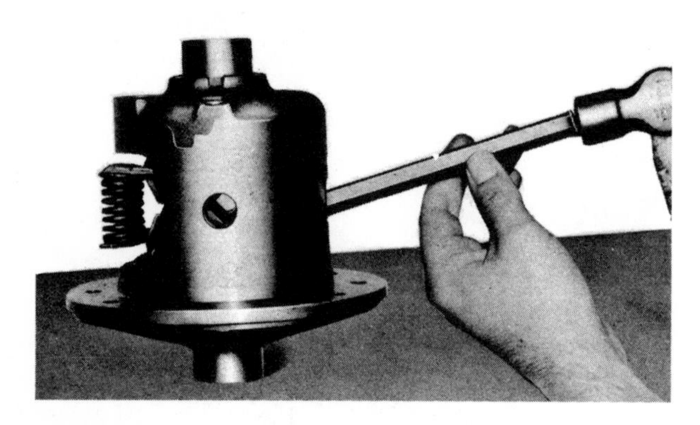

Figure 22 First step in removing the preloaded spring pack. *(Chevrolet Motor Division of General Motors Corporation.)*

Figure 23 Installing bolts to retain springs. *(Chevrolet Motor Division of General Motors Corporation.)*

■ 4-6-9 Servicing Spring-Loaded Clutch and Cone Nonslip Differentials

One type of nonslip differential, the type with cones, is a Borg-Warner unit and is not repairable. If it becomes defective, Chevrolet specifies replacement with either the Eaton or Chevrolet unit they supply.

The service procedures for the nonslip differential will now be described. Overhaul procedures are the same as for the differentials described previously, with the following exceptions.

1. DISASSEMBLING THE EATON NONSLIP DIFFERENTIAL
Remove the ring gear and side bearings in the same manner as for other differentials. Remove the pinion shaft. Then remove the preloaded spring retainer and springs by tapping on the spring retainer through the observation hole (Fig. 22). Drive the spring retainers out far enough to permit installation of ¼-inch (6.35-mm) bolts through the spring. Secure the bolts with nuts to hold the springs in compression (Fig. 23). Then tap the spring retainers out enough so that you can put a clamp on the retainers (Fig. 24).

Use bar stock, as shown, to avoid damaging the retainers. Tighten the clamp enough to compress the other springs so that the assembly can be removed from the differential case. To disassemble this assembly, clamp it in a vise. Remove the nuts and bolts. Then alternately loosen the vise and C clamp until spring pressure is relieved.

For truck models, roll out the differential pinions and thrust washers. For passenger-car models, remove the pinion gears by rotating them in one direction only. Rotate the differential case clockwise (viewed from inside) to remove the first gear. Then rotate the case counterclockwise to remove the other gear. It may be necessary to pry on the gear, as shown, to remove the second gear.

Figure 24 Using a C-clamp and bar stock to remove spring pack. *(Chevrolet Motor Division of General Motors Corporation.)*

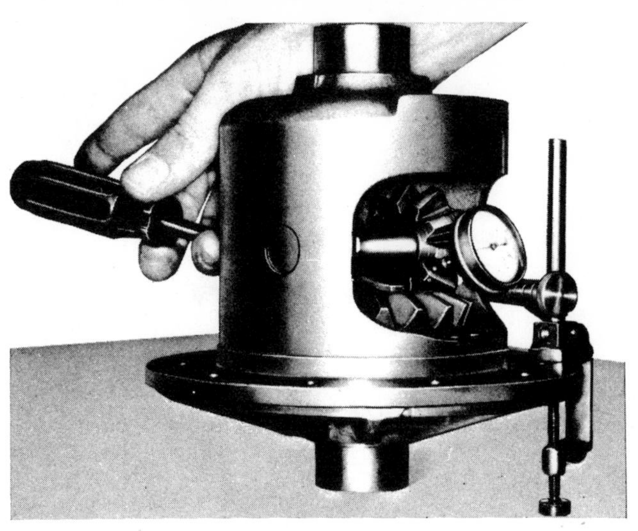

Figure 25 Measuring pinion-gear-tooth clearance. *(Chevrolet Motor Division of General Motors Corporation.)*

Next, remove the side gears, clutch packs, shims, and guides from the case. To remove one side gear, tap on the assembly using a brass drive. Reverse the case and remove the second side gear.

2. INSPECTING AND ASSEMBLING THE EATON NONSLIP DIFFERENTIAL First, inspect parts. Check clutch plates and disks for wear and signs of overheating. If some plates or disks look questionable, install a complete new clutch pack. Inspect springs for weakness or distortion. Make sure the spring retainers are in good alignment and are not worn excessively at the spring seats.

To reassemble, lubricate the plates and disks with special lubricant and assemble the pack on the side gear. Install clutch-pack guides. Select shims of the same thickness as those removed (or use the old shims if they are still in good condition). Install them over the side-gear hub. Lubricate and assemble the opposite clutch pack on the other side-gear hub.

Install one side gear with clutch pack and shims in the case.

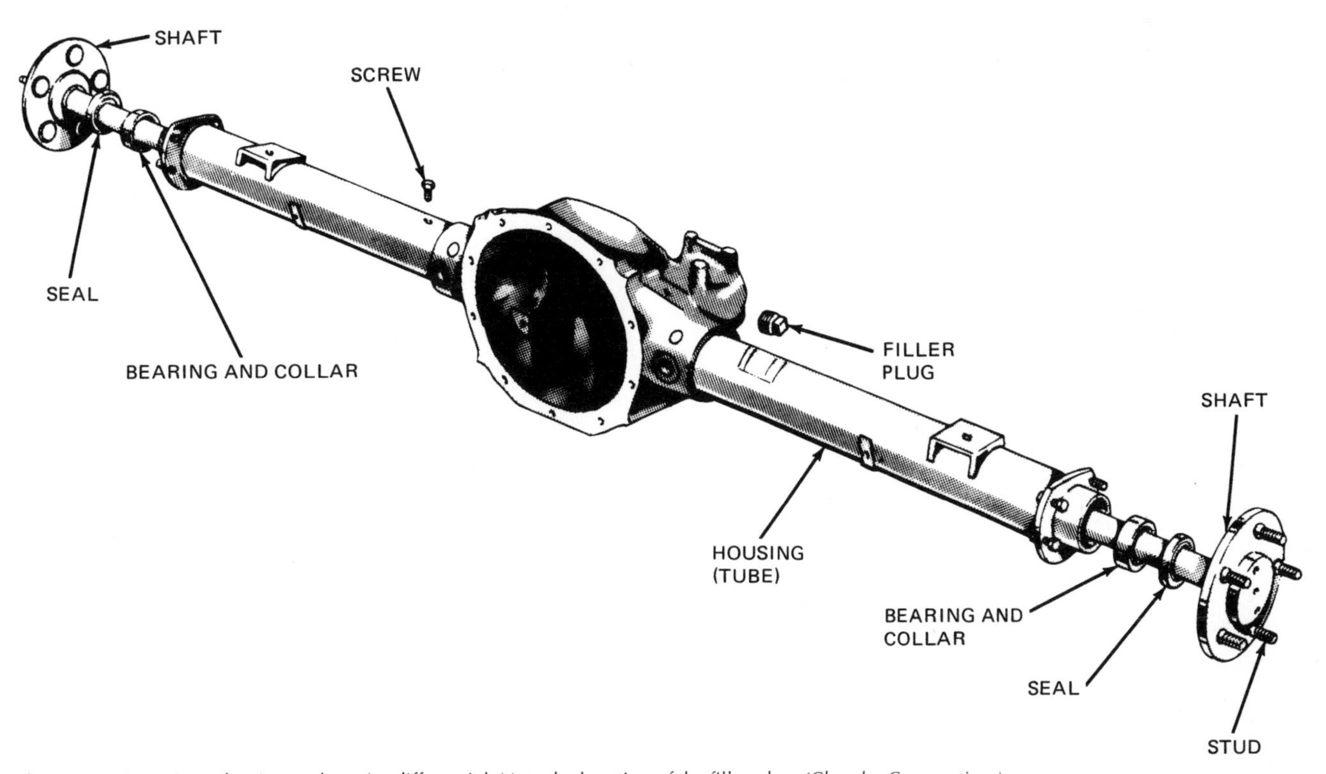

Figure 26 Rear view of an integral-carrier differential. Note the location of the filler plug. *(Chrysler Corporation.)*

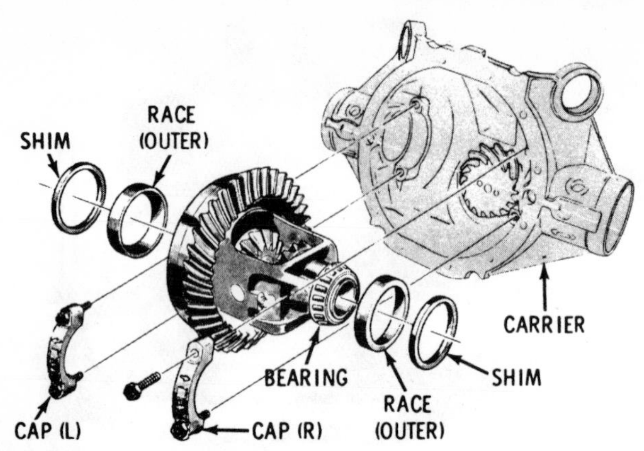

Figure 27 Differential case and bearings. *(Oldsmobile, Division of General Motors Corporation.)*

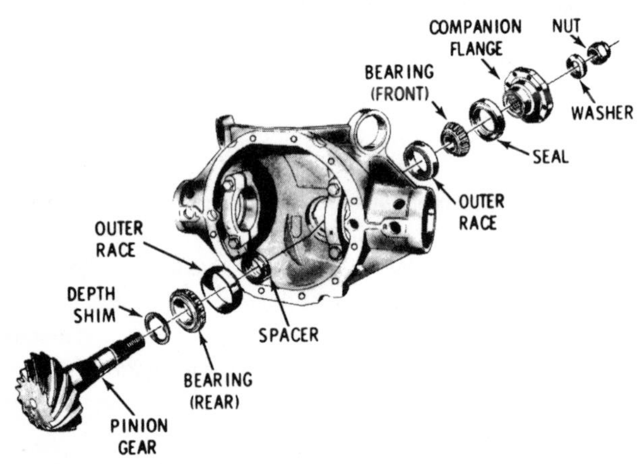

Figure 28 Differential pinion gear and companion flange. *(Oldsmobile Division of General Motors Corporation.)*

Position the pinion gears and thrust washers on the side gear. Install the pinion shaft. Position a dial indicator with the contact button pinion gear (Fig. 25). Compress the clutch pack with a screwdriver, as shown. Move the pinion gear to check tooth clearance. If required, change shims to get proper clearance. Remove the side gear and repeat the clearance-check procedure for the other side gear. Then remove the pinion shaft, gears, and thrust washers.

Install the two side gears with clutch packs and shims. Install the pinion gears and thrust washers. With springs and retainers assembled with C clamp and nuts and bolts, as shown in Fig. 24, drive the assembly partly into the case. Then remove the C clamp and bolts to complete the installation. The next step is to install the pinion shaft and lock screw.

Check the alignment of spring retainers with side gears. The spring pack may require some adjustment to secure proper alignment. Install the side bearings and ring gear to the case. Then place the differential in the carrier and adjust the bearings in the same manner as for the other differentials previously described.

3. CHECKING OPERATION The operation of the unit can be checked while it is in the car by raising the car so that both drive wheels are off the ground. Then remove one wheel-and-tire assembly. Use the special adapter and torque wrench to check the torque required to turn the axle. With the other wheel held firmly so that it cannot turn, the torque required should be no less than 40-pound-feet (5.528 kg-m).

■ 4-6-10 Servicing Integral-Carrier Differentials

Many late-model cars use a rear-axle assembly from which the differential carrier cannot be removed. Ford calls this type of rear axle an integral-carrier axle, while Buick calls it a Salisbury-type axle housing. This rear-axle housing is made by pressing and welding tubes (which then become the axle housing) into each side of the differential carrier (Fig. 26). A stamped bolt-on cover is used, and the filler plug is threaded into the front part of the carrier casting (Fig. 26). Usually, the differential can be serviced without removing the axle housing from the car.

To remove the differential case and bearings for service, first remove the axle shafts (see ■4-6-3). Check the ring-gear-to-pinion backlash. Then mark and remove the differential side-bearing caps. Pull the differential case from the carrier (Fig. 27). Some manufacturers recommend the use of a special slide hammer to pull the case.

Remove the companion-flange nut and companion flange. Drive out the pinion gear (Fig. 28). Cleaning, inspection, and service procedures on the ring gear, pinion gear, and case assembly generally follow those covered in ■4-6-6. However, always refer to the applicable shop manual before attempting to service a specific make and model of differential.

To assemble an integral-carrier differential, install the pinion gear, following the procedure in the manufacturer's shop manual for adjusting pinion depth. Then, before installing the pinion in the carrier, install the case and make the differential-side-bearing-preload adjustment. Some integral-carrier differentials use adjusters. In integral-carrier differentials that do not use adjusters, the differential-side-bearing preload is adjusted by changing the thickness of the right and left shims (Fig. 27).

PART 5 Automatic Transmissions

SECTION 5-1 Automatic-Transmission Fundamentals

This section discusses the fundamentals of automatic-transmission action. Later sections describe specific models and makes of automatic transmissions.

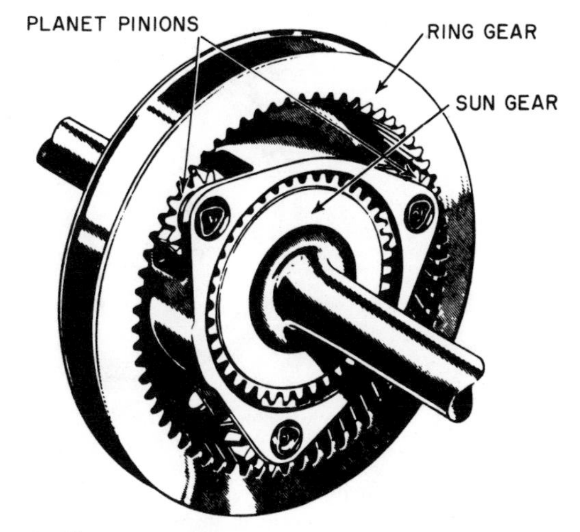

Figure 1 Planetary gearset.

■ **5-1-1 Automatic Transmissions** Automatic transmissions do the job of shifting gears without assistance from the driver. They start out in low as the car begins to move forward. Then they shift from low gear into intermediate (where present) and then high gear as the car picks up speed. The actions are produced hydraulically, that is, by oil pressure.

There are two basic parts to the automatic transmission: the torque converter and the gear system. The torque converter passes the engine power to the gear system, that is, to the planetary-gear system (Figs. 1 and 2).

Although there are several variations of automatic transmissions, all work in the same general manner. All have selector levers on the steering column or console, or buttons on the steering column or instrument panel. In some automatic transmissions, there are five selector-lever positions: P (park), R (reverse), N (neutral), D (drive), and L (low). In addition, most transmissions have a second D position so that there are D1 and D2 positions (D2 is called S, or super range). In P, the transmission is locked up so that the car cannot move. In N, no power flows through the transmission but the locking effect is off. In L, there is a gear reduction through the transmission, which provides extra torque at the wheels for a hard pull or for braking when going down a long hill. In the D position (or positions), the transmission automatically shifts up or down according to car speed and throttle position. All these positions are covered on later pages.

Some automatic transmissions have a select-shift feature which enables the driver to select the desired gear. The transmission will then stay in this gear until the driver manually shifts out of it.

■ **5-1-2 Planetary Gears in Automatic Transmissions** Planetary gears (Fig. 1) consist of a ring gear, a sun gear, and planet pinions held in a planet-pinion carrier. Some automatic-transmission planetary gears are compound planetary gears. These are discussed later. They consist of a sun gear, two sets of planetary gears with carriers, and two ring gears.

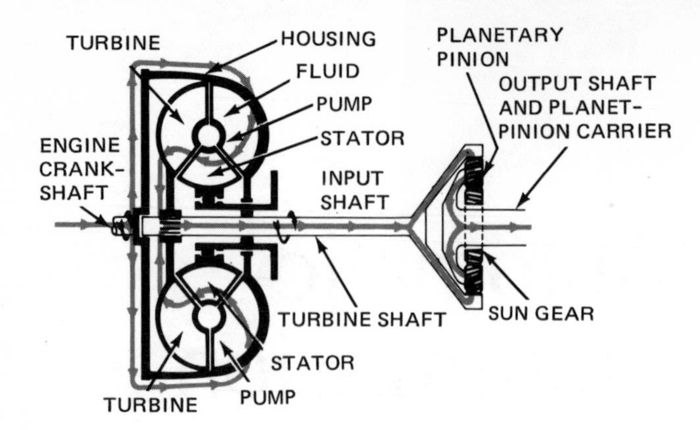

Figure 2 Power flow through the torque converter to the planetary gears.

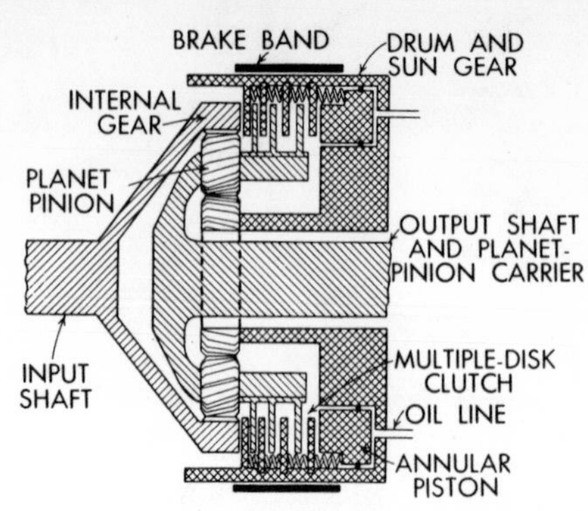

Figure 3 Schematic sectional view of the two controlling mechanisms used in the front planetary gearset in one model of automatic transmission. One controlling mechanism consists of a brake drum and brake band; the other is a multiple-disk clutch.

Holding one of the three members of the simple planetary gearset (sun gear, planet-pinion cage, or ring gear) stationary turns the assembly into a speed-reducing or speed-increasing unit (according to which member is held stationary). Also, locking up two of the members together produces direct drive through the gearset. In addition, if the planet-pinion cage is held stationary and the ring gear or sun gear is turned, the planet pinions act as reverse-idler gears. The direction of rotation is reversed through the gearset. These, briefly, are the three actions of the planetary gears in the automatic transmission. They produce either gear reduction, direct drive, or reverse.

Figure 2 shows one arrangement for carrying the power flow from the torque converter into the planetary gears. This is only one of three possible arrangements. The power can flow to the ring gear, the carrier, or the sun gear.

■ 5-1-3 Planetary-Gear-System Control

Holding one member of the planetary-gear system stationary can produce gear reduction or reverse. Also, locking up two members can produce direct drive. Now let us examine the means used to hold one or another of the members stationary and lock two members together to establish a 1 : 1 gear ratio (both input and output shafts turning at the same speed) through the system.

Figure 3 illustrates the two mechanisms used in a planetary-gear system to achieve the various conditions: a multiple-plate clutch and a brake band and brake drum. Note that the input shaft has the internal gear (ring gear) on it, and the planet-pinion cage (or carrier) is attached to the output shaft. The sun gear is separately mounted, as it has a brake drum as part of the sun-gear assembly. The sun gear and the brake drum turn together as a unit.

The brake band is operated by a servo, as shown in Fig. 4. The servo consists of two pistons on a single stem (or rod) all mounted in a cylinder and linked to the brake band positioned around the brake drum. Without pressure on either side of the servo pistons, the spring force holds the brake band away from the brake drum. The sun gear is, therefore, not held stationary. However, under the proper operating conditions, oil under pressure is admitted to the left part of the cylinder, as shown in

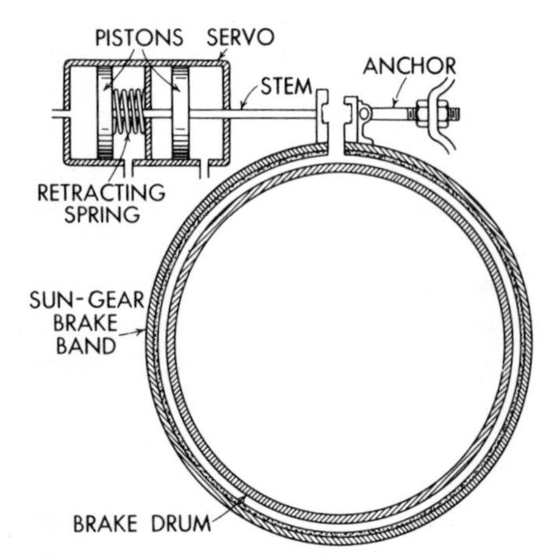

Figure 4 Arrangement of the servo, brake band, and brake drum.

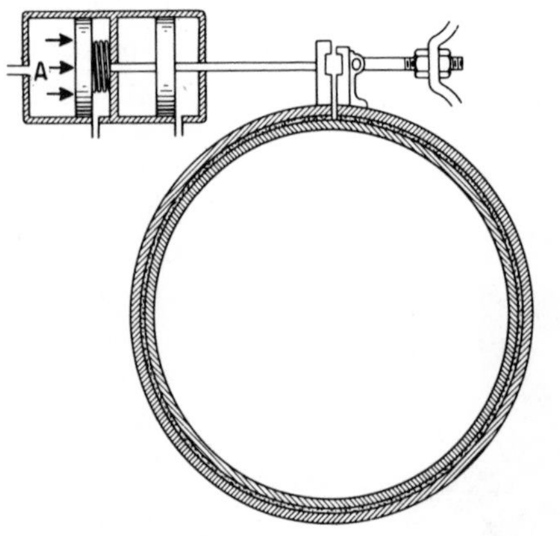

Figure 5 When hydraulic pressure is applied behind the piston at *A*, the piston and rod move to the right (in the illustration) to cause the band to tighten on the drum. The brake drum (and sun gear) is held stationary.

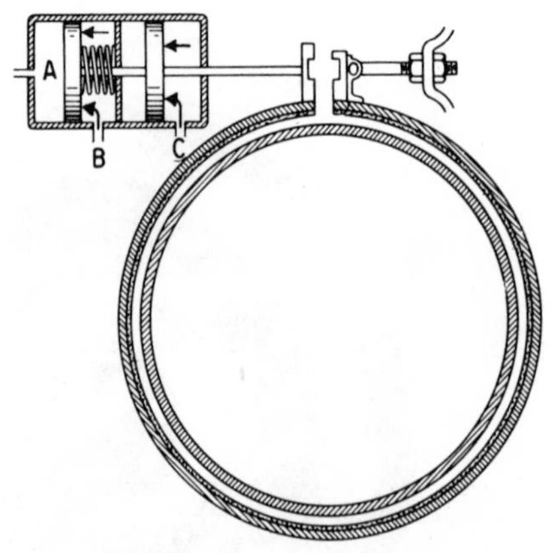

Figure 6 When the hydraulic control system admits oil under pressure at *B* and *C*, the pressure forces the pistons to the left (in the illustration). This action causes the band to release the drum and sun gear so that the sun gear can rotate.

Fig. 5, forcing the piston to the right. This action compresses the spring and tightens the brake band on the drum, thus bringing the drum and the sun gear to a halt. The sun gear is, therefore, held stationary. With the ring gear turned and the sun gear held stationary, there is speed reduction, or gear reduction, through the system.

NOTE: The arrangement described here (the brake band holding the sun gear stationary) is only one of several arrangements used in automatic transmissions. In some transmissions, when the brake band is applied, it holds the ring gear or the planet-pinion carrier stationary. Different transmissions may lock different members together when the clutch is applied. The principle is the same in all transmissions, however. There is gear reduction when the band is applied, and there is direct drive when the clutch is applied. Note also that in some transmissions the brake-band function is taken over by another clutch.

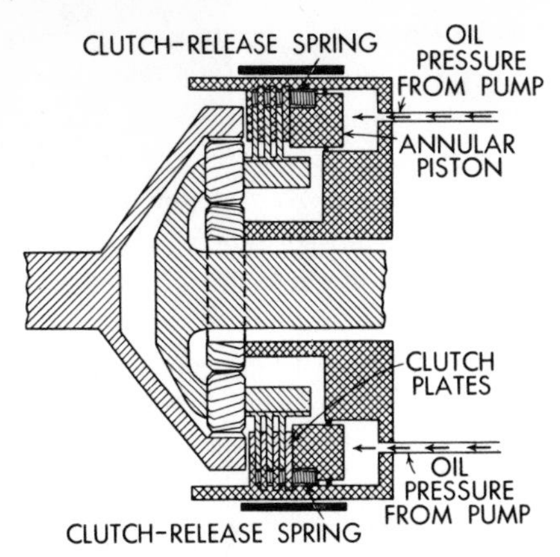

Figure 7 One set of clutch plates is splined to the sun-gear drums. The other set is splined to the planet-pinion carrier. When the hydraulic control system directs oil behind the annular piston, as shown by the arrows, the clutch plates are forced together so that the sun gear and planet-pinion carrier are locked together.

Under certain other conditions, the brake band must be released. This action takes place when the hydraulic control system directs oil into the right-hand chambers of the servo cylinder. This forces the pistons to move to the left (Fig. 6). At the same time, the clutch is actuated so as to lock the sun gear and planet-pinion cage together. The clutch consists of a series of clutch plates alternately splined to the cage and to the inner face of the brake drum. When the clutch is disengaged, these plates are held apart. However, simultaneously with the releasing of the brake band, as explained above, oil is directed into the chamber back of the annular (ring-like) piston in the brake-drum-sun-gear assembly. This action forces the piston to the left (Fig. 7) so that the clutch plates are forced together. Then, friction between the plates locks the sun gear and planet-pinion cage together. When this happens, the planetary-gear system acts like a direct-drive coupling, and both the input and output shafts turn at the same speed (1:1 gear ratio).

To achieve reverse in the planetary-gear system shown in Figs. 1 to 7, it would be necessary to hold the planet-pinion cage stationary and allow both the ring gear (on the input shaft) and the sun gear and drum to rotate. With this arrangement, the sun gear would rotate in reverse. Actually, more complex arrangements are used in automatic transmissions.

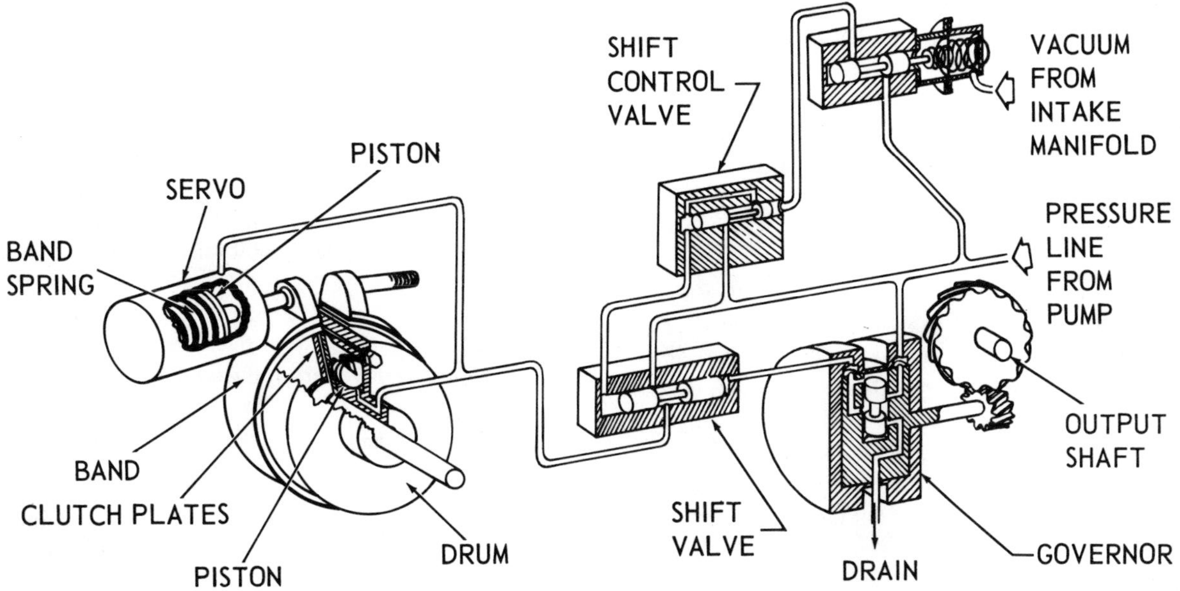

Figure 8 Schematic diagram of the hydraulic control system for the band servo and clutch. In the system shown, the band is normally on, and the clutch off; this arrangement produces gear reduction. But when the shift valve is moved, pressure from the oil pump is admitted to the front of the band piston and to the clutch piston. This movement causes the band to release and the clutch to apply. Now, with the clutch locking two planetary members together, the planetary system goes into direct drive.

■ **5-1-4 Shift Control** Figure 8 is a simplified diagram of a hydraulic control circuit for a single planetary gearset in an automatic transmission. Later we shall look at the circuits for automatic transmissions that use two or more planetary gearsets. As we have noted, automatic transmissions use more than one planetary gearset.

The major purpose of the hydraulic circuit is to control the shift from gear reduction to direct drive. The shift must take place at the right time, and this depends on car speed and throttle opening. These two factors produce two varying oil pressures that work against the two ends of the shift valve.

The shift valve is a spool valve inside a bore, or hole, in the valve body. Figure 9 shows the spool valve. Pressure at one end of the spool valve comes from the governor.

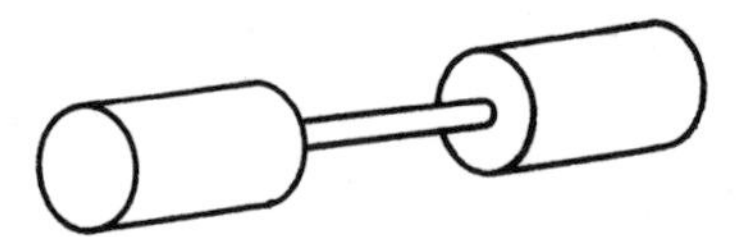

Figure 9 Spool valve for a shift valve.

> **NOTE:** A governor is a device that controls, or governs, another device. In the hydraulic circuit, the governor controls pressure on one end of the shift valve.

Pressure at the other end of the spool valve changes as vacuum in the intake manifold changes. Let us explain. First, the governor pressure changes with car speed. The governor is driven from the transmission by the output shaft. As output-shaft speed and car speed increase, the governor pressure increases proportionally. This pressure works against the right end of the shift valve, as shown in Fig. 8.

The governor pressure is actually a modified line pressure. That is, a pump in the transmission produces the line pressure. This line pressure passes into the governor. The governor then releases part of the pressure to the right end of the shift valve. The higher the car speed, the more pressure released by the governor. It is this modified pressure, the governor pressure, that works on one end of the shift valve.

Working on the left end of the shift valve is a pressure that changes as intake-manifold vacuum changes. Line pressure enters the modulator valve at the upper right in Fig. 8. The modulator valve contains a spool valve attached to a spring-loaded diaphragm. Vacuum increases in the intake manifold when the throttle is partly closed. This vacuum pulls the diaphragm in and moves the modulator spool valve to the right. The motion cuts off the line pressure going to the shift-control valve. When this happens, the shift-control valve moves to the right, cutting off pressure from the left end of the shift valve. This means that the shift valve is pushed to the left by the governor pressure. As a result, line pressure can pass through the shift valve. Therefore, line pressure is applied to the clutch and servo at the planetary gearset. With this condition, the band is released and the clutch is applied. This puts the planetary gearset into direct drive.

1. SHIFT ACTION Now let's see how the hydraulic control circuit works. To start with, there is no pressure going to the planetary-gear controls. The clutch is released, and the band is applied by the heavy spring in the servo.

> **NOTE:** Figure 8 is a simplified version of the actual system found in modern automatic transmissions. In modern transmissions oil pressure is used to help the spring hold the band tight. However, the basic principles are as shown in Fig. 8.

With the clutch released and the band applied, the planetary gearset is in gear reduction or low. As car speed increases, the governor releases more and more pressure. This pressure is applied to one end of the shift valve, as mentioned. The pressure on the other end of the shift valve depends on intake-manifold vacuum, that is, on engine speed plus throttle opening. As long as the throttle is held open, there is little manifold vacuum. The pressure on the left end of the shift valve is high. This high pressure holds the planetary gearset in low for good acceleration. However, as car speed continues to increase, the governor pressure becomes great enough to push the shift valve to the left. This lets line pressure through to the planetary gearset. Now the band is released and the clutch is applied. This shifts the planetary gearset into direct drive.

The upshift will also take place if the throttle is partly closed after the car reaches intermediate speed. Closing the throttle increases the intake-manifold vacuum. The vacuum cuts off line pressure to the shift-control valve. When this happens, the shift-control valve moves to the right, cutting off pressure to the left end of the shift valve. The shift valve then moves to the left, pushed by governor pressure. This applies line pressure to the planetary gearset. The clutch applies and the band releases. Now the planetary geatset shifts into direct drive.

There is a reason for this roundabout way of getting pressure to the left end of the shift valve. It is to vary the point of upshift according to driving conditions. When the vehicle is accelerating, the driver wants high engine torque. The gears must stay in low. Then, when the vehicle reaches the desired cruising speed, less torque is needed, and so the driver eases up on the throttle. This action increases the intake-manifold vacuum so that the upshift takes place. As you can see, the upshift can take place at any speed from medium to high. Also, for fast acceleration, the driver opens the throttle. This action reduces the intake-manifold vacuum. As a result, the planetary gearset drops into gear reduction to increase torque.

2. OTHER VALVES The preceding discussion is a very simplified description of how the upshifting is accomplished. The actual valves are more complicated, having springs for initial loading of the valves. There are other valves besides the ones mentioned to ease the shifts, regulate pressures, time downshifts, and so on. There is also a manual-shift valve.

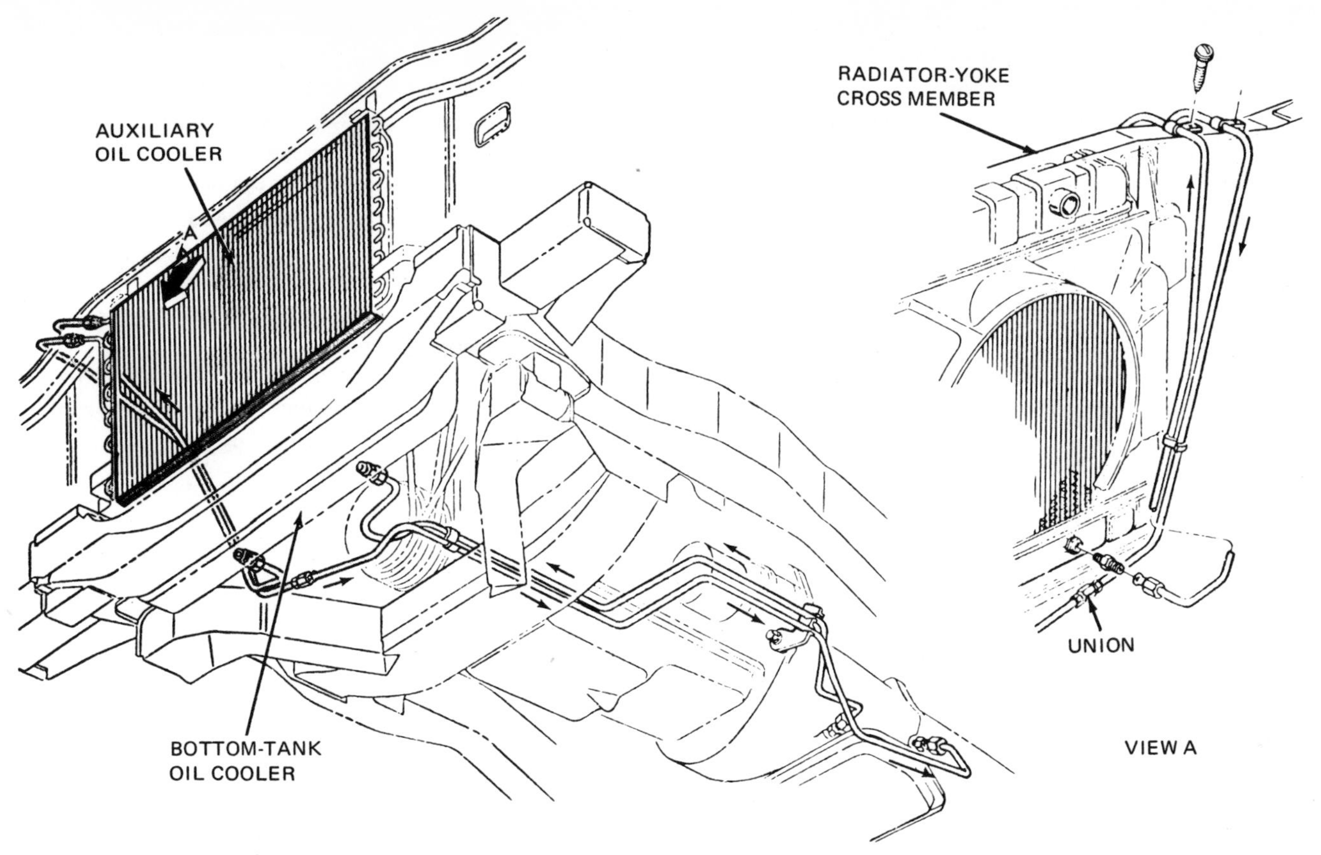

Figure 10 Two views of the connections of the tubes from the transmission to the oil cooler in the bottom tank of the cooling-system radiator. *(Chrysler Corporation.)*

3. MANUAL-SHIFT VALUE The manual-shift valve is controlled by the driver by movement of a shift lever on the steering column or console. As the manual valve is moved, it opens or closes various lines that direct oil pressure to the valves in the transmissions. For example, when the valve is moved to D, or drive, oil pressure is directed to the transmission valves so that they are ready to shift into D whenever the speed and throttle conditions are right. (This action has already been discussed in previous paragraphs.) If the manual-shift valve is placed in L, or low, the oil pressure is directed to the valves so that the modulator valve is blocked from producing an upshift.

■ 5-1-5 Transmission Fluid

We have used the term "oil" throughout our discussion of transmission operation. Transmission fluid could be considered a form of oil, but it is a very special sort of oil. Transmission fluid has several additives, such as viscosity-index improvers, oxidation and corrosion inhibitors, extreme-pressure and antifoam agents, detergents, dispersants, friction modifiers, pour-point depressants, and fluidity modifiers. The oil is dyed red so that it will not be confused with other automotive lubricants. Also, if leakage occurs, it is easy to tell whether it is engine oil or transmission fluid that is leaking.

NOTE: It is extremely important to use the proper transmission fluid recommended by the automobile manufacturer. Use of a transmission fluid that is not on the recommended list can cause serious transmission trouble.

■ 5-1-6 Transmission-Fluid Coolers

Transmission fluid may become very hot, especially under severe operating conditions. Thus, cars are equipped with transmission-fluid

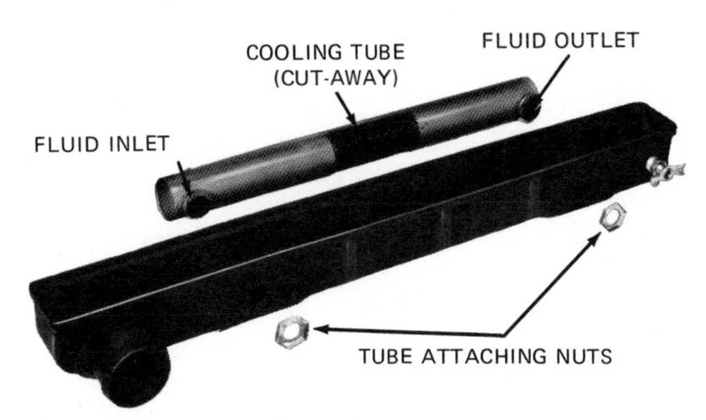

Figure 11 Lower tank of the radiator and oil-cooler tube, showing how the tube fits into the lower tank. *(Chrysler Corporation.)*

coolers, as shown in Figs. 10 and 11. The transmission fluid circulates through a tube located in the engine-cooling-system radiator. Heat from the transmission fluid passes to the coolant circulating through the engine cooling system. This process cools the transmission fluid. In addition, a vehicle used for towing or trailering is frequently equipped with an auxiliary transmission fluid cooler.

■ 5-1-7 Automatic-Transmission Variations A basic automatic-transmission model may be used, with small variations, with a variety of engines and automobiles. The operation of the clutches and brake bands in a transmission is due to hydraulic pressure. The timing and amount of pressure can be changed by changing valve spring, hydraulic connections, and servos. In this way, a basic model can be adapted to suit a particular engine and automobile. In other words, the planetary-gear system, clutches, and brake bands can remain essentially the same. But valves and other components of the hydraulic system can be altered to suit engine requirements. For example, when the transmission is used with one engine, the shift points might be designed to be on the high side. But with another engine having a different torque output curve, best car operation might require that the transmission shift at a somewhat lower speed.

Also, the clutches may differ with different engines. For example, with a high-output engine, the transmission clutches may have more plates for greater holding power to handle the higher engine outputs.

SECTION 5-2

General Service Instructions on Automatic Transmissions

In this section, we outline the general servicing instructions that apply to all automatic transmissions. All automatic transmissions work in a similar way. All have planetary gearsets, torque converters, brake bands, clutches, and hydraulic systems. Valves, accumulators, oil pumps, and other parts are similar in all automatic transmissions. However, the basic construction of the various automatic transmissions differs in many details, as do the arrangements of the bands and clutches. This means that the servicing procedures also differ. In following sections, therefore, we describe the servicing procedures that apply to specific automatic transmission models. There are several basic procedures, however, that apply, in general, to all models. These general instructions are the subject of this section.

■ **5-2-1 Towing Instructions** Never tow a car equipped with the automatic transmission in any driving range. If it is necessary to tow a disabled car with its rear wheels on the ground, make sure the transmission, drive line, and differential are okay. Shift the lever into N (neutral) and drive slowly. Manufacturers specify the maximum distance and speed it is safe to drive under these conditions. A typical specification is 50 miles (80 km) and 35 mph (56 km/h). Exceeding these specifications can ruin the transmission.

If the transmission is damaged, or if the distance the car must be towed exceeds the maximum allowable, disconnect the drive shaft. An alternative is to tow the car on its front wheels. In this case, the steering wheel must be secured in the straight-ahead position. However, if the ignition key is not available (on late-model cars which lock the steering wheel and shift lever when the key is removed), you will have to tow the car with the front wheels on a dolly and the rear wheels hoisted.

NOTE: Prior to about 1966, it was possible to push-start some cars with automatic transmissions. These transmissions had rear pumps which operated when the rear wheels turned so as to provide pressure and lubrication to the transmission parts. Thus, when the car was being pushed, the transmission would back-drive the engine, and so push-starting would work. However, late-model automatic transmissions do not have rear pumps and cannot be push-started.

■ **5-2-2 Operating Cautions** For mountain driving, either with heavy loads or when pulling a trailer, use second or low when on upgrades requiring a heavy throttle for more than ½ mile (0.8 km). This reduces the possibility that the transmission or converter will overheat and also eases the load on the engine.

■ 5-2-3 General Servicing Instructions

All manufacturers supply instructions on checking fluid level and adding fluid, and making adjustments to the transmission and linkage. Some manufacturers recommend periodic fluid changes, others say that no fluid change is necessary except if the transmission is overhauled, or if the car is in exceptionally heavy service. Disassembly and reassembly procedures vary from model to model. However, transmission-service precautions, cleaning and inspection of transmission assemblies are similar in all models. In this present section we cover these general instructions. Following sections discuss servicing procedures for specific models.

■ 5-2-4 Fluid Changes

Some manufacturers recommend changing the fluid periodically. Others say no change is ever necessary with a certain qualification. This is: If the vehicle is used in heavy service (police car, taxicab, pulling a trailer), then the fluid should be changed periodically. Table 1 lists the recommendations for various automatic transmissions.

Table 1 Automatic transmission fluid change intervals

Transmission	Check fluid, miles	Change fluid—regular service, miles	Change fluid—severe service, miles
Powerglide	6,000	24,000	12,000
Borg-Warner	12,000	24,000	12,000
GM Type 350	7,500	60,000	15,000
GM Type 400	7,500	60,000	15,000
TorqueFlite	Every 6 months	Not recommended	24,000
Ford (all)	Occasionally	Not required	22,500

■ 5-2-5 General Cautions on Fluid Checks and Changes

There are certain precautions to observe when changing or adding transmission fluid.

1. Use only the transmission fluid recommended by the manufacturer. Use of the wrong fluid can cause complete transmission failure.

2. Do not overfill. If the fluid level is checked with the transmission cold, chances are the dipstick will show low fluid. However, this is normal because the fluid level will rise as it reaches operating temperature. If the fluid level is too high, the planetary gears will run in the fluid, causing the fluid to aerate and foam. This will produce loss of drive, improper clutch and band application, and overheating of the transmission. In addition, fluid can be lost through the vent. The result could be transmission failure. So don't overfill!

3. The old fluid should be drained with the transmission hot. This gets out any substances that may have formed owing to deterioration of the fluid. Remember that the fluid can be very hot—up to 350°F (177°C).

4. Mechanics often check the color of the transmission fluid and smell it to get an idea of whether the fluid has been overheated and there is trouble inside the transmission. The older type of transmission fluid would turn darker and take on a strong odor from overheating and transmission damage. However, the newer type of fluid can darken and take on an odor without this meaning there has been overheating or damage.

5. If the oil has been contaminated by a transmission failure, the torque converter must be flushed out after draining. This requires removal of the converter so it can be laid on its side. Then 2 quarts (1.9 liters) of solvent or kerosine is poured into it. The converter should then be shaken and the turbine and stator rotated. Special tools are available to assist in this operation. The solvent or kerosine should then be drained out. This procedure should be repeated at least once more.

> **NOTE:** Some manufacturers say that if serious internal damage has occurred, as for example a clutch failure, it will be impossible to flush out all the debris. The torque converter will have to be replaced.

■ 5-2-6 Checking Fluid Level

Check the fluid level with the car on level ground. Start the engine and run it at fast idle until it reaches operating temperature. Then put your foot on the brake and shift the selector lever through all positions, finally returning it to PARK. Then remove the dipstick to check fluid level. If it is too low, add enough fluid to bring the level to the full mark on the dipstick.

■ 5-2-7 Changing Fluid

Raise the car on a hoist and position a container to catch the draining fluid. Remove the oil pan and gasket. Throw away the gasket. Drain the fluid from the oil pan. Clean the oil pan with solvent and dry it with compressed air.

Remove the filter or strainer, discarding the filter gasket, if present. Clean strainers with solvent and dry with compressed air. Install a new filter on transmissions using filters.

On those models having an intake pipe, remove and discard the old O-ring seal. Install an O-ring seal on reassembly.

Install a new filter or strainer gasket and install the cleaned strainer or new filter. Put a new gasket on the oil pan and install the oil pan, torquing the attaching bolts to the specified tension.

Lower the car and add the specified quantity of transmission fluid through the filler pipe. Start the engine and with it running at fast idle, move the selector lever through each range, returning it to park. Check the fluid level as previously described. Add fluid if necessary.

■ 5-2-8 Transmission Service Precautions

Cleanliness is of the upmost importance in transmission work. The slightest, almost invisible, piece of dirt or lint from a cleaning rag can cause a valve to hang up and prevent normal transmission action. Under some conditions, this situation could cause serious damage to the transmission. Other things to watch out for include:

1. Never mix parts between transmissions. Keep all parts belonging to the transmission you are working on in one place so that they will not get mixed with parts from another transmission.

2. Clean the outside of the transmission thoroughly before starting to work on it. One recommendation is to plug all openings and use steam to clean the transmission.

3. The workbench, tools, your hands, and all parts must be kept clean at all times. Do not allow dust to blow in from outside or from other shop areas and settle on the transmission parts. Keep them covered with a clean cloth when you are away from the workbench for any length of time.

4. Before installing screws into aluminum parts such as the case, dip the screws in transmission fluid to lubricate them. This prevents their galling the threads and seizing.

5. If the threads in an aluminum part are stripped, repair can be made with a Heli-Coil, or similar device, as shown in Fig. 1. First, the hole is drilled and then tapped with a special Heli-Coil tap. Finally, a Heli-Coil is installed to bring the hole back to its original thread size.

6. Special care and special tools must be used to protect the seals during the assembly procedure to prevent damage to the seals. The slightest flaw in a seal or a sealing surface can result in an oil leak and transmission trouble.

7. The aluminum case and other parts are relatively soft and can be easily scratched, nicked, or burred. Use great care in handling them.

8. Discard all old O sealing rings, gaskets, and oil seals that are removed, and use new ones on reassembly.

9. During disassembly, clean and inspect all parts as explained in the following paragraphs.

10. During reassembly, lubricate all internal parts with transmission fluid.

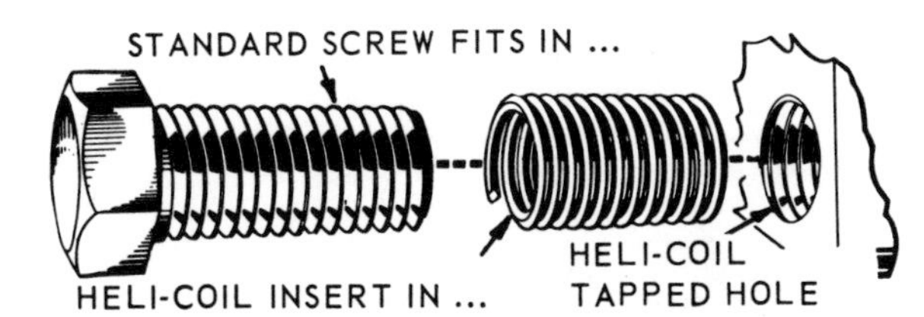

Figure 1 Heli-Coil installation. *(Chrysler Corporation.)*

■ 5-2-9 Cleaning and Inspecting Transmission Parts

As parts are removed from the transmission, clean and inspect them as explained below. Wash all metal parts in solvent and blow them dry with compressed air. Do not use solvents that could damage clutch facings. Never wipe parts with shop cloths or paper because these could leave lint that could cause transmission trouble. Check small passages with small wire such as tag wire. Inspect parts as follows:

1. Check linkage and pivot points for excessive wear.

2. Check bearing and thrust faces for wear and scoring.

3. Check mating surfaces of castings and end plates for burrs or irregularities that could cause poor seating and oil leaks. To remove burrs, lay a piece of crocus cloth on a very flat surface such as a piece of glass. Then put the part to be worked on on the crocus cloth, flat surface down. Move the part back and forth in a figure-8 pattern. This procedure is called *lapping* and will bring the metal to a smooth finish. Clean the part of all grit and filings.

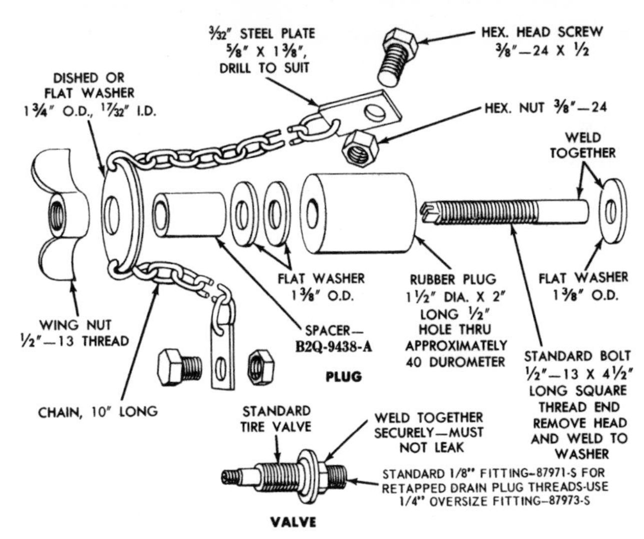

Figure 2 Special tools needed to check the converter for leakage. *(Ford Motor Company.)*

4. Check for damaged grooves or lands where O-rings seat. Irregularities here can cause serious oil leaks.

5. Check castings for cracks and sand holes and for damaged threads. Thread repairs can often be made with Heli-Coils, as already noted and shown in Fig. 2.

6. Check gear teeth for chipping, scores, or wear.

7. Make sure valves are free of burrs and that the shoulders are square and sharp. Burrs can be removed from bores by honing. Valves must slide freely in the bores.

8. Check the facings on composition clutch plates for damaged surfaces and loose facings. If you can remove flakes of facing with your thumbnail or if the plates look scored, worn, or burned, replace the plates. Some discoloration is normal, however, and is not a sign of failure.

9. Inspect springs for distortion or collapsed coils.

10. Check bushings and test for wear by inserting the mating parts into the bushings and noting the amount of looseness. Worn, scored, or galled bushings should be replaced. You will need special tools to remove and replace bushings.

11. If the transmission shows evidence that foreign material has been circulating in the fluid, all the old fluid must be removed from the transmission, torque converter, and oil cooler. All parts must be cleaned and the oil cooler, oil-cooler lines, and torque converter must be flushed out.[1] Install a new filter on reassembly.

[1] If clutch failure has occurred, most manufacturers recommend replacement of the torque converter. The old converter probably contains so much debris that it cannot be flushed out.

■ 5-2-10 Transmission Removal

A typical procedure for removing an automatic transmission from a car follows. The procedure may vary somewhat from car to car because of individual differences in engine and accessory mounting arrangements.

1. Raise vehicle on hoist and remove drain plug to drain oil. Draining the oil can also be done after the transmission is removed.

2. Disconnect oil-cooler lines (where present), the vacuum-modulator line, and the speedometer drive cable, and tie the lines up out of the way.

3. Disconnect the manual and TV (throttle valve) control-lever rods from the transmission.

4. Scribe marks on the universal joint so it can be reattached in the same relationship. Disconnect the drive shaft from the transmission.

5. Put the transmission jack in position under the transmission.

6. Disconnect the engine rear mount from the extension housing. Disconnect the transmission-support cross member and slide it rearward.

7. Remove the converter underpan. Mark the flywheel and converter so that they can be reattached in the same relationship. Remove the flywheel-to-converter attaching bolts.

8. Support the engine at the oil-pan rail with a jack or other suitable brace capable of supporting the engine when the transmission is removed.

9. Lower the rear of the transmission slightly so that the upper transmission-housing-to-engine attaching bolts can be reached. Remove upper bolts.

> **NOTE:** On V-8 engines, do not lower the engine too far or the distributor may be forced against the fire wall and damaged. Have an assistant topside to watch.

10. Remove the rest of the transmission-housing-to-engine attaching bolts.

11. Move the transmission to the rear and downward to remove it from the car. Mount the transmission on a repair fixture to work on it.

> **NOTE:** Watch the converter when moving the transmission rearward. If the converter does not move, gently pry it loose from the flywheel.

Keep the front end of the transmission up to prevent the converter from falling off. Install a C clamp or similar tool to prevent the converter from falling off the transmission while moving it from the car to the repair fixture.

■ 5-2-11 Disassembly Procedures

The procedures required to disassemble automatic transmissions vary from one model to another. Following sections of the Handbook describe typical disassembly procedures. Disassembly procedures are also to be found in the manufacturer's manuals.

When you are disassembling an automatic transmission, carefully note the exact location of each part you remove. Make notes and rough sketches if you are not sure you can remember. If you do this, and follow the general disassembly and reassembly procedures, you should have no trouble putting the transmission back together again.

■ 5-2-12 Transmission Tests

Different manufacturers call for different tests of their transmissions. For example, Ford and Chrysler shop manuals call for stall testing their transmissions. This is a test for slippage. General Motors does not recommend stall testing their transmissions.

Some manufacturers call for testing the operation of clutches by applying air to the appropriate holes in the assemblies. These and other tests are covered in following sections.

■ 5-2-13 Converter Test

Manufacturers recommend testing the torque converter, while it is removed from

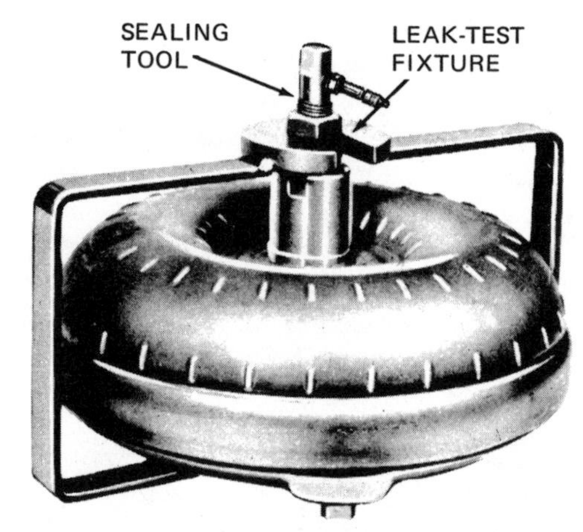

Figure 3 Setup to check the converter for leaks. *(Oldsmobile Division of General Motors Corporation.)*

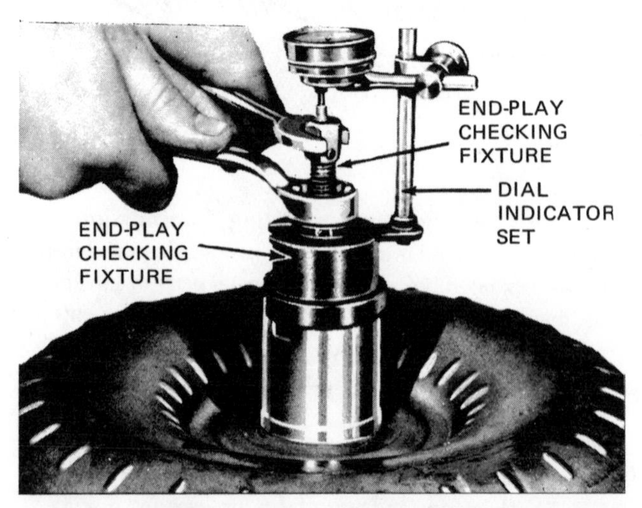

Figure 4 Test setup to check converter end play. *(Oldsmobile Division of General Motors Corporation.)*

the vehicle, for leakage and for end play. To check it for leakage, it must be sealed and air pressure applied. Tools to seal one model of torque converter are shown in Fig. 2. Note that the tools include a standard tire valve, especially prepared to fit with the tools so that air pressure can be applied to the torque converter. Figure 3 shows a torque converter sealed for the test.

After the converter is sealed, air pressure is applied. Different manufacturers recommend different pressures. Ford says 20 psi (1.406 kg/cm²). Oldsmobile (typical of General Motors) recommends 80 psi (5.625 kg/cm²).

The converter is then submerged in water to see if there are any leaks. A leak would show itself as a flow of air bubbles from the converter. If the converter leaks, it should be discarded.

To check for end play, use a dial indicator and the special tools as shown in Fig. 4. Tighten the hex nut and zero the dial indicator. Loosen the hex nut and note the indicator reading. This is the end play and should not exceed the manufacturer's specifications. If the end play is excessive, the converter must be discarded.

■ **5-2-14 Transmission Installation** Mount the transmission on the transmission jack and remove the converter holding tool.

NOTE: Do not allow the converter to move forward after the tool is removed.

1. Raise the transmission into place at the rear of the engine and install the transmission-case-to-engine upper mounting bolts. Then install the rest of the mounting bolts, torquing them to the correct specifications.

2. Remove the support from under the engine and raise the rear of the transmission up to the final position. Align the scribe marks on the flywheel and converter cover. Install the attaching bolts and torque them to specifications.

3. Install the converter under the pan.

4. Reinstall the transmission-support cross member, if it has been removed, to the transmission and frame.

5. Remove the transmission jack.

6. Connect the drive shaft, aligning the scribe marks that had been made during transmission removal.

7. Connect the throttle and selector lever linkages.

8. Connect oil-cooler lines (if used), vacuum modulator line, and speedometer cable to the transmission.

9. Refill the transmission with the proper amount of fluid, following the procedure outlined previously.

10. Make sure the starting motor will operate.

11. Check the transmission for proper operation. If necessary, adjust the linkages.

12. Lower the vehicle and remove it from the hoist.

SECTION 5-3 | Borg-Warner Three-Speed Automatic-Transmission Service

This section covers the trouble-diagnosis and service procedures for the Borg-Warner three-speed automatic transmission with a compound planetary gearset. The section is divided into three parts: "Normal Maintenance and Adjustments," "Trouble Diagnosis," and "Transmission Overhaul."

NORMAL MAINTENANCE AND ADJUSTMENTS

Refer to Part 5, Sec. 2, for procedures of checking and adding transmission fluid and towing instructions.

NOTE: Bands must be adjusted every time the transmission fluid is changed.

■ **5-3-1 Band Adjustments** The two brake bands must be adjusted as follows every time the fluid is changed, and also if transmission checks indicate the bands are not being applied correctly.

1. FRONT-BAND ADJUSTMENT The oil pan must be removed for front-band adjustment. Loosen the locknut (Fig. 1). Pivot the servo lever away from the servo and insert the

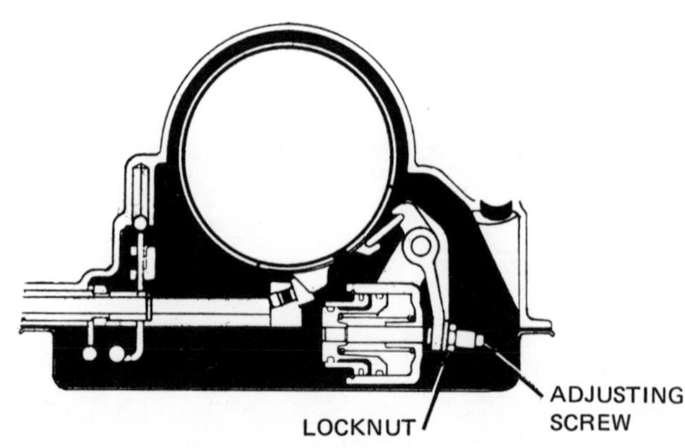

Figure 1 Adjustment of front band. *(Chrysler Corporation.)*

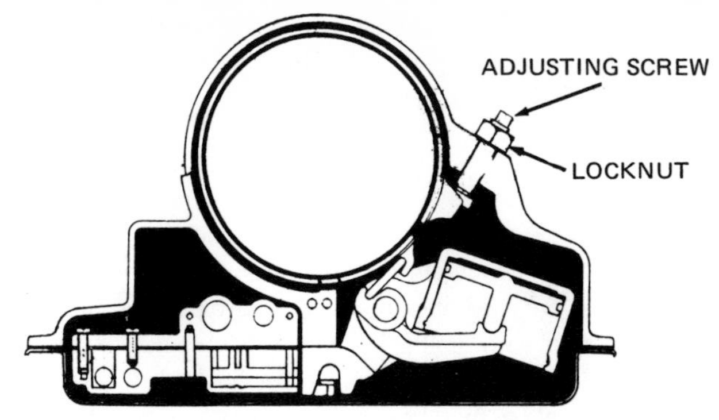

Figure 2 Adjustment of rear band. *(Chrysler Corporation.)*

special 0.250-inch (6.35-mm) gauge between the adjusting screw and the servo piston pin. Then, using the special adapter, spin the torque screw-driver to tighten the adjusting screw to the correct tension [10-pound-inches (11.5 kg-cm) torque for one model]. Tighten the locknut to the specified tension.

2. REAR-BAND ADJUSTMENT Rear-band adjustment (Fig. 2) is made by turning the adjusting screw located on the right-hand side of the outside wall of the transmission case. Loosen the locknut. Then, using the special socket tool, tighten the adjusting screw to the proper torque [10 pound-feet (1.38 kg-m)]. Then back off the adjusting screw ¾ turn. Tighten the locknut to the specified tension.

TROUBLE DIAGNOSIS

The chart and the list that follow will enable you to relate Borg-Warner transmission troubles with possible causes. The chart lists transmission trouble followed by numbers. The numbers refer to the list of possible trouble causes given after the chart.

■ 5-3-2 Transmission Troubles

After each trouble given in the following chart you will find a series of numbers. The numbers refer to the list of possible trouble causes. For example, "Rough engagement in R, D, or L" could be caused by conditions 1, 2, 3, 4, 5, 6, or 7 in the list.

BORG-WARNER TROUBLE-DIAGNOSIS CHART

TROUBLE	POSSIBLE-CAUSE NUMBER
Engagement Problems	
1. Rough engagement in R, D, or L	1, 2, 3, 4, 5, 6, 7
2. Delayed engagement in D and L	1, 3, 5, 6, 8, 9, 10, 11, 12, 13, 14
3. Delayed engagement in R	1, 3, 5, 7, 8, 9, 10, 11, 12, 13, 14, 15
4. No engagement	3, 5, 8, 9, 10, 11, 13, 16, 17, 18
5. No drive in forward direction	6, 8, 9, 11, 13, 18, 19
6. Dragging D and L engagement	6, 8, 11
Engagement Problems (continued)	
7. No drive in reverse	7, 8, 9, 11, 15
8. Transmission does not go into neutral	6
9. Car not held in P	20, 21
Upshift Problems	
10. No 1-2 upshift	5, 9, 10, 11, 22, 23, 24, 25, 26
11. No 2-3 upshift	7, 9, 10, 11, 25, 26, 27, 28, 29, 30
12. Too-high speed required to upshift	3, 5, 11, 22, 24, 25, 27, 28, 31
13. Upshift occurs at too-low speed	2, 4, 5, 11, 22, 28
Abnormal Upshifts	
14. Slipping in 1-2 upshift	2, 3, 4, 5, 8, 9, 10, 11, 22
15. Slipping in 2-3 upshift	2, 3, 4, 5, 7, 8, 9, 10, 11, 22
16. Shock in 1-2 upshift	2, 3, 4, 5, 6, 19, 22, 26, 32
17. Shock in 2-3 upshift	2, 3, 4, 5, 7, 22
18. Tied up in 1-2 upshift	5, 7, 11, 15, 19, 32
19. Tied up in 2-3 upshift	5, 10, 11, 22
Downshift Problems	
20. No 2-1 downshift	2, 15, 22, 24
21. No 3-2 downshift	2, 7, 22, 23, 24
22. Unexpected 3-2 downshift	7, 8, 10
23. Downshift at too-high speed	2, 5, 11, 23, 25, 28
24. Downshift at too-low speed	2, 5, 11, 24, 25, 27, 28
Abnormal Downshift	
25. Slipping in 2-1 down-shifting	32
26. Slipping in 3-2 down-shifting	3, 4, 5, 10, 11, 22, 28
27. Shock in 2-1 downshift	6, 11, 19
28. Shock in 3-2 downshift	3, 4, 5, 7, 22
Kickdown Problems	
29. No 3-2 kickdown	24, 27, 29, 30, 31
30. No 2-1 kickdown	24, 27, 29, 30
Reverse Problems	
31. Slipping or dragging	6, 7, 11, 15
32. Tied up in R	6, 11
Line-Pressure Problems	
33. Too low at idle	1, 2, 3, 5, 8, 9, 10, 11, 12, 13, 18
34. Too high at idle	1, 2, 3, 4, 33
35. Too low at stall	2, 3, 4, 5, 6, 8, 10, 11, 26
36. Too high at stall	3, 4, 5, 26
Engine Speed at Stall	
37. Too low	18
38. Too high in D position	3, 5, 6, 8, 9, 10, 11, 15, 16, 18, 19
39. Too high in R position	7, 8, 9, 15, 16, 18
Noises	
40. In neutral	6, 7, 13, 18
41. In parking position	6, 18
42. In all speed positions	13, 18, 34
43. In 1 and 2 only	6, 34

(continued)

BORG-WARNER TROUBLE-DIAGNOSIS CHART

TROUBLE	POSSIBLE-CAUSE NUMBER
Overheating	
44. Overheating	8, 15, 18, 22
Shifting Problems	
45. Selector lever operates roughly or hard	35, 36
46. Starter will not operate in N or P	37, 38, 39

■ **5-3-3 Possible Trouble Causes** The list that follows is related by numbers to the troubles listed in the chart. In every case, the cure of the trouble is obvious. You either make an adjustment, replace a part or an assembly, or tighten a screw or other part—whatever is required.

1. Engine speed wrong
2. Vacuum diaphragm maladjusted
3. Primary regulator inoperative
4. Throttle valve inoperative
5. Valve-body screw loose or missing
6. Front clutch malfunctioning—seized, slipping, etc.
7. Rear clutch malfunctioning—seized, slipping, etc.
8. Oil level low
9. Manual linkage improperly installed or out of adjustment
10. Oil tube not installed or installed incorrectly
11. Sealing ring not installed or damaged
12. Pump-check valve not installed or inoperative
13. Pump worn or damaged
14. Converter check valve not installed or inoperative
15. Rear band slipping, damaged, or worn, or servo defective
16. Input shaft defective
17. Converter-pump driving hub damaged
18. Converter defective
19. One-way clutch slipping or improperly installed
20. Parking linkage defective
21. Output shaft defective
22. Front band slipping, damaged, or worn, or servo defective
23. Governor valve inoperative
24. 1-2 shift valve inoperative
25. Throttle valve inoperative
26. Modulator valve inoperative
27. 2-3 shift valve inoperative
28. 2-3 shift-valve plunger inoperative
29. Kickdown switch faulty or connection defective
30. Kickdown solenoid, switch, or wiring faulty
31. Vacuum diaphragm maladjusted or faulty
32. One-way clutch seized
33. Secondary regulator valve inoperative
34. Planetary-gear assembly defective
35. Linkage maladjusted or worn
36. Detent worn
37. Neutral safety switch defective or maladjusted
38. Circuit defective
39. Interlock system inoperative

■ **5-3-4 Line-Pressure Check** To check the line pressure, make sure the engine is in good operating condition and at operating temperature. Attach an oil-pressure gauge to the transmission case after removing the pipe plug (Fig. 3). Install a vacuum gauge in the line to the vacuum diaphragm.

Set the selector lever at R. Apply the brakes and place blocks under the wheels so that the car does not move. The oil-gauge readings should be as noted in the specifications in the shop manual for the unit being serviced. If the line pressure is low, remove the vacuum-diaphragm hose and turn the adjusting screw clockwise (Fig. 3). If the line pressure is high, turn the adjusting screw counterclockwise. One turn of the screw changes the adjustment about 10 psi (0.703 kg/cm²). If you cannot get the correct line pressures, check the vacuum diaphragm (■ 5-3-5).

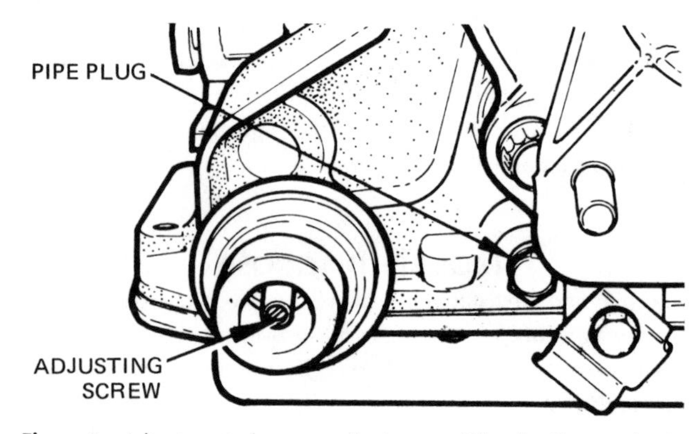

Figure 3 Adjustment of vacuum diaphragm. *(Chrysler Corporation.)*

If the oil pressure is normal in R, check the pressure in D and L with the throttle open just enough to give 12 inches (304.8 mm) of vacuum. If the oil pressure is low in D and L but normal in R, check for sticking or other troubles in the governor valve.

If the line pressure is normal in all ranges, but upshift takes place in D, the governor valve is probably sticking closed. Make a road test (or use a chassis dynamometer) to check the shifts.

■ **5-3-5 Vacuum-Diaphragm Check** If the pressure cannot be corrected by adjusting the vacuum diaphragm as explained in ■ 5-3-4, check the diaphragm further. Look for external damage. Remove the vacuum hose and check the hose and tube for oil or gasoline. If there is visible damage or if oil or gas is found, replace the vacuum diaphragm.

If the vacuum diaphragm looks okay, remove it and test it with a source of variable vacuum. Put the rod in place. Increase the vacuum slowly and note the movement of the rod. It must retract completely with a vacuum of 18 inches (457.2

mm). Next, clamp the vacuum hose to prevent escape of the vacuum in the diaphragm. The rod should remain stationary. Failure of the vacuum diaphragm in either of these tests indicates a leak, which requires replacement of the unit.

■ 5-4-6 Kickdown-Switch and Solenoid Checks

To check the kickdown switch, disconnect the lead wire from the solenoid terminal and connect a voltmeter from the lead clip to ground. With the ignition switch at ON and the engine not running, push the accelerator pedal to the floor. If the meter shows no voltage, then the switch requires adjusting or replacing.

To check the kickdown solenoid, use the following procedures:

1. NO 2-3 UPSHIFT Disconnect the lead to the solenoid and test the car either on the road or on a chassis dynamometer. If the 2-3 upshift now occurs, the kickdown switch is faulty. If no 2-3 upshift takes place, oil is probably leaking into the solenoid. Replace it.

2. NO FORCED DOWNSHIFT Disconnect the wire from the solenoid. Connect a jumper lead from the battery insulated terminal to the solenoid terminal. If the solenoid does not click, it is defective. If the solenoid does click, the trouble is in the switch or circuit to the solenoid.

■ 5-3-7 Torque-Converter Check

If the converter seems to be defective, check it in the following manner.

1. With the selector lever in L or D and blocks under the rear wheels of the car, apply the brakes and open the throttle fully. Check the stall speed of the converter with a tachometer.

> **NOTE:** Limit the stall check to not more than 10 seconds. Then return the selector lever to N to cool the transmission.

If the stall speed is 300 rpm below the specified value, there is trouble in the torque converter.

2. If the car has poor acceleration or fails to start up a steep slope, either the stator or the stator one-way clutch may be defective. The stator is probably turning backward, and so no torque multiplication results.

Check the stall speed and if it is about 600 rpm below specifications, replace the torque converter.

3. If the car has poor acceleration over 30 mph (48 km/h) and low top speed, chances are the stator one-way clutch is locked up, preventing the stator from freewheeling. Replace the torque converter.

4. If the stall speed is too high, the converter fluid may be low, or the clutches in the transmission may be slipping.

TRANSMISSION OVERHAUL

See Part 5, Sec. 2, for various precautions, cleaning and inspecting transmission parts, and removal procedures.

■ 5-3-8 Transmission Disassembly

In the following order, remove:

1. Vacuum tube and hose.
2. Torque converter. Be careful not to damage the oil-pump-driving finger, gear slot, and oil seals.
3. Converter housing.
4. Speedometer-driven-gear assembly and gasket.
5. The 15 oil-pan attaching bolts, loosening them in the numbered order shown in Fig 4. Then remove the oil pan.

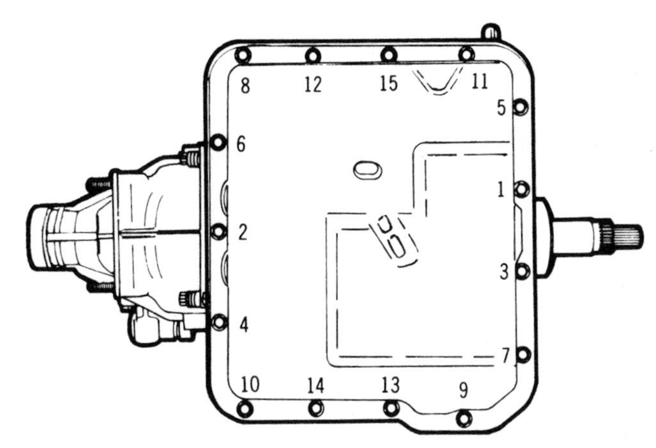

Figure 4 Order in which oil-pan attaching bolts should be loosened when the oil pan is removed. *(Chrysler Corporation.)*

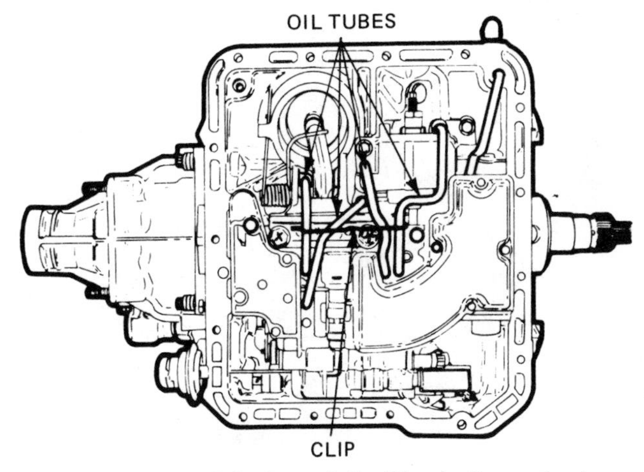

Figure 5 Locations of oil tubes and clip. *(Chrysler Corporation.)*

6. Oil-tube clip and four oil tubes (Fig. 5). If the tubes stick, pry them loose, being careful not to damage them or the transmission parts.
7. Magnet, vacuum diaphragm, and rod.
8. Kickdown wiring.
9. The three-valve-body bolts and valve body. Lift the valve body off carefully so that you do not damage the oil-feed tube.
10. Extension housing.
11. Oil pump. First measure the end play of the input shaft with a dial gauge or special tool and feeler gauge (Fig. 6). If the

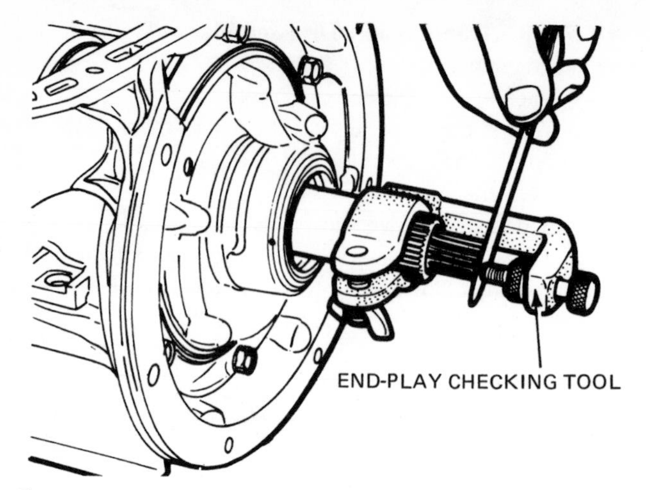

Figure 6 Measuring input-shaft end play. *(Chrysler Corporation.)*

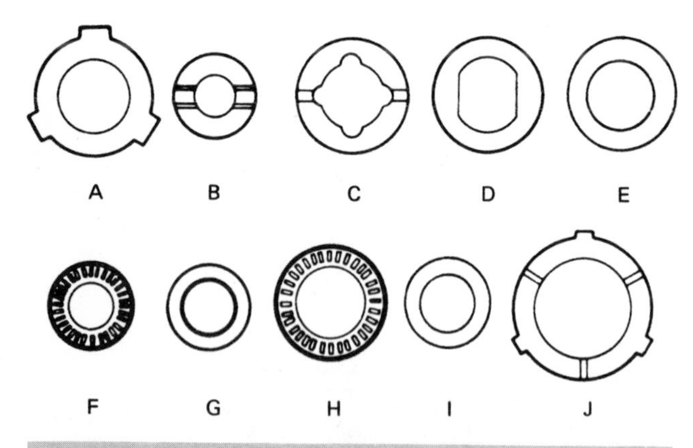

A. Input-shaft thrust washer (selective adjustment)—between pump adapter and converter support and input shaft
B. Front-clutch-hub thrust washer—between input shaft and front-clutch hub
C. Front-clutch-cylinder thrust washer (bronze)—between front-clutch cylinder and rear-clutch spring seat
D. Front-clutch-cylinder thrust washer (steel)—between front-clutch cylinder and rear-clutch spring seat
E. Thrust washer—between reverse sun gear and forward sun gear
F. Needle thrust bearing—between forward sun gear and planet cover
G. Needle-thrust-bearing plate—between forward sun gear and planet cover
H. Needle thrust bearing—between planet cover and output shaft
I. Needle-thrust-bearing plate—between planet cover and output shaft
J. Output-shaft thrust washer—between output shaft and transmission case

Figure 7 Types of thrust washers, thrust bearings, and plates. *(Chrysler Corporation.)*

end play is not correct [0.010 to 0.030 inch (0.25 to 0.76 mm)], replace the old input-shaft thrust washer with a new one that will give the proper end play. Thrust washers come in various thicknesses. See *A* in Fig. 7.

Next, remove the oil tube from the pump adapter. Do not drop the O ring. Then remove the six oil-pump attaching bolts. Press the input shaft in and pull off the pump assembly. Remove the gasket.

12. Front clutch. Pull it out together with the input-shaft thrust washer. Take out the two front-clutch thrust washers.

13. Rear clutch. Pull off the rear clutch with the sun gear. Then remove the two sealing rings and separate the forward sun gear from the clutch.

14. Front servo. Remove the two bolts. They are of different lengths. The long bolt (to the rear) is a dowel bolt. Remove the front brake band by squeezing the ends together.

15. Rear servo. Remove the two bolts, rear servo, and strut.

16. Planetary gear and center support. Remove two screws from the two sides of the transmission case. Pull off the center support, planetary gearset, needle bearing, and washers. Remove the center support and clutch from the planetary gearset. Then remove the snap ring and one-way clutch outer race from the gearset.

17. Rear brake band. Squeeze the band together and take it out from the front of the case.

18. Speedometer drive gear and ball by removing the snap ring.

19. Governor and ball by removing the snap ring.

20. Air-breather baffle plate and adapter.

21. Output shaft and ring gear with thrust washer (*J* in Fig. 7) from front of case.

NOTE: Do not damage the white metal bushing at the rear of the case.

22. Shaft lever and parking brake. See Fig. 8. Pull out the roll pin, anchor pin, and toggle pin. To remove the anchor pin, use a magnet or shake it out. Then pull the toggle pin to the rear.

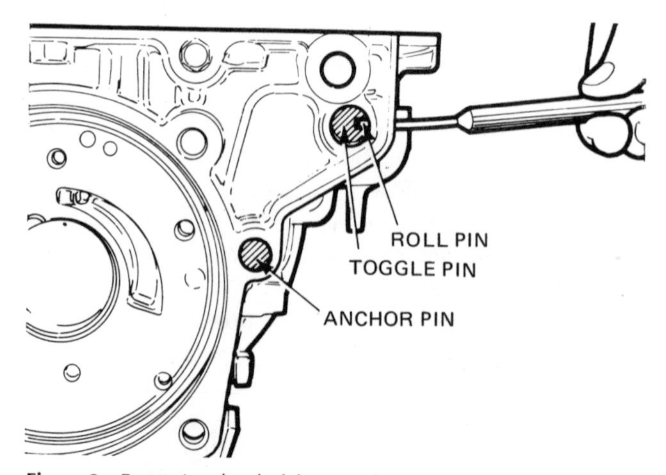

Figure 8 Removing the shaft lever and parking brake, step 1. *(Chrysler Corporation.)*

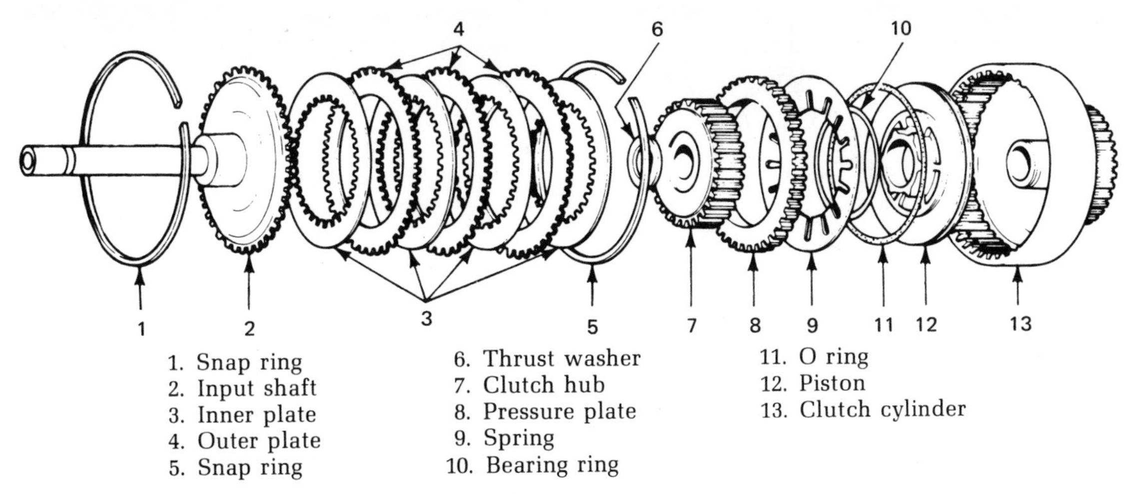

Figure 9 Disassembled front clutch. *(Chrysler Corporation.)*

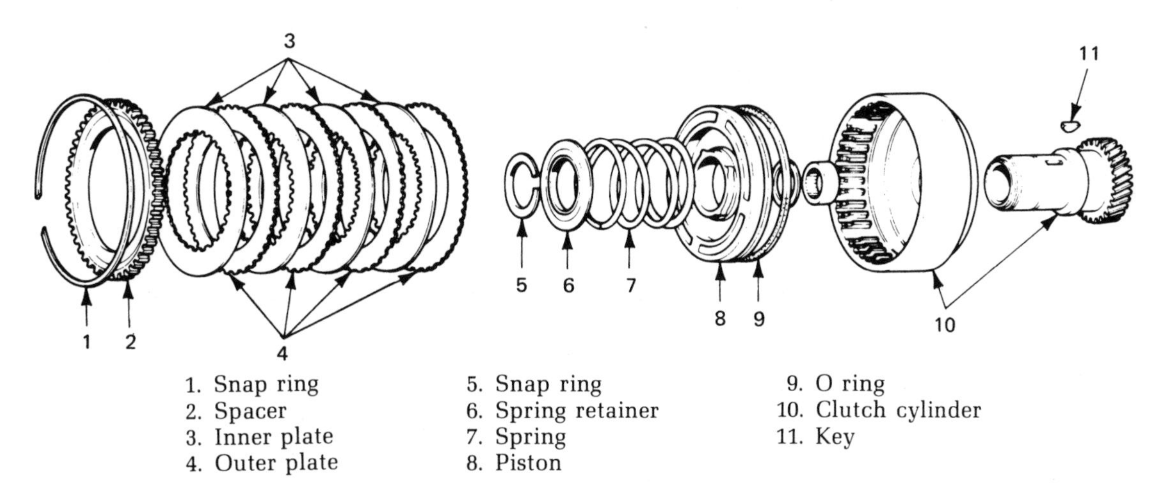

Figure 10 Disassembled rear clutch. *(Chrysler Corporation.)*

Loosen the nut and remove the inside manual lever with the manual control rod. Pull out the taper pin and draw the manual shaft out. Remove the retainer spring and washer from the torsion-lever pin and then remove the torsion lever, toggle lever, and toggle-lever assembly with spring. Then pull out the taper pin and pull the torsion-lever pin out from the case.

23. The two oil-cooler connectors, rear-band adjusting screw, and pipe plugs.

NOTE: The preceding list is the complete disassembly procedure. As a rule, the complete procedure is not necessary. Only the major parts need be removed for cleaning, inspection, and replacement.

■ **5-3-9 Front-Clutch Service** Figure 9 shows the disassembled front clutch. To disassemble the clutch, remove the two snap rings (1 and 6). Check the plates and thrust washer for wear and damage. Also, check the sealing rings, O rings, and piston check valve for defects. Replace defective parts.

To reassemble the front clutch, install the sealing ring in the piston groove. Insert the O ring in the cylinder-ring groove. Use the special piston tool to install the piston. Then install the other parts in the order shown in Fig. 9.

■ **5-3-10 Rear-Clutch Service** Figure 10 shows the disassembled rear clutch. Note the key (11) that locks the gear to the clutch cylinder (10). To disassemble the clutch, remove the snap ring, spacer, and clutch plates. Note that the inner plates are identical to the inner plates of the front clutch. However, the outer plates are slightly conical and are different from the front-clutch outer plates. To remove the spring, use the spring compressor, as shown in Fig. 11, so that the snap ring can be removed. Then remove the other parts, as shown.

Inspect all parts for wear or damage. Replace defective parts.

To reassemble the rear clutch, use the spring to compress the spring compressor and then assemble all parts in the order shown in Fig. 10. When installing the slightly conical outer plates, be sure they all face in the same direction.

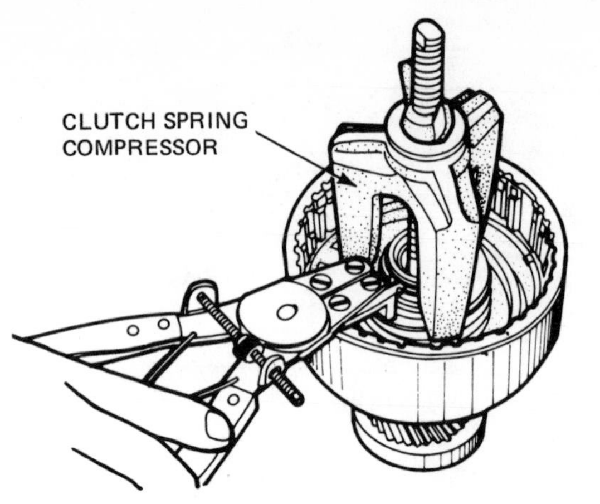

Figure 11 Using a clutch-spring compressor to disassemble the rear clutch. *(Chrysler Corporation.)*

■ **5-3-11 Front Servo** To disassemble the front servo, remove the snap ring.

■ **5-3-12 Rear Servo** To disassemble the rear servo, remove the spring and pull out the piston pin.

■ **5-3-13 Governor** Removing the screws and retainer permits complete disassembly of the unit. Inspect the valve for free movement in the body.

■ **5-3-14 Oil Pump** Remove five bolts and one screw to separate the oil pump from the support. Place a mark across the driven and drive gears before removing them. The mark will permit realignment of the parts in the original order on reassembly. Check the oil seal and O ring, and check the pump housing and gears for wear or damage.

■ **5-3-15 Planetary Gearset** Note that the planet-pinion carrier, with the planet pinions, is serviced as a com-

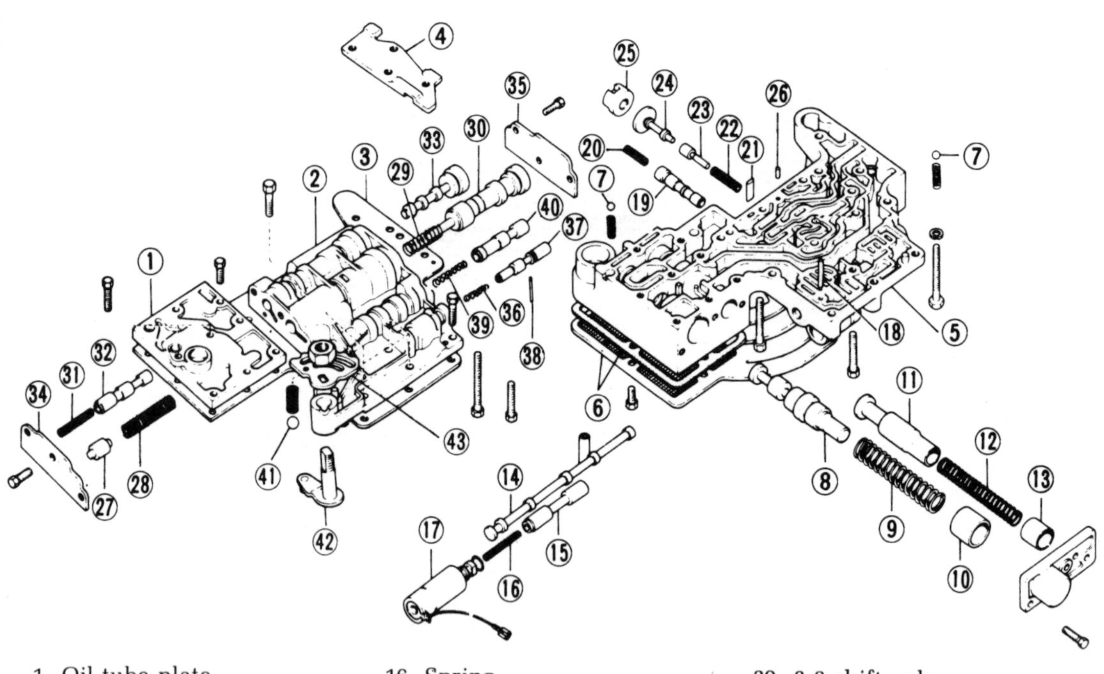

1. Oil-tube plate
2. Upper valve body
3. Separating plate
4. Governor line plate
5. Lower valve body
6. Oil strainer
7. Check ball
8. Primary regulator valve
9. Spring
10. Sleeve
11. Secondary regulator valve
12. Spring
13. Sleeve
14. Manual control valve
15. Downshift valve
16. Spring
17. Solenoid
18. Dowel pin
19. Servo-orifice control valve
20. Spring
21. Stopper
22. Spring
23. Modulator plunger
24. Modulator valve
25. Modulator-valve spacer
26. Stopper
27. 2-3 shift plunger
28. Spring
29. Spring
30. 2-3 shift valve
31. Spring
32. 1-2 shift plunger
33. 1-2 shift valve
34. End plate
35. End plate
36. Spring
37. Throttle valve
38. Dowel pin
39. Spring
40. Range control valve
41. Detent ball
42. Manual valve lever
43. Detent lever

Figure 12 Disassembled valve body. *(Chrysler Corporation.)*

plete unit and should not be disassembled.

Inspect the bearings, gears, and one-way clutch for damage or wear. Replace defective parts.

■ **5-3-16 Output Shaft and Ring Gear** Check the oil-seal ring and ring gear for damage. Replace defective parts.

■ **5-3-17 Control Valve Body Assembly** Figure 12 shows the completely disassembled valve body. If it is necessary to disassemble the body, proceed carefully so that you do not mix the parts. Handle parts with care because any nick or scratch on the valves or plungers can cause serious trouble in the transmission. Make sure the valves move freely in the valve body. With valves and valve body dry, put valves in place and turn the valve body vertically. Valves should fall out of their own weight. Check oil passages in the valve body to make sure they are clean. On reassembly, apply automatic-transmission fluid to all parts.

■ **5-3-18 Transmission Reassembly** Note the transmission-service precautions listed in Part 5, Sec. 2. Lubricate parts with transmission fluid on reassembly. To hold thrust washers and other parts in place, coat them lightly with petroleum jelly—not grease! Tighten all screws, bolts, and nuts to the proper specifications. Handle parts with care because some are made of relatively soft material and can be nicked and scratched easily. Proceed as follows:

1. Install the parking pawl and lever (Fig. 13). Note the relationship between the inside manual lever and the toggle-lift lever. Secure the parts with pins.

2. Install the solenoid terminal if it was removed, being sure to use the O ring.

3. Install the oil-cooler connections, rear-band adjusting screw, and pipe plug if they were removed.

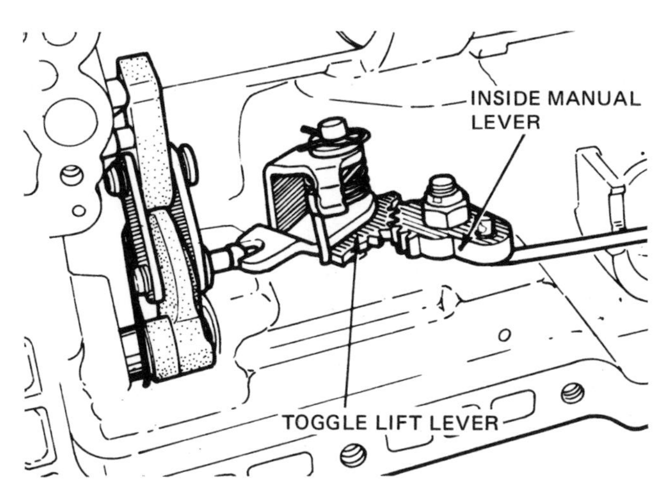

Figure 13 Installing the parking pawl and lever. *(Chrysler Corporation.)*

4. Install the output shaft. Hold the thrust washer in place with petroleum jelly. A thrust washer of the right thickness (previously selected) must be used to ensure correct end play (Fig. 6).

5. Install the adapter. Tighten five bolts to the correct tension.

6. Install the air-breather baffle plate.

7. Install the governor. Put a ¼-inch (6.35-mm) ball on the output shaft and slide the governor into place. The cover plate should face the rear. Secure with a snap ring.

8. Install the speedometer drive gear using a 3/16-inch (4.76-mm) ball. Secure with a snap ring.

9. Install the rear brake band. Make sure the band seat is lined up with the adjusting screw. Note that the rear brake band is narrower than the front brake band.

10. Install the planet-pinion carrier. Stick the needle thrust bearing on the planet-pinion carrier with petroleum jelly. Make sure the one-way-clutch flange faces the front when installing it. Then install the carrier.

11. Install the center support. Make sure the one-way-clutch lubricating hole and rear-clutch feed hole are visible from underneath. Tighten the two bolts to the specified tension.

NOTE: The center-support-screw lock washers are also oil retainers. Make sure the screws are tightened enough so that the flat rims contact the case.

12. Install the rear servo. Hold the strut in place with petroleum jelly while installing the servo. Install the magnet on the bolt head.

13. Install the front band, making sure the seat is in line with the case anchor pin.

14. Install the clutches. With thurst washers held in place by petroleum jelly and the sealing rings installed, bring the two clutches together. Then install the assembly in the transmission case.

15. Install the front servo. Attach the strut to the servo lever with petroleum jelly. Then install the servo. Make sure the strut fits properly into the brake-band slot.

16. Install the oil pump. Use a new gasket between the oil pump and the transmission case. Stick the input-shaft thrust washer to the oil pump with petroleum jelly. Install the pump and tighten the six bolts to specifications. Recheck the input-shaft end play (Fig. 6). If end play is not correct, replace the thrust washer with a thrust washer of the correct thickness.

17. Install the extension housing. Use a new gasket.

18. Install the drive-gear assembly with a new gasket.

19. Install the oil tubs (Fig. 14).

20. Install the valve body. Make sure the manual control rod is fitted properly in the detent lever. Connect the solenoid wire to the terminal on the case. Tighten three bolts to specifications. Do not tighten too much!

21. Install the four oil tubes shown in Fig. 5. Install the clip.

22. Install the oil pan, tightening the screws in the sequence shown in Fig.15.

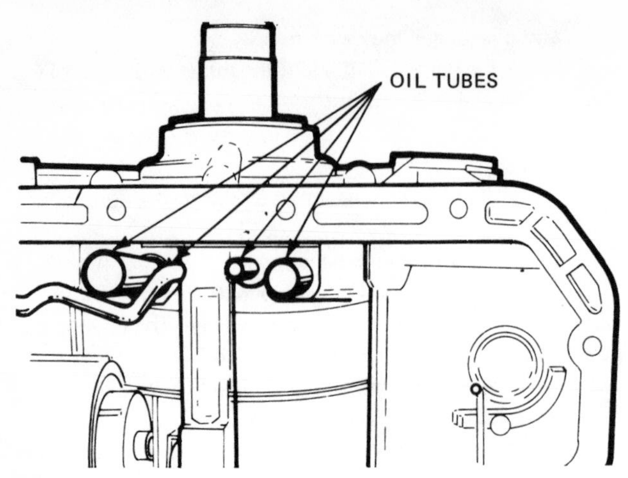

Figure 14 Installing the oil tubes. *(Chrysler Corporation.)*

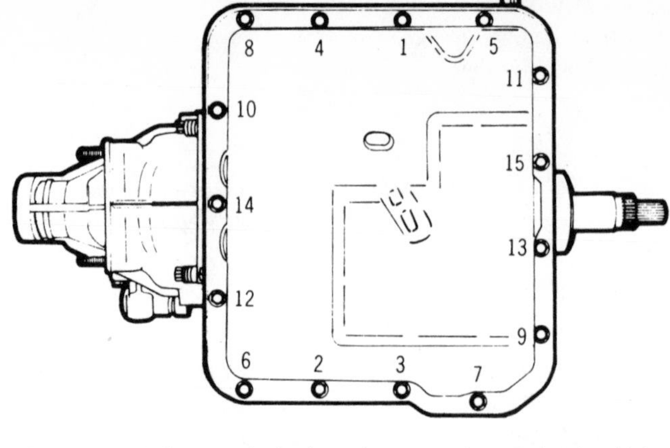

Figure 15 Order in which the oil-pan attaching bolts should be tightened when the oil pan is installed. *(Chrysler Corporation.)*

23. Install the converter housing with six bolts.

24. Install the torque converter, making sure to properly align the converter-hub finger with the slot in the oil-pump drive gear.

■ 5-3-19 Transmission Installation

When installing the transmission, observe the following procedure:

1. Use a transmission jack to raise the transmission into place.

2. Tighten the insulator bolts and nuts to the specified torque.

3. With the selector lever in N or P, turn the ignition switch on and make sure the starting motor operates.

4. See also the general installation instructions given in Part 5, Sec. 2.

■ 5-3-20 Transmission Control

Adjust selector lever and linkage as detailed in the shop manual for the vehicle.

SECTION 5-4 | Type 350 Turbo Hydra-Matic Transmission Service

This section discusses the trouble-diagnosis and service procedures for the Type 350 Turbo Hydra-Matic automatic transmission. The section is divided into four parts: "Normal Maintenance and Adjustments," "Trouble Diagnosis," "On-the-Car Repair," and "Transmission Overhaul."

■ **5-4-1 Type 350 Transmission Variations** The Type 350 transmission is used on many cars with a wide variety of engines, both sixes and eights. Some minor modifications of the transmission are made so that it will operate properly with the engine. These modifications have no effect on the service procedures, but they do give the characteristics the transmission needs for engine torque and output curves. For example, the transmission used on Buick six-cylinder engines has fewer plates in the clutches than the transmission used on Buick eight-cylinder engines. Fewer plates are required to handle the lower torque of the smaller engine. Also, springs and valves may be changed so as to provide different shift points. But the service procedures are essentially the same for all models of the Type 350 Turbo Hydra-Matic transmission.

NORMAL MAINTENANCE AND ADJUSTMENTS

Refer to Part 5, Sec. 2, for instructions on checking and adding fluid, and towing the vehicle.

■ **5-4-2 Adjustments** Only two adjustments are required with the transmission in the car: linkage to the selector lever and linkage to the accelerator (for the detent downshift). The adjustments are different for different cars, and so you should always refer to the appropriate shop manual for the car you are working on. There, you will find the instructions that apply.

TROUBLE DIAGNOSIS

Although the transmission is fairly complex and packs a considerable number of moving parts in a small space, causes of troubles are usually easy to spot. A specific trouble can have only certain specific causes.

PROBLEM — CAR ROAD TEST

LEGEND
X–PROBLEM AREA VS. CAUSE
*–@ "O" VACUUM ONLY
O–BALLS/#2/3/4 ONLY
L–LOCKED
S–STUCK

POSSIBLE CAUSE	ALL RANGES–SLIPS	DRIVE–SLIPS–NO 1ST GEAR	LINE PRESSURE–ALL LOW	LINE PRESSURE–ALL HIGH	1-2 INTERM. CL. PRES. HIGH	1-2 INTERM. CL. PRES. LOW	2-3 DIRECT CL. PRES. HIGH	2-3 DIRECT CL. PRES. LOW	NO 1-2 UPSHIFT	1-2 U.S. EARLY/LATE	1-2 UPSHIFT @ W.O.T. ONLY	SLIPS–1-2 UPSHIFT	ROUGH–1-2 UPSHIFT	NO 2-3 UPSHIFT	2-3 U.S.–EARLY/LATE	SLIPS–2-3 UPSHIFT	ROUGH–2-3 UPSHIFT	NO WOT. 1-2 UPSHIFT	NO–PART TH. DOWN SHIFT	NO–FULL TH. DOWN SHIFT	2-3 UPSHIFT–W.O.T. ONLY	HARSH–DOWN SHIFT	L1 RANGE–NO ENG. BRAKING	L2 RANGE–NO ENG. BRAKING	NEUTRAL–DRIVES IN NEUTRAL	REVERSE–NO REVERSE	SLIPS IN REVERSE	PARK–NO PARK–RATCHETS	NOISY–ALL RANGES	1-2 2-3 SHIFT NOISY	REV. & D. L1 & L2 NOISY	LOW COOLER–FLOW	SPEWS OIL OUT BREATHER	HUNTS BETWEEN 2 & 3 AND 3 & 2
LOW OIL LEVEL/WATER IN OIL	X	X	X			X		X				X				X											X		X	X		X	X	
VACUUM LEAK				X	X		X		X	X	X		X		X		X				X													
MODULATOR &/OR VALVE	X	X	*	X	X							X	X		X	X	X										X							
STRAINER &/OR GASKET	X	X	X			X		X																			X		X			X	X	
GOVERNOR–VALVE/SCREEN			X	X					X	X					X																			
VALVE BODY–GASKET/PLATE	X	X	X			X		X	X	X		X		X	X	X											X		X					
PRES. REG. &/OR BOOST VALVE	X	X	X	X	X	X	X	X	X			X	X			X	X						X	X		X	X							
BALL (#1) SHY	X	X	*			X				X		X			X	X						O				X	X							
1-2 SHIFT VALVE						X			X	X	X	X											X				X							
2-3 SHIFT VALVE								X						X	X	X	X		X															
MANUAL LOW CONT'L. VALVE																							X											
DETENT VALVE & LINKAGE				X							X				X				X	X	X													S
DETENT REG. VALVE																		X																
2-3 ACCUMULATOR						X						X					X																	
MANUAL VALVE/LINKAGE	X	X	X																				X	X		X	X							
POROSITY/CROSS LEAK	X	X	X	X	X	X	X	X	X	X	X	X	X	X	X	X	X	X					X	X		X	X							
PUMP–GEARS	X	X	X			X		X				X				X													X					
PRIMING VALVE SHY	X	X	X																														S	
COOLER VALVE LEAK																																X	X	
CLUTCH SEAL RINGS	X	X	X			X		X	X			X		X		X							X	X		X	X							
POROUS/CROSS LEAK	X	X	X			X		X	X			X	X	X		X		X								X	X					X	X	
GASKET SCREEN–PRESSURE	X	X	X																							X	X		X			X		
BAND–INTERM. O.R.																								X										
CASE–POROUS/X LEAK	X	X	X	X	X	X	X	X	X	X	X	X	X	X	X	X	X						X			X	X					X		
1-2 ACCUMULATOR	X	X	X			X			X			X	X																					
INTERMED. SERVO		X	X			X						X												X										
FORWARD CLUTCH ASS'Y		X																					X	X	X	L								
DIRECT CLUTCH ASS'Y								X						X		X										X	X			X				
INTERMED. CL. ASS'Y						X			X			X																		X				
L & REV. CL. ASS'Y																							X			X	X							
INT. ROLLER CL. ASS'Y									X			X												X										
L. & R. ROLLER CL. ASS'Y		X																																
PARK PAWL/LINKAGE																												X						
CONVERTER ASS'Y																													X		X			
GEAR SET & BEARINGS																													X	X				

Figure 1 Type 350 Turbo Hydra-Matic transmission trouble-diagnosis chart. *(Chevrolet Motor Division of General Motors Corporation.)*

All the various car manufacturers who use the Type 350 automatic transmission recommend that oil-pressure checks be made with the transmission in operation to help locate causes of trouble. The procedures recommended, as well as the pressures specified under different operating conditions, vary somewhat from manufacturer to manufacturer. Thus, always refer to the shop manual that specifically covers the car and transmission you are checking. A typical diagnosis procedure follows.

■ **5-4-3 Trouble Diagnosis** The chart shown in Fig. 1 will help you to locate causes of trouble in the Type 350 transmission. Before we look at the chart, however, here is a typical diagnosis procedure as outlined by one of the car manufacturers using the transmission:

1. Check and correct the oil level.
2. Check and correct the detent-cable adjustment.
3. Check the vacuum line and fittings for leakage.

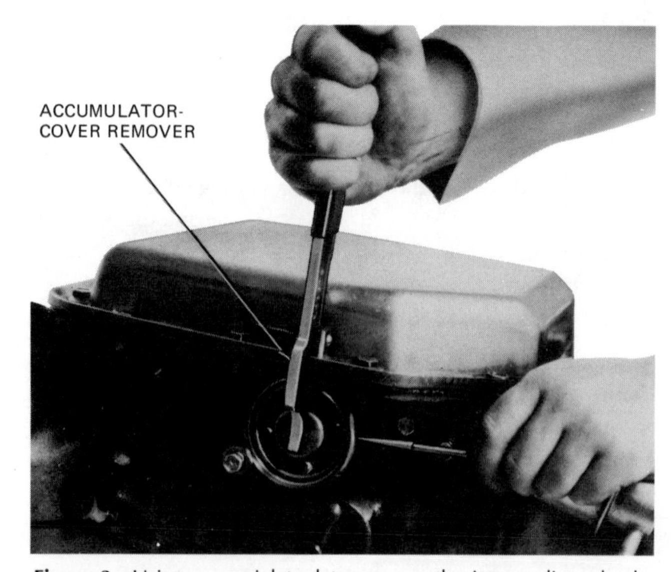

Figure 2 Using a special tool to remove the intermediate-clutch-accumulator retaining ring.

4. Check and adjust the manual linkage as necessary.

5. Shop-test and road-test the car, as follows. Install the oil-pressure gauge by connecting it to the transmission line-pressure tap located to the left of the 1-2 accumulator cover (shown being removed in Fig.2). Then test the car in the shop and on the road, using all the selector-lever positions and noting transmission operation and oil pressure under different conditions.

> **NOTE:** If the engine is not performing satisfactorily, it should be tuned and given whatever service is necessary to bring it up to normal operating conditions. Poor engine performance can result in faulty transmission shift and can make the transmission look bad even though it is in normal condition.

6. The tabulation that follows is the recommendation of one car manufacturer for the test procedure and pressure readings, in pounds per square inch, that should be obtained.

Car stationary
Parking brake applied—wheels blocked

Range	Min. psi at 1,000 rpm with vacuum line connected	Max. psi at 1,200 rpm with vacuum line disconnected
Park and neutral	60	156
Reverse	85	240
Drive	60	156
Super	85	156
Low	85	156

Road or dynamometer test
Vacuum line and pressure gauge installed

Throttle drive range	Idle	Wide open
First	60	153
Second	60	153
Third	60	
Reverse	85	239
Low (coast at 3 mph)	85	
Super (coast at 30 mph)	85	

7. Refer to the trouble-diagnosis chart (Fig. 1) to determine causes of possible troubles that show up during the tests. In most cases, the chart will help you locate the causes so that you can make the necessary repairs. Sometimes, it will be necessary to remove the transmission from the car for disassembly so that defective parts can be replaced. Other troubles, however, may be solved by replacement of parts without removal of the transmission.

■ 5-4-4 In-Car Transmission Repairs

Some parts can be removed and replaced without removing the transmission from the car. These include:

Oil pan and gasket
Oil screen
Valve-body assembly
Direct-clutch accumulator and servo
(after valve body is removed)
Manual control linkage and parking pawl
Extension housing and seal
Vacuum modulator
Speedometer drive gear
Transmission-control-spark switch
Governor assembly
Intermediate-clutch accumulator

These parts, with the exception of the last two, require the same procedure used during complete disassembly and reassembly of the transmission. Thus, these removal-and-replacement procedures are described on later pages where complete transmission disassembly and reassembly are described. Governor assembly and intermediate-clutch-accumulator removal and replacement require different procedures if the transmission is not removed from the car, and these procedures are described next.

■ 5-4-5 Governor-Assembly Removal and Replacement

The governor assembly can be removed and replaced with the transmission of the car, as follows:

1. Put the car on a hoist and disconnect the speedometer cable at the transmission.

2. Remove the governor cover retainer and cover. Do not damage the O-ring seal.

3. Remove the governor. Check weights and valve to make sure they move freely. If they do not, repair or replace the parts as necessary.

4. To replace the governor, slip it into place and install the cover, using a brass drift around the outside flange of the cover. Do not distort the cover, and be sure the O-ring seal is not cut or damaged.

5. Replace the retainer and connect the speedometer cable. Lower the car from the hoist and check the fluid level.

■ 5-4-6 Intermediate-Clutch Accumulator Removal and Replacement

The intermediate-clutch accumulator can be removed and replaced with the transmission on the car, as follows:

1. Remove the two transmission oil-pan bolts below the intermediate-clutch cover. Install a special tool, as shown in Fig. 2, in place of the bolts removed.

2. Press in on the tool handle and use an awl to remove the retaining ring, as shown in Fig. 2.

3. Remove the cover O-ring seal, spring, and intermediate-clutch accumulator.

4. To replace, put the intermediate-clutch accumulator into place. Lubricate the rings. Rotating the piston slightly will help start the rings into the piston bore.

5. Put the spring, O-ring seal, and cover into place. Press in

on the cover and replace the retaining ring.

6. Remove the tool and replace the oil-pan bolts.

TRANSMISSION OVERHAUL

See Part 5, Sec. 2, for service precautions, cleaning and inspecting transmission parts, and the removal procedure.

■ 5-4-7 Transmission Disassembly None of the moving parts requires forcing when disassembling or reassembling the transmission. Bushing removal and replacement do require driving or pressing, of course. The cases might fit tightly, and you can loosen them with a rawhide or plastic mallet. Never use a hard hammer.

As a first step, the transmission must be placed in a holding fixture. Proceed as follows:

1. Turn the transmission so that the oil pan is up. If you have used a torque-converter holding tool, remove it. Then slip off the torque converter.

2. Remove the vacuum-modulator-assembly attaching bolt and retainer. Now, remove the vacuum-modulator assembly, O-ring seal, and modulator valve. The vacuum modulator is checked as explained in ■5-4-16.

3. Remove the extension housing by taking out the four attaching bolts. Remove the square-cut O-ring seal. Use a screwdriver to remove the extension-housing lip seal from the housing. If it is necessary to replace the housing bushing, use a screwdriver to collapse it, as shown in Fig. 3. Clean the housing carefully and inspect it for any damage. Then install a new housing bushing with special tools. A new housing lip seal can then be installed with the special tool. The extension housing is now ready for reinstallation on the transmission case and can be set aside until the rest of the transmission has been disassembled and reassembled.

4. To remove the yoke seal from the end of the output shaft, install the special tool, as shown in Fig. 4, to keep the seal from cocking. Then tap the seal off with a screwdriver, as shown. Next, take off the speedometer-drive gear by depressing the retaining clip. The gear can be slid off the shaft with the clip depressed. Remove the clip.

5. Next, remove the governor by first prying off the governor retaining wire with a screwdriver. Remove the governor cover and O-ring seal from the case. Use a screwdriver to pry between the cover flange and the case. But be extremely careful to avoid denting or bending the cover or gouging the transmission case. The dimple in the end of the cover provides the proper end play for the governor. If the cover is bent or damaged in any way, it must be discarded and a new cover installed. Remove the O-ring seal from the cover. Now, the governor assembly can be withdrawn from the case.

6. Now, remove the oil pan, strainer, and valve body. First, take out 13 attaching-screw-and -washer assemblies and lift off the oil pan and gasket. Then remove the two screws attaching the oil-pump strainer to the valve body. Take the oil-pump-strainer gasket off the valve body.

Next, remove the detent-spring-and-roller assembly from the valve body. See Fig. 5. Remove the bolts attaching the valve body to the case. Now, lift the valve body from the case, carefully guiding the manual-valve link from the range-selector inner lever. Remove the detent-control-valve link from the detent actuating lever. Lay the valve body aside on a clean surface in preparation for further disassembly.

Remove the following from the case: valve-body-to-spacer-plate gasket, spacer-support-plate bolts, and the spacer support plate. Then remove the valve-body spacer plate and gasket.

7. From the case, remove the oil-pump pressure screen from the pressure hole, and the governor screens. Clean the screens and lay them aside in a clean, safe place. Remove the four check balls from the case face. Their locations are shown in Fig. 6.

8. Next, remove the manual shaft, inner lever, and parking pawl. First, take off the manual-control-valve-link retainer from the range-selector-inner lever. Then use a screwdriver to remove the manual-shaft-to-case retainer. Next, use a wrench

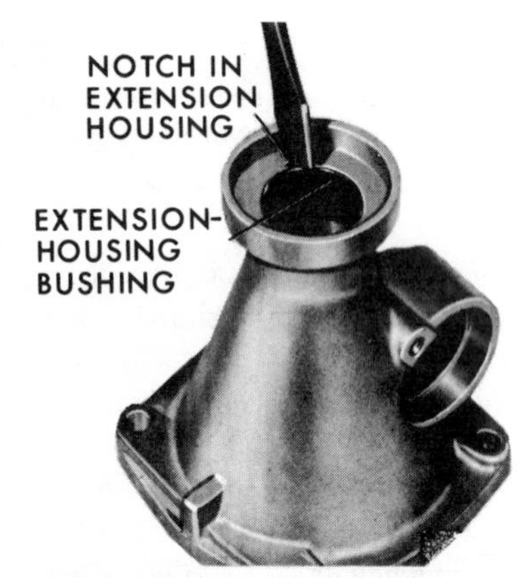

Figure 3 Removing the extension-housing bushing with a screwdriver. *(Buick Motor Division of General Motors Corporation.)*

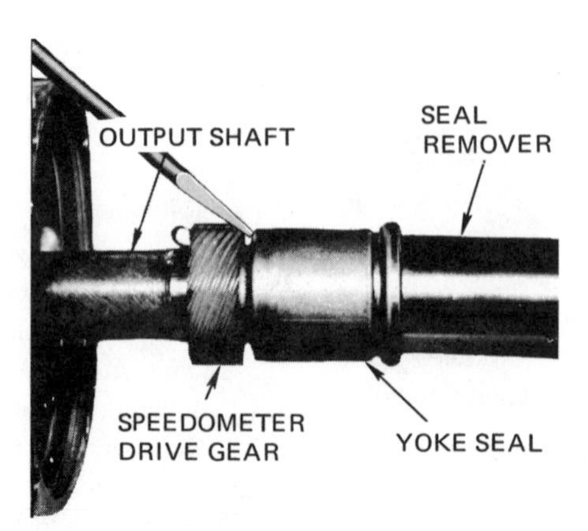

Figure 4 Removing the yoke seal from the end of the transmission output shaft. *(Oldsmobile Division of General Motors Corporation.)*

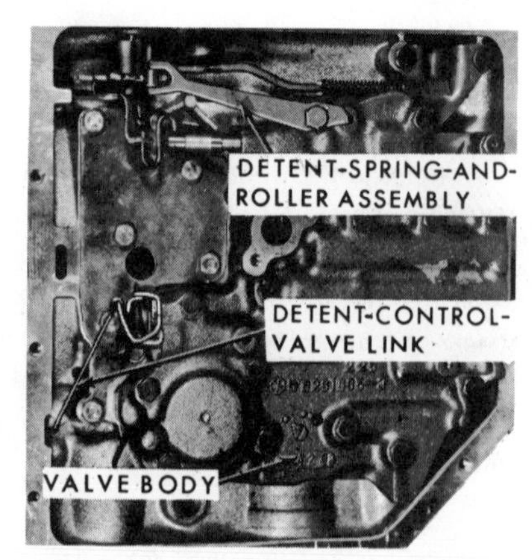

Figure 5 Locations of the detent-spring-and-roller assembly and the detent-control-valve link on the valve body. *(Buick Motor Division of General Motors Corporation.)*

Figure 6 Locations of the four check balls in case. *(Buick Motor Division of General Motors Corporation.)*

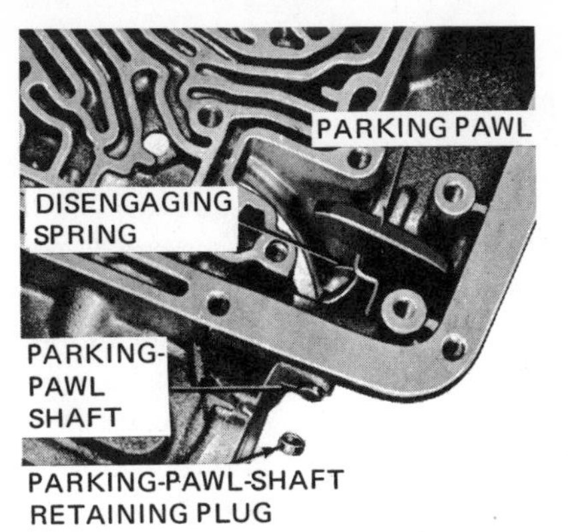

Figure 7 Locations of the parking pawl, parking-pawl shaft, parking-pawl-shaft retaining plug, and disengaging spring. *(Buick Motor Division of General Motors Corporation.)*

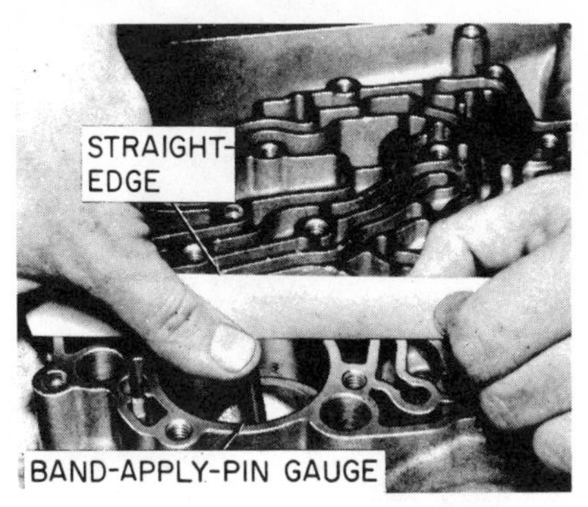

Figure 8 Using a special gauge and straightedge to determine what apply pin to use on reassembly. *(Buick Motor Division of General Motors Corporation.)*

to remove the jam nut holding the range-selector inner lever to the manual shaft. Now, remove the manual shaft from the case. Remove the range-selector inner lever and parking-pawl actuating rod. If the manual-shaft-to-case lip seal is damaged, remove it with a screwdriver.

If necessary to remove the parking pawl or shaft, proceed as follows: Remove the parking-lock bracket. Then remove the retaining plug, parking-pawl shaft, parking pawl, and disengaging spring. These parts are shown in Fig. 7.

9. Remove the intermediate-servo piston and metal oil-seal ring. Then remove the washer, spring seat, and apply pin. Now, check to see if a new long or short apply pin is required on reassembly. Do this by using a special apply-pin gauge and straightedge, as shown in Fig. 8. Press down on the gauge and note whether the upper end of the gauge is above or below the straightedge. There are two replacements apply pins: long and short. If the gauge is below the straightedge, the long pin should be used; if above, the short pin should be used. Selecting the proper length of pin is equivalent to adjusting the brake band. Make a note of which pin is required so that it can be installed on reassembly.

10. Remove the pump as follows: With the transmission turned, pump end up, remove the eight pump attaching bolts and washer-type seals. Discard the seals. Install two threaded slide hammers into the threaded holes in the pump body and tighten the jam nuts. Carefully use the slide hammers to draw the pump up and out of the case. Remove and discard the pump-assembly-to-case gasket. Lay the pump aside on a clean surface for later disassembly.

11. Remove the intermediate-clutch plates and band as follows: First take out the intermediate-clutch cushion spring, and then remove the intermediate-clutch plates. Inspect the plates. (See Part 5, Sec. 2.) Next, remove the intermediate-clutch pressure plate and the overrun brake band.

12. Next, remove the forward- and direct-clutch assemblies from the case. Lay them aside in a clean place to await further disassembly.

13. Remove the front input-ring-gear thrust washer, and then remove the input ring gear. Check the bushing in the ring gear. If it is worn or galled, use a special tool to remove and replace is. Thread the tool onto the drive handle and use the tool to remove the bushing. The same tool is used to install the new bushing.

14. To remove the output-carrier assembly, first remove the input-ring-gear-to-output-carrier thrust washer. Then remove and discard the output-carrier-to-output-shaft snap ring. Now the output-carrier assembly will slide out. Lay it aside on a clean surfact to await further disassembly.

15. Next, remove the sun-gear-and-drive-shell assembly by pulling it out.

16. Remove the low-and-reverse-clutch-support assembly by first prying out the retaining ring. Now, grasp the output shaft and pull up until the low-and-reverse-roller-clutch-support assembly clears the low-and-reverse-clutch-support retainer spring. The support assembly will then slide out. Now, use pliers to remove the retainer spring.

17. Now reach into the case and remove the low-and-reverse-clutch plates, followed by the reaction carrier. Inspect the clutch plates. (See Part 5, Sec. 2.) If the reaction-carrier bushing is worn or galled, replace it with the special tool.

18. Remove the output-ring-gear-and-shaft assembly from the case. Remove the output-ring-gear-to-case needle bearing from either the case or the output shaft. Then take the tanged thrust washer from the assembly. Next, take off the output-ring-gear-to-output-shaft snap ring and discard it. Slip the output shaft from the output ring gear.

Remove the output-ring-gear-to-case needle-bearing assembly.

Check the output-shaft bushing. If it is worn or galled, replace it with special tools. The procedure is to assemble the special tool into the adapter and then assemble them to the slide hammer. Thread the assembly into the bushing and clamp the slide hammer in a vise. Then grasp the output shaft to remove the bushing. Use the special tool, assembled into the drive handle, and press the new bushing into place 0.140 inch (3.56 mm) below the end surface of the output shaft.

Figure 9 Pencil points to the passage at which compressed air is applied to aid in removal of the low-and-reverse-clutch piston. *(Buick Motor Division of General Motors Corporation.)*

19. To remove the low-and-reverse-clutch piston, the springs behind the piston must be compressed by installing a special compressor tool. Then the piston retaining ring and spring retainer can be removed. Remove the 17 piston return springs. Now, the low-and-reverse-clutch-piston assembly can be removed. Use compressed air to aid in the removal of the piston assembly. Apply compressed air in the passage shown pointed out by a pencil in Fig. 9. The low-and-reverse-clutch-piston assembly has three seals: the outer seal, center seal, and inner seal. All three seals should be removed and discarded.

20. If the case bushing is worn or otherwise damaged, remove it by using the special removing tool installed on the drive handle. Note that the bushing is driven inward. The same tools are then used to drive the new bushing into place. The bushing should be pressed in to 0.195 inch (4.95 mm) below the chamfered edge of the case. Make sure that the split on the bushing is opposite the notch on the case.

21. Removal and replacement of the intermediate-clutch accumulator have already been discussed (■5-4-6). A disassembled view of the intermediate-clutch accumulator with retaining ring, cover and seal, spring, and piston is shown in Fig. 10.

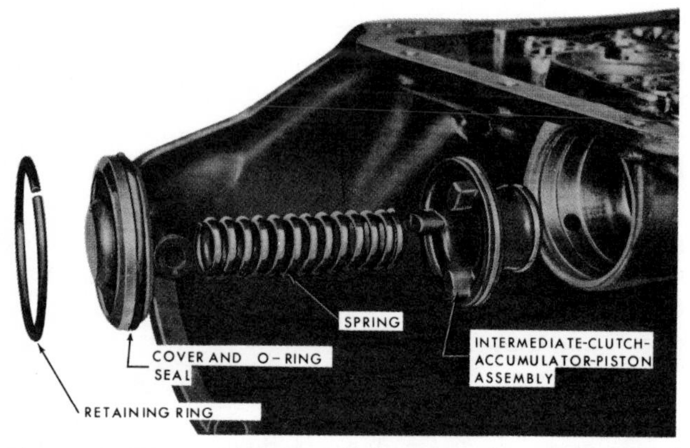

Figure 10 Disassembled view of the intermediate clutch. *(Buick Motor Division of General Motors Corporation.)*

■ 5-4-8 Oil-Pump-Assembly Service

The oil-pump assembly is shown in exploded view in Fig. 11. Note that the assembly includes the intermediate-clutch-piston assembly and related parts.

Disassembly

To disassemble the oil-pump assembly, put it on the bench with the shaft through a hole in the bench.

1. Remove the five pump-cover-to-pump-body bolts. This

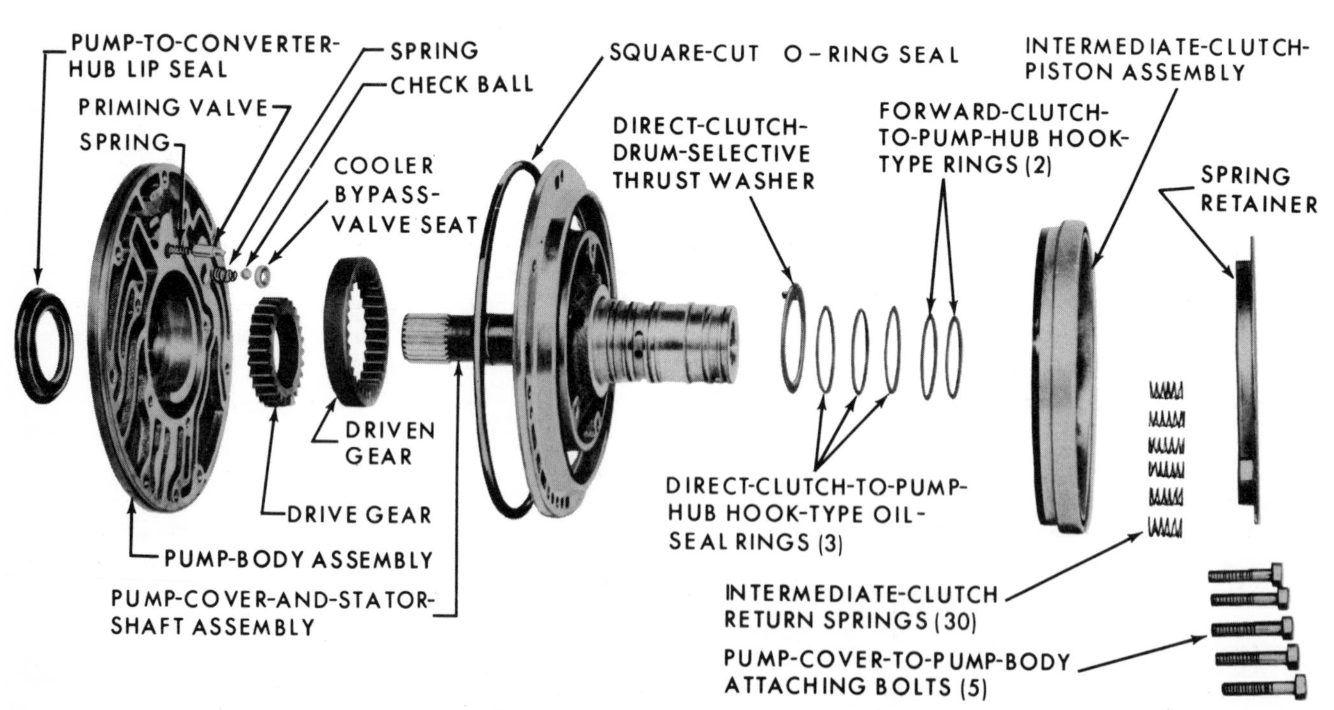

Figure 11 Exploded view of the oil-pump assembly. *(Chevrolet Motor Division of General Motors Corporation.)*

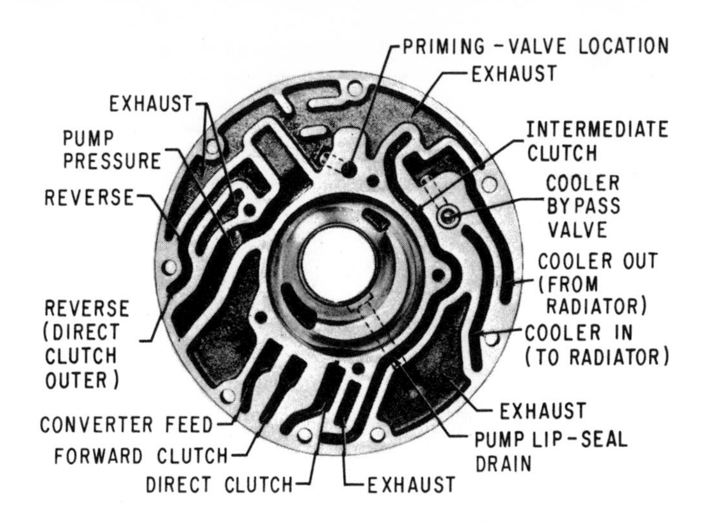

Figure 12 Pump-body oil passages. *(Chevrolet Motor Division of General Motors Corporation.)*

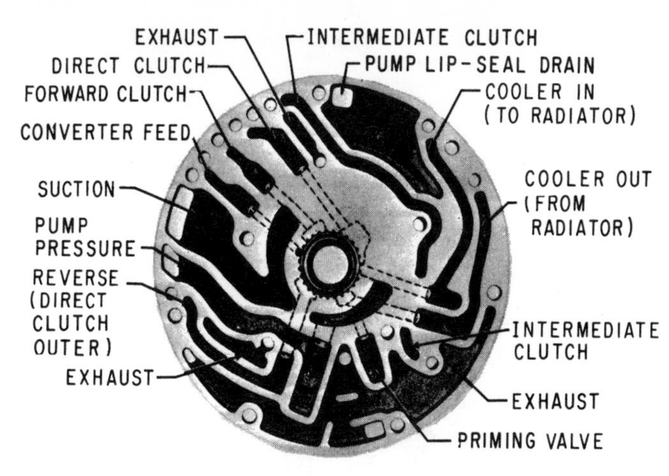

Figure 13 Pump-cover oil passages. *(Chevrolet Motor Division of General Motors Corporation.)*

permits removal of the spring retainer, 30 springs, and intermediate-clutch-piston assembly, all shown in Fig. 11. The intermediate-clutch piston has two seals: an inner seal and an outer seal. Both seals should be removed and discarded so that new seals can be installed.

2. There are five hook-type oil-seal rings on the pump hub. These are removed by unhooking the ring ends and lifting them up and off the hub. The selective thrust washer can now be removed. Note that this thrust washer comes in various thicknesses. The correct thickness must be selected to produce the proper end play in the transmission.

3. Lift the pump-cover-and-stator-shaft assembly from the pump body. Remove the pump drive and driven gears from the pump body. Remove and discard the large square-cut O-ring seal.

4. Turn the pump body over on two wood blocks to prevent damage to the surface, and remove the pump-to-converter-hub lip seal. Turn the pump body inner face up, and remove the priming valve and spring.

5. Then remove the cooler bypass-valve seat, the check ball, and the spring. Two methods for removal are given. In one method, a bolt extractor is used. In the other, the bypass passage is filled with grease and a special tool is driven into the passage to force out the valve seat, the check ball, and the spring.

Inspection of Parts

Clean and inspect parts as explained in Part 5, Sec. 2.

Reassembly

1. If the pump-to-converter-hub lip seal has been removed, replace it by using a special driver tool.

2. Turn the gear body over and install the gears, making sure that the driving tang on the driving gear is up and that the marks on the gears, where present, align.

3. Install the priming valve and spring, cooler bypass-valve seat, check ball, and spring. These are all shown in Fig. 11. When installing the valve seat, tap it down with a soft hammer or brass drift until it is flush to 0.010 inch (0.25 mm) below the surface.

4. To the hub on the pump cover, install five hook-type oil seal rings. These are shown in Fig. 11.

5. Install the inner seal and outer seal on the intermediate-clutch piston. Now carefully install the intermediate-clutch piston assembly in the pump cover, being careful not to damage the seals. Install 30 clutch return springs. Put the intermediate-clutch-spring seat retainer into place and install five bolts.

6. Bring the pump-cover-and-stator-shaft assembly down onto the pump body. Be sure to align them properly. Figures 12 and 13 show the various passages in the faces of the pump body and cover. One convenient alignment procedure is to align the priming valve in the pump body with the priming-valve cavity in the pump cover. Install the square-cut O-ring seal. Tighten the five attaching bolts to 18 pound-feet (2.487 kg-m) torque.

■ **5-4-9 Direct-Clutch Service** The direct-clutch assembly, with overrun-clutch parts, is shown in Fig. 14. To remove the overrun parts, pry out the retaining ring with a screwdriver. The retainer, outer race, and roller-clutch assembly can then be lifted off. Next, the direct-clutch assembly itself can be disassembled.

Disassembly

1. Start by removing the clutch-drum-to-forward-clutch-housing special thrust washer.

2. Use a screwdriver to remove the retaining ring, pressure plate, and clutch plates.

3. Use the special tool to compress the springs. Then remove the retaining ring, spring seat, 17 clutch return springs, and direct-clutch-piston assembly.

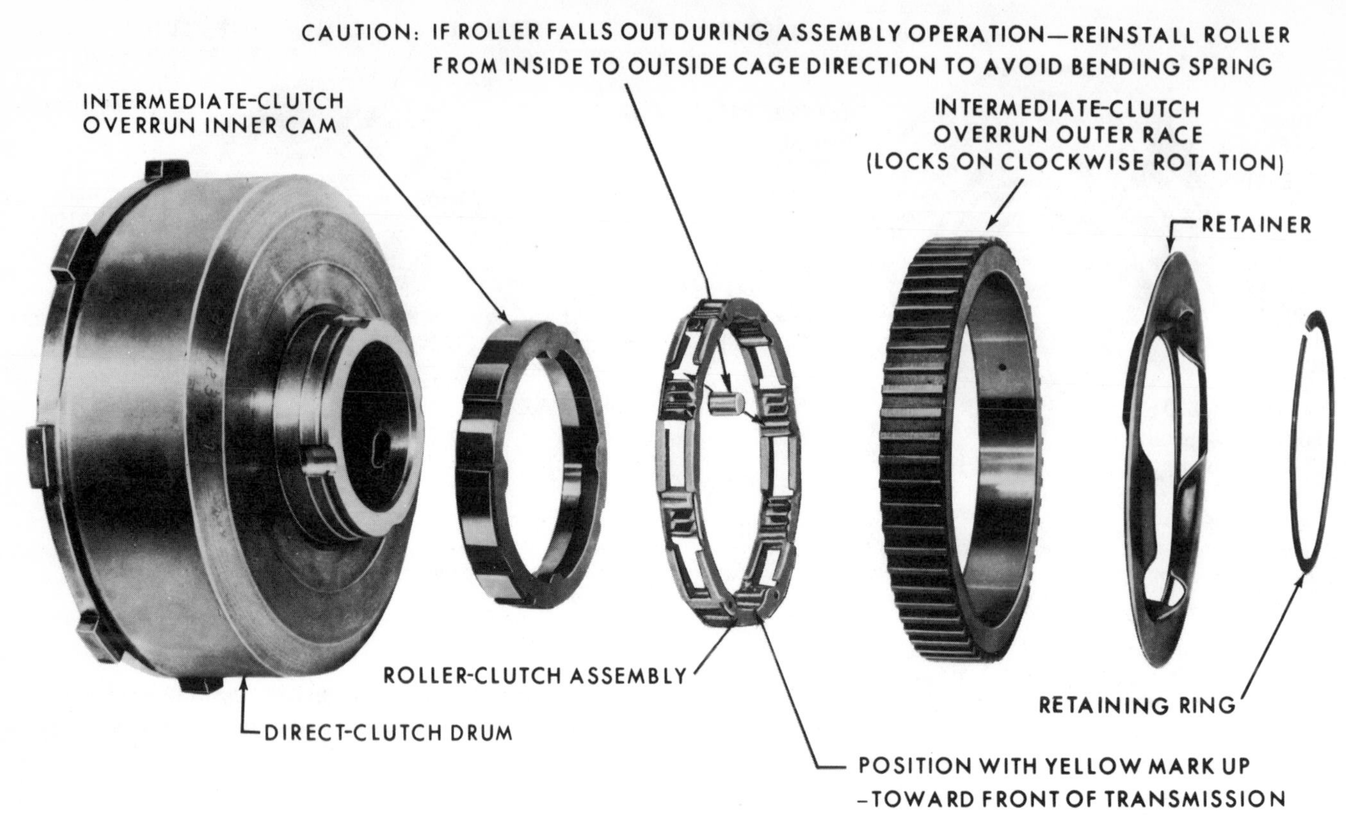

Figure 14 Direct-clutch assembly with intermediate-overrun-clutch parts. *(Chevrolet Motor Division of General Motors Corporation.)*

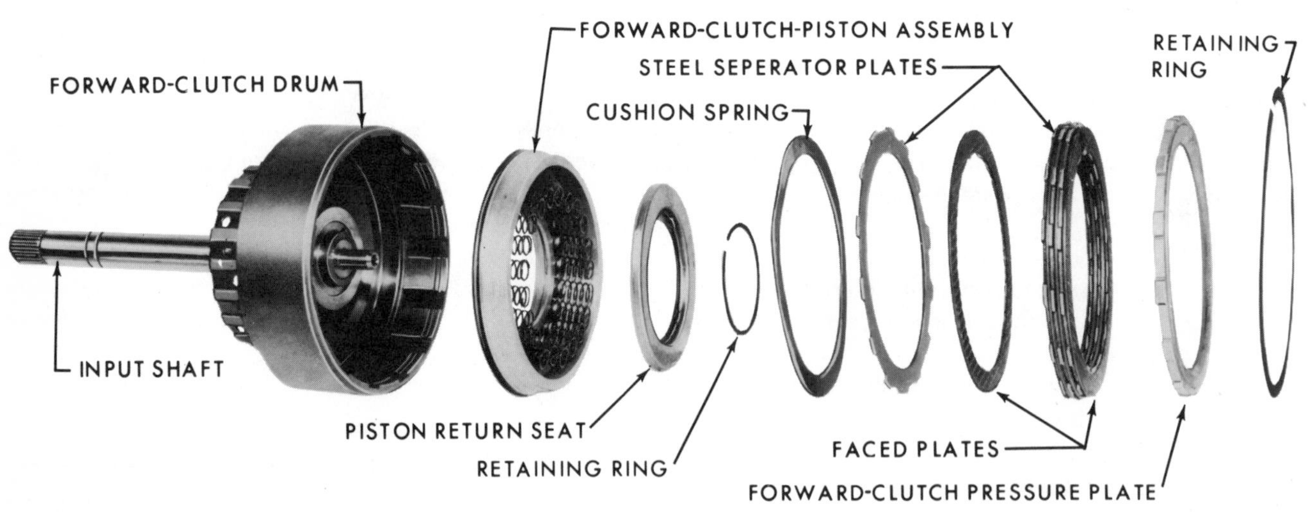

Figure 15 Exploded view of the forward-clutch assembly. *(Chevrolet Motor Division of General Motors Corporation.)*

Inspection

Check clutch plates for signs of burning, wear, or scoring. Check springs for collapsed coils or distortion. Check the piston and clutch housing for wear and scores. Make sure all oil passages are open and that the ball check works freely. Make sure roller-clutch inner and outer races are free of scratches, indentations, or other signs of wear. The roller cage should be free of excessive wear, and roller springs should be in good condition.

Reassembly

1. Install new inner and outer seals on the direct-clutch piston.

2. Install the direct-clutch-piston center seal on the drum with the lip facing upward.

3. Install the direct-clutch piston in the drum using a piece of 0.020-inch (0.51-mm) piano wire crimped into copper tubing, to help get the seal into place.

4. Install 17 clutch return springs and put the spring retainer into position. Compress springs with a special tool and install the retaining ring.

5. Lubricate the clutch plates with transmission fluid and install them, alternating faced and steel plates.

6. Install the pressure plate and retaining ring.

7. Install the roller-clutch assembly, outer race, retainer, and retainer ring (all shown in Fig. 14). Make sure that the outer race can freewheel in a counterclockwise direction only.

■ 5-4-10 Forward-Clutch Service

Figure 15 shows the forward-clutch assembly in exploded view.

Disassembly

1. Remove the pressure-plate-to-drum retaining ring, pressure plate, clutch plates, and cushion spring. These are all shown in Fig. 13.

2. Use the special compressing tool to compress springs so

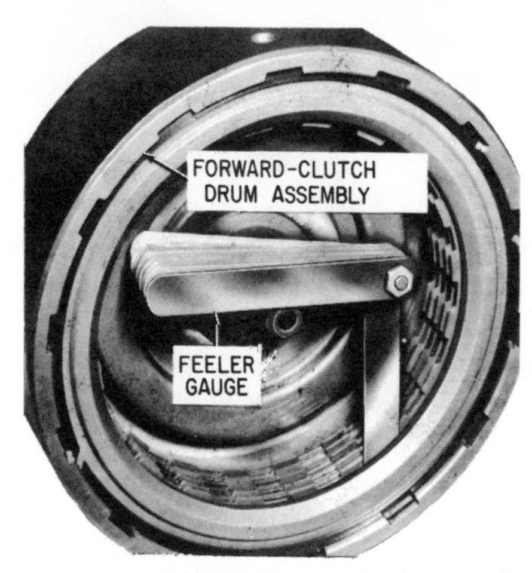

Figure 16 Measuring clearance between the pressure plates and the nearest clutch plate. *(Buick Motor Division of General Motors Corporation.)*

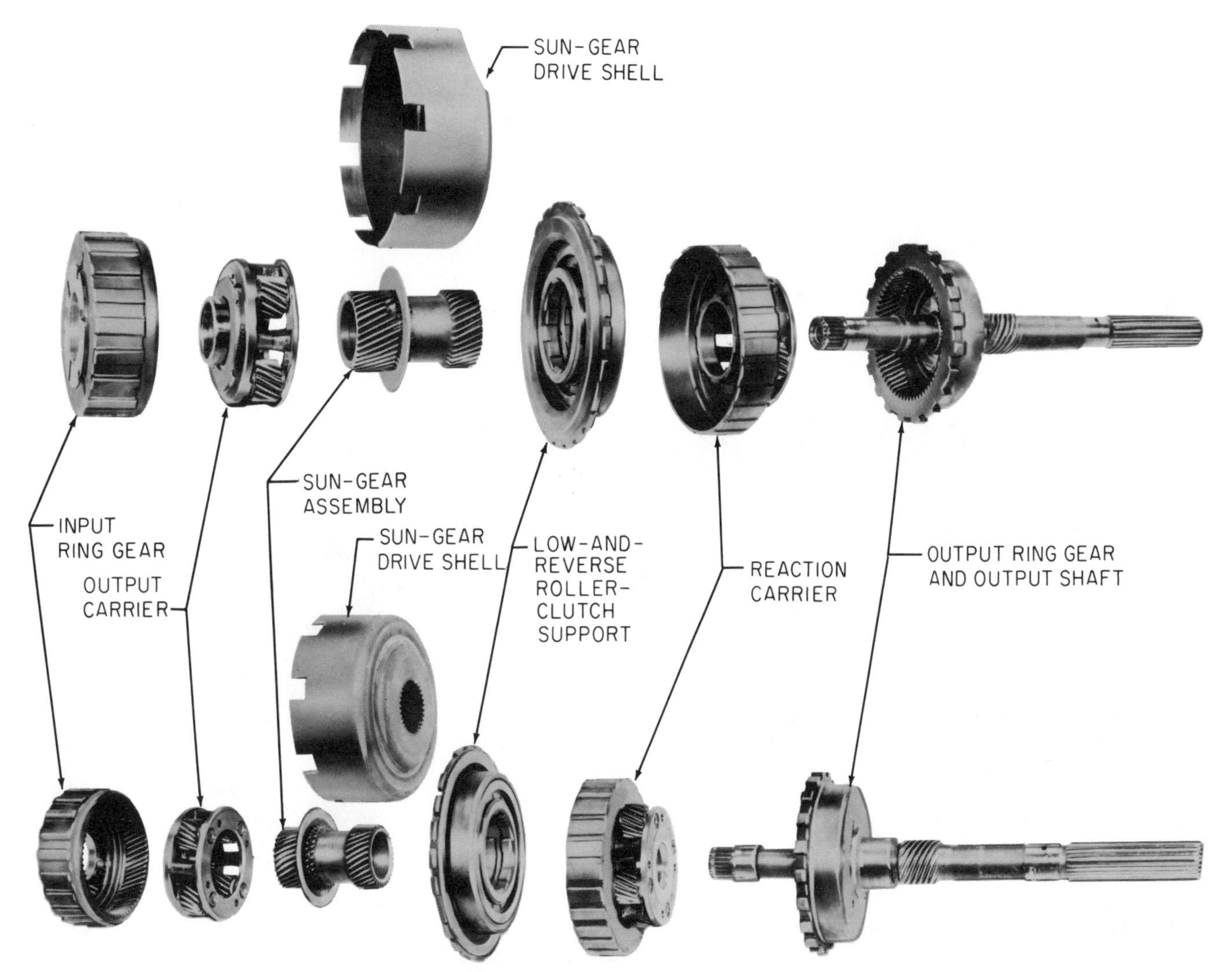

Figure 17 Planetary-gear train in exploded view. Note that there are two views of each part. *(Chevrolet Motor Division of General Motors Corporation.)*

that the retaining ring can be removed. Now, the piston return seat, 21 springs, and forward-clutch-piston assembly can be removed.

3. Remove the piston inner and outer seals.

Inspection

Check clutch plates for signs of wear, burning, or scoring. Check springs for collapsed coils or signs of distortion. Check the piston and clutch drum for signs of wear or other damage. Make sure oil passages are open. Inspect the input shaft for damaged splines, worn bushing journals, cracks, or other damage, and make sure the oil passages are open. Check the ball-check exhaust to make sure it is free.

Reassembly

1. Install the inner and outer seals on the piston. Then install the forward-clutch-piston assembly in the clutch drum, using a piece of 0.020-inch (0.51-mm) piano wire crimped into copper tubing. This procedure is similar to the procedure for installing the direct-clutch piston.

2. Install the 12 springs and the spring retainer. Compress the springs with a special tool and install the retaining ring.

3. Lubricate the clutch plates with transmission oil and install the cushion spring, clutch plates, forward-clutch pressure plate, and retaining ring.

4. Use a feeler gauge to check the clearance between the pressure plate and the clutch plate, as shown in Fig. 16. If the clearance is less than 0.0105 inch (0.263 mm), a thinner pressure plate should be used. If the clearance is greater than 0.082 inch (2.08 mm), a thicker pressure plate should be used. The correct clearance is between 0.0105 and 0.082 (0.263 and 2.08 mm). Pressure plates of three thicknesses are available.

■ 5-4-11 Sun-Gear and Drive-Shell Service

The sun gear and drive shell, along with the other components of the planetary-gear train, are shown in exploded view in Fig 17.

1. Remove the sun-gear-to-drive-shell rear retaining ring. Then lift off the rear flat-steel thrust washer. Then remove the front retaining ring.

2. Check the gear and shell for wear.

3. On reassembly, use new retaining rings.

NOTE: If sun-gear bushings require replacement, they may be removed with a cape chisel, and the new bushings pressed in with the special tool required.

■ 5-4-12 Low-and-Reverse-Roller-Clutch Service

This assembly is shown in exploded view in Fig. 18. The parts

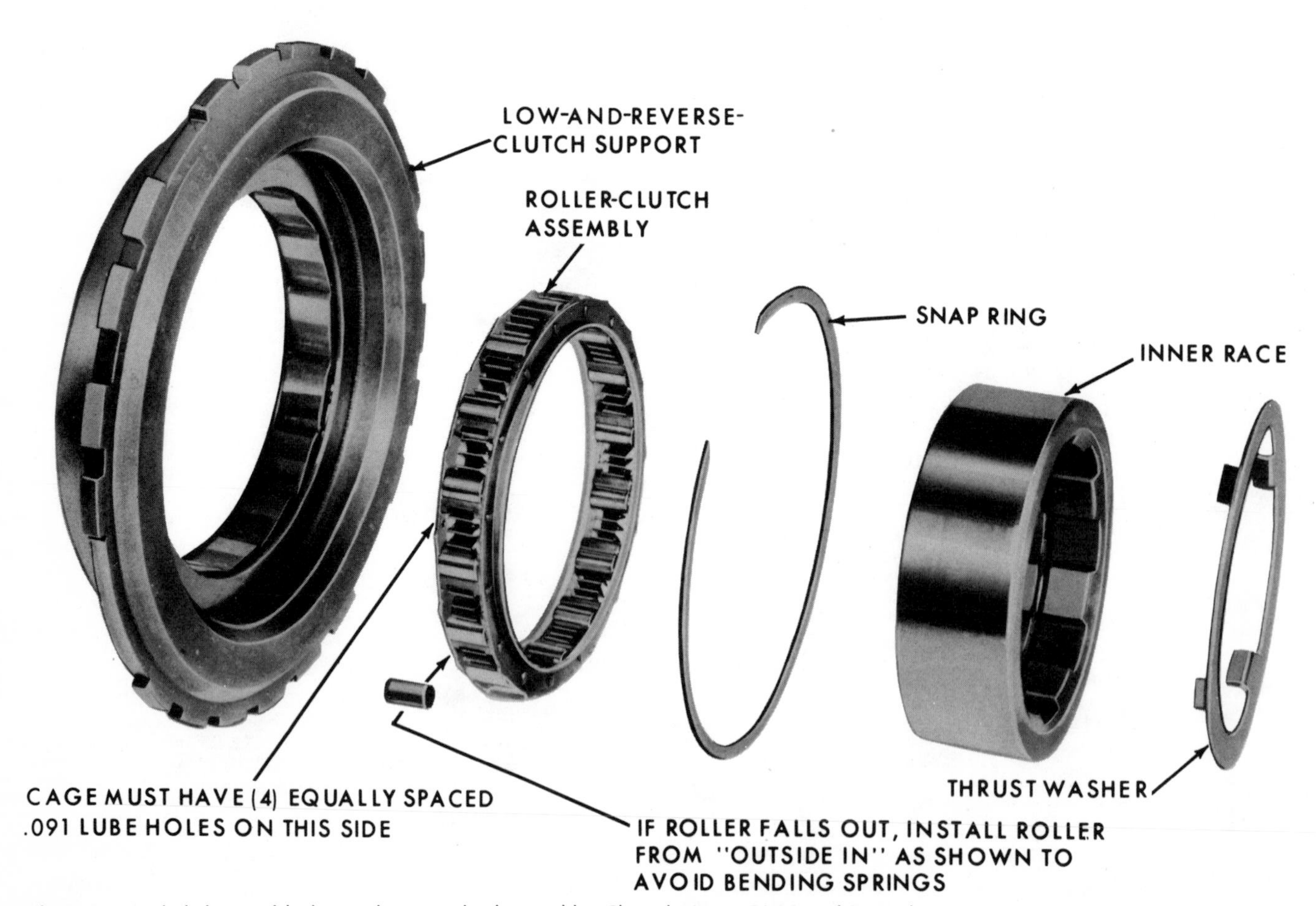

Figure 18 Exploded view of the low-and-reverse-clutch assembly. *(Chevrolet Motor Division of General Motors Corporation.)*

are separated by removing the thrust washer and retaining ring. Inspect the roller races and rollers for wear, scratches, or other damage. Check the springs for distortion.

When reassembling, be sure that the roller-clutch assembly is installed in the support with oil holes to the rear of the transmission. Make sure that the inner race freewheels in a clockwise direction only.

■ 5-4-13 Governor Service

The governor is serviced by disassembling it completely, with the exception of the driven gear, which can be replaced. The reason for this is that the parts are selectively fitted and each assembly is carefully calibrated to give the required performance. If drive-gear replacement is required, or if foreign matter has gotten into the governor so that it does not perform properly, the governor can be disassembled, as follows.

Refer to Fig 19. Cut off one end of each governor weight pin and remove the pins, thrust cap, weights, and springs. Remove the valve from the governor sleeve.

Wash all parts in cleaning solvent and air-dry. Blow out all passages. Inspect the sleeve and valve for nicks, burrs, or other damage. Check the governor sleeve for free operation in the bore of the transmission case. The governor valve should slide freely in the bore of the sleeve. Springs and weights should be in good condition. If the driven gear is damaged, it may be replaced as follows.

A special service package is available, containing a new driven gear, two weight-retaining pins, and a gear-retainer split pin. To replace the driven gear, drive out the old split pin with a small punch. Support the sleeve on 3/16-inch (4.762-mm) plates installed in the exhaust slots of the sleeve, and press the gear out of the sleeve in an arbor press. Clean the governor sleeve. Press the new driven gear into the sleeve until it is nearly seated. Remove any chips that may have been shaved off the gear, and press the gear on in until it bottoms on the shoulder. Drill a new pinhole 90° from the old one. Install the split retaining pin. Wash the sleeve off to remove any chips or dirt.

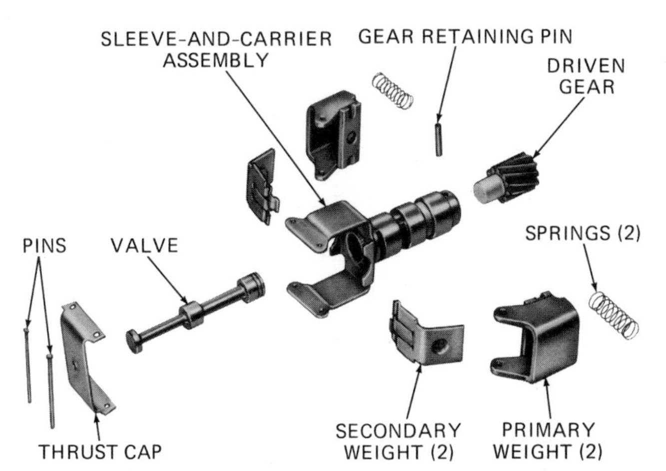

Figure 19 Disassembled view of the governor. *(Chevrolet Motor Division of General Motors Corporation.)*

Reassemble the governor by installing the valve in the sleeve, large-land end first. Install the weights, springs, and thrust cap and secure with new pins. Crimp both ends of the pins to keep them from falling out. Check for free operation of weights and valve in the sleeve.

■ 5-4-14 Valve-Body Service

There is nothing especially difficult about disassembling the valve body, although extreme care must be used to avoid dirt and damage to finished surfaces. The various valves and springs are held in place by retaining pins. The direct-clutch-accumulator piston is held in place by a retaining ring. Extreme cleanliness is essential in working on the valve body and valves. The slightest piece of lint or dirt can cause a valve to hold up, and this could cause the transmission to malfunction and even be severely damaged. Be sure to identify all springs as they are removed so that they can be replaced in the proper positions.

Handle the valves with great care in order to avoid damaging the operating surfaces. Here, again, any dent or burr can cause the valve to hold up with possible serious consequences.

Clean all parts in cleaning solvent and air-dry them. Make sure all oil passages in the valve body are clear.

■ 5-4-15 Transmission Reassembly

Cleanliness is extremely important when handling any transmission parts. Hands, tools, and working area must be clean. If work is stopped before reassembly is complete, cover all openings with clean cloths.

During reassembly, lubricate all bushings with transmission oil. Coat thrust washers, both sides, with petroleum jelly.

Use all new seals and gaskets. Do not take chances on old ones.

Tighten all parts evenly and in the proper sequence when replacing screws or bolts. Use new retaining rings, as called for. Be careful not to overstress retaining rings. This could cause them to loosen in service with possible disastrous results. The reassembly procedure follows.

1. Install the low-and-reverse-clutch piston, with new seals to place, with the notch in the piston adjacent to the parking pawl.

2. Install 17 piston return springs and the spring retainer. Use the compressor tool to compress the springs so that the retaining ring can be installed.

3. Install the output ring gear on the output shaft. Install the retaining ring. Install the reaction-carrier-to-output-ring-gear thrust washer into the output-ring-gear-support. This thrust washer has three tangs.

4. Put the output-ring-gear-to-case needle bearing into position and install the output-shaft assembly in the case.

5. Install the reaction-carrier assembly.

6. Oil and install the low-and-reverse-clutch plates. Start with a steel plate and alternate with faced plates. Secure with a retainer spring.

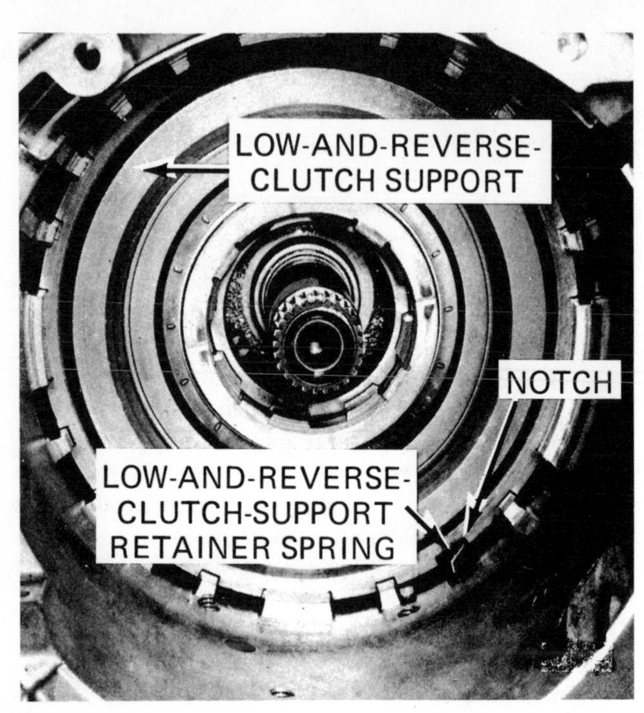

Figure 20 Location of notch in the retainer spring. *(Chevrolet Motor Division of General Motors Corporation.)*

7. Install the low-and-reverse-clutch-support assembly. The notch of the retainer spring should be located as shown in Fig. 20.

> **NOTE:** The splines in the inner race of the roller clutch must align with the splines on the reaction carrier.

8. Install the low-and-reverse-roller-clutch-inner-race-to-sun-gear-shell thrust washer. Install the retaining ring.

9. Install the sun-gear-and-drive-shell assembly.

10. Install the output-carrier assembly. Secure with a retainer ring and install the thrust washer.

11. Install the input ring gear and the thrust washer.

12. Install the direct-clutch assembly and special thrust washer to the forward-clutch assembly. There are two designs here. One design uses a thrust washer between the forward and direct clutches. The second design uses a Torrington needle bearing. When replacing the first design, use the new design parts. That is, use a new direct clutch, forward-clutch housing, and needle bearing.

13. Install the clutch assemblies in the case. Make sure that the forward-clutch face plates are positioned over the input ring gear and that the tangs on the direct-clutch housing are installed into the slots on the sun-gear drive shell.

14. Install the intermediate-overrun brake band.

15. Install the intermediate-clutch pressure plate.

16. Oil and install the intermediate-clutch plates, starting with a face plate and alternating steel and face plates. The notch in the steel reaction plates is installed toward the selector-lever inner bracket.

17. Install the intermediate-clutch cushion spring.

18. The pump is installed next, but during this procedure, the end play of the input shaft must be checked. If the end play is incorrect, the pump must be removed so that a selective thrust washer of the proper thickness can be installed. The procedure is as follows:

Install a selective-fit thrust washer, oil-pump gasket, and oil pump. Use two guide pins in two opposing holes in the case to align the oil pump as it is brought into position. Install and tighten the pump-to-case bolts. Mount a dial indicator. Pull out on the input shaft and set the dial indicator to zero. Push in on the input shaft to read the end play. The end play should be between 0.032 and 0.064 inches (0.81 and 1.63 mm). If it is not, then a different selective-fit thrust washer should be used. This means removal and reinstallation of the pump. Selective-fit washers are available in three thicknesses: 0.066, 0.083, and 0.100 inch (1.68, 2.11, and 2.54 mm).

19. After the proper selective-fit thrust washer is determined, the complete pump-installation procedure is as follows:

a. Install the correct thrust washer, first covering both sides with petroleum jelly.

c. Install a new square-cut oil-seal ring.

d. Install the pump, using two guide pins, as in item 18 above, to align it. Attach with bolts, using new washer-type seals.

> **NOTE:** Check the rotation of the input shaft as the pump is pulled down into place. If the input shaft cannot be rotated freely, the direct- and forward-clutch housings have not been properly installed. That is, the clutch plates are not indexing. Remove the necessary parts to secure proper indexing. Otherwise, parts will break as the pump is pulled down into place.

20. Put the drive-gear retainer clip into the hole in the output shaft, align the slot in the speedometer-drive gear with a retainer clip, and install the gear on the shaft.

21. Install the extension-housing-to-case square-cut ring seal, and attach the extension housing to the case with attaching bolts. Torque to 25 pound-feet (3.46 kg-m).

22. Install the parking pawl, with the tooth toward the inside of the case. Then install the disengaging spring on the pawl and slide the shaft into place. See Fig. 7. Drive the retainer plug flush to 0.010 inch (0.25 mm) below the case, using a 3/8-inch (9.53-mm) rod. Stake the plug in three places.

23. Install the park-lock bracket and torque bolts to 29 pound-feet (4.01 kg-m).

24. With the actuating rod attached to the range-selector inner lever, put the assembly into place.

25. Install the manual shaft through the case and the range-selector inner lever. Install the retaining nut on the manual shaft and torque to 25 pound-feet (3.46 kg-m). Install the manual-shaft-to-case spacer clip.

26. Next, install the intermediate-servo piston, washer, spring seat, and apply pin. We have already explained how to check the band apply pin for correct length. See Fig. 8. When installing the piston, use a new metal oil-seal ring.

27. Install the four check balls in the transmission-case

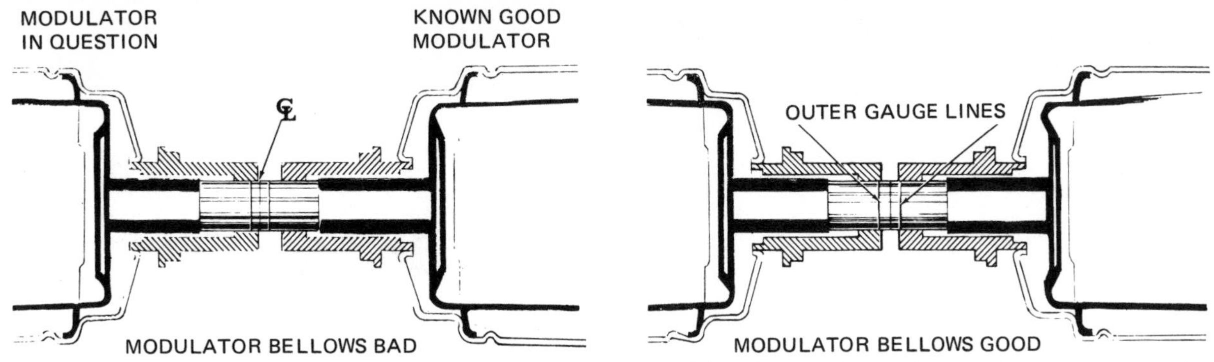

Figure 21 Checking a possible defective modulator bellows against a modulator known to be good. *(Chevrolet Motor Division of General Motors Corporation.)*

pockets, as shown in Fig. 6.

> **NOTE:** If check balls are missing, complete transmission failure may occur.

28. Install the oil-pump pressure screen and governor screens in the case.

29. Install the valve-body spacer-plate-to-case gasket and spacer plate.

30. Install the valve-body-to-spacer-plate gasket and spacer support plate. Torque the support-plate bolts to 13 pound-feet (1.80 kg-m).

31. Connect the detent-control-valve link to the actuating lever. See Fig. 5.

32. Install the valve body. Connect the manual-control-valve link to the range-selector inner lever. Torque bolts in random sequence to 13 pound-feet (1.80 kg-m). Leave a bolt loose for the detent-spring-and-roller assembly. See Fig. 5.

> **NOTE:** When handling the valve body, be careful that the retainer pins do not fall out.

33. Install the manual-shaft-to-case retainer ring and detent-spring-and-roller assembly, as shown in Fig. 5.

34. Install the strainer-assembly gasket and strainer.

35. Install the new gasket and oil pan.

> **NOTE:** The intermediate-clutch-accumulator assembly must be installed, as explained in ■ 5-4-6, before the oil pan is installed.

36. Install the governor assembly, cover, seal, and retainer wire.

37. Install the vacuum-modulator valve and retainer clip. Lubricate the O-ring seal to prevent damaging it. Torque the clip bolt to 12 pound-feet (1.66 kg-m).

38. Before installing the converter, check it for leaks and end play (Part 5, Sec. 2).

39. Transmission installation is essentially the reverse of removal except for the following added steps: Before replacing the flex-plate-to-converter bolts, make sure that the attaching lugs on the converter are flush with the flex plate and that the converter rotates freely by hand in this position. Then, hand-start all three bolts and tighten them finger tight before torquing to specifications. This ensures proper alignment of the converter. After replacement is complete, remove the car from the hoist and check the linkage for proper adjustment. Check the fluid level as explained in Part 5, Sec. 2, and add fluid as necessary.

■ 5-4-16 Vacuum-Modulator Check Turn the vacuum modulator so that the vacuum side points down. If oil comes out, the diaphragm is defective and the modulator must be replaced. Make a bellows-comparison check with a vacuum modulator known to be good, as shown in Fig. 21. Using the gauge as shown, install the two modulators on either end of the gauge. Hold the modulators horizontal, and push them toward each other until either modulator sleeve end just touches the line in the center of the gauge. The gap between the other modulator sleeve end and the line should be 1/16 inch (1.6 mm) or less. If it is more, the modulator being checked should be discarded.

SECTION 5-5 | TorqueFlite Transmission Service

This section covers the trouble-diagnosis and service procedures for the Chrysler TorqueFlite transmission used on Chrysler, Imperial, Dodge, and Plymouth automobiles. There are two basic models of the TorqueFlite, the A-727 and the A-904, as explained below.

■ **5-5-1 Basic Models of the TorqueFlite** There are two basic models of the TorqueFlite transmission: The A-727 and the A-904. They are used with the engines shown in the chart in Fig. 1. Note that the A-904 is used with small-output engines while the A-727 is used with high-output engines. There are a number of internal differences that we shall illustrate and describe when we discuss the transmissions. For example, the A-904 has one large spring in its front clutch while the A-727 has several small springs. There are also differences in the rear clutches, planetary-gear trains, and overrunning clutches. We discuss these differences later.

■ **5-5-2 Operating Cautions** See Part 5, Sect. 2, for operating cautions and towing instructions.

TROUBLE DIAGNOSIS

■ **5-5-3 Transmission Trouble Diagnosis** Figures 2 to 5 are trouble-diagnosis charts for the TorqueFlite transmission. Figure 2 is a general chart, listing possible trouble conditions in the left-hand column. Possible causes are listed horizontally at the top of the chart. To find the causes of a trouble, locate the trouble in the column to the left. Then run across the chart horizontally, noting the X's on the horizontal line. Each X indicates a possible cause.

Figure 3 is a diagnosis guide to follow if the car will not move in any selector-lever position. Figure 4 is a diagnosis guide to follow if there is abnormal noise that seems to come from the transmission. Figure 5 is a diagnosis guide to follow if the transmission leaks fluid.

The chart in Fig. 6 lists the shift patterns of the TorqueFlite transmission as used on different engines. Note that the figures

TORQUEFLITE TRANSMISSION APPLICATION AND STALL SPEED

TRANSMISSION ASSEMBLY NO.*	ENGINE in^3	TRANSMISSION TYPE	CONVERTER DIAMETER, in	STALL rpm	APPLICATION
3681841	198	A-904	$10\frac{3}{4}$	1,625-1,925	Any models
3681841	225	A-904	$10\frac{3}{4}$	1,800-2,100	equipped with
3681843	318	A-904-LA	$10\frac{3}{4}$	2,125-2,425	these engines
3681861	225	A-727	$11\frac{3}{4}$	1,400-1,700	Police & taxi
3681862	318	A-727	$11\frac{3}{4}$	1,725-2,025	Police & taxi
3681863	360-4 hp	A-727	$10\frac{3}{4}$	2,200-2,500	(VLBJRW)
3681862	360-2 360-4	A-727	$10\frac{3}{4}$	2,300-2,600	(PDC)
3681864	400-2 400-4	A-727	$11\frac{3}{4}$	1,875-2,175	(BJRWPDC)
3681865	400-4 hp	A-727	$10\frac{3}{4}$	2,400-2,700	Hi. Perf. (BJRWPDC)
3681866	440-4	A-727	$11\frac{3}{4}$	1,975-2,275	(PDCY)
3681867	440-4	A-727	$10\frac{3}{4}$	2,600-2,900	Hi. Perf. (RW)
3681867	440-4	A-727	$11\frac{3}{4}$	2,100-2,400	Hi. Perf. (PDC)

*Part numbers subject to change during model year. Number is found on left side of transmission oil-pan flange.

Figure 1 Table of TorqueFlite transmission applications and stall speeds. *(Chrysler Corporation.)*

POSSIBLE CAUSE

1. Engine idle speed too high
2. Hydraulic pressures too low
3. Low-reverse band out of adjustment
4. Valve-body malfunction or leakage
5. Low-reverse servo, band or linkage malfunction
6. Low fluid level
7. Incorrect gearshift-control-linkage adjustment
8. Oil filter clogged
9. Faulty oil pump
10. Worn or broken input-shaft seal rings
11. Aerated fluid
12. Engine idle speed too low
13. Incorrect throttle-linkage adjustment
14. Kickdown band out of adjustment
15. Overrunning clutch not holding
16. Output-shaft bearing and/or bushing damaged
17. Governor-support seal rings broken or worn
18. Worn or broken reaction-shaft-support seal rings
19. Governor malfunction
20. Kickdown servo band or linkage malfunction
21. Worn or faulty front clutch
22. High fluid level
23. Breather clogged
24. Hydraulic pressure too high
25. Kickdown-band adjustment too tight
26. Faulty cooling system
27. Insufficient clutch-plate clearance
28. Worn or faulty rear clutch
29. Rear clutch dragging
30. Planetary gear sets broken or seized
31. Overrunning clutch worn, broken or seized
32. Overrunning clutch inner race damaged

CONDITION	1	2	3	4	5	6	7	8	9	10	11	12	13	14	15	16	17	18	19	20	21	22	23	24	25	26	27	28	29	30	31	32
HARSH ENGAGEMENT FROM NEUTRAL TO D OR R	X			X																				X				X				
DELAYED ENGAGEMENT FROM NEUTRAL TO D OR R		X		X	X	X	X	X	X	X	X	X						X			X							X				
RUNAWAY UPSHIFT		X		X		X		X			X		X					X		X	X											
NO UPSHIFT		X		X		X	X						X				X	X	X	X	X											
3-2 KICKDOWN RUNAWAY		X		X		X					X		X	X				X		X	X											
NO KICKDOWN OR NORMAL DOWNSHIFT				X									X						X	X												
SHIFTS ERRATIC		X		X		X	X	X	X		X		X				X	X	X	X	X											
SLIPS IN FORWARD DRIVE POSITIONS		X		X		X	X	X	X	X	X		X		X													X			X	
SLIPS IN REVERSE ONLY		X	X	X	X	X	X		X		X							X			X											
SLIPS IN ALL POSITIONS		X		X		X		X	X	X	X																					
NO DRIVE IN ANY POSITION		X		X		X		X	X																					X		
NO DRIVE IN FORWARD DRIVE POSITIONS		X		X		X				X					X													X		X	X	
NO DRIVE IN REVERSE		X	X	X	X		X											X			X							X		X		
DRIVES IN NEUTRAL				X			X																				X	X	X			
DRAGS OR LOCKS			X																						X					X	X	
GRATING, SCRAPING GROWLING NOISE			X											X		X														X	X	
BUZZING NOISE				X		X					X																					X
HARD TO FILL, OIL BLOWS OUT FILLER TUBE								X			X											X	X									
TRANSMISSION OVERHEATS	X	X				X	X		X																X	X	X					
HARSH UPSHIFT		X											X	X										X								
DELAYED UPSHIFT													X	X			X	X	X	X	X											

Figure 2 Diagnosis chart for the TorqueFlite transmission. *(Chrysler Corporation.)*

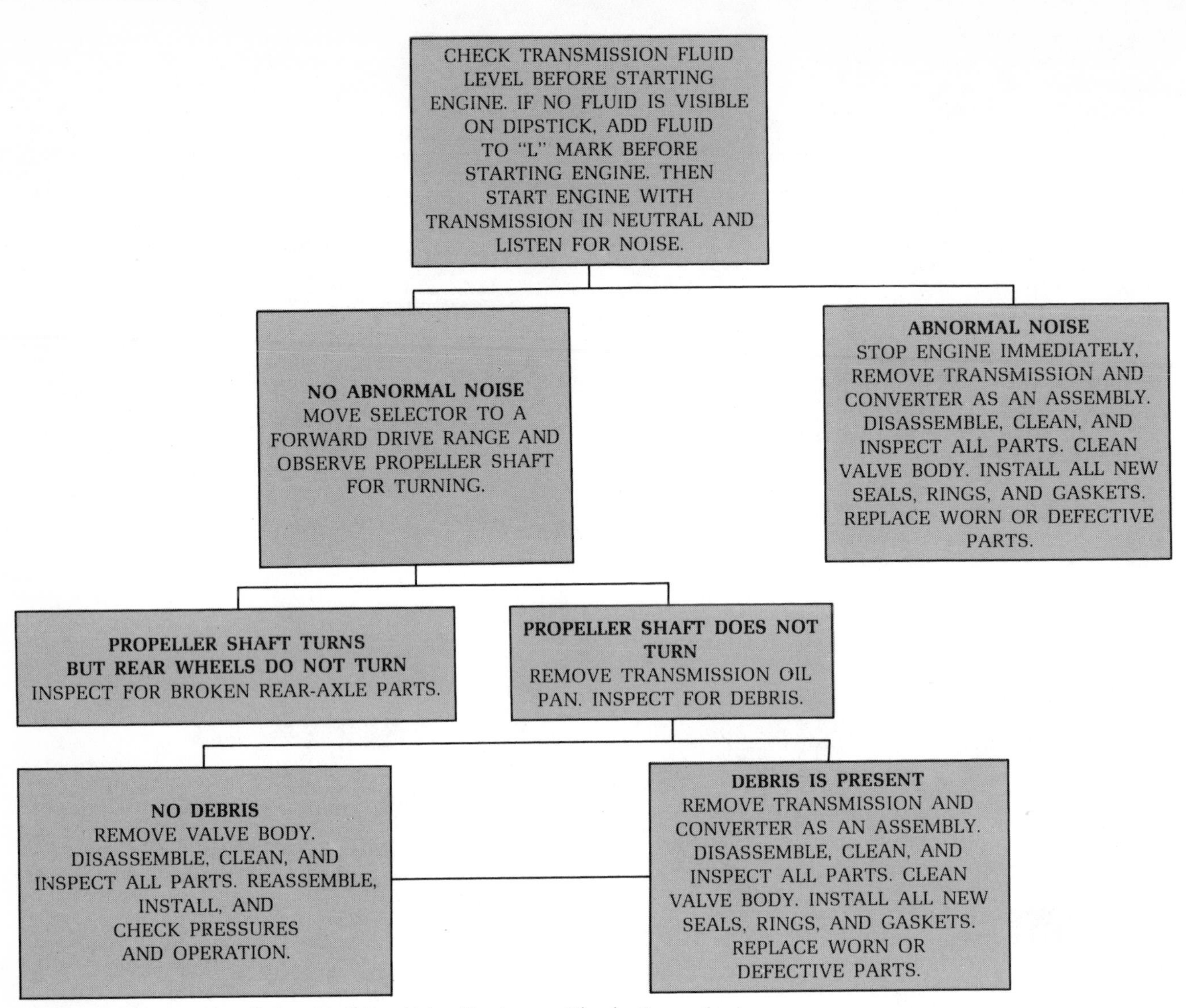

Figure 3 Diagnosis guide to find trouble if the vehicle will not move. *(Chrysler Corporation.)*

vary somewhat, but this is not important as long as the shifts are smooth and responsive and there is no noticeable engine runaway.

Three tests are made on the TorqueFlite transmission for diagnostic purposes: the stall test, hydraulic-control pressure tests, the air-pressure tests. These are covered in following sections.

■ **5-5-4 Stall Test** The stall test consists in determining engine speed obtained at full throttle in the D (drive) range. This test checks the torque-converter stator clutch and the holding ability of the transmission clutches. Check the transmission oil level and bring the engine up to operating temperature before beginning the stall test.

Do not hold the throttle wide open for more than 5 seconds at a time! If you have to make more than one stall check, run the engine at 1000 rpm in neutral for 20 seconds between runs

> **NOTE:** Both the parking and service brakes must be fully applied and both front wheels blocked while making this test. Do not allow anyone to stand in front of the car during the test!

to cool the transmission. If engine speed exceeds the maximum limits shown in the chart in Fig. 1, release the throttle at once since this condition indicates clutch slippage.

To make the stall test, connect a tachometer that can be read from the driver's seat, block the front wheels, apply both brakes, and open the throttle wide. Read the top engine speed and compare it with the reading on the chart (Fig. 1) for the model being tested.

> **NOTE:** Make the test in 5 seconds or less!

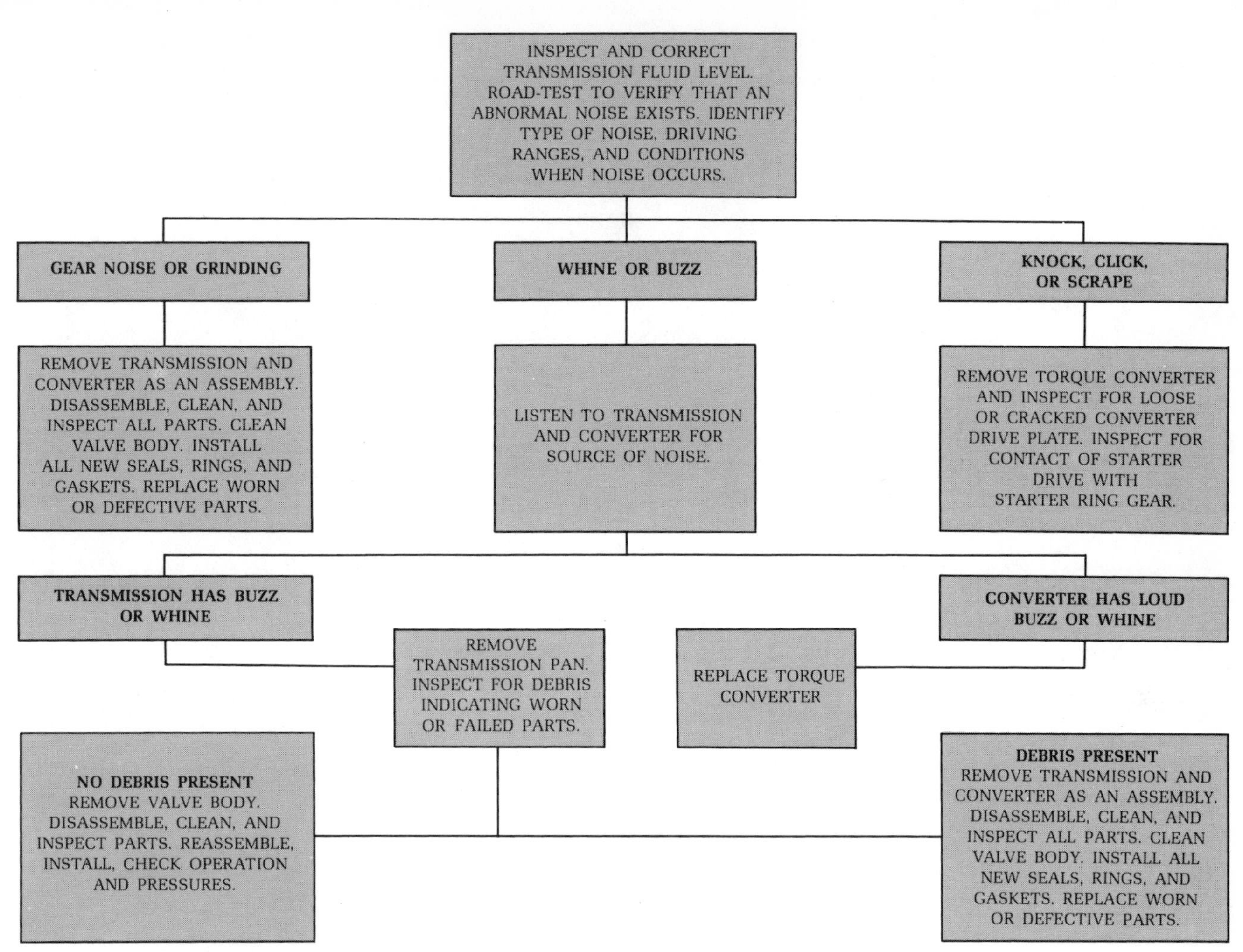

Figure 4 Diagnosis guide to find trouble if the transmission has abnormal noises. *(Chrysler Corporation.)*

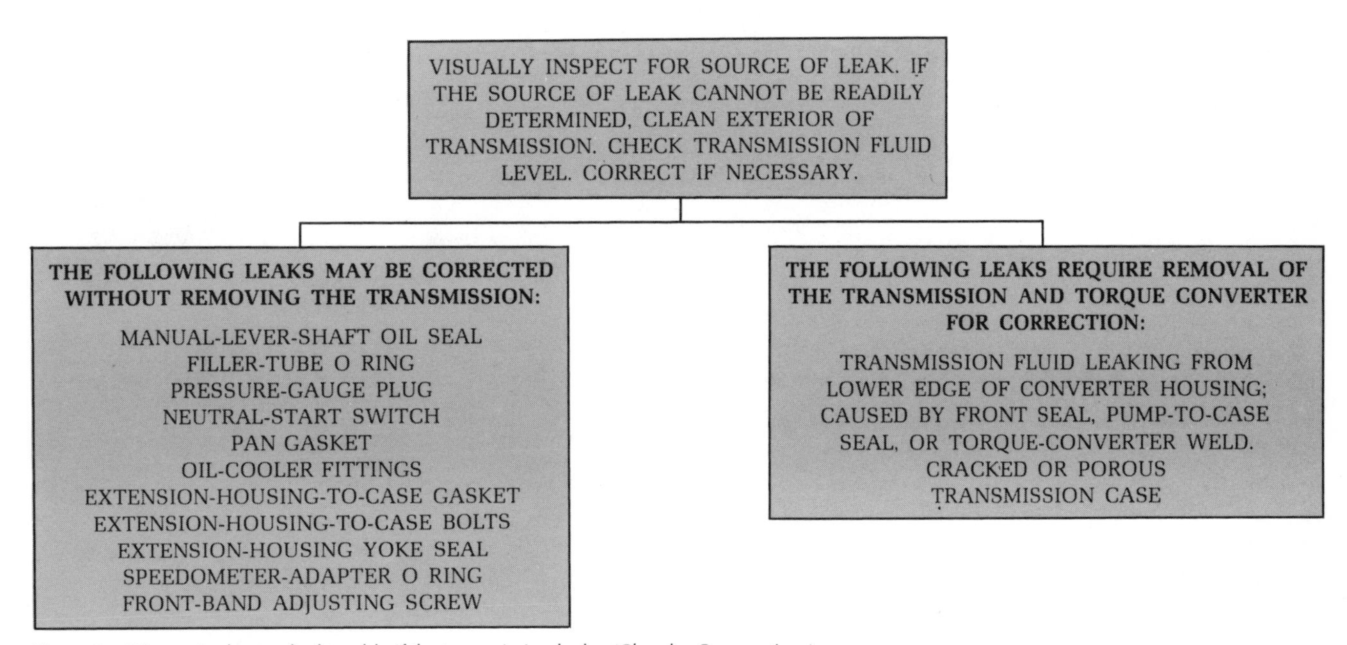

Figure 5 Diagnosis chart to find trouble if the transmission leaks. *(Chrysler Corporation.)*

CARLINE	VL	RW	BJ	PDC	PDC	PDC	Y
Engine in^3	198 225	318	360-4 Hi. Perf.	360-2 360-4	400-2 400-4	400-4 & 440 Hi. Perf.	440
Axle ratio	2.76	2.71	3.23	2.71	2.76	3.23	3.23
Tire size	6.95 X 14	E78 X 14	F70 X 14	F78 X 15	G78 X 15	G78 X 15	L84 X 15
Throttle minimum							
1-2 upshift	9–16	8–16	8–15	9–16	9–16	8–15	8–16
2-3 upshift	15–25	15–25	15–23	17–25	15–25	15–23	16–25
3-1 downshift	9–13	8–12	7-10	8–11	9–12	8–13	8–11
Throttle wide open							
1-2 upshift	31–43	35–48	33–44	37–51	37–51	36–47	33–46
2-3 upshift	65–75	72–89	62–71	77–89	76–88	62–77	68–80
Kickdown limit							
3-2 W.O.T. downshift	62–72	70–79	60–68	73–83	73–83	60–72	66–75
3-2 part-throttle downshift	47–57	26–52	26–46	27–54	28–54	27–50	25–45
3-1 W.O.T. downshift	28–33	27–37	28–35	28–38	28–38	28–38	25–34
Governor pressure*							
15 psi	20–22	20–22	17–18	20–22	21–22	16–19	18–20
40 psi	38–43	44–50	40–45	46–50	46–50	42–46	41–46
60 psi	57–62	66–71	56–61	68–73	68–73	59–63	60–65

*Governor pressure should be from 0 to 1.5 psi at standstill, or downshift may not occur.

Note: Figures given are typical for other models. Changes in tire size or axle ratio will cause shift points to occur at corresponding higher or lower vehicle speeds.

Figure 6 Chart showing automatic-transmission shift speeds and governor pressures. Miles per hour are only approximate and will vary somewhat from one model to another. *(Chrysler Corporation.)*

1. STALL SPEED ABOVE SPECIFICATIONS If the engine speed increases by more than 200 rpm above the specification in the chart, clutch slippage is indicated. Release the throttle at once to avoid damage to the transmission. Clutch slippage requires further checking, and the transmission hydraulic-control- and air-pressure checks should be made, as explained in ■5-5-5 to ■5-5-7.

2. STALL TEST BELOW SPECIFICATIONS Low stall speed with a properly tuned engine indicates torque-converter stator-clutch problems, and a road test is necessary to determine what is wrong. If stall speeds are 250 to 350 rpm below specifications and the vehicle operates properly at highway speeds but has poor through-gear acceleration, the stator clutch is slipping. If the stall speed and acceleration are normal, but abnormally high throttle opening is required to maintain highway speed, the stator clutch has seized. With either of these stator defects, the torque converter must be replaced.

■ 5-5-5 Hydraulic-Control Pressure Tests

These tests check the pressures in the hydraulic system during different operating conditions and can reveal certain defects.

1. LINE PRESSURE AND KICKDOWN-SERVO RELEASE PRESSURE This check is made in D with the rear wheels free to turn. Transmission fluid must be at operating temperature [150 to 200°F (65.6 to 93.8°C)]. Install an engine tachometer, raise the car on a hoist that leaves the rear wheels free, and position the tachometer so it can be read from under the car.

a. Connect two 0- to 100-psi (0- to 7.031-kg/cm^2) pressure gauges to the pressure-takeoff plugs to check line pressure and kickdown-servo release pressure. See Fig. 7 for connection points.

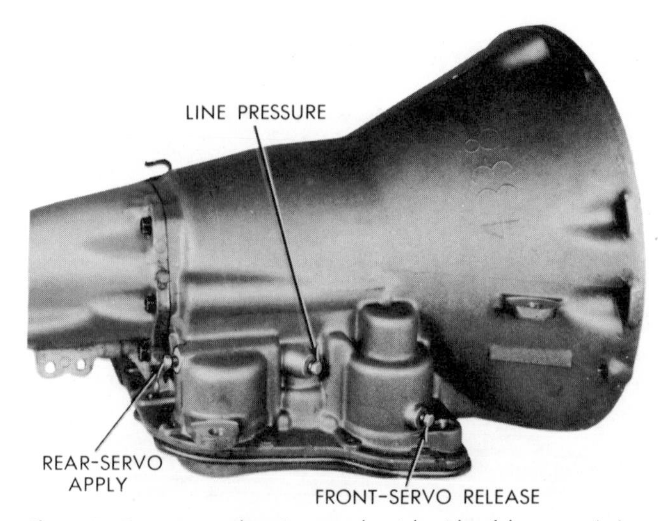

Figure 7 Pressure-test locations on the right side of the transmission case. *(Chrysler Corporation.)*

b. With the control in D, speed up the engine slightly so that the transmission shifts into direct gear. Reduce the engine slowly to 1,000 rpm. Now, line pressure must be 54 to 60 psi (3.797 to 4.219 kg/cm²). Kickdown-servo release pressure must not be more than 3 psi (0.21 kg/cm²) below line pressure.

c. Disconnect the throttle linkage from the transmission throttle lever and move the transmission throttle lever gradually to the full-throttle position. Line pressure must rise to a maximum of 90 to 96 psi (6.328 to 6.750 kg/cm²) just before or at kickdown into low gear. Kickdown-servo release pressure must follow line pressure up and should be not more than 3 psi (0.021 kg/cm²) below it.

If the line pressure is not 54 to 60 psi (3.797 to 4.219 kg/cm²) at 1,000 rpm, make adjustments as explained in ■5-5-6. This requires removal of the valve body. If the kickdown-servo release pressures are below specifications, with line pressures okay, there is excessive leakage in the front clutch or in the kickdown-servo circuit.

NOTE: Always check the external transmission throttle lever for looseness on the valve-body shaft when making the pressure check.

2. LUBRICATION PRESSURE This check is made by installing a "tee" fitting at the cooler return line, shown in Fig. 8. Connect a 0- to 100-psi (0- to 7.031-kg/cm²) pressure gauge to the "tee" fitting. At 1,000 engine rpm, with the throttle closed and the transmission in D, lubrication pressure should be 5 to 15 psi (0.352 to 1.055 kg/cm²). It will just about double as the throttle is opened to maximum line pressure.

3. REAR-SERVO APPLY PRESSURE Connect a 0- to 300-psi (0- to 21-kg/cm²) gauge to the rear-servo apply-pressure takeoff, shown in Fig. 8. With the transmission in R and the engine running at 1,600 rpm, the pressure should be 230 to 300 psi (16.171 to 21.090 kg/cm²).

4. GOVERNOR PRESSURE Connect a 0- to 100-psi (0- to 7.031-kg/cm²) gauge to the governor-pressure takeoff point, shown in Fig. 8. Governor pressure should fall within the limits shown in the chart in Fig. 6. If it does not, or if pressure does not fall to 0 to 1.5 psi (0 to 0.106 kg/cm²) when the car stops, the governor valve or weights are sticking and the valve assembly must be removed for service.

■ 5-5-6 Hydraulic-Control Pressure Adjustments

There are two pressure adjustments that can be made: line pressure and throttle pressure. We explained how to check line pressure in ■5-5-5. If it is not correct, then the throttle pressure must be adjusted first, followed by an adjustment of line pressure. These adjustments require removal of the valve body, as we shall explain. The valve body should be mounted in a valve-body repair stand. Also, note the cautions about cleanliness in Part 5, Sec. 2.

1. THROTTLE PRESSURE Loosen the locknut on the throttle-lever stop screw. Back the screw off 5 turns. Use the

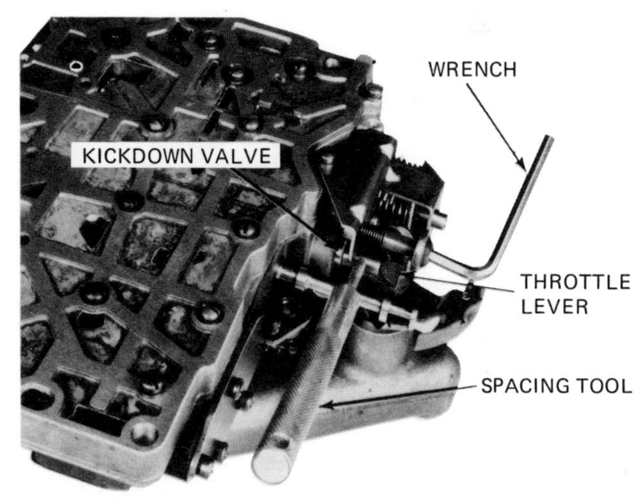

Figure 9 Throttle-pressure adjustment. *(Chrysler Corporation.)*

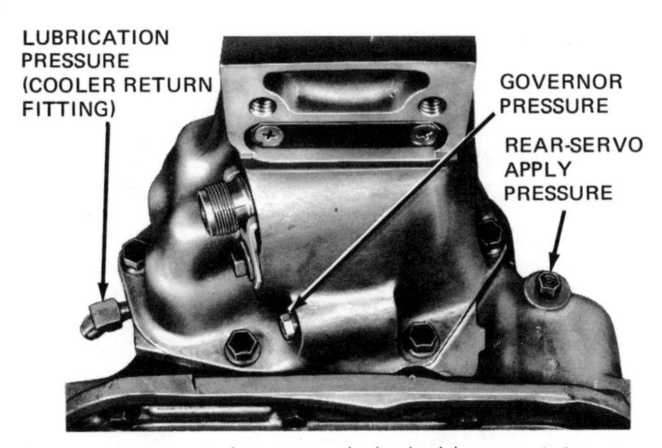

Figure 8 Pressure-test locations at the back of the transmission case. *(Chrysler Corporation.)*

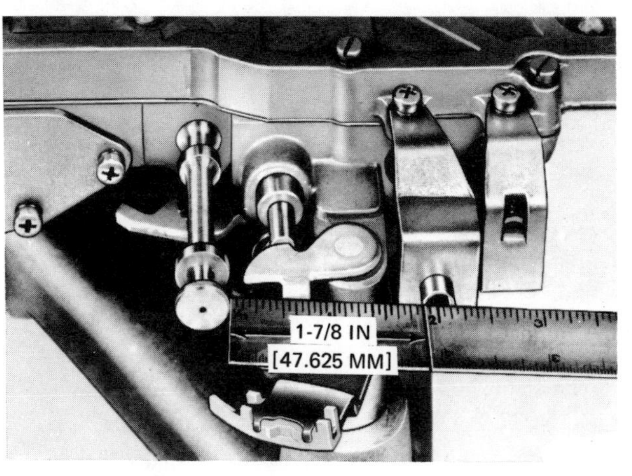

Figure 10 Measuring spring-retainer location. *(Chrysler Corporation.)*

gauge pin, as shown in Fig. 9, between the throttle-lever cam and the kickdown valve. Push in on the tool to push the kickdown valve all the way in so that the throttle valve will bottom in the valve body. Now tighten the stop screw finger tight against the tang with the throttle-lever cam touching the gauge pin, as shown. Be sure the kickdown valve is pushed in as far as it will go. Remove the tool and tighten the locknut without turning the stop screw.

2. *LINE PRESSURE* First, check the distance between the manual valve and the line-pressure adjusting screw, as shown in Fig. 10. This distance should measure 1⅞ inches (47.625 mm) with the manual valve in L (low). If the measurement is off, it means the spring retainer is not square with the valve body; the spring, hitting the pressure-regulator valve at an angle, may cause it to cock and hang up, thus preventing normal pressure regulation. You can correct the measurement by loosening the spring-retainer screws and moving the retainer as necessary. Tighten the screws and recheck the measurement to make sure it is correct.

Next, measure the distance between the valve body and the inner edge of the adjusting nut, as shown in Fig. 11. This distance should be approximately 1 5/16 inches (33.3 mm). Adjustment can be made to obtain the proper line pressure by turning the adjusting screw with an allen wrench. One complete turn of the adjusting screw represents about 1⅔ psi (0.117 kg/cm²). Turn the screw clockwise to decrease pressure, and counterclockwise to increase pressure.

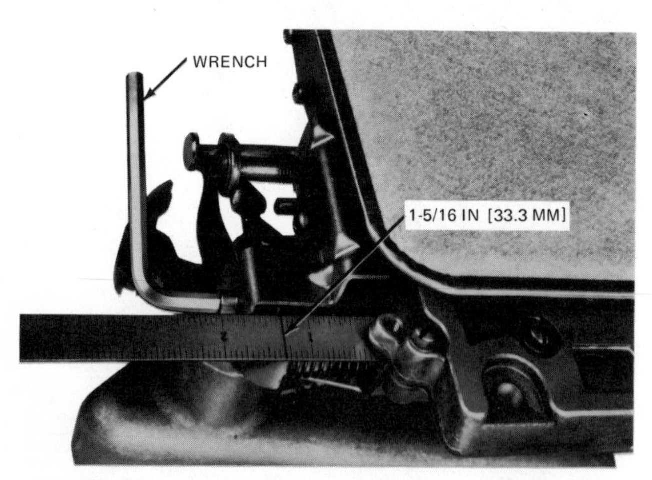

Figure 11 Line-pressure adjustment. *(Chrysler Corporation.)*

■ **5-5-7 Air-Pressure Tests** The clutches, bands, and servos can be checked with air pressure to determine whether they are working. First, remove the valve body. Then apply air pressure at 30 to 100 psi (2.109 to 7.031 kg/cm²) to the proper oil passages in the transmission. These passages are shown in Fig. 12.

NOTE: Compressed air must be clean and dry!

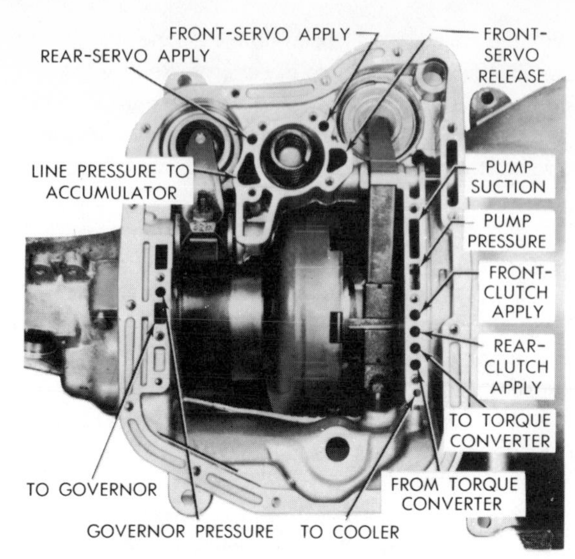

Figure 12 Air-pressure tests. *(Chrysler Corporation.)*

1. *FRONT CLUTCH* Apply air pressure to the front-clutch apply passage and listen for a dull thud, which indicates that the clutch has engaged. Hold pressure for a few seconds and check for oil leakage.

2. *REAR CLUTCH* Apply air pressure to the rear-clutch apply passage and listen for a dull thud, which indicates clutch engagement. Inspect for oil leaks.

NOTE: If you cannot hear the thud, touch the clutch housing with your fingertips as you apply air pressure. If the clutch engages, you can feel it.

3. *KICKDOWN SERVO AND LOW-AND-REVERSE SERVO* Apply air pressure to the kickdown-servo and low-and-reverse-servo passages, in turn, and note whether the related brake band tightens. It should tighten, and when air pressure is released, spring pressure should release the band.

NOTE: If clutches and servos operate properly, but shifting is incorrect, the trouble is probably in the valve body itself.

TRANSMISSION ADJUSTMENTS

In addition to the hydraulic-control pressure adjustments described in ■5-5-6, other adjustments to be made include gearshift linkage, throttle-rod linkage, and brake band. Gearshift and throttle-rod linkage adjustments vary according to the application and car model. Refer to the applicable car shop manual for details.

■ **5-5-8 Band Adjustments** The two bands are adjusted as follows:

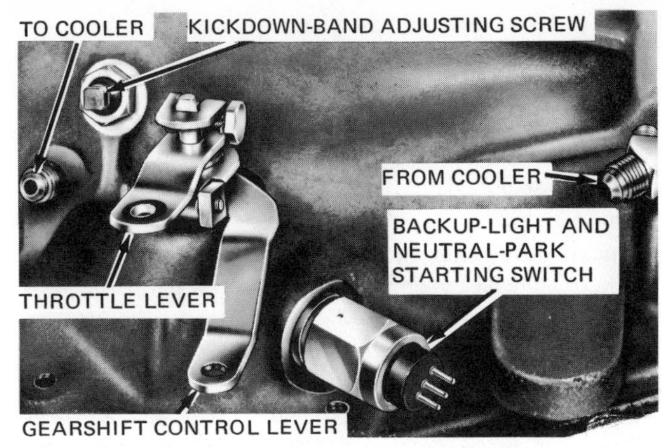

Figure 13 External controls and adjustments. *(Chrysler Corporation.)*

1. KICKDOWN BAND The kickdown-band adjusting screw is on the left side of the transmission case, as shown in Fig. 13. It is adjusted by loosening the locknut and backing off the screw about 5 turns, making sure it is backed off enough to be free of the band. Next, take a torque wrench and tighten the band adjusting screw to 72 pound-inches (2.29 kg-mm). Then back off the adjusting screw 2 turns, hold the screw, and tighten the locknut to 35 pound-feet (4.837 kg-m). (On the A-727 model used on the 426 engine, back off 1½ turns only.)

2. LOW-AND-REVERSE BAND Raise the car, drain the transmission fluid, and remove the oil pan. Note the position of the adjusting screw in Fig. 14. Loosen the locknut and back off the screw about 5 turns. Make sure the screw is backed off enough to be free of the band. Tighten the adjusting screw to 72 pound-feet (2.29 kg-m). Then, on the A-904, back off the adjusting screw 3¼ turns, or 4 turns for the 318 cubic inch [5,211 cc (cubic centimeter)] engine. On the A-727, back off 2 turns. Hold the adjusting screw and tighten the locknut to 30 pound-feet (4.146 kg-m).

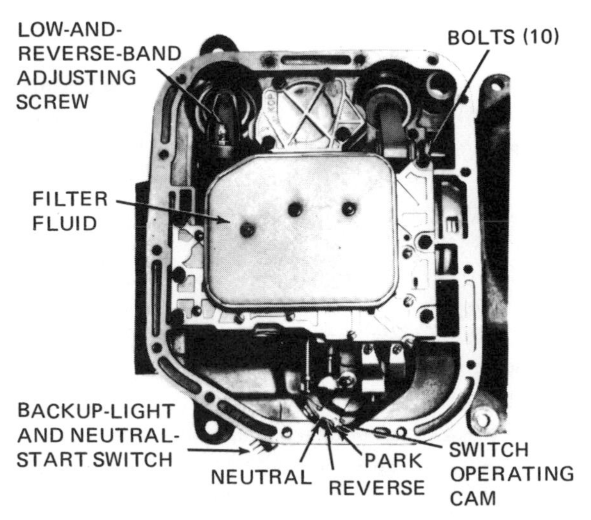

Figure 14 Bottom view of a transmission with the oil pan removed. *(Chrysler Corporation.)*

Reinstall the oil pan, using a new gasket. Tighten the pan bolts to 150 pound-inches (2.70 kg-mm). Fill the transmission with Dexron automatic-transmission fluid, as explained in Part 5, Sec. 2.

IN-CAR SERVICE

A number of services can be performed in the car without removing the complete transmission. These include lubrication, replacing the backup and neutral starting switch, replacing the speedometer pinion, some seals, the governor, and so on. We shall discuss each of these services in following sections. See Part 5, Sec. 2 for checking and changing fluid, service precautions, and cleaning and inspecting transmission parts.

■ 5-5-9 Backup and Neutral Starting Switch

The location of the neutral starting switch is shown in Fig. 14. To check the switch, remove the wiring connector and check for continuity with a low-voltage test light between the center pin of the switch and the transmission case. The light should go on only when the transmission is in P or N. If the switch tests bad, check the gearshift-linkage adjustment before replacing the switch.

To replace the switch, unscrew it and allow fluid to drain into a container. Move the selector lever to P and then N. Check to see that the switch-operating-lever fingers are centered in the switch opening in the case. Install a new switch, tightening it to 24 pound-feet (3.316 kg-m). Retest the switch and add fluid to replace the fluid lost. See Part 5, Sec. 2.

The backup-light-switch circuit extends through the two outside terminals of the switch. To test the switch, remove the wiring connector from the switch and check for continuity between the two outside pins. Continuity should exist only with the transmission in R. No continuity should exist from either pin to the transmission case. If the switch is defective, replace it, as previously explained.

■ 5-5-10 Speedometer Pinion

To replace the pinion, remove the bolt and retainer and carefully work the adapter and pinion out of the extension housing. If you find transmission fluid in the housing, replace the small oil seal in the adapter. The seal and retainer ring must be pushed in with a

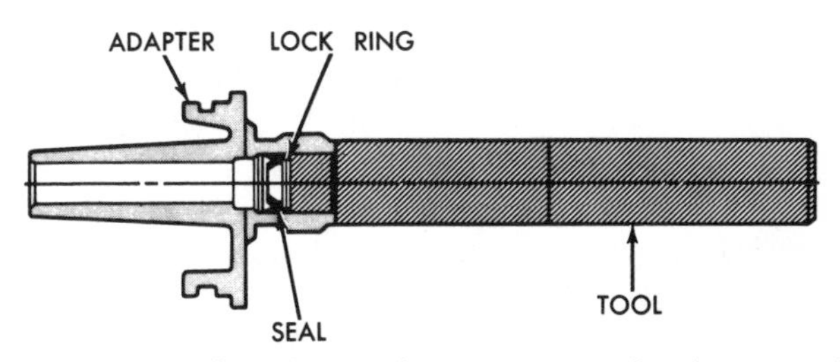

Figure 15 Installing the speedometer-pinion seal with a special tool. *(Chrysler Corporation.)*

tool, as shown in Fig. 15 until the tool bottoms.

NOTE: All parts must be clean!

Count the number of teeth on the pinion. Then rotate the adapter so that the number of the adapter which corresponds with the number of teeth will be at the bottom, or 6 o'clock position. For example, if the number of teeth were 34, then you would locate the 32-38 at 6 o'clock, as shown in Fig. 16.

Install the retainer and bolt, with the retaining tangs in the adapter-positioning slots. Tap the adapter firmly into the extension housing, and tighten the retainer bolt to 100 pound-inches (1.8 kg-mm).

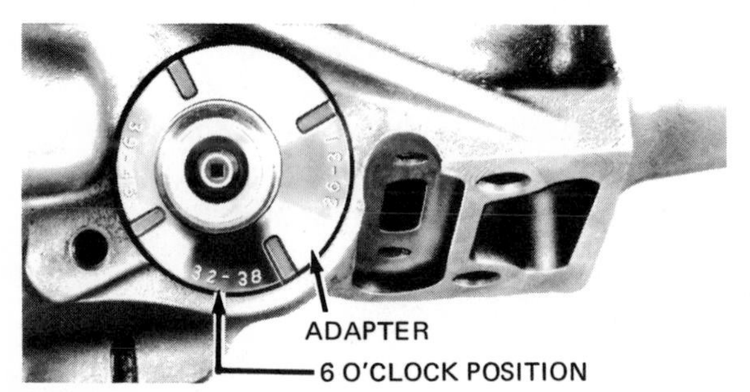

Figure 16 Speedometer pinion and adapter installed but with retainer removed. *(Chrysler Corporation.)*

■ 5-5-11 Extension-Housing Yoke Seal

To replace this seal, mark the parts for reassembly in the same relative positions and disconnect the drive shaft at the rear universal joint. Pull the shaft yoke out of the extension housing. Do not nick or scratch finished surfaces!

Then use special tools to remove the old seal and install a new one. Reattach the drive shaft after pushing the shaft yoke carefully into the extension housing and onto the main-shaft splines.

■ 5-5-12 Extension Housing and Output-Shaft Bearing

To replace this bearing, the extension housing must be removed from the transmission. This requires detachment of the drive shaft.

With the extension housing off, use snap-ring pliers to remove the rear snap ring. Slide the old bearing off the output shaft and install a new bearing. Secure it with the rear snap ring. Then install the housing, as explained in ■ 5-5-18 and reconnect the drive shaft.

NOTE: With the transmission in the car, the transmission must be raised slightly with a jack, and the center cross-member-and-support assembly must be removed before the extension housing can be removed.

■ 5-5-13 Governor Service

To remove the governor, the extension-housing-and-output-shaft bearing must be removed. Governor parts are held together by snap rings. Remove the small snap rings to slide the valve and valve shaft from the governor body. Remove the other snap rings to complete disassembly. The governor body is held to the governor-support-and-parking gear by bolts. Both can be slid off the output shaft by removing the shaft snap ring.

Thoroughly clean and inspect all governor parts. The major trouble in governors is sticking valves or weights. You can remove rough surfaces with a crocus cloth. Clean parts before reassembly.

When reinstalling the governor body and support on the output shaft, make sure the valve-shaft hole in the output shaft aligns with the hole in the governor body. Assemble all parts in their original places, and secure with snap rings.

■ 5-5-14 Parking-Lock Components

The parking-lock components are shown in Fig. 17. To replace them, the extension housing must be removed, as already explained. Follow Fig. 17 in removing and replacing parts.

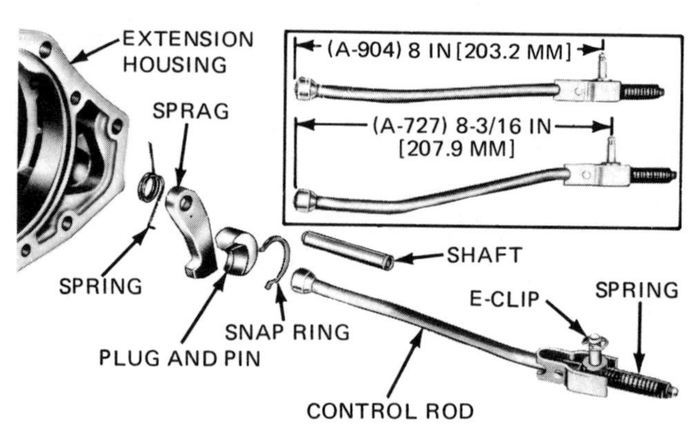

Figure 17 Parking-lock components. *(Chrysler Corporation.)*

■ 5-5-15 Valve-Body Assembly and Accumulator Piston

To remove the valve body, raise the vehicle on a hoist and remove the transmission oil pan. Then proceed as follows:

1. Disconnect the throttle and gearshift linkage from the transmission levers. Loosen the clamp bolts and remove the levers. They are shown in Fig. 13.

2. Remove the E clip, shown in Fig. 18. Remove the back-up-light and neutral starting switch.

3. With the drain pan to catch oil, remove the 10 valve-body-to-transmission-case bolts, and lower the valve body from the case. Disconnect the parking-lock rod from the lever while lowering the valve body.

4. Withdraw the accumulator piston from the transmission case, and inspect the piston for scoring and the rings for wear or damage. Replace as necessary.

Figure 18 Location of the parking-lock control-rod-retaining E clip. *(Chrysler Corporation.)*

5. If the valve-body manual-lever-shaft seal requires replacement, drive it out of the case with a punch and use a special tool to install a new seal.

> **NOTE:** Service the valve body and internal parts as explained in ■5-5-20.

To reinstall the valve body:

1. If the parking-lock rod was removed, insert it through the opening in the rear of the case with the knob positioned against the plug and sprag (see Fig. 17). Force the plug past the sprag, rotating the drive shaft if necessary.

2. Install the accumulator piston and position the accumulator spring in the valve body.

3. Put the manual lever in L and lift the valve body into approximate position. Connect the parking-lock rod to the manual lever and secure with an E clip. Then install the valve-body bolts finger tight.

4. Install the neutral starting switch. Put the manual lever in N. Shift the valve body as necessary to center the neutral finger over the neutral-switch plunger. Then snug bolts down evenly and tighten to 100 pound-inches (1.8 kg-mm).

5. Install the gearshift lever and tighten the clamp bolt. Make sure it is free to move in all lever positions. If binding exists, loosen the valve-body bolts and realign the body to correct the problem.

6. Make sure the throttle-shaft seal is in place. Install the flat washer and throttle lever, and tighten the clamp bolt. Reconnect the linkage and check linkage adjustments, as already explained.

7. Install the oil pan, using a new gasket. Add transmission fluid, as explained in Part 5, Sec. 2, to bring fluid up to the proper level.

OUT-OF-CAR SERVICE

The following sections describe transmission removal, disassembly, servicing of subassemblies, reassembly, and installation.

> **NOTE:** The transmission and torque converter must be removed and replaced as an assembly. Otherwise, the converter drive plate, pump bushing, and oil seal will be damaged. The drive plate cannot support a load. None of the transmission weight must be allowed to rest on the plate at any time.

■ **5-5-16 Transmission Removal** First, connect a remote-control starter switch to the starting-motor solenoid so that the engine can be rotated from under the car. Disconnect the lead from the negative terminal of the ignition coil. This is the lead that goes to the distributor. Disconnecting this lead prevents the engine from starting and also protects the ignition coil from high voltage. Raise the car on a hoist. Proceed as follows:

1. Remove the cover plate from in front of the converter. Rotate the engine with the remote-control switch to bring the drain plug to the 6 o'clock position. With the container in place, remove the drain plug and drain converter and transmission.

2. Mark the converter and drive plate to aid in reassembly. One bolt hole is offset so that parts must go back in original position. This arrangement retains the original balance of the converter and engine.

3. Rotate the engine to locate two converter-to-drive-plate bolts at the 5 and 7 o'clock positions. Remove the two bolts, rotate the engine again, and remove the other two bolts.

> **NOTE:** Do not rotate the converter or drive plate by prying with a screwdriver or other tool, as this could ruin the drive plate. Also, do not use the starting motor if the drive plate is not attached to the converter by at least one bolt. Do not use the starting motor if the transmission-case-to-engine bolts have been loosened. Either condition could cause transmission damage.

4. Disconnect the ground cable from the battery and remove the starting motor.

5. Disconnect the wire from the neutral starting switch.

6. Disconnect the gearshift rod from the transmission lever. Remove the gearshift-torque shaft from the transmission housing and left side rail.

7. Disconnect the throttle rod from the throttle lever on the transmission.

8. Disconnect oil-cooler lines from the transmission and remove the oil-filler tube. Disconnect the speedometer cable.

9. Mark parts for reassembly and disconnect the drive shaft at the rear universal joint. Pull the shaft assembly from the extension housing.

10. Remove rear-mount-to-extension-housing bolts.

11. Install the engine-support fixture and raise the engine slightly.

> **NOTE:** Some models have exhaust systems that will interfere and will have to be partly removed for adequate clearance.

12. Remove the frame cross member.

13. Place the transmission-service jack under the transmission to support it.

14. Attach a small C clamp to the edge of the converter housing to hold the converter in place during transmission removal.

15. Remove converter-housing-to-engine retaining bolts. Carefully work the transmission rearward off the engine-block dowels and disengage the converter hub from the end of the crankshaft.

16. Lower the transmission jack and remove the converter assembly by taking off the C clamp. Then slide the converter off.

17. Mount the transmission in a repair stand for further service.

■ 5-5-17 Starting-Motor Ring Gear

The starting-motor ring gear is welded in four places to the outer diameter of the torque converter. If the ring gear must be replaced, these welds must be cut with a hacksaw or grinding wheel. Then the ring gear must be driven off with a brass drift and hammer.

> **NOTE:** Do not allow the converter to rest on its hub during this operation. This could ruin the converter.

The new ring gear must be heated so that it expands slightly, and then it can be driven onto the torque converter. Finally, the ring gear must be welded in place, with the new welds in the same places as the old welds.

■ 5-5-18 Transmission Disassembly

Before disassembling the transmission, plug all openings and thoroughly clean the exterior, preferably by steam. We emphasized in Part 5, Sec. 2, the importance of cleanliness when servicing automatic transmissions. Do not wipe parts with a shop towel. Instead, wash them in solvent and air-dry them. Do not scratch or nick finished surfaces; this could cause valve hang-ups or fluid leakage and faulty transmission operation. Proceed with disassembly as follows:

1. First, measure the drive-train end play by mounting a dial indicator, as shown in Fig. 19. Move the input shaft in and out to check end play. Specifications are 0.030 to 0.089 inch (0.762 to 2.260 mm) for the A-904 transmission and 0.037 to 0.084 inch (0.939 to 2.134 mm) for the A-727 transmission. Write down the indicator reading for reference when reassembling the transmission.

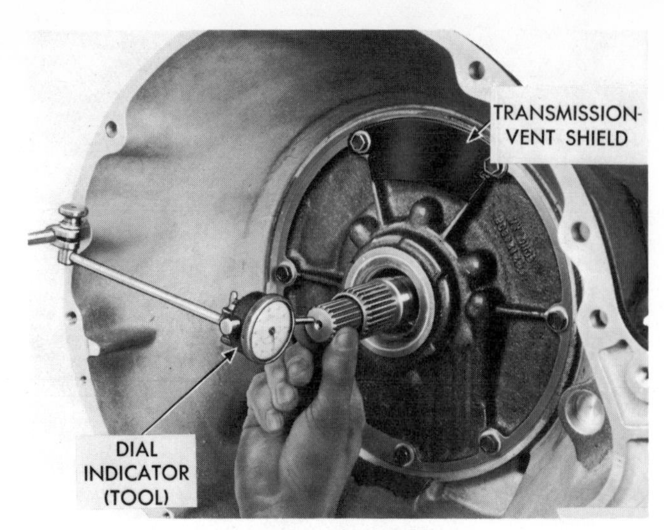

Figure 19 Measuring drive-train end play with a dial indicator. *(Chrysler Corporation.)*

2. Remove the oil pan and gasket.

3. Remove the valve body and accumulator piston and spring, as explained in ■ 5-5-15.

4. To remove the extension housing, pull the parking-lock rod forward out of the case. Rotate the output shaft if necessary to align the parking gear and sprag to permit the knob on the end of the control rod to pass the sprag. Then proceed as follows:

a. Remove the speedometer and adapter assembly.

b. Remove extension-housing-to-transmission bolts.

c. Remove two screws, plate, and gasket from the bottom of the extension-housing mounting pad. Spread the large snap ring on the output-shaft bearing with a special tool, as shown in Fig. 20. With the snap ring spread as much as possible, carefully tap the extension housing off the output shaft and bearing.

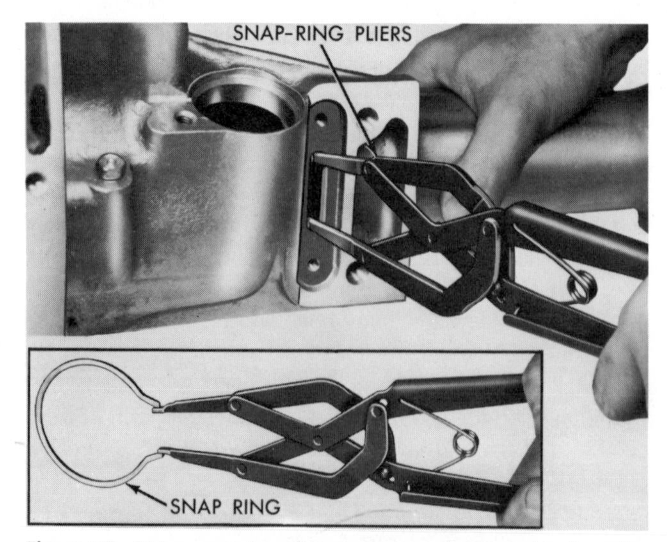

Figure 20 Using snap-ring pliers to remove the snap ring from the output-shaft bearing. *(Chrysler Corporation.)*

5. We have explained how to remove the governor and support in ■ 5-5-13. This is the next assembly to come off the transmission.

6. The pump and reaction-shaft support come out next. First, tighten the front-band adjusting screw until the band is tight on the front-clutch retainer. This adjustment will hold the retainer when the pump is removed and thereby prevent damage to the clutch.

Next, remove the oil-pump-housing retaining bolts and use two slide hammers to remove the pump.

7. Loosen the front-band adjuster, remove the band strut, and slide the band from the case.

8. Slide the front-clutch assembly from the case.

9. Pull on the input shaft to slide the input-shaft-and-rear-clutch assembly out of the case.

10. Support the output shaft and driving shell with your hands, and slide the assembly forward and out through the case.

NOTE: Be very careful to avoid damaging the ground surfaces on the output shaft.

11. Remove the low-and-reverse drum. Then loosen the rear-band adjuster, and remove the band strut and link and the band. On the double-wrap band (A-904LA), loosen the band adjusting screw to remove the band and then the low-and-reverse drum.

12. Note the position of the overrunning-clutch rollers and springs before disassembly so that you can reassemble everything in the original positions. Slide out the clutch hub and remove the rollers and springs. If the overrunning-clutch cam or spring retainer is damaged, refer to ■ 5-5-6 for the repair procedure.

13. Next, remove the kickdown servo. The servo spring must be compressed by an engine-valve-spring compressor so that the snap ring can be removed. This allows removal of the rod guide, springs, and piston rod. Do not damage these parts during removal. Now, the piston can be withdrawn from the transmission case.

14. Remove the low-and-reverse servo by compressing the piston spring with the engine-valve-spring compressor so that the snap ring can be removed. Then remove the spring retainer, spring, and servo piston and plug from the transmission case.

■ 5-5-19 Reconditioning Subassemblies

We have already mentioned the necessity of keeping everything clean when working on transmissions. Also, care must be used to avoid scratching or nicking finished surfaces. Crocus cloth can be used, within reason, to remove burrs and rough spots. When using it on valves, take great care to avoid rounding off sharp edges. The sharp edges on valves are essential to proper valve operation. They help prevent dirt particles from getting between the valve and body and possibly causing the valve to stick.

Use new seal rings when reconditioning an automatic transmission. Also, check all bushings and replace those that are worn or galled. Use the special bushing removal-and-replacement tools supplied by Chrysler.

The following subsections describe the service procedure for the various subassemblies removed from the TorqueFlite transmission.

■ 5-5-20 Valve Body

Use a special valve-body repair stand to work on the valve body. Never clamp any part of the body in a vise. Doing so can distort the body and cause leakage, valve hangups, and serious transmission trouble. Slide valves and plugs in and out of the valve body with great care to avoid damage. Proceed as follows:

1. With the valve body on the repair stand, as shown in Fig. 21, remove three screws and the filter.

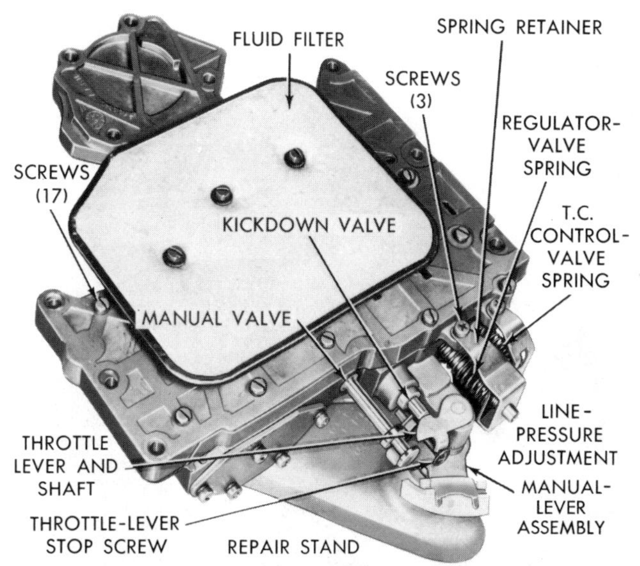

Figure 21 Valve body mounted on a repair stand. *(Chrysler Corporation.)*

2. Hold the spring retainer against the spring pressure and remove the three screws so that the spring retainer can be removed.

3. With the spring retainer off, remove the torque-converter valve spring and valve and the line-pressure adjusting screw, spring, and regulator valve. See Fig. 22.

NOTE: Do not change the setting of the line-pressure adjusting screw.

4. Remove the transfer-plate attaching screws and lift the transfer plate and steel separator plate off the valve body. Invert the transfer plate and take off the small stiffener plate.

5. Remove and note locations of the seven steel balls and one spring from the valve body. (See Fig. 23.)

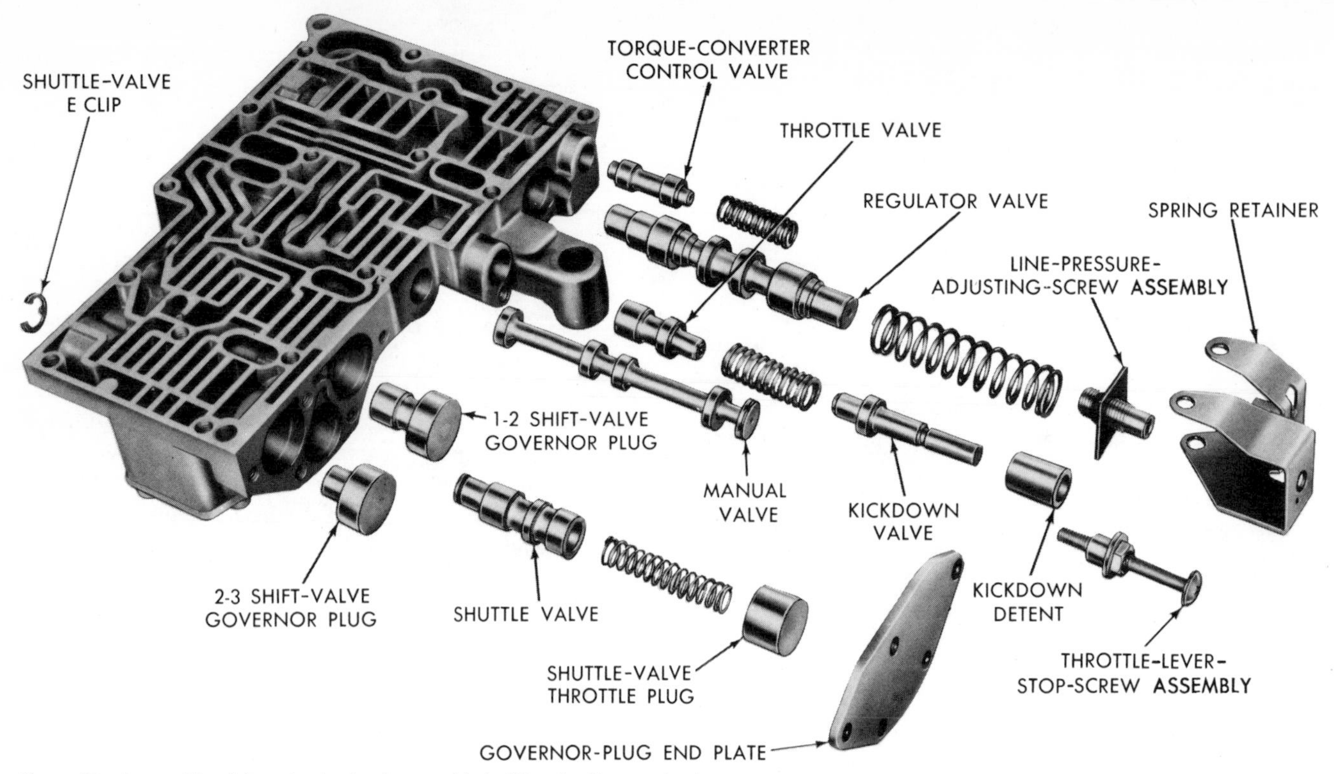

Figure 22 Lever side of the valve body, disassembled. *(Chrysler Corporation.)*

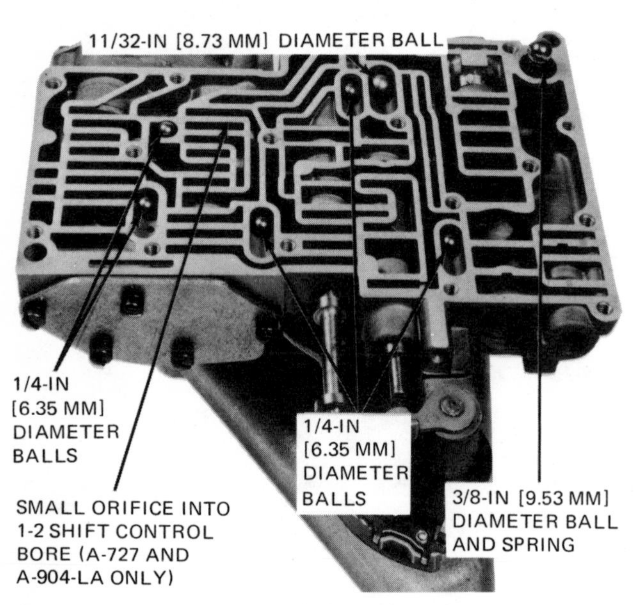

Figure 23 Locations of steel balls in the valve body. *(Chrysler Corporation.)*

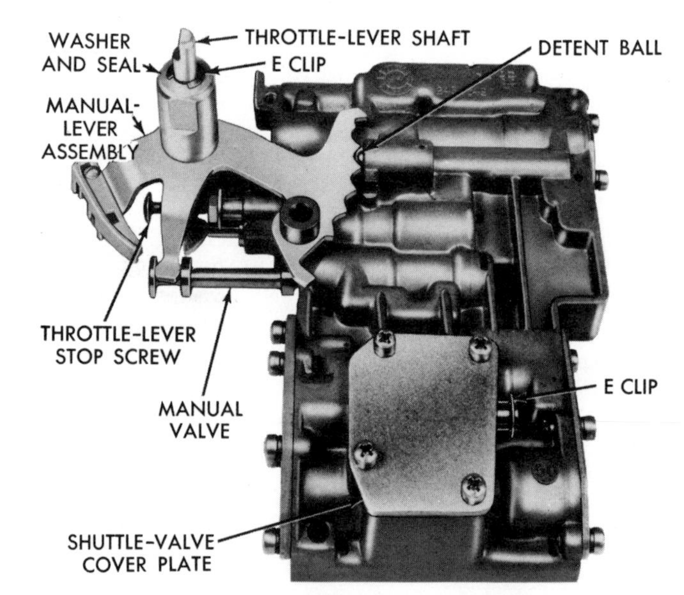

Figure 24 Valve-body controls. *(Chrysler Corporation.)*

NOTE: Do not mix the balls. The five small balls are the same size [¼ inch (6.35 mm)], but there is one 11/32-inch (8.73-mm) ball and one ⅜-inch (9.53-mm) ball with a spring behind it.

6. Invert the valve body and lay it on a clean cloth. Remove the E clip and washer from the throttle-lever shaft. See Fig. 24. Hold the detent ball in its bore and slide the manual-lever assembly off the shaft. Remove the detent ball and spring.

7. Remove the manual valve by sliding it carefully out of the valve body with a rotating motion.

8. Remove the throttle lever and shaft.

9. Remove the shuttle-valve cover plate. See Fig. 24 for location. Then remove the E clip from the exposed end of the shuttle valve.

10. Remove the throttle-lever-stop-screw assembly, being careful not to disturb its setting. Then remove the kickdown detent, kickdown valve, throttle-valve spring, and throttle valve.

11. Remove the governor-plug end plate, and tilt the valve body to allow the throttle plug, spring, shuttle valve, and two governor plugs to slide out in your hand. Note that the 1-2 shift-valve governor plug has a longer stem.

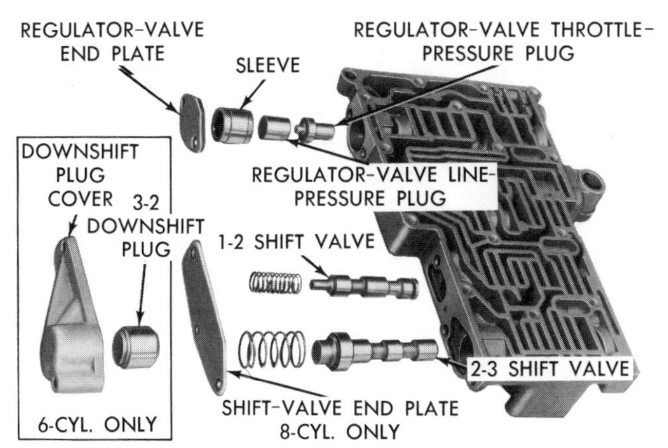

Figure 25 Shift-valve side of the valve body, disassembled. *(Chrysler Corporation.)*

12. Remove the shift-valve end plate or downshift-plug cover (on six-cylinder engines), and slide out the springs and valve (Fig. 25). Figure 26 shows a similar valve body with the same basic parts. It also shows parts that are included in the valve body for the A-727 and A-904-LA transmissions used with eight-cyclinder engines. These parts are shown inside the dashed line. They include the limit valve and the throttle plug.

13. Clean and inspect parts. Soak parts in a suitable solvent for several minutes. Air-dry. Make sure all passages are clean. Check operating levers and shafts for wear, looseness, or bending. Check mating surfaces for burrs, nicks, and scratches. Check valve springs for distortion and collapsed coils. Make sure all valves and plugs fit their bores freely. They should fall freely in the bores.

14. Reassembly is essentially the reverse of disassembly. Refer to Figs. 24 and 25. Stiffener-plate screws should be tightened to 28 pound-inches (0.504 kg-mm). Also, the governor-plug-end-plate screws, shuttle-valve-cover-plate screws, shift-valve-end-plate (eight cylinder) or downshift-plug-cover (six-cylinder) screws, and regulator-valve-end-plate screws should also be tightened to 28 pound-inches (0.504 kg-mm).

To install the spring retainer, tighten the three retaining screws to 28 pound-inches (0.504 kg-mm). Measure and correct spring-retainer alignment, as shown in Fig. 10. Then adjust throttle and line pressures, as shown in Figs. 9 and 11.

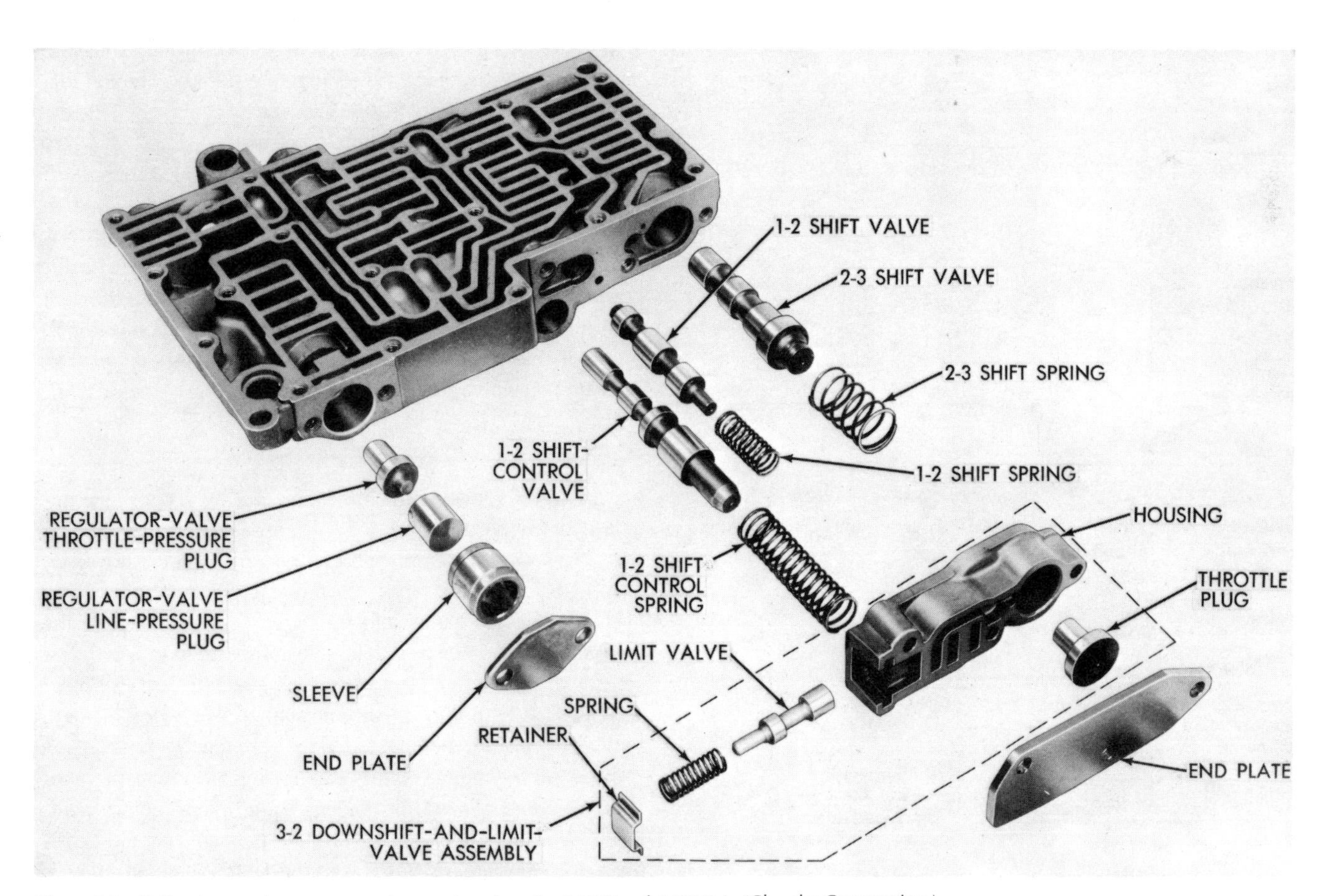

Figure 26 Shift valves and pressure-regulator valve plugs for A-727 and A-904LA. *(Chrysler Corporation.)*

■ 5-5-21 Other Subassemblies

In previous subsections, we have described the removal and replacement of the accumulator piston, extension-housing oil seal, parking-lock sprag, and governor-and-support assembly. Other subassemblies that we shall look into in following subsections are the oil pump, clutches, and planetary-gear train.

■ 5-5-22 Oil Pump and Reaction-Shaft Support

These are different for the A-904 and A-727 transmissions. Both are disassembled as follows:

1. Remove bolts from the rear side of the reaction-shaft support and lift the support off the pump.

2. Remove the rubber seal ring from the pump-body flange.

3. Drive out the oil seal with a blunt punch.

4. Inspect parts as follows:

a. Check the interlocking seal rings on the reaction-shaft support for wear or broken locks. Replace if necessary.

b. On the A-904, check the thickness of the thrust washer, which should be 0.043 to 0.045 inch (0.992 to 1.133 mm). Replace if worn.

c. Check the machined surfaces for nicks and burrs. Check pump rotors for scores or pitting. Clean the rotors and pump body, and install the rotors to check clearances. Put a straightedge across the surface of the pump face and measure with a feeler gauge to the rotors. Clearance limits are 0.0015 to 0.003 inch (0.0381 to 0.0762 mm). Rotor-tip clearance between rotor teeth should be 0.005 to 0.010 inch (0.127 to 0.254 mm). Clearance between the outer rotor and its bore should be 0.004 to 0.008 inch (0.916 to 0.203 mm). Replace the rotors and body if worn.

5. Replace the oil-pump-body bushing, if worn, as shown in Fig. 27 for the A-904 and as shown in Fig. 28 for the A-727. Be careful not to cock the removal or replacement tools because this could damage the bore in the oil-pump body. Stake the new bushing in place. A gentle tap at each stake is all that is necessary. Use a narrow-bladed knife to remove high points around the stake that could interfere with the shaft.

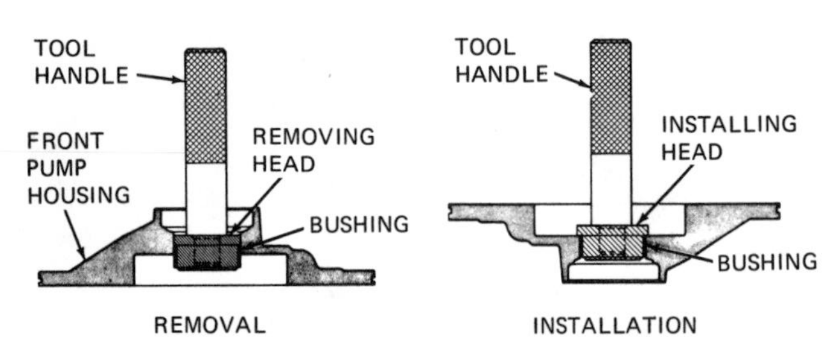

Figure 27 Removal and installation of the pump-body bushing on the A-904. *(Chrysler Corporation.)*

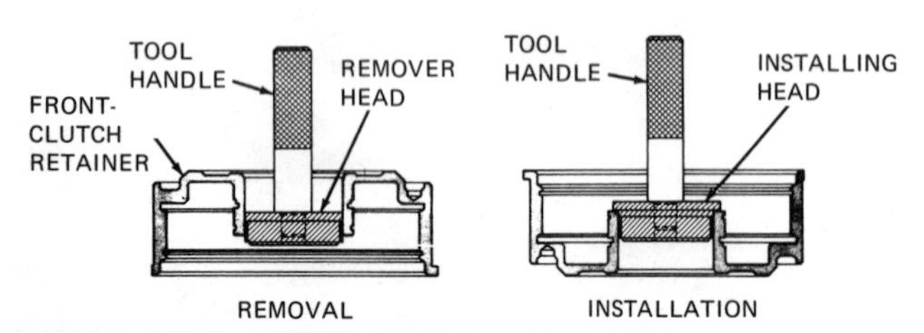

Figure 28 Removal and installation of the pump-body bushing on the A-727. *(Chrysler Corporation.)*

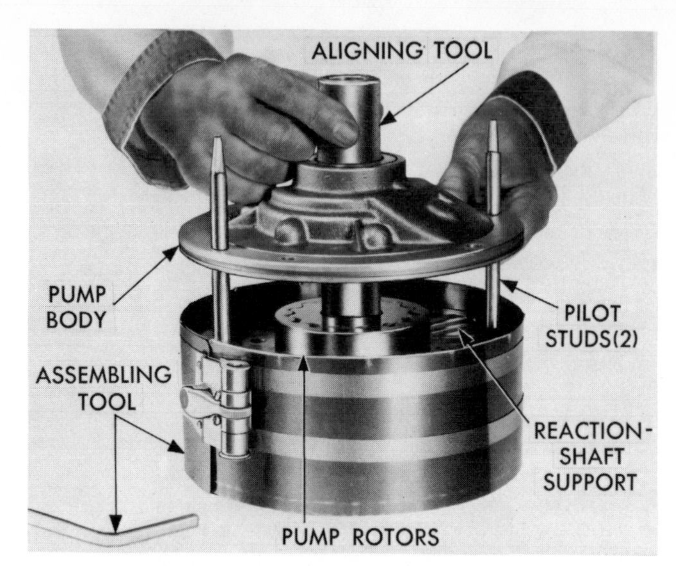

Figure 29 Assembling the pump and reaction-shaft support for the A-904. *(Chrysler Corporation.)*

6. Replace the reaction-shaft bushing if necessary.

7. Assemble the A-904 pump, as shown in Fig. 29. Note that two pilot studs are used to align the pump body and that the rotors are installed in the support and aligned with the aligning tool. Rotate the aligning tool as the pump is brought down into place. Tighten pump-body bolts to 160 pound-inches (2.88 kg-mm). Install a new pump-body oil seal, lip facing in, using a special installing tool.

8. Assemble the A-717 pump by putting the rotors in the housing and installing the reaction-shaft support with the vent baffle over the vent opening. Tighten the retaining bolts to 160 pound-inches (2.88 kg-mm). Install a new pump-body oil seal, lip facing in, with a special installing tool.

■ 5-5-23 Front Clutch

The front clutches are different for the A-904 and A-727 transmissions. See Figs. 30 and 31. The disassembly procedures are similar, however, except for the piston spring compressor that must be used. First, remove the large selective snap ring and remove the pressure plate and clutch plates. Next, use the spring compressor to remove the small snap ring, spring retainer, and spring or springs. Finally, bump the piston retainer on a wood block to remove the piston. Remove the seal rings from the piston.

Inspect the clutch plates and facings. Facings that are charred, pitted, glazed, or flaking require plate replacement. Steel plates that are burned, scored, or damaged should be replaced. Steel-plate-lug-grooves in the clutch retainer must be smooth so that plates can move freely. The brake-band surface

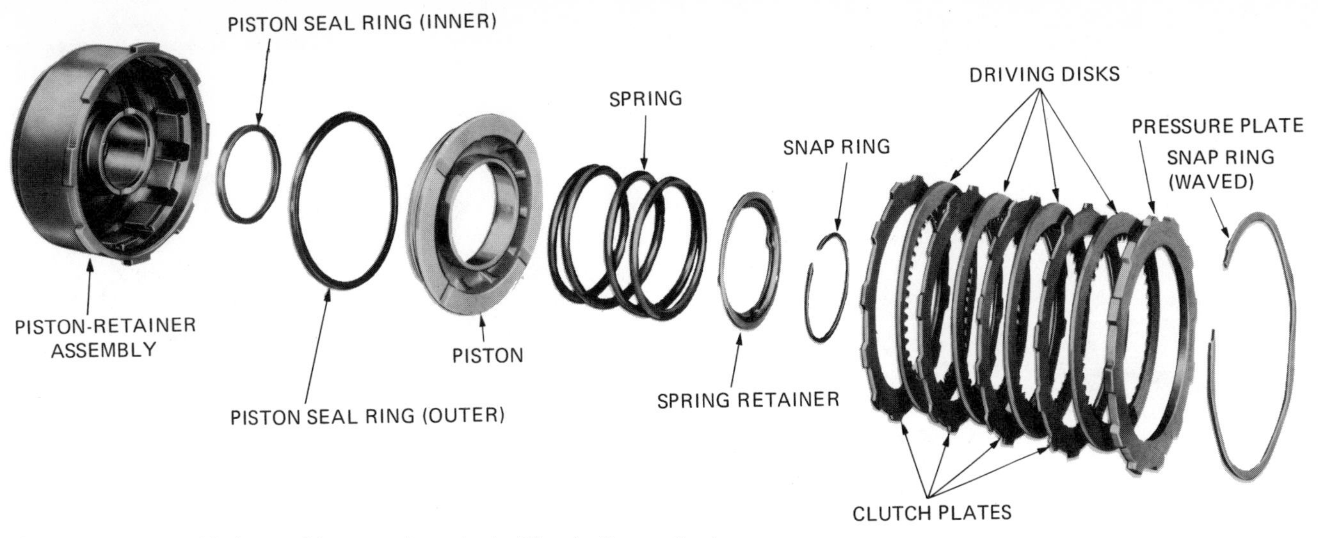

Figure 30 Disassembled view of the A-904 front clutch. *(Chrysler Corporation.)*

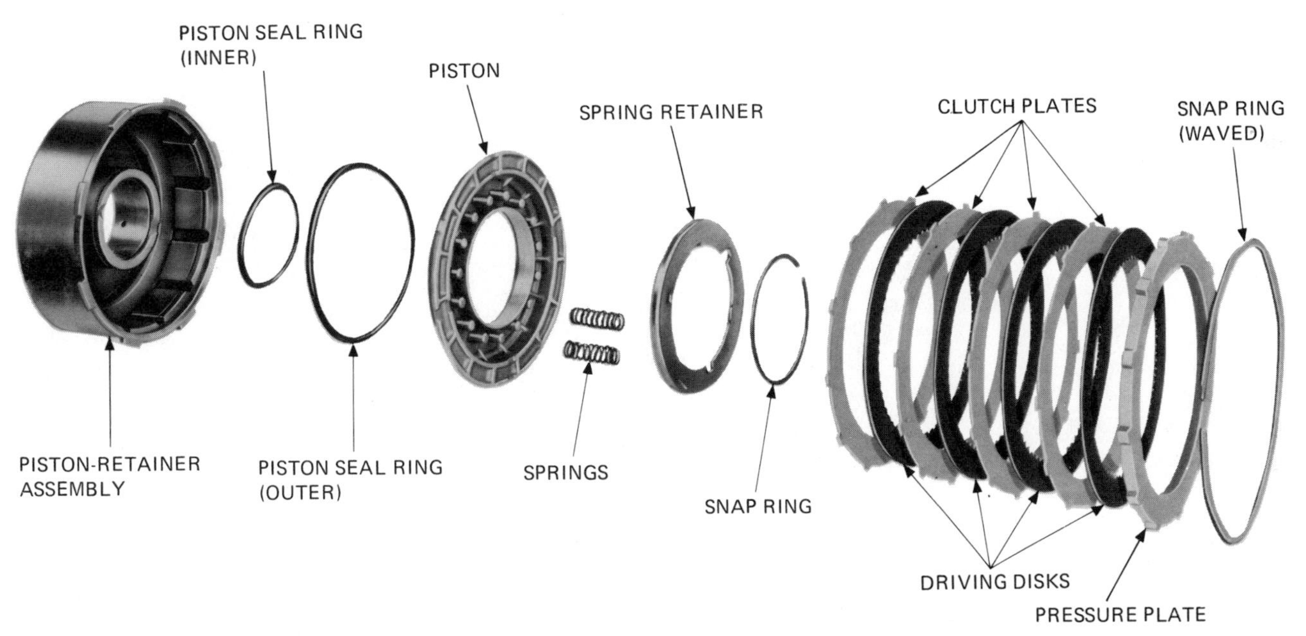

Figure 31 Disassembled view of the A-727 front clutch. Only 2 of the 15 springs required are shown. *(Chrysler Corporation.)*

on the outside of the piston retainer must be smooth, as must surfaces *in* the retainer on which the piston seals slide. Use new seals on reassembly. The ball check must be free.

If the retainer bushing needs replacement, see Fig. 32. Special tools are needed to remove and replace the bushing. The procedure is similar for the A-904 and the A-727.

On reassembly, make sure the lips on the seal rings face down, or into the piston retainer, when installed on the piston. Lubricate all parts with transmission fluid for easier installation. Use the spring compressor to compress the spring or springs so that the snap ring can be installed. Make sure the spring or springs are in the same location as on the original assembly. Note that on the A-727, there may be from six to twelve springs.

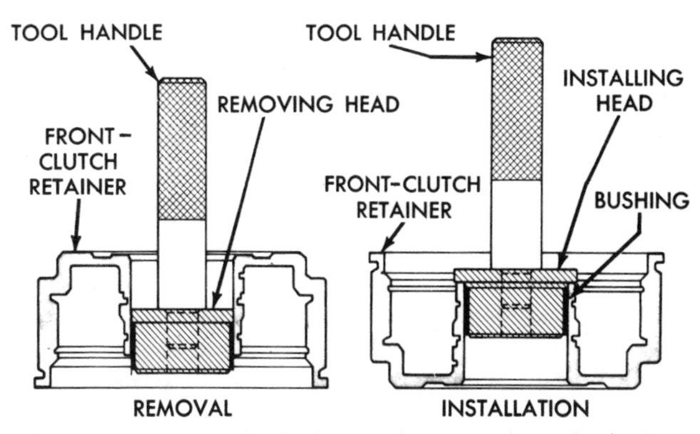

Figure 32 Replacing the bushing in the A-904 front clutch piston retainer. *(Chrysler Corporation.)*

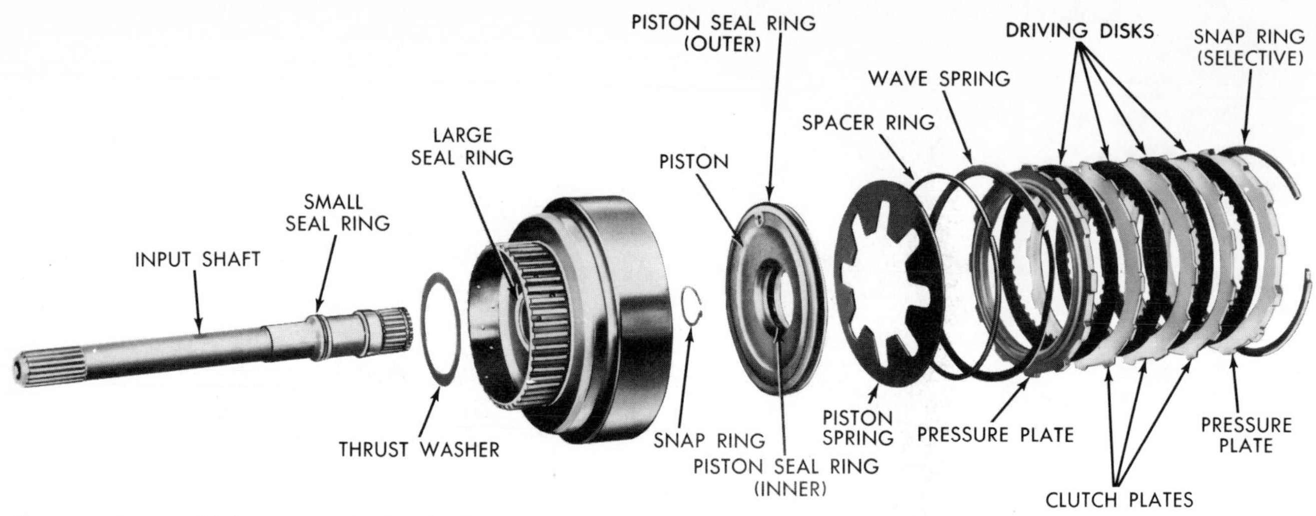

Figure 33 Disassembled A-904 rear clutch. *(Chrysler Corporation.)*

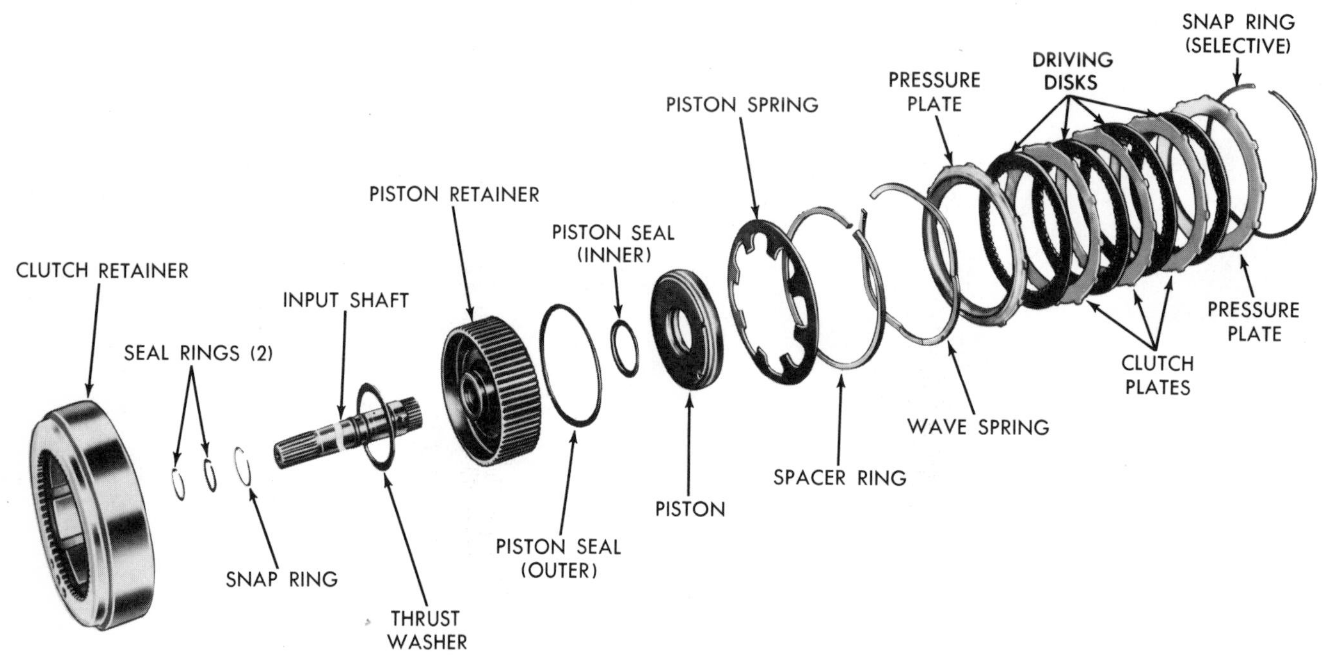

Figure 34 Disassembled A-727 rear clutch. *(Chrysler Corporation.)*

After reassembly, check the clearance between the pressure plate and the selective snap ring. The clearance varies with different engines. Check the shop manual for the proper specifications. There are snap rings of different thicknesses which can be installed to produce the correct clearance.

■ 5-5-24 Rear Clutch

Figures 33 and 34 show the rear clutches for the A-904 and A-727 transmissions in disassembled views. To disassemble the rear clutch, remove the large selective snap ring and lift the pressure plate, clutch plates, and inner pressure plate out of the retainer. Then carefully pry one end of the wave spring out of its groove in the clutch retainer and remove the wave spring, spacer ring, and clutch-piston ring. Tap the retainer on a wood block to remove the piston. Take off the piston seals, noting the direction of the seal lips.

Inspect parts as for the front clutch, as explained in ■ 5-5-23.

On reassembly, lubricate parts with transmission fluid. To install the wave spring, start one end in the groove and then work the ring into the groove from that end to the other end. Check the clearance on the clutch by having an assistant press down firmly on the outer pressure plate. Then measure with a feeler gauge between the selective snap ring and the pressure plate. If the clearance is not correct, install a snap ring of the correct thickness that will give the proper clearance. See the appropriate shop manual for specifications.

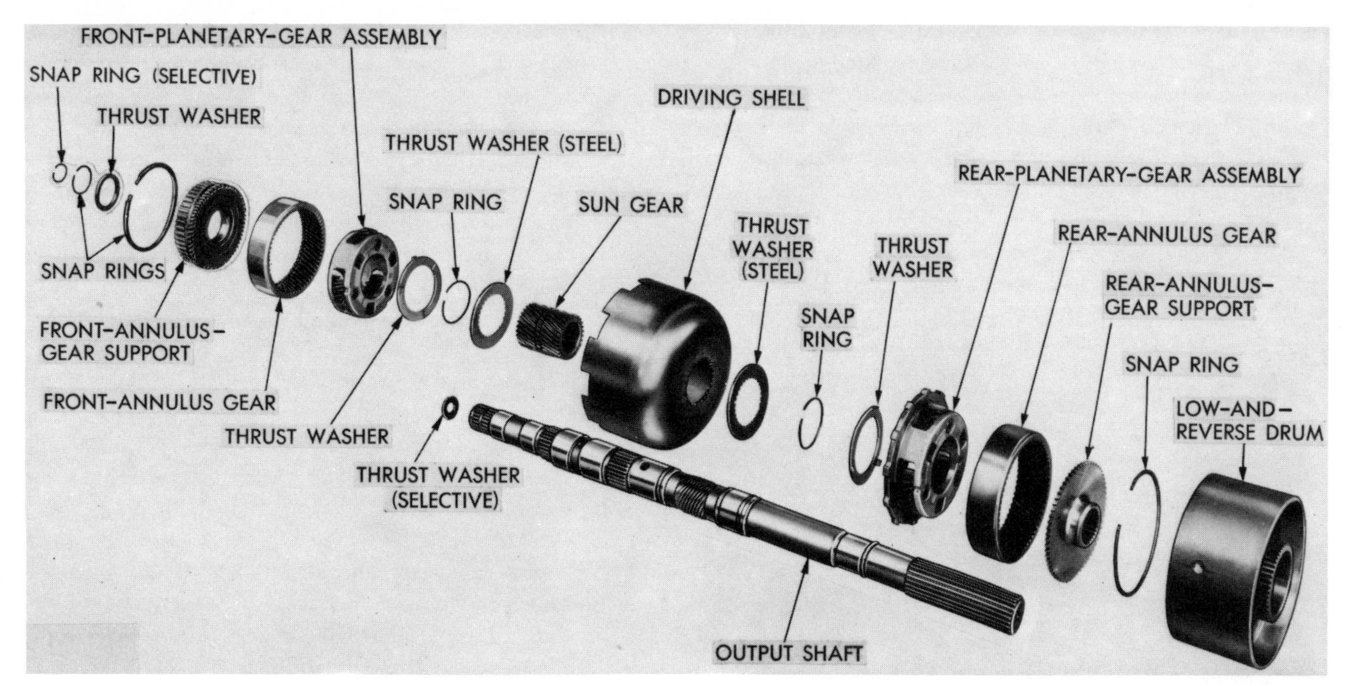

Figure 35 Disassembled A-904 planetary-gear train. *(Chrysler Corporation.)*

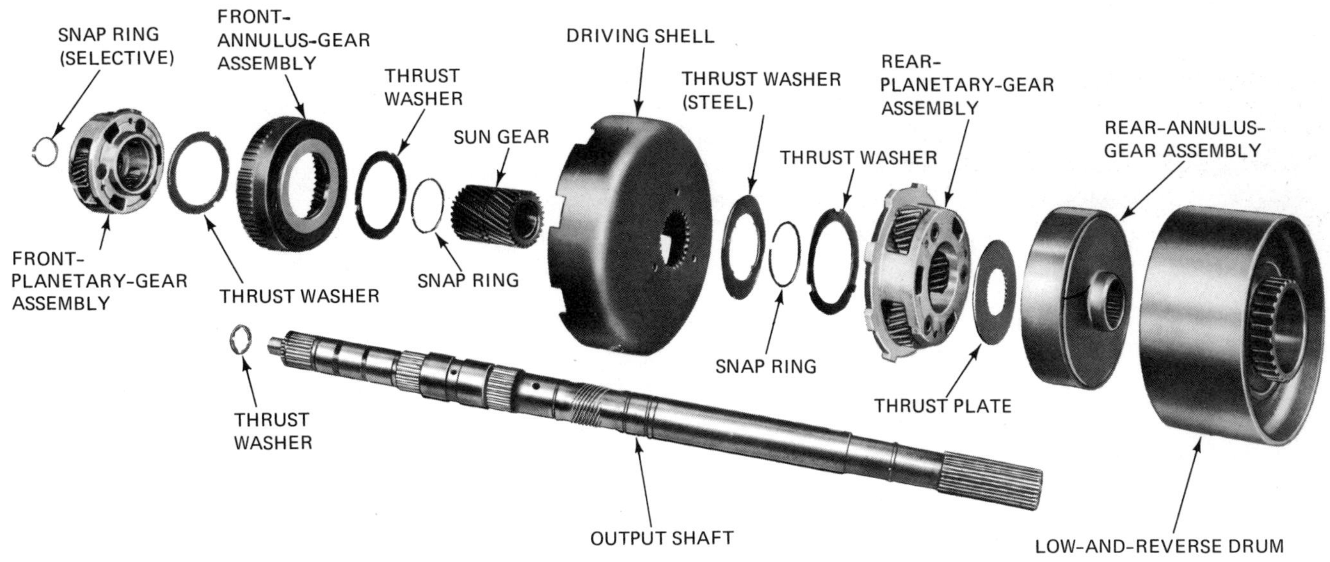

Figure 36 Disassembled A-727 planetary-gear train. *(Chrysler Corporation.)*

■ **5-5-25 Planetary-Gear Trains** Figures 35 and 36 are disassembled views of the planetary-gear trains used in the A-904 and A-727 transmissions. With both, disassembly is essentially a process of removing the snap rings and sliding parts off the shaft. Before disassembly, however, measure the clearance between the shoulder on the output shaft and the rear-ring-gear-support hub. This clearance is the gearset end play. If it is excessive, another selective snap ring of the proper thickness must be used to correct the end play.

See Figs. 35 and 36 for proper relationship of parts during reassembly. Make sure all parts are in good condition and not burred, nicked, or worn.

■ **5-5-26 Overrunning-Clutch Cam** If the cam is worn, a condition which is rare, it can be replaced. On the A-904, it is held in place with rivets, which must be driven out. The new cam is then installed with retaining bolts. On the A-727, there is a set screw that must be removed, followed by four bolts that hold the output-shaft support in place. The cam is then driven out of the transmission case by a punch inserted through the bolt holes.

■ **5-5-27 Servos** The kickdown and low-and-reverse servos are disassembled by removing the snap rings.

■ 5-5-28 Transmission Reassembly Procedure

Keep everything clean. Use transmission fluid to lubricate parts during reassembly of the transmission. Do not use force to install mating parts. Everything should slide into place easily. If force is required, something is not properly installed. Remove parts to find the trouble. Reassemble the transmission as follows:

1. Insert the clutch hub and install the overrunning-clutch rollers and springs exactly as shown in Fig. 37.

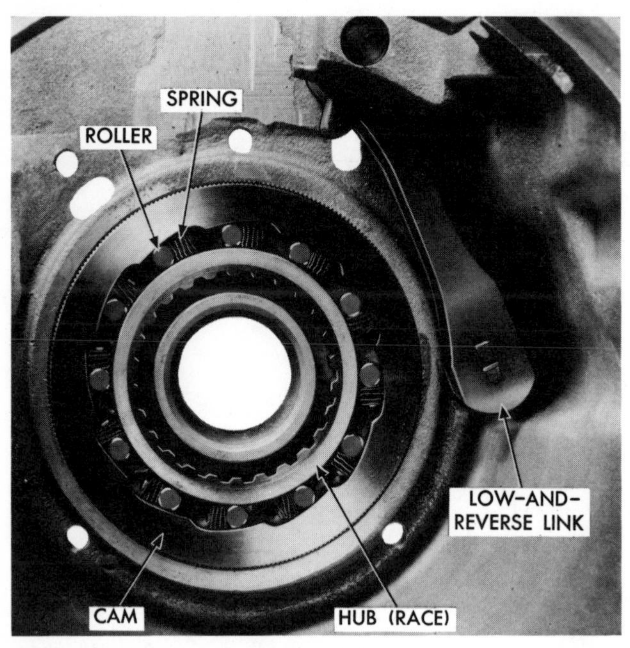

Figure 37 Overrunning clutch and low-and-reverse band link in place. *(Chrysler Corporation.)*

2. Install the low-and-reverse-servo piston in the case with a twisting motion and put the spring, retainer, and snap ring over the piston. Use a compressor tool to compress the spring so that the snap ring can be installed.

3. Put the rear band in the case and install a short strut. Connect the long link and anchor to the band. Screw in the band adjuster just enough to hold the strut in place. Install the low-and-reverse drum. Make sure the link is installed as shown in Fig. 37.

4. Install the kickdown-servo piston with a twisting motion, followed by the other parts. Use a spring compressor to compress the spring so that the snap ring can be installed.

5. Install the planetary-gear assembly with the sun gear and driving shell, as follows: Support the assembly in the case and insert the output shaft through the rear support. Carefully work the assembly into the case, engaging the rear planetary lugs into the low-and-reverse-drum slots.

> **NOTE:** Do not damage finished surfaces on the output shaft!

6. The front and rear clutches, front band, oil pump, and reaction-shaft support are more easily installed with the transmission in an upright position. Proceed as follows:

a. On the A-904 transmission, if the end play is not correct, a selective thrust washer of a different thickness will be required. Stick this thrust washer to the end of the output shaft with a coat of grease. On the A-727, apply a coat of grease on the input-to-output-shaft thrust washer (Fig. 36) to hold it on the end of the output shaft.

b. Align the front-clutch-plate inner splines and put the assembly in position on the rear clutch. Make sure the front-clutch-plate splines are fully engaged on the rear-clutch splines.

c. Align the rear-clutch-plate inner splines, grasp the input shaft, and lower the two clutch assemblies into the transmission case.

d. Carefully work the clutch assemblies in a circular action to engage the rear-clutch splines over the splines of the front annulus gear. Make sure the front-clutch drive lugs are fully engaged in the slots in the driving shell.

7. The front band and associated parts are shown in Fig. 38. Slide the band over the front-clutch assembly and install the parts, tightening the adjusting screw tight enough to hold the strut and anchor in place.

8. Install the oil pump by first installing two pilot studs. Put a new gasket over the studs. Put a new seal ring in the groove on the outer flange of the pump housing. Coat the seal with grease for easy installation. Install the pump in the case, tapping it down with a wood mallet if necessary. Put a deflector over the vent opening and install the pump attaching bolts. Remove two studs and install the other two bolts. Rotate the input and output shafts to make sure nothing is binding. Then, tighten the bolts to 175 pound-inches (3.15 kg-mm).

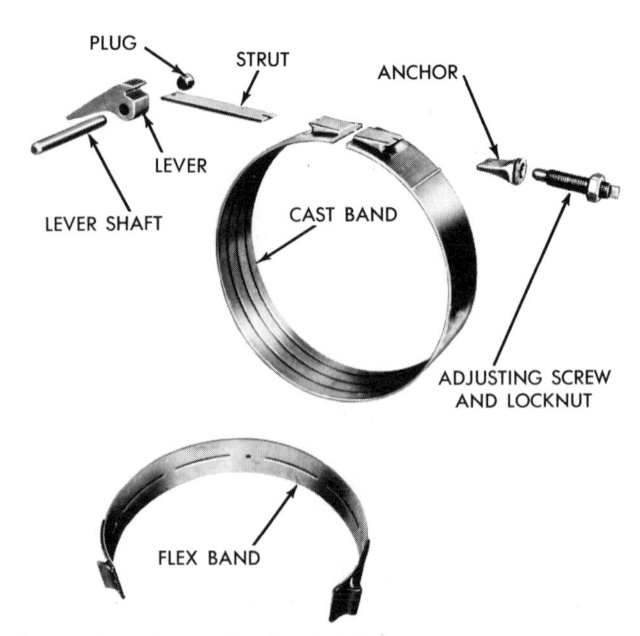

Figure 38 Kickdown band and linkage with flex band for the A-727. *(Chrysler Corporation.)*

9. Install the governor and support, as explained in ■5-5-13.

10. Install the extension-housing and output-shaft bearing, as explained in ■ 5-5-12.

11. Install the valve-body assembly, as explained in ■5-5-15.

12. Install the torque converter as follows:

a. Use a special tool to turn the pump rotors until the holes in the tool are vertical. Remove the tool.

b. Make sure converter-impeller-shaft slots are vertical so that they will engage with the oil-pump inner-rotor lugs. Then slide the converter into place.

c. Check for full engagement by placing a straightedge on the face of the case and measuring from the straightedge to one of the front-cover mounting lugs. The distance should be at least 1/2 inch (12.7 mm).

d. Attach a small C clamp to hold the converter in place.

■ **5-5-29 Transmission Installation** To install the transmission on the car, proceed as follows:

1. Check the converter drive plate for distortion or cracks. If it is replaced, torque the bolts attaching it to the crankshaft to 55 pound-feet (7.602 kg-m).

2. Coat the converter-hub hole in the crankshaft with wheel-bearing grease. Put the transmission assembly on a jack and raise it up under the car, aligned for installation. Rotate the converter so that the mark on it will align with the mark on the drive plate.

3. Carefully work the transmission assembly forward so that the converter hub enters the crankshaft hole.

4. Install and tighten the converter-housing bolts to 28 pound-feet (3.869 kg-m).

5. Install and tighten the two lower drive-plate-to-converter bolts to 270 pound-inches (4.86 kg-mm).

6. Install the starting motor and connect the battery ground cable. Use the remote-control-switch to rotate the converter and install and tighten the other two drive-plate-to-converter bolts to 270 pound-inches (4.86 kg-mm).

7. Install the cross member and also tighten the exhaust system if it was loosened for transmission removal.

8. Check and adjust pressure, linkages, and bands, as described previously. Add fluid as necessary.

SECTION 5-6

Ford C6 Transmission Service

This section describes the maintenance, trouble-diagnosis, and service procedures for the Ford C6 automatic transmission. The service procedures for the Ford C6 automatic transmission are similar to those used for the Ford C4 and FMX automatic transmissions. However, there are differences among the various models. Therefore, you should always refer to the manufacturer's shop manual that covers the specific model you are working on.

NORMAL MAINTENANCE AND ADJUSTMENTS

Normal maintenance includes periodic checking of fluid level, checking throttle and shift linkages, and possibly band adjustment. See Part 5, Sec. 2, for procedures on checking and adding fluid, and towing instructions.

■ **5-6-1 Throttle-Linkage Adjustment** The linkage between the throttle and the transmission actuates the transmission downshift valve to cause downshift when the throttle is open wide. Adjustment is made by holding the downshift rod against the stop and adjusting the downshift screw to provide proper clearance. The linkage is then reconnected.

■ **5-6-2 Selector-Lever Linkage Adjustment** The linkage between the selector lever and transmission is different on different models. Check the shop manual whenever you have an adjustment to make.

■ **5-6-3 Neutral-Switch Adjustment** The neutral start switch should be closed only with the selector lever in P or N to permit starting only in these positions. If the switch does not do its job, chances are it is out of adjustment. Adjustment is made by loosening the attaching screws and sliding the switch back and forth as necessary to obtain the correct action.

■ **5-6-4 Band Adjustment** There is only one band on the C6 transmission: the intermediate band. It is adjusted as follows: Raise the car on a hoist and clean all dirt from around the band-adjustment-screw area. Remove and discard the locknut. Install a new locknut and tighten the adjusting screw to 10 pound-feet (1.382 kg-m) torque. Then back off the adjusting screw exactly 1½ turns. Hold the adjusting screw and tighten the locknut to specifications. Lower the car.

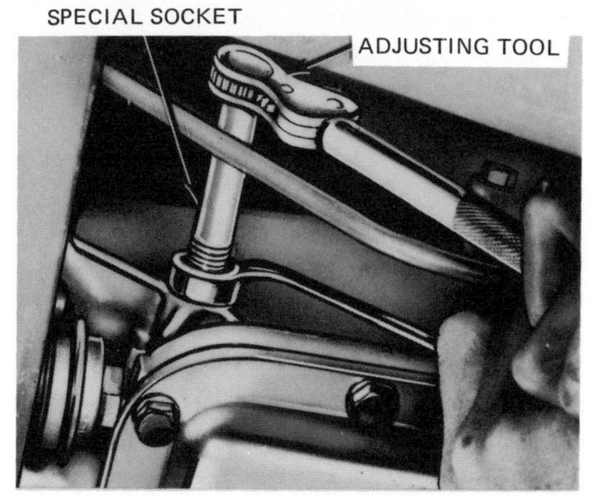

Figure 1 Adjusting the low-reverse band on the C4. *(Ford Motor Company.)*

On the C4 transmission, there is an additional band: the low-reverse band, which is used instead of a clutch as on the C6. On the C4, the intermediate band is adjusted in the same way as in the C6. The low-reverse band on the C4 is adjusted in a similar way, but with a special tool. Figure 1 shows the special tools required for different cars using the C4. With a new locknut installed in place of the old one, tighten the adjusting screw until the tool handle clicks. It is preset to click at 10 pound-feet (1.382 kg-m) torque. Then back off the adjusting screw 3 turns. Tighten the locknut to the proper tension, holding the screw stationary.

The FMX transmission has both a front and rear band. To adjust the front band, you must remove the oil pan and drain the fluid. Then remove the fluid screen and clip. Next, loosen the locknut, pull back on the actuating rod, and insert a 1/4-inch (6.35-mm) spacer between the adjusting screw and the servo-piston stem (Fig. 2). Tighten the adjusting screw to 10 pound-inches (11.5 kg-cm) torque. Remove the spacer and

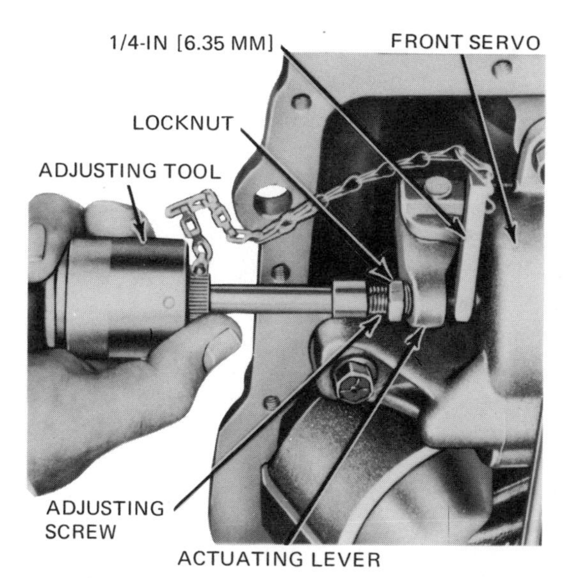

Figure 2 Adjusting the front band on the FMX. *(Ford Motor Company.)*

tighten the screw an additional 3/4 turn. Hold the adjusting screw stationary and tighten the locknut. Reinstall the fluid screen and clip. Then install the oil pan using a new gasket. Refill the transmission as described in Part 5, Sec. 2.

To adjust the rear band on the FMX, remove all dirt from the adjusting-screw threads and oil the threads. Then loosen the locknut. Use the special torque wrench, as shown in Fig. 3, and tighten the screw until the tool clicks. Then, back off the screw 1 1/2 turns. Hold the screw and tighten the locknut to specifications.

NOTE: The transmission can be severely damaged if the adjusting screw is not backed off exactly 1 1/2 turns!

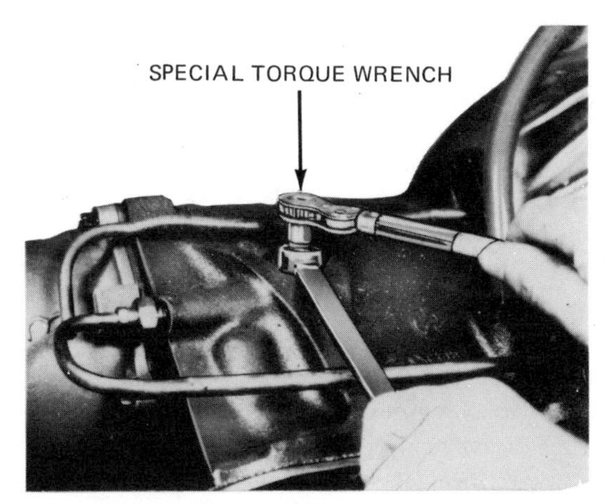

Figure 3 Adjusting the rear band on the FMX. *(Ford Motor Company.)*

ON-THE-CAR REPAIRS

A number of C6 transmission parts can be removed from the car without removing the complete transmission. These include the governor and extension housing, the servo, and the valve body.

■ **5-6-5 Governor and Extension-Housing Removal and Installation** First, raise the car on a hoist. Then disconnect the parking-brake cable from the equalizer. On the Lincoln Continental, remove the equalizer. Proceed as follows:

1. Disconnect the drive shaft from the rear-axle flange and remove it from the transmission.

2. Disconnect the speedometer cable from the extension housing.

3. Remove the engine-rear-support-to-extension-housing attaching bolts. On the Lincoln, remove the reinforcement plate from under the transmission oil pan as well.

4. Place a jack under the transmission and raise it just enough to remove the weight from the engine rear support.

5. Remove the bolt that attaches the engine rear support to the cross member and remove the support.

6. Put a drain pan under the transmission.

7. Lower the transmission and remove the extension-housing attaching bolts. Slide the housing off the output shaft and allow the fluid to drain.

8. Remove the governor attaching bolts and slide the governor off the output shaft.

9. Clean the governor parts with solvent and air-dry them. Check valves and bores for scores. Minor scores can be removed with crocus cloth. Heavier scores or other damage require replacement of the governor assembly. Valves should slide through the bores of their own weight when dry. Fluid passages should be free. Mating surfaces should be smooth and flat.

10. On the C4, the oil screen should be removed from the collector body, cleaned, and air-dried.

11. Check the extension-housing bushing and rear seal. If either needs replacement, use the special tools required to remove the old part and install the new one.

12. To reinstall the governor and extension housing, first attach the governor to the distributor flange and secure it with the attaching bolts, torqued to specifications.

13. Next, make sure the matching surfaces of the extension housing and transmission case are clean. Use a new gasket and install the housing, securing it with the attaching bolts.

14. Raise the transmission high enough to position the engine rear support on the cross member. Secure the support with the attaching bolt and nut, torqued to specifications.

15. Lower the transmission and remove the jack. Install and torque the engine rear-support-to-extension-housing attaching bolts. On the Lincoln, install the reinforcing plate with attaching bolts.

16. Attach the speedometer cable and connect the parking-brake cable to the equalizer. On the Lincoln, connect the parking-brake equalizer. Adjust the parking brakes.

17. Install the drive shaft. Fill the transmission to the correct level with the specified transmission fluid.

■ 5-6-6 Servo Removal and Installation Remove the servo by raising the car on a hoist. Then:

1. Remove the engine rear-support-to-extension-housing attaching bolts. Raise the transmission high enough to remove the weight from the engine rear support and remove the bolt that secures the engine rear support to the cross member. Remove the support.

2. Lower the transmission and remove the jack. Put a drain pan under the servo. Remove the bolts that attach the servo cover to the transmission case.

3. Remove the cover, piston, spring, and gasket from the case, screwing the band adjusting screw inward as the piston is removed. This will place enough tension on the band to keep the struts in place when the piston is removed.

4. To change the piston seals, apply air pressure to the port in the servo cover to remove the piston. Then remove the seals from the piston and the seal from the cover. Dip new seals in transmission fluid and install them. Coat two new gaskets with petroleum jelly and install them on the cover. Dip the piston in transmission fluid and install it in the cover.

5. Put the servo spring on the piston rod and insert the piston rod in the case. Secure the cover with the attaching bolts, taking care to back off the band adjusting screw as the cover bolts are tightened. Make sure the vent-tube retaining clip and service-identification tag are in place.

6. Raise the transmission high enough to install the engine rear support. Secure the support to the extension housing with the attaching bolts. Lower the transmission to install the support to the cross member. Torque the attaching bolt to specifications.

7. Remove the jack. Adjust the band as previously explained.

8. Lower the car and replenish the fluid as necessary.

■ 5-6-7 Valve-Body Removal and Installation

Raise the car on a hoist and put a drain pan under the transmission. Loosen the transmission-pan bolts and allow the fluid to drain. Then:

1. Remove the transmission-pan attaching bolts from both sides to complete draining. Remove the rest of the bolts and the pan. Remove and discard the nylon shipping plug from the filler-tube hole. This plug is used to retain transmission fluid during shipping and should be removed when the pan is off.

2. Remove the valve-body attaching bolts and take the valve body off.

3. Service the valve body, as described in ■5-6-18.

4. When reinstalling the valve body, make sure that the selector and downshift levers are engaged. Then install and torque the attaching bolts to specifications.

5. Clean the pan and gasket surfaces thoroughly. Use a new pan gasket and attach the pan with the bolts tightened to specifications.

6. Lower the car and add fluid as necessary.

TROUBLE DIAGNOSIS

To diagnose transmission troubles, a series of checks are made. These include checks of the shift points and hydraulic control pressures, as well as air-checks of the clutches and servo. In addition, the technician diagnosing the trouble can use one of the diagnosis guides given later in this section to help pinpoint the trouble.

■ 5-6-8 Shift-Point Checks The engine should be in good condition, linkages to the transmission should be properly adjusted, and the transmission fluid should be at the proper height. The shift points can be checked on the road or in the shop if a dynamometer or a source of vacuum, such as a hand vacuum pump, is available. Without the dynamometer, engine loading can be simulated by applying a varying vacuum to the vacuum diaphragm of the transmission throttle control. By varying the vacuum to simulate closed to open throttle conditions and varying engine speeds, you can make all the checks you need in the shop. Ford furnishes diagnostic guides, as shown in Fig. 4. They have spaces in which

Automatic Transmission Diagnosis Guide
Ford Customer Service Division

General: This form must be completely filled in throughout the steps required to diagnose the condition covering transmission malfunction complaints (e.g., erratic shifting, slippage during shifts, failure to shift, harsh and delayed shifts, noise, etc.). It is not necessary to complete this form on complaints involving external leaks.

Transmission Model ______ Transmission Date Code/or Serial No. ______

R.O. No. ______ Axle Ratio ______ Tire Size ______

DIAGNOSIS PROCEDURE

Following steps will provide complete data necessary to perform an accurate diagnosis of transmission difficulties.

1. Check transmission fluid level ☐ Room Temp. ☐ Operating Temp. ☐ OK ☐ Overfilled ☐ Low
2. Engine (CID) and Calibration Number ______
   Idle RPM in Drive ______ Specification ______ As Received ______ Set To
   Check EGR System (if so equipped)
   Valve Operation ☐ OK ☐ Other (Explain) ______
   Restriction ☐ OK ☐ Other (Explain) ______
3. Check downshift and manual linkage ☐ OK ☐ Other (Explain) ______
4. Drive the car in each range, and through all shifts, including forced downshifts, observing any irregularities of transmission performance.

Throttle Opening	Range	Shift	Shift Points (MPH) Record Actual	Shift Points (MPH) Record Spec.
Minimum (Above 12" Vacuum)	D	1-2		
	D	2-3		
	D	3-1		
	1	2-1		

Throttle Opening	Range	Shift	Shift Points (MPH) Record Actual	Shift Points (MPH) Record Spec.
To Detent (Torque Demand)	D	1-2		
	D	2-3		
		3-2		
Thru Detent (WOT)	D	1-2		
	D	2-3		
	D	3-2		
	D	2-1 or 3-1		

5. Control Pressure Test ______ AND ______ Stall Speed Data
   Transmission fluid must be normal operating temperatures. DO NOT hold throttle open over five seconds during tests.
   CAUTION: Release throttle immediately if slippage is indicated.
   After each stall test move selector lever to neutral with engine running at 1000 RPM to cool the transmission.

Engine RPM	Manifold Vacuum In-Hg	Throttle	Range	PSI Record Actual	PSI Record Spec.
Idle	Above 12	Closed	P		
			N		
			D		
			2		
			1		
			R		
As Required	10 ①	As Required	D, 2, 1		
As Required	Below 3	Wide Open	D		
			2		
			1		
			R		

Above Specified Engine RPM
1. Transmission slippage
2. Clutches or bands not holding

Below Specified Engine RPM
1. Poor engine performance, such as need for tune-up
2. Converter one way clutch slipping or improperly installed

Specified Engine RPM	Record Actual Engine RPM

① On units equipped with a dual area diaphragm, the front port of diaphragm must be vented to atmosphere (hose disconnected and plugged) during this check only.

After the tests, you should know the following items:

- CONTROL PRESSURE – Does the transmission have the CORRECT CONTROL PRESSURE? ☐ Yes ☐ No
- CONTROL VALVES – Beyond the manual valve are all the CONTROL VALVES FUNCTIONING? ☐ Yes ☐ No
- HYDRAULIC CIRCUITS – If the first two items check out good, then check the transmission's internal hydraulic circuits that are beyond the VALVE BODY. These circuits must be checked during transmission disassembly.

6. TORQUE CONVERTER AND OIL COOLER (where applicable)
   - Was torque converter flushed with a mechanical cleaner? ☐ Yes ☐ No
   - Was oil cooler flushed with a mechanical cleaner? ☐ Yes ☐ No
7. The problem was diagnosed to be: ______
8. If it was necessary to disassemble the transmission, record the actual problem found: ______

Figure 4 Automatic transmission diagnosis guide. *(Ford Motor Company.)*

to record test data on shift points, stall speed, and pressure tests. Note that there are spaces in which to record the specifications that are to be picked up from the shop manual. The actual test results are then compared with the specifications. This comparison usually shows up any trouble in the transmission.

1. To make the shift-point test in the shop, raise the car on jacks or a hoist that will allow the wheels to turn. Then disconnect the vacuum line from the transmission and plug it. Connect the vacuum hose from the vacuum source to the transmission. Now start the engine and move the selector lever through all positions. Adjust the vacuum to 18 inches (457.2 mm) to simulate a light throttle. Move the lever to D and gradually increase engine speed. Note the upshift points. You can tell these because the speedometer needle will surge momentarily, and you can feel the slight bump indicating the upshift. Slow the engine to idle speed.

NOTE: Do not exceed 60 mph (97 km/h) on the speedometer!

2. Now simulate a high engine load or wide-open throttle by reducing the vacuum to 0 to 2 inches (0 to 50.8 mm). Accelerate the engine slowly and note the 1-2 upshift point. You don't need to check the 2-3 shift point because you already checked this in the previous test. Do not exceed 60 mph (97 km/h)!

3. Next, test the kickdown system. You do not want to run an unloaded engine at wide-open throttle because this could damage it. So you need another way to check kickdown. You can do this by leaving the vacuum adjusted to 0 to 2 inches (0 to 50.8 mm) and manually holding the downshift linkage in the wide-open-throttle position. Accelerate the engine just enough to cause a 1-2 upshift. Do not exceed 60 mph (97 km/h). Note that the wide-throttle 1-2 shift should be at a higher mph than the high-engine-load test. This indicates that the kickdown system is working.

4. To make the shift-point tests on the highway, operate the car at various speeds and in the different selector-lever positions to note whether all shifts take place properly.

■ 5-6-9 Control-Pressure and Stall Checks

These checks consist in measuring the control pressure in the hydraulic system under varying operating conditions and also seeing if there is transmission slippage. Ford recommends the tests in the shop with a dynamometer or with a special transmission tester. The transmission tester has a pressure gauge, vacuum gauge, and tachometer. We shall describe the use of the transmission tester to make the checks.

First, connect the tachometer to the ignition system so that you can measure engine speed.

Next, connect the vacuum hose from the tester into the manifold vacuum line by means of a T fitting. The third connection is the pressure hose to the control-pressure port. The control-pressure port has different locations in other transmissions; check the shop manual. With the three connections made, proceed as follows:

1. It is assumed that the engine is in satisfactory condition and that the intake-manifold vacuum will read around 18 inches (457.2 mm) at idle.

2. The Stall Speed Data Chart in the diagnosis guide of Fig. 4 has spaces in which to record the specified engine rpm at which the stall test should be made, and spaces in which to record the stall-test results.

3. The Control Pressure Test Chart in Fig. 4 has spaces in which to record the specified pressures under different conditions, and places to record the results of the pressure tests.

4. Prior to the test, you should refer to the shop manual and find the specifications for the transmission and car being tested. These should be recorded on the diagnosis guide.

5. Now, with the transmission at normal operating temperature, apply the foot brake. Make the stall check by shifting into the indicated selector-lever position and increasing the engine speed to the specified value.

NOTE: Do not hold the throttle open more than 5 seconds! After each stall check, return the selector lever to N and idle the engine for a minute or so to cool the transmission. Release the throttle instantly if the transmission slips, that is, if the speed goes beyond specifications.

6. Excessive speed in any selector position indicates transmission slippage.

7. Now, make a pressure check by adjusting the engine idle to the specified speed. With a closed throttle, move the selector lever to all positions and note the pressures. See Fig. 4.

8. Next, with a source of vacuum connected to the transmission instead of the intake manifold of the engine, make the pressure tests at 10 and 1 inches (254.0 and 25.4 mm) of vacuum. These tests can be made with the engine idling and only the vacuum changed. In other words, it is not necessary to open the throttle wide to get the vacuums needed for the test. Note that the pressures should be checked in D, D2, and D1 with 10 inches (254 mm) of vacuum and at D, D2, D1, and R with 1 inch (25.4 mm) of vacuum.

9. The chart in Fig. 5 tells you what to suspect if the pressures are not within the specifications. Improper pressures usually require looking into the transmission itself to find the actual unit causing the trouble.

■ 5-6-10 Air-Pressure Checks

Further information on the condition of the clutches and servo can be obtained by using air pressure to operate them. This procedure requires removal of the oil pan and control-valve body and draining of the fluid, as explained in ■5-6-7. Then air pressure can be directed into the appropriate "apply" hole to see whether or not the brake band or the clutch will apply. Figure 6 shows the transmission case for the C6 with the various fluid passages identified. Figure 7 shows the FMX transmission case with all fluid passages identified.

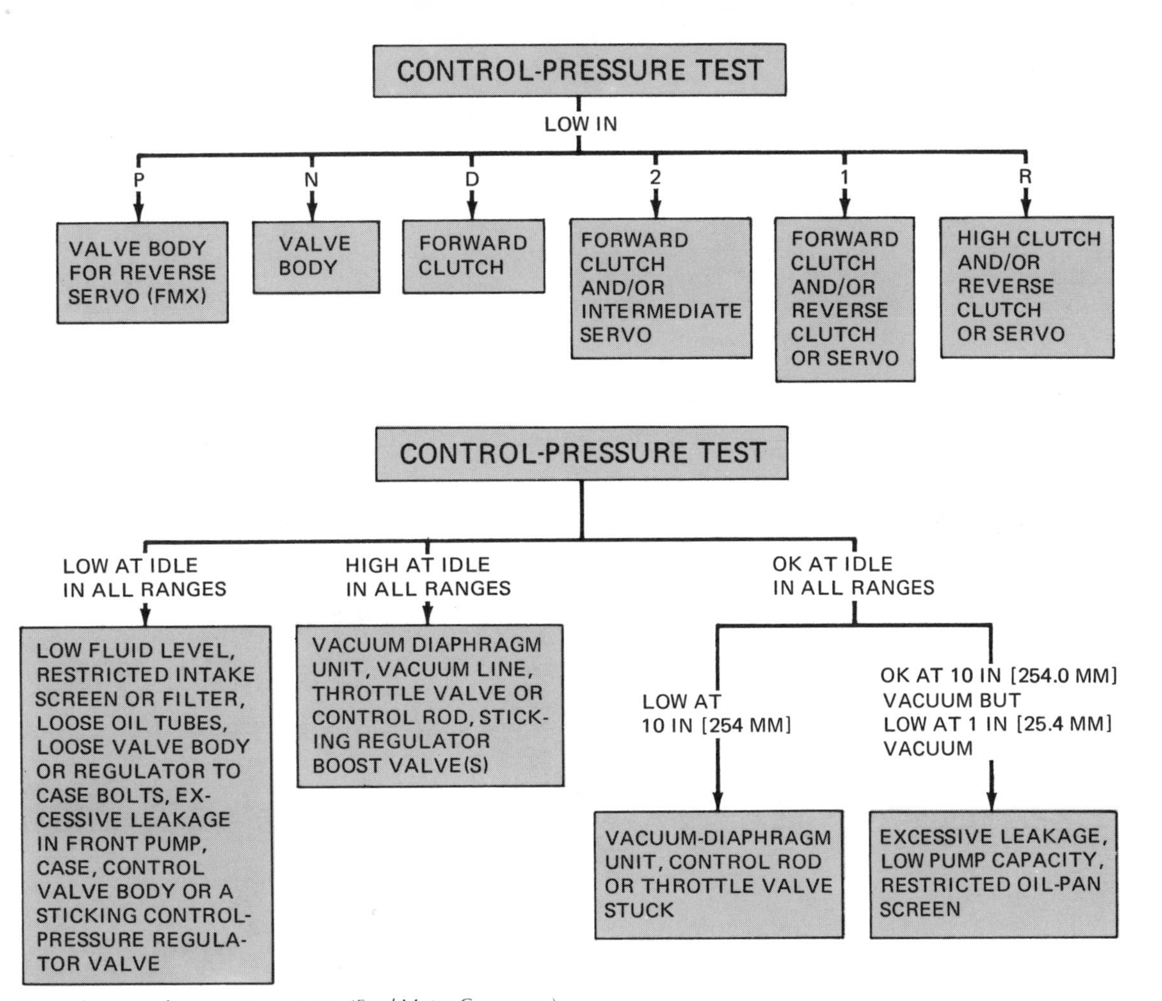

Figure 5 Chart of causes of incorrect pressures. *(Ford Motor Company.)*

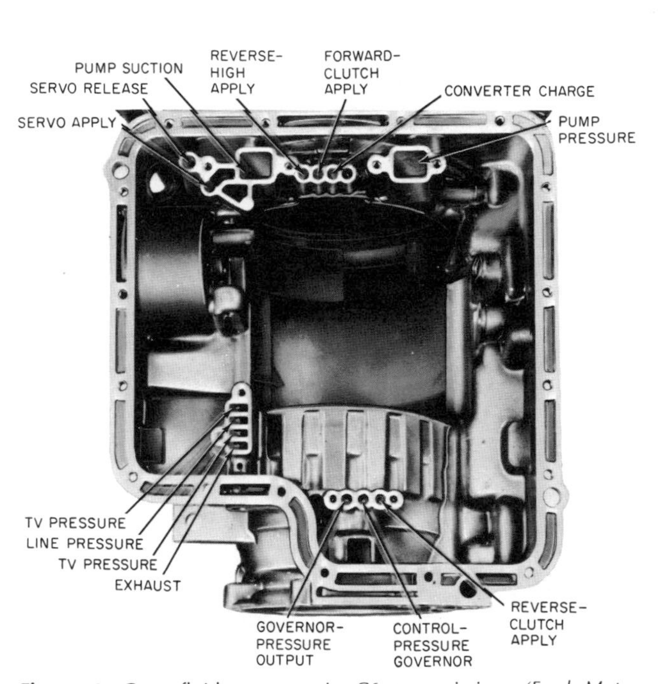

Figure 6 Case fluid passages in C6 transmission. *(Ford Motor Company.)*

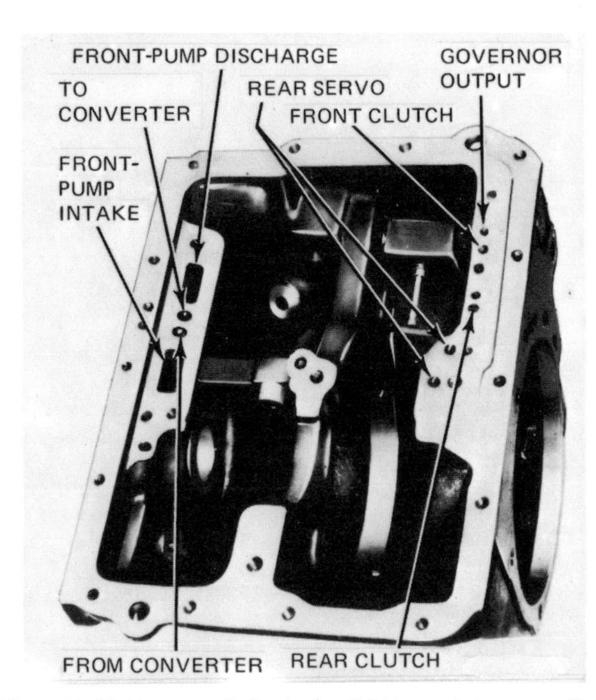

Figure 7 Fluid passage holes in the FMX transmission case. *(Ford Motor Company.)*

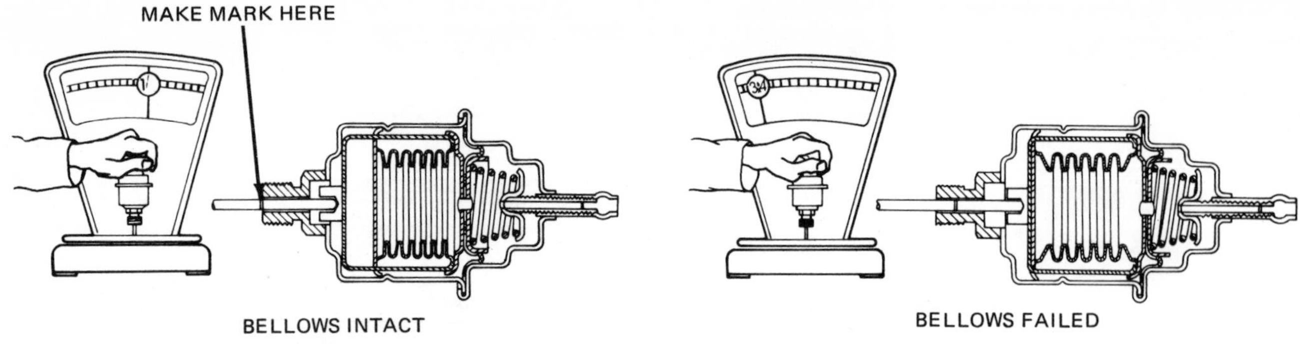

Figure 8 Checking vacuum-unit bellows. *(Ford Motor Company.)*

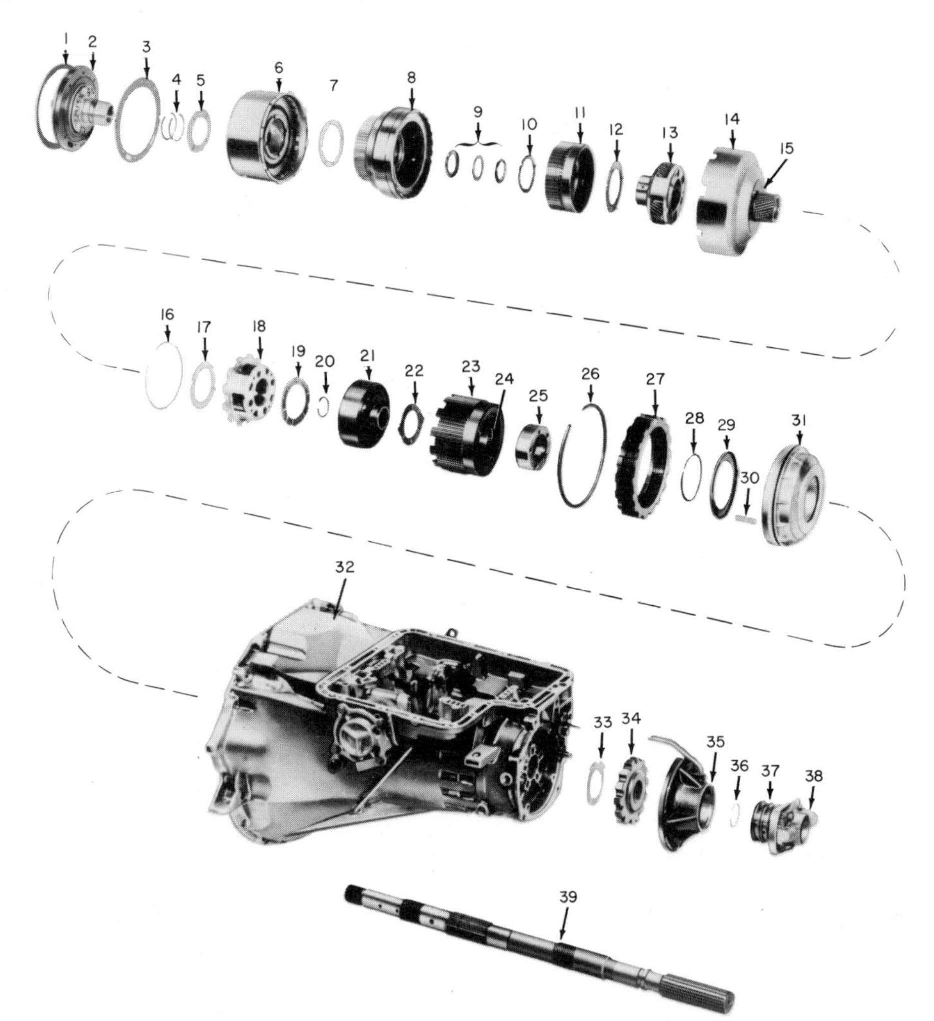

1. Front-pump seal ring
2. Front pump
3. Gasket
4. Seal
5. No. 1 thrust washer (selective)
6. Reverse-high-clutch assembly
7. No. 2 thrust washer
8. Forward clutch assembly
9. No. 3 thrust washer
10. No. 4 thrust washer
11. Forward-clutch-hub assembly
12. No. 5 thrust washer
13. Forward planet assembly
14. Input shell and sun-gear assembly
15. No. 6 thrust washer
16. Snap ring
17. No. 7 thrust washer
18. Reverse planet assembly
19. No. 8 thrust washer
20. Reverse ring gear and hub-retaining ring
21. Reverse ring gear and hub
22. No. 9 thrust washer
23. Low-reverse clutch hub
24. One-way clutch
25. One-way clutch inner race
26. Snap ring
27. Low-reverse clutch
28. Snap ring
29. Low-reverse piston-return-spring retainer
30. Return spring
31. Low-reverse piston
32. Case
33. No. 10 thrust washer
34. Parking gear
35. Governor-distributor sleeve
36. Snap ring
37. Governor distributor
38. Governor
39. Output shaft

Figure 9 Disassembled view of the transmission drive train. *(Ford Motor Company.)*

■ 5-6-11 Vacuum-Unit Checks and Adjustments

The vacuum unit actuates the primary throttle valve. The unit should be checked for leakage and for bellows failure. To check for leakage, connect the unit to a source of vacuum, such as a vacuum pump on a distributor tester. Apply 18 inches (457.2 mm) of vacuum to the vacuum unit and see if it will hold this vacuum. If it does not, the diaphragm is leaking.

Next, check the bellows, as shown in Fig. 8. Insert a rod in the unit, as shown, and make a reference mark on the rod with the rod bottomed in the hole. Then press down on the unit with the rod resting on a scale, as shown. Increase pressure to 12 pounds (5.443 kg). If the mark remains visible, the bellows is okay. If the mark disappears before 4 pounds (1.814 kg) is exerted, the bellows is defective and the complete vacuum unit must be replaced.

The vacuum unit can be adjusted by turning the adjusting screw in or out. Adjustment is desirable if the control pressure is high or low and if upshifts or downshifts are high or low. One complete turn of the adjusting screw changes idle control pressure approximately 2 to 3 psi (0.141 to 0.210 kg/cm^2). If the pressure readings are low, turn the adjusting screw in. If the readings are high, turn the screw out.

■ 5-6-12 Diagnosis Guides

The guide in Fig. 4 explains how to make various diagnostic tests of the transmission to determine what might be wrong and what is causing the trouble. In addition to these, there are diagnosis guides for specific models. These guides can help you pinpoint every cause of trouble in the transmission.

TRANSMISSION OVERHAUL

If there are troubles in the transmission that require its removal and overhaul, proceed as follows.

■ 5-6-13 Transmission Removal and Installation

There are many variations in engine-compartment arrangements and methods of transmission support in different car models. Thus, you should always check the shop manual for the car you are working on before proceeding with transmission removal. See also the general instructions in Part 5, Sec. 2, which also list service precautions and describe the cleaning and inspecting of transmission parts.

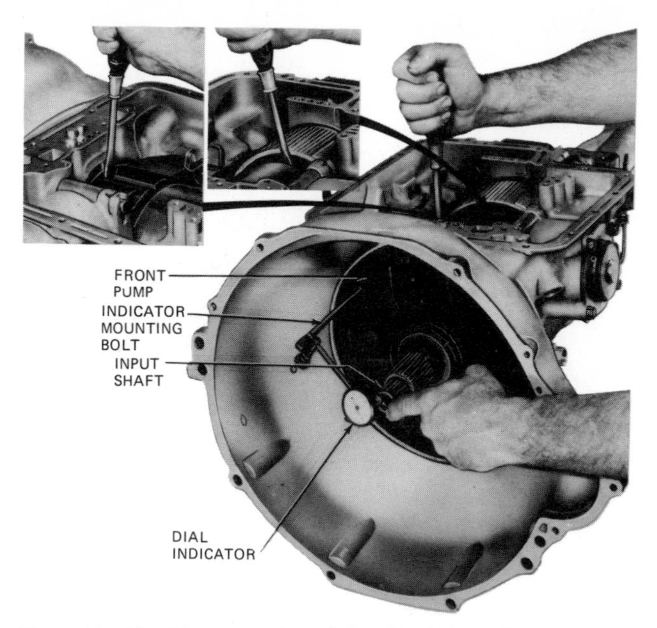

Figure 10 Checking gear-train end play. *(Ford Motor Company.)*

■ 5-6-14 Transmission Disassembly

First, mount the transmission in a holding fixture. The transmission drive train is shown in disassembled view in Fig. 9. Proceed with disassembly as follows:

1. Remove the 17 oil-pan attaching screws and the oil pan.

2. Remove the eight valve-body attaching screws and the valve body.

3. Attach a dial indicator to the front pump, as shown in Fig. 10. Install a special tool in the extension housing to center

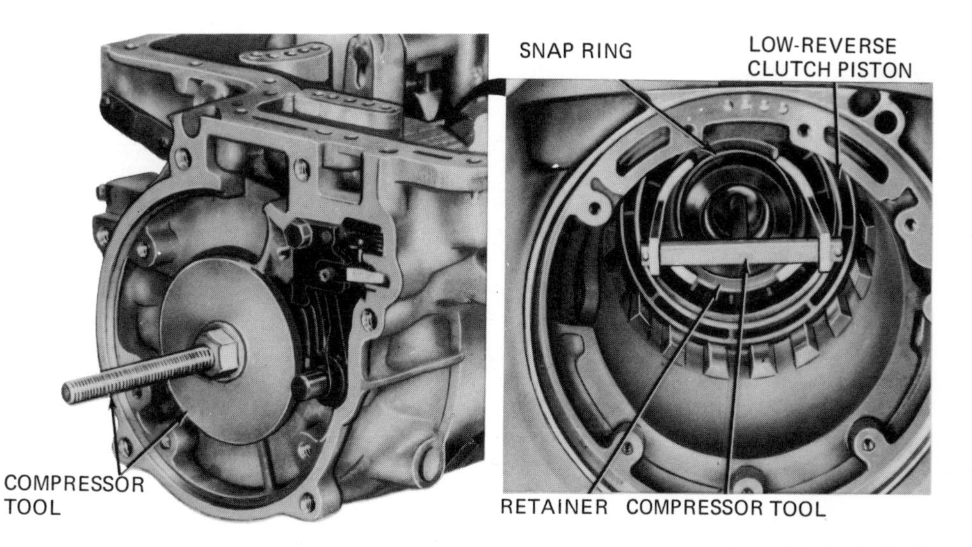

Figure 11 Compressing the low-reverse-clutch spring. *(Ford Motor Company.)*

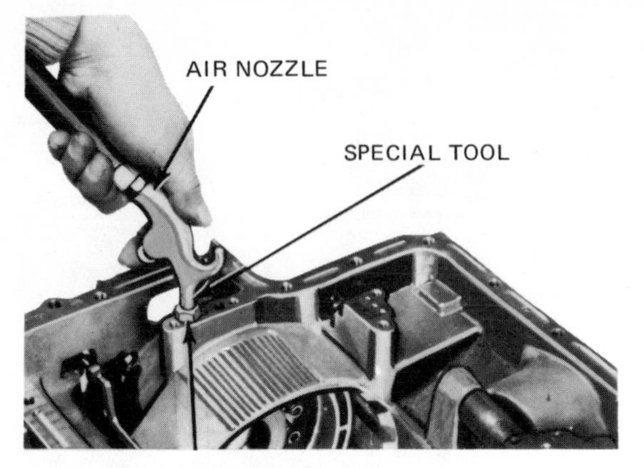

Figure 12 Removing the low-reverse-clutch piston with compressed air. *(Ford Motor Company.)*

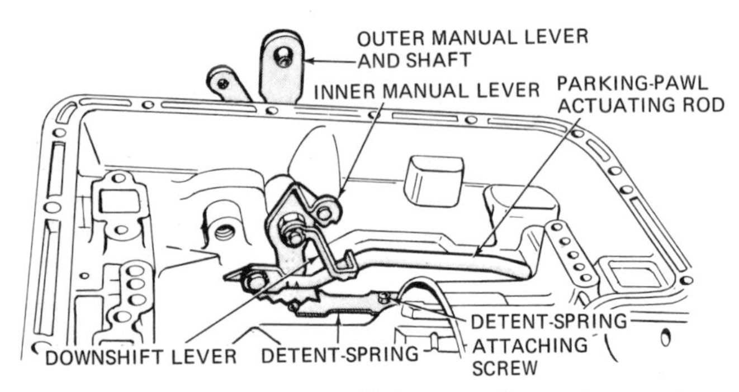

Figure 13 Downshift and manual linkage. *(Ford Motor Company.)*

the shaft. Then pry the gear train to the rear of the case, as shown, and press the input shaft inward until it bottoms. Set the dial indicator to zero.

4. Pry the gear train forward and note the amount of gear-train end play as registered on the dial indicator. Record the end play. You will need this figure on reassembly.

5. Remove the vacuum unit, rod, and primary throttle

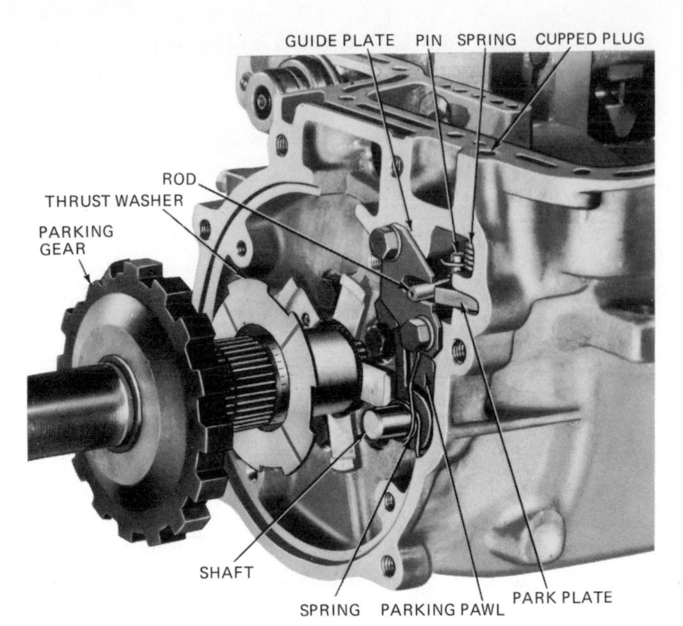

Figure 14 Parking-pawl mechanism. *(Ford Motor Company.)*

valve. Slip the input shaft out of the pump.

6. Remove the front-pump attaching bolts. Pry the gear train forward to remove the pump.

7. Loosen the band adjustment screw and remove the two struts. Rotate the band 90° counterclockwise to align the ends with the slot in the case. Then slide the band off the clutch drum.

8. Remove the forward part of the gear train as an assembly.

9. Remove the large snap ring that holds the reverse planet carrier in the low-and-reverse clutch hub. Lift the planet carrier from the drum.

10. Remove the snap ring that secures the reverse ring gear and hub to the output shaft. Slide the ring gear and hub off the shaft.

11. Rotate the low-and-reverse clutch hub in a clockwise direction and at the same time withdraw it from the case.

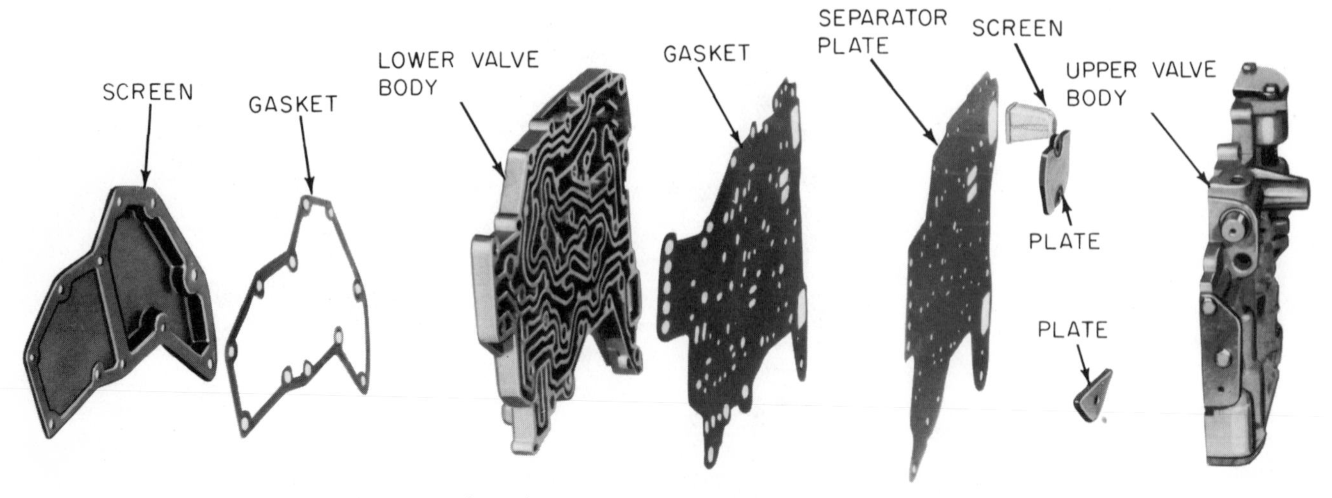

Figure 15 Upper and lower valve bodies separated. *(Ford Motor Company.)*

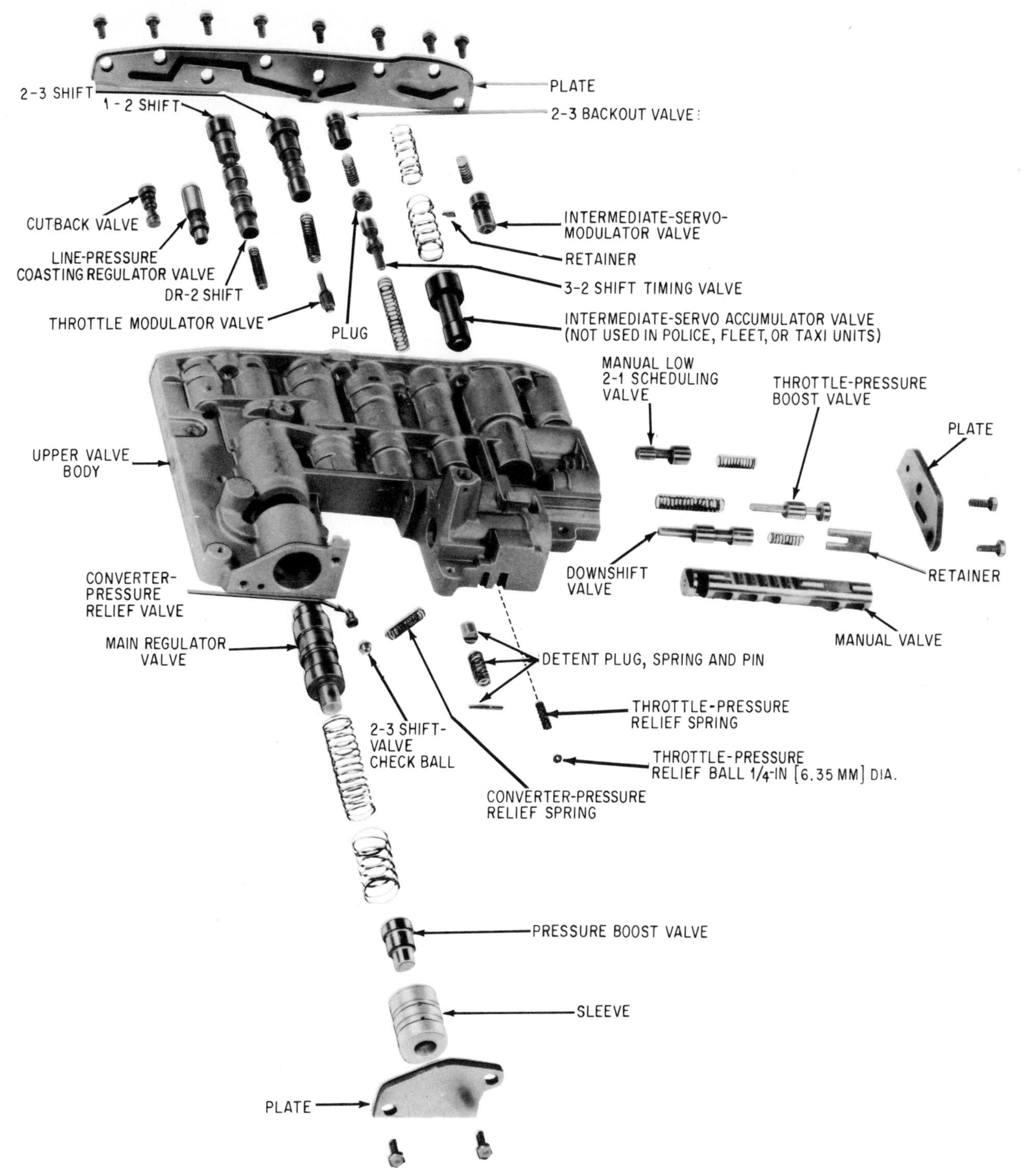

Figure 16 Disassembled view of the upper valve body. *(Ford Motor Company.)*

12. Remove the reverse-clutch snap ring from the case, and then remove the clutch disks, plates, and pressure plate from the case.

13. Remove the extension-housing attaching bolts and vent tube from the case. Remove the extension housing and gasket.

14. Slide the output-shaft assembly from the case.

15. Remove the distributor-sleeve attaching bolts and remove the sleeve, parking pawl gear, and thrust washer. If the thrust washer is staked in place, use a sharp chisel and cut off the metal from behind the washer. Clean up the rear of the case with air pressure and solvent to remove any metal particles.

16. Compress the reverse-clutch-piston spring with a compressor tool, as shown in Fig. 11. Remove the snap ring, tool, and spring retainer.

17. Remove the one-way-clutch inner-race attaching bolts and the inner race. Then remove the reverse-clutch piston from the case, using air pressure, as shown in Fig. 12.

■ **5-6-15 Downshift and Manual Linkages** The downshift and manual linkages are shown in the case in Fig. 13. Follow this illustration if the parts must be removed. If they are removed, remove the shaft seal from the case and install a new seal by using a special tool to drive it in place.

■ **5-6-16 Parking-Pawl Linkage** The parking-pawl linkage is shown in Fig. 14. Refer to this illustration if the parts must be removed. Drill a ⅛-inch (3.175-mm) hole in the cupped plug and pull it out with a wire hook. Then, after the spring is lifted off the park-plate pin, thread a ¼-20 screw into the shaft and pull it out. You will need a new cupped plug to retain the shaft when you reassemble the parts.

■ **5-6-17 Servo-Apply Lever** If the servo-apply lever requires replacement, drive the lever shaft from inside the case to drive out the cup plug. Then the shaft can be pulled out. Use a new plug on reinstallation, and coat it with a special sealant, such as Loctite.

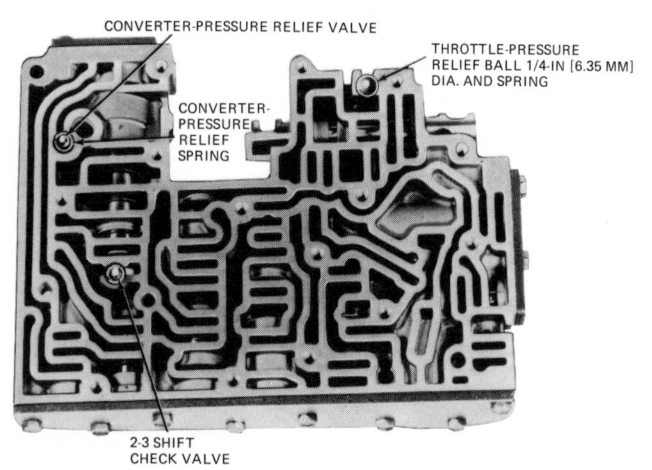

Figure 17 Location of check balls in the valve body. *(Ford Motor Company.)*

■ **5-6-18 Valve Body** Figure 15 shows the upper and lower valve bodies separated. Figure 16 shows the upper valve body disassembled. Follow these illustrations to disassemble and reassemble the valve body. To remove the manual valve, you will need a special tool to depress the manual-valve detent spring. Note, also, the locations of the relief balls and springs, as shown in Fig. 17.

■ **5-6-19 Pump** To disassemble the pump, remove the selective thrust washer and the two seal rings, the large square-cut seal ring, and the five bolts that secure the pump support and the drive and driven gears from the housing.

When reassembling the pump, make sure that the gears are installed with the identification marks facing the front of the pump housing. Also, make sure that the two locking seal rings on the support are locked. Use new seal rings on reinstallation.

Finally, make sure that the correct thickness of selective thrust washer is used to produce the correct gear-train end play. If the end play is not within the specifications given in the car shop manual, select a thrust washer of the different thickness to give the correct end play.

■ **5-6-20 Reverse-and-High Clutch** Separate the drive train into its major component parts, as shown in Fig. 9. Then remove the pressure-plate snap ring so that the internal parts can be taken out of the clutch drum, as shown in Fig. 18. Next, use the special compressor tool, as shown in Fig. 19, to compress the springs so that the snap ring can be removed. Then, the tool can be removed along with the spring retainer and springs. Compressed air can then be used to remove the piston, as shown in Fig. 20. The piston seals, shown in Fig. 18, should be removed from the piston and drum.

If the front bushing is worn, it can be removed by cutting along the bushing seam with a cape chisel. The rear bushing is removed with a removal tool. New bushings can then be pressed into place.

To reassemble the reverse-and-high clutch, dip new seals in transmission fluid and install one on the piston and one in the

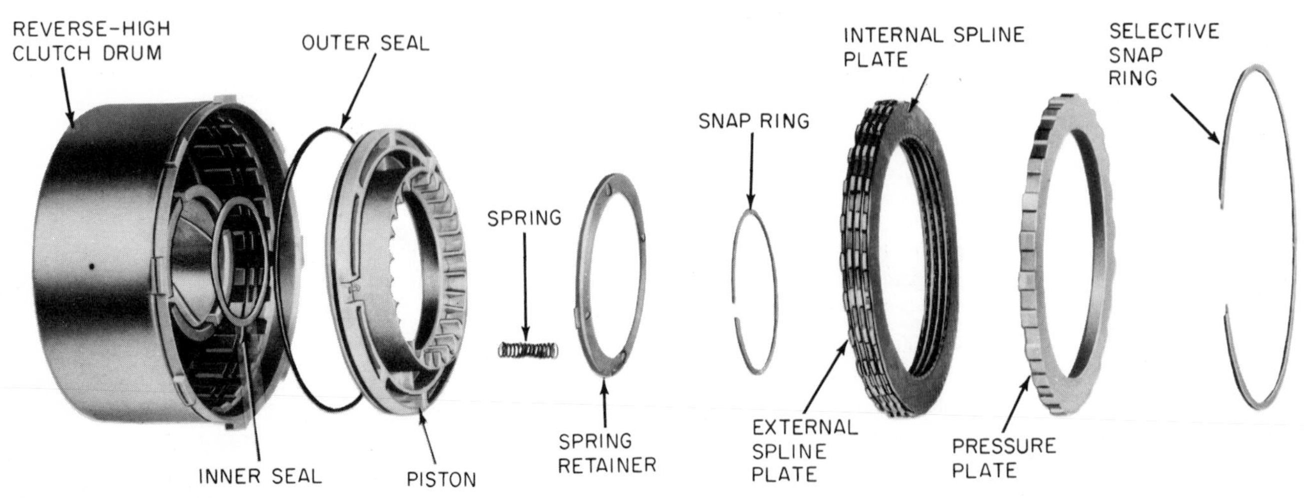

Figure 18 Disassembled view of the reverse-high clutch. *(Ford Motor Company.)*

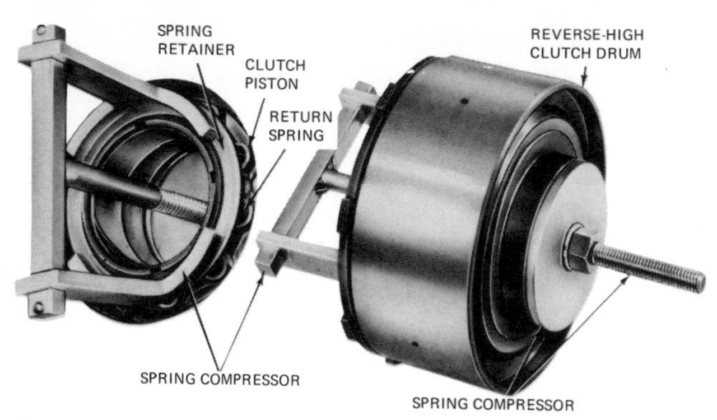

Figure 19 Using a spring compressor to remove the clutch-piston snap ring. *(Ford Motor Company.)*

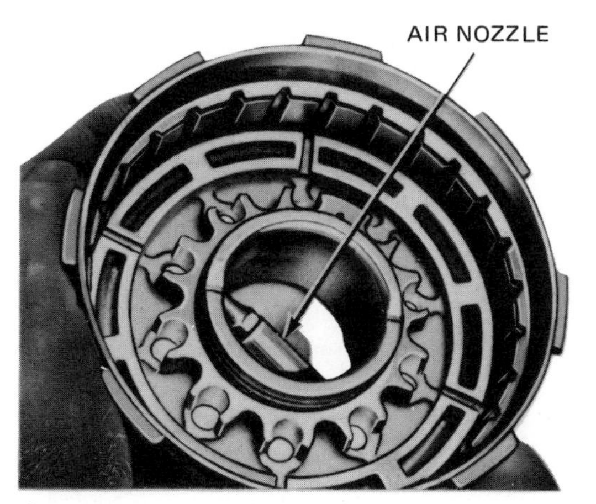

Figure 20 Removing the clutch piston with air pressure. *(Ford Motor Company.)*

drum. Put the piston in the drum. Put the piston springs in the piston sockets and place the spring retainer on the springs. Compress the springs with the special tool, as shown in Fig. 19, and install the snap ring. Make sure the snap ring is inside the four snap-ring guides on the spring retainer.

Install the clutch plates, starting with a steel drive plate and alternating with the composition plates. Soak the composition plates in transmission fluid for 15 minutes before installing them. Then, install the pressure plate and secure it with the pressure-plate snap ring.

Check the clearance between the pressure plate and snap ring with a feeler gauge. If the clearance is not within specification, replace the snap ring with another snap ring of the correct thickness to produce the proper clearance. Selective snap rings of three thicknesses are available.

■ **5-6-21 Forward Clutch** The forward clutch is shown in disassembled view in Fig. 21. It is disassembled in the same way as the reverse-and-high clutch. The snap ring is removed so that the pressure plate and disks can be removed. This clutch also has a forward pressure plate and disk spring, as shown. After these parts are removed, the disk spring must be compressed by a compressor so that the snap ring and spring can be removed. Then the piston can be removed by air pressure applied to the passage in the cylinder.

On reassembly, clearance must be checked between the snap ring and the pressure plate, just as in the forward clutch. Also, there are snap rings of different thicknesses so that the correct one can be installed to provide the proper clearance.

■ **5-6-22 Input Shell and Sun Gear** The sun gear is held in place in the input shell by two snap rings and a thrust washer. Removal of the snap rings permits separation of the parts.

■ **5-6-23 One-Way Clutch** The one-way clutch is shown disassembled and separated from the low-and-reverse clutch hub in Fig. 22. This clutch is disassembled by removing

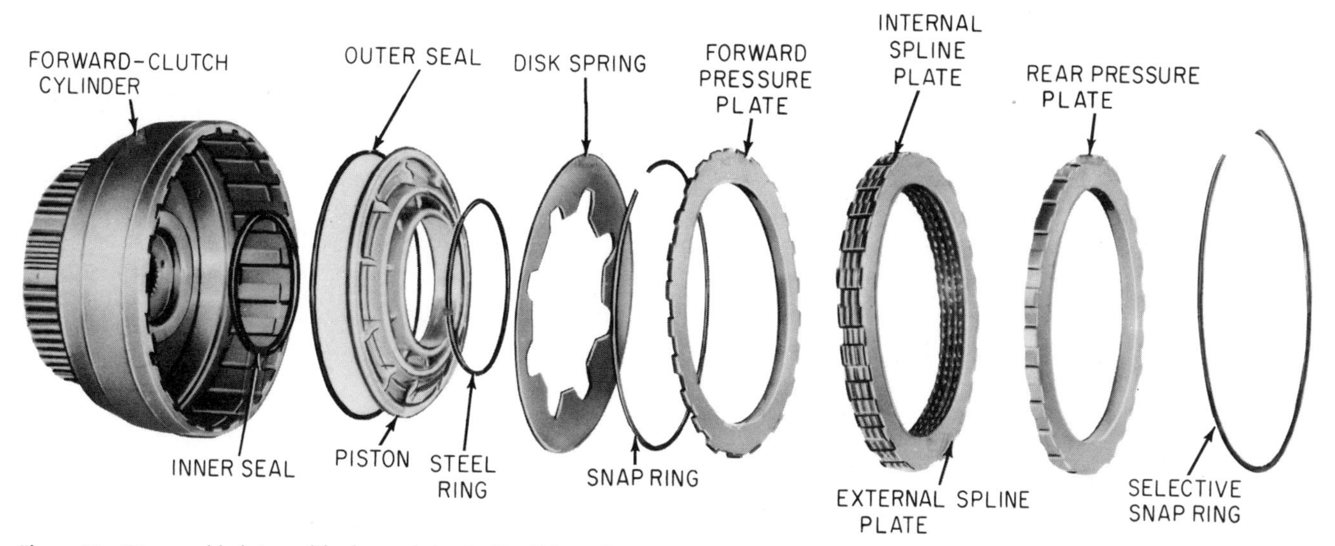

Figure 21 Disassembled view of the forward clutch. *(Ford Motor Company.)*

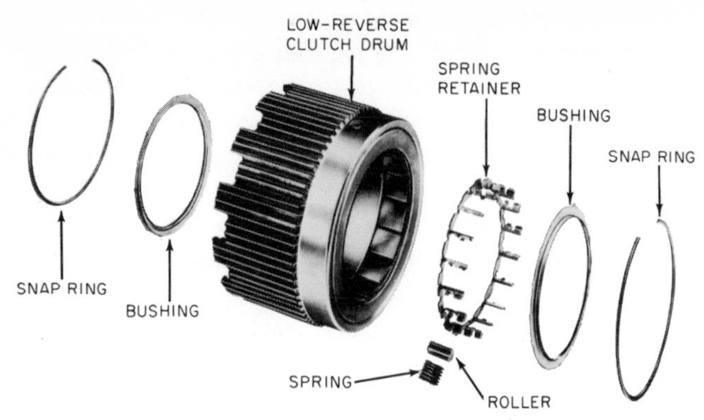

Figure 22 Disassembled view of the one-way clutch. *(Ford Motor Company.)*

the snap rings. On reassembly, first install a snap ring in the forward-snap-ring groove of the clutch hub. Then put the hub forward-end down. Put the forward-clutch bushing into place against the snap ring with the flat side up. Install the spring retainer on top of the bushing. Be sure to install it in the hub so that the springs load the rollers in a counterclockwise direction when one is looking down at the unit. Install a spring and roller into each of the spring-retainer compartments by slightly compressing each spring and positioning the roller between the spring and spring retainer. Install the rear bushing, flat side down, and install the snap ring to secure the assembly.

■ **5-6-24 Output Shaft** The output shaft contains the governor and governor distributor. The governor is attached by bolts, and the distributor is held on the shaft by snap rings. Remove bolts and snap rings to remove these parts.

■ **5-6-25 Converter Checks** The converter is checked for leakage and for end play and stator-clutch action as explained in Part 5, Sec. 2.

■ **5-6-26 Transmission Reassembly** On reassembly, lubricate the parts with transmission fluid. Use petroleum jelly to hold washers in place during reassembly. Proceed as follows, after the case has been installed in a repair fixture:

1. Position the low-and-reverse-clutch piston so that the check ball is at the 6 o'clock position—at the bottom of the case—and tap it into place with a clean rubber hammer.

2. Hold the one-way-clutch inner race in position and install and torque the attaching bolts to specifications.

3. Install the low-and-reverse-clutch return springs into the pocket in the piston. Press the springs firmly into place so that they will not fall out.

4. Put the spring retainer over the springs and put the snap ring above it. Use a compressor tool to compress the springs and install the snap ring.

5. Put the case on the bench, front end down.

6. Put the parking-gear thrust washer and gear on the case. Do not stake the washer.

7. Position the oil distributor and tubes on the rear of the case, and torque the attaching bolts to specifications.

8. Install the output shaft and governor.

9. Put a new gasket on the rear of the case and install the extension housing, torquing the bolts to specifications.

10. Put the case back in the repair fixture.

11. Align the low-and-reverse clutch hub and one-way clutch with the inner race at the rear of the case. Rotate the low-and-reverse-clutch hub clockwise while applying pressure to seat it on the inner race.

12. Install the low-and-reverse-clutch plates, starting with a steel plate and following alternately with composition and steel plates. Retain them with petroleum jelly. New composition plates should be soaked in transmission fluid for 15 minutes before installation. Test the operation of the clutch with compressed air.

13. Install the reverse-planet-ring-gear thrust washer and the ring-gear-and-hub assembly. Insert the snap ring in the groove in the output shaft.

14. Assemble the front and rear thrust washers onto the reverse-planet assembly. Retain them with petroleum jelly. Insert the assembly into the ring gear and secure with the snap ring.

15. Set the reverse-and-high clutch on the bench, front end facing down. Install the thrust washer on the rear end, retaining it with petroleum jelly. Insert the splined end of the forward clutch into the open end of the reverse-and-high clutch so that the splines engage the direct-clutch plates.

16. On the front end of the forward planet ring gear and hub, install the thrust washer and retain it with petroleum jelly. Insert the assembly into the ring gear. Install the input-shell-and-sun-gear assembly.

17. Install the reverse-and-high clutch, forward clutch, forward-planet assembly, and input shell and sun gear as an assembly into the transmission case.

18. Insert the intermediate band into the case around the direct-clutch drum. Install the struts and tighten the band adjusting screw enough to hold the band.

19. Place a selective-thickness washer of the proper thickness as determined by the end-play check during disassembly (see Fig. 10) on the shoulder of the stator support. This is the selective thrust washer referred to in ■5-6-19. Retain the washer with petroleum jelly.

20. Lay a new gasket on the rear mounting face of the pump and bring the pump into place. Be careful not to damage the large seal on the outside diameter of the pump housing. Install six of the seven pump mounting screws and torque them to specifications.

21. Adjust the intermediate band, as already noted, and install the input shaft with the long splined end inserted into the forward-clutch assembly.

22. Install the special tool with the dial indicator in the seventh pump bolt hole and recheck the end play. If the end play is correct, remove the tool and install the seventh bolt. If it is incorrect, remove the pump and install a selective thrust washer of the correct thickness.

23. Install the control-valve body in the case, making sure the levers engage the valves properly. Install the primary throttle valve, rod, and vacuum unit.

24. Install a new oil-pan gasket and pan.

25. Install the converter and install the transmission in the car, as explained in Part 5, Sec. 2. Attach and adjust linkages.

26. Add transmission fluid, as explained in Part 5, Sec. 2, to bring the fluid up to the correct level.

27. Start the engine and check the operation of the transmission in all selector-lever positions.

PART 6

Steering and Suspension

SECTION 6-1 | Chassis Fundamentals

This section describes the various components or subassemblies that make up the automobile. Later sections explain how they operate, and how to service and repair them. Figure 1 shows an automotive chassis. The chassis is made up of the engine, frame, power train, wheels, and steering and brake systems.

Figure 1 Chassis of a passenger car. The chassis contains the source of power, or engine; the frame, which supports the engine, wheels, and body; the power train, which carries the engine power to the rear wheels; and the steering and braking systems. *(Oldsmobile Division of General Motors Corporation.)*

■ 6-1-1 Frame

The frame (Fig. 1) supports the engine, body, wheels, and power-train members. It is usually made of box, tubular, and channel members carefully shaped and then welded or riveted together. Cross members reinforce the frame and also support the engine and wheels. The frame is extremely rigid and strong so that it can withstand the shock blows, twists, vibrations, and other strains to which it is subjected on the road.

The engine is attached to the frame in three or four places. Noise and some vibrations are inherent in engine operation. To prevent this noise and vibration from passing to the engine frame, and from there to the occupants of the car, the engine is insulated from the frame by some form of rubber pad or washer at each point of support. One type of engine mounting support is shown in Fig. 2. In this engine, there are two rubber mountings at the front, and a single, long, narrow, rubber mounting pad at the back. Engine mounting bolts pass through these rubber mountings so that there is no metal-to-metal contact. As a result, the rubber absorbs vibration and engine noise so that they are not carried to the engine frame.

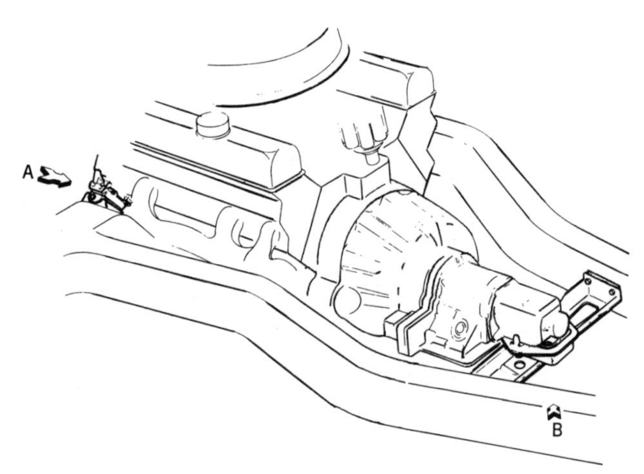

Figure 2 Engine supports, indicated by arrows. *(Buick Motor Division of General Motors Corporation.)*

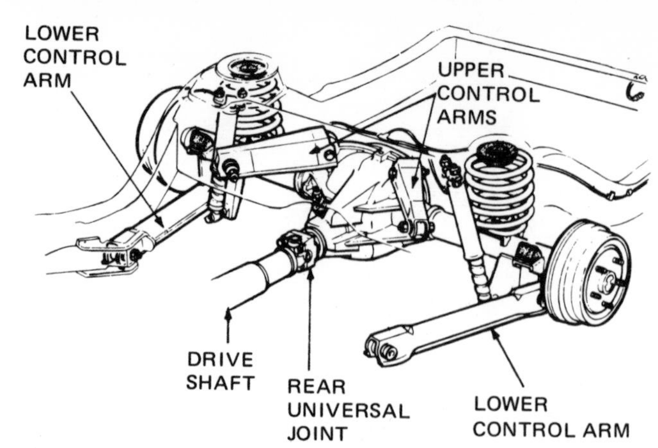

Figure 3 Rear-suspension system using coil springs. *(Buick Motor Division of General Motors Corporation.)*

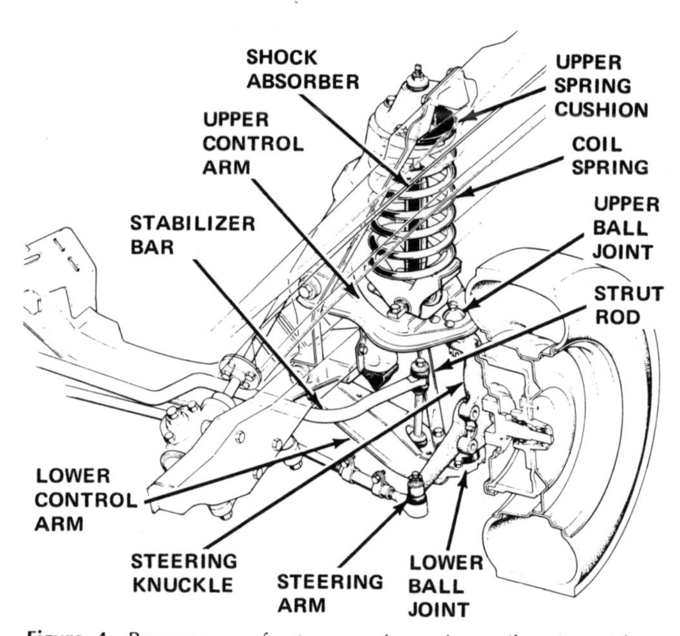

Figure 4 Passenger-car front suspension using coil springs. The frame, wheel, and other components are partly cut away to show suspension parts. *(American Motors Corporation.)*

■ 6-1-2 Springs

The car wheels are suspended on springs that support the weight of the vehicle (Figs. 3 and 4). The springs absorb road shock as the wheels encounter holes or bumps and prevent, to a large extent, any consequent jarring action or up-and-down motion from being carried through the frame and body. Springs are coil type, leaf type, torsion bar, or air suspension. Figure 4 shows one of the coil springs used in a front-suspension system. The coil spring is a heavy steel coil. The weight of the frame and body puts an initial compression on the spring. The spring will further compress when the wheel passes over an obstruction in the road. It will expand if the wheel encounters a hole in the road.

The leaf spring has been made in a number of forms, but the one most commonly used is the semi-elliptical type (Fig. 5). The leaf spring is made up of a series of flat plates, or leaves, of graduated length, one on top of another. The spring assembly

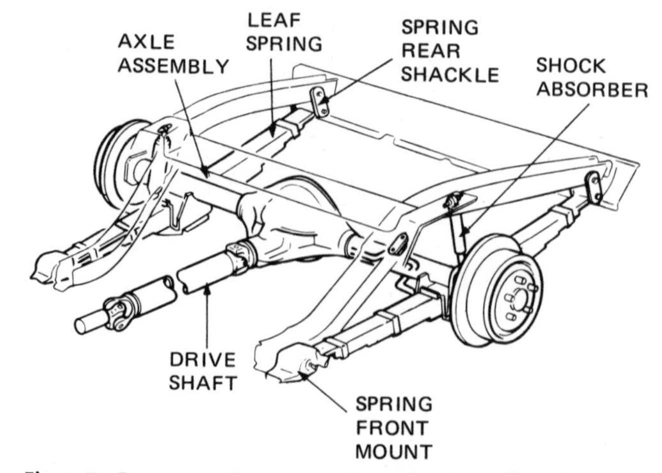

Figure 5 Rear-suspension system using leaf springs. *(Chevrolet Motor Division of General Motors Corporation.)*

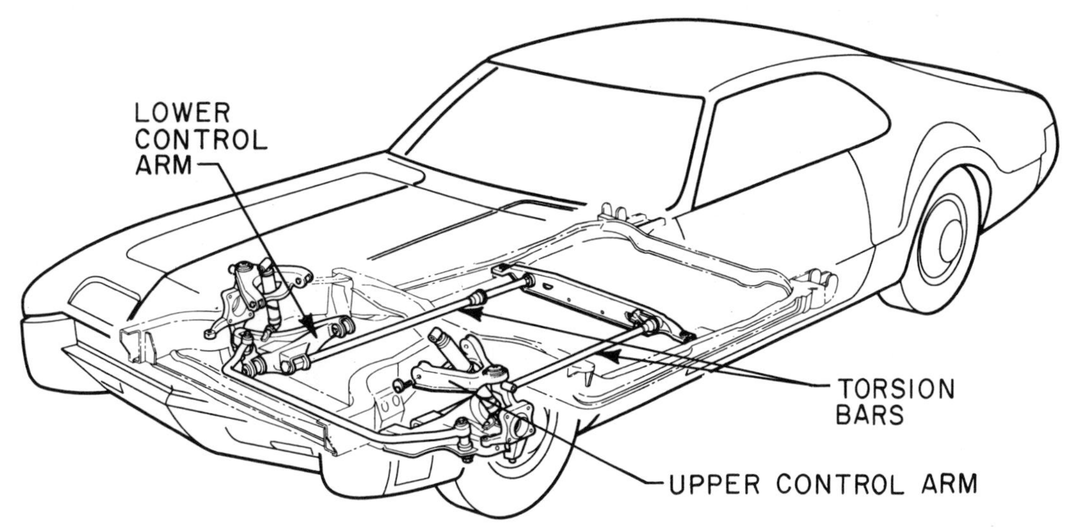

Figure 6 Front suspension of a car with front-wheel drive using torsion bars. The bars are locked to the frame at the rear. They are attached at the front to the inner ends of the lower control arms. The torsion bars twist varying amounts as varying loads are applied. This allows the front wheels to move up and down. The action is similar to that of other springs. *(Oldsmobile Division of General Motors Corporation.)*

acts as a flexible beam and is usually fastened at the two ends to the car frame and at the center to the wheel axle. Some cars have used only one leaf spring at the rear and one at the front, each spring supporting two wheels. With this design, the center of the spring is attached to the frame, and each end of the spring supports a wheel. The action is similar on all leaf springs. When the wheel encounters a bump, the spring bends upward to absorb the blow. When the wheel drops into a hole, the spring bends downward. Thus, the leaf spring does the same job as the coil spring in the vehicle.

The torsion-bar suspension system (Fig. 6) uses bars connected between the suspension of control arms and the frame. Movement of the wheels up and down twists the bars more or less to provide the springing action.

Springs are usually insulated mechanically from the frame by means of rubber bushings and pads. This prevents road vibration from being transmitted to the frame and body.

■ **6-1-3 Shock Absorbers** Springs alone cannot provide a satisfactorily smooth ride. Therefore, an additional device, called a "shock absorber," is used with each spring. To understand why springs alone would not give smooth riding qualities, let us consider the action of a coil spring. The same actions would take place with a leaf type of spring. The spring is under an initial load provided by the car weight. This gives the spring an original amount of compression. When the wheel passes over a bump, the spring becomes further compressed. After the bump is passed, the spring attempts to return to its original position. However, it overrides its original position and expands too much. This behavior causes the car frame to be thrown upward. Having expanded too much, the spring attempts to compress so that it will return to its original position; but in compressing, it again overrides. In doing this the wheel may be raised clear of the road, and the car frame consequently drops. The result is an oscillating motion of the spring that causes the wheel to rebound, or bounce up and down several times, after a bump has been encountered. If, in the meantime, another bump is encountered, a second series of reboundings will be started. On a bumpy road, and particularly in rounding a curve, the oscillations might be so serious as to cause the driver to lose control of the car.

Shock absorbers (Fig. 3) prevent these spring oscillations. Figure 7 shows one type of shock absorber in sectional view. This is the direct-acting, or telescope, shock absorber. One end of the shock absorber is attached to the frame, the other to

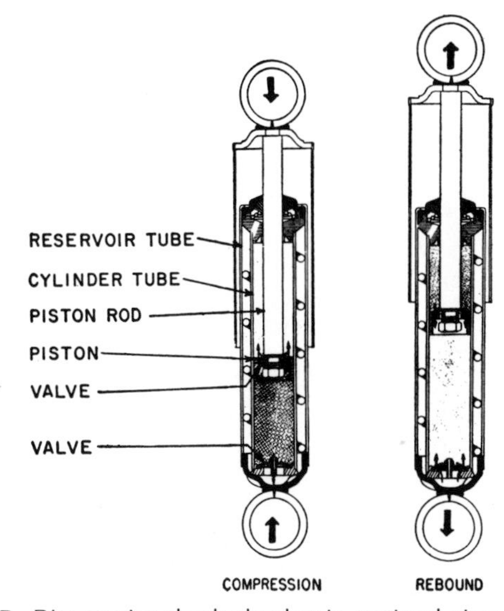

Figure 7 Direct-acting shock absorber in sectional view, showing what happens during compression and rebound. Fluid movement is shown by arrows. Fluid under pressure is shown darker than fluid not under pressure. *(Chrysler Corporation.)*

the lower control arm (at front as shown in Fig. 4) or to the axle housing or spring (at rear, as shown in Figs. 3 and 5). Thus as a wheel moves up or down in relation to the frame, the shock absorber will shorten or lengthen (see Fig. 7). When the shock absorber shortens, the piston rod forces the piston down into the cylinder tube, thereby putting fluid below the piston under high compression. The fluid is forced through small orifices, or openings, in the piston and into the upper part of the cylinder tube. On rebound, when the wheel moves downward after passing a bump or dropping into a hole in the road, the shock absorber is extended (Fig. 7). As this happens, the piston moves into the upper part of the cylinder tube, thereby forcing fluid from the upper into the lower part of the tube.

As the fluid is forced in one direction or the other, it must pass through small orifices. This slows the motion of the piston and tends to place restraint on the spring action. In this way, the shock of the wheel meeting a bump or hole is absorbed. The orifices have spring-loaded valves which open varying amounts to allow varying speeds of fluid movement through the orifices. This permits rapid spring motion while still imposing a restraining action. At the same time, it prevents excessive pressure rise in the fluid that might otherwise occur when large bumps in the road are encountered by the wheels. Also, the restraining action prevents excessive oscillations of the wheel after it passes a bump or hole.

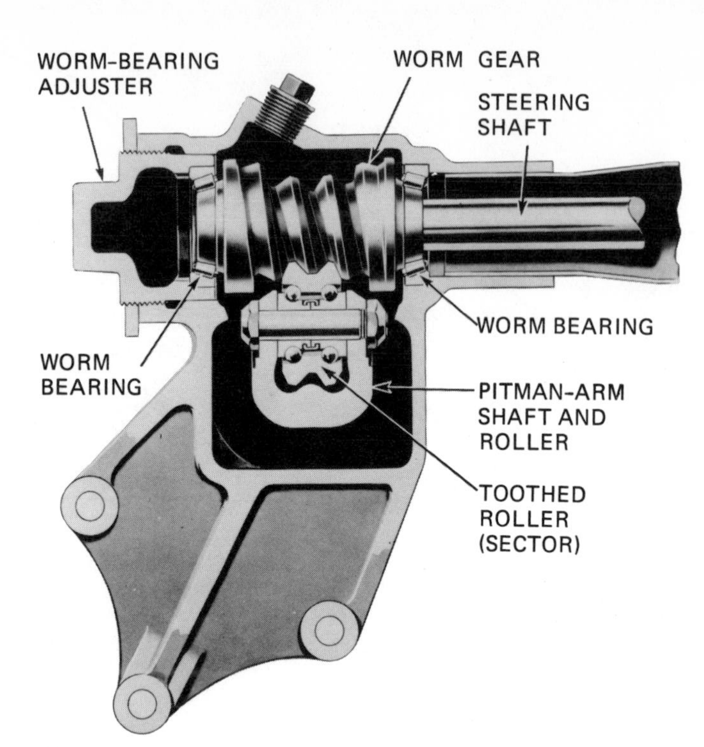

Figure 9 One type of steering gear (in sectional view) using a roller sector with an hourglass worm gear. *(Chevrolet Motor Division of General Motors Corporation.)*

■ 6-1-4 Steering System

To guide the car, some means of turning the front wheels is necessary so that the car can be pointed in the direction the driver wants to go. The steering wheel in front of the driver is linked by gears and levers to the front wheels for this purpose. A simplified drawing of a steering system is shown in Fig. 8. The front wheels are supported on pivots so that they can be swung to the left or right. They are attached by steering-knuckle arms to tie rods. The tie rods are, in turn, attached to a pitman arm. As the steering wheel is turned in one direction or the other, gearing in the steering-gear assembly causes the end of the pitman arm to swing to the left or right. This movement is carried by the tie rods to the steering-knuckle arms, and wheels, causing them to swing to the left or right.

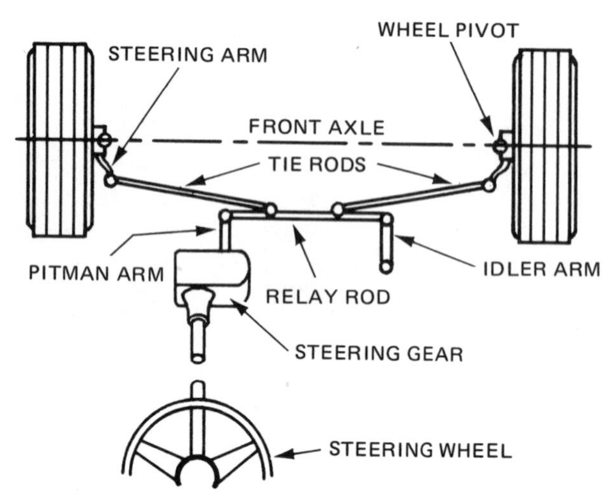

Figure 8 Simplified drawing of a steering system as seen from above.

Various arrangements of linkage are used. Although they are considerably different in general arrangement, all operate basically in the same manner. Linkage arrangements are covered in following sections.

Figure 9 shows, in cutaway view, a steering-gear assembly. The steering shaft has a special sort of worm gear on its lower end. Meshing with the teeth of this worm gear is a special gear called a "sector." The sector is attached to one end of a shaft. The other end of the shaft carries the pitman arm. When the steering wheel is turned, the worm on the steering shaft rotates. This causes the sector to move toward one end or the other of the worm. The sector movement causes the sector shaft to rotate. This rotary motion is carried to the pitman arm, causing it to swing to the left or right as already described.

Most steering systems use a worm gear on the lower end of the steering shaft. But there are several types of devices on the pitman-arm shaft. Some steering gears use studs that ride between the worm-gear teeth; others use a half nut, a plain gear, ball bearings, and so on. A different arrangement uses a pinion on the end of the steering shaft. The pinion is meshed with a rack which moves to the right or left as the shaft and pinion turn to provide the steering action. In addition, several devices that use hydraulic pressure assist in steering. These are called power-steering devices, and they take most of the effort out of steering; hydraulic pressure supplies most of the effort. Steering and power-steering mechanisms are covered in the sections on steering systems.

■ **6-1-5 Brakes** Brakes are necessary to slow or stop the car. Practically all cars use hydraulic brakes (which operate by applying pressure to a fluid). Most modern brake systems have a fluid-filled cylinder, called the "master cylinder," containing two separate sections. There is a piston in each section, and both pistons are connected to a brake pedal in the driver's compartment. When the brake pedal is pushed by the driver, the two pistons move in the two sections of the master cylinder. This forces brake fluid out and through the brake lines, or tubes, to the brake mechanisms at the wheels. In a typical system, the brake fluid from one section of the master cylinder goes to the two front-wheel brakes. The brake fluid from the other section goes to the two rear-wheel brakes. The purpose of having two sections is that, if one section fails, the other section will still provide braking.

There are two different types of brake mechanisms at the wheels: the drum-and-shoe type and the disk type. The drum-and-shoe type has a wheel brake cylinder with two pistons. When brake fluid is forced into the brake cylinder by the action at the master cylinder, the two pistons are forced outward. This causes the curved brake shoes to move into contact with the brake drum. The brake shoes apply friction to the brake drum, forcing it, and the wheel, to slow or stop.

In the disk type, a rotating disk attached to the wheel is positioned between flat brake shoes. One or more pistons, actuated by the brake fluid from the master cylinder, force the shoes into contact with the rotating disk, and slow or stop the car.

Many vehicles use power brakes. In these, vacuum and air pressure supply most of the brake-applying effort. As the driver pushes down on the brake pedal, vacuum is applied on one side of a piston and air pressure is applied on the other. This causes the piston to move in a cylinder. The piston then takes over most of the effort required to build up the hydraulic pressure in the lines to the wheel cylinders. Details of this and other braking mechanisms are discussed in Part 7.

■ **6-1-6 Tires** Tires are of the air-filled, or pneumatic, type. Their function is to transmit the driving power of the wheels to the road through frictional contact. They also absorb a considerable part of the road shock resulting from small bumps and holes and prevent these shocks from being carried to the frame and the body of the car. As the tires roll over small bumps, they flex; the outer surface, or tread, moves inward against the cushion of air inside the tires.

Pneumatic tires are of two types: those with inner tubes and those without. Tubeless types are in general use today, although years ago all pneumatic (air) tires had inner tubes. The tubeless tire mounts on the wheel rim in such a way that the tire beads seal airtight against the rim (Fig. 10). In tires with inner tubes, the air is held in the inner tube itself.

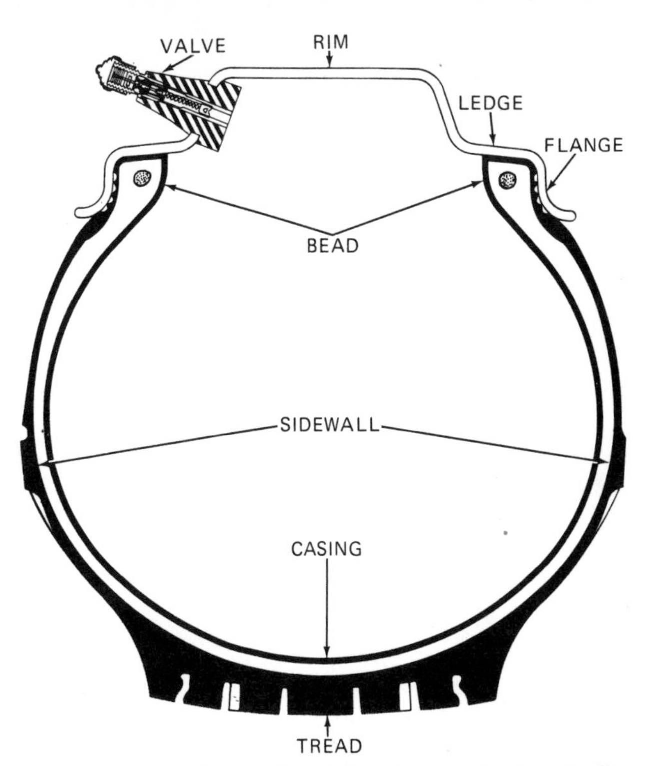

Figure 10 Sectional view of a tubeless tire, showing how the tire bead rests between the ledge and flange of the rim. This arrangement produces a good seal. *(Pontiac Motor Division of General Motors Corporation.)*

The tire casing has an outer coating of rubber which is baked, or vulcanized, onto an inner structure of fabric. The fabric is built up in layers, or plies (a four-ply tire has four layers, for example). The tread, which is the thickest part of the rubber coating, is supplied in a number of different patterns which provide good traction under various operating conditions, such as driving on a turnpike, in mud or snow, or off the highway.

Air is introduced into the tire or tube through a valve. The valve closes after the air has entered, sealing against a seat and preventing leakage of air.

SECTION 6-2 Springs and Suspension Systems

This section describes the various springs and suspension systems used in automotive vehicles, with the exception of shock absorbers.

■ **6-2-1 Function of Springs** The car frame supports the weight of the engine, power-train components, body, and passengers. The frame, in turn, is supported by the springs. The springs are placed between the frame and the wheel axles. Regardless of the type of spring, all work in a similar manner. The weight of the frame, body, and so on applies an initial compression to the springs. The springs will further compress, or will expand, as the car wheels encounter irregularities in the road. Thus, the wheels can move up and down somewhat independently of the frame. This allows the springs to absorb a good part of the up-and-down motion of the car wheels. This motion, therefore, is not transmitted to the car frame and from it to the passengers.

■ **6-2-2 Types of Springs** The automobile uses three types of springs: coil, leaf, and torsion bar. Air suspension was offered at one time as optional equipment for passenger cars; it is now used on some buses. Most automobiles use either coil springs or torsion bars at the two front wheels. Some cars use coil springs at the rear wheels (Fig. 3 in Part 6, Sec. 1, shows coil springs at the rear wheels). Other cars use leaf springs at the rear wheels (Fig. 5 in Part 6, Sec. 1). In addition, some General Motors front-drive cars (Cadillac Eldorado and Oldsmobile Tornado), as well as certain foreign cars, use torsion-bar front suspension.

■ **6-2-3 Coil Springs** The coil spring is made of a length of special spring steel (usually round in cross section) which is wound in the shape of a coil. The spring is formed at high temperature while the steel is white-hot. It is then cooled and properly heat-treated so as to give it the proper characteristics of elasticity and "springiness." Spring characteristics are discussed in a later subsection.

■ 6-2-4 Leaf Springs

There are two types of leaf spring: the multileaf and the single-leaf. The latter is also called a "tapered-plate spring."

1. MULTILEAF SPRING The multileaf spring is made up of a series of flat steel plates of graduated length placed one on top of another. The plates, or leaves, are held together at the center by a center bolt which passes through holes in the leaves. Clips placed at intervals along the spring keep the leaves in alignment. Instead of clips, some leaf springs are sheathed in a metal cover. The longest, or master, leaf is rolled at both ends to form spring eyes through which bolts are placed to attach the spring ends. On some springs, the ends of the second leaf are also rolled partway around the two spring eyes to reinforce the master leaf.

The leaves are of graduated length. To permit them to slip, various means of applying lubricant between the leaves are used. In addition, some leaf springs have special inserts of various materials placed between the leaves to permit easier slipping.

2. SINGLE-LEAF SPRING The single-leaf spring, also called the "tapered-plate spring," is made of a single steel plate which is thick at the center and tapers to the two ends. The methods of mounting and operation are generally the same as with the multileaf spring.

■ 6-2-5 Torsion-Bar Suspension

Figures 6 (in Part 6, Sec. 1) and 1 (this section) show torsion-bar front-suspension systems. In the system shown, the rear end of the torsion bar is rigidly attached to the cross member of the car frame so it is held stationary. The front end is attached to the lower control arm at a point halfway between the arm pivots. Thus, as the lower control arm moves up and down, pivoting on the frame, the torsion bar twists more or less. The car weight places an initial twist on the bar, just as it places an initial compression on the coil springs of the car with coil-spring compression. The twisting of the torsion bar provides the springing effect.

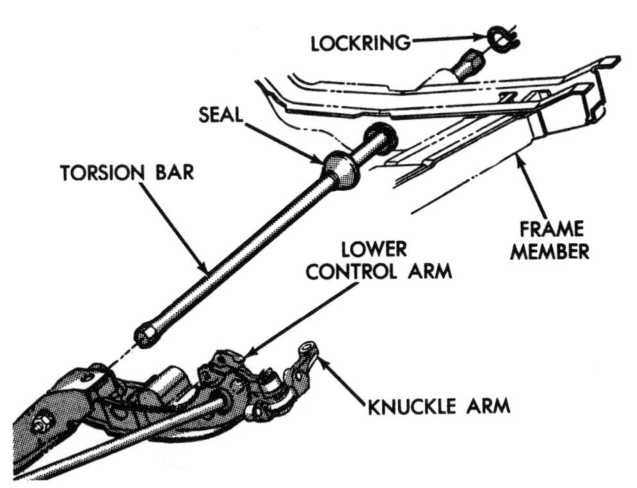

Figure 1 Torsion bar in a front-suspension system. *(Chrysler Corporation.)*

The torsion-bar suspension system includes a means of height adjustment. Thus if sag has occurred due to a change in the torsion-bar characteristic, correction can be made by turning an adjuster bolt. On some cars, the adjustment is made at the rear of the torsion bar, where the bar is attached to the frame cross member. On other cars, the adjustment is made at the lower control arm where the torsion bar is attached to the control arm.

■ 6-2-6 Sprung and Unsprung Weight

In the automobile the terms "sprung weight" and "unsprung weight" refer to the part of the car that is supported on springs and the part that is not. The frame and the parts attached to the frame are sprung; that is, their weight is supported on the car springs. However, the wheels, wheel axles, rear-axle housing, and differential are not supported on springs; they represent unsprung weight.

Generally, unsprung weight should be kept as low as possible because the roughness of the ride increases as unsprung weight increases. For example, consider a single wheel. If it is light, it can move up and down as road irregularities are encountered without causing much reaction to the car frame. But if the weight of the wheel is increased, its movement will become more noticeable to the car occupants. This is the reason for keeping the unsprung weight as low as possible so that it represents only a small portion of the total weight of the car.

■ 6-2-7 Characteristics of Springs

The ideal spring for automotive suspension would be one that would absorb road shock rapidly and then return to the normal position slowly. Such an ideal is not possible, however. An extremely flexible, or soft, spring would allow too much movement, and a stiff, or hard, spring would give too rough a ride. However, satisfactory riding qualities are attained by using a fairly soft spring combined with a shock absorber.

Softness or hardness of a spring is referred to as its "rate." The rate of a spring is the weight required to deflect it 1 inch (25.4 mm). The rates of automotive springs are almost constant throughout their operating range, or deflection, in the car. This is an example of Hooke's law as applied to coil springs: The spring will compress in direct proportion to the weight applied. Thus, if 600 pounds (272.2 kg) will compress the spring 3 inches (76.2 mm), 1,200 pounds (544.3 kg) will compress the spring 6 inches (152.4 mm).

■ 6-2-8 Hotchkiss and Torque-Tube Drives

Before we discuss rear-suspension systems further, we should note that the rear springs may have an additional job to do besides supporting the car load. This additional job is to absorb a

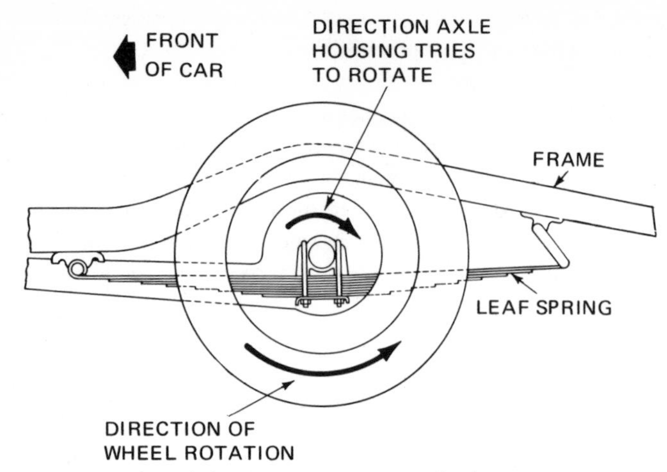

Figure 2 The axle housing tries to rotate in the direction opposite to that of wheel rotation.

kind of force known as "rear-end torque." Whenever the rear wheel is being driven through the power train by the engine, it rotates as shown in Fig. 2 (for forward car motion). A fundamental law of nature states that for every action there must be an equal and opposite reaction. Thus, when the wheel rotates in one direction, the wheel-axle housing tries to rotate in the opposite direction, as shown (Fig. 2). The twisting motion thus

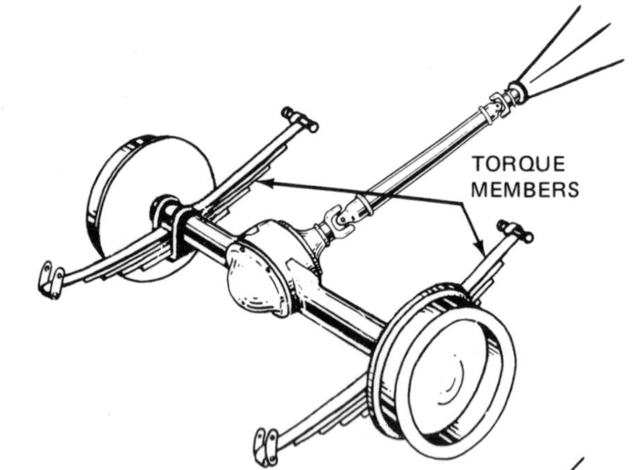

Figure 3 Hotchkiss drive (top) compared with torque-tube drive (bottom).

applied to the axle housing is called "rear-end torque." Two different rear-end designs are used to combat this twisting motion of the axle housing, the Hotchkiss drive and the torque-tube drive (Fig. 3).

1. HOTCHKISS DRIVE In the Hotchkiss drive, the twisting effect, or torque, is taken by the springs. Note that the spring (Fig. 2) is firmly attached to the axle housing. The torque applied by the housing to the spring tends to lift the front end of the spring (Fig. 4). At the same time, it tends to lower the rear end of the spring. The spring does flex a little to permit a slight amount of housing rotation, thus absorbing the rear-end torque, or twisting effort.

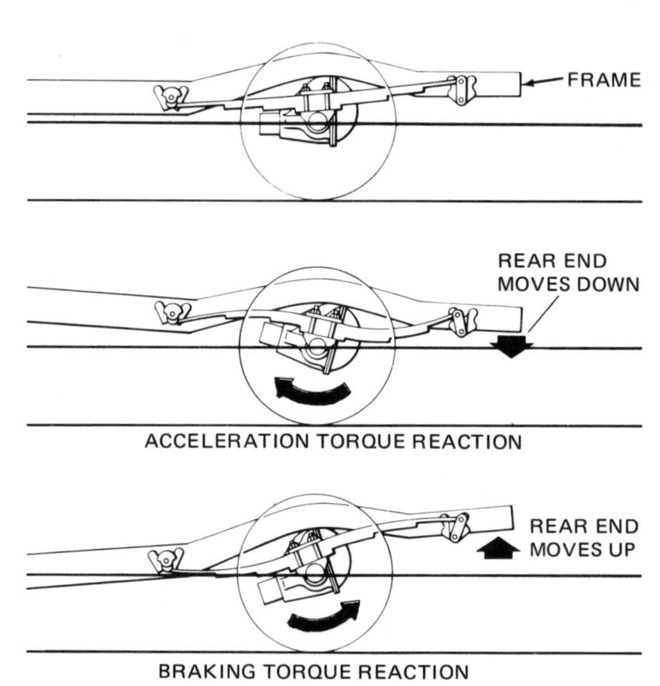

Figure 4 Actions of the spring and rear end when the car is accelerated or braked. *(Ford Motor Company.)*

2. TORQUE-TUBE DRIVE The torque-tube drive is no longer used on cars. It consists of a rigid tube (Fig. 3) that surrounds the propeller shaft. (The propeller shaft carries the power developed by the engine from the transmission to the rear-wheel axles.) The rigid tube is attached to the transmission at the front and to the axle housing—actually the differential housing—at the rear. The axle housing, in attempting to rotate, tries to bend the tube, but the tube resists this effort. The twisting effort of the housing, or rear-end torque, is thus absorbed by the torque tube.

■ 6-2-9 Rear-End Torque

When the rear wheels are driving the car, the wheel-axle housing tries to rotate in a direction opposite to wheel rotation (Fig. 4), causing a motion called "rear-end torque." In a leaf-spring rear suspension, the leaf springs absorb the rear-end torque. On the coil-spring rear suspension, the control arms absorb the rear-end torque. See

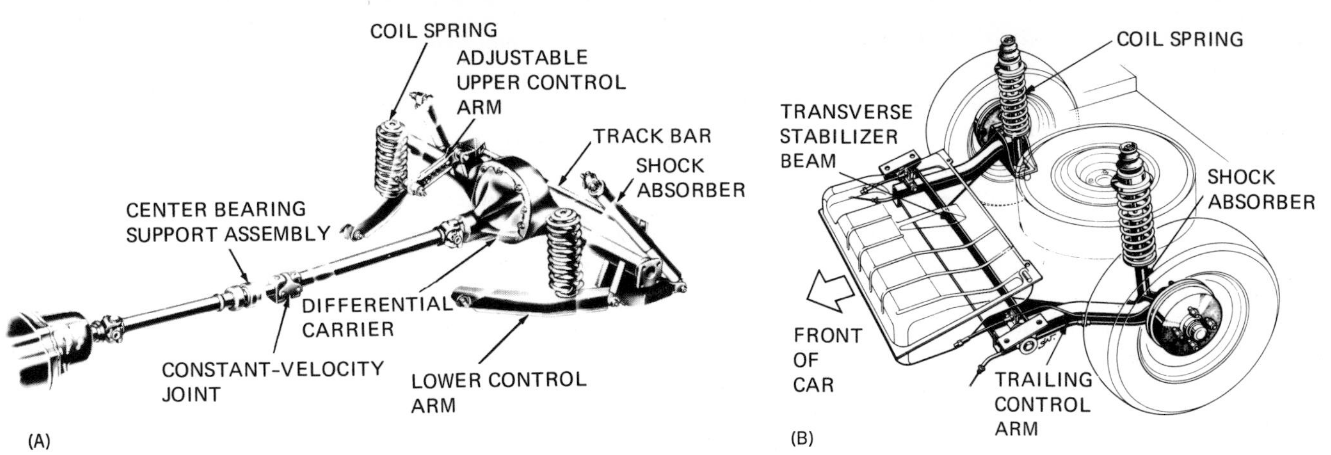

Figure 5 *(a)* Coil-spring rear-suspension system in which coil springs are located between the frame and the lower control arms; *(b)* coil-spring rear suspension in which coil springs are connected to the frame through seats on the shock absorbers. *(Buick Motor Division of General Motors Corporation; Volkswagen of America, Inc.)*

■6-2-10 and ■6-2-11 for details of these two types of rear-end suspension systems.

One effect of rear-end torque is rear-end "squat" on acceleration (Fig. 4). When a car is accelerated from a standing start, the drive pinion in the differential tries to climb the teeth of the differential ring gear. Thus, the drive pinion and differential move upward, and the springs are twisted and compressed by the differential action. In other words, the rear end of the car moves down, or squats, when the car is accelerated. On deceleration, or braking, the rear of the car moves upward, owing to the inertia of the car (Fig. 4).

■ 6-2-10 Coil-Spring Rear Suspension

In some rear-suspension systems using coil springs, the springs are placed between spring housings in the car frame and brackets on the rear-axle housing (Fig. 3 in Part 6, Sec. 1). Note how the spring fits between a circular depression in the frame and a bracket mounted on the axle housing. Somewhat different arrangements are shown in Fig. 5. In these designs, the coil springs are installed between the frame and the lower control arms.

The purpose of the control arms or links, the track bar, and the control yoke is to hold the rear-axle housing and assembly, with the wheels in proper alignment with the frame. The axle housing must be permitted to move up and down in relation with the frame. But it must not be allowed to move forward or backward, or sideways, with respect to the car frame. The control arms permit the rear-axle housing to move upward and downward as the springs compress or expand. At the same time, they keep the axle in proper alignment with the frame. On some cars, control arms are also used to prevent sideward movement of the axle housing. Other cars use a track bar (Fig. 5) connected between the axle housing and the frame to prevent sideward movement. Other designs use a control yoke to prevent sideward movement.

In all these designs, the shock absorbers are connected between the car frame and axle housing.

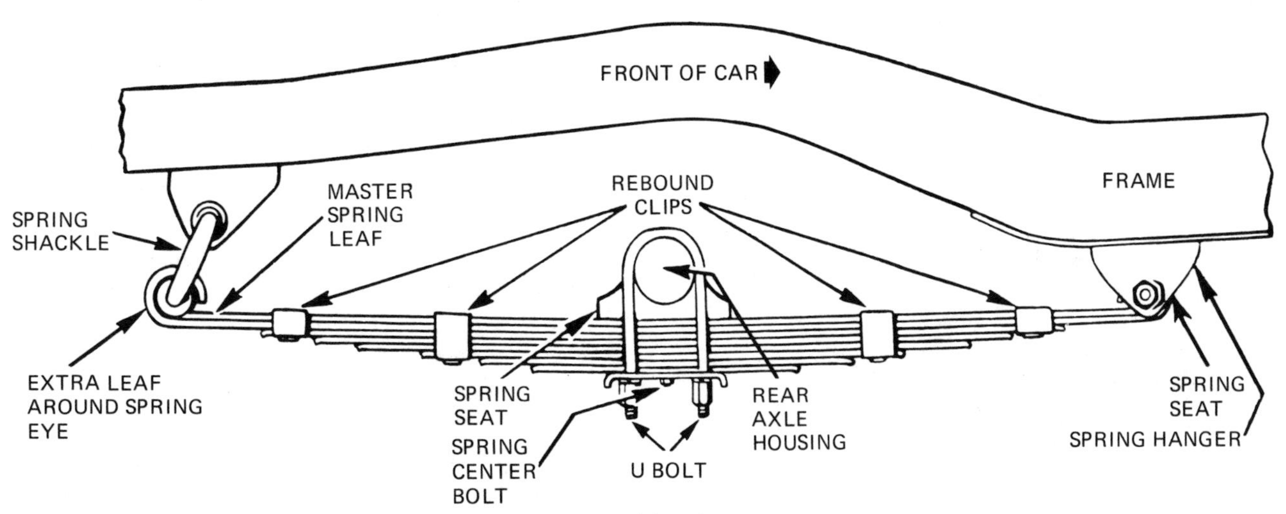

Figure 6 Typical leaf spring, showing how it is attached to the frame and the axle.

■ 6-2-11 Leaf-Spring Rear Suspensions

A considerable variety of leaf-spring rear-suspension systems have been used. The leaf spring most commonly used in automotive vehicles is a semielliptical spring. It has the shape of half an ellipse, and that is the reason for its name.

Note the methods shown in the illustrations for attaching the spring to the car frame and the rear-axle housing. The usual method is to attach the center of the spring to the axle housing with two U bolts so that the spring is, in effect, hanging from the axle housing. A spring plate or straps are used at the bottom of the spring (Fig. 6). Some installations include insulating strips or pads of rubber to reduce noise transfer from the axle housing to the spring.

Note that leaf-spring rear-suspension systems do not require control arms, as do coil-spring rear suspension systems. The leaf springs absorb rear-end torque and side thrust (as when rounding a corner). The exception to this is the system using a transverse leaf spring (■6-2-12).

On some vehicles, the spring is placed on top of the axle housing, rather than under it. This is a common arrangement in heavy-duty suspension (■6-2-13).

The two ends of the spring are attached to the frame by a spring hanger (usually at the front) and by a spring shackle (usually at the rear). A typical installation is shown in Fig. 6. Note the construction and arrangement of the hanger and shackle.

NOTE: In some heavy-duty installations, no shackle or hanger attachment is used. Instead, the two ends of the spring are straight and ride on hangers on the frame. This permits the spring ends to move back and forth as the effective length of the spring changes.

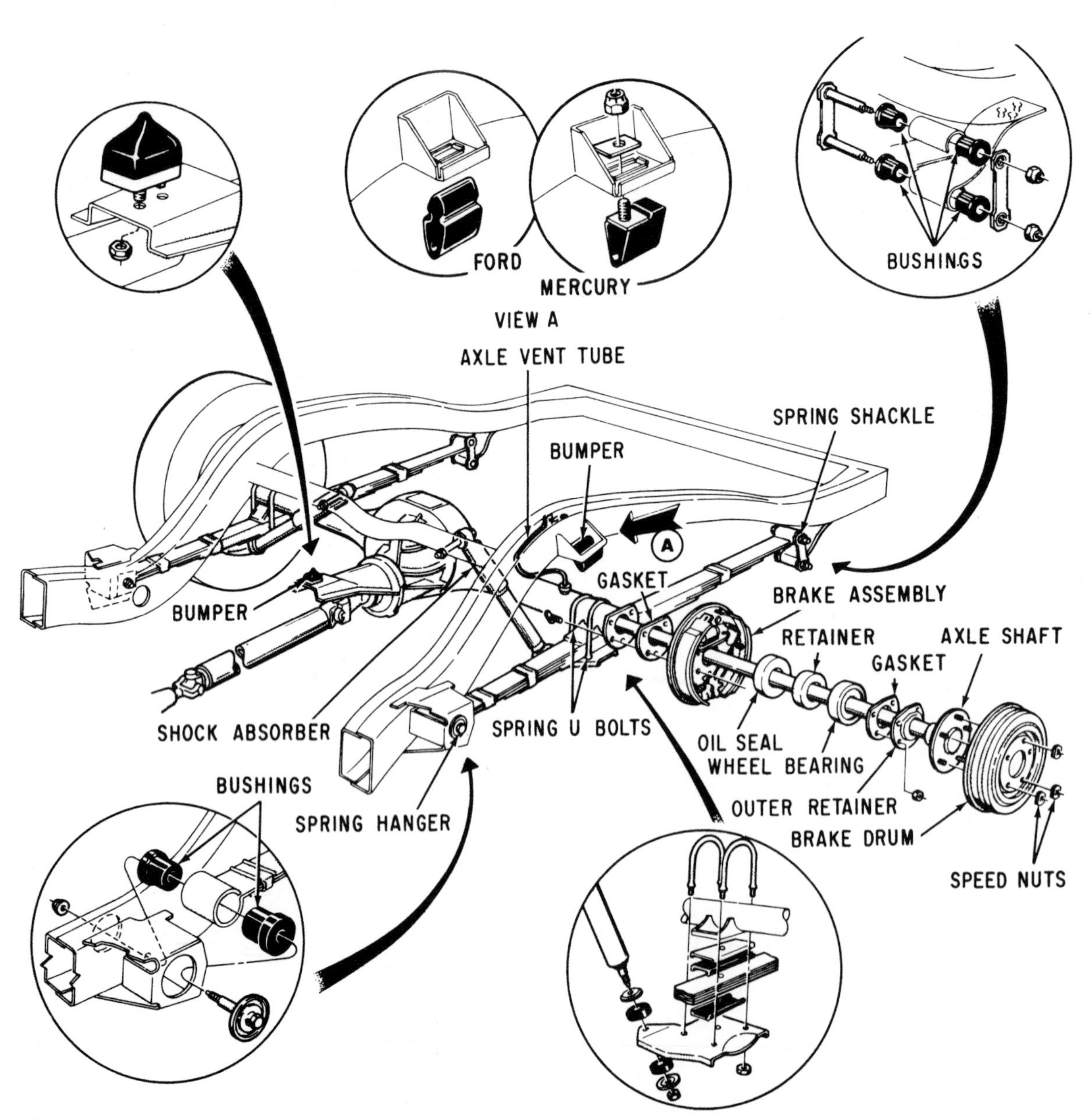

Figure 7 Partial disassembled view of a rear-suspension system using leaf springs. *(Ford Motor Company.)*

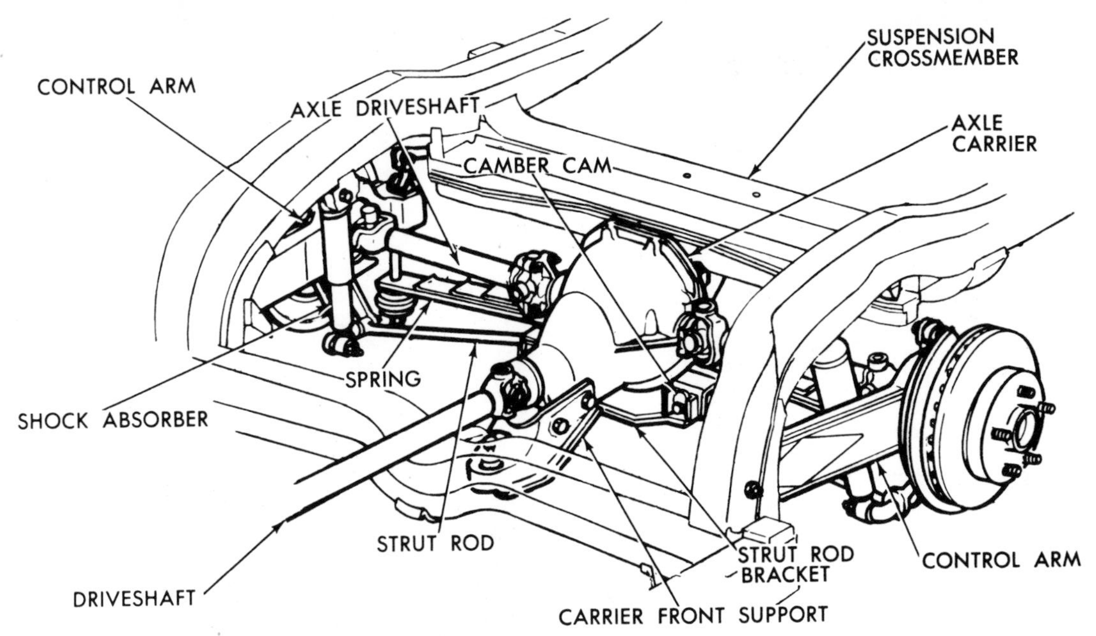

Figure 8 Rear-suspension and drive-line components in the Corvette. Note the transverse leaf spring and the axle driveshafts with their two universal joints each. *(Chevrolet Motor Division of General Motors Corporation.)*

1. SPRING HANGER One end of the spring is attached to a hanger on the frame by means of a bolt and bushings in the spring eye. The spring, as it bends, causes the spring eye to turn back and forth with respect to the spring hanger. The attaching bolt and bushing must permit this rotation. Some forms have a hollow spring bolt with a lubrication fitting that permits lubrication. Some designs have a bushing made up of an inner and an outer metal shell. Between these two shells is a molded rubber bushing. The weight is carried through the rubber bushing. The rubber also acts to dampen vibration and noise and thus prevents them from entering the car frame. These mountings require no lubrication.

2. SPRING SHACKLE As the spring bends, the distance between the two spring eyes changes. If both ends of the spring were fastened rigidly to the frame, the spring would not be able to bend. To permit bending, the spring is fastened at one end to the frame through a link called a "shackle." The shackle is a swinging support attached at one end to the spring eye and at the other end to a supporting bracket on the car frame. Spring shackles can be seen in Figs. 2 and 6. A spring shackle is shown in disassembled view in Fig. 7. The two links provide the swinging support that the spring requires, and the bolts attach the links to the shackle bracket on the frame and the spring eye. The rubber bushings insulate the spring from the frame to prevent transfer of noise and vibration between the two. A link-type shackle is very similar to this unit.

■ 6-2-12 Transverse-Leaf-Spring Rear Suspension

Some rear-suspension systems use a single multileaf spring mounted transversely so that each rear wheel is independently suspended by one end of the spring (Fig. 8). On the system shown, each rear wheel is driven by a separate shaft which includes two universal joints. These universal joints are necessary to permit the power from the engine to be carried through the differential and the shafts to the rear wheels.

■ 6-2-13 Heavy-Duty Rear Suspension

Figure 9 shows the spring arrangement used at the rear of heavy-duty trucks. Note that the spring is above the axle housing (not slung below it, as in other suspension systems previously described). Note also that there is an auxiliary, or helper, spring above the main spring (Fig. 9). This helper spring comes into action only when the truck is heavily loaded or when the

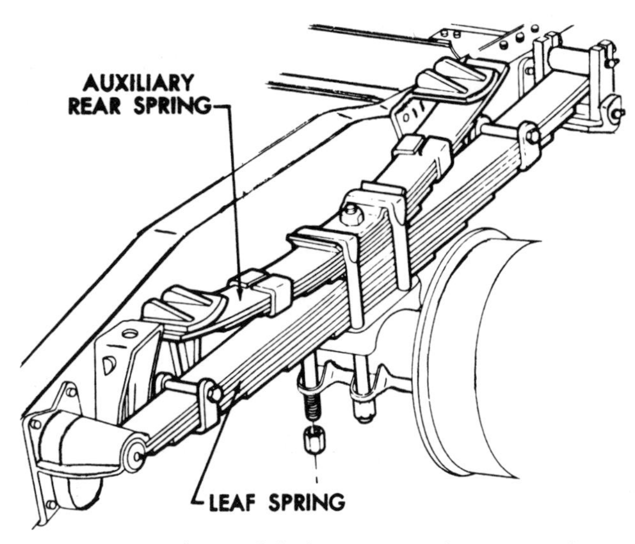

Figure 9 Heavy-duty truck leaf-spring suspension system using an auxiliary spring. *(Chevrolet Motor Division of General Motors Corporation.)*

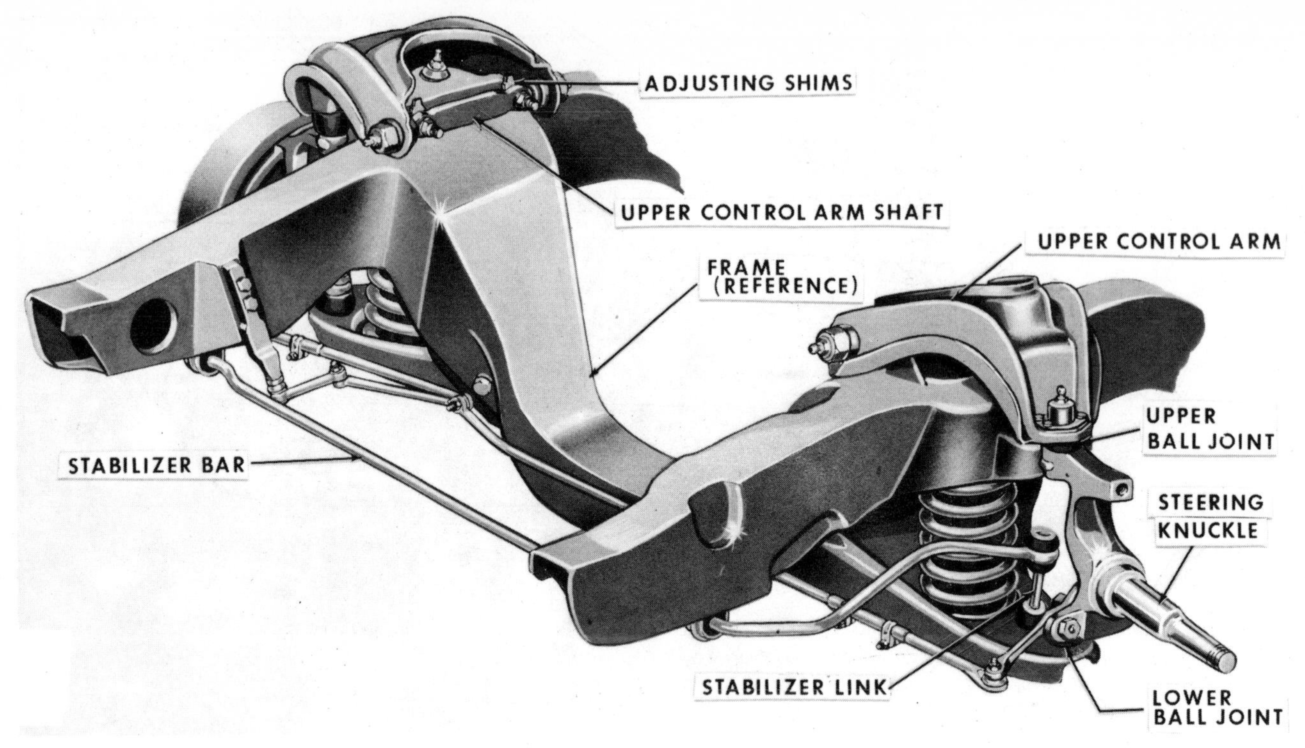

Figure 10 Coil-spring front suspension, showing only the front end of the frame and the suspension parts. *(Buick Motor Division of General Motors Corporation.)*

wheel encounters a large road bump. Then, as the main spring goes through a large deflection, the ends of the helper spring encounter the two bumpers on the frame. The auxiliary spring then deflects and adds its tension to the tension of the main spring.

Some heavy-duty leaf springs are not attached at either end. Instead, the two ends bear on spring hangers attached to the frame. The radius leaf maintains forward-and-back relationship of the axle with the frame.

■ **6-2-14 Front Suspension** The suspension of the front wheels is more complicated than the suspension for the rear wheels. Not only must the front wheels move up and down with respect to the car frame for spring action, but they must also be able to swing at various angles to the car frame for steering.

To permit the front wheels to swing to one side or the other for steering, each wheel is supported on a spindle which is part of a steering knuckle. The steering knuckle is supported, through ball joints, by upper and lower control arms which are attached to the car frame.

■ **6-2-15 Independent Front Suspension** Practically all passenger cars now use the independent type of front-suspension system in which each front wheel is independently supported by a coil, torsion bar, or leaf spring. The coil-spring arrangement is the most common. There are three general types of coil-spring front suspension. In one, the coil spring is located between upper and lower control arms (Fig. 10). The lower control arm has two points of attachment to the car frame. This control arm is called the "A," or "wishbone-type," arm because of its shape. In the second type, the coil spring is located between the upper and lower control arms (Fig. 11). The lower control arm has one point of attachment to the car frame. This is called a "beam-type arm." In the third type, the coil spring is between the upper control arm and the

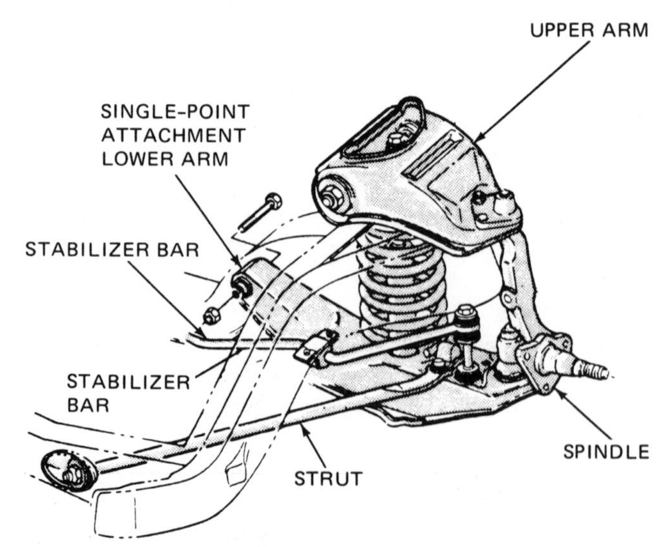

Figure 11 Front-suspension system at the left front wheel. The lower arm has a single point of attachment to the frame. A strut connects the lower arm to the frame. *(Ford Motor Company.)*

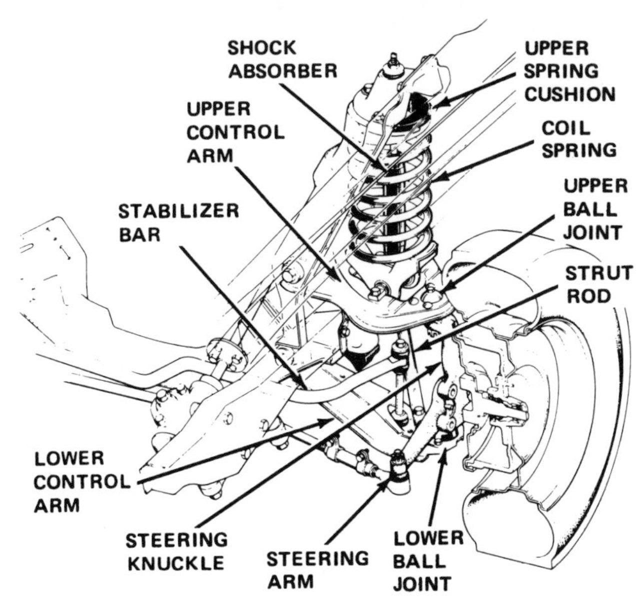

Figure 12 Coil-spring suspension system with coil spring above the upper control arm. The lower control arm has a single point of attachment to the frame. The strut rod is located back of the arm. *(American Motors Corporation.)*

spring tower or housing that is part of the front-end sheetmetal (Fig. 12).

In the beam type with a single point of attachment for the lower control arm (Fig. 11), a strut, or brake reaction rod, is used to prevent forward or backward movement of the lower control arm. This strut, or rod, can also be seen in Fig. 12. It is attached between the outer end of the lower control arm and the car frame. This construction prevents forward or backward movement of the outer end of the lower control arm but allows it to move up or down. Note that, in Fig. 12, the strut is behind the control arm. In other designs, it is in front of the control arm. The A, or wishbone type, with its two points of attachment (Fig. 10), does not require this extra bracing. In the design shown in Figs. 10 to 12, the shock absorber is the telescoping type and is located inside the coil spring.

The brake assembly is mounted on the spindle, or steering knuckle. It is attached rigidly to the steering knuckle. The brake drum and wheel are mounted, by bearings, on the tapered spindle shaft. The wheel can turn freely on the bearings. At the same time, the steering knuckle can be swung back and forth on the two ball joints. This turns the attached wheel in or out so the car can be steered.

■ **6-2-16 Rubber Bumpers** Rubber bumpers are placed on the frame and lower suspension arm. This prevents metal-to-metal contact between frame and arms as limits of spring compression or expansion are reached.

■ **6-2-17 Stabilizer Bar** A stabilizer bar, or sway bar, is used on most cars to interconnect the two lower suspension arms (Figs. 10 to 12). The bar is a long steel rod. Its purpose is to reduce "lean out," or body roll, when the car goes around a curve. When the car is moving around a curve, centrifugal force tends to keep the car moving in a straight line. The car, therefore, leans out. With lean out, or body roll, additional weight is thrown on the outer springs on the turn. This puts additional compression on the outer spring, and the lower control arm pivots upward. As the control arm pivots upward, it carries the end of the stabilizer bar with it. At the inner wheel on the turn, the opposite happens. There is less weight on the spring. Weight has shifted to the outer spring because of centrifugal force. Therefore, the inner spring tends to expand and allow the lower control arm to pivot downward, carrying the end of the stabilizer downward.

The outer end of the stabilizer bar is carried upward by the outer control arm. The inner end of the stabilizer bar is carried downward by the inner control arm. This combined action twists the stabilizer bar. The resistance of the bar to twisting combats the tendency of the car to lean out on turns. Thus, there is less body roll, or lean out, than there would be without the stabilizer bar.

■ **6-2-18 Kingpin** Earlier passenger-car front-suspension systems used a kingpin (Fig. 13). Notice, in this design, that the knuckle support is attached by pivots, top and bottom, to the two control arms. The knuckle is supported on the knuckle support by means of the kingpin. The knuckle can swing back and forth on the kingpin for steering. In later designs, the support, kingpin, and knuckle have been combined into a single part, the steering knuckle, which is supported at the top and bottom by ball joints (see Figs. 10 to 12). Note how this reduces the unsprung weight (■ 6-2-6) and thus improves the riding qualities of the car.

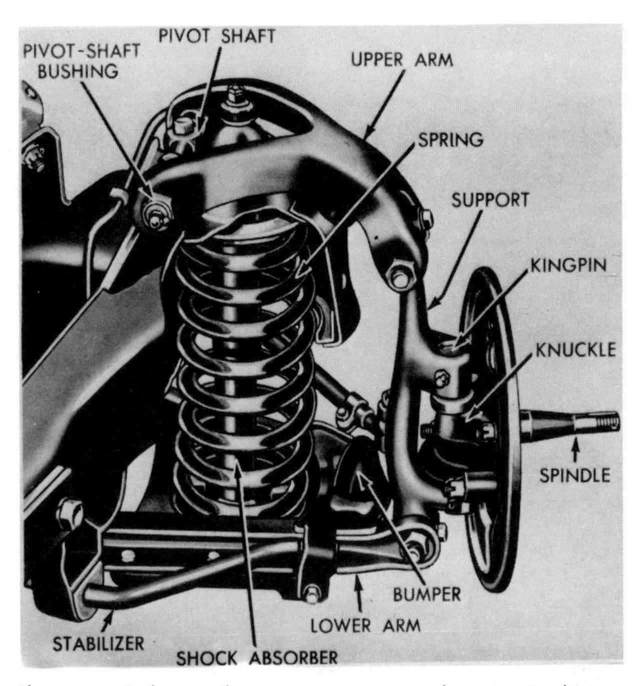

Figure 13 Coil-spring front suspension using a kingpin. *(Ford Motor Company.)*

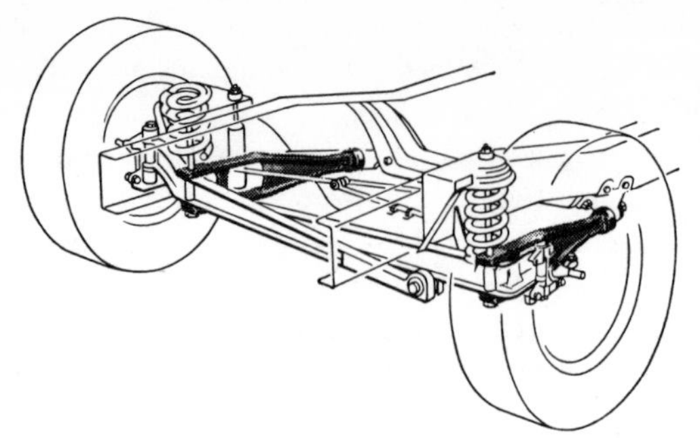

Figure 14 Twin I-beam front suspension using coil springs. *(Ford Motor Company.)*

Many front-suspension systems, especially the heavy-duty types, still use kingpins. In wheel-alignment work, where measuring and changing various angles are important, the inclination, or angle from vertical, of the kingpin (where present) is usually measured. This is the center line around which the front wheel swings for steering. When the system has no kingpin, the steering-axis inclination is measured. The steering axis is an imaginary line drawn through the centers of the two ball joints; the front wheel swings around this line for steering.

■ **6-2-19 Twin I-Beam Front Suspension** Figure 14 illustrates a twin I-beam front suspension with coil springs

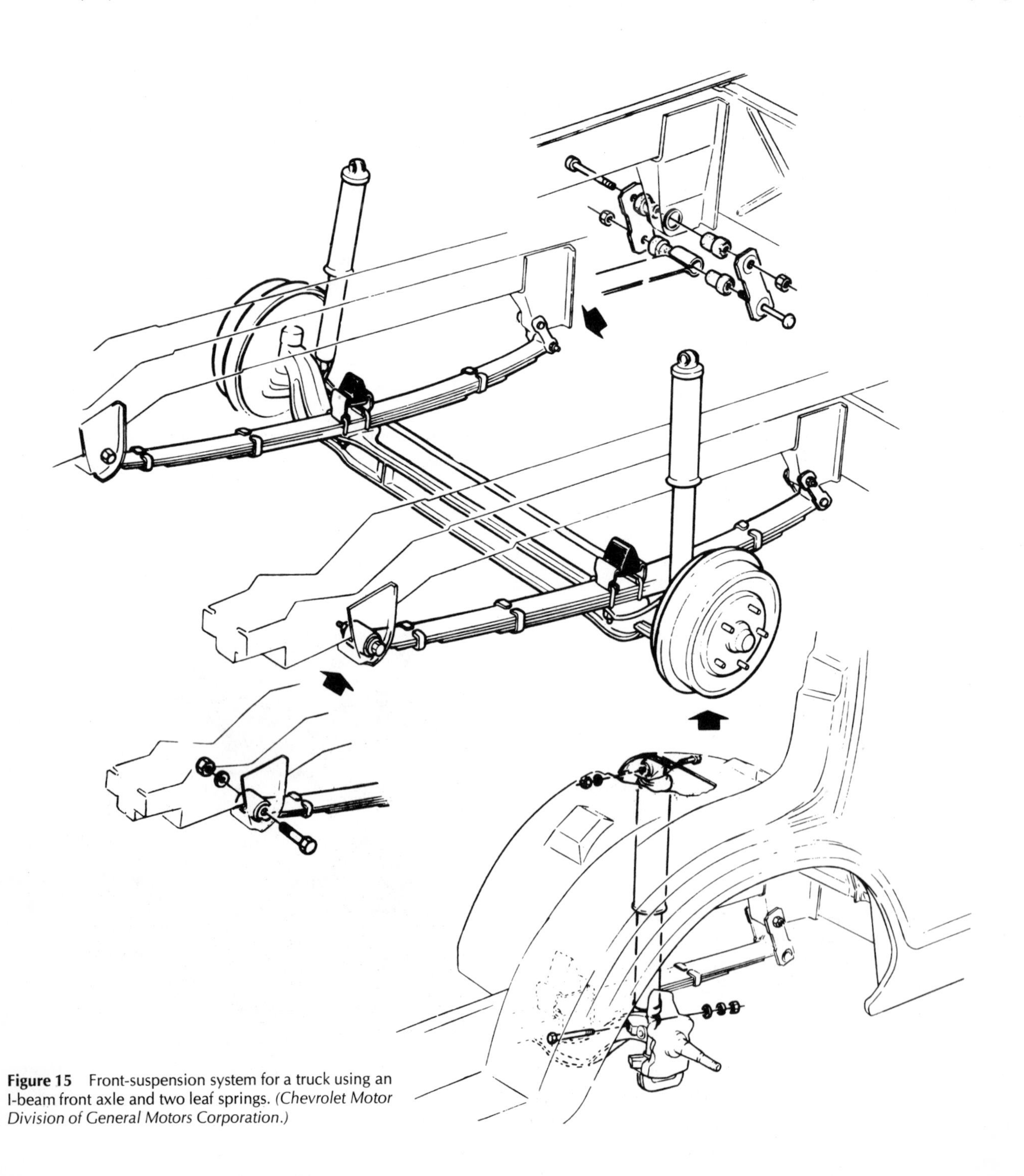

Figure 15 Front-suspension system for a truck using an I-beam front axle and two leaf springs. *(Chevrolet Motor Division of General Motors Corporation.)*

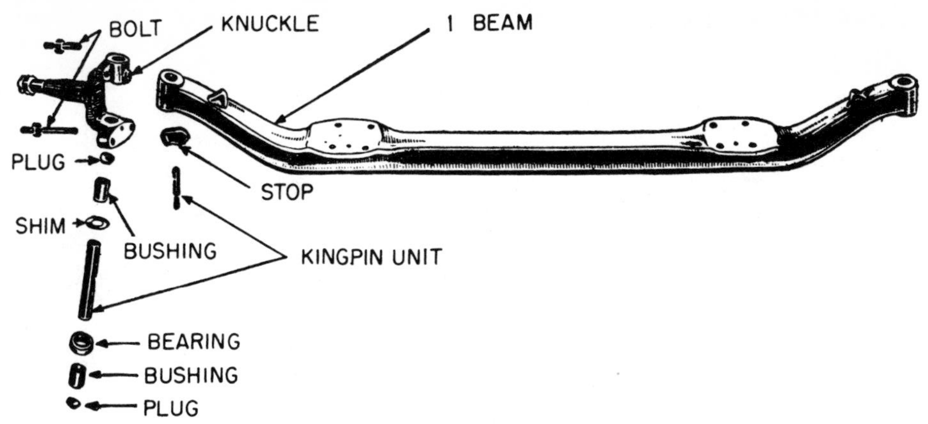

Figure 16 Beam-type front axle, showing the method of supporting the steering knuckle on the end of the beam. *(Chevrolet Motor Division of General Motors Corporation.)*

used on some Ford trucks. Each front wheel is supported at the end of a separate I beam. The opposite ends of the I beams are attached to the frame by pivots. The wheel ends of the two I beams are attached to the frame by radius arms which prevent backward or forward movement of the wheels. The arrangement provides adequate suspension flexibility with the added strength of the I-beam construction.

■ **6-2-20 Leaf-Spring Front Suspension** Most passenger cars today use either coil-spring or torsion-bar front-suspension systems. Some cars manufactured outside the United States use leaf-spring front-suspension systems. Many trucks and other heavy-duty equipment also use leaf springs at the front.

In a front-suspension system using a single-transverse leaf spring, the spring is not fastened to the frame at its center point. Instead, it is fastened at two intermediate points. The two ends of the spring support the two front wheels. In effect, each end of the spring becomes the lower control arm of the system, with the lower end of the steering knuckle attached to it.

Many trucks and other heavy-duty equipment use a solid one-piece axle, or I beam, at the front instead of independent front suspension (Fig. 15). Generally, this arrangement uses two leaf springs, one at each wheel. Figure 16 shows the manner in which the steering knuckle is supported on the end of the axle beam. The springs normally rest on top of the axle instead of being suspended from underneath, as in passenger-car rear-suspension systems using leaf springs. The front ends of the leaf springs are attached to the frame hangers. In some designs, the rear end of the spring is attached to the frame by a shackle. In others, the rear end of the spring is straight and rides in a hanger on the frame that permits it to move back and forth as the effective length of the spring changes. Figure 15 illustrates a heavy-duty front-suspension system.

■ **6-2-21 MacPherson Strut-Type Front Suspensions** The MacPherson strut-type front suspension (Fig. 17), also called a "strut suspension," is used on many foreign cars (Toyota, Datsun, Porsche, Volkswagen, Plymouth Cricket, Mercury Capri, and others). The struts (shock absorbers) are inside the coil springs. On most cars, the top supporting bearing is an oilless ball bearing. The bottom has a ball joint. The assembly includes a stabilizer, as do other independent front suspensions.

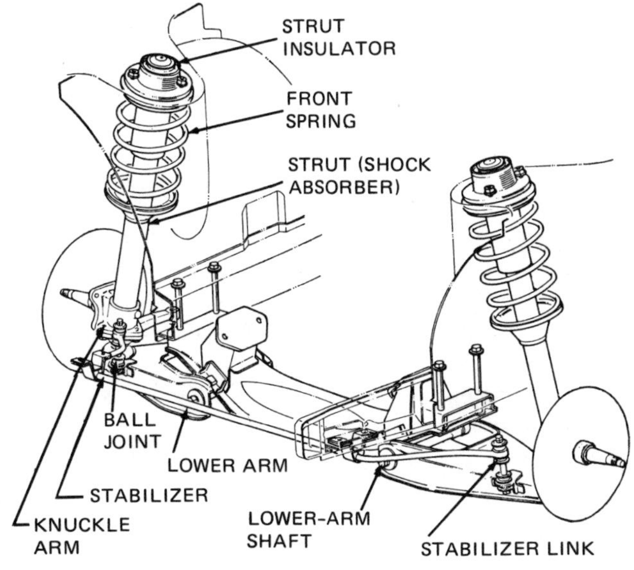

Figure 17 MacPherson strut type of front-suspension system.

■ **6-2-22 Air Suspension** Air suspension was at one time widely offered by automobile manufacturers as optional equipment. It was not generally accepted and is no longer available (except on a few foreign cars and some heavy-duty equipment such as trailers and buses). A modification of the system has been adopted on some cars, however, which provides leveling of the car. This system, called "automatic level control," brings the car back to level as the load changes.

In air suspension, the four conventional springs are replaced by four air bags or air-spring assemblies. Figure 18 is a schematic diagram of a complete system.

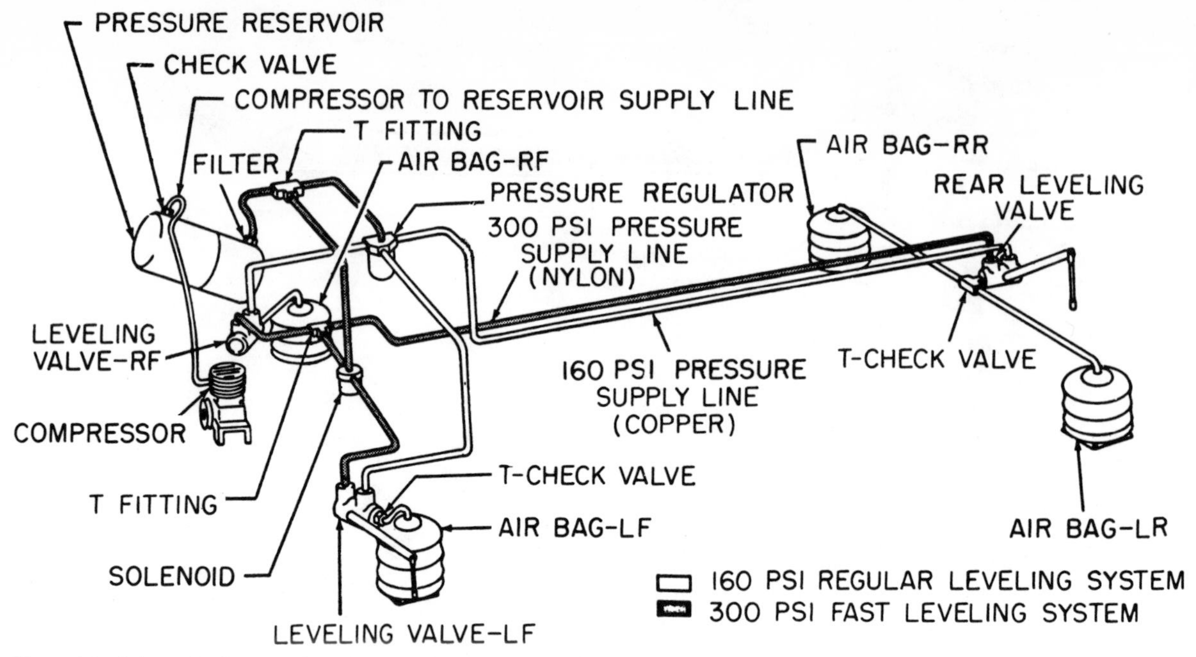

Figure 18 Schematic diagram of an air-suspension system. *(Ford Motor Company.)*

Essentially each air-spring assembly is a flexible bag enclosed in a metal dome, or girdle. The bag is filled with compressed air, which supports the car weight. When a wheel encounters a bump in the road, the air is further compressed and absorbs the shock.

An air compressor, or pump, supplies air to the system (Fig. 18). On the system shown, the compressor is driven by a belt from the water-pump pulley. Pressure is maintained in the reservoir at about 300 psi (21.09 kg/cm²). The air then passes through the two circuits to the four air bags. In one circuit the air pressure is reduced to 160 psi (11.25 kg/cm²) by a pressure regulator. This pressure is admitted to the four air bags through height-control or leveling valves. When there is insufficient air in an air bag, that side of the car will ride low. This causes the linkage to move the leveling arm so that the valve is opened, admitting more air.

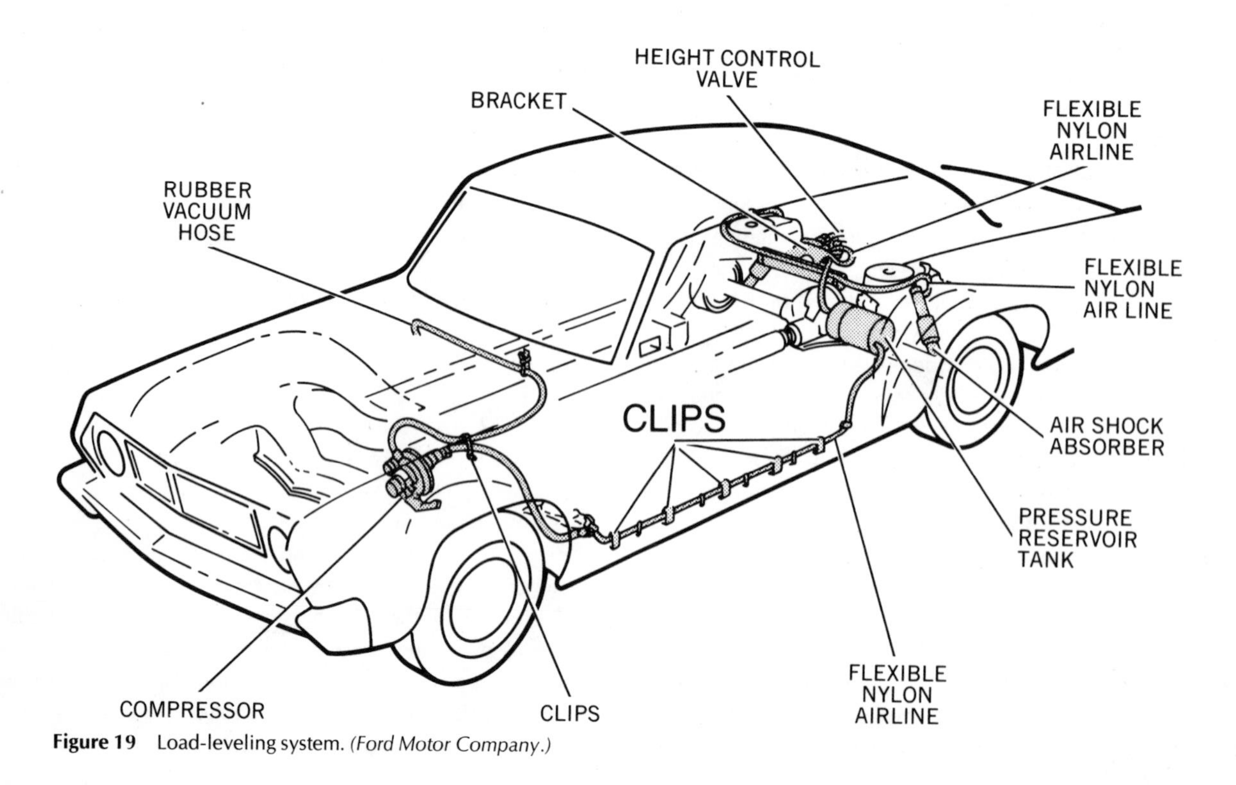

Figure 19 Load-leveling system. *(Ford Motor Company.)*

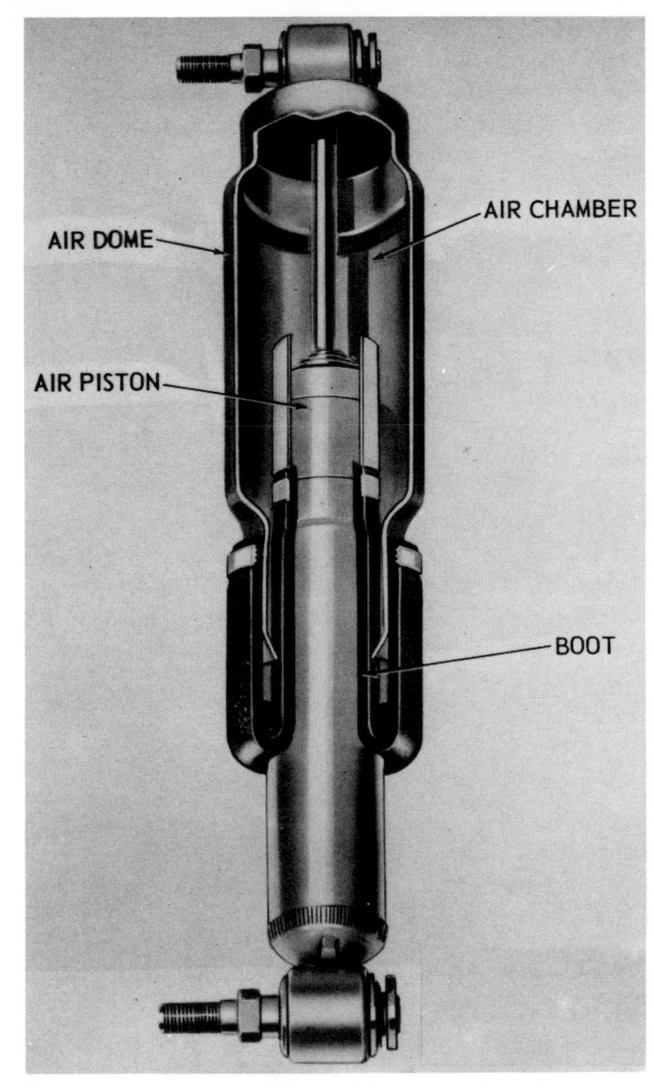

Figure 20 Cutaway view of the special shock absorber with air chamber used in the automatic level control. *(Cadillac Motor Car Division of General Motors Corporation.)*

The 300-psi (21.09-kg/cm²) air supply is used to correct the additional loading of the car. This keeps the car level the same, regardless of whether there are passengers or not. The action is as follows: When a car door is opened, the door switch closes, turning on the courtesy light. At the same time, the air-suspension solenoid is connected to the battery through the switch, and the solenoid valve opens. Now air at 300 psi (21.09 kg/cm²) is admitted to the leveling valves. If the air bag has been compressed by added weight, as when a passenger climbs in, the leveling valve quickly feeds additional air pressure to the low air bag, and it is brought up to the proper level. On the other hand, if a passenger has gotten out, the air bag is high. Now the leveling valve releases air to lower the bag to the proper level.

■ 6-2-23 Automatic Level Control

Automatic level control, which is standard equipment on some cars and optional equipment on others, compensates for variations in load in the rear of the car. When a heavy load is added to the trunk or rear seat, the springs will give and allow the rear end to settle. This changes the handling characteristics of the car and also causes the headlights to point upward. The automatic level control prevents all this by automatically raising the rear back to level when a load is added, and automatically lowering the rear back to level when the load is removed. The system consists of a compressor (with reservoir and regulator), a height-control valve, two special shock absorbers or two rubber air cylinders, and air-pressure lines connecting the components (Fig. 19).

1. TYPE WITH SHOCK ABSORBERS The compressor is operated by engine intake-manifold vacuum. The vacuum actuates a pump which builds up air pressure in the compressor reservoir. When a load is added to the rear of the car, this air pressure is passed through the height-control valve to the two special rear shock absorbers. Each shock absorber contains an air chamber (Fig. 20). The air pressure, entering this chamber, will raise the upper shell of the shock absorber to bring the rear of the car back up to level again.

The height-control valve (Fig. 19) has a linkage to the rear suspension. When this linkage is raised by the addition of a load, it opens the intake valve, thus allowing compressed air to flow to the shock absorbers. When the load is removed, and the rear of the car is thus raised, the linkage operates the exhaust valve, allowing air to exit from the shock absorber until the correct level is achieved. The height-control valve has a time-delay mechanism that allows the valve to respond only after several seconds. This eliminates fast valve action, which would tend to cause the system to function every time a wheel encountered a bump in the road. Thus the system functions on load changes only, and not on road shocks.

The compressor, mounted at the front end of the car, works on the difference in pressure between atmospheric pressure

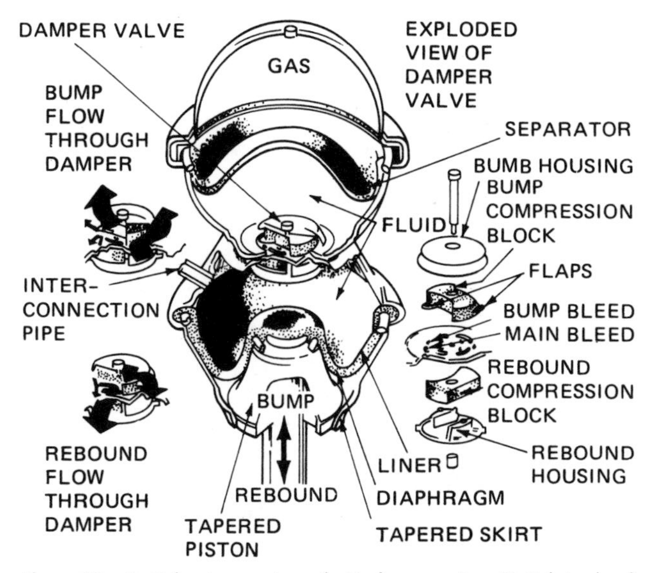

Figure 21 Partial cutaway view of a Hydragas spring. *(British Leyland Ltd.)*

and intake-manifold vacuum. Air pressure is applied to one side of a diaphragm in the compressor; intake-manifold vacuum is applied to the other side of the diaphragm. This difference in pressure moves the diaphragm. A piston attached to the diaphragm is made to move by this action. A pulsating action of the diaphragm is set up by means of a small valve which opens each time the diaphragm has moved to the vacuum side. This valve now admits air to the vacuum side and vacuum to the other side, so the diaphragm moves to the opposite side. The pulsations of the diaphragm move the piston, and the piston pumps air into the reservoir, building up a pressure that may go as high as 275 psi (19.33kg/cm^2). A relief valve prevents excessive pressure.

2. TYPE WITH RUBBER AIR CYLINDERS This type, no longer in common use for passenger cars, uses rubber air cylinders enclosed within the coil springs. The height-control valve and compressor work in a manner similar to those already described. When the rear of the car is lowered by the addition of a load, as when someone climbs in, the height-control valve directs air from the compressor to the rubber air cylinders within the rear coil springs. The rubber air cylinders expand and raise the rear of the car back to level again. When the load is removed so the rear of the car goes above level, the height-control valve releases air from the rubber air cylinders. This allows the car to settle back down to level.

■ **6-2-24 Hydraulic Suspension** The hydraulic suspension system uses gas-filled spring units, one at each wheel (Fig. 21). Each unit has a sealed chamber containing a quantity of nitrogen gas at high pressure. Below this chamber is a displacement chamber filled with water-based fluid. When the wheel meets a bump, the fluid is pushed upward, compressing the gas. This action provides the springing effect. In addition, the two units on each side of the car are interconnected front to back. Therefore, when the left front wheel meets a bump, for example, part of the fluid from the left front unit is forced through a pipe to the left rear unit. This action raises the left rear wheel also. The shock is thus distributed between left front and left rear wheels. This is claimed to improve the ride.

SECTION 6-3 Steering Systems

This section covers the various types of steering systems used in automotive vehicles. The requirements of a steering system, as well as types of steering gears and linkages, are described. There are many varieties of steering gears, both manually and hydraulically operated. The latter type is known as "power steering." Most cars produced today have power steering.

■ **6-3-1 Function of the Steering System** A simplified drawing of a steering system is shown in Fig. 8 (Part 6, Sec. 1). There are various methods of supporting the front-wheel spindles (Part 6, Sec. 2), so that the wheels can be swung to the left or right for steering. This movement is produced by gearing and linkage between the steering wheel in front of the driver and the steering knuckle or wheel. The complete arrangement is called the steering system. Actually, the steering system is composed of two elements: a steering gear at the lower end of the steering column, and the linkage between the gear and the wheel steering knuckle.

■ **6-3-2 Front-End Geometry** Front-end geometry is the angular relationship among the front wheels, the front-wheel attaching parts, and the car frame. The angle of the steering axis or kingpin away from vertical, the pointing in (toe-in) of the front wheels, the tilt of the front wheels from vertical—all these are involved in front-end geometry. Every one of them influences the steering ease, steering stability, and the riding qualities of the car and has a direct effect on tire wear. The various factors that enter into front-end geometry are classified under the following terms: camber, steering-axis inclination (kingpin inclination), caster, toe-in, and toe-out on turns. These are discussed in detail below.

NOTE: Even though most late-model cars do not use kingpins, they are treated as though they have kingpins during the front-alignment checks and adjustments. On these cars, reference is made to the "apparent," or theoretical, kingpin inclination (actually the steering-axis inclination).

■ **6-3-3 Camber** Camber is the tilting of the front wheels from the vertical (Fig. 1). When the tilt is outward so that the wheels are farther apart at the top than at the bottom, the camber is positive. Positive camber is shown in Fig. 1. When the tilt is inward so that the wheels are closer together at the top than at the bottom, the camber is negative. The amount of tilt is measured in degrees from the vertical, and this mea-

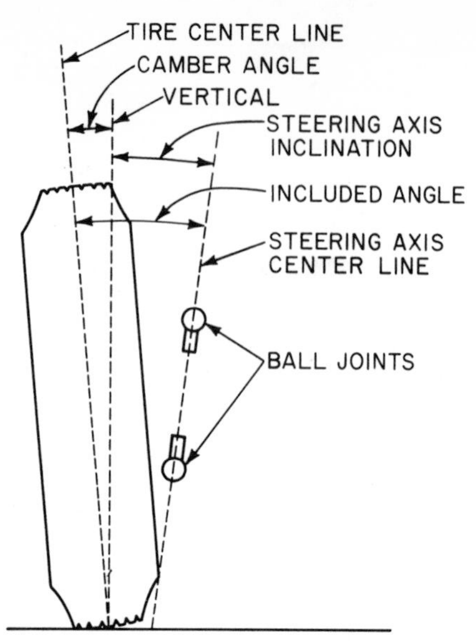

Figure 1 Camber angle and steering-axis inclination. Positive camber is shown.

surement is called the "camber angle." The wheels are given a slight outward tilt to start with so that when the vehicle is loaded and rolling along on the road, the load will just about bring the wheels to a vertical position. If you started with no camber angle—wheels vertical—loading the car might give them a negative camber. Any amount of camber—positive or negative—tends to cause uneven or more rapid tire wear, since the tilt puts more of the load on one side of the tread than on the other.

If the vehicle were rolling on a perfectly level road, the ideal camber would be the same for both front wheels. This ideal camber would be just sufficient to bring the front wheels to the vertical position when the vehicle is loaded and moving. However, roads are seldom perfectly level. Many roads are crowned slightly; that is, they are higher at the center than on the two sides. The result is that when a car is moving along on one side of the road, it tends to lean out slightly. This could ultimately cause the outside of the tread on the right front tire to wear excessively because this part of the tread would be carrying more of the weight of the car. On some vehicles, the right front wheel is set with less positive camber than the left front.

■ 6-3-4 Steering-Axis (or Kingpin) Inclination

At one time, all steering systems had a kingpin which attached the steering knuckle to a support (Fig. 13 in Part 6, Sec. 2). Later, ball-joint supports were adopted (Figs. 10 to 12 in Part 6, Sec. 2). In this design, the steering knuckle and the steering-knuckle support have, in effect, been combined into a single part, called the "steering knuckle," or "spindle"; no kingpin is used. The steering knuckle is supported at top and bottom by the control arms and is attached to the arms by ball joints.

The inclination from the vertical of the center lines of the ball joints, or of the kingpin, is a very important factor in steering action. This is the center line around which the front wheel swings for steering. This inclination is called the "steering-axis inclination" (on ball-joint systems) or "kingpin inclination" (on systems with kingpins). It is also called the "ball-joint angle." This inclination is the inward tilt of the ball-joint center line, or kingpin, from the vertical (Fig. 1). This inward tilt is desirable for several reasons. First, it helps provide steering returnability by tending to return the wheels to the straight-ahead position after any turn. Second, it reduces steering effort, particularly when the car is stationary. Third, it reduces tire wear.

The inward tilt, or inclination, of the steering axis tends to keep the wheels straight ahead. It helps recovery, or the return of the wheels to the straight-ahead position after a turn has been made. As the wheel is swung away from straight ahead, the ball joints and supporting parts are moved upward. This means that the car body is actually lifted. In other words, steering-axis inclination causes the car to be raised every time the front wheels are swung away from straight ahead. Then the weight of the car brings the wheels back to straight ahead after the turn is completed and the steering wheel is released.

■ 6-3-5 Included Angle

The included, or combined, angle is the camber angle plus the steering-axis inclination angle (Fig. 1). The included angle is important because it determines the point of intersection of the wheel and the ball-joint center line (Fig. 2). This, in turn, determines whether the wheel will tend to toe out or toe in. "Toe-out" is a term used to describe the tendency for the wheel to point outward. A wheel that toes in tries to point inward as it rolls. Figure 4 shows what toe-in is on a vehicle. The tire on a wheel that is toed in or toed out will wear more rapidly. The tire has to go in the direction that the car is moving. But, since the tire is not pointed in that

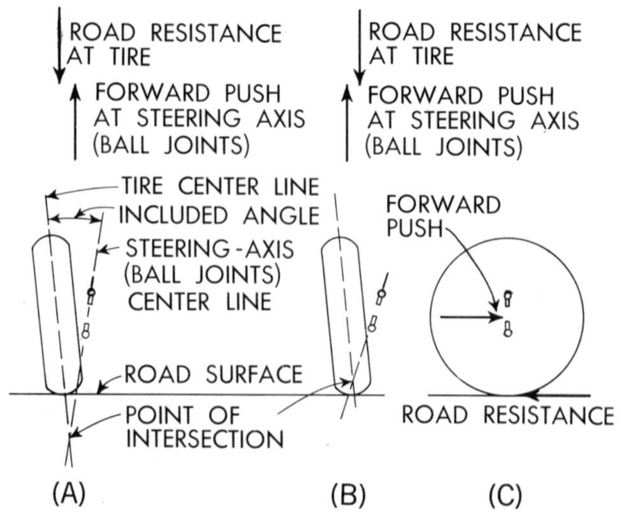

Figure 2 Effect when the point of intersection is below the road surface *(A)* and above the road surface *(B)*. The left front wheel as viewed from the driver's seat is shown in *A* and *B*. *C* is a side view of the wheel to show two forces acting on the wheel and ball joints.

direction—it is toed out or toed in—it is dragged sideways as it rolls forward. The more toe-out or toe-in, the more it is dragged sideways and the faster the tire wears.

When the point of intersection (Fig. 2) is below the road surface, the wheel will tend to toe out. This is because the forward push, which is through the center line of the ball joints, is inside the tire center line at the road surface. In the right illustration in Fig. 2, the two opposing forces working on the wheel are shown. One is the forward push through the ball joints; the other is the road resistance to the tire. If these two forces are exactly in line, the wheel will have no tendency to toe out or toe in. The two forces will be in line with each other only when the point of intersection is at the road surface. When it is below the road level, as shown at *A* in Fig. 2, the wheel attempts to swing outward, or toe out. When the point of intersection is above the road level, as shown at *B* in Fig. 2, the wheel attempts to swing inward, or toe in.

■ **6-3-6 Caster** In addition to being tilted inward toward the center of the car, the steering axis may also be tilted forward or backward from the vertical (Fig. 3). Backward tilt from the vertical is called "positive caster." Positive caster aids directional stability, since the center line of the ball joints passes through the road surface ahead of the center line of the wheel. Thus, the push on the ball joints is ahead of the road resistance to the tire. The tire is trailing behind, just as the caster on a table leg "trails behind" when the table is pushed.

Caster has another effect that is important. When both front wheels have positive caster, the car tends to roll out or lean out on turns. But if the front wheels have negative caster, the car tends to bank, or lean in, on turns.

As a right turn is made, the wheel pivots on the road surface, causing the ball joints to be lifted. The right side of the car is lifted. When the left side of the car is lowered and the right side of the car is lifted as a right turn is made, the car rolls, or leans out, on the turn. This is just the opposite of what would be most desirable, since it adds to the effect of centrifugal force on the turn. By using negative caster—tilting the center line of the ball joints forward—the car can be made to lean in on a turn and thus decrease the effect of centrifugal force. For example, with negative caster the left side of the car would lift during a right turn, and the right side of the car would drop. This would combat the roll-out effect of centrifugal force.

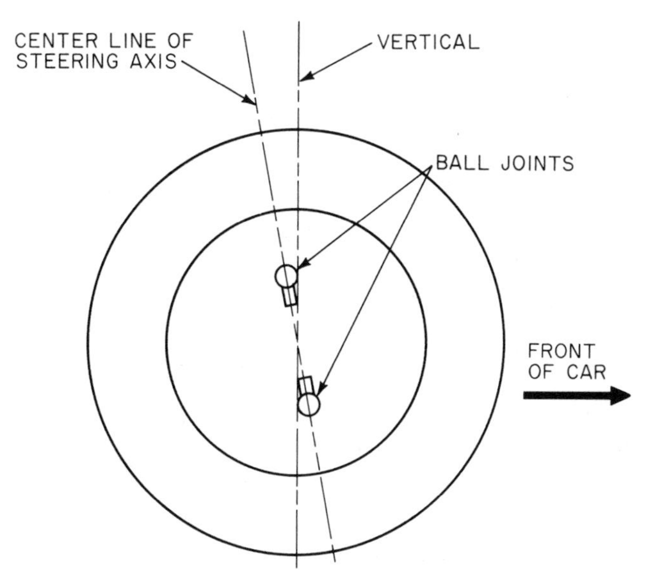

Figure 3 Left front wheel (as viewed from driver's seat). The view is from inside so that the backward tilt of steering axis from the vertical can be seen. This backward tilt is called "positive caster."

Caster has another important effect. Positive caster tends to make the front wheels toe in. With positive caster, the car is lowered as the wheel pivots inward. Thus, the weight of the car is always exerting force to make the wheel toe in. With negative caster, the wheels would tend to toe out.

Note that positive caster increases the effort required to steer. Positive caster tries to keep the wheels straight ahead. In order to make a turn, this tendency must be overcome. Note that steering-axis inclination also tries to keep the wheels straight ahead. Thus, to make a turn, the effects of both caster—when positive—and steering-axis inclination must be overcome. Late-model vehicles, particularly heavy-duty trucks, tend to have a negative caster. This makes steering easier, and a sufficient tendency toward recovery, or the return of the wheels to straight ahead, is still provided by steering-axis inclination.

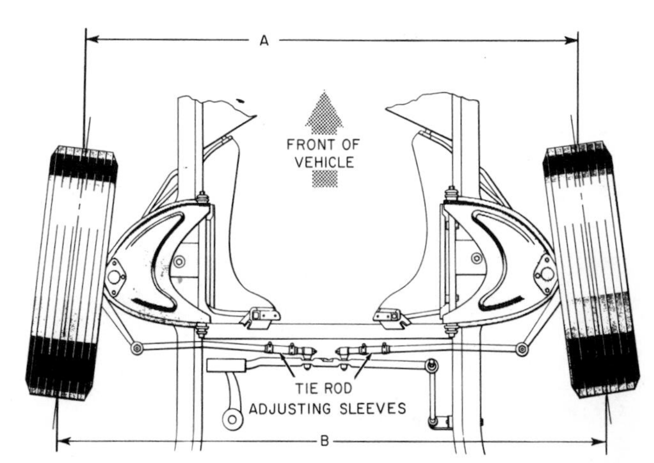

Figure 4 Toe-in. The wheels are viewed from above; the front of the car is at the top of the illustration. *A* is less than *B*. Toe-in angles are shown greatly exaggerated. *(Bear Manufacturing Company.)*

■ **6-3-7 Toe-In** Toe-in is the turning in of the front wheels; they attempt to roll inward instead of straight ahead. On a car with toe-in (Fig. 4), the distance between the front wheels is the less at the front *(A)* than at the rear *(B)*. The actual amount of toe-in is normally only a fraction of an inch. The purpose of toe-in is to ensure parallel rolling of the front wheels, to stabilize steering, and to prevent sideslipping and excessive wear of tires. The toe-in on the front wheels of a car serves to offset the small deflections in the wheel-support sys-

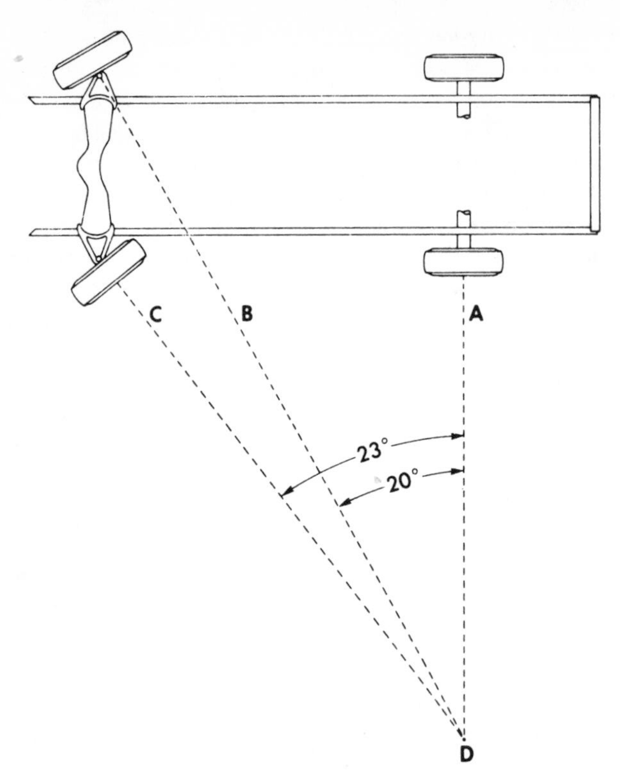

Figure 5 Toe-out on turns, or turning radius.

tem, which come about when the car is moving forward. These deflections are due to the rolling resistance of the tires of the road. In other words, even though the wheels are set to toe in slightly when the car is standing still, they tend to roll parallel on the road when the car is moving forward.

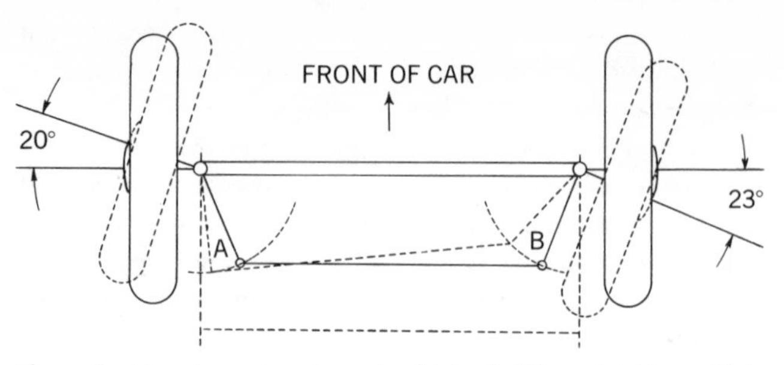

Figure 6 How toe-out on turns is obtained. *(Chevrolet Motor Division of General Motors Corporation.)*

■ 6-3-8 Toe-Out during Turns

Toe-out during turns, also called "turning radius," "front-wheel turning angle," and "cornering wheel relationship," refers to the difference in angles between the two front wheels and the car frame during turns. Since the inner wheel is rotating on, or following, a smaller radius than the outer wheel when the car is rounding a curve, its axle must be at a sharper angle with the car frame; that is, it must toe out more. This condition is shown in Fig. 5. When the front wheels are steered to make the turn illustrated, the inner wheel turns at an angle of 23° with the car frame, while the outer wheel turns at an angle of only 20° with the car frame. This permits the inner wheel to follow a shorter radius than the outer wheel, and the circles on which the two front wheels turn are concentric: their centers are at the same place *(D)*. Toe-out is secured by providing the proper relationship between the steering knuckle arms, tie rods, and pitman arm. This relationship is such that the inner wheel on a curve always toes out more than the outer wheel. Figure 6

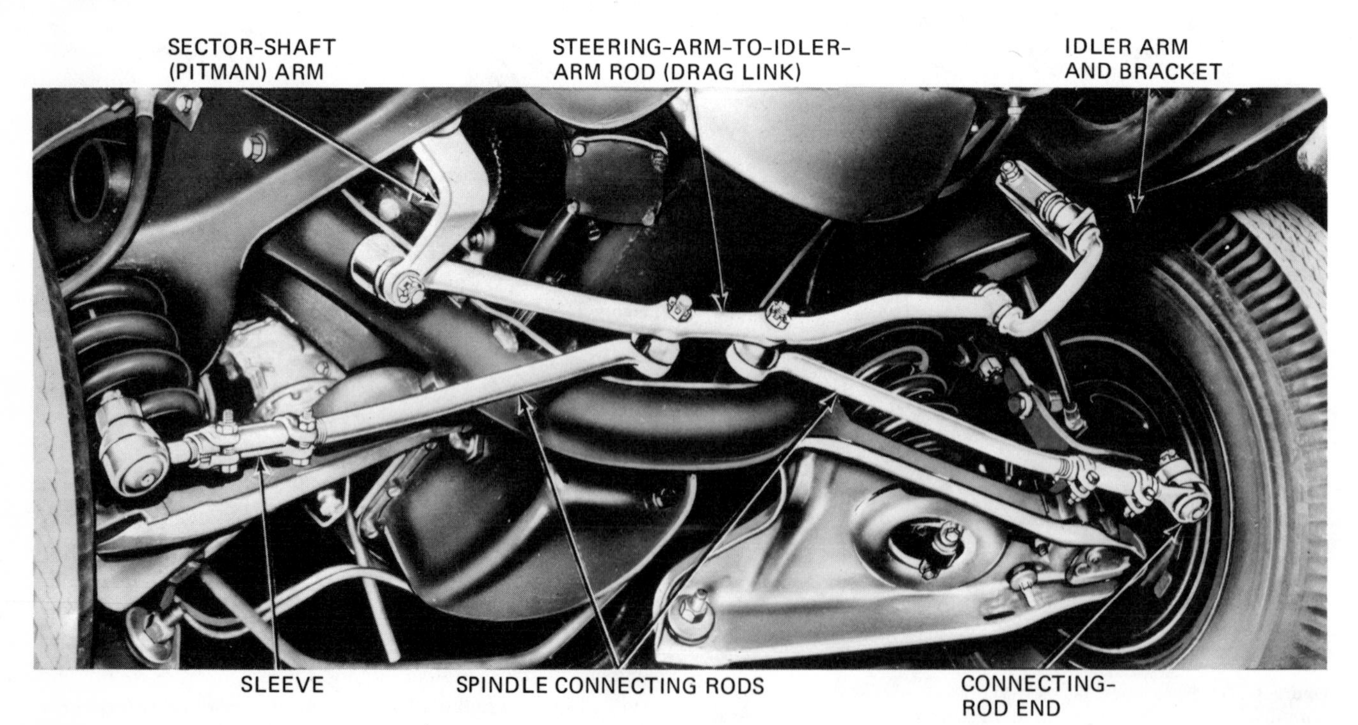

Figure 7 Steering linkage with traverse drag link (relay rod). *(Ford Motor Company.)*

illustrates the manner of securing this condition. When the tie rod is moved to the left during a right turn, it pushes at almost a right angle against the left steering-knuckle arm. The right end of the tie rod, however, not only moves to the left but also swings forward (as shown by the dotted line) so that the right wheel is turned an additional amount. When a left turn is made, the left wheel is turned an additional amount over that which the right wheel turns. Figure 6 shows a parallelogram type of linkage (see ■6-3-9). Other types of linkage give a similar effect and provide a similar toe-out on turns.

■ 6-3-9 Steering Linkages Many types of steering linkages have been made to connect the steering knuckles of the front wheels and the pitman arm of the steering gears. The pitman arm swings from one side to the other—or forward and backward, on some cars—as the steering wheel is turned. This movement must be carried to the steering knuckles at the wheels by some form of linkage. All linkages have some means of adjusting the lengths of the tie rods or links so that proper alignment of the front wheels can be established. This alignment gives the front wheels a slight toe-in when the car is at rest. When the car begins to move forward, the toe-in practically disappears as all looseness in the steering system is taken up.

The most commonly used type of steering linkage is some form of the parallelogram system. Figure 7 is a modified form of the parallelogram type of steering linkage. Points of attachment between the metal parts of the rods, pitman and idler arms, and steering spindles (knuckles) are insulated by bushings. The connecting-rod (or tie-rod) ends are attached to the spindles (knuckles) by ball joints. The sleeves that connect the spindle connecting rods to the connecting-rod ends are threaded, as are the mating ends of the rods, permitting adjustment of the toe-in. The sleeves can be turned one way or the other to change the effective length of the connecting rods, thus altering the toe-in adjustment at the wheels.

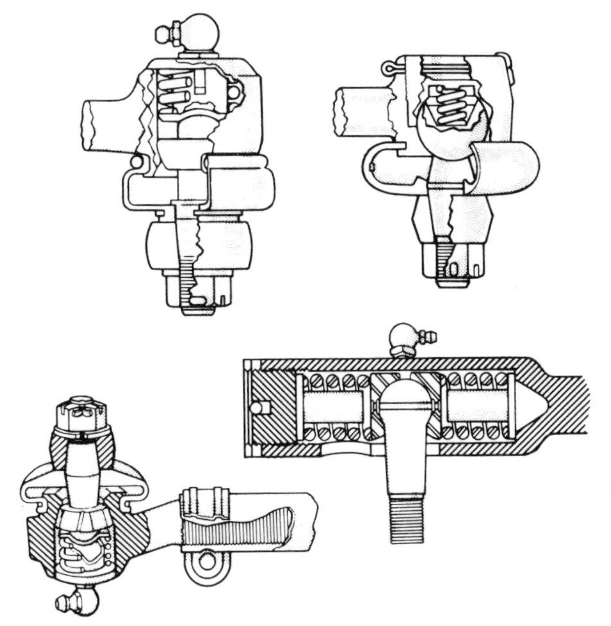

Figure 8 Ball sockets and tie-rod ends. *(Ford Motor Company.)*

■ 6-3-10 Ball Sockets and Ball Joints The various parts of the steering linkage are connected by ball sockets or ball joints of several kinds (Fig. 8). Some have provisions for lubrication; others are prelubricated at the factory and require no lubrication for the life of the car. On many cars, the idler arm is connected through rubber bushings. These bushings twist as the idler arm swings to one side or the other. They then supply some force to help return the wheels to center after a turn is completed.

■ 6-3-11 Steering Gears The steering gear converts the rotary motion of the steering wheel into straight-line motion of the linkage. Essentially, on most cars, the steering gear consists of two parts: a worm on the end of the steering shaft and a pitman-arm shaft (or cross shaft) on which there is a gear sector, a toothed roller, or a stud.[1] The gear sector, toothed roller, or stud meshes with the worm as shown in Fig. 9. In

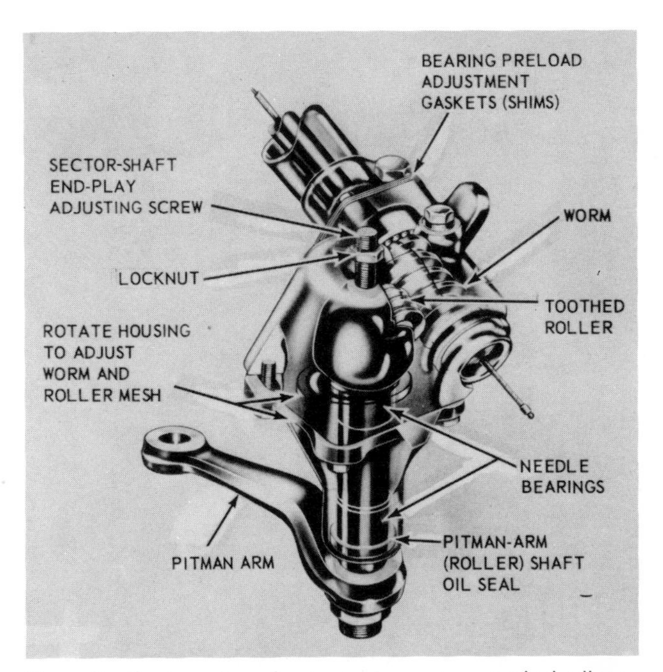

Figure 9 Phantom view of a steering gear using a toothed roller attached to the pitman-arm shaft. The worm and roller teeth mesh. *(Ford Motor Company.)*

this illustration, the steering gear uses a toothed roller. The roller and worm teeth mesh. When the worm is rotated (by rotation of the steering wheel), the roller teeth must follow along. This action causes the pitman-arm shaft to rotate. The other end of the pitman-arm shaft carries the pitman arm;

[1] Some foreign and small domestic cars use a rack-and-pinion steering gear, as explained in ■6-3-12.

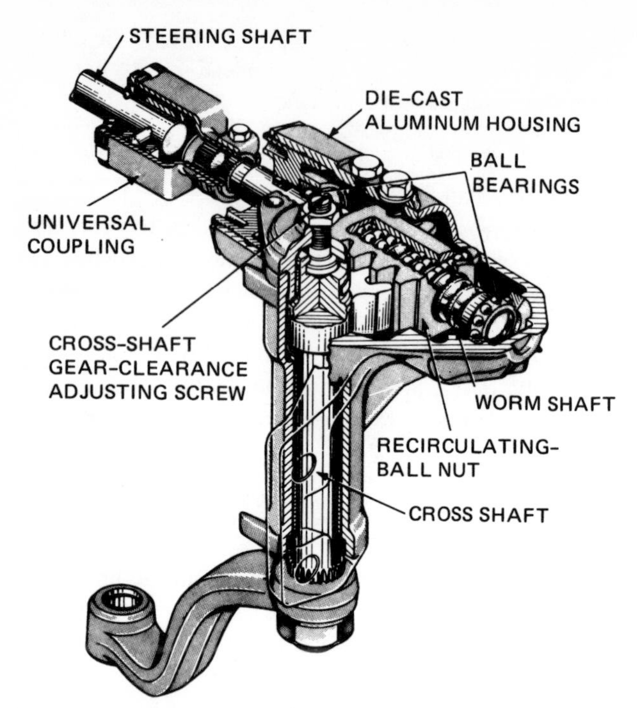

Figure 10 Cutaway view of the Chrysler recirculating ball steering gear. *(Chrysler Corporation.)*

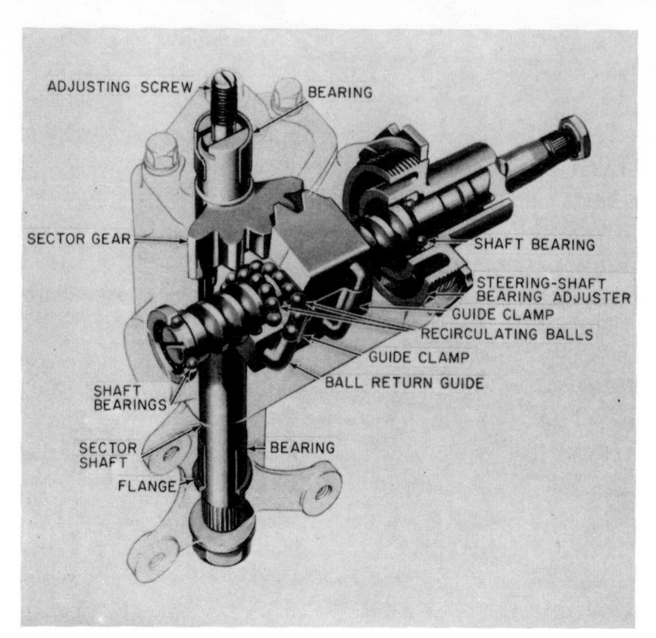

Figure 11 Phantom view of the Ford recirculating-ball steering gear. *(Ford Motor Company.)*

rotation of the pitman-arm shaft causes the arm to swing in one direction or the other. This motion is then carried through the linkage to the steering knuckles at the wheels.

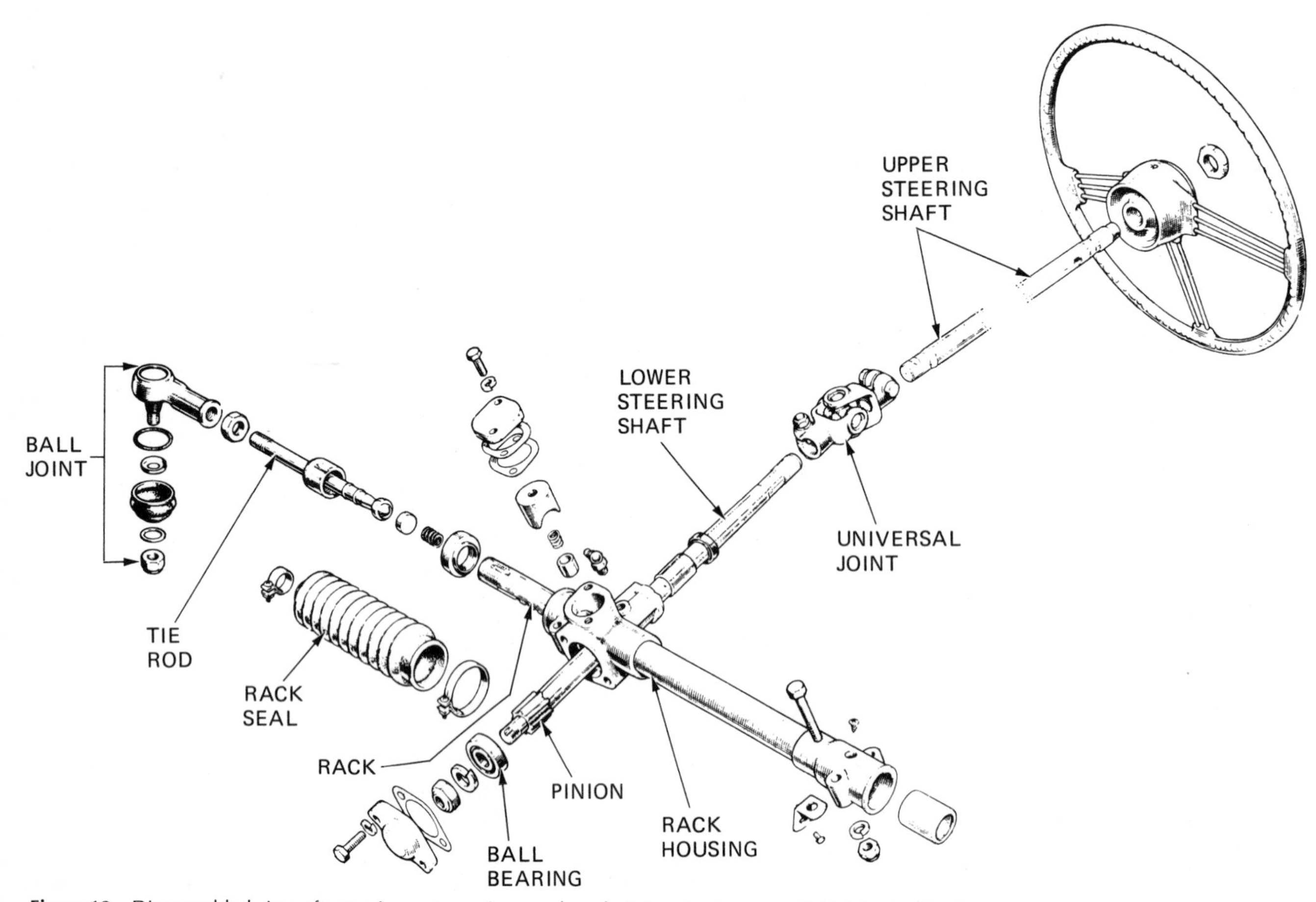

Figure 12 Disassembled view of a steering system using a rack-and-pinion steering gear. *(British Leyland, Ltd.)*

NOTE: The pitman-arm shaft is also called the "cross shaft," "pitman shaft," "roller shaft," "steering-arm shaft," and "section shaft."

Two versions of the recirculating-ball steering gear are shown in Figs. 10 and 11. In these units, friction is kept exceptionally low by interposing balls between the major moving parts or between the worm teeth and grooves cut in the inner face of a ball nut. The rotation of the worm gear causes the balls to roll in the worm teeth. The balls also roll in grooves cut in the inner face of the nut. Thus as the worm rotates, the balls cause the nut to move up or down along the worm. The up-or-down motion is carried to the gear sector by teeth on the side of the ball nut. This then forces the gear sector to move along with the ball nut so that the pitman-arm shaft rotates.

The balls are called "recirculating balls" because they can continuously recirculate from one end of the ball nut to the other through a pair of ball return guides. For example, suppose that the driver makes a right turn. The worm gear is rotated in a clockwise direction—viewed from the driver's seat—and this causes the ball nut to move upward. The balls roll between the worm and ball nut. As they reach the upper end of the nut, they enter the return guide and then roll back to the lower point, where they reenter the groove between the worm and the ball nut.

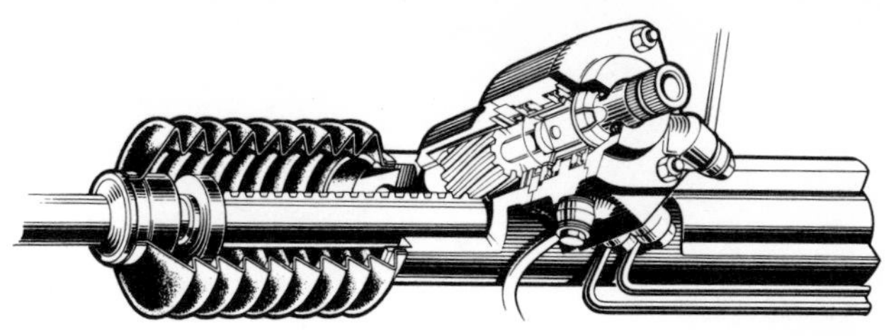

Figure 13 Cutaway view of a rack-and-pinion steering gear. *(Burman and Sons, Ltd.)*

■ **6-3-12 Rack-and-Pinion Steering Gear** The rack-and-pinion steering gear (Figs. 12 and 13), used on some imported cars and small domestic cars such as the Ford Pinto, has a pinion on the end of the steering shaft. The pinion meshes with a rack which is the major cross member of the steering linkage. When the steering wheel and shaft are turned for steering, the gear causes the rack to move to the left or right in the housing. This motion, carried through the tie rods and ball joint, causes the front wheels to pivot for steering. This is a satisfactory arrangement for small cars where the steering forces are light. For larger cars, a greater mechanical advantage is necessary. A worm on the end of the steering shaft, engaging a ball nut and gear sector, toothed roller, or stud, is used to gain this mechanical advantage.

Still other types of steering gears are in use. All are very similar in operation.

SECTION 6-4 Diagnosing Steering and Suspension Troubles

This section discusses various steering and suspension troubles and relates them to possible causes and corrections; that is, it describes trouble-diagnosis procedures on steering and suspension systems. It gives you the information you need to understand the various effects produced by different kinds of trouble in the steering and suspension. In addition, it tells you what corrections should be made. Later sections explain how these corrections are made.

■ 6-4-1 Steering and Suspension Trouble-Diagnosis Chart The chart that follows tells you where to look when various complaints are made regarding the steering or suspension. Following the chart are detailed explanations of the checking procedures to use with each trouble complaint.

A variety of steering and suspension troubles will bring the driver to the mechanic, but it is rare that the driver will have a clear idea of what causes the trouble. The driver can detect an increase in steering difficulty, hard steering, or excessive play in the steering system, but probably does not have a very good idea of what would cause those conditions. The chart that follows lists possible causes of these and other steering and suspension troubles, and refers to numbered sections after the chart for explanations of the way in which to locate and eliminate the troubles.

NOTE: The troubles and possible causes are not listed in the chart in the order of frequency of occurrence; that is, item 1 does not necessarily occur more frequently than item 2, not does item *a* under "Possible Cause" necessarily occur more frequently than item *b*.

STEERING AND SUSPENSION TROUBLE-DIAGNOSIS CHART

(See ■ 6-4-2 to 6-4-16 for detailed explanations of trouble causes and corrections listed below.)

COMPLAINT	POSSIBLE CAUSE	CHECK OR CORRECTION
1. Excessive play in steering system (■ 6-4-2)	a. Looseness in steering gear	Readjust, replace worn parts
	b. Looseness in linkage	Readjust, replace worn parts

(Continued)

STEERING AND SUSPENSION TROUBLE DIAGNOSIS CHART *(Continued)*

(See ■ 6-4-2 to 6-4-16 for detailed explanations of trouble causes and corrections listed below.)

COMPLAINT	POSSIBLE CAUSE	CHECK OR CORRECTION
1. *(Continued)*		
	c. Worn ball joints or steering-knuckle parts	Replace worn parts
	d. Loose wheel bearings	Readjust
2. Hard steering (■ 6-4-3)	a. Power steering inoperative	See Part 6, Sec. 10
	b. Low or uneven tire pressure	Inflate to correct pressure
	c. Friction in steering gear	Lubricate, readjust, replace worn parts
	d. Friction in linkage	Lubricate, readjust, replace worn parts
	e. Friction in ball joints	Lubricate, replace worn parts
	f. Alignment off (caster, camber, toe-in, steering-axis inclination)	Check alignment and readjust as necessary
	g. Frame misaligned	Straighten
	h. Front spring sagging	Replace or adjust
3. Car wander (■ 6-4-4)	a. Low or uneven tire pressure	Inflate to correct pressure
	b. Linkage binding	Readjust, lubricate, replace worn parts
	c. Steering gear binding	Readjust, lubricate, replace worn parts
	d. Front alignment off (caster, camber, toe-in, steering-axis inclination)	Check alignment and readjust as necessary
	e. Looseness in linkage	Readjust, replace worn parts
	f. Looseness in steering gear	Readjust, replace worn parts
	g. Looseness in ball joints	Replace worn parts
	h. Loose rear springs	Tighten
	i. Unequal load in car	Readjust load
	j. Stabilizer bar ineffective	Tighten attachment, replace if damaged
4. Car pulls to one side during normal driving (■ 6-4-5)	a. Uneven tire pressure	Inflate to correct pressure
	b. Uneven caster or camber	Check alignment, adjust as necessary
	c. Tight wheel bearings	Readjust, replace parts if damaged
	d. Uneven springs (sagging, broken, loose attachment)	Tighten, replace defective parts
	e. Wheels not tracking	Check tracking, straighten frame, tighten loose parts, replace defective parts
4. *(Continued)*		
	f. Uneven torsion-bar adjustment	Adjust
5. Car pulls to one side when braking (■ 6-4-6)	a. Brakes grab	Readjust, replace brake lining, etc. (see Part 7, Sec. 2)
	b. Uneven tire inflation	Inflate to correct pressure
	c. Incorrect or uneven caster	Readjust
	d. Causes listed under item 4	
6. Front-wheel shimmy at low speeds (■ 6-4-7)	a. Uneven or low tire pressure	Inflate to correct pressure
	b. Loose linkage	Readjust, replace worn parts
	c. Loose ball joints	Replace worn parts
	d. Looseness in steering gear	Readjust, replace worn parts
	e. Front springs too flexible	Replace, tighten attachment
	f. Incorrect or unequal camber	Readjust
	g. Irregular tire tread	Replace worn tires, match treads
	h. Dynamic imbalance	Balance wheels
7. Front-wheel tramp (high-speed shimmy) (■ 6-4-8)	a. Wheels out of balance	Rebalance
	b. Too much wheel runout	Balance, remount tire, straighten or replace wheel
	c. Defective shock absorbers	Repair or replace
	d. Causes listed under item 6	
8. Steering kickback (■ 6-4-9)	a. Tire pressure low or uneven	Inflate to correct pressure
	b. Springs sagging	Tighten attachment, replace
	c. Shock absorbers defective	Repair or replace
	d. Looseness in linkage	Readjust, replace worn parts
	e. Looseness in steering gear	Readjust, replace worn parts
9. Tires squeal on turns (■ 6-4-10)	a. Excessive speed	Take curves at slower speed
	b. Low or uneven tire pressure	Inflate to correct pressure
	c. Front alignment incorrect	Check and adjust
	d. Worn tires	Replace
10. Improper tire wear (■ 6-4-11)	a. Wear at tread sides from underinflation	Inflate to correct pressure
	b. Wear at tread center from overinflation	Inflate to correct pressure
	c. Wear at one tread side from excessive camber	Adjust camber

(Continued)

STEERING AND SUSPENSION TROUBLE-DIAGNOSIS CHART *(Continued)*

(See ■ 6-4-2 to 6-4-16 for detailed explanations of trouble causes and corrections listed below.)

COMPLAINT	POSSIBLE CAUSE	CHECK OR CORRECTION
10. *(Continued)*		
	d. Featheredge wear from excessive toe-in or toe-out on turns	Correct toe-in or toe-out on turns
	e. Cornering wear from excessive speeds on turns	Take turns at slower speed
	f. Uneven or spotty wear from mechanical causes	Adjust brakes, align wheels, balance wheels, adjust linkage, etc.
	g. Rapid wear from speed	Drive more slowly for longer tire life
11. Hard or rough ride (■ 6-4-12)	a. Excessive tire pressure	Reduce to correct pressure
	b. Defective shock absorbers	Repair or replace
	c. Excessive friction in spring suspension	Lubricate, realign parts
12. Sway on turns (■ 6-4-13)	a. Loose stabilizer bar	Tighten
	b. Weak or sagging springs	Repair or replace
	c. Caster incorrect	Adjust
	d. Defective shock absorbers	Replace
13. Spring breakage (■ 6-4-14)	a. Overloading	Avoid overloading
	b. Loose center or U bolts	Keep bolts tight
	c. Defective shock absorbers	Repair or replace
	d. Tight spring shackle	Loosen, replace
14. Sagging springs (■ 6-4-15)	a. Broken leaf	Replace
	b. Spring weak	Replace
	c. Coil spring short	Install shim
	d. Defective shock absorber	Repair or replace
15. Noises (■ 6-4-16)	Could come from any loose, worn, or unlubricated part in the suspension or steering system	

■ 6-4-2 Excessive Play in Steering System

Excessive play or looseness in the steering system means that there will be excessive free movement of the steering wheel without corresponding movement of the front wheels. A small amount of steering-wheel play is desirable in order to provide easy steering. But when the play becomes excessive, it is considered objectionable by most drivers. Excessive play can be due to wear or improper adjustment in the steering linkage, to worn ball joints or steering-knuckle parts, or to loose wheel bearings.

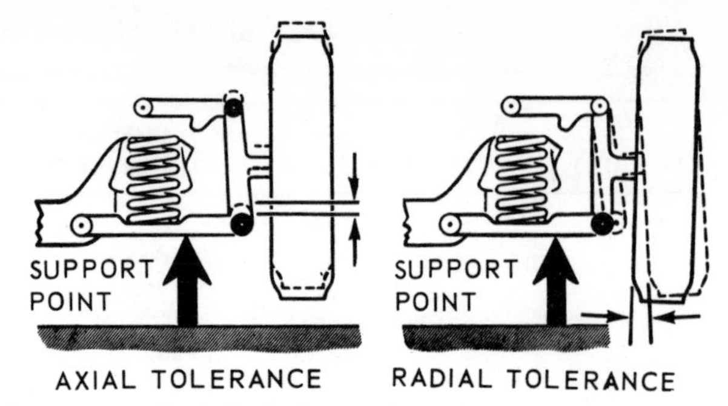

Figure 1 To check the ball joints for wear on a suspension system with the spring on the lower arm, support the wheel under the arm as shown.

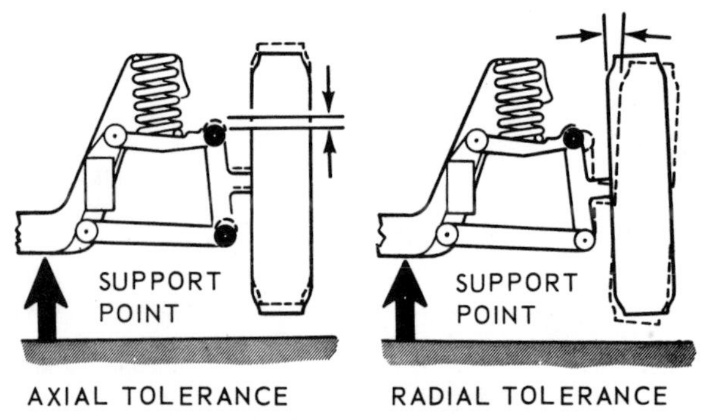

Figure 2 To check the ball joints for wear on a suspension system with the spring on the upper arm, support the front end of the frame, as shown.

The tie rods and linkage may be checked for looseness by jacking up the front end of the car, grasping both front wheels, pushing out on both at the same time, and then pulling in on both at the same time. Excessive relative movement between the two wheels means that the linkage connections are worn or out of adjustment.

Worn steering-knuckle parts and loose wheel bearings can be detected by jacking up the front end of the car, grasping the wheel top and bottom, and checking it for side play. Try to see how much you can wobble the wheel. Excessive looseness indicates worn or loose parts, either in the steering knuckle or in the wheel bearing. The bearing should be readjusted to see whether the looseness is in the bearing or in the knuckle.

Ball joints can be checked for wear by supporting the wheel as shown in Figs. 1 and 2. Axial play is checked by moving the wheel up and down. Radial play is measured by rocking the wheel back and forth.

On the suspension with the spring on the lower arm (Fig. 1), the upper ball joint should be replaced if there is any noticeable looseness at the joint.[1] The lower ball joint should be re-

[1] Some manufacturers (Chevrolet, for example) specify replacement of the lower ball joint, also, when the upper ball joint is replaced.

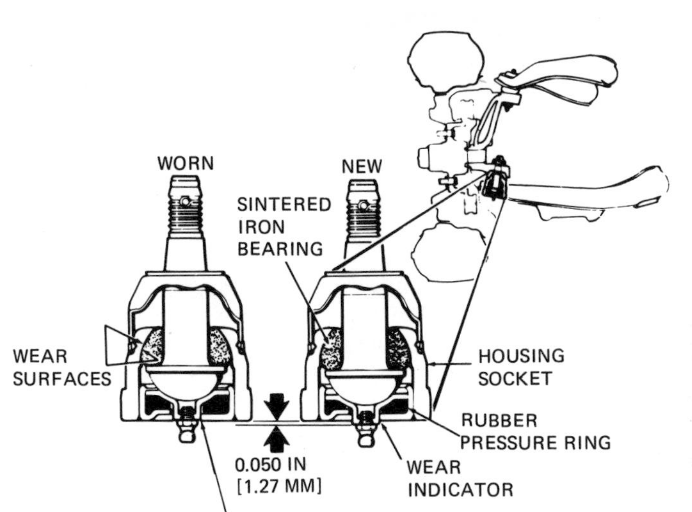

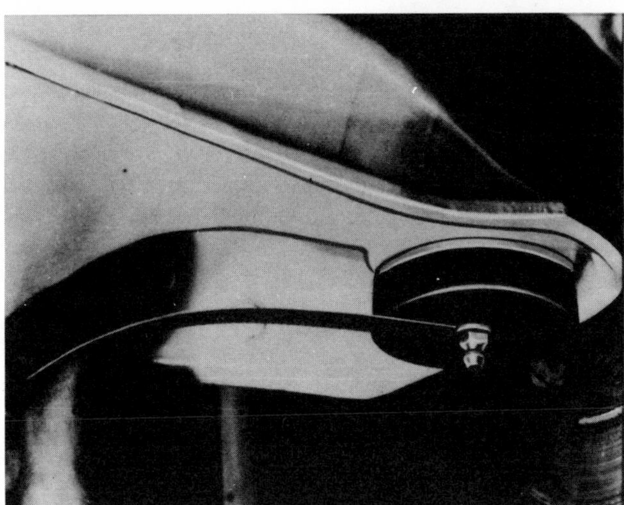

Figure 3 Wear-indicating ball joint. Left, sectional views showing a ball joint in good condition with a ball joint worn to the point where it requires replacement. Right, checking with a scale to see how much the nipple protrudes. *(Chevrolet Motor Division of General Motors Corporation.)*

placed if radial play exceeds 0.250 inch (6.35 mm). The lower ball joint should be replaced if axial play between the lower control arm and the spindle exceeds the tolerance specified by the vehicle manufacturer. This specification may vary from zero to 0.200 inch (5.08 mm), so always refer to the manufacturer's shop manual.

Many ball joints have wear indicators (Fig. 3). On these, the lower ball joints can be checked by visual inspection alone. Wear is indicated by the recession of the grease-fitting nipple into the ball-joint socket, as shown. The nipple protrudes from the socket 0.050 inch (1.27 mm) when new. As the ball joint wears, the nipple recedes into the socket. If the wear has caused the nipple to recede as much as 0.050 inch (1.27 mm), it will be level with the socket, and the ball joint should be replaced. Figure 3 shows the nipple being checked with a steel scale, but it can be checked with a screwdriver or even a fingernail. Replacement procedures are covered in Part 6, Sec. 6.

On the suspension with the spring on the upper arm (Fig. 2), the lower ball joint should be replaced if there is any noticeable looseness at the joint. The upper ball joint should be replaced if radial play exceeds 0.250 inch (6.35 mm). The upper ball joint should be replaced if axial play between the upper control arm and spindle exceeds the tolerances specified by the vehicle manufacturer. This specification may vary from zero to 0.200 inch (5.08 mm), so always refer to the manufacturer's shop manual.

> **NOTE:** Some lower ball joints are not internally preloaded. When the car weight is removed from these, they will exhibit some looseness due to normal operating clearance. But such looseness does not necessarily mean the ball joint should be replaced. A method of checking these non-preloaded ball joints is described in ■6-6-1 (item 10).

A rough check for looseness in the steering gear can be made by watching the pitman arm while an assistant turns the steering wheel one way and then the other with the front wheels on the floor. If, after reversal of steering-wheel rotation, considerable initial movement of the steering wheel is required to set the pitman arm in motion, the steering gear is worn or in need of adjustment.

■ 6-4-3 Hard Steering

If hard steering occurs just after the steering system has been worked on, chances are it is due to excessively tight adjustments in the steering gear or linkages. If hard steering develops at other times, it could be due to low or uneven tire pressure, abnormal friction in the steering gear, in the linkage, or at the kingpin or ball joints, or to improper wheel or frame alignment.

On a car equipped with power steering, failure of the power-steering mechanism will cause the steering system to revert to straight mechanical operation and a considerably greater steering effort. In such a case, the power-steering unit and the hydraulic pump should be checked as outlined in Part 6, Sec. 10.

The steering system may be checked for excessive friction by jacking up the front end of the car, turning the steering wheel, and observing the steering-system components to locate the source of excessive friction. Disconnect the linkage at the pitman arm. If this eliminates the frictional drag that makes it hard to turn the steering wheel, the friction is either in the linkage itself or at the steering knuckles. If the friction is not eliminated when the linkage is disconnected at the pitman arm, the steering gear is probably at fault. Steering-gear service is discussed in Part 6, Sec. 9, and linkage service is described in Part 6, Sec. 5.

If the trouble does not seem to be due to excessive friction in the steering system, chances are it is due to incorrect front-wheel alignment or to a misaligned frame or sagging springs. Excessive caster especially causes hard steering (see Part 6, Sec. 8, "Front-End Alignment").

■ 6-4-4 Car Wander

Car wander is experienced as difficulty in keeping the car moving straight ahead; frequent steering-wheel movements are necessary to prevent the car from wandering from one side of the road to the other. Inexperienced drivers may sometimes complain of car wander because they tend to oversteer. They keep moving the wheel back and forth unnecessarily to stay on their side of the road.

A variety of conditions can cause car wander. Low or uneven tire pressure, binding or excessive play in the linkage or steering gear, or improper front-wheel alignment will cause car wander. Any condition that causes tightness in the steering system will keep the wheels from automatically seeking the straight-ahead position. The driver has to correct the wheels constantly. This condition would probably also cause hard steering (■6-4-3). Looseness or excessive play in the steering system might cause car wander, too. This would tend to allow the wheels to waver somewhat and would permit the car to wander.

Excessively low caster, uneven caster, or a point of intersection too far above or below the road surface (due to the wrong camber angle) will tend to cause the wheels to swing away from straight ahead. The driver must steer continually. Excessive toe-in will cause the same condition. Front-end alignment is covered in Part 6, Sec. 8.

■ 6-4-5 Car Pulls to One Side (Normal Driving)

If the car persistently pulls to one side so that pressure must constantly be applied to the steering wheel to maintain forward movement, the trouble could be due to uneven tire pressure, uneven caster or camber, a tight wheel bearing, uneven springs, uneven torsion-bar adjustment, or to the wheels not tracking (rear wheels not following in the tracks of the front wheels). Anything that would tend to make one wheel drag or toe in or toe out more than the other would make the car pull to that side. The methods used to check tracking and front-wheel alignment are covered in Part 6, Sec. 8.

■ 6-4-6 Car Pulls to One Side (When Braking)

The most likely cause of pulling to one side when braking is grabbing brakes. Such brake action could be due to the brake linings becoming soaked with oil or brake fluid, to brake shoes that are unevenly or improperly adjusted, to a brake backing plate that is loose or out of line, or to other conditions that would cause the brake at one wheel to apply harder than the brake at the corresponding wheel on the other side. Section 3, Part 7, covers brake service. The other conditions listed in ■6-4-5 could also cause pulling to one side when braking, since the condition, from whatever cause, tends to become more noticeable when the car is braked.

■ 6-4-7 Front-Wheel Shimmy (Low Speed)

Front-wheel shimmy and front-wheel tramp (■6-4-8) are sometimes confused. Low-speed shimmy is the rapid oscillation of the wheel on the steering-knuckle support. The wheel tries to turn in and out alternately. This action causes the front end of the car to shake from side to side. On the other hand, front-wheel tramp, or high-speed shimmy, is the tendency for the wheel-and-tire assembly to hop up and down and, under severe conditions, actually to leave the pavement. Even when the tire does not leave the pavement, tramp can be observed as a rapid flexing-unflexing action of the part of the tire in contact with the pavement. That is, the bottom of the tire first appears deflated (as the wheel moves down) and then inflated (as the wheel moves up).

Low-speed shimmy can result from low or uneven tire pressure, loose linkage, excessively soft springs, incorrect or uneven wheel camber, dynamic imbalance of the wheels, or from irregularities in the tire treads.

■ 6-4-8 Front-Wheel Tramp

Front-wheel tramp is often called "high-speed shimmy." This condition causes the front wheels to move up and down alternately. One of the most common causes of front-wheel tramp is unbalanced wheels, or wheels that have too much runout. An unbalanced wheel is heavy at one part; as it rotates, the heavy part sets up a circulating outward thrust that tends to make the wheel hop up and down. A similar action occurs if the wheel has too much runout. Runout is the amount the wheel is out of line with the axle so that one part of the wheel "runs out," or moves to the side more than other parts of the wheel. Defective shock absorbers, which fail to control natural spring oscillations, also cause wheel tramp. Any of the causes described in the previous section may also cause wheel tramp. Later sections describe the servicing of the wheel and tire so that they can be restored to proper balance and alignment.

■ 6-4-9 Steering Kickback

Steering shock, or kickback, consists of sharp and rapid movements of the steering wheel that occur when the front wheels encounter obstructions in the road. Normally, some kickback to the steering wheel will always occur; when it becomes excessive, an investigation should be made. This condition could result from incorrect or uneven tire inflation, sagging springs, defective shock absorbers, or looseness in the linkage or steering gear. Any of these defects could permit road shock to carry back excessively to the steering wheel.

■ 6-4-10 Tires Squeal on Turns

If the tires skid or squeal in turns, the cause may be driver-related—excessive speed on the turns. If this is not the cause, however, it is probably low or uneven tire pressure, worn tires, or misalignment of the front wheels—particularly camber and toe-in (see ■6-3-3 and 6-3-7).

■ **6-4-11 Improper Tire Wear** Various types of abnormal tire wear can be experienced. The type of tire wear found is often a good indication of a particular defect in the suspension or steering system, or improper operation or abuse. For example, if the tire is operated with insufficient air pressure—underinflated—the sides will bulge over, and the center of the tread will be lifted clear of the road. The sides of the tread will take all the wear; the center will barely be worn (Fig. 4). The uneven tread wear shortens tire life. But even more damaging is the excessive flexing of the tire sidewalls that takes place as the underinflated tire rolls on the pavement. The repeated flexing causes the fabric in the sidewalls to crack or break and the plies to separate. This seriously weakens the sidewalls and may soon lead to complete tire failure. Aside from all this, the underinflated tire is unprotected against rim bruises. Thus if the tire should strike a rut or stone on the road, or if it should bump a curb a little too hard, the tire will flex so much under the blow that it will actually be pinched on the rim. This causes plies to break and leads to early tire failure.

NOTE: The radial tire applies a much larger area of tread to the pavement. Therefore, a radial tire appears to be running underinflated, when compared with the bias-ply tire used on cars for many years. The information in the previous paragraph applies more to bias-ply tires than to radial-ply tires.

Continuous high-speed driving on curves, both right and left, can produce tread wear that looks almost like underinflation wear. The side thrust on the tires as they round the curves causes the sides of the tread to be worn. The only remedy here is to reduce car speed on turns.

Overinflation causes the tire to ride on the center of its tread so that only the center of the tread wears (Fig. 4). The uneven tread wear shortens tire life. But equally damaging, the overinflated tire does not have normal "give" when it meets a rut or bump in the road. Instead of giving normally, the tire fabric takes the major shock of the encounter. As a result, the fabric may crack or break so that the tire quickly fails.

Excessive toe-in or toe-out on turns causes the tire to be dragged sideways while it is moving forward. The tire on a front wheel that toes in 1 inch (25.4 mm) from straight ahead will be dragged sideways about 150 feet (45.7 mm) every mile (1.6 km). This sideward drag scrapes off rubber as shown in Fig. 4. Characteristic of this type of wear are the featheredges of rubber that appear on one side of the tread design. If both front tires show this type of wear, the front system is misaligned. But if only one tire shows this type of wear—and if both tires have been on the car for some time—a bent steering arm is indicated. This causes one wheel to toe in more than the other.

Excessive camber of a wheel causes one side of the tread to wear more rapidly than the other (Fig. 4). If the camber is positive, the tires will tilt outward and the heavy tread wear will be on the outside. If the camber is negative, the tires will tilt inward and the heavy tread wear will be on the inside.

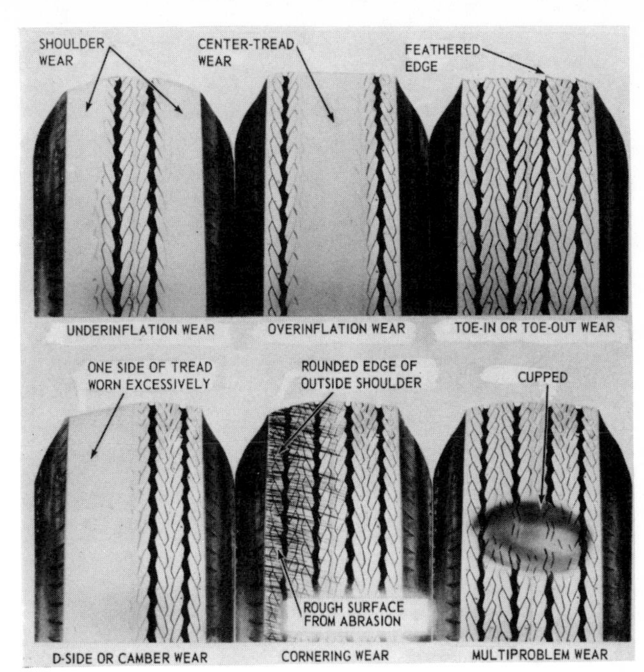

Figure 4 Patterns of abnormal tire-tread wear. *(Buick Motor Division of General Motors Corporation.)*

Cornering wear, caused by taking curves at excessively high speeds, may be mistaken for camber wear or toe-in or toe-out wear (Fig. 4). Cornering wear is due to centrifugal force acting on the car and causing the tires to roll, as well as skid, on the road. This produces a diagonal type of wear, which rounds the outside shoulder of the tire and roughens the tread surface near the outside shoulder. In severe cornering wear, fins or sharp edges will be found along the inner edges of the tire treads. There is no adjustment that can be made to correct the steering system for this type of wear. The only preventive is for the driver to slow down on curves.

Uneven tire wear (such as shown in Fig. 4), with the tread unevenly or spottily worn, can result from a number of mechanical conditions. These include misaligned wheels, unequal or improperly adjusted brakes, unbalanced wheels, overinflated tires, out-of-round brake drums, and incorrect linkage adjustments.

High-speed operation causes much more rapid tire wear because of the high temperature and greater amount of scuffing and rapid flexing to which the tires are subjected. The chart (Fig. 5) shows just how much tire wear increases with car speed. According to the chart, tires wear more than three times faster at 70 mph (113 km/h) than they do at 30 mph (48 km/h). More careful, slower driving and correct tire inflation will increase tire life greatly.

■ **6-4-12 Hard or Rough Ride** A hard or rough ride could be due to excessive tire pressure, improperly operating shock absorbers, or excessive friction in the spring suspension. The spring suspension can be checked easily for excessive friction in leaf-spring-suspension systems. Place strips of masking

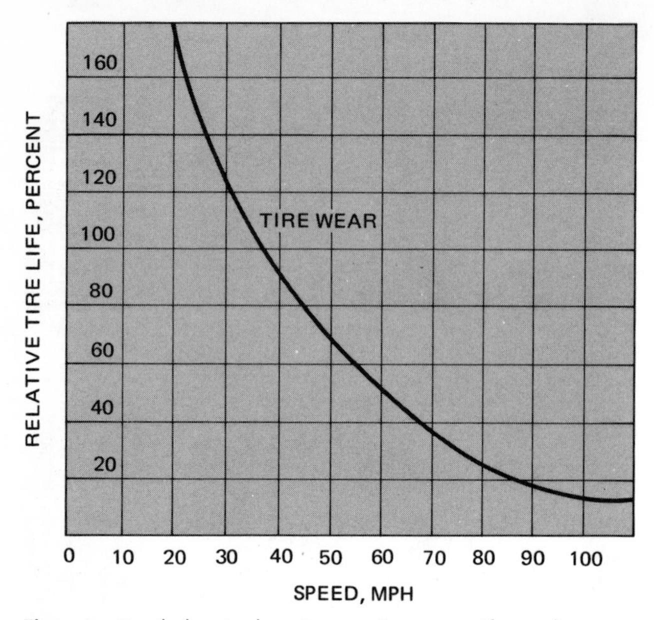

Figure 5 Graph showing how tire wear increases with speed.

tape at the lower edges of the car body, front and back. Lift the front end of the car as high as possible by hand, and very slowly let it down. Carefully measure from the floor to the tape and note the distance. Then push down on the car bumper at the front end, and again slowly release the car. Remeasure the distance from the floor to the tape, and note the difference in measurements. Repeat this action several times to obtain accurate measurements. The difference is caused by the friction in the suspension system and is called "friction lag." After determining friction lag at the front end, check it at the back end of the car. Make correction by lubricating the springs, shackles, and bushings (on types where lubrication is specified) and by loosening the shock-absorber arm linkages, shackle bolts, and U bolts. Then retighten the U bolts, shackle bolts, and shock-absorber linkages, in that order. Such a procedure permits re-alignment of parts that might have slipped and caused excessive friction.

Shock-absorber action on cars giving a hard or uneven ride may be roughly checked by bouncing each corner of the car in turn. This is done by seizing the bumper, pulling up and pushing down on it several times so that the car bounces, and then releasing the bumper.[1] If the shock absorber is operating normally, the car will come to rest immediately. If the car continues to bounce after the bumper is released, the shock absorber is probably defective. A more accurate check can be made by disconnecting the shock absorber at one end and then noting its resistance to shortening and lengthening. If the resistance is small or is not uniform through the full stroke, or if the movement is very stiff, the shock absorber will require additional attention.

[1] Some direct-acting shock absorbers cannot be tested in this way, since they are valved to permit slow spring oscillations in the interest of smoother riding.

■ **6-4-13 Sway on Turns** Sway of the car body on turns or on rough roads may be due to a loose stabilizer bar or shaft. Their attachments to the frame, axle housing, or suspension arms should be checked. Weak or sagging springs could also cause excessive sway. If the shock absorbers are ineffective, they may permit excessive spring movement, which could cause strong body pitching or sway, particularly on rough roads. If the caster is excessively positive, it will cause the car to roll out, or lean out, on turns. This requires front-wheel alignment.

■ **6-4-14 Spring Breakage** Breakage of leaf springs can result from (1) excessive overloading; (2) loose U bolts, which cause breakage near the center bolts; (3) loose center bolt, which causes breakage at the center-bolt holes; (4) improperly operating shock absorber, which causes breakage of the master leaf; or (5) tight spring shackle, which causes breakage of the master leaf near or at the spring eye. Determining the point at which breakage has occurred will make the cause obvious.

■ **6-4-15 Sagging Springs** Springs will sag if they have become weak—as they might, for example, from habitual overloading. Loss of the shim from the coil-spring seat on coil-spring suspension—due to failure to return it during overhaul—will also cause the spring to sag and to seem shorter. Not all coil springs require or use shims. If a torsion-bar suspension system sags, the torsion bars can be adjusted to restore normal car height. Defective shock absorbers may tend to restrict spring action and thus make them appear to sag more than normal.

■ **6-4-16 Noises** The noises produced by spring or shock-absorber difficulties will usually be either rattles or squeaks. Rattling noises can be produced by looseness of such parts as spring U bolts, metal spring covers, rebound clips, spring shackles, or shock-absorber linkages or springs. These can generally be located by a careful examination of the various suspension parts. Spring squeaks can result from lack of lubrication in the spring shackles, at spring bushings (on the type requiring lubrication), or in the spring itself (leaf type requiring lubrication). Shock absorber squeak could result from tight or dry bushings. Steering-linkage rattles may develop if linkage components become loose. Under exceptional circumstances, squeaks during turns could develop because of lack of lubrication in steering-linkage joints or bearings. This would also produce hard steering.

Some of the connections between steering-linkage parts are with ball joints that can be lubricated. Others are permanently lubricated on original assembly and have no provision for further lubrication. If the latter develop squeaks or excessive friction, they must be replaced. Lubricating and replacing steering-linkage ball joints are covered in Part 6, Sec. 5.

SECTION 6-5 Servicing Steering Linkage

This section discusses the servicing procedures required for various types of steering linkages. Later sections describe front-wheel alignment service and steering-gear service (manual and power). It is extremely important always to check and correct front-wheel alignment whenever any work has been done on the front suspension that might disturb alignment. Always refer to the shop manual covering the specific car model you are working on when servicing steering linkage and front- and rear-suspension systems.

■ **6-5-1 Steering Linkage Service** The only service that steering linkages normally require is periodic lubrication of the connecting joints between the links. The connecting joints are ball joints. Figure 1 shows a typical arrangement. The joints arrowed are ball joints and have a means of lubrication. Note that the joints at the pitman arm and the idler arm are not arrowed. These joints are permanently lubricated on assembly and do not require lubrication. The arrangement shown in Fig. 1 is for a specific model of car. Other cars may have different arrangements.

The lubricating procedure varies slightly, according to whether the ball joints have plugs to be removed (Fig. 2) or regular grease fittings. Typical recommendations (Ford and Chrysler) are that the seals at the ball joints should be inspected at least every 6 months and lubricated every 3 years. Chevrolet recommends lubricating the linkage every 6,000 miles (9,656 km) or 4 months with water-resistant chassis lubricant.

1. BALL JOINT WITH PLUG (FIG. 2) First, wipe the plug and area around the plug so no dirt will get into the ball joint. Then use a rubber-tipped, hand-operated grease gun, filled with the proper lubricant. Apply the tip to the plug hole and operate the grease gun at low pressure. This forces lubricant into the joint. When the joint boot (dust cover) begins to swell, stop. Do not overlubricate or you will destroy the weathertight seal.

2. BALL JOINT WITH GREASE FITTING First, wipe the grease fitting so no dirt will get into the ball joint. Then take a hand-operated grease gun with the proper applicator for the fitting, and fill it with the proper lubricant. Operate the grease gun at low pressure. Chrysler says to "fill and flush" the joint with lubricant. Stop filling when the grease begins to flow freely from the bleed area at the base of the seal or if the seal begins to balloon.

NOTE: Some ball joints cannot be lubricated.

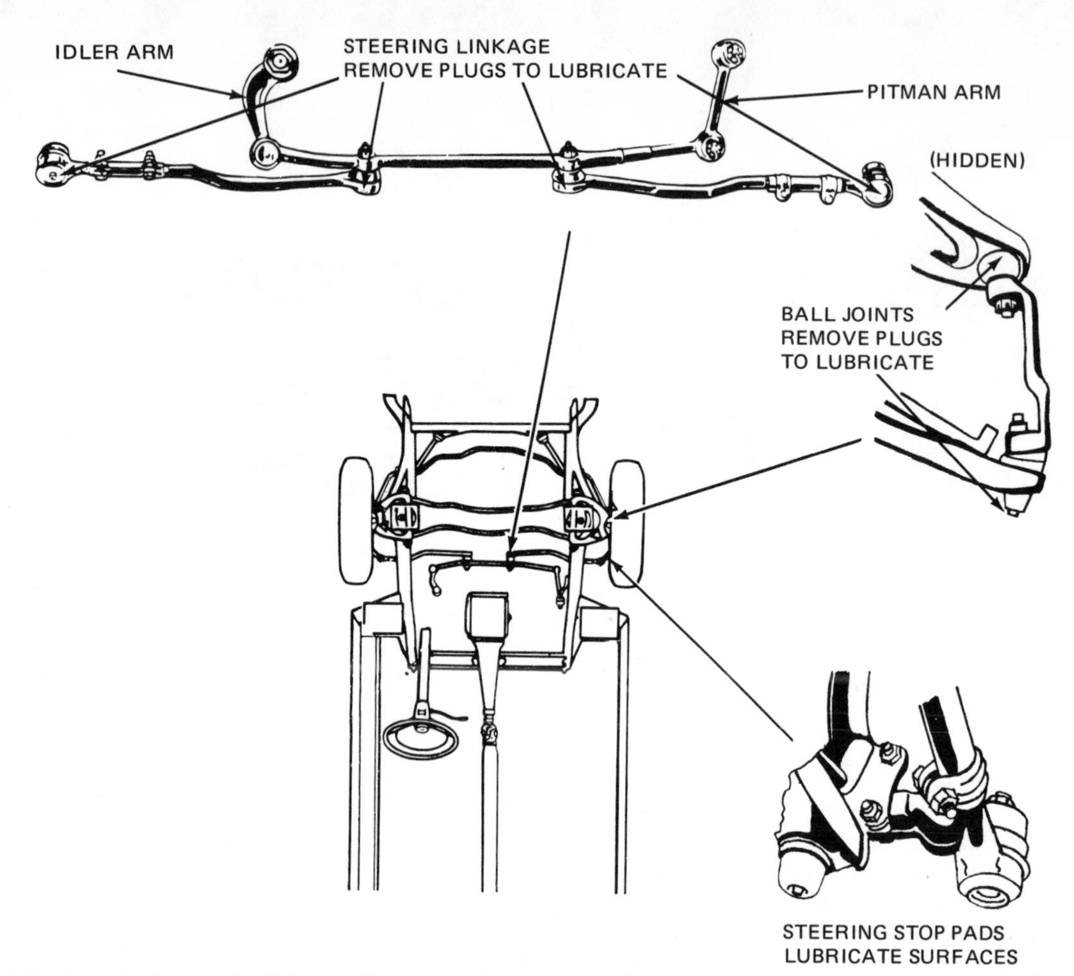

Figure 1 Lubrication points in a steering-linkage and front-suspension system. *(Ford Motor Company.)*

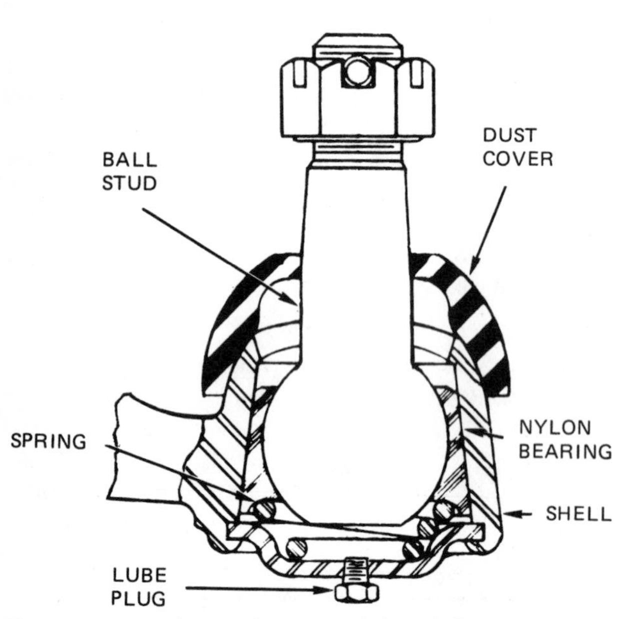

Figure 2 Sectional view of a steering-linkage ball joint. *(American Motors Corporation.)*

Figure 3 Freeing the ball stud from the tie rod. *(Chevrolet Motor Division of General Motors Corporation.)*

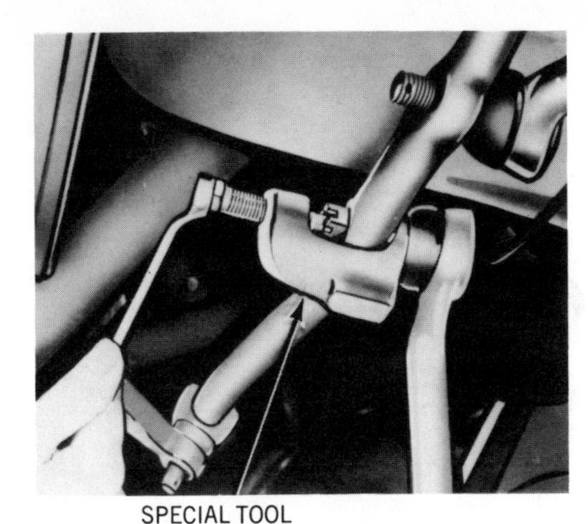

Figure 4 Removing the ball stud from the rod. *(Ford Motor Company.)*

If ball joints or other parts are worn or have been bent or damaged, they should be replaced. Never try to straighten and reuse bent steering-linkage parts. This could lead to failure later, causing an accident.

If the linkage is disassembled, check the front alignment after all parts have been put back together again (Part 6, Sec. 8). Following pages describe the servicing of steering linkages and front- and rear-suspension systems, including wheel-bearing inspection, lubrication, and adjustment.

NOTE: Always inspect the steering linkage and suspension when working on a car on the lift for whatever purpose. It takes only a moment to check seals and note the conditions of the ball joints and links. A steering-linkage system in good condition is necessary to the safe operation of the car. Therefore, you should make sure that the steering linkage of every car you service is in good shape.

■ 6-5-2 Chevrolet Steering-Linkage Service

Steering linkages for Chevrolet, Ford, Plymouth, American Motors, and other vehicles are similar although not the same. Parts that can be removed and reinstalled include: Tie rods, relay rod, idler arm, pitman arm, and the steering arms. To remove the ball studs from the tie rods, use a heavy hammer as a backing and tap on the steering arm as shown in Fig. 3. Ford and Plymouth recommend the use of special screw-type tools (Fig. 4). When replacing tie rods or sleeves, lubricate the threads with EP chassis lubricant. Tie-rod bolts and clamps must be installed downward with the bolts facing forward. Use new cotter pins.

Whenever working on a specific model of vehicle, always refer to the shop manual that applies. A great variety of steering-linkage arrangements have been used. Servicing procedures may vary from car to car.

SECTION 6-6 Front-Suspension Service

In this section, we describe typical front-suspension servicing procedures, with emphasis on Chevrolet, Ford, and Plymouth. These procedures are illustrative only. When you are working on a specific model of vehicle, refer to the shop manual that applies.

■ 6-6-1 Chevrolet Front-Suspension Service

Figure 1 shows a front-suspension system of the type described in following paragraphs. Servicing procedures are outlined below for front-wheel bearings, hubs, shock absorbers, coil springs, and upper and lower control arms.

1. BRAKE-DRUM REMOVAL To remove the brake drum, with the vehicle jacked up take off the wheel and pull off the brake drum. You may need to back off the brake adjustment. Check and service the drum (Part 7, Sec. 3). On reinstallation, make sure the alignment dowel pin on the drum web indexes with the hole in the wheel hub. The brakes may require readjustment after the installation is completed (Part 7, Sec. 3).

2. BRAKE-DISK REMOVAL Removal requires detaching of the disk caliper so that the disk (or "rotor" as Ford calls it) can be removed. (See Part 7, Sec. 3.)

3. FRONT-WHEEL-BEARING ADJUSTMENT The bearings should be lubricated and adjusted every 24 months or 24,000 miles (38,624 km). Proper adjustment is extremely important. Improper adjustment can cause poor steering stability, wander or shimmy, and excessive tire wear. Tapered roller bearings are used on all late models. These bearings must never be preloaded. Cones must be a slip fit on the spindle, and the inside diameters of the cones should be lubricated so that the cones can creep. The spindle nut must be a free-running fit on the threads.

To check the adjustment, raise the car and support it at the front lower control arm. Spin the wheel to check for unusual noise or roughness. If bearings are noisy, tight, or too loose, they should be cleaned, inspected, and, if okay, relubricated. To check for looseness, grip the tire at top and bottom. Push and pull with both hands to see if you can move the hub on the spindle. If you cannot move it 0.001 inch (0.025 mm), or if it moves more than 0.005 inch (0.127 mm), adjust the bearings.

To adjust, jack up the front end and remove the hubcap or wheel disk and the dust cap. Take out the cotter pin. Tighten the spindle nut to 12 pound-feet (1.66 kg-m) torque while rotating the wheel. Back off the adjustment nut one flat or to the "just loose" position. Insert the cotter pin. If the slot and the cotter pin do not align, back off the adjustment nut just barely enough to get alignment. When bending back ends of the cot-

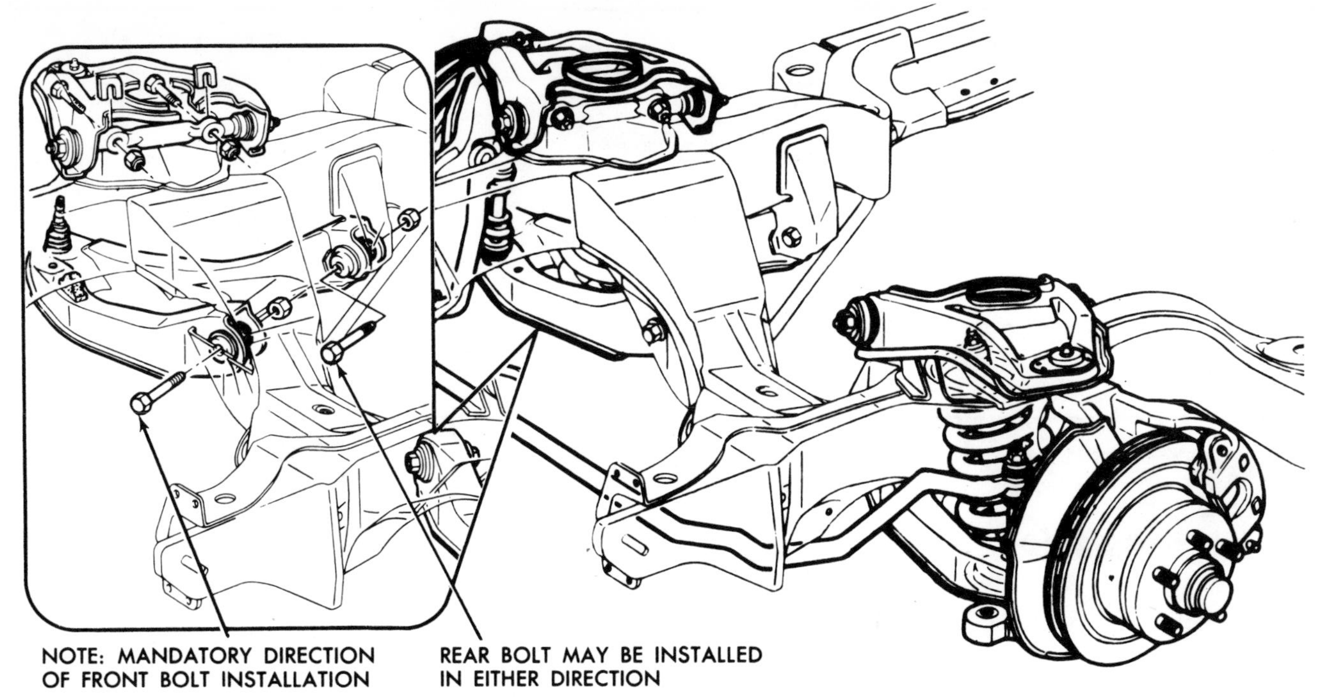

Figure 1 Front suspension in Chevrolet, Chevelle, Monte Carlo, and Camaro. *(Chevrolet Motor Division of General Motors Corporation.)*

ter pin, bend them inboard or cut ends off to avoid the possibility of their damaging the static collector in the dust cap. Reinstall the dust cap and the hubcap.

4. FRONT-WHEEL-BEARING REPLACEMENT Remove the wheel, brake drum, dust cap, cotter pin, spindle nut, and washer. Discard the old cotter pin. With your fingers, remove the outer bearing assembly. Pry out the lip-seal assembly and remove the inner bearing assembly from the hub. Discard the seal. Wash the bearings in clean solvent and inspect them for damaged roller separators, worn or cracked rollers, and pitted or cracked races (see Fig. 2). Races can be removed and replaced with a special tool. After reassembly of the bearings, adjust them (see item 3, above).

NOTE: You must have clean hands, clean tools, and a clean work area when you work on bearings. Hands must be not only clean but dry. Chevrolet recommends wearing clean canvas gloves. The slightest trace of dirt in a bearing can quickly ruin it. As soon as you wash a bearing, oil it lightly and wrap it in clean oilproof paper to protect it from dirt or rusting. Never spin a bearing with compressed air. Do not spin an uncleaned bearing even by hand.

5. FRONT-WHEEL HUB If the hub bore is out of round or the flange is distorted, the hub must be replaced. If the trouble is due only to bent hub bolts, they can be pressed out and new bolts pressed in.

6. SHOCK ABSORBERS Hold the upper stem with an open-end wrench to keep it from turning. Remove the retaining nut, retainer, and rubber grommet. Remove the two bolts at the lower end which attach the pivot to the lower control arm, and pull the shock absorber down and out. During reinstallation, tighten the upper stem nut to the specified torque.

7. FRONT STABILIZER BAR The front stabilizer bar is attached at four places: at the two frame side rails and to the two lower control arms. Detaching it from these four points will permit its removal. Reach through the hole in the frame side rail to hold the bolt heads while unscrewing the nuts attaching the stabilizer support.

If new insulators are necessary, coat the stabilizer with the recommended rubber lubricant, and slide the bushings into position. Never get lubricant on the outside of the frame-stabilizer-bar bushings, or they may slip out of the brackets. Connect the brackets to the frame and attach the stabilizer ends to the lower control arms. Torque the bracket bolts and link nuts to specifications.

8. STRUT ROD Put the car on the hoist and remove the nut, retainer, and rubber bushing from the front end of the strut rod. Remove the two bolts attaching the rear end of the strut rod to the lower control arm. Pull the strut rod from the bracket.

If the rear nut on the front end of the strut rod has been removed, turn it on uptil it is about 3/4 inch (19.05 mm) from the end of the threads. Install the rear retainer, sleeve, and bushing on the rod so the pilot diameter faces forward. Insert the rod into the bracket. Install the front bushing on the sleeve so the raised pilot diameter faces the rear to enter the hole in the bracket and rear bushing. Install the forward retainer and nut on the rod. Attach the strut rod to the top of the lower control arm with two bolts, washers, and nuts. Torque to specifications. Check the caster, camber, and toe-in.

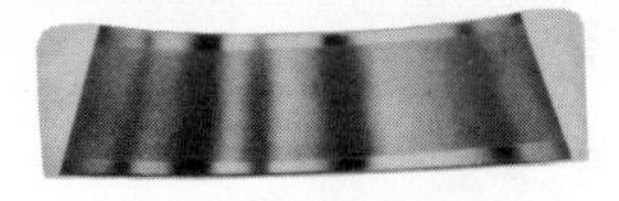

ABRASIVE ROLLER WEAR

PATTERN ON RACES AND ROLLERS CAUSED BY FINE ABRASIVES.

CLEAN ALL PARTS AND HOUSINGS. CHECK SEALS AND BEARINGS AND REPLACE IF LEAKING, ROUGH OR NOISY.

GALLING

METAL SMEARS ON ROLLER ENDS DUE TO OVERHEAT, LUBRICANT FAILURE, OR OVERLOAD (WAGON'S).

REPLACE BEARING. CHECK SEALS AND CHECK FOR PROPER LUBRICATION.

ETCHING

BEARING SURFACES APPEAR GRAY OR GRAYISH BLACK IN COLOR WITH RELATED ETCHING AWAY OF MATERIAL USUALLY AT ROLLER SPACING.

REPLACE BEARINGS, CHECK SEALS AND CHECK FOR PROPER LUBRICATION.

BENT CAGE

CAGE DAMAGE DUE TO IMPROPER HANDLING OR TOOL USAGE.

REPLACE BEARING.

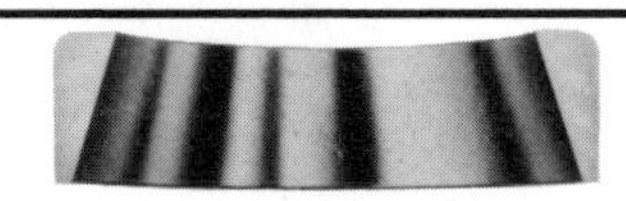

INDENTATIONS

SURFACE DEPRESSIONS ON RACE AND ROLLERS CAUSED BY HARD PARTICLES OF FOREIGN MATERIAL.

CLEAN ALL PARTS AND HOUSINGS. CHECK SEALS AND REPLACE BEARINGS IF ROUGH OR NOISY.

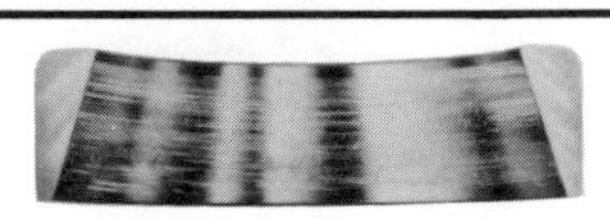

CAGE WEAR

WEAR AROUND OUTSIDE DIAMETER OF CAGE AND ROLLER POCKETS CAUSED BY ABRASIVE MATERIAL AND INEFFICIENT LUBRICATION.

CLEAN RELATED PARTS AND HOUSINGS. CHECK SEALS AND REPLACE BEARINGS.

MISALIGNMENT

OUTER RACE MISALIGNMENT.

CLEAN RELATED PARTS AND REPLACE BEARING. MAKE SURE RACES ARE PROPERLY SEATED.

CRACKED INNER RACE

RACE CRACKED DUE TO IMPROPER FIT, COCKING, OR POOR BEARING SEATS.

REPLACE BEARING AND CORRECT BEARING SEATS.

FATIGUE SPALLING

FLAKING OF SURFACE METAL RESULTING FROM FATIGUE.

REPLACE BEARING. CLEAN ALL RELATED PARTS.

BRINELLING

SURFACE INDENTATIONS IN RACEWAY CAUSED BY ROLLERS EITHER UNDER IMPACT LOADING OR VIBRATION WHILE THE BEARING IS NOT ROTATING.

REPLACE BEARING IF ROUGH OR NOISY.

FRETTING

CORROSION SET UP BY SMALL RELATIVE MOVEMENT OF PARTS WITH NO LUBRICATION.

REPLACE BEARING. CLEAN RELATED PARTS. CHECK SEALS AND CHECK FOR PROPER LUBRICATION.

HEAT DISCOLORATION

HEAT DISCOLORATION CAN RANGE FROM FAINT YELLOW TO DARK BLUE RESULTING FROM OVER LOAD OR INCORRECT LUBRICANT

EXCESSIVE HEAT CAN CAUSE SOFTENING OF RACES OR ROLLERS.

TO CHECK FOR LOSS OF TEMPER ON RACES OR ROLLERS A SIMPLE FILE TEST MAY BE MADE. A FILE DRAWN OVER A TEMPERED PART WILL GRAB AND CUT METAL, WHEREAS, A FILE DRAWN OVER A HARD PART WILL GLIDE READILY WITH NO METAL CUTTING.

REPLACE BEARINGS IF OVER HEATING DAMAGE IS INDICATED. CHECK SEALS AND OTHER PARTS.

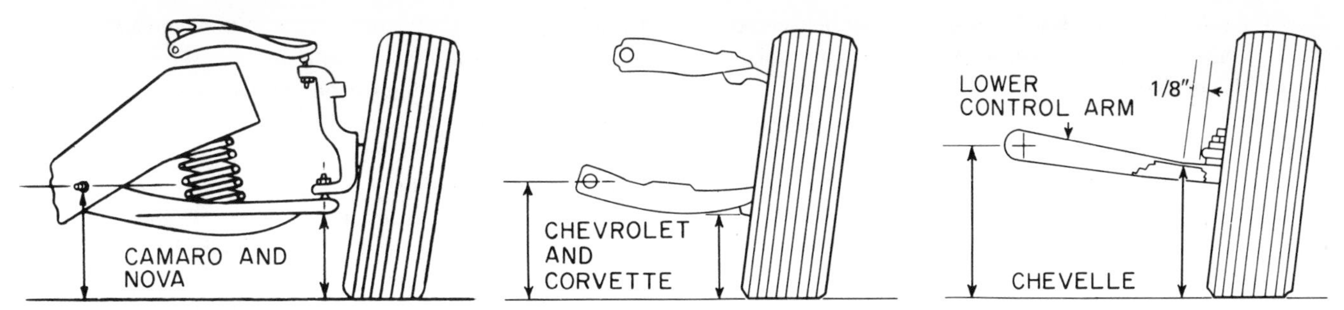

Figure 3 Measurements to check for front-spring sag. *(Chevrolet Motor Division of General Motors Corporation.)*

9. FRONT-COIL-SPRING CHECK To check for spring sag, position the car on a smooth, level surface, bounce the front end several times, raise up on the front end, and allow it to settle. Then take the measurements as shown in Fig. 3. The differences should be as noted in the specifications for the car being checked. Next, take the measurements on the other side. The difference between the two sides should be no greater than ½ inch (12.7 mm). To make a correction, the springs must be replaced. Shimming up under a spring is not recommended.

a. *Removal* Raise the car on a hoist. Remove the two shock-absorber attaching screws and push the shock up through the control arm and into the spring. The car should be supported so the control arms hang free. Put the special tool or adapter shown in Fig. 4 into position so it cradles the inner bushings. Note that the adapter must be attached to a suitable jack.

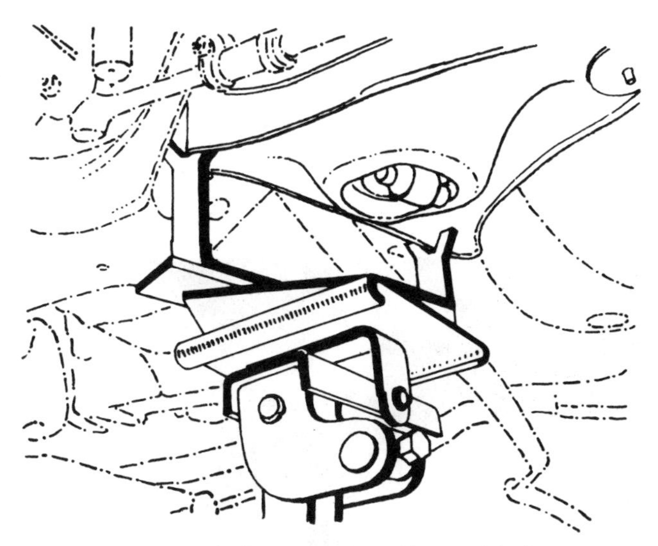

Figure 4 Removing the front coil spring with a special adaptor.

Detach the stabilizer bar from the lower control arm. Raise the jack to remove the tension in the lower-control-arm pivot bolts. Install a chain around the spring and through the control arm so the spring cannot jump out as the tension is released. Remove the rear bolt and nut, and then the front bolt and nut. Lower the jack to lower the control arm. When all spring compression is removed, take off safety chain and spring.

CAUTION: Do not apply pressure on the lower control arm and ball joint as you remove the spring. Maneuver the spring so it will come out easily.

b. *Replacement* Position the spring properly on the control arm and lift the control arm with the special tool shown in Fig. 4. Position the control arm into the frame and install the pivot bolts (front bolt first) and nuts. See Fig. 1 for mandatory bolt directions. Torque to specifications and lower the jack. Reattach the stabilizer bar and shock absorber.

10. UPPER-CONTROL-ARM BALL-JOINT CHECK Part 6, Sec. 4, described how to check ball joints for wear. A second method, which requires partial disassembly, follows. Raise the car to take weight off the control arms. Remove the tire and wheel assembly. Remove the upper ball-stud cotter pin and

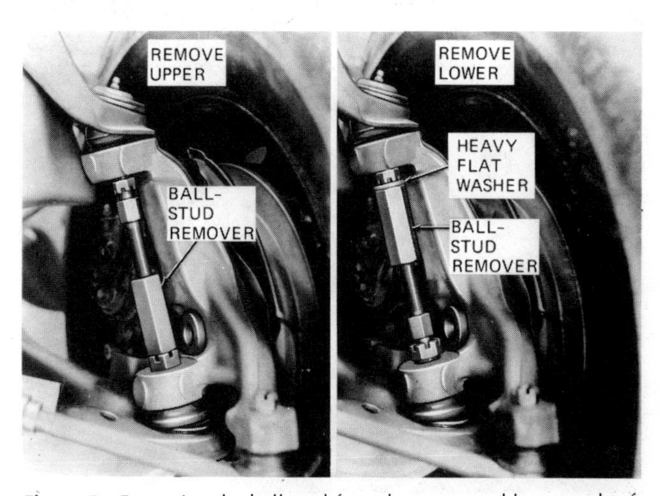

Figure 5 Removing the ball stud from the upper and lower ends of the steering knuckle with a special tool. *(Chevrolet Motor Division of General Motors Corporation.)*

Figure 2 (Opposite page) Front-wheel-bearing trouble diagnosis. When diagnosing bearing condition: (1) Check the general condition of all parts during disassembly and inspection. (2) Classify the failure with the aid of the illustrations. (3) Determine the cause. (4) Make all repairs following recommended procedures. *(Chevrolet Motor Division of General Motors Corporation.)*

loosen the nut one turn. Install the special tool between ball studs as shown in Fig. 5. Turn the threaded end of the tool until the stud is free of the steering knuckle.

Remove the upper ball-joint-stud nut and allow the steering knuckle to swing out of the way. Lift the upper arm and put a block of wood between the frame and arm to act as a support.

Check the ball joint for wear and looseness. If the stud has any preceptible lateral shake, or if it can be twisted in its socket with the fingers, replace the ball joint.

a. *Replacement* Use a grinding wheel to grind off the rivet heads. Do not damage the control arm or ball-joint seat. Then install the new ball joint in the arm. Attach it with the bolts and nuts supplied with the replacement ball joints. Install the bolts pointing up. Torque to specifications. Turn the ball-stud cotter-pin hole fore and aft (pointing toward front of car).

 Remove the block of wood which you placed there as a support. Inspect the steering-knuckle tapered hole into which the stud fits. It must be clean and round. If it is not round, or if you note other wear or damage, install a new knuckle.

b. *Attachment to Steering Knuckle* Mate the ball stud with the steering-knuckle hole and install the stud nut. Torque the nut and install a new cotter pin.

NOTE: Never back off the nut to align it with the cotter-pin hole. Instead, tighten it to the next slot that lines up with the hole. Install a lubrication fitting and lubricate the joint. Install the tire and wheel.

11. LOWER-CONTROL-ARM BALL-JOINT CHECK Late-model cars are equipped with lower-control-arm ball joints with wear indicators as explained in ■6-4-2 and illustrated in Fig. 3 (Part 6, Sec. 4). On earlier models, the lower ball joint can be checked for wear by measuring from the top of the lubrication fitting to the bottom of the ball stud with a micrometer. Take the measurement with the car supported on its wheels. Then support the car on the outer ends of the lower control arms and remeasure. If the difference is greater than 1/16 inch (1.59 mm), the joint is worn and must be replaced.

a. *Removal* Raise the car on a hoist. Remove the lower ball-stud cotter pin. Loosen the stud nut one turn. Install the special tool as shown in Fig. 5 between the ball studs. Turn the threaded end of the tool until the stud is free of the steering knuckle. Remove the stud nut. Pull outward on the bottom of the tire and at the same time push the tire upward to free the knuckle from the ball stud. Remove the wheel and tire.

 Lift the upper control arm, with the knuckle and hub assembly attached. Put a block of wood between the frame and the upper control arm.

NOTE: Do not pull on the brake hose when lifting the assembly!

 If the tie-rod end of the steering knuckle is in the way, detach it. If it is not in the way, leave it attached.

 Put the tools shown in Fig. 6 in position. Turn the bolt until the lower ball joint is pushed out of the control arm.

b. *Inspection* On most late-model Chevrolet cars, a look at the wear indicators (Fig. 3 in Part 6, Sec. 4) tells you whether the ball joint is worn. The ball-stud tightness in the knuckle can be checked by shaking the wheel and noting if there is any movement of the stud or nut in the knuckle, or by removing the cotter pin and checking torque.

c. *Replacement* Position the ball joint in the lower control arm with the special tools as shown in Fig. 7. Position the bleed vent of the new ball joint facing inward. Turn down the bolt until the new ball joint is seated in the control arm. Remove the tools. Turn the stud cotter-pin hole fore and aft.

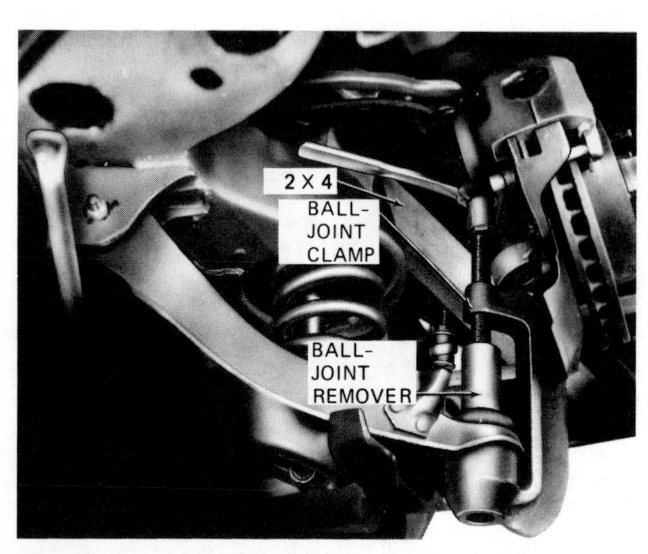

Figure 6 Removing ball joints from a car. *(Chevrolet Motor Division of General Motors Corporation.)*

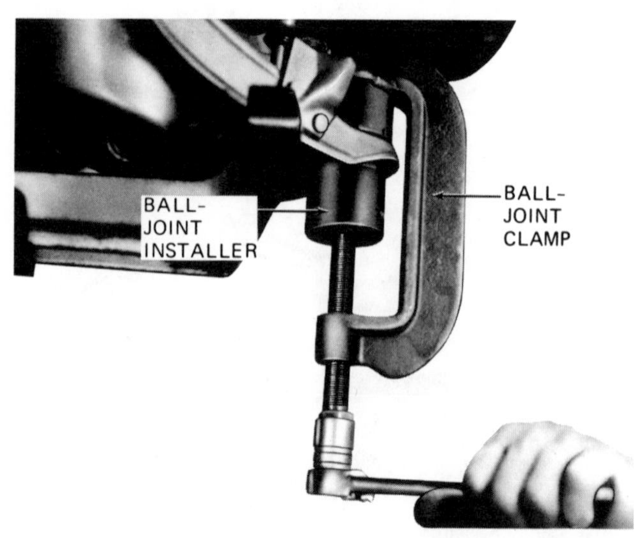

Figure 7 Installing ball joints on a car. *(Chevrolet Motor Division of General Motors Corporation.)*

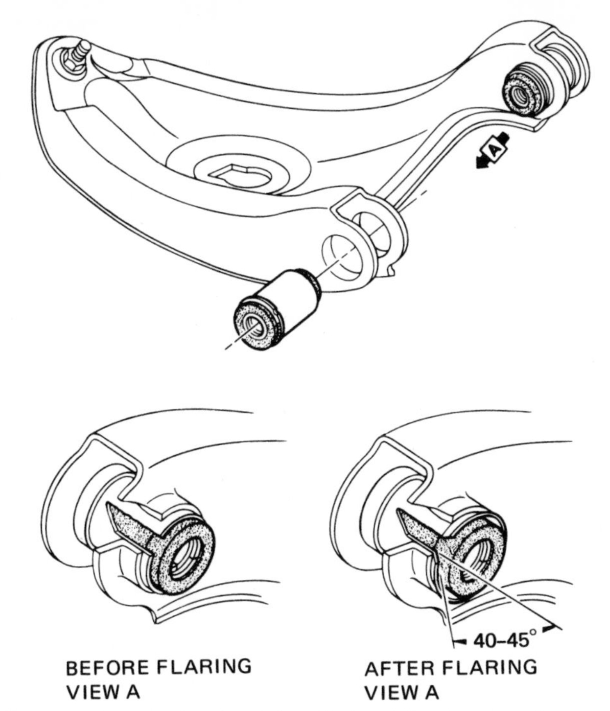

Figure 8 How the bushing is installed and flared. *(Chevrolet Motor Division of General Motors Corporation.)*

Remove the block of wood holding the upper control arm out of the way.

Inspect the tapered hole in the steering knuckle. If it is out of round or otherwise damaged, replace the steering knuckle. Mate the stud with the hole and install the stud nut. Torque the nut and install the cotter pin.

> **NOTE:** Never back off the nut to align it with the cotter-pin hole. Instead, tighten the nut to the next slot that lines up with the stud hole.

Install a lubrication fitting and lubricate the joint. Then install the wheel and tire, if they have been removed from the steering knuckle.

12. CONTROL-ARM BUSHINGS The upper-control-arm bushings are removed and replaced with special tools. Note that when the second bushing is installed, the cross shaft must be in place.

The lower-control-arm bushings are removed and replaced with special tools. Note that the metal collars on the bushings are flared on the inner ends after installation. This flare must be removed by tapping on the edge with a hammer before the bushing is pressed out. Then, when the new bushing is in place, flare it with special tools. See Fig. 8.

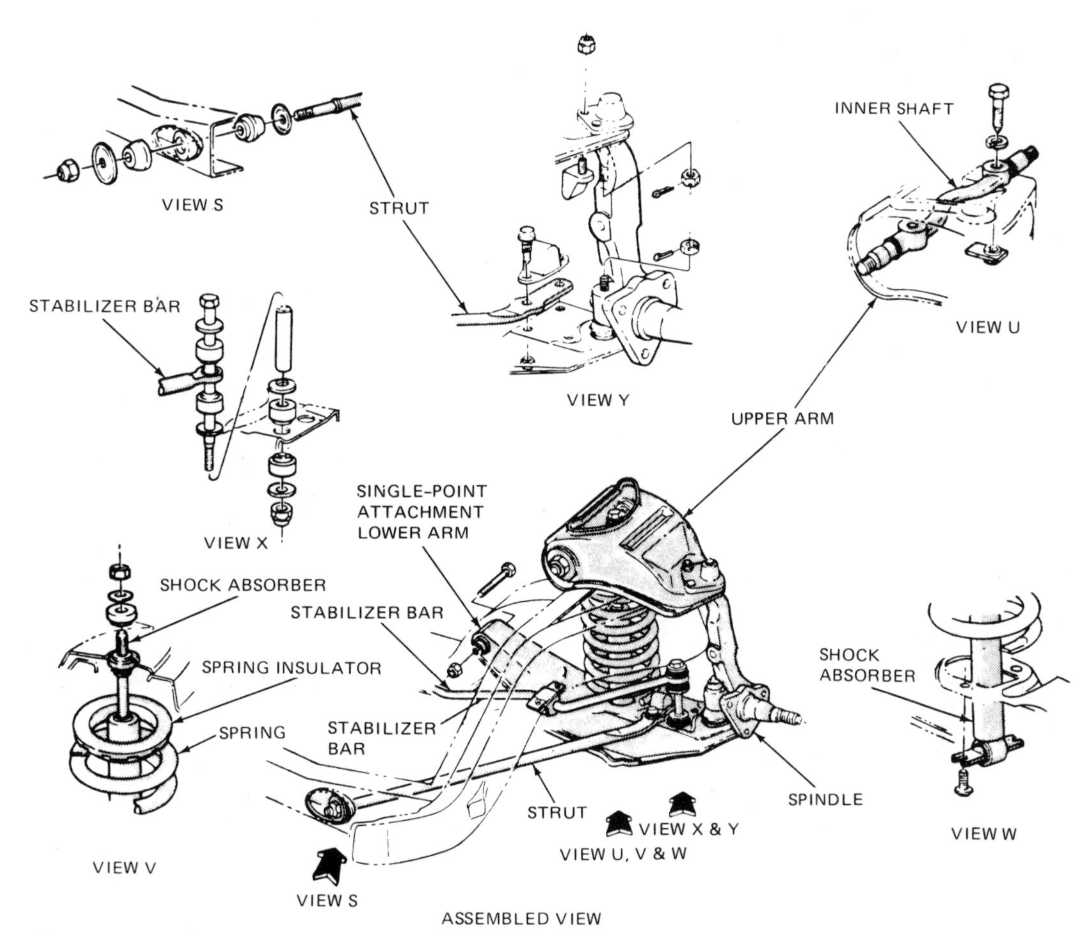

Figure 9 Details of the front suspension for most Ford Motor Company cars. *(Ford Motor Company.)*

■ 6-6-2 Ford Front-Suspension Service

The Ford upper or lower suspension (control) arm must be serviced as a unit. You do not install new ball joints or other components in used suspension arms. Figure 9 shows various views of a front-suspension system used in Ford cars. The following two subsections describe servicing procedures for front-suspension systems with the spring between the two suspension arms and the procedures for systems with the spring above the upper suspension arms.

■ 6-6-3 Ford Front-Suspension Service—Spring between Arms

The eight necessary procedures are detailed below.

1. FRONT-WHEEL-BEARING ADJUSTMENT AND LUBRICATION Bearings should be lubricated and adjusted every 24 months or 24,000 miles (38,624 km). Figure 10 shows a front-wheel bearing and related parts. Procedures are different for drum and disk brakes.

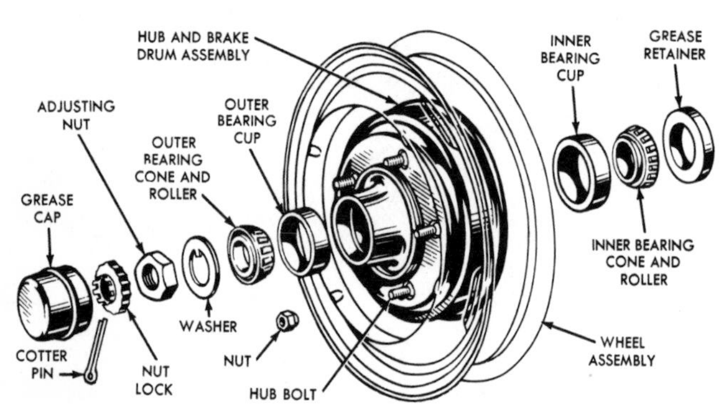

Figure 10 Disassembled view of front-wheel bearings. *(Ford Motor Company.)*

a. *Adjustment (Drum Brakes)* Hoist the car and remove the wheel cover and grease cap. Wipe away excess grease and remove the cotter pin and locknut. Rotate the wheel and at the same time torque the adjusting nut to 17 to 25 pound-feet (2.3 to 3.5 kg-m). Loosen the adjusting nut ½ turn. Then retighten it to 10 to 15 pound-inches (0.18 to 0.27 kg-mm), all the time rotating the wheel. Install the locknut with a new cotter pin. Recheck wheel rotation. If it is rough and noisy, disassemble for inspection and lubrication.

b. *Bearing Service (Drum Brakes)* Hoist the car and remove the wheel cover, grease cap, cotter pin, locknut, adjusting nut, flat washer, and outer bearing cone and roller assembly (Fig. 10). Pull the wheel, hub, and drum assembly off the spindle. Use the special tool to remove the grease retainer. Discard it. Clean the bearing cups and inspect them (see Fig. 2). If cups are worn or damaged, remove them. Install new cups with special tools after cleaning all lubricant from inside the hub.

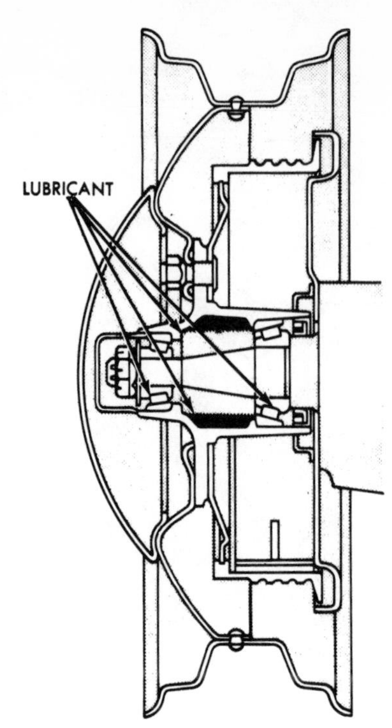

Figure 11 Front-wheel-bearing lubrication. *(Ford Motor Company.)*

Thoroughly clean and inspect the rollers (Fig. 2), handling the bearings as detailed in ■ 6-6-1, item 4. Brush all loose dirt from the brake assembly. Clean the spindle. Pack the inside of the hub with the specified wheel grease. Do not overlubricate. Add grease until it is flush with the inside diameters of the bearing cups (Fig. 11).

Pack the bearings with the specified grease, using a bearing packer. Grease the cone surfaces. Install a new grease retainer. Then install other parts and adjust the bearings as previously noted.

c. *Adjustment (Disk Brakes)* Disk-brake adjustment is similar to that of drum brakes with these exceptions. Loosen the adjusting nut 3 turns (not ½ turn). Rock the wheel and rotor assembly several times to push the shoes and linings away from the rotor. Then tighten the adjusting nut while rotating the wheel. Finish the adjustment as previously explained. Before driving the car, pump the brake pedal several times to restore braking.

d. *Bearing Service (Disk Brakes)* Disk-brake service is similar to that of drum brakes except that the caliper must be detached and wired up out of the way. On reassembly, after lubrication and bearing adjustment, install the caliper to the anchor plate. Finally, pump the brake pedal several times before driving the car to restore braking.

2. STABILIZER-BAR ATTACHMENTS The stabilizer bar is attached at its two ends to the lower suspension arms through bushings (see view *X* in Fig. 9). It is attached at two points to the frame through insulators. Bushings can be replaced by removing the attaching nut and bolt. Note carefully the relationship of washers, insulators, and spacers so all parts can be returned in their correct positions. Use a new nut and bolt.

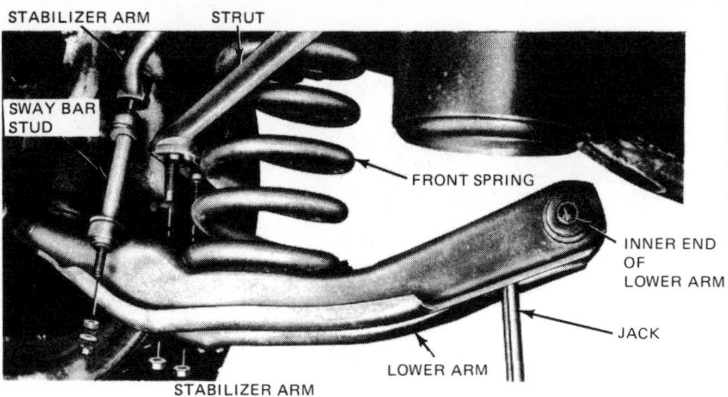

Figure 12 Removing or installing a front spring. *(Ford Motor Company.)*

To replace insulators, remove the stabilizer bar from the car. Coat the ends of the bar with Ruglyde or similar lubricant and slide the new insulators into place. Use new bolts to attach the ends of the bar to the suspension arms. Attach the insulators to the frame.

3. LOWER-ARM-STRUT BUSHING See Fig. 9. The strut must be removed from the car to replace the bushing. After reinstalling the strut, check caster, camber, and toe-in.

4. FRONT-SPRING REMOVAL AND REPLACEMENT With the car on a hoist, disconnect the lower end of the shock absorber from the suspension arm. You may need a pry bar to free the shock absorber from the arm. (On some models—Pinto and Mustang—you must remove the shock absorber.) Put a jack under the lower arm. Remove the bolts attaching the strut and stabilizer bar to the control arm (Fig. 12). Disconnect the inner end of the lower arm from the frame. Then slowly and carefully lower the jack to relieve the spring pressure (Fig. 12). You may need to use a pry bar to free the spring.

To replace the spring, tape the insulator to the spring and position the spring on the lower arm. The end of the spring must be no more than ½ inch (12.7mm) from the end of the depression in the arm. Raise the lower arm carefully to compress the spring and attach the inner end to the frame with nut and bolt. Reattach the shock absorber, strut, and stabilizer bar to the lower control arm. Then remove the jack and lower the car.

5. LOWER-SUSPENSION-ARM REMOVAL AND REPLACEMENT Raise the front of the car and support it with safety stands under both sides of the frame just behind the lower arms. Remove the wheel-and-tire assembly, caliper and brake hose, and hub-and-rotor assembly. Disconnect the lower end of the shock absorber and push it up out of the way. Disconnect the stabilizer bar and strut. Remove the cotter pins from the ball joints. Loosen the lower ball-joint-stud nut 1 or 2 turns. Install the special tool between the upper and lower ball-joint studs (Fig. 5). Make sure the tool is seated on the studs and not on the nuts. Turn the adapter screw to place the stud under pressure. Tap the spindle near the lower stud with a hammer to loosen the stud in the spindle. Do not loosen the stud with tool pressure (Fig. 13). Remove the stud nut, then lower the arm, as shown, and detach it from the frame.

To install the arm, loosely attach it to the spindle. Do not tighten the stud nut. Position the spring and insulator to the upper spring pad and lower arm. Use a floor jack and raise the control arm to align with the frame connection for the inner end of the arm. Attach the arm with through-bolt and nut. Remove the jack. Tighten the ball-joint attaching nut to specifications. Secure with the cotter pin. Attach the shock absorber, strut, and stabilizer bar. Install the hub and rotor, caliper, and wheel and tire. Then adjust wheel bearing. Install the grease cap and wheel cover. If necessary, check caster, camber, and toe-in.

6. UPPER-ARM REMOVAL AND REPLACEMENT Raise the car and support it with jack stands under both sides of the frame just in back of the lower arm. Remove the wheel cover, wheel and tire, and cotter pin from the upper ball-joint-stud nut. Loosen the nut 1 or 2 turns. Use the special tool as shown in Fig. 5 to loosen the upper ball-joint stud from the spindle. Do not loosen the stud by tool pressure alone. Tap the spindle

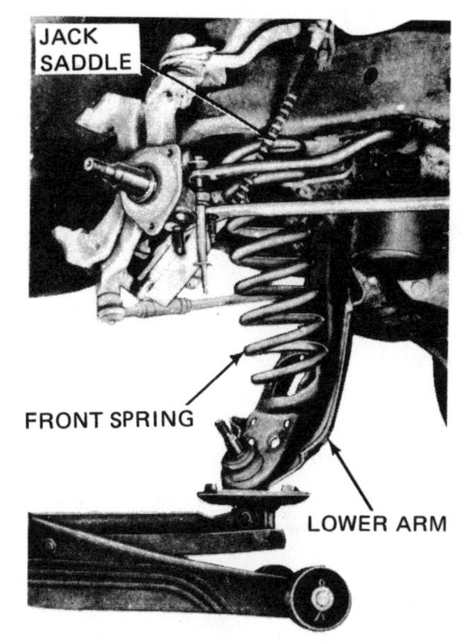

Figure 13 Removing the coil spring so that the lower control arm can be removed. *(Ford Motor Company.)*

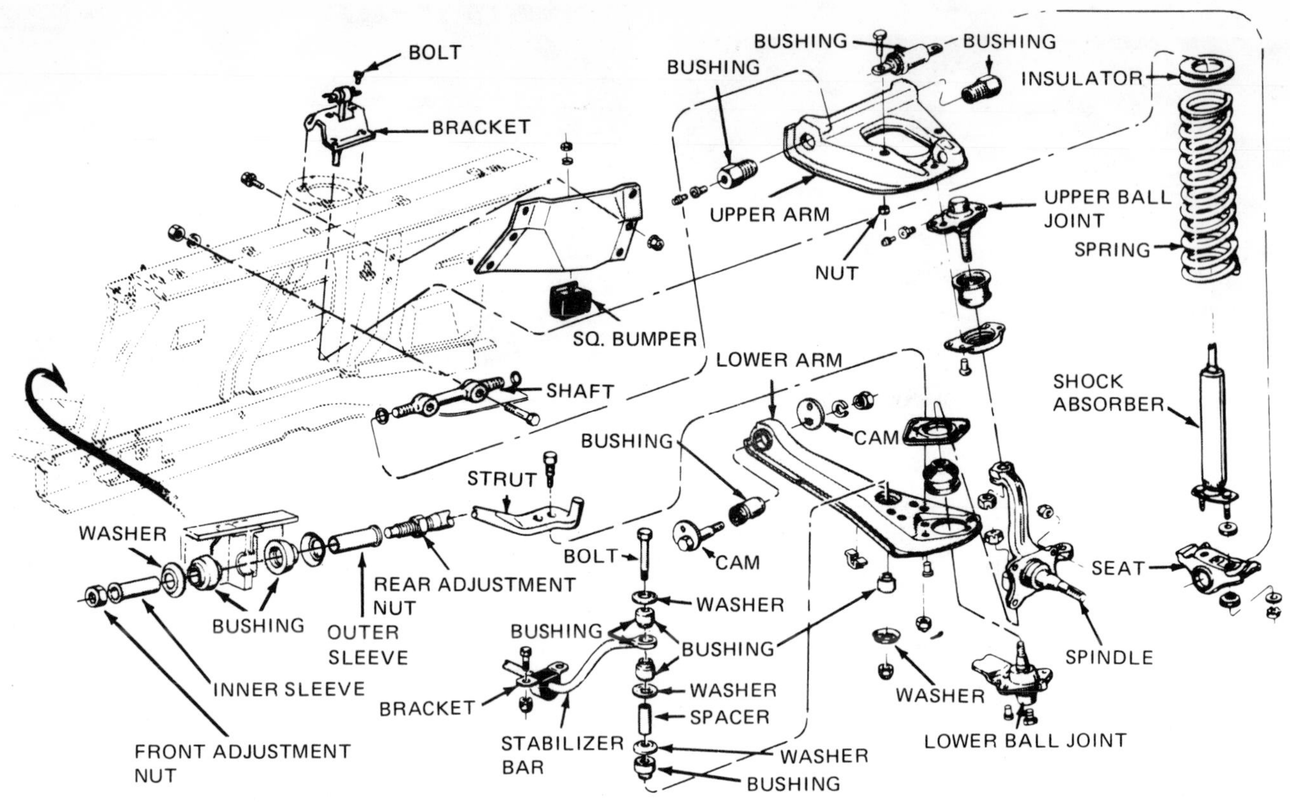

Figure 14 Disassembled view of a front-suspension system which has the spring above the upper control arm. *(Ford Motor Company.)*

near the stud with a hammer while the stud is under pressure from the tool. Put a floor jack under the lower arm and raise it to relieve the pressure from the upper ball joint. Remove the nut, then remove the attaching bolts of the upper arm inner shaft. Now take off the arm as an assembly.

To replace the arm, attach the inner end to the frame bracket and the ball-joint stud at the outer end to the spindle. Tighten the nut to specifications. Tighten further to align the cotter-pin-hole in the stud with the nut slots. Install the cotter pin. Then install the wheel and tire and adjust the wheel bearings. Install the wheel cover. Remove the jack stands and lower the car. Adjust caster, camber, and toe-in.

7. SHOCK ABSORBER Remove the shock absorber through the lower suspension arm after removing the attaching nuts and screws. Install it with the new nuts and screws supplied with the replacement shock-absorber kit.

8. UPPER-ARM BUSHING SERVICE If the bushings require replacement, remove the nuts and washers from both ends of the upper-arm shaft. Then use a special tool to press the bushings out. Force the lower bushing out by putting pressure on the tool from above with an arbor press. Then install the new bushings with a special tool.

■ 6-6-4 Ford Front Suspension Service—Spring above Upper Arm

An upper or lower suspension arm must be installed as a unit. Replace the stabilizer bar bushings and insulators, and the strut-rod bushing, as for the suspension system with the spring between the arms (■ 6-6-3). Figure 14 shows the assembly in exploded view.

1. UPPER-ARM BUSHING SERVICE Remove the shock absorber. Raise and support the car on jack stands. Remove the wheel cover, grease cap, cotter pin, locknut, adjusting nut, and outer bearing from the hub. Pull the wheel, tire, hub, and drum from the spindle. On disk brakes, detach the caliper before removing the disk assembly.

Compress the spring with the special tool (Fig. 15). Remove the two upper-arm-to-spring-tower attaching nuts and swing the upper arm out. Rotate the shaft and remove the studs by tapping them out with a soft mallet. Unscrew the bushings from the shaft and suspension arm. Remove the shaft.

To replace the bushings, position the shaft, grease the new bushings and O rings, and install the bushings loosely on the shaft and arm. Turn the bushings in so the shaft is exactly centered. Make a spacer of 3/4-inch pipe 8 1/16 inches long and position it parallel to the shaft. If it will not fit, the arm is distorted and must be discarded.

With the spacer positioned, torque the bushings to specifications. Make sure the arm can move on the shaft. Then remove the spacer. Attach the upper suspension arm to the underbody. Release the spring. Install the parts removed and adjust the wheel bearing. Lower the vehicle, install the shock absorber, and adjust caster, camber, and toe-in.

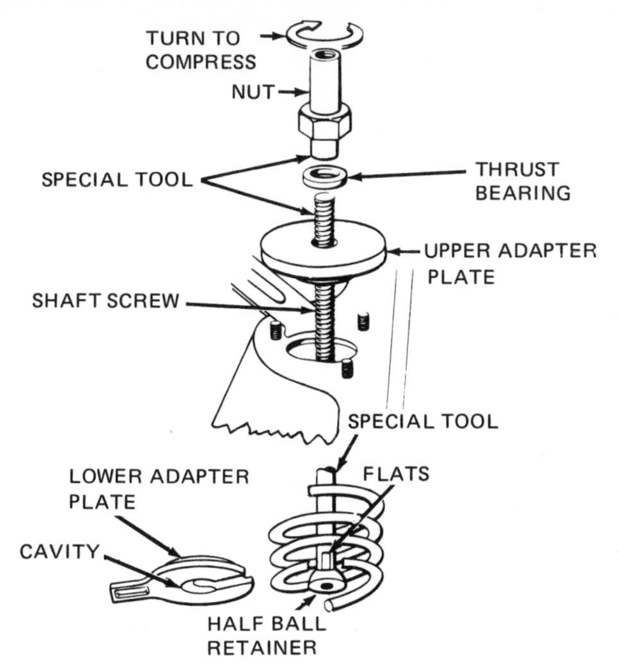

Figure 15 Spring-compressor tool and installation method. *(Ford Motor Company.)*

2. FRONT SPRING REMOVAL AND REPLACEMENT Proceed as for replacement of upper-arm bushings, detailed above, to get the upper arm out of the way. Then replace the spring-compressor tool and remove the spring. Installation is the reverse of removal.

3. LOWER-ARM REMOVAL AND REPLACEMENT With the car raised and supported on car stands, remove the wheel and tire. Disconnect the stabilizer bar and strut. Remove the cotter pin from the nut on the lower ball-joint stud and loosen the nut 1 or 2 turns. Use the ball-joint-stud loosening tool (Fig. 5) to put pressure on the lower stud. Tap the spindle to loosen the stud from the spindle. Remove the nut from the stud and lower the arm. Detach the arm from the underbody by removing the cam bolt, nut, and washer.

To install the arm, reattach the arm to the underbody and spindle.

4. UPPER-ARM REMOVAL AND REPLACEMENT With the car raised and supported on car stands, remove the wheel and tire. Remove the shock-absorber-attaching nuts and lift the shock absorber out. On eight-cylinder cars, remove the air cleaner. Install the compressor tool and compress the spring (Fig. 15). Disconnect the upper-ball-joint stud from the spindle using the special tool (Fig. 5) and a hammer as already explained. Now detach the upper-arm-shaft nuts and remove the arm.

Installation is just the reverse of removal. Use the specified keystone-type lock washers to attach the shaft-bolt nuts.

5. FRONT-WHEEL SPINDLE REMOVAL AND REPLACEMENT Removal and replacement procedures vary a little because of the different steps required for drum and disk brakes. Basically, the procedure is to detach the wheel-and-tire assembly

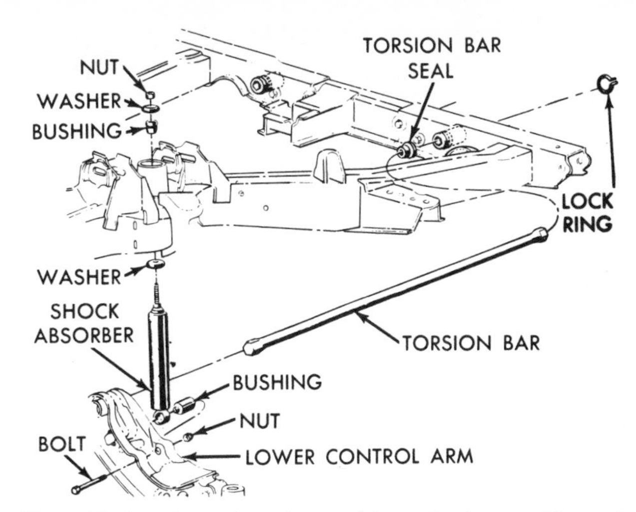

Figure 16 Location and attachment of the torsion bar on a Plymouth. *(Chrysler Corporation.)*

and the brake assembly from the spindle and move them out of the way. Then loosen the upper and lower ball-joint studs with the special tool (Fig. 5) and a hammer. With the studs detached from the spindle, the spindle is free for removal. Installation is the reverse of removal.

■ 6-6-5 Plymouth Front-Suspension Service

The Plymouth front-suspension system uses torsion bars (Fig. 16) instead of coil springs. Service operations include height adjustment, torsion-bar replacement, upper- and lower-control-arm replacement, and ball-joint and sway-bar replacement.

1. HEIGHT ADJUSTMENT With the vehicle on a level floor, the tires at the proper pressure, a full tank of gas, and no passengers, jounce the car a few times to settle the suspension.

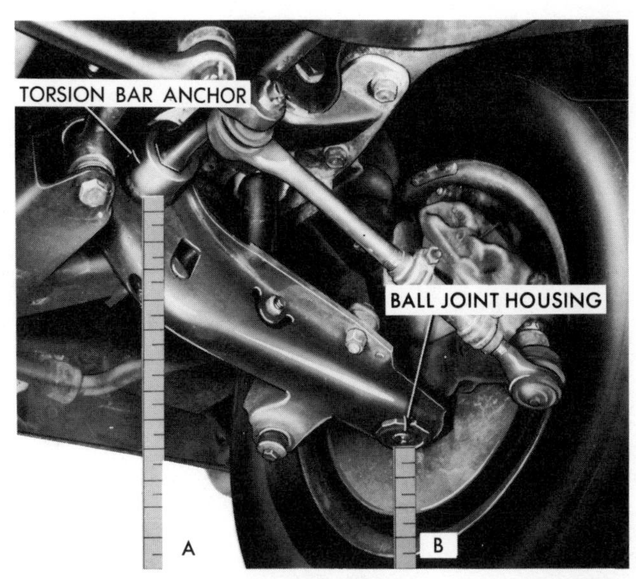

Figure 17 Measuring front-suspension height. *(Chrysler Corporation.)*

Release the car on the downward motion.

Measure the distance between the adjustment blade to the floor and the lowest point of the steering knuckle to the floor(*A* and *B* in Fig. 17). The difference varies with different models, but a typical Plymouth specification is 1⅝ to 1⅞ inches (41.28 to 47.63 mm). Also, the difference between the two sides of the car should be not more than ⅛ inch (3.17 mm). To correct, turn the torsion-bar adjustment bolt. After each adjustment, jounce the car before rechecking the measurement.

2. TORSION-BAR REPLACEMENT The torsion bars are not interchangeable between left and right. They are marked either right or left by an R or L stamped on one end of the bar. To remove a torsion bar, raise the front of the car. If you use a hoist, it should be on the body so that the front suspension is under no load. If you use jacks, you must place a support under the frame cross member first to avoid damaging the cross member.

Release the load from the torsion bar (Fig. 16) by backing off the adjustment bolt. Remove the lock ring from the rear end of the torsion bar. Attach the special striking tool to the torsion bar and knock the bar loose. Then remove the tool, slide the rear-anchor balloon seal off the anchor, and slide the bar out through the rear of the anchor. Try not to damage the balloon seal.

Check the torsion bar for scratches or nicks. Dress them down and paint the repaired area with rustproof paint. Check the bar attachments (anchors) and replace any damaged parts. Clean all parts.

Install the torsion bar by sliding it forward through the rear anchor. Slip the balloon seal over the front of the torsion bar (cupped end toward the rear). Coat both ends of the bar with special lubricant and slide the bar forward so that the hex head enters the opening in the lower control arm. Install the lock ring at the rear. Pack the annular opening in the rear anchor completely full of multipurpose grease. Position the balloon seal on the rear anchor so that the lip engages in the groove of the anchor. Tighten the adjustment bolt to place a load on the torsion bar. Lower the vehicle to the floor and adjust its height (item 1, above). Replace the upper bumper.

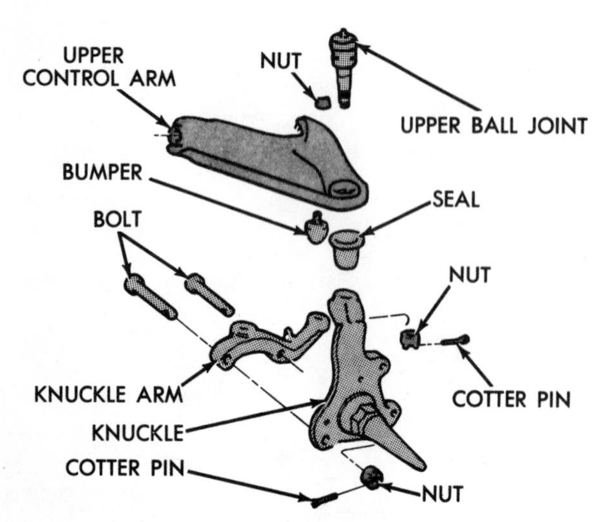

Figure 18 Steering knuckle and upper control arm on car lines P, D, C, and Y. *(Chrysler Corporation.)*

3. STEERING-KNUCKLE REMOVAL Figure 18 shows, in disassembled view, a typical arrangement. To replace a steering knuckle, turn the ignition switch to OFF or UNLOCKED. Remove the rebound bumper. Raise the vehicle to remove all load from the front suspension. Place jack stands under the frame. Remove the wheel cover, wheel, and tire assembly.On cars with disk brakes, remove the brake caliper and support it with a piece of wire so it does not hang from the brake hose. Remove the hub and disk or drum assembly and brake splash shield. Remove all load from the torsion bar by backing off the adjusting bolt.

Remove the upper ball joint from the steering knuckle by removing the cotter pin and nut from the upper ball joint. Force out the ball joint with the special tool (Fig. 19). Remove the bolts attaching the steering arm to the steering knuckle. Take the steering knuckle off. Note that the lower ball joint is in the steering arm.

4. STEERING-KNUCKLE REPLACEMENT Attach the steering knuckle to the steering arm. Then install the upper ball-joint stud in the steering knuckle and secure with the nut properly tightened. Install the cotter pin. Put the load on the torsion bar by turning the adjusting bolt. Replace parts removed (splash shield, hub and disk or drum, and caliper if so equipped). Adjust wheel bearings. Install the wheel and cover. Then lower the car to the floor. Install the rebound bumper. Adjust front-suspension height and wheel alignment.

5. STEERING-KNUCKLE-ARM REMOVAL Turn the ignition switch to OFF or UNLOCKED. Remove the rebound bumper. Raise the vehicle so that the front suspension is unloaded. Put jack stands under the frame. Remove the wheel cover, wheel, and tire. Remove the brake caliper (where present) and hang it by a wire to prevent damage to the brake hose. Remove the hub and brake disk or drum assembly. Remove the brake splash shield. Unload the torsion bar. Disconnect the tie rod from the steering-knuckle arm by removing the cotter pin and nut. Remove the lower ball-joint stud from the knuckle arm (Fig. 19) and detach the arm from the knuckle.

6. STEERING-KNUCKLE-ARM REPLACEMENT Install the ball-joint stud and attach it with nut and cotter pin. Attach the tie rod. Load the torsion bar. Install the brake splash shield, hub, and brake disk or drum assembly. Install the caliper (if present). Adjust wheel bearings, install the wheel and cover, then lower the car. Install the rebound bumper and adjust height and alignment.

7. LOWER-CONTROL-ARM AND SHAFT REMOVAL With ignition switch at OFF or UNLOCKED and car supported as previously explained, remove the rebound bumper, wheel cover, wheel, brake caliper, hub-and-rotor assembly (or brake drum), and splash shield.

Disconnect the lower end of the shock absorber. Disconnect the strut and sway (stabilizer) bar. On some models, the strut is removed with the control arm as an assembly. Also, on some

Figure 19 Using the special tool to loosen the ball-joint stud. *(Chrysler Corporation.)*

models, the automatic-transmission gearshift torque-shaft assembly must be removed. Measure the depth of the torsion-bar anchor bolt in the lower control arm, then unwind the torsion bar. Remove the torsion bar as explained above.

Separate the lower ball joint from the knuckle arm (Fig. 19). Remove the nut from the lower control-arm shaft and push the shaft out of the frame cross member. Tap the threaded end of the shaft with a soft hammer if necessary to loosen it. Remove the lower control arm and shaft as an assembly. If the shaft bushing is worn, replace it.

8. LOWER-CONTROL-ARM AND SHAFT REPLACEMENT Position the lower control arm with the shaft in the frame cross member. Install and tighten the nut finger-tight. Attach the lower ball-joint stud to the knuckle arm with the nut properly tightened. Install the torsion bar and load it by returning the adjusting bolt to its original position. Replace the transmission torque shaft if it was removed. Reattach the strut and sway bar. Reinstall other parts that were removed. Adjust the wheel bearing and check height and front alignment.

9. LOWER-BALL-JOINT REMOVAL Figure 20 shows the procedure of measuring the lower-ball-joint axial travel. With the weight of the car on the lower control arm, as shown, raise and lower the wheel with a pry bar under the center of the tire. The removal of the ball joint requires all the preliminary steps already outlined up to the point of installing the removal tool (Fig. 19) with the cotter pins and nuts removed from both the upper- and lower-ball-joint studs. The removal tool now will rest on the lower stud. Tighten the tool enough to put pressure on the stud, but do not try to remove the ball joint by pressure alone. Strike the knuckle arm with a hammer to loosen the ball joint stud. The ball joint can then be pressed out of the lower control arm with a special tool (Fig. 20).

10. LOWER-BALL-JOINT REPLACEMENT Press the new ball joint in the lower control arm with the special tool (Fig. 20). Install a new seal over the ball joint, if necessary, using the special tool which is essentially a collar of the proper size. Insert the stud into the hole in the knuckle arm. Install the retainer nut and tighten as specified. Secure with the cotter pin. Lubricate the new ball joint (■6-5-1). Load the torsion bar and install the parts you removed. Lower the vehicle to floor and adjust height and front alignment as needed.

11. UPPER-CONTROL-ARM AND BALL-JOINT REMOVAL To remove the upper control arm, position ignition switch at OFF or UNLOCKED. Raise the front of the car with a jack and remove the wheel cover and wheel. Position a short stand under the lower control arm near the splash shield, and lower the jack. Make sure the stand does not touch the shield and that the rebound bumpers are under no load. Remove the cotter pin and nut from both ball joints. Slide the special tool in place with the lower end resting on the steering-knuckle arm and the upper end on the upper ball-joint stud. Then strike the steering knuckle with a hammer to loosen the stud. Do not loosen the stud with tool pressure alone.

Remove the tool and disengage the ball joint from the steering knuckle. Remove the rubber engine splash shield and pivot-shaft-bolt nuts or bolts. Lift the upper control arm with the ball joint and pivot bar as an assembly from the bracket. Remove the pivot bar nuts, retainers, and bushings. Install new bushings if the old ones are worn. Unscrew the ball joint from the upper arm with the special tool.

12. UPPER-CONTROL-ARM AND BALL-JOINT REPLACEMENT Install the new ball joint with the special tool.

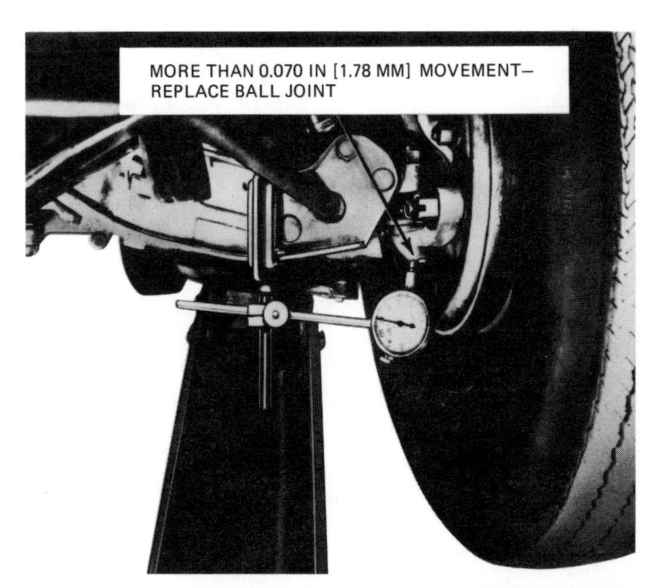

Figure 20 Measuring lower-ball-joint axial travel. *(Chrysler Corporation.)*

The ball joint will cut threads into a new arm. Install new bushings into the control arm. Press the old bushings out from inside out. Press new bushings from outside in until the tapered part seats on the arm. Install new ball-joint seal with the special collar tool. Put the control arm in the support bracket and install cams, cam bolts, lock washers, and nuts. Position the stud in the steering knuckle and install the nut. Tighten the end nut and install the cotter pin. Lubricate the ball joint (■ 6-5-1). Reinstall nut and cotter pin on the lower ball-joint stud. Install the wheel and wheel cover. Lower the vehicle and adjust height and front-wheel alignment.

13. SHOCK ABSORBERS The front shock absorbers can be taken out by removing the upper nut and washer (accessible from the engine compartment). Then raise the front end of the car and remove the pivot bolt and nut from the lower shock-absorber eye. Compress the shock absorber to take it off the vehicle. Install new upper and lower bushings if necessary. A special tool is required to press out the lower bushing and install a new one. Replace the shock absorber by attaching the two ends with the pivot bolt and nuts and washers.

14. FRONT-WHEEL BEARINGS The front-wheel bearings are very similar to those in Ford cars, shown in Fig. 10. They are checked, removed, cleaned, replaced, and adjusted in a similar manner.

SECTION 6-7 Rear-Suspension Service

This section discusses typical rear-suspension servicing procedures, with emphasis on Chevrolet, Ford, and Plymouth. These procedures are illustrative only. When you are working on a specific vehicle model, refer to the shop manual that applies.

■ **6-7-1 Rear-Suspension Service** Generally, rear suspensions require no special service. If parts are worn or broken, they must be replaced. Subsections that follow describe specific replacement procedures for Chevrolet, Ford, and Plymouth cars; these are typical for all cars. Possibly the parts that most often require replacement are the rubber grommets in spring eyes, control arms, and track bars. In addition, cars using independent rear suspensions, such as the Corvette (Fig. 8 in Part 6, Sec. 2), require periodic rear-end alignment as explained in ■ 6-8-13.

■ **6-7-2 Chevrolet Rear-Suspension Service** Chevrolet models use two general types of rear suspension: coil and leaf. See Figs. 3 and 5 in Part 6, Sec. 1.

1. COIL-SPRING REPLACEMENT Raise the rear of the car with a hoist under the axle housing, and put jack stands under the frame. Remove both rear wheels. Disconnect the lower ends of the shock absorbers. Loosen the upper-control-arm pivot bolt and both the left and right-lower-control-arm rear attachments (loosen only, do not disconnect).

Remove the rear-suspension tie rod from the stud on the axle housing. At the lower seat of both rear coil springs, slightly loosen the nut on the retaining bolt.

> **NOTE:** Do not remove nuts!

Slowly lower the hoist so as to allow the axle housing to swing down. Springs and insulators can now be removed by removing the lower seat-attaching parts.

To replace, position the springs and upper insulators in the upper seats. Install the lower seat parts on the control arm, and tighten the nuts finger-tight.

> **NOTE:** Omit lock washers so sufficient bolt thread will be available to start the nuts.

Alternately raise the axle slightly and resnug the bolt until the vehicle is fully supported on the hoist. Then, torque the nuts to specifications. Reconnect the shock absorbers, torque

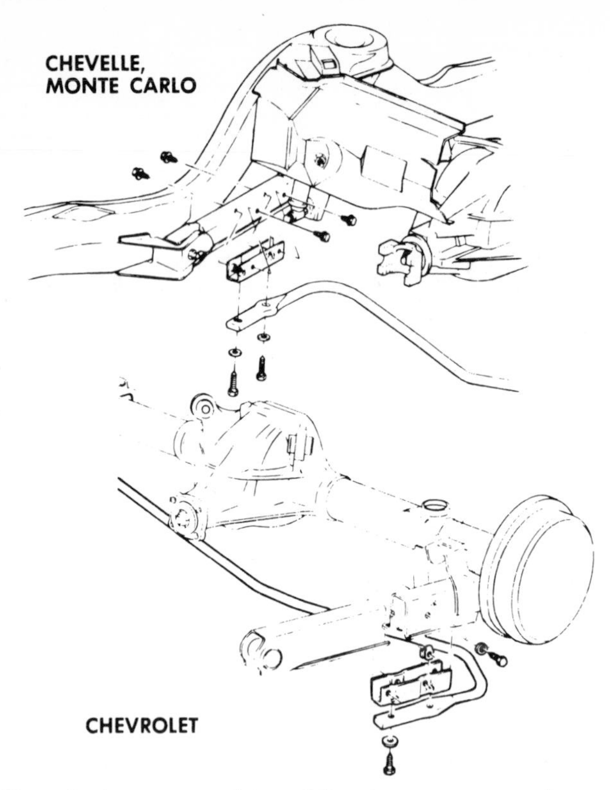

Figure 1 Arrangement of the stabilizer bar on rear-suspension system. *(Chevrolet Motor Division of General Motors Corporation.)*

the upper- and lower-control-arm attachments, and reconnect the axle tie rod.

Finally, install the lock washers by removing the nuts (one at a time), putting the lock washers on, and torquing the nuts to specifications. Install the rear wheels and lower the car to the floor. Check riding height between the top of the axle tube and the frame.

2. LEAF-SPRING REPLACEMENT (See Fig. 6 in Part 6, Sec. 2.) Raise the rear of the car so the axle assembly hangs free. Then support the car at both frame side rails near the front eye of the spring. Lift the axle housing so all tension is removed from the spring. Detach the lower end of the shock absorber.

Loosen the spring-eye-to-bracket retaining bolt and remove the screws attaching the bracket to the underbody of the car. Lower the axle assembly enough to allow you to remove the bracket from the spring.

Pry the parking-brake cable from the retainer bracket mounted on the spring plate. Remove the nuts from under the car that attach the spring to the axle housing.

Support the spring and remove the lower bolt from the spring rear shackle. Now, the spring can be removed from the car.

If a spring leaf requires replacement, both it and any damaged spring-leaf insert can be replaced by removing the center-bolt nut.

To install the leaf spring, loosely attach the bracket to the spring eye. Put the spring in place and attach the rear of the spring to the shackle. Then loosely attach the front bracket to the underbody. Loosely attach the spring to the mounting pad on the axle housing.

NOTE: Be sure all insulators and cushions are in place.

Attach the parking-brake cable. Remove the jack stands and lower the car to the floor. Torque all parts to specifications.

3. SHOCK-ABSORBER REPLACEMENT Refer to Figs. 3 and 5 in Part 6, Sec. 1, which show typical mounting arrangements. When removing a shock absorber, make sure that the stud on the shock absorber is prevented from turning when the nut is loosened. The hex on the thread end of the stud will enable you to hold the stud stationary when the nut is loosened or tightened. If the stud turns, it will damage the rubber grommet in which the stud is mounted.

4. CONTROL ARM Figures 5 in Sec. 1 and 5 and 6 in Sec. 2, all in Part 6, show the control-arm attaching points. Note that the rear axle must be supported in such a way as to prevent the housing from rotating when the control arm is detached.

5. STABILIZER BAR Figure 1 shows the stabilizer bar attaching points. Removing and replacing the bar is a simple job. To provide sufficient working space, raise the car on a hoist.

6. CORVETTE REAR SUSPENSION The Corvette rear suspension is independent with a transverse leaf spring (Fig. 8 in Part 6, Sec. 2). There is nothing very complicated about removing and replacing the parts in it. However, the rear wheels must be checked for alignment. Camber and toe-in can be adjusted (Part 6, Sec. 8).

■ 6-7-3 Ford Rear-Suspension Service Ford has two general types of rear-suspension systems: coil and leaf-spring. The procedures for replacing shock absorbers, springs, control arms, tracking bars, and other parts are very similar to those on the Chevrolet cars, discussed in ■6-7-2. Special points to watch include:

1. In some models, it is necessary to remove an access cover in the luggage compartment to get at the shock-absorber upper attaching nut.

2. The rear-suspension lower arms on the coil-spring suspension are not interchangeable. The lower arm on the left side is identified by the notches in the bushing flange.

3. One check that can be made on the leaf-spring suspension pertains to tracking. This determines whether the rear wheels are following, or tracking, properly. To make the check, drive straight ahead on pavement, part of which is wet, and stop about 10 feet (3.05 m) beyond the wet area. Check the wet tracks of the tires. Rear-wheel tracks should be an equal distance inside the front tracks (Fig. 2). If they are not, the spring tie-bolt head possibly is not centered in the locating hole on the spring mounting pad of the axle housing. This may be checked by measuring *A* in Fig. 3 at both springs. The measurement is taken from the locating hole in the side frame member and the forward edge of the axle housing. If the measurements differ more than 1/8 inch (3.17 mm), it will be necessary to reposition the tie bolt, as follows.

Loosen the four spring-clip nuts and use a jack to push the axle housing into position. Then move the spring clip into line and tighten the clip nuts to the specified torque. If this does not correct the tracking, consider the possibility that the frame may be out of line because of a collision.

The dimension *B* in Fig. 3 is a measurement to be taken to determine whether the front hanger should be replaced. If this dimension is not correct, cut off the old hanger with a cutting torch and weld a new hanger to the frame. (Some hangers are attached with nuts and bolts.)

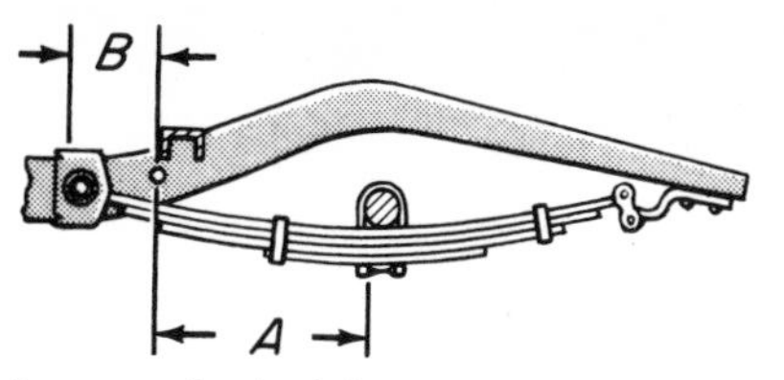

Figure 3 Alignment check of the rear suspension. *A* should be the same [or within 1/8 inch (3.18 mm)] at both springs. *(Ford Motor Company.)*

■ 6-7-4 Plymouth Rear-Suspension Service

Following paragraphs describe the various service operations on this suspension system.

1. MEASURING SPRING HEIGHT Jounce the car several times, first at the front and then at the back, releasing the bumpers at the same point in each cycle. Locate the highest point on the underside of the rear-axle bumper strap (at the rear of the bumper), and measure from here to the top of the axle housing. Take measurements on both sides. If the distance is more than 3/4 inch (19 mm), one of the rear springs needs replacement.

2. REAR-SPRING REMOVAL Disconnect the rear shock absorbers at the lower mounting studs. Raise the vehicle at the lifting points so that the rear springs hang free. Use a jack to support the axle housing in this position. Remove the nuts that attach the spring front hanger to the frame. Remove the U-bolt nuts and the spring plate. Remove the rear hanger bolts and take the spring off the car. Take out the front pivot bolt to remove the front hanger from the spring. Remove the rear shackle and bushings from the spring.

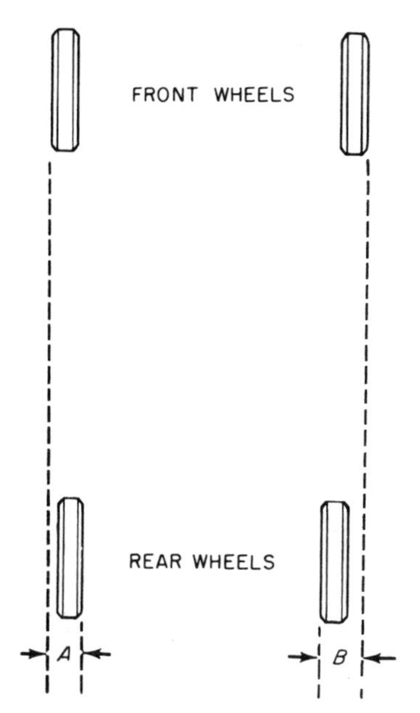

Figure 2 Alignment check of the rear suspension. *A* should equal *B*. *(Ford Motor Company.)*

3. REAR-SPRING INSTALLATION If the front-pivot-bolt bushing needs replacement in the spring, use a special tool to remove the old bushing and install a new one.

Attach the front hanger with the front pivot bolt and run on the nut, but do not tighten it. Assemble the rear shackle and bushings. Do not lubricate the rubber bushings. Start the shackle-bolts nuts, but do not tighten them.

Now, put the spring in place on the car and attach the hangers to the car frame, tightening the bolts and nuts to the proper tension. Remove the axle support and put the center hole of the axle-spring seat over the head of the spring center bolt. Put the spring plate under the spring and install the U bolts, tightening the nuts to the specified tension. Lower the vehicle and reconnect the shock absorbers.

Jounce the car several times and recheck the spring height. Tighten the front pivot bolt and the shackle nuts to the proper tension.

4. REAR-SPRING FRONT-PIVOT-BUSHING REPLACEMENT This bushing may be replaced without removing the spring from the car. The vehicle should be raised just enough so that the spring is relaxed and the rear wheels are just touching the floor. Never allow the weight of the rear axle to be suspended on the fully extended shock absorbers. This could damage them. Now the front hanger can be detached from the car frame and taken off the spring so that the new bushing can be installed. A special tool is needed to remove the old and install the new bushing.

5. INTERLAYS Zinc interleaves are used between the spring leaves to reduce corrosion and improve spring life. To replace the interleaves, the spring must be removed from the car and disassembled.

SECTION 6-8 Front-End Alignment

This section discusses the various procedures required to check and adjust front-end alignment. It explains how caster, camber, toe-in, toe-out on turns, and steering-axis inclination are checked. It also explains how to adjust caster, camber, and toe-in, where possible. On some cars, caster and camber are preset at the factory and no adjustment is possible. The section also discusses the preliminary checks and adjustments that precede a front-end alignment job. In addition, it tells how to adjust the rear-wheel alignment of independent rear-suspension systems.

■ **6-8-1 Front-Wheel Alignment** Numerous devices have been used to check front-wheel alignment, varying from lines marked on the floor to complete wheel-alignment machines using light beams and electronic meters. Different alignment-checking devices vary in complexity and construction, but they all check the same fundamental factors on the front end of the car.

Several interrelated factors besides wheel alignment influence steering control. Before caster, camber, toe-in, toe-out on turns, and steering-axis (or kingpin) inclination are checked, these other factors should be investigated. They include tire pressure, wheel-bearing condition, wheel balance, wheel runout, shock-absorber action, frame alignment, and steering-knuckle and ball-joint condition. If any of these factors is off, the wheel-alignment checks and adjustments will mean little; they may actually make conditions worse. Even though you adjusted caster and camber exactly to specifications in a car with loose wheel bearings or worn ball joints, it would mean little. As soon as the car went out on the road, the looseness or wear would probably throw the adjustments off.

■ **6-8-2 Preliminary Checks** The first step in wheel alignment is to make sure that all tires are inflated to the proper air pressure. Next, jack up the front end of the car. Check the tie rods and linkages for looseness and the ball joints or kingpin and wheel bearings for wear and adjustment. (See ■ 6-4-2.) Correct wheel alignment cannot be maintained if steering-system parts are worn or out of adjustment. A worn wheel bearing can often be detected by spinning the wheel and placing a finger on the car bumper. If the wheel bearing is worn, a slight vibration or grinding may be felt as the wheel is spun. Front-wheel-bearing adjustment is described in ■ 6-6-1, item 3, and ■ 6-6-3, item 1.

Wobble, or runout, of the tire should be checked to determine whether the tire wobbles sideways (has lateral runout) or whether it is out of round (has radial runout). Spin the wheel and slowly bring a piece of chalk to the sidewall of the tire. If the tire is wobbling (or has lateral runout), the chalk mark will not be uniform around the sidewall. It will be wide where the side of the tire is out from the center, and will be narrow or miss where the side is in from the center.

Figure 1 Left, bubble type of static wheel balancer; right, tire and wheel on balancer in readiness for balance check. *(John Bean Division of FMC Corporation.)*

Out-of-roundness (radial runout) can be checked by spinning the tire slowly and bringing a pointer or piece of chalk toward the center of the tread until it touches. If it touches uniformly all around, the tire tread is centered. If the tread is off-center, or out of round (radial runout), the pointer will touch some places and miss others.

If wobble or out-of-roundness exceeds $\frac{1}{16}$ to $\frac{1}{4}$ inch (1.58 to 6.35 mm) (specifications vary), correction must be made.

To correct excessive tire runout, it may be necessary only to deflate the tire and work it around to another position on the rim. In some cases of excessive radial runout, it may be necessary to remove some of the rubber from the tread by the use of a special machine that trims off the excess. This trues the tread.

If the excess runout is due to a bent wheel rim, the rim must be replaced or straightened.

Wheel balance should be checked and corrected if necessary (see ■6-8-13). Condition of the shock absorbers should be checked ■6-4-12). Another factor that should be considered is alignment, or tracking. Tracking is the following of the rear wheels directly behind, or in the tracks of, the front wheels. Failure to track usually means that the frame or rear springs are out of alignment; this causes rapid tire wear and poor steering control. If tracking is bad, it can be readily detected by following the car on the highway and observing the tracks. A check of alignment, or tracking, is described in ■6-7-3, item 3, along with the procedure for realigning the rear leaf springs.

> **NOTE:** Never attempt to straighten any suspension part by heating or bending it. Either of these procedures could cause the part to fail later.

■ 6-8-3 Wheel Balance If a wheel-and-tire assembly is out of balance, the car will be hard to steer, riding will be rough, and tire wear will be rapid. Wheel balance can be checked in several ways.

Both front and rear wheels can be checked for balance, and balanced, either on or off the car, depending on the type of balancing equipment available. Fasten weights to the wheel rim to balance heavy spots in the tire or wheel.

> **NOTE:** Wheels with disk brakes are harder to spin on the car than wheels with drum brakes. The reason is that the disk-brake shoes are nearly in contact with the disk. Therefore, wheel spinners with greater power are required for wheels with disk brakes. The electric motor in earlier spinners was designed for wheels with drum brakes. Older spinners may burn out if they are used on wheels with disk brakes.

Wheels can be checked for balance in two ways, statically and dynamically. A wheel that is statically out of balance is heavier in one section than in another. When it is suspended on a spindle in a vertical plane (as on the car), it will rotate until the heaviest section is at the bottom. A dynamically out-of-balance wheel does not have an even distribution of weight in a plane vertical to the wheel axle. A wheel that is statically in balance can be dynamically out of balance. For example, a wheel with a heavy spot on one side can be balanced, statically, by a heavy spot 180° from it. When this wheel starts to rotate, it will try to wobble, or run out, because the heavy spots have a greater centrifugal force working on them.

■ 6-8-4 Wheel Balancing off the Car There are twc general types of off-the-car wheel balancers: one that balances statically only and one that balances both statically and dynamically.

1. STATIC BALANCER Figure 1 shows one type of static balancer. It has a bubble under a convex glass that will center under the crossmarks when the floating wheel support is balanced. To use the balancer, the wheel-and-tire assembly is placed on the support. Any lack of balance of the assembly will show up by causing the bubble to move off center. The amount and direction of displacement indicate how much and where weight must be added to the rim, as explained below.

> **NOTE:** This wheel balancer is less accurate than other types described below, particularly in the hands of inexperienced operators.

2. STATIC-AND-DYNAMIC BALANCER This balancer (Fig. 2) can be used to check both static and dynamic balance. As previously noted, a wheel that is statically balanced may be dynamically out of balance. Thus, many technicians prefer to check both items.

a. *Checking Static Balance* First, remove all weights and make sure that all stones have been removed from the tire tread. Then mount the wheel on the balancer in a vertical position and spin it. Allow it to come to rest. The heaviest part of the tire will come to rest at the bottom. Make a chalk mark at the top of the tire to indicate the point opposite the heaviest part.

Figure 2 Wheel balancer in operation. The balancer is spinning the wheel to check it for dynamic balance. A device in the balancer indicates where and how much the wheel is out of dynamic balance. *(Bear Manufacturing Company.)*

Static balance is corrected by placing weights on the wheel rim. Add sufficient weight at the chalk mark to balance the wheel. Balance is good if the wheel will not turn from any position at which it is stopped. If more than 2 ounces [56.70 g (grams)] is required, put the additional weight on the other side of the tire rim. If two 2-ounce (56.70 g) weights are not enough, increase both weights an equal amount.

NOTE: Tap the weights on lightly during the location tests so they can be removed or slid along the rim.

If you cannot achieve exact static balance with weights placed exactly opposite the heavy spot (at the chalk mark), then use two weights which total slightly more than the amount needed to achieve balance. Put one weight inside the wheel, the other one outside the wheel, both at the chalk mark. Then, move them slightly apart, equal amounts, and recheck static balance (Fig. 3). Repeat this until balance is achieved. Tap weights firmly into position.

b. *Dynamic Balance* To check balance, spin the wheel and read the indicating device in the wheel balancer to learn the place and approximate amount the wheel is dynamically out of balance. Balance is then achieved by putting additional weights on the indicated spots on the rim.

NOTE: Make sure all stones are removed from the tire tread before spinning the tire!

It may happen that a weight will be required for dynamic balance on a spot on a rim that is near a weight installed for static balance. For example, suppose a weight A is added (as shown in Fig. 4) to achieve static balance. For dynamic balance, another weight B is required on the other side of the rim, as shown. Adding the second weight throws the wheel out of static balance. But static balance can be restored by a weight at C (Fig. 4). The weight at C does not throw dynamic balance off, since it is on the same side as weight B. A better way to take care of the balance is to combine the effect of weights A and B. For example, if weight A is 4 ounces (113 g) and weight B is 2 ounces (57 g), approximately correct static and dynamic balance can be achieved by using only one weight, at B, of 2 ounces (57 g). In such a case, no weight would be needed at C. Other combining arrangements are possible. The reason they are desirable is that they keep the total amount of weight added to the rim to a minimum. The less weight added the better, so long as static and dynamic balance are achieved. In any event, no more than 8 ounces (227 g) should be added to a rim, according to authorities.

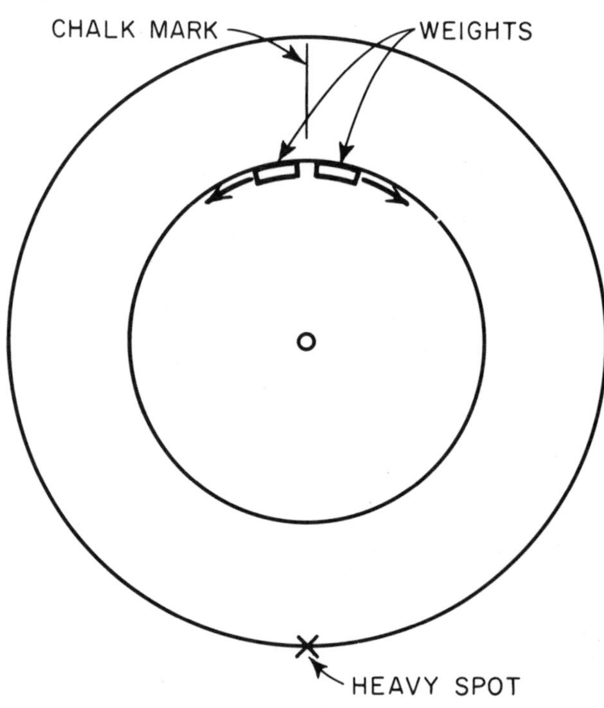

Figure 3 Using two weights—one on each side of wheel—to achieve static balance. Move the weights apart equal amounts until static balance is attained.

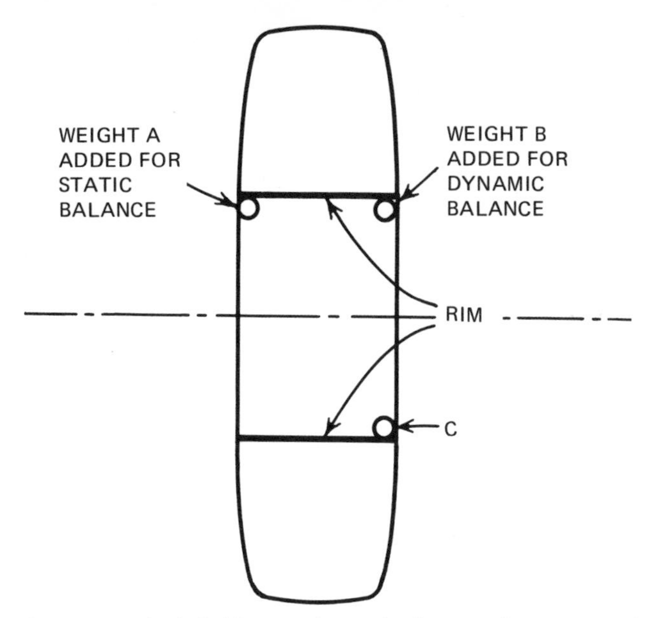

Figure 4 Method of adding weights to wheel rim to achieve static and dynamic balance.

> **NOTE:** After each readjustment of weights for dynamic balance, recheck the static balance, as previously explained.

■ **6-8-5 Wheel Balancing on the Car** A variety of dynamic wheel-balancing devices are available for checking wheel balance on the car. One type consists of a wheel spinner and a vibration indicator, or jiggler (Fig. 5). The wheel spinner contains an electric motor and a driving wheel which is held against the tire to cause the car wheel to spin. The jiggler is installed under the bumper or bumper bracket and adjusted so that the pointer is in a horizontal position. The pointer is connected through a lever to the vertical shaft so that a slight up-and-down motion of the shaft, due to car vibration, will cause the pointer to jiggle. The technician watches the pointer as the wheel spins to note how much it moves and thus how much out of balance the wheel is.

Instead of a jiggler, some systems use an electronic device

Figure 5 Checking the balance of the left front wheel on a car. *(Bear Manufacturing Company.)*

that sends out a signal with each movement of the suspension system. Both systems are discussed below.

NOTE: Some technicians merely open the car door nearest the wheel being checked and watch it while the wheel is spun. Door movement then takes the place of the jiggler or electronic device.

1. BALANCING FRONT WHEELS WITH JIGGLER The wheel is spun with the spinner. The technician runs it with increasing speed while watching the jiggler, as already noted. If jiggling is noticeable, a special adapter and detecting device are mounted on the wheel. First, remove all weights. Then install the adapter as shown in the wheel in Fig. 5.

NOTE: Adapters and installation procedures vary with different makes and models of balancers. Carefully follow the detailed instructions for the balancer you are using. Make sure the adapter is securely in place.

Put the balancer unit on the wheel adapter (Fig. 5), making sure it is securely in place. There are two knobs on the balancer shown. The outer knob is a weight control knob. It controls the amount of unbalanced weight that is added to the wheel. The inner knob is the position control knob. It controls the position around the wheel rim where the unbalanced weight is applied. Thus, with the wheel spinning, unbalanced weight can be added or subtracted, and moved around the rim, until the exact amount of weight, and its proper location to produce balance, can be determined. When the pointer on the vibration indicator is quiet, the wheel is in balance. Then, with the wheel stopped, the amount and position of the weight required are shown on the indicator scale of the balancer unit. Figure 5 shows the technician checking wheel balance.

2. BALANCING REAR WHEELS WITH JIGGLER To balance a rear wheel, the adapter, balancer, and jiggler are installed in the same manner as for a front wheel. However, for checking rear wheels, use the car engine to drive the wheels. The transmission should be in high, or drive. With the standard differential, only one wheel is raised from the floor at a time and balanced. Then, the other wheel is raised for the balance check, and the first wheel is lowered to the floor.

NOTE: Never exceed 35 mph (56 km/h) on the speedometer. This is equivalent to 70 mph (113 km/h) at the wheel owing to the differential action. Do the job fast. Never spin the wheel more than 2 minutes or you may damage the differential!

3. BALANCING REAR WHEELS WITH NO-SLIP DIFFERENTIAL On these wheels, a different procedure is required. Raise both wheels, remove one wheel-and-tire assembly, and then replace the wheel nuts to hold the brake drum in place. Reverse the nuts so the flat face contacts the brake drum. Do not use an impact wrench!

Then balance the wheel remaining on the car. Do not exceed 70 mph (113 km/h) on the speedometer! When the first wheel is balanced, reinstall the other wheel and balance it. The first wheel can be left in place because it has been balanced and will not disturb the balancing check of the second wheel.

NOTE: Never take longer than 2 minutes to balance drive wheels on the car.

4. BALANCING WITH ELECTRONIC DETECTOR Certain types of wheel balancers have an electronic-detector test for checking the dynamic balance of a wheel. The signal-pickup unit is placed under the car, as near the wheel as possible. The magnet is placed on a flat surface such as the underside of the lower control arm. This pickup will detect suspension movement caused by an out-of-balance condition in the wheel and tire. Every movement will cause the pickup to send out a signal. The signal will activate the strobe (stroboscopic light), which is a flasher that produces a powerful flash of light on signal. (A strobe is used for timing the ignition on engines.) The system works as described below.

An unbalanced wheel will tend to move up and down as it is spun. This causes the pickup to send out a signal every time the wheel moves up. The signal causes the strobe to flash. When the strobe is pointed at the wheel, it will strongly illuminate the wheel in the position at which the upward motion occurs. Since the strong light is on only a fraction of a second, the wheel will appear to stand still.

Now, you see how the system works. To begin, you make a mark on the tire sidewall with a piece of chalk. (Also, remove all weights from the rim and stones from the tread.) Then you spin the tire and point the strobe light at the sidewall. The chalk mark will appear to stand still. Note its position. An easy way is to think of the hour hand of a clock. Suppose the mark is at the 5 o'clock position. Stop the wheel and position the mark at 5. Then put a weight at the 12 o'clock position. The size of weight will be indicated by a meter on the top of the strobe. The meter needle moves more or less, depending on how much the wheel is unbalanced. Recheck balance after adding weight.

The above procedure corrects for up-and-down movement. To check for lateral runout, place the pickup so that the magnet will be in contact with the backing plate at the front edge, as close to the horizontal center line as possible. Spin the wheel and point the strobe at the tire. Note the location of the chalk mark when the light flashes. Stop the wheel and position it so the mark is in the same location (same "o'clock"). Add weights inside and outside to correct lack of balance. The inside weight should go as close to the pickup as possible, the outside weight 180° away (Fig. 6). Recheck balance.

5. BALANCING WHEELS ON ALEMITE VIBRATEC ANALYZER This analyzer, shown in Fig. 7, is a fully automated electronic balance analyzer. The analyzer includes a hydraulic jacking system to lift the front or rear of the car, as required, for spinning the wheels. It has wheel spinners built into the floor, as shown. Pendant controls, hanging from the ceiling, enable the operator, while seated at the car wheel, to drive onto the analyzer and then make the complete test without leaving the seat. The meters record the condition of balance at the wheels so that corrections can be quickly made.

■ **6-8-6 Dynamic-Alignment Indicators** A number of dynamic-alignment indicators are available that give evidence of any out-of-line conditions when the car is driven over them. The Weaver Sign-Align has a pair of test plates over which the car front wheels are driven. If the wheels are out of line, they will exert a sideward push on the plates, and this sideward push registers on the dial. Further, it actuates the display-board lights to show either green (for okay), yellow (for caution, which means that alignment is required to reduce excessive tire wear), or red (which means the misalignment is so bad that immediate service is required). Further, a record of the findings can be punched out on a card by pressing a button.

Another dynamic-alignment tester, known as a "scuff gauge," uses indicating blades instead of test plates. With either tester, the procedure is simple. After a 20-foot (6-m) or more straight-ahead approach, drive the front wheels, in the straight-ahead position, over the tester blades or plates. Stop before the rear wheels cross the tester platform. Record the misalignment reading. Back the car so that the front wheels roll back over the platform for a few inches. Then drive the car forward again. Record the misalignment reading once again. The first reading indicates the amount of misalignment. The difference between the first and second reading indicates the amount of looseness in the suspension and steering system. If the difference is excessive, the car will require a complete front-end check so that the cause of the excessive looseness can be found and eliminated.

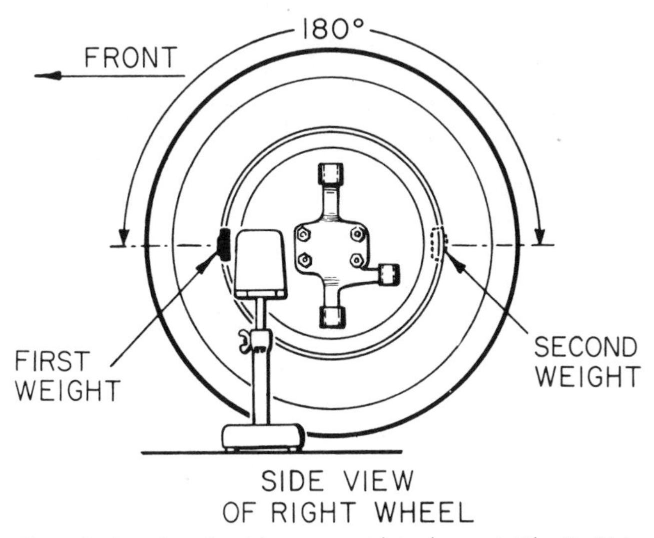

Figure 6 Location of weights to correct lateral runout. *(Alemite Division of Stewart-Warner Corporation.)*

Figure 7 A floor-mounted wheel balancer with rollers and electronic pickup devices to detect balance conditions as wheels are spun. *(Alemite Division of Stewart-Warner Corporation.)*

NOTE: The rear wheels can also be checked for misalignment with the dynamic-alignment tester. Excessive misalignment would indicate a bent rear axle or housing, a misaligned spring, or worn or bent attachment parts or control arms.

Although these dynamic-alignment testers do give an indication of front-end or rear-end misalignment, they do not accurately measure the amount of misalignment or pinpoint the cause. They simply indicate that something is wrong and that further checking is required to find and correct the trouble.

■ **6-8-7 Front-Alignment Testers** There are several alignment testers that will show the type and amount of front-end misalignment. They vary from relatively simple spirit-level (or bubble) devices that are mounted on the wheel hub or rim, to more complex instruments that use beams of light or that report the alignment conditions directly on meters. With the spirit-level devices, the position of the bubble in the level indicates the alignment condition being checked. With the beam-of-light instruments, the position of the beam on a wall chart or similar scale indicates the alignment condition. The tester that reports alignment conditions on meters picks up the alignment angles through two sets of rollers in the floor. Regardless of type, the alignment testers check caster, camber, and steering-axis inclination (or kingpin angle). In addition, toe-in is checked with a gauge that measures the amount that the tires point inward at the front of the car. Toe-out on turns is measured with turntables or turning-radius gauges placed under the front wheels to measure the degrees of turn at each front wheel as the steering wheel is rotated in one direction and the other.

NOTE: All the preliminary checks and adjustments to the tires, wheel bearings, wheels (for runout and balance), and suspension and steering linkages must be made, as already described, before wheel alignment is checked. The instructions for the operation of the tester being used, as well as the special instructions and specifications for the model of car being checked, must be carefully followed.

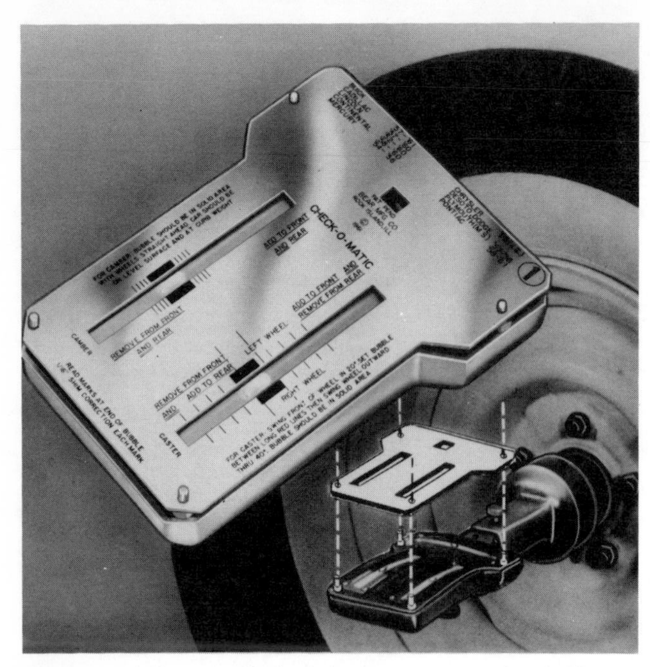

Figure 8 A hub-mounted wheel alignment gauge used to check camber and caster. *(Bear Manufacturing Company.)*

■ 6-8-8 Camber-Caster Testers

Some camber-caster testers mount on the wheel hub; others mount on the wheel rim. Some use a beam of light that spotlights a viewing screen. Others use a spirit level. These are described below.

1. HUB-MOUNTED SPIRIT-LEVEL TYPE This type is shown in Fig. 8. It contains three curved spirit levels and a magnetic attachment to hold it in place on the wheel hub. It also has a series of templates, each of which is calibrated to apply to certain models of automobile. Figure 8 shows the tester attached to the wheel hub with a template in position above the tester, ready to be placed down over the four screw studs.

To use the tester, roll the car forward until the front wheels are centered on the turning-radius gauges. Turning-radius gauges are a part of wheel-alignment racks and are also available separately. Their purpose is to measure the number of degrees that a front wheel is turned in or out as the steering wheel is turned.

With the front wheels straight ahead, remove the hub and the dust cap, wipe off excess grease from the end of the spindle, and clean the face of the wheel hub. Install the brake-pedal depressor so that the brake pedal is held down to lock all four wheels. Make sure all tires are inflated to the proper pressure.

Select the template for the make and model of car being checked. Put it on the four stud screws (Fig. 8). Install the tester on the wheel hub, centering it on the spindle with the centering pin so that it is horizontal, as shown by the bubble being centered in the small window closest to the wheel hub.

a. *Checking Camber* Camber can now be checked by noting the location of the camber bubble. It should lie entirely within the solid area of the camber scale (Fig. 8). If the bubble is not entirely within the solid area, the amount that lies outside will determine the amount and direction of adjustment required. For example, if the end of the bubble lies two graduations, or marks, outside the solid area, this means that, on cars adjusted by shims, the camber adjustment must be changed by two 1/16-inch (1.59-mm) shims. If the bubble is on one side, the shims must be added; if on the other, they must be removed. ■6-8-9 describes camber adjustments.

b. *Checking Caster* With the tester in place and the wheel straight ahead, set the turning-radius gauge to zero. Turn the wheel in (front of wheel moving in) until the turning-radius gauge reads 20°. With the thumbscrew, adjust the caster level until the bubble lies squarely between the two long red crosslines on the caster scale. Now turn the wheel back in the opposite direction, stopping it when the turning-radius gauge reads 20° (this is a 40° total swing). Now the entire bubble should lie in the solid area on the left side of the caster scale when the left wheel is being checked (Fig. 8). It should lie entirely in the solid area at the right side of the caster side when the right wheel is being checked.

If the bubble is not properly located, the amount and direction that it is off indicate the amount and direction of correction that need to be made. ■6-8-9 describes caster adjustment.

2. RIM-MOUNTED SPIRIT-LEVEL TYPE This alignment gauge mounts on the wheel rim. After being mounted, the spirit level and attached pointer are adjusted until the bubble is centered. The pointer then indicates on the scale the number of camber or caster degrees. The checking procedures are similar to those outlined above for the hub-mounted alignment gauge.

3. LIGHT-BEAM TYPE There are several variations of the light-beam type of alignment checker. Figure 9 shows one of

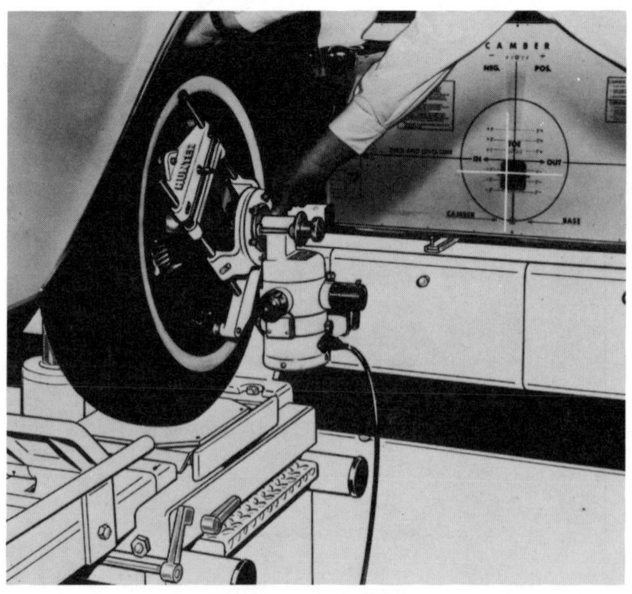

Figure 9 Checking wheel alignment with a rim-mounted light projector. Note the horizontal and vertical light lines shining on the screen. *(Hunter Engineering Company.)*

Figure 10 Dynamic wheel-alignment tester. With this tester, you can check camber, caster, and toe-in in 1 minute. *(Hunter Engineering Company.)*

these, the ramp type. It has a ramp on which the car must be driven for checking. (There are also the pit type and the lift type.) The system includes two light projectors, one on each side, plus screens straight ahead hung in shadow boxes for easier viewing. In addition, there are two turntables, or turning-radius gauges, on which the front wheels rest, as well as gauges to mount on the wheel rims. Figure 9 shows the system in operation, checking the right front wheel. The principle of the system is this: A light inside the projector is directed to a mirror on the wheel-mounted gauge. It passes through aiming lenses and then strikes the screen ahead of the car. The position of the spot or lines of light indicates the camber and caster angles. Checking procedures are similar to those outlined above for the hub-mounted alignment gauge.

4. FLOOR-ROLLER TYPE The floor-roller alignment tester is shown in Fig. 10. This figure shows a car on the aligner, being tested. There is a pair of rollers for each wheel. Each roller pair is free to tilt sideways and also swing through the horizontal plane. In operation, the rollers are driven so the wheel spins. As it spins, it assumes normal operating position. The rollers align with the wheel, and their position is sensed and reported to the console. The console contains solid-state circuits with computerized read-out meters. These meters report camber and caster of both wheels. Pushing the control buttons and turning the steering wheel are the only operations required (see Fig. 10). The tester checks not only caster and camber, but also toe-in.

■ 6-8-9 Caster and Camber Adjustments

Some cars have eccentric pins, or bushings, which are rotated to move the upper or lower control arm and thus change caster and camber. Other cars have shim-type adjustments of caster and camber. The locations of the shims on one car are shown on Fig. 10 (in Part 6, Sec. 2). The shims are located between the upper-control-arm shaft (or pivot shaft) and the frame bracket. When shims are added or removed from between the shaft and the frame bracket, the upper control arm is moved in relation to the frame. This changes the position of the upper ball joint and thus the caster and camber. Another adjustment method requires changing the effective length of the strut rod attached to the lower arm, thus moving the end of the arm back or forward. Also, some cars have an eccentric bushing in which the upper ball stud mounts. This bushing can be turned in its upper-arm mounting to move the ball joint in or out to change the camber. In addition, many cars have elongated bolt holes for attaching the upper-arm inner shaft to the frame. The bolts are loosened so the upper-arm shaft can be moved to change camber and caster. These various adjustment methods are described below.

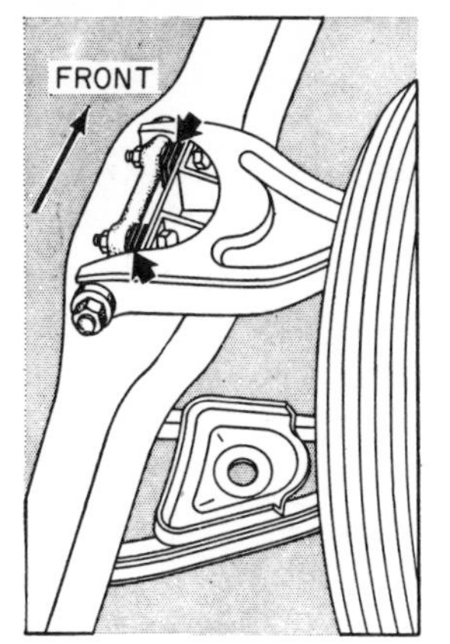

Figure 11 Location of caster- and camber-adjusting shims (indicated by heavy arrows). Note that the shims and upper-control-arm shaft are inside the frame bracket. *(Bear Manufacturing Company.)*

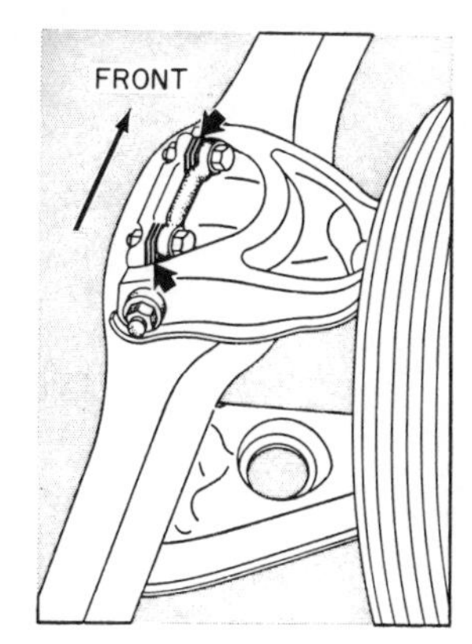

Figure 12 Location of caster- and camber-adjusting shims (indicated by heavy arrows). Note that the shims and upper-control-arm shaft are outside the frame bracket. *(Bear Manufacturing Company.)*

1. SHIM ADJUSTMENTS Figures 11 and 12 show the locations of the shims on many makes of car. Note that on some cars, the shims are inside the frame bracket (Fig. 11). On others, the shims are outside the frame bracket (Fig. 12). When the shims and shaft are inside the frame bracket (Fig. 11), adding shims will move the upper-control arm inward and thus bring the top of the wheel inward. This decreases positive camber. When the shims and upper-control-arm shaft are outside the frame bracket (Fig. 12), adding shims will move the upper control arm outward and thus tilt the wheel outward more to increase the positive camber.

Caster is changed by adding shims at one of the upper-control-arm attachment bolts and removing shims from the other. Refer again to Fig.11. If a shim is taken away at the front attachment bolt (the upper bolt in the picture) and added at the rear bolt, the outer end of the upper control arm will be shifted forward. Thus, positive caster will be decreased. Positive caster is the backward tilt of the steering axis (ball-joint center lines) from the vertical.

Caster and camber adjustments are made by loosening the shaft attachment bolts and installing or removing the correct number of shims. The alignment tester will indicate how far off the camber and caster angles are and thus the amount of correction (number of shims) to add or subtract.

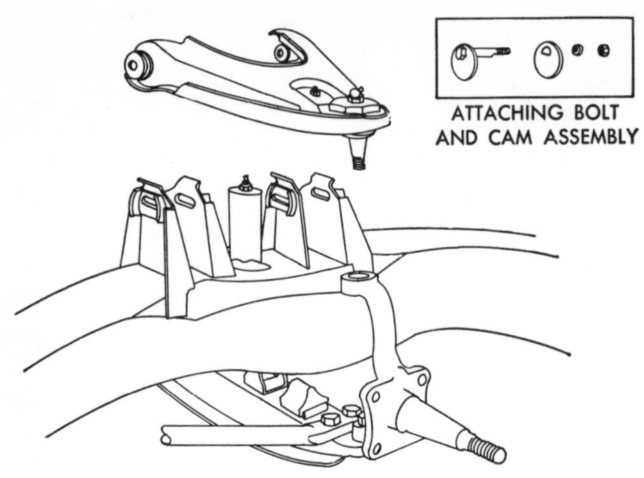

Figure 13 The upper control arm is attached to the frame brackets by two bolt and cam assemblies so that the two attachment bushings can be shifted back and forth for caster and camber adjustments. *(Bear Manufacturing Company.)*

2. ADJUSTMENTS WITH CAMS A variety of eccentric bushing, or pin, arrangements have been used to provide camber and caster adjustment of the front wheels. One widely used method, found on many Chrysler Corporation cars, is illustrated in Fig. 13. The two bushings at the inner end of the upper control arm are attached to the frame brackets by two attachment bolt and cam assemblies. When these cam assemblies are turned, the camber and caster are changed.

If both cam assemblies are turned the same amount and in the same direction, the control arm is moved in or out to change the camber. If only one cam is turned, or if the two are turned in opposite directions, the outer end of the control arm is shifted back or forward to change the caster.

To make the adjustments, after the direction and type of correction needed are determined, the bolt nuts are loosened and the cam bolts are turned. Caster should be adjusted first. Then, camber is adjusted by turning both cam bolts the same amount.

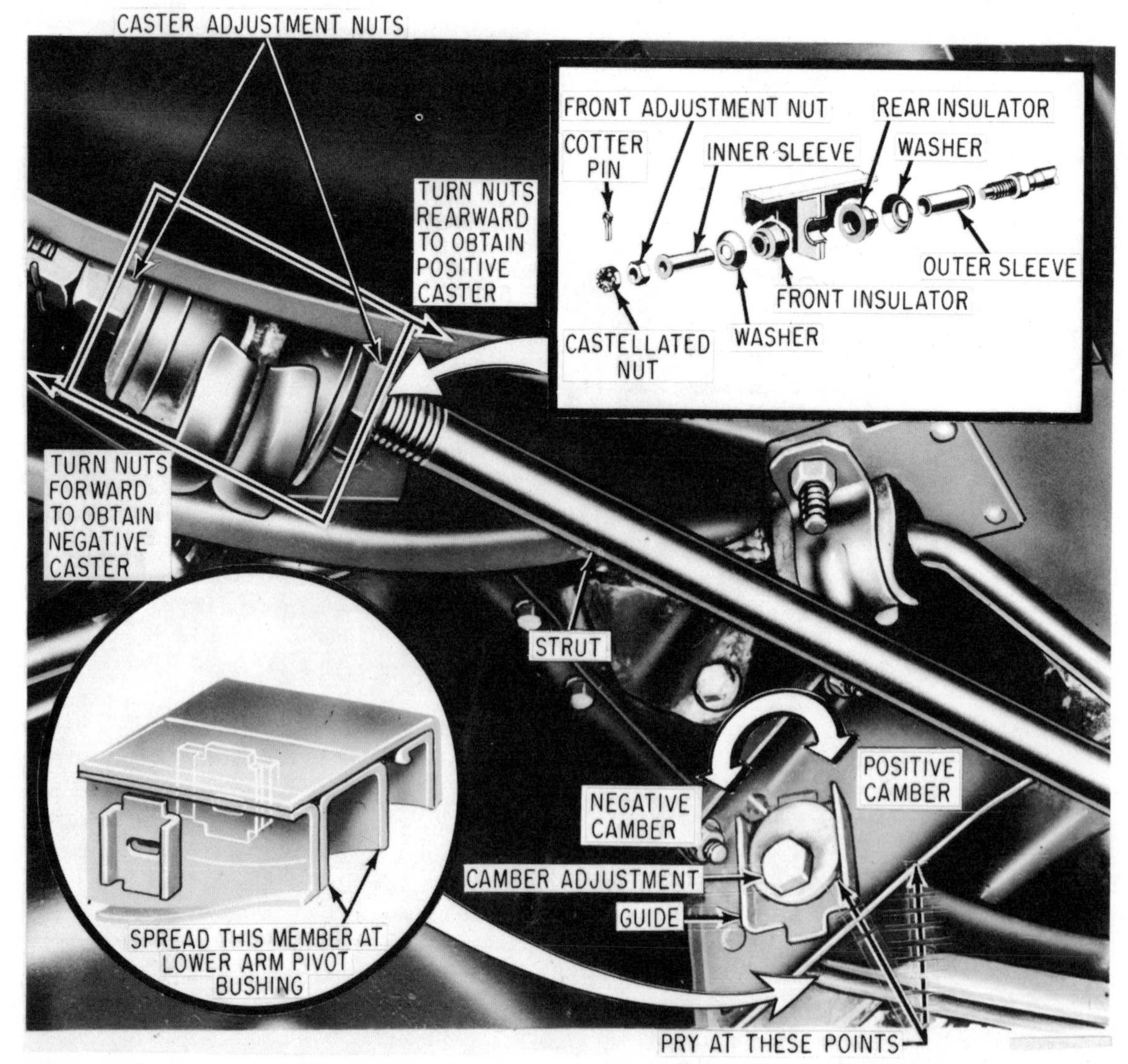

Figure 14 Caster and camber adjustments on the Cougar, Fairlane, Falcon, Montego, and Mustang. *(Ford Motor Company.)*

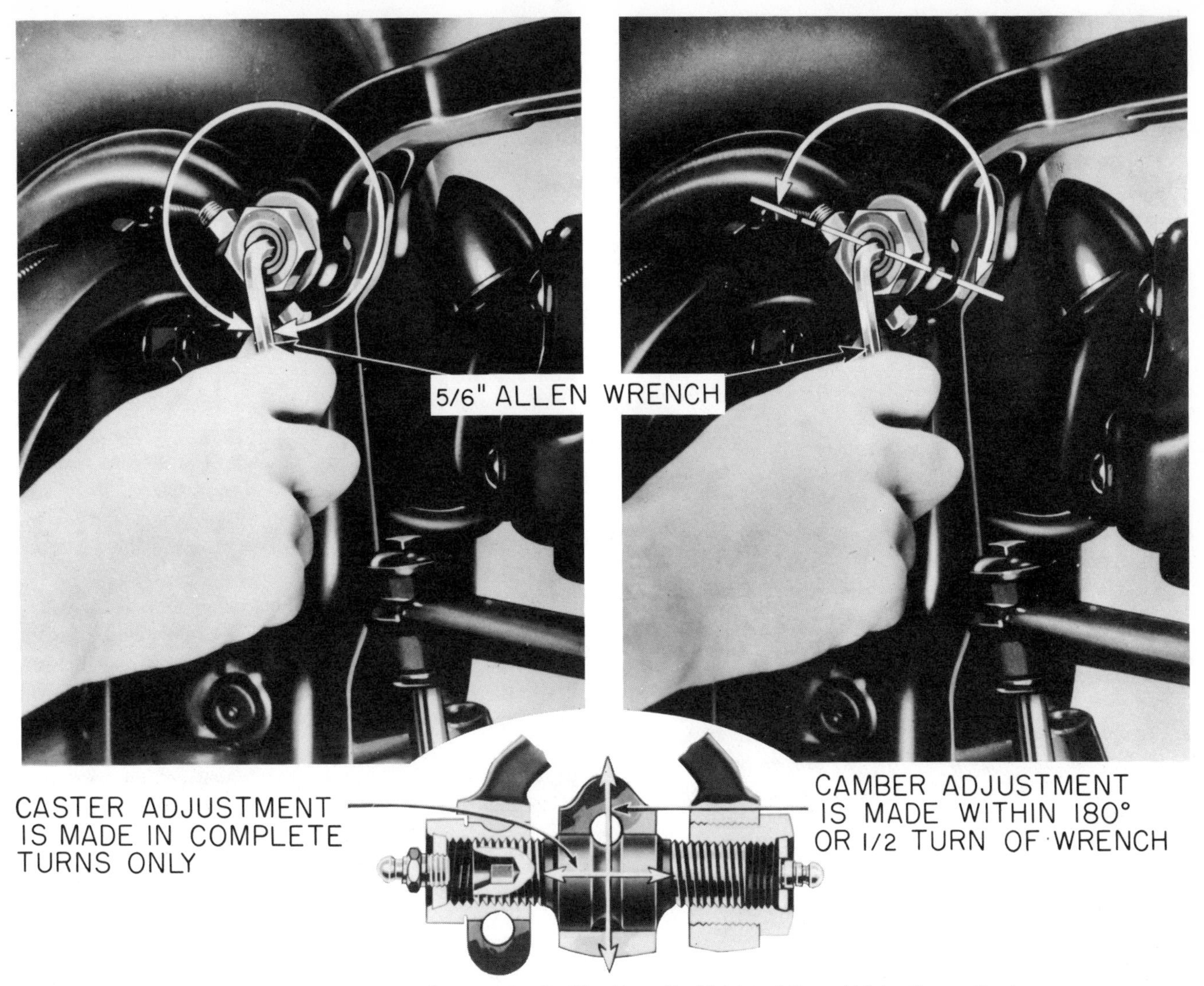

Figure 15 Adjusting caster and camber by turning the pivot pin. *(Cadillac Motor Car Division of General Motors Corporation.)*

NOTE: One complete rotation of a cam bolt represents the full amount of possible adjustment.

Always recheck the final caster and camber settings after retightening the cam-bolt nuts.

3. ADJUSTMENT BY SHIFTING INNER SHAFT This system uses elongated holes in the frame at the two points where the inner shaft of the upper arm is attached. Thus, if the attaching bolts are loosened and the inner shaft shifted inward or outward, the caster and camber are changed because this movement will move the upper arm. First, however, special alignment spacers must be installed at both front wheels. To do this, lift the car enough to allow the spacers to be placed between the lower arms and the frame spring pocket. Then, when the car is lowered so that it rests on the wheels, the proper curb height is established by the spacers. Adjust caster and camber by shifting the inner shaft with a special tool after loosening the shaft attaching bolts. If both ends of the inner shaft are moved in or out together, the camber is changed. But if only one end is moved, the caster is changed. This is very similar to installing or removing shims as in the type adjusted with shims. After making the adjustment, tighten the attaching bolts and check the adjustment again. Then, if it is okay, remove the spacers.

4. ADJUSTMENT WITH STRUT ROD AND CAM This arrangement (Fig. 14) shortens or lengthens the strut rod to change the caster angle. When the strut rod is shortened, for example (by turning the nuts at the front of the rod), the outer end of the lower control arm is pulled forward, thus increasing the caster.

Camber is adjusted by turning the cams on which the inner end of the lower control arm is mounted (Fig. 14). This action moves the lower control arm in or out to change the camber.

5. ADJUSTMENT WITH ECCENTRIC PIVOT PIN On this older system, the upper control arm is attached to the upper end of the steering-knuckle support by an eccentric pivot pin. Caster and camber are adjusted together by turning the upper-control-arm pivot pin with an allen wrench (Fig. 15).

The pivot pin changes both the caster and the camber of the wheel when it is turned. Both ends of the pivot pin are threaded in the front and rear bushings in the upper control arm. Thus, when the pivot pin is turned with an allen wrench, the pin and upper end of the steering-knuckle support are shifted backward or forward with respect to the upper control arm. This causes the kingpin to tilt backward or forward to change the caster angle. Change of the camber is effected by an eccentric section of the pivot pin on which the upper end of the steering-knuckle support pivots. As the pivot pin is turned with an allen wrench, this eccentric center section rotates, moving the upper end of the steering-knuckle support in toward, or out away from, the car. This moves the top of the wheel in to decrease, or out to increase, the camber. One rotation of the pivot pin represents the full range of camber adjustment. The adjustment procedure, in detail, follows:

a. Loosen the clamp bolt at the top of the steering-knuckle support (Fig. 12).
b. Remove the lubrication fitting from the upper front pivot-pin bushing.
c. Use an allen wrench and turn the pivot pin clockwise to increase the caster or counterclockwise to decrease the caster. If the pin is turned one or more full turns, the eccentric will always be brought back to the same position to provide the same camber angle.
d. To change camber, turn the pivot pin only part of a turn. If the caster angle has been adjusted to the approximately correct value, adjusting the camber by turning the pivot pin a part turn will change the caster angle slightly but not enough to throw the caster angle out of specifications.
e. Recheck caster and camber adjustments and, if they are correct, tighten the clamp bolt and install the lubrication fitting.

6. *ADJUSTMENT BY STRUT ROD AND STEERING-KNUCKLE ECCENTRIC* With this system, caster is adjusted by shortening or lengthening the strut rod that is attached between the frame and the outer end of the lower control arm. Camber is adjusted by turning an eccentric bushing in the upper end of the steering knuckle. The ball joint mounts in this steering knuckle, and it can be shifted back and forth by turning the eccentric bushing to change the camber.

7. *OTHER ADJUSTMENT METHODS* Several other adjustment methods have been used. Essentially, all are similar in that the adjustments move the control-arm attachments in such a way as to alter the caster and camber angles.

On the solid, or I-beam, front axle, camber and kingpin-inclination-angle adjustment must be made by bending the axle with special correction tools. Caster adjustments can be made by inserting wedge-shaped shims between the spring seat on the axle and the spring or by use of correction tools that bend the axle. These tools slightly bend the axle to make the correction. Correction can be made by this method only when both camber and kingpin inclination are off the same amount. When one is off more than the other, the wheel spindle is bent and should be replaced; in addition, the axle may require bending to bring the two angles within specifications.

NOTE: The axle should be replaced if excessive bending is required. A significant distortion of the axle may have caused invisible cracks or weakening of the beam. Such an axle is unsafe to use.

■ 6-8-10 Toe-In

Toe-in is the amount, in fractions of an inch or millimeters, that the front wheels point inward. It is measured in various ways, but the adjustment procedure is similar on all cars.

To adjust the toe-in, change the effective lengths of the two tie rods by loosening the clamp bolts on the adjustment sleeves and turning the sleeves as required. The sleeves and the matching ends of the rod and tie-rod end have right-hand and left-hand threads. Thus, turning the sleeve one direction increases the effective length of a tie rod. Turning the sleeve the other direction shortens the length.

Adjustment of the sleeves can also affect the steering-wheel position in straight-ahead driving. For example, if both sleeves are turned in the same direction and the same amount, the toe-in will remain unchanged but the steering-wheel position will be changed (see ■6-8-12).

A very accurate method of checking toe-in makes use of gauge bars that measure the distance between the backs and fronts of the tires. The difference in the two is due to toe-in. To use the toe gauge, drive the front wheels onto turning-radius gauges. Attach the parallel bars to the front-wheel spindles. Level the parallel bars (with the use of their built-in spirit levels). Then attach the gauge bar to the parallel bars at the back, behind the wheels. Set the reading on the scale to zero. Next, transfer the gauge bar to the front of the parallel bars and note the reading on the scale.

A somewhat simpler toe-in gauge also can be used. To use this gauge, mark the center lines of the tires with chalk. Roll the car ahead to settle the linkage in the running position. Then measure the distance between the two center lines accurately with the gauge at the back of the tires, hub high. Next, roll the car forward until the two points that have been measured come around to the front, hub high. Now measure them with the gauge at the front of the tires. The difference between the two measurements is the toe-in.

The floor-roller type of alignment tester (Fig. 10) reads the toe-in along with caster and camber. No separate check is required to measure toe-in when this tester is used.

■ 6-8-11 Steering-Axis Inclination and Toe-out on Turns

These two factors, described in ■6-3-4 and ■6-3-8, are not adjustable. They are, however, factors to be checked during an alignment job. If they are not within specifications after the camber and caster are adjusted to specifications, then wheel-supporting parts or a steering arm is bent.

Figure 16 Straight-ahead-position marks. *(Ford Motor Company.)*

Toe-out on turns is easily checked by rolling the front wheels onto turning-radius gauges. Then turn the steering wheel until one front wheel is angled at 20°. Measure the amount of turning of the other wheel on the other turning-radius gauge. A typical specification, for certain Fords, is that with power steering, when the inside wheel (the left wheel in a left turn, for example) is turned 20°, the outside wheel should be turned 17°30′ (minutes) (17°21′ with manual steering).

If the toe-out is not correct, it means that a steering arm is bent and must be replaced. Then, front alignment must be rechecked.

> **NOTE:** Never attempt to straighten a bent steering or suspension part! This could weaken the part to the point where it might break in operation.

Steering axis (or kingpin) inclination is checked with a tester attached to the wheel spindle. It is leveled until the bubble in the steering-axis-inclination scale is at zero. Then, camber and caster should be checked as already explained for another tester (■6-8-8). Camber is read directly from the camber scale on the face plate. Caster is checked by turning the wheel 20° in (as measured on the turning-radius gauge). Then the caster spirit level should be set to zero and the wheel turned 40° so that it is pointed out at a 20° angle. Caster can now be read directly from the caster point.

At the same time that caster is checked, the steering-axis inclination can also be checked. This is done by adjusting the steering-axis-inclination scale so that the bubble is at zero when the wheel is turned in 20°. Then when the wheel is turned out 20° (a total of 40° of turn), the steering-axis inclination scale will indicate the inclination angle.

If the steering-axis inclination is incorrect but other factors

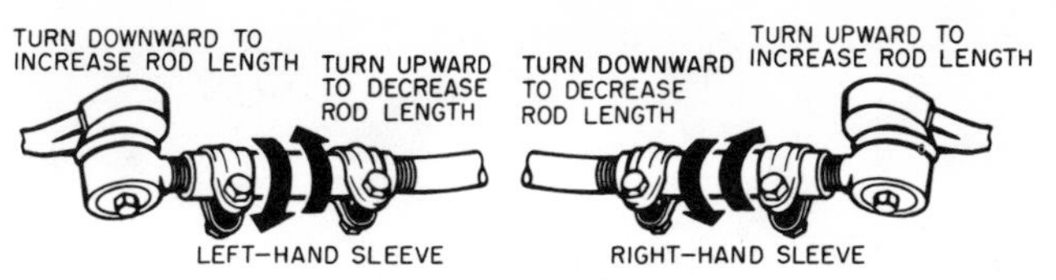

Figure 17 Spindle-connecting-rod (tie-rod) adjustments. *(Ford Motor Company.)*

check out okay, the spindle probably is bent and must be replaced.

■ 6-8-12 A Typical Alignment Procedure

Here is the alignment procedure and the steps required to check and adjust alignment on a typical automobile.

All the preliminary steps must be taken before the alignment checks start. These include checking tire inflation, wheel bearings, wheel runout, wheel balance, linkages and ball joints for looseness, suspension for height and looseness, shock absorbers, and tracking.

Drive the car forward far enough to establish the straight-ahead position of the front wheels. Then mark the steering-wheel hub and column (Fig. 16). This establishes the position that the steering wheel actually takes when the front wheels are pointed straight ahead. If the wheel spokes are not in a balanced position, adjustment will have to be made when the toe-in is adjusted.

Adjust caster and camber. After completing adjustment, tighten the nuts to the proper torque.

Figure 17 shows the two spindle-connecting-rod (tie-rod) sleeves and how to adjust the sleeves to increase or decrease the rods' effective length.

Figure 18 shows the adjustments to be made to get the steering-wheel spokes centered. It is important to center the spokes because this means that the steering gear will then also be centered.

■ 6-8-13 Rear-Wheel Alignment

On cars with independent rear suspension such as the Corvette (Fig. 8 in Part

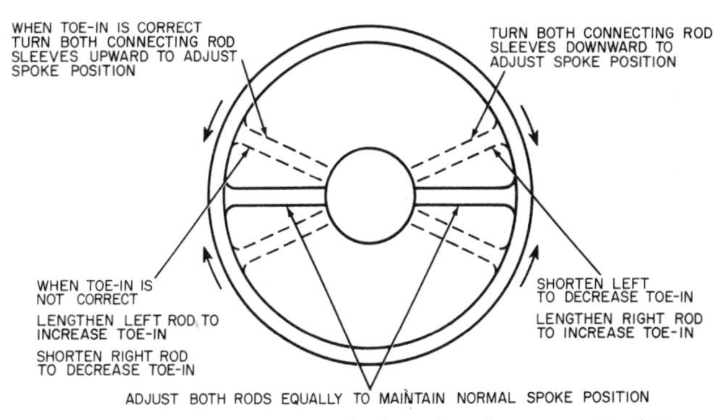

Figure 18 Toe-in and steering-wheel-spoke adjustments. *(Ford Motor Company.)*

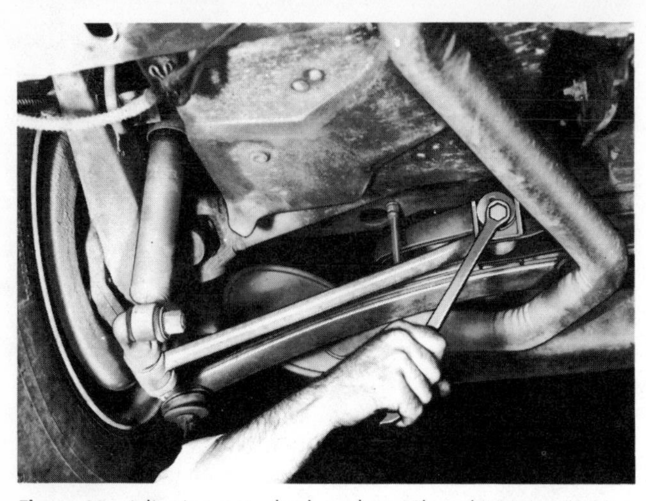

Figure 19 Adjusting rear-wheel camber. *(Chevrolet Motor Division of General Motors Corporation.)*

6, Sec. 2), the wheel alignment should be checked periodically. To do this, back the car onto the machine that is normally used to align front suspension. Camber will read in the normal manner. But toe-in will now read as toe-out, while toe-out will read as toe-in.

Make sure the strut rods are straight. If they are bent, they should be replaced.

1. CAMBER ADJUSTMENT Adjust camber by turning the eccentric cam and bolt (Fig. 19). Loosen the cam-bolt nut and turn the cam-and-bolt assembly to get the correct camber. The location of the cam can be seen in Fig. 8 (in Part 6, Sec. 2). It is shown to the lower right of the differential. Tighten the locknut after making the adjustment.

2. TOE-IN ADJUSTMENT Adjust toe-in by inserting shims inside the frame side member on both sides of the torque-control-arm pivot bushing.

SECTION 6-9 Manual-Steering-Gear Service

This section explains how to check, adjust, and repair various types of manually operated steering gears used on passenger cars. Section 4 of this part described trouble-diagnosis methods for determining the causes of different steering and suspension troubles. Following subsections discuss the adjustments and repairs required to eliminate causes of trouble in manually operated steering gears. The next section describes power-steering checks, adjustments, and repairs.

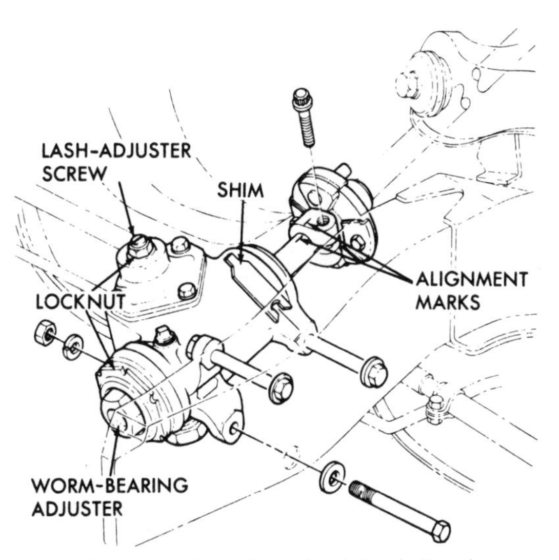

Figure 1 Adjustment points of a recirculating-ball-and-nut manual-steering gear. *(Chevrolet Motor Division of General Motors Corporation.)*

■ **6-9-1 Steering-Gear Adjustments** A variety of manual steering-gear designs have been used on automobiles. All have two basic adjustments: one for taking up the worm-gear and steering shaft end play and the other for removing backlash between the worm and the sector (or roller or lever studs). In addition, some designs have a means of adjusting the sector-shaft (pitman-arm-shaft) end play.

Before attempting to adjust a steering gear to take up excessive end play or to relieve binding, make sure the condition is not the result of faulty alignment or of wear in some other components of the linkage or front suspension. Adjustment and repair procedures on various manual steering gears follow.

■ **6-9-2 Saginaw (General Motors) Steering-Gear Service** The Saginaw manual steering gear, used on General Motors cars since 1961, is shown in exterior view in Fig. 1. This steering gear is filled at the factory with steering-gear lubricant. No lubrication is required for the life of the steering gear. This means that it should never be drained and refilled with lubricant if it continues to operate normally. However, the gear should be inspected every 36,000 miles (57,369 km) for leakage (actual solid grease, not just oily film). If a seal is replaced or the gear is overhauled, the housing should be filled with the specific lubricant called for by General Motors. Do not overfill!

Adjustment will be required if the steering is too loose (too much lash) or too tight (requiring too much turning effort). Before any adjustment is made, however, be sure that all other front-end factors are up to specifications. Check tires, wheel balance, absorbers, and make any corrections that are required. Then steering-gear adjustments can be made.

■ **6-9-3 Saginaw Steering-Gear Adjustments** Two adjustments can be made: pitman-shaft lash and worm-shaft bearing end play (see Fig. 1). Follow this sequence.

1. Disconnect the battery ground cable. Raise the car. Remove the pitman-arm nut and mark the relationship of the pitman arm to the pitman shaft.

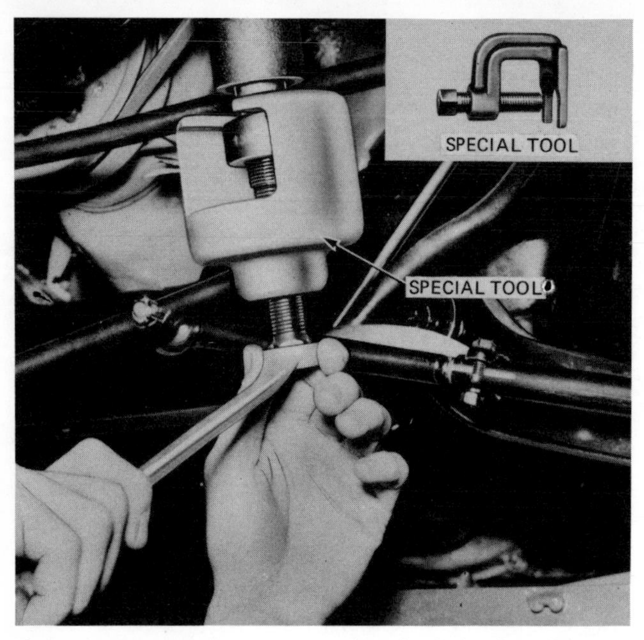

Figure 2 Removing the pitman arm from the shaft. *(Chevrolet Motor Division of General Motors Corporation.)*

2. Remove the pitman arm with the special tool as shown in Fig. 2.

3. Loosen the lash-adjuster-screw locknut and back off the screw 1/4 turn.

4. Measure the worm-shaft-bearing drag with a spring scale. On earlier models, the procedure was to hook the spring scale to the steering wheel. On later models, remove the horn button or shroud and use a 3/4-inch (19-mm) socket on a torque wrench to measure the torque required. In either case, take the measurements with the steering gear centered. Do this by turning the steering wheel gently in one direction until it is stopped by the gear. Turn it all the way to the other extreme, counting the turns. Then turn the wheel back exactly one-half of the total turns.

NOTE: Do not turn the steering wheel hard against the stops. This could damage the steering gear.

5. If the pull or torque is not correct, adjust the worm bearings. Loosen the worm-bearing-adjuster locknut and turn the worm-bearing adjuster to obtain the proper bearing preload

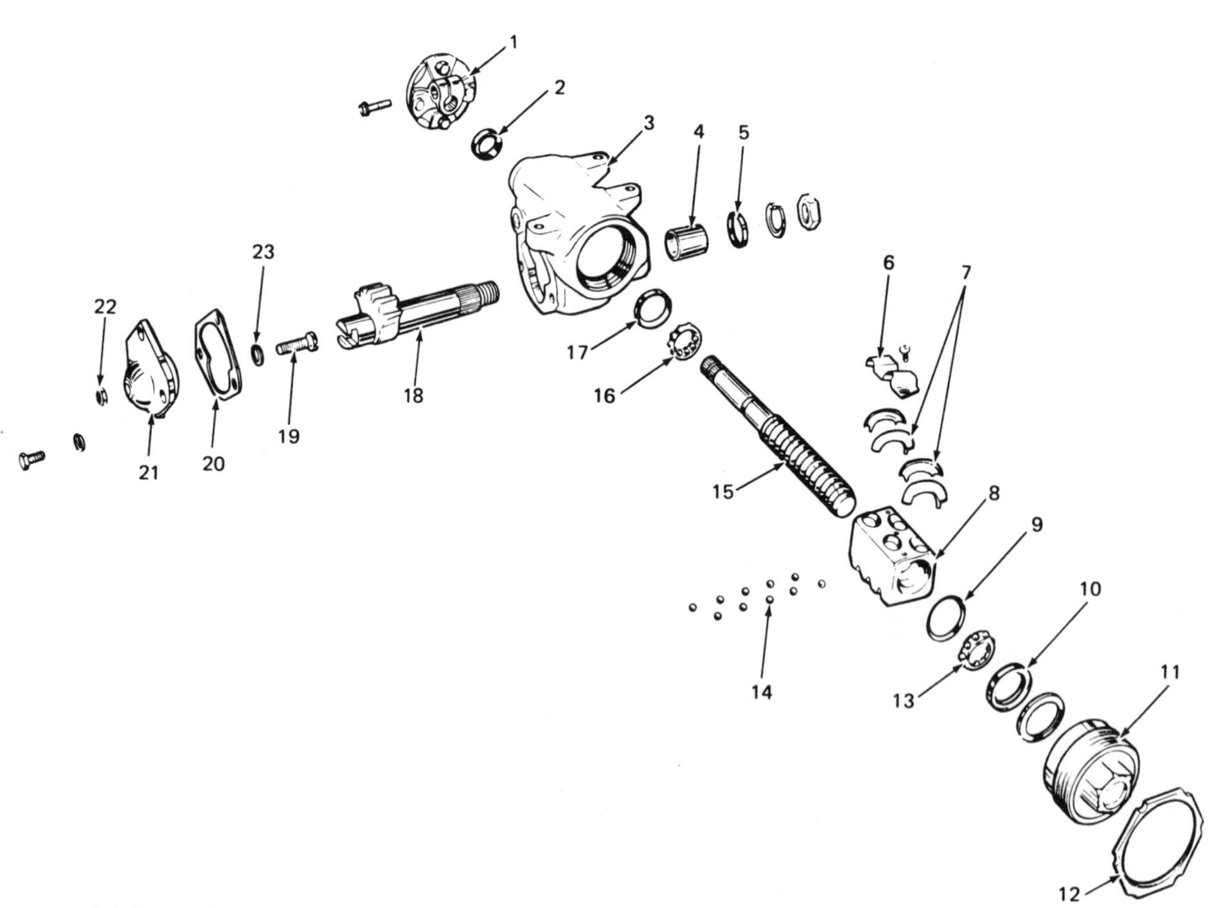

Figure 3 Exploded view of a Saginaw manual-steering gear. (1) Coupling and lower flange; (2) seal; (3) housing; (4) bushing; (5) seal; (6) clamp; (7) guide; (8) ball nut; (9) retainer; (10) bearing race; (11) adjuster; (12) locknut; (13) bearing; (14) balls; (15) worm shaft; (16) bearing; (17) bearing race; (18) shaft and sector; (19) screw, lash adjuster; (20) gasket; (21) cover; (22) locknut; (23) shims, lash adjuster. *(Pontiac Motor Division of General Motors Corporation.)*

(pull or torque on wheel). Then tighten the locknut and re-check the pull or torque.

NOTE: If the gear feels "lumpy" or rough after adjustment, the bearings probably are damaged. This will require disassembly of the gear for replacement of the defective parts.

6. Check the pitman-shaft lash, also called the "over-center preload," with the steering wheel centered, as explained above. Then, turn the lash-adjuster screw to take up all lash between the ball nut and pitman-shaft sector gear. Next tighten the locknut. Now check the pull on the steering wheel or torque as the wheel is turned through the center position. Adjust, if necessary, by loosening the locknut and readjusting the lash-adjuster screw.

NOTE: If you go above the maximum specification, back off the screw. Then come back up on adjustment by turning the adjuster locknut in.

7. Reassemble the pitman arm to the pitman shaft, lining up the marks made during disassembly. Tighten the pitman shaft nut to specifications. If you removed the horn button cap or shroud, install it.

■ **6-9-4 Saginaw Steering-Gear Overhaul** Figure 1 is an exterior view of the Saginaw steering gear discussed in this section. Figure 3 is a disassembled view of the steering gear.

1. REMOVAL Raise the car so that you can get under it conveniently. Disconnect the pitman arm from the shaft as already described (■6-9-3 and Fig. 2). Remove the splash-pan attachment bolts and the pan. Remove the nuts and lock washers from the steering-gear attachment bolts and take out the bolts (and shims, where present). The steering gear is now loose from the frame and can be taken off the car as soon as the gear is detached from the intermediate shaft. This is done by loosening the bolt on the lower universal-joint clamp.

2. DISASSEMBLY Clamp one of the steering-gear mounting tabs in a vise with the worm shaft horizontal. Rotate the worm shaft from one extreme to the other. Then turn it back exactly halfway so the gear is centered. Now, loosen the locknut and back off the lash-adjuster screw (Fig. 2) several turns. Then loosen the locknut and back off the worm-bearing adjuster a few turns.

Put a pan under the unit to catch the lubricant. Remove the three bolts and washers attaching the side cover to the housing (Fig. 3). Pull the side cover with the pitman (sector) shaft from the housing. If the sector does not clear the housing opening, turn the worm shaft by hand until it does.

Remove the worm-bearing adjuster, locknut, and lower ball bearing from the housing. Then, draw the worm shaft and nut from the housing (Fig. 3). Remove the upper ball bearing.

NOTE: Do not allow the ball nut to run down to either end of the worm. This could damage the ends of the ball guides.

Unscrew the lash-adjuster locknut and adjuster from the side cover and slide the adjuster and its shim from the slot in the end of the sector shaft. Pry out and discard the pitman shaft and worn shaft seals from the housing.

Do not disassemble the ball nut unless it is tight, binds, or runs roughly up and down the worm. In such cases, disassemble it by removing the screw and clamp-retaining ball guides in the nut and pull the guides from the nut. Turn the nut upside down and rotate the worm shaft back and forth until all the balls have fallen out of the nut. Have a clean pan handy in which to catch the balls. Now, the nut can be slid off the worm.

3. INSPECTION Carefully inspect the ball bearings, balls, bearing cups, worm, and nut for signs of wear, dents, cracks, chipping, etc. Replace any part that shows signs of wear or damage. Check the fit of the sector shaft in the bushing. Examine the bushing in the side cover; if this bushing is worn, replace the side cover and bushing as an assembly. Examine the ends of the ball guides; if they are bent or damaged, replace the guides.

4. REPAIRS Replace the sector-shaft bushing in the housing by pressing out the old bushing with an arbor press and a special tool and pressing in the new bushing. New bushings are already bored by size and need no reaming.

Replace the worm-shaft seal if necessary. Always replace the sector-shaft packing whenever the steering gear is torn down. If the worm-shaft bearing cup in the bearing adjuster requires replacement, remove it with a special puller and press a new cup into place.

5. REASSEMBLY Adjustment procedures are as follows:

a. *Ball Nut* The model of steering gear used on most General Motors cars has ball guides with holes in the top through which all balls can be installed. Twenty balls go into each guide. The worm must be turned back and forth to get the balls to run down into the circuits and fill them. Before assembly, the worm and the inside of the nut should be coated with steering-gear lubricant. When the balls are all in place, the guide clamp should be attached with screws.

On some Saginaw steering gears, there are no holes in the ball guides. A different method of installing the balls is required. On these, some of the balls must be installed in the nut circuits by slipping the nut over the worm with the ball holes up and the shallow end of the rack teeth to the left (from the steering-wheel position). Align the worm and nut grooves by looking into a ball hole. Count out 27 balls. Start feeding balls into one of the guide holes and turning the worm away from this hole at the same time. Continue until the circuit is filled in the nut. Then lay one-half of the ball guide down, groove up, and put the rest of the 27 balls into it. Put the other half of the guide on top and plug the

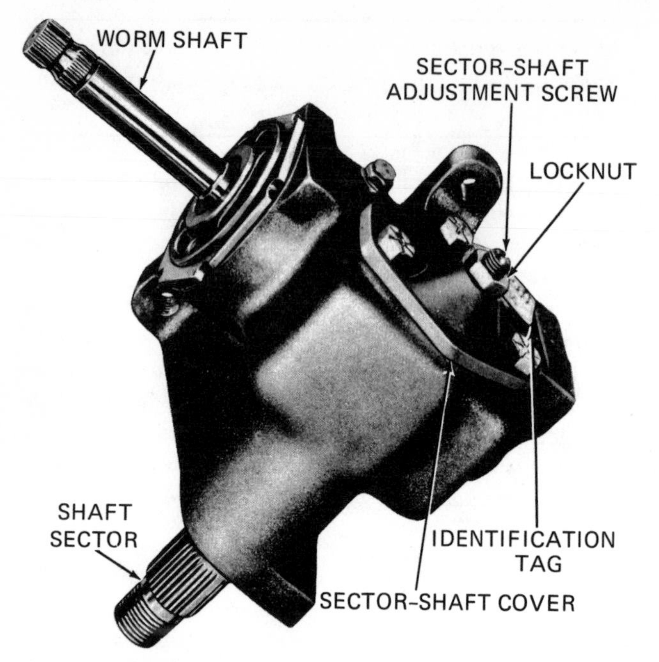

Figure 4 Manual-steering gear. *(Ford Motor Company.)*

two ends with petroleum jelly so that the balls will not fall out. Push the guide into place in the ball holes. Tap it down if necessary with the wooden handle of a screwdriver. Fill the other ball circuit in the nut the same way. Install the guide clamp. Check the assembly by rotating the worm to make sure that the nut can move freely from one end of the worm to the other.

b. *Steering Gear* Cleaning the parts will remove the sealing compound from the screw threads. Thus, the threads on the adjuster, side-cover bolts, and lash adjuster should be coated with a sealing compound, such as Permatex #2. Do not get compound on the worm-shaft bearing in the adjuster. Apply grease to the worm bearings, sector-shaft bushings and ball-nut teeth.

With the worm-shaft seal, bushings, and bearing cups installed, slip the upper ball bearing over the worm shaft. Insert the worm-shaft-and-nut assembly into the housing. Put the ball bearing in the adjuster cup, press the retainer into place, and install the adjuster and locknut in the lower end of the housing.

Assemble the lash adjuster with a shim in the slot in the end of the sector shaft. End clearance between the bottom of the slot and the head of the lash adjuster should be no greater than 0.002 inch (0.05 mm). If it is greater, install another shim.

Start the end of the sector shaft into the side-cover bushing. Pull the shaft into place by turning the lash adjuster. Rotate the worm shaft to put the nut in the center of its travel. This is to make sure that the rack and sector will mesh properly with the center tooth of the sector entering the center-tooth space in the rack on the nut.

Put a new gasket on the side cover. Push the cover-and-sector-shaft assembly into the housing, making sure that the teeth mesh properly. Make sure that there is some lash between the sector and the rack. Then secure the side cover with screws.

c. *Adjustment on Bench* The steering gear can be adjusted on the bench by tightening the worm bearing adjuster to remove all shaft end play, tightening the locknut, and then installing the steering wheel on the worm shaft.

NOTE: Do not force the steering wheel on the shaft, but tap it into place lightly. Forcing the wheel on would damage the bearings.

The adjustment procedure is the same as that already described (■6-9-3).

■ 6-9-5 Ford Steering-Gear Adjustments Figure 11 (in Part 6 Sec. 3) is a phantom view of the recirculating-ball-and-nut steering gear described in this section. Figure 4 (in this section) is an exterior view. Two adjustments are required to provide minimum worm-shaft end play (also called steering-shaft end play) and minimum backlash between the sector and the ball nut. Adjustments are to be made in the following order.

1. Disconnect the pitman arm from the steering-arm-to idler-arm rod (see Fig. 11 in Part 6, Sec. 3). On cars with power steering, disconnect the arm from the valve ball stud.

2. Loosen the locknut on the sector-shaft adjustment screw. Turn the adjustment screw counter-clockwise. This relieves the load on the teeth.

3. Use a torque wrench on the steering-wheel nut to measure the worm-bearing preload. With the steering wheel off center, read the pull required to move the shaft at points about 1½ turns to either side of center. If it is not within specifications, adjust by loosening the bearing-adjuster locknut and tightening or backing off the adjuster. Tighten the locknut and recheck the pull.

4. Adjust the backlash next. Turn the steering wheel slowly to either stop. Do not bump it against the stop because this could damage the ball guides. Then rotate the wheel to center the ball nut. Turn the sector-shaft adjustment screw clockwise, repeatedly checking the pull required to pull the steering wheel through center. When the correct pull is attained, hold the adjustment screw and tighten the locknut. Recheck the pull.

NOTE: There should be no perceptible backlash at 30° on either side of center.

5. Connect the pitman arm to the steering-arm-to-idler-arm rod (or control-valve ball stud, on power steering).

■ 6-9-6 Ford Steering-Gear Service Figure 11 (in Part 6, Sec. 3) is a phantom view of the steering gear described in this section.

1. REMOVAL If the steering column is of the movable type, remove the three steering-column pivot-plate bolts.

Then, on all types, remove the bolt that attaches the flex coupling to the worm shaft of the steering gear. Raise the front end of the car, disconnect the pitman arm from the sector shaft. Remove the bolts that attach the steering gear to the frame. It may be necessary on some cars to disconnect the muffler inlet pipe. It may also be necessary to disconnect the clutch linkage (on cars so equipped).

2. DISASSEMBLY Rotate the worm shaft to the center position. Remove the locknut from the sector-shaft adjustment screw and the three cover bolts. Now the cover and sector shaft can be taken from the housing.

Loosen the locknut and back off the worm-shaft-bearing-adjuster nut so that the shaft and ball nut can be withdrawn from the housing.

NOTE: Do not let the nut run down to the end of the worm. This could damage the ball guides.

Remove the ball-guide clamp, turn the nut upside down over a clean pan, and rotate the worm shaft back and forth until all 50 balls fall out. The nut will now slide off the shaft.

Remove the needle bearings only if they require replacement. They can be pressed out with an arbor press and special tools. The bearing cups can be removed from the housing and adjuster by tapping the housing or adjuster on a wooden block to jar them loose.

3. REASSEMBLY Install new needle bearings and oil seal if the old ones have been removed. Apply steering-gear lubricant to the bearings. Install sector-shaft bearing cups in the housing and adjuster. Install a new seal in the adjuster.

Insert the ball guides into the holes in the ball nut, tapping them lightly with the wood handle of a screwdriver if necessary to seat them. Put the ball nut into position on the steering shaft. Drop 25 balls into the hole in the top of each ball guide. Rotate the shaft slightly back and forth to distribute the balls.

Install ball-guide clamps. Check the steering shaft to make sure it is free to turn in the ball nut.

Coat the threads of the steering-shaft bearing adjuster, housing-cover bolts, and sector adjustment screw with oil-resistant sealing compound. Do not get sealer on the internal threads or on the bearings. Coat the worm bearings, sector-shaft bearings, and gear teeth with steering-gear lubricant.

Clamp the housing in a vise, sector-shaft axis horizontal, and position the worm-shaft lower bearing in its cup. Install the worm shaft, with its nut, in the housing. Put the upper bearing in place on the worm. Then run the bearing adjuster (with cup in place) down. Adjust the worm-bearing preload as already described (■6-9-5).

Put the sector-shaft adjustment screw, with a shim, in the slot in the end of the sector shaft. Clearance should be less than 0.002 inch (0.05 mm) between the end of the screw and the bottom of the slot in the shaft. If it is greater, add shims.

Install a new gasket on the housing cover. Start the adjustment screw into the cover. Apply enough lubricant to fill the pocket in the housing between the sector-shaft bearings (about 30 percent full). Rotate the worm shaft so that the ball nut will mesh properly with the sector teeth.

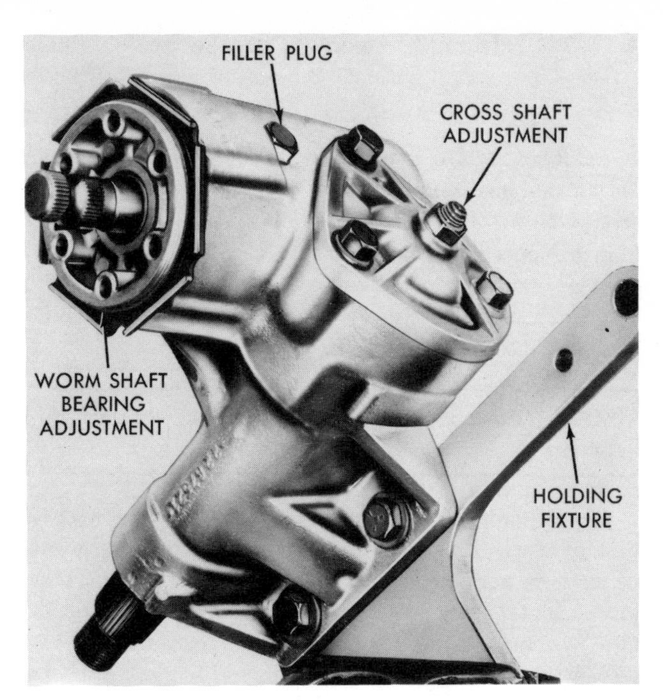

Figure 5 Steering-gear adjustments. *(Chrysler Corporation.)*

Put the sector shaft, with its cover, into place, turn the cover out of the way, and pack about 0.7 pound (0.32 kg) of lubricant into the gear. Push the sector shaft and cover into place and install the top two cover bolts, but do not tighten them until you are sure that there is some lash between the teeth. Then tighten the top two cover bolts and adjust the lash as already explained (■6-9-5). The lower bolt goes in after final lubrication of the steering gear.

5. INSTALLATION With the steering wheel and the sector shaft in their center, or straight-ahead, positions, attach the steering gear to the frame. Tighten the attachment bolts to the specified torque. Connect the pitman arm to the sector shaft (the front wheels must be straight ahead). Reconnect the muffler inlet pipe (if it was disconnected).

Reinstall the flex-coupling bolt (and pivot-plate bolts on the movable-column type).

Turn the steering wheel to the left to move the ball nut away from the filler hole. Now fill the steering gear with lubricant until it comes out the lower cover-bolt hole. Then install this lower bolt and tighten it to the specified tension.

■ 6-9-7 Plymouth Steering-Gear Adjustments

The steering gear described in this section is illustrated in Fig. 10 (in Part 6, Sec. 3). There are two adjustments: for worm-shaft-bearing preload and for ball-nut-rack and sector-shaft teeth mesh (Fig. 5). These are the same as required on the two steering gears previously described.

■ 6-9-8 Plymouth Steering-Gear Service

Figure 10 (in Part 6, Sec. 3) illustrates the steering gear described in this section.

1. REMOVAL To remove the steering gear, first remove the pitman-arm nut. Pull the arm from the sector shaft (or cross shaft) with a special tool. Remove the coupling-clamp bolt from the upper end of the worm shaft.

To get enough room to remove the steering gear, loosen the column-jacket clamp bolts. Slide the column assembly up far enough to disengage the coupling from the worm shaft.

NOTE: Do not scratch the steering column on the clamps!

Remove the three mounting bolts and take off the steering gear. On cars with six-cylinder engines, the steering gear can be removed from the engine compartment. On eight-cylinder models, the steering gear must be removed from underneath. On some models, the left-front engine mount must be detached and the engine raised 1½ inches (38 mm). Also, the starting motor may require removal.

2. DISASSEMBLY AND REASSEMBLY The disassembly and reassembly procedures for this steering gear are about the same as for the steering gears previously described. Special tools are required to remove and replace oil seals, bearings, and bearing cups.

3. INSTALLATION The steering wheel, steering gear, and front wheels must all be in the straight-ahead position when the steering gear is reinstalled on the car. First, attach the steering gear to the frame. Then, slide the steering column down far enough to permit the worm shaft to enter the flexible coupling. The master serration must be aligned with the notch mark on the coupling housing. When the grooves in the coupling and worm shaft are aligned, install and tighten the coupling bolt and nut.

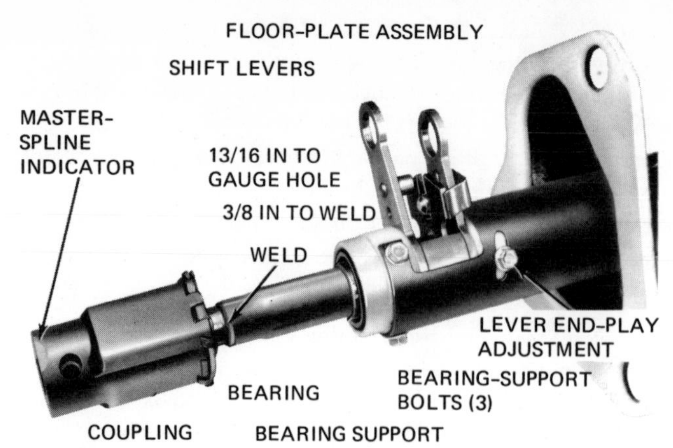

Figure 6 Steering-column adjustments. *(Chrysler Corporation.)*

Position the column assembly so that the steering-shaft coupling is centered at the midpoint of its travel, as determined by the ³⁄₁₆-inch (4.76-mm) gauge hole in the steering shaft (Fig. 6). Then tighten the column clamp bolts.

With the steering gear, steering wheel, and front wheels in the straight-ahead position, install the pitman arm on the sector shaft.

SECTION 6-10 Saginaw Rotary-Valve Power-Steering Service

This section describes the trouble-diagnosis, adjustment, removal, repair, and reinstallation of the Saginaw rotary-valve power-steering gears used on late-model General Motors cars. Section 4 in this part discussed trouble-diagnosis procedures on steering and suspension generally.

■ 6-10-1 In-Line and Rotary-Valve Power-Steering Trouble-Diagnosis Chart The list below of trouble symptoms, causes, and checks or corrections is provided to give you a means of logically analyzing trouble and quickly locating the cause. Once the cause is known, the trouble can be cured. Following the trouble chart are several sections that describe repair procedures on the Saginaw power-steering gears.

> **NOTE:** The troubles and possible causes are not listed in the chart in the order of frequency of occurrence. That is, item 1 does not necessarily occur more often than item 2, nor does item *a* under "Possible Cause" necessarily occur more often than item *b*.

IN-LINE AND ROTARY-VALVE POWER-STEERING TROUBLE-DIAGNOSIS CHART

(See ■6-10-2 to 6-10-12 for details of checks and corrections listed.)

COMPLAINT	POSSIBLE CAUSE	CHECK OR CORRECTION
1. Hard steering	a. Tight steering-gear adjustment	Readjust
	b. Pump drive belt loose	Tighten
	c. Low oil pressure	Check (see item 3, below)
	d. Air in hydraulic system	Bleed system
	e. Low oil level	Add oil
	f. Lower coupling flange rubbing on adjuster plug	Loosen flange bolt and adjust to 1/16-inch (1.59-mm) clearance
	g. Internal leakage	Check pump pressure (see item 3, below)
	h. Tire pressure low	Inflate to correct pressure
	i. Frame bent	Repair

(Continued)

IN-LINE AND ROTARY-VALVE POWER-STEERING TROUBLE-DIAGNOSIS CHART *(Continued)*
(See ■6-10-2 to 6-10-12 for details of checks and corrections listed.)

COMPLAINT	POSSIBLE CAUSE	CHECK OR CORRECTION
1. *(Continued)*	j. Front springs weak	Check standing height; replace springs
2. Poor centering (or recovery from turns)	a. Valve sticky	Free
	b. Steering shaft binding	Align, replace bushings
	c. Incorrect steering-gear adjustments	Readjust
	d. Lower coupling flange rubbing on adjuster plug	Loosen flange bolt, adjust to $1/16$-inch (1.59-mm) clearance
	e. Front end needs alignment	Align
	f. Steering gear out of adjustment	Adjust
	g. Steering linkage or ball joints binding	Replace affected parts
3. Low oil pressure	a. Loose pump belt	Tighten
	b. Low oil level	Add oil
	c. Mechanical trouble in pump	Check relief valve, rotor parts
	d. Oil leaks, external	Check hose connections, O sealing rings at cover, etc.
	e. Oil leaks, internal	Replace cylinder adapter, valve cover, or upper housing seal
	f. Engine idling too slowly	Set idle speed to specifications, check speedup control
4. Excessive wheel kickback or loose steering	a. Steering-linkage ball joints loose	Replace
	b. Steering-gear adjustments loose	Adjust
	c. Front-wheel bearings out of adjustment or worn	Adjust or replace
	d. Air in system	Fill, bleed
	e. Steering gear loose on frame	Tighten attaching bolts
	f. Flexible coupling loose	Tighten pinch bolts
5. Pump noise	a. Oil cold	Oil will warm up in a few minutes after starting the engine
	b. Air in system	Bleed
	c. Oil level low	Add oil
	d. Air vent plugged	Open
	e. Dirt in pump	Clean
	f. Mechanical damage	Disassemble pump, replace defective parts
6. Gear noise	a. Loose over-center adjustment	Adjust
	b. Loose thrust-bearing adjustment	Adjust
	c. Air in system	Bleed
	d. Oil level low	Add oil
	e. Hose rubbing body or chassis part	Relocate hose

■ 6-10-2 Trouble Diagnosis (Rotary-Valve Power Steering) The chart above lists possible troubles, causes, and corrections. When trouble is reported in the steering system, the following checks should be made in an attempt to pinpoint the trouble. Often, it may be some such simple thing as a loose belt that can be corrected without difficulty.

1. CHECK BELT TENSION As noted in the chart, low belt tension can cause low oil pressure and hard steering. A quick check of belt tension can be made—while the engine and pump are warm—by turning the steering wheel with the front wheels on a dry floor. As the wheel is turned, maximum pressure is built up. This imposes a full load on the belt. If the belt now slips, the tension is too low. To check tension more accurately, turn the engine off and push in on the belt midway between the pulleys. The specifications for one car state that the belt should deflect $1/2$ to $3/4$ inch (12.7 to 19.05 mm) with a push of 15 pounds (6.81 kg) halfway between the fan and pump pulleys. Loosen the mounting bolts and move the pump out to increase tension. Then tighten the bolts.

Some adjustment procedures call for the use of a belt-tension gauge (Fig. 1). The gauge fits on the belt as shown and measures the pull required to deflect the belt a standard distance.

2. CHECK OIL LEVEL If the oil level is low, add oil to bring the level up to the marking on the side of the reservoir. Use only the special oil recommended. If the oil level is low, the possibility exists that there is an oil leak; check all hose and power-steering connections for signs of a leak. Leakage may occur at various points in the power-steering unit if the seals are defective. Check around the piston and valve housings for leakage signs. Replace the seals or tighten the connections to eliminate leaks.

3. CHECK STEERING ACTION A check of the power-steering action can be made with a pull scale hooked to the

Figure 1 Checking pump-belt tension with a belt-tension gauge. *(Chevrolet Motor Division of General Motors Corporation.)*

wheel rim. Oil in the system must be warm before the test is made, and the front wheels must be resting on a level, dry floor. If the oil is cold, set the parking brake, start the engine, and allow it to idle for several minutes. While the engine is idling, turn the steering wheel back and forth so as to build up pressure in the system; this hastens the warming of the oil. With the oil warm, hook the pull scale on the steering-wheel rim, and see how much pull is required to turn the front wheels first in one direction and then in the other. The amount of pull specified varies with different models (because of tire and wheel size, linkage design, and so on). In general, if the pull exceeds about 10 pounds (4.54 kg), the unit is not working properly and the oil pressure should be checked.

> **NOTE:** Be sure the engine is idling at the specified speed. If it is idling too slowly, it may not be driving the pump fast enough to build up normal pressure.

4. CHECK OIL PRESSURE A special hydraulic-pressure gauge is required to check oil pressure from the pump. To use the gauge, disconnect the pressure hose from the pump and connect the gauge between the pressure fitting on the pump and the pressure hose (Fig. 2). To make the test, the pump reservoir must be filled, the tires inflated to the correct pressure, and the engine idling at specified speed. Hold the steering wheel against one stop and check connections at the gauge you just installed for leaks. Bleed the system (■6-10-3). Insert a thermometer in the pump reservoir. Move the steering wheel from one stop to the other several times until the thermometer registers 150 to 170°F (65.6 to 76.7°C).

> **NOTE:** To prevent scrubbing wear and flat spots on tires, move the car if you have to turn the steering wheel more than five times.

Hold the wheel against the stop and read the pressure. If it is below specifications, check further to find the trouble, as follows.

Slowly turn the shutoff valve to the closed position and read the pressure. Quickly reopen the valve to prevent damage to the pump. If the pressure is low, the pump is at fault. If the pressure comes up to normal, the trouble is in the hoses, connections, valve, or steering gear.

■ 6-10-3 Bleeding Hydraulic System

Air will enter the hydraulic system while oil lines are being disconnected and reconnected, after the pump or steering gear has been removed and replaced, or possibly because of a low oil level in the reservoir. The air must be removed; otherwise the unit will operate noisily and unsatisfactorily. To bleed the system, fill the oil reservoir to the proper level and allow the car to sit for at least 2 minutes. Start the engine and let it run for about 2 seconds. Add oil if necessary. Repeat until the oil level remains constant.

Raise the car so the front wheels are off the ground. Start the engine and run it at about 1,500 rpm. Turn the steering wheel right and left. Turn to stops, but avoid banging them hard. Add more oil if necessary. Lower the car to the ground and turn the wheel right and left. Add more oil if necessary.

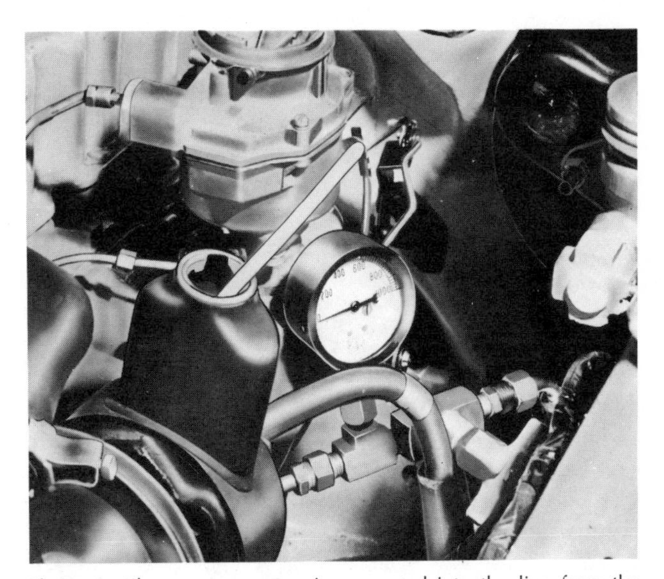

Figure 2 The pressure gauge is connected into the line from the pump to check maximum pump pressure. *(Chevrolet Motor Division of General Motors Corporation.)*

If the oil is foamy, wait for a few minutes and repeat the procedure. Then check the pulley for wobble and hoses and connections to make sure they are tight and not leaking. Fomay oil may indicate air leadage into the system, so check all points at which this could occur.

■ 6-10-4 Adjusting Steering Gear on Car At one time, an overcenter adjustment could be made on the car. Today, however, the manufacturers discourage adjustment of the steering gear in the car. Getting to the steering gear is difficult, and the hydraulic fluid tends to confuse the adjustment. It is, therefore, recommended that the steering gear be removed from the vehicle before any adjustments are attempted.

■ 6-10-5 Adjusting Steering Gear off Car With the steering gear off the car (■6-10-6) and drained of fluid, clamp it in a vise. Make adjustments as follows.

1. Adjust worm thrust-bearing preload by backing off the locknut and pitman-shaft adjuster screw 1 ½ turns. Then loosen the adjuster-plug locknut. Use a spanner wrench to bottom the adjuster plug by turning it clockwise. Avoid excessive torque! Then back off the adjuster plug 5 to 10°, or about 3/16 inch (4.76 mm) at the outside diameter of the adjuster plug. Use the torque wrench to make sure the torque required to turn the worm shaft is within specifications. Then hold the adjuster plug with the spanner and tighten the locknut.

2. Overcenter preload is adjusted by turning the pitman-shaft adjusting screw while turning the worm shaft through its center position with a torque wrench. First, check the torque with the adjusting screw backed out all the way. Then turn the adjusting screw in slowly, all the time swinging the torque wrench through center. Adjustment is correct when the torque wrench reads 4 to 8 pound-inches (4 to 8 kg-cm) more than the torque with the adjusting screw backed out. When adjustment is correct, tighten the locknut.

> **NOTE:** The permissible additional torque for a used gear [400 miles (643.7 km) or more] is 4 to 5 pound-inches (4 to 5 kg-cm). But the total torque should not exceed 14 pound-inches (14 kg-cm).

■ 6-10-6 Removing Steering Gear from Car The removal procedure varies somewhat from car to car because of variations in the installation. A typical removal procedure follows.

Disconnect the pressure and return hoses and elevate the ends of the hoses so that the oil will not run out. Cap both the hoses and the steering gear outlets to keep dirt from getting in. Remove the two nuts that attach the coupling lower flange to the steering-shaft coupling. Jack up the car and remove the pitman arm from the pitman shaft. Loosen the three bolts that attach the steering gear to the frame and remove the steering gear.

■ 6-10-7 Disassembly Figure 3 is a disassembled view of the steering gear. Mount the steering gear on a holding fixture which can be clamped in a vise. Never clamp the housing in a vise; this could distort it. Clean the steering gear. Drain out all lubricant, turning the worm shaft through its entire range several times to assist drainage.

It is not always necessary to completely disassemble the steering gear to find and fix a trouble. Most of the components can be removed from the housing without complete disassembly. However, the complete procedure follows.

> **NOTE:** When disassembling a steering gear, the work area, tools, and parts must be kept absolutely clean. Even a trace of dirt can cause malfunctioning of the steering gear. If a broken component or dirt is found in either the steering gear or pump, the entire hydraulic system must be disassembled and cleaned. Then the system must be flushed out and fresh oil added after everything is back together again.

1. Use a punch and a screwdriver to remove the end-plug retaining ring. Turn the worm shaft to push the end plug out. Discard the O ring. Do not turn the shaft farther than necessary; this could allow the balls to drop out of the ball nut. Remove the rack-piston end plug with an extension attached to a ½-inch drive ratchet from your socket set.

2. Remove the side-cover screws and washers. Move the cover around so that you can see the location of the sector. Turn the worm shaft until the sector is centered so that the pitman shaft and cover can be removed. Discard the side-cover O ring.

3. Remove the rack piston by using a special arbor held in the end of the piston while turning the worm shaft. The tool prevents the balls from falling out while the worm is threaded out of the rack nut.

4. Take the coupling flange off the worm shaft by removing the locking bolt. Remove the adjuster-plug locknut with a punch or a spanner wrench and then remove the adjuster plug. Push on the end of the worm with a hammer handle while turning the shaft to slip the assembly out of the housing. Pull the adjuster plug off the shaft. Pull the worm shaft from the rotary valve and discard the O ring. Discard the O ring from the adjuster plug.

5. If necessary, separate the side cover from the pitman shaft by removing and discarding the locknut and backing out the lash adjuster from the cover. Do not disassemble the lash adjuster from the pitman shaft; these parts are serviced as a single assembly.

6. The rotary valve should be disassembled only if necessary. If a "squawk" has developed in the steering gear, the valve-spool-dampener O ring probably needs replacement. This can be done by working the spool spring onto the bearing diameter of the shaft so that the spring can be removed. Tap

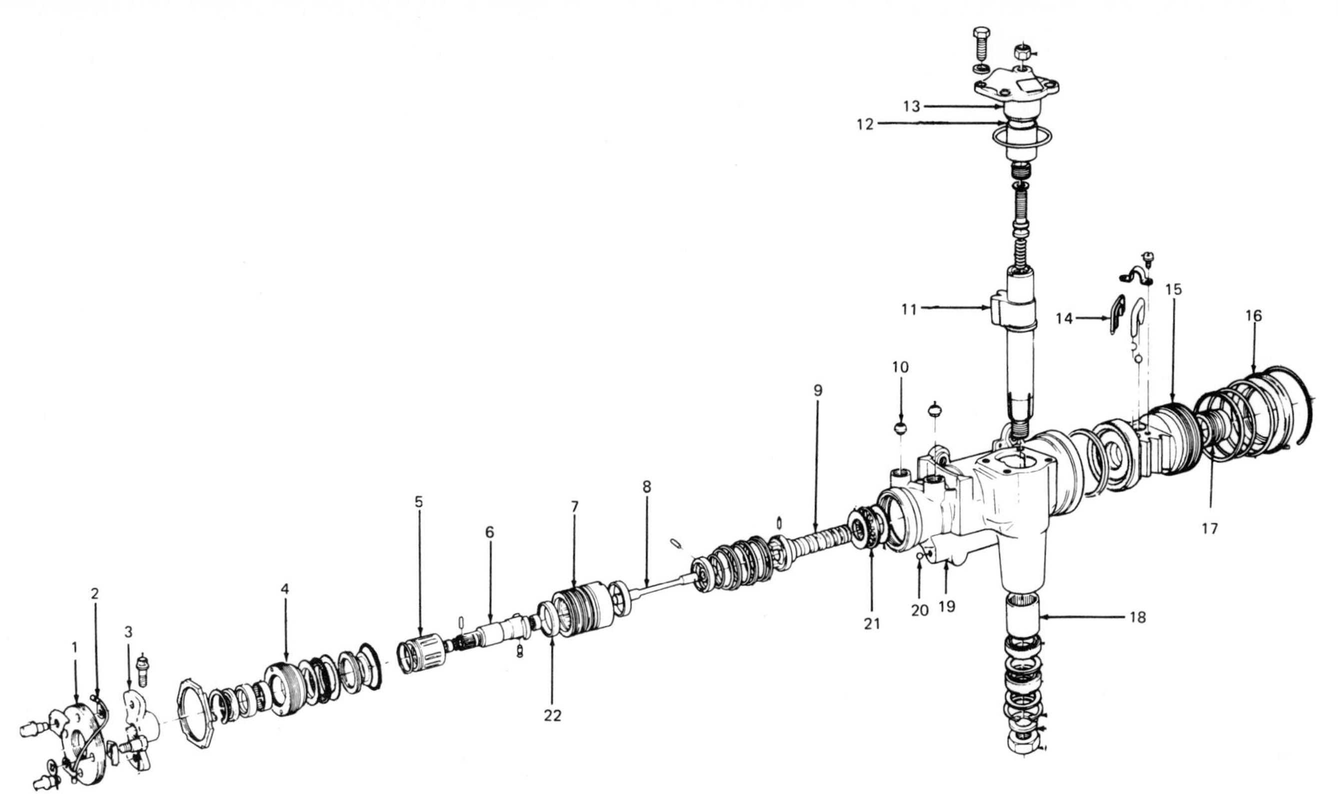

Figure 3 Exploded view of a power-steering gear. (1) Flange coupling; (2) horn ground strip; (3) lower flange; (4) adjuster plug; (5) spool valve; (6) stub shaft; (7) valve body; (8) torsion bar; (9) steering worm; (10) hose connector; (11) pitman-shaft gear; (12) housing-side-cover bushing; (13) housing side cover; (14) ball-return guide; (15) piston rack; (16) end cover; (17) piston end plug; (18) bearing, needle bearing; (19) steering-gear housing; (20) ball, oil-passage plug ball; (21) thrust bearing; (22) valve-body sleeve. *(Pontiac Motor Division of General Motors Corporation.)*

the end of the shaft gently down against the workbench so that the spool comes off.

> **NOTE:** Use great care because the clearance is small and the spool could cock and jam in the valve body.

Remove and discard the O ring. Put a new O ring in the spool groove, lubricate with type-A hydraulic fluid, and install the spool in the valve body. Do not allow the O ring to twist in the groove. Extreme care is required to prevent damage to the O ring! The notch in the spool must align with the pin in the stub shaft.

7. On the housing, the pitman-shaft lower seal and bearing can be replaced, if necessary, by using special tools to drive out the old and drive in the new bearing.

■ **6-10-8 Inspection** If the pitman-shaft bearing in the side cover is worn, replace the side-cover assembly. Likewise, replace the pitman-shaft-and-lash-adjuster assembly if the sector teeth or bearing surfaces are worn or damaged or if the lash adjuster has end play in the shaft.

The worm groove and rack-piston interior grooves and balls should be checked for wear. If replacement is required, both the worm and rack piston must be replaced as a match assembly.

Check the ball-return guides, making sure the ends, where the balls enter and leave, are not damaged. Replace the lower thrust bearing and races if they are worn or otherwise damaged.

If the rotary valve is damaged, the valve must be replaced as an assembly. The valve parts are matched and are not serviced separately.

The housing will require replacement if there are defects in the piston bore or rotary-valve bore. A slight polishing of the bores is normal.

■ **6-10-9 Reassembly** Lubricate all parts as they are assembled.

1. Screw the lash adjuster through the side cover until the cover bottoms on the shaft. Install but do not tighten the locknut.

2. Use great care when assembling the rotary valve, making sure the valve spool does not cock and jam in the valve body. The notch in the spool must line up with the pin in the shaft.

3. The pitman-shaft seals and washers can be installed, if the old ones are removed, by using special driving tools.

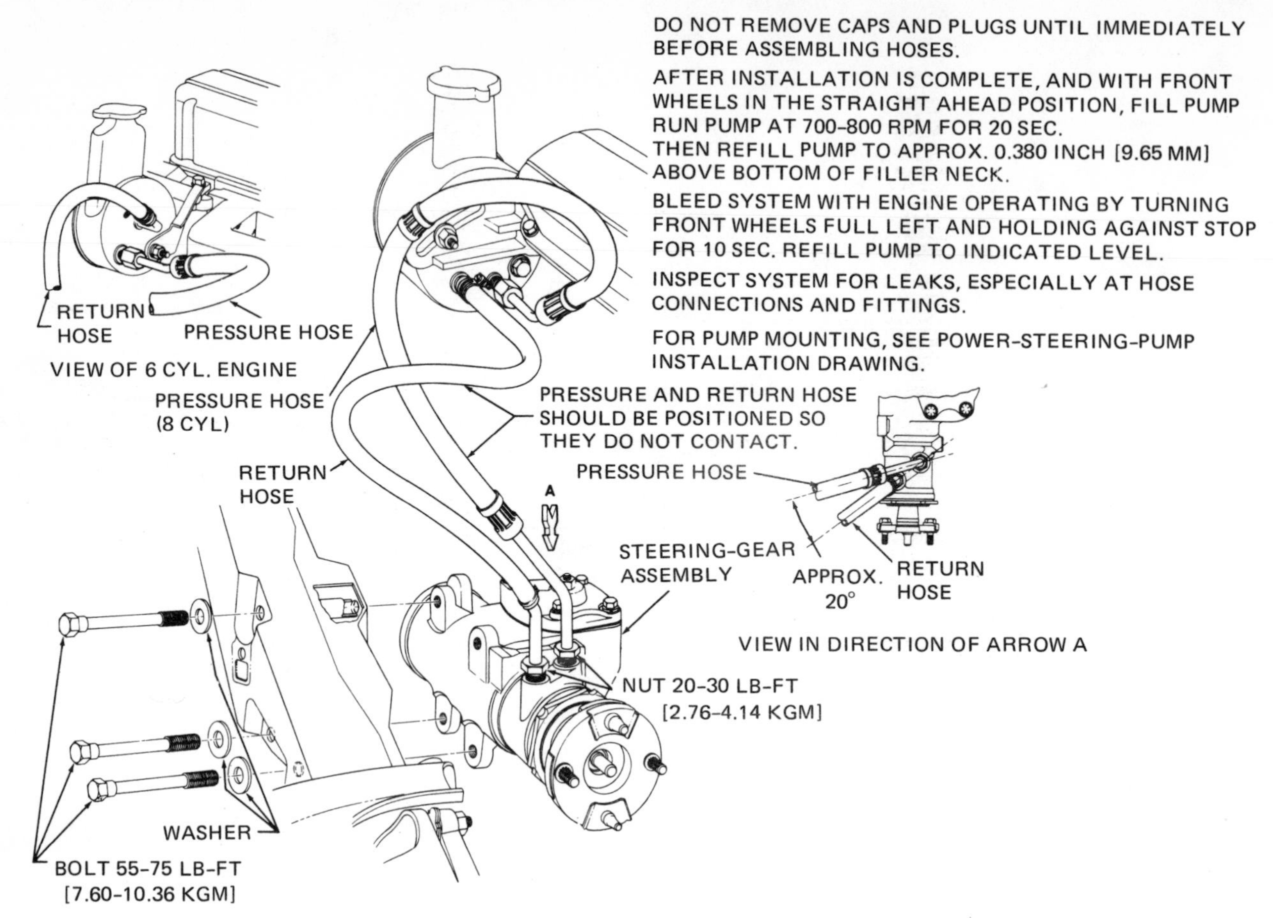

Figure 4 Details of power-steering-gear installation. *(Pontiac Motor Division of General Motors Corporation.)*

4. Working on the rack piston, lubricate and install the O and piston rings. Insert the worm into the rack piston all the way. Align the ball-return guide holes with the worm groove. Load 15 balls into the guide hole nearest the piston ring while slowly rotating the worm to the left. Alternate black and silver balls. Fill one-half of the ball-return guide with 7 balls. Place the other guide over the balls and plug the ends with grease. Insert the guide into the guide holes. Secure with a guide clamp and screws.

5. Check the worm preload. The worm has a high point at the center which should cause a small increase in torque when the rack piston passes over this point. If this torque is not as specified in the manufacturer's instructions, it may be necessary to fit smaller or larger balls. Note, however, that this is not necessary unless a complaint of loose steering has been received. Normally, a thrust and overcenter adjustment will correct the problem (see ■6-10-5). Put a special arbor into the end of the rack piston and turn the worm out of the rack piston. Keep the arbor in contact with the worm so that the balls do not fall out.

6. Install the lower thrust bearing and races on the worm and assemble the valve assembly to the worm, making sure the slot aligns with the pin on the worm head. Make sure the O ring is between the valve body and the worm head. Install a new O ring on the adjuster plug and put the plug on the shaft.

7. Put the worm-valve assembly into the housing and turn the adjuster plug into the housing until it is snug. Back it off about 1/8 turn. Use a torque wrench to check the torque required to turn the worm shaft. Tighten the adjuster plug to obtain the correct reading. Install and tighten the locknut and recheck the torque.

8. Put the coupling flange on the worm shaft. Use a special piston-ring compressor so that the ring will go into the housing. Push the rack piston into the housing until the special arbor contacts the end of the worm. Hold the arbor tightly against the end of the worm and turn the coupling flange to draw the rack piston onto the worm and into the housing. Do not drop the balls out of the rack piston!

9. Replace the pitman shaft and the side cover. Make sure the center tooth of the shaft sector aligns with the center groove of the rack piston. Use a new O ring on the side cover and make sure it is in place before pushing the cover against the housing. Install and tighten the side-cover screws.

Install the end plug in the rack piston with a 1/2-inch drive extension from your socket set. Tighten to the proper torque.

10. Replace the housing lower end plug with a new O ring and secure with a retainer ring.

11. Adjust the pitman-shaft preload at the center point. Remove the coupling flange and use a torque wrench to check the preload at the center point. Adjust the lash adjuster to in-

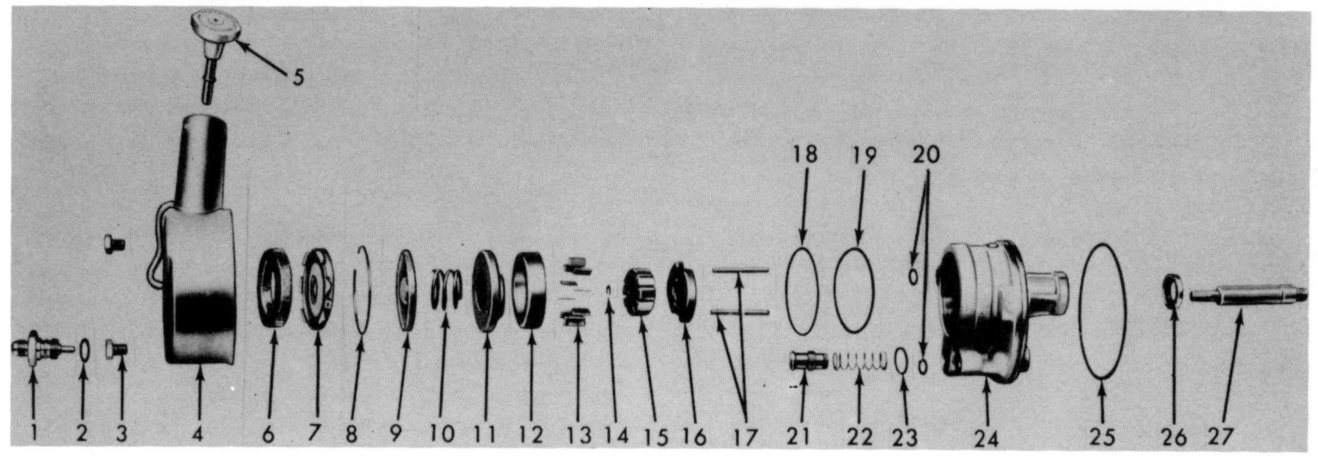

1. Union
2. Union O-ring seal
3. Mounting studs
4. Reservoir
5. Dipstick and cover
6. Element (Corvette only)
7. Filter assembly (Corvette only)
8. End-plate retaining ring
9. End plate
10. Spring
11. Pressure plate
12. Pump ring
13. Vanes
14. Drive-shaft retaining ring
15. Rotor
16. Thrust plate
17. Dowel pins
18. End-plate O ring
19. Pressure-plate O ring
20. Mounting-stud square ring seals
21. Flow-control valve
22. Flow-control-valve spring
23. Flow-control-valve-spring ring seal
24. Pump housing
25. Reservoir O ring seal
26. Shaft seal
27. Shaft

Figure 5 Exploded view of a power-steering pump. *(Chevrolet Motor Division of General Motors Corporation.)*

crease the torque to the specified reading. Tighten the locknut and recheck it.

12. Replace the coupling flange and secure it with a clamp bolt.

■ **6-10-10 Installation** Figure 4 illustrates the details of installation of the power-steering gear on one vehicle. Details may vary in some installations, so always check the shop manual of the specific car being worked on before attempting installation. Be sure to replace the shims between the steering-gear housing and the car frame in the original positions. The steering gear should align properly with the steering shaft. Tighten the attachment bolts.

After installation is complete, check the fluid level in the pump reservoir. Add fluid as necessary to bring it up to the mark. With the car wheels off the floor, start the engine and turn the steering wheel back and forth to the limit several times to bleed out all air.

Make a final check of the through-center pull after the installation is complete to make sure there is no misalignment.

■ **6-10-11 Oil-Pump Removal** To remove the pump from the engine, disconnect the hoses from the pump and fasten them in an elevated position so they will not drain. Put caps on all pump connections. Take off the pump-mounting bolts. Then remove the pump. Drain all oil from the reservoir after removing the cover.

■ **6-10-12 Vane-Type Pump Service** The vane-type pump, widely used in power-steering systems, has a series of vanes assembled in slots in a rotor. A typical overhaul procedure follows.

1. DISASSEMBLY Clean the outside of the pump with solvent. Remove the pulley retaining nut with a special tool. Clamp the pump in the soft jaws of a vise (lightly to avoid distortion) and remove: Union (1 in Fig. 5), O-ring seal (2), mounting studs (3), and reservoir (4). Tap lightly on the outer edge of the reservoir to break it loose. Remove the reservoir O-ring seal (25) and discard it.

Remove the stud square ring seals (20) and discard them. On the Corvette, remove the filter assembly (7) and discard it.

Remove the end-plate ring (8), using a small punch to compress the ring and a screwdriver to pry it out. Remove the end plate (9). The end plate is spring-loaded and will usually rise above the housing when the ring is removed. If it sticks, tap it lightly with a soft hammer or rock it.

With the end plate off, remove the spring (10) and shaft woodruff key. Then take out the impeller unit as an assembly. This includes parts numbered 11 through 16 plus the shaft (27) in Fig. 5. These parts can then be separated. Discard old O rings and seals, including the shaft seal (26), which must be pried out of the housing.

2. INSPECTION OF PARTS After cleaning all parts in solvent, check the following.

The flow-control valve must slide freely in the housing bore. The cap screw in the end of the flow-control valve must be tight. The pressure-plate and pump-plate surfaces must be flat and free of cracks and scoring. The vanes must be installed with rounded edges toward the pump ring, and they must move freely in the rotor slots. Check the drive shaft for worn splines and cracks.

3. REASSEMBLY Make sure all parts are clean during reassembly. Install a new shaft seal in the pump housing with a special tool. Put dowel pins in the pump housing and install a new pressure-plate O ring lubricated with transmission fluid. Install the thrust plate (16 in Fig. 5) on the shaft with ports facing toward the splined end of the shaft.

Install the rotor on the shaft with the countersunk side toward the thrust plate. Install the new shaft retaining ring, tapping it onto the shaft with a drift punch. Then tap it into place with a ⅜-inch (9.53-mm) socket. Put the housing in the vise and install the shaft, thrust plate, and rotor assembly. Align the holes in the thrust plate with the dowels in the housing. Install the pump ring on the dowels with the arrow showing the direction of rotation to the rear of the housing. Install the vanes in the rotor slots with rounded edges out. Lubricate the pressure plate with transmission fluid and install it with ports toward the pump ring. Seat the plate by pressing down with a large socket on top of the plate. Put the pressure-plate spring in place.

Lubricate a new end-plate O ring with transmission fluid and install it in the housing groove. Lubricate the outer diameter of the end plate with transmission fluid and install it in the housing, using an arbor press to hold it down while the retaining ring is installed. The end of the ring should be near the hole in the housing.

Install the flow-control spring and valve. The hex-head screw goes into the bore first. On the Corvette, install the cage and new filter. Install new square ring seals and a new reservoir O-ring seal. Lubricate the sealing edge of the reservoir with transmission fluid and put the reservoir on the housing. Install the new union O ring, union, and studs.

Support the drive shaft on the opposite side and tap the woodruff key into place. Slide the pulley onto the shaft, install the pulley nut, and then tighten the nut to 60 pound-feet (8.29 kg-m).

SECTION 6-11 Tire Service

This section covers the removal and replacement of tires and tire and tube repair.

■ **6-11-1 Tire Service** Tire service includes periodic inflation to make sure the tire is kept at the proper pressure, periodic tire inspection so that small damages can be detected and repaired before they develop into major defects, and tire removal, repair, and replacement. These services are covered below.

■ **6-11-2 Tire Inflation and Tire Wear** Incorrect tire inflation can cause many types of steering and braking difficulties. Low pressure will cause hard steering, front-wheel shimmy, steering kickback, and tire squeal on turns. Uneven tire pressure will tend to make the car pull to one side. ■6-4-11 covers, in detail, the effects of improper tire inflation on the tires themselves. Low pressure wears the sides of the treads (Figs. 4 in Part 6, Sec. 4, and 1 in this section), causes excessive flexing of the sidewalls, and results in ply separation. A tire with insufficient pressure is also subject to rim bruises; this could break plies and lead to early tire failure. Excessive pressure also causes uneven tread wear: the tread wears in the center. Also, a tire that is excessively inflated will give a hard ride and is subject to fabric rupture, since the pressure may be so high that the tire does not give normally. Thus, when the tire meets a rut or bump, the fabric takes the shock and cannot give, or flex, in a normal manner. This can result in weakened or even broken tire fabric.

■ **6-11-3 Toe-In or Toe-Out Tire Wear** Excessive toe-in or toe-out on turns causes the tire to be dragged sideways as it is moving forward. For example, a tire on a front wheel that toes in 1 inch (25.4 mm) from straight ahead will be dragged sideways about 150 feet (45.72 m) every mile (1.60 km). This sideward drag scrapes off rubber, as shown in Fig. 1. Note the featheredges of rubber that appear on one side of the tread. If both sides show this type of wear, the front end is misaligned. If only one tire shows this type of wear, the steering arm probably is bent. This condition can cause one wheel to toe in more than the other.

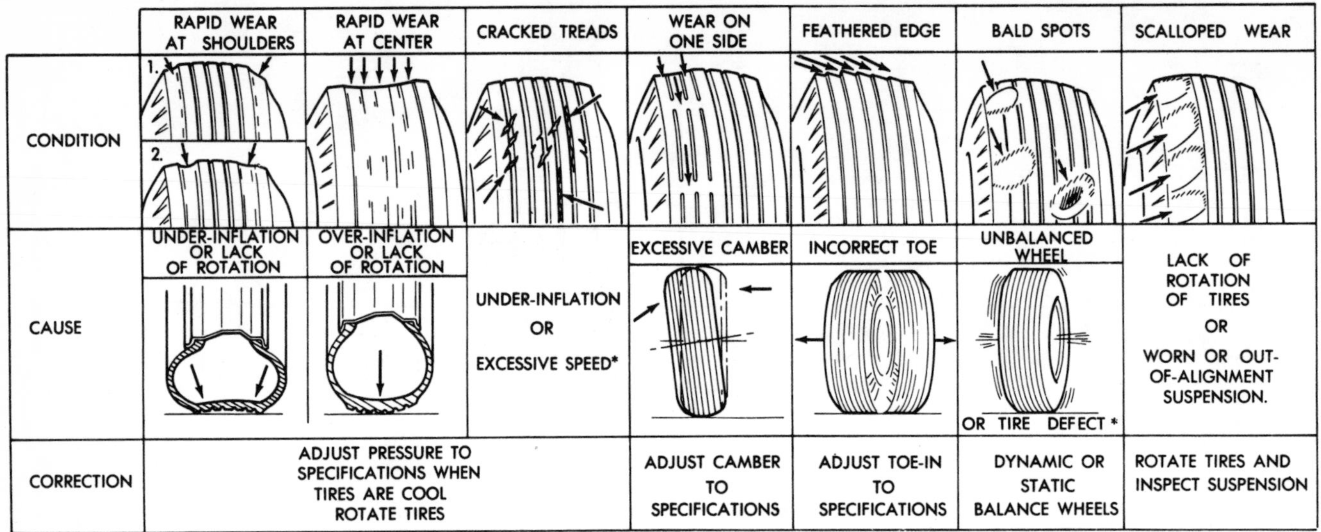

Figure 1 Types of tire wear and their causes and corrections. *(Chrysler Corporation.)*

■ 6-11-4 Camber Wear

If a wheel has excessive camber, the tire runs more on one shoulder than the other. The tread will wear excessively on that side, as shown in Fig. 1.

■ 6-11-5 Cornering Wear

Cornering wear, shown in Fig. 1, is caused by taking curves at excessive speeds. The tire not only skids, but it tends to roll, producing the diagonal types of wear shown. This is one of the more common causes of tire wear. The only remedy is to slow down around curves.

■ 6-11-6 Uneven Tire Wear

Uneven tire wear, with the tread unevenly or spottily worn, is shown in Fig. 1. It can result from several mechanical problems. These problems include misaligned wheels, unbalanced wheels, uneven or "grabby" brakes, overinflated tires, and out-of-round brake drums.

■ 6-11-7 High-Speed Wear

Tires wear more rapidly at high speed than at low speed. Tires driven consistently at 70 to 80 mph (113 to 129 km/h) will give less than half as many miles as tires driven at 30 mph (48 km/h).

■ 6-11-8 Checking Tire Pressure and Inflating Tires

To check tire pressure and inflate the tire, you must know the correct tire pressure for the tire you are servicing. You find this specification on the tire sidewall (on many tires), in the shop manual, in the driver's operating manual, and also on one of the door jambs (or at some similar place) on the car. Specifications are for cold tires. Tires that are hot from being driven or from sitting in the sun will have an increased air pressure because air expands when hot. Tires that have just been driven on a highway may show an increase of as much as 5 to 7 psi (0.35 to 0.49 kg/cm²).

As a hot tire cools, it loses pressure. Never bleed a hot tire to reduce the pressure. If you do, when the tire cools, its pressure could drop well below the specified minimum.

There are times when the tire pressure should be on the high side. For instance, one tire manufacturer recommends adding 4 psi (0.28 kg/cm²) for highway speed, trailer pulling, or extra-heavy loads. But never exceed the maximum pressure specified on the tire sidewall.

If the tire valve has a cap, always replace the cap after checking pressure or adding air.

■ 6-11-9 Tire Rotation

The amount of wear a tire gets depends on its location on the car. For example, the right rear tire wears about twice as fast as the left front tire. To equalize wear, manufacturers recommend rotating the tires every 5,000 miles (8,046 km). Figure 2 shows the recommended procedure for bias-belted, bias-ply, and radial tires. Note that bias-belted and bias-ply tires can be switched from one side of the car to the other. Belted radial tires should not be switched from one side to the other. Doing this would reverse their direction of rotation which could result in handling and wear problems (see Fig. 2).

Always check tire pressures after switching tires. Many cars require that the front tires carry different pressures from the rear tires. Thus, when you switch tires from front to back, the pressures will require adjustment to meet the specifications.

> **NOTE:** Studded tires should never be rotated. A studded tire should be put back on the wheel from which is was removed.

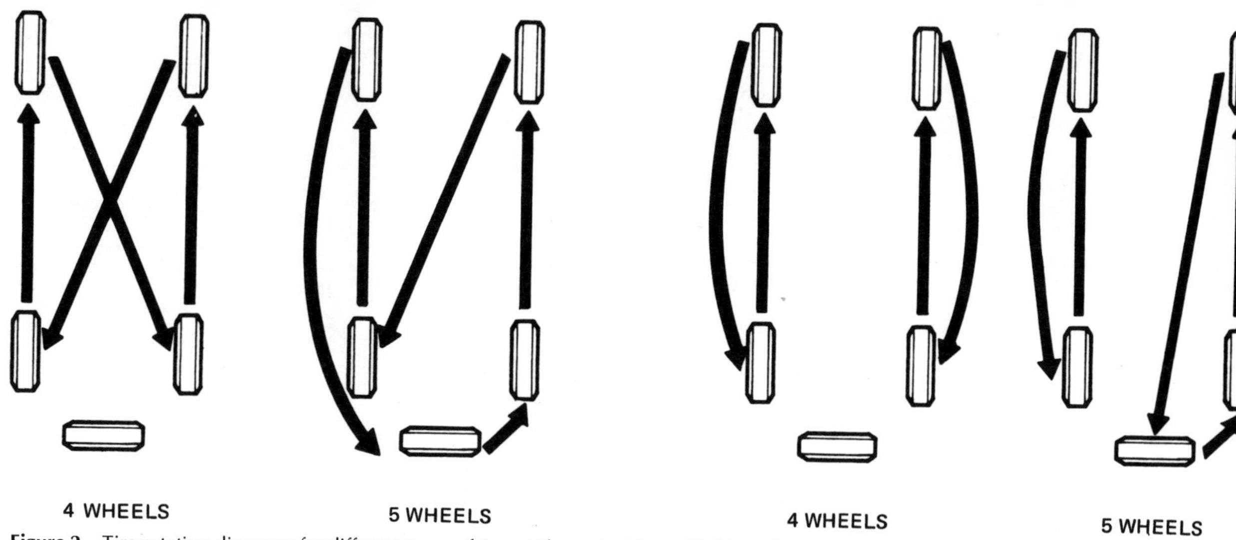

Figure 2 Tire rotation diagrams for different types of tires. *(Chevrolet Motor Division of General Motors Corporation.)*

■ 6-11-10 Tire Inspection

When inspecting a tire, remove all stones from the treads to make sure they are not hiding some damage. Check for bulges in the sidewalls. A bulge is a danger signal, since it can mean that the plies are separated or broken and that the tire is about ready to blow out. A tire with a bulge should be removed from the rim so that it can be checked inside and out. If the plies are broken or separated, the tire should be thrown away.

Many tires have wear indicators, which are filled-in sections of the tread grooves. When the tread has worn down enough to show the indicators (see Fig. 3), the tire should be replaced. There are also gauges that can be inserted into the tread grooves to measure how much tread is left. A simple way to check tread wear is with a Lincoln penny, as shown in Fig. 4. If at any point you can see all of Lincoln's head, the tread is excessively worn. Some state laws require a tread depth of at least 1/32 inch (0.79 mm) in any two adjacent grooves at any location on the tire. A tire with little or no tread has little holding power on the highway and will produce poor braking action.

> **NOTE:** A tire can look okay from the outside and still have internal damage from rim bruises or fabric breaks. The only way to completely inspect a tire is to remove it from the rim and look at it closely inside and out.

■ 6-11-11 Tube Inspection

Tubes usually give little trouble if correctly installed. However, careless installation can cause trouble. For example, if the wheel rim is rough or rusty, or if the tire bead is rough, the tube may wear through. Dirt in the casing can cause the same trouble. Another condition that can cause trouble is installing a tube that is too large in the tire. Sometimes an old tube (which may have stretched a little) is put into a new tire. When this is done, the tube can overlap at some point; the overlap will rub and wear and possibly cause early tube failure.

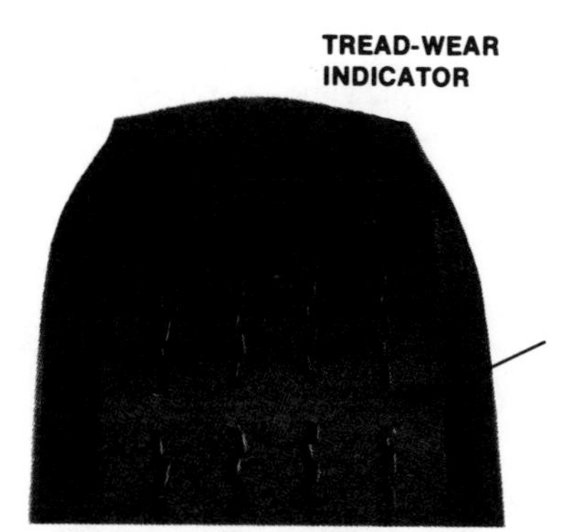

Figure 3 Tire tread, worn down so much that the tread-wear indicator is visible. *(Chevrolet Motor Division of General Motors Corporation.)*

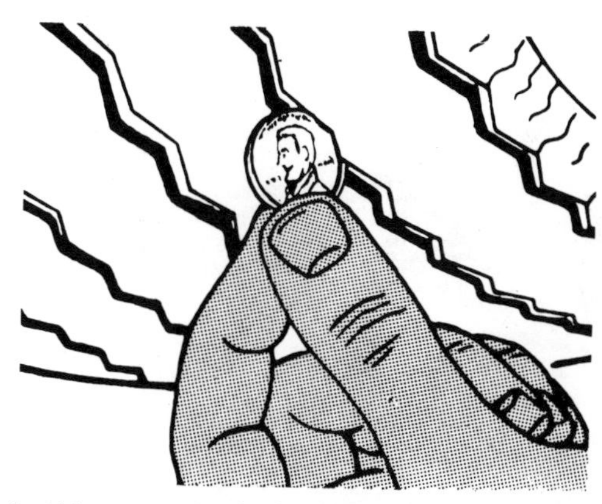

Figure 4 Using a penny to check tire-tread wear.

■ 6-11-12 Removing a Wheel from the Car

To repair a tire, first remove the wheel from the car (except for small-hole repairs on tubeless tires). Loosen the nuts before jacking up the car. It is easier to do it this way because the wheel will not turn if the car weight is on it. On some cars the lug nuts on the right-hand side of the car have right-hand threads, and the lug nuts on the left-hand side have left-hand threads. With this arrangement, the forward rotation of the wheels tends to tighten the nuts, not loosen them.

> **NOTE:** When using an impact wrench, use an impact socket with it. An ordinary socket is likely to break when used on an impact wrench.

■ 6-11-13 Removing a Tire from a Drop-Center Rim

With the wheel off the car, make a chalk mark across the tire and rim so you can put the tire back in the same position. This preserves the balance of the wheel and tire. Next, release the air from the tire by holding the tire valve open or removing the valve core. Then remove the tire from the rim, using the shop tire changer. At one time tire irons—flat strips of steel—were used to remove and install tires on rims. Today, however, they are not recommended because they can damage the tire bead and ruin the tire.

■ 6-11-14 Demounting Tools Demount or remove the tire from the rim using the special demounting tool that is part of the tire changer, as shown in Fig. 5. First, place the tire-and-rim assembly outside down in the tire changer. Then, push both beads down off the rim flanges into the drop-center well of the rim. Using the center post of the tire changer as a pivot, move the tool around to lift the bead off the rim. Repeat the procedure to lift the lower bead up and off the rim.

Figure 5 Using a special tire-removing tool as the first step in removing a tire from a rim. *(Jack P. Hennessy Company, Inc.)*

Figure 6 Powered tire changer. *(Jack P. Hennessy Company, Inc.)*

■ 6-11-15 Powered Tire Changers Where many tires are changed, as in a tire dealer's shop, an air-powered tire changer is used. It is similar to the manual tire changer. A powered tire changer is shown in Fig. 6. It has two major moving parts: the bead loosener and the rotating center post for demounting and mounting the tire. The bead loosener is brought down into position after the tire-and-rim assembly has been placed on the center post. The rim is held firm by a positioning pin and an adapter cup that screws down on the center post. When the bead loosener is operating, a hydraulic cylinder is actuated to force the loosener shoe down onto the bead. At the same time, a lower shoe pushes upward on the lower bead to loosen it. Next, the demounter tool is placed over the center post with the demounting end under the bead. Then, the technician starts the center post revolving. The demounting tool is carried all the way around to lift the bead above the rim. The lower bead is lifted off the rim in the same way.

To remount the tire, use the same procedure but in reverse, also reversing the double-ended demounting-mounting tool. As the center post revolves and carries the tool around with it, the bead is slid over the edge of the rim and down into place.

■ 6-11-16 Inspecting the Wheel When the tire is off the wheel, check the wheel rim for dents or roughness. Use coarse steel wool to clean off rust spots. File off nicks or butts. Clean the rim to remove all fillings and dirt. A wheel or rim that has been bent by an accident or by slamming into a curb, for example, should be discarded. Generally, do not straighten a bent wheel. Even if you do get the wheel straightened, it may be weakened so that it could fail when put under stress on the highway.

■ **6-11-17 Remounting Tires** The tire using a tube requires one mounting procedure. Tubeless tires require a different mounting procedure.

1. TIRE WITH TUBE Before replacing a tire that uses a tube, inflate the tube until it is barely rounded and put it into the casing. The inside and outside of the tire bead should be coated with tire-mounting lubricant to make it easier for the beads to slide over the rim. Do not use a nondrying lubricant; this would allow the tire to "walk around" on the rim so that balance would be lost. Never use grease or oil—these will damage the rubber. When mounting the tire on the rim, install one bead first, following with the second. After the tire is in place on the rim, make sure the beads are up on the bead seats in the rim and that the beads are uniformly seated all around the rim. Inflate the tube, making sure that it is properly centered in the tire and that the valve stem is square in the rim valve-stem hole. Deflate and then reinflate the tube. This last operation ensures good alignment of the tire, tube, and rim.

If a tire has been deflated, never inflate it while the car weight is on the tire. Always jack up the car before inflating the tire so that the tube can distribute itself around the tire evenly. If this is not done, some parts of the tube will be stretched more than other parts. This puts a strain on the tube that might cause it to blow out.

2. TUBELESS TIRE In mounting the tubeless tire, make sure that the rim flange, where the tire bead seats, is clean, smooth, and in good condition (■6-11-16). The tire bead seals the air in at this point, and so the rim flange must be smooth enough to permit a good seal.

If the valve in the wheel rim requires replacement, remove the old valve and install a new one. There are two types: the snap-in type, shown in Fig. 7, and the type that is secured with a nut. To remove the snap-in type, drive the valve into the rim with a soft hammer or cut the base off. Then use a valve-installing tool to install the new valve. Coat the new valve with tire-mounting lubricant. Then push the valve through the hole enough so that you can screw the tool onto the stem. Give the tool a sharp pull to seat the valve.

To mount the tire, install the two beads over the rim, as noted above (for a tire with a tube). Coating the beads and rim flanges with tire-mounting lubricant makes the mounting procedure easier. Do not use a nondrying lubricant. This would allow the tire to "walk around" on the rim so that balance would be lost. Never use grease or oil, since they will damage

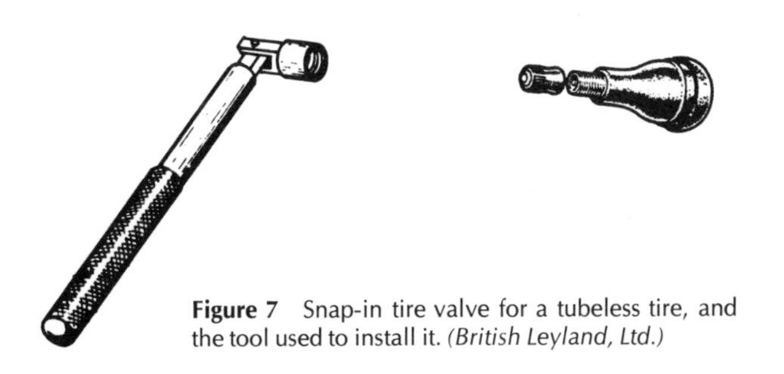

Figure 7 Snap-in tire valve for a tubeless tire, and the tool used to install it. *(British Leyland, Ltd.)*

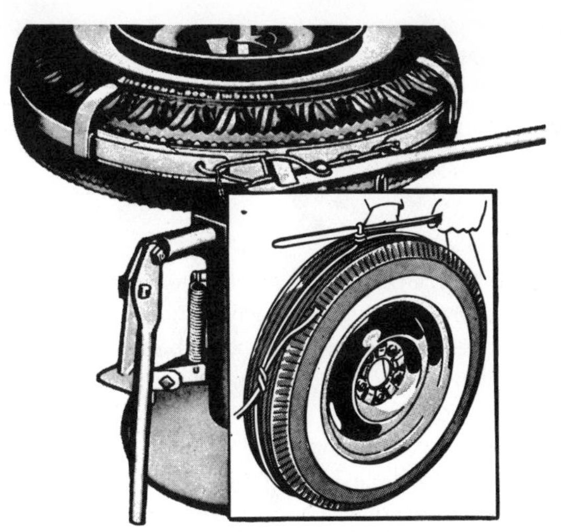

Figure 8 Using a commercial tire-mounting band or a rope tourniquet to spread the beads during mounting of a tubeless tire.

the rubber. After mounting the tire on the rim, use a commercial tire-mounting band or a simple rope tourniquet to spread the beads (Fig. 8). Then give the tire a few quick bursts of air to seat the beads properly. After the beads are seated, inflate the tire to 40 psi (2.81 kg/cm^2) for most passenger-car tires.

CAUTION: Do not stand over the tire while inflating it! If it bursts, you could be seriously injured!

If the bead-positioning rings on the tire (the outer rings near the sidewalls) are evenly visible all around the rim, the beads are seated properly. If the positioning rings are not evenly visible, deflate the tire completely and then reinflate it.

After the beads are properly positioned, deflate the tire to the recommended pressure.

■ **6-11-18 Tube Repair** If a tire tube has been punctured but is otherwise good, it can be repaired with a patch. First, you have to find the hole. Inflate the tube after it is out of the tire, then submerge it in water. Bubbles will appear where the leak is. Mark the spot with anything that will make a light scratch on the rubber. Deflate the tube and dry it.

There are two ways to patch a tube leak: the cold-patch and the hot-patch methods. With the cold-patch method, first make sure the rubber is clean, dry, and free of oil or grease. Then roughen the area around the hole, and cover the area with cement. Let the cement dry until it is tacky. Peel the back off a patch and apply the patch firmly. Recheck the tire for leaks by reinflating it and submerging it in water.

With the hot-patch method, prepare the tube in the same way as for the cold patch. Put the hot patch into place and clamp it. Then, with a match, light the fuel on the back of the patch. The heat ensures a good bond of the patch to the tube. After the patch has cooled, recheck the leaks by submerging the inflated tube in water.

Another kind of hot patch uses a vulcanizing hot plate, which supplies the heat required to bond the patch to the tube.

> **NOTE:** The hot-patch is the preferred method of tube repair by many technicians.

■ **6-11-19 Tire Repair** No attempt should be made to repair a tire that has been badly damaged. If plies are torn or have holes in them, the tire should be thrown away. Even though you might be able to patch the tire to hold air, using it would be dangerous and illegal. The tire might blow out at high speed and cause an accident.

Repairing small holes in a tubeless tire is simple. First make sure that the object that caused the hole is removed. While the tire is off, check it for other puncturing objects. Tubeless tires can carry a nail for miles without losing air.

> **NOTE:** You find leaks from a tubeless tire the same way you find leaks from a tube. With the tire on the wheel and inflated, submerge the tire and wheel in water. Bubbles will show the location of any leaks. If a water tank is not available, you can coat the tire with soapy water. Bubbles will show the location of leaks.

If air leaks around the spoke welds of the wheel, you can repair the leaks as follows: Clean the area and apply two coats of cold-patching cement on the inside of the rim. Allow the first coat to dry before applying the second coat. Then cement a strip of rubber over the area.

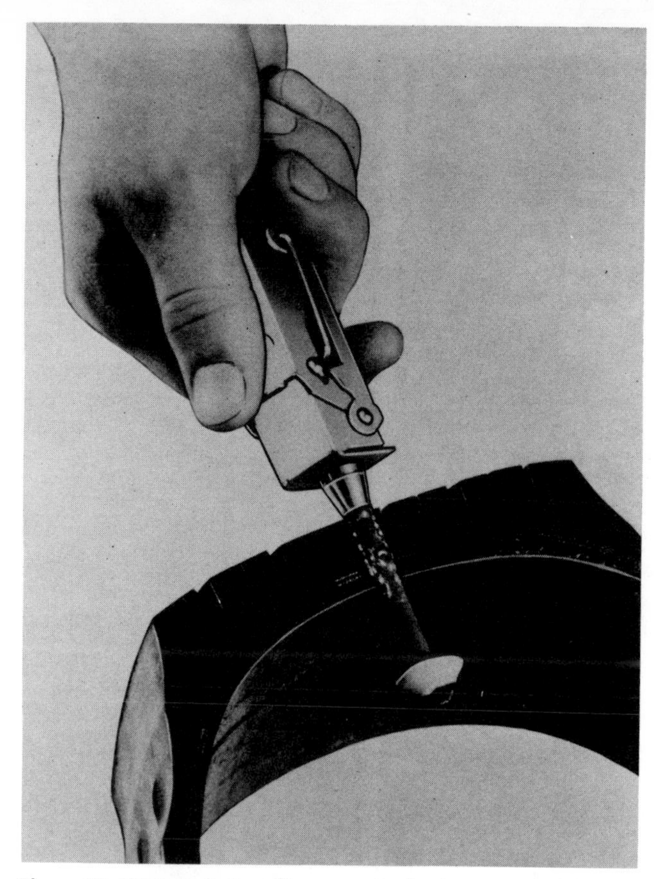

Figure 10 First step in installing a repair plug in a tire. The plug has been inserted by the applicator far enough to allow the cup on the end to clear the inside of the tire. *(General Motors Corporation.)*

■ **6-11-20 Repairing a Puncture with a Rubber Plug—Tire on Rim** A temporary repair of a small puncture can be made with the tire still mounted on the rim, as described in the next paragraph. However, this repair is only a temporary fix. At the first opportunity the tire must be removed from the rim and repaired from the inside, as explained in ■6-11-21.

Figure 9 Tire cut away to show the needle being used to insert the rubber plug in the hole.

Remove the puncturing object and clean the hole with a rasp. Apply rubber cement to the outside of the hole. Push the snout of the can of rubber cement into the hole to get some inside the tire. There are different kinds of rubber plugs. The kind shown in Fig. 9 is installed with a special needle. To use this plug, first cover the hole with rubber cement. Then select a plug of the right size for the hole. The plug should be at least twice the diameter of the hole. Roll the small end of the plug into the eye of the needle. Dip the plug into rubber cement. Push the needle and plug through the hole. Then pull the needle out. Trim off the plug 1/8 inch (3.2 mm) above the tire surface. Check for leakage. If there is no leakage, the tire is ready for service after it is inflated.

Another type of plug and its applicator are shown in Fig. 10. When using this plug, first clean the hole with a rasp. Coat the hole on the inside with rubber cement. Then place the plug on the applicator, and coat the plug with rubber cement. Next, insert the applicator through the hole, as shown in Fig. 10. Pull the plug back out enough to force the cap on the end of the plug to seat on the inside of the tire. Finally, remove the applicator and cut off the plug about 1/8 inch (3.2 mm) from the tire surface.

used. After the repair is done, mount the tire on the rim, inflate it, and test it for leakage, as explained in ■6-11-19.

■ 6-11-21 Repairing a Tire—Removed from Rim

There are three methods of repairing holes in tires: the rubber-plug, the cold-patch, and the hot-patch methods. Permanent repairs are made from inside the tire—with the tire off the rim.

1. RUBBER-PLUG METHOD Rubber plugs can be used in the same way as explained in ■6-11-20. The basic difference is that the repair is made from inside the tire, and the inside area around the hole is buffed and cleaned. Then the plug is installed from inside the tire.

2. COLD-PATCH METHOD In the cold-patch method, first clean and buff the inside area around the hole. Then pour a small amount of rubber cement around the hole and allow it to dry for 5 minutes. Next, remove the backing on the patch. Place the patch over the hold, rolling it down with the roller. Start rolling at the center and work out, making sure to roll down the edges.

NOTE: Be sure no dirt gets on the cement or patch during a repair job. Dirt could allow leakage.

3. HOT-PATCH METHOD The hot-patch method is very similar to the cold-patch method. The essential difference is that heat is applied after the patch has been put into place over the area. This is done by lighting the patch with a match, or with an electric hot plate, according to the type of patch being used. After the repair is done, mount the tire on the rim, inflate it, and test it for leakage, as explained in ■6-11-19.

■ 6-11-22 Recapping

Recapping is a special process. It involves applying new tread material to the old casing and vulcanizing it into place. Only casings that are in good condition should be recapped. Recapping cannot repair a casing with broken or separated plies or other damage. Recapping requires a special recapping machine.

The tire is first cleaned and the tread area is roughened by rasping it or buffing it on a wire wheel. Then a strip of new rubber tread, called "camel-back," is placed around the tread. The casing with the camelback then goes into the recapping machine. The machine is clamped shut, and heat is applied for the specified time. A new tread is formed and vulcanized onto the old casing.

■ 6-11-23 Repairing a Tire that Uses a Tube

If a tire that uses a tube has a small hole, clean out the hole. The tube will hold air, if it has not been punctured. However, if the hole is very large, repair it with a patch on the inside of the tire. This prevents dirt or water from working in between the tire and tube and causing trouble.

■ 6-11-24 Balancing the Wheel

After a tire change or repair, the tire-and-wheel assembly should be checked for balance. Balancing is covered in Part 6, Sec. 8.

PART 7 Brakes

SECTION 7-1 Automotive Brakes

This section describes the construction and operation of the various types of brakes used on automobiles. The sections that follow explain how to service brakes. Since the great majority of brakes in use today are hydraulically actuated, the section reviews hydraulic principles and explains their application to brakes. There are two general types of hydraulic brakes: drum and disk (also spelled "disc"). In the drum type, curved brake shoes move against the inner surfaces of brake drums. In the disk type, flat brake pads or shoes move in against a flat disk.

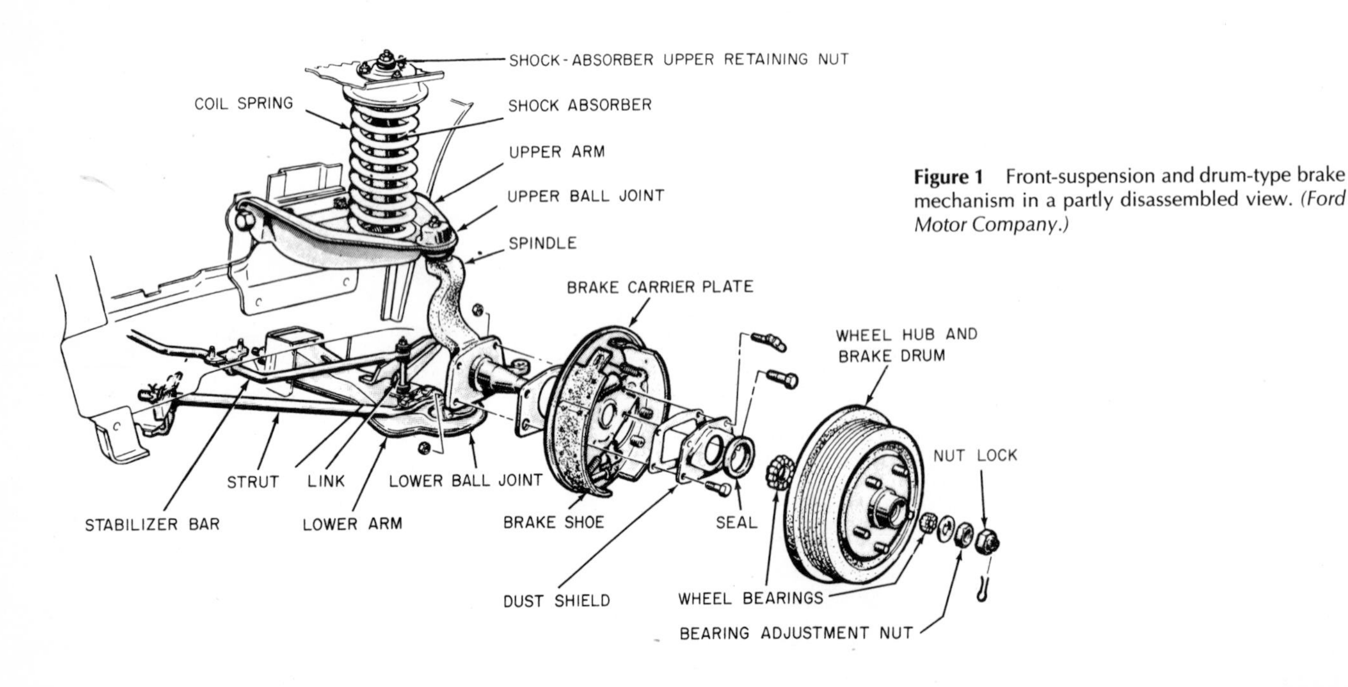

Figure 1 Front-suspension and drum-type brake mechanism in a partly disassembled view. *(Ford Motor Company.)*

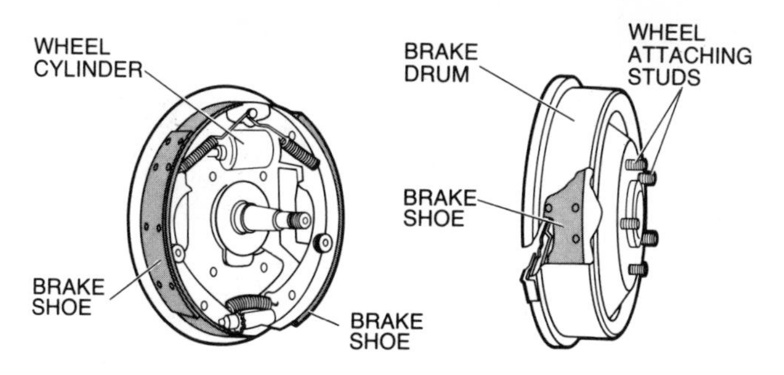

Figure 2 Brake-shoe assembly (left) and brake drum in place on the assembly (right). The drum is partly cut away to show a shoe. The studs are for attaching the wheel to the drum. *(Oldsmobile Division of General Motors Corporation.)*

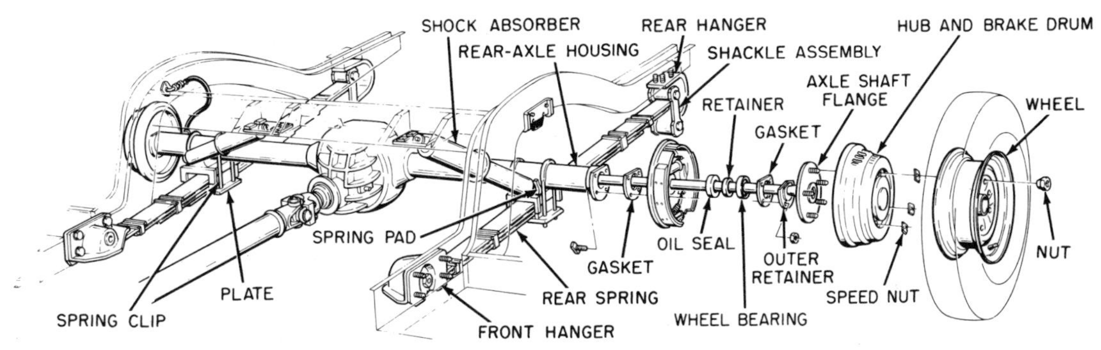

Figure 3 Rear-suspension and drum-type brake mechanism in partly disassembled view. *(Ford Motor Company.)*

■ 7-1-1 Function and Types of Brakes

Brakes slow and stop the car. They may be operated by mechanical, hydraulic, air-pressure, or electrical devices. Essentially, however, all function in the same manner. The operating device forces brake shoes or pads against the rotating brake drums or disks at the wheels when the driver operates the brake pedal. Friction between the brake shoes or pads and the brake drums or disks then slows or stops the wheels so that the car is braked.

Figure 1 shows a front-wheel brake mechanism of the drum type in disassembled view so that the relationship of the parts can be seen. When the mechanism is assembled, the brake drum fits around the brake shoes as shown in Fig. 2. Figure 3 shows a rear-wheel brake mechanism in disassembled view.

The brake shoes are lined with an asbestos material that can withstand the heat and dragging effect imposed when the shoes are forced against the brake drum or disk. During hard braking, the shoe may be pressed against the drum or disk with a pressure of as much as 1,000 psi (70.31 kg/cm²). Since friction increases as the load, or pressure, increases, a strong frictional drag is produced on the brake drum or disk and a strong braking effect results on the wheel.

A great deal of heat is produced, also, by the frictional effect between the brake shoes and the drum or disk. When you rub your hands together vigorously, they become warm. In a similar manner, when the drum or disk rubs against the shoe, the drum or disk and shoe get warm. In fact, under extreme braking conditions, temperatures may reach 500° F (260° C). The heat is disposed of in different ways in drum and disk brakes. In the drum type, some of the heat goes through the brake linings to the shoes and backing plate, where it is radiated to the surrounding air. But most of it is absorbed by the brake drum. Some brake drums have cooling fins that provide additional radiating surface for dispelling the heat more readily. Excessive temperature is not good for brakes, since it may char the brake lining; also, with the lining and shoes hot, less effective braking action results. This is the reason that brakes "fade" when they are used continuously for relatively long periods, as they are, for example, when the car is coming down a mountain or long slope.

Some special-performance vehicles, such as racing cars, are equipped with metallic brakes. Instead of linings of asbestos material, these brakes have a series of metallic pads attached to the brake shoes. These brakes can withstand more severe braking and higher temperatures and have less tendency to fade.

The disks in disk brakes are ventilated to improve cooling and reduce fade. For example, the disk shown in Fig. 4 has cooling louvers or fins to aid in the dissipation of heat. Also, note that only a small part of the disk is in contact with the brake shoes or pads during braking. The rest of the disk is dissipating heat. Disk brakes are described in detail in ■ 7-1-12.

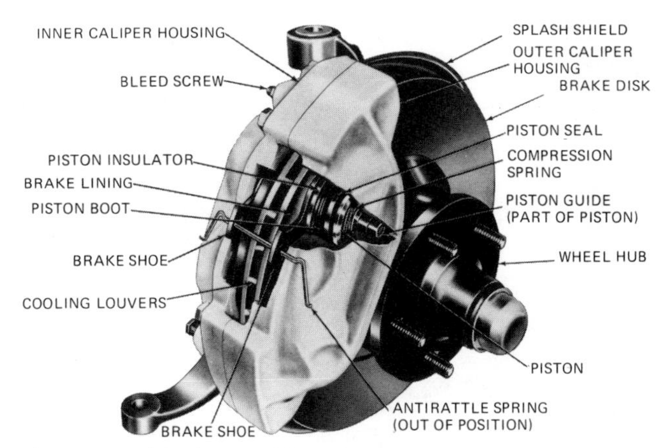

Figure 4 Disk-brake assembly (Budd) partly cut away so that the piston and shoe can be seen. *(Chrysler Corporation.)*

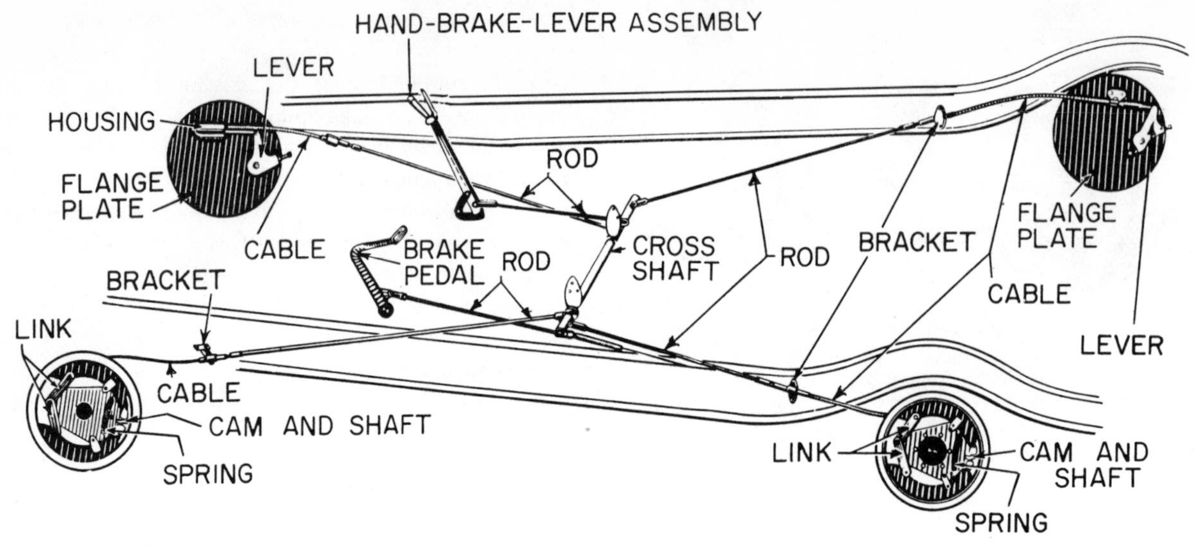

Figure 5 Mechanically operated four-wheel brake system.

■ 7-1-2 Mechanical Brakes

Mechanical brakes are no longer widely used for braking or stopping the car, although almost all cars have a mechanically operated parking brake. Mechanical brakes incorporate cables that link the brake pedal with the brake-shoe operating devices. Figure 5 illustrates a mechanically operated four-wheel brake system. Pressing down on the brake pedal pulls against cables attached to the brake-shoe expanding devices. The brake-shoe expanding device consists of a lever or cam that is actuated or rotated to push one end of the brake shoe out. The other end of the brake shoe is attached to the brake backing plate by an anchor pin. Figure 6 illustrates one type of cam-operated brake shoe.

Mechanically operated parking brakes on most cars make use of a foot or hand brake connected by cables to the rear-wheel brake shoes or to a separate brake that is part of the transmission shaft. Figure 7 illustrates the layout of a parking brake that makes use of the two rear-wheel brakes. The hand lever, when pulled, pulls cables that operate levers in the two rear-wheel brake mechanisms. The levers, as they operate, force the brake shoes apart and into contact with the brake drum. In many cars, the parking brake is released by a vacuum cylinder when the engine is started and the transmission selector lever is moved out of PARK.

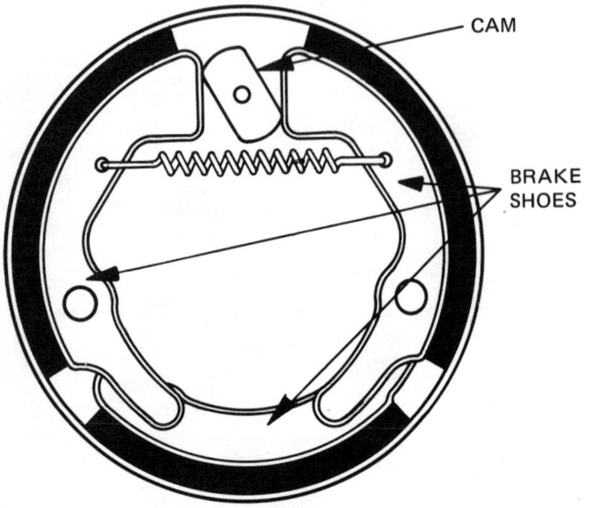

Figure 6 Brake-shoe actuating device. The pull of a cable from the brake pedal rotates the cam. The cam, as it rotates, forces the ends of the shoes outward and into contact with the brake drum.

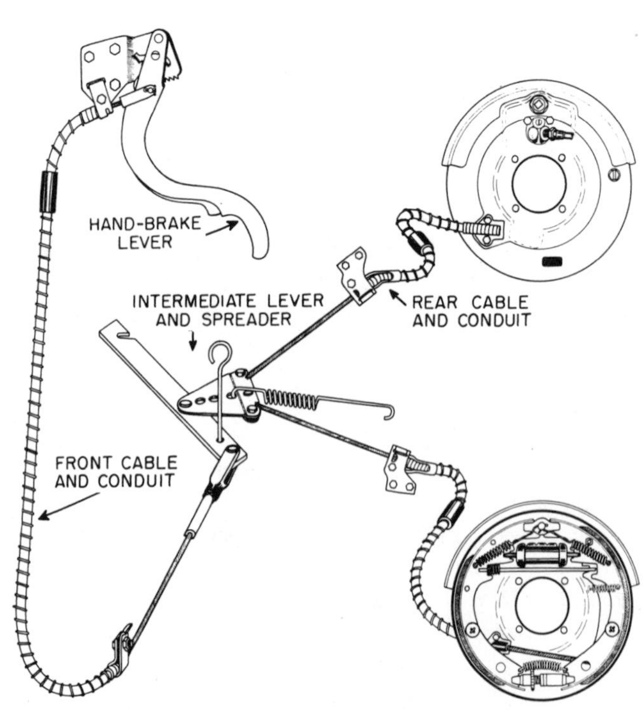

Figure 7 Schematic layout of a parking-brake system. Operation of the hand-brake lever causes the intermediate lever to pivot forward. This pulls on the two rear cables so that the rear brakes are mechanically applied. *(Pontiac Motor Division of General Motors Corporation.)*

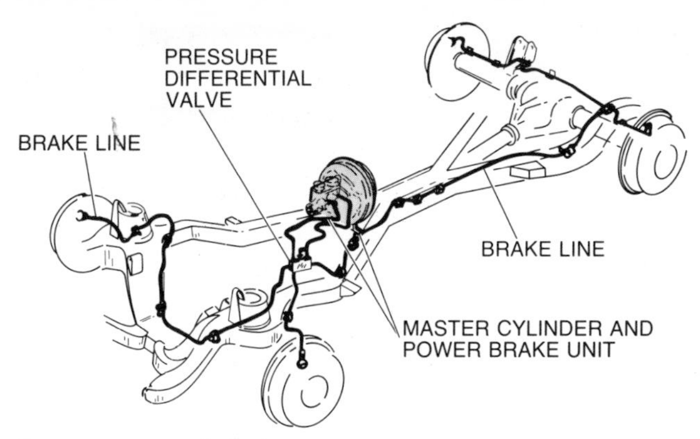

Figure 8 Layout of a hydraulic-brake system, showing the brake line and components.

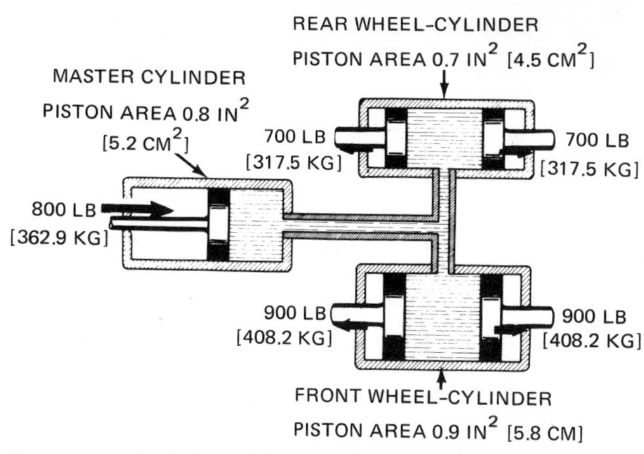

Figure 9 As the brake pedal is moved, the piston in the master cylinder applies pressure to the liquid. This pressure forces the liquid into the wheel cylinders. *(Pontiac Motor Division of General Motors Corporation.)*

■ **7-1-3 Hydraulic Principles** Since most brakes are hydraulically operated, we review briefly the hydraulic principles that cause them to operate. Fluid is not compressible. Pressure on a fluid will force it through a tube and into chambers or cylinders where it can force pistons to move. This is the principle on which hydraulic brakes work.

■ **7-1-4 Hydraulic-Braking Action** Hydraulic-type brakes use the pressure of a fluid (hydraulic pressure) to force the brake shoes outward and against the brake drums or disk. Figure 8 illustrates a typical hydraulic-brake system. The system consists essentially of two components: the brake pedal with master cylinder, and the wheel brake mechanisms, together with the connecting tubing or brake fluid lines and the supporting arrangements.

In operation, movement of the brake pedal forces a piston to move in the master cylinder. This applies pressure to fluid ahead of the piston, forcing the fluid—under pressure—through the brake lines to the wheel cylinders (Fig. 9). On the drum type,[1] each wheel cylinder has two pistons, as shown. Each piston is linked to one of the brake shoes by an actuating pin. Thus, when the fluid is forced into the wheel cylinders, the two wheel-cylinder pistons are pushed outward. This outward movement forces the brake shoes outward and into contact with the brake drum.

Note that in Fig. 9, piston sizes and hydraulic pressures are given as examples of the pressures involved. The piston in the master cylinder has an area of 0.8 square inch (5.2 cm^2). A push of 800 pounds (362.9 kg) is being applied to the piston. This gives a pressure of 1,000 psi (70.31 kg/cm^2) in the system. This pressure at the rear wheels gives an outward force of 700 pounds (317.5 kg) on each piston. The pistons are 0.7 square inch (4.5 cm^2) in area. At the front wheels, the piston area is shown to be 0.9 square inch, so that a pressure of 900 pounds (408.2 kg) is applied by the pistons to the front brake shoes.

The pistons are usually larger at the front wheels because when the brakes are applied, the forward momentum of the car throws more of the weight on the front wheels. A stronger braking effort at the front wheels is, therefore, necessary to achieve balanced braking effort.

■ **7-1-5 Dual Brake System** In older-model cars, the master cylinder contained only one piston, and its movement forced brake fluid to all four wheel cylinders. Now, however, the hydraulic system has been split into two sections, a front section and a rear section (Fig. 10). With this arrangement, if one section fails owing to damage or leakage, the other section will still provide braking. This system also includes a warning light that comes on when one section has failed.

■ **7-1-6 Master Cylinder** In the older braking system, the master cylinder has but one piston. The dual-brake system has a master cylinder with two pistons, set in tandem. Figures 11 to 13 illustrate the two types. The operation is similar in both systems, except that in the dual system there are two separate sections functioning independently. The master-cylinder pistons are linked to the brake pedal through a lever arrangement that provides a considerable mechanical advantage. That is, the push on the brake pedal is multiplied several times by the lever arrangement. For example, in the arrangement shown in Fig. 11, a push of 100 pounds (45.4 kg) on the brake pedal will produce a push of 750 pounds (340.2 kg) at the piston.

As the piston in the master cylinder moves in (from the position shown in Fig. 11 to the position shown in Fig. 13), it moves past the compensating port. This traps the fluid in the

[1] Disk brakes are described in ■7-1-12.

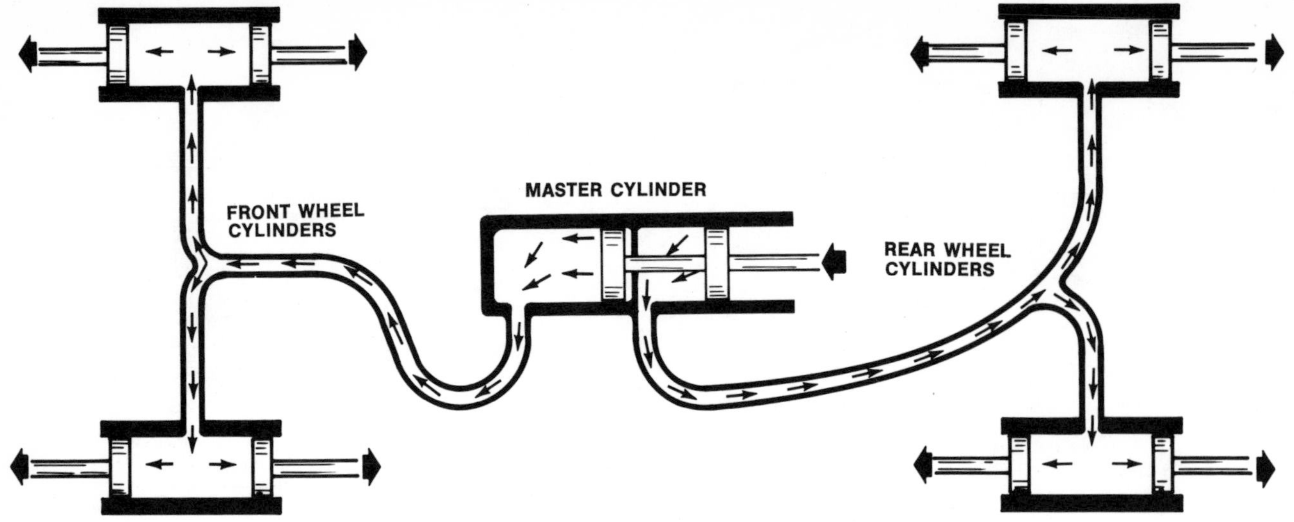

Figure 10 Flow of brake fluid to the four wheel cylinders when the pistons are pushed into the master cylinders.

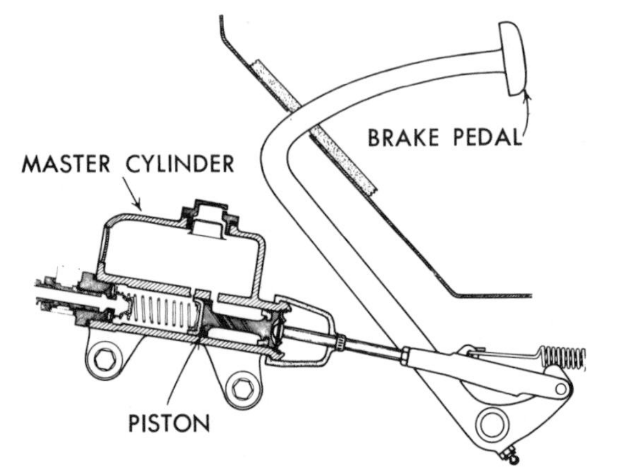

Figure 11 Relationship between the brake pedal and the single-piston master cylinder. *(Pontiac Motor Division of General Motors Corporation.)*

cylinder that is ahead of the piston. Pressure rises rapidly, and fluid is forced through the brake lines to the wheel cylinders. This action is shown in Fig. 13.

■ 7-1-7 Wheel Cylinders

Figure 14 shows the construction of a wheel cylinder for a drum-type brake. Hydraulic pressure applied between the two piston cups forces the pistons out. Thus, the brake-shoe actuating pins force the brake shoes into contact with the brake drums. The piston cups are so formed that the hydraulic pressure forces them tightly against the cylinder wall of the wheel cylinder. This produces a good sealing action that holds the fluid in the cylinder. For a description of the arrangement used at the wheels in the disk-type brake, see ■7-1-12.

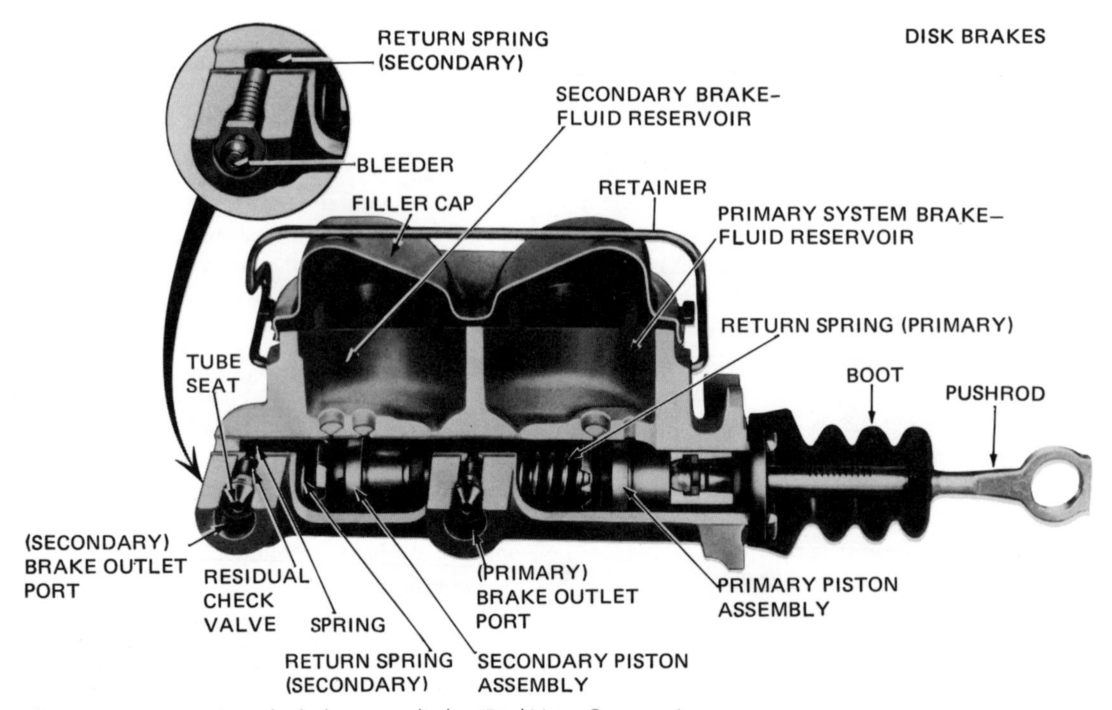

Figure 12 Cutaway view of a dual master cylinder. *(Ford Motor Company.)*

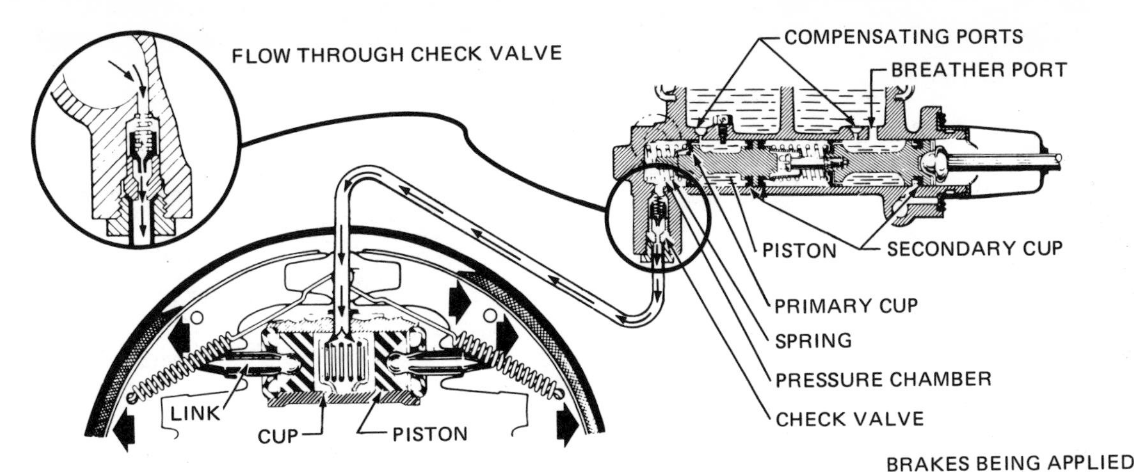

Figure 13 Conditions in a drum-type brake system with the brakes applied. Brake fluid flows from the master cylinder to the wheel cylinder, as shown. There the fluid causes the wheel-cylinder pistons to move outward and thereby apply the brakes.

■ **7-1-8 Self-Energizing Action** When the brakes are applied, as shown in Fig. 13, the wheel cylinder pushes the brake shoes toward the rotating drum. The primary shoe—the shoe toward the front of the car—comes into contact with the drum first. The friction between the primary shoe and the drum forces the brake assembly to shift in the direction of drum rotation. It can shift only a little, because the anchor pin permits only limited movement (Fig. 15). This movement forces the primary shoe more tightly against the revolving drum, greatly increasing the braking action (Fig. 16).

At the same time, the adjusting screw and pin are forced to move as the primary shoe moves. In Fig. 16 we see how this shifts the adjusting screw in the direction of drum movement. Thus, the secondary shoe is forced against the drum by the wheel cylinder and the shifting of the adjusting screw. As a result, the secondary shoe provides about twice as much braking effect as the primary shoe. For this reason, the lining in the secondary shoe is larger (Fig. 17).

Always remember, when doing a brake job, that the primary shoe, with the smaller lining, is toward the front of the car. The secondary shoe, with the larger lining, is toward the rear.

■ **7-1-9 Return Stroke** On the return stroke, spring tension on the brake linkage and spring pressure against the master-cylinder piston force the piston to move back in its cylinder. Fluid now flows from the wheel cylinders to the master cylinder, as shown in Fig. 18. The tension of the brake-shoe springs forces the brake shoes away from the brake drums and thus pushes the wheel-cylinder pistons inward. Fluid is thus

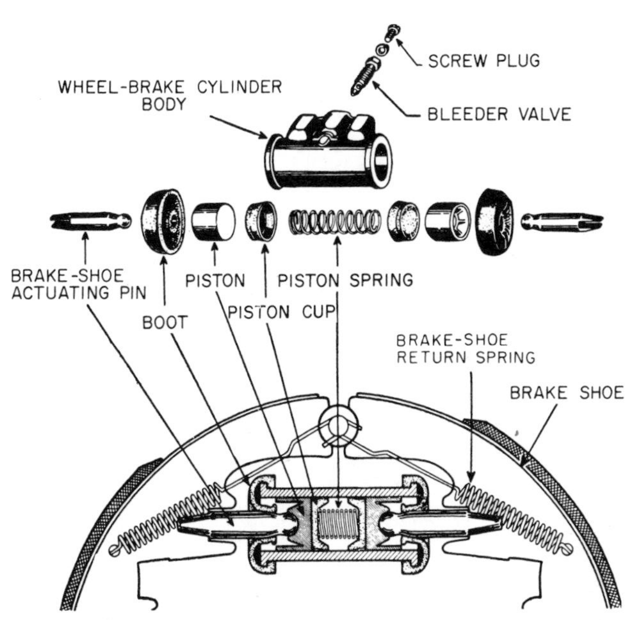

Figure 14 Disassembled and sectional views of a wheel cylinder. *(Pontiac Motor Division of General Motors Corporation.)*

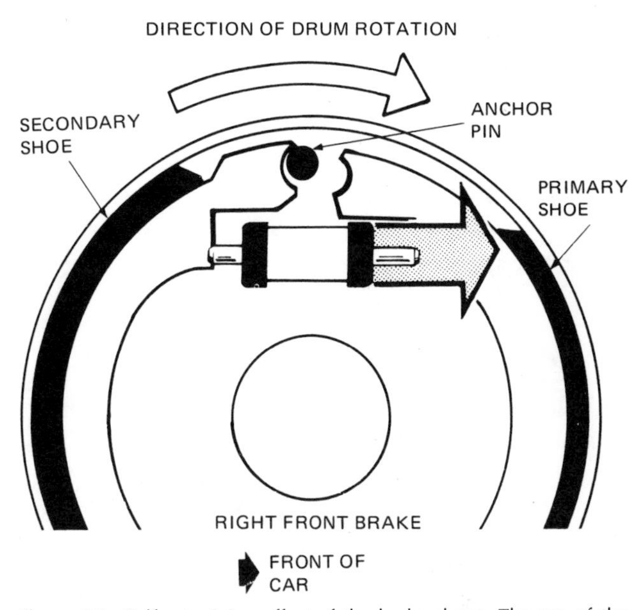

Figure 15 Self-energizing effect of the brake shoes. The top of the primary shoe is forced against the rotating drum as the first effect. *(Ford Motor Company.)*

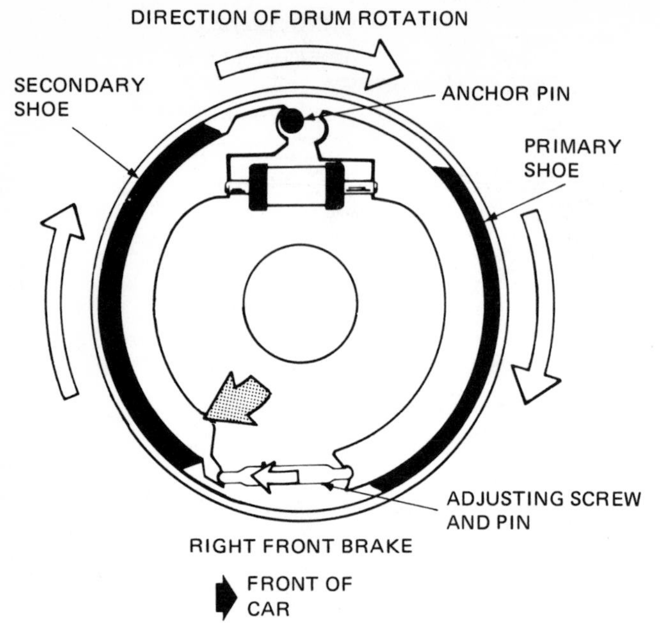

Figure 16 The shifting of the primary shoe downward pushes the adjusting screw and pin to the left so that the bottom of the secondary shoe is forced against the drum. *(Ford Motor Company.)*

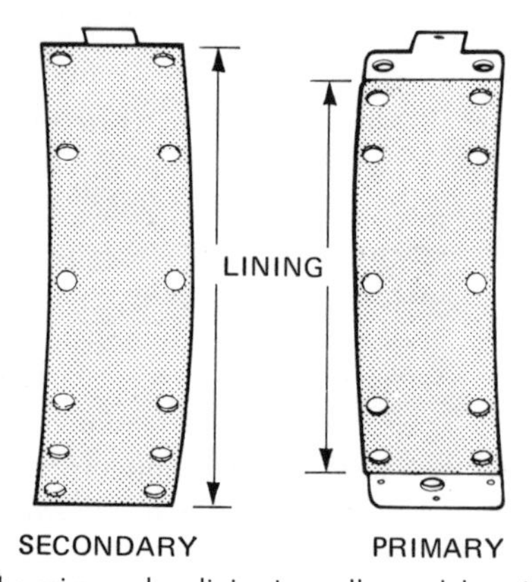

Figure 17 The primary shoe lining is smaller, and the primary shoe is installed toward the front of the car. The secondary shoe lining is larger, and the secondary shoe is installed toward the rear of the car. *(Ford Motor Company.)*

returned from the wheel cylinders to the master cylinder, as shown by the arrows. However, some pressure is trapped in the lines by the check valve at the end of the master cylinder (see Fig. 13). As the pressure drops, the check valve closes, trapping a slight pressure in the lines and wheel cylinders. This pressure serves the purpose of keeping the wheel cylinders from leaking and also of reducing the chances of air leaking into the system.

■ 7-1-10 Warning Light

In the dual-brake system, a pressure differential valve is used to operate a warning-light switch. Figure 19 is a schematic view of the system. The valve (Fig. 20*a*) has a piston that is centered when both front and rear brakes are operating normally. However, if one section should fail, there will be low pressure on one side of the piston. The high pressure, from the normally operating section, will then move the piston and cause it to push the switch plunger upward (Fig. 20*b*). This closes contacts, which turns on the warning light on the instrument panel. The driver is thus warned that either the rear-wheel or the front-wheel brakes have failed.

Some switches have a tripping arrangement that causes the light to remain on, even though the brakes are not used again, until the trouble is fixed and the switch is reset.

■ 7-1-11 Self-Adjusting Brakes (Drum Type)

Automotive brakes now have a self-adjusting mechanism that automatically adjusts the brakes when they need it as a result of brake-lining wear. Figure 21 illustrates a typical arrangement. The adjustment takes place only when the brakes are applied as the car is moving rearward. When this happens, an adjustment is made only when the brake linings have worn enough to make adjustment necessary.

As the brakes are applied with the car moving backward, friction between the primary shoe and the brake drum forces the primary shoe against the anchor pin. Then hydraulic pressure from the wheel cylinder forces the upper end of the sec-

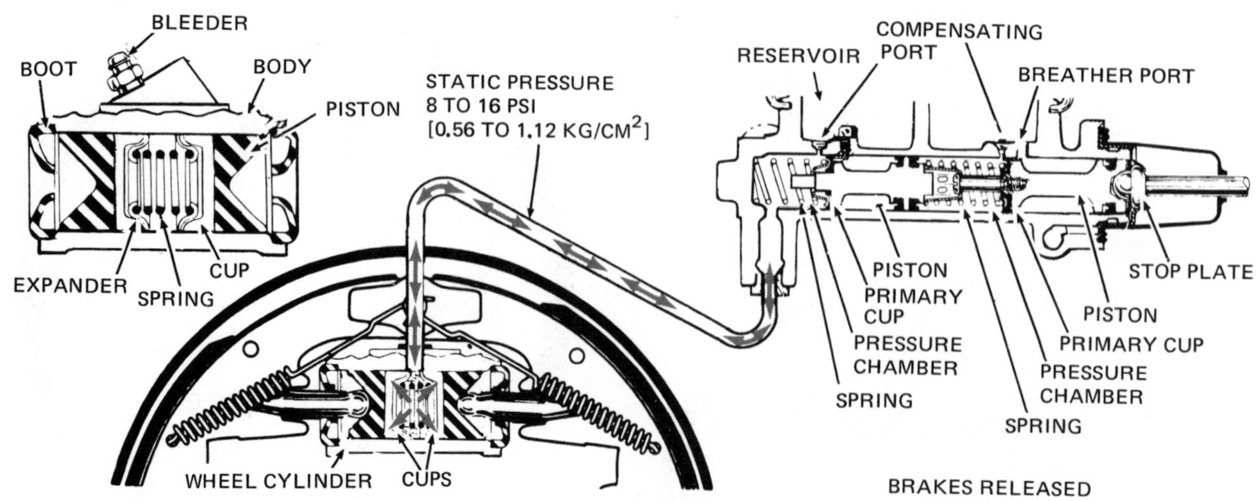

Figure 18 Conditions in a drum-brake system when the brakes are released. Brake fluid flows back to the master cylinder, as shown. *(Buick Motor Division of General Motors Corporation.)*

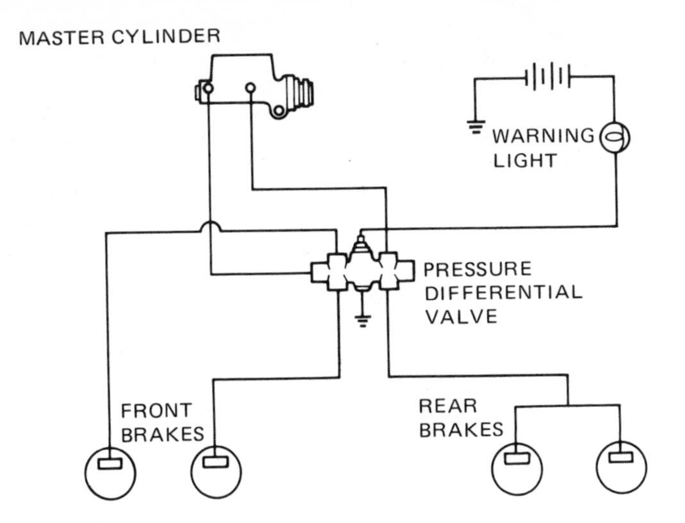

Figure 19 Schematic drawing of dual-brake system with a pressure-differential valve. *(Chevrolet Motor Division of General Motors Corporation.)*

ondary shoe away from the anchor pin and downward (Fig. 22). This causes the adjuster lever to pivot on the secondary shoe so that the lower end of the lever is forced against the sprocket on the adjuster screw. If the brake linings have worn enough, the adjuster screw will be turned a full tooth. This spreads the lower ends of the brake shoes a few thousandths of an inch—enough to compensate for lining wear.

On some cars, the self-adjustment mechanism operates with the car moving forward when the brakes are applied.

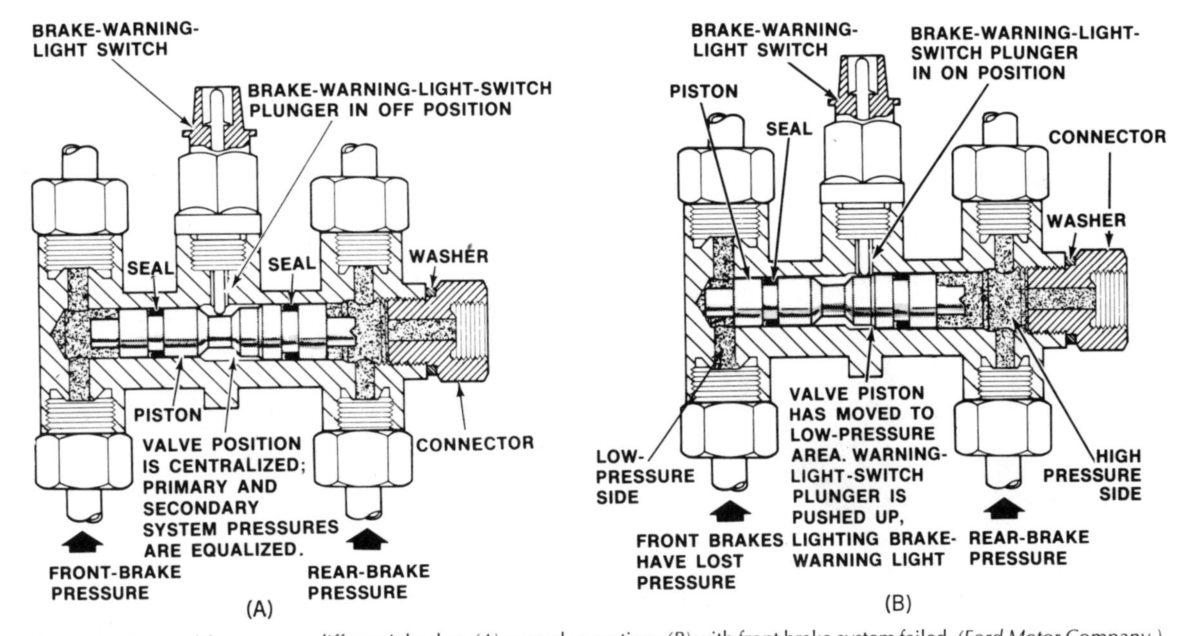

Figure 20 The two positions of the pressure-differential valve: *(A)* normal operation; *(B)* with front brake system failed. *(Ford Motor Company.)*

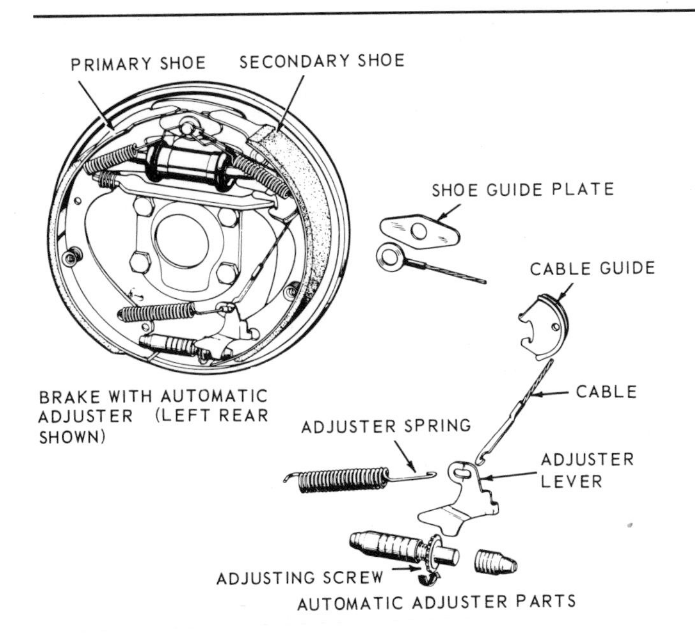

Figure 21 Brake assembly of the drum type with the automatic self-adjuster and adjuster parts disassembled. *(Bendix Corporation.)*

■ 7-1-12 Disk Brakes

The disk, or caliper, brake has a metal disk instead of a drum, and a pair of pads, or flat shoes, instead of the curved shoes used with the drum brakes. There are three general types, fixed-caliper, sliding-caliper, and floating-caliper. The caliper is the assembly in which the brake shoes are held. It contains the flat shoes or pads, which are positioned on the two sides of the disk (Fig. 23). In operation, the shoes are forced inward against the two sides of the disks by the movement of pistons in the caliper assembly (Fig. 24).These pistons are actuated by the hydraulic pressure developed in the master cylinder as the brake pedal is pushed down by the driver. The effect is to clamp the disk between the

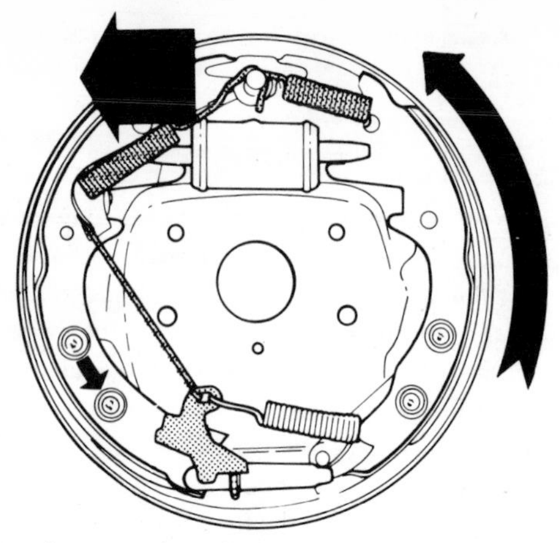

Figure 22 Illustrating the self-adjustment of brakes. When the brakes are applied as the car is being backed, the shifting of the brake shoes actuates the adjusting lever. *(Ford Motor Company.)*

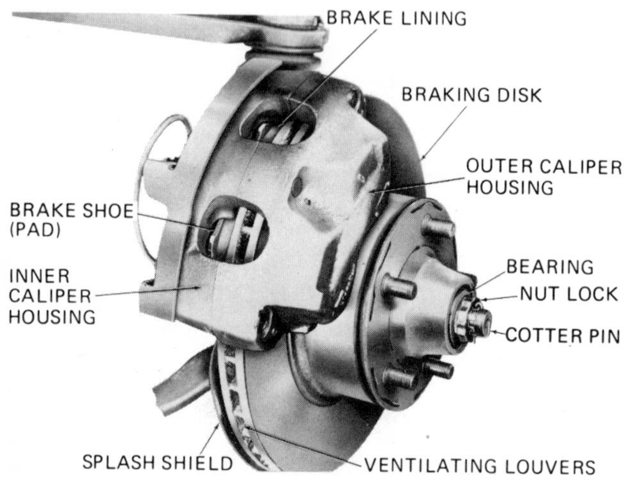

Figure 23 Disk-brake assembly of the fixed-caliper type. *(Chrysler Corporation.)*

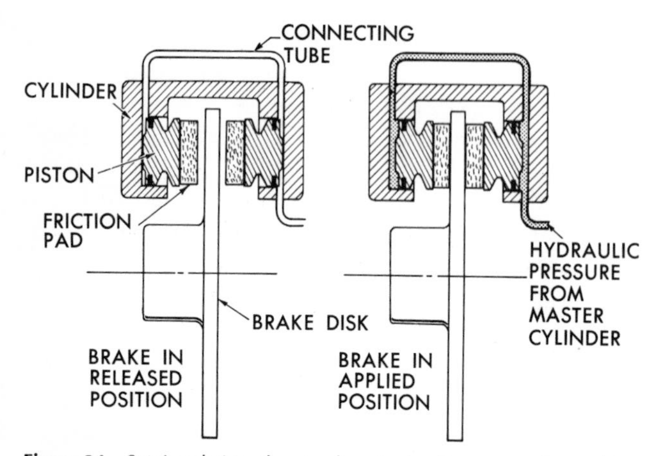

Figure 24 Sectional view showing how hydraulic pressure forces friction pads inward against the brake disk to produce braking action.

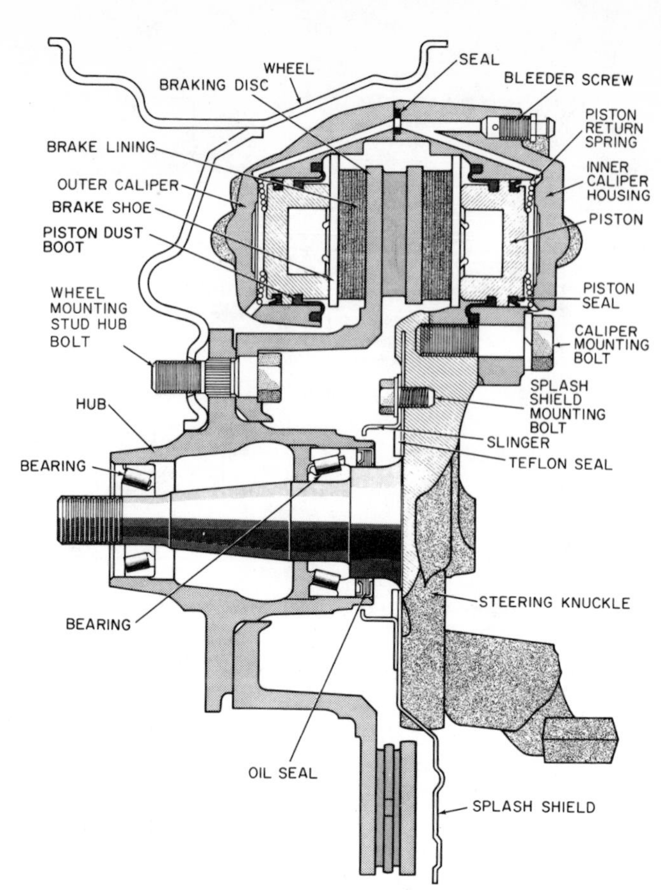

Figure 25 Sectional view of a disk-brake assembly of the fixed-caliper type. *(Chrysler Corporation.)*

shoes. This is the same action you get when you pick up a piece of paper; your fingers and thumb clamp on both sides of the paper to hold it. In the same way, the shoes apply friction to the disk and attempt to stop its rotation. This provides the braking action.

1. FIXED CALIPER The fixed-caliper disk brake (Figs. 23 to 25) has pistons on both sides of the disk (two on each side). The caliper is rigidly attached to a stationary car part. With front disk brakes, for example, the caliper is attached to the steering knuckle (or spindle), as shown in Fig. 25. On rear disk brakes, the caliper is attached to the rear-axle-housing flange. In operation, all four pistons are forced inward by hydraulic pressure, thus causing the two shoes to move in against the rotating disk.

2. FLOATING CALIPER The floating, or swinging, caliper (Fig. 26) can pivot, or swing in or out. It is mounted through rubber bushings which give enough to permit this movement. The caliper has only one piston. In operation, hydraulic pressure forces the piston to move toward the disk, thus forcing the inner brake shoe against the disk. At the same time, the pressure of the shoe against the disk causes the caliper to swing inward slightly so that the fixed brake shoe on the opposite side is brought into contact with the other side of the disk.

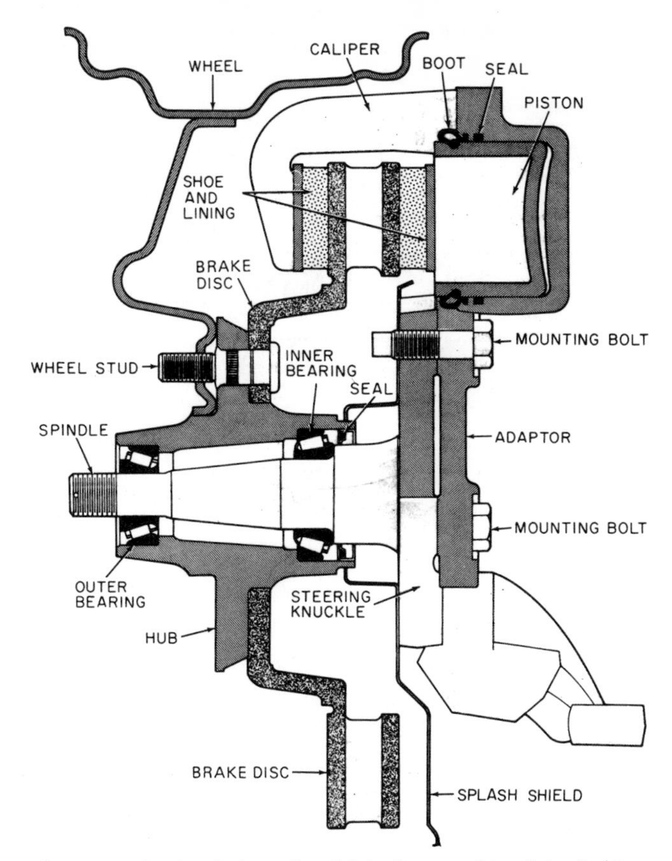

Figure 26 Sectional view of a disk-brake assembly of the floating-caliper type. *(Chrysler Corporation.)*

Now, braking action is the same as with the fixed-caliper type.

3. SLIDING CALIPER The sliding caliper is similar to the floating caliper. The difference is that the sliding caliper is suspended from rubber bushings on bolts (Fig. 27). When hydraulic pressure is applied back of the piston, the piston pushes the inboard shoe into hard contact with the rotating brake disk. At the same time, the hydraulic pressure on the bottom end of the piston cylinder forces the caliper to slide inward. This brings the outboard shoe into hard contact with the outer surface of the rotating disk. The pressure of the shoes on the two sides of the disk provides the braking effect.

It is important to remember that the brake lining on the shoes is actually in contact with the brake disk at all times. This is not heavy contact (except when braking). It is a light sliding contact that keeps the disk wiped clean of foreign matter. Because of this "zero" clearance, relatively little brake pedal movement is required to produce braking action.

4. TELLTALE TABS Some brake shoes have telltale tabs (Fig. 28) which come into action when the brake linings are worn down to where they must be replaced. When this happens, the tabs rub against the disk and give off a scraping noise. This noise warns the driver that the brake shoes must be replaced.

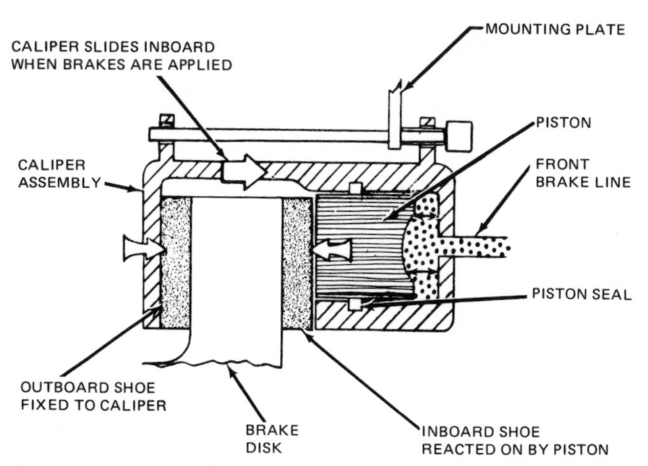

Figure 27 Sliding disk-brake operation. *(Chevrolet Motor Division of General Motors Corporation.)*

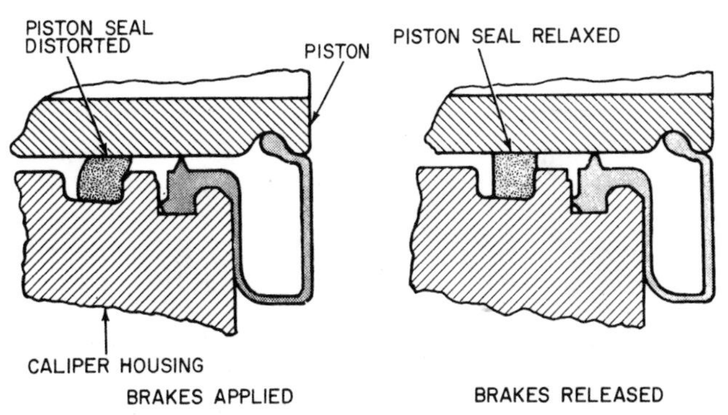

Figure 28 Disk-brake piston and shoe-and-lining assembly. *(Chrysler Corporation.)*

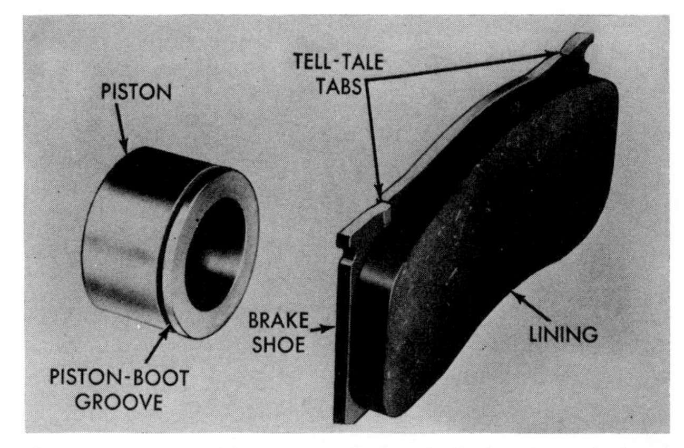

Figure 29 Action of the piston seal when the brakes are applied and released. *(Ford Motor Company.)*

■ 7-1-13 Self-Adjustment of Disk Brakes

Disk brakes are self-adjusting. On some types, there is a piston-return spring back of each piston. This is a light spring that keeps the piston in the forward position and holds the brake lining lightly against the disk when the brakes are released.

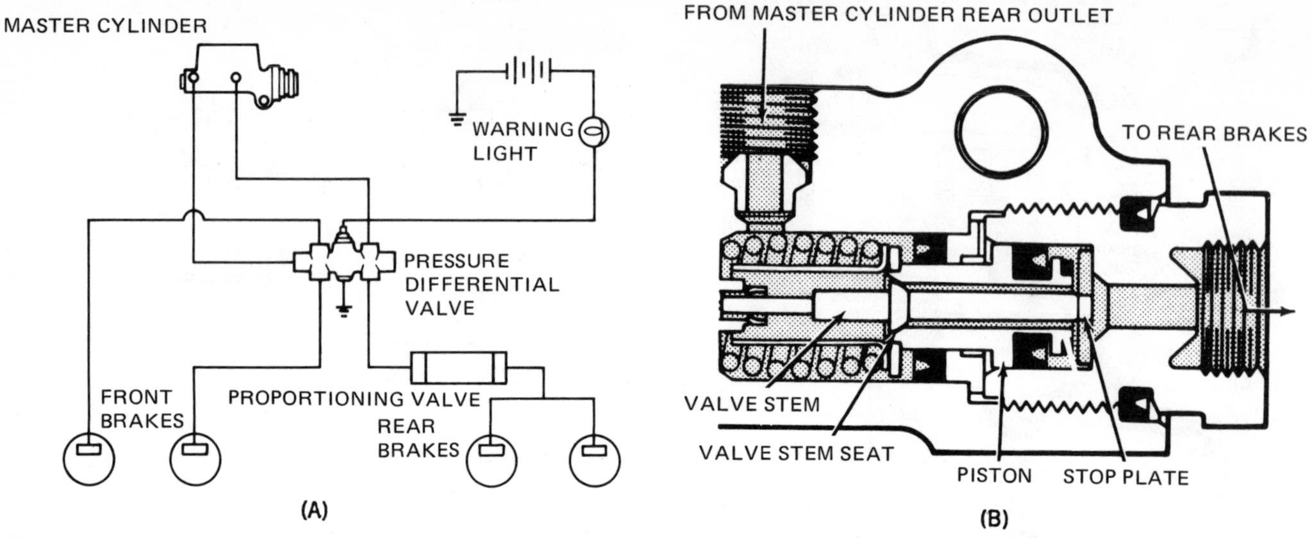

Figure 30 *(A)* Schematic drawing of a brake system with proportioning valve, and *(B)* sectional view of the valve. *(Chevrolet Motor Division of General Motors Corporation.)*

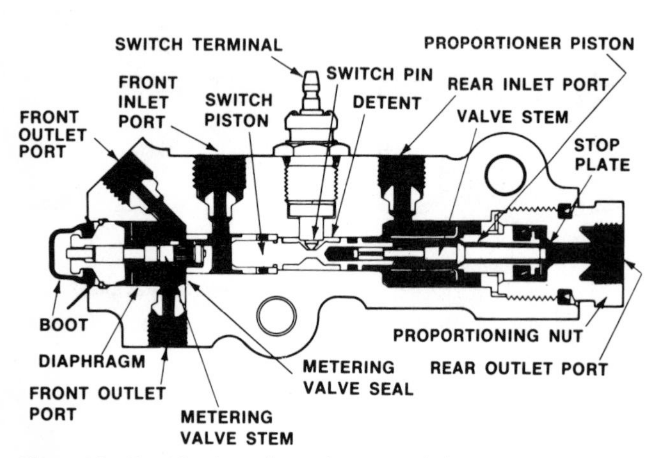

Figure 31 Combination valve with warning-light, metering, and proportioning valves all in the same assembly. *(Chevrolet Motor Division of General Motors Corporation.)*

In this position, only a small additional movement of the pistons will bring the lining up hard against the disk for quick braking. Another system provides automatic self-adjustment by means of the piston seals. When the brakes are applied, the piston slides toward the disk, distorting the piston seal as shown in Fig. 29. Then, when the brakes are released, relaxation of the seal draws the piston slightly away from the disk, as shown. As the brake linings wear, piston travel tends to exceed the limit of deflection of the seal. The piston, therefore, slides outward through the seal to the precise extent necessary to compensate for lining wear.

■ 7-1-14 Metering Valve

Disk-brake systems have a metering valve. This valve keeps the front brakes from applying until the rear brakes apply. If the front brakes were applied first, the car could be thrown into a rear-end skid.

■ 7-1-15 Proportioning Valve

The proportioning valve improves braking action during hard braking when more of the car weight is transferred to the front wheels. As a result, more braking is needed at the front wheels and less at the rear wheels. If normal braking continued, the rear wheels could skid and could throw the entire car into a rear-end skid. The proportioning valve reduces the pressure to the rear wheel brakes when hard braking and high fluid pressures develop. Figure 30 is a schematic view of the system and a sectional view of the proportioning valve.

■ 7-1-16 Combination Valve

In many cars the warning-light valve (■7-7-10), the metering valve, and the proportioning valve are combined into a single unit. Figure 31 is a sectional view of this combination valve.

■ 7-1-17 Parking Brake for Rear Disk Brakes

As explained in ■7-1-2, the drum brake shoes at the rear wheels can be actuated by a mechanical pull from a hand-brake lever in the driver's compartment. This arrangement provides sufficient braking to hold the car stationary when it is parked. However, the disk brakes cannot be directly actuated by a mechanical pull. The disk brakes at the rear wheels, therefore, must have a separate parking-brake arrangement. This arrangement consists of a brake drum and pair of brake shoes. The assembly is much like that used with the regular drum brakes described in ■7-1-1. The major difference is that the parking brakes are actuated by a mechanical pull, whereas the hydraulic brakes are actuated by hydraulic pressure.

Figure 32 is a disassembled view of a rear disk-brake assembly, showing the shoes. The brake drum for these shoes is inside the disk-drum brake rotor. A cam or lever is located between the tops of the two brake shoes. When the cable from the parking-brake system is pulled, it rotates the cam or moves

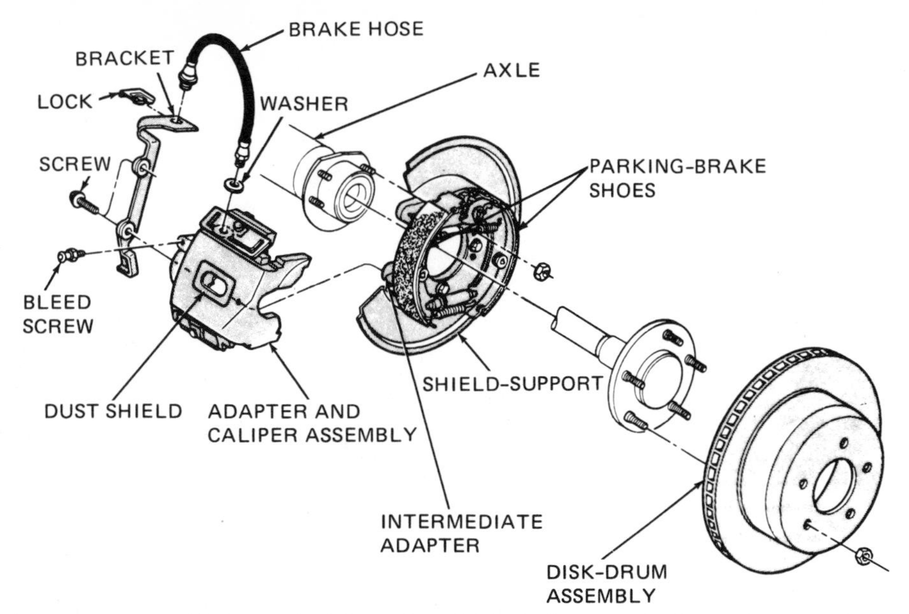

Figure 32 Disassembled view of a sliding-caliper disk brake for a rear wheel. Note the parking-brake shoes. *(Chrysler Corporation.)*

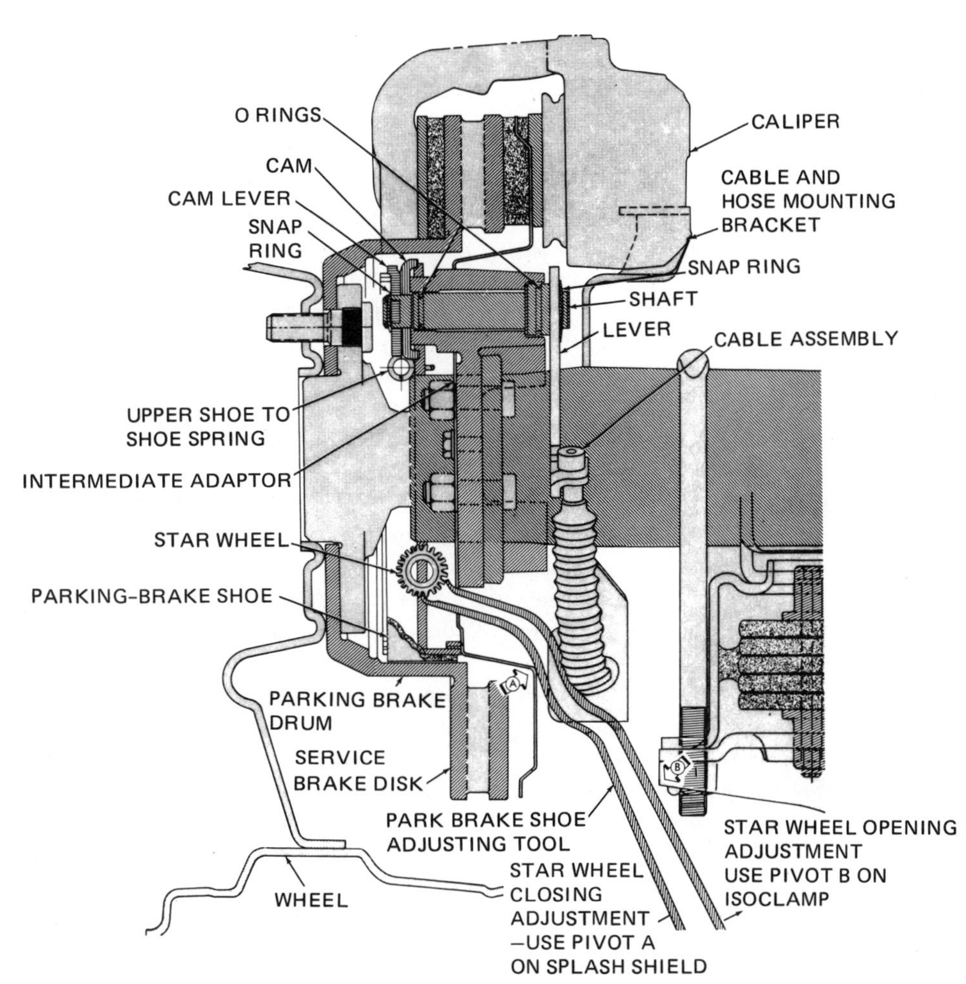

Figure 33 Sectional view of a sliding-caliper disk brake assembly for a rear wheel. The two positions of the parking-brake-shoe adjusting tool for turning the adjusting star wheel one way or the other are shown. *(Chrysler Corporation.)*

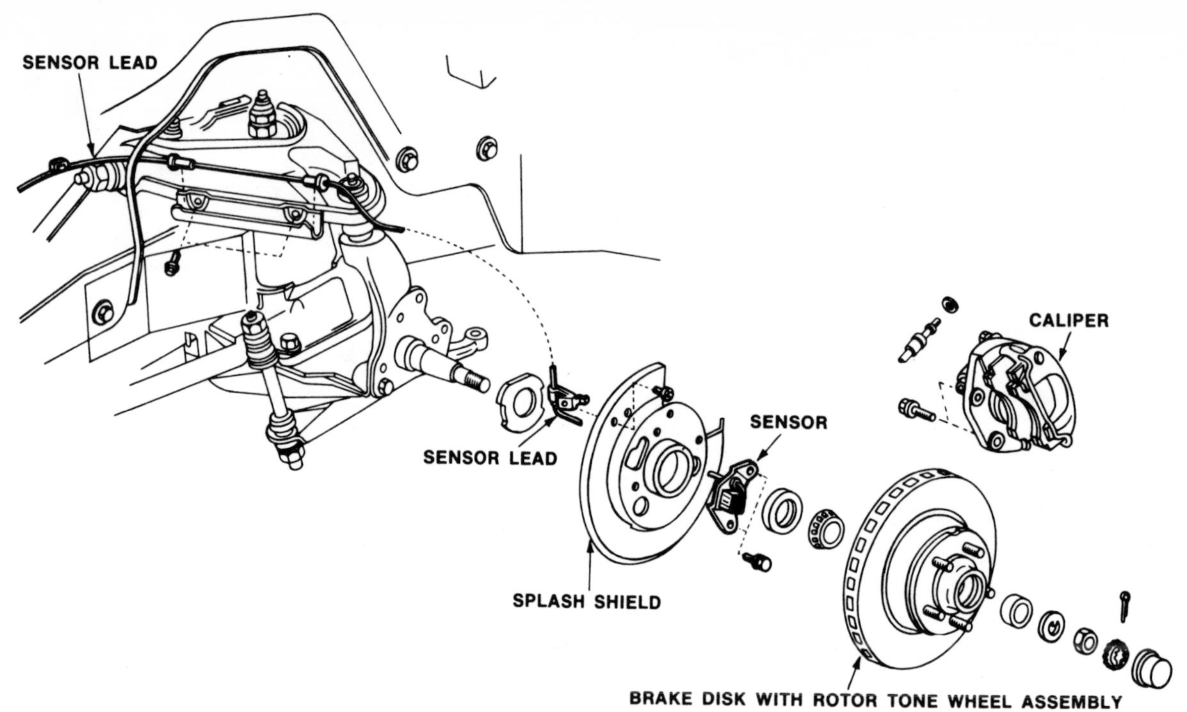

Figure 34 Antilock mechanism for the Chrysler Sure-Brake system at a front wheel. *(Chrysler Corporation.)*

the lever to force the brake shoes tightly against the drum on the inside of the disk-drum rotor. With the brake shoes tightly applied, the rotor and wheel are held stationary for parking. Figure 33 is a sectional view of the assembly, showing how a parking-brake-shoe adjusting tool is used to get to the star (adjusting) wheel and turn it. This action moves the brake shoes closer to, or farther away from, the drum, thus establishing the proper parking-brake adjustment.

■ 7-1-18 Antilock Devices

The most efficient braking takes place when the wheels are still revolving. If the brakes lock the wheels so that the tires skid, kinetic friction results and braking is much less effective. To prevent locking and thus provide maximum effective braking, several antilock devices have been proposed. Some provide skid control of the rear wheels only. Others provide control at all four wheels. The meaning of "control" is this: As long as the wheels are rotating, the antilock device permits normal application of the brakes. But if the brakes are applied so hard that the wheels tend to stop turning, and a skid starts to develop, the device comes into operation and partly releases the brakes so the wheels continue to rotate. However, braking continues. But it is held just below the point where a skid would start. The result is maximum braking effect.

■ 7-1-19 Buick Max Trac

The Buick antilock device is called "Max Trac." It uses two sensing devices, one for the rear wheels and one for the left front wheel. The rear-wheel sensing device is actually located at the transmission output shaft. The two sensing devices feed data to a solid-state computer located under the instrument panel. The computer is constantly comparing wheel speeds. If at any time the rear-wheel speed gets to be 10 percent greater than the front-wheel speed—which indicates a skid is starting—the computer repeatedly interrupts the ignition-system action for a brief moment (1/100 second). This of course slows the rear wheels. Depending on the severity of the rear-wheel spin, or skid, the interruptions take place up to 50 times a second. They continue until there is less than 10 percent difference between the rear- and front-wheel speeds. There is no risk of stalling the engine with such short interruptions of the ignition-system actions.

With less than 10 percent difference, the rear wheels are assumed to have adequate traction to stop the skid, or wheel spin.

The rear-wheel speed sensor, located in the speedometer drive opening in the transmission housing, has a gear which spins when the transmission output shaft, and the rear wheels, are turning. Surrounding the gear is a housing with internal splines, and a coil. A magnet is located within the coil. The rotating gear causes the magnetic lines of forces to change, or weave, as the gear teeth pass the splines in the housing. This moving magnetic field creates an alternating current (ac) in the coil. This ac flows to the computer. The higher the speed, the higher the frequency of the ac.

At the same time, the left front wheel is sending ac to the computer. This ac originates from a round metal plate with 30 elongated holes in it that rotates with the wheel. A magnetic pickup is mounted directly opposite the holes. As the wheel turns, the holes alternately allow and prevent the magnetic

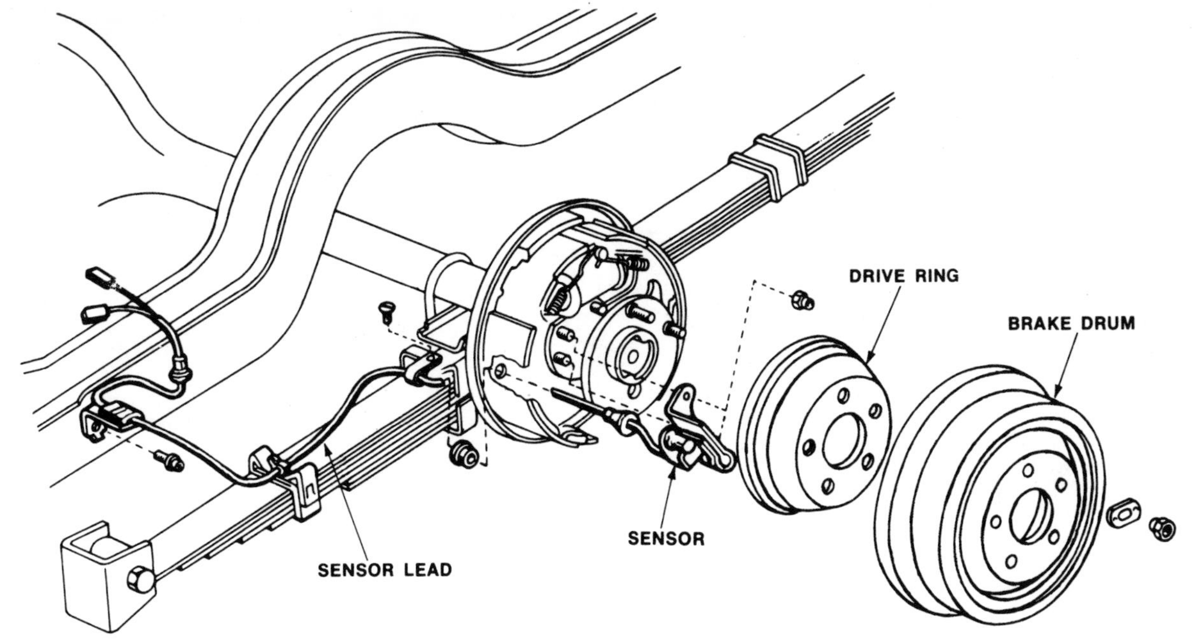

Figure 35 Antilock mechanism for the Chrysler Sure-Brake system at a rear wheel. *(Chrysler Corporation.)*

field from acting on a coil. This produces ac which is fed to the computer. The faster the wheel turns, the higher the frequency of the ac.

Actually, the computer is comparing the frequencies of the ac from the two sensors, and it acts when the frequency of the rear-wheel sensor ac shows that the rear wheels are turning 10 percent or more faster than the front wheels. Not only does this inhibit rear-wheel skid or spin, it also prevents wheel spin when accelerating on dry pavement.

■ 7-1-20 Chrysler Sure-Brake

The antilock system used on cars manufactured by Chrysler Corporation is called the "Sure-Brake" system. Figure 34 shows the antilock mechanism at the front wheel. Figure 35 shows the mechanism at a rear wheel. The action is the same at both wheels. At the front wheel there is a magnetic wheel attached to the brake disk. As the wheel and disk revolve, the magnetic wheel produces alternating current (ac) in the sensor. The sensor is a coil of wire, or a winding. A similar action takes place at the other wheels. These ac signals from the car wheels are fed into a logic control unit, located in the trunk, as shown in Fig. 36.

When the brakes are applied, the logic control compares the ac signals from the wheels. The frequency of the ac increases with speed. As long as the frequency of the ac from all wheels is about the same, normal braking will take place. However, if the ac from any wheel is slowing down too rapidly, it means that the wheel is also slowing down too rapidly. It is beginning to skid.

When the logic control unit senses a rapid drop in the frequency of the ac, it signals modulators at the front of the car. Figure 37 shows the locations of the front-wheel and rear-wheel modulators. The hydraulic pressure from the master cylinder to the wheel cylinder or calipers passes through these

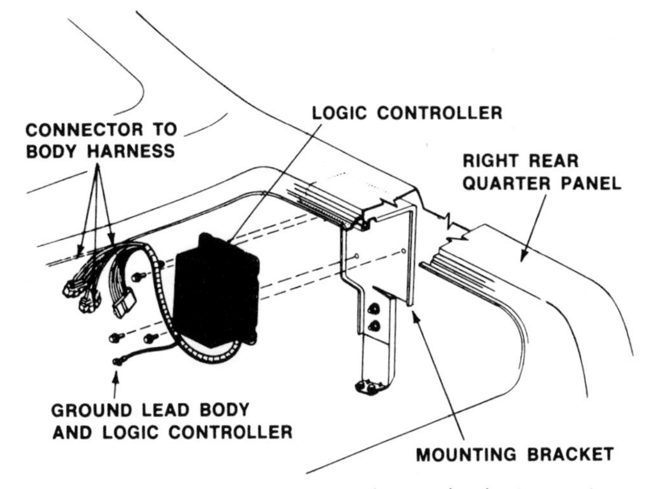

Figure 36 Location of the logic control unit. *(Chrysler Corporation.)*

modulators. When the logic control unit senses that a wheel is about to skid, it signals the modulator for that wheel to "ease up." It "tells" the modulator to reduce the hydraulic pressure to the brake for that wheel. When the pressure is reduced, the braking effect at that wheel is reduced, and so the skid is prevented.

■ 7-1-21 Brake Fluid

The liquid used in the hydraulic-brake system is called brake fluid. Brake fluid must have very definite characteristics. It must be chemically inert, it must be little affected by high or low temperatures, it must provide lubrication for the master-cylinder and wheel-cylinder pistons, and it must not attack the metallic and rubber parts in the braking system. Therefore, only the brake fluid recommended by the car manufacturer must be used when the addition of brake fluid becomes necessary.

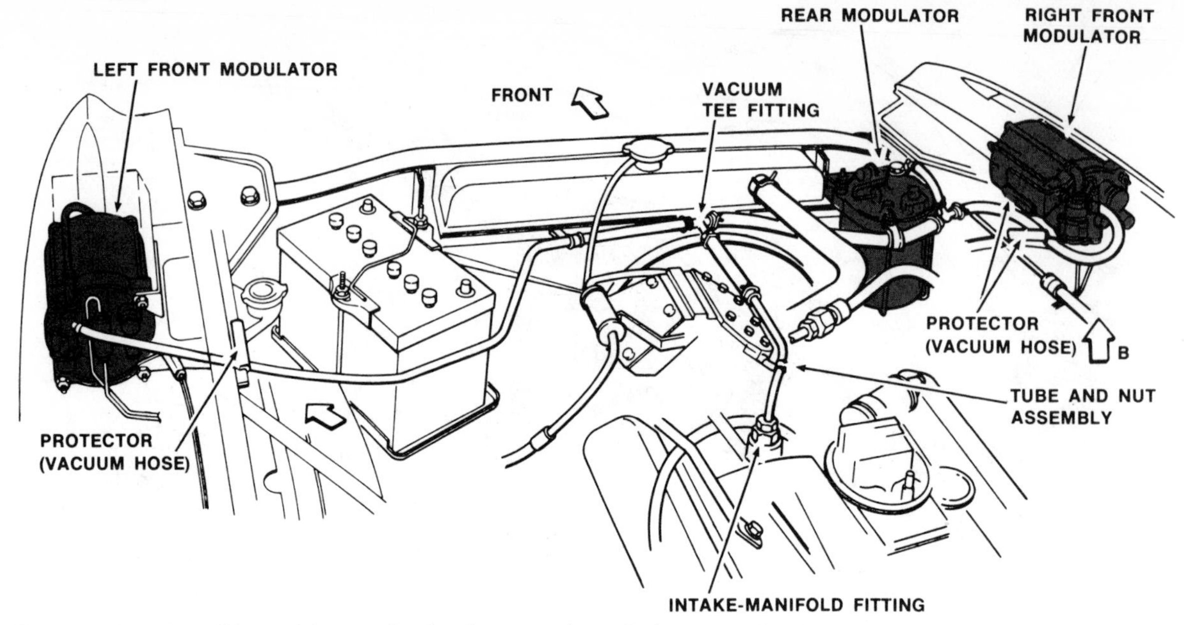

Figure 37 Locations of the modulators in the Chrysler Sure-Brake antilock system. *(Chrysler Corporation.)*

NOTE: Engine oil must never be put into the brake system. Engine oil will cause the rubber parts in the system, including the piston cups, to swell and disintegrate. This would, of course, cause faulty braking action and possibly complete brake failure. Nothing except the fluid recommended by the manufacturer must be put into the hydraulic-brake system.

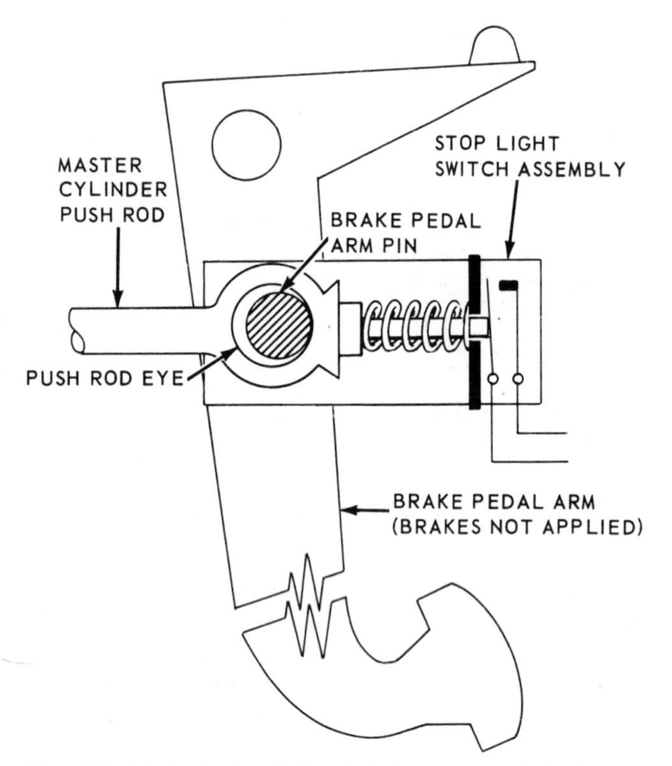

Figure 38 Mechanical stoplight switch shown open, with brakes not applied. *(Ford Motor Company.)*

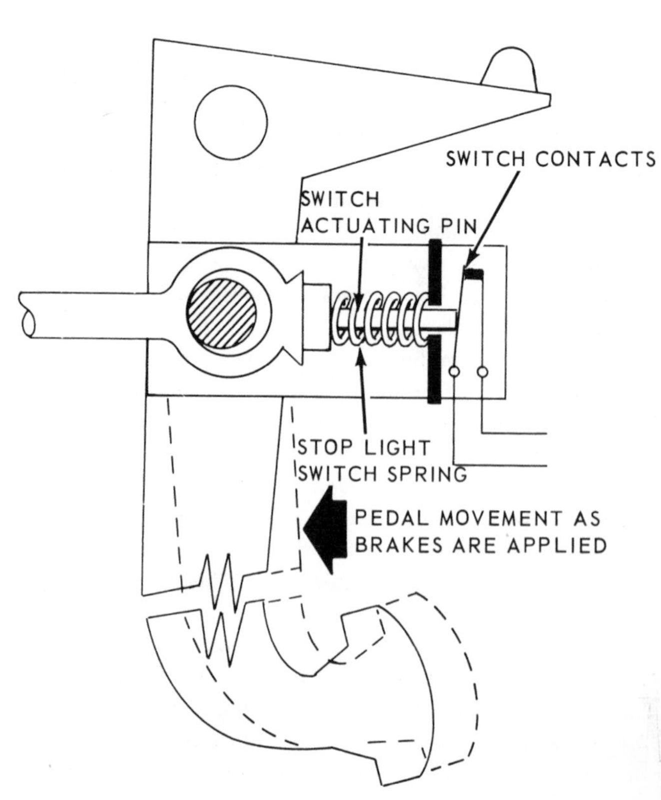

Figure 39 Mechanical stoplight switch shown closed, with brakes applied. *(Ford Motor Company.)*

■ **7-1-22 Brake Lines** Steel pipe is used between the master cylinder and the frame connections, and between the rear-axle T (or "tee") fitting and the rear-wheel cylinders. Flexible hose connects the brake pipe to the front-wheel cylinders and to the rear-axle fitting. These various hoses and pipes can be seen in Fig. 8. If a section of pipe or a hose becomes damaged, replace it with the proper pipe or hose specified by the manufacturer. Since these lines are required to withstand considerable pressure, they are special. Ordinary copper tubing, for example, is not satisfactory. The steel pipe, or tubing, must be double-flared when it is installed.

■ **7-1-23 Stoplight Switch** Until the introduction of the dual-brake system, most stoplight switches were hydraulic. They contained a small diaphragm that was moved by hydraulic pressure when the brakes were applied. This action closed a switch which connected the stoplights to the battery.

When the dual-brake system was introduced, however, the hydraulic switch could no longer be used. With this system, there are two separate hydraulic systems: one for the front wheels and one for the rear wheels. If the hydraulic switch were connected into one system, and if that system failed, the car would have no stoplights even though the other system was still working and stopping the car.

Thus, the mechanical switch came into use. Figures 38 and 39 illustrate one design. When the pedal is pushed for braking, it carries the switch contacts with it (to left in Fig. 39). This brings the switch contacts together, and thus the stoplights come on.

SECTION 7-2 Power Brakes

In this section, we describe the construction and operation of power brakes. Following sections cover troubleshooting and servicing brakes and power brake assemblies.

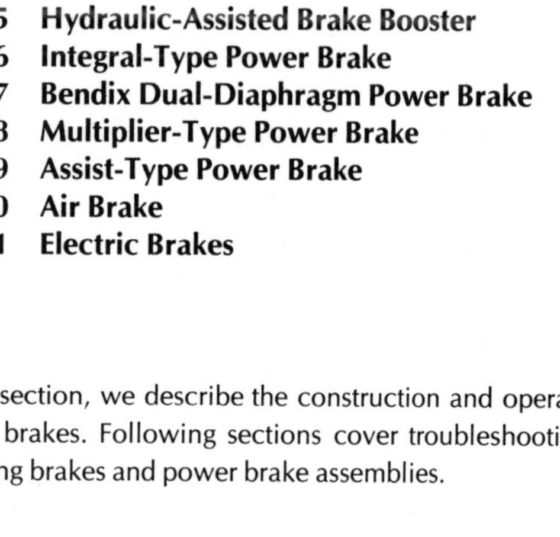

ATMOSPHERIC PRESSURE
VACUUM
PISTON

Figure 1 If atmospheric pressure is applied on one side of a piston and vacuum on the other side, the piston will move toward the vacuum side, as shown.

■ **7-2-1 Power Brakes** For hard braking and fast stops, a considerable pressure must be exerted on the brake pedal with the brake system described above. Also, the heavier the vehicle, the greater the braking effort required. For many years, buses and trucks have used special equipment that assists the driver to brake the vehicle. This equipment may use either compressed air or vacuum. When the driver applies the brake, the compressed air or vacuum supplies most of the effort required for braking. There is another system that uses an electrical means of braking.

Most passenger cars are supplied with vacuum-assisted braking systems, called "power brakes." Essentially, they all operate in a similar manner. When the brake pedal is moved to apply the brakes, a valving arrangement is actuated. The valves admit atmospheric pressure on one side of a piston or diaphragm and apply vacuum to the other side. The piston or diaphragm then moves toward the vacuum side; this movement transmits most of the hydraulic pressure, through the brake fluid, to the wheel cylinders.

■ **7-2-2 Atmospheric Pressure and Vacuum** Atmospheric pressure is about 15 psi (1.05 kg/cm^2) at sea level. Vacuum is an absence of air. If we arranged a simple cylinder and piston (as shown in Fig. 1) and then applied atmospheric pressure to one side and vacuum to the other, the piston would move toward the vacuum side, as shown. If we held the piston stationary, we could calculate the pressure, or push, being exerted on it, provided we knew the area of the piston, the atmospheric pressure, and amount of vacuum. Suppose the piston had an area of 50 square inches (about 8 inches in diameter). We'll assume also that the atmospheric pressure is 15 psi (1.05 kg/cm^2) and the vacuum is great enough to have brought the pressure down to only 5 psi (0.35 kg/cm^2). With 15 psi (1.05 kg/cm^2) on one side, and only 5 psi (0.35 kg/cm^2) on the other, the difference in pressure is 10 psi (0.70 kg/cm^2); that is, there is an effective pressure of 10 pounds on every square inch of the piston area. Since there are 50 square inches of piston area, the push on the piston urging it to the vacuum side is 500 pounds (50×10). It is this effective pressure, or push, that it utilized in power brakes. The vacuum is supplied

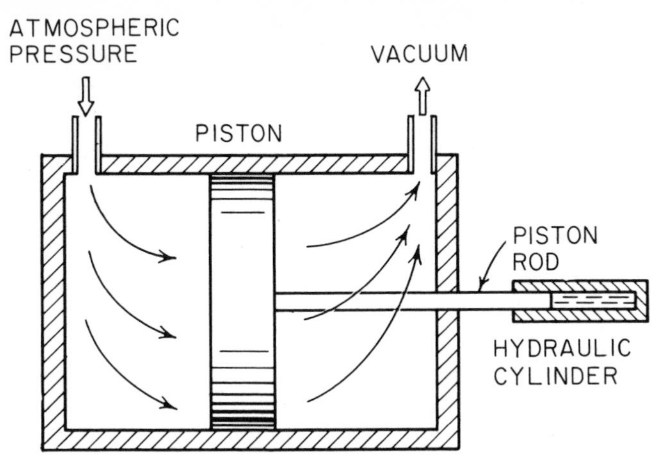

Figure 2 If the piston rod is placed in a hydraulic cylinder, the pressure on the piston in the atmospheric-pressure cylinder will be translated into hydraulic pressure.

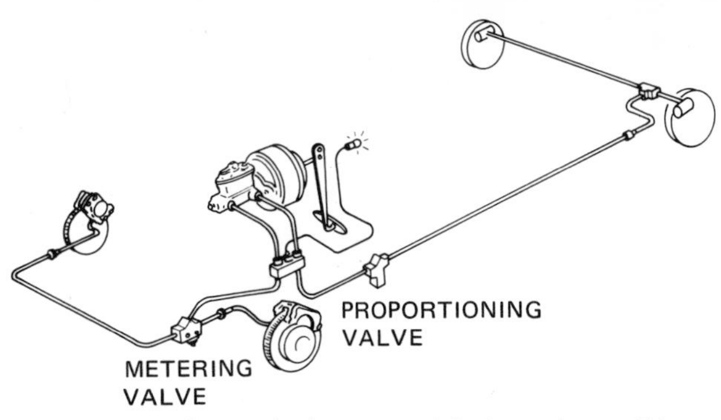

Figure 3 Typical power-brake system of the integral type. *(Wagner Lockheed.)*

by the automobile engine. The engine is a vacuum pump in one sense of the word. With every intake stroke, the downward-moving piston produces a partial vacuum in the cylinder and thus in the intake manifold. The vacuum side of the power-brake cylinder (Fig. 1) is connected to the intake manifold so that it can utilize intake-manifold vacuum.

■ 7-2-3 Putting the Vacuum to Work

If we add a hydraulic cylinder to the cylinder and piston of Fig. 1 as shown in Fig. 2, we can utilize the push on the piston to produce hydraulic pressure. All the pressure on the piston is carried through the piston rod and into the hydraulic cylinder. Thus, in the example described above, the piston rod would push into the hydraulic cylinder with a 500-pound force. If the end of the piston rod had an area of 0.5 square inch, the pressure in the hydraulic fluid would be 1,000 psi (70.31 kg/cm²) (or 500 pounds divided by the area, 0.5 square inch). The hydraulic pressure can be altered by changing the size of either the piston or the rod (with the same pressure differential acting on the piston). For example, a piston with an area of 100 square inches and a rod of 0.2 square inch area would produce a hydraulic pressure of 5,000 psi (351.54 kg/cm²) (or 1,000 pounds divided by 0.2 square inch).

If the hydraulic cylinder is connected to the wheel cylinders, the hydraulic pressure produced will result in braking action. Even if the hydraulic cylinder has been increased in diameter, the piston rod entering it still displaces liquid; and it still produces the same pressure increase as it would if the cylinder were the same size as the rod (as shown in Fig. 2).

■ 7-2-4 Types of Vacuum-Assisted Power Brakes

Vacuum-assisted power brakes can be divided into two general categories: vacuum-suspended and atmospheric-suspended. In the vacuum-suspended type, intake-manifold vacuum is applied to both sides of a piston or diaphragm in the power assembly when no braking action is taking place. To produce braking, atmospheric pressure is admitted to one side of the piston or diaphragm; the difference in pressures causes the piston or diaphragm to move, producing the braking action. Most automotive power-brake systems are of this type.

In the atmospheric-suspended type, atmospheric pressure is applied to both sides of the diaphragm or piston. To produce braking action, one side must be connected to a source of vacuum such as the intake manifold. This type of power brake will not operate, however, if the engine is not running, unless there is a reserve vacuum supply. In some applications of this type of power brake, a small vacuum tank is included to provide enough vacuum for several brake applications after the engine has stopped.

Both of these types of brake can be operated even though the power assistance is not operating. In other words, even though the power diaphragm or piston does not operate, braking can still be achieved. However, a much heavier brake-pedal application is necessary.

Thus vacuum-assisted power brakes can be classified in another way, as the integral type, the multiplier type, and the assist type.

1. INTEGRAL TYPE The integral-type power-brake system (Fig. 3) has the brake master cylinder as an integral part of the power-brake assembly. When the brake pedal is operated, it actuates a valve in the power-brake assembly that applies atmospheric pressure to one side of a piston or diaphragm and vacuum to the other side. This causes the piston or diaphragm to move, and the movement forces a piston to move into the master cylinder and thus apply the brakes. An integral-type system is described in ■7-2-6. Most passenger cars and light trucks use this type of system.

2. MULTIPLIER TYPE The multiplier-type power-brake system (Fig. 4) multiplies the pressure produced by the master cylinder. The pressure from the master cylinder is directed to the multiplier unit through a brake tube. In the multiplier unit, the pressure of the brake fluid actuates a valve. The valve causes atmospheric pressure to be directed to one side of a piston or diaphragm and vacuum to the other side. The piston or diaphragm thus is forced to move, and the movement causes a piston to move in a hydraulic cylinder that is part of the multi-

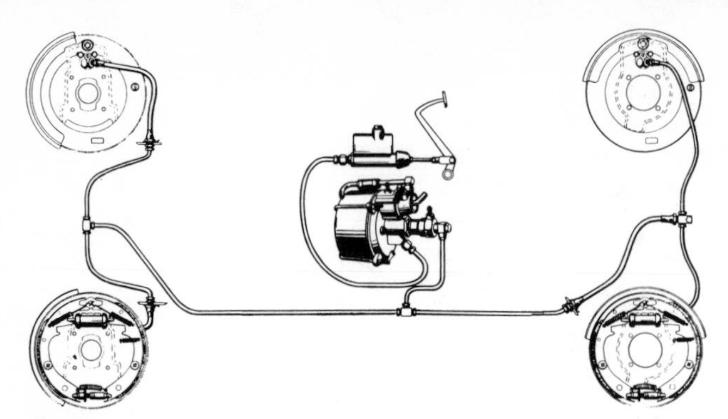
Figure 4 Typical power-brake system of the multiplier type. *(Bendix-Westinghouse Automotive Air Brake Company.)*

plier unit. This produces a high hydraulic pressure which is carried by brake lines to the wheel cylinders. To sum up, the relatively low pressure from the master cylinder, produced by brake-pedal movement, is multiplied to a high pressure by the multiplier unit. Thus, a relatively light brake-pedal pressure produces heavy braking action. A multiplier-type power-brake system is described in ■7-2-8.

3. ASSIST TYPE The assist-type power-brake system (Fig. 5) has a power-cylinder assembly that assists in applying the brakes through a mechanical linkage. When the brake pedal is moved, linkage to the power cylinder is actuated, causing valve action and thus movement of a diaphragm or bellows within the cylinder. This movement is carried through linkage to the master cylinder, thereby increasing the total force being applied, which in turn increases the braking action. A power-brake system of this type is described in ■7-2-9.

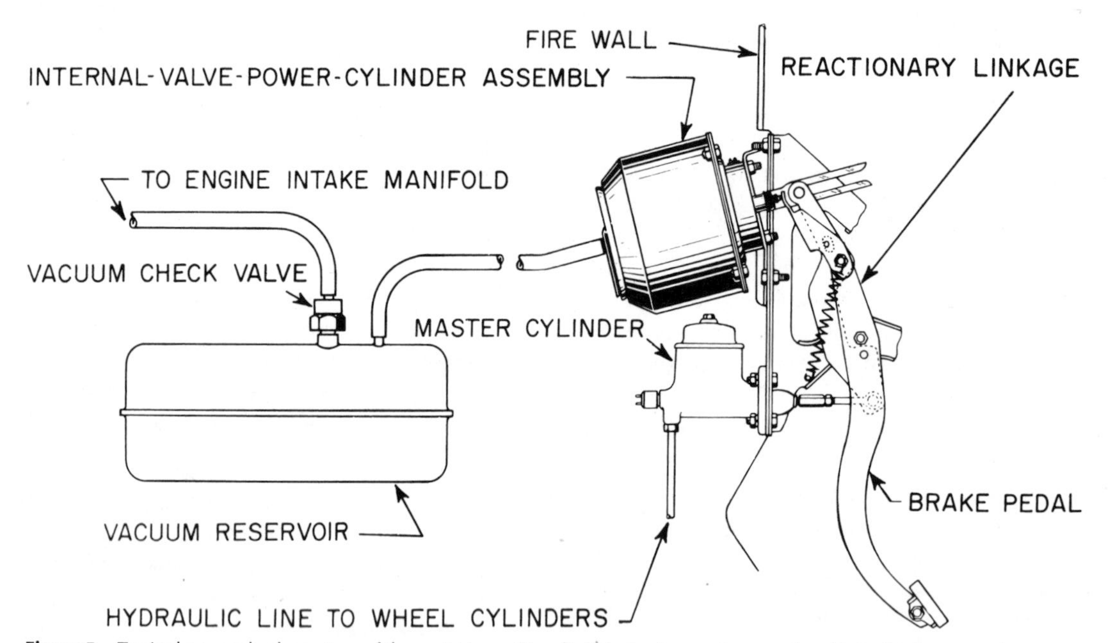

Figure 5 Typical power-brake system of the assist type. *(Bendix-Westinghouse Automotive Air Brake Company.)*

■ 7-2-5 Hydraulic-Assisted Brake Booster The hydraulic-assisted brake booster (Fig. 6) uses hydraulic pressure supplied by the power-steering pump to assist in applying the brakes. Figure 7 is a sectional view of the booster unit. The four ports (pressure, accumulator, return, and gear) are connected to the power-steering system. When the power-steering pump is running, there is always pressure in the smaller cylinder of the assembly. As the brakes are applied, the pressure through the input rod moves the lever. This forces the spool assembly to move off center. The spool assembly now admits hydraulic pressure back of the large piston in the large cylinder. This pressure is applied to the output pushrod, which is pressing against the pistons in the master cylinder. Then the master-cylinder pistons move to send brake fluid to the wheel cylinders or calipers, thus producing braking.

■ 7-2-6 Integral-Type Power Brake Figure 3 illustrates the integral-type power-brake system schematically. A sectional view of one model is shown in Fig. 8. This unit has a tandem master cylinder for a dual-brake system.

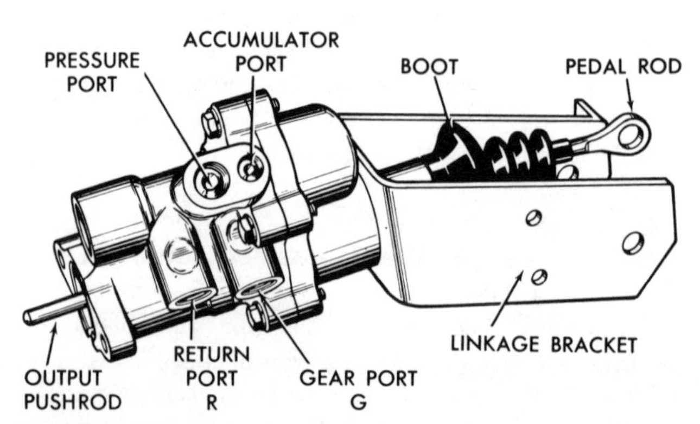

Figure 6 Bendix Hydro-Boost brake booster. *(Chevrolet Motor Division of General Motors Corporation.)*

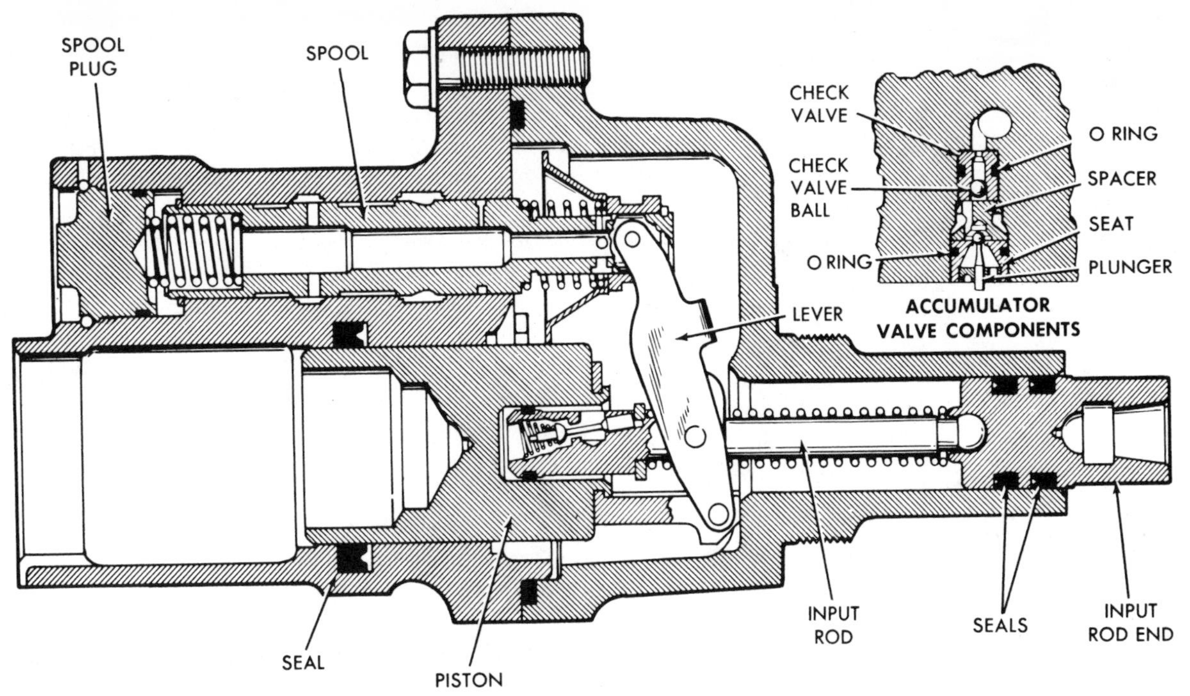

Figure 7 Sectional view of a Bendix Hydro-Boost brake booster. *(Chevrolet Motor Division of General Motors Corporation.)*

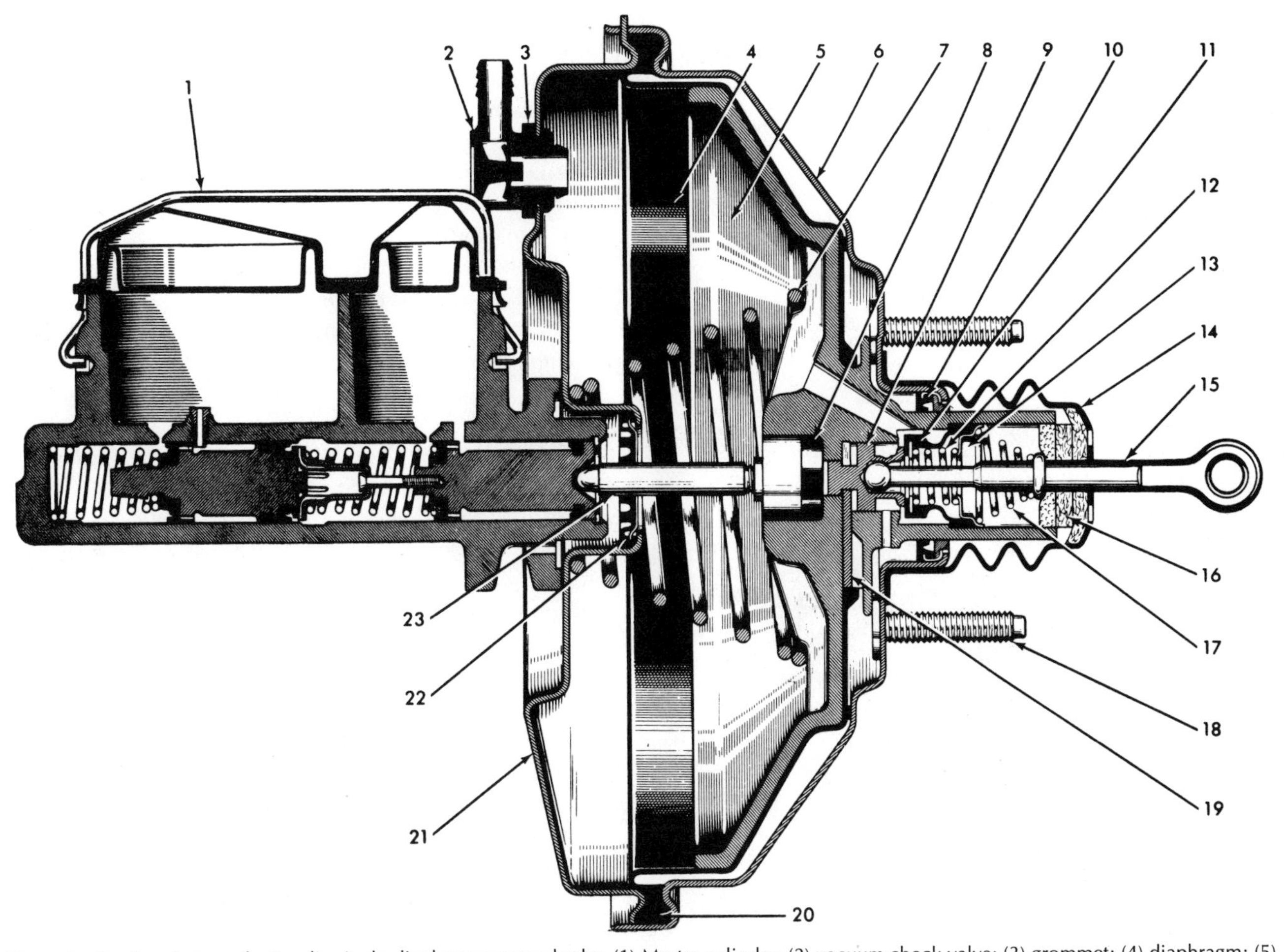

Figure 8 Sectional view of a Bendix single-diaphragm power brake. (1) Master cylinder; (2) vacuum check valve; (3) grommet; (4) diaphragm; (5) diaphragm plate; (6) rear housing; (7) diaphragm spring; (8) reaction disk; (9) air valve; (10) front-housing seal; (11) poppet valve; (12) poppet-valve spring; (13) poppet retainer; (14) dust boot; (15) valve pushrod; (16) filter and silencers; (17) valve-return spring; (18) mounting study; (19) air-valve lock plate; (20) diaphragm lip; (21) front housing; (22) front-housing seal; and (23) piston rod. *(Chevrolet Motor Division of General Motors Corporation.)*

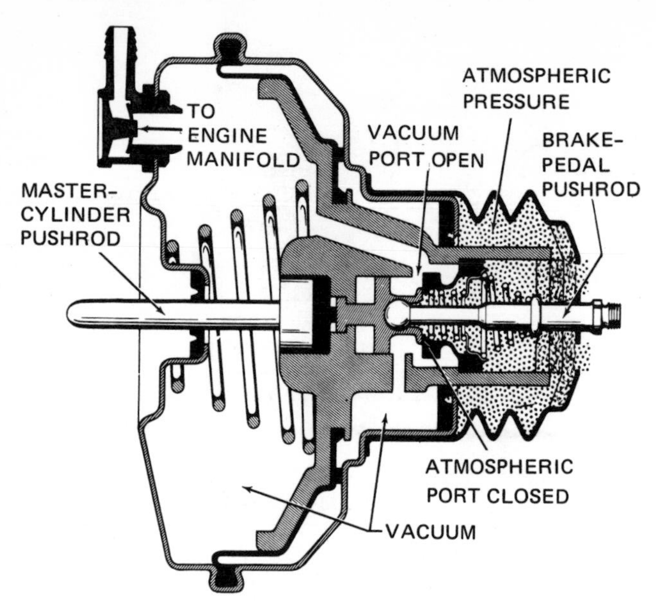

Figure 9 Sectional view of a Bendix single-diaphragm power brake in the released position. *(Chevrolet Motor Division of General Motors Corporation.)*

Let us examine the operation of a typical integral-power-brake assembly. Figure 9 shows the assembly in the released position, that is, with the brakes not applied. In this position, there is intake-manifold vacuum on both sides of the diaphragm. Spring action has moved the piston in the master cylinder and the diaphragm all the way to the right. The atmospheric valve is closed.

When the brake pedal is depressed for braking action (Fig. 10), the brake-pedal pushrod is moved forward (to the left in Fig. 10). This action causes the valve to close the vacuum port

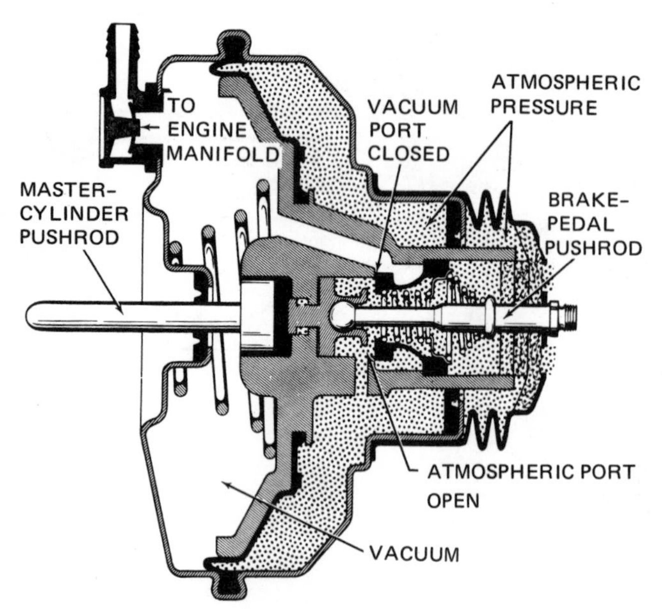

Figure 10 Sectional view of a Bendix single-diaphragm power brake in the applying position. *(Chevrolet Motor Division of General Motors Corporation.)*

and open the atmospheric port. Now atmospheric pressure can enter on the right side of the diaphragm and exert a pressure on the diaphragm. The diaphragm is forced to move to the left, and this causes the pushrod to push the master-cylinder piston to the left. Hydraulic pressure now develops in the master cylinder, forcing brake fluid through the brake lines to the wheel cylinders. The brakes are, therefore, applied. The harder the driver presses on the brake pedal, the wider the atmospheric port is opened, and the harder the diaphragm presses on the pushrod to produce braking.

As hydraulic pressure develops in the hydraulic system, a reaction counterforce acts against the reaction disk (see Fig. 8). This disk then transmits the reaction force back through the valve pushrod and the brake pedal. The reaction, or "push-back," force is proportional to the hydraulic pressure and thus to the actual braking taking place. The reaction, therefore, gives the driver a feel of the braking action. The higher the hydraulic pressure and thus the harder the brakes are applied, the stronger will be the reaction on the brake pedal.

When the brake-pedal movement is stopped and the driver holds the pedal in the braking position, the valve pushrod stops its movement of the control-valve plunger. However, the unbalanced pressures on the two sides of the diaphragm will continue to move the outer sleeve of the control-valve plunger forward, keeping the vacuum port closed. At the same time, the reaction force acting on the reaction disk will tend to move the atmospheric valve to the closed position. When these forces reach a balance, the vacuum port will remain closed and the atmospheric valve will cut off any further passage of atmospheric pressure to the right-hand side of the diaphragm. Thus, the hydraulic pressure will be maintained at a constant value so that the braking effect continues.

When the brake pedal is released (Fig. 9), the spring action closes the atmospheric port and opens the vacuum port so that vacuum is applied to both sides of the diaphragm. The brakes, therefore, are released.

■ 7-2-7 Bendix Dual-Diaphragm Power Brake

The Bendix dual-diaphragm assembly, shown in Fig. 11, is similar to the unit previously discussed. However, it has a second diaphragm and plate. The purpose of the secondary diaphragm is to provide additional braking power. The unit works in the same manner as the power-brake assembly described in ■7-2-6.

■ 7-2-8 Multiplier-Type Power Brake

Figure 4 shows a multiplier-type brake system schematically. Figure 12 shows a brake assembly of this type. In operation, when the brakes are applied, the hydraulic pressure from the master cylinder is applied to the control valve. This action causes the valve to admit atmospheric pressure to one side of the power diaphragm. With intake-manifold vacuum on the other side of the power diaphragm, the diaphragm is forced to move. This motion forces the piston into the hydraulic cylinder so that brake fluid is forced from the hydraulic cylinder to the wheel

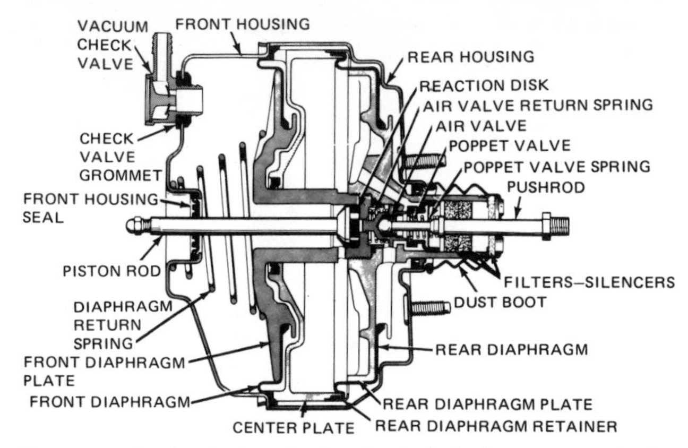

Figure 11 Sectional view of a Bendix dual-diaphragm power brake. *(Chevrolet Motor Division of General Motors Corporation.)*

cylinders. Thus, braking takes place. The relatively light brake-pedal pressure and the hydraulic pressure in the master cylinder are multiplied several times by the power brake.

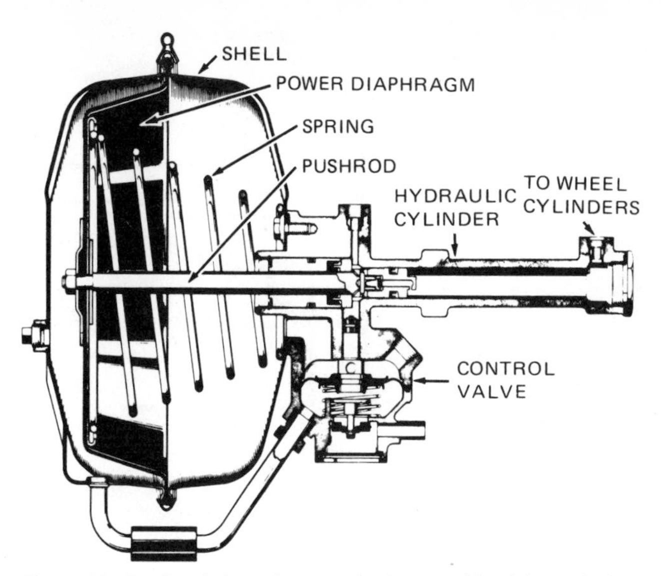

Figure 12 Sectional view of a power-brake assembly of the multiplier type. *(Chevrolet Motor Division of General Motors Corporation.)*

■ 7-2-9 Assist-Type Power Brake

Figure 5 shows a typical installation of an assist-type power brake. Figures 13 and 14 show sectional views of a specific model. This type of power brake uses a bellows which is mechanically linked to the brake pedal and the master cylinder. When the brake is applied, a valve in the power-brake assembly admits vacuum into the bellows. This collapses the bellows and causes the upper end of the power lever to move (to the left, in Fig. 13). The brake-pedal pushrod is also pushing on the power lever. This combined push is applied to the master cylinder pushrod, forcing it to push the master-cylinder piston into the master cylinder so that the brakes are applied.

Figure 13 shows the assembly in the unapplied position. The vacuum valve is closed and the air valve is open. The bellows is fully extended because it is filled with atmospheric pressure.

When the brake pedal is moved, applying the brakes (Fig. 14), the linkage to the bellows assembly causes the vacuum valve to open and the air valve to close. Now the vacuum applied in the bellows causes it to collapse, or shorten, and this motion is carried through the power lever to the master-cylinder pushrod. Thus, both the brake-pedal pushrod and the bellows work together to move the master-cylinder pushrod and to apply the brakes. However, most of the braking effort comes from the bellows.

This power-brake system includes a brake "feel" arrangement similar to those described previously for other power-brake systems. The increasing hydraulic pressure in the master cylinder, resulting from increased application of the brakes, causes a reaction through the reaction disk and the piston. This reaction is carried through a secondary lever (the reaction or actuating lever) to the valves in the bellows. The reaction causes a small movement of the vacuum valve, which shuts it. The reaction force, which is proportional to the hydraulic pressure in the master cylinder (and therefore braking effort), thus provides the driver with brake "feel."

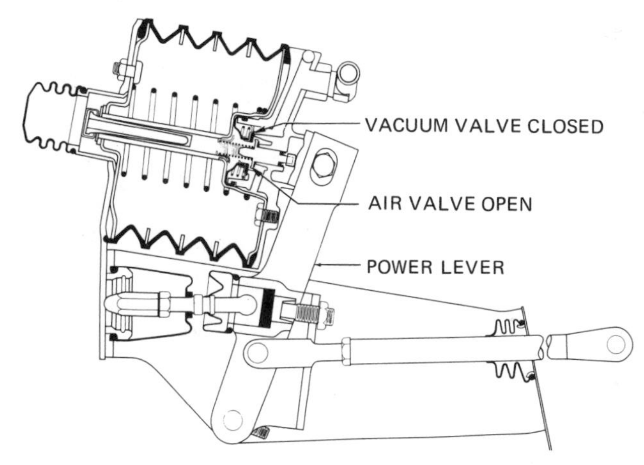

Figure 13 Assist type of power brake in the released position. *(Buick Motor Division of General Motors Corporation.)*

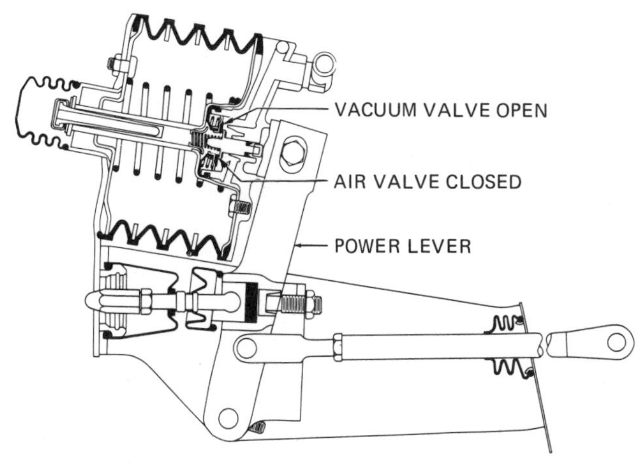

Figure 14 Assist type of power brake in the applied position. *(Buick Motor Division of General Motors Corporation.)*

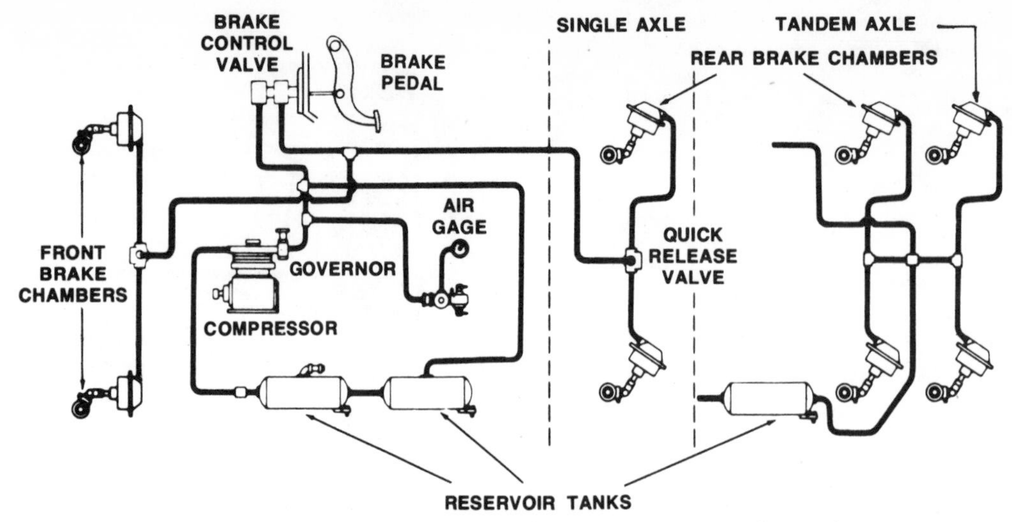

Figure 15 Schematic layout of a typical air-brake system. *(Chevrolet Motor Division of General Motors Corporation.)*

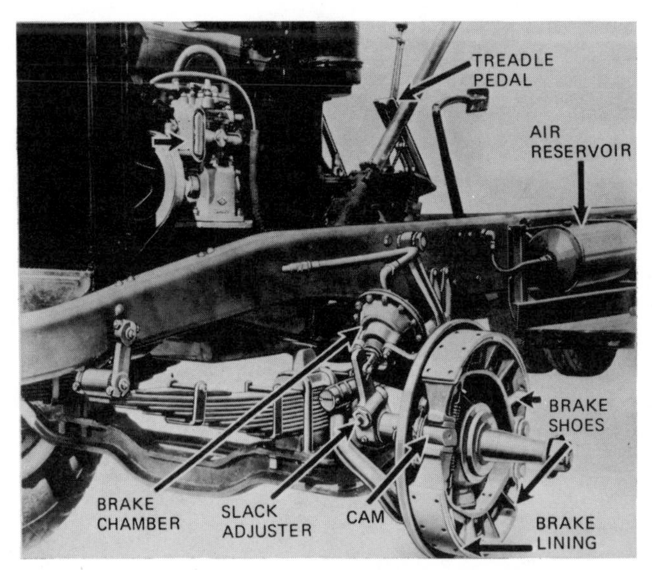

Figure 16 Installation of an air-brake system on a heavy-duty truck. *(International Harvester Company.)*

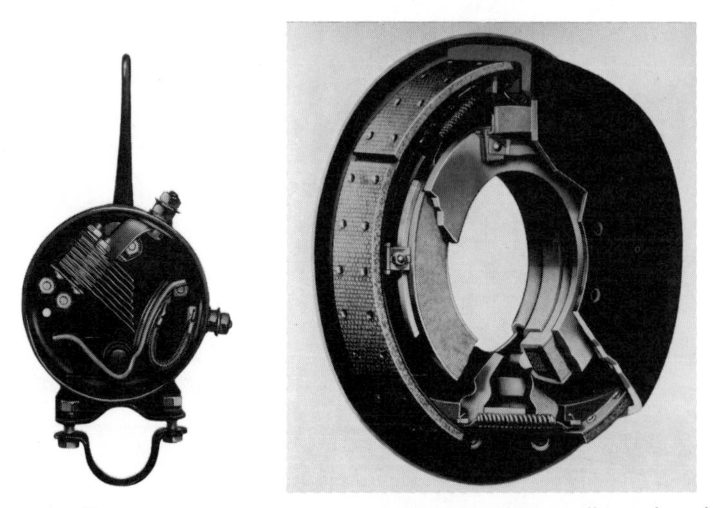

Figure 17 Construction of an electric-brake mechanism. Left, controller; right, wheel-braking mechanism. *(Warner Electric Brake Manufacturing Company.)*

Note that this system includes a vacuum reserve tank to ensure that vacuum will be available for braking when the engine is not running. Vacuum is built up in the tank from the intake manifold when the engine is running. The reserve thus stored permits the power brakes to be applied several times after the engine has stopped. Even though the vacuum is exhausted, however, the brakes can still be applied, but there will be no power assist. The brake-pedal pressure must be considerably greater to achieve braking.

■ **7-2-10 Air Brake** The air brake uses compressed air to apply the braking force to the brake shoes. A typical air-brake-system layout is illustrated in Fig. 15. The compressor unit, air-reservoir tank, brake chamber, and wheel mechanism are shown in Fig. 16. Air-reservoir tanks are necessary in order to maintain adequate braking power at all times, even when the engine is not running. The air compressor, which is a small air pump, maintains air pressure in the tanks. When the air pressure is applied to the brake chambers by operation of the treadle pedal, the brake chamber rotates the cam. This causes the brake shoes to push outward against the brake drum.

■ **7-2-11 Electric Brakes** Electric brakes use electromagnets to provide the braking force against the brake shoes. Each wheel contains a semistationary circular electromagnet and an armature disk that revolves with the wheel (Fig. 17). The electromagnet operates from the battery current. A controller in the driver's compartment enables the driver to connect the electromagnets to the battery and to vary the amount of current flowing from the battery to the electromagnets in order to vary the amount of braking action. When the brakes are not applied, there is no magnetic attraction between the electromagnet and the armature disk in the wheel. When the driver applies the brakes, current begins to flow through the electromagnets. This builds up a magnetic field, causing magnetic attraction between the semistationary electromagnet and the rotating armature disk. The electromagnet is thus forced to shift through a limited arc in the direction of the wheel rotation. A lug on the electromagnet is connected to a cam; movement of the electromagnet and the lug causes the cam to press against the end of the brake shoes and forces the brake shoes outward against the brake drum. The greater the current flowing through the electromagnet, the greater the braking effect.

SECTION 7-3 Brake Service

This section discusses trouble diagnosis, adjustments, and servicing of the various components in automotive hydraulic-brake systems.

■ **7-3-1 Brake Trouble Diagnosis** The charts and the subsections that follow them give you a means of tracing troubles in the brakes to their causes. This permits quick location of causes and, thus, quick correction of troubles. If the cause is known, the trouble is usually easy to correct. Following the trouble-diagnosis charts are several subsections that cover the adjustment and repair procedures on different types of automotive brakes.

■ **7-3-2 Drum-Brake Trouble-Diagnosis Chart** A variety of braking problems bring the driver to the mechanic. It is a rare driver who will know exactly what is causing a trouble. The chart that follows lists possible troubles in drum-brake systems, their possible causes, and checks or corrections to be made. Following subsections describe the trouble and causes or corrections in detail. The chart in ■7-3-15 covers possible disk-brake troubles.

NOTE: The troubles and possible causes are not listed according to how often they occur. That is, item 1 (or item *a* under "Possible Cause") does not necessarily occur more often than item 2 (or item *b*).

DRUM-BRAKE TROUBLE-DIAGNOSIS CHART

(See ■7-3-3 to 7-3-14 for detailed explanations of the trouble causes and corrections listed in the chart.)

COMPLAINT	POSSIBLE CAUSE	CHECK OR CORRECTION
1. Brake pedal goes to floorboard (■7-3-3)	a. Linkage or shoes out of adjustment	Adjust
	b. Brake linings worn	Replace
	c. Lack of brake fluid	Add fluid; bleed system (see item 10 below)
	d. Air in system	Add fluid; bleed system (see item 9 below)
	e. Worn master cylinder	Repair
2. One brake drags (■7-3-4)	a. Shoes out of adjustment	Adjust
	b. Clogged brake line	Clear or replace line
	c. Wheel cylinder defective	Repair or replace
	d. Weak or broken return spring	Replace
	e. Loose wheel bearing	Adjust bearing
3. All brakes drag (■7-3-5)	a. Incorrect linkage adjustment	Adjust
	b. Trouble in master cylinder	Repair or replace
	c. Oil in system	Replace damaged rubber parts; use only recommended brake fluid
4. Car pulls to one side when braking (■7-3-6)	a. Brake linings soaked with oil	Replace linings and oil seals; avoid overlubrication
	b. Brake linings soaked with brake fluid	Replace linings; repair or replace wheel cylinder
	c. Brake shoes out of adjustment	Adjust
	d. Tires not uniformly inflated	Inflate correctly
	e. Brake line clogged	Clear or replace line
	f. Defective wheel cylinder	Repair or replace
	g. Brake backing-plate loose	Tighten
	h. Mismatched linings	Use same linings all around
5. Soft, or spongy, pedal (■7-3-7)	a. Air in system	Add brake fluid; bleed system (see item 9 below)
	b. Brake shoes out of adjustment	Adjust
6. Poor braking action requiring excessive pedal pressure (■7-3-8)	a. Brake linings soaked with water	Will be all right when dried out
	b. Shoes out of adjustment	Adjust
	c. Brake linings hot	Allow to cool
	d. Brake linings burned	Replace
	e. Brake drum glazed	Turn or grind drum
	f. Power-brake assembly not operating	Overhaul or replace
7. Brakes too sensitive or grab (■7-3-9)	a. Shoes out of adjustment	Replace
	b. Wrong linings	Install correct linings
	c. Brake linings greasy	Replace; check oil seals; avoid overlubrication
	d. Drums scored	Turn or grind drums
	e. Backing plates loose	Tighten
	f. Power-brake assembly malfunctioning	Overhaul or replace
	g. Brake linings soaked with oil	Replace linings and oil seals; avoid over-lubrication
	h. Brake linings soaked with brake fluid	Replace linings; repair or replace wheel cylinders
8. Noisy brakes (■7-3-10)	a. Linings worn	Replace
	b. Shoes warped	Replace
	c. Shoe rivets loose	Replace shoe or lining
	d. Drums worn or rough	Turn or grind drums
	e. Loose parts	Tighten
9. Air in system (■7-3-11)	a. Defective master cylinder	Repair or replace
	b. Loose connections, damaged tube	Tighten connections; replace tube
	c. Brake fluid lost	See item 10 below
10. Loss of brake fluid (■7-3-12)	a. Master cylinder leaks	Repair or replace
	b. Wheel cylinder leaks	Repair or replace

(Continued)

DRUM-BRAKE TROUBLE-DIAGNOSIS CHART
(Continued)

(See ■7-3-3 to 7-3-14 for detailed explanations of the trouble causes and corrections listed in the chart.)

COMPLAINT	POSSIBLE CAUSE	CHECK OR CORRECTION
10. *(Continued)*		
	c. Loose connections; damaged tube	Tighten connections; replace tube

NOTE: After repair, add brake fluid and bleed system.

COMPLAINT	POSSIBLE CAUSE	CHECK OR CORRECTION
11. Brakes do not self-adjust (■7-3-13)	a. Adjustment screw stuck	Free and clean up
	b. Adjustment lever does not engage star wheel	Repair; free up or replace adjuster
	c. Adjuster incorrectly installed	Install correctly
12. Warning light comes on when braking (dual system) (■7-3-14)	a. One section (front or back) has failed	Check both sections for braking action; repair defective section
	b. Pressure-differential valve defective	Replace

■ 7-3-3 Brake Pedal Goes to Floorboard When the brake pedal goes to the floorboard, there is no pedal reserve. Full pedal movement does not produce adequate braking. This would be a very unlikely situation with a dual-brake system. One section (front or rear) might fail, but it would be rare for both to fail at the same time. It is possible that the driver has continued to operate the car with one section out. (Either the driver ignores the warning light or the light or pressure-differential valve has failed.) Causes of failure could be linkage or brake shoes out of adjustment, linings worn, air in the system, lack of brake fluid, or a worn master cylinder.

■ 7-3-4 One Brake Drags If one brake drags, this means that the brake shoes are not moving away from the brake drum when the brakes are released. This trouble could be due to a number of problems. It could be caused by incorrect shoe adjustment or a clogged brake line which does not release pressure from the wheel cylinder. It could also be due to sticking pistons in the wheel cylinder, to weak or broken brake-shoe return springs, or to a loose wheel bearing which permits the wheel to wobble so that the brake drum comes in contact with the brake shoes even though they are retracted.

■ 7-3-5 All Brakes Drag When all brakes drag, it may be that the brake pedal does not have sufficient play. In that case, the pistons in the master cylinder do not fully retract. This would prevent the lip of the piston cup from clearing the compensating port. Hydraulic pressure would not be relieved as it should be. As a result, the wheel cylinders would not release the brake shoes. A similar condition could result if oil had been added to the system. Oil is likely to cause the piston cup to swell. If it swelled enough, it would not clear the compensating port even with the piston in the "fully retracted" position. A clogged compensating port would have the same result. Do not use a wire or drill to clear the port—you might produce a burr that would cut the piston cup. Instead, clear it with alcohol and compressed air. Clogging of the reservoir vent might also cause dragging brakes by trapping pressure in the reservoir which would prevent release of pressure. But this would be just as likely to cause leakage of air into the system (see ■7-3-11 below).

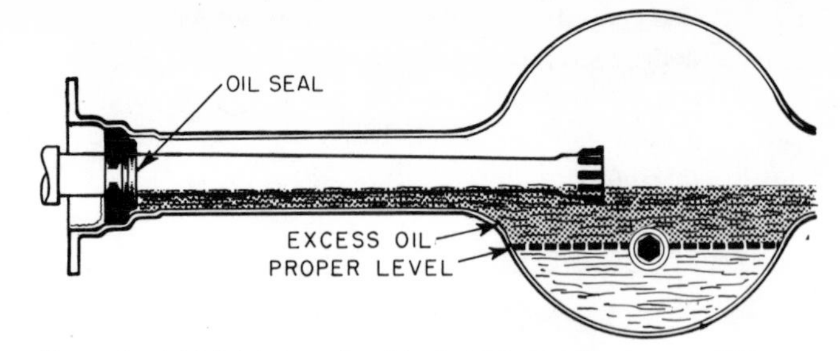

Figure 1 A high lubricant level in the differential and rear-axle housing may cause leakage past the oil seal. This would result in oil-soaked brake linings. *(Pontiac Motor Division of General Motors Corporation.)*

■ 7-3-6 Car Pulls to One Side If the car pulls to one side when the brakes are applied, more braking pressure is being applied to one side than to the other. This happens if some of the brake linings have become soaked in oil or brake fluid, if brake shoes are unevenly or improperly adjusted, if tires are not evenly inflated, or if defective wheel cylinders or clogged brake lines are preventing uniform braking action at all wheels. A loose brake-backing plate or the use of two different types of brake lining will cause the car to pull to one side when the brakes are applied. A misaligned front end or a broken spring could also cause this problem.

Linings will become soaked with oil if the lubricant level in the differential and rear axle is too high. This usually causes leakage past the oil seal (Fig. 1). At the front wheel, brake linings may become oil soaked if the front-wheel bearings are improperly lubricated or if the oil seal is defective or not properly installed. Wheel cylinders will leak brake fluid onto the brake linings if they are defective or if an actuating pin has been improperly installed (see ■7-3-12). If the linings at a left wheel become soaked with brake fluid or oil, for example, the car pulls to the left because the brakes are more effective on the left side.

■ 7-3-7 Soft, or Spongy, Pedal If the pedal action is soft, or spongy, the chances are that there is air in the system.

Out-of-adjustment brake shoes could also cause this. Refer to ■7-3-11 for conditions that could allow air to get into the system.

■ **7-3-8 Poor Braking Action Requiring Excessive Pedal Pressure** Excessive pedal pressure could be caused by improper brake-shoe adjustment. The use of the wrong brake lining could cause the same trouble. Sometimes, brake linings that have become wet after a hard rain or after driving through water will not hold well. Normal braking action is usually restored after the brake linings have dried out.

Another possible cause of poor braking action is excessive temperature. After the brakes have been applied for long periods, as in coming down a long hill, they begin to overheat. This overheating reduces braking effectiveness so that the brakes "fade." Often, if brakes are allowed to cool, braking efficiency is restored. However, excessively long periods of braking at high temperature may char the brake linings so that they must be replaced. Further, this overheating may glaze the brake drum so that it becomes too smooth for effective braking action. In this case, the drum must be ground or turned to remove the glaze. Glazing can also take place even though the brakes are not overheated. Failure of the power-brake assembly will considerably increase the amount of pedal pressure required to produce braking.

■ **7-3-9 Brakes Too Sensitive or Grab** If linings are greasy, or soaked with oil or brake fluid, the brakes tend to grab with slight pedal pressure. In any case, the linings must be replaced. If the brakes shoes are out of adjustment, if the wrong linings are used, or if drums are scored or rough, grabbing may result. A loose backing plate may cause the same condition. As the linings come into contact with the drum, the backing plate shifts to give hard braking. A defective power-brake assembly can also cause grabbing.

■ **7-3-10 Noisy Brakes** Brakes become noisy if the brake linings wear so much that the rivets come into contact with the brake drum; if the shoes become warped so that pressure on the drum is not uniform; if shoe rivets become loose so that they contact the drum; or if the drum becomes rough or worn. Any of these conditions is likely to cause a squeak or squeal when the brakes are applied. Loose parts, such as the brake backing plate, also may rattle.

■ **7-3-11 Air in System** If air gets into the hydraulic system, poor braking and a spongy pedal will result. Air can get into the system if the filler vent becomes plugged (Fig. 2), since this may tend to create a partial vacuum in the system on the return stroke of the piston. Air could then bypass the rear piston cup, as shown by the arrows, and enter the system. It is possible accidentally to plug the vent when the filler plug or cover is removed. Always check the vent and clean it when the

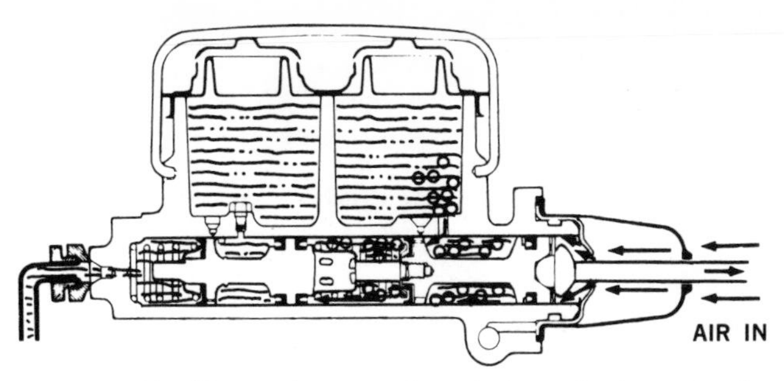

Figure 2 If the filler vent becomes plugged, air may be drawn into the system on the return stroke of the piston, past the rear piston cup. This is shown by the small arrows and bobbles. *(Pontiac Motor Division of General Motors Corporation.)*

plug or cover is removed. Air can also get into the hydraulic system if the master-cylinder valve is leaky and does not hold pressure in the system. A leak could allow air to seep in around the wheel-cylinder piston cups, since there would be no pressure holding the cups tight against the cylinder walls. Probably the most common cause of air in the brake system is insufficient brake fluid in the master cylinder. If the brake fluid drops below the compensating port, the hydraulic system will draw air in as the piston moves forward on the braking stroke. Air in the system must be removed by adding brake fluid and bleeding the system, as described in ■7-3-40.

■ **7-3-12 Loss of Brake Fluid** Brake fluid can be lost if the master cylinder leaks, if the wheel cylinder leaks, if the line connections are loose, or if the line is damaged. One possible cause of wheel-cylinder leakage is incorrect installation of the actuating pin (Fig. 3). If the pin is cocked, as shown, the side thrust on the piston may permit leakage past the piston. Leakage from other causes at the master cylinder or wheel cylinder requires removal and repair, or replacement, of the defective parts.

■ **7-3-13 Brakes Do Not Self-Adjust** Brakes do not self-adjust if the adjustment screw is stuck, the adjustment

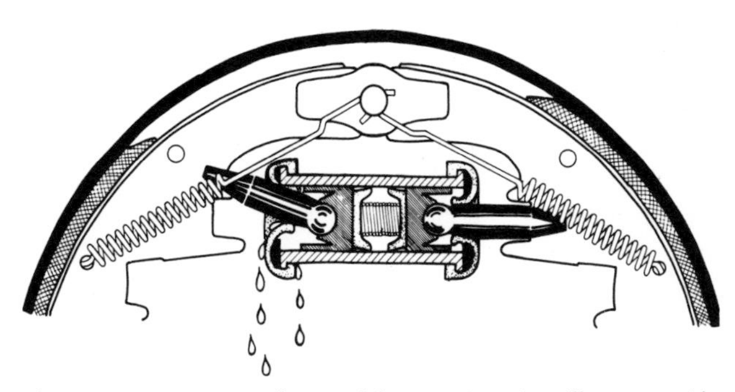

Figure 3 Incorrect installation of the actuating pin will cause a side thrust on the piston which will permit leakage of brake fluid from the wheel cylinder. The pin must always align with the notch in the brake shoe. *(Pontiac Motor Division of General Motors Corporation.)*

lever does not engage the star wheel, or the adjuster was incorrectly installed. It is necessary to get into the brake to find and correct the trouble.

■ 7-3-14 Warning Light Comes On When Braking (Dual System) If the warning light comes on when braking, it means that one of the two braking sections has failed. Both sections (front and rear) should be checked so that the trouble can be found and eliminated. It is dangerous to drive with this condition, even though the car brakes, because only half the wheels are being braked.

■ 7-3-15 Disk-Brake Trouble-Diagnosis Chart The chart that follows lists disk-brake troubles, their possible causes, and checks or corrections to be made. Following sections describe the troubles and causes or corrections in detail.

> **NOTE:** The troubles and possible causes are not listed according to how often they occur; item 1 (or item a under "Possible Cause") does not necessarily occur more often than item 2 (or item *b*).

DISK-BRAKE TROUBLE-DIAGNOSIS CHART

(See ■7-3-16 to 7-3-24 for detailed explanations of the trouble causes and corrections listed in the chart.)

COMPLAINT	POSSIBLE CAUSE	CHECK OR CORRECTION
1. Excessive pedal travel (■7-3-16)	a. Excessive disk runout	Check runout; if excessive, install new disk
	b. Air leak, or insufficient brake fluid	Check system for leaks
	c. Improper brake fluid (boil)	Drain and install correct fluid
	d. Warped or tapered shoe	Install new shoe
	e. Loose wheel-bearing adjustment	Readjust
	f. Damaged piston seal	Install new seal
	g. Power-brake malfunction	Check power unit
2. Brake roughness or chatter (pedal pulsation) (■7-3-17)	a. Excessive disk runout	Check runout; if excessive, install new disk
	b. Disk out of parallel	Check runout; if excessive, install new disk
	c. Loose wheel bearing	Readjust
3. Excessive pedal effort, grabbing, or uneven braking action (■7-3-18)	a. Power-brake malfunction	Check power unit
	b. Brake fluid or grease on linings	Install new linings
	c. Lining worn	Install new shoe and linings
	d. Incorrect lining	Install correct lining
	e. Frozen or seized pistons	Disassemble caliper and free-up pistons; install new caliper and pistons, if necessary
4. Car pulls to one side (■7-3-19)	a. Brake fluid or grease on linings	Install new linings
	b. Frozen or seized pistons	Disassemble caliper and free pistons
	c. Incorrect tire pressure	Inflate tires to recommended pressures
	d. Distorted brake shoes	Install new brake shoes
	e. Front end out of alignment	Check and align front end
	f. Broken rear spring	Install new rear spring
	g. Restricted hose or line	Check hoses and lines and correct as necessary
	h. Unmatched linings	Install correct lining
5. Noise (■7-3-20): Groan	Brake noise when slowly releasing brakes (creep-groan). Not detrimental to function of disk brakes—no corrective action required. This noise may be eliminated by slightly increasing or decreasing brake-pedal efforts.	
Rattle	Brake noise or rattle at low speeds on rough roads may be due to excessive clearance between the shoe and the caliper. Install new shoe and lining assemblies to correct.	
Scraping	a. Mounting bolts too long	Install mounting bolts of correct length
	b. Disk rubbing housing	Check for rust or mud buildup on caliper housing; check caliper mounting and bridge bolt tightness
	c. Loose wheel bearings	Readjust
	d. Linings worn, allowing telltale tabs to scrape on disk	Replace linings
6. Brakes heat up during driving and fail to release (■7-3-21)	a. Power-brake malfunction	Check and correct power unit
	b. Sticking pedal linkage	Free sticking pedal linkage
	c. Driver riding brake pedal	Instruct driver

COMPLAINT	POSSIBLE CAUSE	CHECK OR CORRECTION
	d. Frozen or seized piston	Disassemble caliper, clean cylinder bore, clean seal groove, and install new pistons, seals, and boots
	e. Residual pressure valve in master cylinder	Remove valve from cylinder
7. Leaky caliper cylinder (■7-3-22)	a. Damaged or worn piston seal	Install new seal
	b. Scores or corrosion on surface of piston	Disassemble caliper, clean cylinder bore; if necessary, install new pistons or replace caliper
8. Brake pedal can be depressed without braking effect (■7-3-23)	a. Piston pushed back in cylinder bores during servicing of caliper (and lining not properly positioned)	Reposition brake shoe and lining assemblies. Depress pedal a second time and if condition persists, look for the following causes:
	b. Leak in system or caliper	Check for leak, repair as required
	c. Damaged piston seal in one or more of the cylinders	Disassemble caliper and replace piston seals as required
	d. Air in hydraulic system, or improper bleeding procedure	Bleed system
	e. Bleeder screw opens	Close bleeder screw and bleed entire system
	f. Leak past primary cup in master cylinder	Recondition master cylinder
9. Fluid level low in master cylinder (■7-3-24)	a. Leaks in system or caliper	Check for leak, repair as required
	b. Worn brake-shoe linings	Replace shoes
10. Warning light comes on when braking (dual system) (■7-3-14)	a. One section (front or back) has failed	Check both sections for braking action; repair defective section
	b. Pressure-differential valve defective	Replace

■ **7-3-16 Excessive Pedal Travel** Anything that requires excessive movement of the caliper pistons will require excessive pedal travel. For example, if the disk has excessive runout, it will force the pistons farther back in their bores when the brakes are released. Thus additional pedal travel is required when the brakes are applied. Of course, warped or tapered shoes, a damaged piston seal, or a loose wheel bearing could cause the same problem. In addition, air in the lines, insufficient fluid in the system, or incorrect fluid, which boils, will cause a spongy pedal and excessive pedal travel. If the power brake is malfunctioning, it also could produce excessive pedal travel.

■ **7-3-17 Brake-Pedal Pulsation** Brake-pedal pulsation is probably due to a disk with excessive runout or to a loose wheel bearing.

■ **7-3-18 Excessive Pedal Effort** The first cause you might think of for excessive pedal effort is that the power brake is not operating properly. In addition, if the linings are worn they will not produce normal braking, so that high pedal pressure is required. Also, if the pistons are jammed in the calipers, high pedal effort will be required.

■ **7-3-19 Car Pulls to One Side** Pulling to one side is due to uneven braking action. It could be caused by incorrect front-end alignment, uneven tire inflation, or a broken or weak suspension spring. Within the braking system itself, such things as brake fluid on the linings, unmatched linings, warped brake shoes, jammed pistons, or restrictions in the brake lines could cause the car to pull to one side when braking.

■ **7-3-20 Noise** The chart (■7-3-15) covers various noises and their causes. Refer to it for details.

■ **7-3-21 Brakes Fail to Release** Brake-release failure could result from anything from a sticking pedal linkage or malfunctioning power brake to pistons stuck in the calipers. It could also be due to the driver's riding the brake pedal or to failure of the master cylinder to release the pressure when the brakes are released.

■ **7-3-22 Leaky Caliper Cylinder** A leaky caliper cylinder could be due to a damaged or worn piston seal or to

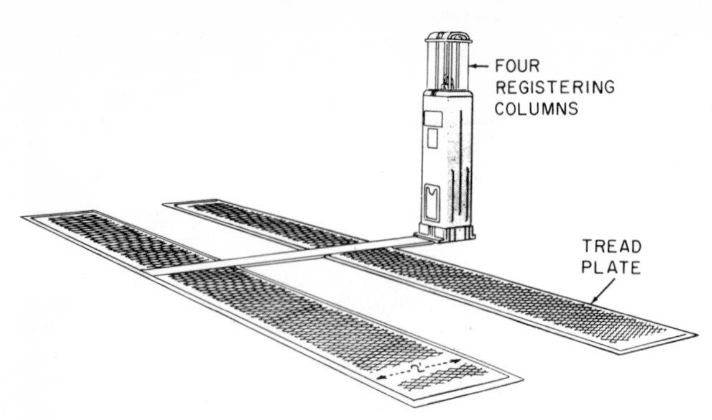

Figure 4 Automatic brake tester. *(Weaver Manufacturing Company.)*

roughness on the surface of the piston as a result of scores, scratches, or corrosion.

■ 7-3-23 Brake Pedal Can Be Depressed without Braking Effect

If the brake calipers have been serviced, the pistons may be pushed back so far in their bores that a single full movement of the brake pedal will not produce braking. Thus, after any service on disk brakes, the brake pedal should be pumped many times, and the master-cylinder reservoir properly filled, before the car is moved. Pumping the pedal several times gradually moves the pistons into normal position so that normal brake-pedal application causes braking.

Of course, other conditions can prevent braking action when the pedal is depressed, among them leaks or air in the system. Leaks can occur at the piston seals, bleeder screws, brake-line connections, or in the master cylinder.

Consider the possibility that the pressure-differential valve is stuck, or that the warning light may be burned out if both the front and rear sections have failed. The driver might have been driving for some time with one section defective, and the warning system might not have worked to warn of the trouble.

■ 7-3-24 Fluid Level Low in Master Cylinder

Low fluid level in the master cylinder could be due to leaks in the system or caliper (see ■7-3-23). Worn disk-brake shoe linings also can cause this problem. As the linings wear, the fluid level drops in the master cylinder.

■ 7-3-25 Drum-Brake Service

Any complaint of faulty brake action should always be analyzed to determine its cause, as noted in previous subsections. Sometimes, all that is required (on earlier drum-type brakes) is a minor brake adjustment to compensate for lining wear. On later brakes with the self-adjuster (Fig. 21 in Part 7, Sec. 1), the brakes automatically adjust themselves to compensate for lining wear. Other brake services include addition of brake fluid, bleeding the hydraulic system to remove air, repair or replacement of master cylinder and wheel cylinders, replacement of brake linings, and refinishing of brake drums or disks.

Some automotive shops have automatic brake testers which quickly check brake action and efficiency. Visual inspection may reveal some troubles, but the only way to really check brake action is to operate the brakes and see how they perform.

One automatic brake tester is shown in Fig. 4. With this tester, you simply drive the car onto the four tread plates at about 5 mph (8 km/h) and then apply the brakes hard. The braking effort at each wheel is registered on four dials or in four glass columns (in which colored liquid rises in proportion to the braking effort). The four tread plates are supported on rollers and are spring-loaded in a horizontal direction. When a rolling wheel on a tread is suddenly stopped by brake application, the tread is moved forward against the spring tension. This movement causes the needle on a dial to turn or the liquid in a glass column to rise to register the amount of braking action. The use of this type of brake tester gives graphic proof of the amount of braking at each wheel. If it is inadequate, the brakes should be checked and serviced as necessary.

A dynamic brake analyzer using two pairs of motor-driven rollers is shown in Fig. 5. The principle of this analyzer is simple: Either the front or the rear wheels of the car are placed on the rollers, as shown. Then, the operator turns on the electric motors which drive the rollers (see Fig. 6). Now, with the wheels being turned by the rollers at medium to high speed, the operator applies the car brakes. The braking effort at each wheel is registered on a dial (Fig. 7) so that there is no question as to how well the brakes are operating. Note that there are two hands on the meter dial (Fig. 7). One, which is the color red, is for the right wheel; the black is for the left wheel. Not only does the analyzer indicate brake efficiency, but it also shows up imbalance between the left and right brakes. This is important because if one brake takes hold well and the other does not, the car will tend to be thrown sideways.

Note that, while the brake tester shown in Fig. 4 will test brake stopping power at only low speed, the brake analyzer shown in Fig. 5 will test the brakes at all speeds.

If the brake test shows low braking efficiency, or braking imbalance between wheels, the brakes should be checked further, as explained in later subsections.

NOTE: The analyzer shown in Fig. 5 is also supplied with a dynamometer as an integral part of the assembly.

NOTE: This type of tester gives only an indication of braking efficiency and does not pinpoint causes of low efficiency. For an accurate analysis of the braking system, checking procedures outlined later should be followed.

■ 7-3-26 Adjustment of Brakes

On the early models of brakes without the self-adjustment feature, two types of adjustment are required: minor and major. Minor adjustments are required to compensate for brake-lining wear and are made without removing the car wheels. Major adjustments require removal of the brake drums or shoes for service. With self-ad-

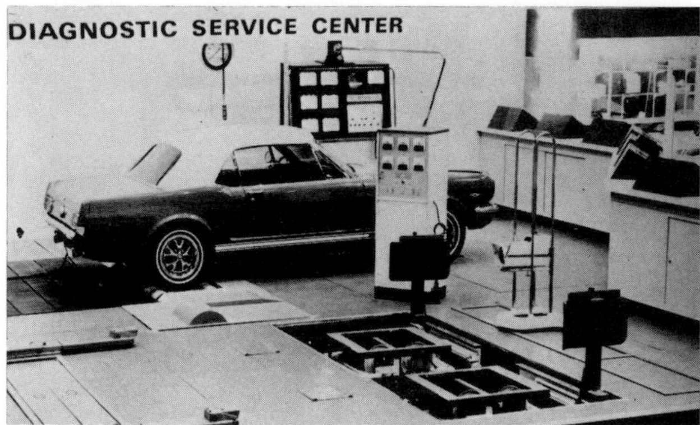

Figure 5 Car on dynamic brake tester, ready for a test of the brakes at the rear wheels. The two sets of rollers in the foreground are for testing front alignment dynamically. *(Clayton Manufacturing Company.)*

justing brakes, however, no adjustment is normally required except after such brake services as brake-shoe replacement or brake-drum grinding or replacement. Adjustments on different types of brakes are described in following subsections. Disk-type brakes are self-adjusting.

Before any adjustment is attempted, the fluid level in the master cylinder, the brake-pedal toe-board clearance, and brake-lining and brake-drum conditions should be checked. Fluid should be added and the brake-pedal linkage adjusted, as needed. It is usually not necessary to remove all four wheels to check the brake-lining condition, since similar conditions should be found at each wheel. Thus, as a rule, only one drum and wheel need be removed. Remove a front wheel, since front-wheel linings wear faster than rear-wheel linings. However, for a thorough inspection all four wheels are removed so that all brake linings and drums can be checked. Linings

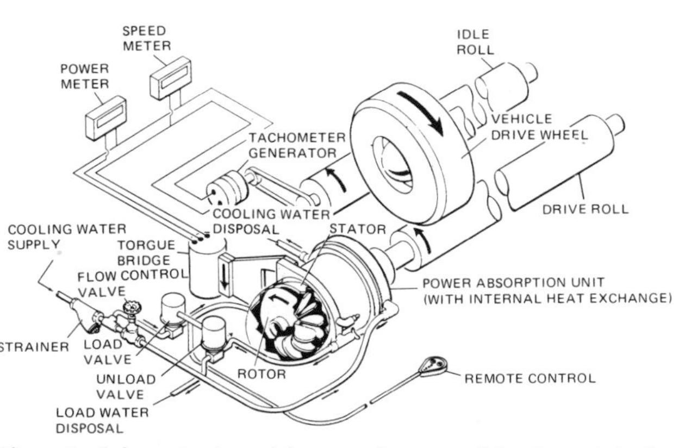

Figure 6 Schematic view of the operating parts of the dynamic brake analyzer. The rollers are driven by the motors, which drive the wheels. When brakes are applied, the wheels attempt to stop the rollers. This effect causes the motors to swing, changing the air pressure through the pneumatic weighing units. This moves the positions of the needles on the dial. *(Clayton Manufacturing Company.)*

In the first, or rolling resistance test, the technician does not touch the brake pedal. The solid hand records action of left brake, while the dash indicates operation of right. A wide spread of the hands indicates presence of a dragging brake or uneven tire pressures.

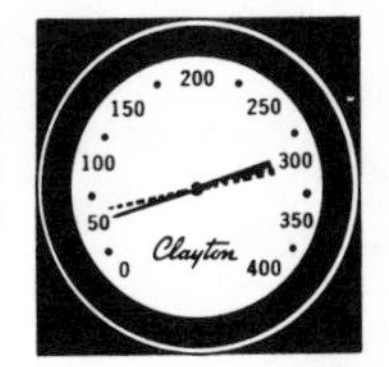

This test determines mechanical application of the brakes. A light application is made to observe first contact of brake shoes with the drums. Often revealed are such things as sticking wheel cylinders, corrosion or ledges between shoes and mounting plates, and/or unhooked or broken return springs.

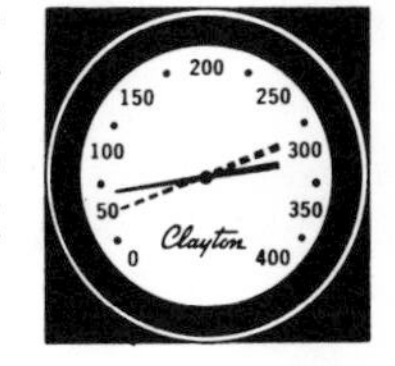

Hydraulic application (the difference in braking power between the two wheels under test) is found by making two short applications of the brakes. Slow application—shown here—reveals brake balance at moderate pressures.

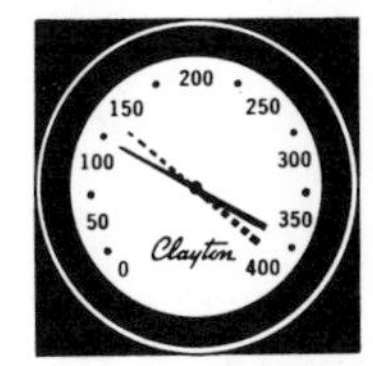

A rapid application is shown here. Any hydraulic restrictions are indicated by a lag in one hand or the other. Hydraulic lag creates momentary imbalance that may cause a car to react wildly during an emergency stop at freeway speeds.

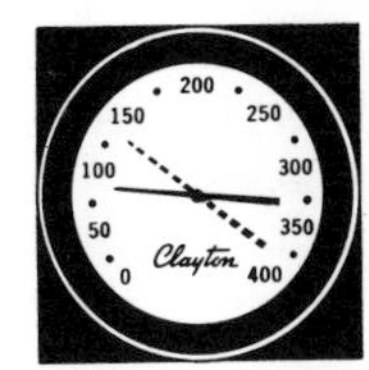

A high effort application on very good brakes. Note closeness of hands.

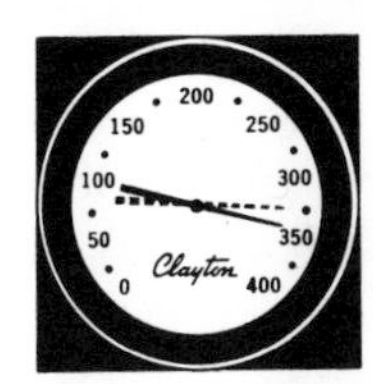

The same hydraulic test on brakes with modest imbalance, but within acceptable limits.

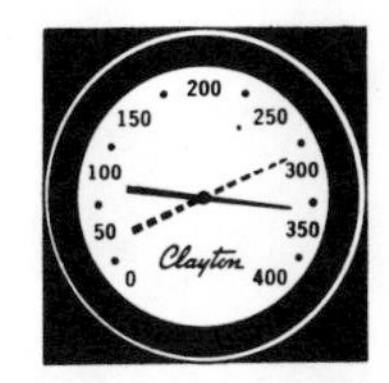

A high effort application or simulated stop from high speeds. These brakes are marginal and can be dangerous in a panic stop. Condition could be improved by repair.

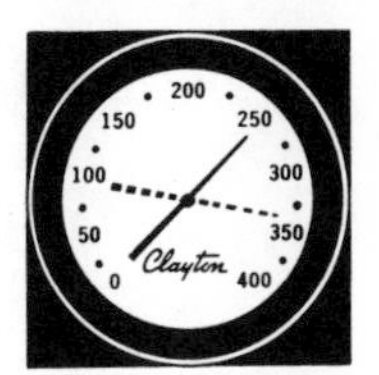

These brakes could cause a fatal accident if not repaired. Note wide spread of the hands. With hydraulic imbalance like this, a car could be literally jerked into another lane of traffic . . . a divider . . . or into a head-on collision. This car is unsafe in any driving situation.

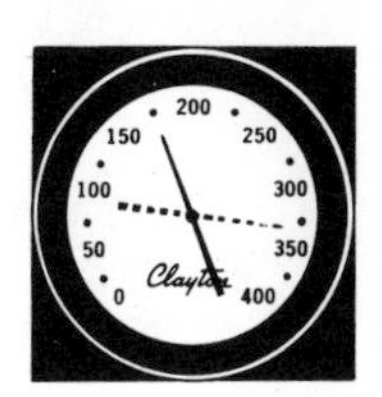

Figure 7 Various readings of the two needles on the dial and their meanings. *(Clayton Manufacturing Company.)*

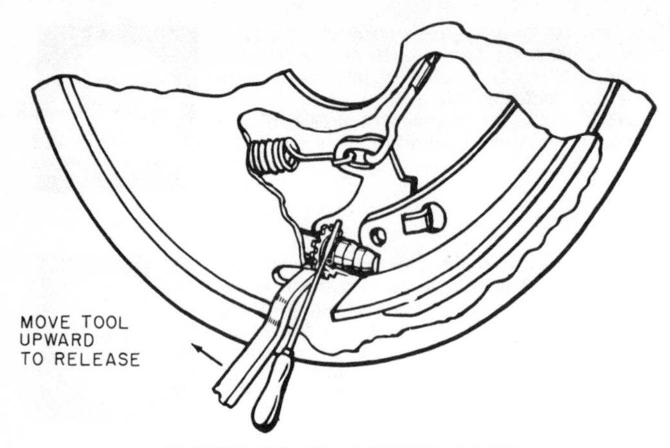

Figure 8 Holding the adjusting lever off the adjusting screw with a screwdriver, while turning the screw. *(Bendix Corporation.)*

should be inspected for wear or contamination with grease or oil. Drums should be inspected for roughness or scoring. See ■7-3-35 and 7-3-36 for lining and drum service.

> **NOTE:** Handle brake linings with care to avoid getting grease on them. Even slight amounts of grease—from greasy fingers—may cause uneven brake action.

■ 7-3-27 Self-Adjusting-Brake Adjustments (Drum Type)

Drum-type self-adjusting brakes require adjustment only after replacement of brake shoes, grinding of brake drums,

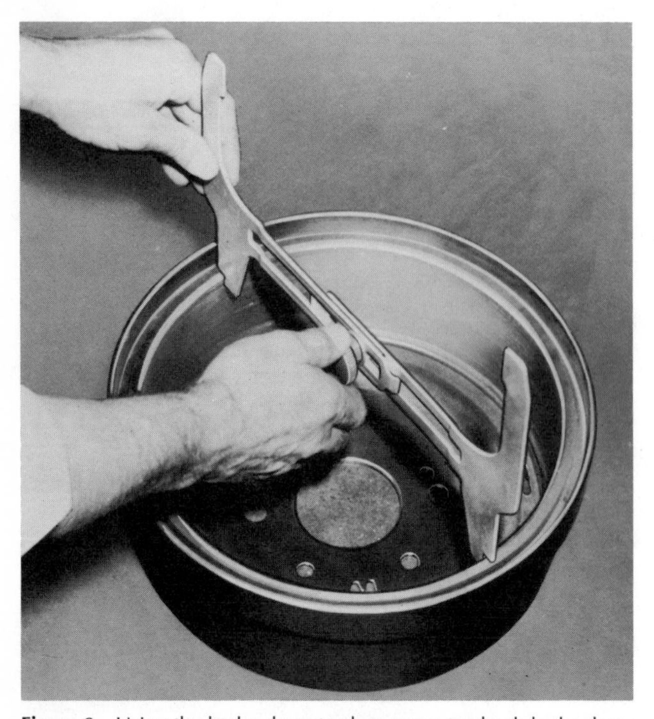

Figure 9 Using the brake drum-to-shoe gauge to check brake-drum diameter. *(Chevrolet Motor Division of General Motors Corporation.)*

Figure 10 Using the brake drum-to-shoe gauge to check the diameter of the brake-shoe linings. *(Chevrolet Motor Division of General Motors Corporation.)*

or other service in which disassembly of the brakes was performed. (Disk-type brakes require no adjustment.) Two typical procedures for drum-type brakes follow.

1. BENDIX BRAKE WITH AUTOMATIC ADJUSTER The Bendix brake and its automatic adjuster parts are illustrated in Fig. 21 in Part 7, Sec. 1. To adjust, remove the adjustment-hole cover from the brake backing plate. Expand the brake shoes by moving the outer end of the tool downward until the wheel drags heavily when it is turned. Then insert an ice pick or a thin-blade screwdriver into the adjustment hole as shown (Fig. 8) to hold the lever away from the adjustment screw. Back off the adjustment screw until the wheel and the drum turn freely. Replace the adjustment-hole cover.

> **NOTE:** On this type of brake, do not attempt to back off the adjustment screw without holding the adjuster lever away from the screw. To do this would damage the adjuster.

An alternative initial adjustment procedure, described below, is recommended by some service people as being somewhat quicker. It requires a special gauge. With the drum off, use the gauge to check the drum braking-surface diameter (Fig. 9). Set the gauge at this diameter and lock with the screw. Then fit it over the brake-shoe linings (Fig. 10) to check their diameter. If this is incorrect, turn the adjustment screw. When the gauge will just fit over the linings at all points, the clearance between the linings and the drum will be approximately correct.

Complete the adjustment, after the drum and wheel have been installed, by driving the car back and forth and firmly applying the brakes. Repeat this several times until the brake-pedal height at which the braking takes place is correct.

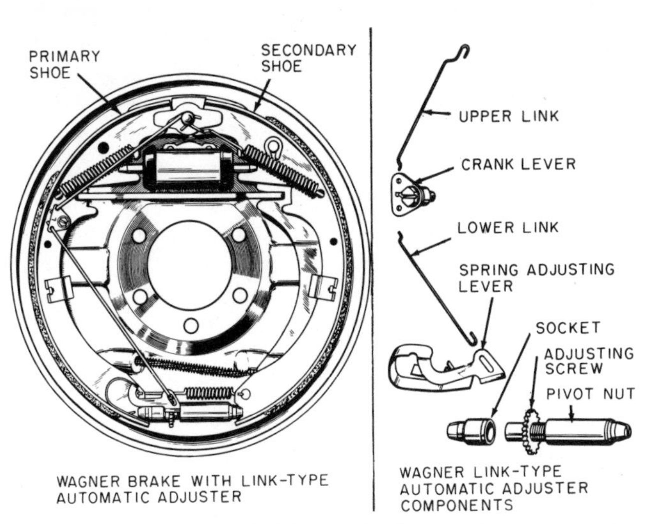

Figure 11 Wagner brake (at left rear wheel) with link-type automatic adjuster and adjuster components. *(Bendix Corporation.)*

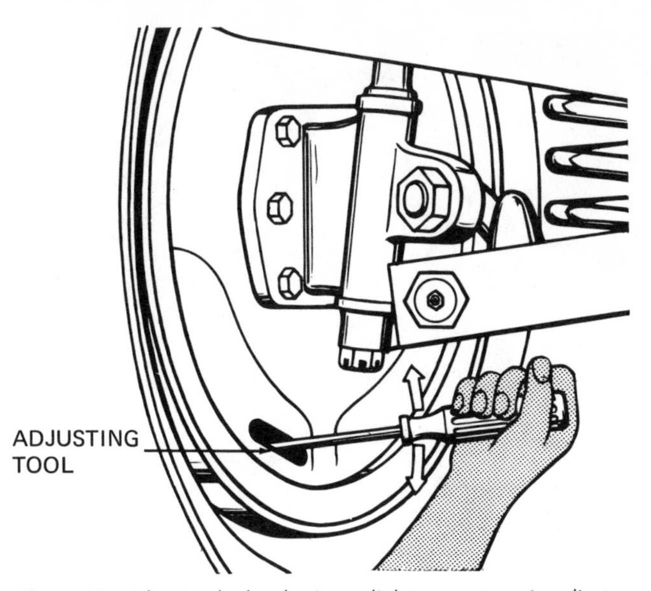

Figure 12 Adjusting brakes having a link-type automatic adjuster. *(Bendix Corporation.)*

2. WAGNER BRAKE WITH LINK-TYPE AUTOMATIC ADJUSTER The Wagner brake (Fig. 11) can be adjusted by turning the adjustment screw without using an ice pick or screwdriver to hold the adjustment lever off the screw (Fig. 12). Do not use a tool to force the adjustment lever off the adjustment screw because this would damage the lever.

■ **7-3-28 Drum-Type Minor Brake Adjustments (Non-Self-Adjusting)** The brake shown in Fig. 13 does not have the self-adjustment feature. It was widely used until supplanted by the later type with the self-adjuster. In this assembly, the brake shoes are held in position by hold-down cups and springs. An expanding adjustment screw (star-shaped) at the bottom (see Fig. 3) can be turned to move the brake shoes outward toward the brake drum and thus compensate for brake-lining wear. In addition, the anchor pin is either eccentric or assembled in a slotted hole. This arrangement makes it possible to shift the upper ends of the brake shoes to the front or back, or up or down, so that the clearances between the linings and the drum will be equalized when the brakes are released. Normally, the anchor pin will not require adjustment unless parts have been replaced or repaired.

To make a minor adjustment, raise the car until all four wheels clear the floor. Loosen or disconnect the parking-brake cables at the parking-brake equalizer, and remove the adjustment-hole covers at all wheels. Expand the brake shoes by turning the star adjustment screw. Do this by moving the outer end of the tool upward repeatedly until you feel a heavy drag on the wheel as it is turned. Then back off the adjustment screw approximately 14 to 16 notches. Brake adjustment should then be correct. If a heavy drag is still felt at the wheel, it will be necessary to readjust the anchor pin as explained in ■7-3-30 below. If this is not necessary, replace the adjustment-hole covers and then adjust the parking-brake cables.

■ **7-3-29 Parking-Brake Adjustments** In adjusting the parking brakes, the objective is to tighten them sufficiently to ensure adequate braking when the brake handle is pulled most of the way out. There should be some reserve; that is, it should not be necessary to pull the handle all the way out to secure full braking. On the other hand, the adjustment should not be so tight as to cause the brake shoes to be shifted toward the brake drum with the brake handle all the way in (retracted). Parking brakes are adjusted in different ways, depending on the type of linkage used between the brake handle and the

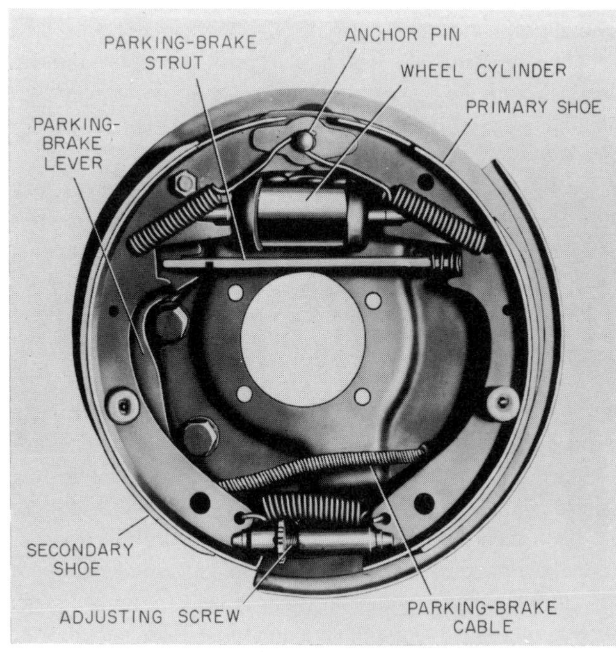

Figure 13 Details of a Bendix rear-wheel brake mechanism. *(Oldsmobile Division of General Motors Corporation.)*

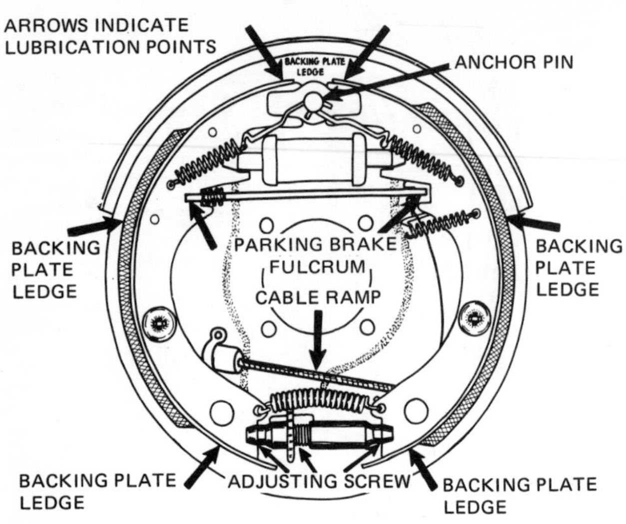

Figure 14 Lubrication points in the wheel-brake mechanism are indicated by arrows. The backing-plate ledges are areas on which the brake shoes ride as they move toward or away from the brake drum. *(Pontiac Motor Division of General Motors Corporation.)*

cables leading to the parking-brake levers at the wheels. One specification, for example, is that first the parking-brake handle should be pulled out for seven clicks of the pawl (not seven notches). Then, the check nuts at the cable ends should be loosened, the forward check nuts should be turned against the clevis plates to draw each brake cable up until a moderate drag is felt when the wheel is rotated, and the check nuts should be tightened securely. To check, set the parking-brake handle back two clicks from full release; no brake-shoe drag should be felt.

On another make of car, the parking brake is adjusted by first checking the position of the equalizer lever pin with the handle in the released position. The lever pin should align horizontally with the frame cross member. If it does not, adjust the equalizer lever nut until it is correctly positioned. Then remove the slack from the brake cables by turning the adjustment nuts on the equalizer rod. But do not tighten the cables too much; the shoes will be pulled off their anchors.

On disk brakes, the parking-brake shoes themselves may also require adjustment. Figure 33 in Part 7, Sec. 1, shows this procedure. The adjusting tool is inserted through the backing plate, as shown. It is pivoted on either the splash shield or on the clamp to turn the adjusting star wheel one way or the other.

■ 7-3-30 Drum-Type Major Brake Adjustments (Non-Self-Adjusting) There are still some non-self-adjusting drum brakes in operation, although the self-adjusting feature (Fig. 21 in Part 7, Sec. 1, and Fig. 11 in this section) has been incorporated in automotive brakes for many years. To make a major adjustment, jack up the car and remove the wheels, wheel hubs, and brake drums. Check the brake linings for wear and the brake-drum braking surfaces for smoothness. Worn brake linings should be replaced (■7-3-35), and excessively rough drums should be turned or ground (■7-3-36). Disconnect the brake-shoe return springs, and remove the brake-shoe hold-down cups, springs, and brake shoes. Examine the shoes for defects as noted in ■7-3-35. Clean the parts that are dirty or rusty, taking extreme care to avoid getting grease on the brake linings. Even slight traces of grease—from greasy fingers—might be sufficient to cause eccentric braking action and might require brake-lining replacement. If wheel cylinders give any indication of leakage or other defect, they should be removed for servicing or replacement (■7-3-37).

Lubricate all metal contact points with special lubricant (Fig. 14). Reinstall the brake shoes and brake-drum assemblies. Adjust the front-wheel bearings as required. Add brake fluid to the master cylinder and adjust the brake-pedal toeboard clearance as already noted (■7-3-26). With these preliminaries out of the way, adjust the anchor pin as necessary. The procedure for making these adjustments varies to some extent. Typical procedures follow.

1. SLOTTED-ANCHOR-PIN-HOLE TYPE Loosen the anchor-pin nut (Fig. 15) just enough to permit the pin to shift in the slotted hole—but no more than this or the pin will tilt. Turn the brake adjustment screw (star screw) to expand the shoes so that a heavy drag is felt as the drum is turned. Tap the pin and the backing plate lightly to center the shoes in the drum. If the drag on the drum is reduced, tighten the star screw a few notches to restore the drag. Again tap the pin and the backing plate. Repeat if necessary until the drag remains constant. This means the shoes are now centered. Tighten the anchor nut just enough to hold it without shifting.

Figure 15 Loosening the anchor-pin nut in preparation for pin adjustment. *(Buick Motor Division of General Motors Corporation.)*

Back off the adjustment screw 10 notches and check the clearance at the toe and heel of the secondary (rear) shoe with a 0.010-inch (0.254-mm) feeler gauge (Fig. 16). If the clearances at the ends of the shoe are not equal, tap the anchor pin up or down to equalize the clearance. Then tighten the nut to 60 to 80 pound-feet (8.29 to 11.06 kg/m) torque. Finally, replace the wheels and then make the minor adjustment, as above (■7-3-28). Back off each star adjustment screw 14 notches from the light-drag position. Install the hole covers, adjust the parking brakes, and road-test the brakes.

2. ECCENTRIC-ANCHOR-PIN TYPE Loosen the handbrake cable so that the levers are free at the rear wheels. Then insert a 0.015-inch (0.38-mm) feeler gauge at the lower end of the secondary (rear shoe) and wedge the shoe forward by moving the gauge up. Expand the shoes by turning the star adjustment screw until the primary shoe is tight against the drum and the secondary shoe is snug on the feeler gauge. Back it off just enough to establish a 0.015-inch (0.38-mm) clearance 1½ inches (38 mm) from each end of the secondary shoe. If a 0.015-inch (0.38-mm) clearance cannot be obtained, loosen the anchor-pin locknut. Turn the eccentric anchor pin as required to equalize clearances. For example, if clearance is excessive at the top, turn the anchor pin in the direction that the wheel rotates as the car moves forward. Tighten the locknut, recheck the clearances, and road-test the brakes.

Figure 16 Checking the clearance between the shoe and the brake drum by inserting a feeler gauge through the checking slot in the drum. *(Buick Motor Division of General Motors Corporation.)*

■ 7-3-31 Disk-Brake Service (Fixed-Caliper Type)

The chart in ■7-3-15 lists troubles and possible causes in disk-brake systems. Although all disk brakes work in much the same manner, their design and construction vary with different manufacturers. There are three general types, as described in ■7-1-12: fixed caliper, floating caliper, and sliding caliper. In this subsection, we describe the servicing of the fixed-caliper disk brake. Following subsections discuss the servicing of the other two types.

1. REMOVING THE BRAKE SHOES Raise the vehicle on a hoist or jack stand. Remove wheel covers and the wheel-and-tire assembly. Remove bolts holding the splash shield, and remove the shield and antirattle spring. Now, use two pliers to grip the tabs on the shoe and pull the shoe out (Fig. 17). If the shoe hangs up on the pistons, push the piston in with slip-joint pliers as shown in Fig. 17. Watch for master-cylinder reservoir overflow when pushing the pistons in. Mark the shoes so you can return them to the same side of the caliper from which you removed them.

On disk brakes that have spring-loaded pistons, a special piston-compressing tool is used. It pushes pistons back into their bores and holds them in that position during the time that the brake shoe is out.

With the brake shoes out, check the caliper and pistons for possible leaks and wipe all parts clean. If brake fluid is present, remove the caliper as explained below for replacement of piston seals.

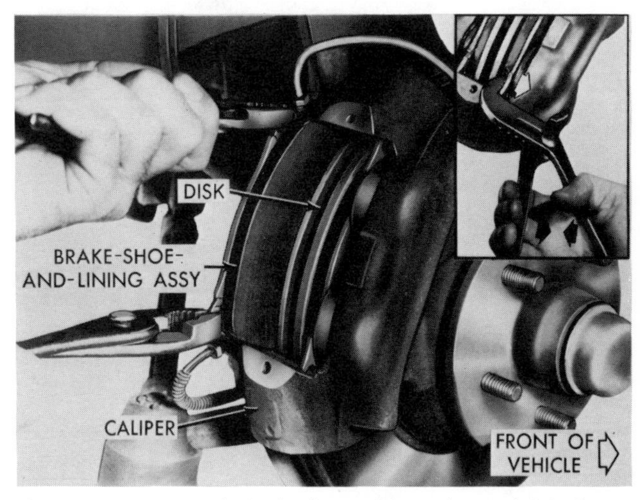

Figure 17 Removing the brake shoe and lining from a disk-brake assembly. Upper right, forcing the piston into the bore with slip-joint pliers. *(Chrysler Corporation.)*

2. INSTALLING THE BRAKE SHOES Push pistons back into their bores to allow room for installation of new thicker shoes and linings. Then slide the new shoe into the caliper with the ears of the shoe resting on the bridges of the caliper. Be sure the shoe is fully seated with lining facing the disk. Install the other shoe. Install the caliper splash shield and antirattle spring assembly. Pump the brake several times until a firm

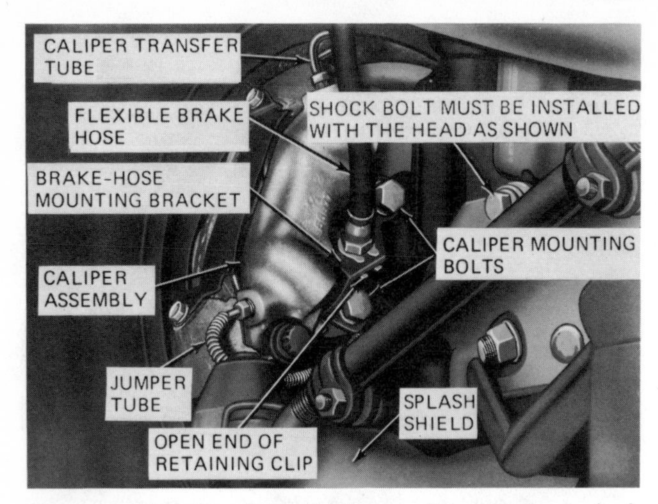

Figure 18 Mounting of the disk-brake caliper at a front wheel. *(Chrysler Corporation.)*

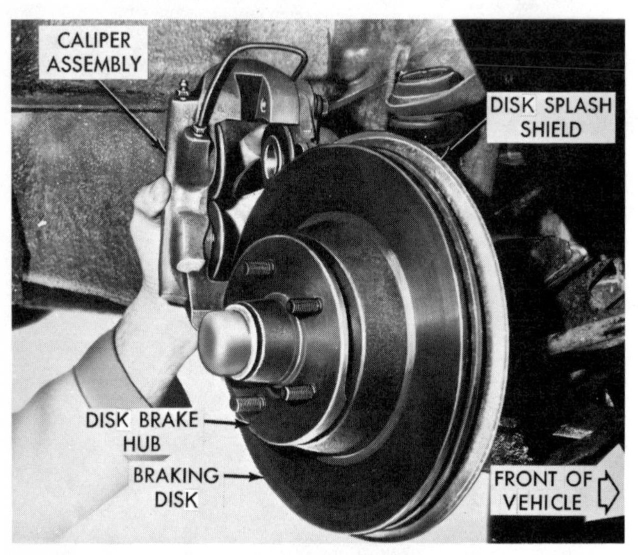

Figure 19 Removing the disk-brake caliper. *(Chrysler Corporation.)*

pedal is obtained. This ensures proper seating of the shoes. Install the wheel and tire. Check and refill the master cylinder if necessary.

NOTE: Road-test the car and make several heavy braking stops from about 40 mph (64.37 km/h) to ensure good seating of the brake lining on the disk. Unless this is done, initial braking may cause the car to pull to one side or the other.

3. REMOVING THE CALIPER Refer to Fig. 18 and proceed as follows. Raise the car on a hoist or jack stand and remove the wheel cover and wheel-and-tire assembly. Disconnect the brake flexible hose from the brake tube at the frame mounting bracket and plug the brake tube to prevent loss of

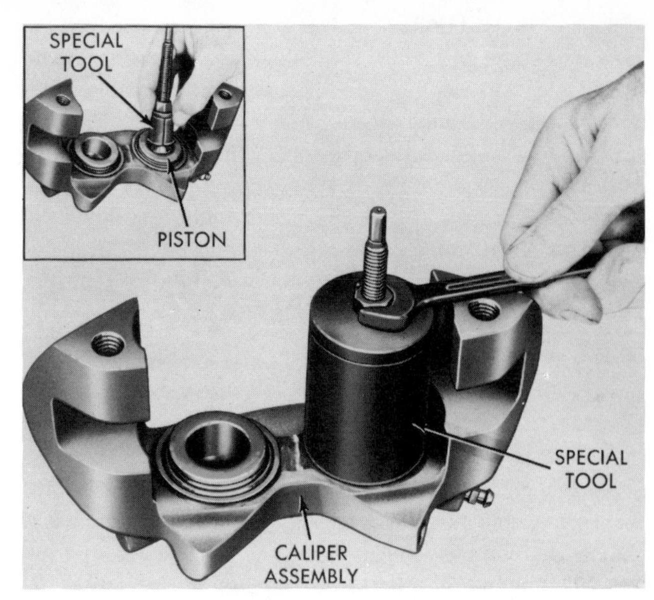

Figure 20 Removing pistons from the caliper. *(Chrysler Corporation.)*

fluid. Remove attaching bolts and lift the caliper assembly up and out (Fig. 19).

4. DISASSEMBLING THE CALIPER Remove the splash shield and antirattle spring assembly. Clamp caliper mounting lugs in the soft jaws of a vise and remove the transfer tube and jumper tube (armored). Remove shoes. Separate the two halves of the caliper by removing two bolts. Peel dust boots off the caliper and pistons. Use a special tool (Fig. 20) to remove pistons, being very careful to avoid scratching the pistons and bores. Then use a small pointed wood or plastic stick to remove piston seals from grooves in the piston bores. Do not scratch bores!

5. CLEANING CALIPER PARTS Clean all parts, except shoes and linings, in brake fluid and wipe dry with lint-free towels. Blow out drilled passages and bores with compressed air. Discard old piston seals. Also, discard dust boots and pistons that appear damaged in any way. If piston bores are scratched, clean them with crocus cloth or a hone. However, if more than about 0.002 inch (0.051 mm) must be removed to clean up deep scratches, discard the old caliper. Carefully clean the caliper to remove traces of dust or dirt.

6. REASSEMBLING THE CALIPER Clamp the inner half, by the mounting lugs, in the soft jaws of a vise. If a new dust-boot retainer ring is necessary, clean the boot-retainer groove in the caliper. Apply a special sealing compound to the retainer groove in the caliper and to the retainer ring where it will seat in the housing. Then install the ring. Dip new piston seals in brake fluid and install them in the grooves in the piston bores. Be sure the seals are not twisted or rolled. Coat outside of pistons with brake fluid and slide them into the bores, using slow, steady pressure. Install new dust boots, making sure they seat over the retaining rings and in piston grooves. Reattach

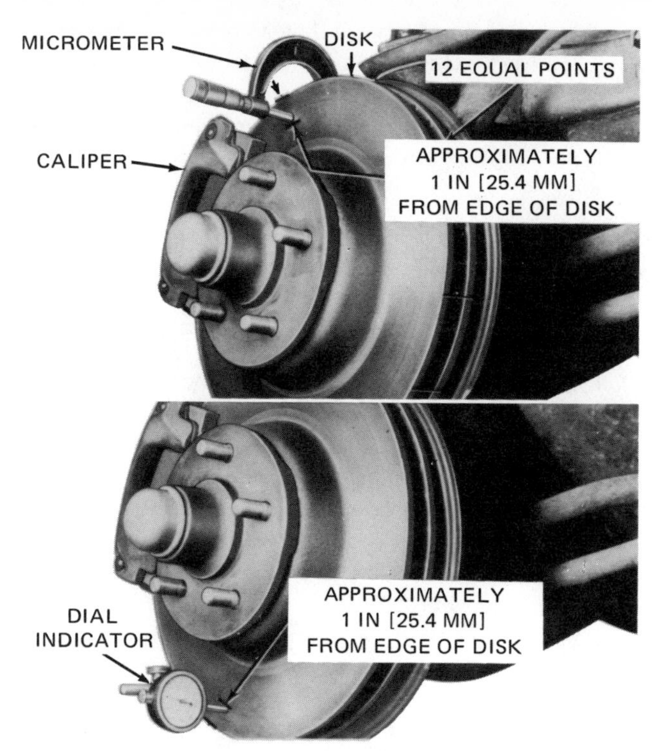

Figure 21 Checking brake-disk thickness and runout. *(Chrysler Corporation.)*

the two halves of the caliper with special bolts, tightened to 70 to 80 pound-feet (9.67 to 11.06 kg-m) torque. Install transfer and jumper tubes. Install the bleeder screw (but do not tighten).

7. CHECKING DISK FOR THICKNESS AND RUNOUT
Before reinstalling the caliper, check the disk for runout and thickness, as follows. Use a micrometer (Fig. 21 top) and measure thickness at 12 equal points about 1 inch (25.4 mm) from the edge. If thickness varies excessively [Plymouth says more than 0.0005 inch (0.0127 mm)], discard the disk and install a new one. Measure runout by first adjusting the wheel bearing to zero end play and then mounting a dial indicator as shown in Fig. 21, bottom. Rotate the disk and check runout. If it is excessive [Plymouth says more than 0.0025 inch (0.635 mm)], discard the disk and install a new one.

NOTE: Readjust wheel bearings after the check.

Light scores and wear of the disk are okay, but if the scores are fairly deep, the disk should be refinished (Fig. 22). For rust spots or lining deposits, a grinder may be used. But if the scores or wear marks are deep, the disk must first be refaced with a cutting tool, then given a final grinding with the grinder to remove tool marks.

Machining disks produces considerable noise. Several different kinds of silencers are available. One is shown attached to the disk in Fig. 22. Another view of this damper, or silencer, is shown in Fig. 23. In this figure you can see how it is held in

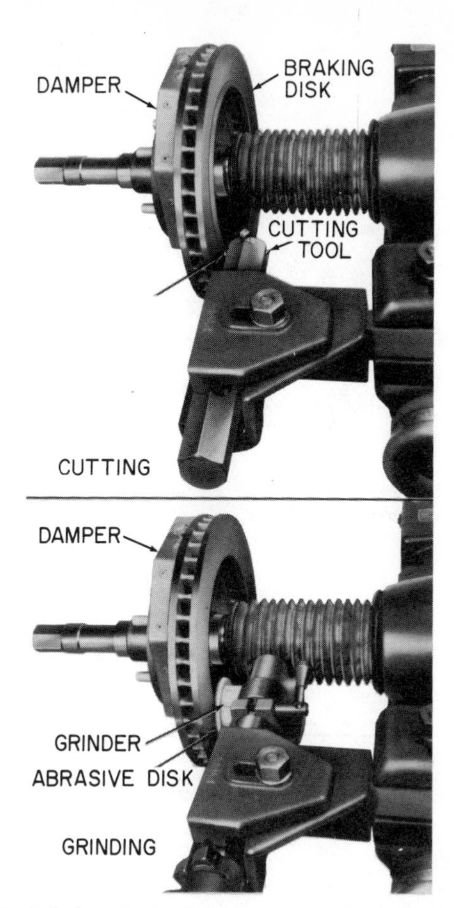

Figure 22 Refacing a brake disk. Top, turning the disk with a cutting tool. Bottom, using a grinder on the disk. *(Chrysler Corporation.)*

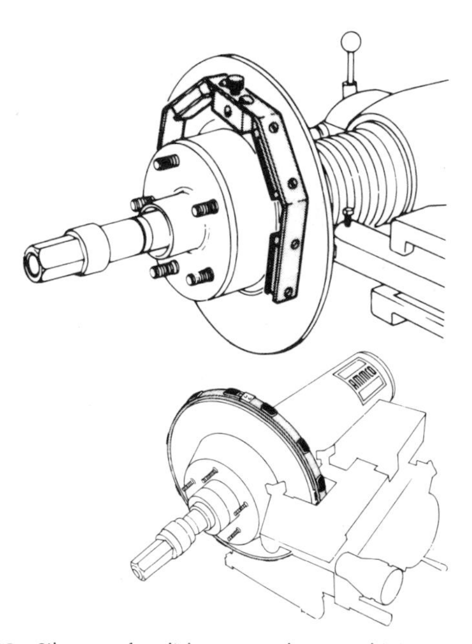

Figure 23 Silencers for disk rotors when machining rotor faces. *(Ammo Tools, Inc.)*

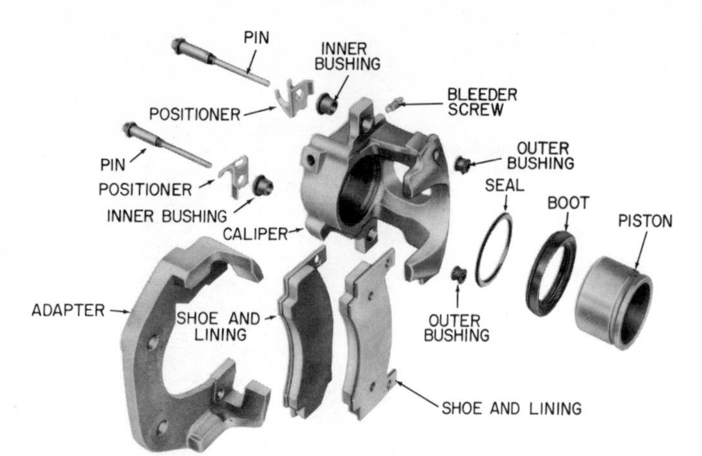

Figure 24 Disassembled view of a floating-caliper assembly. *(Chrysler Corporation.)*

place by magnets. Another silencer is also shown in Fig. 23. This one is a heavy rubber band that is wrapped around the disk before it is machined.

> **CAUTION:** Disks usually have a dimension (a number) cast into them. This dimension is the minimum to which the disk can be finished. If it is necessary to refinish the disk to a smaller dimension, discard it, because the disk would be too thin to use safely.

8. INSTALLING THE CALIPER After the disk has been reinstalled (if it had been removed for service) and the wheel bearings adjusted, install the caliper assembly. Tighten mounting bolts to 45 to 60 pound-feet (6.22 to 8.29 kg-m) torque. Make sure the disk runs square with the caliper opening. Install the shoes and splash shield. Open the bleeder screw and reconnect the brake line. Allow fluid to flow until all air is pushed out of the caliper (until air bubbles stop flowing out of bleeder). Tighten the bleeder screw. Replenish the reservoir in the master cylinder.

■ 7-3-32 Disk-Brake Service (Floating-Caliper Type)

The chart in ■7-3-15 lists troubles and possible causes in disk-brake systems. Although all disk brakes work in the same manner, their design and construction vary with different manufacturers. There are three general types, already described in ■1-1-12: fixed caliper, sliding caliper, and floating caliper. In this section, we describe the servicing of the floating-caliper disk brake. (Figure 24 is a disassembled view of this type of unit.) The preceding subsection described the servicing of the fixed-caliper disk brake.

1. REMOVING THE BRAKE SHOES Raise the car on a hoise or jack stand and remove the front-wheel covers and the wheel-and-tire assemblies. Remove the caliper guide pins and positioners that attach the caliper to the adapter. Now, you can slide the caliper up and away from the disk (Fig. 25). Support the caliper firmly so you don't damage the brake hose.

Slide outboard and inboard shoe-and-lining assemblies out (Fig. 26). Mark shoes so you can put them back in the same places in the caliper. Push outer bushings from the caliper with a wooden or plastic stick (Fig. 27). Throw the bushings away. Slide the inner bushings off the guide pins and discard them.

2. INSPECTING CALIPER PARTS Check for piston-seal leaks (brake fluid in or around boot area and inboard lining). If the boot is damaged or fluid has leaked, disassemble the caliper to install new parts as explained in item 5, below. Inspect the brake disk and service it if necessary (■7-3-31, item 7).

3. INSTALLING BRAKE SHOES New positioners and inner and outer bushings will be required (see Fig. 24). Slowly and carefully push the piston back into the bore until it bottoms. Watch for possible reservoir overflow at the brake master cylinder. Install new bushings, noting their proper relationship as shown in Fig. 24. Slide new shoe-and-lining assemblies into position (Fig. 26). Make sure the metal part of the shoe is fully in the recess of the caliper and adapter. Hold the outboard lining in position and slide the caliper down into place over the disk (Fig. 25). Align guide-pin holes of the adapter, and inboard and outboard shoes (see Fig. 28).

Install new positioners over guide pins with the open ends toward the outside and the stamped arrows pointing upward.

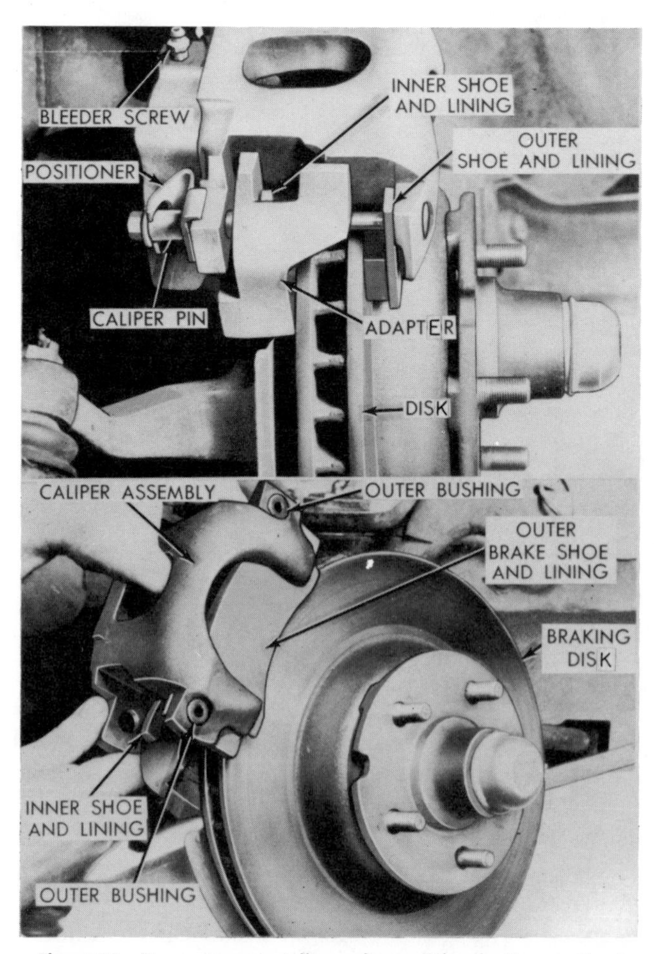

Figure 25 Removing or installing calipers. *(Chrysler Corporation.)*

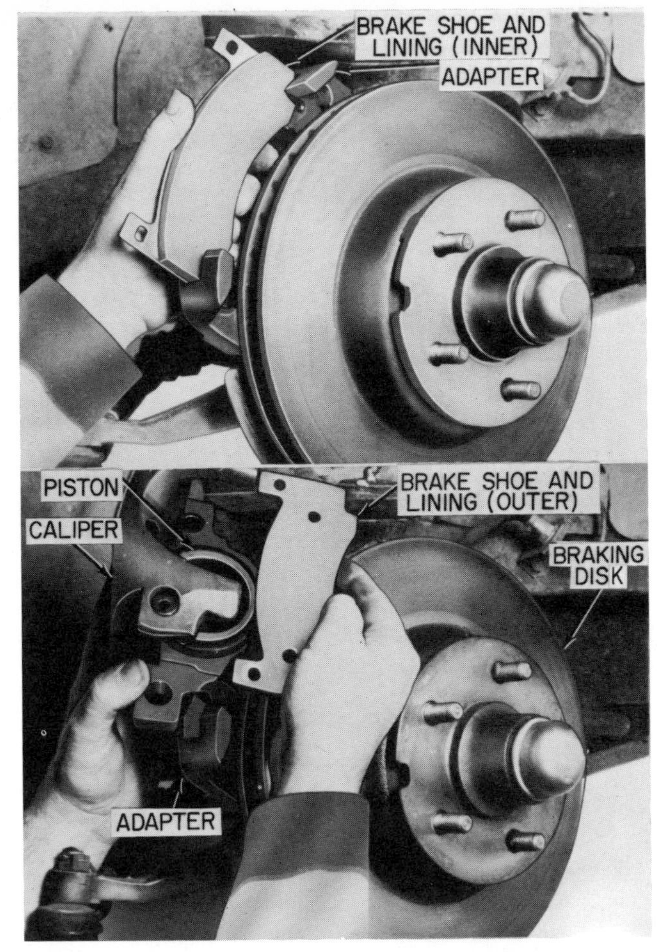

Figure 26 Removing or installing brake shoes and linings. *(Chrysler Corporation.)*

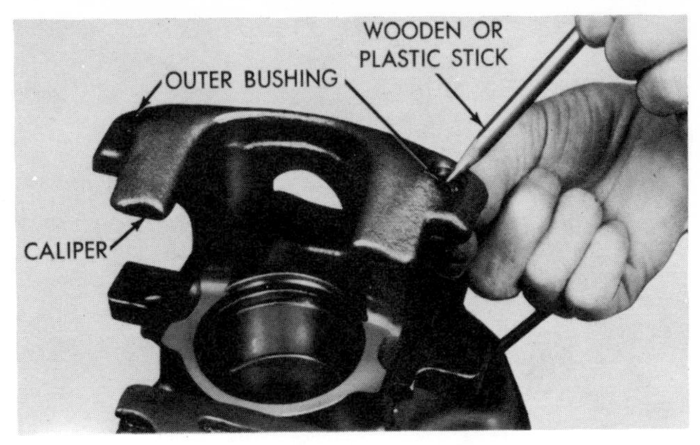

Figure 27 Removing outer bushings. *(Chrysler Corporation.)*

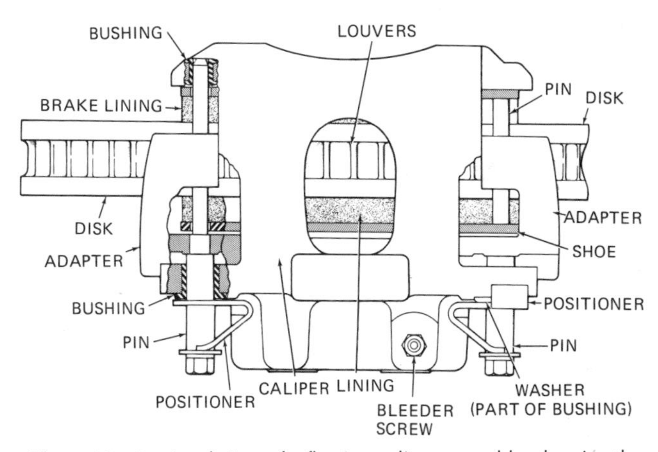

Figure 28 Sectional view of a floating-caliper assembly, showing the positions of the adapter, pins, bushings, and positioners. *(Chrysler Corporation.)*

Install each guide pin through the bushing, caliper, adapter, inboard shoe, outboard shoe, and outer bushing (Fig. 28). Press in on the end of the guide pin and thread the pin into the adapter. Use great care to avoid cross-threading. Tighten to specifications. Make sure tabs of positioners are over the machined surfaces of the caliper.

Pump the brake pedal several times until a firm pedal has been obtained. Check and refill the master-cylinder reservoir if necessary. If you cannot get a firm pedal, you may have to bleed the brake system and add brake fluid to the reservoir ■7-3-40).

Install the wheel-and-tire assemblies and wheel covers. Remove the car from the hoist or jack stands.

4. REMOVING THE CALIPER If a new piston seal or boot is required, the caliper must be removed. Proceed as already outlined in item 1 above, with the additional step that the flexible hose must be disconnected from the tube at the frame (tube must then be plugged to prevent loss of fluid).

5. DISASSEMBLING THE CALIPER Clamp the caliper lightly in the soft jaws of a vise, and remove the dust boot. Use a special tool (Fig. 29) to remove the piston from the caliper.

Use a pointed wood stick to work the seal out of its groove

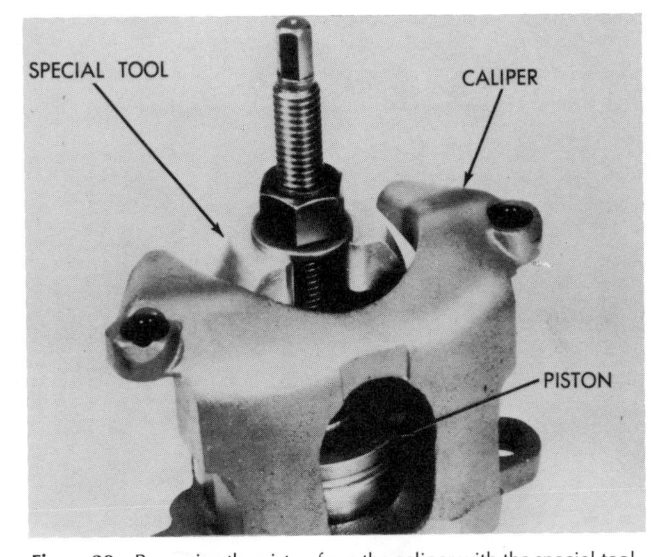

Figure 29 Removing the piston from the caliper with the special tool. *(Chrysler Corporation.)*

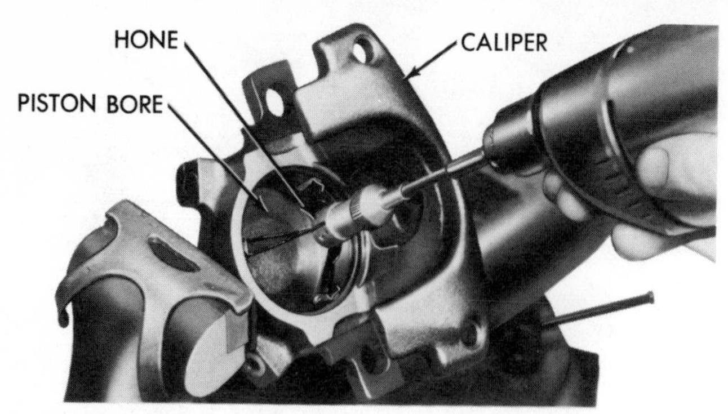

Figure 30 Honing the piston bore in the caliper. *(Chrysler Corporation.)*

in the piston bore. Never use a screwdriver or metal tool; it could scratch the bore or burr the edge of the seal groove, thus ruining the caliper.

6. CLEANING AND INSPECTING CALIPER PARTS Clean parts with alcohol or other solvent and blow dry with compressed air. Inspect the bore for pits or scoring. Install a new piston if the old one is pitted or scored or if the plating is worn off. Light score marks in the bore can be cleaned off with crocus cloth. Deeper scores require honing (Fig. 30), provided no more than 0.002 inch (0.051 mm) is removed. If the bore does not clean up, discard the old caliper.

> **NOTE:** After using crocus cloth or honing, clean the caliper thoroughly with brake fluid, including drilled passages. Wipe the bore with a clean, lintless cloth. Continue wiping until the cloth shows no sign of dirt.

7. ASSEMBLING THE CALIPER Clamp the caliper in the soft jaws of a vise and install the new piston seal in the groove in the bore. (Never reuse the old seal!) Lubricate the seal in special lubricant supplied in the service kit. Position the seal in one area and carefully work it into the groove, using clean fingers. Make sure the seal is not twisted or rolled.

Coat the new piston boot with lubricant, leaving plenty on the inside circumference. Install it in the caliper (Fig. 31), working it into place with the fingers (clean) only. Temporarily plug the fluid inlet to the caliper and bleeder-screw hole. Coat the piston with a generous amount of lubricant. Spread the boot with the fingers of one hand and push the piston straight down into the bore. The trapped air under the piston will force the boot around the piston and into its groove as the piston is pushed down. Remove the plug and push the piston down until it bottoms. Apply force uniformly all around the piston to keep it from cocking.

Reinstall the caliper as described, with the additional step of reconnecting the flexible brake hose.

8. CHECKING THE DISK FOR THICKNESS AND RUNOUT This has already been covered in ■7-3-31, item 7.

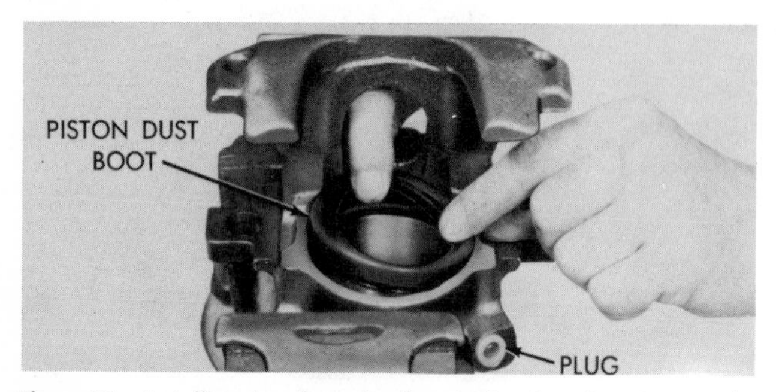

Figure 31 Installing the piston dust boot in the piston bore in the caliper. *(Chrysler Corporation.)*

■ 7-3-33 Disk-Brake Service (Sliding-Caliper Type)

The chart in ■7-3-15 lists troubles and possible causes in disk-brake systems. Although all disk brakes work in the same general manner, their design and construction vary from one model to another. In this section, we describe servicing of the sliding-caliper disk brake. Figure 18 (in Part 7, Sec. 1) shows how this brake works, and Fig. 32 in this section gives a disassembled view. Note that it is somewhat simpler in construction than the other disk brakes previously described.

1. INSPECTING SHOES AND LININGS Linings should be inspected for wear every 6,000 miles (9,656 km) and also whenever a wheel is removed. The outboard shoe should be checked at both ends as shown by the two arrows in Fig. 33. The inboard lining can be checked through the inspection hole as shown by the single arrow. If a lining is worn down to within 0.020 inch (0.51 mm) of the rivet at either end, all shoe-and-lining assemblies should be replaced.

2. REMOVING SHOES AND LININGS Remove two-thirds of the brake fluid from the master cylinder section feeding the disk brakes. Discard, do not reuse, the fluid.

Raise the car and remove the wheel covers and wheels. Use a 7-inch (178-mm) C clamp as shown in Fig. 34. The solid end of the clamp rests against the inside of the caliper. The screw end rests against the metal part of the outboard shoe. Tighten the C clamp to move the caliper out far enough to push the piston to the bottom of the piston bore. This produces clearance between the disk and shoes.

Remove the two mounting bolts (Fig. 35). Lift the caliper off the disk. Support it with a wire hook so it does not hang from the brake hose. Remove the shoes. Mark the shoes so you can return them on the same side of the caliper from which they were removed. Next, remove the sleeves and bushings from the four caliper ears (Fig. 36). A special tool is used to remove the sleeves. The bushings fit into grooves in the ears.

3. CLEANING AND INSPECTION Clean the holes and grooves in the caliper ears and wipe dirt from the mounting bolts. Replace the bolts if they are corroded or damaged. Wipe the inside of the caliper clean while inspecting it for brake-fluid leakage. If leakage is noted, remove the caliper for overhaul (see below). Make sure the dust boot is in good con-

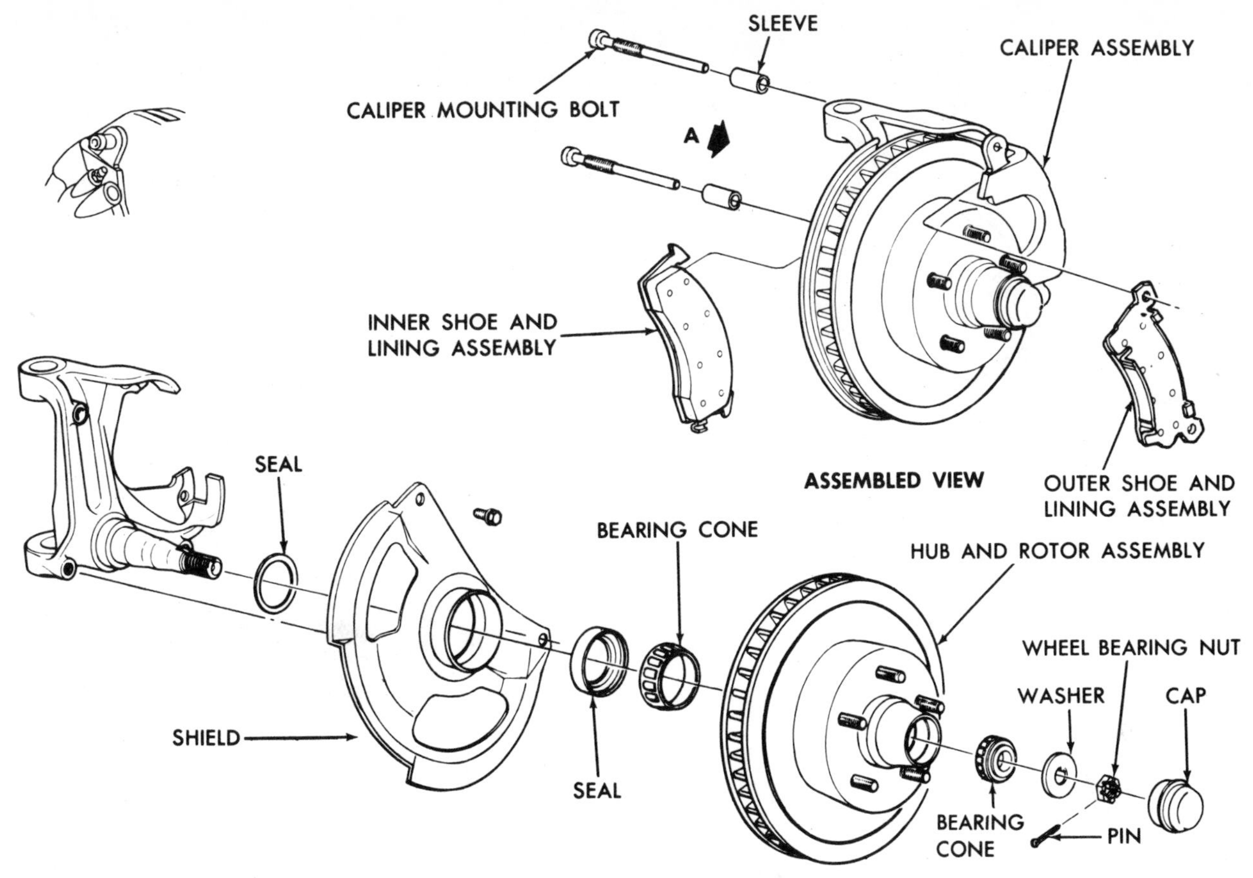

Figure 32 Disassembled view of a sliding-caliper disk-brake assembly. *(Chevrolet Motor Division of General Motors Corporation.)*

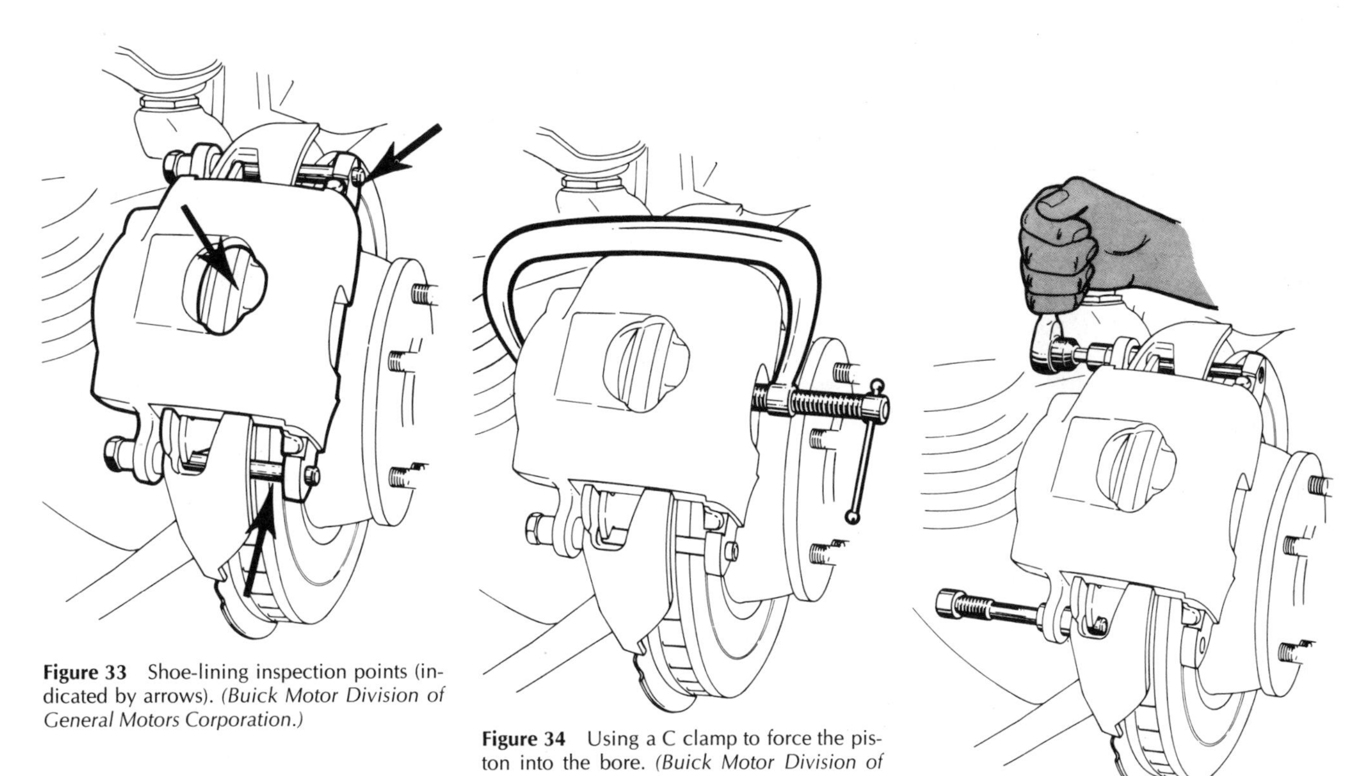

Figure 33 Shoe-lining inspection points (indicated by arrows). *(Buick Motor Division of General Motors Corporation.)*

Figure 34 Using a C clamp to force the piston into the bore. *(Buick Motor Division of General Motors Corporation.)*

Figure 35 Using a ratchet wrench to remove the mounting bolts. *(Buick Motor Division of General Motors Corporation.)*

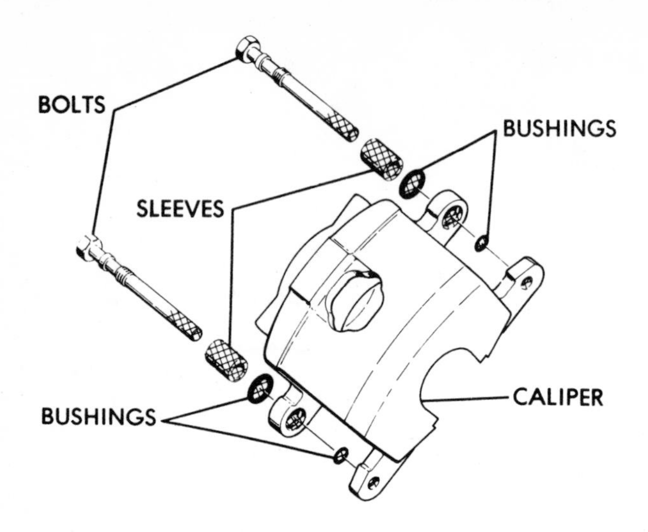

LUBRICATE AREAS INDICATED

Figure 36 Relationship of the mounting bolts to the sleeves and bushings. The areas to be lubricated with silicone lubricant are indicated. *(Buick Motor Division of General Motors Corporation.)*

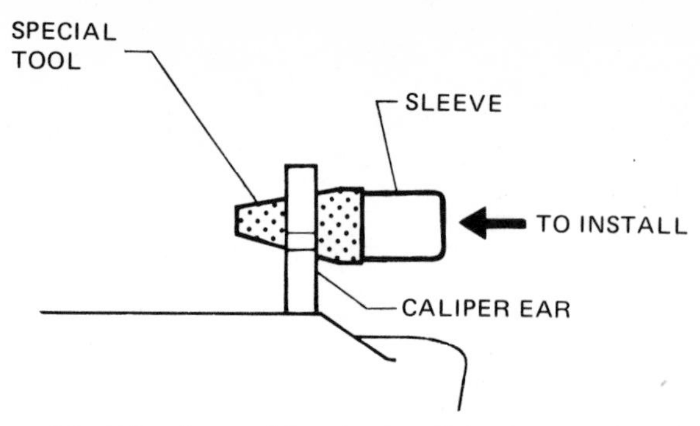

Figure 38 Using the special tool to install the sleeve in the caliper ear. *(Buick Motor Division of General Motors Corporation.)*

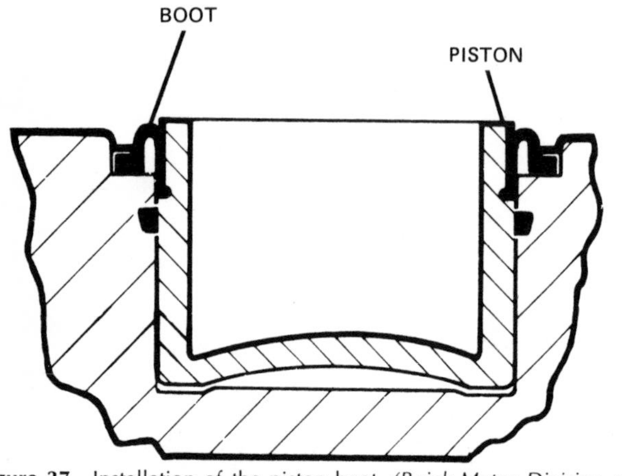

Figure 37 Installation of the piston boot. *(Buick Motor Division of General Motors Corporation.)*

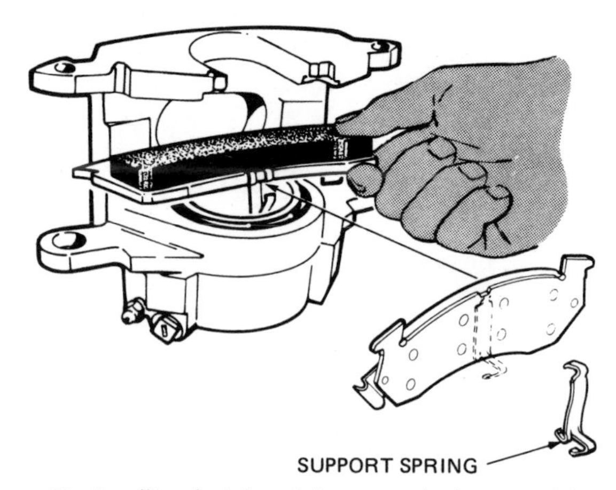

Figure 39 Installing the inboard shoe. Note the location of the support spring. *(Chevrolet Motor Division of General Motors Corporation.)*

dition and is properly installed in the piston and caliper (Fig. 37). Check the rotor for wear and runout (■ 7-3-31, item 7). If it needs service, remove it.

4. INSTALLING SHOES AND CALIPER Use special silicone lubricant on the new sleeves and bushings, the bolts, and the bushing holes and grooves in the caliper ears (Fig. 36).

NOTE: Always use new sleeves and bushings, properly lubricated, to ensure easy sliding of the caliper.

Install the four bushings in the caliper ears. Use the special tool as shown in Fig. 38 to install the sleeves. The outer ends of the sleeves should be flush with the surface of the ears.

Install the shoe support spring and the inboard shoe in the center of the piston cavity as shown in Fig. 39. Install the outboard shoe as shown in Fig. 40.

Now position the caliper over the disk, making sure the brake hose is not twisted or kinked. Start the bolts through the sleeves, making sure the bolts pass under the retaining ears on the inboard shoes (Fig. 41). Push the bolts on through, making sure they go through the holes in the outboard shoe and the ears in the caliper. Screw the bolts into the mounting holes and tighten the bolts to the proper tension.

Add fresh brake fluid to the reservoir and pump the brake pedal to seat the linings against the disk. Now clinch the upper ears of the outboard shoe with Channellock pliers as shown in Fig. 42. After clinching, the ears should be flat against the caliper.

5. OVERHAULING CALIPER To remove the caliper, first detach the caliper and remove the shoes as previously noted. Then disconnect the hose from the steel brake line and cap the fittings to keep dirt out. Detach the hose from the frame support bracket and take the caliper to the workbench.

NOTE: Bench, tools, and hands must be clean.

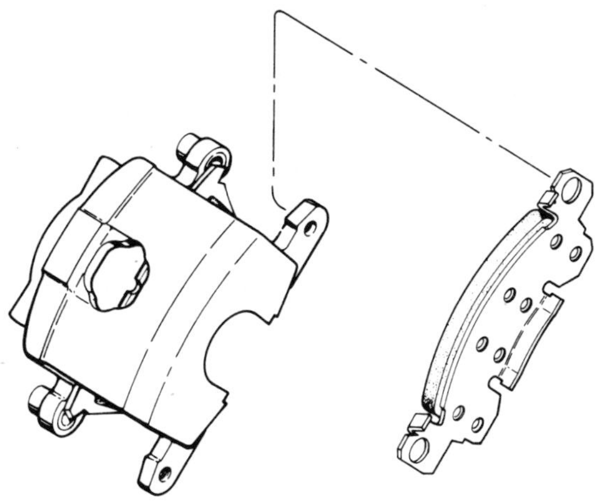

Figure 40 Position of the outboard shoe in the caliper. *(Buick Motor Division of General Motors Corporation.)*

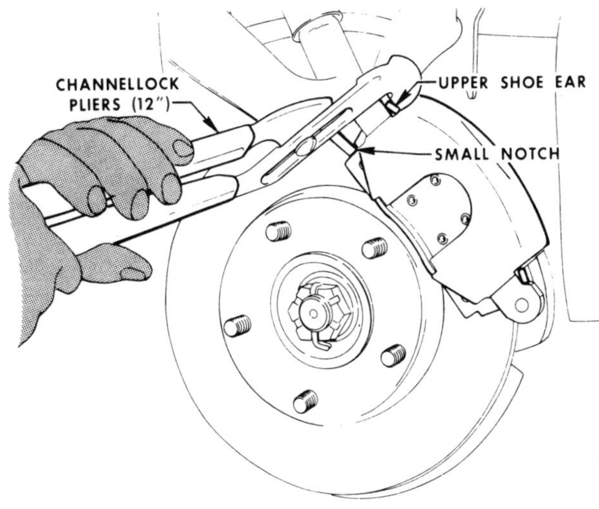

Figure 42 Clinching ears on the outboard shoe. *(Buick Motor Division of General Motors Corporation.)*

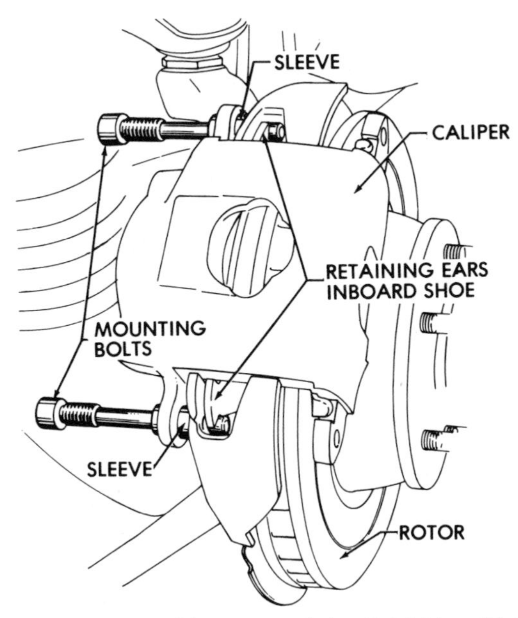

Figure 41 Installation of the mounting bolts. *(Buick Motor Division of General Motors Corporation.)*

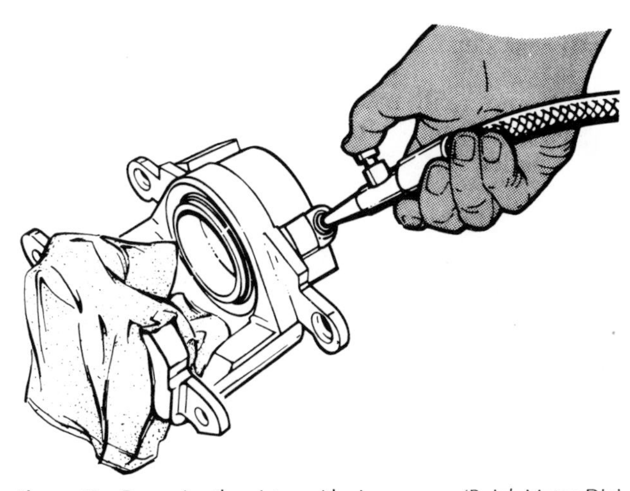

Figure 43 Removing the piston with air pressure. *(Buick Motor Division of General Motors Corporation.)*

Disconnect hose from the caliper, discarding the copper gasket; discard the hose, too, if it appears damaged. Drain fluid from caliper. Use a clean shop towel to pad the inside of the caliper as shown in Fig. 43. Apply air pressure to force the piston out.

CAUTION: Use only enough pressure to force the piston out! Excessive pressure may drive the piston out so hard that it will be ruined. Also, never use your fingers to catch the piston. It can fly out with enough speed to mash your fingers!

Use a screwdriver to pry the boot out of the caliper. Do not scratch the bore! Use a plastic toothpick to remove the seal from the groove in the bore. Do not use a metal tool! It could ruin the bore. Remove the bleeder valve.

Discard the boot, piston seal, rubber bushings, and sleeves. Use new parts on reassembly. Clean piston and caliper with brake cleaner. Blow out all passages with compressed air.

NOTE: Lubricated shop air can leave a film of oil on the metal parts. This oil will damage the rubber parts.

Discard the piston if it has any nicks, scratches, or worn spots. Examine the bore. Minor corrosion or stains can be polished away with crocus cloth (not emery cloth!). If the bore cannot be cleaned up, discard it.

To install the piston, first lubricate the bore and new piston

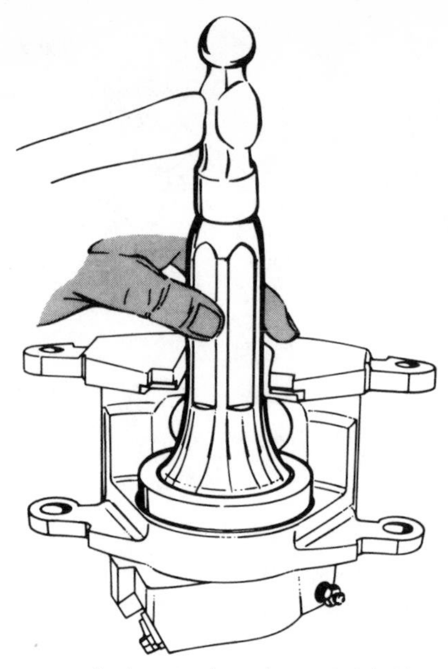

Figure 44 Seating the boot in the caliper. *(Buick Motor Division of General Motors Corporation.)*

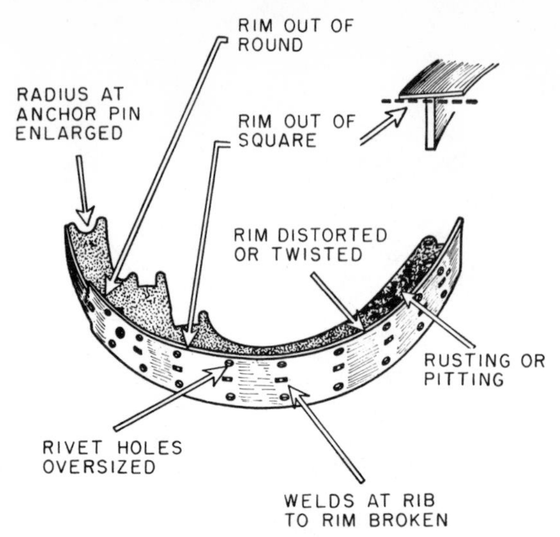

Figure 45 Various types of brake-shoe defects. *(Pontiac Motor Division of General Motors Corporation.)*

seal with brake fluid. Install the seal in the groove. Lubricate the piston and assemble a new boot into the piston groove. Install the piston in the bore, being careful not to unseat the seal. Push the piston to the bottom of the bore. This will require a push of 50 to 100 pounds (22.68 to 45.40 kg). Put the outside of the boot into the caliper counterbore and seat it with the special tool as shown in Fig. 44.

Now reconnect the brake hose using a new copper gasket. Install the caliper, attach the hose to the frame bracket, and reconnect it to the steel tube.

Finish installation as already noted above (in item 4). Bleed the system (see ■7-3-40).

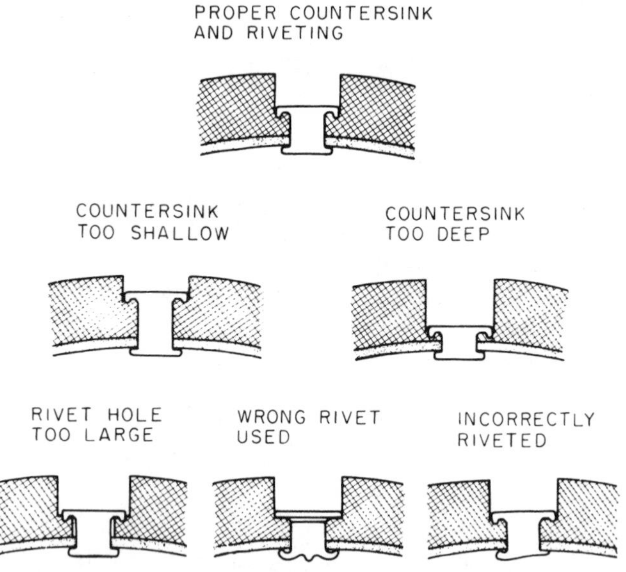

Figure 46 The proper method contrasted with several wrong methods of installing brake-shoe rivets. *(Pontiac Motor Division of General Motors Corporation.)*

■ **7-3-34 Other Brake Services** Disk-brake services have been covered in previous subsections, so far as the wheel mechanisms are concerned (calipers, shoes, and disks). In addition, brake lines and the master cylinder may require service. With drum-type brakes, the procedures include servicing the brake lines and master cylinder. In addition the brake linings may require replacement and the brake drums may need reboring or grinding. All systems may require flushing and bleeding if other services have been performed. All these servicing procedures are covered in following subsections.

■ **7-3-35 Brake Linings (Drum-Type)** As a first step in replacing brake linings, the brake shoes must be removed (as already explained). Brake linings can be checked by removing the right front wheel and noting their condition (the brake drum can be checked at the same time). It can normally be assumed that the brake linings at the other three wheels are in about the same condition. If the linings are oil- or brake-fluid-soaked, or if they are worn down to the replacement point, the linings at all wheels should be replaced.

NOTE: If the drums are in good condition, standard-size linings may be installed. But if the drums require grinding to a larger inside diameter (■7-3-36), oversize linings should be installed.

1. INSPECTING SHOES When the shoes have been removed, they should be cleaned and checked for distortion, cracks, or other defects (Fig. 45). You can check a shoe for distortion or warping by laying the web on a flat surface plate. Put it on the corner of the surface plate so that you can see how

Figure 47 Brake-shoe grinder. *(Ammco Tools, Inc.)*

snugly the web lies on the surface. It the web is twisted, the shoe is bent. It is somewhat difficult to straighten accurately a bent or warped shoe. Such conditions, and other shoe defects, require installation of new shoes. Shoes may become distorted from high temperature owing to excessive braking or from improper lining installation.

> **NOTE:** If some shoes and linings require replacement, be sure to replace all shoes on an axle with the same type of lining. For example, don't have riveted linings on the left rear and bonded linings on the right rear.

2. REPLACING LININGS Brake linings are either riveted or cemented (bonded) to the brake shoes. Manufacturers recommend that on the bonded type no attempt should be made to install new linings on the shoes. The shoes should be replaced when the linings have become worn.

On the riveted type, drill out the rivets to remove the old lining. Do not punch them out, since this may distort the shoe. Avoid using too large a drill because this would enlarge the rivet holes in the shoe and make it hard to do a good reinstallation job. Clean the shoe surfaces and file off any burrs or rough spots. Wash the shoe in degreasing compound and wipe it dry. Then put the new lining in place and attach it with the two center rivets. Use a roll type of set to set the rivets. A pointed punch might split the rivets. Figure 46 shows the right way contrasted with several wrong ways of installing rivets.

> **NOTE:** Be sure your hands are dry and free of grease or oil. Remember, even a slight trace of grease on a brake lining may cause erratic braking action that would require installation of another lining.

3. GRINDING BRAKE-LINING RADIUS To ensure more nearly perfect brake operation when new linings are installed, many manufacturers recommend the use of a brake-lining-radius grinder (Fig. 47). With this device, the shoe is swung in an arc in front of a grinding wheel which levels off lining irregularities and gives the lining the same radius, or contour, as the brake drum. This avoids poor contact (see Fig. 48), which could result in brake squeal, fade, and drum hot spots. These, in turn, would produce hard or glazed spots on the drum.

Another type of grinder, shown in Fig. 49, is used after the brake shoes are installed on the car and brake adjustment has been completed. It is mounted on the wheel spindle or axle and is moved around the brake linings as the grinding wheel spins.

> **NOTE:** Some automotive manufacturers supply preground linings which require no further grinding. On these, they recommend that the linings be installed without grinding. One preground type of lining has a slight crown (Fig. 50). During initial operation, this slight crown wears flat to ensure good shoe seating against the drum.

■ **7-3-36 Brake Drums** Brake drums should be inspected for distortion, cracks, scores, roughness or excessive glaze, or smoothness. Glaze lowers friction and, therefore, braking efficiency. Figure 51 shows various drum conditions that can be corrected by the drum grinder. Drums that are distorted or cracked should be discarded and new drums installed. Light score marks can be removed with fine emery cloth. All traces of emery must be removed after smoothing the drum. Deeper scores and roughness, as well as glaze, can be removed by turning or grinding the drum.

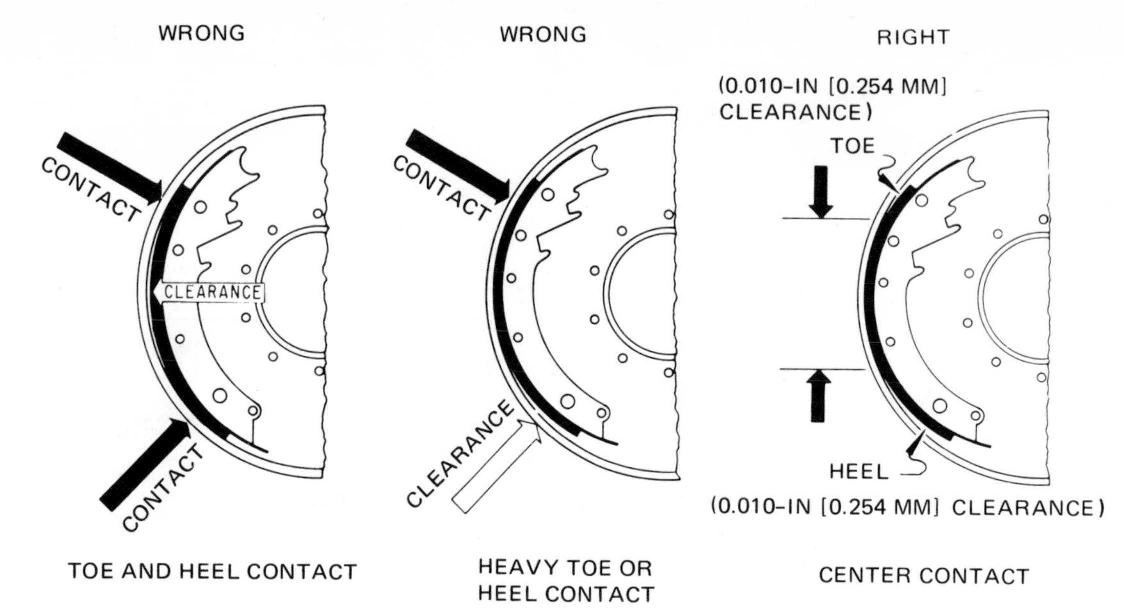

Figure 48 Contact between the lining and the brake drum. *(Bear Manufacturing Company.)*

> **NOTE:** After grinding or turning a drum, be sure all traces of cuttings or abrasives are removed. Do not touch the finished surface or get any oil or grease on it. This would prevent normal braking action.

Cast-iron drums can be either turned or ground, but steel drums, because of their hardness, usually require grinding.

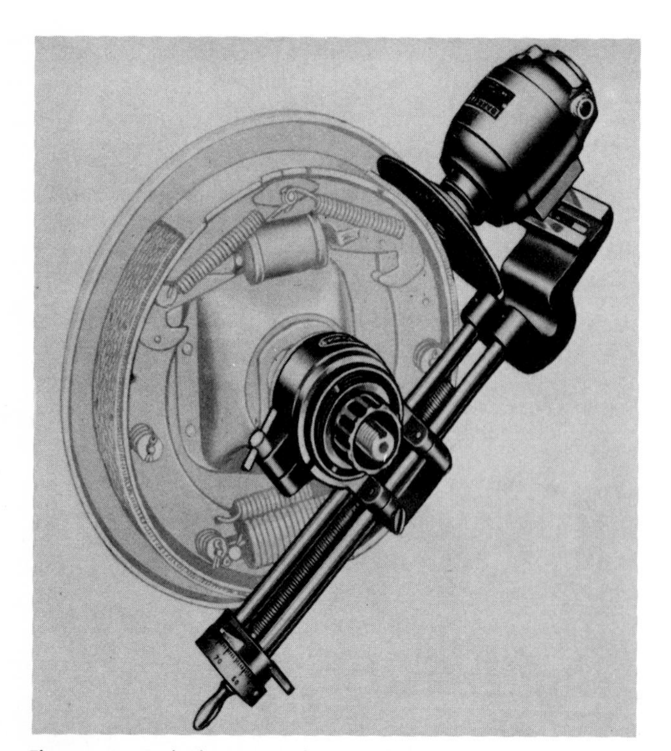

Figure 49 Brake-lining grinder installed on the wheel spindle. *(Barrett Equipment Company.)*

Figure 50 Some replacement shoes are slightly crowned and do not need to be ground before installation. *(AC Delco Division of General Motors Corporation.)*

Many automobile manufacturers recommend turning in preference to grinding. A ground drum does not wear in so readily as a turned drum and is more liable to cause uneven braking when new. Figure 52 illustrates a typical drum lathe. Figure 53 shows a portable brake-service table with a brake-shoe grinder and a drum grinder.

In servicing drums, only enough material should be removed to smooth up the braking surface. However, if it is necessary to take off considerable material, the drum should be turned oversize, and oversize brake linings should be installed. For example, one car manufacturer recommends the following. If the drum has to be turned to more than 0.010 inch (0.25 mm) oversize, it should be turned to 0.030 inch (0.76 mm) oversize so that the regularly supplied linings that are 0.030 inch (0.76 mm) oversize can be installed.

> **NOTE:** Removing excessive amounts of material will result in overheating of the drum during braking action, possible warping, and faulty brake action. Many brake drums have a dimension (a number) cast into them. This dimension is the maximum allowable diameter. If it is necessary to turn or grind the drum to a larger diameter, discard it. The drum would be too thin to use safely. It would probably warp or crack when heated up and produce faulty braking.

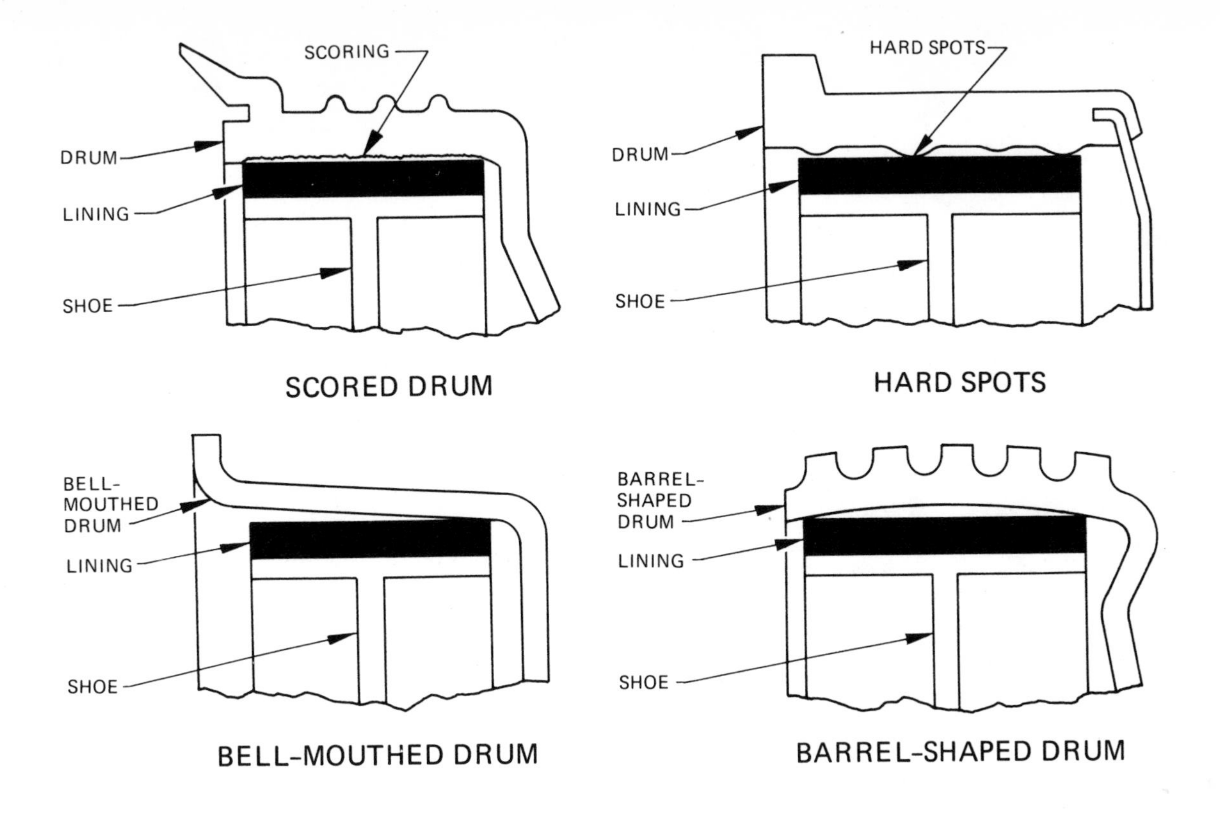

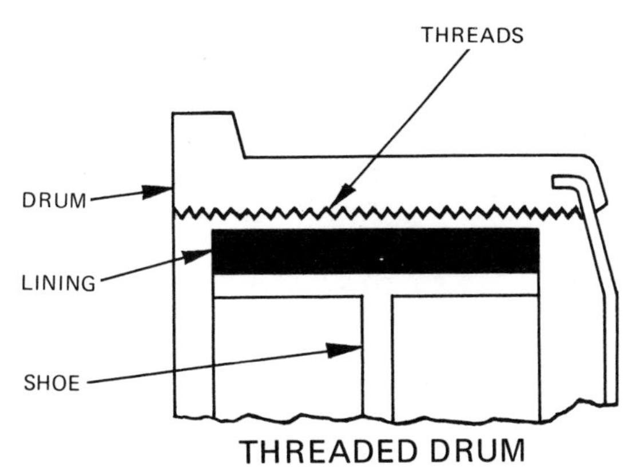

Figure 51 Various types of brake-drum defects that require drum service. *(Bear Manufacturing Company.)*

> **NOTE:** The diameters of the left and right drums on the same axle should be within 0.010 inch (0.254 mm) of each other. When the drum diameters on the same axle differ more than this, replace both drums.

■ 7-3-37 Wheel Cylinders (Drum-Type Brakes)

Wheel cylinders must be disassembled and assembled with extreme care in order to avoid getting the slightest trace of grease or dirt in them. Hands must be clean—washed with soap and water, not gasoline, since any trace of oil or gasoline on the cylinder parts may ruin them. Also, the bench and the tools must be clean.

To remove a wheel cylinder from the car, first remove the wheel and the drum. Then block up the brake pedal to prevent its operation. Next, disconnect the tube or hose from the cylinder and remove the cylinder by taking out the attachment bolts. The tube end at the wheel should be taped closed to prevent the entrance of dirt. The cylinder can be disassembled by rolling off the rubber boots or taking off the covers (see Fig. 54). All parts should be washed in brake-system cleaning fluid. Old boots and piston cups should be discarded if they are not in excellent condition. Some manufacturers recommend replacement of these parts every time the cylinder is disassembled. If the cylinder is scored, polish it with crocus cloth (not sandpaper or emery cloth). Some manufacturers permit the use of a hone if the diameter of the cylinder is not increased more than a few thousandths of an inch. If scores do not come out, replace the cylinder. Cylinder and pistons should also be replaced if the clearance between them is excessive. When reassembling the cylinder, lubricate all parts with brake fluid.

NOTE: Never allow any grease or oil to come in contact with rubber parts of the brake system. This would cause them to swell and might destroy braking action.

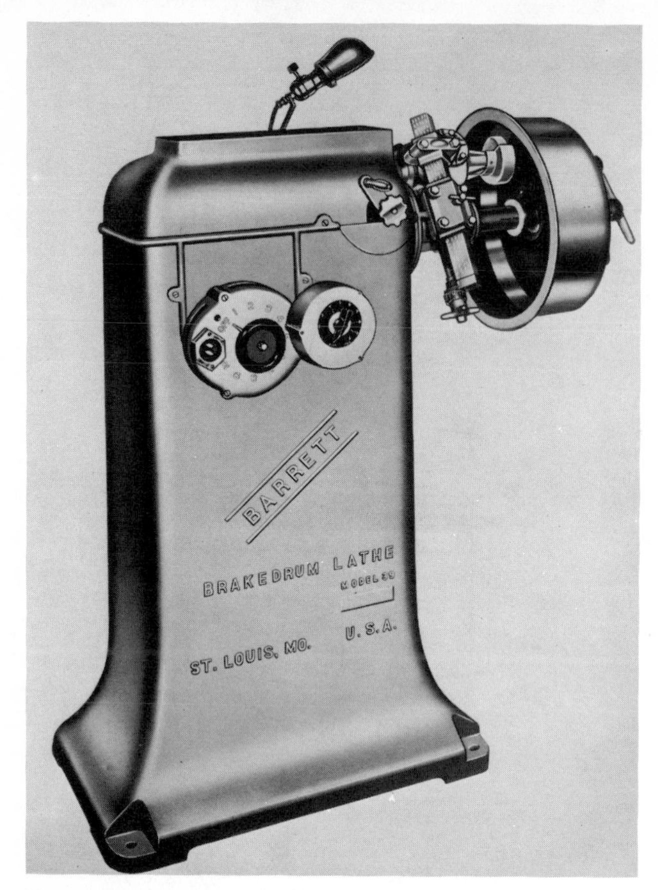

Figure 52 Brake-drum lathe for reconditioning brake drums. *(Barrett Equipment Company.)*

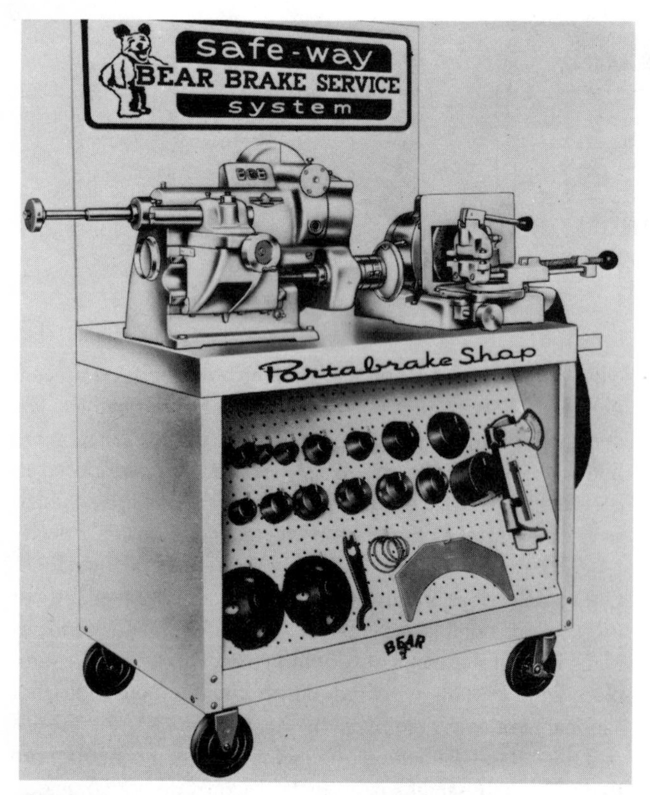

Figure 53 Portable brake-service stand with brake-lining-radius grinder and drum grinder. *(Bear Manufacturing Company.)*

■ 7-3-38 Master-Cylinder Service

The service procedures for master cylinders used with disk brakes and drum brakes are very similar. The major difference is that with the disk-brake system a larger brake-fluid reservoir is required. That is, disk brakes require more brake fluid than drum brakes. Refer to Fig. 55, which is a disassembled view of a master cylinder used with a braking system that has drum brakes at the rear and disk brakes at the front. Note that one of the reservoirs is larger than the other. A typical servicing procedure follows.

1. DISASSEMBLY (See Fig. 55). Clean the outside of the master cylinder and remove the filler cover and gasket. Pour out any remaining brake fluid. Remove the secondary-piston stop bolt from the bottom of the cylinder. Remove the bleeder screw. Depress the primary piston. Use snap-ring pliers to remove the snap ring from the retaining groove at the rear of the master-cylinder bore. Remove the pushrod and primary piston assembly from the master-cylinder bore. Do not remove the screw that retains the primary-return-spring retainer, return spring, primary cup, and protector on the primary piston. This assembly is factory preadjusted and must not be disassembled. Remove the secondary piston assembly. For some models, the service instructions state that you must not remove the outlet tube seats, check valves, and springs because they are permanent parts of the master cylinder. The service instructions for other models of master cylinders tell you to remove these parts if they need service.

NOTE: Disk brakes do not use check valves. See Fig. 55.

2. INSPECTION AND REPAIR Clean all parts in alcohol and inspect parts for chipping, scores, or wear. When using a master-cylinder repair kit, install all parts supplied. Make sure all passages are clean. Blow them out with compressed air. If the master cylinder is scored, rusted, or pitted, it may be necessary to hone the cylinder. If the scoring or wear is deep, install a new master cylinder.

3. REASSEMBLY Dip all parts into brake fluid (except the master cylinder itself). Insert the complete secondary piston assembly, with return spring, into the master-cylinder bore. Put the primary piston assembly into the bore. Depress the primary piston and install the snap ring in the bore groove. Install the pushrod, boot, and retainer on the pushrod, if so equipped. Install the pushrod assembly into the primary piston. Make sure the retainer is properly seated and holding the pushrod securely.

Position the inner end of the pushrod boot (if so equipped) in the retaining groove in the master cylinder. Install the second-

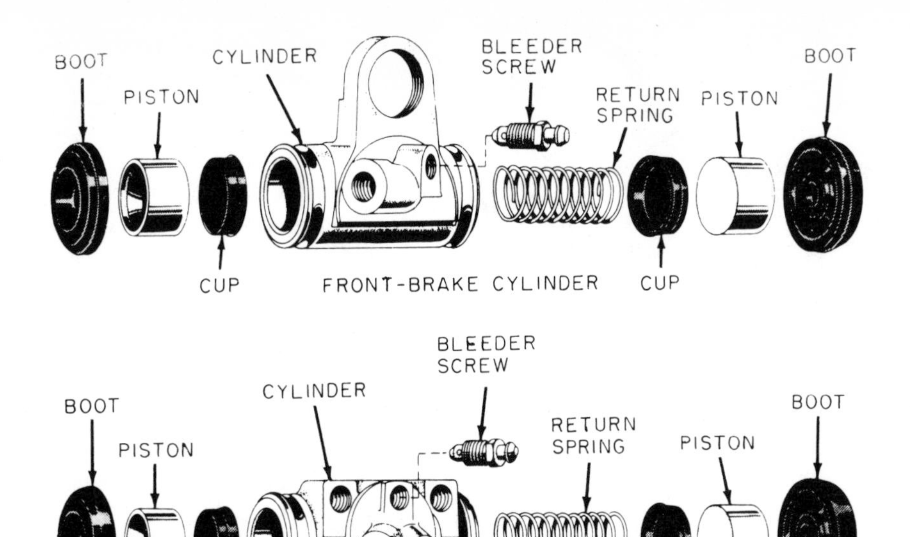

Figure 54 Disassembled view of a front- and rear-wheel cylinder. *(Ford Motor Company.)*

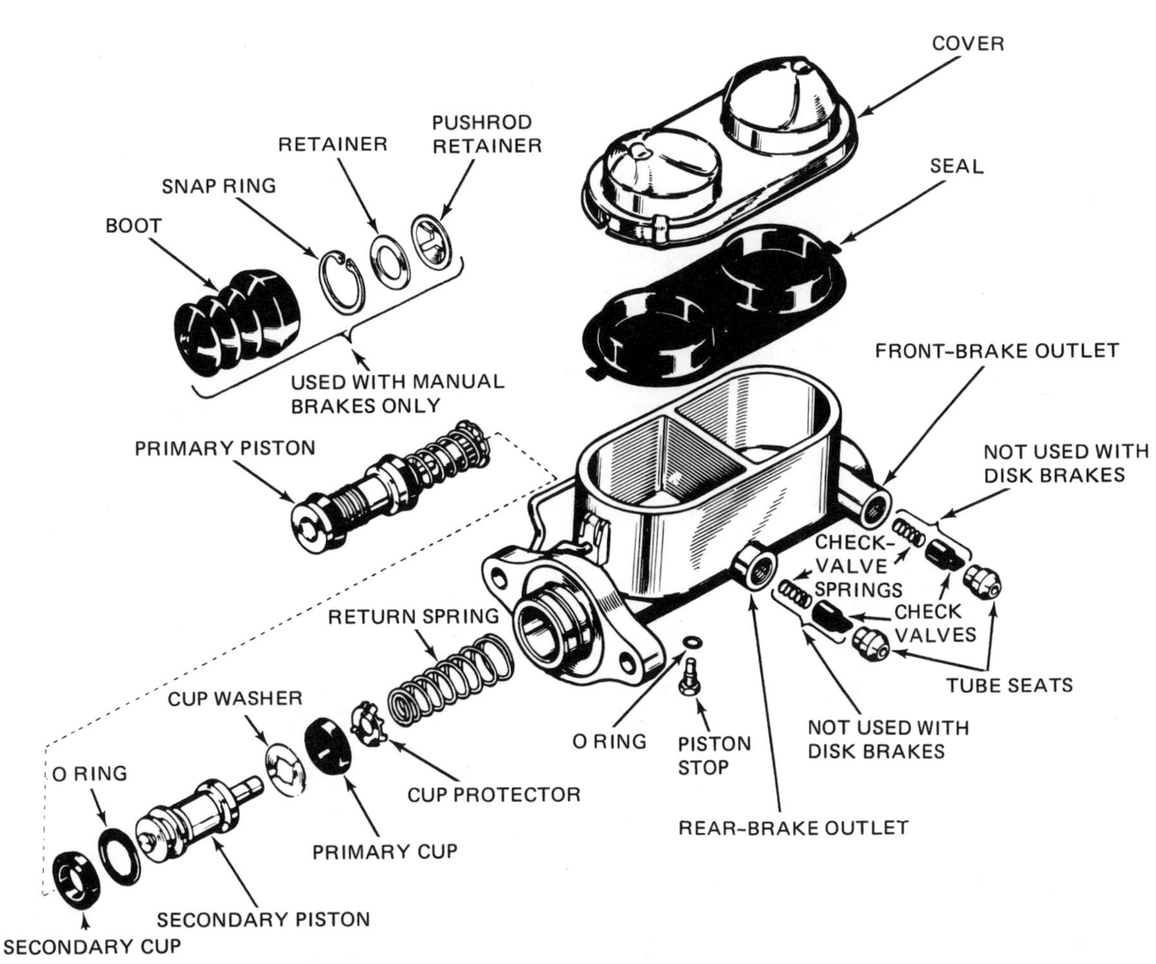

Figure 55 Disassembled view of a dual master cylinder. *(American Motors Corporation.)*

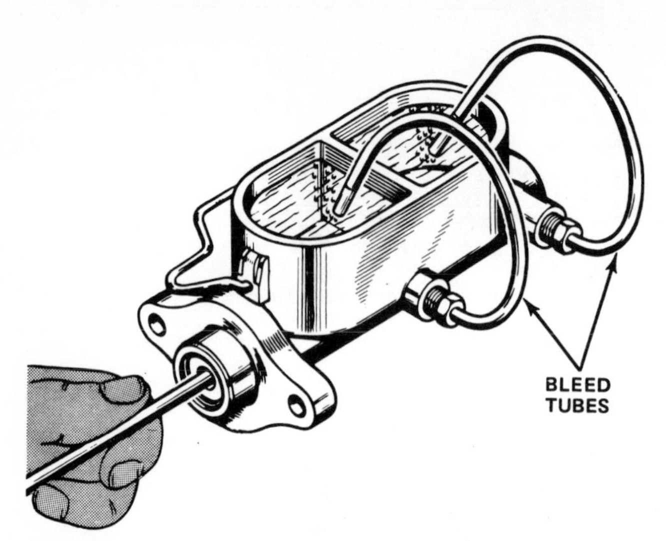

Figure 56 Bleeding the master cylinder with bleed tubes. *(American Motors Corporation.)*

ary-piston-stop bolt and the O ring in the bottom of the master cylinder. Install the bleeder screw. Put the gasket into the cover and install the cover on the master cylinder, securing it with the retainer.

NOTE: The master cylinder must be bled before it is installed on the car. Install plastic plugs at both outlet ports. Clamp the cylinder in a vise with the front end tilted slightly downward. Avoid excessive pressure as this could damage the cylinder. Fill both reservoirs with clean brake fluid. Slowly push the piston assemblies in with a wood dowel or smooth rod. Release the pressure and watch for bubbles. Repeat as long as bubbles appear. Then tilt the master cylinder so the front end is slightly raised. Repeat the push on the pistons, release the pistons, and watch for bubbles. Continue until no bubbles appear. Then install the seal and cover.

An alternative bleeding method uses two bleed tubes as shown in Fig. 56. With this method, install a master-cylinder check valve on the bleed tube connected to the reservoir that feeds the disk brakes. Note that, in Fig. 55, check valves are not used with disk brakes.

■ 7-3-39 Preparing Hydraulic-Brake Tubing for Installation Special steel tubing must be used for hydraulic brakes, since it is best able to withstand the high pressures developed in the system. Tubing must be cut off square with a special tube cutter. Tubing must not be cut with a jaw-type cutter or with a hacksaw. Either of these methods may distort the tube and leave heavy burrs that would prevent normal flaring of the tube. After the tube has been cut off, a special flaring tool must be used to flare the tube. This operation is shown in Fig. 57.

■ 7-3-40 Flushing, Filling, and Bleeding the Hydraulic System

1. FLUSHING If dirt or damaging liquid has been introduced into the hydraulic system, the system must be flushed. Oil should never be put into the system. It will cause the rubber parts to swell and deteriorate; braking action may be completely lost. When flushing the system, use only the special flushing compound recommended by the car manufacturer or new brake fluid. Anything else is apt to cause damage to the rubber, fabric, or metal parts in the system.

To flush the system, remove the cover from the bleeder valve and install a bleeder hose over the bleeder valve.

NOTE: Clean away dirt and grease from around the valves so as to avoid getting any dirt into the cylinders. Any dirt at a valve or in a bleeder hose may get drawn into the cylinder on the brake-pedal return stroke. This could cause subsequent failure of the wheel cylinder and brakes at the wheel.

Put the lower end of the bleeder hose into a clear plastic container (a hose in a container is shown in Fig. 58). Unscrew the bleeder valve about 3/4 turn. If the system is being bled manually, operate the brake pedal with full strokes to force all fluid from the system. Close the valve before allowing the pedal to return after each stroke. When all fluid is out, fill the master cylinder with new brake fluid. Again, operate the brake pedal with full strokes until all brake fluid draining from the valve appears clean and clear.

Then use dry, clean air—applied through the master cylinder—to blow out all the fluid from the system. Do not apply too much air pressure. Finally, add new brake fluid and bleed the system as outlined below.

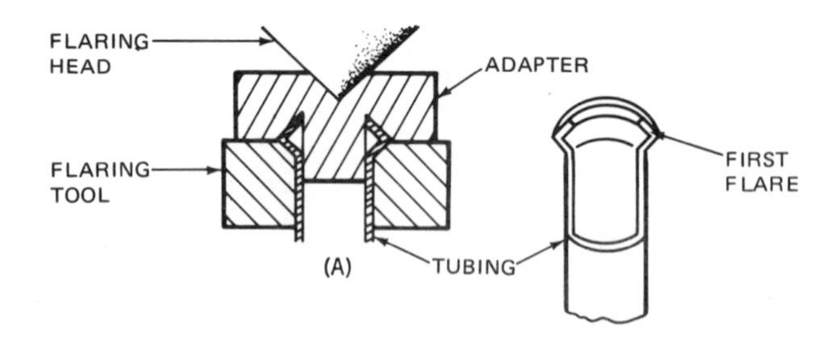

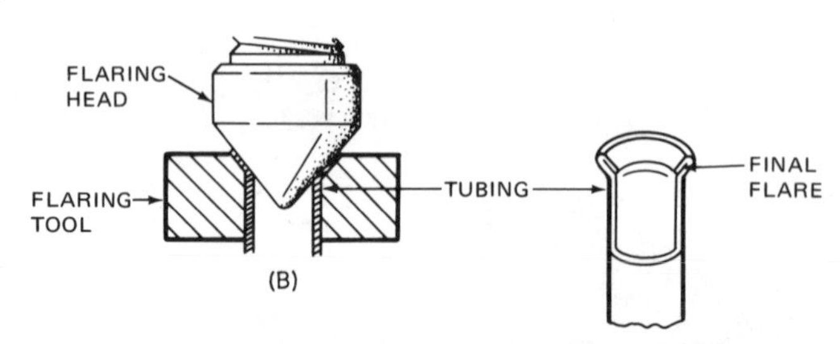

Figure 57 Steps required in double-flaring hydraulic-brake tubing. *(Ford Motor Company.)*

> **NOTE:** Do not use the power brakes when flushing or bleeding the hydraulic system. Stop the engine and reduce the vacuum reserve to zero by applying the brakes several times before starting to flush or bleed the system. If the vehicle is equipped with disk brakes, the metering valve must be held in the open position while the hydraulic system is bled.

2. FILLING AND BLEEDING Whenever a brake system has been flushed, when the fluid has become low, or when air has leaked into the system, the system must be bled to eliminate the air. Air in the system will cause a soft or spongy brake-pedal action. The air will compress when the brakes are applied, and poor braking action will result. Air is eliminated by adding brake fluid and bleeding off a little of the fluid from each wheel cylinder. To add brake fluid, first make sure that the bleeder valves are closed at all cylinders. Then, either fill the master-cylinder reservoir manually or use a pressure tank as shown in Fig. 58. In either case, use only approved brake fluid.

When the reservoir is filled, install a bleeder hose and container at one wheel cylinder. Make sure all dirt is cleaned from around the connection so that dirt will not get into the wheel cylinder. Open the bleeder valve. When not using the pressure bleeder, have an assistant get into the car and pump the brake pedal with full strokes. Allow it to return slowly only after the bleeder valve has been closed. Continue until the fluid flows from the bleeder hose into the container in a solid stream that is free of air bubbles. Make sure the end of the hose is below the liquid level in the container to prevent air from being drawn into the system on the brake-pedal return strokes. Tighten the bleeder valve, remove the hose, and install the cover on the valve. Repeat the operation at the other wheel cylinders. Be sure to maintain the proper fluid level in the master-cylinder reservoir. When the bleeding operation is complete, make sure the fluid level in the reservoir is correct. Then install the master-cylinder cover and gasket.

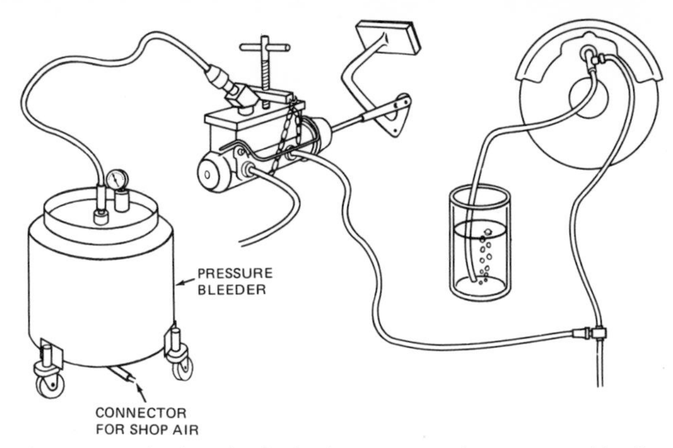

Figure 58 Bleeding the hydraulic system with a pressure bleeder. *(Pontiac Motor Division of General Motors Corporation.)*

When the pressure tank is used (Fig. 58), no assistant is needed. First, partly fill the pressure tank with brake fluid. Then, add compressed air to the tank with the tire-inflating equipment. The brake fluid is, therefore, under pressure in the tank. When the tank is connected to the master cylinder as shown in Fig. 58 and the valve is turned on, brake fluid flows from the tank, under pressure, to the master-cylinder reservoir. When the bleeder valve is opened, brake fluid is forced through the brake line and wheel cylinder. Brake fluid is allowed to flow until it runs from the bleeder hose in a solid stream without air bubbles. Then, the bleeder valve is tightened, the hose removed, and the valve cover installed. The operation is repeated at each wheel cylinder.

Do not attempt to reuse the brake fluid that drains into the container during bleeding. It is likely to be contaminated or dirty.

SECTION 7-4 Power-Brake Service

This section discusses the trouble diagnosis, adjustment, removal, repair, and installation of power brakes. The previous section described the servicing procedures on all hydraulic-brake components except the power unit. Note that this section includes overhaul instructions on the Bendix dual-diaphragm power-brake unit (illustrated in Fig. 11 in Part 7, Sec. 2). This is the unit used on many General Motors cars, and the service manuals for these cars carry overhaul instructions. However, the service manuals for American Motors Corporation, Chrysler Corporation, and Ford Motor Company cars do not carry overhaul instructions. They simply state that, if the power-brake unit is defective, it should be replaced with a new assembly.

■ 7-4-1 Power-Brake Trouble-Diagnosis Chart

The chart below relates various power-brake troubles to their possible causes and corrections. This chart gives you a means of logically tracing troubles to their actual causes and permits quick location of causes and their rapid correction. The chart and the sections that follow pertain to power-brake units only. Generally, the trouble-diagnosis charts in ■7-3-2 and ■7-3-15, which cover hydraulic brakes, also apply to power-brake systems. Thus, the troubles listed in the charts, as well as the trouble corrections described in Part 7, Sec. 3, also apply to power brakes.

NOTE: The troubles and possible causes are not listed in the chart in the order of frequency of occurrence. That is, item 1 does not necessarily occur more often than item 2, nor does item *a* under "Possible Cause" necessarily occur more often than item *b*.

POWER-BRAKE TROUBLE-DIAGNOSIS CHART

(See 7-4-2 and 7-4-3 for details of checks and corrections listed. Not all the possible causes and checks or corrections listed apply to all models of power brakes described in the chapter; this is because of individual variations among models.)

COMPLAINT	POSSIBLE CAUSE	CHECK OR CORRECTION
1. Excessive brake pedal pressure required	a. Defective vacuum check valve	Free or replace
	b. Hose collapsed	Replace
	c. Vacuum fitting plugged	Clear, replace
	d. Binding pedal linkage	Free
	e. Air inlet clogged	Clean
	f. Faulty piston seal	Replace
	g. Stuck piston	Clear, replace damaged parts
	h. Faulty diaphragm	Replace (applies to diaphragm type only)

POWER-BRAKE TROUBLE-DIAGNOSIS CHART *(Continued)*

(See 7-4-2 and 7-4-3 for details of checks and corrections listed. Not all the possible causes and checks or corrections listed apply to all models of power brakes described in the chapter; this is because of individual variations among models.)

COMPLAINT	POSSIBLE CAUSE	CHECK OR CORRECTION
	i. Causes listed under item 6 in chart in ■7-3-2 or under item 3 in chart in ■7-3-15	
2. Brakes grab	a. Reaction, or "brake-feel," mechanism damaged	Replace damaged parts
	b. Air-vacuum valve sticking	Free, replace damaged parts
	c. Causes listed under item 7 in chart in ■7-3-2 or item 3 in chart in ■7-3-15	
3. Pedal goes to floorboard	a. Hydraulic-plunger seal leaking	Replace
	b. Compensating valve not closing	Replace valve
	c. Causes listed under item 1 in chart in ■7-3-2 or item 8 in ■7-3-15	
4. Brakes fail to release	a. Pedal linkage binding	Free up
	b. Faulty check-valve action	Free, replace damaged parts
	c. Compensator port plugged	Clean port
	d. Hydraulic-plunger seal sticking	Replace seal
	e. Piston sticking	Lubricate, replace damaged parts as necessary
	f. Broken return spring	Replace
	g. Causes listed under item 3 in ■7-3-2 or item 6 in ■7-3-15	
5. Loss of brake fluid	a. Worn or damaged seals in hydraulic section	Replace, fill and bleed system
	b. Loose line connections	Tighten, replace seals
	c. Causes listed under item 10 in ■7-3-2 or items 7 and 9 in chart in ■7-3-15	

■ **7-4-2 Servicing Power-Brake Units** Even though the different types of power-brake units operate in a similar manner and have a similar exterior appearance, each model requires a special disassembly and reassembly procedure. Thus, before you make any attempt to service a specific model, refer to the shop manual covering that model.

Keep the workbench and tools clean. Small particles of dirt in the valves could cause malfunctioning of the power brakes. Examine the rubber parts as the unit is disassembled. Discard any part that appears cracked, cut, or worn. The rubber seals and other parts must be in good condition for normal valve and power-brake action. Replace those that you have the slightest doubt about. As a rule, the manufacturer's instructions call for replacement of all old seals during an overhaul.

As an example of disassembly and reassembly procedures, one model of power brakes is described in the following section.

■ **7-4-3 Chevrolet Power Brakes** Chevrolet has used a variety of power brakes in recent years. One that has been very popular is the Bendix unit (Fig. 1).

1. REMOVAL To remove the unit, disconnect the pushrod clevis from the brake-pedal arm. If the clevis will not pass through the hole in the fire wall, take the clevis off the rod, first noting its approximate location. Disconnect the vacuum hose from the power unit and the hydraulic lines from the master cylinder. Cap the lines to keep dirt out. Remove the nuts and the lock washers that attach the power-brake assembly to the fire wall and take the assembly out of the engine compartment.

2. DISASSEMBLY Take the master cylinder off the power unit and lay it aside. The master cylinder is serviced as already described in ■7-3-38.

Scribe lines across the flanges of the front and rear housings, in line with the master-cylinder cover, to provide guidelines for reassembly. Pull the piston rod from the front housing. (See Figs. 1 in Part 7, Sec. 2, and 1 in this section for the locations and appearance of the parts described.) The seal will come off with the piston rod. Pull the vacuum check valve out. Discard the valve and rubber grommet.

If the pushrod has a clevis, remove the clevis. Unseat the dust boot from the housing and remove it and the silencer. Use a thin-bladed screwdriver to pry the silencer retainer off the

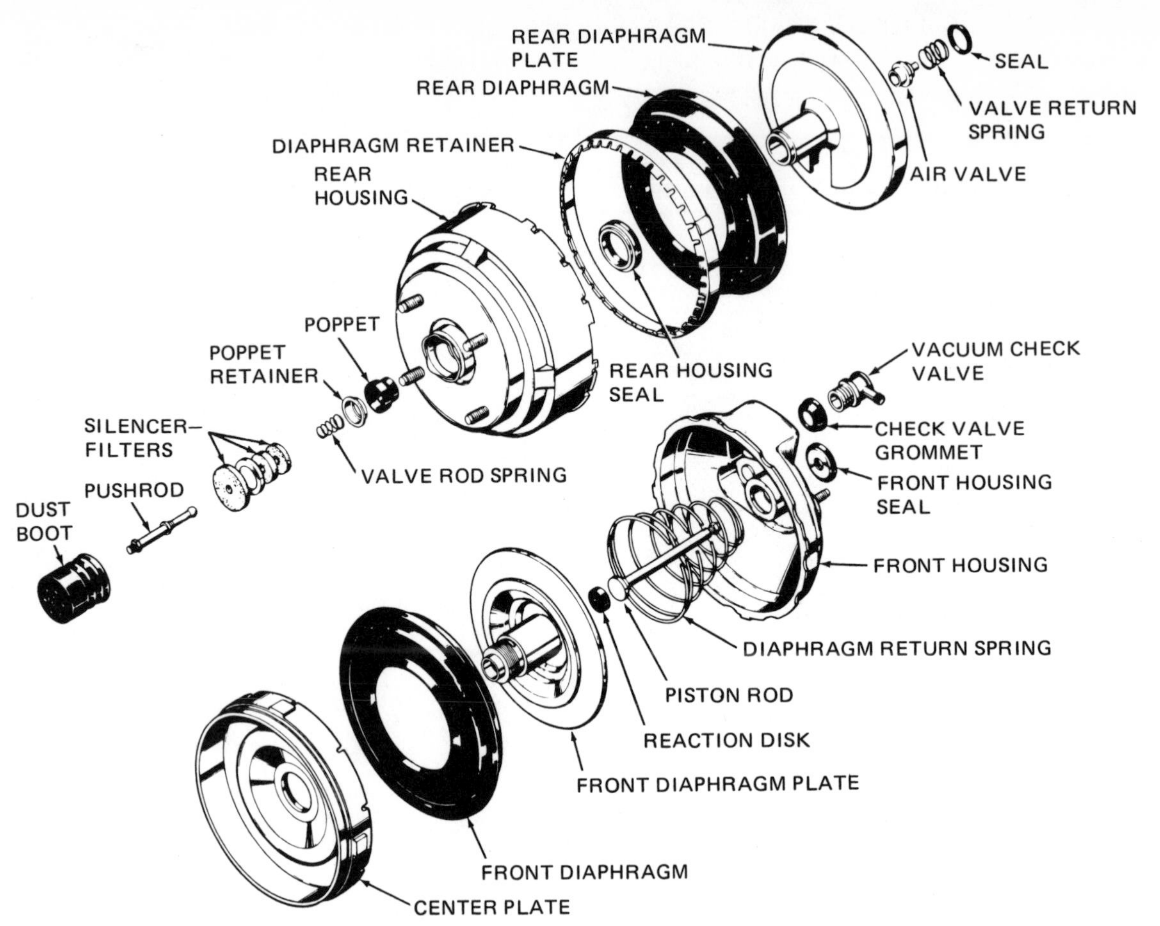

Figure 1 Disassembled view of a Bendix dual-diaphragm power brake. *(Chevrolet Motor Division of General Motors Corporation.)*

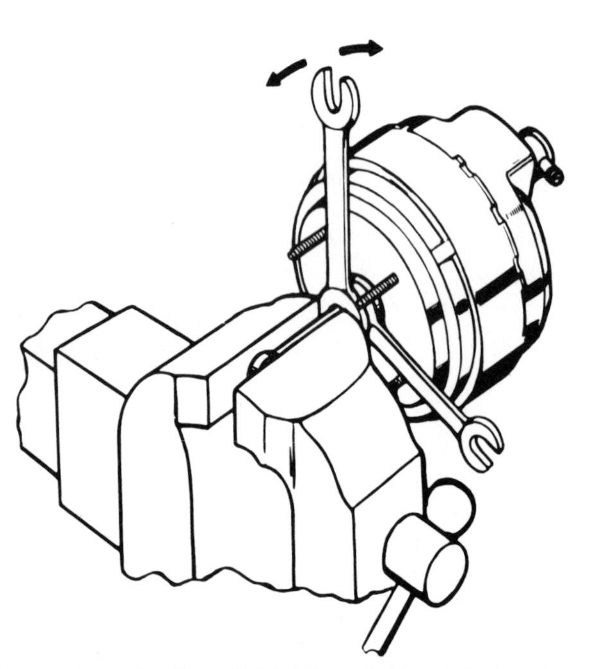

Figure 2 Removing the pushrod. *(Chevrolet Motor Division of General Motors Corporation.)*

end of the hub of the rear diaphragm plate. Do not chip the plastic. Squirt denatured alcohol down the pushrod to lubricate the rubber grommet in the air valve.

Clamp the end of the pushrod in a vise, leaving enough room to position two open-end wrenches between the vise and the retainer on the hub of the rear plate (Fig. 2). Using the wrench nearest the vise as a pry, force the air valve off the ball end of the pushrod. Do not damage the plastic hub or allow the power unit to fall to the floor.

Slide the air filter and air silencer from the pushrod. Remove the poppet spring, retainer, and poppet (Fig. 1).

Figure 3 shows the two types of lances on the edge of the rear housing. Four are the deep type . The metal that forms these must be partly straightened out so the lances will clear the cutouts on the front housing. If the metal tabs break, the housing must be replaced. After straightening the lances, attach a holding fixture to the front housing with nuts and washers drawn tight to eliminate bending of studs. Put the holding fixture in an arbor press (Fig. 4) with rear housing up. Use a 1-½ inch wrench, as shown, to keep the lower unit from turning. It will turn a little, but when the wrench comes up tight against the arbor press, the unit cannot turn further.

Fasten the special spanner to studs on the rear shell with

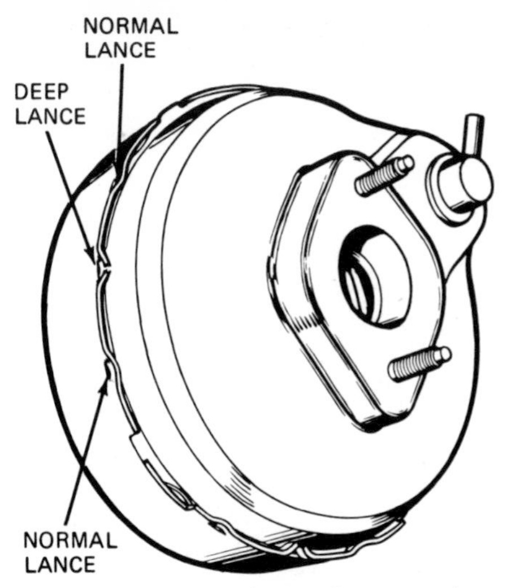

Figure 3 Locations of lances in the rear housing. *(Chevrolet Motor Division of General Motors Corporation.)*

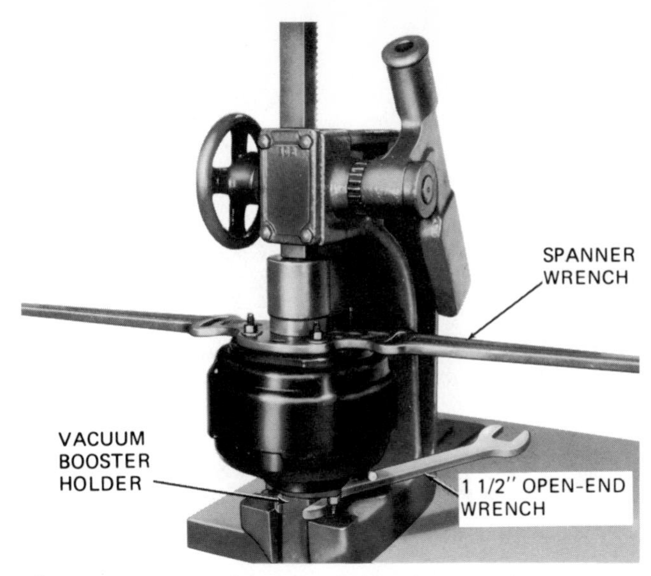

Figure 4 Using special fixtures to hold and separate the housings in an arbor press. *(Chevrolet Motor Division of General Motors Corporation.)*

nuts and lock washers. Place a piece of 2-inch (50.8-mm) pipe about 3 inches (76.2-mm) long over the plastic hub of the diaphragm. Put a piece of flat steel stock over the end of the pipe. Press the housing down with the arbor press to relieve the spring pressure. Rotate the spanner counterclockwise to unlock the shells.

Release the arbor press and remove the diaphragm return spring. Detach the spanner and the holding fixture. Work the edges of the front diaphragm from under the lances of the rear housing and remove the complete vacuum assembly. Bosses on the center plate (Fig. 1) must align with cutouts in the rear housing to permit removal.

Wet the rear diaphragm retainer with denatured alcohol and remove it with your fingers only. Do not use any tool.

Clamp the special tool (Fig. 5) in a vise, hex head up. Put the diaphragm-and-plate assembly on the tool with the tool seated in the hex opening in the front plate. Twist the rear diaphragm plate counterclockwise, using hand leverage on the outer edge of the plate. Remove the plates from the tool and place them, front plate down, on a bench. Unscrew the rear plate completely and lift it off, catching the air valve and return spring as the parts are separated.

Remove the square ring seal from the shoulder of the front-plate hub. Remove the reaction disk from inside the front diaphragm plate. Slide the center plate off the hub of the front plate. The vacuum seal may stay in front of the center diaphragm plate. If the seal assembly is defective, the center-plate-and-seal assembly must be replaced as a unit.

Remove the diaphragms from the plates. If the rear-housing seal requires replacement, use a blunt punch or 1¼ inch socket to drive the seal out.

3. CLEANING AND INSPECTION Clean all parts with denatured alcohol. Blow out all passages and holes with compressed air. Air-dry parts. If slight rust is found on the inside surface of the power-cylinder housing, polish it with crocus cloth and clean with denatured alcohol.

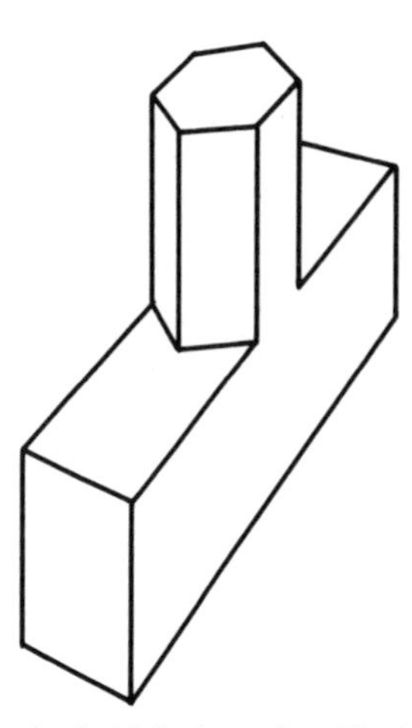

Figure 5 Special tool to hold the front plate. The hex head fits into the hex opening of the front plate. *(Chevrolet Motor Division of General Motors Corporation.)*

> **NOTE:** Never use gasoline, kerosine, or other liquid to clean power-brake parts. These liquids will damage the rubber parts.

Rubber parts must be in good condition, or the brake will not work properly. Replace them if there is the slightest trace of damage.

4. REASSEMBLY Be sure all parts are clean. Rewash them before reassembly if there is any doubt about their being clean.

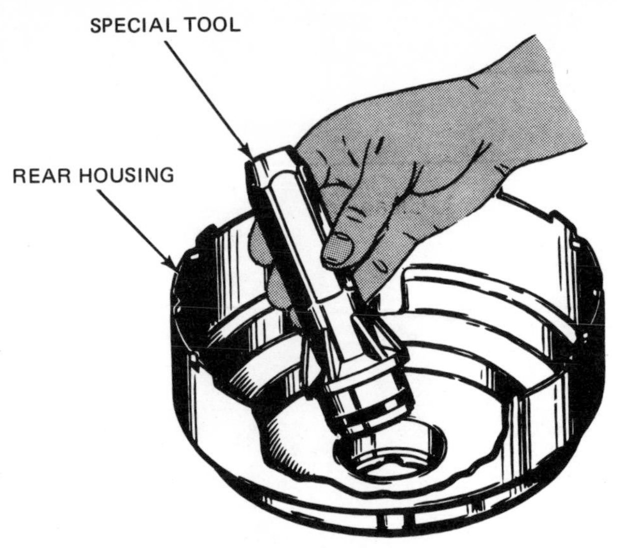

Figure 6 Installing the rear-housing seal with the special tool. *(Chevrolet Motor Division of General Motors Corporation.)*

Figure 8 Installing the air-valve assembly. *(Chevrolet Motor Division of General Motors Corporation.)*

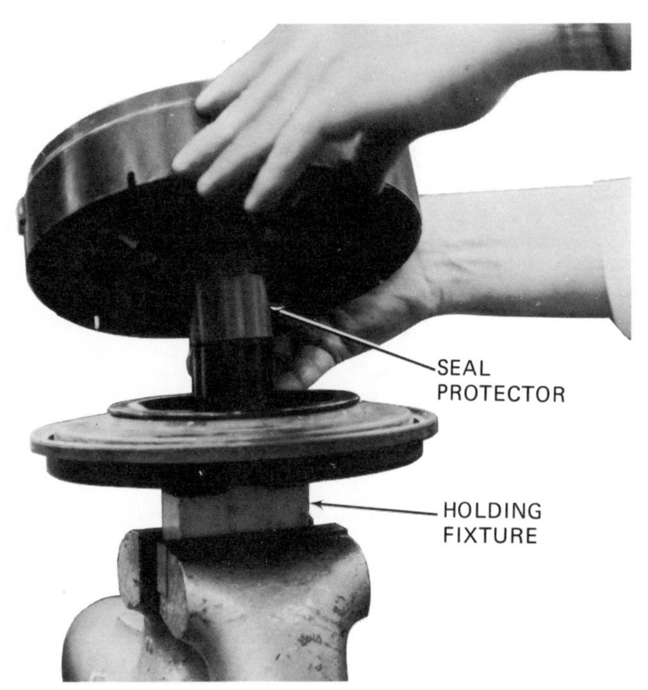

Figure 7 Seal protector installed to protect the seal from threads on the front-plate hub. *(Chevrolet Motor Division of General Motors Corporation.)*

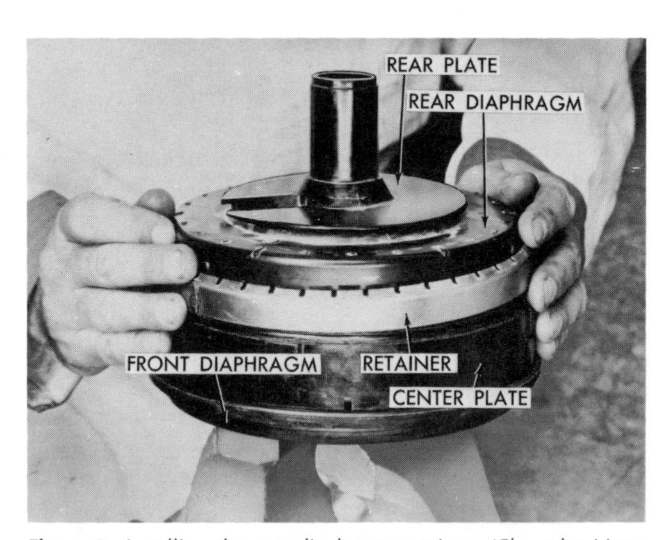

Figure 9 Installing the rear-diaphragm retainer. *(Chevrolet Motor Division of General Motors Corporation.)*

Lubricate rubber, plastic, and metal friction points with special silicone lubricant.

If the rear housing seal was removed, press a new seal into place with the special tool (Fig. 6). Install a reaction disk in the front-plate hub, small tip side first. Use a rounded rod to seat it.

Clamp the special tool (Fig. 5) in a vise. Put the front plate on the tool with hex head of tool in front plate. Put the front diaphragm on the front plate with the long fold of diaphragm facing down. Install the seal protector over the threads on the front-plate hub (Fig. 7). Apply a light film of silicone lubrication on the seal, and then guide center plate, seal first, onto the front-plate hub. Remove the seal protector.

Apply a light film of silicone lubricant to the front and rear bearing surfaces of the air valve, but not to the rubber grommet inside the valve. Install the square ring seal on the front-plate hub. Then install the return spring and air valve in the base of the front-plate hub (Fig. 8).

Set the rear plate over the hub of the front plate. Use your hands only and screw the plate onto the hub, making sure that the valve and spring are properly aligned. Use your index finger to check travel of the valve plunger. It should be free. Plates should be tight, but do not overtorque.

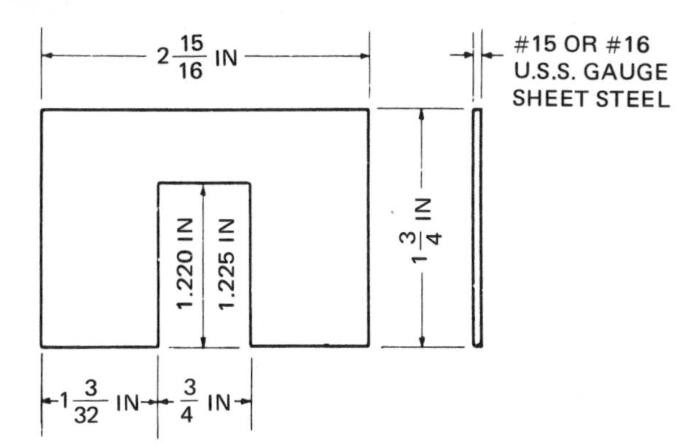

Figure 10 Piston-rod gauge. *(Chevrolet Motor Division of General Motors Corporation.)*

Assemble the rear diaphragm to the rear plate and put the lip of the diaphragm in the groove in the rear plate. Install the diaphragm retainer, using your fingers to press the retainer until it seats on the shoulder of the center plate (Fig. 9).

Apply talcum powder to the inside wall of the rear housing and silicone lubricant to the scalloped cutouts of the front housing and to the seal in the rear housing. Assemble the diaphragm-and-plate assembly into the rear housing. Bosses on center plate must align with cutouts in the rear housing during assembly. Work the outer rim of the front diaphragm into the rear housing with a screwdriver blade so that the rim is under the lances in the housing.

With the setup shown in Fig. 4, compress housings in the arbor press until the diaphragm edge is fully compressed with tangs on the front housing against the slots in the rear housing. Rotate the spanner clockwise until tangs butt against rear-housing stops.

Bend lanced areas in to secure the assembly. (If tangs break, that half of the housing must be replaced.) Remove the assembly from the press and detach tools.

Wet the poppet valve with denatured alcohol, install a retainer inside the poppet, and put it into the hub. Install silencers and filters over the ball end of the pushrod (see Fig. 1). Put the spring over the end of the rod, then push the rod into place. Tap the end of the rod with a plastic hammer to seat the ball in the poppet. Seat the filters and silencers into the hub and install the retainer on the end of the hub. Assemble the silencer in the dust boot, wet the dust-boot opening with denatured alcohol, and assemble over the plate hub and rear-housing hub.

If the pushrod has a clevis, attach it. Dip a new check-valve grommet in denatured alcohol and install it in front housing. Dip a new check valve in denatured alcohol and install it in the grommet.

Apply silicone lubricant to the piston end of the piston rod and insert the rod into the front plate. Twist it to eliminate air bubbles between it and the reaction disk. Assemble the seal over the rod and press it into the recess in the front housing.

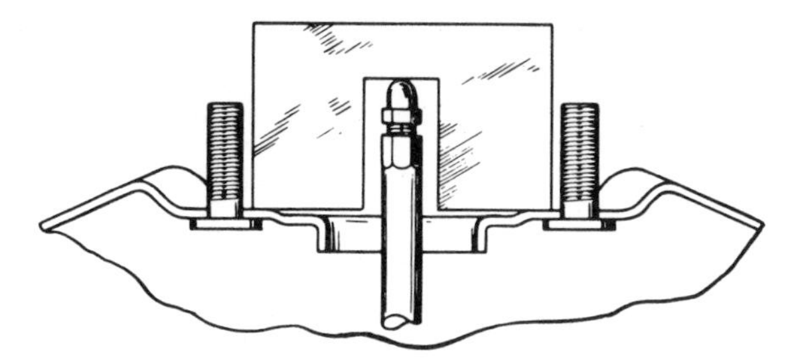

Figure 11 Checking the adjustment of the piston rod with the gauge. *(Chevrolet Motor Division of General Motors Corporation.)*

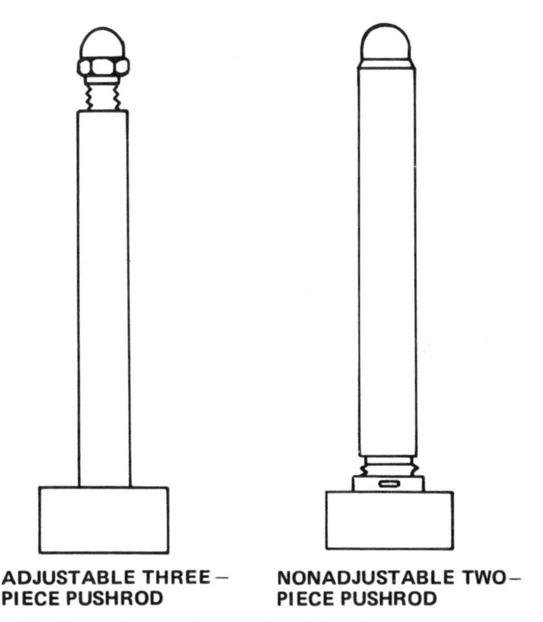

Figure 12 Some piston rods are adjustable, others are not. *(American Motors Corporation.)*

To adjust the piston rod, use the special rod gauge shown in Fig. 10 in the manner demonstrated in Fig. 11. To adjust, grasp the serrated end of the piston rod with pliers and turn the adjusting screw either in or out as necessary. The adjustment screw is self-locking.

Install the master cylinder and then install the assembly in the car. Bleed the hydraulic system after connecting the tubes to the master cylinder (■7-3-40).

■ 7-4-4 Adjustments of Other Power-Brake Units

American Motors Corporation, and Ford Motor Company no longer supply overhaul instructions on power-brake units. They specify that if trouble occurs in the unit, replace it with a new assembly. Many do have a pushrod adjustment as shown in Fig. 11. However, some pushrods are not adjustable (Fig. 12). On these, if the height is not correct, the complete unit must be replaced.

PART 8

Heating and Air Conditioning

SECTION 8-1 Air-Conditioner Fundamentals

In this section, we describe the fundamentals of automotive air conditioners. We also explain how the components of a typical system operate. Later sections take up specific types of automotive air conditioners and describe their operation in detail.

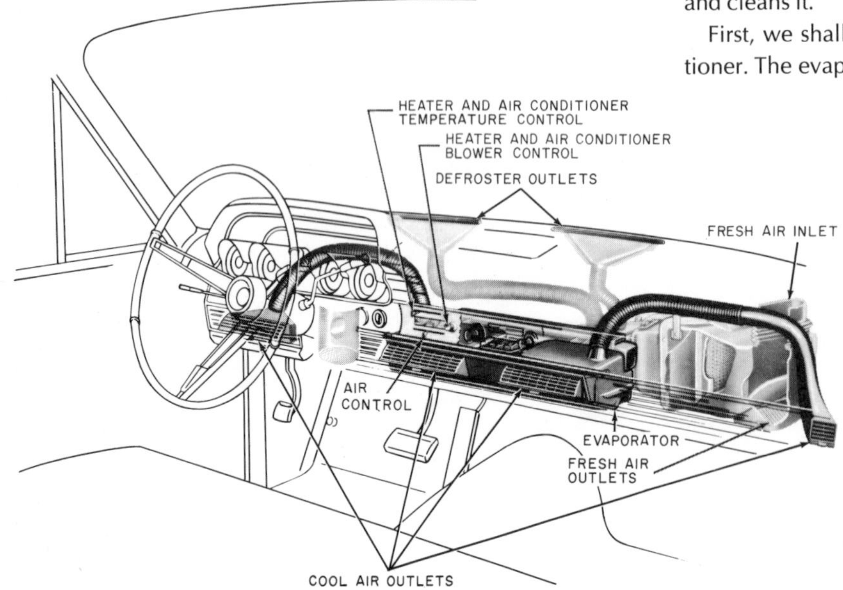

Figure 1 Air-conditioner installation in phantom view, as it appears from the front seat of the car. *(Ford Motor Company.)*

■ **8-1-1 Humidity** When the weather forecaster says, "Today will be hot and humid," you know you are in for an uncomfortable day. One of the keys is the word "humid." It means that the air has a lot of water vapor in it. Sometimes the weather report says "90 percent humidity." That is, the air contains 90 percent of the water vapor it is capable of holding. There is not much room for additional water vapor.

However, if the air is dry (has very little water vapor in it), you feel more comfortable, even on very hot days. For instance, if the humidity is only 30 percent, the air has plenty of room for water vapor. The air is 70 percent empty of water vapor.

Dry air feels much more comfortable than moist or humid air. And that is one thing the air conditioner does: It dries the air. Also, the air conditioner circulates the air. Every air conditioner, including those in cars, has a fan or blower to circulate the air through the cooled space.

■ **8-1-2 Cooling the Air** The air conditioner cools the air that it dries and circulates. In operation, the air conditioner does four things with the air: cools, dries, circulates, and cleans it.

First, we shall describe the cooling action of the air conditioner. The evaporator does this job. The evaporator is located

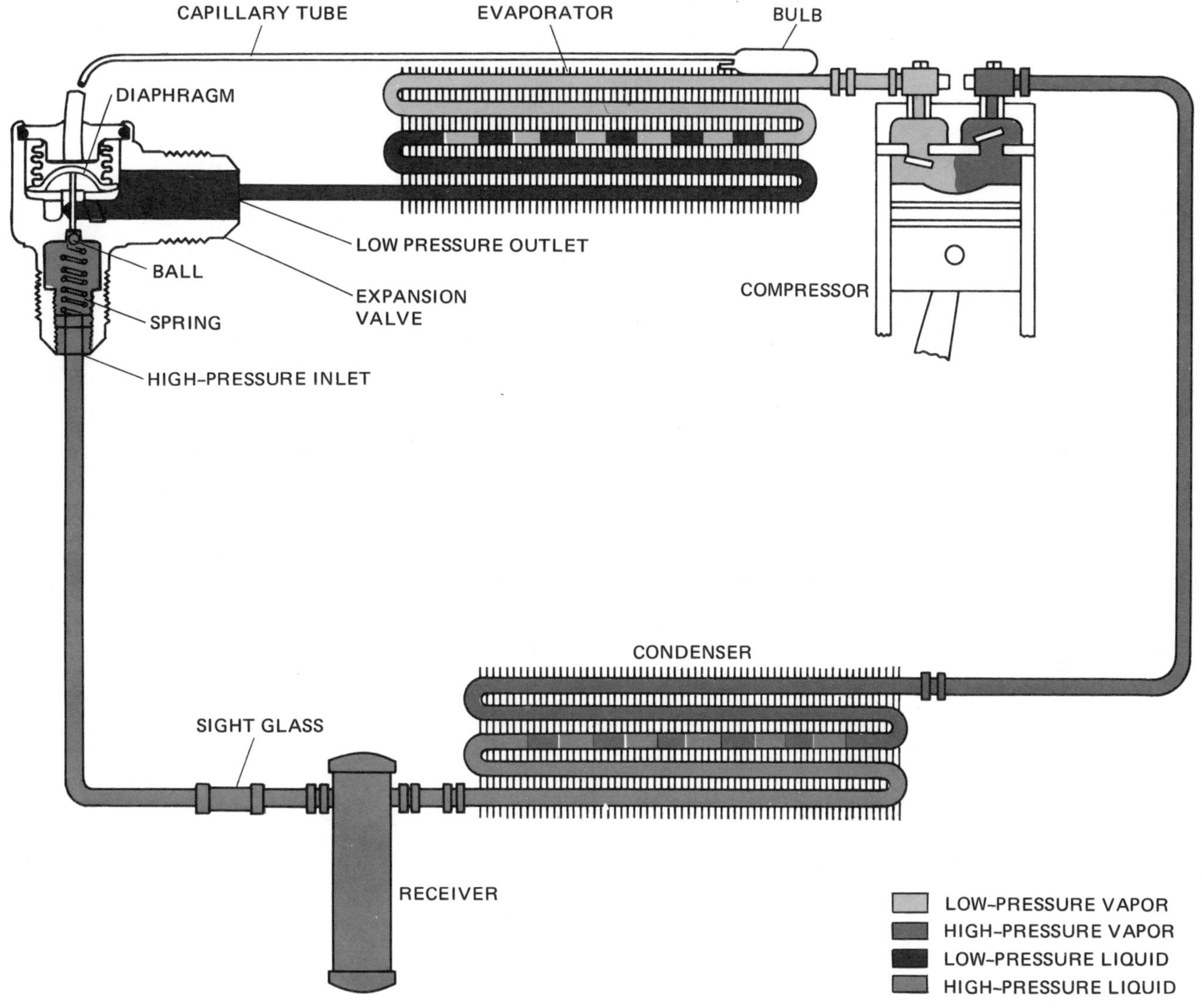

Figure 2 Simple refrigeration system.

in a box (sometimes called the "plenum chamber") in or under the instrument panel of the car (Fig. 1). Figure 2 shows the complete air-conditioner system in simplified form. The typical air-conditioning or refrigeration system contains a condenser, an evaporator, and a compressor. It also contains a valve, or restriction, between the condenser and evaporator. This valve is the thermostatic expansion valve. It passes the proper amount of refrigerant to meet the cooling requirements.

In operation, the compressor pulls vaporized refrigerant from the evaporator. It compresses this vapor and sends it to the condenser. The condenser takes heat from the hot compressed vapor, causing it to condense back into liquid again. This liquid then flows to the evaporator. In the evaporator, the liquid vaporizes, thereby taking heat from the surrounding air. The vapor then is pulled back through the compressor, and the "cycle" is repeated. Compressor action is described in ■8-1-6.

The evaporator looks very much like the condenser (Fig. 3). It includes a tube and fins. The liquid refrigerant flows into the bottom of the tube and begins to vaporize as it moves up the tube. The action is the reverse of what happens in the condenser. In the evaporator, the fins pick up heat from the air around them in the hot passenger compartment. They transfer this heat, through the tube, to the refrigerant. The refrigerant, as it vaporizes, takes up this heat. The vapor then carries the heat through the compressor to the condenser. In the condenser, the vapor gives up its heat and turns back to a liquid again.

■ 8-1-3 Drying and Cleaning the Air

As the air passes through the evaporator, moisture condenses on the cool tube and fins. You have seen this effect many times, when moisture condenses on the outside of a cold glass or bottle. Water-vapor molecules from the warm air are trapped by the cold metal of the evaporator. They clump together to form water on the metal surface. The water then drips off the evaporator.

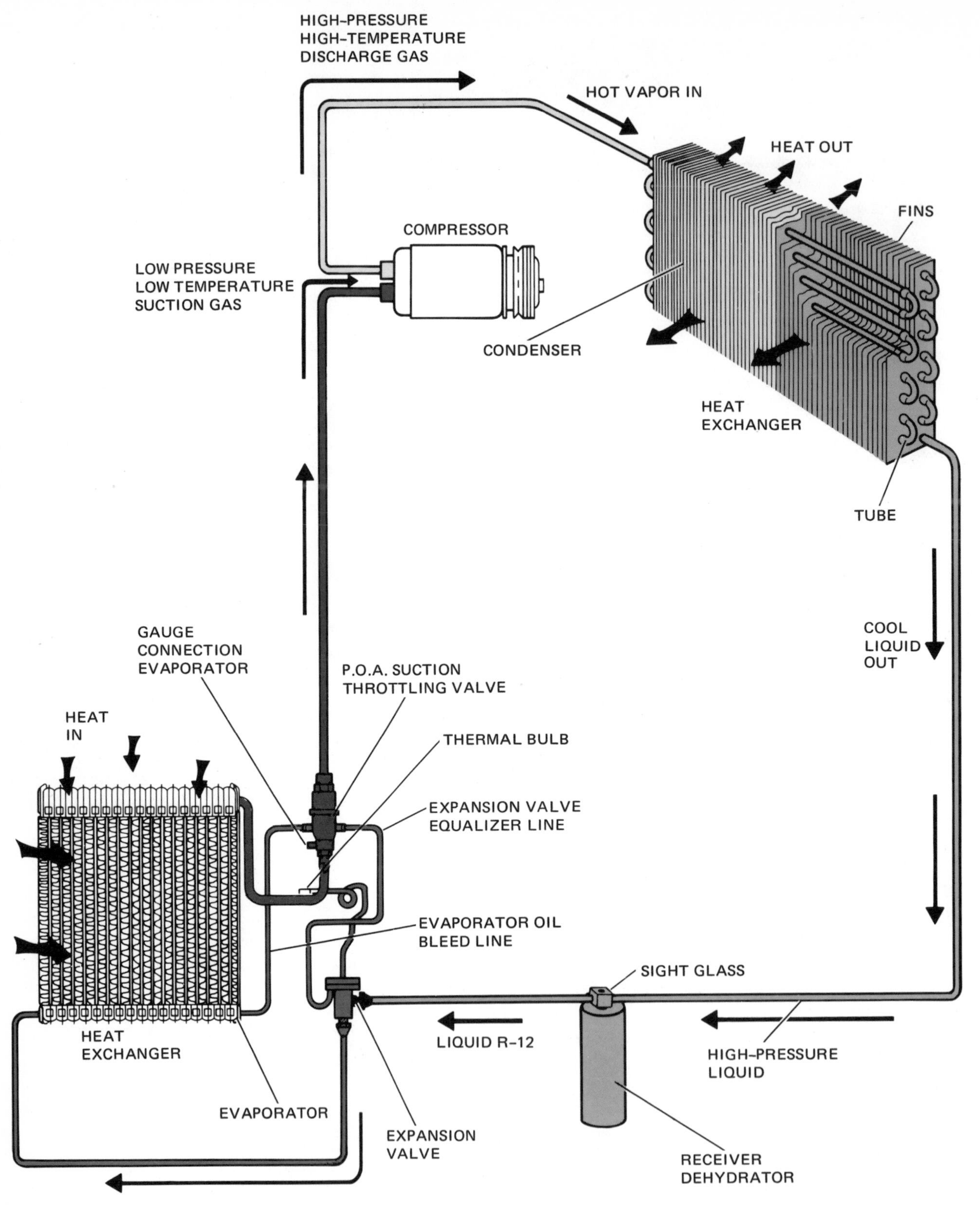

Figure 3 Schematic layout of a refrigeration system. The evaporator is to the left. The valves and other parts are explained later. *(Harrison Radiator Division of General Motors Corporation.)*

Dirt particles in the air passing through the evaporator are trapped on the wet surface. As the water drops off the evaporator, it carries the dirt particles with it.

Thus, the air conditioner does four things to keep you comfortable in the car. It dries the air so the air can pick up moisture from your skin. It cools the air so the air can take heat from your skin. It circulates the air, sending fresh, cool, dry air to you. And it helps remove dust particles from the air.

■ **8-1-4 Expansion Valve** There is a valve located between the condenser and the evaporator (Figs. 2 and 3). This valve acts like a restriction. In an air conditioner, there must be some restriction between the condenser and evaporator. If there were no restriction, the refrigerant would circulate freely in the system. There would be no pressure difference, and thus no refrigerating action. The pressure must be high in the condenser, in order for the heated vapor to lose heat and condense to a liquid. The pressure must be low in the evaporator, in order for the liquid refrigerant to vaporize and pick up heat.

The expansion valve regulates the flow of liquid refrigerant from the condenser to the evaporator. The expansion valve is connected by a capillary tube to a gas-filled bulb. The bulb is located on top of the evaporator. When the temperature of the bulb rises high enough, the gas pressure is great enough to push down the diaphragm in the expansion valve. This gas-tight diaphragm, as it is pushed down, forces the valve (the ball) to move down. This allows liquid refrigerant to flow through the expansion valve to the evaporator.

The expansion valve thus allows liquid refrigerant to flow to the evaporator if the evaporator gets too warm. It shuts off the flow of liquid refrigerant to the evaporator if the evaporator starts to get too cold.

■ **8-1-5 Receiver and Sight Glass** There is a receiver between the condenser and the expansion valve. See Fig. 2. The purpose of the receiver is to hold excess liquid refrigerant as it leaves the condenser. To the left of the receiver (in Fig. 2) is the sight glass. This is an inspection glass that allows the air-conditioning technician to see the condition of the refrigerant in the system. The receiver and the sight glass are discussed in detail in ■8-2-6 and 8-2-7. In many automobile air-conditioning systems, the expansion valve and the sight glass are mounted on the receiver. However, some late-model automotive air-conditioning systems do not use a sight glass.

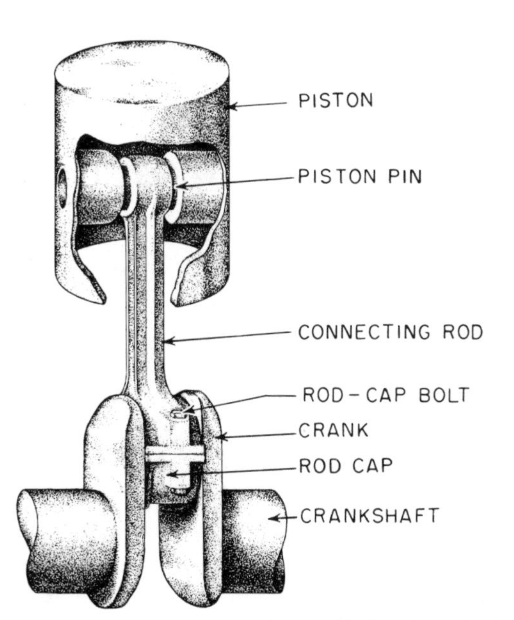

Figure 4 Piston and connecting rod assembled and attached to the crankpin on the crankshaft.

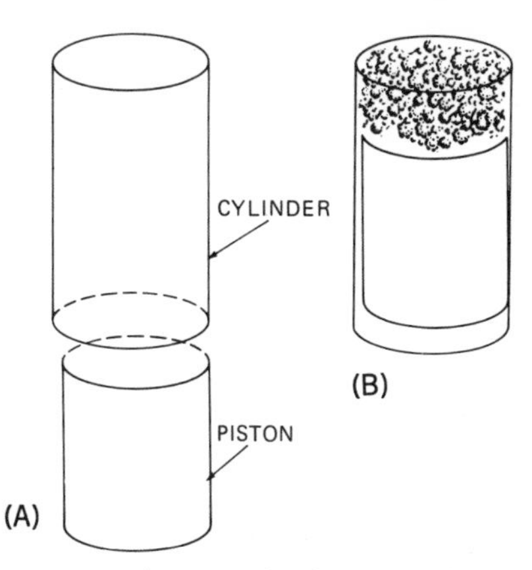

Figure 5 Two views showing what happens when the piston is pushed up into the cylinder. Air is trapped ahead of the piston and compressed. The cylinder is drawn transparent so that the piston can be seen.

■ **8-1-6 Compressor** There are various types of air-conditioning-system compressors. Figure 2 shows a simple version. The purpose of the compressor is to take in low-pressure vapor and send out high-pressure vapor.

The major parts of the compressor are the piston, the connecting rod, the crankshaft, the cylinder, and the valves. The piston, connecting rod, and crankshaft are shown in Fig. 4.

The cylinder is like a tin can with the bottom cut out. The piston is like a slightly smaller tin can that fits snugly into the cylinder (Fig. 5). When the piston is pushed up into the cylinder, it traps air ahead of it. The air is compressed, or squeezed, into a smaller volume. This increases the pressure of the air. Suppose, for example, there are 10 cubic inches (163.87 cc). The pressure is then 150 psi (10.55 kg/cm^2).

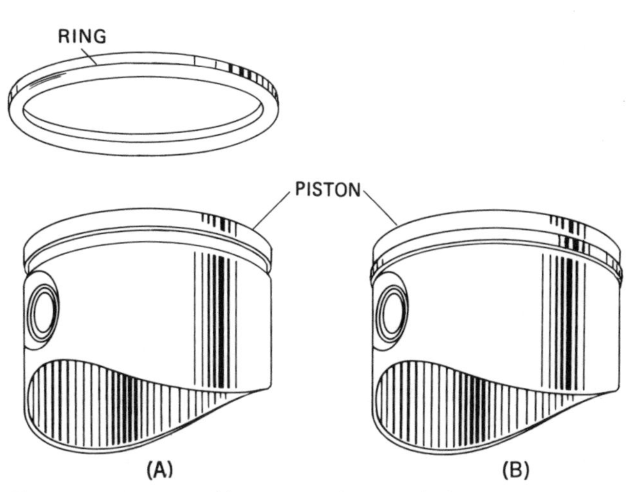

Figure 6 Two views of the piston and ring: with the ring off, and with the ring installed.

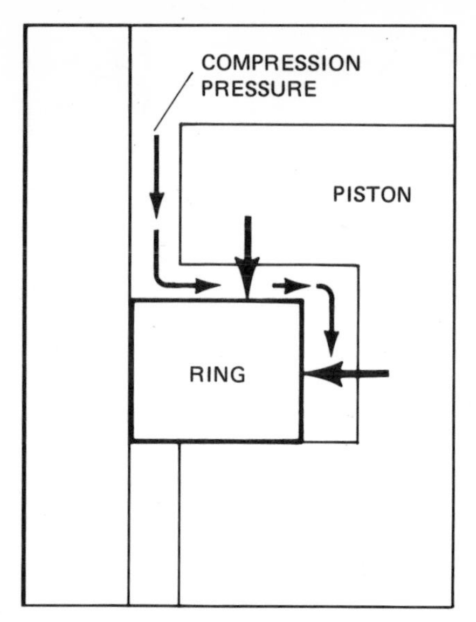

Figure 7 On the upward, or compression, stroke of the piston, the pressure pushes the ring out against the cylinder wall and down against the lower side of the piston-ring groove. Thus, both points are sealed.

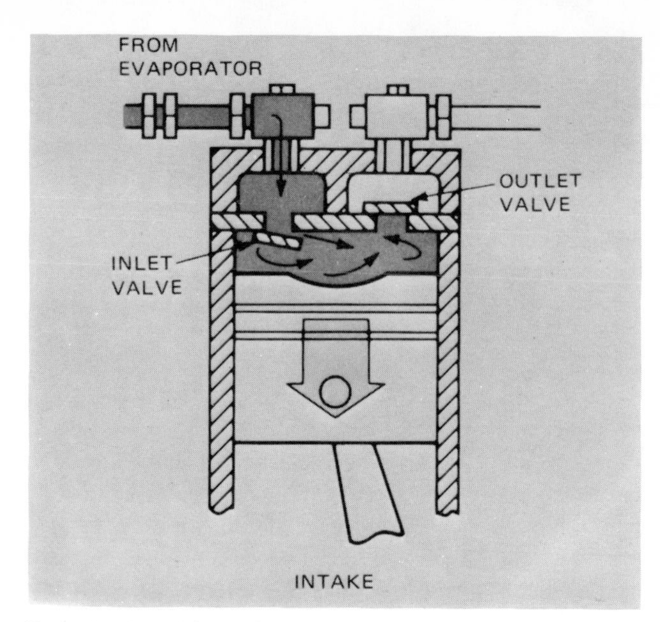

Figure 8 During the intake stroke, the inlet valve opens to allow vapor to flow from the evaporator into the cylinder. *(Ford Motor Company.)*

NOTE: The temperature of the air also goes up as the air is compressed.

The piston, by itself, does not fit very tightly in the cylinder. It has to be loose if it is to slide up and down easily. But if it is too loose, most of the air can leak past it during its upward (compression) movement. Equipping the piston with a piston ring solves this problem.

Figure 6 shows a piston with the ring both off and on. The ring is made of cast iron and is split at one point. To install it, the ring is expanded, and then slid down over the head of the piston and into the groove in the piston. The ring is compressed into its groove when the piston is installed in the cylinder. Then, since it is under tension like a compressed spring, it presses tightly against the cylinder wall. During the compression stroke (or upward movement) of the piston, there is pressure on the side and back of the ring. This presses the ring down against the lower side of the groove and out against the cylinder wall (Fig. 7). This provides a seal at these two places and keeps air from leaking past the piston.

■ 8-1-7 Compressor Action

When the piston moves down, a partial vacuum is produced above the piston. See Fig. 8. The pressure at the top of the evaporator is greater than the pressure above the piston. The evaporator pressure can push the inlet flapper valve down off its seat. At the same time, pressure from the condenser keeps the outlet valve closed. The inlet valve is often called the "suction valve," because it opens as the piston "sucks" vapor into the cylinder. As the piston moves down and the inlet valve opens, vapor from the evaporator moves into the cylinder.

When the piston starts back up again, the conditions are as shown in Fig. 9. That is, the piston compresses the vapor. The increasing pressure on the vapor causes the inlet valve to close and the outlet valve to open. The vapor is then pushed out of the cylinder and into the condenser. Figure 10 shows the actions in a two-cylinder compressor during the intake and compression strokes.

The vapor may be compressed to a pressure as high as 200 psi (14.06 kg/cm²). The hot vapor, under high pressure, then passes through the condenser, losing heat and condensing to a liquid.

■ 8-1-8 Refrigerant

The refrigerant is a very special substance. It is liquid at very low temperature, and a vapor at fairly low temperatures. The refrigerant used in automotive air conditioners boils at −22°F (−30°C) at atmospheric pressures. The ideal refrigerant must be nontoxic (not poisonous), nonflammable, and nonexplosive. It must be reasonably inert (not causing damage to any metal, rubber, or other substances it touches). The refrigerant that has all these desirable qualities is a special substance created by chemists and engineers. It is called "dichlorodifluoromethane" and is commonly known as Freon-12, or R-12 (for Refrigerant-12), or simply Freon. It has the chemical formula CCl_2F_2.

CAUTION: Although R-12 is safe if handled properly, it is dangerous if it is handled carelessly or improperly. If you should get R-12 on your hand, it could freeze the flesh and cause you pain, suffering, and possible permanent injury. If you get R-12 in your eye, it could freeze the eye and cause loss of sight. Also, if R-12 comes in contact with a flame, it turns into a poisonous gas. However, R-12 is a safe refrigerant if handled properly. There is more safety information in the sections on automotive air-conditioning service.

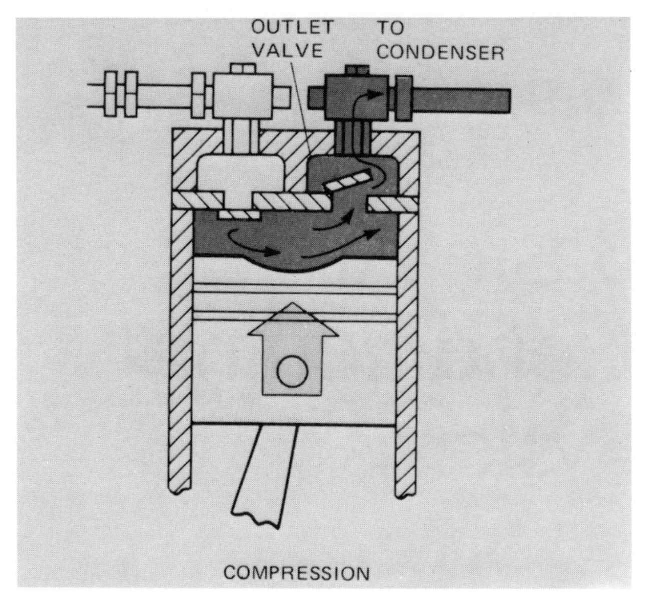

Figure 9 During the compressor stroke, the inlet valve is closed. The outlet valve is open to allow compressed refrigerant vapor to flow to the condenser. *(Ford Motor Company.)*

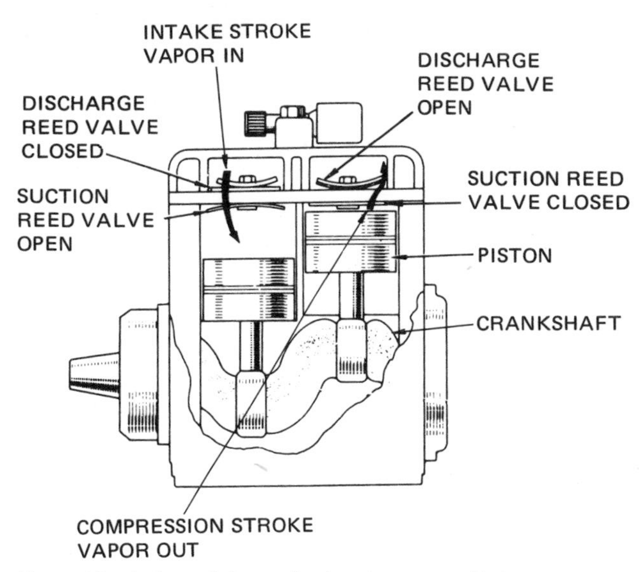

Figure 10 Actions of the reed valves in a two-cylinder compressor during the intake stroke (shown in the left cylinder) and during the compression stroke (shown in the right cylinder). *(Toyota Motor Sales Company, Ltd.)*

■ **8-1-9 Refrigerant Oil** The air-conditioning system needs oil to keep its moving parts and seals lubricated. Since there is no provision for adding oil, it must be put into the air-conditioning refrigerant system when the system is first assembled. Refrigerant oil is a special oil. It is nonfoaming and highly refined, with all impurities, such as wax, moisture, and sulfur, removed.

The compressor has a sump in which a reserve of oil is kept. Oil is pumped from this sump to lubricate the compressor. Some of the oil mixes with the refrigerant and circulates in the system. Therefore, when a part is replaced in the system, it is necessary to measure how much oil the old part has in it. Then, put that same amount of new oil back into the system when the new part is installed.

The oil is supplied in special airtight containers. Refrigerant oil rapidly picks up moisture from the air if the container is left open. The container should be opened only as long as necessary to remove the amount of oil required for adding to the system.

■ **8-1-10 Moisture in the Air-Conditioning System** Even a trace of moisture can cause trouble in an air-conditioning system. Moisture can combine with the metals in the system, producing oxides. Moisture can combine with R-12 and produce a variety of acids. Oxides and acids can cause the valves and compressor to malfunction, and the system to cool poorly. Moisture can also cause the valves to freeze up. This can cause the system to fail.

The receiver (see Fig. 2) contains a bag of a moisture-absorbing chemical. Under normal conditions, this chemical absorbs any moisture that gets into the system when it is first assembled. However, if the system is opened improperly for service, or if leaks develop, then more moisture can enter and cause system failure.

SECTION 8-2 Basic Air-Conditioning Systems

In this section, we describe the basic air-conditioning systems used in automobiles, trucks, and vans. We discuss the types of compressors, valves, and other components used in different systems. In following sections, we discuss specific systems and describe their operation in detail. Many automotive air-conditioning systems include both a heater and an air conditioner.

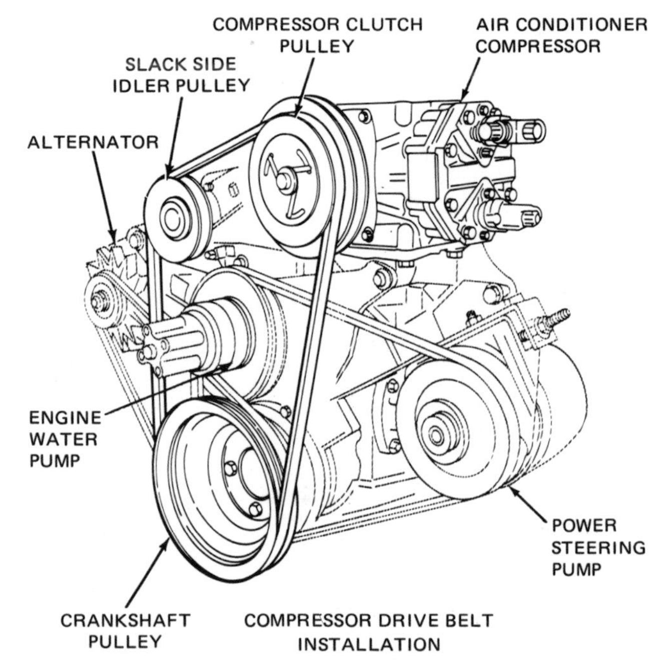

Figure 1 Belt drive of the air-conditioner compressor and other belt-driven accessories. *(Ford Motor Company.)*

■ **8-2-1 Types of Systems** There are two basic types of automotive air-conditioner systems. In one system, the compressor is turned on or off automatically by signals from a temperature sensor in the passenger compartment. This system is called a "cycling-clutch system." In the other system, the compressor runs continuously when the dash controls are set at the A/C, or air-conditioning, position. This system is called the "evaporator-pressure-control-valve" system. Both systems use a magnetic clutch which engages or disengages the compressor to suit the cooling requirements.

■ **8-2-2 Magnetic Clutch** The compressor is driven by a belt from the engine crankshaft pulley (Fig. 1). The com-

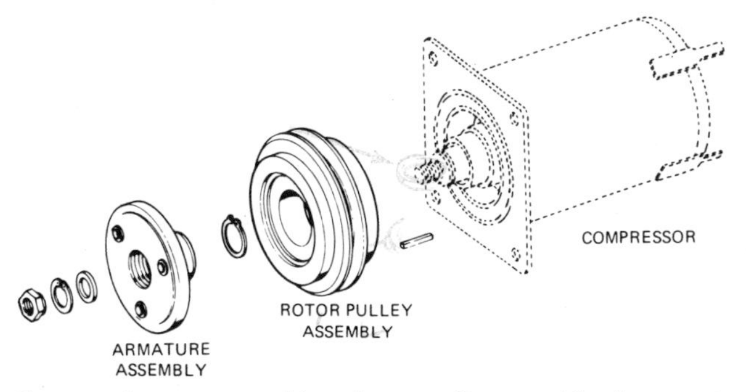

Figure 2 Armature assembly and outer-pulley assembly of a magnetic clutch. *(Warner Electric Brake and Clutch Company.)*

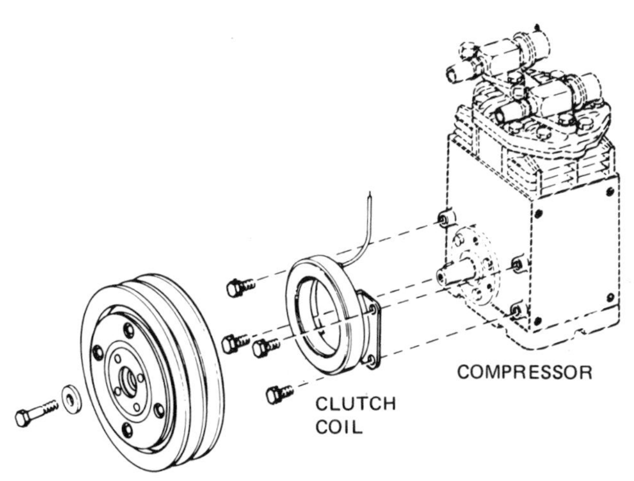

Figure 3 Clutch coil and outer-pulley assembly for a magnetic clutch. *(Warner Electric Brake and Clutch Company.)*

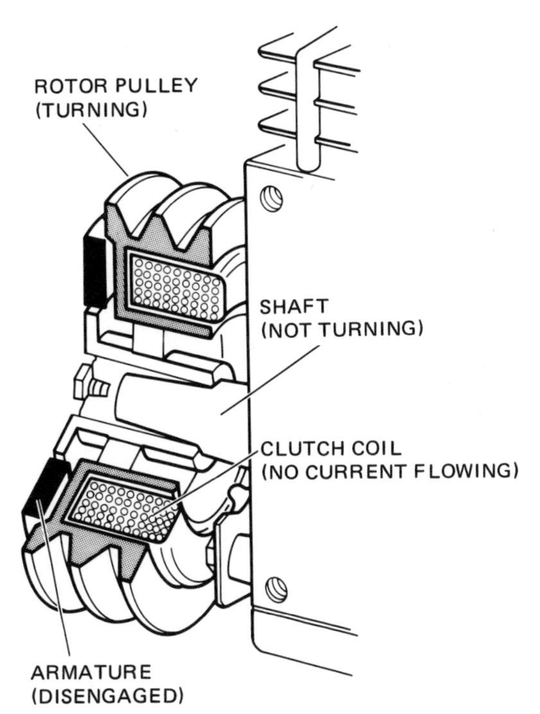

Figure 4 Cutaway view of magnetic clutch in the OFF position. *(Warner Electric Brake and Clutch Company.)*

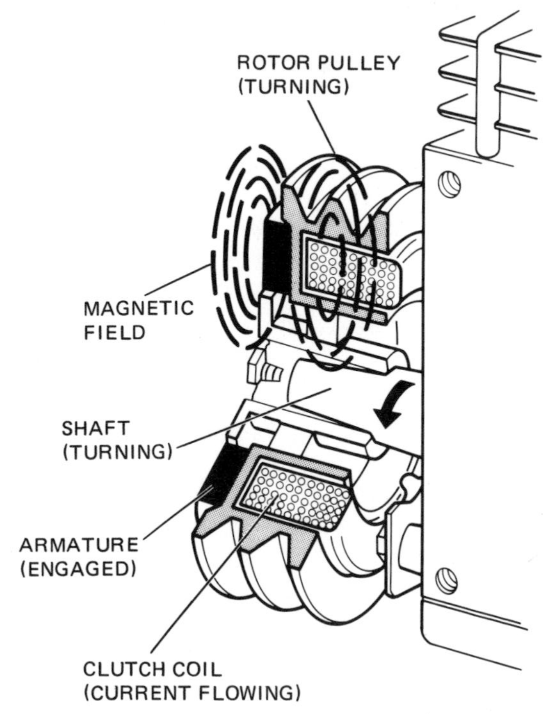

Figure 5 Cutaway view of magnetic clutch in the ON position. *(Warner Electric Brake and Clutch Company.)*

pressor pulley is really two pulleys in one. The outer pulley is driven by a belt from the engine crankshaft pulley. The inner pulley is called the "armature assembly" (Fig. 2). It is attached to the compressor shaft by a key or by screws. There is a third part to the magnetic clutch—the clutch coil (Fig. 3).

Whenever the engine is running, the outer pulley is turning, driven by the belt. The pulley is mounted on ball bearings so it can turn independently. When no cooling is required, the pulley spins freely on the ball bearings. The armature and compressor shaft do not turn. See Fig. 4.

When the air-conditioner control system calls for cooling, the armature and compressor shaft turn together. Here is how it happens: The clutch coil is mounted on the compressor, as shown in Fig. 3. This coil has many turns of wire. When it is connected to the car battery, current from the battery flows

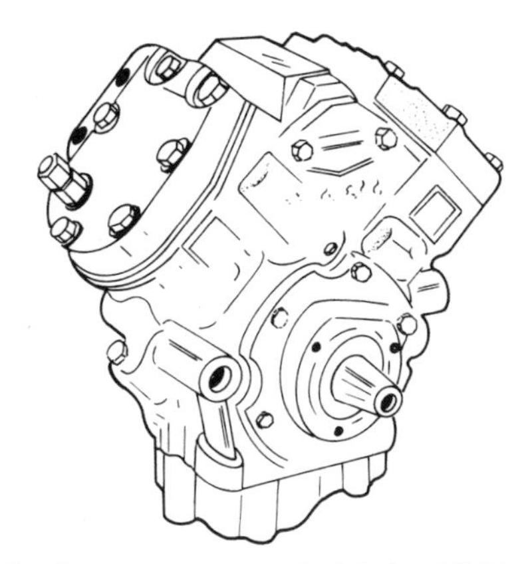

Figure 6 Chrysler compressor. *(United Delco Division of General Motors Corporation.)*

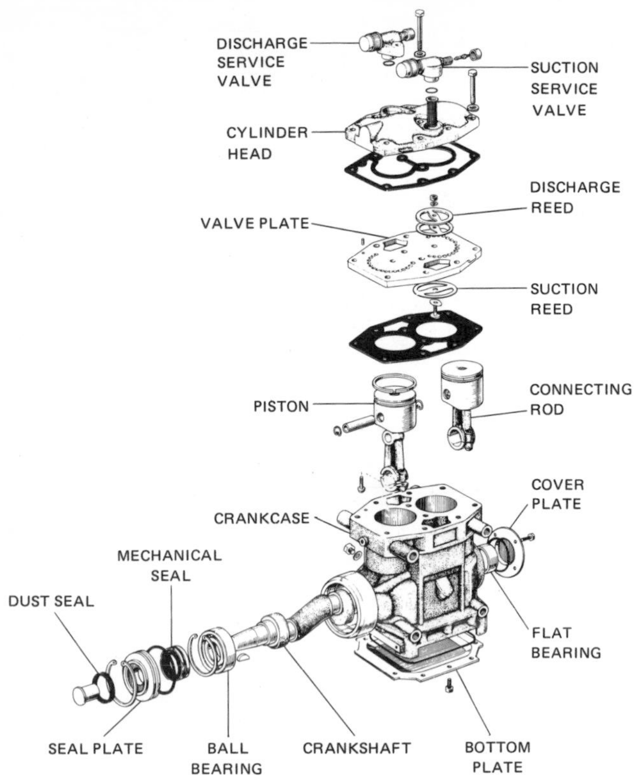

Figure 7 Exploded view of a square two-cylinder compressor used on imported cars. *(Toyota Motor Sales Company, Ltd.)*

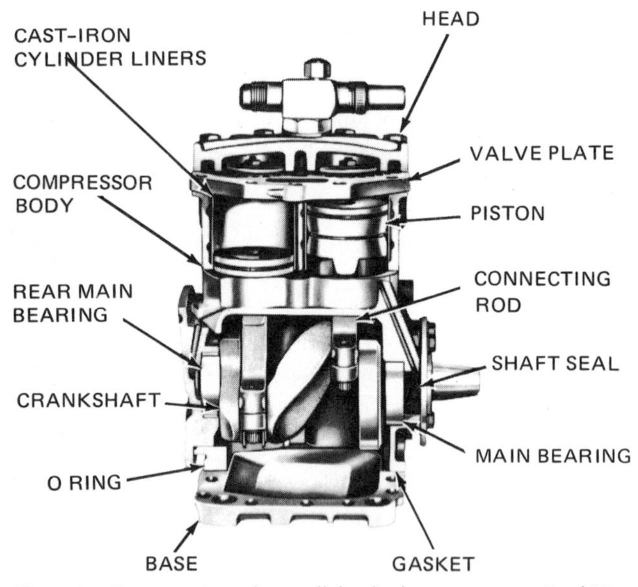

Figure 8 Cutaway view of a parallel-cylinder compressor. *(Ford Motor Company.)*

through the clutch coil. Current flowing through through a coil of wire produces a magnetic field.

In the magnetic clutch, this magnetic field "locks" the armature to the pulley. See Fig. 5. Both are made of iron. The magnetic field from the clutch coil permeates (goes through) both the armature and the pulley. The result is that the magnetism

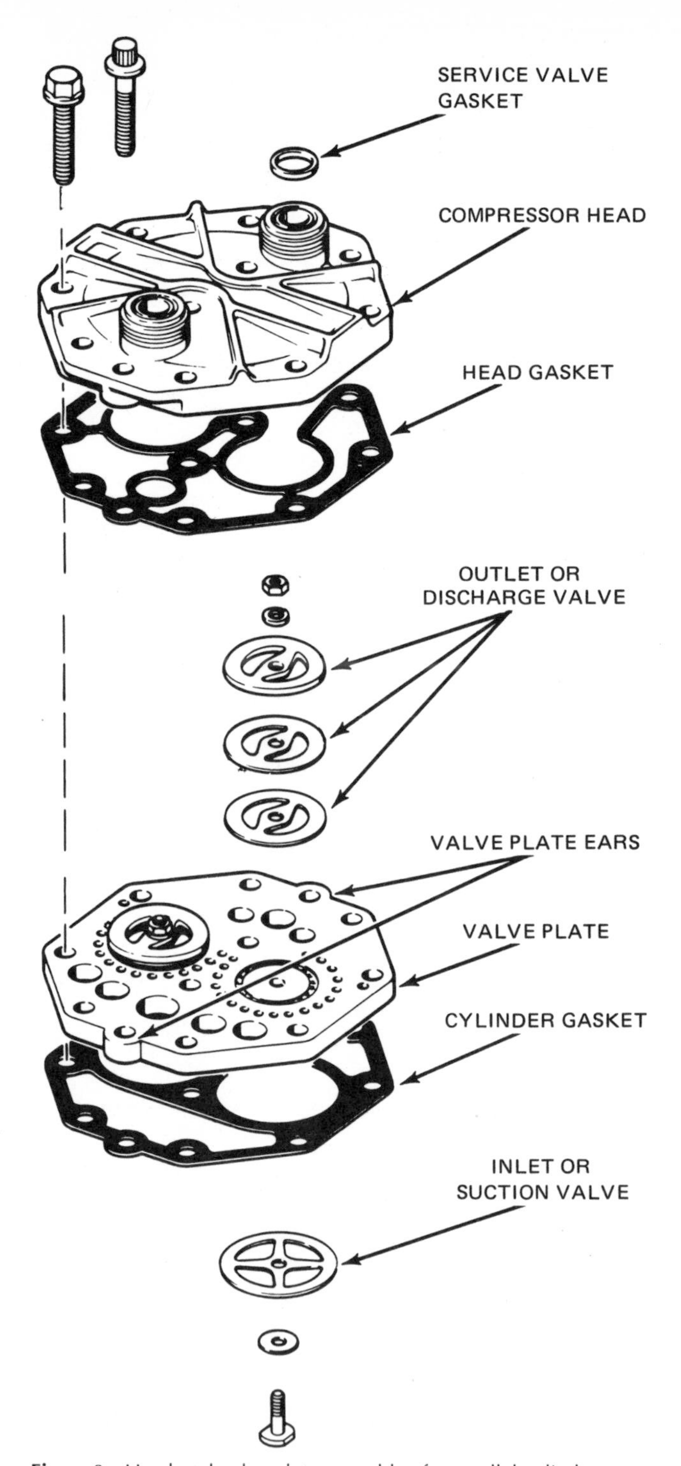

Figure 9 Head-and-valve-plate assembly of a parallel-cylinder compressor, with valves. *(American Motors Corporation.)*

locks the two together, so both turn together. The compressor shaft turns, and cooling takes place.

■ 8-2-3 Types of Compressors

From the outside, there appear to be three general types of automotive air-conditioner compressors: round (Fig. 2), square (Fig. 3), and V-shaped (Fig. 6). All compressors for automotive air-condi-

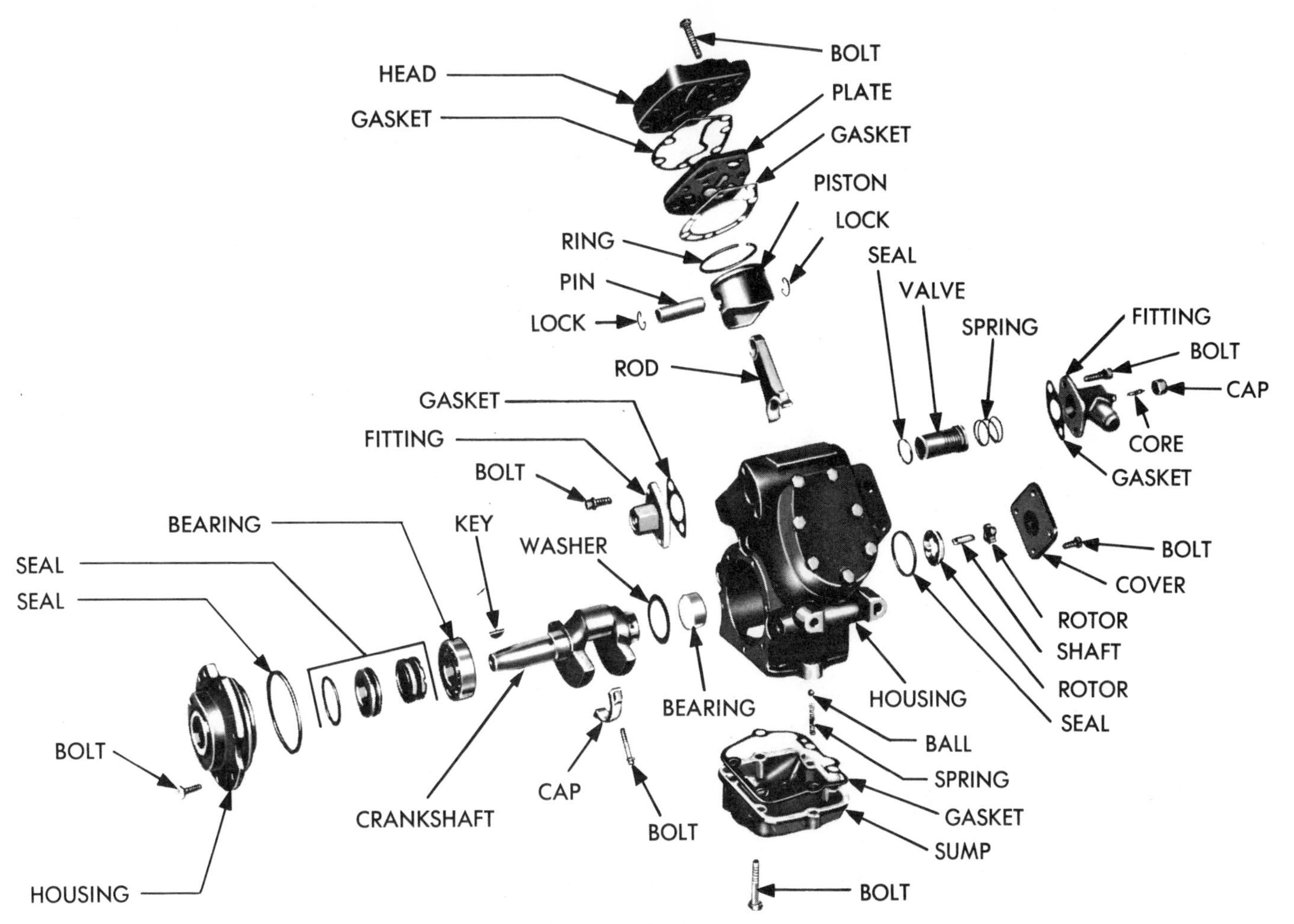

Figure 10 Disassembled view of a V-type compressor. *(Chrysler Corporation.)*

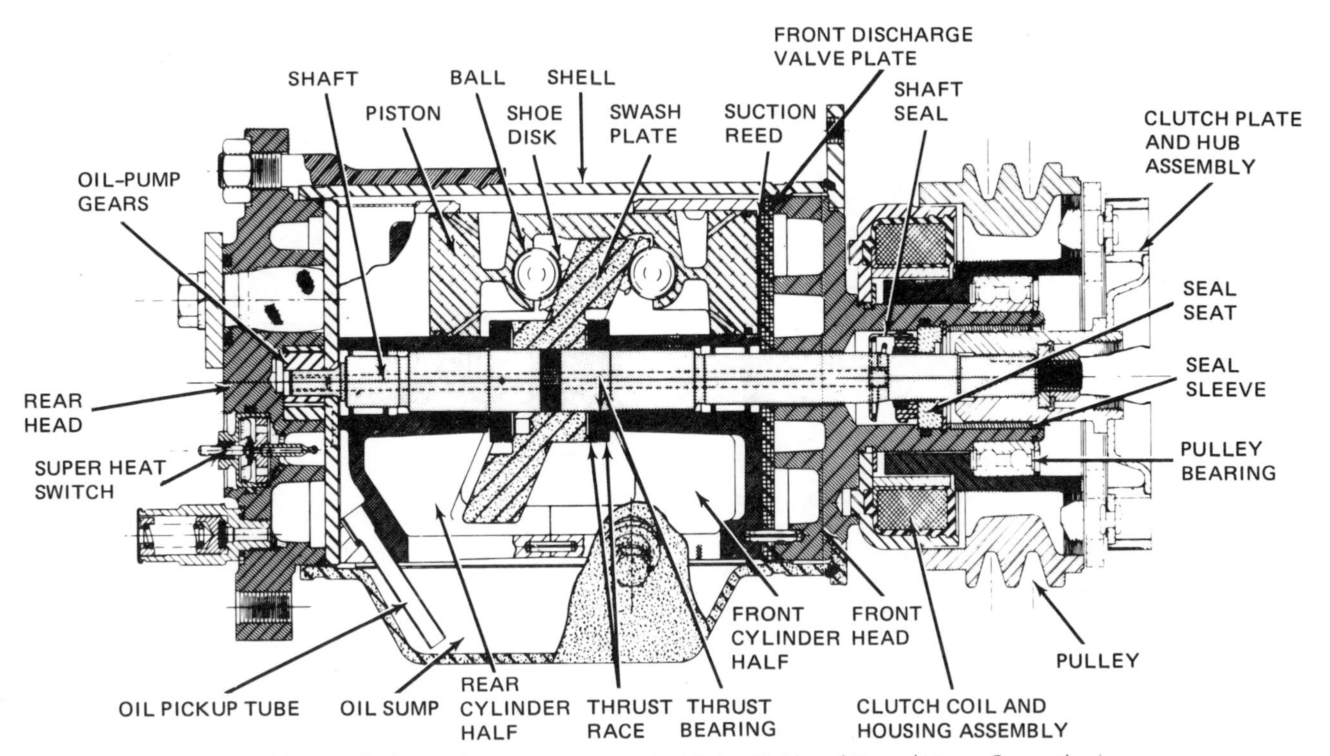

Figure 11 Sectional view of the six-cylinder Frigidaire compressor. *(United Delco Division of General Motors Corporation.)*

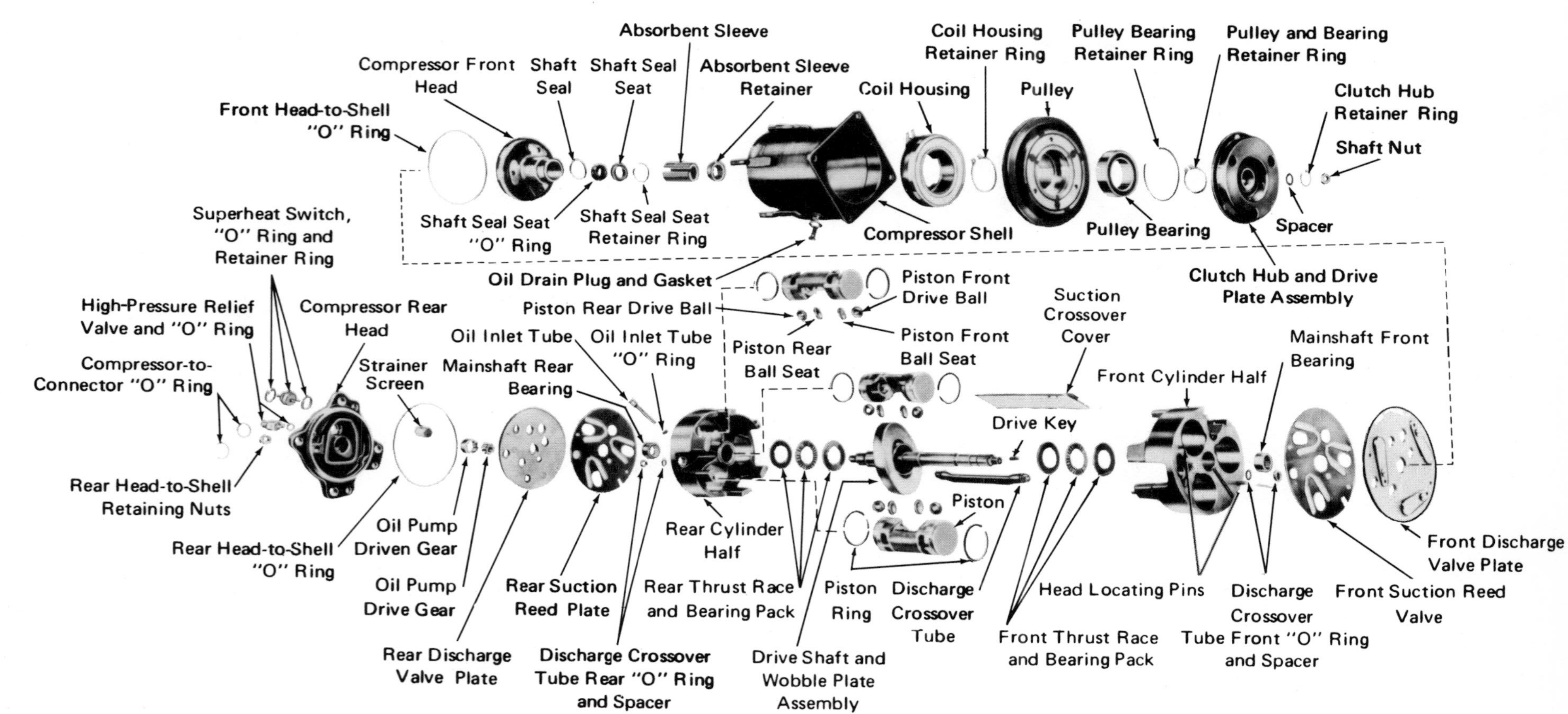

Figure 12 Disassembled view of the Frigidaire compressor. *(Chevrolet Motor Division of General Motors Corporation.)*

tioning systems have two or more pistons, rather than the single piston shown in Part 8, Sec. 1.

1. TECUMSEH AND YORK COMPRESSOR Figure 3 shows this type of compressor. Figure 7 shows an exploded view of a similar compressor. It has two pistons working in parallel cylinders to a crankshaft with two crankpins. Figure 8 is a cutaway view of this type of compressor. The two pistons, in effect, work alternately. That is, while one piston is going down to pull in refrigerant vapor from the evaporator, the other piston is moving up to push hot, high-pressure vapor into the condenser. Two separate pistons operating in this manner give a steadier flow of refrigerant vapor than a single piston. Also, the compressor is better balanced, so that it vibrates less when it runs.

Figure 9 shows the valve plate and compressor head in a disassembled view. Note the locations of the inlet and outlet valves. These valves are called by other names by various car manufacturers. The valves shown removed from the valve plate are for only one of the two cylinders. Each cylinder has two valves.

Figure 1 shows how this type of compressor is mounted on the engine.

2. CHRYSLER COMPRESSOR Figure 6 shows this type of compressor. Its two cylinders are set at an angle to form a V. Each cylinder has its own piston and connecting rod. Both connecting rods are attached to the single crankpin on the crankshaft. Figure 10 shows this compressor in a partly disassembled view. Only one of the two cylinders has been disassembled in the picture. Note the oil sump at the bottom of the picture.

3. ROUND (FRIGIDAIRE) SIX-CYLINDER COMPRESSOR This compressor, shown in Fig. 2, is made by the Frigidaire Division of General Motors. It is used by the car divisions of General Motors and by other car manufacturers.

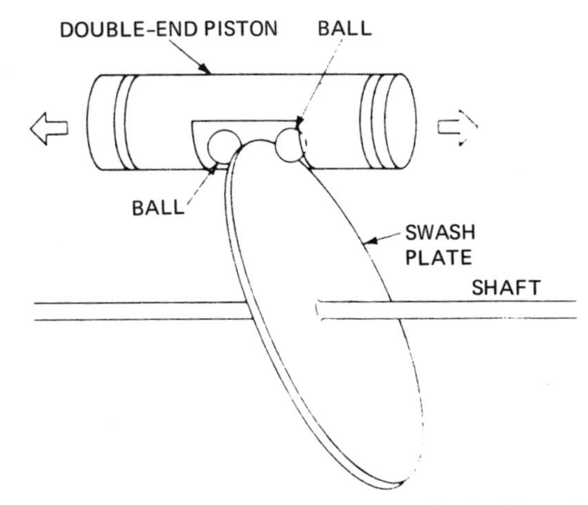

Figure 13 As a swash plate wobbles, it causes the double-ended piston to move back and forth in its cylinders.

Figure 11 is a sectional view of the compressor. Figure 12 is a disassembled view of the compressor. This compressor has six cylinders and three double-acting pistons that are, in effect, six pistons. The pistons are moved back and forth in the cylinders by a swash plate. It is also called a "wobble plate" because it does just that. The plate wobbles as the shaft rotates (Fig. 13).

The pistons fit around the plate as shown in Fig. 13. They ride on balls, on both sides of the swash plate, and cause the pistons to move back and forth. The three double-ended pistons work in three cylinders. Thus, there are actually six pistons in all. As the pistons move back and forth in their cylinders, they pump refrigerant vapor from the evaporator to the condenser.

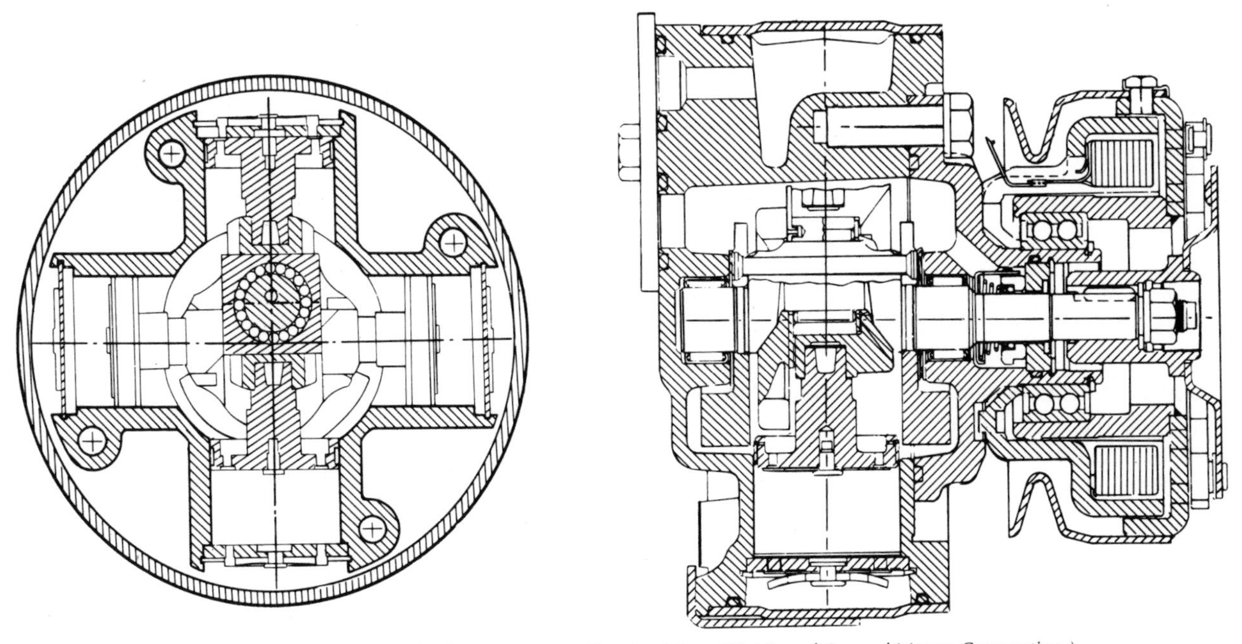

Figure 14 Sectional views of the R-4 four-cylinder compressor. *(Pontiac Motor Division of General Motors Corporation.)*

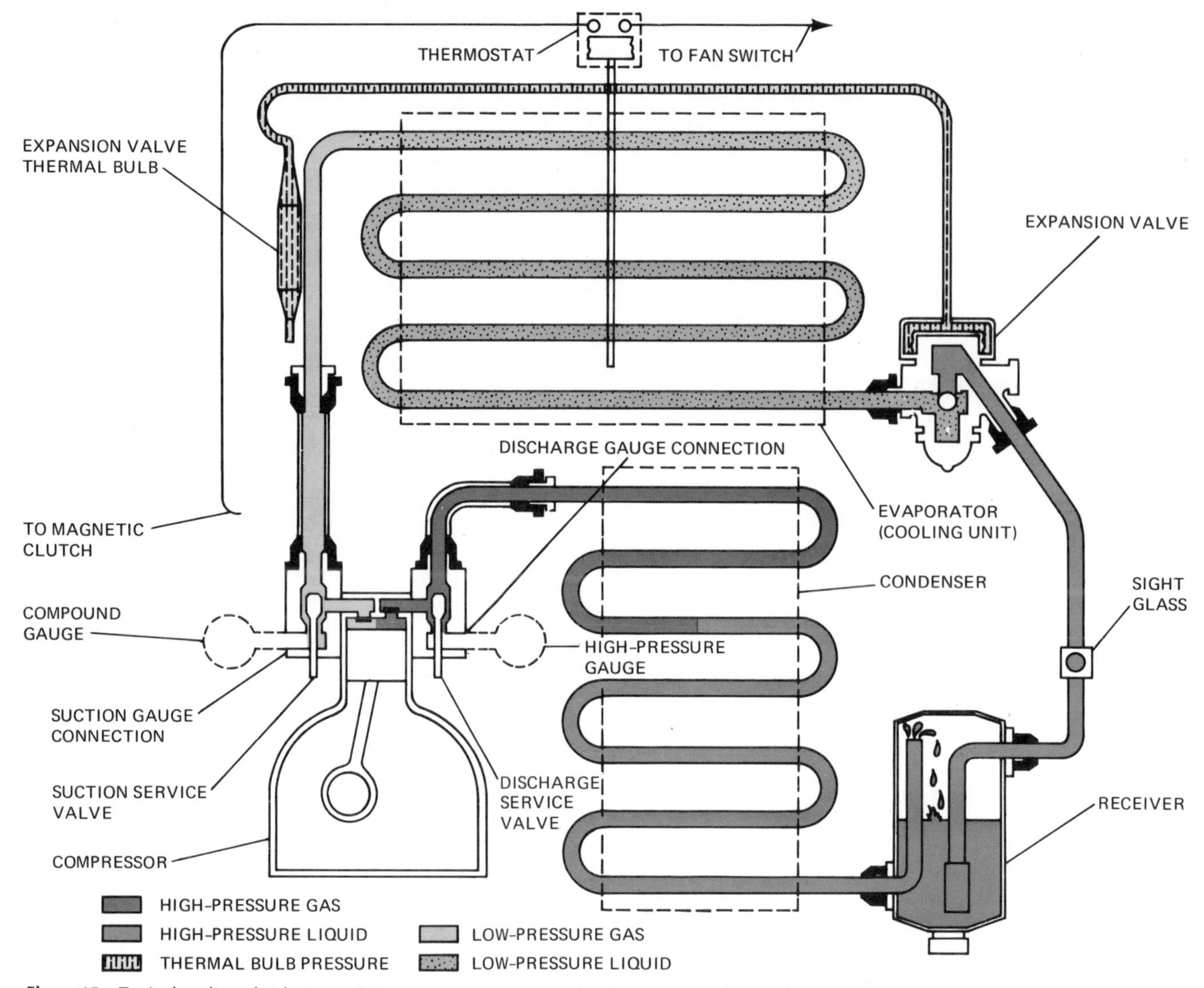

Figure 15 Typical cycling-clutch air-conditioner arrangement. *(United Delco Division of General Motors Corporation.)*

There is an oil sump in the bottom of the compressor (Fig. 11). A gear-type pump (left in Fig. 11) circulates oil from this sump through the compressor. Some oil also travels through the system along with the refrigerant vapor and liquid.

4. ROUND FOUR-CYLINDER COMPRESSOR This compressor, known as the R-4 type, has four cylinders set radially around an eccentric on the compressor shaft (Fig. 14). As the shaft rotates, the four pistons are moved back and forth in their cylinders. Refrigerant vapor enters the compressor through a connection at the rear. Each piston has a reed valve in its top. During the inward motion of a piston, the reed valve opens to allow refrigerant vapor to pass through the valve top and into the outer end of the cylinder. Then, on the outward stroke of the piston, the reed valve is closed by the developing pressure. The refrigerant is, therefore, compressed. This pressure causes a reed valve in the valve plate to open. The valve plate closes off the outer end of the cylinder. The refrigerant vapor, under pressure, is forced out of the cylinder through the opened reed valve in the valve plate, and into the space surrounding the cylinders. This space is connected to the condenser. On the return, or inward, stroke of the piston, the reduced pressure in the cylinder causes the reed valve in the valve plate to close. At the same time, the reed valve in the piston top opens to admit more refrigerant vapor into the cylinder. The cycle is repeated continuously. Thus, each of the four cylinders draws in refrigerant vapor, compresses it, and sends it to the condenser.

■ 8-2-4 Cycling-Clutch Air-Conditioning System

The most common use for cycling-clutch air-conditioners is in "hang-on" or field-installed units. These units are designed for the automotive aftermarket to make field installation as easy as possible. For example, the evaporator, thermostatic expansion valve, and thermostatic control valve are all contained in a single assembly that is installed under the car dash.

In the cycling-clutch system, the clutch is repeatedly applied and released (cycled) to control the flow of refrigerant in the

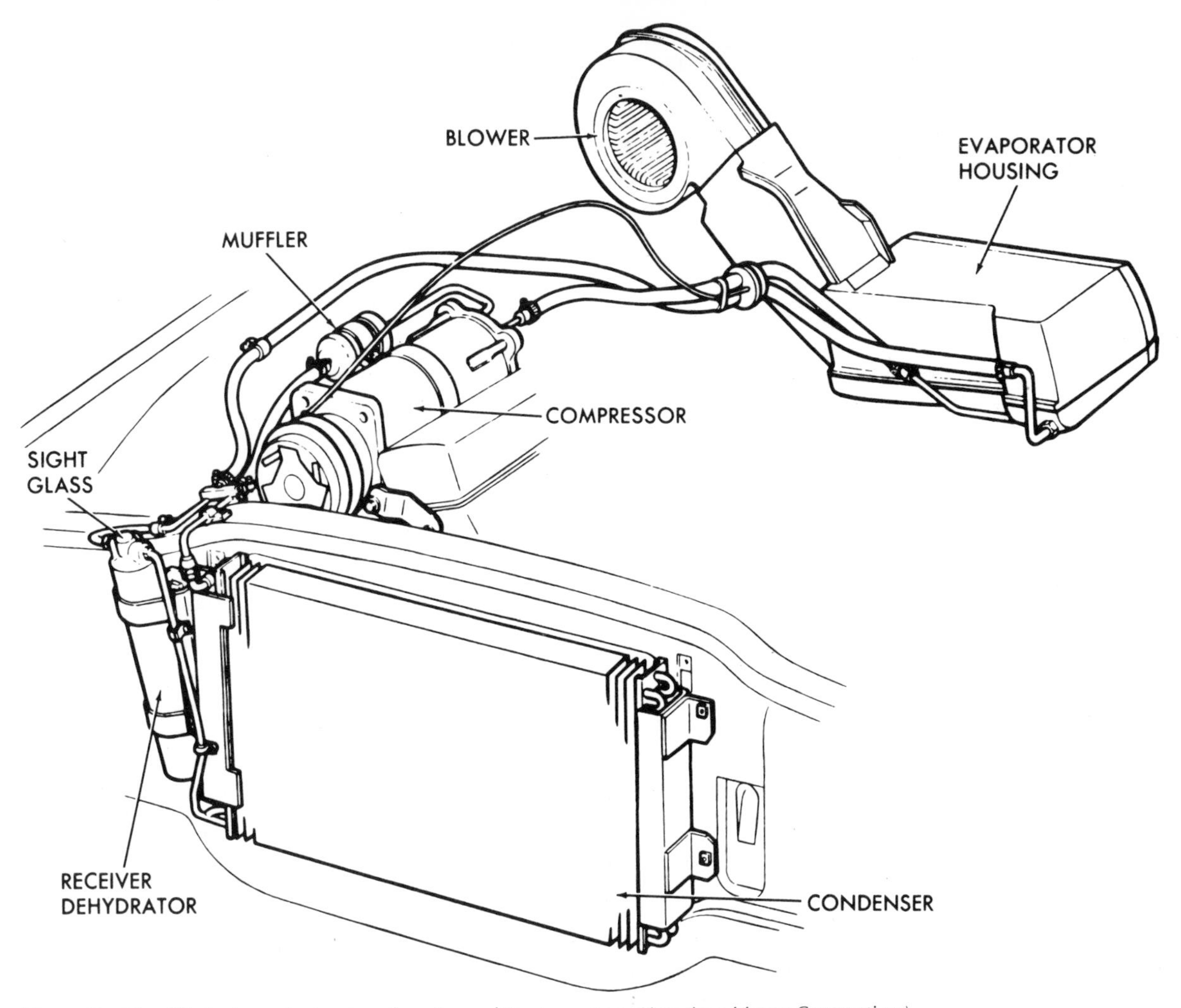

Figure 16 Simplified schematic drawing of an air-conditioning system. *(American Motors Corporation.)*

system. See Fig. 15. Figure 16 shows how the components are located in the automobile. Notice that the condenser is located in front of the car radiator. The cooled and liquefied refrigerant flows from the bottom of the condenser to the receiver-dehydrator. From there the liquid refrigerant flows to the evaporator, where the refrigerant evaporates. When the compressor is operating, the refrigerant vapor flows from the evaporator to the compressor. In the compressor, the vapor is compressed (and heated). Then the vapor is forced from the compressor to the condenser. Meanwhile, the blower pulls air through the evaporator and sends it, cooled and dried, to the passenger compartment of the car.

On the side of some compressors, there is a muffler mounted. See Fig. 16. Its purpose is to smooth out the surges of refrigerant vapor coming from the compressor. This reduces the otherwise annoying compressor noise.

The cycling-clutch system is controlled by a thermostatic switch located in the passenger compartment or in the evaporator. When the temperature goes too high, the switch closes contacts that connect the magnetic clutch to the battery. This energizes the clutch coil, and the compressor operates. When the temperature drops to the thermostat setting, the contacts

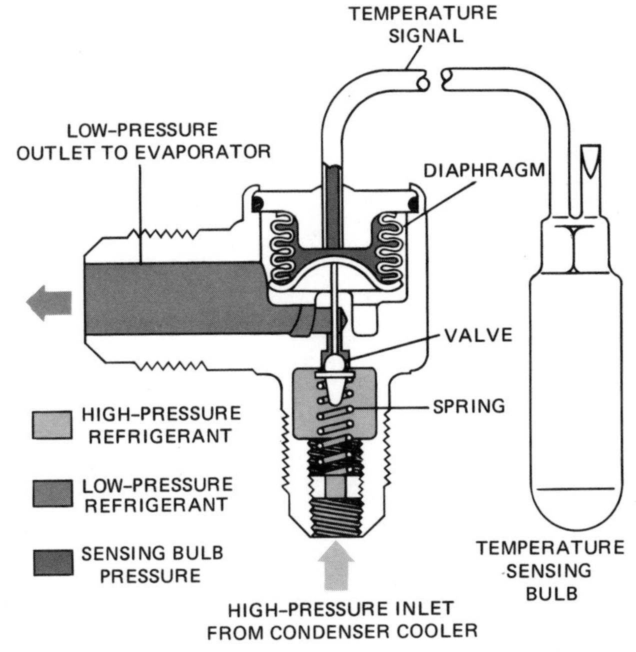

Figure 17 Sectional view of an expansion valve. *(Ford Motor Company.)*

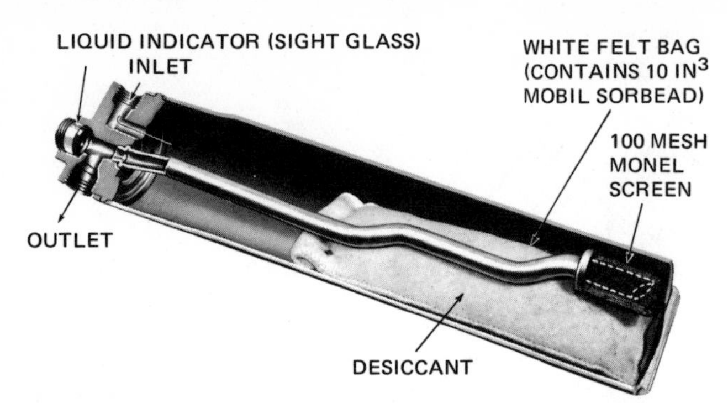

Figure 18 Sectional view of a receiver-dehydrator assembly. *(Buick Motor Division of General Motors Corporation.)*

open. This disconnects the magnetic clutch from the battery, and the compressor stops operating. In normal operation, the compressor comes on and goes off, or cycles, frequently.

■ 8-2-5 Expansion-Valve Operation The system includes an expansion valve (see Figs. 2 in Part 8, Sec. 1, and 17 in this section). This valve controls the flow of refrigerant from the condenser to the evaporator (actually to the receiver). Figure 17 is a schematic view of the expansion-valve assembly. The temperature-sensing bulb is at the top or outlet tube of the evaporator. It senses the temperature of the vaporized refrigerant leaving the evaporator. If this temperature goes too high, the evaporator itself has warmed up too much. It is then not sufficiently cooling the air passing through it. When this happens, the gas inside the bulb expands enough to force the diaphragm down in the valve. The diaphragm pushes down on a rod that pushes the spring-loaded ball off its seat. When the ball is pushed down, high-pressure liquid refrigerant can pass through the valve to the evaporator.

The evaporator, now receiving more liquid refrigerant, increases its cooling activity. This lowers the temperature of the vaporized refrigerant leaving the evaporator. This lowered temperature causes the gas inside the bulb to contract and to release the pressure on the diaphragm. The spring now pushes the ball back up into the ball seat, shutting off the flow of refrigerant to the evaporator.

In actual operation, the valve stays slightly open. It passes just enough refrigerant to keep the evaporator at a relatively even temperature.

■ 8-2-6 Receiver-Dehydrator Assembly The receiver-dehydrator (Fig. 18) ensures that there is a solid column of liquid refrigerant supplying the thermostatic expansion

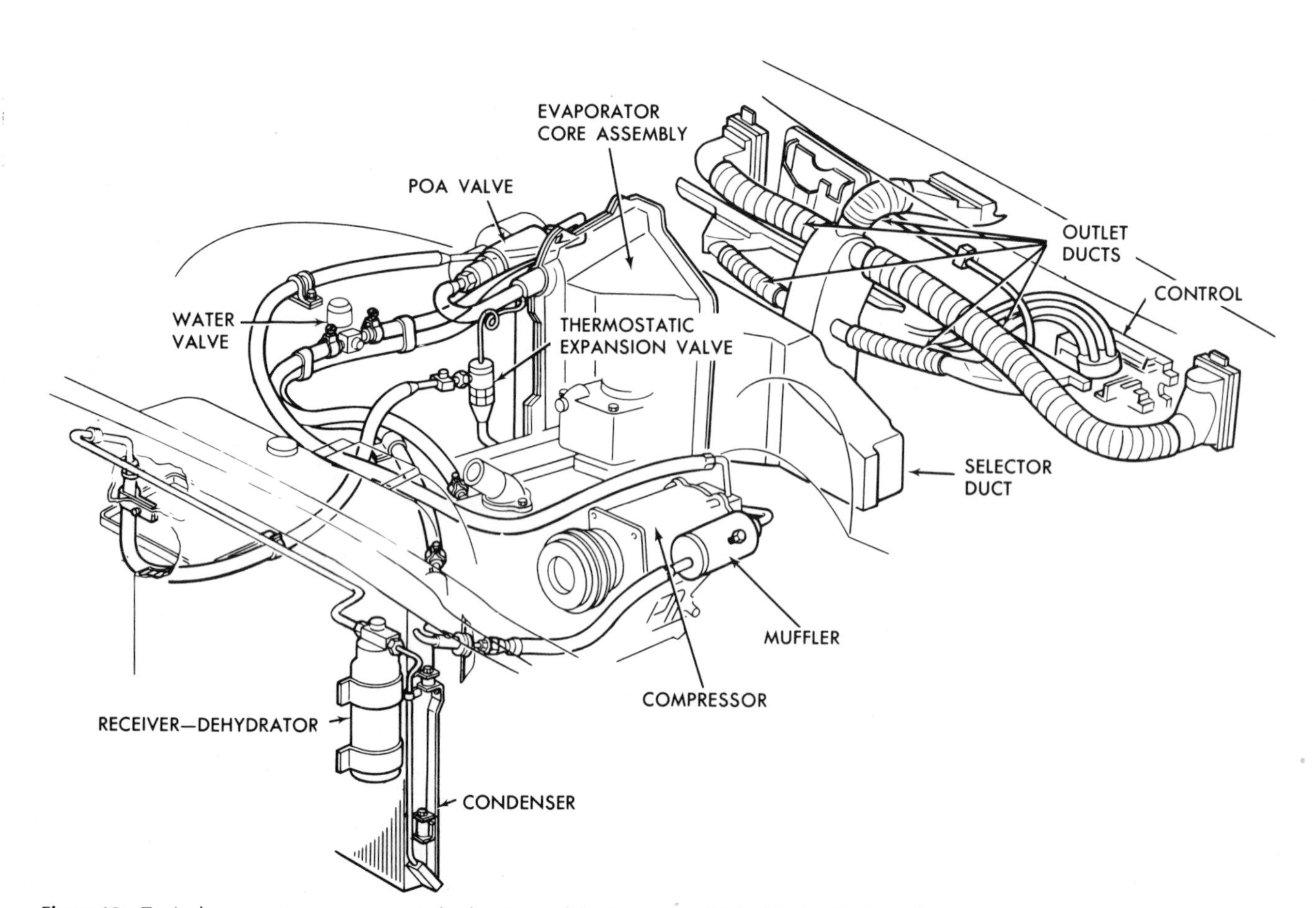

Figure 19 Typical evaporator-pressure-control-valve air-conditioning system. *(United Delco Division of General Motors Corporation.)*

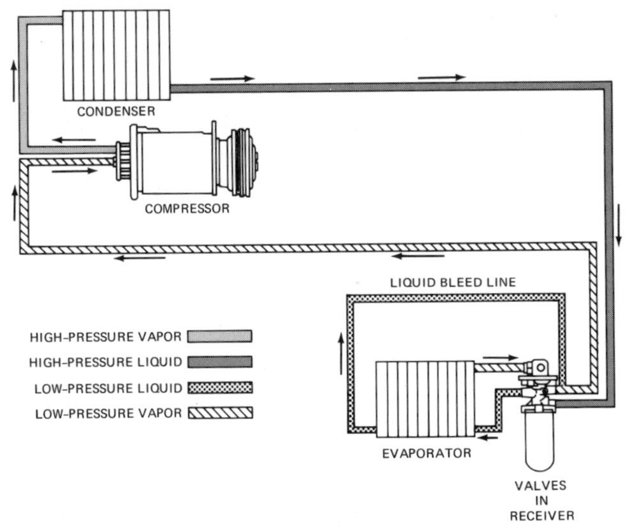

Figure 20 Basic refrigeration layout of an air-conditioning system with valves in receiver (VIR). *(Chevrolet Motor Division of General Motors Corporation.)*

valve. Any vapor that leaves the condenser gathers at the top of the receiver. The receiver outlet tube extends to the bottom of the receiver. The bottom of the tube has a filter screen. It is installed to remove any dirt particles that might have gotten into the system during original assembly. The receiver also contains some water-absorbent material (in the bag to the right of Fig. 18, labeled "desiccant"). This material removes any moisture that gets into the system during original assembly or during service.

■ 8-2-7 Sight Glass

At the top of the receiver-dehydrator, there is a sight glass, or liquid indicator (Fig. 18). This device is for the diagnosis of troubles. If bubbles or foam (or no bubbles at all) can be seen in the glass, then something is wrong. Use of the sight glass in trouble diagnosis is covered in ■8-8-2 and 8-8-3. However, some air-conditioners on late-model cars do not have a sight glass.

■ 8-2-8 Evaporator-Pressure-Control-Valve System

This system is widely used as a factory option. That is, it is installed at the factory during the original assembly of the car. Figure 19 shows how the system fits into a car. Note that this system contains the same components as the cycling-clutch system. They are the compressor, the condenser with receiver-dehydrator, the thermostatic expansion valve, and the evaporator, along with a blower to circulate air through the evaporator. The system has several outlet ducts spaced along the dash. There is also an additional valve, called the pilot-operated absolute (POA) valve, in the system.

The compressor in an evaporator-pressure-control-valve system operates continuously, as long as the dash controls are set for the A/C, or air-conditioning, mode. In this mode, the control contacts connect the magnetic clutch to the battery. The evaporator-outlet-air temperature is automatically con-

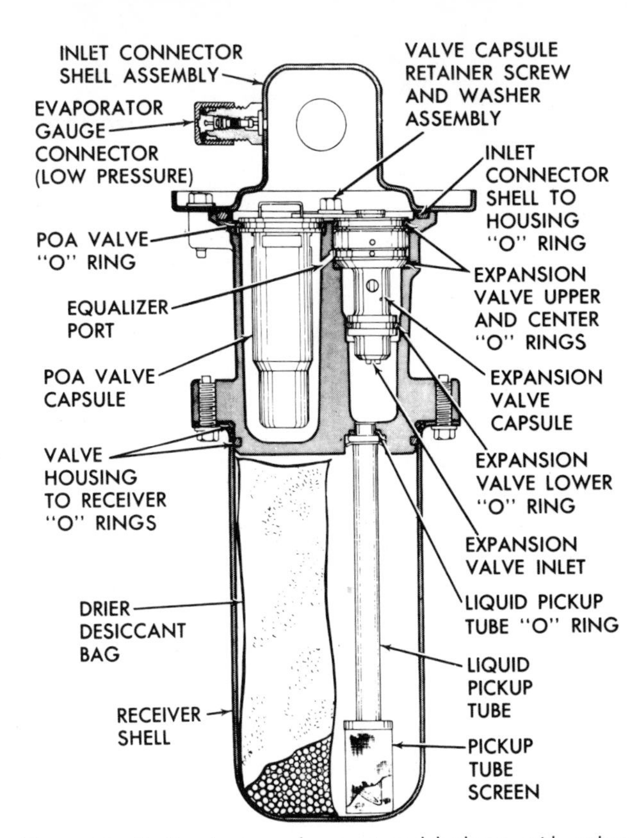

Figure 21 Sectional view of a receiver-dehydrator with valves. *(Chevrolet Motor Division of General Motors Corporation.)*

trolled by the POA valve, which is described in ■8-2-11. Air continually circulates between the passenger compartment of the car and the evaporator. However, the amount of cooling that the air gets depends on the actions of the control valves.

Figure 20 shows the basic components of the system. The compressor, condenser, receiver-dehydrator, and evaporator are the same as in the cycling-clutch system. In the system shown in Fig. 20, the valves have been put into the receiver-dehydrator. This is somewhat different from the system shown in Fig. 19, where the valves are outside the receiver-dehydrator. Both arrangements have been used. The system shown in Fig. 20, with the valves inside the receiver-dehydrator, is used in many General Motors cars, and by other automotive manufacturers.

■ 8-2-9 Valves in Receiver (VIR)

The valves-in-receiver, or VIR, assembly contains the thermostatic expansion valve, a second valve called the "POA suction throttling valve," the receiver-dehydrator, and the sight glass. Figure 21 shows the assembly in a sectional view.

Figure 22 shows the flow of liquid and vaporized refrigerant through the assembly. Note that there are four connections to the VIR assembly. Connection 1, to the center right, runs from the condenser. Liquid refrigerant enters the VIR assembly through this connection. The refrigerant then moves down past the dehydrator bag and up, through the pickup tube, to the expansion valve. The expansion valve controls the flow of re-

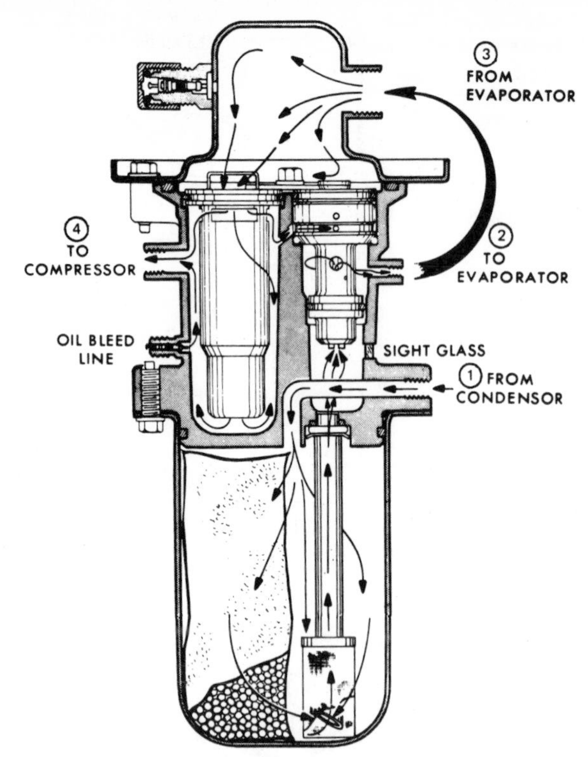

Figure 22 Refrigerant flow through the receiver-dehydrator. *(Cadillac Motor Car Division of General Motors Corporation.)*

frigerant to the evaporator to suit operating requirements. The liquid refrigerant flows out connection 1 to the evaporator. The vaporized refrigerant then returns from the evaporator and enters the VIR assembly through connection 3. It passes through and around the POA valve and then flows to the compressor through connection 4.

The purpose of the two valves is twofold. First, to feed the right amount of liquid refrigerant to the evaporator, to provide the required cooling. Second, to control the flow of refrigerant vapor out of the evaporator, to maintain an evaporator pressure of about 30 psi (2.11 kg/cm²). At this pressure, the evaporator coil stays about 32°F (0° C). Below this temperature, the water that collects on the evaporator would freeze. The frost would block the flow of air through the evaporator and keep it from cooling properly.

■ **8-2-10 VIR Expansion Valve** This valve is shown in Fig. 23 in both the closed and opened positions. The valve does the same job as the externally mounted valve in Fig. 17. That is, it controls the flow of liquid refrigerant to the evaporator. However, as you can see by comparing Figs. 17 and 23, the two valves are quite different in construction. The VIR expansion valve does not have a temperature-sensing bulb and tube. The upper end of the expansion valve is exposed directly to the refrigerant vapor coming from the evaporator, so no sensing bulb is needed.

During the original assembly of the valve, the space above the power diaphragm is filled with a carefully measured amount of refrigerant. The opening is then sealed with the steel ball. This refrigerant senses the temperature of refrigerant vapor entering the VIR expansion valve from the evaporator. Figure 22 shows how the vapor coming in at connection 3 flows over the top of the expansion valve.

The charcoal and the filter keep the refrigerant clean and in pure condition. They remove any foreign material from the original refrigerant charge.

The sealed-in refrigerant acts on the diaphragm from above. It tends to push down on the diaphragm disk, the operating pin, and the valve seat. The round ball on the end of the pin is called the "valve seat" in this assembly (Fig. 23). The adjusting spring opposes this downward push on the valve seat.

As the temperature of the refrigerant vapor from the evaporator goes up, the pressure above the power diaphragm increases. As the temperature of the refrigerant vapor from the evaporator goes down, the pressure above the power diaphragm is reduced. The temperature of the vaporized refrigerant coming from the evaporator controls the pressure on the power diaphragm.

When the compressor first starts, the pressures in the system have equalized. That is, the condenser pressure has dropped, and the evaporator pressure has increased. This allows the compressor to start up easily, without operating against a high condenser pressure. If the pressure differential remained high, it would put a considerable start-up strain on the compressor and drive belt.

The expansion valve is closed when the compressor starts. It has been closed by a combination of the adjusting spring and the evaporator pressure. The evaporator pressure is transmitted to the bottom of the power diaphragm through the equalizer tube. You can see the equalizer tube in Figs. 21 and 22. It connects the POA-valve cavity with the expansion-valve equalizer port (near the top right in Fig. 23). The evaporator pressure in a warm, inoperative system can be higher than 70 psi (4.92 kg/cm²). This pressure is higher than the pressure above the diaphragm (produced by the sealed-in refrigerant vapor), and so the valve is closed.

With the expansion valve closed, the compressor builds up pressure when it starts. The compressor begins to send pressurized refrigerant vapor to the condenser. There, it condenses and flows, in liquid form, to the receiver. It flows in through connection 1 (see Fig. 22). It begins to collect in the receiver. Meantime, the evaporator pressure has fallen because the compressor has taken refrigerant vapor from it. As the evaporator pressure is reduced, the pressure below the diaphragm in the expansion valve is also reduced. (This pressure is evaporator pressure introduced through the equalizer port.)

The pressure above the power diaphragm is the pressure of the relatively warm sealed-in refrigerant. As the pressure below the diaphragm is reduced, the pressure above the diaphragm takes over. It overcomes the adjusting-spring pressure and pushes the valve seat down off the port. The valve opens (left in Fig. 23), and liquid refrigerant flows to the evaporator (through connection 2 in Fig. 22). The air-conditioning system is in operation.

Now the expansion valve begins to exercise control. The

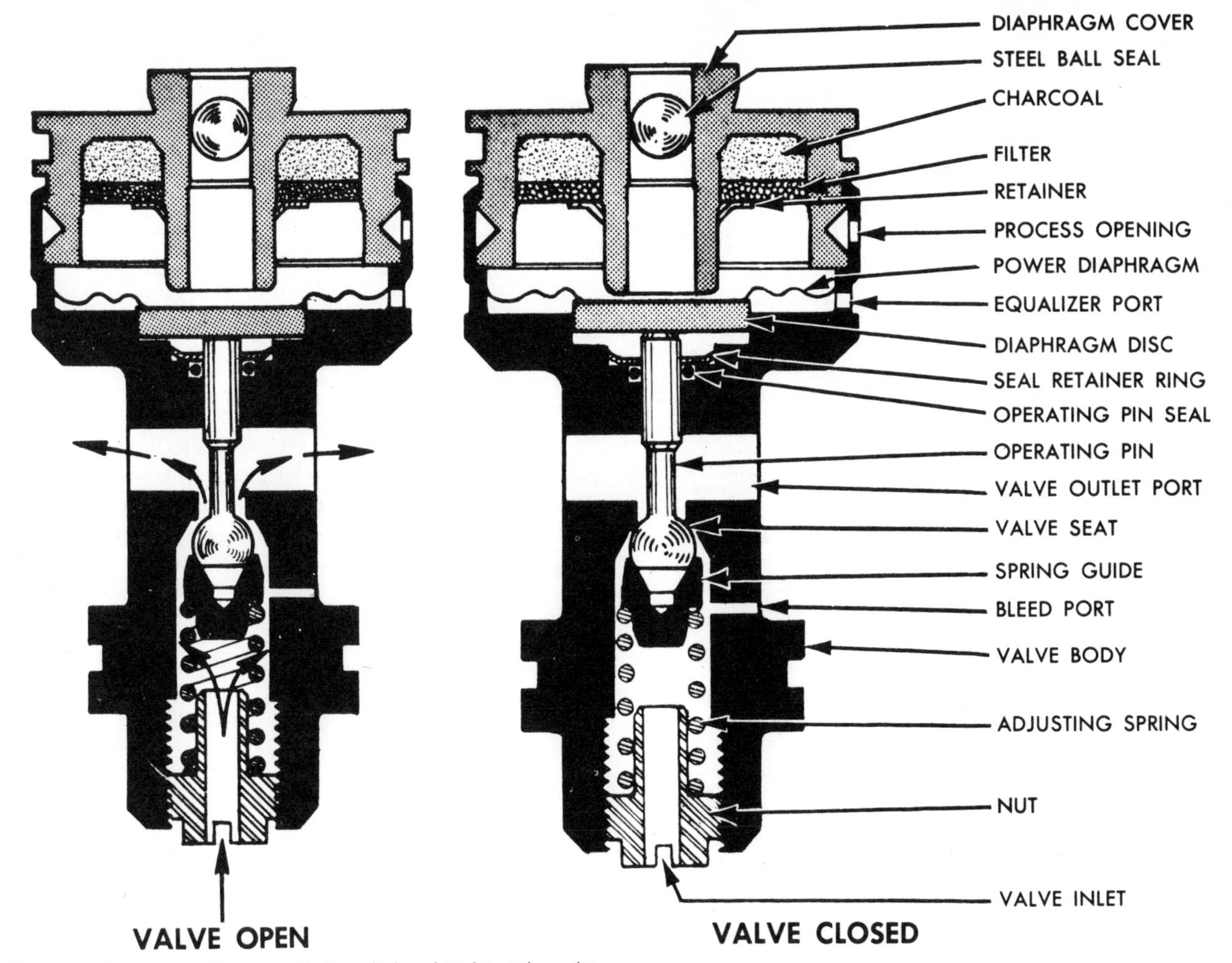

Figure 23 Expansion valve open (left) and closed (right). *(Chevrolet Motor Division of General Motors Corporation.)*

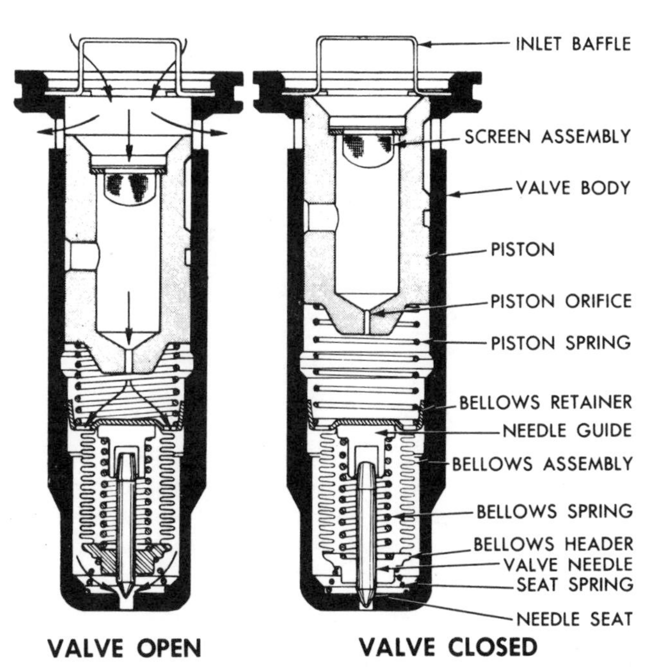

Figure 24 POA valve open (left) and closed (right). *(Chevrolet Motor Division of General Motors Corporation.)*

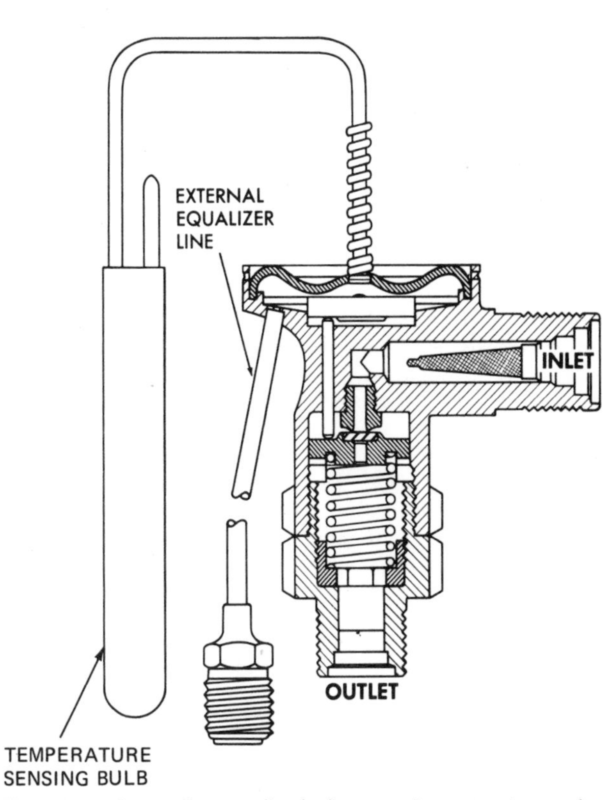

Figure 25 Externally equalized thermostatic expansion valve. *(United Delco Division of General Motors Corporation.)*

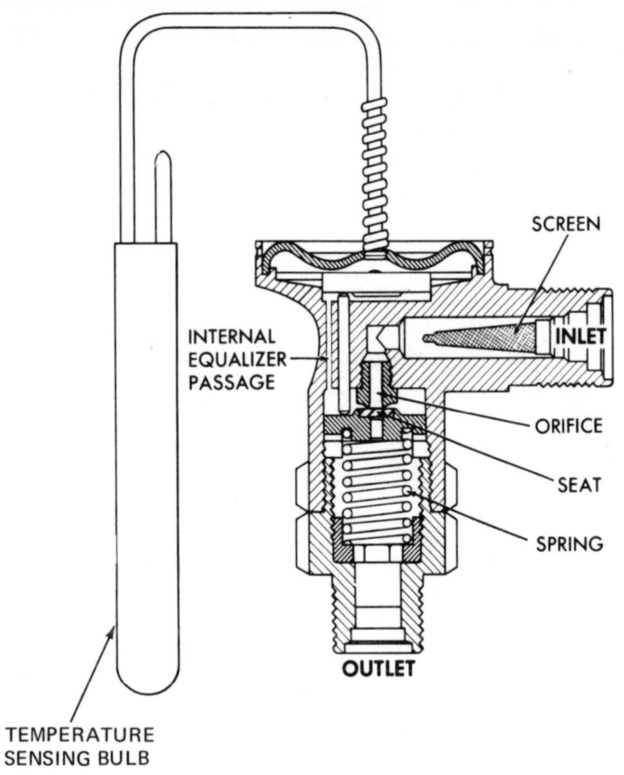

Figure 26 Sectional view of an internally equalized thermostatic expansion valve. *(United Delco Division of General Motors Corporation.)*

upper end of the valve is exposed to the refrigerant vapor coming from the evaporator (through connection 3 in Fig. 22). If the evaporator does not get enough liquid refrigerant, the temperature of the refrigerant vapor goes up. Then the sealed-in refrigerant above the diaphragm expands. This forces the diaphragm, the rod, and the valve seat down, allowing more refrigerant to pass to the evaporator. If the evaporator gets too much refrigerant, vapor coming from the evaporator is too cold. Then the sealed-in refrigerant contracts. The adjusting spring takes over and pushes the valve seat toward the closed position. Now, less refrigerant can pass to the evaporator.

The VIR expansion valve is not adjustable or serviceable in the field. It can only be replaced.

■ **8-2-11 VIR POA Suction Valve** The POA suction valve controls the pressure of the refrigerant vapor coming from the evaporator. It maintains this pressure at around 30 psi (2.11 kg/cm^2). At this pressure, the evaporator temperature is above 32°F (0°C). The evaporator temperature should be kept high enough to prevent freezing of water on the evaporator. Otherwise, ice could form and block the air circulation through the evaporator.

Figure 24 shows the valve in sectional view. When the system is in operation, evaporator pressure is applied to the upper end of the valve piston. It enters through connection 3, as shown in Fig. 22. The vapor passes through the screen assembly and the piston orifice, and into the chamber around the bellows assembly. The bellows contains a high vacuum. Variations in pressure around the bellows cause it to shorten or elongate. High pressure shortens it. Low pressure allows the spring inside the bellows to elongate it.

As the evaporator pressure goes up, it reaches a pressure that overcomes the piston spring. The piston is pushed down, as shown to the left in Fig. 24. Now, refrigerant vapor from the evaporator can pass through the valve and exit through connection 4 (in Fig. 22). This vapor goes to the compressor, where it is compressed and sent back through the condenser and evaporator.

With the valve open and refrigerant vapor flowing to the compressor, the evaporator pressure falls to 30 psi (2.11 kg/cm^2). Now the pressure on the top of the piston is reduced. This allows the piston spring (plus refrigerant-vapor pressure below the piston) to push the piston up. This decreases the flow of refrigerant to the compressor. The evaporator pressure goes up.

Evaporator pressure is transmitted through the piston orifice to the bellows chamber. This pressure affects the movement of the needle valve. If the pressure goes too high, the bellows is collapsed by the pressure. This raises the needle valve, so that refrigerant can flow through the piston orifice and the needle-valve seat. It flows into the cavity in which the POA valve is

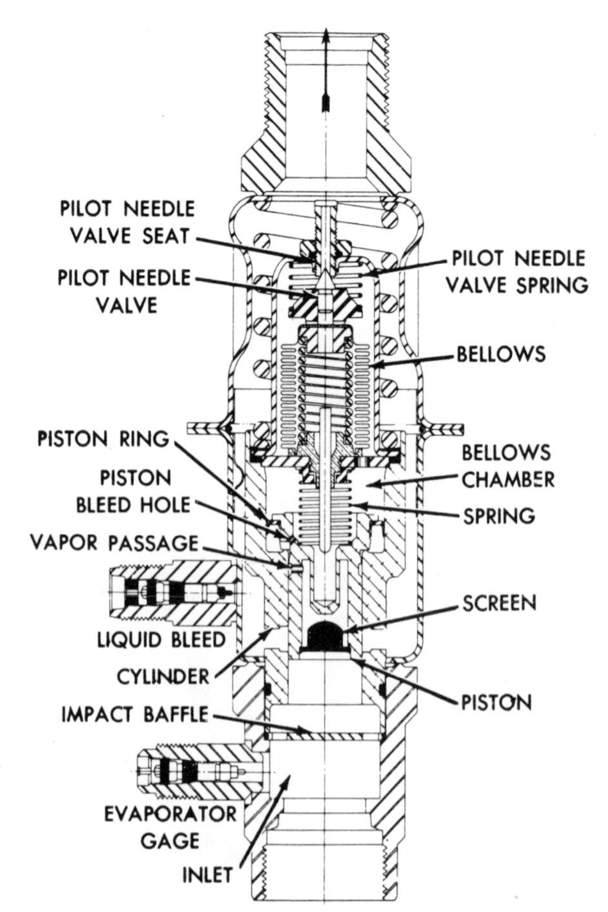

Figure 27 Sectional view of a suction throttling valve. *(Cadillac Motor Car Division of General Motors Corporation.)*

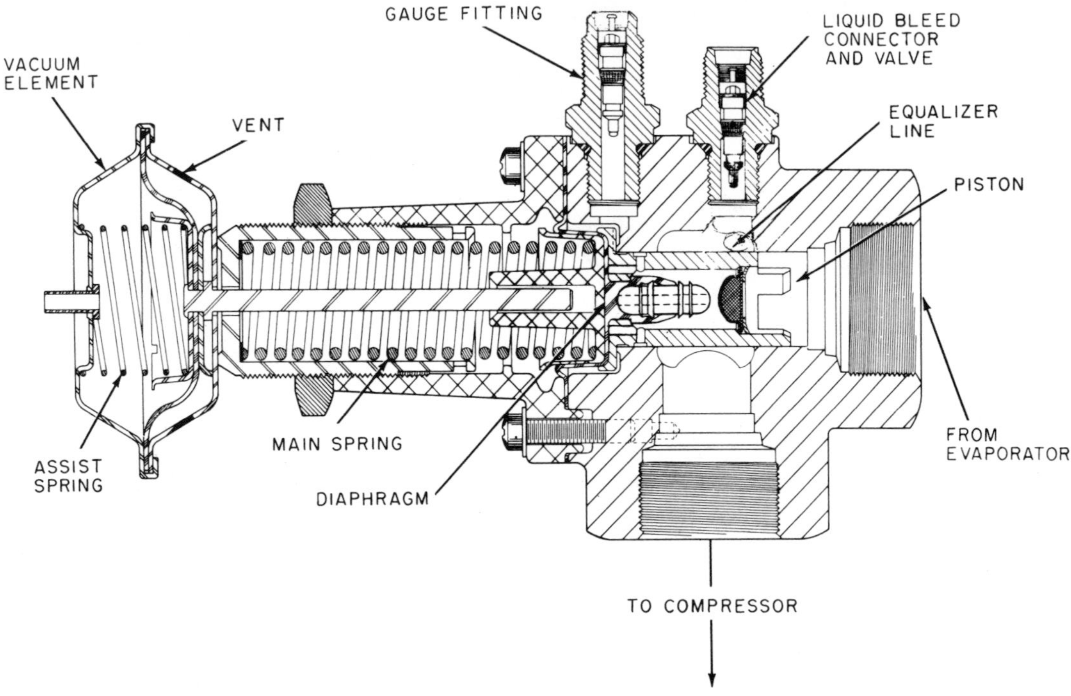

Figure 28 Cutaway view of a suction throttling valve. *(Pontiac Motor Division of General Motors Corporation.)*

mounted. This is the same cavity into which the refrigerant flows when the piston valve is open. The refrigerant can then leave through connection 4 (Fig. 24).

The second valve (the needle valve controlled by the bellows) gives finer control, to maintain a more even pressure in the evaporator. In operation, the piston and needle valve assume the positions required to maintain a steady flow of refrigerant vapor from the evaporator.

The POA valve is not adjustable or serviceable in the field. It can only be replaced.

■ 8-2-12 Other Expansion Valves

Other expansion valves have been used in automotive air-conditioning systems. Figure 25 shows an externally mounted type in sectional view. This expansion valve is much like the one in Fig. 17, but the valve shown in Fig. 25 has an additional control. This is an equalizer line that runs to the separately mounted POA valve. Recall that the expansion valve controls the flow of liquid refrigerant to the evaporator. The POA valve controls the evaporator pressure, maintaining it around 30 psi (2.11 kg/cm²) so that the evaporator temperature will not go below 32°F (0°C).

The expansion valve in Fig. 25 works like the one described above. That is, the pressure in the temperature-sensing bulb increases with increasing temperature. This pressure causes the diaphragm to unseat the valve and allow liquid refrigerant to flow to the evaporator. The equalizer line brings evaporator pressure into the valve, below the diaphragm. If this pressure is high, it and the spring pressure prevent the sensing bulb from opening the valve. This is the situation when the system is off. However, once the compressor starts, the valve never completely shuts off the flow of refrigerant to the evaporator.

The expansion valve in Fig. 26 works like the valve in Fig. 25. The major difference is that the pressure of the entering liquid refrigerant is applied to the bottom of the diaphragm, once the valve has opened. This pressure is applied through the internal equalizer passage. Its effect is the same as that of the refrigerant-vapor pressure in the valve in Fig. 23.

Other expansion valves have been used, but all function similarly. They all control the flow of liquid refrigerant into the evaporator.

■ 8-2-13 Other Suction Valves

All suction valves work in the same general manner to control the pressure of the refrigerant leaving the evaporator. This valve maintains a pressure that prevents freeze-up. That is, it prevents the evaporator temperature from falling below 32°F (0°C). A separately mounted POA suction valve is shown in sectional view in Fig. 27. Compare it with the POA valve shown in Fig. 24. The two valves are constructed similarly. The valve in Fig. 27 is inverted, relative to the one in Fig. 24. But both work in the same manner.

Another suction throttling valve is shown in Fig. 28. This is also a separately mounted valve. It is located in the evaporator outlet (Fig. 29). Even though it looks different from other evaporator-pressure-regulator valves, it works the same way. Spring pressure and atmospheric pressure (working through the vent in the diaphragm assembly) oppose the evaporator pressure. When the evaporator pressure exceeds about 30 psi (2.11 kg/cm²), it overcomes the spring and atmospheric pressures

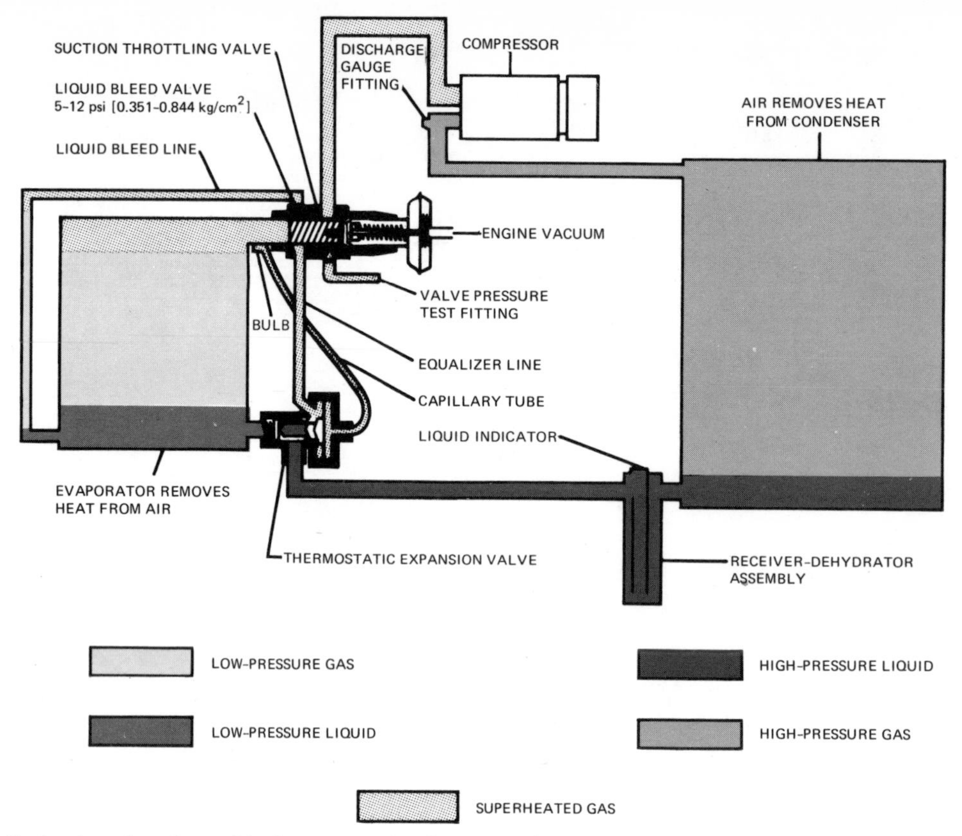

Figure 29 Schematic drawing of an air-conditioning system using the suction throttling valve shown in Fig. 28. *(Pontiac Motor Division of General Motors Corporation.)*

and opens the valve. Refrigerant vapor then flows from the evaporator to the compressor.

The vacuum element comes into play when the control is turned to full cooling by the driver of the car. In this mode, vacuum from the engine is admitted to the end of the vacuum element. This causes the diaphragm to move (to the left in Fig. 28). It carries the diaphragm rod with it, so the piston can move further. This allows more refrigerant to flow through the evaporator, for more cooling.

■ 8-2-14 Automotive Air-Conditioning Controls

Several special devices are used to control the operation of automotive air conditioners, and to protect the components if something goes wrong. Some air conditioners have a manual control which permits the driver to turn the air conditioner on or off to suit the cooling needs. Other air conditioners are completely automatic. They work with the car heater to provide the temperature that the driver has set on the control panel. On these, the car heater comes on if heat is required to maintain the preset temperature. If cooling is required, the air conditioner comes on. Included in many systems are an ambient switch, a thermal limiter and superheat switch, a low-pressure cutoff switch, and a high-pressure relief valve.

Figure 30 shows the compressor-clutch wiring circuit including the ambient switch and low-pressure cut-off switch.

1. AMBIENT SWITCH The ambient switch senses outside temperatures and prevents the clutch from engaging under certain conditions. For example, its contacts open at temperatures below 32°F (0°C), so that the clutch will not engage. This prevents operation of the system when air conditioning is not required or when operation might damage seals and other internal compressor parts. The ambient switch is used with systems that have an evaporator pressure control (a POA or similar valve). It is located in the air-inlet duct of the air-conditioning system. At that point, it can sense the temperature of the air entering from outside the car.

2. LOW-PRESSURE CUTOFF SWITCH This switch is installed on top of the receiver-dehydrator (Fig. 31). It senses the evaporator pressure, and disengages the compressor clutch if the pressure drops too low. A very low evaporator pressure usually means the system has lost refrigerant. If refrigerant has been lost, then refrigerant oil has also been lost. Loss of oil could cause fatal damage to the compressor, if it continued to operate. The low-pressure cutoff switch guards against this damage by shutting off the compressor when the pressure falls too low.

3. HIGH-PRESSURE RELIEF VALVE The high-pressure relief valve (Fig. 31) is located on the receiver-dehydrator, opposite the low-pressure cutoff switch. Its purpose is to prevent damage due to excessive pressure. Excessive pressure could

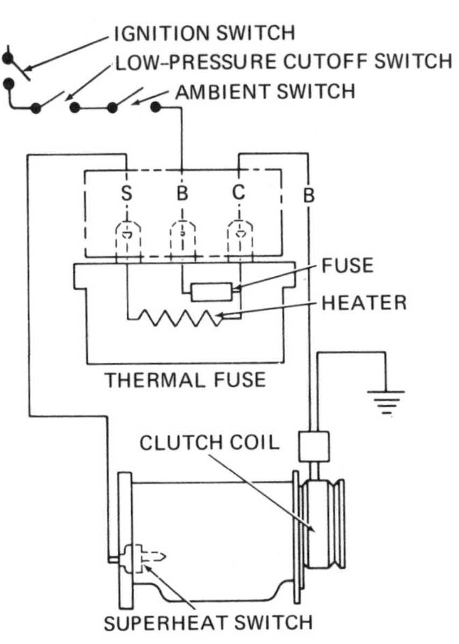

Figure 30 Wiring circuit of the magnetic clutch, showing the safety devices. *(United Delco Division of General Motors Corporation.)*

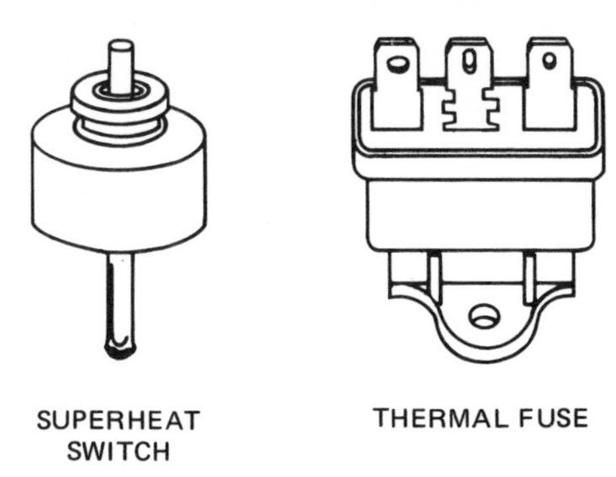

Figure 32 Superheat switch and thermal limiter. *(United Delco Division of General Motors Corporation.)*

Figure 31 Receiver-dehydrator with low-pressure cutoff switch and high-pressure relief valve. *(Chrysler Corporation.)*

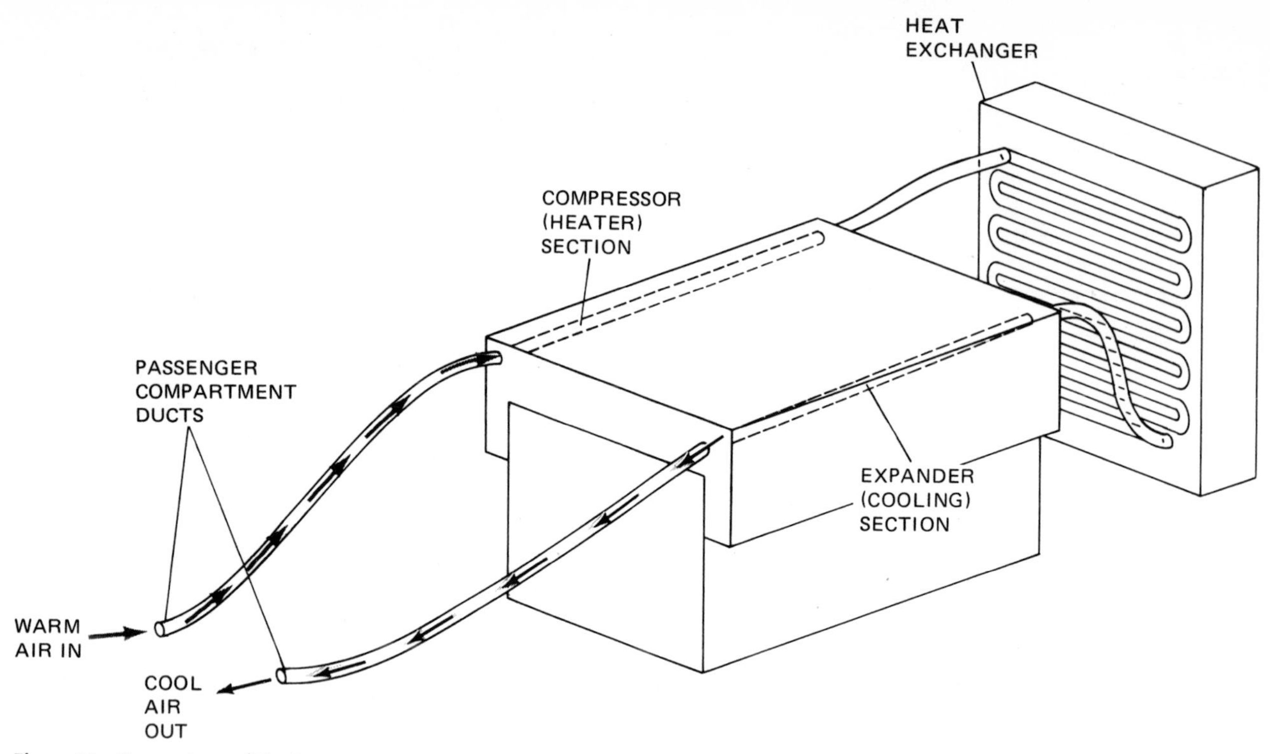

Figure 33 Rovac air-conditioning system.

develop, for example, if the airflow through the condenser were restricted by newspapers, leaves, or other trash. An overcharge of refrigerant could also cause excessive pressure in the air-conditioning system.

4. THERMAL LIMITER AND SUPERHEAT SWITCH Another protection for the compressor is illustrated in Figs. 30 and 32. A superheat switch is installed in the end of the compressor, as shown in Fig. 30. The superheat switch (Fig. 32) contacts are open at all times, except when the system loses some or all of its refrigerant. Then the switch senses the low pressure and the high refrigerant temperature. Its contacts close, and current flows through the heater in the thermal limiter (fuse). See Fig. 32. The heat melts the fuse, opening the compressor clutch circuit. This stops the compressor and prevents its damage.

> **NOTE:** Before the thermal fuse is replaced, the reason for the refrigerant loss must be found and corrected.

5. OTHER CONTROLS Other protective devices are used in air-conditioning systems. Not all the devices described above will be found in any one system. For example, if a system has a low-pressure cutoff switch, it does not need a thermal limiter and superheat switch.

■ **8-2-15 Rovac System** This is an air-conditioning system that uses no refrigerant other than ordinary air. The system is simple (Fig. 33). A vane-type pump, driven by a belt from the crankshaft pulley, compresses air and sends it to a heat exchanger. When the air is compressed, it gets hot. The air approaches 250°F (121°C) in temperature. When the hot air passes through the heat exchanger, it loses heat. Then the cooler (but still compressed) air goes into an expansion chamber. There the air expands and, in doing so, turns still cooler. In fact, the expanding air turns so cold that it can freeze moisture surrounding it.

There is a simple comparison between the Rovac system and a standard air-conditioning system. The heat exchanger in the Rovac system compares with the condenser in the standard system. The expansion chamber compares with the evaporator. The Rovac system is still under development.

SECTION 8-3

Manually Controlled Air-Conditioner–Heater Systems

In this section, we describe air-conditioner–heater systems that have manual controls. These controls are operated by the driver to select either heating or cooling and to set the car temperature. These systems are closely tied in with the car heater as shown in Fig. 1. The heat comes from the engine cooling system. Figure 2 shows a typical control panel for this type of system.

■ **8-3-1 Heater–Air-Conditioner System** Figures 1 and 3 show how the air-conditioner evaporator and the heater core are assembled into a typical heater–air-conditioner system. Both are heat exchangers. The evaporator takes in heat from the air that passes through it. The heater core puts heat into the air that passes through it.

In Fig. 1, the airflow is shown with the system set to heat and defrost. The air is taken in from the outside, because the outside-air door is open. It passes through the evaporator, as shown. However, the air is not cooled, because the air conditioner is not working. It then goes through the heater core, where heat is added to the air (from the engine cooling system). As shown, the heated air then goes up past the opened defroster door, to heat and defrost the windshield. Some of the heated air also exits through the vents that heat the car interior.

Figure 3 shows a similar system schematically. Note, to the right, the doors that admit air to the system. These are the outside-air door and the inside, or recirculate, door. When one of these doors is open, the other is closed. The blower pulls in the air and sends it through the evaporator core.

If the controls are set for heat, the heater core adds heat to the air. The air takes any of several paths, depending on which doors are open and closed. If the restrictor door is open, the air passes through the heater core. If this core is hot, the air is heated. If the driver wants only a little heat, he or she adjusts the temperature-blend door so that some heated air bypasses the heater core. It then mixes with the heated air coming through the heater core, and cools it somewhat.

If the driver has adjusted the controls for heat inside the car, the air-conditioner–heat door is open (not closed as shown). This allows the heated air to blow out through the air-conditioner registers. If the driver has set the controls for floor heat, the air-conditioner–heat door is closed, and the air-conditioner–defrost door is in the UP position. All the heated air then exits through the floor-heat vents.

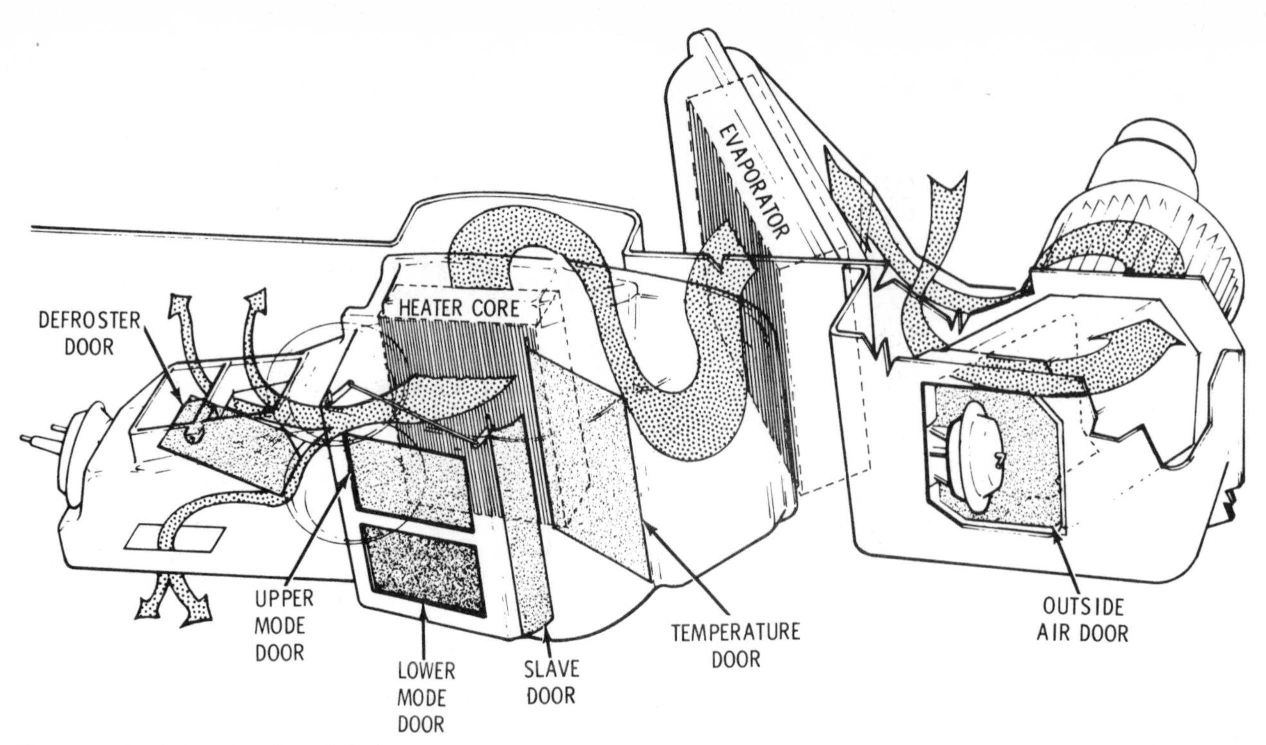

Figure 1 Circulation of air through the heater–air-conditioner system with the temperature selector lever set for heat. *(United Delco Division of General Motors Corporation.)*

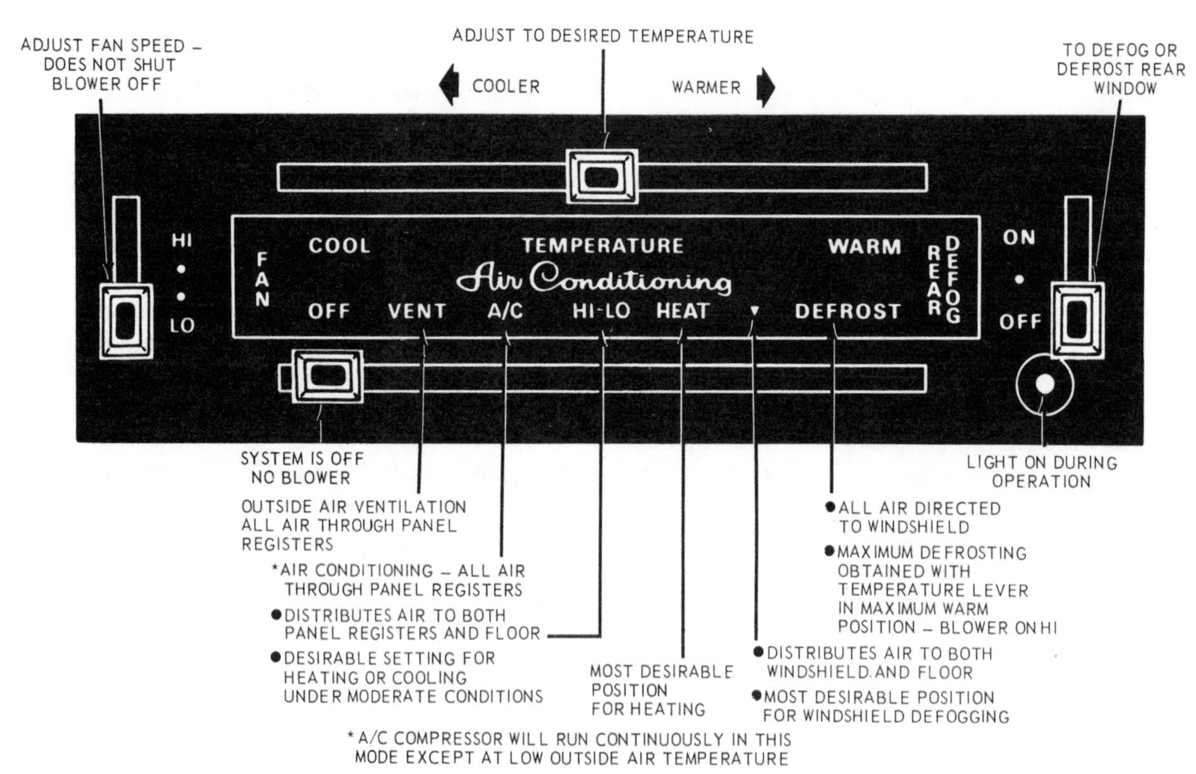

Figure 2 Control panel for a manually controlled air-conditioner–heater system. *(Ford Motor Company.)*

To vary the amount of heated air sent to the defroster vents, the driver adjusts the air-conditioner–defrost door.

If the driver sets the controls for air conditioning, the air-conditioning system goes into operation. At the same time, the heater water-control valve closes. This shuts off the flow of hot water (coolant) from the engine cooling system. Figure 4 is a sectional view of a water control valve. It consists of a sealed diaphragm chamber with a spring, and a piston-valve arrange-

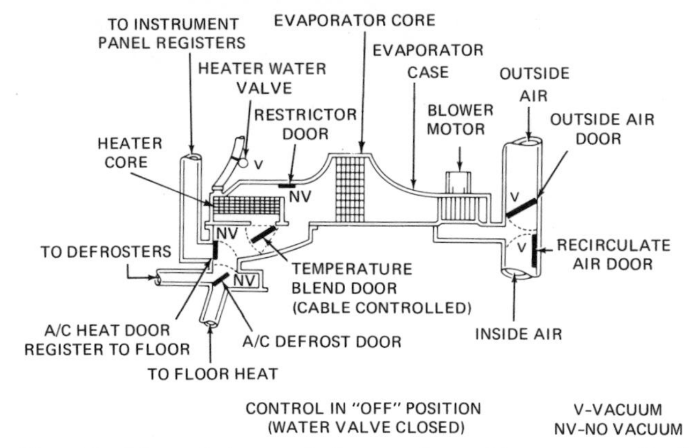

Figure 3 Schematic layout of a heater–air-conditioner system. *(Ford Motor Company.)*

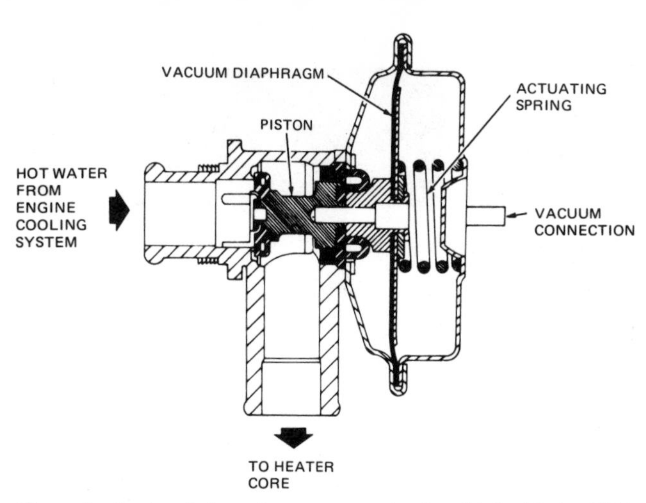

Figure 4 Sectional view of a water control valve. *(United Delco Division of General Motors Corporation.)*

ment. The assembly is called a "vacuum motor." The vacuum comes from the engine intake manifold when the engine is running.

In the water control valve (Fig. 4), vacuum is applied when heating is called for. This pulls the diaphragm to the right. The diaphragm moves the piston away from the port. This allows hot coolant from the engine heating system to flow through the heater core. However, when air conditioning is called for, the vacuum is cut off. Now, the spring pushes the piston back on its seat. This closes off the flow of hot water from the engine cooling system.

With the air conditioner working, the air passing through the evaporator core is cooled. The restrictor door is closed, so the cooled air bypasses the heater core. It goes either to the defroster vents or the air-conditioner registers, depending on the positions of the doors.

■ 8-3-2 Ford Manually Controlled Air-Conditioner–Heater System

The Ford manually controlled air-conditioner–heater system has a heater core, the complete air-conditioning system described in Part 8, Sec. 2, an electric control system, and a vacuum control system.

Figure 5 shows the general layout of the system. We have already described, in ■8-3-1, how the system works. The temperature-blend door is controlled by a cable from the temperature lever (top in Fig. 2). As the lever is moved to the left or right, the temperature-blend door (Fig. 2) swings one way or the other. This allows more or less air to pass through the heater core. In the COOL position, the temperature-blend door is all the way up, so no air can pass through the heater core. The air conditioner is of the evaporator-pressure-control-valve type (■8-2-8).

■ 8-3-3 Operating Modes

Figures 6 to 11 show the air flow through the system with different control settings. To identify the different parts in these illustrations, refer to Fig. 5, where they are all named.

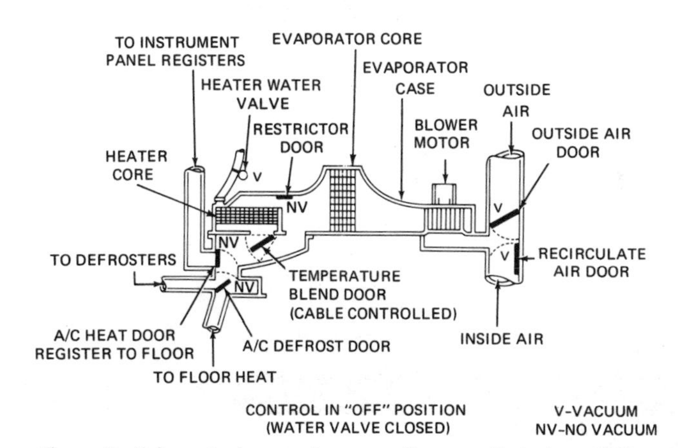

Figure 5 Schematic layout of a manually controlled air-conditioner–heater system. *(Ford Motor Company.)*

> **NOTE:** Ford calls the functional control lever the "mode lever." Another name for it is the "selector control lever." We shall continue to call it the functional control lever in our explanations.

In Fig. 6, the functional control lever is set at VENT. The temperature control lever is set at COOL. Neither the air conditioner nor the heater is working. Outside air enters and, as shown by the arrows, passes through the system without being heated or cooled. It exits through the instrument-panel registers.

In Fig. 7, the functional control lever is set at A/C for air conditioning. The temperature control lever is set at COOL for maximum cooling. The vacuum motor that controls the flow of coolant from the engine cooling system has closed the water valve. That is, moving the functional-control lever to A/C connects vacuum to the water-valve vacuum motor; it operates to close the valve. The temperature control lever can be moved to the right, toward WARM, to change the position of the temperature-blend door. Since the restrictor door is closed, this

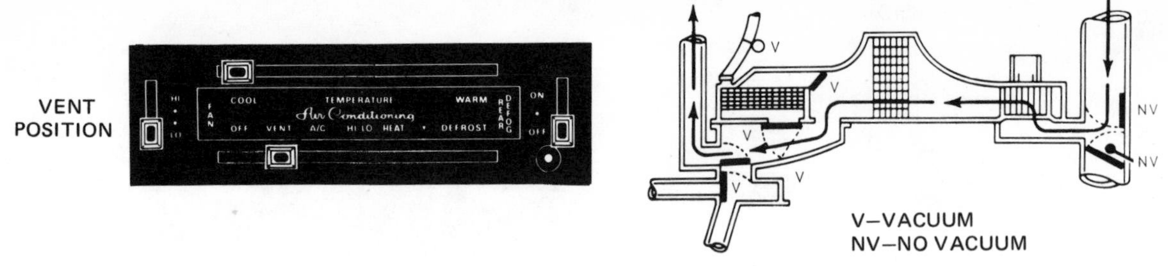

Figure 6 Operation of system in the VENT position. *(Ford Motor Company.)*

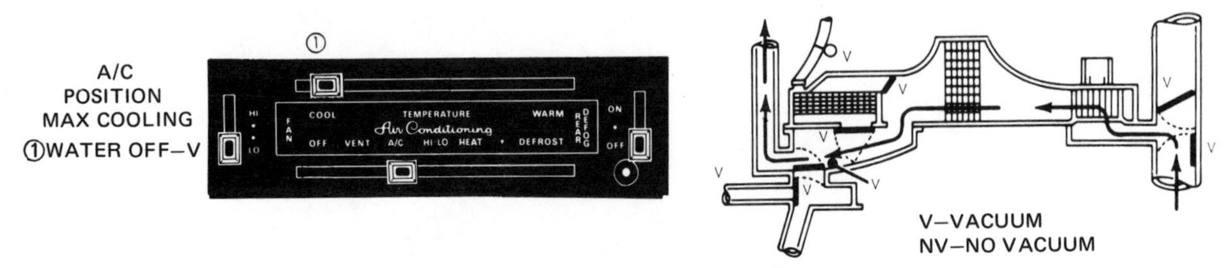

Figure 7 Operation of system in the A/C position. *(Ford Motor Company.)*

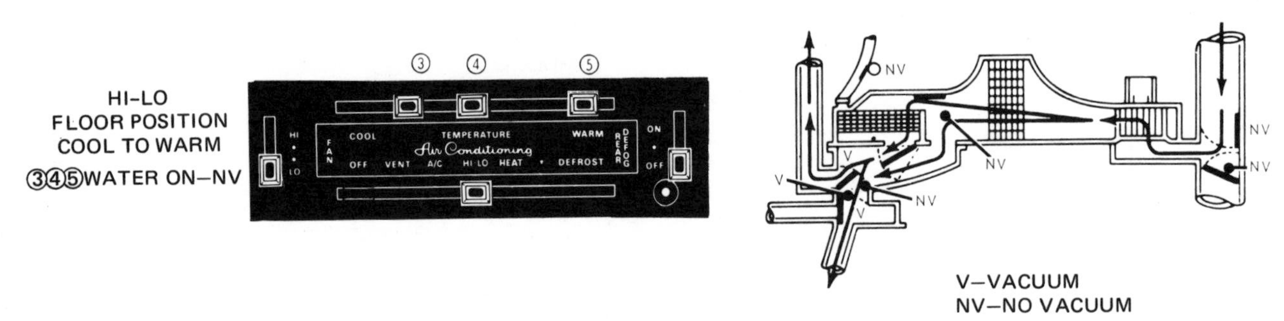

Figure 8 Operation of system in the HI-LO position. *(Ford Motor Company.)*

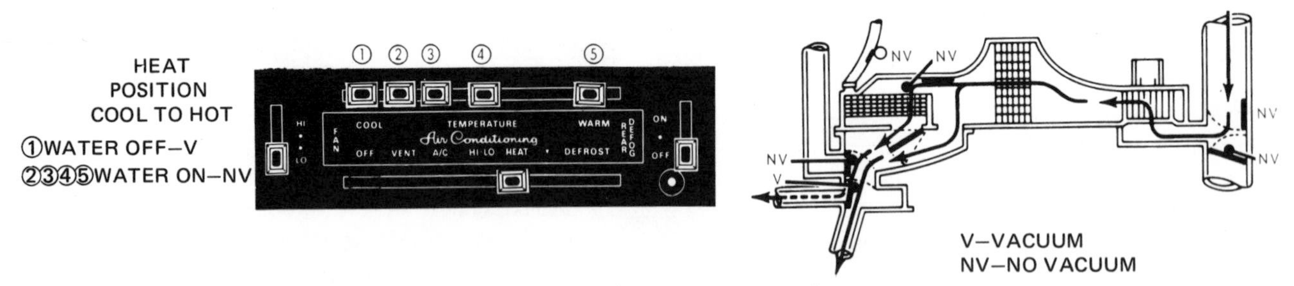

Figure 9 Operation of system in the HEAT position. *(Ford Motor Company.)*

causes the temperature-blend door to decrease the flow of air. This reduces the cooling.

In Fig. 8, the functional control lever has been moved to HI-LO. This means that air is discharged through both the floor registers and the instrument-panel registers. This is the most desirable setting for heating or cooling under moderate conditions. Note that three temperature positions are shown at (3), (4), and (5). These indicate varying amounts of heating. The air conditioner is off. The restrictor door is open. The water valve is also open. In the temperature-control-lever positions shown, vacuum has been cut off from the water-valve vacuum motor. The vacuum motor, therefore, allows the water valve to open. Now, a flow of hot coolant can pass through the heater core. The temperature-blend-door position changes as the tempera-

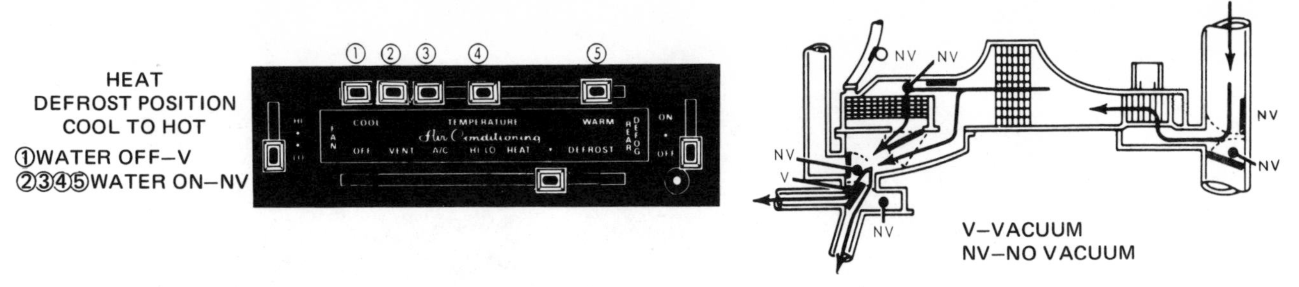

Figure 10 Operation of system in the HEAT-DEFROST position. *(Ford Motor Company.)*

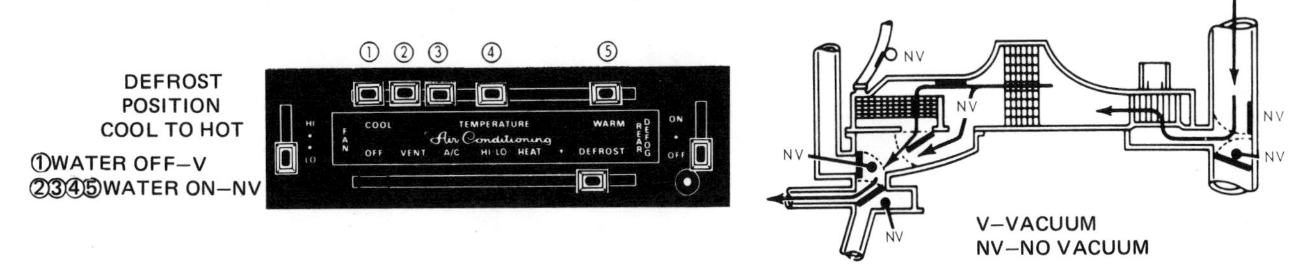

Figure 11 Operation of system in the DEFROST position. *(Ford Motor Company.)*

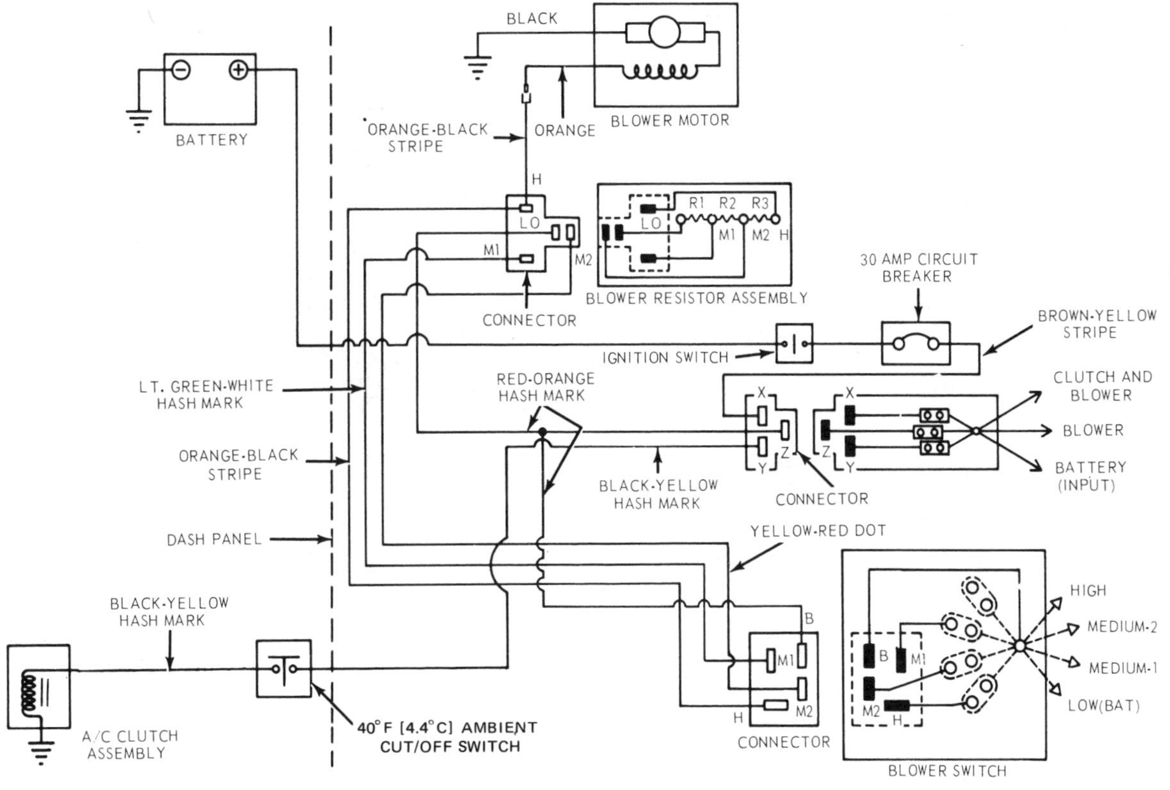

Figure 12 Electric system for manually controlled air-conditioner system. *(Ford Motor Company.)*

ture control lever is moved across the control panel. In position (3), it is open only a little. In position (4), it is open much more. In position (5), it is wide open so that all the air goes through the heater core.

Figure 9 shows the situation with the functional control lever set at HEAT. This is very much like the situation shown in Fig. 8, with the lever set at HI-LO. The difference is that, at HEAT, the vacuum motors controlling the air-conditioner–heat door

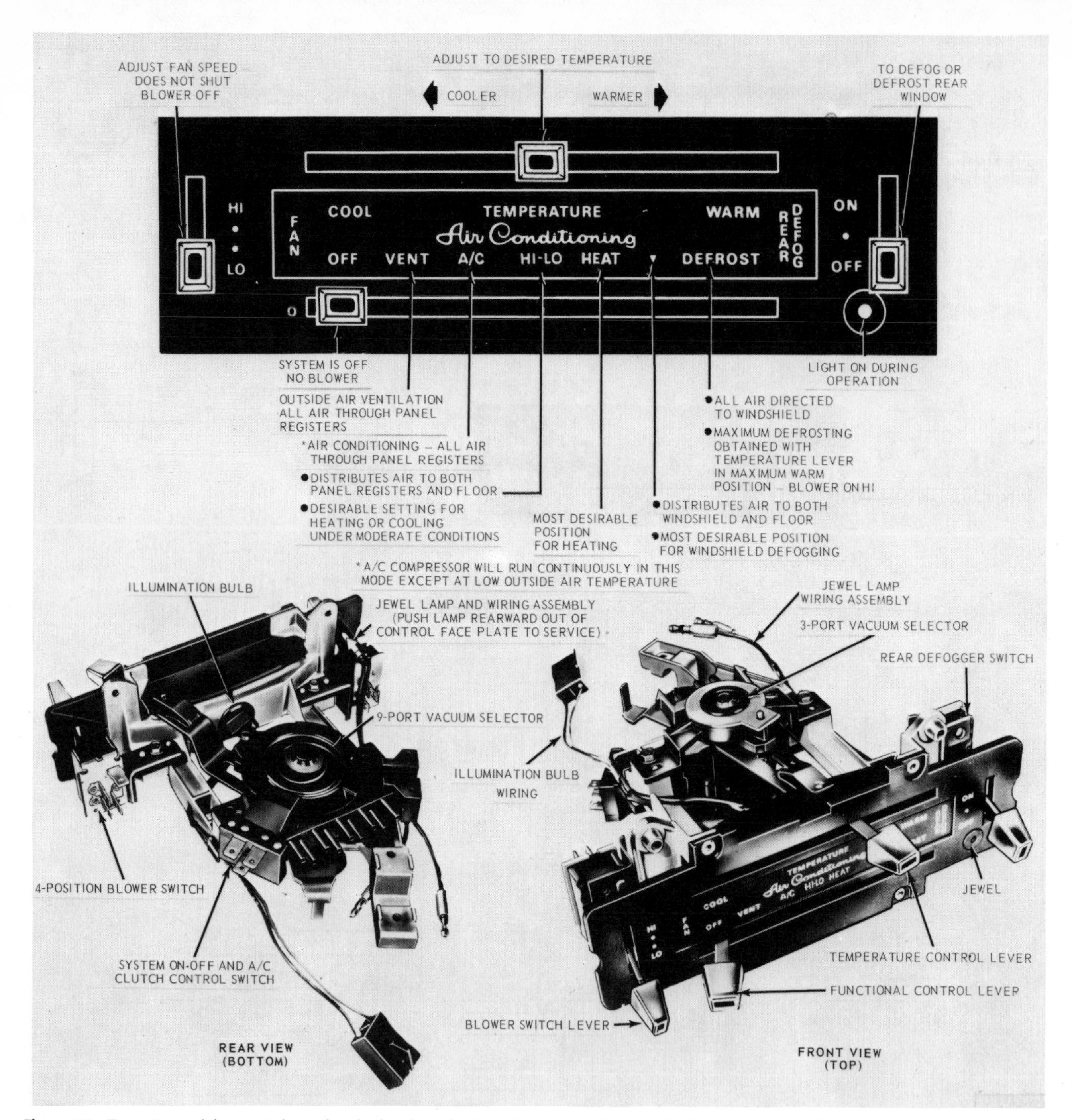

Figure 13 Two views of the control panel and related mechanisms for a manually controlled air-conditioner–heater system. *(Ford Motor Company.)*

and the air-conditioner–defrost door operate to put the doors in the positions shown. Now, almost all the heated air is directed to the floor registers. A small amount of heated air does get past the air-conditioner–defrost door and to the defrost vents.

Figure 10 shows the situation with the functional control lever moved halfway between HEAT and DEFROST. In this position, the vacuum motor holds the heat door halfway open. Now, heated air flows to both the defrost vents and the floor registers.

Figure 11 is the same as Fig. 10, except that the functional control lever is set at DEFROST. The vacuum motor has moved the heat door so that all the heated air is directed to the defrost vents.

■ **8-3-4 Electric System** Figure 12 is the electric wiring diagram for the heater–air-conditioner system. Basically, the system provides several blower-motor speeds, and con-

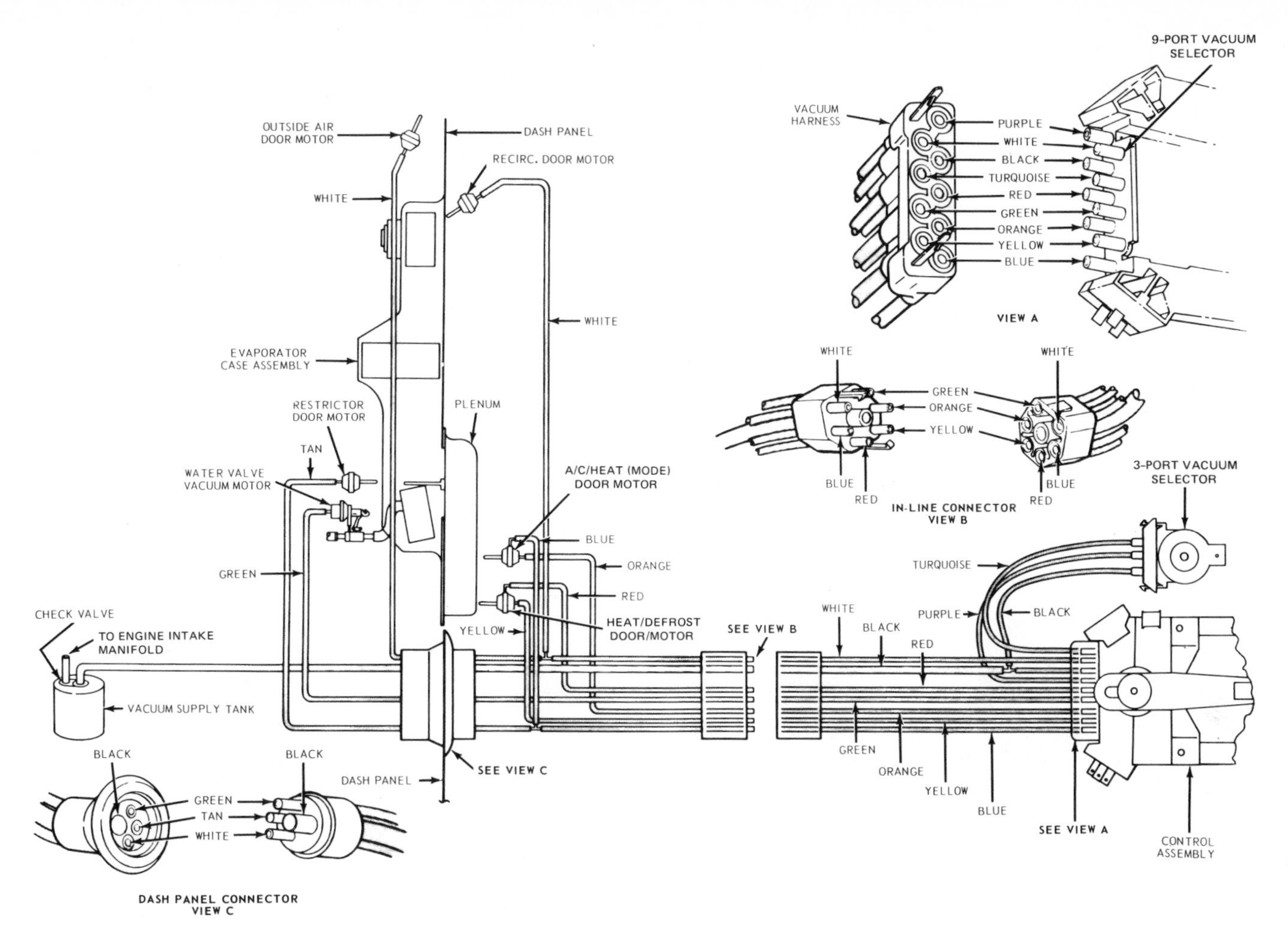

Figure 14 Vacuum diagram for a manually controlled air-conditioner – heater system. *(Ford Motor Company.)*

nects or disconnects the compressor clutch and the battery. You will recall that there are two basic types of air-conditioner systems, the cycling-clutch type and the evaporator-pressure-control-valve system. In the cycling-clutch type, the clutch is connected and disconnected repeatedly, to control the cooling action. In the evaporator-pressure-control-valve system, control is provided by the expansion valve and the suction valve (■8-2-5 to 8-2-8). The expansion valve controls the flow of liquid refrigerant to the evaporator. It always supplies the evaporator with enough refrigerant to provide adequate cooling. The suction valve prevents excessive pressure in the evaporator which could cause the evaporator temperature to fall below freezing. At temperatures below 32°F (0°C), ice forms on the evaporator and blocks the airflow.

The suction valve keeps the evaporator at a fairly constant low temperature. Therefore, the amount of cooling it does depends mostly on the amount of air that flows through the evaporator. This airflow depends on how fast the blower motor is turning and on the positions of the various doors in the system (see Figs. 5 and 7).

When the functional control lever is moved to A/C, an electric switch connects the compressor clutch to the battery. The clutch engages and drives the compressor. The compressor operates whenever the functional control lever is in the A/C position. How hard the compressor works depends on how much cooling is needed. If the cooling needs are small, the expansion valve allows only a little liquid refrigerant to flow to the evaporator. The compressor then works against a light load. However, if the cooling needs are great, the expansion valve lets much more liquid refrigerant flow to the evaporator. The compressor then has to work much harder to maintain the necessary flow.

■ 8-3-5 Vacuum Circuits

The air-conditioner – heater control assembly is shown in top and bottom views in Fig. 13. The temperature control lever is connected by a cable to the temperature-blend door. As the control lever is moved, the temperature-blend door is moved up or down, as previously explained.

The functional control lever controls the more complex electric and vacuum systems. We have already discussed the electric system (■8-3-4). Now let us look at the vacuum system.

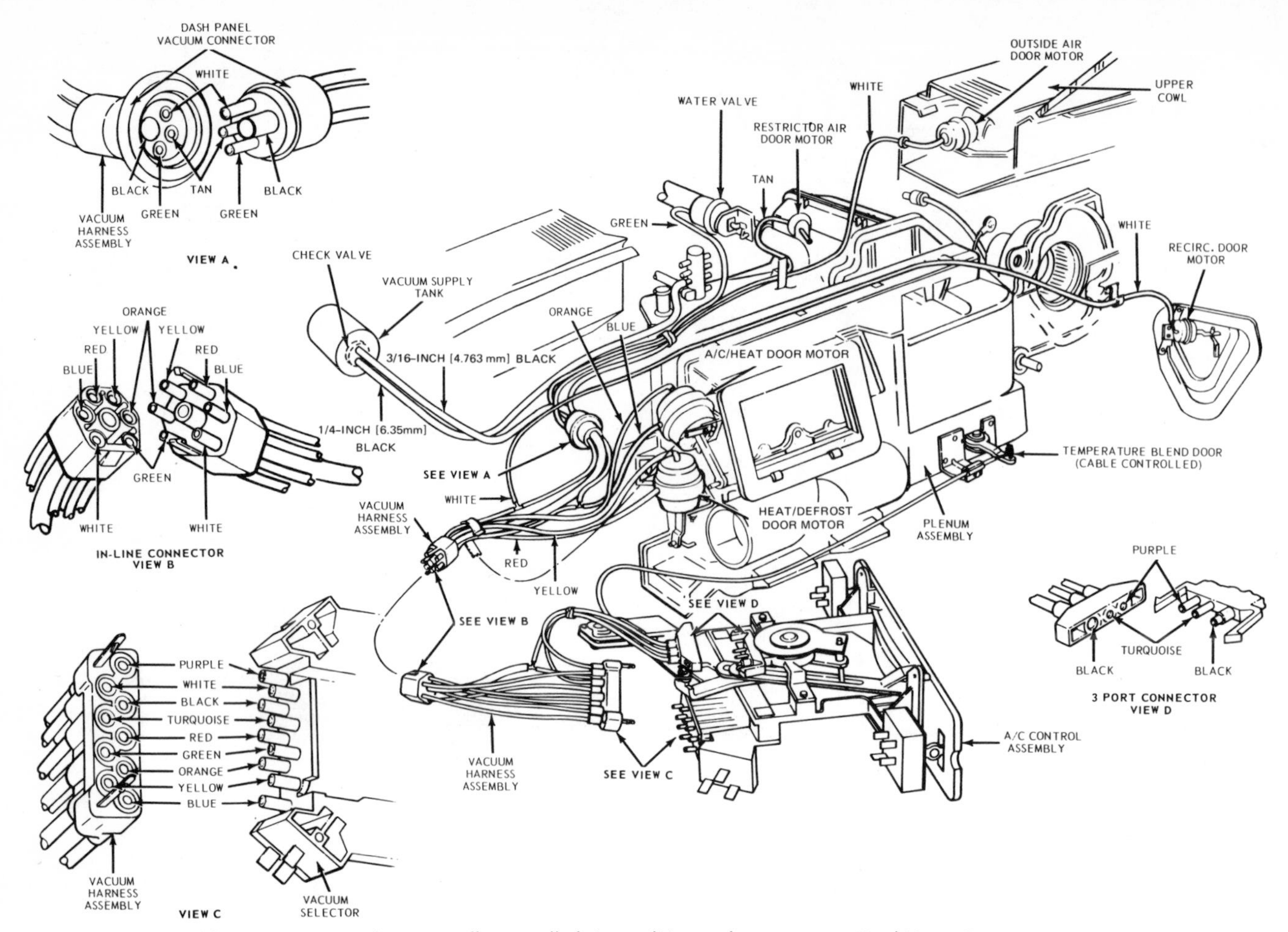

Figure 15 Layout of the vacuum system for a manually controlled air-conditioner–heater system. *(Ford Motor Company.)*

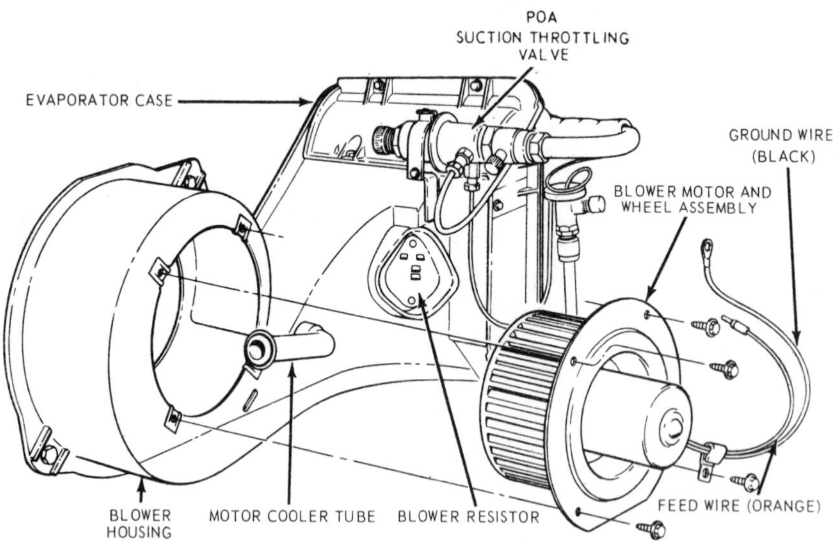

Figure 16 Blower motor. *(Ford Motor Company.)*

Figure 14 is a vacuum diagram showing the connections between the control assembly and the vacuum motors. Identify the various vacuum motors and count them. Refer back to Fig. 5 to see which doors are operated by the vacuum motors. Notice that there are actually six vacuum motors. But there are nine vacuum connections to the control assembly. One of these is the main connection to the vacuum source. Note also that the heat-defrost-door vacuum motor has a separate vacu-

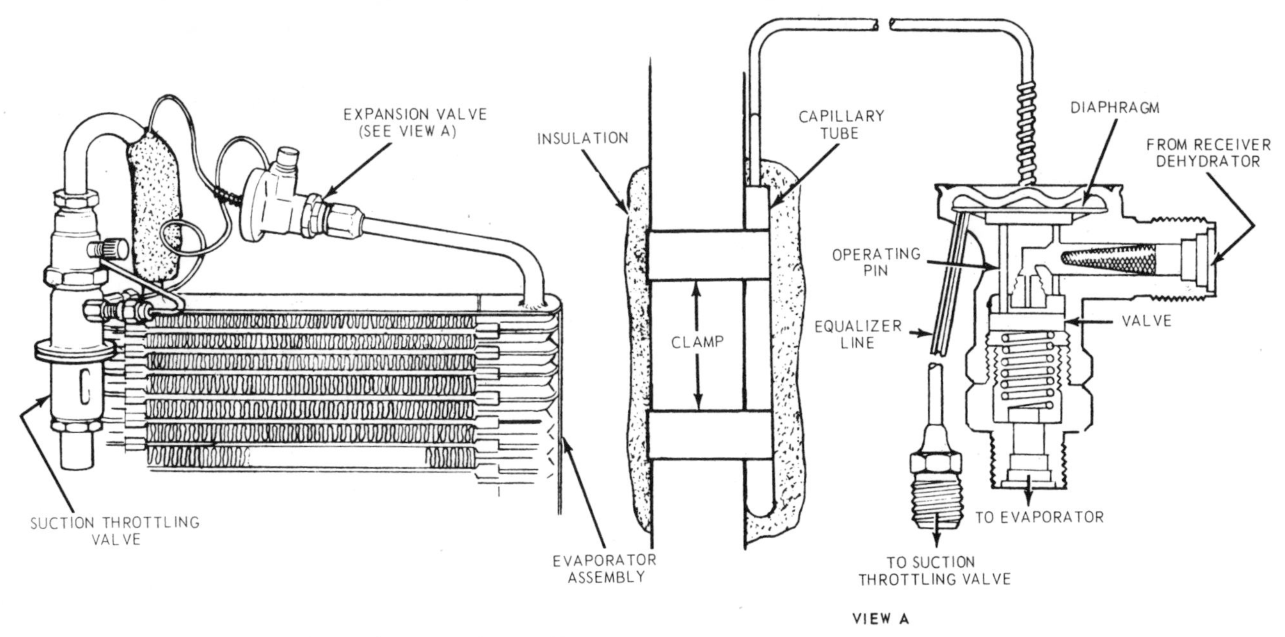

Figure 17 Left, installation of valves; right, sectional view of the expansion valve.

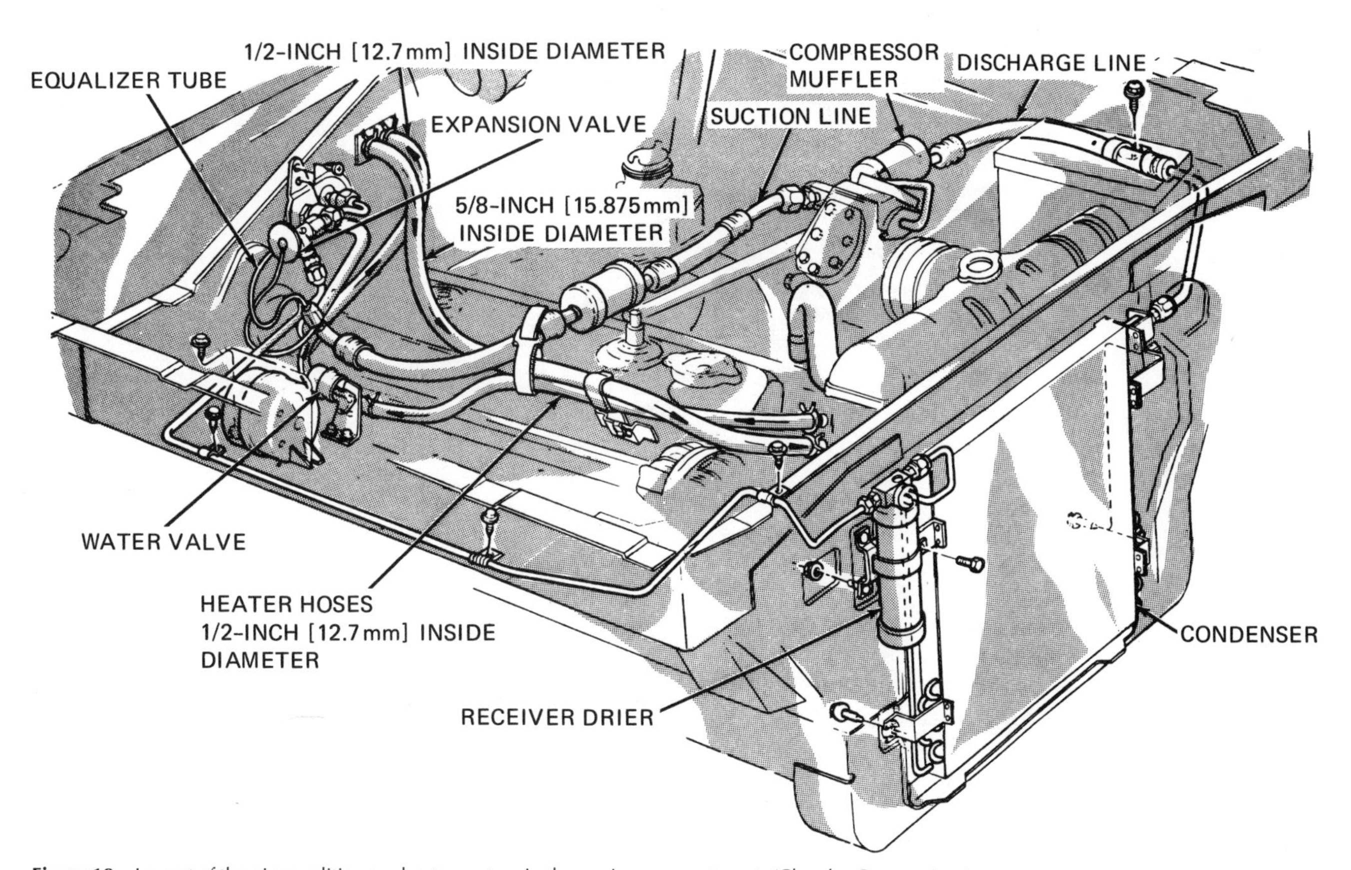

Figure 18 Layout of the air-conditioner – heater system in the engine compartment. *(Chrysler Corporation.)*

um connection to the control assembly. This extra connection is needed because the vacuum motor has three functions. It is used to do the following:

1. Close off the defrost vents and send all the heated air to the floor registers.

2. Send half the air to the defrost vents and half to the floor registers.

3. Send all the heated air to the defrost vents.

The vacuum motor is thus either all the way on (HEAT position), half on (halfway between HEAT and DEFROST), or off

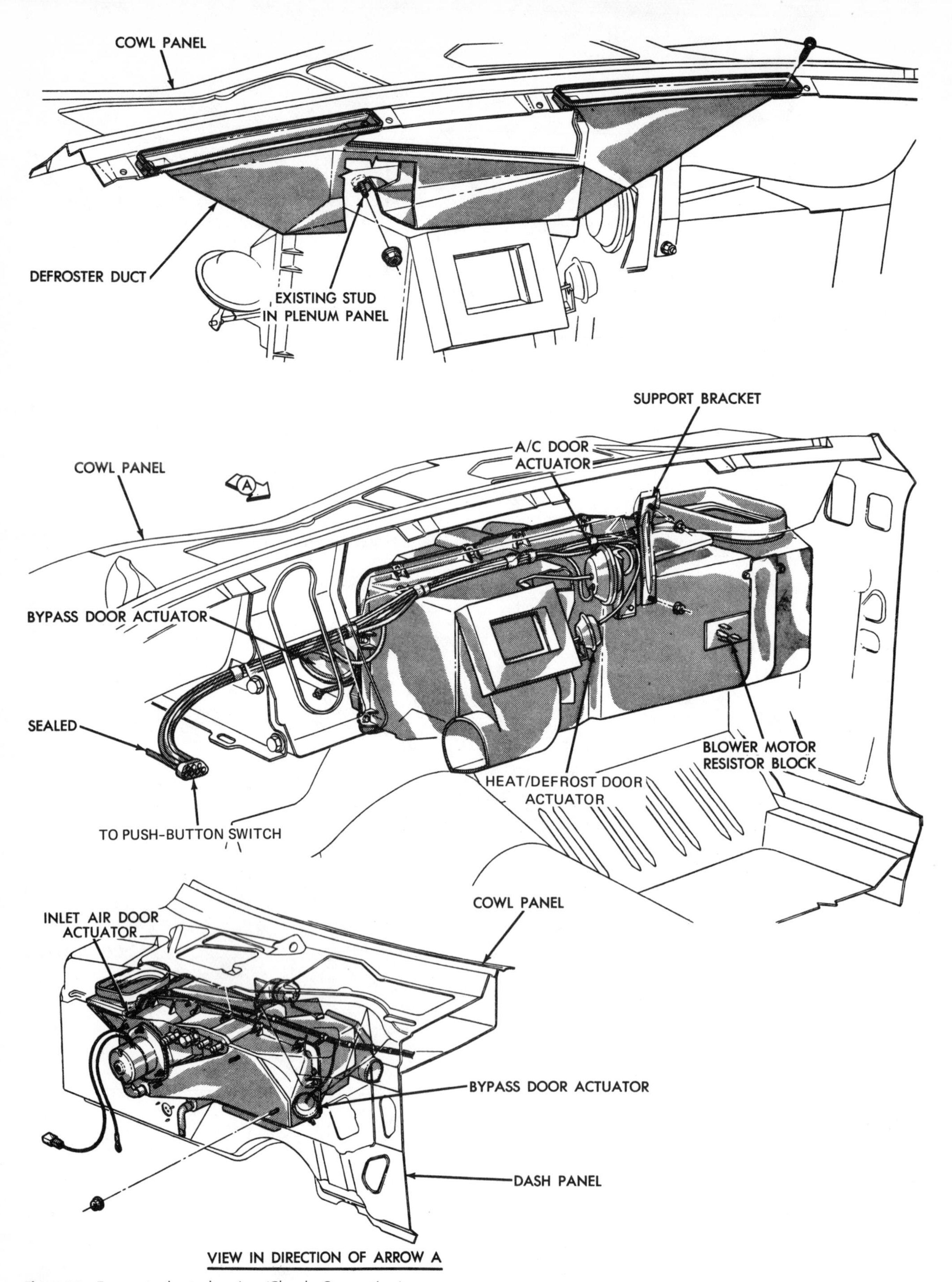

Figure 19 Evaporator-heater housing. *(Chrysler Corporation.)*

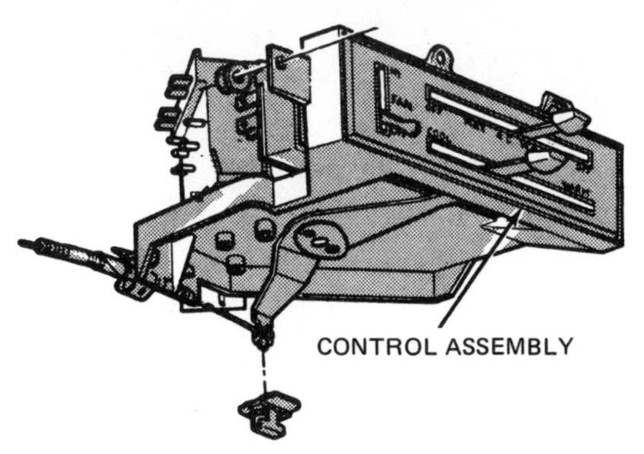

Figure 20 Control panel for manually controlled air-conditioner – heater system. *(Chrysler Corporation.)*

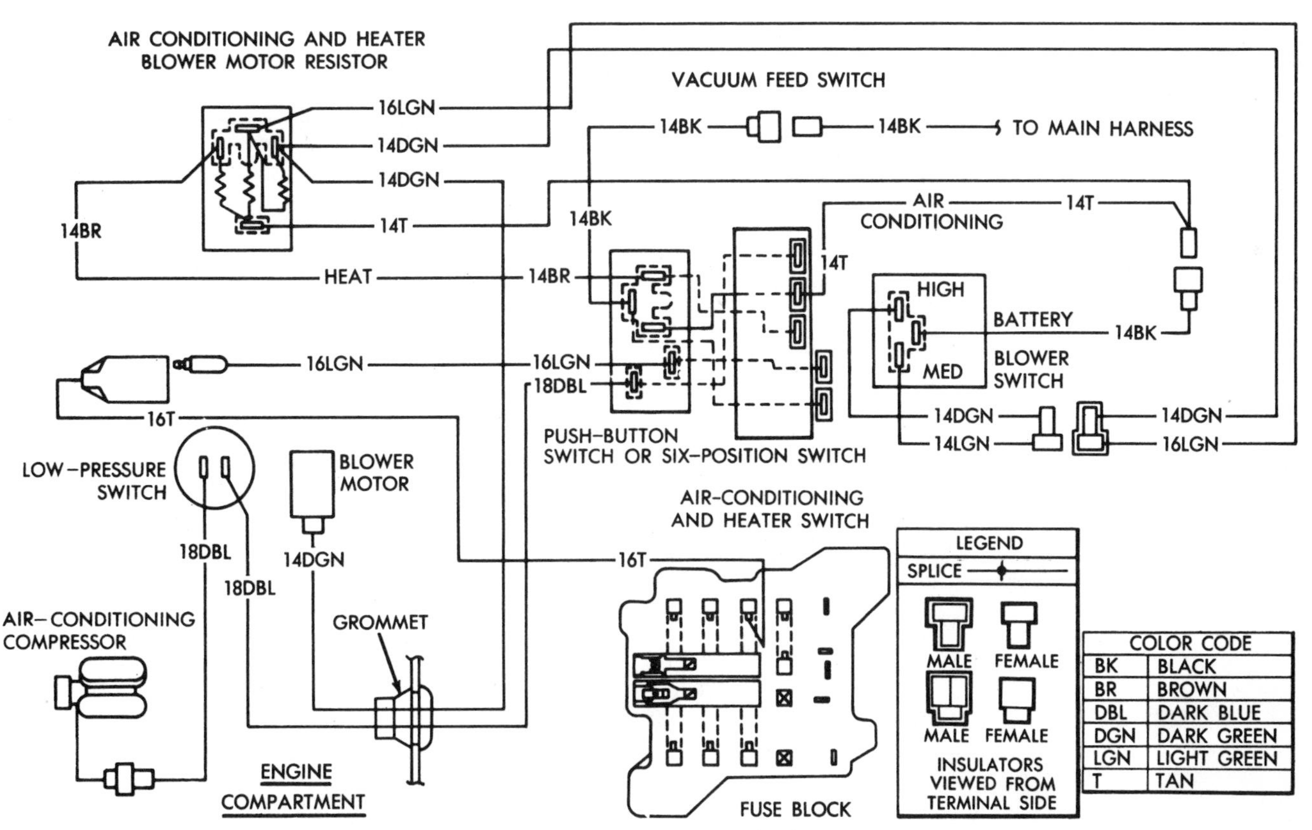

Figure 21 Electric system for manually controlled air-conditioner – heater system. *(Chrysler Corporation.)*

(DEFROST position). See Figs. 9 to 11. This type of vacuum motor is called a "two-step unit."

Note, in Fig. 14, that the system includes a vacuum-supply, or reserve, tank with a check valve. The tank holds a reserve of vacuum. The check valve closes to prevent the loss of vacuum if the engine-manifold vacuum drops off excessively.

Figure 15 shows the complete assembly, as it looks installed in the car. The views around the edge show how the connectors go together.

■ **8-3-6 Blower** Figure 16 shows the blower motor and wheel for the system. Note the evaporator case in the background. The POA suction throttling valve is mounted on top of it. Figure 17 shows how the suction throttling valve is attached, and how the expansion valve is mounted on the evaporator assembly. Figure 17 also shows the expansion valve in sectional view. We covered the operation of these valves in detail in ■8-2-5 to 8-2-8. Note that the valves in Fig. 17 are of the separately mounted type. That is, they are not mounted within the receiver-dehydrator (■8-2-9).

■ **8-3-7 Chrysler Manually Controlled Air-Conditioner – Heater System** This system is very similar to the Ford system discussed in ■8-3-2 to 8-3-6. Figure 18 shows the

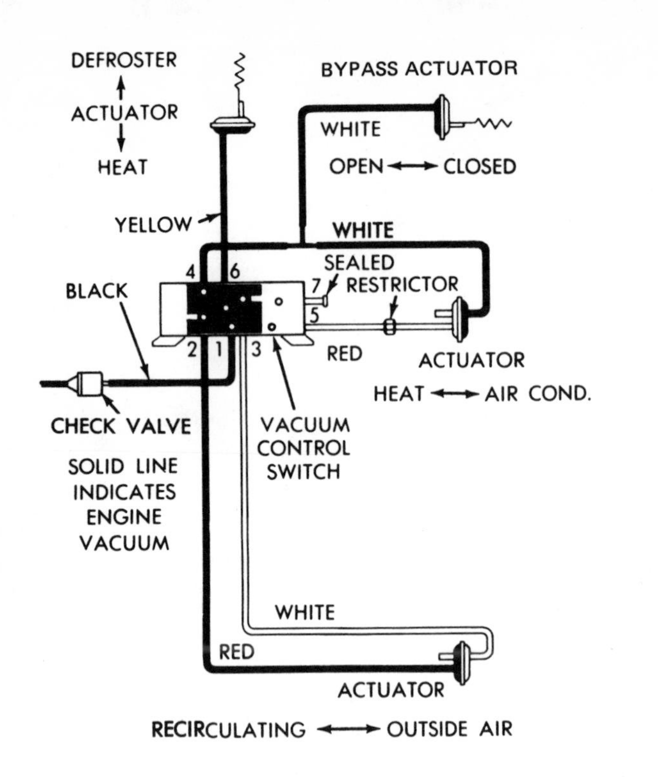

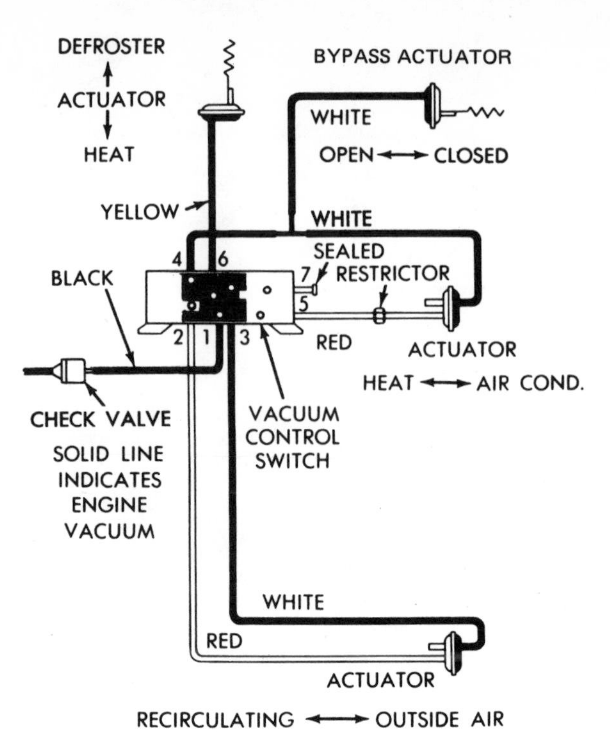

OFF MAX-A/C

A/C-VENT

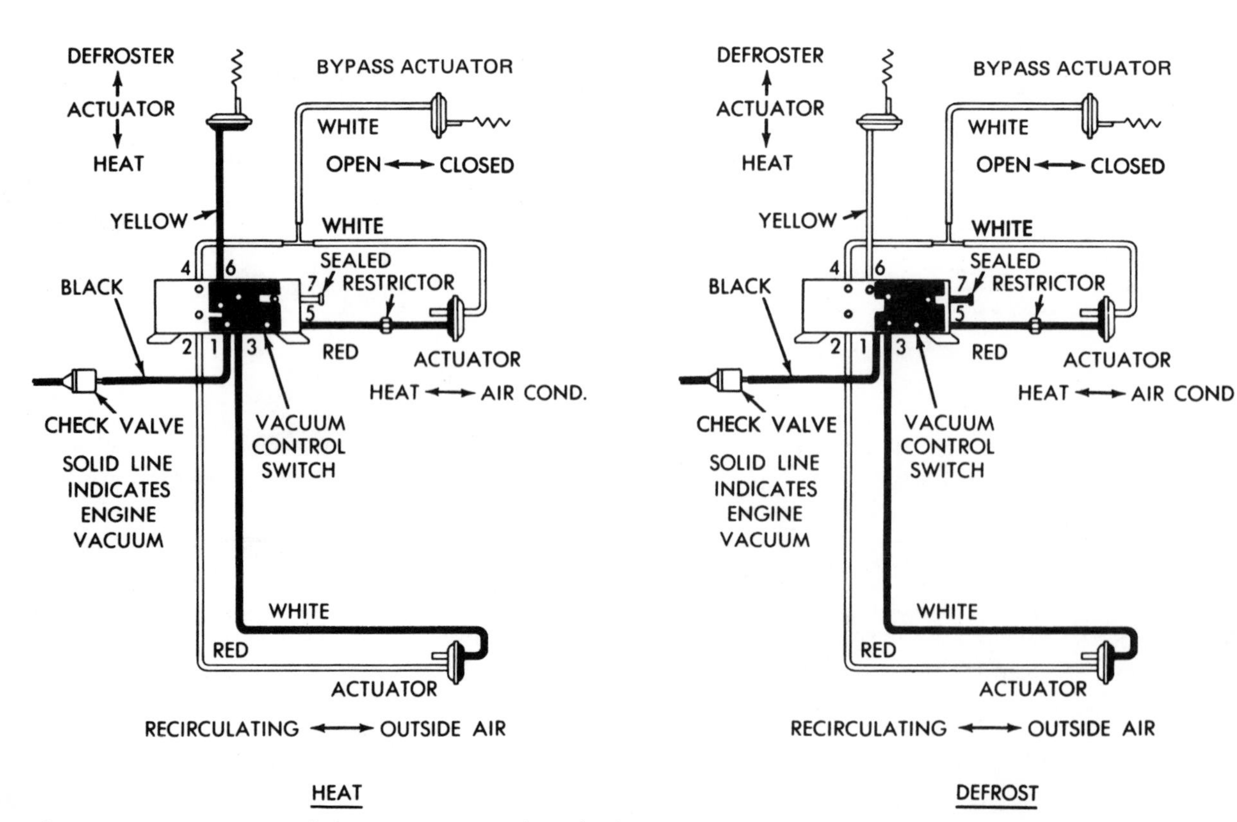

Figure 22 Vacuum circuits in the various operating modes. *(Chrysler Corporation.)*

Table 1. Positions of the doors in the various operating modes

Functional lever control position	OFF	MAX A/C	A/C	VENT	HEAT	DEFROST
Inlet air door (open to)	Inside	Inside	Outside	Outside	Outside	Outside.
Mode door (open to)	A/C	A/C	A/C	A/C	Heat/Def.	Heat/Def.
Heat defrost (open to)	Heat	Heat	Heat	Heat	Heat	Defrost
Bypass door	Open	Open	Open	Open	Closed	Closed
Compressor clutch	Off	On	On	Off	Off	Off
Blower	Off	On	On	On	On	On

Source: Chrysler Corporation.

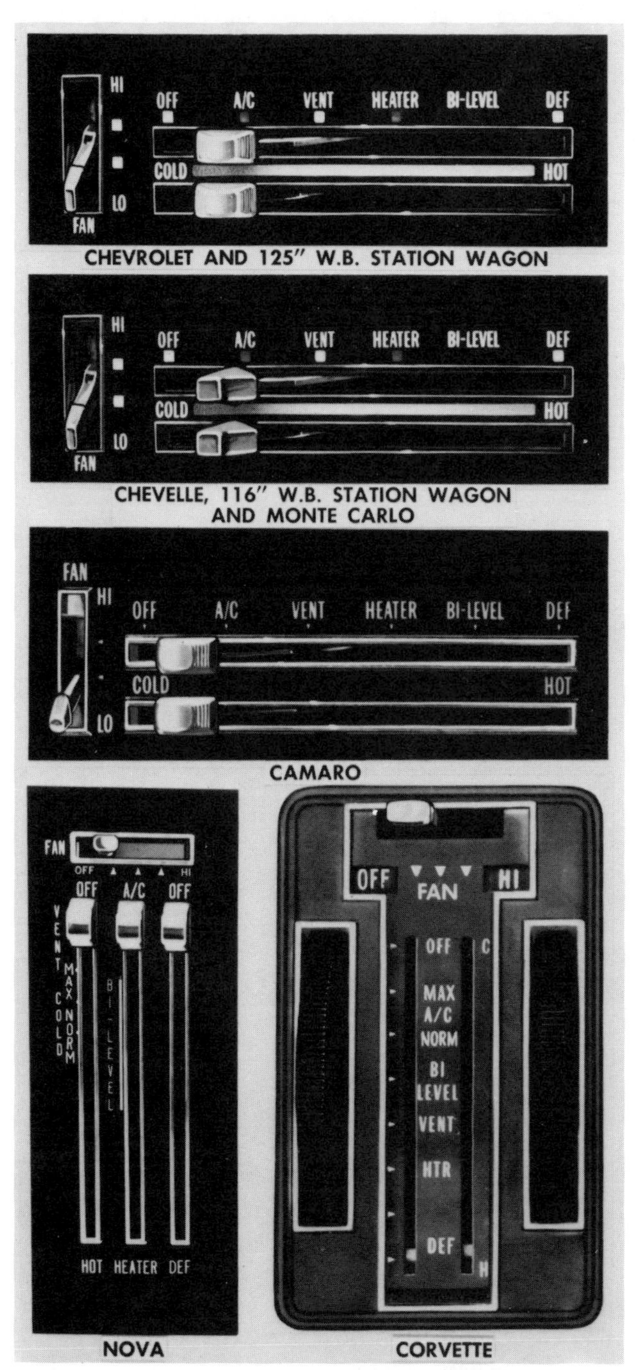

Figure 23 Control panels for various Chevrolet models using manually controlled air-conditioner–heater systems. *(Chevrolet Motor Division of General Motors Corporation.)*

general layout of the system in the engine compartment. As you can see, it has the usual receiver-dehydrator (called the "receiver-drier" by Chrysler), condenser, compressor, muffler, water valve, and expansion valve. The air conditioner is of the evaporator-pressure-control-valve type. Note that the compressor is of the V type described in ■8-2-3. Figure 19 shows how the heater–air-conditioner assembly mounts under the instrument panel. The instrument panel has been removed in this picture so the assembly can be seen.

The control panel looks much like the Ford panel (Fig. 20). The electric circuit for one model is shown in Fig. 21. The circuit looks a little complicated, but you can see that it includes the blower switch, the motor resistor assembly, the control-assembly electric switch, and the connections to the compressor magnetic switch. This circuit is wired through the low-pressure switch (discussed in ■8-2-14).

One difference between the Chrysler and the Ford systems is in the operation of the temperature control lever. This lever controls the water valve (Chrysler) rather than a temperature-blend door (Ford).

Table 1 shows the various operating modes of the system. Note that there are six settings for the functional control lever (see also Fig. 20). These are OFF, MAX A/C, A/C, VENT, HEAT, and DEFROST. As you study the chart, you will see how the lever settings affect the positions of the various doors in the system.

This system does not have as many vacuum motors as the Ford System. Figure 22 shows the vacuum circuits of the Chrysler system in the four basic operating modes. Note that there are four single-step vacuum motors. Study the four operating modes to see which vacuum motors are active in the four functional-lever positions, and what they do. Note the check valve in the line to the engine intake manifold (engine vacuum in Fig. 22). It prevents loss of vacuum in the system in case the manifold vacuum drops off.

This system is of the reheat-cooling type. The air conditioner constantly operates at full capacity when the functional control lever is in the MAX A/C or A/C position. "Full capacity" means the maximum cooling required by the existing temperature and humidity. If the discharge air from the air-conditioning outlets is too cold, the air temperature can be increased. This is done by moving the temperature control lever toward WARM. This opens the water valve. Now, hot coolant from the engine cooling system can flow through the heater core. This warms the cold air coming from the evaporator. The amount of

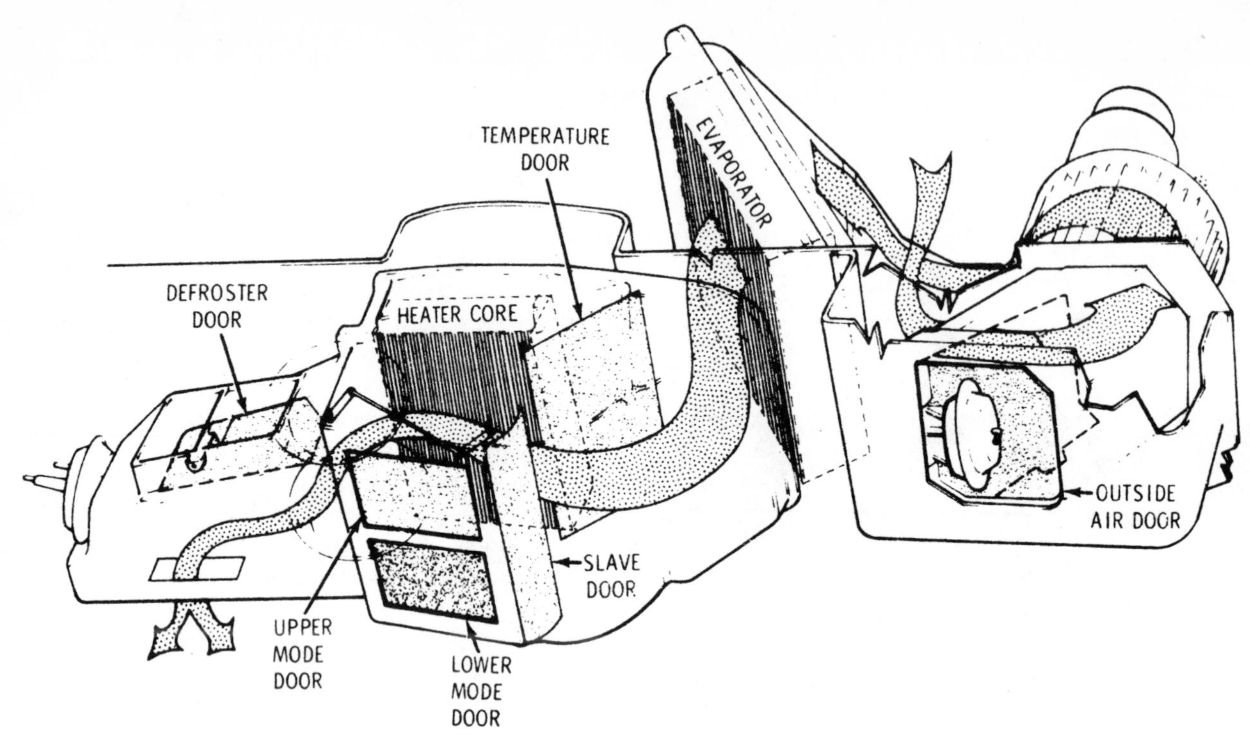

Figure 24 Airflow in the OFF mode. *(Oldsmobile Division of General Motors Corporation.)*

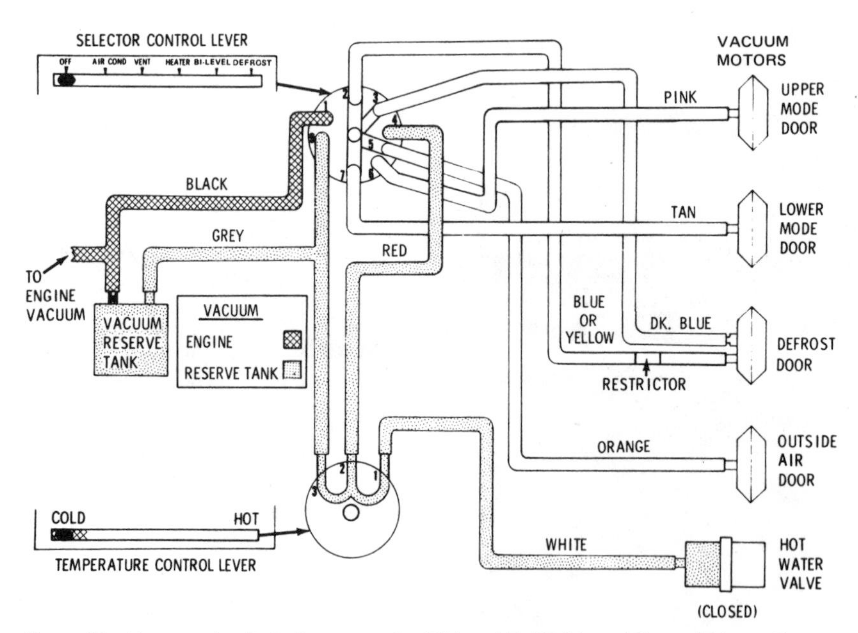

Figure 25 Vacuum circuits in the OFF mode. *(Oldsmobile Division of General Motors Corporation.)*

warming depends on the position of the temperature control lever, since that lever controls the water-valve opening.

■ 8-3-8 General Motors Manually Controlled Air-Conditioner–Heater System

The General Motors (GM) system is very similar to the systems described previously. It is also of the evaporator-pressure-control-valve type. Figure 23 shows the control panels for the various Chevrolet models. The control lever is at the upper left in Fig. 23. The temperature lever is underneath it. The functional control lever has six positions: OFF, A/C, VENT, HEATER, BI-LEVEL, and DEF.

When the functional control lever is placed in the A/C, BI-LEVEL, and DEF positions, the compressor clutch is connected to the battery. This means that the compressor runs when the lever is in these positions – provided the air temperature is above 40°F (4.4°C). Many systems have an ambient switch to prevent compressor operation if the outdoor temperature is too

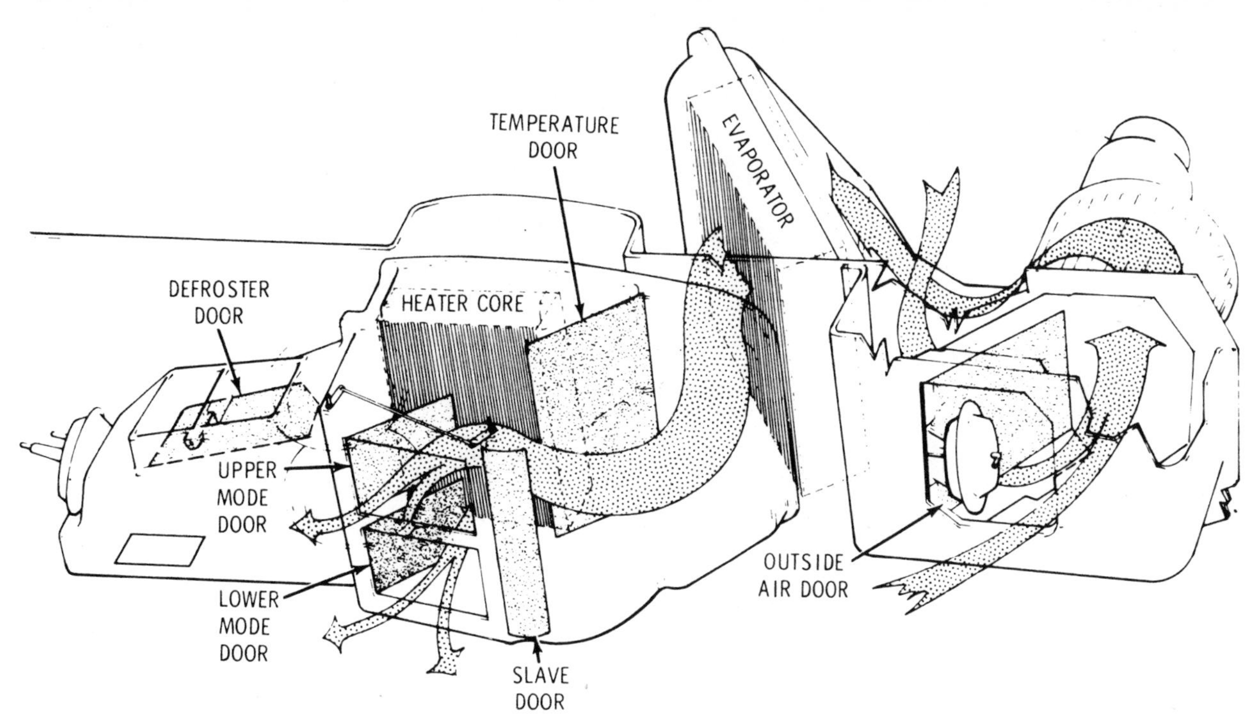

Figure 26 Airflow in the A/C mode. *(Oldsmobile Division of General Motors Corporation.)*

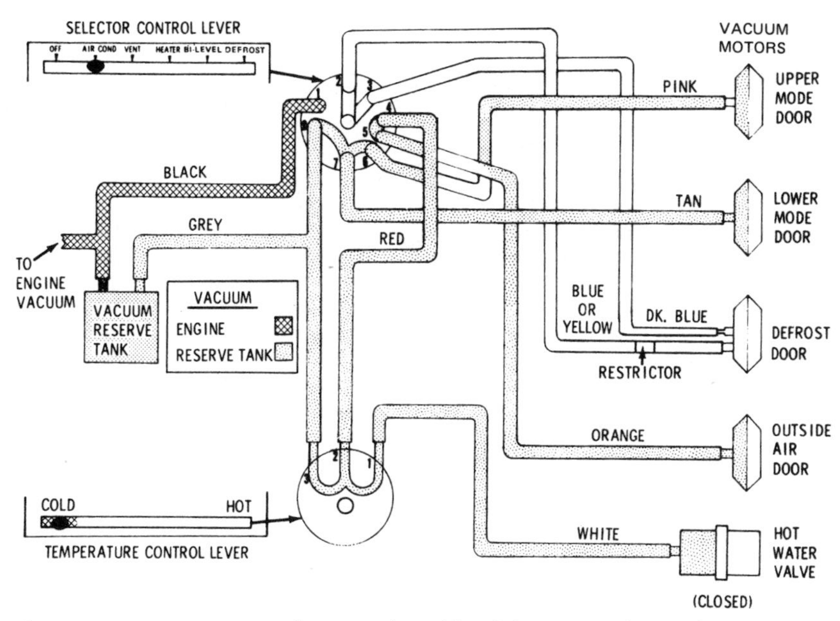

Figure 27 Vacuum circuits in the A/C mode. *(Oldsmobile Division of General Motors Corporation.)*

low. This switch is in the circuit between the battery and the magnetic clutch on the compressor. The switch opens at low temperature, to prevent compressor action.

In the OFF, VENT, and HEATER positions, the compressor magnetic clutch is not energized. Thus, in these positions, there is no compressor action and no air conditioning.

The functional control lever determines the direction in which the air flows through the system. Moving the lever changes the position of the vacuum valve in the control assembly. Depending on its position, the vacuum valve either supplies vacuum to, or cuts vacuum off from, the vacuum motors in the system.

■ **8-3-9 General Motors Manually Controlled System Operation** We shall now look at the operation of the system with the functional control lever in the various operating positions.

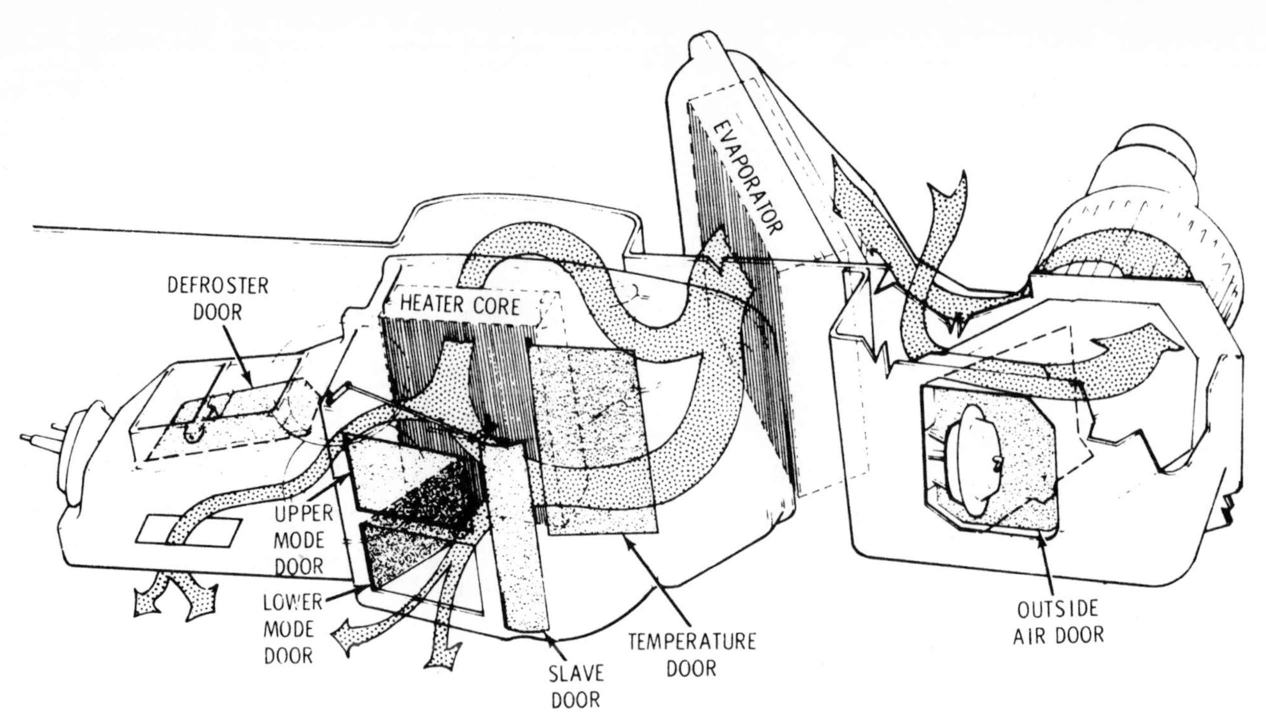

Figure 28 Airflow in the VENT mode. *(Oldsmobile Division of General Motors Corporation.)*

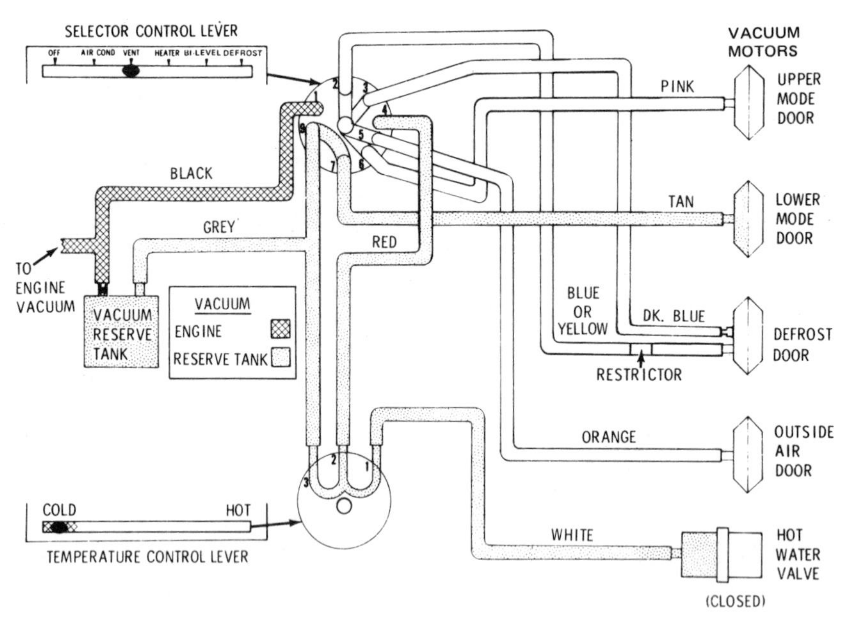

Figure 29 Vacuum circuits in the VENT mode. *(Oldsmobile Division of General Motors Corporation.)*

With the lever in the OFF position, and the blower turned on, the airflow is as shown in Fig. 24. Note which doors are open and which are closed. Now look at Fig. 25, which shows the vacuum circuits with the lever in the OFF position. Note that the only vacuum motor operating is the one controlling the hot-water valve. It has closed the hot-water valve so that no hot coolant can flow from the engine cooling system to the heater core. The temperature control lever controls the hot-water-valve vacuum motor through the three-port vacuum switch. This lever also controls the position of the temperature door through a wire (a Bowden cable) connected between them.

With the functional control lever in the AIR COND (A/C) position, the airflow is as shown in Fig. 26. An electric switch in the control assembly connects the compressor magnetic clutch to the battery. If the other clutch switches in the circuit are also closed (see ■ 8-2-14), the magnetic clutch engages. The compressor operates, and the air-conditioning system goes

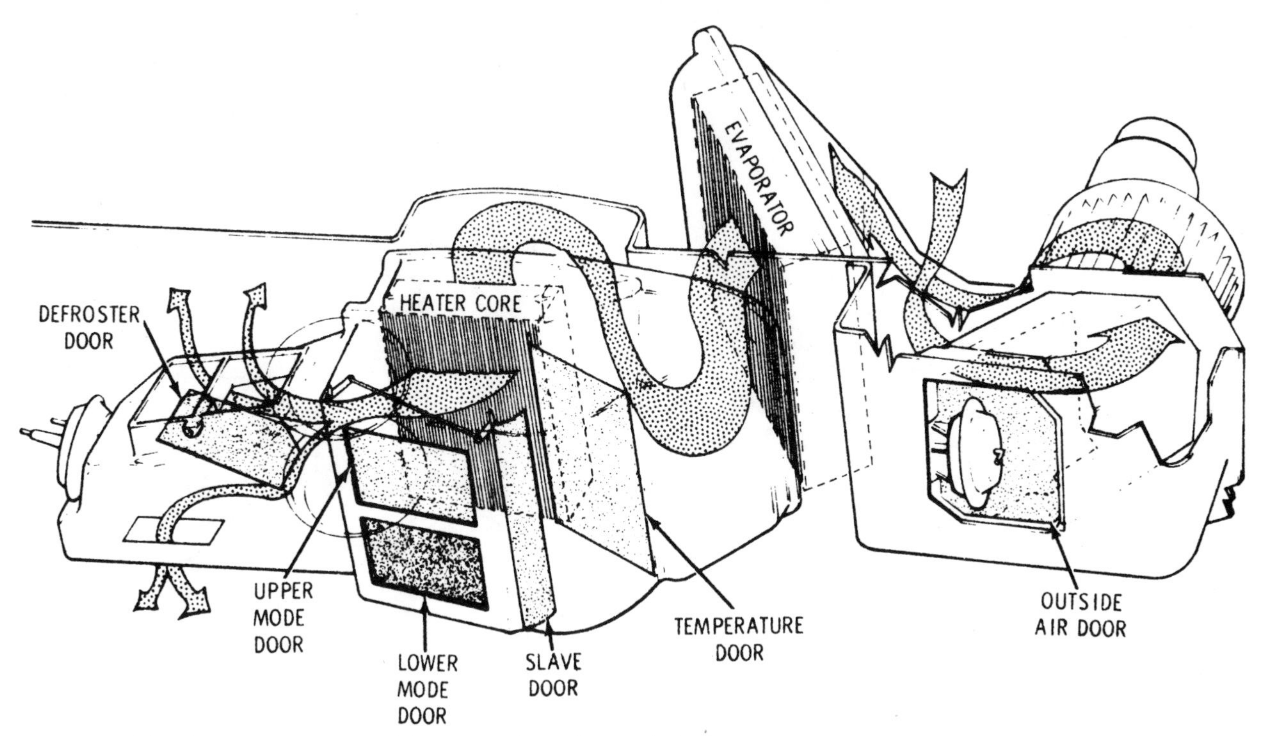

Figure 30 Airflow in the HEATER mode. *(Oldsmobile Division of General Motors Corporation.)*

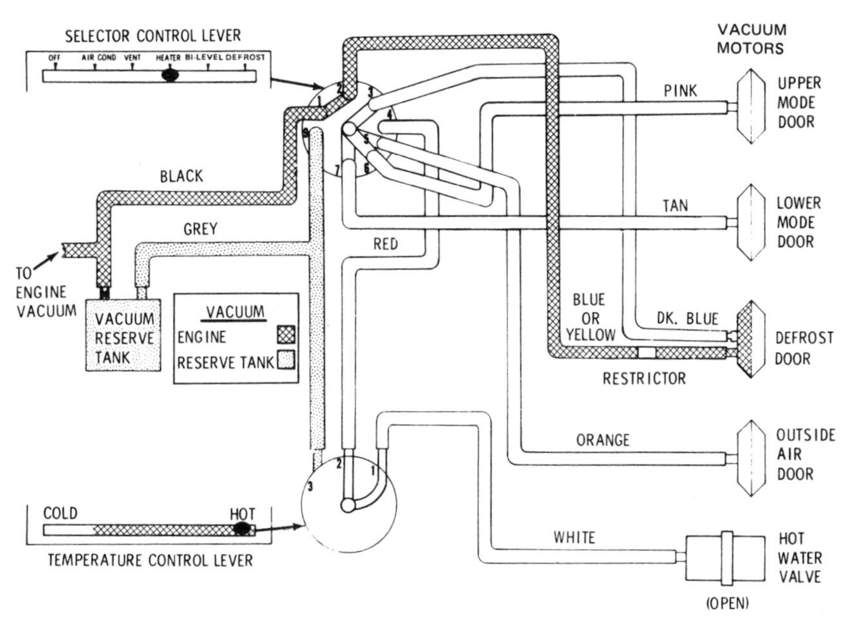

Figure 31 Vacuum circuits in the HEATER mode. *(Oldsmobile Division of General Motors Corporation.)*

to work. The evaporator temperature drops, and the air passing through the evaporator is cooled. Figure 27 shows the vacuum circuits with the lever in the AIR COND position. Note that the vacuum is applied to the vacuum motors of the upper mode door, lower mode door, outside-air door, and hot-water valve. All this causes the doors to take the positions shown in Fig. 27.

Now let us look at the situation with the functional selector lever set at VENT. The airflow is shown in Fig. 28. The situation in the vacuum circuits with the lever in the vent position is as shown in Fig. 29. Note that only the vacuum motors for the lower mode door and the hot-water valve are actuated—that is, have vacuum applied to them. This positions the doors as in Fig. 28, for airflow as shown. The electric circuit to the magnetic clutch is open, so the compressor and air-conditioning system do not work.

Figure 30 shows the airflow through the system when the functional control lever is set at HEATER. Note which doors are open. Now look at Fig. 31, which shows the vacuum cir-

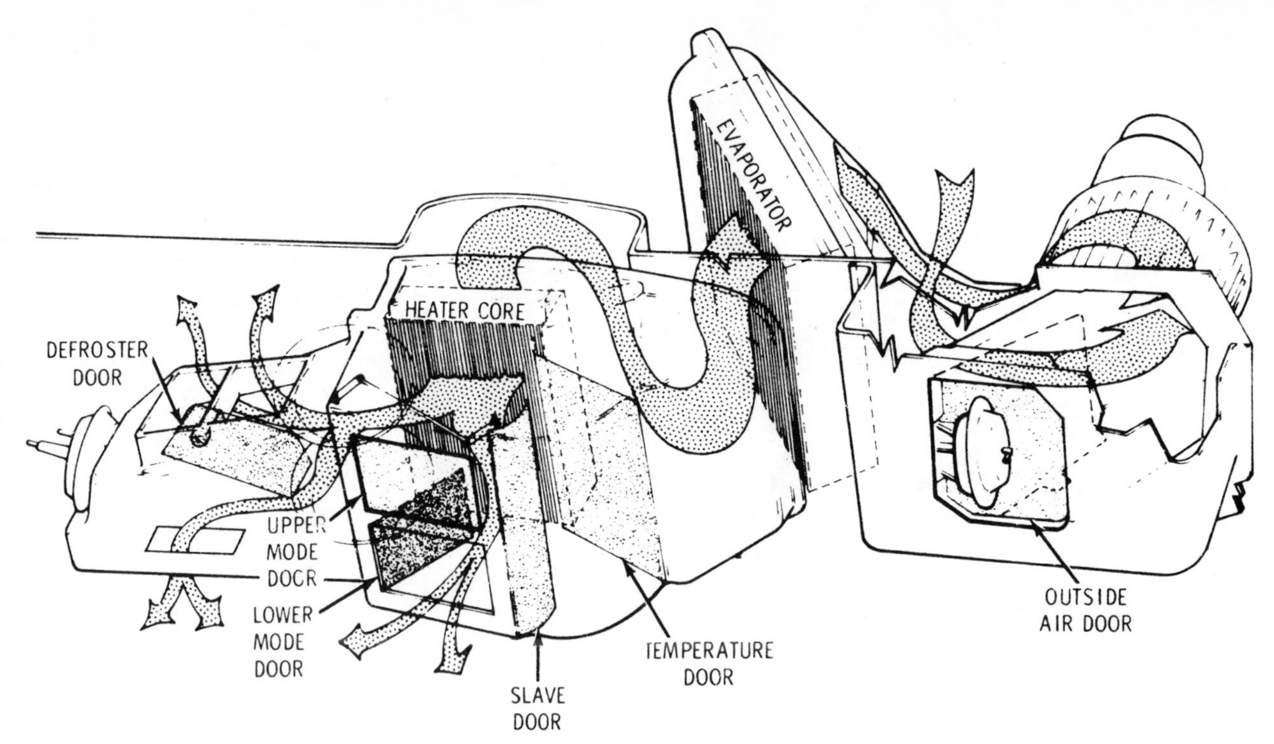

Figure 32 Airflow in the BI-LEVEL mode. *(Oldsmobile Division of General Motors Corporation.)*

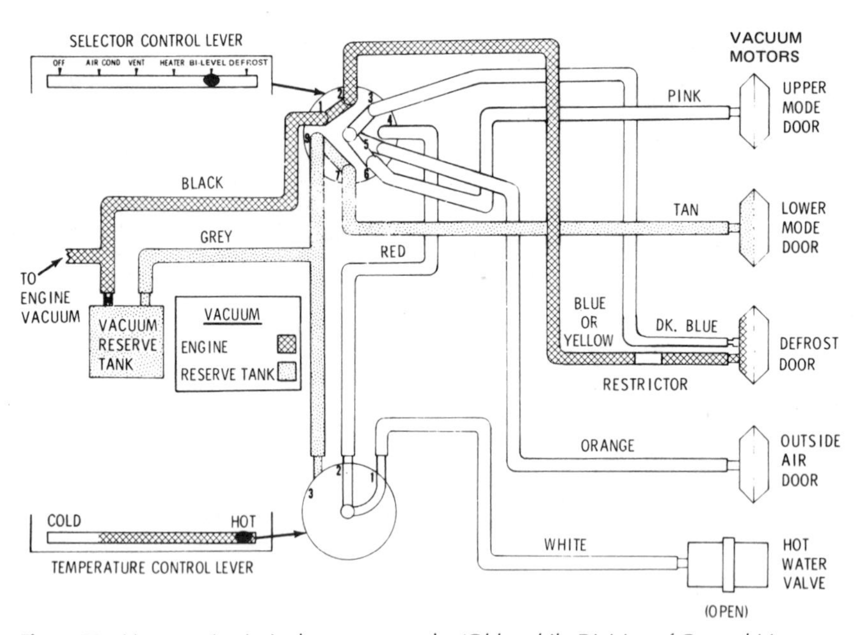

Figure 33 Vacuum circuits in the BI-LEVEL mode. *(Oldsmobile Division of General Motors Corporation.)*

cuits when the functional control lever is set at HEATER. Note that the engine vacuum is applied directly to the defrost door, so it takes the position shown in Fig. 30. The temperature control lever has been moved to HOT. This positions the temperature door as shown. It also cuts off the vacuum to the hot-water-valve vacuum motor. This allows the hot-water valve to open, so hot coolant flows through the heater core. Also, the circuit to the magnetic clutch is open. Thus, when the air flows through the system (Fig. 30), it picks up heat from the heater core. No cooling takes place.

Figure 32 shows the airflow with the functional control lever set at BI-LEVEL. The vacuum circuits are shown in Fig. 33.

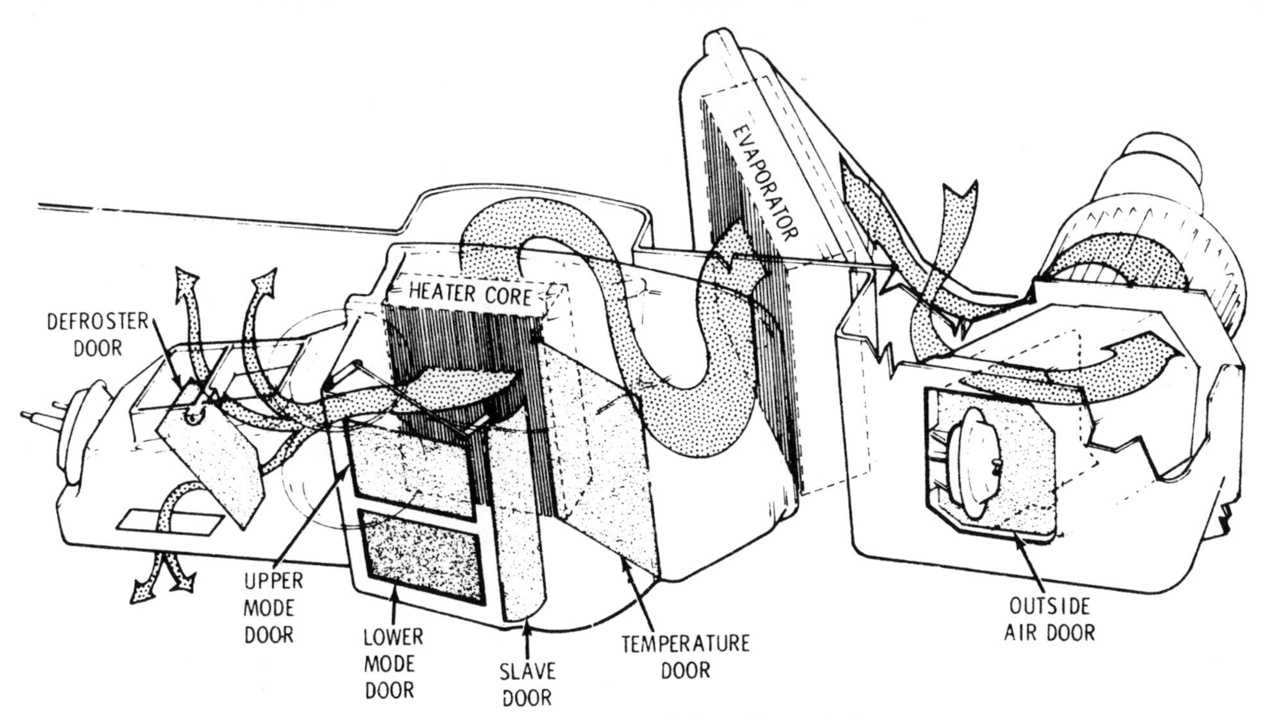

Figure 34 Airflow in the DEFROST mode. *(Oldsmobile Division of General Motors Corporation.)*

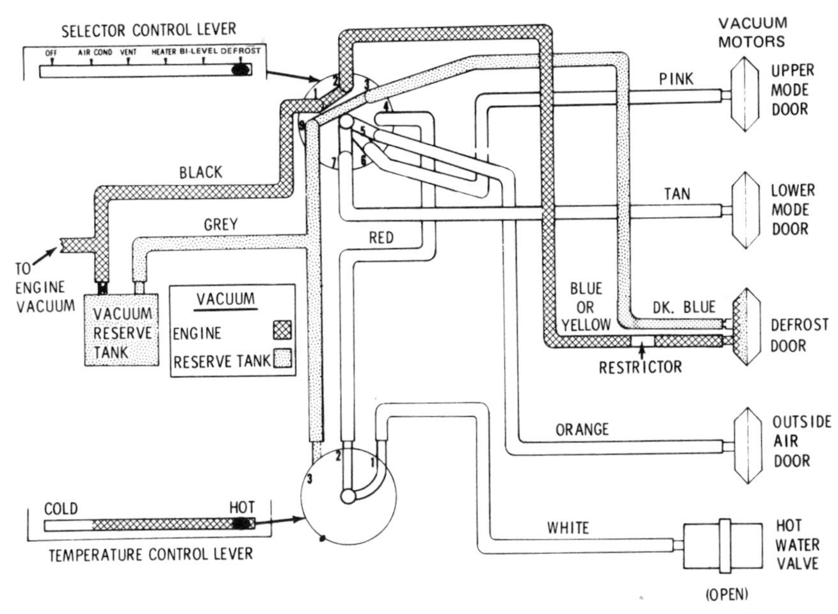

Figure 35 Vacuum circuits in the DEFROST mode. *(Oldsmobile Division of General Motors Corporation.)*

Note that the vacuum switch directs vacuum to the lower mode door and the defrost door, so they take the positions shown in Fig. 32.

When the functional control lever is moved to DEFROST, the airflow is as shown in Fig. 34. The vacuum circuits are as shown in Fig. 35. Note that the vacuum is applied to both vacuum connections for the defrost door. This causes the defrost vacuum motor to swing the door all the way down (Fig. 34). Now, most of the heated air passes up through the defrost vents (Fig. 34). Some air does flow past the notch in the defrost door, so some hot air moves into the car through the hot-air vents.

SECTION 8-4 General Motors Automatically Controlled Air-Conditioner–Heater Systems

This section continues the discussion of automatic temperature-control systems in automobiles. It describes the construction and operation of the systems used in General Motors (GM) cars. These systems have automatic controls that maintain a preset temperature. The driver sets the desired temperature, and the system either heats or cools to maintain that temperature.

■ 8-4-1 General Motors Automatic Air Conditioner

This system is shown in top view, in an automobile, in Fig. 1. Note that it includes all the standard components of the evaporator-pressure-control-valve system. The air-conditioning system is very much like the manually controlled system described in ■8-3-8 and 8-3-9. The basic difference is that it has additional controls to ensure automatic operation. That is, the system heats or cools as required to maintain the preset temperature.

■ 8-4-2 Control-Panel Settings

Figure 2 shows a typical control panel for the GM automatic air-conditioning system. The temperature control is a thumb wheel which can be turned to set the desired temperature. The functional control lever has the seven positions discussed below.

1. OFF In the OFF position, the system is completely shut off when the ignition switch is turned off. When the ignition switch is turned on, the circuit to the air-conditioner electric system is completed. The system then comes on if the engine coolant temperature reaches about 140°F (60°C) or the passenger-compartment temperature reaches 80°F (26.7°C). The fan runs at the low blower speed, and air flows from the heater outlets. However, the compressor does not operate.

2. VENT When the functional control lever is moved to VENT, the system comes on. The blower runs at low speed. Outside air is sent into the passenger compartment through the A/C outlets. The compressor is off, and the outside air comes in unheated and uncooled.

3. LO-AUTO The system comes on only if the car temperature is above 80°F (26.7°C), or the engine coolant tempera-

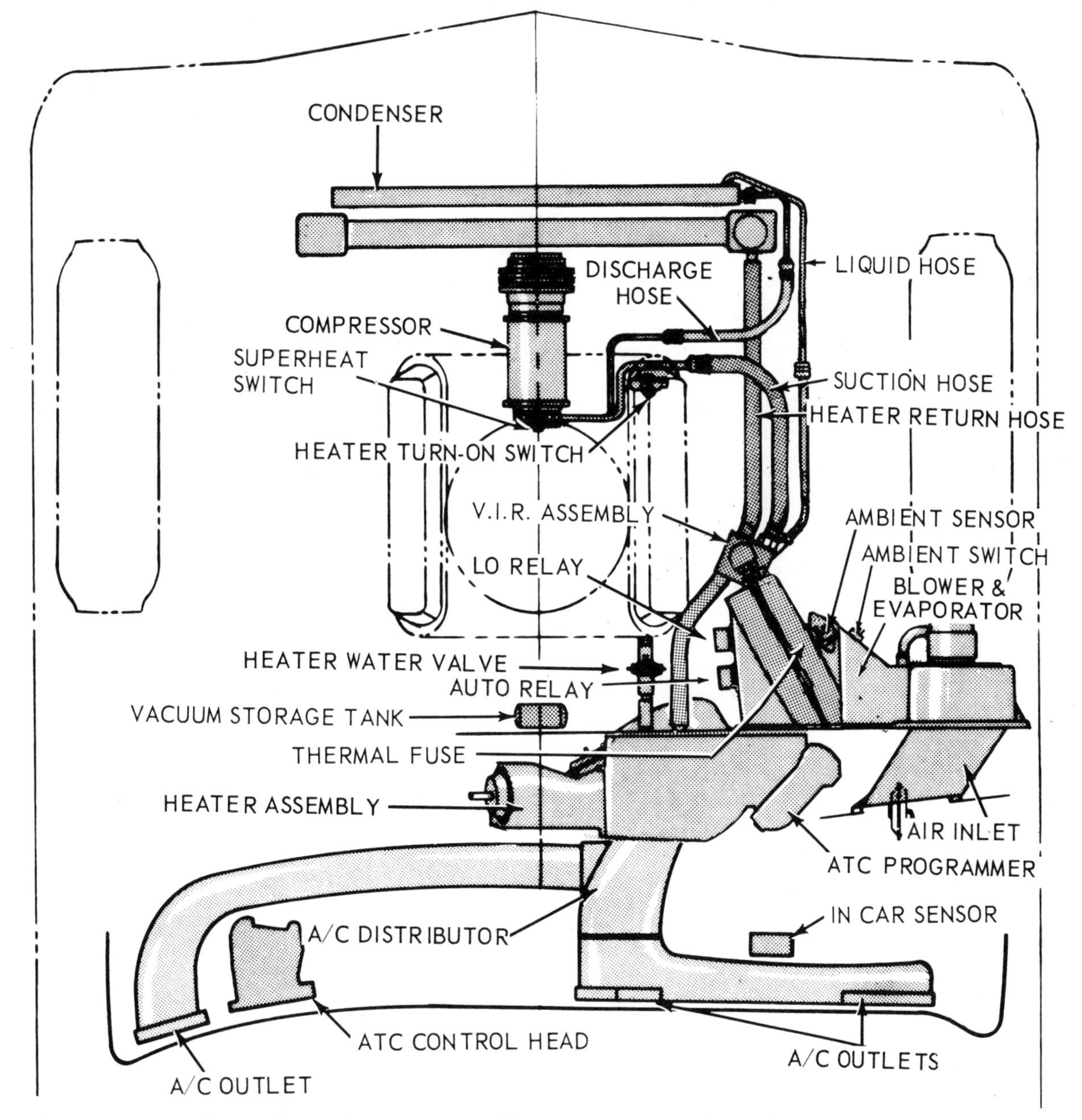

Figure 1 Top view of air-conditioner – heater system. *(Cadillac Motor Car Division of General Motors Corporation.)*

ture is above about 140°F (60°C). The blower then operates at low speed only. Conditioned air flows from the A/C outlets or the heater outlets, depending on whether the system is cooling or heating.

4. *AUTO* When the functional control lever is set at the midpoint between LO-AUTO and HI-AUTO, it is in the AUTO position. Operation is the same as in the LO-AUTO position, except that the blower is not limited to low speed. Instead, it may operate at any of the four speeds (Lo, Med1, Med2, and Hi), according to the temperature in the car.

5. *HI-AUTO* This position is similar to the other two auto positions. However, the blower operates only at the top speed. If maximum air conditioning is demanded the inside air is recirculated through the A/C system for maximum cooling. When the car temperature reaches the preset level, the blower

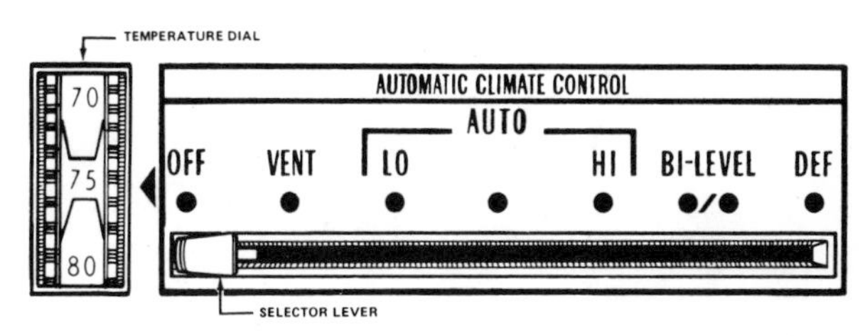

Figure 2 Control panel for automatically controlled air-conditioner – heater system. *(Buick Motor Division of General Motors Corporation.)*

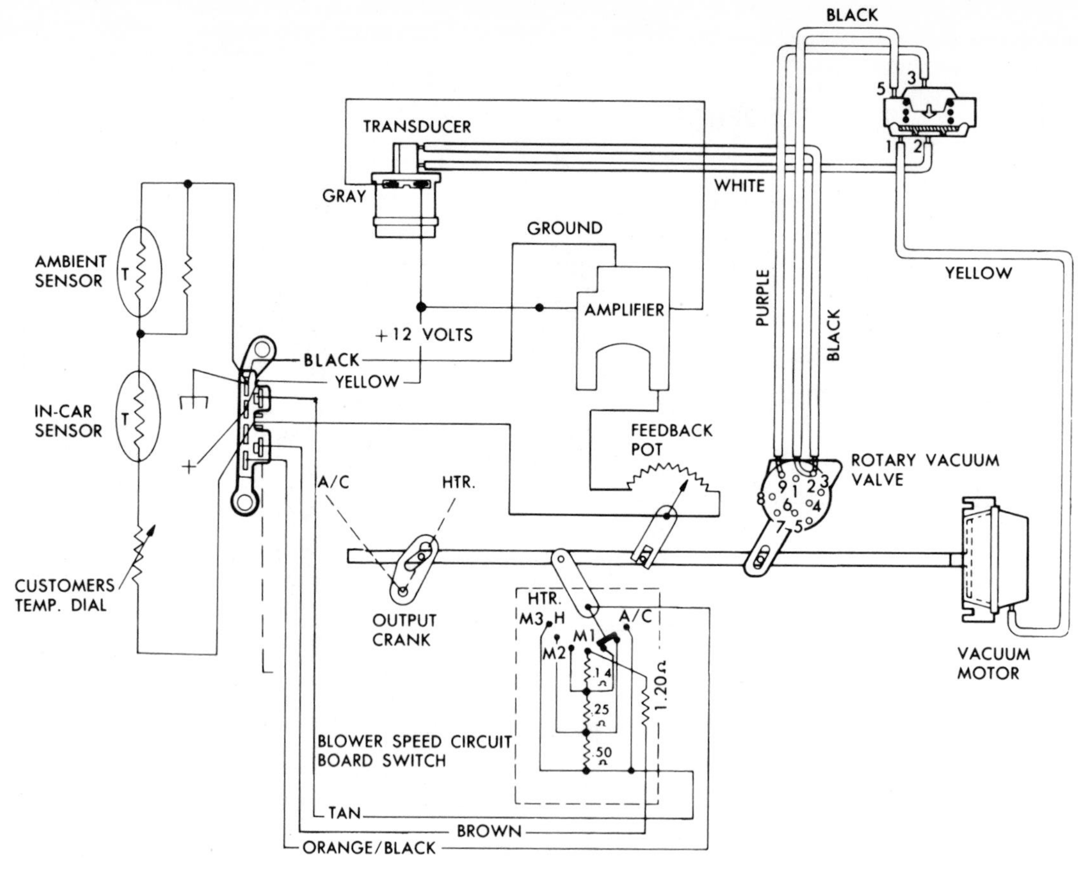

Figure 3 Temperature control circuit for automatically controlled air-conditioner–heater system. *(Cadillac Motor Car Division of General Motors Corporation.)*

speed drops off. The conditioned air flows from both the A/C and the heater outlets.

6. *BI-LEVEL* With the functional control lever in this position, the blower can operate at any of the four speeds. The conditioned air (heated or cooled) flows from the A/C, heater, and defroster outlets.

7. *DEFROST* In this position, the system comes on as soon as the ignition switch is turned on. The blower operates only at top speed. Most of the air is directed up through the defrost vents to the windshield. Some does exit to the floor through the lower vents.

■ 8-4-3 Temperature Control System

This system (Fig. 3) provides the control that maintains the preselected

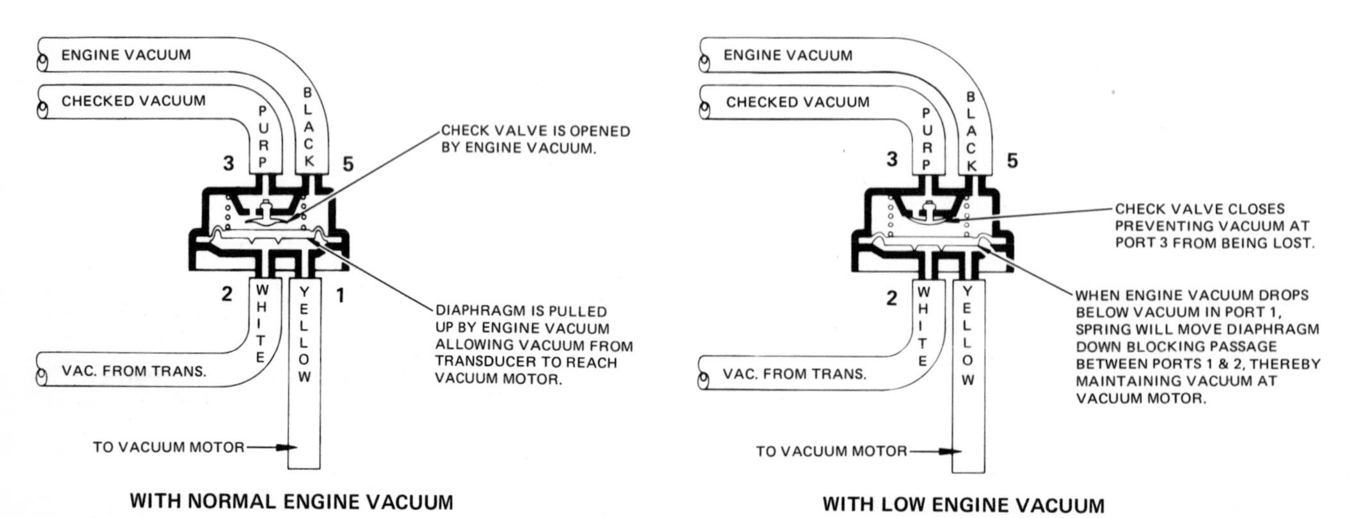

Figure 4 Operation of the vacuum checking valve. *(Cadillac Motor Car Division of General Motors Corporation.)*

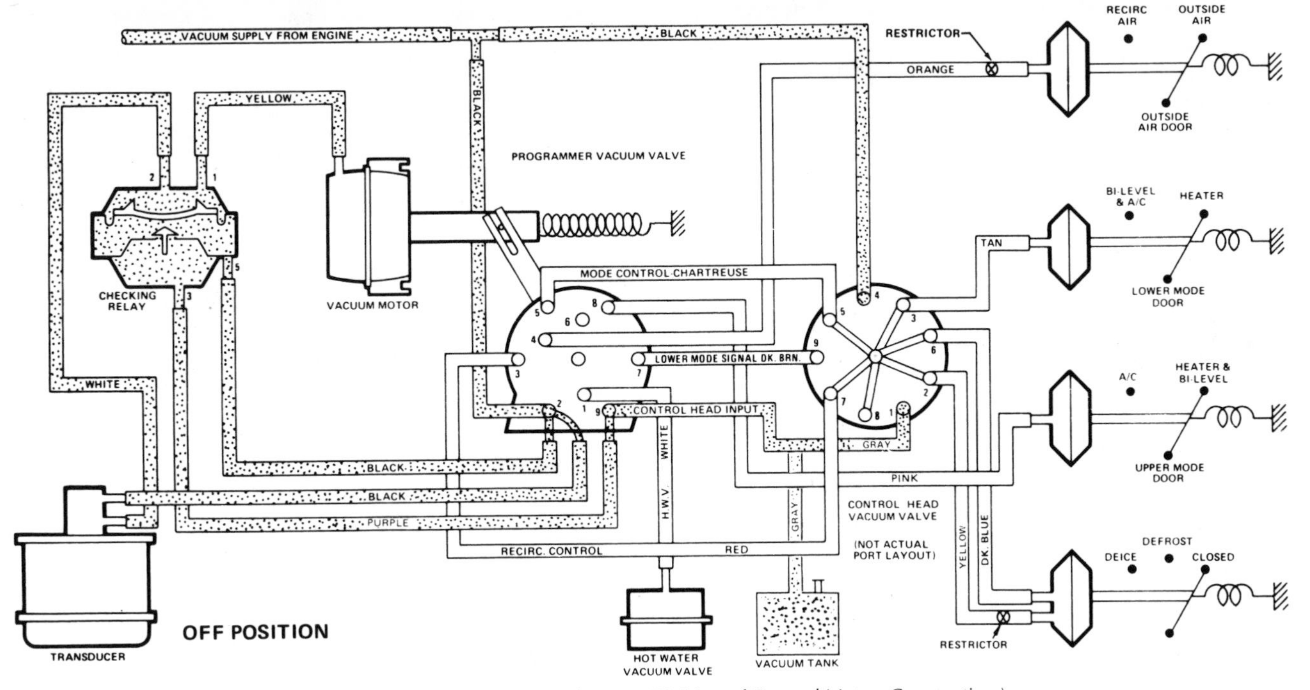

Figure 5 Conditions in the vacuum system in OFF position. *(Buick Motor Division of General Motors Corporation.)*

temperature. Note (to the left) the three resistances, in series, that feed a voltage signal to the amplifier. These three resistances are the temperature dial, the in-car temperature sensor, and the ambient or outside-air temperature sensor. The voltage leaving these three devices "tells" the amplifier what it has to do. The amplifier may increase the heating or cooling, reduce the heating or cooling, change the in-car airflow pattern, and change the blower speed. The control system acts much like the automatic systems discussed earlier.

■ 8-4-4 Vacuum Checking Relay

This relay works with the transducer to produce various actions in the system. The transducer (upper left in Fig. 3) is an electric vacuum device that opens or closes a vacuum line on electric signals from

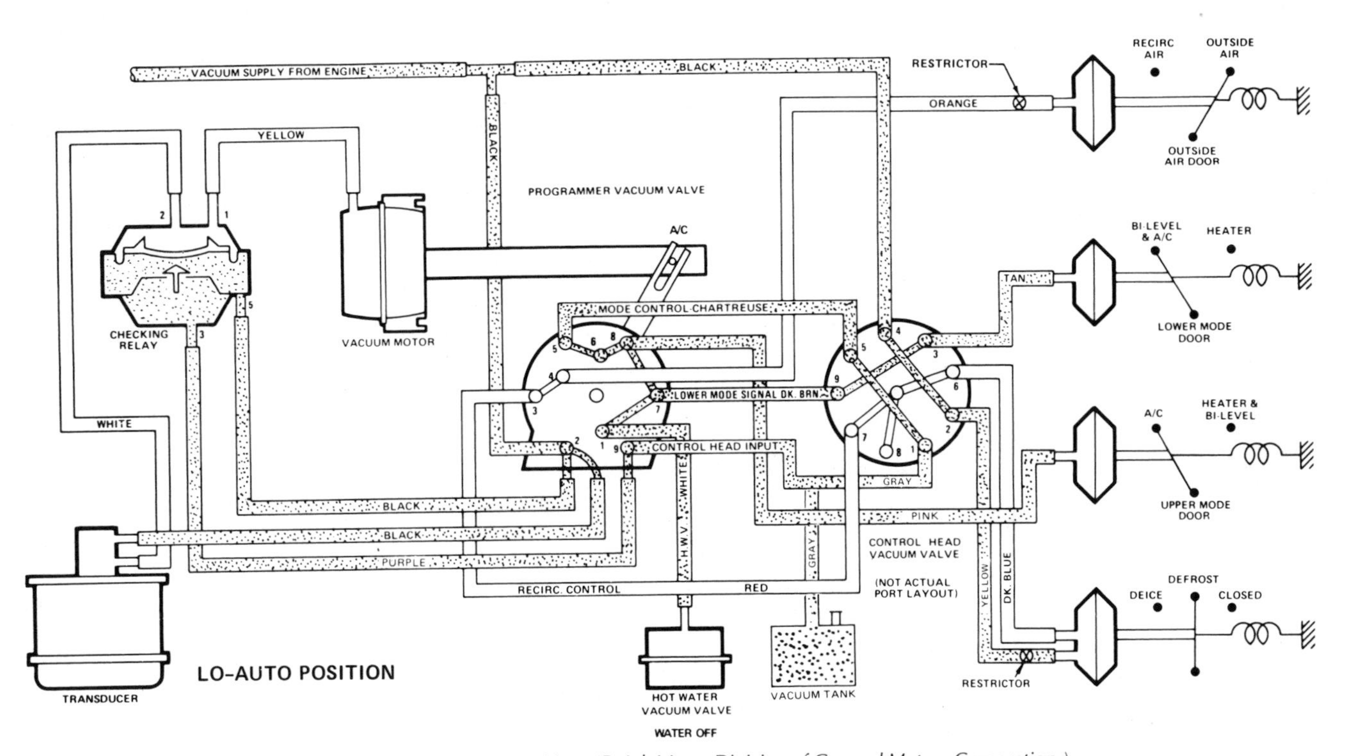

Figure 6 Conditions in the vacuum system in LO-AUTO position. *(Buick Motor Division of General Motors Corporation.)*

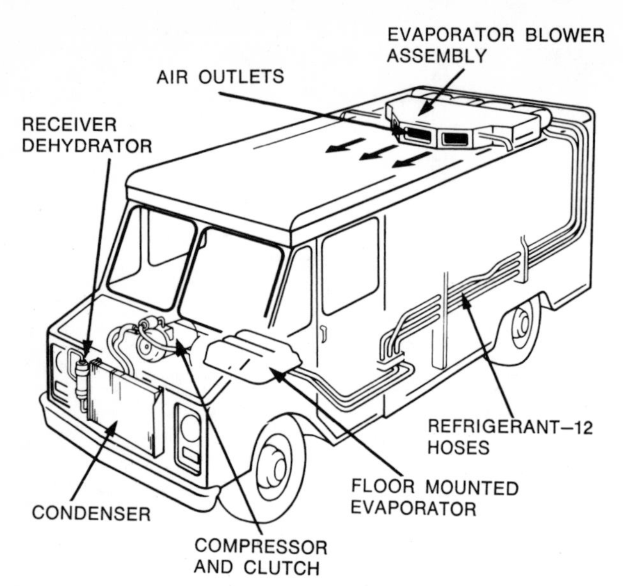

Figure 7 Air-conditioning system in a van. *(Harrison Radiator Division of General Motors Corporation.)*

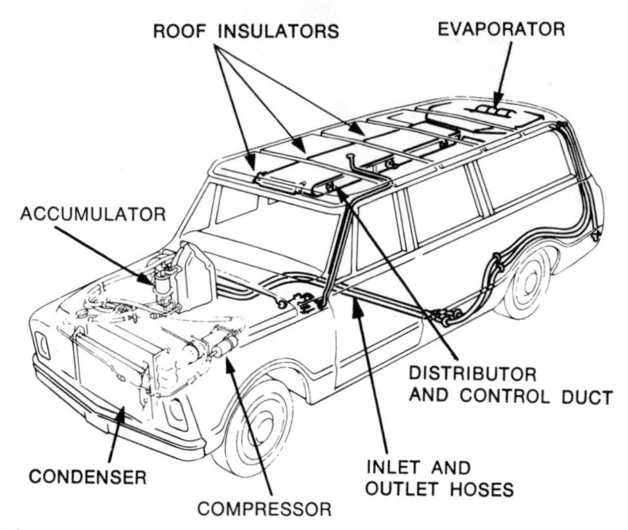

Figure 8 Air-conditioning system in a station wagon. *(Harrison Radiator Division of General Motors Corporation.)*

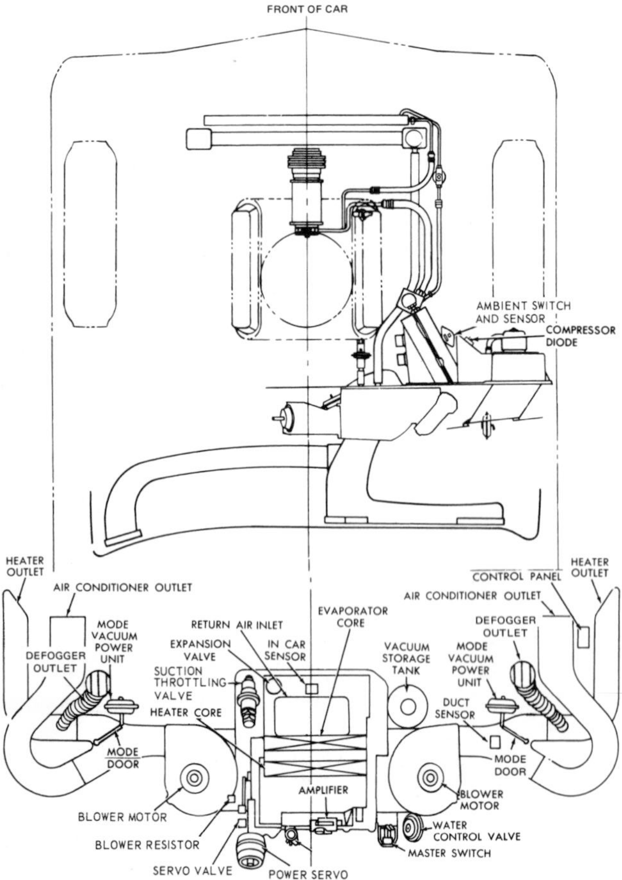

Figure 9 Layout of an air-conditioning system for the rear compartment of a limousine. *(Cadillac Motor Car Division of General Motors Corporation.)*

the amplifier. The checking valve maintains vacuum in certain parts of the system when engine-manifold vacuum drops. Figure 4 shows the operation of the vacuum checking valve.

■ 8-4-5 System Operation

We shall now describe how the system functions in various operating modes. Figure 5 shows the vacuum circuits. Note that the rotary vacuum valve is controlled by the vacuum motor. The motor operating rod has three positions: left (as shown), straight up, and to the right. In Fig. 3, you can see that the vacuum motor also controls a feedback resistance, the blower speed control, and the output crank. The output crank is linked to the temperature-blend door, which serves the same purpose as in other systems. That is, the blend door position depends on how much heating is required. Although Figs. 3 and 5 look quite different, they both show parts of the same system.

When the functional control lever is set at VENT, vacuum is cut off from the vacuum motor. This permits the spring on the end of the operating rod to pull the rod all the way to the right. This, in turn, causes the rotary vacuum valve to make the necessary vacuum connections to change the positions of the doors. Movement of the rotary vacuum valve also moves the blower-control switch and changes the resistance of the feedback resistor. This changes the voltage through the resistor, and this voltage is fed to the amplifier. Now the amplifier puts together all the signals being fed to it, and provides the control needed.

When the functional selector lever is moved to LO-AUTO, the situation is as shown in Fig. 6. Compare this with Fig. 5 to determine which doors have changed their positions. The temperature-blend door is separately operated, to provide the right mix of cool and warm air.

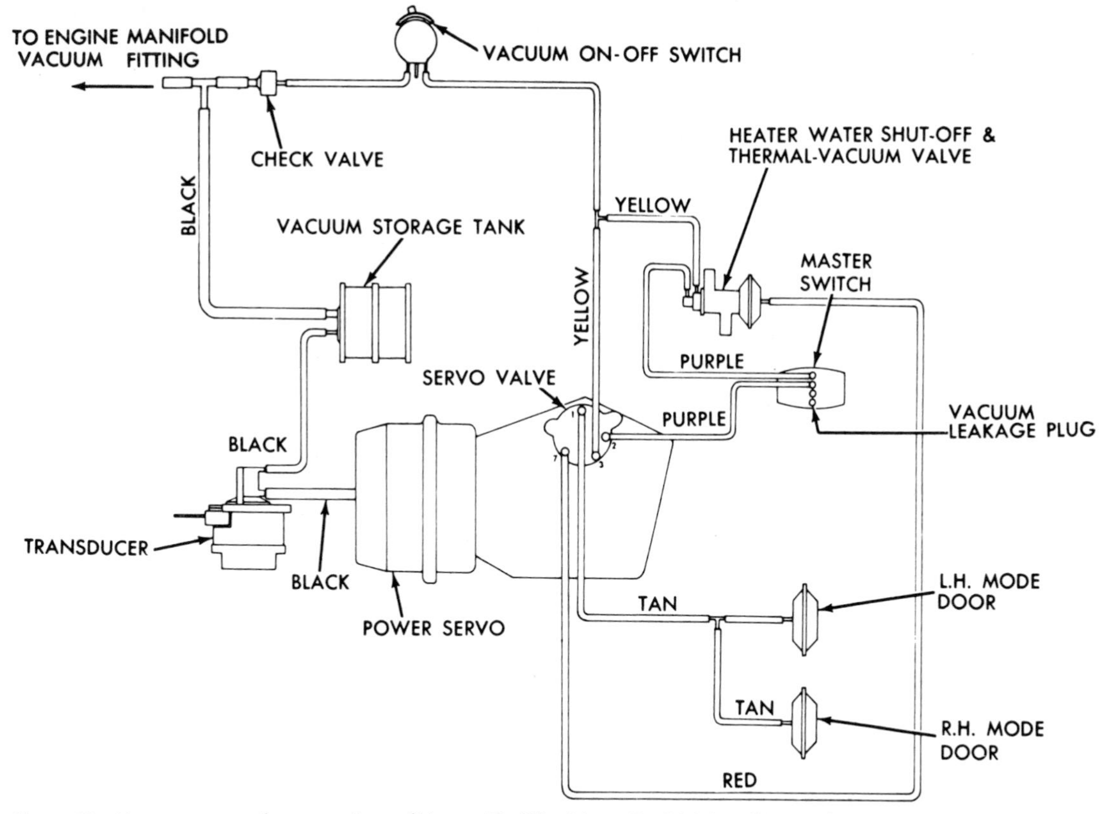

Figure 10 Vacuum system for a rear air conditioner. *(Cadillac Motor Car Division of General Motors Corporation.)*

With the functional control lever in the LO-AUTO modulated position, the system starts out to do a quick cooling or heating job. [But the heater does not come on until the engine coolant has reached 125°F (51.7°C) or more.] However, as the preset temperature is approached, the in-car sensor signals this fact to the amplifier. The amplifier then causes the blower speed to be cut back.

In the HI-AUTO position, however, the blower operates at top speed until the amplifier slows it down.

■ **8-4-6 Rear-Mounted and Auxiliary Air Conditioners** Some vehicles, such as limousines, vans, and station wagons, have an air-conditioning system at the rear. Figure 7 shows an installation in a van. Figure 8 shows an installation in a station wagon. In the van, the evaporator-blower assembly is mounted at the top rear. The station wagon has the evaporator at the rear and a distributor duct along the roof of the vehicle.

Figure 9 shows the layout of the rear A/C system in a limousine. The rear system is similar to the front system, except that the rear system does not have its own compressor and condenser. The rear assembly is installed in the trunk compartment. It feeds heated or cooled air through vents on the package shelf below the back window. Hot coolant and refrigerant are fed to the rear system through tubes and hoses. Figure 10 shows the vacuum circuits for the rear system.

SECTION 8-5 Servicing Car Heaters

This section covers the checking and servicing of car heating systems. Heating problems are usually reported by the driver as: (1) little or no heat, (2) failure of the blower to work, and (3) coolant leaks. Also, the driver may complain of too much heat; that is, the system cannot be turned down so that it produces only a little heat.

■ **8-5-1 Trouble-Diagnosis Chart** The chart that follows relates car-heater troubles with their possible causes and corrections. The chart will help you find the cause of any trouble that a driver reports to you. Explanations of the causes and corrections are given after the chart.

NOTE: The troubles and possible causes are not listed in the order of frequency of occurrence. That is, item 1 does not necessarily occur more often than item 2.

CAR-HEATER-SYSTEM TROUBLE-DIAGNOSIS CHART

(See ■ 8-5-2 to 8-5-7 for details of checks and corrections listed.)

COMPLAINT	POSSIBLE CAUSE	CHECK OR CORRECTION
1. Little or no heat (■ 8-5-2)	a. Air circulation insufficient	Blower motor or switch at fault, air leaks from heater housing, temperature door or cable out of adjustment, loose carpet obstructing airflow
	b. Coolant hose to heater blocked	Unkink hose, replace defective hose
	c. Air in heater core	Bleed air out
	d. Heater core clogged	Repair or replace core
	e. Water valve or vacuum motor malfunctioning	Repair or replace to permit coolant circulation
	f. Coolant level low in engine cooling system	Add coolant, bleed air out of system, check system to locate and repair leaks (Part 1, Sec. 7)
	g. Engine-cooling system thermostat stuck open	Replace thermostat (Part 1, Sec. 7)

CAR-HEATER-SYSTEM TROUBLE-DIAGNOSIS CHART *(Continued)*

(See ■ 8-5-2 to 8-5-7 for details of checks and corrections listed.)

COMPLAINT	POSSIBLE CAUSE	CHECK OR CORRECTION
2. Blower motor inoperative (■ 8-5-3)	a. Blown fuse, poor electrical connections	Check for cause of blown fuse and correct, tighten connections
	b. Motor defective	Replace
	c. Resistor open	Replace
3. Coolant leaks (■ 8-5-4)	Check hoses, hose connections, heater core, water valve	
4. Too much heat (■ 8-5-5)	a. Temperature-door cable out of adjustment	Readjust
	b. Engine-cooling-system thermostat stuck closed	Replace thermostat (Part 1, Sec. 7)
5. Insufficient defrosting (■ 8-5-5)	a. Defrost-door control cable out of adjustment	Readjust cable
	b. Defrost outlets blocked	Remove obstructions
	c. Any cause of little or no heat (■ 8-5-2)	See item 1
6. Vent door does not operate (■ 8-5-5)	Defective vacuum motor, leaky vacuum connections, or a defective control assembly	
7. Controls hard to operate (■ 8-5-5)	Loose or binding control cable or a sticky door	
8. Odors from heater (■ 8-5-5)	Air leaks around blower case, coolant leaks around heater core	Tighten bolts and see that seals and gaskets are in place, remove and repair heater core

■ **8-5-2 Little or No Heat** This can result from insufficient air or coolant circulation. For example, if the blower motor or switch is defective, not enough air will flow through the heater core. If coolant circulation is inadequate, not enough hot coolant will enter the heater core. In either case, little or no heat will come out of the heater vents.

In addition to a defective blower motor or switch, other possible causes of insufficient air circulation include:

1. A loose heater or blower housing that leaks air. This can be repaired by tightening the attaching bolts and making sure that gaskets and seals are in place. Sometimes, leaks around joints allow the blower to pull engine-compartment air into the heater system. This causes an obnoxious engine odor in the car.

2. Bent or battered fins on the heater core. These restrict the flow of air through the heater core. If the fins cannot be straightened, the core should be replaced.

3. A loose carpet that blocks the air exits from the heater vents. The carpet should be repositioned.

4. A temperature door that is out of adjustment. The door cable or lever should be readjusted. See the manufacturer's shop manual.

Possible causes of inadequate coolant circulation include:

1. Blocked coolant hose to the heater core. The hose should be unkinked. If defective, it should be replaced.

2. Air in the heater core. This could block coolant circulation. With this condition, you can often hear a gurgling sound when the heater is turned on. The remedy here is to temporarily disconnect the upper or outlet hose from the heater core. Run the engine until coolant starts to come out the core. Then reconnect the hose.

3. Clogged heater core. This restricts coolant circulation. It should be cleaned out or replaced.

4. Defective water solenoid or vacuum motor. On systems so equipped, this could prevent normal coolant circulation to the heater core. The defective unit should be replaced.

5. Not enough coolant in the engine cooling system. This could prevent normal coolant circulation to the heater core. Add coolant as necessary, to bring the coolant up to the proper level. Also, check the cooling system, to determine why it was low on coolant. If there is a leak, fix it. Part 1, Sec. 7, covers cooling system service in detail.

6. Engine-cooling-system thermostat stuck open. This may cause the coolant to take a long time to warm up. In cold weather, it may never warm up enough to provide adequate heating to the heater core. The remedy here is to replace the thermostat. See Part 1, Sec. 7.

■ **8-5-3 Blower Motor Does Not Work** This could be due to a blown fuse, loose electrical connections, or a defective switch, blower motor, or resistor. Replace the defective part, and tighten the connections (■ 8-5-7). For details, refer to the shop manual covering the car you are working on.

■ **8-5-4 Leaks** Leaks in the car heater system are usually obvious and easily found. Leaks can occur in the hoses, the heater core, and the water valve (in a system so equipped).

■ **8-5-5 Other Problems** Several other problems may occur in car heating systems:

1. Too much heat can result if the temperature door is incorrectly adjusted. This requires readjustment of the cable to the door. Also, if the engine-cooling-system thermostat is stuck in the closed position, the engine will overheat. The coolant coming into the heater core will be too hot. See Part 1, Sec. 17, for details of checking and replacing thermostats.

2. Defrosting is inadequate. This can result if the defrost door does not open fully, or if the defrost outlets are blocked. The door control cable should be adjusted, and any obstruction removed. In addition, any of the causes of little or no heat (■ 8-5-2) will prevent normal flow of hot air to the defective outlets.

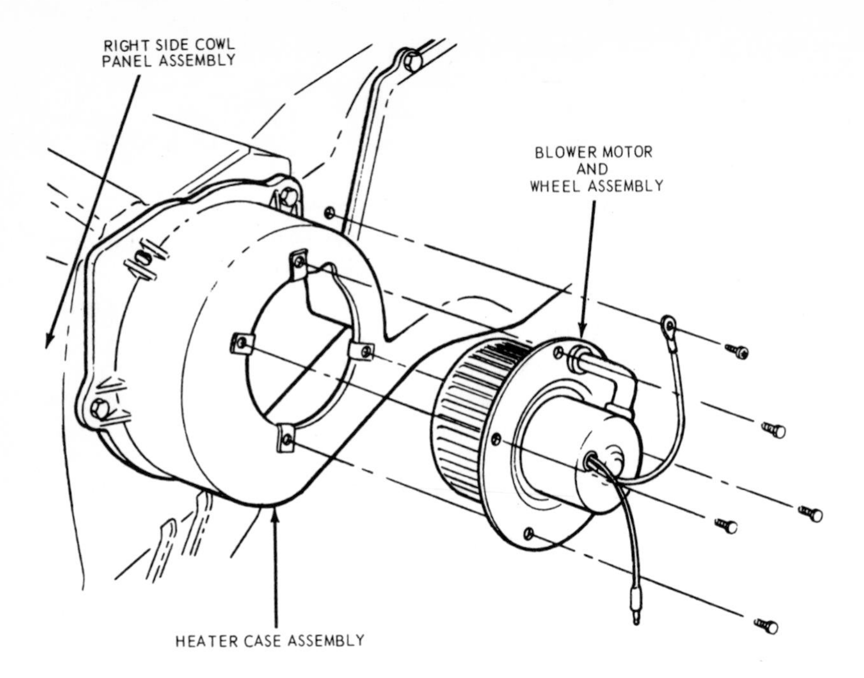

Figure 1 Blower-motor-and-wheel-assembly installation. *(Ford Motor Company.)*

3. Vent door does not operate. This can happen on systems using a vacuum motor to operate the vent door. A defective vacuum motor, leaky vacuum connections, or a defective control assembly could prevent normal operation of the vent door.

4. Controls hard to operate. This could be caused by a loose or binding control cable or a sticky door.

5. Engine odors from the heating system are due to air leaks around the blower case. The leaks allow the blower to pull engine-compartment air into the heater system. The remedy is to make sure gaskets and seals are in place, and to tighten attaching screws. A musty, or "something rotting," type of smell from the heating system is usually due to coolant seepage, or leaks, from the heater core. A radiator shop can repair a leaky core.

■ **8-5-6 Testing Vacuum Control System** To check the vacuum system, connect a vacuum gauge in the vacuum supply line between the check valve and the control assembly. Move the functional control lever to OFF. Start the engine, and let it run until you get a good vacuum reading on the gauge. Then turn the ignition key to the accessory position, to see if the vacuum holds with the engine not running. If vacuum is now lost, there is a leak in the check valve or line.

If the vacuum is held, repeat the test with the functional control lever in the VENT position. In this position, vacuum is applied to the vent-door vacuum motor and the water-valve vacuum motor. If vacuum now leaks (with the ignition key in the accessory position), one or both vacuum motors are leaking and must be replaced.

If vacuum is held with the functional control lever in VENT, check the operation of the doors to make sure they function normally. If the vent door does not open when the control lever is in VENT, disconnect the vacuum tube from the vent-door vacuum motor. Connect it to the vacuum gauge. Now start the engine, and see if the gauge registers a vacuum. If it does not, the line is plugged or there is a defect in the control assembly. If there is vacuum, then either the trouble is in the vacuum motor, or the door is jammed closed. The water-valve vacuum motor can be checked in the same way by checking to see if vacuum is available to the vacuum motor.

■ **8-5-7 Removing and Replacing Assemblies** A variety of mounting arrangements are used to position the control assembly, heater core, and case. This means that no one set of instructions applies to all of them. Generally speaking, there is nothing difficult about replacing the blower switch, the heater core, or the blower itself. Follow the instruction in the manufacturer's shop manual for the car being serviced.

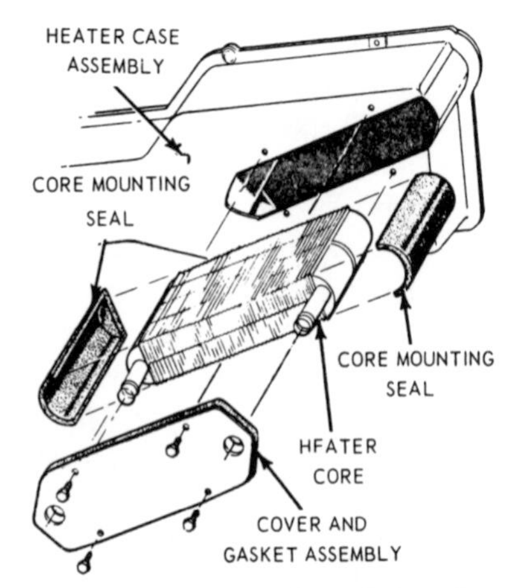

Figure 2 Heater-core removal. *(Ford Motor Company.)*

To remove the blower-motor assembly from many cars, it is necessary to cut an access opening in the inner fender skirt. First, the area must be located and cleaned. Then a hole is drilled in the fender skirt. Finally, snips are used to cut the opening.

> **NOTE:** Do not use a sabre saw or similar tool, as this would probably damage the heater case. Also, be extremely careful when drilling the hole. Avoid push-through, which would allow the drill to hit the case and damage it.

With the opening cut, the motor and blower are accessible. The screws attaching the assembly can be removed, and the assembly taken out through the opening (Fig. 1). Some manufacturers furnish a special adaptor plate for closing the hole in the fender skirt. If an adaptor plate is not available, one can be made from a piece of scrap sheet metal.

The heater core is removed in different ways, according to its location. Figure 2 shows a heater core being removed from its case. The engine cooling system must be drained first.

The control assembly is removed from the engine side of the instrument panel. Before working on it, disconnect the ground lead from the battery. This prevents accidental grounding of an insulated wire, which would cause a direct short across the battery.

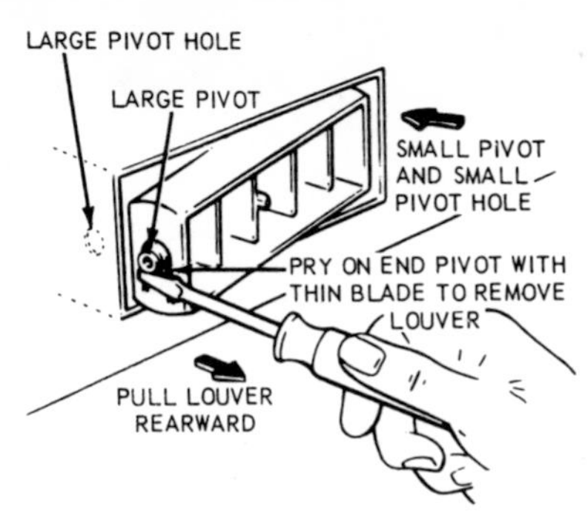

Figure 3 Louver-barrel removal. *(Ford Motor Company.)*

Some heater vents have louver barrels, which can be removed, if necessary, as shown in Fig. 3. A thin-bladed screwdriver is used to separate the pivot from the pivot hole, so the barrel can be pulled out of the instrument panel.

SECTION 8-6 Causes of Air-Conditioner Failure

This section discusses various causes of air-conditioner failure. Following sections describe the troubleshooting of air conditioners, correction of troubles, and servicing of system components.

■ **8-6-1 Enemies of the Air Conditioner** The three worst enemies of the air conditioner are air, moisture, and dirt. Air, moisture, and dirt have no chance to enter a properly operating air conditioner in good condition. However, these enemies can enter if the system is not properly serviced or if parts have deteriorated. For example, they can enter if the system is improperly evacuated and recharged,[1] or if refrigerant is improperly added. Air, moisture, and dirt can also enter the system if compressor seals or refrigerant-hose connections go bad.

■ **8-6-2 Air in the Refrigerant System** Air entering the system can cause trouble. Air usually carries moisture and some dirt with it, so these can enter along with the air. If the system has a leak, refrigerant is lost. Then a vacuum is produced as the compressor continues to operate. This vacuum pulls air into the system. Also, if the system is improperly evacuated or recharged, air can be left in or can enter.

The air blocks the flow of refrigerant, and the compressor can overheat as it tries to move the refrigerant. In addition, the air and its moisture can damage the lubricating oil in the compressor. The combination could result in bearing seizure and serious damage to the compressor.

Leaks can occur at compressor seals or refrigerant-hose connections. In normal operation, compressor seals last a long time. Overheating of the compressor can damage the seals. Also, long periods of inactivity can allow the seals to dry out and leak. This is why drivers are advised to periodically run their air conditioners for a few minutes, even in cold weather. A few minutes of operation circulates the refrigerant and oil.

Here is another reason why the system should be operated briefly at periodic intervals. When the compressor is idle, the

[1]Evacuating the system means using a vacuum pump to pump out all refrigerant, air, and moisture. Recharging the system means putting in a fresh charge of clean refrigerant.

lubricating oil tends to move away from highly polished surfaces, such as the ball bearings and the swash-plate surfaces. Operating the system briefly will return oil to these surfaces. If this is not done periodically, the polished surfaces can stick together so firmly that they prevent the compressor from operating.

One cause of bad hose connections is improper servicing. On the type of hose that has a clamp fitting, the clamp must be tightened properly after the hose has been installed over the sealing flange. The sealing flange should have no nicks or scratches; otherwise a leak could develop. The hose should be installed clear up to the stop flange, but not beyond (see ■8-10-4 which describes hose installations). On the type of connection using the O-ring gasket, the attaching nut should be tightened to the correct tension. Excessive tightening will compress the O ring excessively and cause a leak. Also, the fitting should have no burrs or nicks that could result in a leak (see ■ 8-10-3 which describes O-ring installation).

■ 8-6-3 Effect of Air or Moisture on Refrigerant Oil

Refrigerant oil is a very special sort of oil. It is very clean, highly refined, and has no moisture in it. The oil is supplied in special sealed containers. The oil should never be exposed to the air for any longer than necessary. It will absorb moisture from the air very rapidly. That is why you should recap the container immediately after taking out the amount of oil needed.

If air gets into the system, the oil absorbs moisture from the air. This damages the oil through chemical reactions that produce gum and varnish (Table 1). These products can cause failure of the compressor bearings, pistons, and rings. The moisture can also corrode metal parts in the system, and this can also cause failure.

Air in a system can also prevent the oil from getting back to the compressor. In a normally operating system, oil mixes with the refrigerant leaving the compressor. The refrigerant carries the oil through the system. However, if there is air in the system, the oil leaves the compressor but collects in the evaporator. There is not enough refrigerant to carry it back to the compressor. As a result, the compressor becomes oil-starved and seizes up. This can quickly ruin the compressor. If refrigerant leaks out, it carries oil with it; this can also oil-starve the compressor.

■ 8-6-4 Dirt and Moisture

Dirt must be kept out of the air-conditioner refrigerant system. Dirt can damage the compressor piston, rings, and bearings, and cause the valves to malfunction. Dirt can get into the system only through improper servicing and air leaks into the system.

Moisture getting into the system damages the oil (Table 1). In addition, moisture oxidizes the metals in the system. Moisture combines with the refrigerant to produce a variety of acids. These substances can seriously damage the compressor and the valves. In addition, moisture can cause the valves to freeze up so they stop working. Excessive moisture overloads the desiccant in the receiver, making it useless. Further, the moisture can powder the desiccant, and the powder can circulate with the refrigerant. It may clog the expansion valve so that the system stops functioning.

Table 1. Various air-conditioning-system contaminants and the effects of each

Contaminant	Effects
Moisture	• Causes valves to freeze • Forms hydrochloric and hydrofluoric acid • Causes corrosion and rust
Air	• Causes high head pressure and high temperatures • Accelerates R-12 instability • Oxidizes oil and causes varnish • Brings in moisture • Affects capacity
Dirt	• Causes clogged screens and orifices • Provides reactants to cause acids • Abrasive action
Other oil	• Wax, sludge—plugs screens, orifices, etc. • Poor lubrication • Additives hasten breakdown
Metal particles	• Clog, jam, gall bearings and score moving parts
Alcohol	• Attacks zinc and aluminum • Promotes copper plating • Hastens refrigerant breakdown • Serves no purpose

Source: Ford Motor Company.

■ 8-6-5 High Pressure and Temperature

At normal temperatures, the air-conditioner system can operate without damage. However, if the internal temperatures rise excessively, high pressures and damage can result. One possible cause of an excessive pressure rise is clogging of the condenser. That is, leaves, insects, or other debris gets on the face of the condenser, preventing normal circulation of air through it. As a result, the compressor works harder to send refrigerant vapor to the condenser, and the compressor overheats. Air in the system can also cause the compressor to overheat.

High temperature can cause the hoses to get brittle, and the compressor bearings and other parts to wear rapidly. High temperatures speed up the damaging effect of contaminants on the system components. For example, at higher temperatures moisture oxidizes the metals faster. The moisture produces more acid as it reacts with the refrigerant.

The high pressures resulting from increased temperatures can cause brittle hoses to burst. They can also break the reed valves in the compressor.

High temperature and pressures can overload the compressor, particularly the bearings, and cause compressor failure.

Figure 1 High-pressure relief-valve location on two-cylinder compressor. *(Ford Motor Company.)*

■ **8-6-6 Corrosion** Corrosion can damage any moving part in the system. This includes the reed valves, piston, rings, and bearings in the compressor. Corrosion can also damage the moving parts in the control valves, causing them to malfunction. Under many conditions, the damage to the moving parts can increase the temperature and pressure in the system. This, in turn, can cause still more rapid corrosion.

■ **8-6-7 Other Causes** Several conditions outside of the refrigeration system can also cause air-conditioner failure.

NOTE: Some systems have a high-pressure relief valve. If the system pressure becomes too high, the relief valve opens to allow some refrigerant to escape. This reduces the pressure, which otherwise might damage the compressor. On Fords with two-cylinder compressors, the high-pressure relief valve is located on the compressor (Fig. 1). On Fords with six-cylinder compressors, the valve is located in the discharge line near the compressor.

For example, if the vacuum or electric systems that control the doors, water valve, or compressor clutch fail, the air conditioner can stop doing its job.

All the components of the control system are closely tied together. A seemingly minor problem can cause major trouble. For example, the vacuum lines and the vacuum-line harnesses in Chrysler vacuum control systems are made of a special rubber-like material. This material is very resistant to high temperatures, but it is not compatible with ordinary plastic or electrician's tape. If such tape is used, it causes the vacuum lines to deteriorate. Chrysler recommends the use of a nylon tape, such as MS CH 63 (#361), available from the 3M Company. If you service a Chrysler air-conditioner system and need to tape the vacuum lines or harness, use the Chrysler-approved nylon tape.

The refrigerant system operates efficiently as long as it is completely sealed from the atmosphere. Then the system is dry and clean inside. If the seal is broken and air, moisture, and dirt get in, the system loses efficiency and can fail completely.

The test gauges and gauge-set hoses must be purged of air before they are connected into the air-conditioner refrigerant system. Even the tiny amount of air in them must be replaced by refrigerant vapor to prevent moisture from entering the system.

SECTION 8-7 Troubleshooting the Air-Conditioner–Heater System

This section describes various troubles that an air-conditioner–heater system might have. It also explains how to pinpoint possible causes. Later sections describe the servicing procedures used to correct troubles. This section includes samples of troubleshooting programs found in the shop manuals of different vehicle manufacturers. For example, included is a chart covering the troubleshooting of the Chevrolet Comfortron system. Also included are the American Motors "Diagnosis and Repair Simplification (DARS)" charts.

■ **8-7-1 Air-Conditioner–Heater Troubles** A variety of troubles may be reported by the driver to the service technician. These include not enough heat, not enough cooling, not enough air circulation, mixed-up air circulation (with heat, for example, coming out of the air-conditioner ducts), the system quitting when the car is accelerated, and so on. We describe all these and other troubles on following pages.

Troubles can begin either in the control system or in the air-conditioner or heater system. For example, if the vacuum system is not working properly, the doors may not open or close as they should, or the water valve may not work. On the other hand, if refrigerant has leaked out of the air conditioner, there will not be enough cooling.

The sight glass allows the technician to determine whether or not the air-conditioner system has the proper amount of refrigerant. The gauge set is used to measure refrigerant pressures in various parts of the system when the air conditioner is operating. The pressure is high on the condenser side of the system and low on the evaporator side. Manufacturers' service manuals give specifications for these pressures. Variations from the specified pressures can mean trouble.

In addition to the gauge set, other testing instruments are used to diagnose air-conditioner-heater troubles (Part 8, Secs. 8 to 10). These include leak detectors, voltmeters, ohmmeters, thermometers, test lights, and specially designed testers.

■ **8-7-2 Checking Out a Trouble** The first thing to do when a customer reports a trouble is to check the system to verify the condition. That is, set the controls for the various operating conditions, and note whether or not the system performs properly at each setting. For example, Chevrolet recommends the following for their automatic-temperature-control system (which they call the Comfortron).

The engine must be operating at 2,000 rpm or more, and the engine coolant must be above 95° (35°C). Here is the procedure:

1. Set the control lever to OFF, and the temperature dial at 65. The blower should operate at low speed. Air should flow from the heater outlet.

2. Set the lever to VENT, and the temperature dial at 65. The blower should operate at low speed. Air, neither heated nor cooled, should flow from the air-conditioner outlets.

3. Set the lever to LOW, and the temperature dial at 65. The blower should operate at low speed. Cool air should flow from the air-conditioner outlets.

4. Set the lever to AUTO, and the temperature dial at 65. The blower speed should increase. Cool air should flow from the air-conditioner outlets.

5. With the lever set at AUTO, rotate the temperature dial to 85. The blower speed should decrease to low, then increase to medium or high. The air temperature should change from cold to hot, and flow out the heater outlets. It takes a few seconds for this shift to occur.

6. Set the lever to HI, and the temperature dial at 65. The blower speed should increase to high, and stay there. Air should flow from the air-conditioner outlets.

7. With the lever at HI, rotate the temperature dial to 85. The air temperature should change from cold to hot. The airflow should shift from the air-conditioner outlets to the heater outlets. It takes up to 30 seconds for this shift to occur.

8. Move the lever to BI-LEVEL, and the dial to 65. The blower should run at medium or high speed. Air should flow from the defroster, heater, and air-conditioner outlets.

9. Move the lever to DEF, and the dial to 65. The blower should operate at high speed. Most of the air should come from the defroster outlets. A small amount will flow from the heater outlets.

This procedure puts the system through its paces. This permits you to spot troubles. The chart that follows relates various system malfunctions to possible causes.

NOTE: The procedure described above is for one type of completely automatic air-conditioner–heater system. The procedure for the manually controlled system is simpler. Therefore, it is not necessary to check the actions as the system shifts automatically from one mode (heating, for example) to another (air conditioning, for example).

■ 8-7-3 Air-Conditioner Trouble-Diagnosis Chart

The chart that follows relates various troubles in an air conditioner to possible causes. With the exception of item 4, any of these troubles could occur in a field-installed air conditioner of the cycling-clutch type. All the problems also could occur in an air-conditioner–heater system as well as in an automatic-temperature-control system. There are many other troubles that can occur in the various types of automotive air conditioners. Other sections in this book discuss these additional troubles.

NOTE: The troubles and possible causes are not listed in the chart in the order of frequency of occurrence. That is, item 1 does not necessarily occur more often than item 2. Nor does item *a* necessarily occur more often than item *b*.

AIR-CONDITIONER TROUBLE-DIAGNOSIS CHART

COMPLAINT	POSSIBLE CAUSE	CHECK OR CORRECTION
1. Compressor noise	a. Broken valves	Replace
	b. System over-charged with refrigerant	Discharge, evacuate, and install correct refrigerant charge
	c. Incorrect oil level	Correct oil level
	d. Piston slap	Repair or replace compressor
	e. Broken piston rings	Repair or replace compressor
2. Excessive compressor vibration	a. Incorrect belt tension	Adjust
	b. Magnetic clutch loose	Tighten
	c. System over-charged with refrigerant	Discharge, evacuate, and install correct refrigerant charge
	d. Pulley misaligned	Align
3. Water dripping into passenger compartment	a. Evaporator drain hose plugged or improperly positioned	Clean or replace hose, position properly
	b. Insulation removed or improperly positioned on expansion valve and hoses	Replace insulation
4. Cold, airflow stops on acceleration	a. Defective vacuum storage tank	Replace
	b. Vacuum line disconnected or leaking	Connect or replace vacuum line
	c. Vacuum switch defective	Replace
	d. Vacuum check valve defective	Replace
5. Frozen evaporator coil	a. Faulty thermostat	Replace
	b. Thermostat capillary tube improperly installed	Correct

■ 8-7-4 Comfortron Trouble-Diagnosis Chart

The chart that follows relates various troubles in the Chevrolet Comfortron system to possible causes. While the chart specifically applies only to the Comfortron system, it generally applies to all automatically controlled air-conditioner–heater systems. However, many different types of controls are used by the various car manufacturers. Although they all produce the same result, each operates in its own special way. Therefore, when you are checking out a specific system, refer to the shop manual covering that make of car and that model year. Systems can vary both from car model to car model and from model year to model year.

> **NOTE:** The troubles and possible causes are not listed in the chart in the order of frequency of occurrence. That is, item 1 does not necessarily occur more often than item 2. Nor does item *a* necessarily occur more often than item *b*.

Note how many of the troubles listed below are caused by pinched or disconnected vacuum lines. The lines should not become pinched or disconnected under normal conditions. However, if service work is done around or in the control system, hoses might be knocked loose or pinched.

> **NOTE:** The Comfortron trouble-diagnosis chart is for one model of automatic-temperature-control system. Systems using somewhat different controls would require somewhat different trouble-diagnosis procedures. Also, manually controlled systems are easier to check, because they do not have automatic programmers and related parts.

COMFORTRON TROUBLE-DIAGNOSIS CHART

COMPLAINT	POSSIBLE CAUSE	CHECK OR CORRECTION
1. Blower inoperative	a. Defective fuse	Check for and correct cause of blown fuse, replace fuse
	b. Poor connection to blower	Repair
	c. Defective blower	Replace
	d. Defective switch in programmer	Replace
	e. Blower resistor or wiper assembly defective	Replace
2. Blower, programmer, compressor not operating	a. Air-conditioner 25-amp fuse blown	Check and correct cause of blown fuse, replace fuse
	b. Open circuit in electric system	Locate and correct
3. HI blower only with maximum heat, at HI-AUTO or DEF	Electric plug disconnected at programmer	Reconnect
4. LO blower only with maximum heat	Disconnected plug at control head	Reconnect
5. LO blower only with A/C or heating	a. Disconnected plug at AUTO relay	Reconnect
	b. Defective AUTO relay	Replace
6. No LO blower in OFF, VENT, and LO	a. Disconnected plug at LO relay	Reconnect
	b. Defective LO relay	Replace
7. Blower comes on with cold engine and car temperature below 70°F (21°C)	a. Defective engine thermal switch	Replace
	b. Defective control-head thermal switch	Replace
	c. Engine thermal switch shorted to ground	Replace switch
8. HI blower on DEFROST only, car temperature below 70°F (21°C)	a. Defective engine thermal switch	Replace
	b. Defective connection	Correct
9. Compressor inoperative above 40°F (4.4°C)	a. Disconnected or defective ambient switch	Replace, connect
	b. Open circuit to compressor clutch	Trace circuit, correct open
	c. Control-head switch defective	Replace
	d. Control-head connector disconnected	Reconnect
	e. Compressor belt loose	Tighten, replace defective belt
	f. Compressor frozen	Remove for service (see note below)

> **NOTE:** If the air conditioner is not used for several months, the lubricating oil may drain from the polished metal surfaces such as the wobble plate and bearings. These metal surfaces may then stick together so tightly that the compressor appears to be frozen. However, before removing the compressor, check as follows to see if it is actually seized: Use a wrench to rock the shaft in the direction opposite to normal rotation. If this breaks the compressor loose, rock the shaft back and forth. This should return oil to the polished surfaces, so that the shaft can be turned by hand. Turn the shaft several times to make sure it turns easily. Then start the engine, and operate the compressor for several minutes. If it now works normally, it can be assumed to be okay. This procedure should be tried out on any frozen compressor that has been idle for a month or more. However, if a compressor was operating normally, and then all at once froze up, chances are it does have internal damage and should be removed for service.

(Continued)

COMFORTRON TROUBLE-DIAGNOSIS CHART *(Continued)*

COMPLAINT	POSSIBLE CAUSE	CHECK OR CORRECTION
10. Compressor operates below 25°F (−4°C)	a. Shorted ambient switch	Replace
	b. Short in compressor clutch	Replace clutch winding
	c. Defective clutch	Replace clutch
11. Maximum heat with no temperature control and no automatic blower change in LO or HI-AUTO	a. Disconnected ambient sensor	Connect
	b. Disconnected in-car sensor	Connect

> **NOTE:** The programmer transducer may buzz when the selector lever is moved to VENT.

COMPLAINT	POSSIBLE CAUSE	CHECK OR CORRECTION
12. No temperature control or blower automatic change in AUTO	Vacuum hose in programmer disconnected	Reattach
13. No temperature control or blower change in AUTO (heat mode)	Pinched vacuum harness or disconnected vacuum plug at control head, programmer, or in-line connector	Correct and reconnect as necessary
14. Cold air from heater outlets in maximum-heat mode	a. Disconnected or pinched vacuum hose in programmer or at vacuum source	Correct and reconnect
	b. Temperature-door link loose or out of adjustment	Adjust, tighten
15. Maximum air conditioning in all positions	a. Shorted ambient sensor	Replace
	b. Shorted in-car sensor	Replace
	c. Disconnected or pinched vacuum hose in programmer	Correct, reconnect
16. Maximum heat in all positions	Defective checking relay	Replace
17. Maximum air conditioning in HI-AUTO and LO-AUTO only	a. Disconnected or pinched vacuum hose in programmer	Correct, reconnect
	b. Shorted sensor system	Replace defective sensor
18. Erratic temperature control	a. Kinked or disconnected aspirator hose	Correct, reconnect
	b. Defective programmer or control head	Replace
19. Temperature of discharge air too hot or cold at mode changes	Misadjusted temperature-door linkage	Readjust
20. Insufficient heat	Conditions listed in the chart in ■8-5-1 under "Little or no heat."	
21. Insufficient cooling	In addition to the specific conditions listed above, any troubles in the refrigeration system could decrease the amount of cooling produced by the air conditioner. The refrigeration system should be checked out (Part 8, Sec. 8).	
22. Mode will not change from air conditioning to heating in AUTO	Vacuum lines switched, pinched, or disconnected	Correct, reconnect
23. Excessive temperature difference at outlets in BI-LEVEL	Vacuum lines switched or pinched at upper and lower mode-door vacuum motors	Correct, reconnect
24. Partial airflow to windshield in DEF, and none in BI-LEVEL	Vacuum line to defroster vacuum motor switched, pinched, or disconnected	Correct, reconnect

> **NOTE:** In normal BI-LEVEL operation, there is a delay before the door opens.

COMPLAINT	POSSIBLE CAUSE	CHECK OR CORRECTION
25. No airflow in in windshield in either DEF or BI-LEVEL	Vacuum line to defroster vacuum motor disconnected or pinched	Correct, reconnect

■ 8-7-5 Air-Conditioner and Magnetic-Clutch Diagnosis and Repair Charts The following subsection is a set of air-conditioner and magnetic-clutch diagnosis and repair charts.

Introduction

This section presents American Motors new Diagnosis and Repair Simplification (DARS) charts. These charts provide a graphic method of diagnosing and troubleshooting the AIR CONDITIONER and MAGNETIC CLUTCH. The DARS charts are different from the ones you have used before. They aren't "go—no go" decision trees or tables.

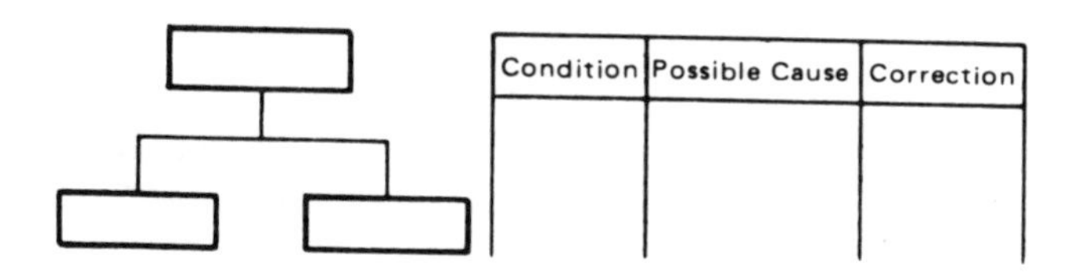

Instead, the new DARS charts use pictures plus a few words to help you solve a problem . . .

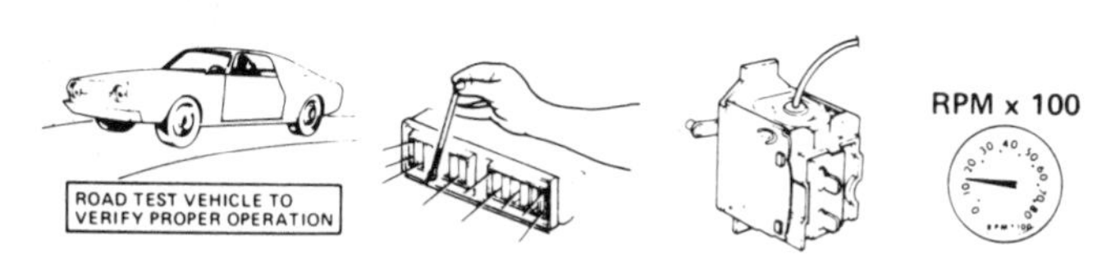

and symbols replace words.

CHECK CONNECT REPAIR OR REPLACE TEST LIGHT ON TEST LIGHT OFF

Using the Charts

The charts are divided into three sections: step, sequence and result.

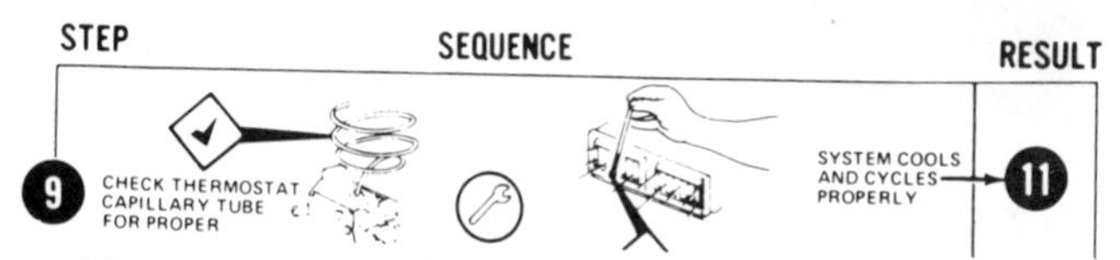

Always start at the first step and go through the complete sequence from left to right.

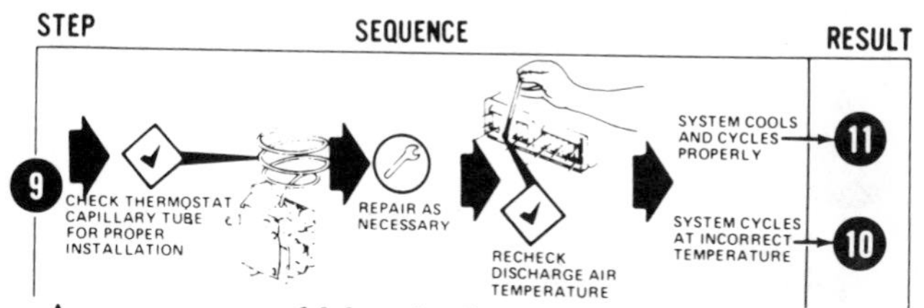

A sequence could be checking the thermostat capillary tube for proper installation and rechecking the discharge air temperature. Each sequence ends with a result and tells you the next step to go to.

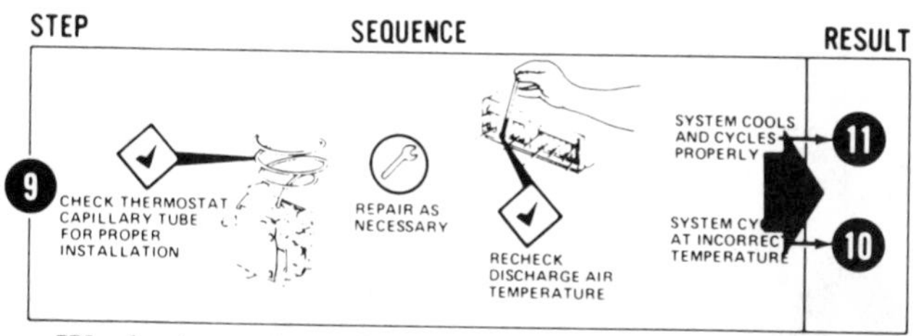

Work through each step of the DARS charts until the system is repaired. (STOP)

PROBLEM: SYSTEM DOES NOT COOL PROPERLY

Chart 1

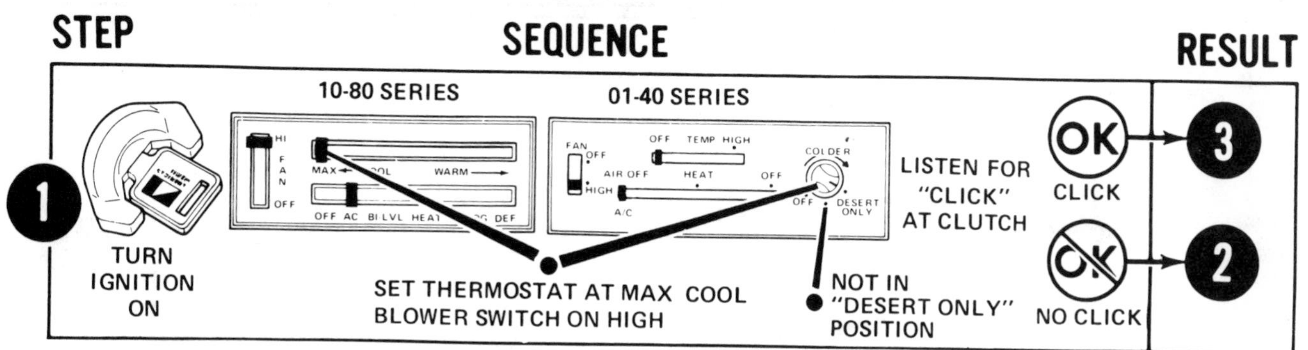

Source: American Motors Corporation.

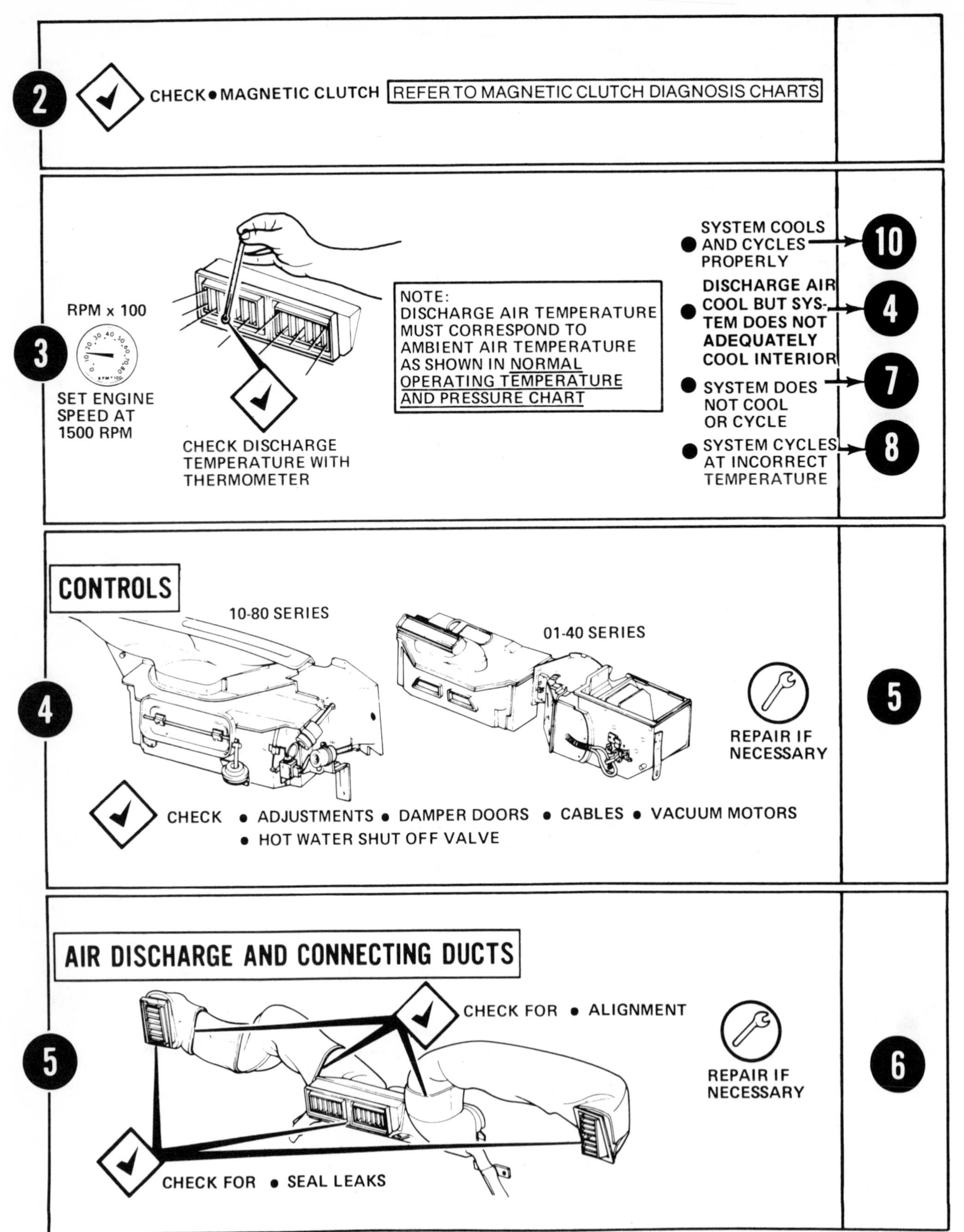

Source: American Motors Corporation.

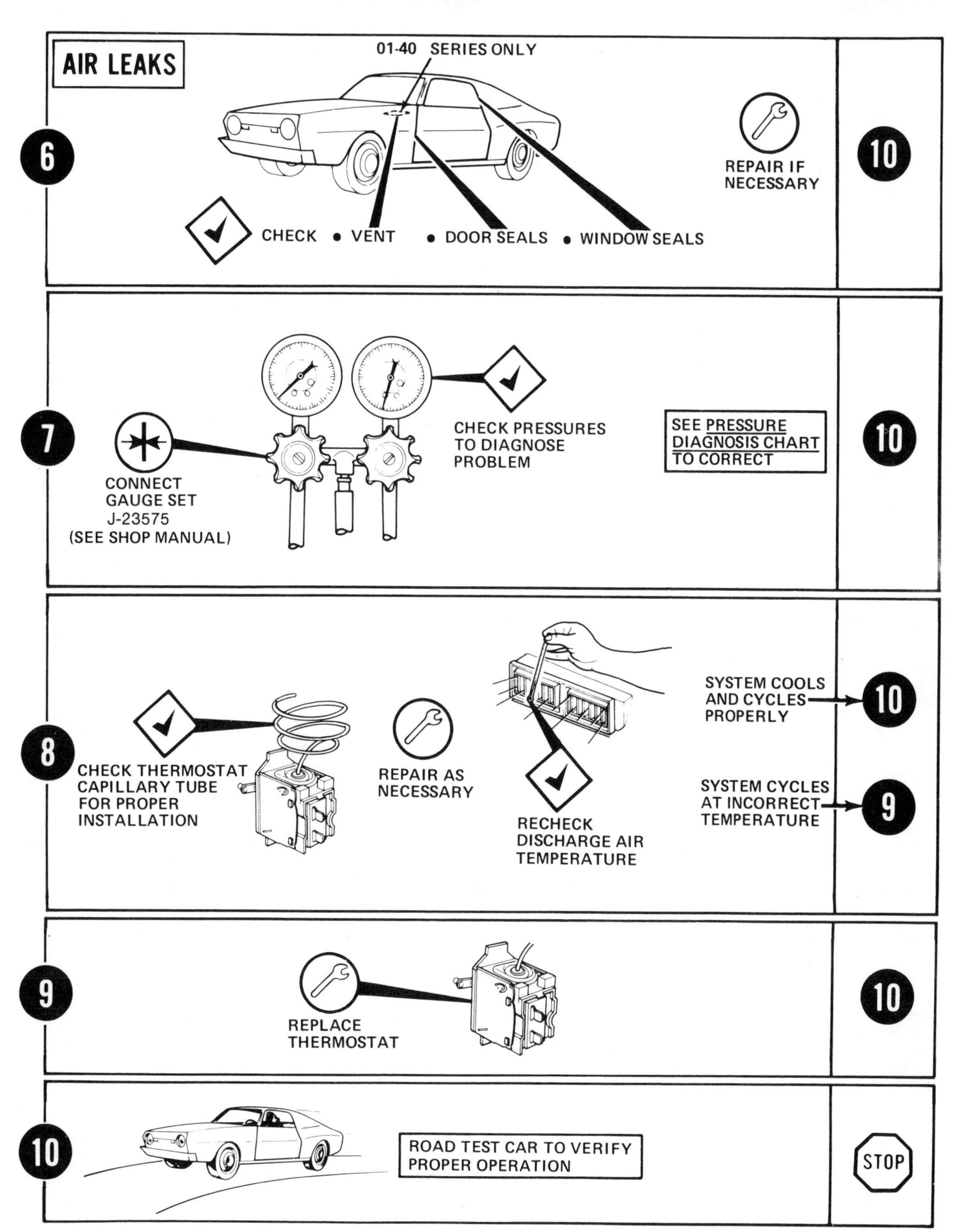

Source: American Motors Corporation.

MAGNETIC CLUTCH DIAGNOSIS 01-40 SERIES

Chart 2

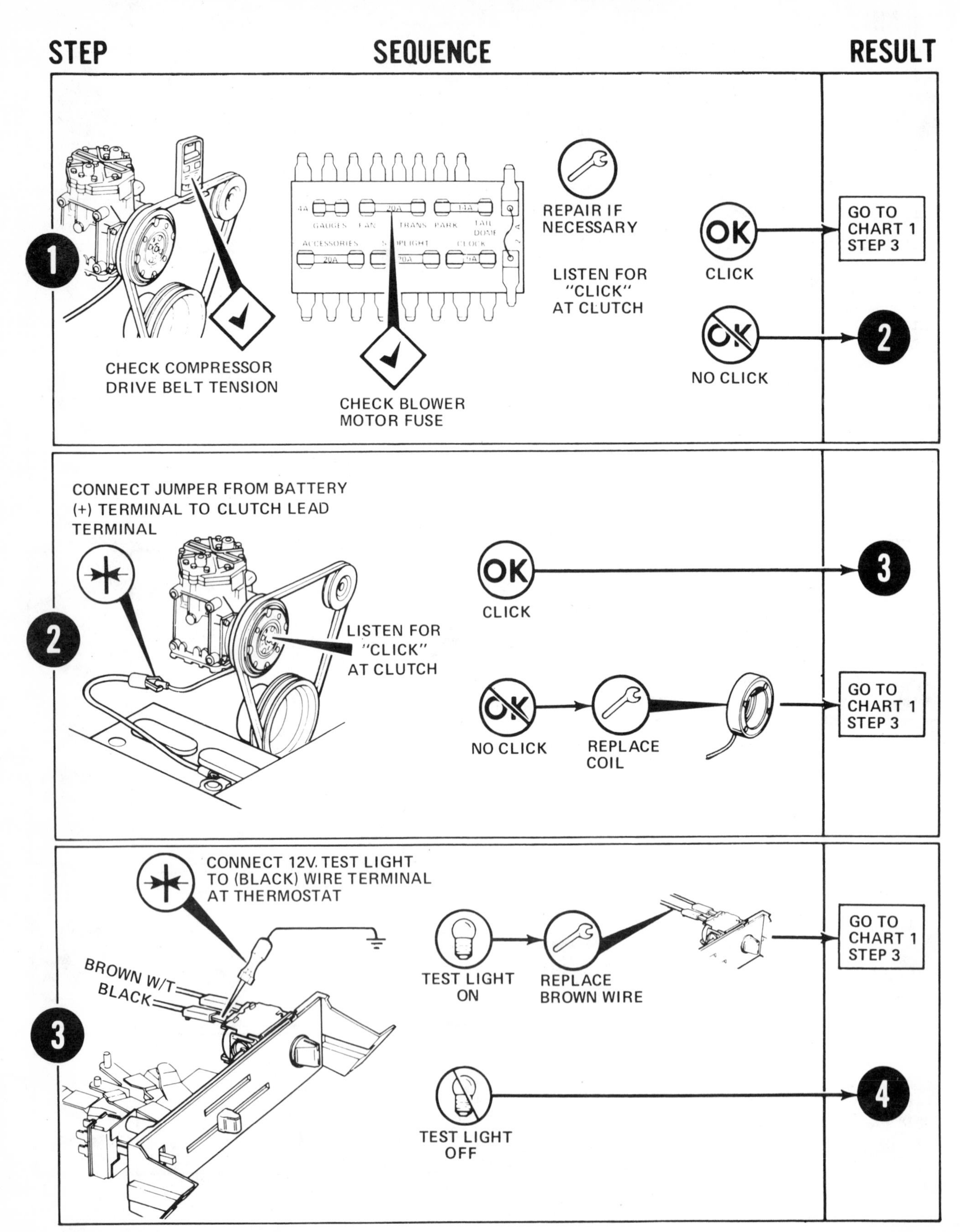

Source: American Motors Corporation.

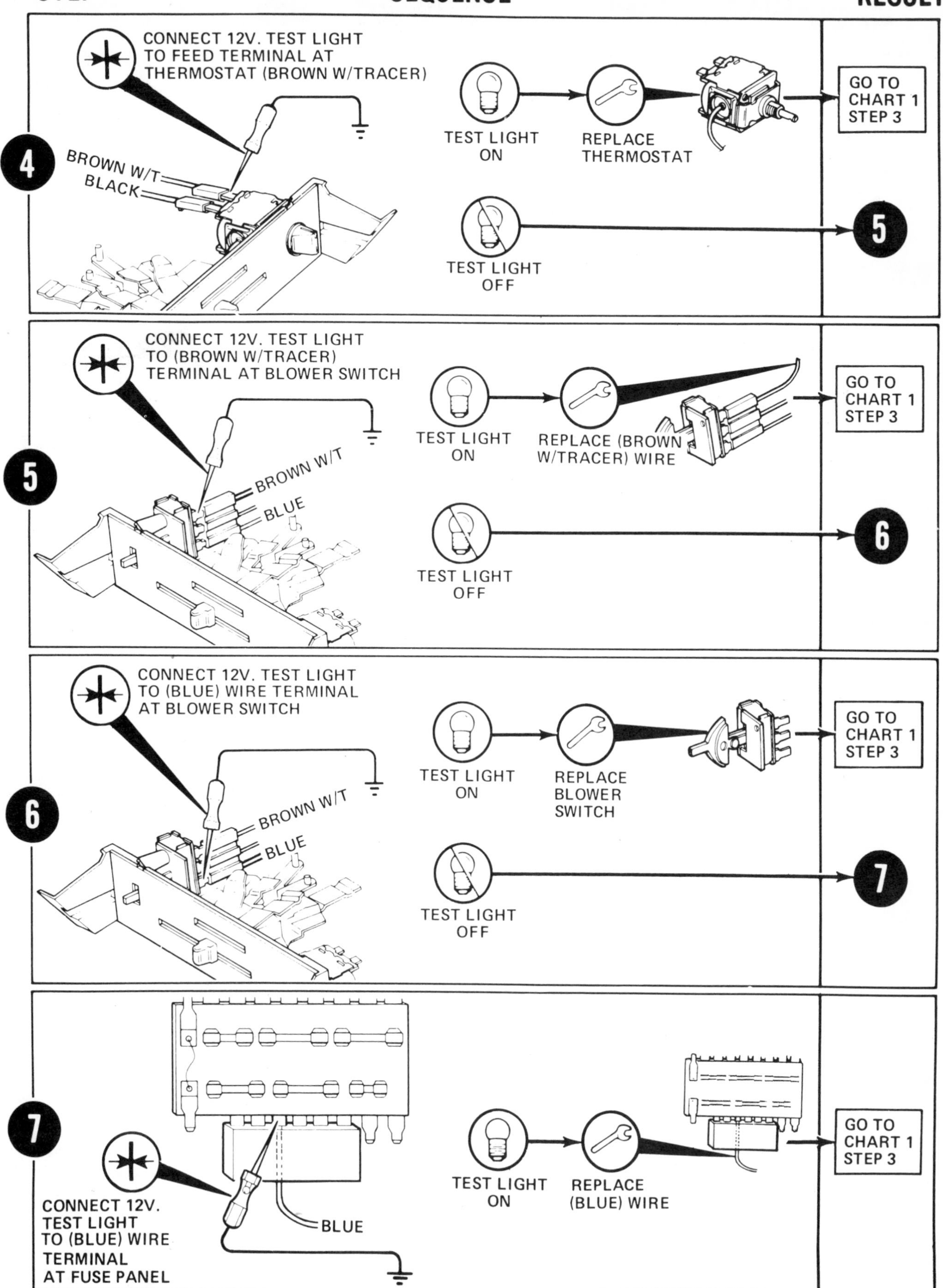

Source: American Motors Corporation.

MAGNETIC CLUTCH DIAGNOSIS 10-80 SERIES

Chart 3

STEP	SEQUENCE	RESULT
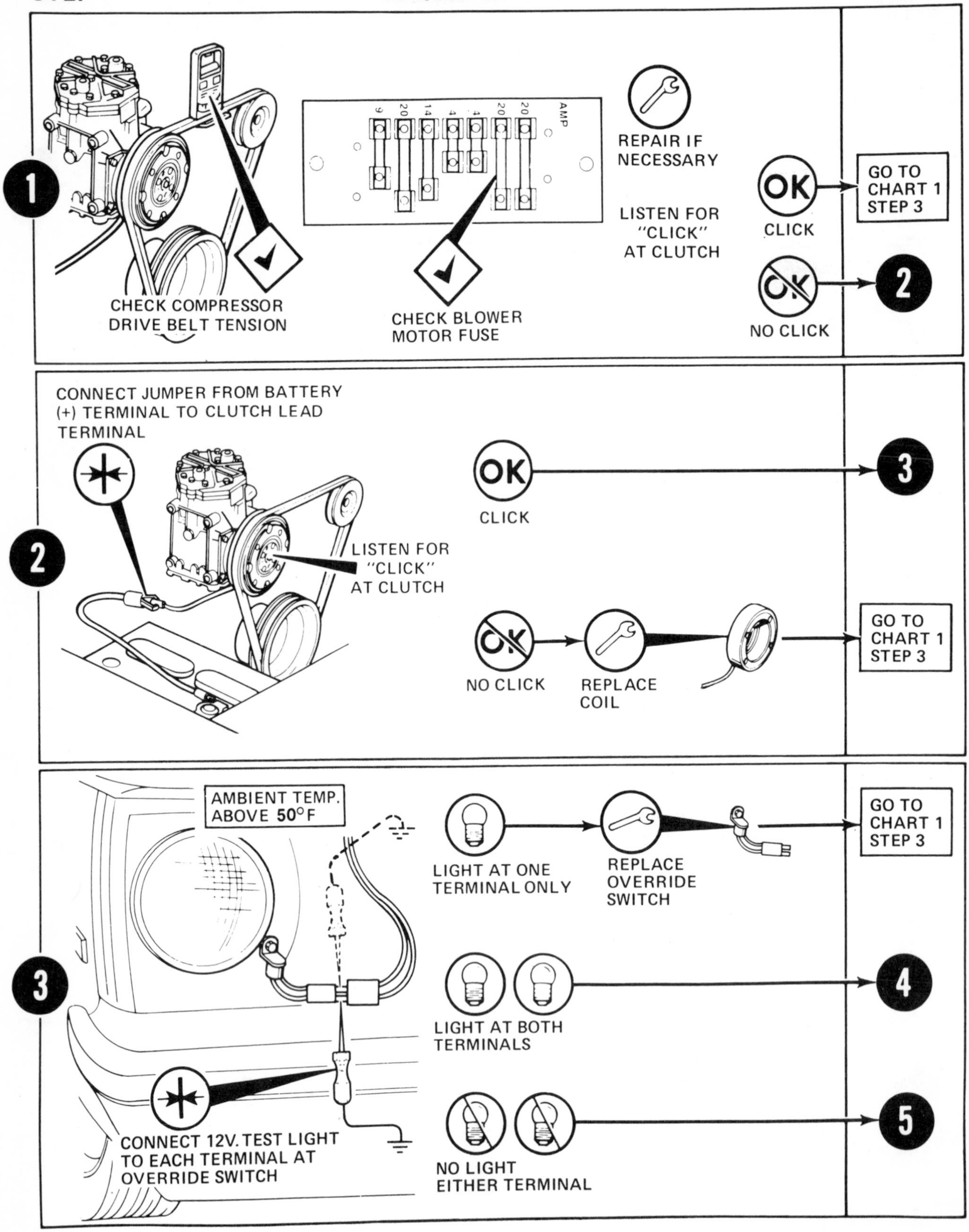 1	CHECK COMPRESSOR DRIVE BELT TENSION; CHECK BLOWER MOTOR FUSE (AMP 20, 20, 4, 4, 14, 20, 9); REPAIR IF NECESSARY; LISTEN FOR "CLICK" AT CLUTCH. OK — CLICK	GO TO CHART 1 STEP 3
	NO CLICK	2
2	CONNECT JUMPER FROM BATTERY (+) TERMINAL TO CLUTCH LEAD TERMINAL; LISTEN FOR "CLICK" AT CLUTCH. OK — CLICK	3
	NO CLICK — REPLACE COIL	GO TO CHART 1 STEP 3
3	AMBIENT TEMP. ABOVE 50°F; CONNECT 12V. TEST LIGHT TO EACH TERMINAL AT OVERRIDE SWITCH. LIGHT AT ONE TERMINAL ONLY — REPLACE OVERRIDE SWITCH	GO TO CHART 1 STEP 3
	LIGHT AT BOTH TERMINALS	4
	NO LIGHT EITHER TERMINAL	5

Source: American Motors Corporation.

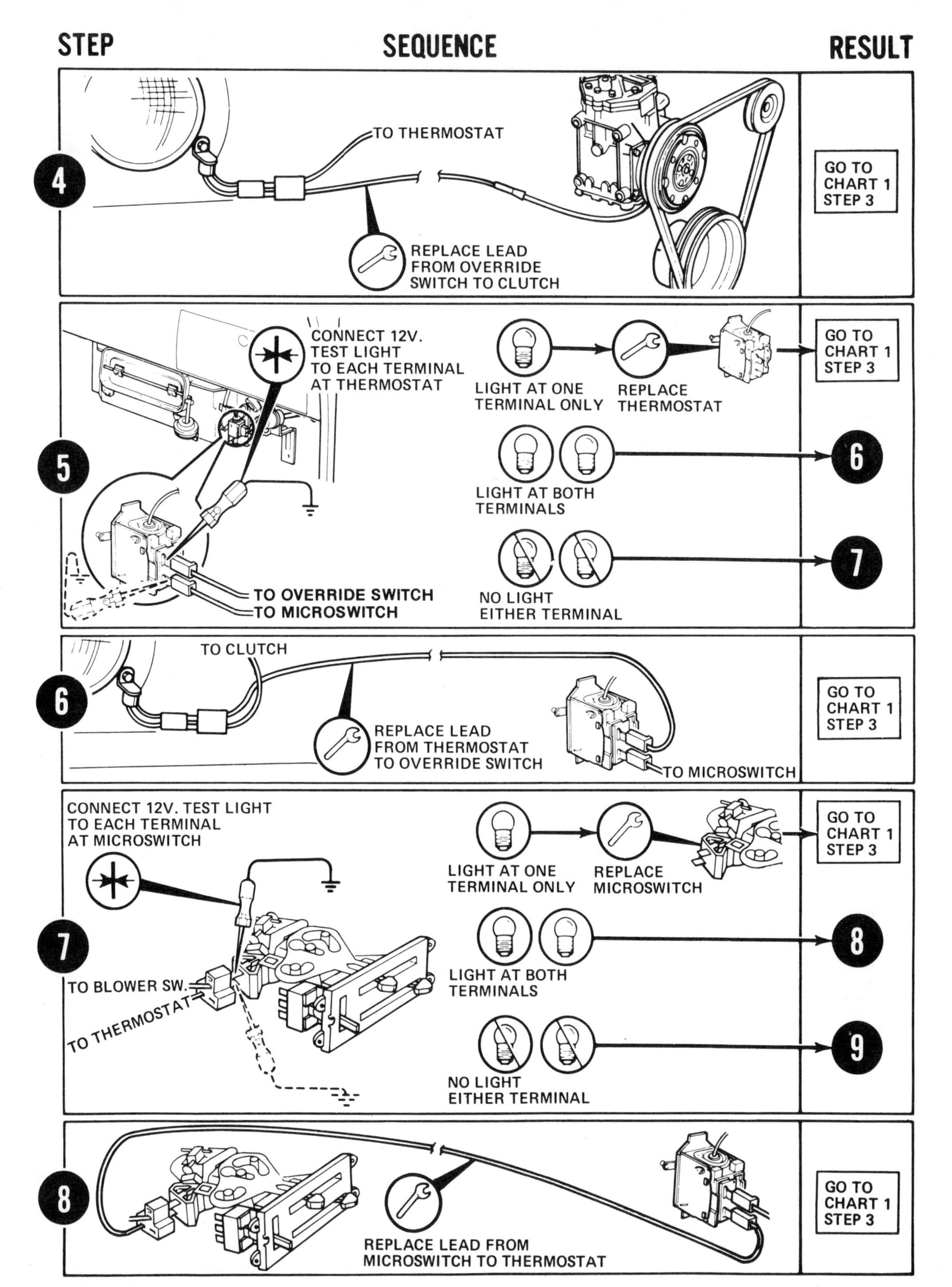

Source: American Motors Corporation.

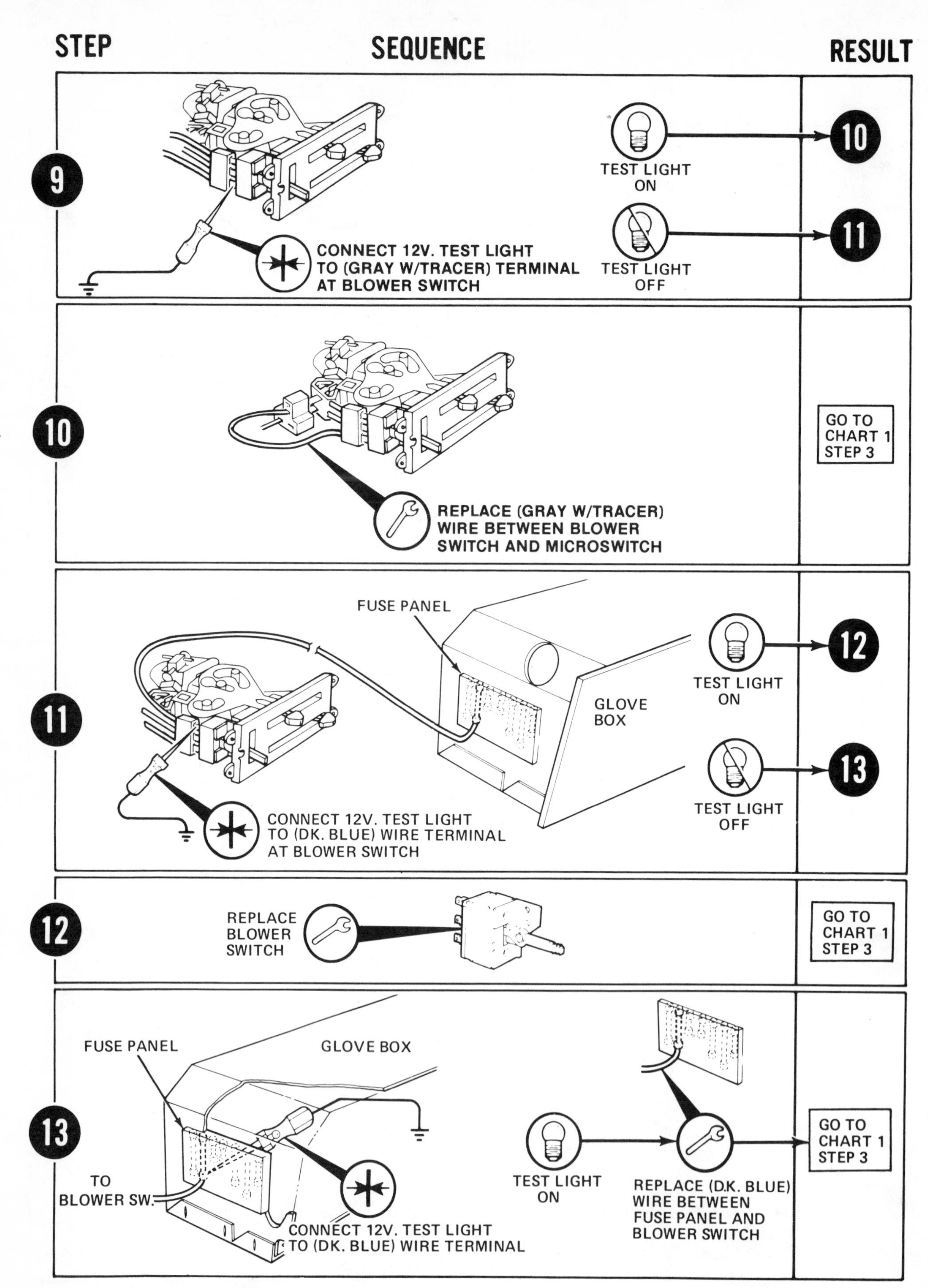

Source: American Motors Corporation.

■ **8-7-6 Thermal-Limiter Diagnosis Chart** The following subsection is a diagnosis chart for a blown thermal limiter on VIR and POA systems.

PICTURES ARE TYPICAL BUT NOT ALL INCLUSIVE.

The following chart provides a systematic method for diagnosing the cause of a blown thermal limiter in both the VIR or POA system. This chart is different from charts you have used before. It is not a'"go-no go" decision tree or table.

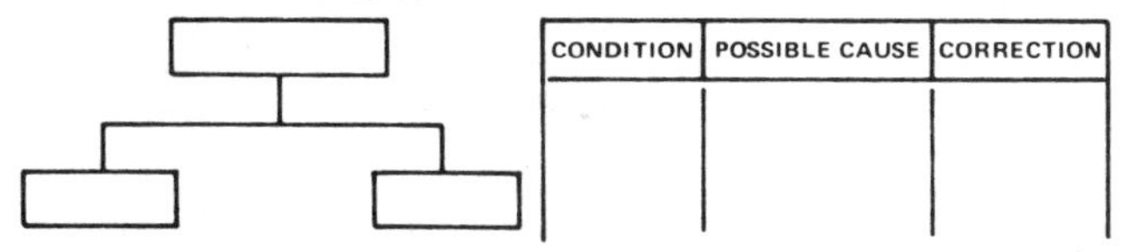

Instead, the chart uses pictures plus a few words to help you solve a problem,

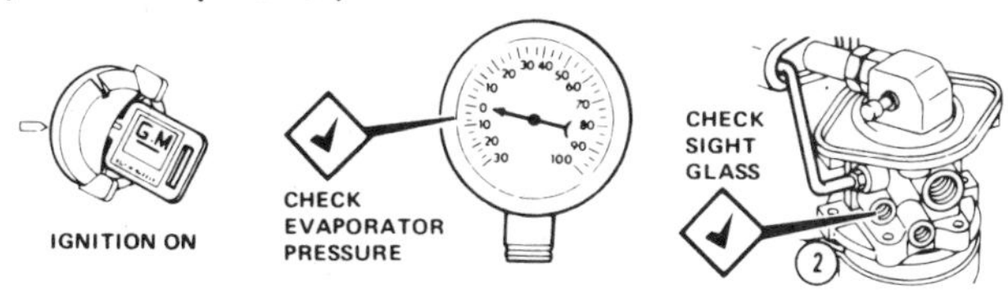

and symbols have replaced words.

How to use the chart

The chart is divided into three sections: STEP, SEQUENCE and RESULT.

Always start at the first step and go through the complete sequence from left to right.

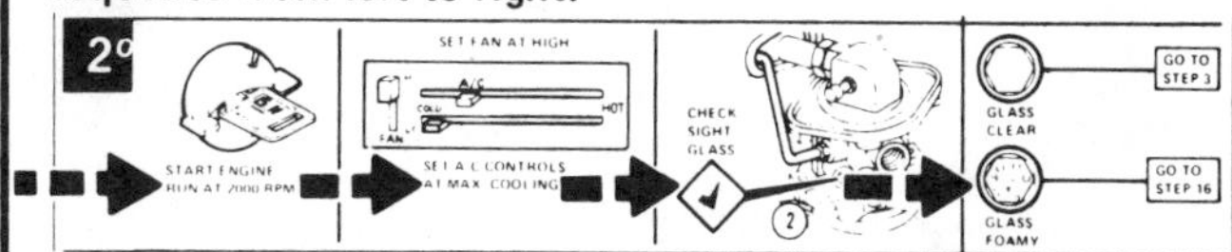

A sequence could be starting engine, then setting A/C controls for maximum cooling, then checking the sight glass. Each sequence ends with a result and tells you the next step to go to.

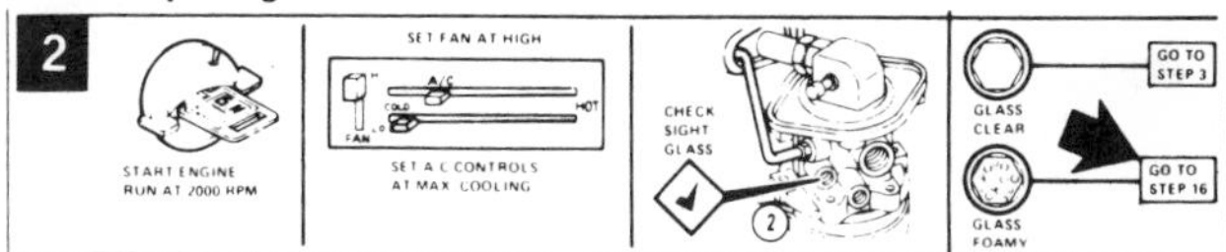

Work through each step of the diagnosis and trouble shooting charts till the system is repaired.

To find where parts are located in either system just look at the parts locator shown below.

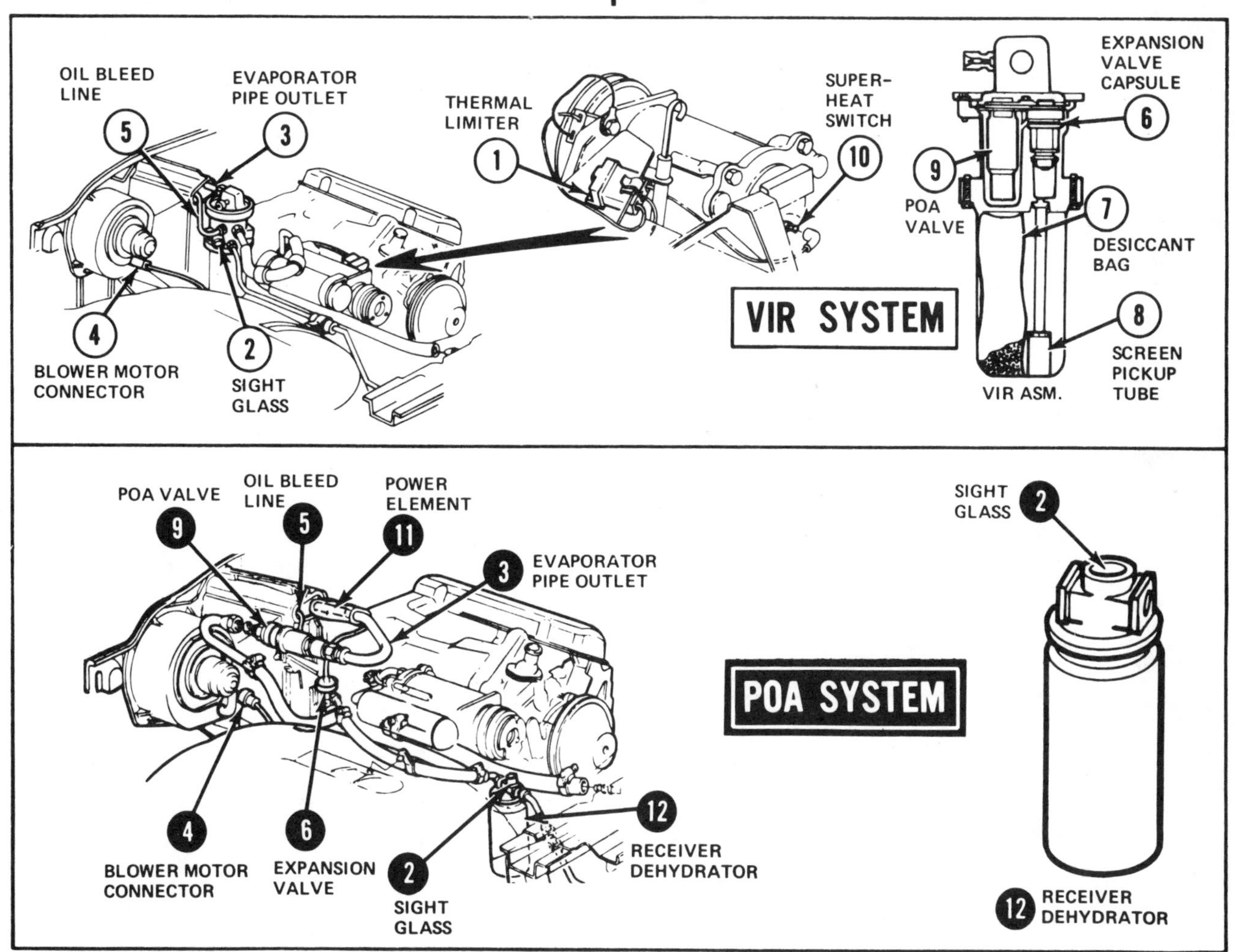

Source: Chevrolet Motor Division of General Motors Corporation.

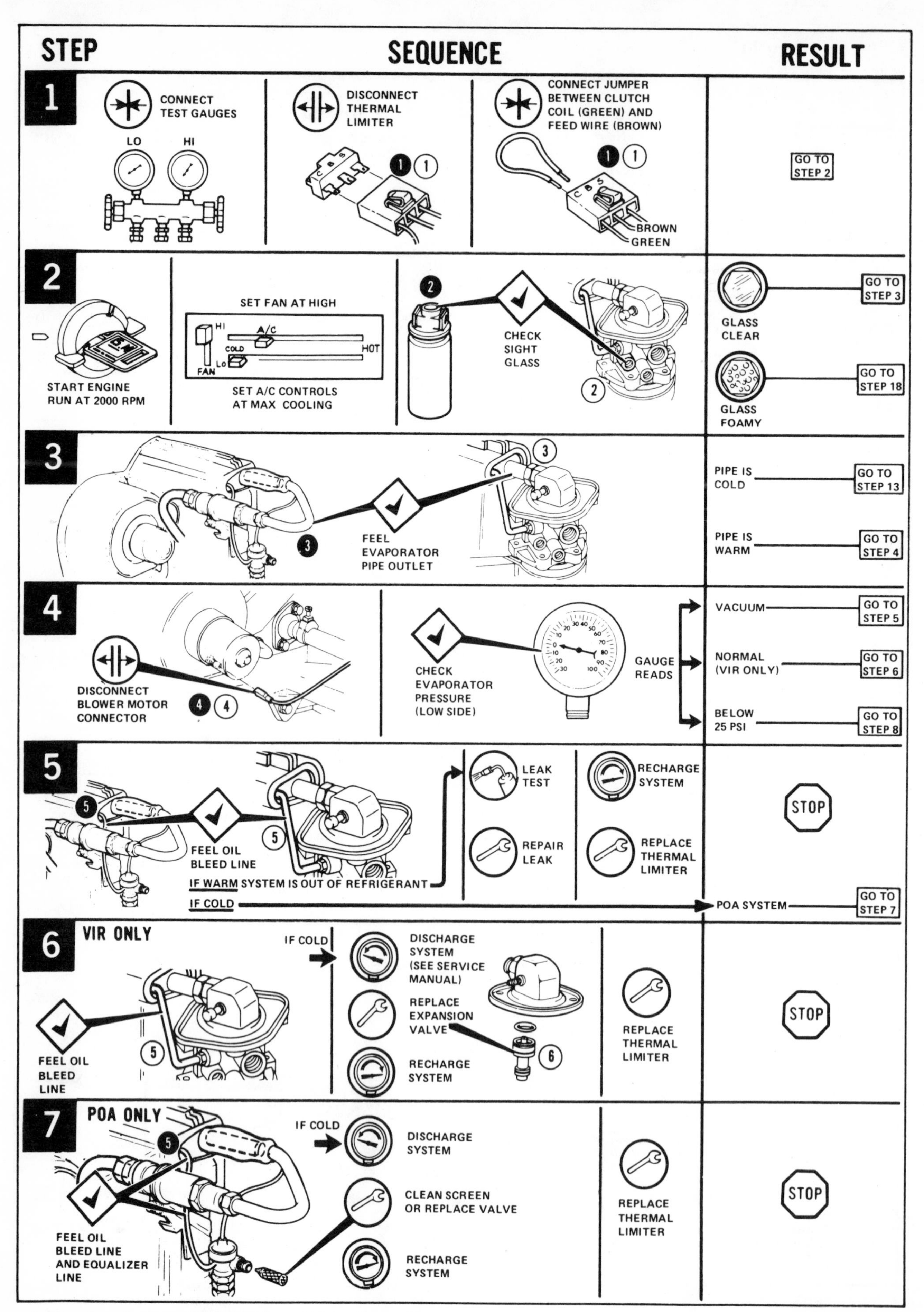

Source: Chevrolet Motor Division of General Motors Corporation.

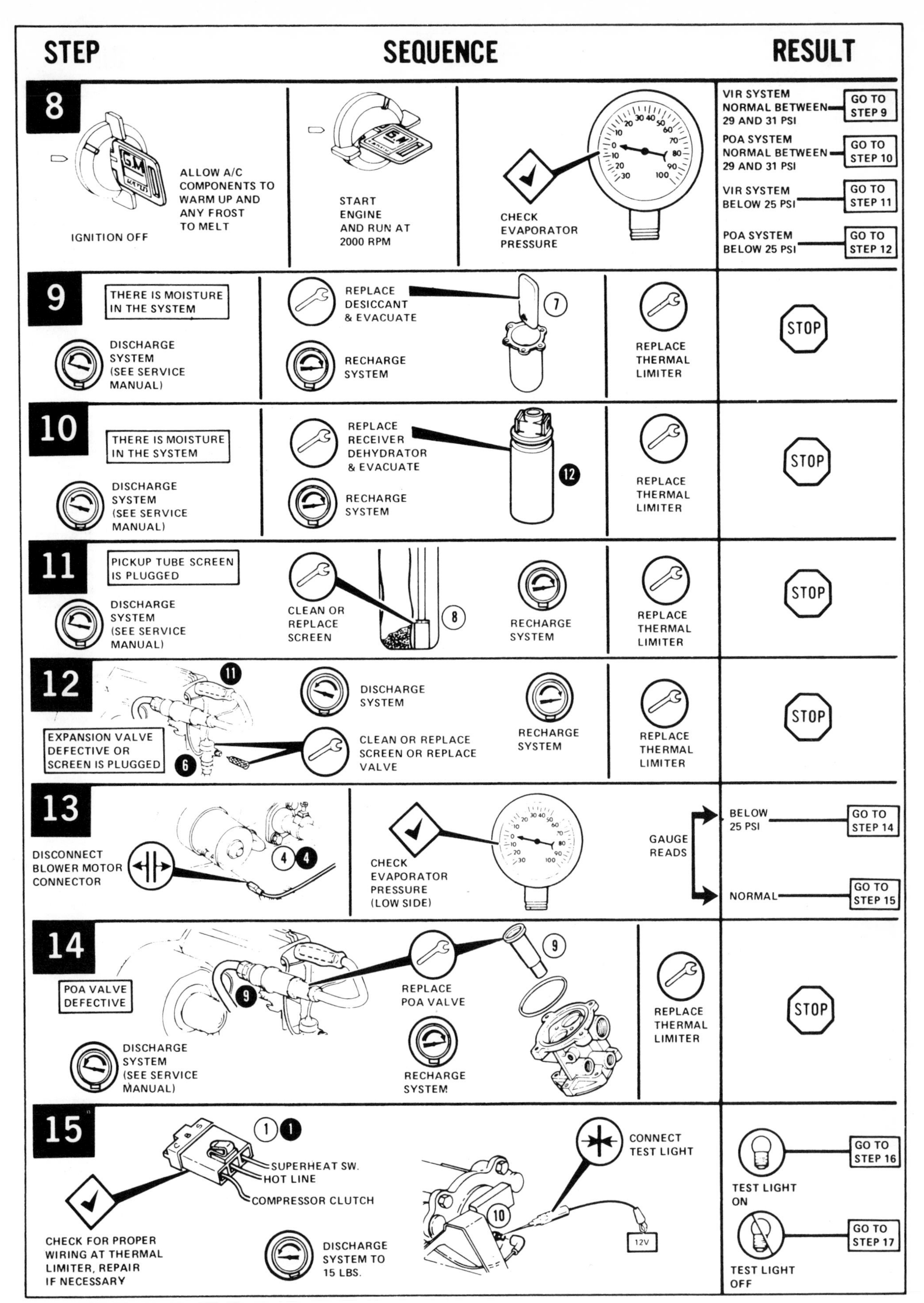

Source: Chevrolet Motor Division of General Motors Corporation.

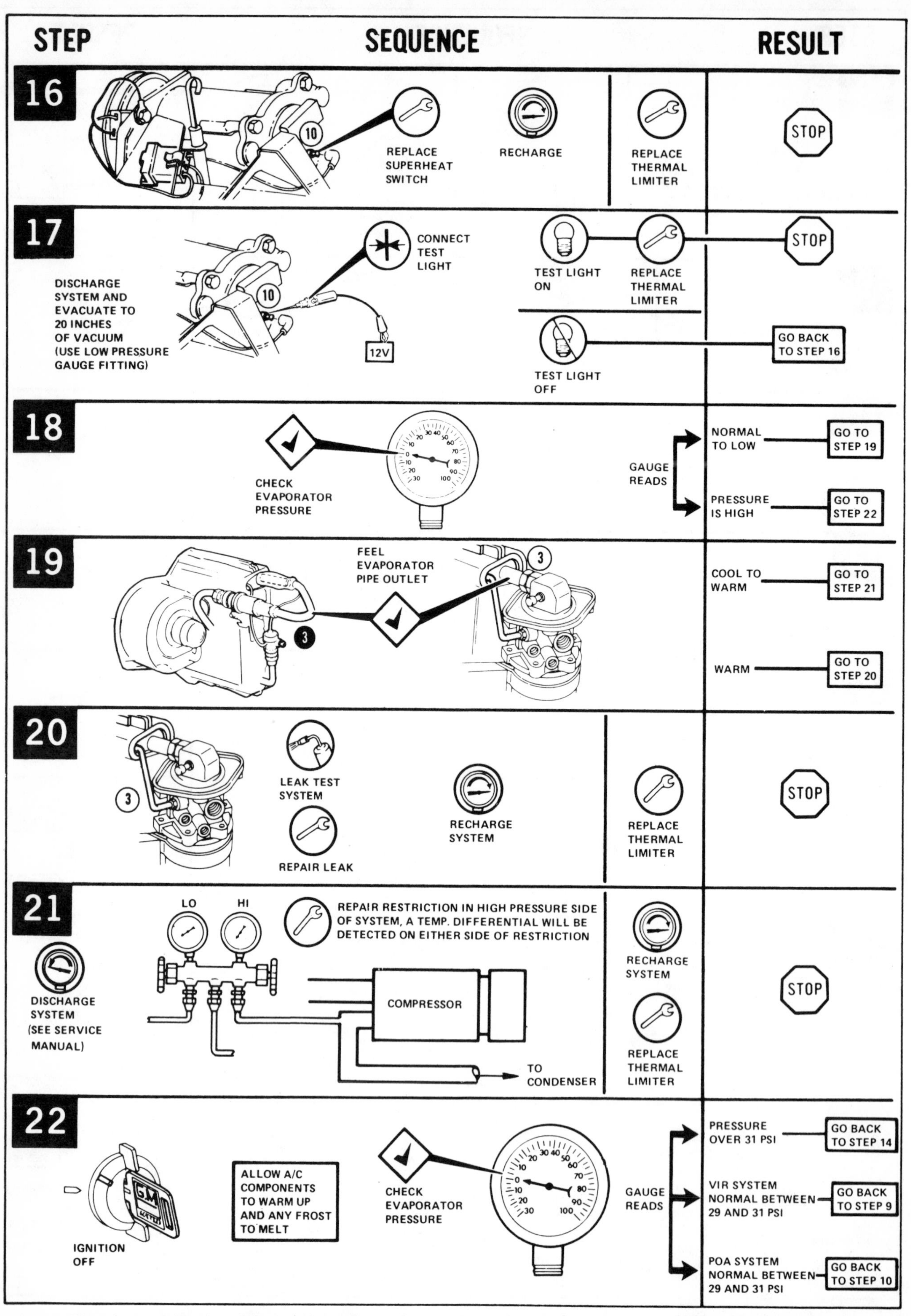

Source: Chevrolet Motor Division of General Motors Corporation.

SECTION 8-8 Checking the Refrigeration System

In this section, we explain how to use the sight glass to determine whether the system contains the right amount of refrigerant. We also describe the use of the leak detector to locate refrigerant leaks. In addition, we discuss the use of pressure gauges to check out the complete system. In a following section we explain how to use the gauge set to evacuate the system (remove the refrigerant, air, and moisture) and recharge it (add a fresh charge of refrigerant).

■ **8-8-1 Cautions** Earlier in this part we pointed out the special cautions you must observe in handling refrigerant. You can handle refrigerant and service refrigerant systems without danger if you heed these cautions. But if you take short cuts or ignore the cautions, you can injure yourself and others. Always wear goggles. Handle the refrigerant with proper respect and according to the safety cautions that apply to working with it.

■ **8-8-2 Using the Sight Glass** All refrigerant leaving the receiver passes under the sight glass (■8-2-7). The appearance (or nonappearance) of the refrigerant gives some indication of whether the system has the proper amount of refrigerant (Fig. 1). The ambient temperature should be 70°F (21.1°C) or above when the sight glass is being checked. Wipe off the sight glass so you can see whether or not there are bubbles in the refrigerant. Operate the system for a few minutes, watching the sight glass. If you observe slow-moving bubbles or a broken column of refrigerant, there is not enough refrigerant in the system. However, it is normal to find a continuous flow of bubbles on a cool day. If the sight glass shows foaming or a broken liquid column, use a piece of heavy cardboard or cloth to partly block off the airflow through the condenser. If the sight glass clears and the air-conditioner performance is otherwise okay, the charge is probably adequate. If the system has lost refrigerant, it should be serviced as explained in Part 8, Sec. 9.

NOTE: On some late-model cars built by Ford, no sight glass is used. The reason given by Ford is that on some systems using a suction throttle valve, the sight glass is not an accurate indicator of the refrigeration-system condition. If there is no sight glass, use a gauge set to check the system (■8-8-5).

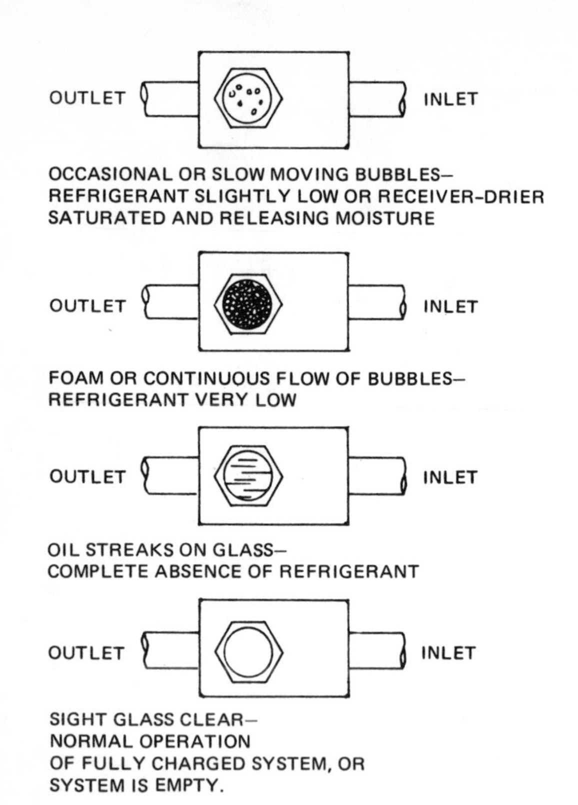

Figure 1 Typical sight-glass indications for various conditions in the refrigeration system. *(Sun Electric Corporation.)*

■ **8-8-3 Checking System with Sight Glass** With the ambient air temperature above 70°F (21.2°C), start the engine, and let it idle fast. Set the air-conditioner controls for maximum cold, with the blower on the high setting. Watch the sight glass for bubbles (Fig. 1). Here are the conditions you may find, and what to do in each case.

1. Bubbles present in sight glass. This probably means the system is low on refrigerant. Check the system with a leak detector (■ 8-8-4). Correct the leak, if any, and evacuate and refill the system (Part 8, Sec. 9).

2. No bubbles, sight glass clear. This means that the system is either fully charged or empty. Feel the high- and low-pressure pipes at the compressor (keep hands away from the belts and engine fan). The high-pressure pipe should be warm, the low-pressure pipe should be cold.

3. No appreciable difference in temperature between the pipes. The system is empty or nearly empty. Turn off the engine, and add about ½ pound [227 g (grams)] of refrigerant to the system. Check the system with a leak detector. Correct the leak, and then evacuate and refill the system (Part 8, Sec. 9).

4. Temperature difference noted between the pipes at the compressor. The system is probably okay as far as refrigerant is concerned. But it could be overcharged. That is, too much refrigerant may have been added, resulting in poor cooling (especially at low speeds). You can check for overcharging by temporarily disconnecting the compressor clutch while the system is operating. Watch the sight glass.

5. If the refrigerant in the sight glass remains clear for more than 45 seconds (before foaming and then settling away from the sight glass), an overcharge is indicated. The excess should be bled off.

6. If the refrigerant foams and then settles away from the sight glass in less than 45 seconds, you can assume that the system has not been overcharged.

NOTE: The sight glass is only a preliminary check. It tells you no more than whether or not the system has the right amount of refrigerant in it. If the system is not functioning properly, other checks may be necessary to locate and correct the trouble. For example, if the sight glass indicates that the system does not have the proper amount of refrigerant, the operating pressure in the system should be checked (■8-8-6).

■ **8-8-4 Using the Leak Detector** A leak detector is a device that is used to locate refrigerant leaks in the system. There are four types. They are the halide or flame torch (Fig. 2), electronic (Fig. 3), soap bubble, and R-12 dye.

The flame type is a small torch that burns a special fuel—either anhydrous methyl alcohol or propane. It has a long tube that is open at one end. When the torch is lighted, air is drawn through the tube to the base of the torch. If the open end of the tube is placed close to a refrigerant leak, the refrigerant vapor is drawn in through the tube. It passes up through the flame. As the refrigerant passes through the flame, it changes the color of the flame. The flame turns green, brilliant blue, or purple, depending on the amount of refrigerant passing through the flame. By moving the open end of the tube around, and holding it close to the connections in the system, you can locate any leak.

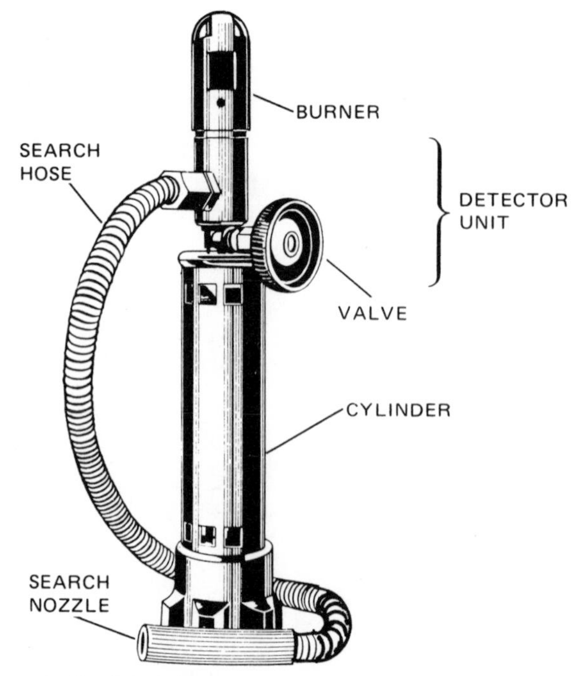

Figure 2 Torch leak detector.

CAUTION: Do not breathe the fumes or black smoke that the torch gives off when a leak has been located. They are poisonous.

If the surrounding air is contaminated with refrigerant vapors, the leak detector will show the presence of refrigerant all the time. Therefore, the torch leak detector should be used only in well-ventilated areas.

CAUTION: Never use a torch-type leak detector in any place where combustible vapor, gas, or dust is present. The flame could set off an explosion or a fire.

The electronic leak detector (Fig. 3) is more sensitive than the flame-type detector. To use the electronic leak detector, proceed as follows: Place the sensitivity switch in the SEARCH position for the first check. Turn the control knob clockwise until a steady ticking sound is heard. Then move the probe tip slowly over and under the places suspected of leaking. These include connections, hoses that look damaged, valves, compressor seal points, receiver, condenser, and evaporator. We move the probe tip under suspected areas because the refrigerant is heavier than air and drops downward toward the floor.

When the probe tip passes a leak, the ticking sound will increase. If the refrigerant vapor is relatively concentrated, the signal will increase to a high-pitched squeal. If you cannot pinpoint the leak, move the sensitivity switch to the PINPOINT position. Then readjust the control knob until you get the steady ticking again. Now, pass the probe tip around the suspected area again. The PINPOINT setting changes the leak-detector sensitivity, so that the ticking will not increase until the probe tip is right at the leak.

The electronic leak detector should be checked occasionally to make sure it has not lost its sensitivity. To do this, remove the screw from the top of the calibrated leak bottle. This allows a small amount of refrigerant vapor to escape from the bottle. Now move the probe tip under the top of the leak bottle. A normal leak detector will begin to tick. The ticking sound will increase to a squeal as the probe tip senses the vapor.

CAUTION: Remove only the screw from the leak bottle, not the top! Refrigerant spilled on the fingers can freeze them!

You can also use soapy water to find leaks. Brush soapy water on the connections, or other places where leaks could occur. Leaks will cause bubbles to appear. This test is not very accurate and will detect only major leaks. Minor leaks would be too slow to blow bubbles while you watch. Small ready-mixed bottles of liquid bubble soap are available from parts stores. It is very safe to use.

Refrigerant dye can also be used to find leaks. Small cans of dye are available which fit the low-pressure side of the gauge set. The dye is then introduced into the refrigerant, turning it red. Any leaks can be seen, or can be located by wiping out-of-sight parts with a white cloth.

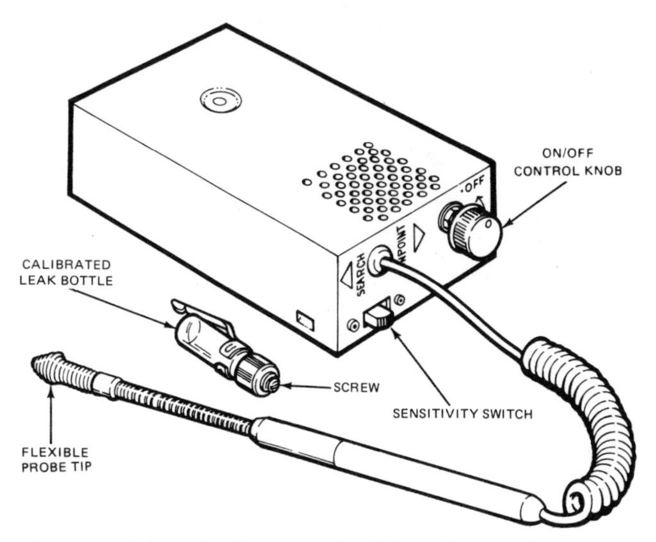

Figure 3 Electronic leak detector. *(Ford Motor Company.)*

CAUTION: The small can of dye must never be connected to the high-pressure side of the refrigerant system. The can could burst and cause serious injury.

■ **8-8-5 Gauge Set** The gauge set (Fig. 4) includes a low-pressure gauge for checking the refrigerant pressure on the low-pressure side of the system. It has a high-pressure gauge for checking the refrigerant pressure on the high-pressure side of the system. Some gauge sets used to check air-conditioning systems in Chrysler Corporation cars also have a third gauge. This gauge is used to check the pressure at the compressor inlet service port (Fig. 5). The gauge set is sometimes called the "manifold gauge set" or the "gauge set manifold."

The low-pressure gauge is often called the "suction gauge." The high-pressure gauge is often called the "discharge gauge." The gauge set is used to measure the refrigerant pressures on

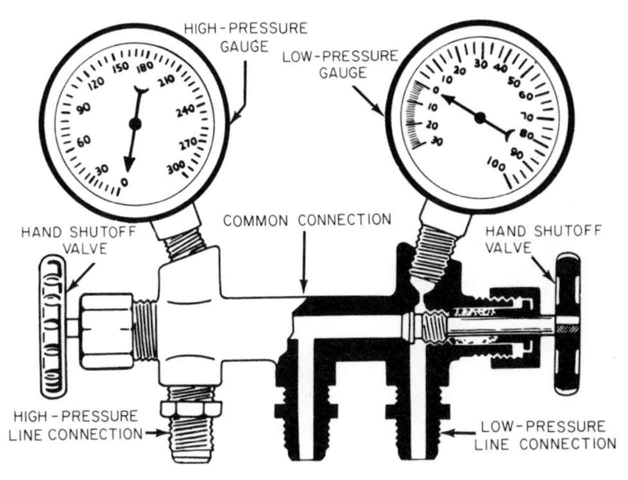

Figure 4 Gauge set.

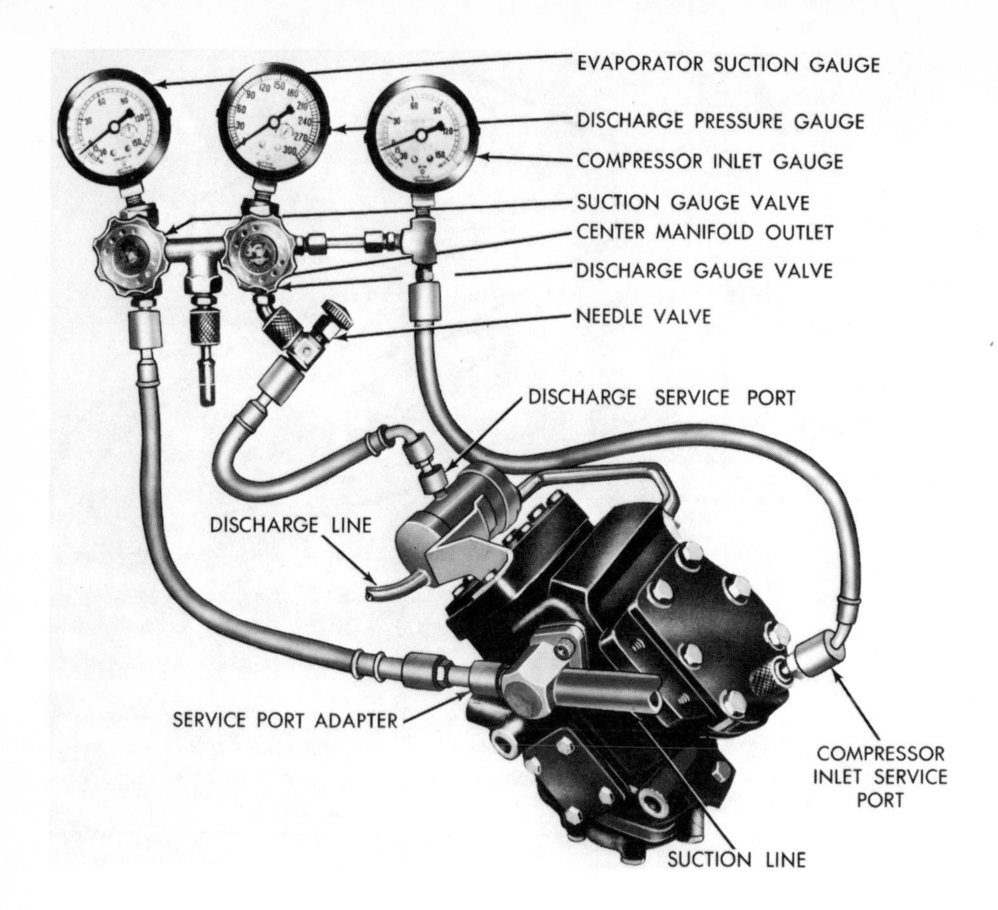

Figure 5 Gauge connections to compressor. *(Chrysler Corporation.)*

the high and low sides of the system and, thereby, to determine how the system is operating. Also, and just as important, the gauge set is used when evacuating and recharging the system. These procedures are covered in detail in Part 8, Sec. 19. An important part of evacuation and recharging is to measure the amount of oil lost during the procedure. Then the same amount of new, fresh oil is added along with the new charge of refrigerant.

The refrigeration system has connection points, or service valves, at which the hoses from the gauges can be connected. These service valves are located in various places in the system. Chrysler Corporation systems, for example, have the service valves at the compressor (Fig. 5). Ford systems have the service valves similarly located. Many General Motors systems using the valves-in-receiver (VIR) assembly have the service valves at the VIR assembly.

Each service valve has a protector cap that guards the valve against dirt and moisture (Fig. 6). The valve is much like the valve used to hold tire pressure. It is often called a "Schrader valve." When the adaptor and hose from a gauge are attached, a pin in the hose adaptor pushes the valve open (Fig. 7). This opens the pressure circuit to the gauge.

Some air-conditioner systems use a manual or hand-shutoff type of service valve (Fig. 8). These valves are opened manually with a special service valve wrench after the hoses from the gauge set are connected to the valve fittings. The valves are protected by caps similar to those used with Schrader-type valves (Fig. 6).

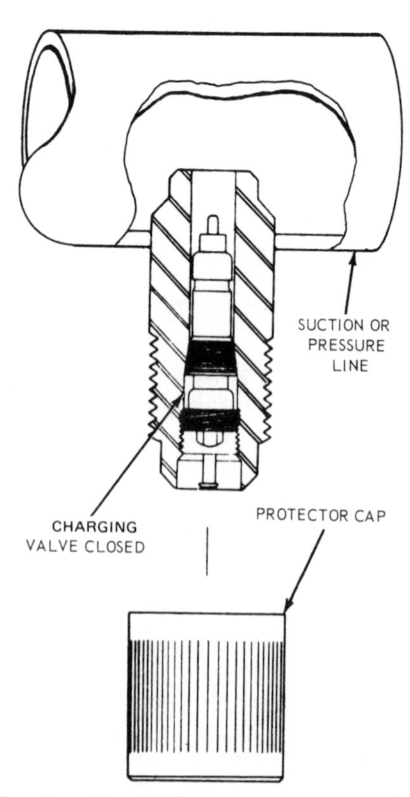

Figure 6 Charging valve with its protector cap removed. *(Ford Motor Company.)*

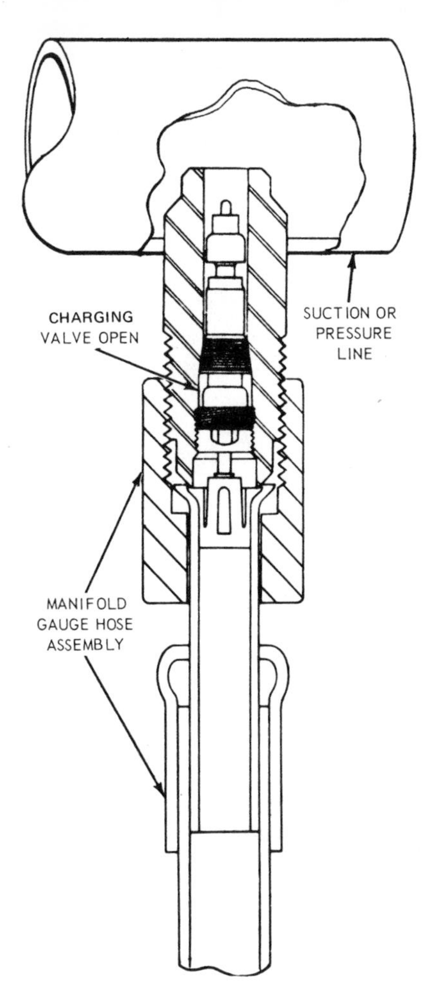

Figure 7 Charging valve with hose from manifold gauge set connected. *(Ford Motor Company.)*

The manually operated valves are mounted on the compressor cylinder head. Each valve is a three-position valve (Fig. 8). The normal operating position for the valve is shown in *B* of Fig. 8. The valve stem is turned fully counterclockwise so the valve is in its back-seated or full-out position. In this position, refrigerant flows from the compressor through the service valve to the refrigerant hose.

When the valve stem is turned clockwise to the front-seated or full-in position, shown in *A* of Fig. 8, the compressor is isolated from the system. With the valve in this position, no refrigerant can flow through the valve. The compressor can be removed from the system or the compressor oil level can be checked without discharging the system.

When the valve is midpositioned or cracked, as in *C* of Fig. 8, the gauge port is open. This is the position the valve must be in for charging, discharging, evacuating, and checking system pressures with a gauge set.

■ 8-8-6 Checking Pressures with the Gauge Set

Here is the way to use the gauge set to check the refrigerant pressures in the air conditioner:

1. Turn the gauge-set valves to the closed positions. That is, the valves should be turned in so the valve needles are seated (see Fig. 4).

2. With the engine not running, remove the protective caps from the gauge fittings (Fig. 6). Attach the adaptors to the gauge hoses (if not already attached).

3. Connect the hose with an adaptor to the high-pressure side of the system. Crack the high-pressure gauge valve (open it slightly) to allow refrigerant vapor to pass through the hoses and gauge set for 3 seconds. This purges all air and moisture from the hoses and gauge set.

4. Close the high-pressure gauge valve. Connect the low-pressure gauge hose to the low-pressure fitting of the system. The system is now ready for pressure checking.

5. Start the engine, and run it at 1,100 to 1,300 rpm. (This is the Ford specification. Other manufacturers may have different specifications. Check their shop manuals.)

6. All controls should be set for maximum cooling, and the front of the car should be at least 5 feet (1.5 m) from any wall.

7. Open the gauge valves, and note the pressures. Compare these with the pressure listed in the specifications (Figs. 9 and

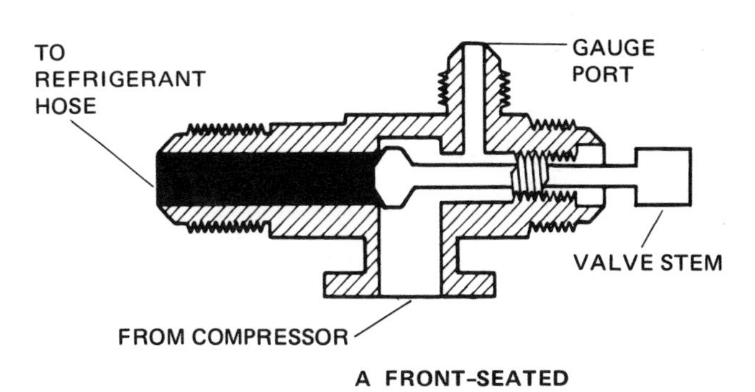

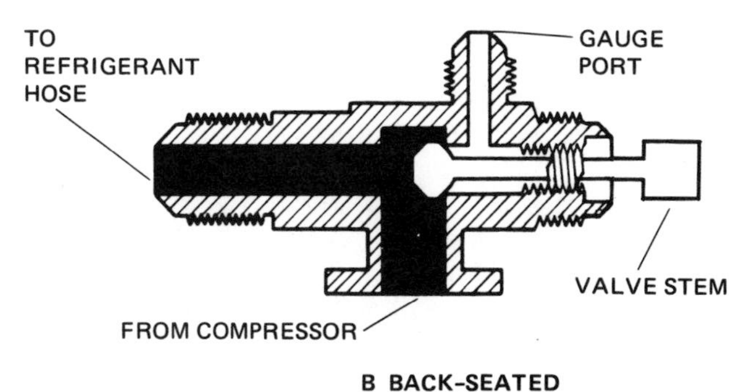

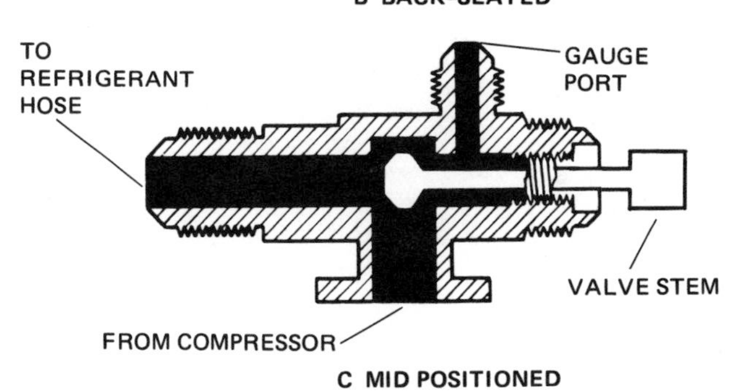

Figure 8 Manual or hand-shutoff type of service valve.

Table 1 Refrigeration-system analysis chart for systems with a suction throttling valve (except Maverick and Comet)

Suction gauge (low pressure)	Discharge gauge (high pressure)	Evaporator gauge (low pressure)	Problem	Suction gauge (low pressure)	Discharge gauge (high pressure)	Evaporator gauge (low pressure)	Problem
10–20 psi (0.703–1.406 kg/cm²) Pressure will normally increase and decrease within this range	120–180 psi (8.437–12.655 kg/cm²) in 70–80°F (21.1–26.7°C)	Refer to pressure/ altitude chart (Table 3)	• Normal	Too high	Too low	(See Note 1) normal or too high	• Expansion valve sticking open • Compressor head gasket blown • Compressor valve problem
				Too low	Too low	Normal or too low	• Undercharged system • Expansion valve inoperative
				Vacuum	Low	Normal	• Expansion valve sticking closed • Plugged receiver (See Note 2) • Iced up (moisture in system) • Undercharged system
Normal	Normal	Too high or too low	• Improperly calibrated gauge • Moisture in system • Suction throttling valve is improperly functioning (See Note 1)	Too high	Normal or too high	(See Note 1) normal or too high	• Expansion valve capillary tube temperature-sensing bulb exposed to engine compartment heat or poor contact with evaporator outlet tube • Expansion valve sticking open
Normal	Too high	Normal	• Restriction in line (See Note 2 Look for frost ring) • Plugged receiver • Plugged condenser • Radiator overheating • Air in system • Overcharged system • Viscous fan inoperative	Normal	Normal	Not constant (complaint of intermittent cooling)	• Moisture in system, passes critical point and clears up but freezes again
Too high	Too high	(See Note 1) Normal or too high	• Very hot shop, no auxiliary fan directed toward condenser • Restricted airflow through condenser • Radiator overheating • Viscous fan inoperative • Overcharged system				

Note 1: If the compressor suction pressure should be higher than the pressure shown in the pressure/altitude chart (see Table 3), the evaporator pressure will also increase. *Do not replace the suction throttling valve.* The problem will usually be elsewhere in the refrigerant system.

Note 2: If the condenser is hot from top to bottom and the receiver is hot but the receiver outlet line is cool, the receiver is restricted. Replace the receiver.

Source: Ford Motor Company.

Table 2 Refrigeration-system analysis chart for systems with a thermostatic switch (Maverick and Comet)

Suction (low pressure)	Discharge gauge (high pressure)	Problem
10–20 psi (0.703–1.406 kg/cm²)	120–180 psi (8.437–12.655 kg/cm²) 70–80°F (21.1–26.7°C)	Normal
Normal	Too high	• Restriction in line (See Note) { Look for frost ring • Plugged receiver (See Note) { Look for frost ring • Plugged condenser • Radiator overheating • Air in system • Overcharged system • Engine fan too small—or viscous fan inoperative
Too high	Too high	• Very hot shop, no auxilary fan directed toward condenser • Restricted airflow through condenser • Radiator overheating • Engine fan too small—or viscous fan inoperative • Temperature-sensing bulb exposed to engine compartment heat or poor contact with evaporator outlet tube • Overcharged system
Too high	Too low	• Compressor valve problem • Compressor head gasket blown • Thermostatic (deicing) switch improperly calibrated or poor sensor tube contact with evaporator fins
Too low	Too low	• Undercharged system • Expansion valve capilliary tube perforated
Vacuum	Normal or low	• Expansion valve stuck closed • Plugged receiver (see Note) • Moisture in system • Undercharged system • Thermostatic (deicing) switch improperly calibrated or poor sensor tube contact with evaporator fins
Too high	Normal or high	• Expansion valve capilliary tube temperature-sensing bulb exposed to engine compartment heat or poor contact with evaporator outlet tube • Expansion valve sticking open
Normal (complaint of intermittent cooling)		• Moisture in system, passes critical point and clears up but freezes again.

Note: If the condenser is hot from top to bottom and the receiver is hot but the receiver outlet line is cool, the receiver is restricted. Replace the receiver.

Source: Ford Motor Company.

10). These charts give the correct pressures and indicate what could be wrong if the measured pressures are not within the specifications given.

NOTE: The actual pressures increase as the surrounding air temperature and humidity go up. Higher temperatures and humidities work the system harder, so the pressures in the system rise. At idle speed, with an ambient temperature of 110°F (43.3°C), the high pressure in the system may go up to 300 psi (21.092 kg/cm²). If it is necessary to test the system when the surrounding air is at a high temperature, use a large fan to blow air through the condenser and the engine radiator.

■ 8-8-7 Pressure-Test Results (Ford) Table 1 shows the correct pressures for Ford systems using a suction throttling valve. Table 2 gives the correct pressures for Ford systems using a thermostatic (deicing) switch. If pressures are incorrect, note what possible causes might produce the incorrect readings. Note that Table 1 has a separate column headed "Evaporator Gauge (Low Pressure)." This pressure is measured separately at the suction throttling valve (see■ 8-8-8).

■ 8-8-8 Evaporator Gauge Pressure This pressure should be measured with a separate additional pressure gauge. It is connected to the suction throttling valve after the protective cap has been removed (Fig. 9). First, however, any defects found during the pressure tests should be corrected. Then, after the low (compound) pressure gauge is connected to the suction throttling valve, the system can stabilize. The evaporator pressure should then be read. Note that the gauge reading is affected by atmospheric pressure. Atmospheric pressure decreases as the altitude increases. To compensate for this, refer to the pressure-altitude chart (Table 3).

Table 3 Pressure-altitude chart showing the relationship of pressure, as regulated by the suction throttling valve, to altitude

Altitude of test site	Required gauge reading ± 1 psi (0.070 kg/cm²)
0 feet (sea level) (0 meters)	28.5 psi (2.004 kg/cm²)
1,000 feet (304.8 meters)	29.0 psi (2.039 kg/cm²)
2,000 feet (609.6 meters)	29.5 psi (2.074 kg/cm²)
3,000 feet (914.4 meters)	30.0 psi (2.109 kg/cm²)
4,000 feet (1,219.2 meters)	30.5 psi (2.144 kg/cm²)
5,000 feet (1,524.0 meters)	31.0 psi (2.180 kg/cm²)
6,000 feet (1,828.8 meters)	31.4 psi (2.208 kg/cm²)
7,000 feet (2,133.6 meters)	31.8 psi (2.236 kg/cm²)
8,000 feet (2,438.4 meters)	32.3 psi (2.271 kg/cm²)
9,000 feet (2,743.2 meters)	32.7 psi (2.299 kg/cm²)
10,000 feet (3,048.0 meters)	33.2 psi (2.334 kg/cm²)

Source: Ford Motor Company.

Table 4 Performance chart for various Chevrolet models

Chevrolet and 125-inch w.b. station wagon

(Refrigerant charge = 3 lb 12 oz)

Temperature of air entering condenser	70°F	80°F	90°F	100°F
Engine speed	2,000 rpm			
Compressor head pressure	115–125 psi	145–155 psi	175–185 psi	210–220 psi
Evaporator pressure @ VIR	29–31 psi			
Discharge air temp. @ right-hand outlet	36–40°F	38–42°F	39–43°F	40–44°F

Chevelle, 116-inch w.b. station wagon and Monte Carlo

(Refrigerant charge = 3 lb 12 oz)

Temperature of air entering condenser	70°F	80°F	90°F	100°F	110°F
Engine speed	2,000 rpm				
Compressor head pressure	135–145 psi	170–180 psi	190–200 psi	220–230 psi	265–275 psi
Evaporator pressure @ VIR	29.0–31.0 psi				
Discharge air temp. @ right-hand outlet	33–37°F	35–39°F	35–39°F	37–41°F	38–42°F

Source: Chevrolet Motor Division of General Motors Corporation.

Table 5 Relationship between pressure and altitude measured at the POA valve

Pressure	Altitude
29.5 psi	Sea level
30.0 psi	1,000 feet
30.5 psi	2,000 feet
31.0 psi	3,000 feet
31.5 psi	4,000 feet
32.0 psi	5,000 feet
32.5 psi	6,000 feet
33.0 psi	7,000 feet
33.5 psi	8,000 feet
34.0 psi	9,000 feet
34.5 psi	10,000 feet

If a valve gives improper readings, it must be replaced. The valve is not adjustable.

■ 8-8-9 Thermostatic (Deicing) Switch Test (Ford) If the test results indicate that the thermostatic switch may be faulty, test it. This should be done with a self-powered test light

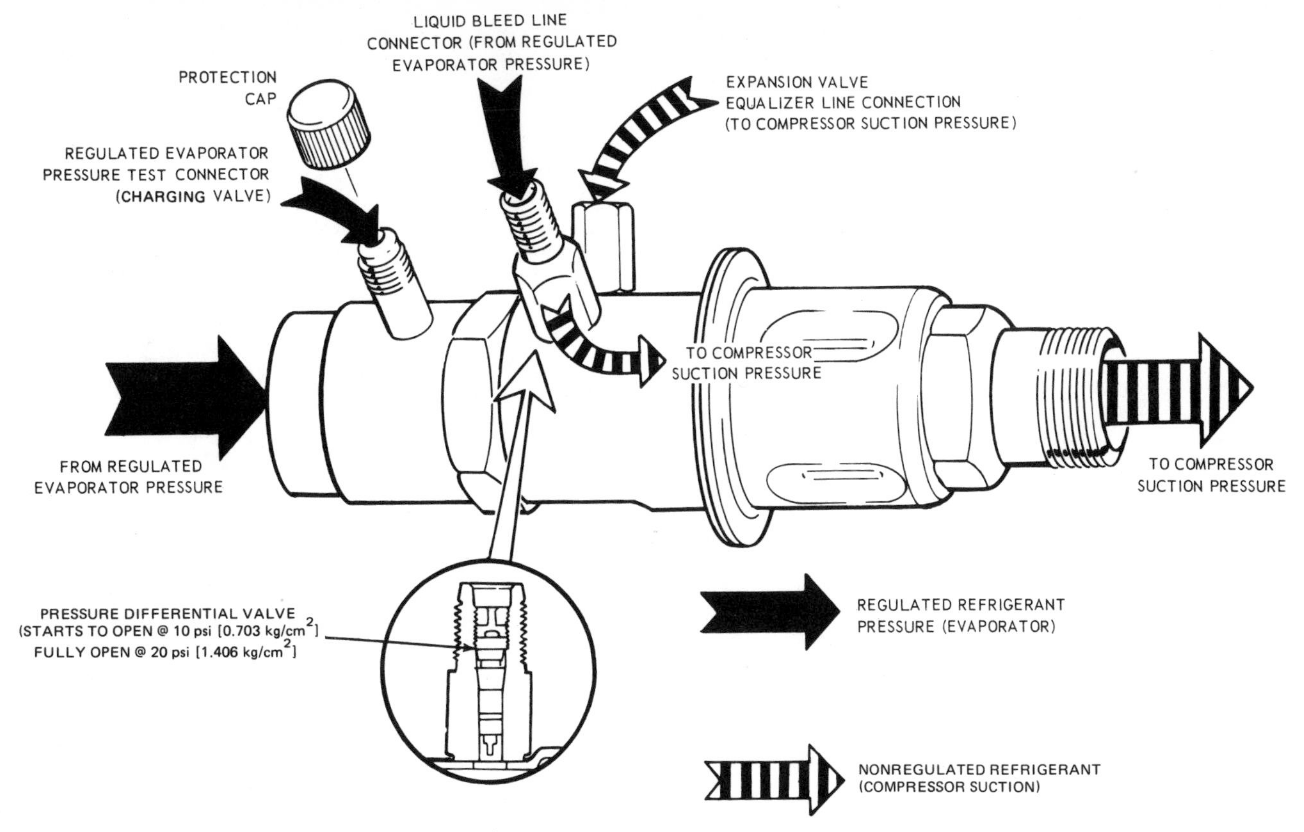

Figure 9 Connections to suction throttling valve. *(Ford Motor Company.)*

connected to the switch terminals. With the capillary tube warm, the switch contacts should be closed, and the light should be on. However, when the tube is cold [20°F (−6.7°C) or lower], the switch should be open, and the light should be off. The capillary tube can be cooled by spraying it with refrigerant.

Another way to cool the capillary tube is to put it in a container packed with ice and salt. Be sure that no salt water gets into the switch.

■ 8-8-10 Checking Pressures with the Gauge Set (Chevrolet)

The performance test that Chevrolet recommends includes more than checking the pressures. It also includes measuring the temperature of the air entering the condenser, and the temperature of the air being discharged from the air-conditioner outlets in the car. Chevrolet also has some recommendations to follow during the test. They state that the car doors and windows should be closed, and the car should be inside or in the shade. A thermometer should be positioned in front of the vehicle grille to check the temperature of air entering the condenser. Thermometers should be used to check the temperature of the cooled air exiting from the air-conditioner outlets. Then gauges are connected.

If the temperature of the air entering the condenser is too high, put a large fan in front of the car grille. This will move more air through the condenser. The performance chart (Table 4) shows the specifications for various late-model Chevrolet cars. Note that a range is given for the evaporator pressure measured at the pilot-operated absolute (POA) valve. This pressure varies with altitude, as does the Ford suction throttling valve (■8-8-7). Table 5 shows the relationship between the pressure and altitude.

SECTION 8-9 Air-Conditioner Maintenance and Service

In this section, we describe the normal maintenance procedures that keep the air conditioner in good running condition. We also explain how a system is evacuated and recharged. In addition, we discuss the problems involved in checking a system on a car that has been in a collision. Later sections explain how to remove and replace system components such as the condenser, evaporator, and compressor.

■ **8-9-1 Cautions** You can handle refrigerant and service refrigerant systems without danger if you heed the cautions pointed out in this part. But, if you take short cuts or ignore the cautions, you can get into serious trouble. You can injure yourself and others. Always wear goggles when handling refrigerant.

■ **8-9-2 Periodic Maintenance** The air conditioner should be operated every week even in cold weather. This keeps the compressor seals from drying out and leaking. It also prevents compressor freeze-up due to loss of lubricating oil from polished surfaces. [See the note in the Trouble-Diagnosis Chart in ■8-7-4, following item 9, "Compressor inoperative above 40°F (4.4°C)."] In addition, note the following.

1. Check the condenser regularly, to make sure that the fins are not plugged with leaves or other trash. Plugged fins reduce the airflow through the condenser and make the system work harder.

2. Check the evaporator drains regularly for dirt and restrictions.

3. Check the hoses for brittleness and damage, and their connections for tightness.

4. Periodically check the sight glass with the system in operation (■8-8-2 and 8-8-3). If the sight glass indicates loss of refrigerant, check the system for leaks (■8-8-4). Then install the gauge set to measure pressures (■8-8-5). Evacuate and recharge the system as necessary, as explained on the following pages.

5. Antifreeze is required in the engine cooling system to protect the coolant from freezing down to 15°F (−9.4°C) for summer operation. This prevents freezing of the coolant in the heater core. However, this is not enough protection against corrosion. For this protection, add enough antifreeze to protect to −15°F (−26.1°C). Chrysler recommends that the engine cooling system be drained and flushed every spring. When draining, flushing, and refilling, set the temperature control to maximum heat, so the heater core is also drained and flushed.

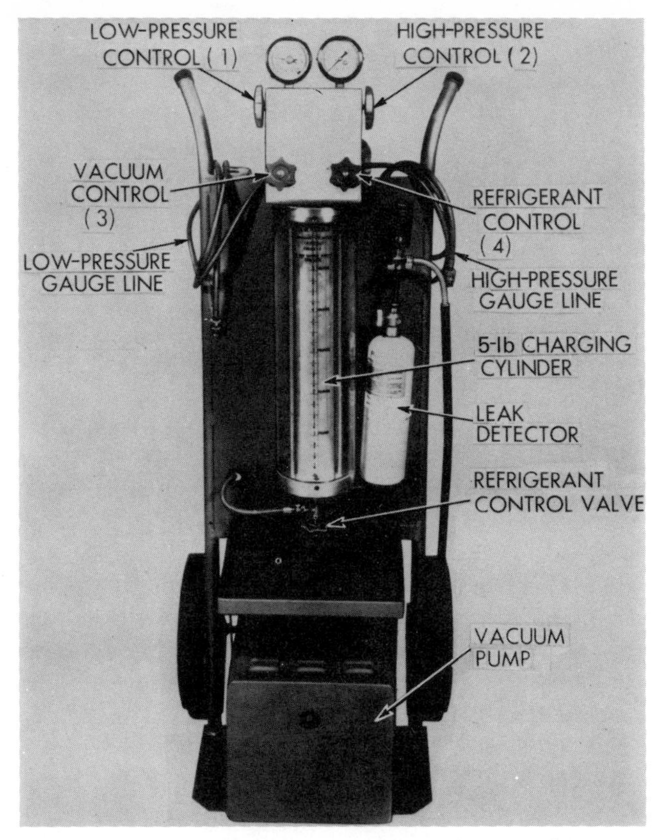

Figure 1 Charging station for servicing air conditioners. The assembly includes low- and high-pressure gauges with control valves, vacuum and refrigerant control valves, a cylinder of liquid refrigerant, a leak detector, and a vacuum pump. *(Chevrolet Motor Division of General Motors Corporation.)*

Old antifreeze should not be reused. Instead, use enough new antifreeze to protect the cooling system to at least −15°F (−26.1°C).

6. Check belt tension and belt condition regularly.

■ **8-9-3 Air-Conditioner Service** A gauge set is required to measure the pressures in the refrigeration system. For complete service, including evacuating and recharging the system, a vacuum pump, a container of refrigerant, and a leak detector are also needed. In addition, a variety of hand and special tools are required if components are to be removed and replaced. Manufacturers have also produced special instruments that are used to check completely automatic heater—air-conditioner systems. These are described in other sections that deal with the servicing of automatic systems.

■ **8-9-4 Charging Station** Many shops that service air conditioners have charging stations (Fig. 1). A typical charging station is assembled on a two-wheeled cart which can be rolled to the car being serviced. It contains the high- and low-pressure gauges, a cylinder of refrigerant, a vacuum pump (Fig. 2), a leak detector, and two valves which are in the lines to the vacuum pump and the refrigerant cylinder (Fig. 3).

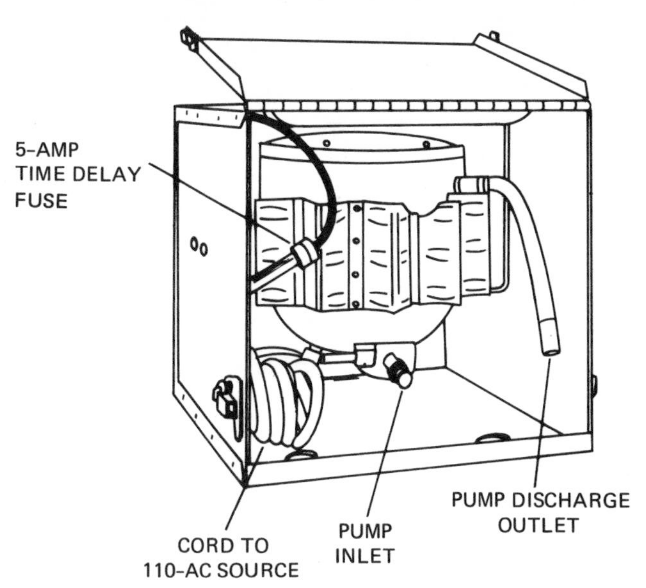

Figure 2 The vacuum pump included in the charging station. *(Chevrolet Motor Division of General Motors Corporation.)*

■ **8-9-5 Vacuum-Pump Service** Chevrolet supplies the following instructions regarding the use and care of the vacuum pump. These instructions apply, in general, to all vacuum pumps used to evacuate air-conditioner refrigeration systems.

1. Keep all openings capped when the pump is not in use. This will prevent moisture from entering the system.

2. Make sure the dust cap is removed from the discharge outlet before operating the vacuum pump.

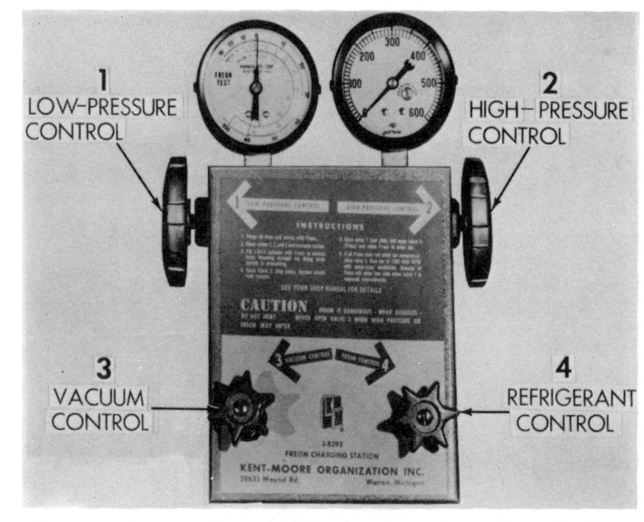

Figure 3 The control panel of the charging station. *(Chevrolet Motor Division of General Motors Corporation.)*

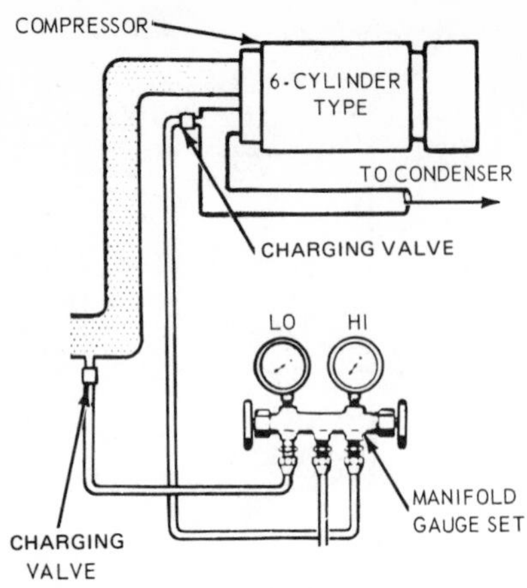

Figure 4 Service connections for a system with a six-cylinder (round) compressor. *(Ford Motor Company.)*

3. Change the vacuum-pump oil every 250 hours of operation.

4. If the pump gets cold, it should be kept in a warm room for several hours before it is used. Otherwise, the cold oil will cause the fuse to blow.

5. Note that the pump uses a 5-amp time-delay fuse. Never use any other kind of fuse. To do so risks damage to the starting windings in the pump.

6. If the pump is used to evacuate a burned-out system, connect a filter in the intake fitting. This will prevent sludge from entering the pump. Such sludge could ruin the pump.

7. Never use the pump as an air compressor.

■ **8-9-6 When to Evacuate the System** If the system has leaked, or damage has occurred, the system must be evacuated and recharged. This is done after the leak or other damage has been repaired. The system must also be evacuated and recharged when new parts are installed.

The vacuum pump is used to evacuate the system. When it operates, it applies vacuum to the system. The vacuum causes refrigerant, water vapor, and air to leave the system.

NOTE: When a refrigerant system has been opened for any purpose, the air conditioner must not be operated until the system has been evacuated to remove the air and moisture that has entered.

The system is evacuated in two steps. First, the refrigerant in the system is discharged or allowed to escape. This is called "discharging" the system. It is very important to measure the amount of oil that comes out of the system along with the refrigerant. New, clean oil must then be put into the system before recharging to replace the oil that was lost. Second, the vacuum pump is used to remove any traces of refrigerant, water vapor, and air that may remain in the system.

NOTE: Chrysler does not require the complete procedure of discharging, evacuating, and recharging the system if only part of the refrigerant has been lost. That is, if the loss is due to a minor leak, and if the leak is fixed without opening the system, it is okay to just add some refrigerant to replace the lost refrigerant. This procedure is covered in ■8-9-15. Refrigerant can be lost due to excessive pressures which open the relief valve. This protects the compressor from damage due to the excessive pressures. High pressures can develop if the air temperature is very high. A temperature of 110°F (43.4°C) can raise the pressure in the refrigerant system to as much as 300 psi (21.092 kg/cm²). High pressures can also develop if the condenser air passages are blocked by leaves, paper, or other trash.

■ **8-9-7 Discharging the System** To discharge the system, connect the high- and low-pressure hoses to the system, as explained in ■8-8-5 and 8-8-6. Both gauge valves should be fully closed.

NOTE: General Motors and Chrysler call for measuring the amount of oil lost with the refrigerant so the same amount of fresh, clean oil can be put back into the system. Ford does not require this. Instead, Ford recommends discharging the system slowly so that very little oil is lost.

1. FORD PROCEDURE With the gauge valves closed, connect the gauge fittings to the system service valves (which Ford calls "charging valves") as in Fig. 4. Place the open end of the gauge-set center hose near an open door or the shop exhaust outlet. Slowly depressurize the system by opening the low-pressure gauge valve slightly. After the system is nearly discharged, open the high-pressure valve. Open it very slowly to avoid losing refrigerant oil.

NOTE: Opening the gauge valves wide or suddenly will cause the refrigerant to discharge quickly carrying refrigerant oil with it.

2. CHEVROLET PROCEDURE This procedure applies, in general, to all General Motors cars. With the gauge valves closed, connect the gauge fittings to the system charging (service) valves. Disconnect the vacuum hose from the vacuum pump, and put the end of the hose into a covered can (Fig. 5). A 3-pound (1.36-kg) coffee can with a plastic top is ideal for this purpose. Slit the top in an X, and insert the end of the hose through the X. The can should be placed close to a garage exhaust outlet.

Fully open the high- and low-pressure gauge valves and allow the refrigerant to discharge from the system at a rapid rate. Watch the hose to make sure it does not blow out of the can.

At a later time, before recharging the system, you will add new oil to replace the oil that has collected in the can. To add

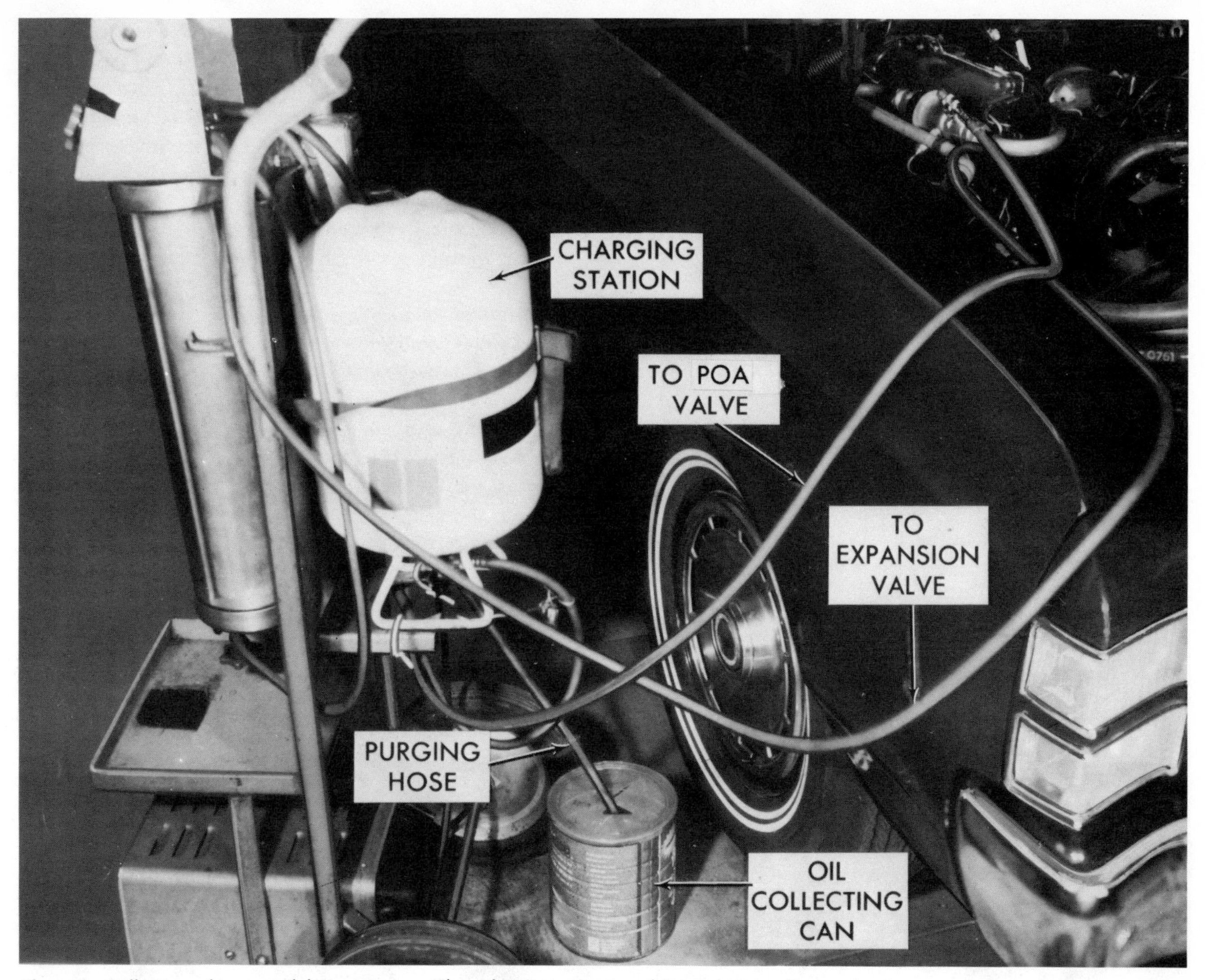

Figure 5 Collecting refrigerant oil during purging. *(Chevrolet Motor Division of General Motors Corporation.)*

the oil, Chevrolet recommends using a tool called an "oil inducer" (Fig. 6). This tool is a hose with connectors at both ends and a manual valve. When the tool is not in use, the two ends of the hose are connected together. This keeps the hose from becoming contaminated with air and moisture.

3. CHRYSLER PROCEDURE The Chrysler procedure is similar to the Chevrolet procedure. However, no special tool is needed to add the oil. Instead, a compressor dipstick is used to measure the level of the oil in the compressor crankcase. This is done near the end of the discharging operation. Then new, fresh refrigerant oil is added to bring the oil in the crankcase up to the proper level.

NOTE: Chrysler recommends that before discharging the system, you should cover the compressor clutch with a cloth. This will prevent oil from getting on the clutch faces as the refrigerant discharges. Oil on these faces could cause clutch slippage.

■ **8-9-8 Adding Refrigerant Oil** Recommendations for adding oil differ for the different manufacturers. There are two times when you should add oil. One is after you have discharged and evacuated the system. You then put new oil into the system to replace oil that was lost during discharging. The other is when you replace a component in the system. Then you add the amount of oil that the old component contained when you removed it. For example, if you replace the condenser in an air conditioner on a Ford, you add 1 fluid ounce (30 cc) of new oil to the condenser just before installing it. The oil circulates through the system with the refrigerant when the system is in operation. Therefore, each component has some oil in it at all times.

1. CHEVROLET PROCEDURE This applies to all General Motors cars. An oil inducer (Fig. 6) is required. This is a long tube with connectors at the ends and a manual shutoff valve. After the system has been discharged, connect the vacuum line to the vacuum pump.

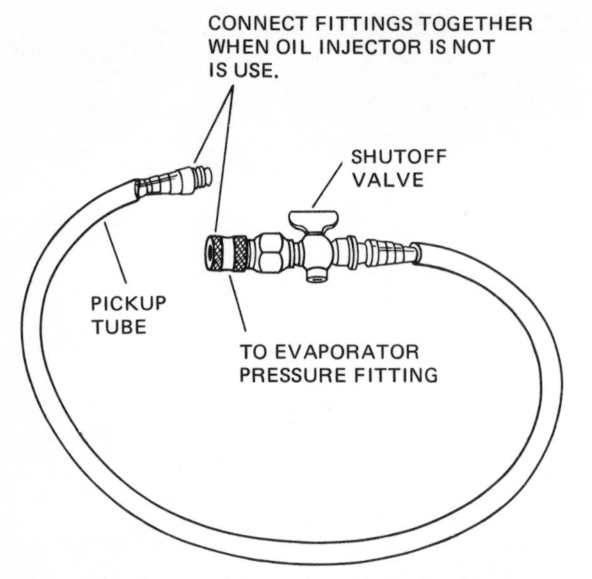

Figure 6 Oil inducer, or injector, for adding oil to the refrigeration system. *(Pontiac Motor Division of General Motors Corporation.)*

Flush out the oil inducer (Fig. 6) as follows: Detach the ends and open the valve on the oil inducer. Disconnect the refrigerant line at the refrigerant container. Crack the valve on the refrigerant container just enough to get a small flow of refrigerant. Hold one end of the oil inducer on the refrigerant-container fitting so the refrigerant vapor flows through the oil inducer. This flushes out any air or moisture. Close the valve on the refrigerant container. Reconnect the ends of the oil inducer and close the oil-inducer valve. Reconnect the refrigerant line to the container.

Measure the amount of oil lost during discharging. The oil inducer will hold about ½ fluid ounce (15 cc) of oil. Add this ½ fluid ounce (15 cc) to the amount lost. Disconnect the low-pressure line from the system service valve. Connect the oil inducer to this valve. Put the other end of the oil inducer into a graduated container of clean refrigerant oil (Fig. 7).

Turn on the vacuum pump, and open the vacuum control valve. Slowly open the high-pressure gauge valve (slowly to avoid pulling oil out of the system).

Now open the valve on the oil inducer, meantime watching

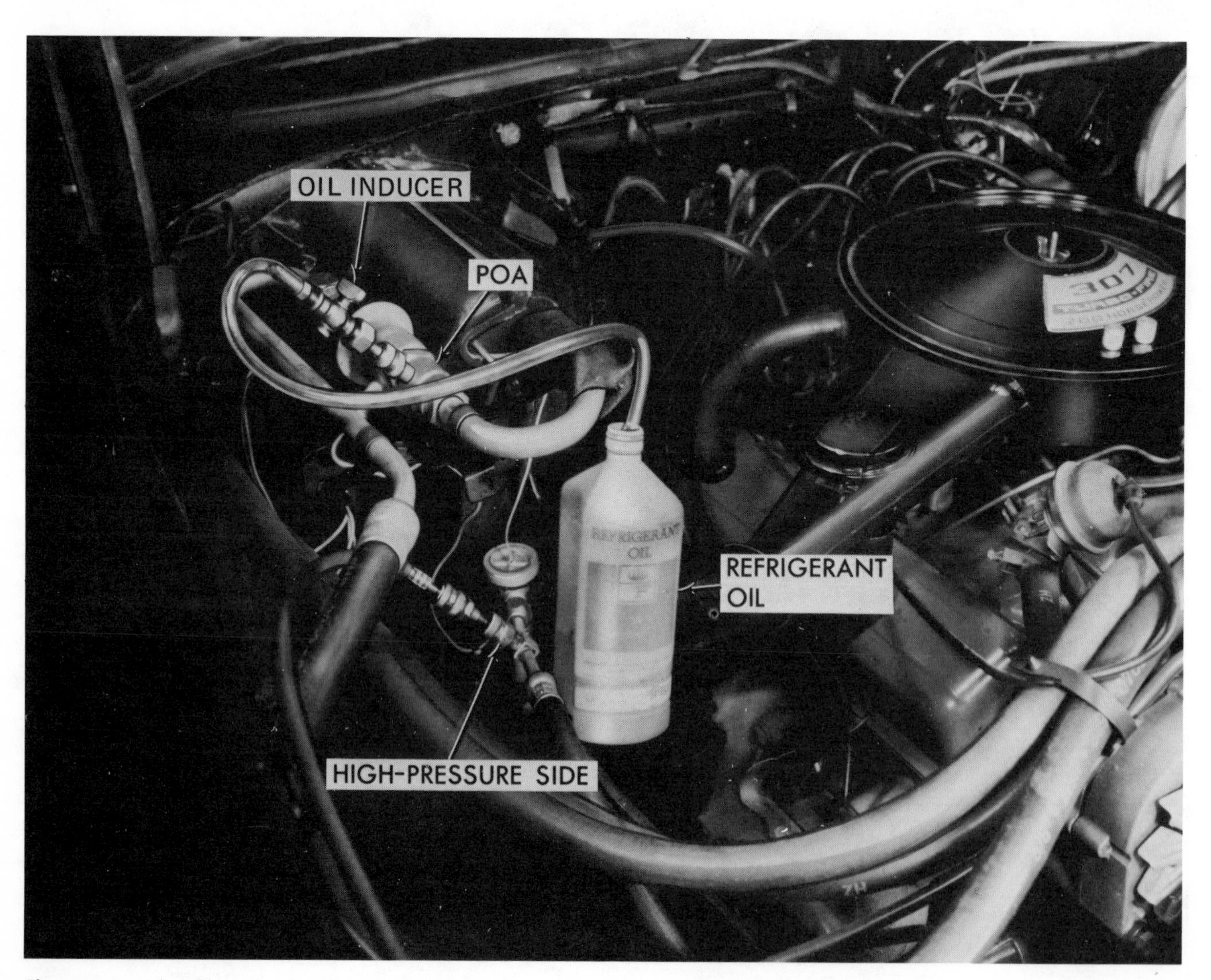

Figure 7 Setup for adding oil to the refrigeration system. *(Chevrolet Motor Division of General Motors Corporation.)*

the graduated container of refrigerant oil. The vacuum will draw oil into the system from the container. When the correct amount has been added, close the oil-inducer valve.

NOTE: Avoid adding more than the correct amount of oil. Too much oil can cause poor air-conditioner operation.

Disconnect the oil inducer. Attach the ends of the oil inducer to each other, and put it away in a safe place.

Reconnect the low-pressure line to the system fitting. The system is now ready for recharging.

NOTE: If a system component is removed and a replacement is installed, oil should be added to the new component. The amount to be added depends on which component is being replaced. See Part 8, Sec. 10.

2. FORD PROCEDURE Ford does not recommend a procedure for adding oil to the system after it is discharged. Instead they list the amounts of oil that the system components normally contain. When any component is removed and discarded, the proper amount of fresh oil should be added to the new component before it is installed. The amounts to be added are as follows:

Evaporator:	3 fluid ounces	(90 cc)
Condenser:	1 fluid ounce	(30 cc)
Receiver:	1 fluid ounce	(30 cc)

For example, if a new evaporator is being installed, 3 fluid ounces (90 cc) of refrigerant oil should be poured into the evaporator just before it is installed.

A different procedure is required if a new six-cylinder compressor is being installed. When the old compressor is removed, the oil should be drained from it and measured. The new compressor is shipped from the factory with 10½ fluid ounces (315 cc) of oil. This oil should be drained out. If the oil drained from the old compressor measures less than 4 fluid ounces (120 cc), put 6 fluid ounces (180 cc) of new oil back into the new compressor. If the old compressor held between 4 to 6 fluid ounces (120 to 180 cc) of oil, then simply put the same amount of new oil back into the new compressor.

NOTE: Never reuse old refrigerant oil. Always add new refrigerant oil to the system or to any of its components.

The procedure for removing and replacing system components is covered in Part 8, Sec. 10.

3. CHRYSLER AND FORD PROCEDURE This procedure applies, in general, to all two-cylinder compressors, including the Chrysler V type and the Ford parallel-cylinder type. The oil level in the compressor crankcase is checked with a special dipstick (Fig. 8). It need not be checked every time the system is discharged. However, the oil should be checked after a new or repaired compressor is installed, if all the refrigerant has

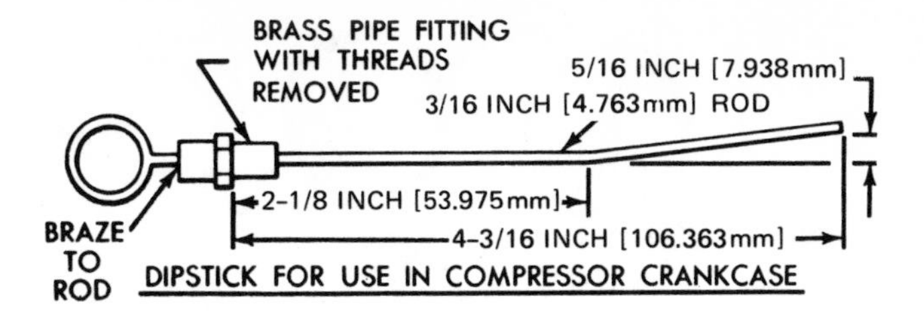

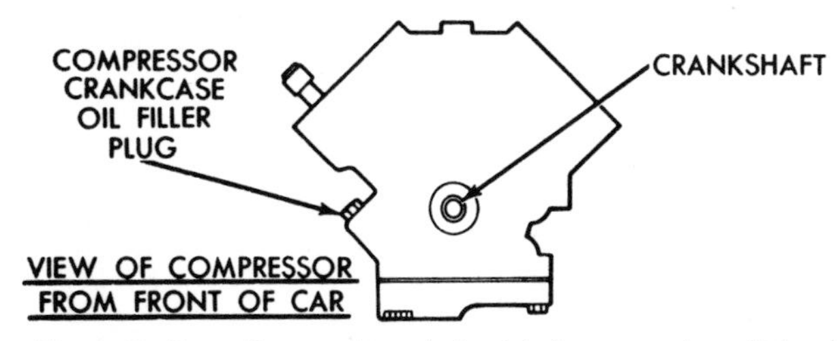

Figure 8 Top: Construction of dipstick for measuring oil level in compressor. Bottom: Location of the compressor-crankcase oil-filler plug. *(Chrysler Corporation.)*

been lost, or if there is evidence of oil loss (oil at the compressor oil seals or connections). Here is how to do it.

Run the engine at fast idle for about 15 minutes. If the room temperature is above 85°F (29.4°C), set the air-conditioner controls on A/C, high blower. If the room temperature is below 85°F (29.4°C), close the car windows and set the controls at MAX A/C, the blower on high, and the temperature at warm.

NOTE: On some Chrysler models, remove and plug the vacuum line to the water valve. This produces the reheat necessary to make the air-conditioning system work at its maximum.

Slowly discharge the refrigeration system. Near the end of the discharge, hold the dipstick in the refrigerant vapor. This flushes and cools the dipstick. When the system is discharged, remove the compressor-crankcase oil-filler plug (Fig. 8). Insert the dipstick into the hole until it bottoms in the crankcase. Remove the dipstick, and check the oil level. The compressor crankcase should hold between 6 and 8 fluid ounces (180 and 240 cc). See Table 1.

Table 1 Specified dipstick readings for compressors on engines and on the workbench

Engine	Dipstick reading: Inches @ 6 ounces minimum	Dipstick reading: Inches @ 8 ounces minimum
All 6-cylinder engines	1¾	2⅜
All 8-cylinder engines	1⅝	2⅜
Compressor set vertically on bench	1⅝	2⅜

Source: Chrysler Corporation.

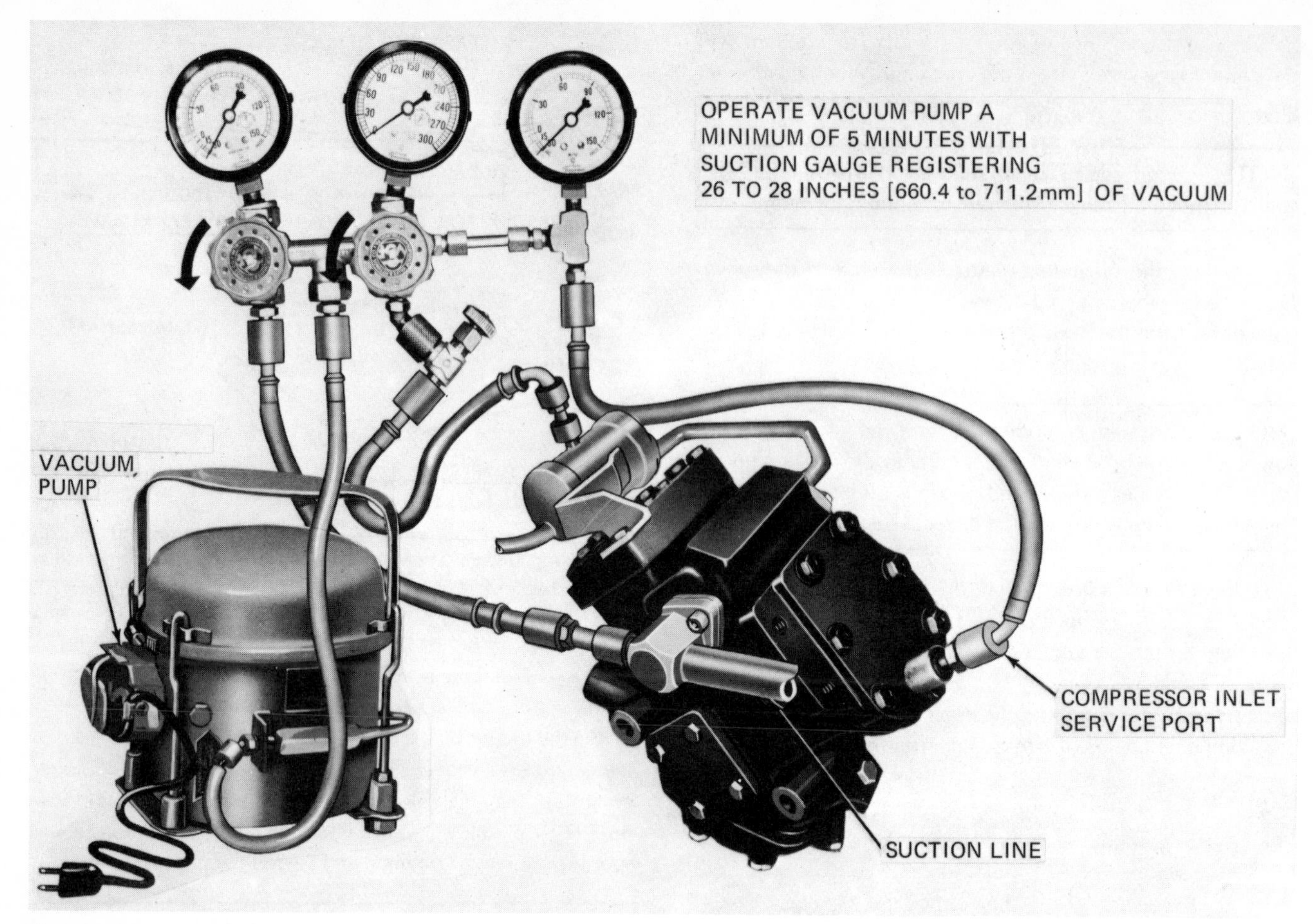

Figure 9 Connections of gauges and vacuum pump to the V-type compressor for evacuating the system. The compressor is shown detached from the system. Actually, the connections shown are made with the compressor mounted on the engine and connected into the refrigeration system. *(Chrysler Corporation.)*

Add oil as necessary to bring the level up to the specified height. Or, if there is too much oil, remove some.

> **NOTE:** Another method of adding oil to the system is by using a small pressure can. A special can of refrigerant, with 2 fluid ounces (60 cc) of oil in it, is available which connects to the gauge set. This can is especially designed for use with the Frigidaire compressor.

■ **8-9-9 Evacuating the System** Any time the system has been opened for any reason, it must be evacuated. That is, vacuum must be applied to the system so that all refrigerant vapor, air, and moisture are pumped out. This is a requirement. Failure to evacuate the system properly leads to poor cooling and possibly expensive damage to the compressor and other components.

The evacuation procedure requires a vacuum pump and the gauge set. The gauge set should be connected, as already described for the discharging procedure (■8-8-5, 8-8-6, and 8-9-6). In addition, a refrigerant tank or several small cans of refrigerant should be available. These will be used to recharge the system after it has been evacuated.

If you are using a charging station (Fig. 1), make sure the charging cylinder contains sufficient refrigerant. The charging cylinder is recharged by connecting a refrigerant tank to the charging cylinder.

Refrigerant comes in small "pound" cans and in large tanks. The procedure for recharging the system is described in ■8-9-10.

After the system has been discharged, connect the vacuum pump. Figure 9 shows the connections for a Chrysler system. The gauges, vacuum pump, and refrigerant supply tank are connected in readiness for evacuating and recharging the system. In Fig. 9, the refrigerant supply is not shown.

With both the high-pressure and low-pressure gauge valves open, operate the vacuum pump. The length of the evacuating period varies with the manufacturer. For example, Chrysler says to operate the pump for at least 5 minutes after the pump has built up a vacuum of at least 26 inches (660.4 mm) as measured on the low-pressure gauge. Chevrolet says to operate the vacuum pump for 10 minutes after the vacuum has reached 28 to 29 inches (711.2 to 736.6 mm). Ford says to run the vacuum pump for 10 minutes after the vacuum goes above 25 inches (635.0 mm). Ford adds that if a component has been replaced, the vacuum pump should be operated for 20 to 30 minutes.

NOTE: The lower the ambient temperature, the longer it takes to properly evacuate the system.

If the specified vacuum cannot be reached, either there is a leak in the system or the vacuum pump is defective. The vacuum pump can be checked by closing the gauge valves. If the vacuum pump then cannot build up the specified vacuum, it is defective. However, if it can build up the specified vacuum, the system has a leak. To check the system, shut off the vacuum pump, and close the line to the pump. Open the refrigerant control valve, and let about ½ pound (227 g) of refrigerant enter the system. Now use the leak detector to locate the leak (■8-8-4). After you locate and repair the leak, discharge the system and reevacuate it.

After the evacuation is completed, turn off the gauge valves and prepare to recharge the system.

■ 8-9-10 Recharging the System with Charging Station If you are using the charging station (Fig. 1), here is the procedure to follow. Before you start, check the sight glass on the charging cylinder. Make sure it has enough refrigerant to give the system a full charge.

Before the system is charged, it must be discharged and evacuated. Then close the vacuum-control valve to the vacuum pump (3 in Fig. 3). The low- and high-pressure valves (1 and 2 in Fig. 3) should still be open. Open the refrigerant control valve (4 in Fig. 3). This allows refrigerant to flow into the system.

If you cannot get a full charge into the system, close the high-pressure gauge valve. Set the A/C controls for maximum cooling and high blower speed. Operate the engine at 2,000 rpm for about 5 minutes. Be sure to vent the engine exhaust to the outside. The operation of the compressor will reduce the pressure on the low side, so that more refrigerant can enter the system.

Close the refrigerant control valve. Make a performance test by checking the high and low pressures, as outlined in ■8-8-10.

■ 8-9-11 Ford Recharging Procedure Here is the recharging procedure recommended by Ford. Discharge and evacuate the system. Close the vacuum-pump valve.

Open the low-pressure gauge valve, and close the high-pressure gauge valve. Open the refrigerant-supply-tank valve to allow refrigerant to flow into the system. When both gauges reach 60 to 80 psi (4.219 to 5.625 kg/cm^2) [temperature about 75°F (23.9°C)], shut off the tank valve.

Check the system for leaks (■8-8-4). Repair any leaks you find. If there are no leaks, proceed as follows. Set the controls for maximum cooling. Start the engine, and open the refrigerant-supply-tank valve. Run the engine at 1,500 rpm until the specified weight of refrigerant has entered the system. To determine how much refrigerant has entered, weigh the supply tank before the recharging starts. Then continue to weigh it during the recharging procedure.

If the temperature is low, enough refrigerant may not enter the system. In that case, put the refrigerant supply tank in a container of hot water at about 150°F (65.6°C). This increases the pressure in the tank and forces more refrigerant out.

CAUTION: Never heat the refrigerant tank with a torch, or heat it above 150°F (65.6°C). If overheated, the tank will explode, possibly seriously injuring or killing anyone standing close by.

NOTE: Keep the tank upright during the charging operation. If the tank is laid on its side or turned upside down, liquid refrigerant will flow into the system. This could overcharge the system and damage the compressor.

During charging, the high-pressure side can build up to an excessive pressure. This could result from overheating of the engine, an overcharge of refrigerant, or high ambient temperatures. Never let the pressure go above 240 psi (16.674 kg/cm^2). If it does, stop the engine and determine what is wrong.

After charging the system, shut off the refrigerant-supply-tank valve. The low-pressure gauge should read 4 to 25 psi (0.281 to 1.758 kg/cm^2), the high-pressure gauge 120 to 210 psi (8.437 to 14.765 kg/cm^2), with the ambient temperature 70 to 90°F (21.2 to 32.2°C). Disconnect the gauge hoses. Install the protective caps on the system charging valves and the gauge hoses.

■ 8-9-12 Ford Charging Procedure with Small Cans Refrigerant comes in 14-ounce (396.89-g) and 15-ounce (425.24-g) cans, as well as in metal drums and tanks of various sizes. The small cans are often used because they are so convenient. There is one special caution that must be followed if the cans are used:

CAUTION: Never try to use cans to charge the system on the high-pressure side—that is, with the high-pressure-gauge valve open. This would admit high pressure to the can, and cause it to explode. Anyone standing nearby could be seriously injured by fragments of the can and by the liquid refrigerant that would fly out. Remember that the liquid refrigerant can freeze anything it touches, including your eyes and your skin.

You must have a special valve and valve retainer to connect to the refrigerant can. Attach the valve retainer to the can by engaging the three tabs of the retainer to the lip on the top of the can. Turn the valve assembly into the threaded hole in the top of the valve retainer.

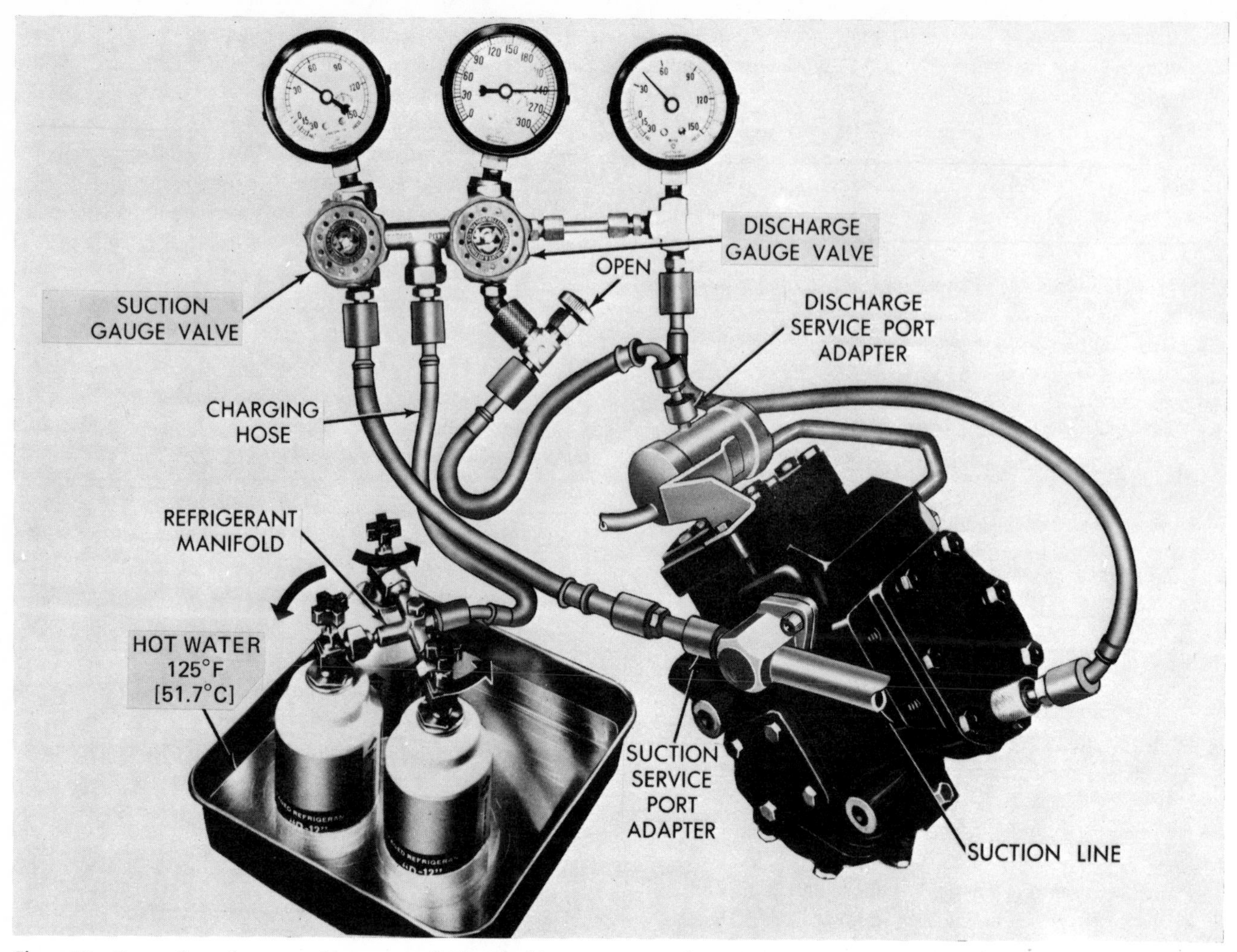

Figure 10 Connections of gauges, refrigerant manifold, and refrigerant cans to recharge the system. *(Chrysler Corporation.)*

Connect the gauge set to the system. Connect the refrigerant hose to the valve on the can. Open the valve, and charge the system as explained in ■ 8-9-11. One can will not be enough. When the first can is empty, disconnect it and connect another can. Repeat until the right amount of refrigerant has been put into the system.

■ **8-9-13 Chrysler Recharging Procedure with Small Cans** Chrysler furnishes a refrigerant-can manifold to which three cans can be attached at one time (Fig. 10). This is convenient because many Chrysler air conditioners require three cans for a complete recharge. However, many require more than three cans, as noted below.

CAUTION: Never connect the cans to the high-pressure side of the system when the system is in operation. This would admit high pressure to the cans, and cause them to explode. Anyone standing nearby could be seriously injured by can fragments and liquid refrigerant.

The refrigerant-can-manifold valves should be capped when the manifold is not in use. This protects the manifold from moisture and dirt. Keep a supply of can-to-manifold gaskets on hand so you can use new gaskets when necessary. The seal between the can and the manifold must be good.

Attach the center hose from the gauge set to the refrigerant-can manifold (Fig. 10). Make sure the gauge valves are closed. Turn the refrigerant-can-manifold valves counterclockwise to open them fully. Remove the protective caps, and screw the refrigerant cans into the manifold. Make sure the gaskets seal tightly.

Turn the three manifold valves clockwise to puncture the cans, and close the manifold valves. To purge the air from the charging hose, first loosen it at the gauge-set manifold. Then turn one of the refrigerant-manifold valves counterclockwise to release refrigerant. When refrigerant vapor starts escaping from the loose connection, tighten the connection.

Both the low-pressure and high-pressure gauge valves on the gauge set must be closed. Fully open all three refrigerant-manifold valves. Place the cans in a pan containing water at 125°F (51.7°C). This will warm the refrigerant and help transfer it from the cans to the system.

Start the engine, and move the controls to the A/C low-blow-

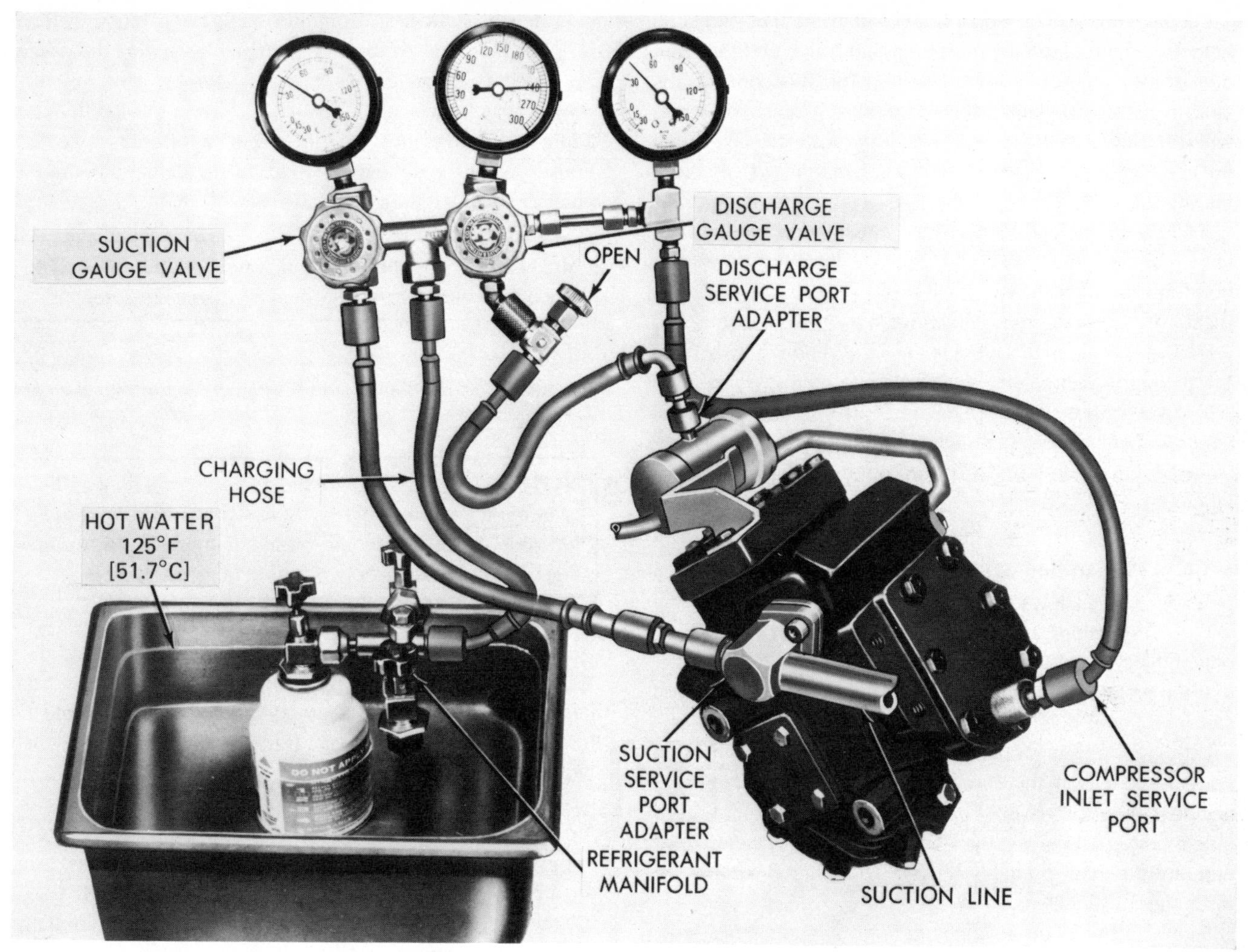

Figure 11 Connections of gauges, refrigerant manifold, and refrigerant can to add a partial charge. *(Chrysler Corporation.)*

er position. The low-pressure cutout switch will prevent the clutch from engaging and driving the compressor until refrigerant is added to the system.

Charge the system through the low-pressure side by slowly opening the low-pressure gauge valve. Adjust the valve as necessary to prevent the charging pressure from exceeding 50 psi (3.515 kg/cm²). The high-pressure gauge valve must be closed. Add warm water as necessary to maintain a water temperature of 125°F (51.7°C) in the pan.

Adjust the engine speed to a fast idle (1,600 rpm on six-cylinder engines, and 1,300 rpm on eight-cylinder engines). When all three cans are completely empty, close the gauge-set valves and the refrigerant-manifold valves. If additional refrigerant is required, use additional cans as necessary. If you are to use only half a can, be sure to weigh the can during the charging process. Only about 7 to 8 ounces (199 to 227 g) of refrigerant is to be added. Adding more could cause high pressures and temperatures in the system.

■ **8-9-14 Chrysler Recharging Procedure with Refrigerant Tank** When a refrigerant tank is used, Chrysler permits charging the system with liquid refrigerant through the compressor discharge muffler.

CAUTION: Never charge the system with liquid refrigerant through the compressor inlet or suction (low pressure) line. This can ruin the compressor. Also, do not operate the compressor while adding liquid refrigerant. The compressor will be damaged.

Make sure the gauge-set valves are closed. Then connect the charging hose to the refrigerant tank. Put the tank in a container of hot water at 125°F (52.7°C).

CAUTION: Never heat the tank with a torch or with excessively hot water. This could cause the tank to explode, possibly seriously injuring or killing anyone standing nearby.

Purge the air from the charging hose by loosening the hose connection at the gauge-set manifold. Then slightly open the valve on the refrigerant tank. When the refrigerant starts to escape from the loose connection, retighten it.

Put the refrigerant tank on a scale in an inverted position and note its weight. Open the refrigerant-tank valve and the compressor-discharge-gauge valve (see Fig. 10). This connects the tank to the compressor discharge muffler. Liquid refrigerant will now flow into the system. Watch the scale closely. When the correct weight of refrigerant has entered the system, close the valves.

If all the refrigerant necessary to charge the system will not enter, close the compressor discharge valve on the gauge manifold. Put the tank in an upright position, so it discharges refrigerant vapor and not liquid refrigerant. Start the engine and set the air-conditioner control in the A/C position. Slowly open the suction (low-pressure) gauge valve. Compressor operation will lower the pressure in the low-pressure side, and refrigerant vapor will enter the system. Open or close the suction-gauge valve so that the low-pressure does not exceed 59 psi (3.515 kg/cm²).

■ **8-9-15 Adding a Partial Charge** Chrysler has a procedure that allows you to correct a low refrigerant level without discharging and evacuating the system. It can be used only if the system has not been opened. Suppose, for example, that the system lost some refrigerant through a leak that you can fix without opening the system. This would be true of a slightly loose hose connection. Tightening the connection corrects the leak. In this case, the system has not been opened, accidentally or otherwise. That is, no air or moisture has been able to enter. Of course, if all the refrigerant has been lost, air and moisture have probably entered. The system then must be discharged, evacuated, and recharged.

Figure 11 shows the setup for adding a partial charge. Note that this is almost the same as the setup for complete charging with the refrigerant manifold (Fig. 10). There are two differences. First, only one can of refrigerant is shown in Fig. 11, rather than the three in Fig. 10. Second, the pan of water, with the refrigerant can, is placed on an accurate scale. This allows you to weigh the amount of refrigerant added. The scale is not shown in Fig. 11.

The partial charging procedure begins like the complete charging procedure (■8-9-13). It differs after the can seal has been pierced, and the air has been purged from the test hoses. After purging the hoses, tighten the hose connections.

Now open the car windows, and raise the hood. Operate the engine at 1,600 rpm for six-cylinder engines, or 1,300 rpm for eight-cylinder engines. Set the air-conditioner control on A/C and the blower on high. The discharge pressure should be between 225 and 250 psi (15.819 and 17.577 kg/cm²). If necessary, block the condenser airflow with a sheet of heavy cardboard or similar material to achieve this pressure.

Slowly open the suction-service-gauge valve. This allows refrigerant to flow from the can into the system. Adjust the suction-service-gauge valve so that the suction-gauge pressure does not exceed 50 psi (3.515 kg/cm²).

NOTE: Keep the refrigerant can upright! Only vapor-charging is permitted with the air-conditioner operating.

Watch the sight glass. Continue to add refrigerant until there is no foam visible. As soon as all foam clears, note the weight registered on the scale.

Now watch the scale carefully. Allow the exact amount of additional refrigerant shown in the manufacturer's specifications to enter the system. As soon as the correct amount has entered, shut off the suction-gauge valve.

NOTE: Do not allow too much refrigerant to enter! Too much can cause excessively high discharge pressures.

Complete the job by closing the valves and disconnecting the hoses. Cap the valves and hose ends with protective caps or seals.

NOTE: Some cars require the addition of 30 ounces (850 g) of refrigerant after the foaming stops. This requires two full cans. The setup would be like that in Fig. 10, except that you would use only two cans of refrigerant.

■ **8-9-16 Checking for Collision Damage** If a car has been in a wreck, the air-conditioner system should be inspected as soon as possible. If the system has been opened by the wreck, it should be repaired without delay. Leaving an air-conditioner system exposed to the atmosphere allows air, moisture, and dirt to enter. The longer the exposure, the greater the amount of air, moisture, and dirt that gets in. Therefore, the greater the damage to the system.

You can often tell at a glance when components are damaged beyond repair, or the whole system is useless. The inspection procedure recommended by Chevrolet follows. Note that the procedure is merely a general guide.

1. Remove the drive belt. Cut it off if necessary.

2. Look at the various components of the system—condenser, evaporator, VIR unit, compressor, mounting brackets, connecting lines, and controls—to determine if any have been damaged. The condenser, being up front, is the most vulnerable and most apt to be damaged in a front-end collision.

NOTE: No repairs of any kind, such as soldering, welding, or brazing, should be attempted on the condenser. If the vapor passages are bent or damaged in any way, or if the fins are mashed together, discard the condenser and install a new one.

3. Inspect the VIR unit for cracks and other damage. If it appears okay, clean it with a suitable cleaner. Dry it thoroughly, and replace the desiccant bag.

4. If the evaporator shows any signs of damage, replace it.

5. Check the control system, connecting wires, vacuum hoses, and vacuum motors for damage. Install new parts as necessary.

6. Check all connecting lines and flexible hoses for damage. Inspect them along their full length. Make sure all connections are in good condition. Replace any lines or hoses that are damaged in any way, and make sure connections are okay.

7. Check the clutch pulley for proper operation.

8. Check the compressor for damage.

9. Install the charging station, and discharge the system.

10. Remove the compressor from the engine. Unscrew the oil test fitting, and pour the oil into a clean glass container. Examine it for dirt, water, metal particles, etc. If any of these are present, discard the compressor and the desiccant bag in the VIR unit. Flush the other system components with liquid refrigerant.

11. If the compressor oil is clean, and free of any harmful substance, discard it. Put the same amount of new, fresh oil into the compressor.

NOTE: If system components have been flushed, replace the full charge of oil. If not, add no more new oil than you poured out.

12. Use a can or supply tank of refrigerant to charge the compressor. Use the leak detector to check the compressor for leaks. If it has no leaks, reinstall it.

13. Evacuate the system (■8-9-9). Put some refrigerant into the system, and leak-test it.

14. If the system passes the leak test, recharge it as explained in ■8-9-10.

SECTION 8-10 Removing and Replacing Components

This section describes the procedures that are common to all systems for removing and replacing heater and air-conditioner components. Following sections cover the servicing of system components.

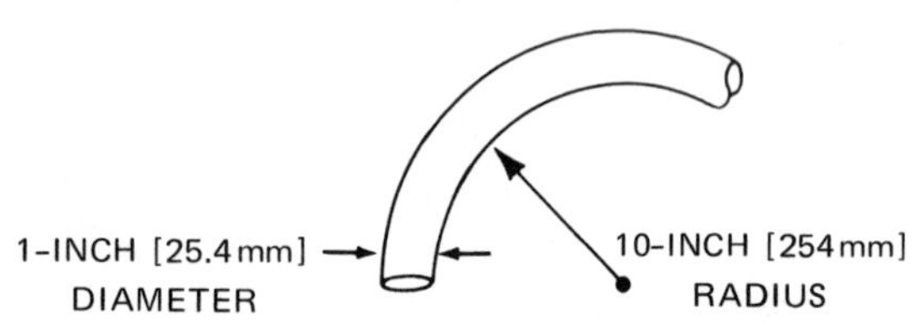

Figure 1 Never bend a hose too sharply, as this will restrict the flow of refrigerant. For example, a 1-inch (25.4-mm) hose should never be bent so sharply that the radius of the bend is less than 10 inches (254 mm), as shown.

■ **8-10-1 Cleanliness** Air, moisture, and dirt in the refrigerant system can damage it. When working with any component of an air-conditioner, be extremely careful to keep all tools, gauges, hoses, workbench, and your hands clean.

Air-conditioner replacement components—condenser, evaporator, compressor, valves, tubes and hoses—are all sealed at the factory. The seals must not be removed until just before the component is installed. Always cap or plug all open lines and fittings when you remove a component.

■ **8-10-2 Handling Tubing and Fittings** Kinks or sharp bends in refrigerant tubes or hoses will restrict the flow of refrigerant. Because the refrigerant is under high pressure in the system, all connections must be tight and leakproof. Before you loosen any connection, you must discharge the system, as explained in ■8-9-7.

NOTE: Open connections carefully, even after discharging the system. There may still be refrigerant under pressure trapped in the system. If you notice any pressure when loosening a connection, allow the trapped refrigerant to bleed off slowly. Do not detach the hose or tube until the pressure has dropped.

If you have to bend a tube, use a tube bender to avoid kinking the tube. Chrysler recommends that for flexible hose lines a good rule is to keep the radius of the bend at least 10 times the diameter of the hose. For a hose 1 inch (25.4 mm) in diameter, the radius of any bend should be at least 10 inches (254 mm) (Fig. 1).

■ **8-10-3 O Rings** Whenever you break an O-ring connection, use a new O ring to reconnect the tube or fitting. Dip the new O ring in clean refrigerant oil before installing it. Use two wrenches to tighten the connection, to avoid twisting the pipe (Fig. 2). Twisting will misalign the pipe and damage

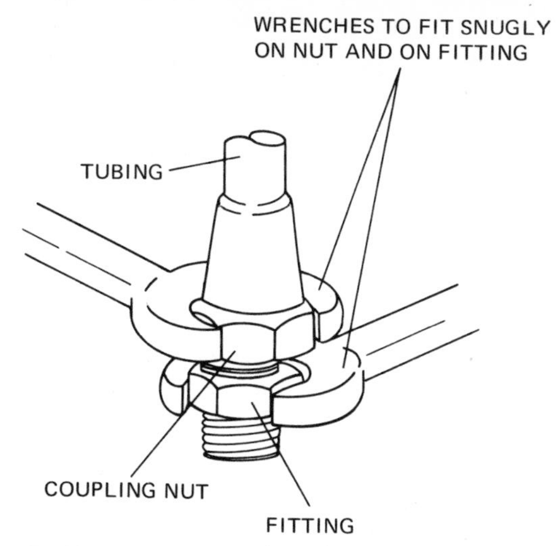

Figure 2 Always use two wrenches to loosen or tighten couplings.

the O ring. Also, when connecting a flexible hose, use wrenches to hold the swaged metal fitting, the flare nut, and the coupling to which the hose is being attached. This requires three separate wrenches. It prevents the fitting from turning and thus damaging the ring seat or O ring. Make sure the fitting is clean and has no burrs or rough spots. These could damage the O ring and produce a leak. Chevrolet recommends the use of a torque wrench to tighten the connection. See Table 1 for the Chevrolet specifications. Note that steel-to-aluminum connections are torqued to the aluminum torque specification.

Table 1 Torque specifications for tightening tube connections (steel and aluminum)

Metal tube o.d., inches	Thread and fitting size, inches	Steel tubing torque, pound-feet	Aluminum tubing torque, pound-feet
1/4	7/16	13 (1.80 kg-m)	6 (0.60 kg-m)
3/8	5/8	33 (4.56 kg-m)	12 (1.66 kg-m)
1/2	3/4	33 (4.56 kg-m)	18 (2.49 kg-m)
5/8	7/8	33 (4.56 kg-m)	24 (3.32 kg-m)
3/4	1 1/16	33 (4.56 kg-m)	30 (4.15 kg-m)

Source: Chevrolet Motor Division of General Motors Corporation.

■ 8-10-4 Hose Clamps

When you work with hose-clamp connections (Fig. 3), take care not to damage the sealing bead on the metal pipe or fitting. When breaking a connection, first remove the clamp. Then use a sharp knife to make an angular cut on the hose, as shown at the top in Fig. 3. This will loosen the hose enough so it can be worked off the fitting. Do not slit the hose endwise. You could nick or scratch the sealing bead on the pipe or fitting. This could cause a leak.

> **NOTE:** Use only approved replacement hoses. Do not use heater hose. It will not hold the pressure, and refrigerant will deteriorate it rapidly.

You can use the old hose again if it is in good condition. To do so, cut off the end where you made the angled cut. To reinstall the hose, coat the fitting and the inside of the hose with clean refrigerant oil. Push the hose over the fitting all the way to the locating bead (Fig. 3). Never use a sealer! Install the clamp on the hose, hooking the locating bead over the cut end of the hose as shown. Tighten the clamp screw to 35 to 42 pound-inches (40.3 to 48.3 kg-cm) of torque. Do not overtighten! Excessive tightening can damage the hose.

■ 8-10-5 Repairing Refrigerant Leaks

Leaks can develop in the hose connections, in the hoses themselves, or around the compressor shaft seals. If your leak detector pinpoints a leak in one of these places, repair it as follows:

1. REPAIRING O-RING LEAKS Check the torque on the fitting. If it is too loose, tighten it (Table 1). Always use two or three wrenches (■8-10-3). Recheck the connection for leaks. If it still leaks, discharge the system, open the connection, and inspect the O ring and fitting. Install a new O ring (■8-10-3), and tighten the connection to the proper torque (Table 1).

2. REPAIRING HOSE LEAKS If a leak develops in a hose, the system must be discharged so the hose can be repaired or replaced. The best remedy is to replace the hose. However, it is possible to cut out the leaky part of the hose and join the two ends with a hose connector and two hose clamps (Fig. 3). ■8-10-4 explains how to use hose clamps.

3. REPAIRING COMPRESSOR SHAFT SEALS This re-

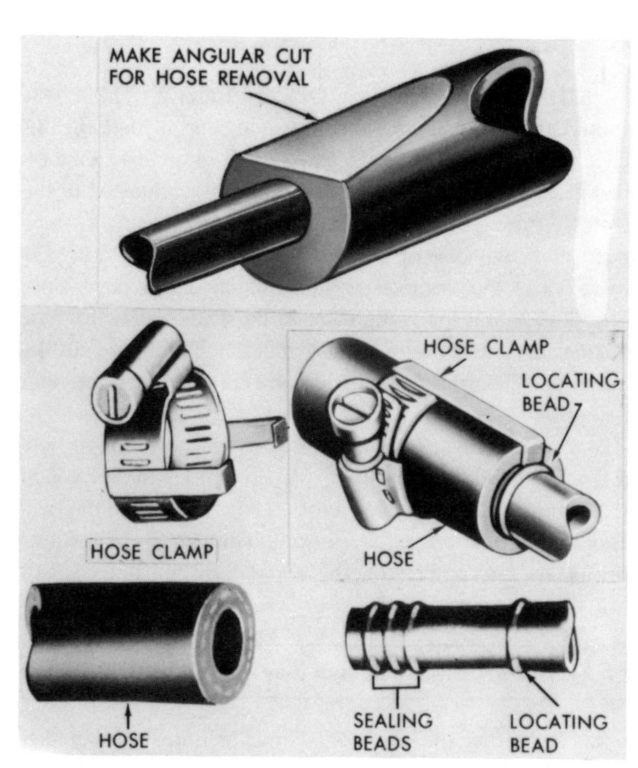

Figure 3 Hose clamps and connections. *(Chevrolet Motor Division of General Motors Corporation.)*

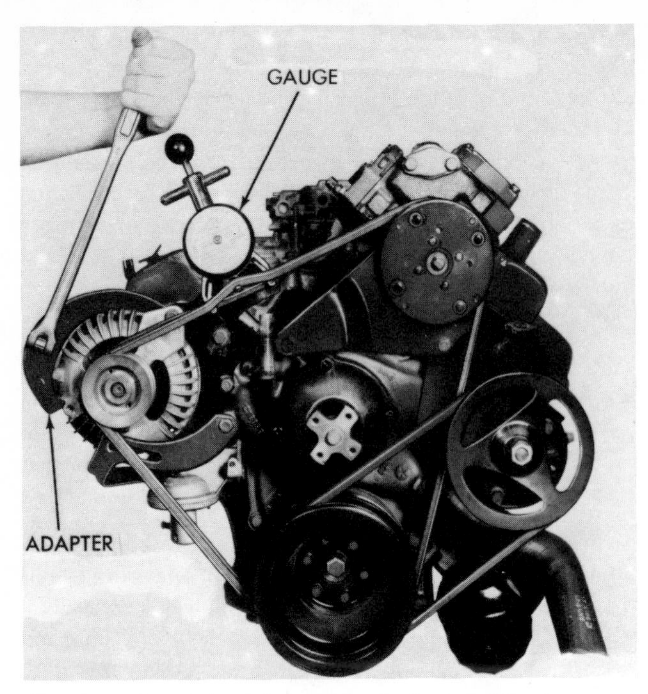

Figure 4 Using a belt-tension gauge and adjusting adaptor to correctly adjust belt tension. *(Chrysler Corporation.)*

quires that you discharge the system so the compressor can be removed for overhaul. Compressor overhaul is covered in Part 8, Sec. 12.

4. EVACUATING AND CHARGING After the repair has been made, and all components reinstalled, the system must be evacuated and recharged, as explained in Part 8, Sec. 9.

■ 8-10-6 Compressor Drive Belts

Drive belts should be checked for condition and tension periodically. Figures 4 and 5 show two different kinds of belt-tension tools being used to check belt tension. Tension is adjusted in different ways, according to the drive arrangement. On some cars, the drive belt or belts drive the compressor only. On these cars, the compressor attaching brackets have slots. The slots permit the compressor to be shifted away from the engine to tighten the belt. First, the attaching bolts must be loosened. Then the compressor can be shifted, and the bolts tightened.

Many compressor mounting brackets have a square hole (called the "belt-tensioning pry-bar slot" in Fig. 6). A ½-inch (12.7-mm) socket wrench or breaker bar is placed in the hole and used to pull the compressor out to tighten the belt. Never pry against the compressor. This could distort the housing and ruin the compressor.

CAUTION: The compressor may be hot.

On some cars, the compressor drive belt runs over an idler pulley. This pulley is shifted to adjust the belt tension (see Fig. 7). On other cars, the drive belt may also drive another device, such as the air pump for the exhaust emission control system. On these, the air pump is shifted to adjust the belt tension. Whatever the method, you must use great care in shifting the component, to avoid damaging it. Applying a pry bar to the housing of a compressor or an air pump can distort the housing and ruin the compressor.

A new belt must be adjusted to a higher tension than a used belt. A belt that has been operated for a minimum of half an hour is considered to be a used belt. The specified belt tensions vary. For the correct tension, always refer to the shop manual of the car being serviced. A typical Chrysler specification is to adjust the tension on cars using the idler pulley to 25 pound-feet (3.46 kg-m) for a new belt, or 15 pound-feet (2.07 kg-m) for a used belt. Chevrolet calls for a reading of 140 pound-feet (19.34 kg-m) for a new belt, and 95 pound-feet (13.13 kg-m) for a used belt. The major differences here are in the type of tester used to check the tension, and the manner of checking it.

If the drive arrangement has two belts, only one belt may go bad. However, both belts must be replaced with new belts at the same time. If only the bad belt is replaced, the new belt will take all the pull to start with. Then it will stretch, and put the load on the other belt. This can cause the old belt to wear out prematurely.

■ 8-10-7 Removing and Replacing the Compressor

The procedure for removing and replacing a compressor varies with the mounting arrangement and the compressor type. (In shop talk, removing and replacing is often called "R and R.") There are certain procedures that are common to all compressor R-and-R work. These include discharging the system, de-

Figure 5 Checking belt tension with a belt-tension gauge. *(Chevrolet Motor Division of General Motors Corporation.)*

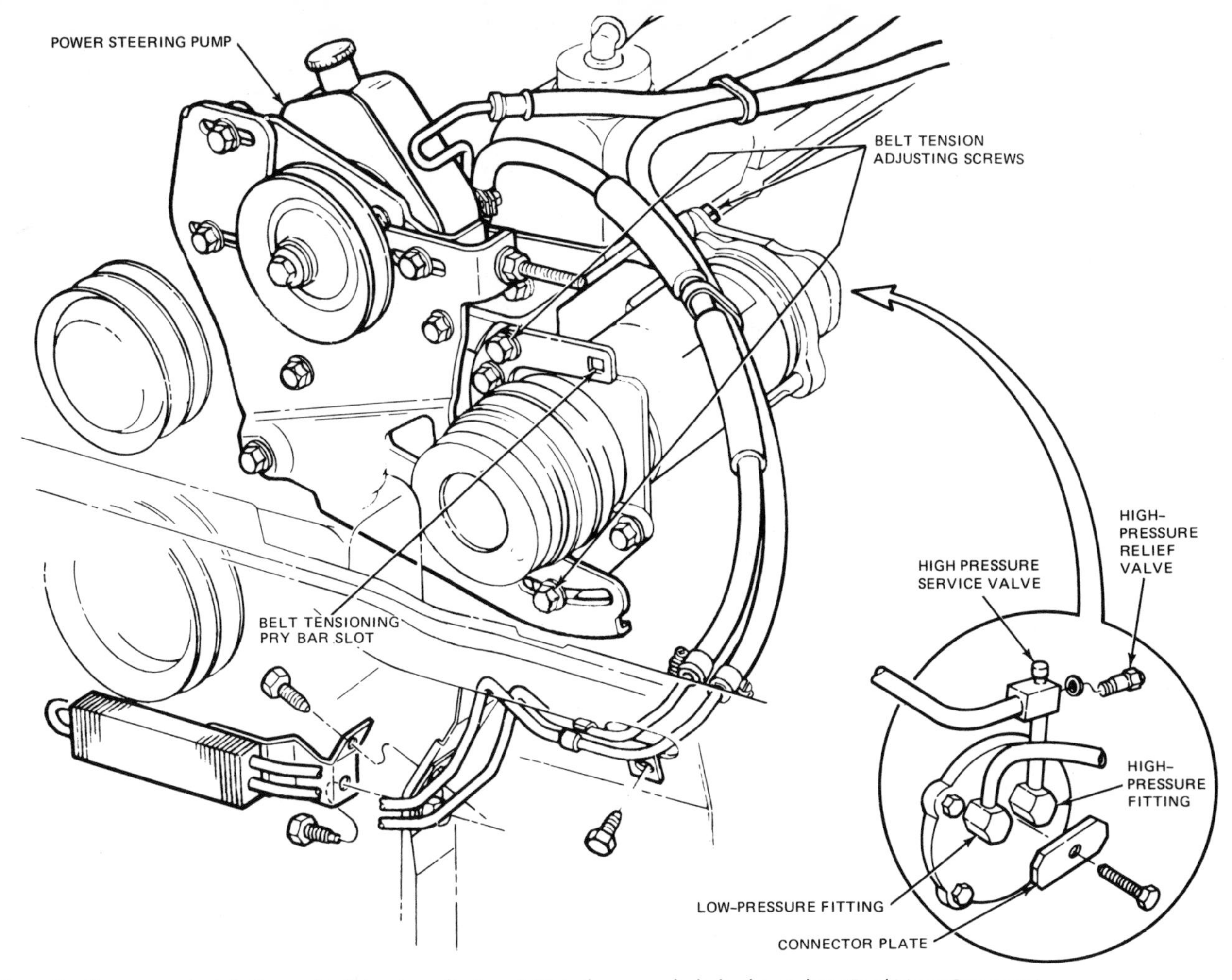

Figure 6 Compressor installation and belt-tension adjustment. Note the square hole for the pry bar. *(Ford Motor Company.)*

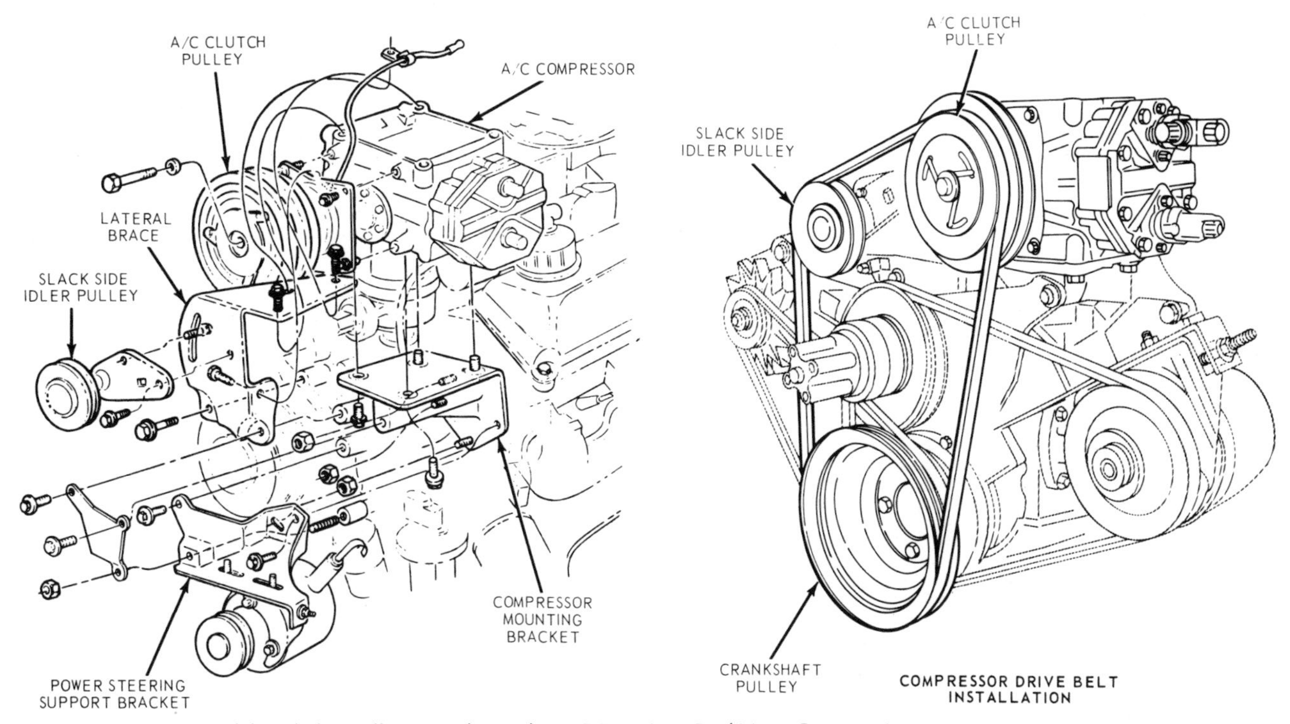

Figure 7 Compressor and drive-belt installation on the Ford 400 CID engine. *(Ford Motor Company.)*

taching all hoses, capping or sealing fittings and hoses, disconnecting electric leads, and draining the compressor oil. After installing a compressor, the drained oil is replaced with new, fresh refrigerant oil, and the system is evacuated and recharged. Specific procedures for round (Frigidaire), parallel-cylinder, and V-type compressors are covered in ■8-11-2 and 8-11-3.

■ 8-10-8 Removal and Replacement of Other Components The other components of the refrigeration system include the condenser, evaporator, receiver, and valves. Removal, servicing, and replacement of these components are covered in other sections. When you remove any of these components, you first discharge the system. Then you remove the component. On a Ford or General Motors car, you add the specified amount of clean, fresh refrigerant oil to the component before installing it. On Chrysler Corporation cars, you add oil to the compressor, as explained in ■8-9-8.

The amount of oil to be added to new components is as follows (for Ford and General Motors cars):

Condenser:	1 fluid ounce	(30 cc)
Evaporator:	3 fluid ounces	(90 cc)
Receiver:	1 fluid ounce	(30 cc)
VIR assembly:	1 fluid ounce	(30 cc)

After the component has been installed, and all connections secured, the system must be evacuated and recharged.

NOTE: A new O ring must be used at any fitting that has been disconnected. The new O ring must be dipped in clean refrigerant oil before it is installed. Flexible hose connections must be properly made. See ■8-10-3 and 8-10-4.

SECTION 8-11 Chevrolet Air-Conditioner Service

This section describes the servicing of the air conditioners used in late-model Chevrolet automobiles. The procedures apply to all General Motors cars.

■ 8-11-1 Air-Conditioner Service Procedures

Other sections describe the servicing of heater systems, causes of air-conditioner failures, troubleshooting of heater-air conditioner systems, checking of refrigeration systems, and removing and replacing components that are common to all air-conditioner systems. In Part 8, Sec. 10, we discussed the handling of tubing and fittings, making connections, and installing and adjusting compressor drive belts. These procedures are the same for all systems. Now we cover removal and replacement of components which require special procedures on Chevrolet and most other cars built by General Motors.

■ 8-11-2 Frigidaire Compressor Removal

These compressors are made in six-cylinder and four-cylinder models (Figs. 11 and 14 in Part 8, Sec. 2). They are often called Frigidaire compressors because they were made by the Frigidaire Division of General Motors. These compressors are used on General Motors cars as well as cars of other companies (Ford, for example). Figure 6 in Part 8, Sec. 10, shows this type of compressor on a Ford car. Figure 1 shows the installation of an air-conditioner in a Pontiac with a V-8 engine. On late-model cars, General Motors uses a connector plate (see Fig. 3). The plate is held in place with a single attaching bolt. The connector plate attaches the high-pressure and low-pressure lines to the compressor. Note that in this installation the compressor has no fittings to which the test gauges can be attached. Instead, the valves-in-receiver (VIR) assembly has the gauge fittings.

The Ford installation (Fig. 6 in Part 8, Sec. 10) uses separate fittings. They are held in place on the compressor connections by the connector plate (see lower right in Fig. 6, Part 8, Sec. 10). Note also that the high-pressure line at the compressor has a high-pressure relief valve. This valve opens to relieve excessive pressure, and thus protects the compressor from damage. Also, the line has the high-pressure service valve. The low-pressure service valve is in the line from the compressor.

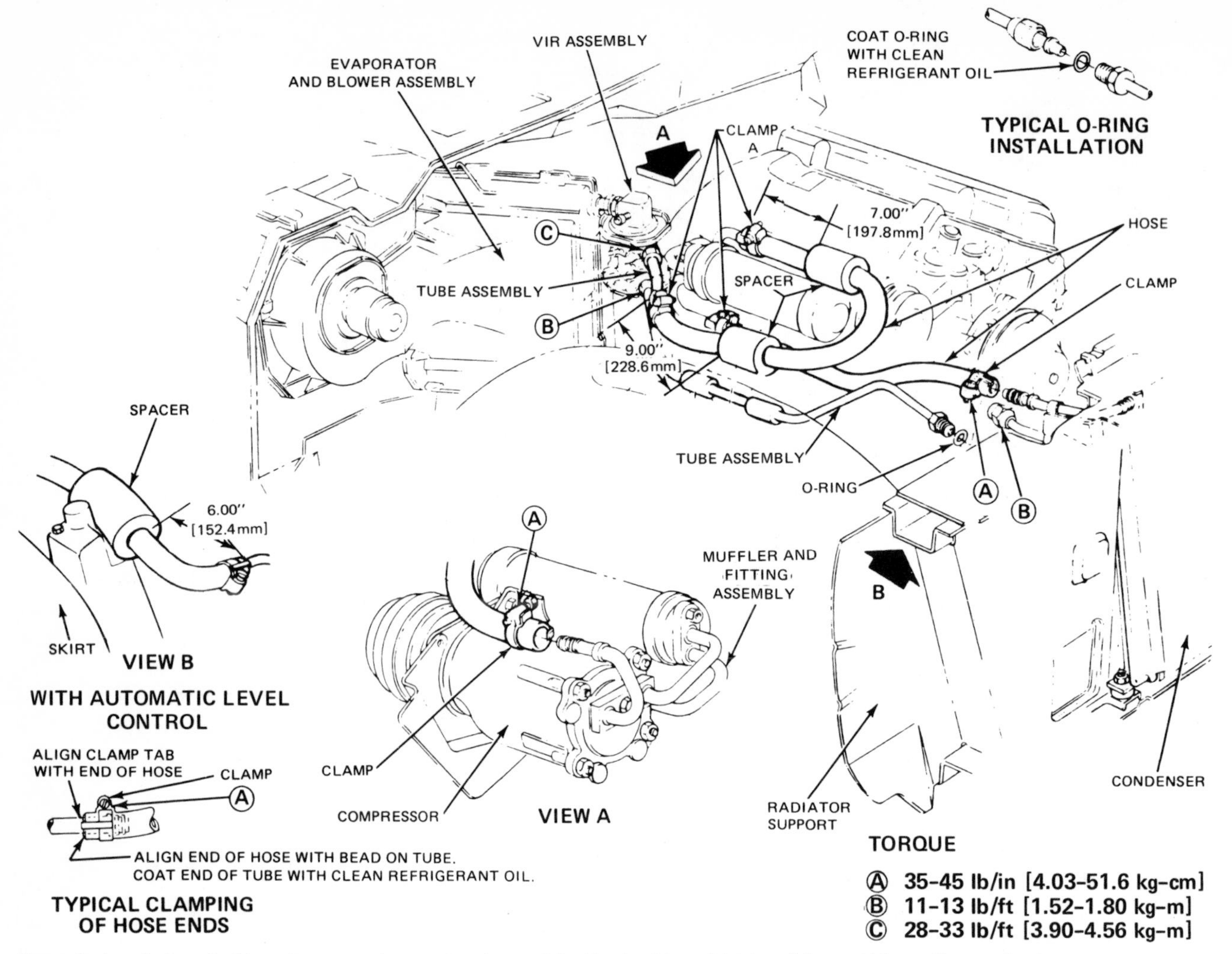

Figure 1 Installation of refrigeration system in some Pontiac models. *(Pontiac Motor Division of General Motors Corporation.)*

Here is the general procedure for removing and replacing the compressor.

Removal

1. Discharge the system as outlined in ■8-9-7. The Ford procedure does not require that you measure how much oil is lost with the refrigerant. However, the Chevrolet procedure requires that the oil lost be measured, as explained in ■8-9-7.

2. Loosen the capscrew holding the connector plate in place. As you loosen the screw, work the fittings back and forth. This will break the seals and allow any remaining refrigerant to bleed off.

CAUTION: Be careful! There may still be high pressure in the compressor. It must be bled off slowly, so that the compressor oil is not blown out.

3. When all pressure is relieved, remove the connector plate. Move the fittings (Ford) or the connector-plate assembly (Chevrolet) out of the way.

4. Immediately install a plate over the compressor openings or fittings. Figure 2 shows the special test plate that Ford recommends. This test plate has a pair of Schrader-type valves. These valves are used to connect the detached compressor to a refrigerant source and test gauges, to check the compressor for leaks. The General Motors recommendation is to use a flat plate with a hole for the screw in its center. The plate can be installed in place of the connector-plate assembly. It will seal against the O rings and protect the compressor from moisture, dirt, and air.

5. Disconnect the electric leads from the clutch and, where present, from the superheat switch.

6. Loosen the mounting bolts. Move the compressor in, so the belt can be removed. Remove the bolts, and take the compressor off the engine.

Checking Compressor Oil

1. Drain all the oil from the compressor into a clean, graduated container. Note the amount of oil. Examine the oil for contaminants such as water, dirt, and metal particles.

2. If the oil shows evidence of contamination (dirt or metal particles), flush the system with refrigerant to remove the contaminants. Disassemble the compressor to determine whether it is damaged, and what repairs should be made. If the compressor has internal damage too severe to be repaired, discard it. Install a new compressor, as explained below.

> **NOTE:** If the system is flushed, all the oil will be removed. In this case, put into the compressor, before installing it, a full charge of fresh refrigerant oil. As soon as the compressor starts to work, the oil will be distributed through the system in a normal fashion.

3. If the oil shows no evidence of contamination, the compressor need not be disassembed. Put into the compressor, just before installing it, the same amount of new refrigerant oil as you poured out of it.

Oil for a New Compressor

1. The new compressor is shipped from the factory with oil in it. If a new compressor is being installed, all this oil should be drained from it. If the oil drained from the old compressor measured between 4 and 6 fluid ounces (120 and 180 cc), put an equal amount of fresh oil into the new compressor.

2. If the oil drained from the old compressor measured 6 fluid ounces (180 cc), or more, put only 6 fluid ounces (180 cc) of new, fresh oil into the new compressor.

Oil for a Repaired Compressor

If a compressor has been repaired, all the oil has been removed from it. Therefore, you must add an additional 1 fluid ounce (30 cc) of oil. That is, if the oil drained from the old compressor measured between 4 and 6 fluid ounces (120 and 180 cc), put back into the compressor that amount, plus 1 fluid ounce (30 cc). If the oil drained from the old compressor measured 6 fluid ounces (180 cc) or more, put in 7 fluid ounces (210 cc) of fresh, new oil.

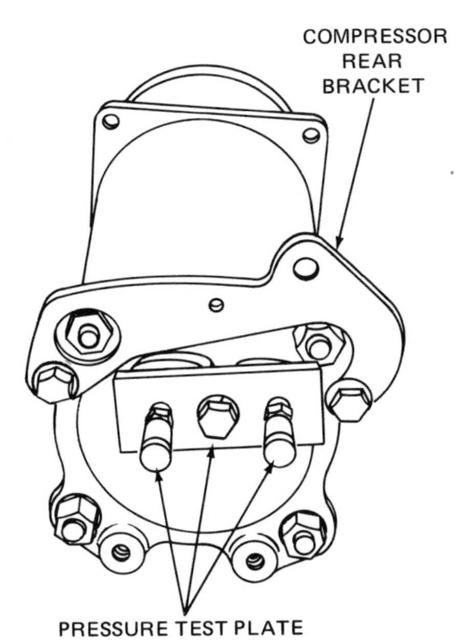

Figure 2 Pressure test plate installed on compressor. *(Ford Motor Company.)*

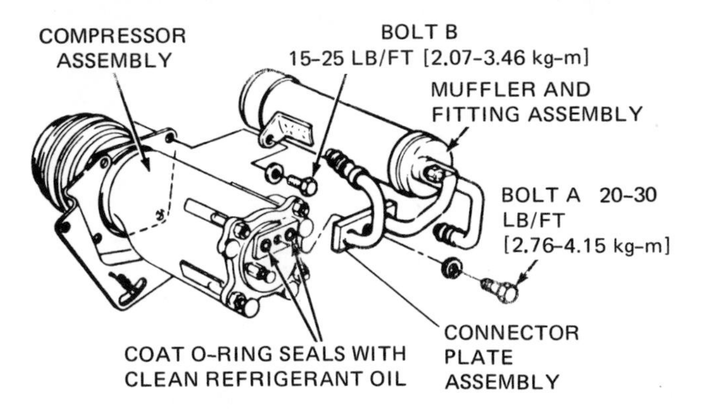

Figure 3 Muffler and fitting assembly on some Pontiac models. *(Pontiac Motor Division of General Motors Corporation.)*

■ 8-11-3 Frigidaire Compressor Replacement

Before installing the compressor, rotate the compressor shaft several times. This distributes the oil on the moving parts and the seals. Before the compressor clutch is mounted to the compressor, wipe the front face of the compressor thoroughly wth a clean, dry cloth. If necessary, use solvent to remove any trace of oil. This is done to keep oil from getting on the clutch surfaces. The oil would cause the clutch to slip and eventually fail. If you are installing a new compressor, stamp the amount of charge specified for the system on the plate attached to the compressor housing. Be sure the protective connector plate is in place.

1. Position the compressor on the engine. Attach the compressor by installing the proper bolts finger-tight.

2. Install the compressor drive belt, and adjust it (■8-10-6).

3. On Ford installations, remove the special test plate (Fig. 2). Remove it very slowly to bleed off any pressure if the compressor is new. (New Ford compressors are shipped partially charged.) If the pressure is released too rapidly, oil will be blown from the compressor. Note how to add oil to a new compressor (■8-11-2). Dip new O rings in refrigerant oil, and install them in the compressor ports. Put the low- and high-pressure fittings in place. Secure them with the connector plate and bolt (Fig. 6 in Part 8, Sec. 10, lower right).

4. On the Chevrolet installation, dip new O rings in refrigerant oil and install them in the compressor ports. Install the connector-plate assembly, making sure the low- and high-pressure lines align properly with the ports (Fig. 3). Secure with bolt A, as shown. Note that this bolt must be tightened first, before the muffler-attaching bolt B and the compressor-mounting bolts are tightened.

5. Connect the electric leads to the clutch coil and, where used, to the superheat switch.

6. Evacuate and recharge the system. Check the leaks and for system performance.

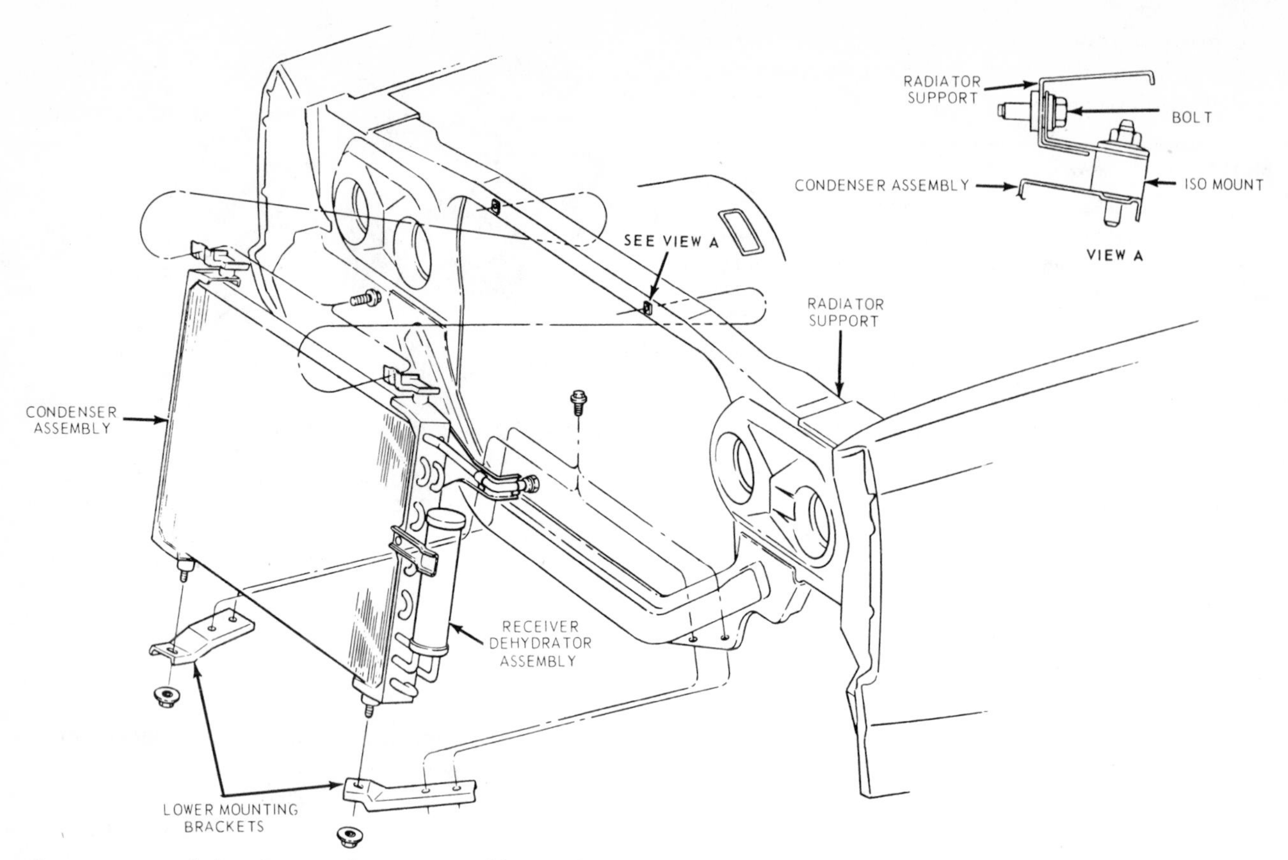

Figure 4 Removal of condenser-and-receiver assembly. Note that the receiver can be removed along with the condenser. *(Ford Motor Company.)*

■ 8-11-4 Condenser Removal and Replacement

The condenser removal-and-replacement procedure is about the same for all cars. On some cars (Ford, for example), the receiver-dehydrator assembly can be removed along with the condenser (Fig. 4). On cars using the valves-in-receiver (VIR) assembly (late-model General Motors), only the condenser is removed. The R-and-R procedure that applies to many Chevrolet models follows. It is typical of the procedure for most cars. Always check the shop manual for the car you are servicing before removing and replacing a condenser.

Removal

1. Disconnect the battery ground cable.

2. Discharge the system.

3. Remove the radiator-shroud upper screws.

4. Remove the radiator upper-retaining-bracket screws, and remove the bracket.

5. Push the upper part of the radiator rearward, and put a 2- by 4-inch (50.8- by 101.6-mm) block of wood between the right upper corner of the radiator and the radiator support. Be careful not to mash the radiator fins or damage the radiator.

6. Remove the screws attaching the upper part of the condenser to the radiator support.

7. From under the car, remove the stud nuts attaching the lower part of the condenser to the radiator support.

8. Disconnect the inlet and outlet lines from the condenser (or from the receiver-dehydrator if it comes off with the condenser). Immediately plug or cap the line and condenser (or receiver-dehydrator) fittings.

9. Lift up on the upper right end of the condenser until the upper bracket on the condenser clears the radiator support. Then move the condenser diagonally up and out. Guide the left end past the radiator, so it does not damage the radiator.

CAUTION: The fins on the condenser are often very sharp and can cut you easily if you are not careful.

NOTE: On many cars, you remove the condenser from the bottom of the car. This means that you must raise the front end of the car and support it safely on jack stands. Various cars use different attachment arrangements, as you will note when you examine different cars and factory shop manuals. Some cars have baffles that must be removed. On other cars (Ford, for example), the radiator must be removed before the condenser can be taken out of the car (Fig. 4). With the radiator removed, the detached condenser is moved rearward, through the radiator support, and lifted up and out.

Replacement

1. Installation of a condenser is just the reverse of removal. If you note carefully just what you did during removal, you will have no trouble installing the condenser. Remember the following:

a. Add 1 fluid ounce (30 cc) of clean, fresh refrigerant oil to the condenser before installing it.

b. Do not uncap or unplug the condenser fitting and lines until just before you are ready to attach the lines.

c. Use new O rings, dipped in fresh refrigerant oil.

d. Use two wrenches to attach the couplings.

2. After installing and connecting the condenser, evacuate and recharge the system. Check the system for leaks and performance.

■ 8-11-5 Evaporator Removal and Replacement

Figure 5 shows evaporator and VIR assemblies being removed from different Chevrolet models. Note that the two components (the evaporator with its blower, and the VIR assembly) can be removed as a unit. However, the evaporator core or the blower motor can be removed separately without removing the entire assembly. Also, the VIR assembly can be removed by itself.

■ 8-11-6 Evaporator-Core Removal and Replacement

First disconnect the battery ground cable, and discharge the system of refrigerant. Then remove the carburetor air cleaner, the VIR pipe at the manifold, the PCV plumbing that may interfere, the carburetor heat stove, and the engine thermal switch, if necessary. Then proceed as follows.

Removal

1. Disconnect the oil bleed line and the core inlet and outlet tubes from the evaporator core. Cap or plug the tubes and core fittings at once.

2. Remove the VIR bracket screws, and lay the VIR unit to one side, out of the way. It is not necessary to detach the condenser and the compressor lines from the VIR assembly.

3. Disconnect the vacuum lines, and remove the vacuum tank and bracket.

4. Disconnect all wires and vacuum hoses attached to the evaporator assembly.

5. Remove the evaporator cover-to-dash-panel stud nuts. Remove the cover-to-evaporator-case screws.

6. Pull the cover up and out. Then remove the core. Be careful not to damage the core.

> **CAUTION:** The core fins are sharp and can cut you. Handle the core carefully.

Replacement

1. Reverse the above procedure to install the core. Add 3 fluid ounces (90 cc) of clean, fresh refrigerant oil to the new core before reconnecting the lines.

2. Evacuate and recharge the system. Check the system for leaks and performance.

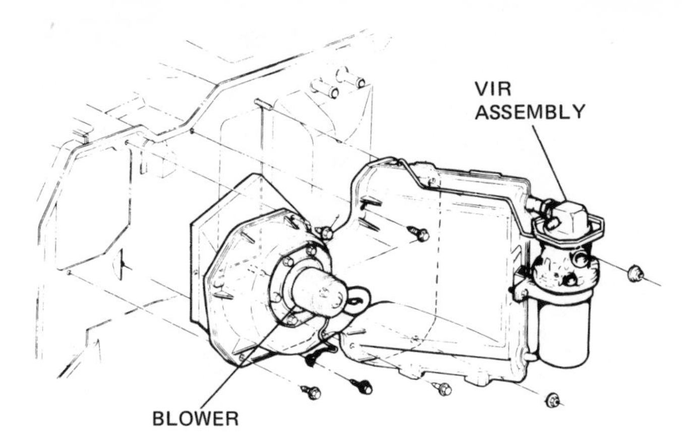

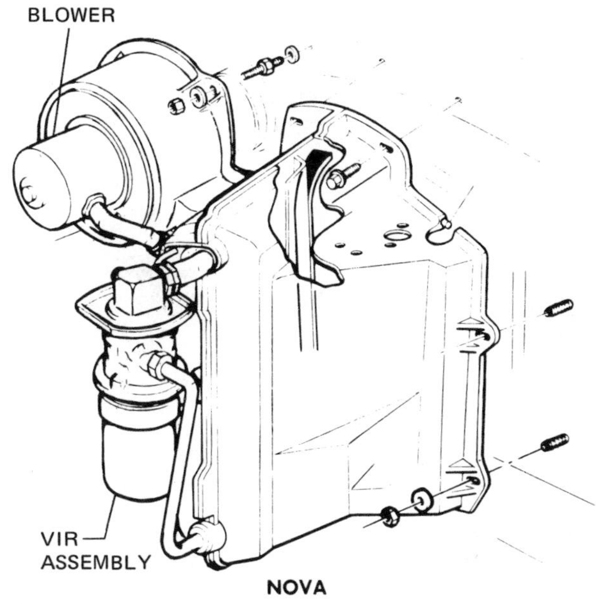

Figure 5 Evaporator and VIR installation on various Chevrolet models. *(Chevrolet Motor Division of General Motors Corporation.)*

■ 8-11-7 Chevrolet Blower-Motor Removal and Replacement

Disconnect the battery ground cable. Remove all heater hoses and wires attached to the fender skirt. Raise the vehicle on a hoist. Remove all fender-skirt attaching bolts, except those attaching the skirt to the radiator support. Pull out, then down, on the fender skirt, and put a 2- by 4-inch (50.8- by 101.6-mm) block of wood between the skirt and the fender. This gives you room to remove the blower and motor.

1. Disconnect the blower-motor cooling tube and electric lead from the motor. Remove the blower-to-case attaching screws, and remove the blower assembly. Pry gently on the flange if the sealer sticks.

2. Remove the blower-wheel retaining nut, and separate the motor and wheel.

3. To replace the assembly, reverse the procedure. Be sure to assemble the blower wheel to the motor with the open end of the blower away from the motor.

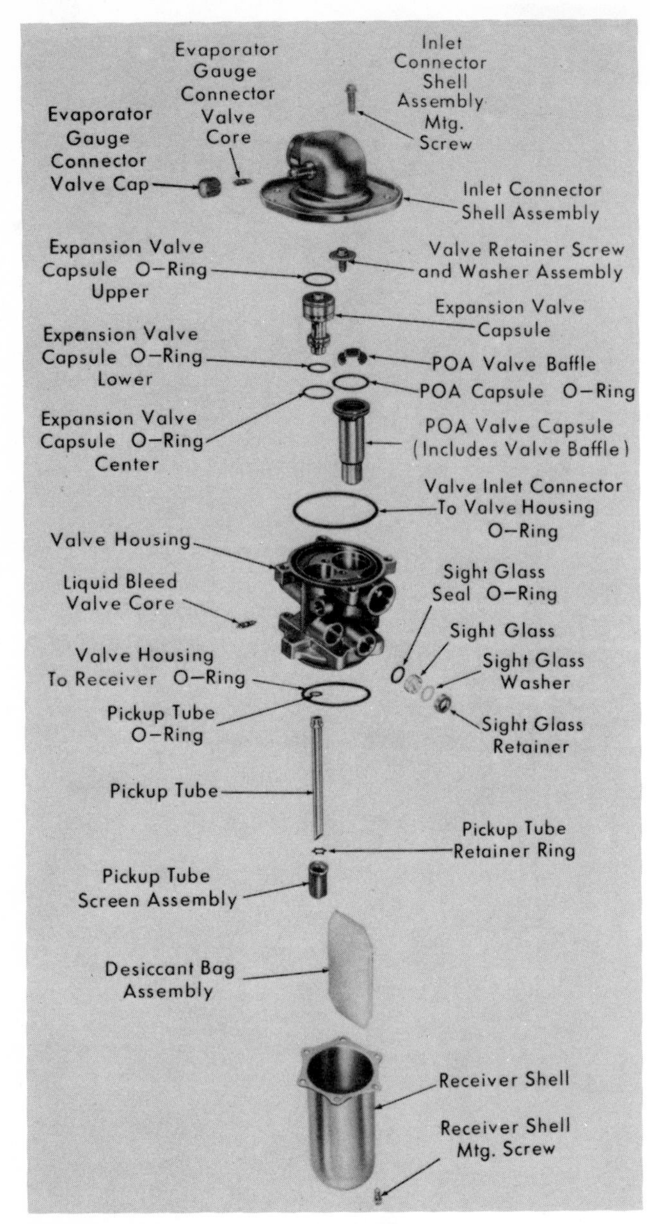

Figure 6 Exploded view of the VIR assembly. *(Chevrolet Motor Division of General Motors Corporation.)*

■ **8-11-8 VIR-Assembly Removal** Figure 5 shows VIR-assembly mounting arrangements for different Chevrolet models. The VIR assembly can be removed separately. It must be removed to replace any internal VIR part, such as the expansion valve or POA-valve capsules (■8-11-10). The procedure follows.

1. Disconnect the battery ground cable, and discharge the system of refrigerant.

2. Clean the surface dirt from the VIR assembly and line connections. Blow away any loose dirt with the air hose.

3. Disconnect the oil bleed line and the inlet and outlet lines from the VIR unit. Cap or plug the hoses and VIR fittings at once.

4. Loosen the evaporator-core inlet and outlet connections. Remove the VIR mounting-clamp screw and the clamp. Slide the VIR assembly off the evaporator outlet line first, and then off the evaporator inlet line. Cap the evaporator lines and VIR fittings at once.

5. Remove and discard all O rings.

■ **8-11-9 VIR-Assembly Replacement** Be sure to use all new O rings, coated with refrigerant oil.

1. Install the new lubricated O rings onto the connecting lines. Make sure the fittings are in good condition. Be careful to avoid cross-threading when making the connections. Remove the plugs or caps just before installing the VIR assembly.

2. Bring the VIR assembly onto the evaporator inlet tube first, and then onto the outlet tube. Start the connections by hand. Then install the VIR mounting clamp. Tighten the evaporator inlet connection to 18 pound-feet (2.49 kg-m), and the evaporator outlet connection to 30 pound-feet (4.15 kg-m).

3. Connect the liquid bleed-line connector to the VIR assembly. Tighten it to 6 pound-feet (0.83 kg-m).

4. Connect the condenser-line connector to the VIR assembly. Tighten it to 12 pound-feet (1.66 kg-m).

5. Connect the compressor-line connector to the VIR assembly. Tighten it to 30 pound-feet (4.15 kg-m).

NOTE: Do not unplug or uncap a fitting or line until just before you make the connection.

6. Evacuate and recharge the system. Test the system for leaks and performance.

■ **8-11-10 VIR-Assembly Service** Several services may be required on the VIR assembly. These include replacing the expansion-valve capsule, the POA-valve capsule, the VIR housing, the desiccant bag, the sight glass, and the liquid bleed-line valve core. These are discussed in following subsections. The first step in replacing any of these subassemblies is to remove the VIR assembly and take it to the repair bench (■8-11-8). After the VIR assembly is reassembled, it is installed as described in ■8-11-9.

■ **8-11-11 Expansion-Valve-Capsule Replacement** Figure 6 is an exploded view of the VIR assembly. If the expansion valve is not working properly, it must be replaced. It is not adjustable. It is not necessary to completely disassemble the unit to replace the expansion-valve capsule. But the VIR assembly must be removed from the car (■8-11-8). Then proceed as follows:

1. Remove the inlet connector-shell mounting screws, and remove the shell. Discard the O ring.

2. Clean the top of the valve housing carefully. Blow away any loose dirt with an air hose.

3. Loosen the two capsule retaining screws. Take one screw and washer off. Leave the other screw in. Back it off no more than 3 turns.

4. Attach the expansion-valve removal tool to the tapered groove on the diaphragm end of the expansion valve (Fig. 7). Position the handle of the tool over the loosened (but still installed) screw. Press down on the tool to lift the expansion valve slightly. This will allow any trapped refrigerant to escape. The reason for leaving one screw and washer in is to keep the valve from being blown out and injuring someone, if there is still pressure back of it.

5. After all refrigerant has escaped, remove the tool and the remaining screw and washer. Lift off the expansion-valve capsule.

6. Use the special O-ring removing tool to remove the O rings from the expansion-valve-capsule cavity. Discard the rings. Wipe the cavity clean with a lint-free cloth.

7. Note that the expansion-valve capsule is sealed in the cavity with three O rings. New O rings must be used when the new expansion-valve capsule is installed. Lubricate the grooves in the valve and in the cavity with clean refrigerant oil. Lubricate, and then install, the O rings. Two rings go on the valve, and one goes in the valve cavity. Install the valve capsule by pressing it down into position by hand.

8. Reinstall the two valve retaining screws and washers. Tighten the screws to 5 to 7 pound-feet (0.69 to 0.97 kg-m) torque.

9. Clean the bottom flange of the inlet connector shell. Clean the mating flange on the valve housing. Check the O-ring grooves and flange mating surfaces to make sure there are no burrs or scratches that could cause a leak. Lubricate the new O ring with refrigerant oil. Install the O ring. Reattach the inlet connector-shell assembly to the valve housing. Tighten the screws to 7 to 12 pound-feet (0.97 to 1.66 kg-m) torque.

10. Replace the desiccant bag (■8-11-13).

11. Install the VIR assembly (■8-11-9). Evacuate and recharge the system. Test the system for leaks and performance.

■ 8-11-12 POA-Valve-Capsule Replacement

Figure 6 is an exploded view of the VIR assembly. If the POA valve is not working properly, a new valve capsule must be installed. The VIR assembly must be removed from the car (■8-11-8). Then proceed as follows:

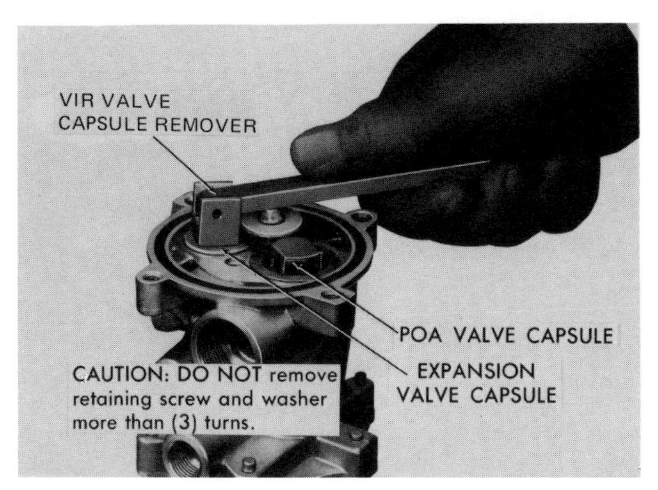

Figure 7 Removing the expansion-valve capsule from the VIR assembly. *(Chevrolet Motor Division of General Motors Corporation.)*

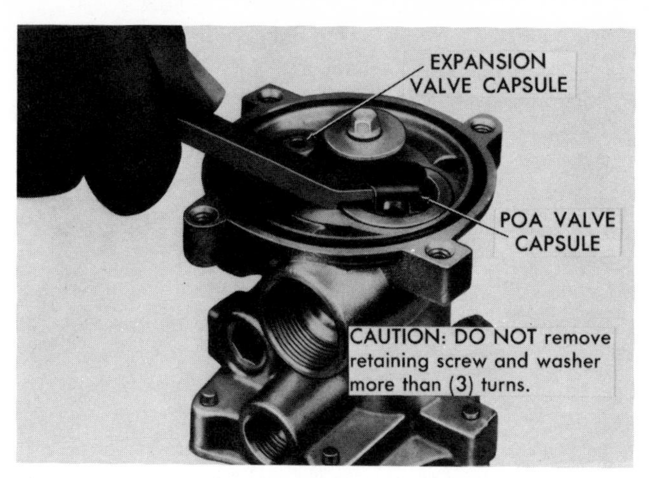

Figure 8 Removing the POA-valve capsule from the VIR assembly. *(Chevrolet Motor Division of General Motors Corporation.)*

1. Remove the inlet connector-shell-assembly screws, the shell assembly, and the O ring. Discard the O ring.

2. Clean the top of the valve housing to remove all dirt. Blow the surface clean with an air hose.

3. Loosen the two screws that retain the expansion-valve capsule and the POA-valve capsule. Loosen one screw 3 turns, and take the other screw off.

4. There may still be pressure in the VIR assembly. This pressure must be released before the POA-valve capsule is removed. The pressure can be released by loosening the expansion valve (steps 3 and 4 in ■8-11-11). To make sure that the pressure in the receiver and inlet side of the expansion valve is released, perform steps 1 and 2 in ■8-11-13.

5. Insert the POA-valve-capsule-removal tool into the valve baffle (Fig. 8) so the step edge of the tool clears the edge of the valve capsule.

> **NOTE:** Position the fulcrum heel of the tool away from the O-ring groove in the valve housing, so you do not damage the ring groove.

6. Press down on the handle of the tool to break the valve capsule free. Remove the tool, the retaining screw and washer, and the valve capsule.

7. Wipe the cavity with a clean, lint-free cloth.

8. Lubricate the new valve-capsule O-ring groove, the ring groove in the valve cavity, and the new O ring with clean refrigerant oil. Install the new O ring on the new POA-valve capsule. Carefully press the valve capsule into place. Then install the two retaining screws and washers. Tighten them to 7 to 12 pound-feet (0.97 to 1.66 kg-m) torque.

9. Clean the bottom flange of the inlet connector shell. Clean the mating flange of the valve housing. Check the O-ring grooves and flange mating surfaces to make sure there are no burrs or scratches that could cause a leak.

10. Lubricate the new O ring and install it. Attach the inlet connector-shell assembly with the attaching screws. Torque them to 5 to 7 pound-feet (0.69 to 0.97 kg-m).

11. Reattach the receiver shell (■8-11-13).

12. Install the VIR assembly (■8-11-9). Evacuate and recharge the system. Test the system for leaks and performance.

■ 8-11-13 Desiccant-Bag Replacement Figure 6 is an exploded view of the VIR assembly. The desiccant bag should be replaced whenever the VIR assembly has been removed from the car (■ 8-11-8). To replace the desiccant bag, proceed as follows:

1. Loosen about 3 turns, but do not remove, the screws that attach the receiver shell.

> **CAUTION:** Do not remove the screws until the shell has been loosened from the valve housing. If there is pressure, it could blow the shell off violently.

2. Hold the valve housing, and push sideways on the receiver shell to loosen it. If the receiver shell sticks, use a flat-bladed screwdriver to pry (carefully!) between the shell mounting flange and the condenser-line connection.

3. Once the shell is free, remove the mounting screws and the shell.

4. Discard the old desiccant bag and the O ring. Wash the liquid pickup-tube filter screen and the receiver shell with clean solvent. Blow them dry with an air hose.

5. Install a new desiccant bag. Replace the filter on the pickup tube.

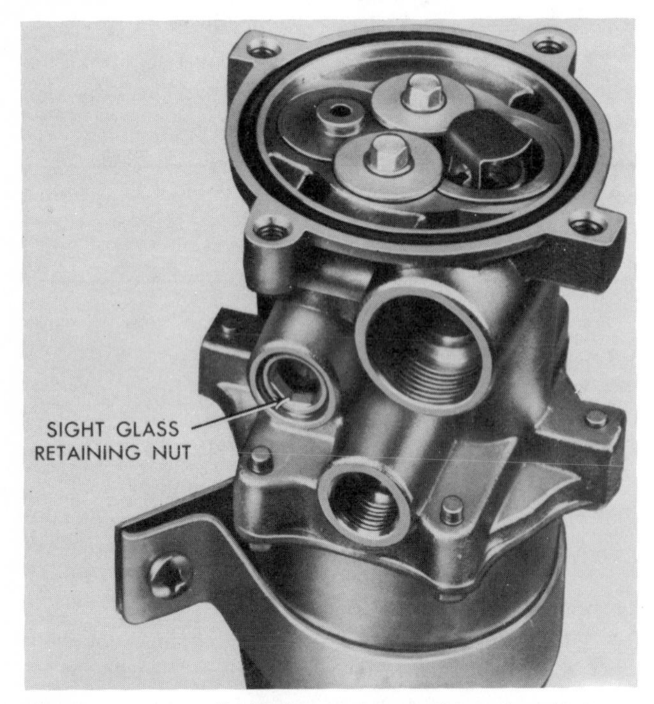

Figure 9 Location of sight glass in VIR assembly. *(Chevrolet Motor Division of General Motors Corporation.)*

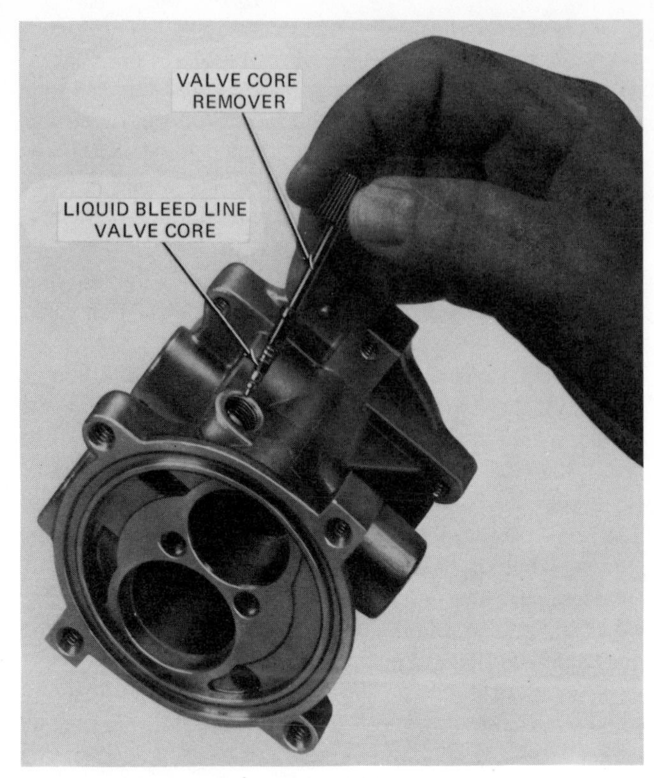

Figure 10 Removing the liquid bleed-line valve core from the VIR assembly. *(Chevrolet Motor Division of General Motors Corporation.)*

6. Lubricate the O ring and the ring groove on the valve housing.

7. Add 1 fluid ounce (30 cc) of new refrigerant oil to the receiver shell.

8. Assemble the receiver shell to the valve housing, tightening the screws to 5 to 7 pound-feet (0.69 to 0.97 kg-m) torque.

9. Reinstall the VIR assembly (■8-11-9). Evacuate and recharge the system. Test the system for leaks and performance.

> **NOTE:** Some cars are equipped with a receiver that cannot be taken apart. If the desiccant bag needs replacement, the complete receiver assembly must be replaced.

■ 8-11-14 Sight-Glass Replacement If the sight glass (Fig. 6) needs to be replaced, the VIR assembly must be removed (■8-11-8). Figure 9 shows the sight glass and retainer. Remove the retainer with a 7/16-inch allen wrench. Then hold the sight glass in place with a finger while applying a slight amount of refrigerant vapor to the assembly. Shift the finger from side to side to help guide the glass out.

Discard all old parts. Lubricate the new O ring, sight glass, nylon thrust washer, and nut with clean refrigerant oil. Install the parts. Torque the nut to 23 pound-inches (26.5 kg-cm). Reinstall the VIR assembly (■8-11-9). Evacuate and recharge the system. Test the system for leaks and performance.

■ 8-11-15 Liquid Bleed-Line Valve-Core Replacement

Replacement of the valve core requires removal of the VIR assembly from the car (■8-11-8). The valve core is removed with a special tool (Fig. 10). Install the new valve core. Turn the core in until the core threads just start to tighten. Note the position of the tool. Then rotate the tool an additional 180°.

> **NOTE:** Be sure to use the correct valve core. They are special and are different from the gauge cores.

Reinstall the VIR assembly (■8-11-9). Evacuate and recharge the system. Test the system for leaks and performance.

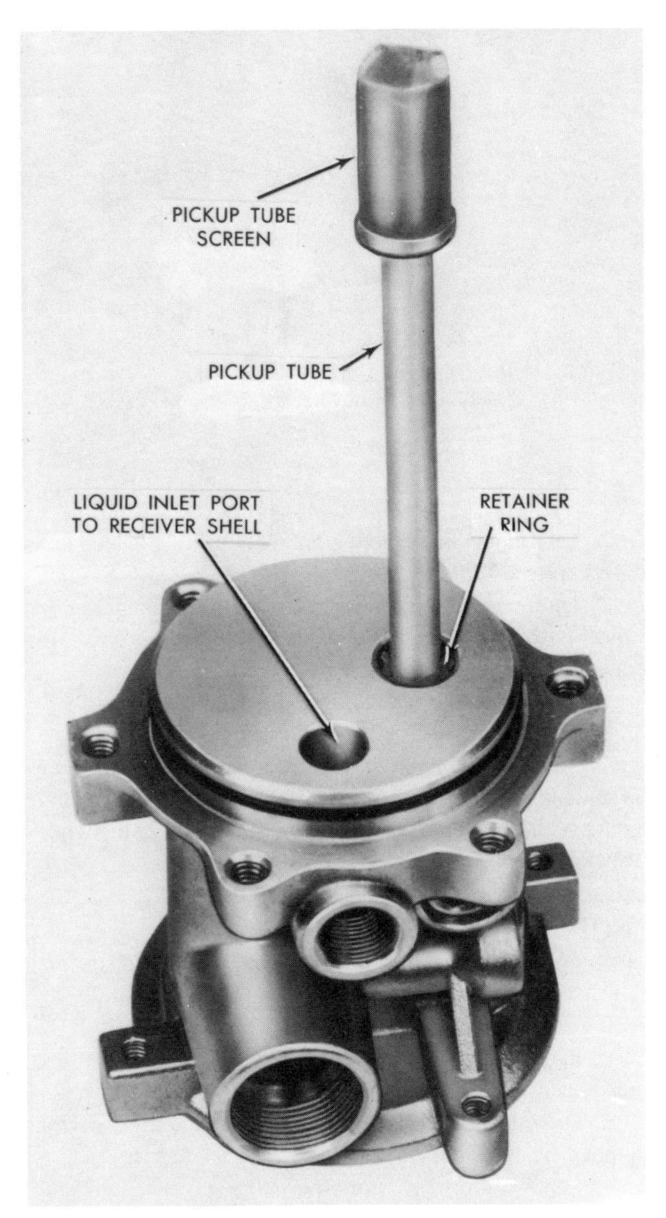

Figure 11 Location of pickup tube and retainer ring in VIR assembly. *(Chevrolet Motor Division of General Motors Corporation.)*

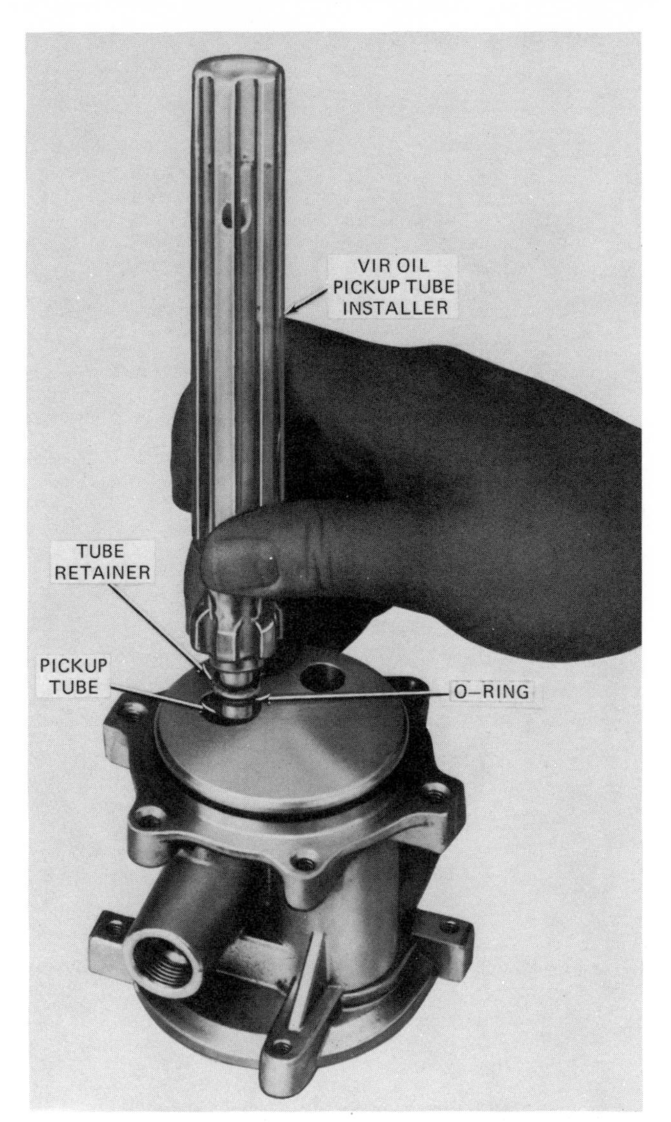

Figure 12 Installing the pickup-tube retainer ring with special tool. *(Chevrolet Motor Division of General Motors Corporation.)*

■ 8-11-16 VIR-Valve-Housing Replacement

If the VIR-valve housing has been damaged, but the valve capsules are in good condition, the capsules can be removed and installed in a new housing.

> **NOTE:** The new housing comes equipped with a new liquid bleed-line valve core and sight glass. Make sure the new housing assembly is clean, inside and out. Wash it in solvent and blow it dry, if necessary. It must be clean.

1. Remove the valve capsules and receiver shell from the old valve housing (■8-11-11 to 8-11-13).

2. Remove the pickup tube (Fig. 11). Use a small screwdriver to raise each tang of the pickup-tube retainer ring, a little at a time. Move around the retainer, raising each tang a little bit each time, until the ring is free. Then remove the pickup tube.

3. Install a new O ring lubricated with refrigerant oil. Install

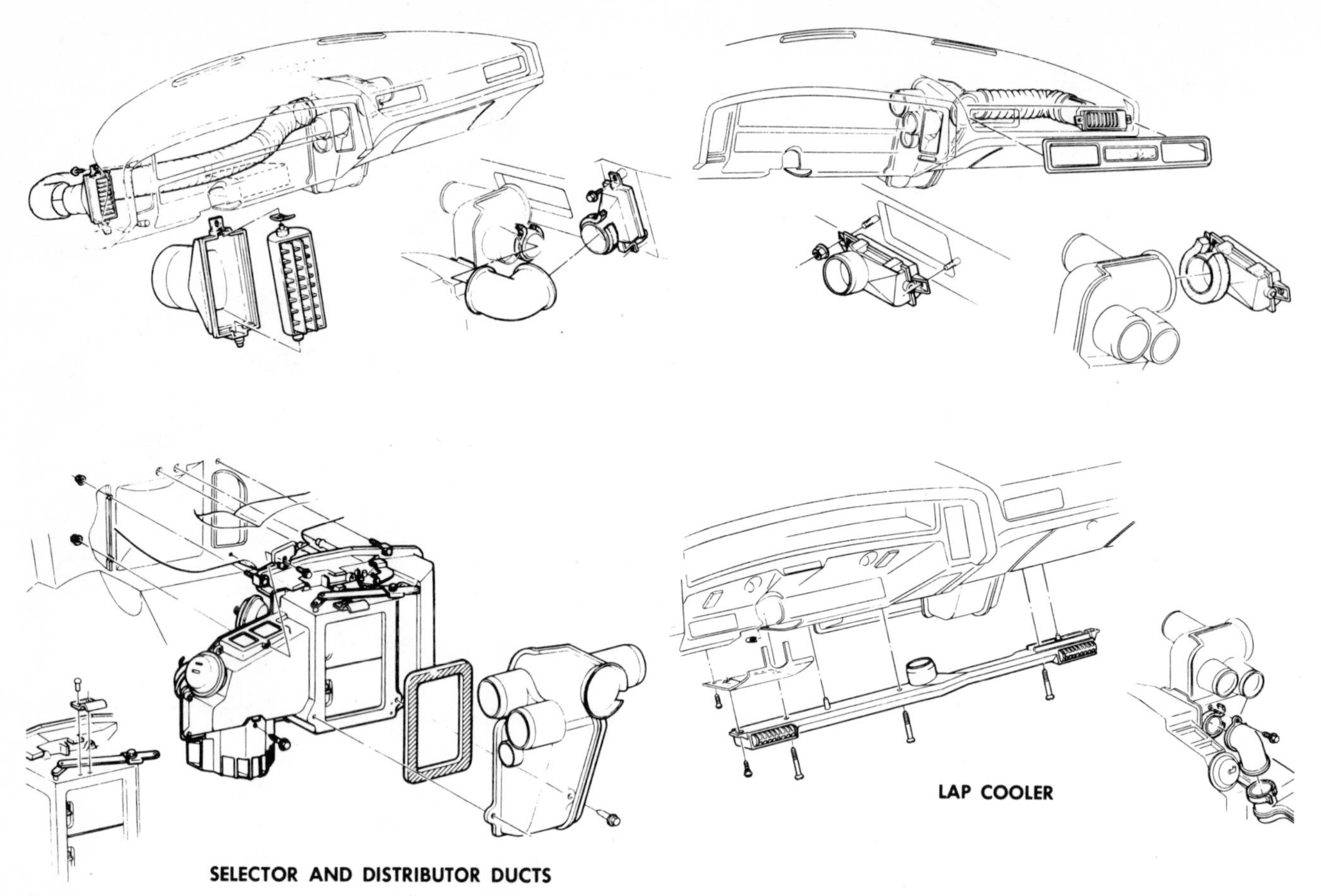

Figure 13 Air-selector and -distributor ducts in various Chevrolet models. *(Chevrolet Motor Division of General Motors Corporation.)*

the pickup-tube retainer on the tube. Use the special tool to install the pickup tube (Fig. 12). Be sure the tube bottoms in the opening. Hold the tool vertically, so the tube will go in correctly. Make sure that no tang is fractured after the retainer ring is seated.

4. Install the valve capsules and the receiver shell, with a new desiccant bag (■8-11-11 to 8-11-13). Be sure to add 1 fluid ounce (30 cc) of clean refrigerant oil, as explained in ■8-11-13.

5. After the assembly is completed, install it (■8-11-9). Evacuate and recharge the system. Test the system for leaks and performance.

■ 8-11-17 Air-Distributor and Heater-Core Replacement

Figure 13 shows the air-distributor tubes and outlets for several models of Chevrolet cars. Here is the procedure for removing and replacing these parts and the heater core.

Removal

1. Drain the engine cooling system. It is not necessary to discharge the refrigerant system because the system does not need to be opened.

2. Disconnect the battery ground cable and the lead from the compressor clutch.

3. Disconnect the vacuum hose from the vacuum check valve. Push the hose grommet through into the passenger compartment.

4. Disconnect the heater hoses from the heater core.

5. Remove the accessible nuts from the studs (three) and screws (two), from the engine side. To remove the last screw on some installations, remove the 10 screws holding the inner fender skirt. Wedge the skirt away from the rear of the wheel well. Remove the screw.

NOTE: On other models, the distributor is mounted differently. It can be detached without wedging the skirt out of the way.

6. Remove the lap-cooler assembly, glove-box door and box, floor outlet duct, and instrument-panel pad.

7. Disconnect the distributor-duct hoses and connector. Remove the duct from the selector.

8. Remove the screw from the defroster duct. Move the duct so you can get to the selector-and-core assembly.

9. Separate the in-line vacuum connector and the vacuum

line feeding the outside-air vacuum motor (diaphragm). Disconnect the Bowden (control) cable from the temperature door.

10. Remove the heater and air-selector duct as an assembly.

11. Remove the screws attaching the heater-core clamps in the selector. The heater core can now be lifted out.

12. The heater core can be checked for leaks by plugging the connector tubes and immersing the core in water. Leaks show up as air bubbles coming out of the leaks. It is not usually worthwhile to repair leaks in the heater core. The factory recommendation is to install a new core.

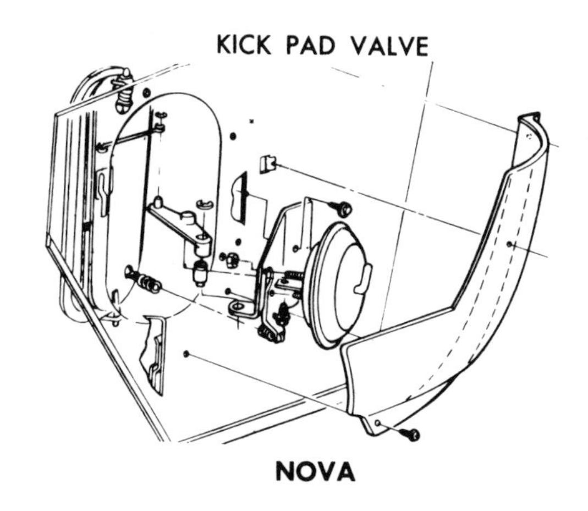

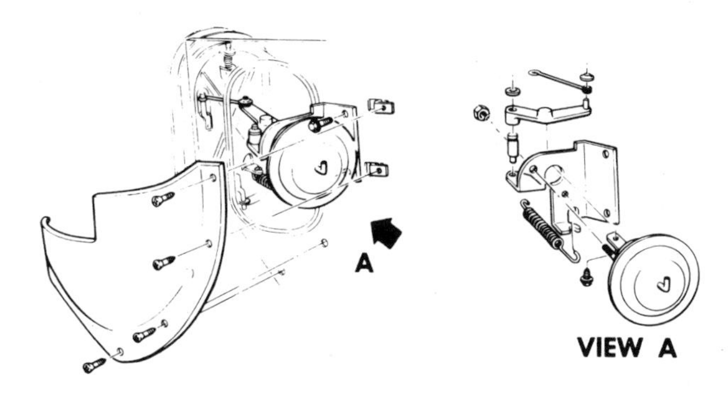

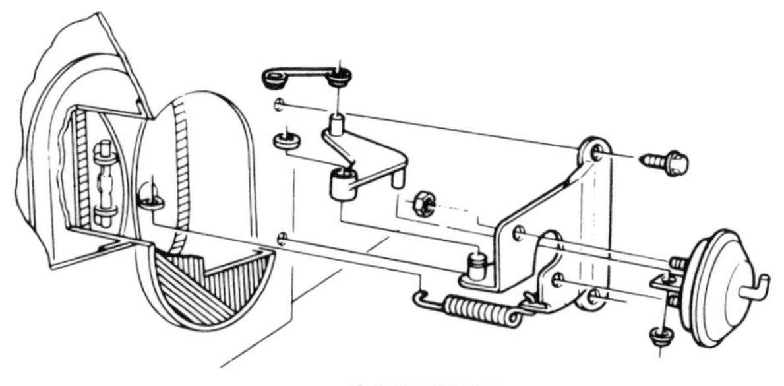

Figure 14 Kick-pad valve in various Chevrolet models. *(Chevrolet Motor Division of General Motors Corporation.)*

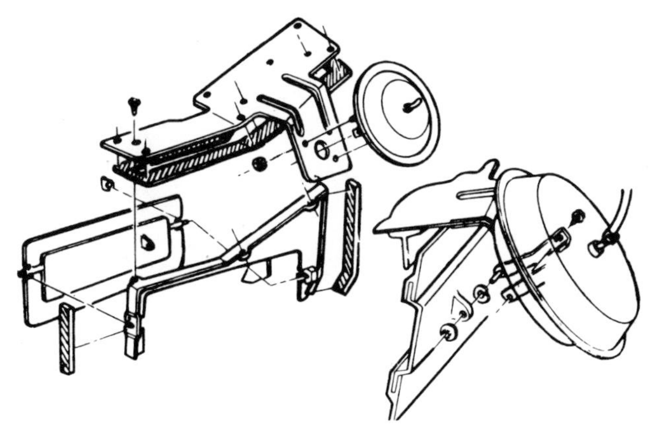

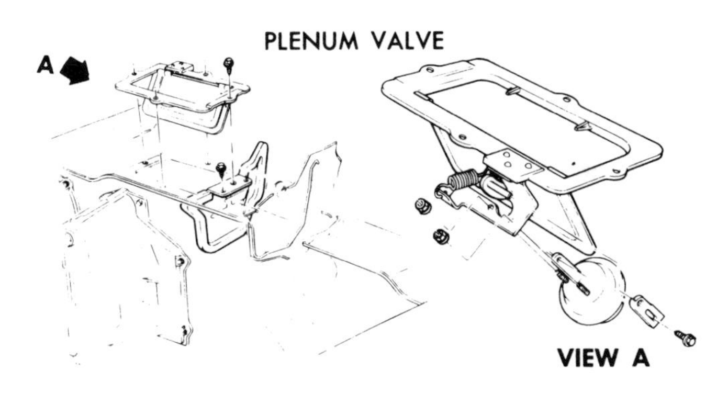

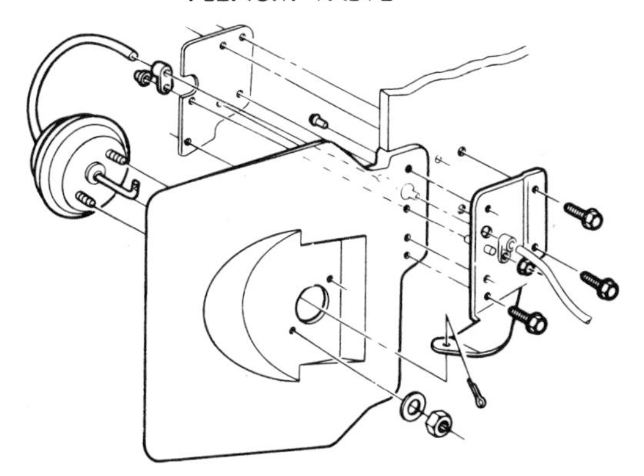

Figure 15 Plenum valve in various Chevrolet models. *(Chevrolet Motor Division of General Motors Corporation.)*

Replacement

To reinstall the heater core and other parts, follow the removal procedure in reverse. Fill the engine cooling system with coolant (water plus the proper amount of antifreeze). Check the heater core and hose connections for leaks.

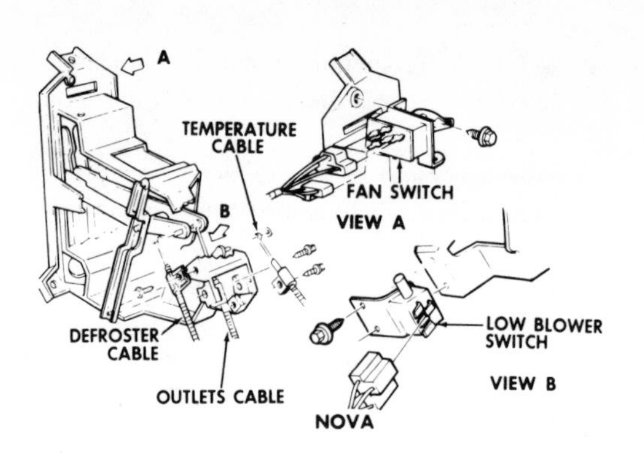

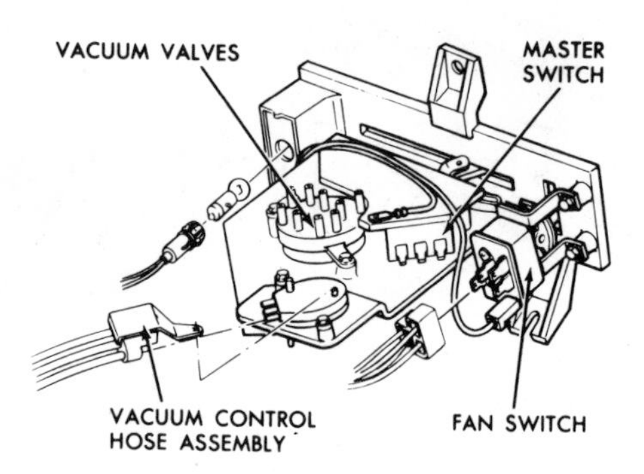

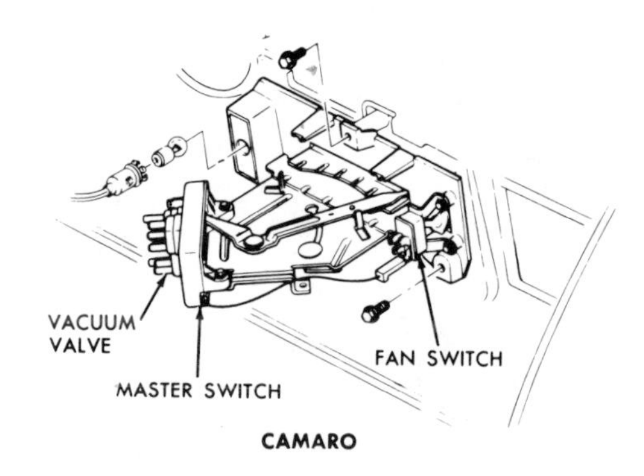

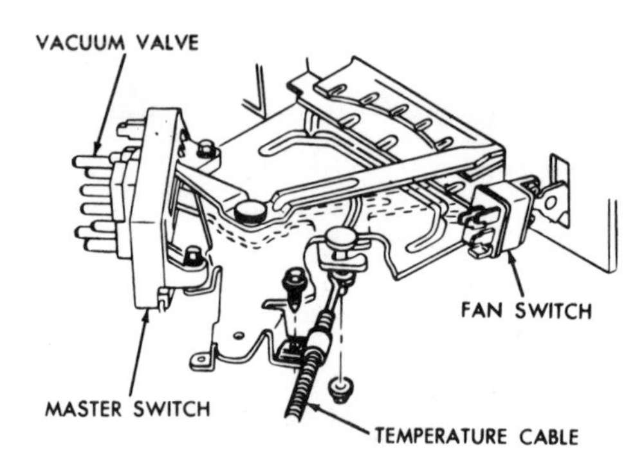

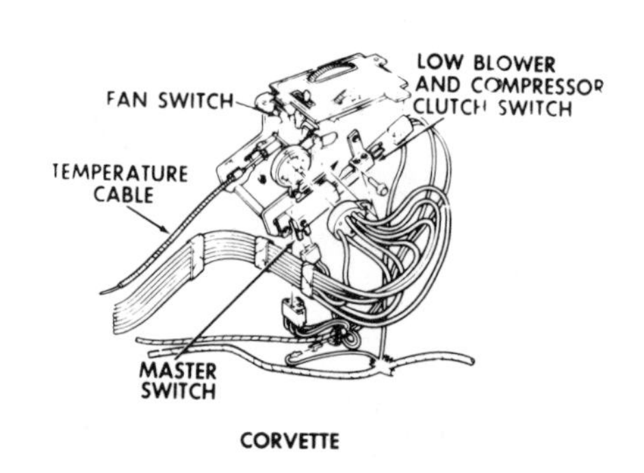

Figure 16 Location of air-conditioning control head in various Chevrolet models. *(Chevrolet Motor Division of General Motors Corporation.)*

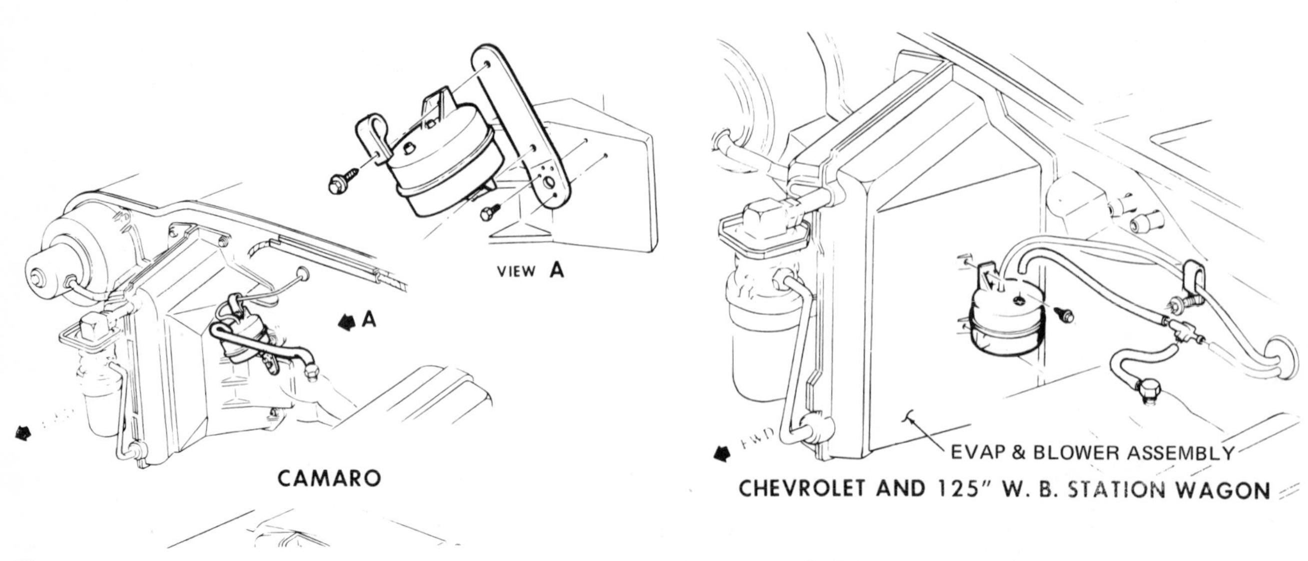

Figure 17 Location of vacuum tank in various Chevrolet models. *(Chevrolet Motor Division of General Motors Corporation.)*

■ **8-11-18 Kick-Pad-Valve Service** Figure 14 shows different kick-pad arrangements. Refer to these illustrations if you have to remove any of the parts shown. On some models, you must adjust the valve before installing the valve cover.

■ **8-11-19 Plenum-Valve Service** Figure 15 shows the plenum valve in different Chevrolet models. Follow these illustrations if you have to service the plenum valve or other parts. On some models, you work from the passenger-compartment side. On others, you work from the engine side, under the hood.

■ **8-11-20 Control-Head-Assembly Service** Figure 16 shows the air-conditioning control heads in various Chevrolet models. The head is easily removed. The ground cable should be disconnected from the battery. Then remove any component that might be in the way, such as the instrument-cluster shroud, radio and headlamp switch knobs, and trim.

Then remove the control-head attaching screws. Disconnect the electric and vacuum lines as shown in Fig. 16. The Bowden (control) cable can then be disconnected, and the control head removed.

■ **8-11-21 Switches** A number of switches are used in air-conditioner systems (Fig. 16). These include the blower switch, the master switch, and the Lo-blower switch. There is no special problem to removing the switches. As a first step, disconnect the battery ground cable. On some models, you have to take off the control head (■8-11-20).

■ **8-11-22 Vacuum-Tank Service** Figure 17 shows the location of the vacuum tank in various Chevrolet models. Disconnect the battery ground cable as a first step. Refer to the illustration for details of how the vacuum-tank is attached on various cars.

■ **8-11-23 Blower-Relay Service** Figure 18 shows the location of the blower-motor relay. To remove it, disconnect the battery ground cable and the electric connector at the switch. Then remove the two screws.

■ **8-11-24 Blower Resistor** Figure 19 shows the location of the blower resistor on many Chevrolet models. To remove it, disconnect the battery ground cable and the wiring-harness connector. Then take out the two mounting screws.

■ **8-11-25 Corvette Discharge-Pressure Switch** This switch (Fig. 20) shuts off the compressor when the re-

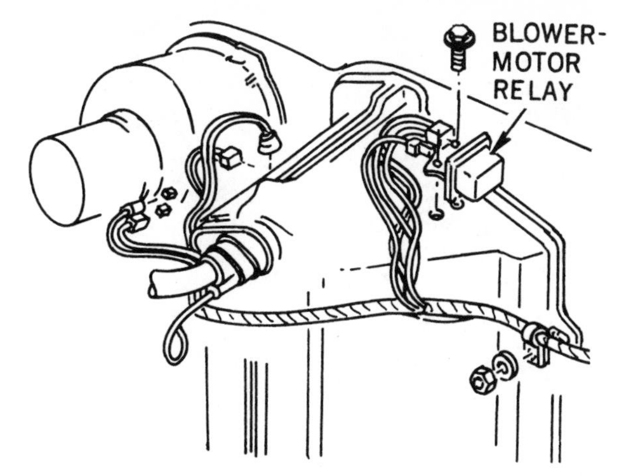

Figure 18 Location of blower-motor relay. *(Chevrolet Motor Division of General Motors Corporation.)*

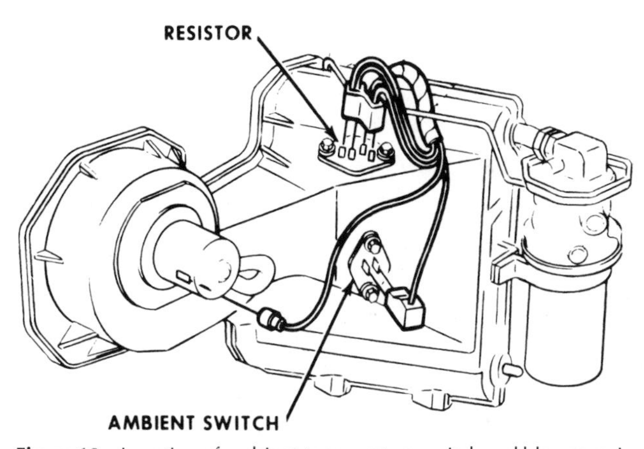

Figure 19 Location of ambient-termperature switch and blower resistor. *(Chevrolet Motor Division of General Motors Corporation.)*

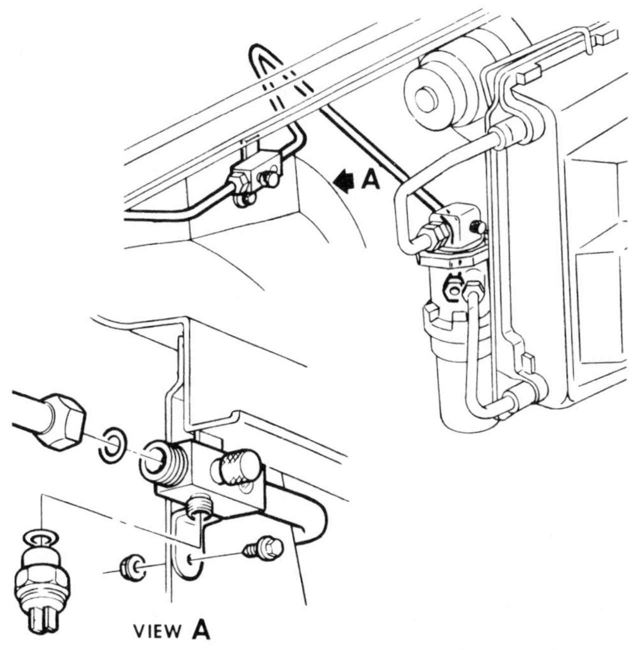

Figure 20 Location of discharge-pressure switch on Corvette. *(Chevrolet Motor Division of General Motors Corporation.)*

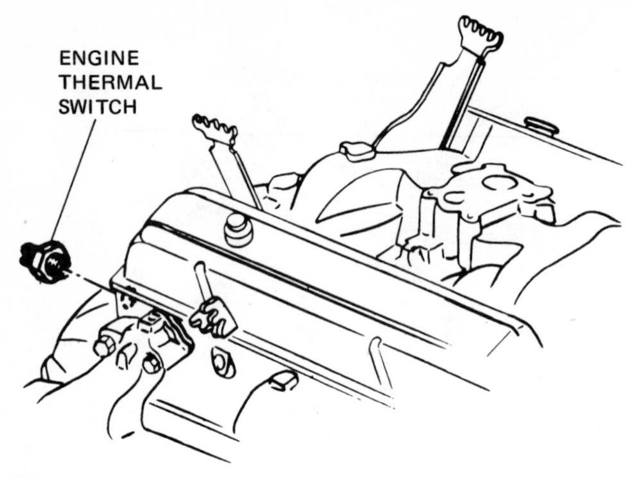

Figure 21 Location of engine thermal switch. *(Chevrolet Motor Division of General Motors Corporation.)*

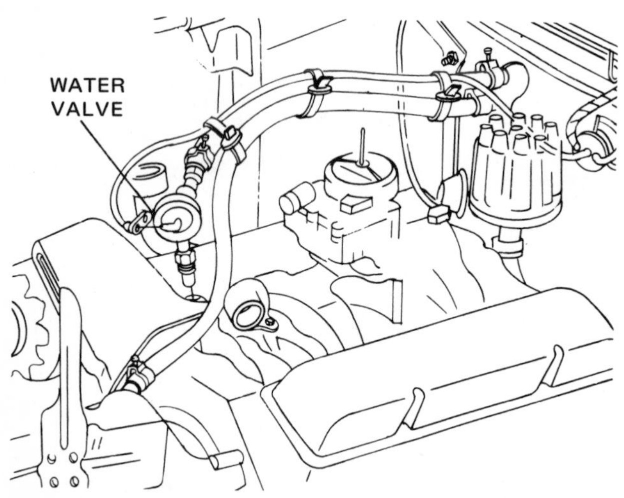

Figure 22 Location of water valve. *(Chevrolet Motor Division of General Motors Corporation.)*

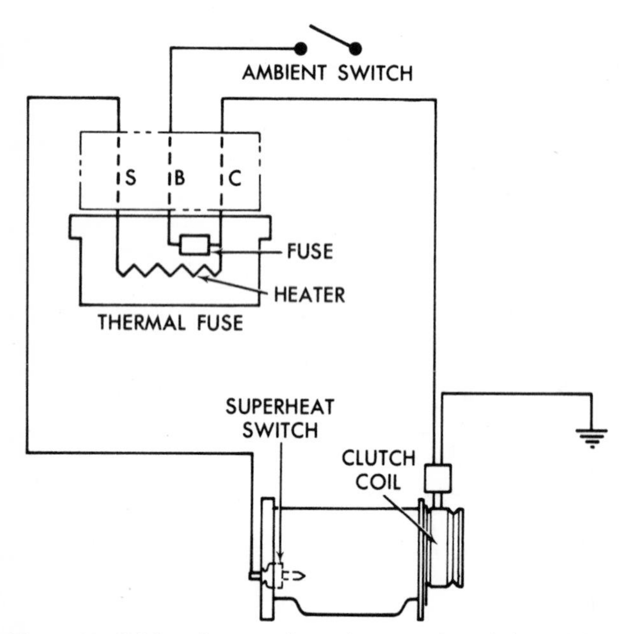

Figure 23 Wiring diagram of superheat switch and thermal fuse. *(Chevrolet Motor Division of General Motors Corporation.)*

frigerant pressure falls too low. This protects the compressor from damage. The switch is connected in series with the compressor clutch, blower switch, and master switch. If the compressor does not operate at ambient temperatures above 45° (7.2°C), check the three switches for continuity with a low-voltage test lamp. If the trouble is in one of the switches, replace it. To replace the discharge-pressure switch, the system must be discharged. Then the old switch is removed, and a new switch installed. Lubricate the new O ring with refrigerant oil. After installing the new switch, evacuate and recharge the system. Check the system for leaks and performance.

■ **8-11-26 Engine Thermal Switch** This switch (Fig. 21) prevents Lo-blower action until the temperature of the engine coolant goes above 95°F (35°C). To remove it, disconnect the battery ground cable and the wiring harness at the switch. Then remove the switch from the cylinder head.

■ **8-11-27 Water Valve** The water valve (Fig. 22) is used in some models to prevent coolant circulation to the heater core when the controls are set at A/C and COLD. With this setting, vacuum is applied to the vacuum motor. The vacuum motor closes the water valve. If the controls are moved to other settings, the vacuum is shut off from the vacuum motor so the water valve opens. This allows coolant to circulate through the heater core.

To remove the water valve, disconnect the battery ground cable. Disconnect the vacuum line from the vacuum motor. Put a drain pan under the vehicle. Disconnect the outlet hose, and drain the coolant into the container. The valve can then be removed from the inlet manifold.

■ **8-11-28 Superheat Switch and Thermal Fuse** These are connected as shown in Fig. 23. Their purpose is to guard the compressor from damage if refrigerant is lost and the system pressure falls off. When this happens, the suction-gas temperature goes up enough to close the superheat switch. This allows current to flow through the heater in the thermal fuse. The heat melts the fuse and opens the circuit to the compressor clutch coil.

To replace the superheat switch, discharge the system. Then remove the superheat switch from the rear of the compressor. Use snap-ring pliers to remove the retainer ring. Clean the cavity in the compressor end, and make sure the O-ring groove is not damaged. Lubricate the new O ring and ring grooves with clean refrigerant oil. Install the new switch, making sure the switch bottoms. Secure it with the snap ring. The high points of the ring should be next to the switch housing. Check the switch for electrical continuity with a low-voltage test lamp. Connect the switch. Evacuate and recharge the system. Test the system for leaks and performance.

If the thermal fuse blows, remove it by disconnecting the wiring harness and removing the attaching screw.

SECTION 8-12 Servicing Compressors

The servicing of air-conditioner compressors is considered by some people as a specialized job requiring special tools and special knowledge. Certain vehicle manufacturers do not provide disassembly and reassembly information. They recommend replacing a defective compressor. Other vehicle manufacturers do provide compressor servicing information. If you have a defective compressor, refer to the vehicle manufacturer's service manual. The following sections contain general information on each type of compressor.

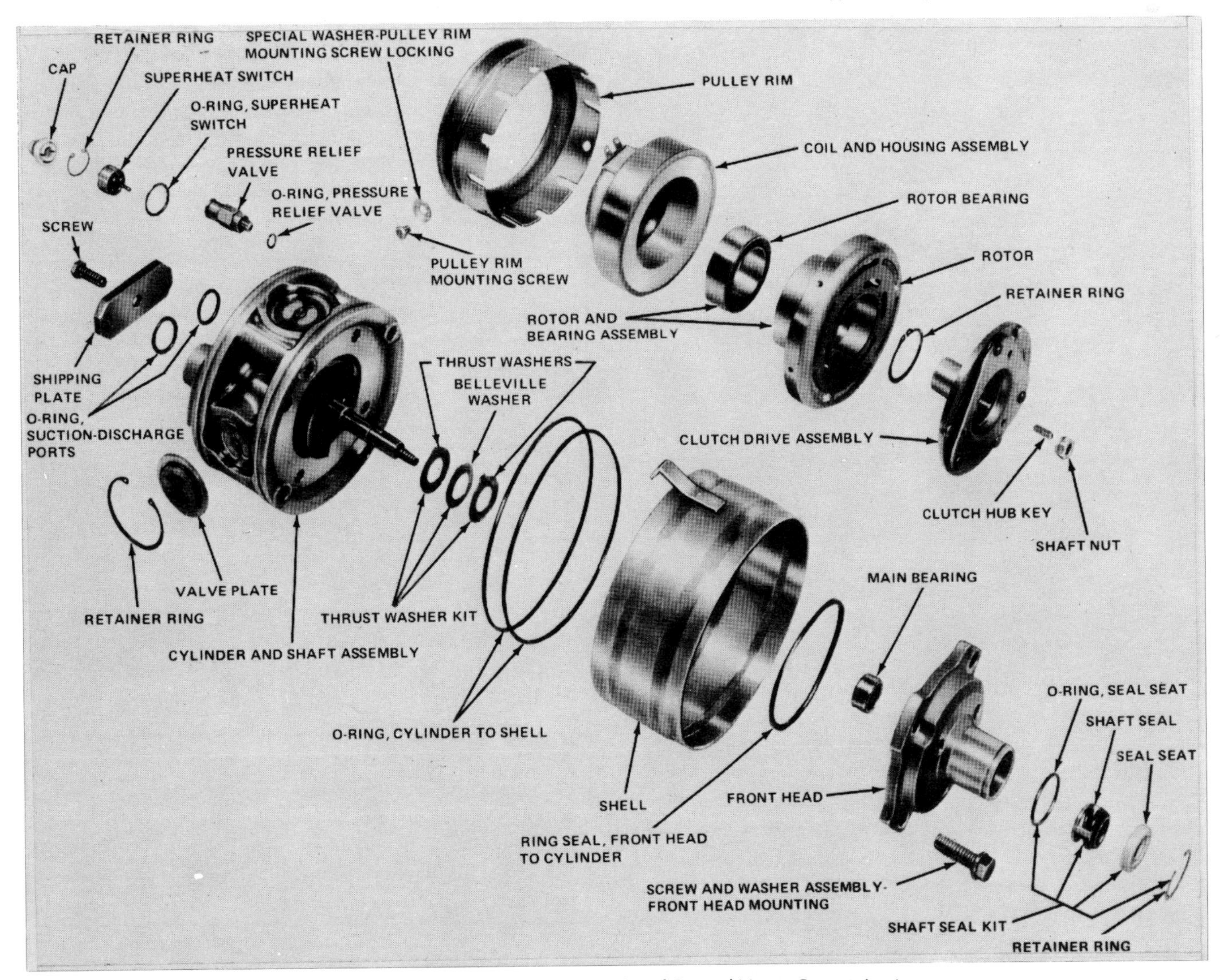

Figure 1 Disassembled view of the R-4 compressor. *(Pontiac Motor Division of General Motors Corporation.)*

■ 8-12-1 Servicing the Frigidaire R-4 Compressor

Figure 1 shows how far this compressor may be disassembled. Note that the cylinder-and-shaft assembly, with the pistons, is not disassembled. This means that if there is trouble within the assembly, it must be replaced as a unit. However, the valve plates can be replaced in the cylinder-and-shaft assembly if they become damaged.

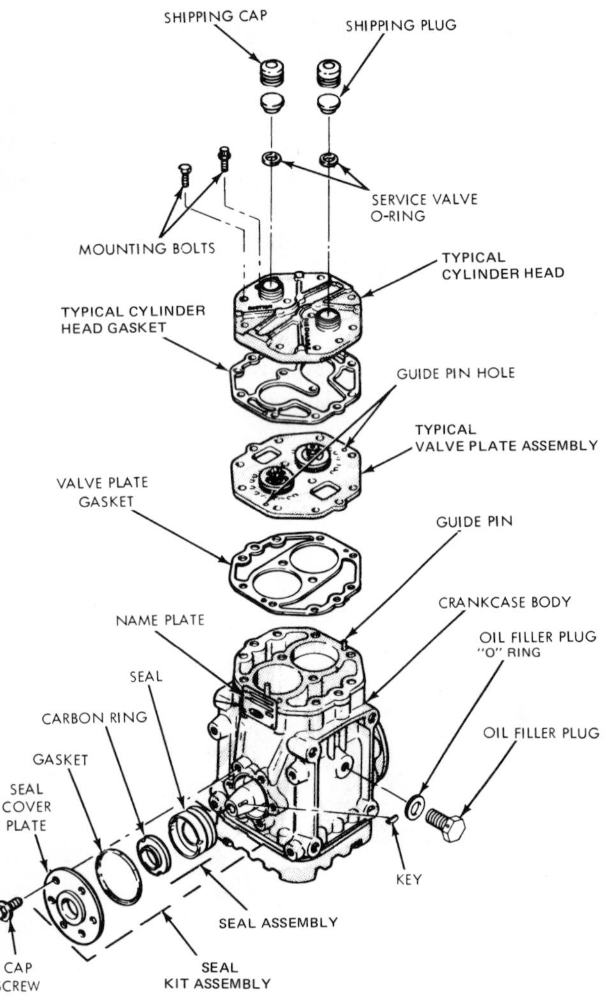

Figure 2 Disassembled view of the York compressor. *(Ford Motor Company.)*

Some servicing operations can be done without completely removing the compressor from the car. The refrigerant system need not be discharged to replace the compressor drive belt, the clutch-drive-plate-and-hub-assembly, the clutch rotor-and-bearing assembly, and the clutch coil and pulley rim. When the crankshaft seal, pressure relief valve, or superheat switch is replaced, the system must be discharged, evacuated, and recharged. However, the compressor need not be removed from the car.

NOTE: When tightening the drive belt, do not pry on the compressor shell. This can damage the shell. Instead, pry on the compressor bracket.

■ 8-12-2 Servicing the Frigidaire R-6 Compressor

Figure 12 (in Part 8, Sec. 2) shows this compressor in disassembled view. The cylinder-and-shaft assembly is not shown disassembled. Some manufacturers' shop manuals give instructions for disassembling this component. Other shop manuals do not. The compressor must be removed from the car for any service operation. This means the system must be discharged. Then, after the repaired compressor is reinstalled on the vehicle, the system must be evacuated and recharged. Then it must be tested for leaks and performance. The removal and replacement procedure is covered in ■8-11-2 and 8-11-3.

■ 8-12-3 Servicing the York and Tecumseh Compressors

Figure 2 shows a partly disassembled York compressor. The construction of the Tecumseh compressor is very similar. Note that the crankcase body, with the crankshaft and pistons, is not shown disassembled. The reason for this is that this subassembly should not be disassembled in the field. If this subassembly is damaged or worn internally, it must be replaced as a unit. Probably a complete new compressor would be installed. Not even the parts that are shown disassembled in the illustration would be saved. However, as shown in Fig. 2, the valve-plate assembly or the seal may be replaced on this type of compressor.

NOTE: When replacing an old compressor with a new one, first check the oil level in the old compressor. Then remove enough oil from the new compressor to make its oil level the same as that in the old unit. If you don't do this, the excess oil in the crankcase could cause compressor troubles.

■ 8-12-4 Servicing the Chrysler V-Type Compressor

Figure 10 (in Part 8, Sec. 2) is a disassembled view of this compressor. Most service operations, as well as complete disassembly of the unit, require removal of the compressor from the vehicle. This means that the system must be discharged. Then, after the compressor has been serviced and reinstalled on the vehicle, the system must be evacuated and recharged.

NOTE: When replacing an old compressor with a new unit, first check the oil level in the old compressor. Then remove enough oil from the new compressor to make its oil level the same as that in the old unit. If you do not do this, the excess oil in the crankcase could cause compressor trouble.

GLOSSARY

GLOSSARY

This glossary of automobile words and phrases provides a ready reference for the automotive technician. The definitions may differ somewhat from those given in a standard dictionary. They are not intended to be all-inclusive but to cover only what specifically applies to the automotive service field. For example, "apexes" is defined as the peaks of the rotor of a Wankel engine. "Air horn" is defined as a tubular passage in a carburetor. The purpose of the glossary is to define frequently used automotive terms.

A

A Abbreviation for **ampere.**

ABDC Abbreviation for after bottom dead center, any position of the piston between bottom dead center and top dead center, on the upward stroke.

abrasive A substance used for cutting, grinding, lapping, or polishing metals.

absolute pressure A pressure measured on a scale having as its zero point the complete absence of pressure (known as a "perfect vacuum"). Atmospheric pressure on the absolute scale is 14.7 psi (1.03 kg/cm^2) or 29.92 inches (760 mm) of mercury (Hg).

absolute zero The temperature indicating the complete absence of heat on the absolute temperature scale; equivalent to −460°F (−273°C).

A/C Abbreviation for **air conditioning.**

AC or ac Abbreviation for **alternating current.**

acceleration An increase in velocity or speed.

accelerator A foot-operated pedal linked to the throttle valve in the carburetor; used to control the flow of gasoline to the engine.

accelerator pump In the carburetor, a small pump (linked to the accelerator) which momentarily enriches the air-fuel mixture when the accelerator is depressed at low speed.

accessories Devices not considered essential to the operation of a vehicle, such as the radio, car heater, and electric window lifts.

accumulator A device used in automatic transmissions to cushion the shock of clutch and servo actions.

additive A substance added to gasoline or oil to improve some property of the gasoline or oil.

adjust To bring the parts of a component or system into a specified relationship, or to a specified dimension, or pressure.

adjustments Necessary or desired changes in clearances, fit, or settings.

adsorb To collect in a very thin layer on the surface of another material.

advance To make faster or to push ahead. To adjust ignition timing so that the spark plug fires earlier or more degrees before TDC; this effect is produced by moving the distributor (initial advance); by centrifugal or vacuum devices in accordance with engine speed and intake-manifold vacuum; or electronically.

afterboil Boiling of fuel in the carburetor or of coolant in the engine immediately after the engine is stopped.

afterburner On an automobile engine, a type of exhaust manifold that burns any hydrocarbon and carbon monoxide remaining in the exhaust gas.

afterrunning The condition in which an engine continues to run after the ignition is turned off. Sometimes referred to as **dieseling.**

aiming screws Horizontal and vertical self-locking adjusting screws used to aim a headlight and keep it in the proper position.

AIR Abbreviation for air-injection reactor, part of a system of exhaust-emission control. See **air-injection system.**

air bags A passive restraint system consisting of balloon-type passenger-safety devices that inflate automatically on vehicle impact.

air bleed An opening into a gasoline passage through which air can pass, or "bleed," into the gasoline as it moves through the passage.

air brakes A brake system that used compressed air to supply the force required to apply brakes.

air cleaner A device, mounted on or connected to the carburetor, for filtering dirt and dust out of air being drawn into the engine.

air compressor An engine-driven pump used to supply air under pressure for operating air brakes and air-powered accessories on a vehicle.

air conditioner Any system or equipment that can provide conditioned air.

air conditioning See **air conditioner** and **air-conditioning system.**

air-conditioning system The system on the car that provides conditioned air for the passenger compartment by cleaning, cooling, and drying the air; consists basically of a compressor, evaporator, condenser, and refrigerant, and a control system.

air-cooled engine An engine that is cooled by the passage of air around the cylinders, and not by the passage of a liquid through water jackets.

air filter A filter that removes dirt and dust particles from air passing through it.

air-fuel mixture The air and fuel traveling to the combustion chamber after being mixed by the carburetor.

air-fuel ratio The proportions (by weight) of air and fuel supplied for combustion; an average mixture is 16 parts of air to 1 part of gasoline.

air gap A small space between parts that are related either magnetically, as in an alternator, or electrically, as between the electrodes of a spark plug.

air horn In the carburetor, a tubular passage on the atmospheric side of the venturi through which the incoming air must pass, and which contains the choke valve.

air-injection system An exhaust-emission control system; injects air at low pressure into the exhaust manifold or thermal reactor to complete the combustion of unburned hydrocarbons and carbon monoxide in the exhaust gas.

air-inlet valve A movable door, or valve, in the plenum blower assembly; permits the selection of outside air or inside air for both the heating and air-conditioning systems.

air line A hose, pipe, or tube through which air passes.

air nozzle In an air-injection system, the tube through which air is delivered to the exhaust gas.

air-outlet valve A movable door, or valve, in the plenum blower assembly or an air conditioner; directs air either into the heater core or into the ducts that lead to the evaporator.

air pollution Contamination of the air by natural and manufactured pollutants, such as smoke, gases, and dust.

air pressure Atomspheric pressure; also the pressure produced by an air pump or by compression of air in a cylinder.

air pump Any device for compressing air. In the air-injection system of exhaust-emission control, an engine-driven (belt-driven) pump incorporating a rotor and vanes.

air resistance The drag on a vehicle moving through the air; increases as the square of the speed of the vehicle.

air starting valve A valve which opens to admit compressed air to an engine cylinder to start the engine, and which closes and remains closed after the engine starts.

air suspension Any suspension system that uses contained air for vehicle springing.

alcohol A colorless, volatile liquid which in some forms can be used as a fuel for racing engines.

alignment The act of lining up; also, the state of being in a true line.

alky Performance term for alcohol used as a fuel for racing engines.

allen wrench A type of hexagonal screwdriver that turns a screw having a matching recessed hex head.

alloy A mixture of two or more metals.

alternating current (ac) Electric current that flows first in one direction and then in the opposite direction.

alternator A device that converts mechanical energy from the engine into electric energy for charging the battery and operating electrical accessories. Also known as an ac generator.

aluminized valve An engine valve with a thin layer of aluminum sprayed on the valve face and sometimes on the top of the valve head; the aluminum provides a thin, hard, corrosion-resistant coating.

aluminum cylinder block An engine cylinder block cast from aluminum or aluminum alloy, usually with cast-iron cylinder sleeves installed as cylinder bores.

ambient compressor switch In an air conditioner, a switch that energizes the compressor clutch when the outside air temperature is 32°F (0°C) or above, and de-energizes it when the outside air temperature drops below 32°F (0°C).

ambient temperature The temperature of the air surrounding an object, such as the car.

ammeter A meter for measuring the amount of current (in amperes) flowing through an electric circuit.

amp Abbreviation for **ampere.**

amperage The amount of current, in amperes.

ampere A measurement of electric current; 1 ampere is equal to a flow of 6.28×10^{18} electrons per second.

ampere-hour capacity A battery rating based on ability to deliver a specified current for a specified length of time.

analyzer A device used to check the internal functioning of a system or component.

aneroid A device with a sealed bellows that provides mechanical movement by extending or retracting in response to varying atmospheric pressure.

antenna Any device used to pick up radio signals.

antibackfire valve A valve used in the air-injection system to prevent backfiring in the exhaust system during deceleration.

antidieseling solenoid See **idle-stop solenoid.**

antifreeze A chemical, usually ethylene glycol, that is added to the engine coolant to raise the coolant boiling point and lower its freezing point.

antifriction bearing Name given to almost any type of ball, roller, or tapered-roller bearing.

anti-icing system A carburetor system designed to prevent the formation of ice on a surface or in a passage.

antiknock compound An additive put into gasoline to suppress spark knock or detonation – usually a lead compound (which becomes an air pollutant in the engine exhaust gas).

antilock brake A system installed with the brakes to prevent wheel lockup during braking, thereby reducing the chance of skidding.

antipercolator A vent in the carburetor that opens to release fuel vapors when the throttle is closed; prevents fuel from being pushed out through the fuel nozzle by pressure build-up.

antisiphon system A small passage designed into a carburetor to prevent fuel from siphoning from the float bowl into the engine.

apexes In a Wankel engine using a triangular-type rotor, the peaks or points on the rotor formed by the meeting of two adjoining rotor faces.

arcing Name given to the spark that jumps an air gap between two electric conductors; for example, the arcing of the distributor contact points.

armature The rotating or stationary assembly that includes the main current-carrying conductor or windings in an electric motor or generator. A part moved by magnetism, or a part moved through a magnetic field to produce current.

asbestos A fiber material that is heat-resistant, and nonburning; used for brake linings, clutch facings, and gaskets.

aspect ratio The ratio of tire height to width. For example, a G78 tire is 78 percent as high as it is wide. The lower the number, the wider the tire.

aspirator A vacuum pump. Any device that uses a vacuum to draw up gases or small, grainy materials; also, the vacuum pump used in catalytic-converter bead replacement.

assembly A component part, itself made up of assembled pieces which form a self-contained, independently mounted unit. For example, in the automobile, the transmission is an "assembly."

ATDC Abbreviation for "after top dead center"; any position of the piston between top dead center and bottom dead center, on the downward stroke.

atmosphere The mass of air that surrounds the earth.

atmospheric pollution See **air pollution.**

atmospheric pressure The weight of the atmosphere per unit area. Atmospheric pressure at sea level is 14.7 psi absolute (101.35 kPa); it decreases as altitude increases.

atom The smallest particle into which an element can be divided.

atomization The spraying of a liquid through a nozzle so that the liquid is broken into a very fine mist.

attrition Wearing down by rubbing or by friction; abrasion.

automatic choke A carburetor choke that positions the choke valve automatically in accordance with carburetor needs.

automatic headlight control A system that electronically selects the proper headlight beam (high or low) for the driving conditions.

automatic level control A suspension system which compensates for variations in load in the rear of the car; it positions the rear at a predesignated level regardless of load.

automatic transmission A transmission in which gear ratios are changed automatically, eliminating the necessity of hand-shifting gears.

automotive air pollution Evaporated and unburned fuel and other undesirable by-products of combustion which escape from a motor vehicle into the atmosphere; mainly carbon monoxide (CO), hydrocarbons (HC), nitrogen oxides (NO_x), sulfur oxides (SO_x), and particulates.

automotive emissions See **automotive air pollution.**

axis The center line of a rotating part, a symmetrical part, or a circular bore.

axle A theoretical or actual crossbar supporting a vehicle and on which one or more wheels turn.

axle ratio The ratio between the rotational speed (rpm) of the drive shaft and that of the driven wheel; gear reduction in the differential, determined by dividing the number of teeth on the ring gear by the number of teeth on the pinion gear.

B

babbitt A metal consisting of tin, antimony, copper, and other metals; used to line bearings.

backfire Noise made by the explosion of air-fuel mixture in the intake or exhaust system, usually during cranking and deceleration.

backfire-suppressor valve An antibackfire valve used in the air-injection system of exhaust-emission control.

backlash In gearing, the clearance between the meshing teeth of two gears.

back pressure Pressure in the exhaust manifold of a running engine; affects volumetric efficiency.

balanced carburetor Carburetor in which the float bowl is vented into the air horn to compensate for the possible effects of a clogged air filter.

balanced valve A type of hydraulic valve that produces pressure changes proportional to the movement of a mechanical linkage, or to variations in spring pressure.

balancing-coil gauge An indicating device (fuel supply, oil pressure, engine temperature) that contains a pair of coils in the instrument-panel unit.

ball-and-nut steering gear See **recirculating-ball-and-nut steering gear.**

ball-and-trunnion joint A type of universal joint that combines the universal joint and the slip joint in one assembly.

ballast resistor A resistor constructed of a special type of wire which tends to increase or decrease voltage in direct proportion to the temperature of the wire, thereby acting as a current limiter.

ball bearing An antifriction bearing with an inner race and an outer race, and one or more rows of balls between them.

ball check valve A valve consisting of a ball and a seat. Fluid can pass in one direction only; flow in the other direction is checked by the ball seating tightly on the seat.

ball joint A flexible joint consisting of a ball within a socket; used in front-suspension systems and valve-train rocker arms.

ball-joint angle The inward tilt of the steering axis from the vertical.

ball-joint suspension A type of front suspension system in which the wheel spindle is attached directly to the upper and lower suspension arms through ball joints. The ball joints pivot for steering, and carry the vertical load of the vehicle.

ball stud A stud with a ball-shaped end; used in steering linkages to connect the pitman arm to the linkage, or to connect tie rods.

band In an automatic transmission, a hydraulically controlled brake band installed around a metal clutch drum; used to stop or permit drum rotation.

barrel Term sometimes applied to the cylinders in an engine; used in referring to the number of throttle bores in a carburetor.

base circle The low portion of each cam of a camshaft, which is not part of the lobe.

battery An electrochemical device for storing energy in chemical form so that it can be released as electricity; a group of electric cells connected together.

battery acid The electrolyte used in a battery, a mixture of sulfuric acid and water.

battery cell A battery element that is covered with electrolyte; a cell has a specific gravity of approximately 1.265 and a voltage of 2.1 volts when fully charged.

battery charging Restoring chemical energy to a battery by passing an electric current from a battery charger through the battery in the reverse direction.

battery element A group of unlike positive and negative plates assembled with separators. There is one element in a cell.

BDC Abbreviation for **bottom dead center.**

bead That part of the tire which is shaped to fit the rim; the bead is made of steel wires, wrapped and reinforced by the plies of the tire.

bearing A part that transmits a load to a support and in so doing absorbs the friction of moving parts.

bearing caps In the engine, caps held in place by bolts or nuts which, in turn, hold bearing halves in place.

bearing crush The additional height (over a full half) which is purposely manufactured into each bearing half to ensure complete contact of the bearing back with the housing bore when the engine is assembled.

bearing groove A channel cut in the surface of a bearing to distribute oil.

bearing oil clearance The space purposely provided between a shaft and a bearing through which lubricating oil can flow.

bearing prelubricator A special tank, attached to an air line; it supplies oil to the engine lubricating system at a predetermined and maintained pressure when the engine is not operating.

bearing roll-out tool A special tool which is basically a small pin with a thin head; when placed in the crankshaft-journal oilhole, it can be used to roll out or roll in the top half of a main bearing while the crankshaft is still in place.

bearing spin A type of bearing failure in which a lack of lubrication overheats the bearing until it seizes on the shaft, shears its locking lip, and rotates in the housing or block.

bearing spread A purposely manufactured small extra distance across the parting faces of the bearing half, in excess of the actual diameter of the housing bore.

bellows A device, usually metal, that can lengthen or shorten much like an accordian. Some cooling-system thermostats are of the bellows type.

bell-shaped wear Condition in which an opening (such as a brake drum) is worn mostly at one end, so that the opening flares out like a bell.

belt In a tire, a layer of fiberglass, rayon, or woven steel located under the tread around the circumference of a tire.

belted-bias tire A tire in which the plies are laid on the bias, diagonally criss-crossing each other, with two circumferential belts on top of them. The rubber tread is vulcanized on top of the belts and plies.

belted-radial tire A tire in which the plies run parallel to each other and perpendicular to the tire bead. Belts running parallel to the tire tread are applied over this radial section.

belt tension The tightness of a drive belt.

Bendix drive An old type of starting-motor drive which screws into mesh with the flywheel teeth as the starting-motor armature begins to turn. It demeshes automatically as the engine speed increases when the engine starts.

bevel gear A gear shaped like the lower part of a cone; used to transmit motion through an angle.

bhp Abbreviation for **brake horsepower.**

bias-belted tire See **belted-bias tire.**

bias-ply tire A conventionally constructed tire in which the plies are laid diagonally, crisscrossing each other at an angle of about 30° to 40°.

big end The crankpin end of the connecting rod.

bimetal A thermostatic element made up of two metals with different heat expansion rates. Temperature changes produce a bending or distortion of the element.

bleed A process by which air is removed from a hydraulic system (brake or power steering) by draining part of the fluid or by operating the system to work out the air.

Bloc-Chek A special measuring device that, when inserted in the radiator filler neck of a running engine, can detect the leakage of exhaust gas into the cooling system.

block See **cylinder block.**

blow Performance term for an engine, transmission, or differential failure, as to "blow an engine."

blow-by Leakage of compressed air-fuel mixture and burned exhaust gases past the piston rings into the crankcase.

blower Performance term for a supercharger or a two-stroke diesel-engine intake-air compressor. Also, the fan motor in a heater or air-conditioning system.

bmep Abbreviation for brake mean effective pressure; the pressure which, acting on the piston, would result in a given brake-horsepower output if there were no losses due to friction and driving the engine accessories.

body On a vehicle, the assembly of sheet-metal sections, together with windows, doors, seats, and other parts, that provides enclosures for the passengers, engine, and luggage compartments.

body mounting Putting a car body onto a car chassis. Also, the placing of rubber cushions at strategic points along the chassis to soak up noise and vibration.

body panels Sheets of steel which are fastened together to form the car body.

boiling Conversion from the liquid to the vapor state, which takes place throughout the liquid. The conversion is accompanied by bubbling as vapor rises from below the surface.

boiling point The temperature at which a liquid begins to boil.

boil tank A very large tank of boiling parts, cleaning solution, usually used for cleaning cylinder blocks, axle housings, and other large metal parts. Also called a "hot tank."

bolt A type of fastener having a head on one end and threads on the other; usually used with a nut.

borderline lubrication Types of poor lubrication resulting from greasy friction; moving parts are coated with a very thin film of lubricant.

bore An engine cylinder, or any cylindrical hole. Also used to describe the process of enlarging or accurately refinishing a hole, as "to bore an engine cylinder." The bore size is the diameter of the hole.

bore out To increase the engine-cylinder diameter by boring it larger; requires the fitting of oversized pistons. In building a high-performance engine, done to obtain greater engine displacement and power.

boring bar An electric motor-powered cutting tool used to machine, or bore, an engine cylinder, thereby removing metal and enlarging the cylinder diameter.

bottom dead center (BDC) The piston position at the lower limit of its travel in the cylinder, such that the cylinder volume is at its maximum.

brake An energy-conversion device used to slow, stop, or hold a vehicle or mechanism. A device which changes the kinetic energy of motion into useless and wasted heat energy.

brake drag A constant, relatively light contact between brake linings and drums when the brakes are not applied. The result is a car that pulls; the brakes destroy themselves by burning up from the generated heat.

brake drum A metal drum mounted on a car wheel to form the outer shell of the brake; the brake shoes press against the drum to slow or stop drum-and-wheel rotation for braking.

brake-drum glaze Excessively smooth brake-drum surface that lowers friction and, therefore, braking efficiency.

brake fade A reduction, or "fading out," of braking effectiveness; caused by overheating from excessively long and hard brake application, or by water reducing the friction between braking surfaces.

brake feel The reaction of the brake pedal against the driver's foot; tells the driver how heavily the brakes are being applied.

brake fluid A special non-mineral-oil fluid used in the hydraulic brake system to transmit pressure through a closed system of tubing known as the **brake lines.**

brake grab A sudden increase in braking at a wheel; usually caused by contaminated brake linings.

brake horsepower (bhp) Power delivered by the engine and available for driving the vehicle; bhp = torque × rpm/5,252.

brake lines The tubes or hoses connecting the master cylinder and wheel cylinders, or calipers, in a hydraulic brake system.

brake lining A high-friction material, usually a form of asbestos, attached to the brake shoe by rivets or a bonding process. The lining takes the wear when the brake shoe is pressed against the brake drum, or rotor.

brake shoes In drum brakes, arc-shaped metal pieces lined with a high-friction material (the brake lining) which are forced against the revolving brake drums to produce braking action. In disk brakes, flat metal pieces lined with brake lining which are forced against the rotor face.

brake system A combination of one or more brakes and their operation and control mechanism.

breaker cam See **distributor cam.**

breakerless ignition system See **electronic ignition system.**

breaker points See **contact points.**

breaker-triggered ignition system Any ignition system which uses conventional contact points to time and trigger the system.

breather On engines without emission-control devices, the opening that allows air to circulate through the crankcase and thereby provides crankcase ventilation.

British thermal unit (Btu) A measure of heat quantity. The amount of heat necessary to raise the temperature of 1 pound of liquid water by 1°F.

brush A block of conducting substance, such as carbon, which rests against a rotating ring or commutator to form a continuous electric circuit.

BTDC Abbreviation for "before top dead center;" any position of the piston between bottom dead center and top dead center, on the upward stroke.

Btu See **British thermal unit.**

bulb An indivisible assembly which contains a source of light; normally used in a lamp.

burr A feather edge of metal left on a part being cut with a file or other cutting tool.

bushing A one-piece sleeve placed in a bore to serve as a bearing surface.

butane A type of liquefied petroleum gas that is liquid below 32°F (0°C) at atmospheric pressure.

butterfly valve A pivoted flat plate used to regulate the flow of air, as in a carburetor.

butyl A type of synthetic rubber used in making tire tubes.

bypass A separate passage which permits a liquid, gas, or electric current to take a path other than that normally used.

bypass valve In an oil filter, a valve that opens when the filter has clogged to allow oil to reach the engine. See **solenoid bypass valve.**

C

cables Conductors composed of strands, usually covered with insulation, used for connections between electric devices.

cadmium-tip tester A battery tester with two cadmium tips which are inserted into the electrolyte of adjacent battery cells to determine cell voltage.

calibrate To check or correct the initial setting of a test instrument.

California Classification of engines for vehicles certified by the Environmental Protection Agency for sale in California; see also **49 state.**

caliper A tool that can be set to measure the thickness of a block, the diameter of a shaft, or the bore of a hole (inside caliper). In a disk brake, a housing for pistons and brake shoes, connected to the hydraulic system; holds the brake shoes so that they straddle the disk.

calorie A measure of heat quantity. The amount of heat needed to raise the temperature of 1 g (gram) of water by 1°C.

cam A rotating lobe or eccentric which can be used with a cam follower to change rotary motion to reciprocating motion.

cam angle See **dwell.**

camber The tilt of the top of the wheel from the vertical; when the tilt is outward, the camber is positive. Also, the angle which a front-wheel spindle makes with the horizontal.

cam follower See **valve lifter.**

cam-ground piston A piston that is ground slightly oval in shape. It becomes round as it expands with heat.

camshaft The shaft in the engine with cam lobes used mainly for operating the valves. It is driven by gears, or by sprockets and a toothed belt or chain from the crankshaft.

camshaft gear A gear, driven by the crankshaft, that is mounted on and rotates the camshaft; it is twice as large G21 as the crankshaft gear.

canister A special container in an evaporative control system that contains charcoal to trap vapors from the fuel system.

capacitor See **condenser.**

capacitor-discharge ignition An ignition system which stores its primary energy in a capacitor, and fires the spark plug as the capacitor discharges through the coil; available for automobiles, and standard on some outboard engines and motorcycles.

capacity The ability to perform or to hold.

capillary tube A tube with a small inside diameter. In air conditioners, a capillary tube is used to produce a pressure differential between the condenser and the evaporator.

carbon (C) A black deposit left on engine parts such as pistons, rings, and valves by the combustion of fuel, and which inhibits their action.

carbon canister See **charcoal canister.**

carbon dioxide (CO_2) A colorless, odorless gas which results from complete combustion; usually considered harmless. The gas absorbed from air by plants in photosynthesis; also used to carbonate beverages.

carbon monoxide (CO) A colorless, odorless, tasteless, poisonous gas which results from incomplete combustion. A pollutant contained in engine exhaust gas.

carbon pile A pile, or stack, of carbon disks enclosed in an insulating tube. When the disks are pressed together, the electric resistance of the pile decreases.

carburetion The actions that take place in the carburetor: converting liquid fuel to vapor and mixing it with air to form a combustible mixture.

carburetor The device in an engine fuel system which mixes gasoline with air in correct proportions and delivers this mixture to the intake manifold.

carburetor insulator A spacer, or insulator, used to prevent excess engine heat from reaching the carburetor.

carburetor kickdown Moderate depressing of the accelerator pedal to change the engagement of the choke-fast-idle-speed screw from the high step to a lower step of the cam.

carcinogen A substance or agent that produces or incites cancer. Also, **carcinogenic,** tending to produce or incite cancer.

Cardan universal joint A ball-and-socket type of universal joint.

case hardening The carburizing method used on low-carbon steel or other alloys to make the case or outer layer of the metal harder than its core.

casing The outer part of the tire assembly, made of fabric or cord to which rubber is vulcanized.

caster The tilting of the steering axis forward or backward to provide directional steering stability. Also, the angle which a front-wheel kingpin makes with the vertical.

catalyst A substance that can speed or slow a chemical reaction between substances without itself being consumed by the reaction. In the catalytic converter, platinum and palladium are the active catalysts.

catalytic converter A mufflerlike device in the exhaust system of an engine that converts harmful exhaust gases into harmless gases by promoting a chemical reaction between a catalyst and the pollutants.

cc Abbreviation for **cubic centimeter.**

CCS Abbreviation for **controlled-combustion system.**

CDI See **capacitor-discharge ignition.**

CEC See **combination emission-control system.**

CEC solenoid A two-position electrically operated solenoid used in some transmission-controlled spark systems; either allows or denies distributor vacuum advance, depending on transmission-gear selection. The solenoid plunger, when extended, maintains a predetermined throttle opening.

cell The separate compartments in a battery which contain positive and negative plates suspended in electrolyte. A fully charged cell has a voltage of 2.1 volts; 6-volt batteries have three cells; 12-volt batteries have six cells.

Celsius A thermometer scale (formerly called "centigrade") on which water boils at 100° and freezes at 0°. The formula °C = 5/9 (°F − 32) converts Fahrenheit readings to Celsius readings.

centigrade See **Celsius.**

centimeter (cm) A unit of linear measure in the metric system; 1 centimeter equals approximately 0.39° inches.

centrifugal See **centrifugal force.**

centrifugal advance A rotating-weight mechanism in the distributor that advances and retards ignition timing through the centrifugal force resulting from changes in engine speed.

centrifugal clutch A clutch that uses centrifugal force to apply a higher pressure against the friction disk as the clutch spins faster.

centrifugal filter fan A filter fan mounted on the air-pump drive shaft; used to clean the air entering the air pump.

centrifugal force The force acting on a rotating body which tends to move it outward and away from the center of rotation. The force increases as rotational speed increases.

ceramic A type of material made from various minerals by baking or firing at high temperatures; can be used as an electric insulator, a filter element, or a catalyst substrate in a catalytic converter.

ceramic filter A filter, for instance, for gasoline, that uses porous ceramic as the filter element.

cetane number An indicator of the ignition quality of diesel fuel. A high-cetane fuel ignites more easily (at a lower temperature) than a low-cetane fuel.

change of state Transformation of a substance from solid to liquid, from liquid to vapor, or vice versa.

charcoal canister A container filled with activated charcoal used to trap gasoline vapor from the fuel tank and carburetor while the engine is off; also called "carbon canister."

charge In an air conditioner, a specific amount of refrigerant, by weight. For a battery, the process of restoring chemical energy to a battery by passing an electric current from a battery charger through the battery in the reverse direction.

charging rate The amperage flowing from the alternator or battery charger into the battery.

charging the system The process of adding refrigerant to an air-conditioning system.

chassis The assembly of mechanisms that make up the major operating systems of the vehicle; usually assumed to include everything except the car body.

check To verify that a component, system, or measurement complies with specifications.

check valve A valve that opens to permit the passage of air or fluid in one direction only, or operates to prevent (check) some undesirable action.

chemical instability An undesirable condition caused by the presence of contaminants in a refrigeration system. Refrigerants are stable chemicals, but in contact with contaminants they may break down into harmful chemicals.

chemical reaction The formation of one or more new substances when two or more substances are brought together.

choke In the carburetor, a plate or valve that is closed when starting a cold engine; it restricts or "chokes off" the airflow through the air horn, producing a partial vacuum that causes greater fuel delivery and a richer air-fuel mixture. Operates automatically on most cars. See also **electric-assist choke.**

chrome-plated ring A piston compression ring or oil ring with its cylinder-wall face lightly plated with hard chrome.

CID Abbreviation for **cubic-inch displacement.**

circuit The complete path of an electric current, including the current source. When the path is continuous, the circuit is closed, and current flows. When the path is broken, the circuit is open, and no current flows. Also used to refer to fluid paths, as in refrigerant and hydraulic systems.

circuit breaker An automatic switch, used as a protective device, that opens an electric circuit to prevent damage when it is overheated by excess current flow. One type contains a thermostatic blade that warps to open the circuit when the maximum safe current is exceeded.

clearance The space between two moving parts, or between a moving and a stationary part, such as a journal and a bearing. The bearing clearance is filled with lubricating oil when the mechanism is running.

closed-crankcase ventilation system A system in which the crankcase vapors (blow-by gases) are discharged into the engine intake system and pass through to the engine cylinders rather than being discharged into the air.

clutch A coupling which connects and disconnects a shaft from its drive while the drive mechanism is running. In an automobile power train, the device which engages and disengages the transmission from the engine. In an air-conditioning system, the device which engages and disengages the compressor shaft from its continuously rotating drive-belt pulley.

clutch disk See **friction disk.**

clutch fork In the clutch, a Y-shaped member into which the throw-out bearing is assembled.

clutch gear See **clutch shaft.**

clutch housing A metal housing that surrounds the flywheel and clutch assembly.

clutch pedal A pedal in the driver's compartment that operates the clutch.

clutch safety switch See **neutral-start switch.**

clutch shaft The shaft on which the clutch is assembled, with the gear that drives the countershaft in the transmission at one end. At the clutch-gear end, the shaft has external splines that can be used by a synchronizer drum to lock the clutch shaft to the main shaft for direct drive.

clutch solenoid In automotive air conditioners, a solenoid that operates a clutch on the compressor drive pulley. When the clutch is engaged, the compressor is driven, and cooling takes place.

cm See **centimeter.**

CO See **carbon monoxide.**

CO_2 See **carbon dioxide.**

coasting-richer system An exhaust-emission control system, controlled by a carburetor solenoid valve, which provides fuel enrichment while the vehicle is coasting; prevents popping in the exhaust manifold due to the operation of the air-injection system. Used on Chevrolet LUV light trucks.

coated ring A piston ring with its cylinder-wall face coated with ferrous oxide, soft phosphate, or tin. This thin coating helps new rings seat by retaining oil and reducing scuffing during break-in.

coefficient of expansion The proportional increase in a dimension of an object per degree of temperature rise.

coil In an ignition system, the transformer used to step up the battery voltage (by induction) to the high voltage required to fire the spark plugs.

coil spring A spring made of an elastic metal such as steel, formed into a wire and wound into a coil.

coil-spring clutch A clutch using coil springs to hold the pressure plate against the friction disk.

cold The absence of heat. An object is considered cold to the touch if its temperature is less than body temperature [98.6°F (37°C)].

cold-cranking rate A battery rating; the minimum amperage maintained by a battery for 30 seconds with a minimum voltage of 1.2 volts per cell, checked at a battery temperature of 0°F (−17.8°C) and at −20°F (−28.9°C).

cold-patching A method of repairing a punctured tire or tube by gluing a thin rubber patch over the hole.

cold rate A battery rating; the number of minutes a battery will deliver 300 amp at 0°F (−17.8°C) before the cell voltage drops below 1.0 volt.

cold-start test A prescribed federal test procedure for measuring emissions from a vehicle before the engine is warmed up. The test is made on the vehicle after a 12-hour cold-soak period at 68 to 78°F (20 to 25°C).

cold welding Repairing a crack in metal by drilling a hole through the crack, threading the hole, and screwing in a section of threaded rod to form a seal.

collapsible spare tire A wheel that mounts a special deflated tire. It is furnished with a can of tire-inflation propellant to use when the tire must be inflated and installed.

collapsible steering column An energy-absorbing steering column designed to collapse if the driver is thrown into it by a severe collision.

combination emission-control system An exhaust-emission control system which combines a transmission-controlled spark system and a deceleration throttle-positioning device.

combustion Burning; fire produced by the proper combination of fuel, heat, and oxygen. In the engine, the rapid burning of the air-fuel mixture in the combustion chamber.

combustion chamber The space between the top of the piston at TDC and the cylinder head, in which the air-fuel mixture is burned.

commutation In a dc generator, the effect produced by the commutator and brushes, in which the alternating current developed in the armature windings is changed to direct current.

commutator A series of copper bars at one end of a generator or starting-motor armature, electrically insulated from the armature shaft and insulated from each other by mica. The brushes rub against the bars of the commutator, which form a rotating connector between the armature windings and brushes.

compact spare tire A special high-pressure spare tire, mounted on a narrow 15 × 4 inch wheel, that can be used on cars without a limited-slip differential.

compensating port A small hole in each section of a brake master cylinder which is closed by piston movement so that fluid is trapped ahead of the piston to apply the brakes. When the brake pedal is released, the piston uncovers the compensating port, allowing the trapped fluid to return to the fluid reservoir.

component A part of a whole, assembly, system, or unit, which may be identified and serviced separately. For example, a bulb is a component of the lighting system.

compound vortex-controlled combustion engine A type of stratified-charge engine built by Honda, and known as a "CVCC" engine.

compression Reducing the volume of a gas by squeezing it into a smaller space. Increasing the pressure reduces the volume and increases the density and temperature of the gas.

compression ignition The ignition of fuel solely by the heat generated when air is compressed in the cylinder; the method of ignition in a diesel engine.

compression pressure The pressure in the combustion chamber at the end of the compression stroke.

compression ratio The volume of the cylinder and combustion chamber when the piston is at BDC divided by the volume when the piston is at TDC.

compression ring The top ring or rings on a piston; designed to hold the burning fuel charge above the piston in the combustion chamber and prevent blow-by.

compression stroke The piston movement from BDC to TDC immediately following the intake stroke, during which both the intake valve and the exhaust valve are closed while the air-fuel mixture in the cylinder is compressed.

compression tester An instrument for testing the amount of pressure, or compression, developed in an engine cylinder during cranking.

compressor A pump that is used to increase the pressure of a gas or vapor.

condensate Water that is removed from air. It forms on the exterior surface of the air-conditioner evaporator.

condensation A change of state during which a gas turns to liquid, usually because of temperature or pressure changes. Also, moisture from the air deposited on a cool surface.

condenser In the ingition system, a device that is also called a "capacitor;" connected across the contact points to reduce arcing by providing a storage place for electricity (electrons) as the contact points open. In an air-conditioning system, the radiatorlike heat exchanger in which refrigerant vapor loses heat and returns to the liquid state.

conditioned air Cool, dry, clean air.

conduction The transfer of heat between the closely packed molecules of a substance or between two substances that are touching.

conductor Any material or substance that allows current or heat to flow easily.

connecting rod In the engine, the rod that connects the crank on the crankshaft with the piston. Sometimes called a "con rod."

connecting-rod bearing See **rod bearing.**

connecting-rod cap The part of the connecting-rod assembly that attaches the rod to the crankpin.

constant-current charging A battery-charging method in which an unchanging amount of current is made to flow into the battery.

constant-velocity universal joint Two closely coupled universal joints arranged so that their acceleration-deceleration effects cancel each other out. This results in an output drive-shaft speed that is always identical with the input drive-shaft speed, regardless of the angle of drive.

constant-voltage charging A charging method in which a constant voltage is applied to the battery. The charging current decreases as the battery becomes fully charged.

contact points In an electric system, a set of replaceable stationary and movable points which open and close to make and break an electric circuit, such as in the ignition distributor. The point faces usually are made of tungsten, platinum, or silver.

contaminants Anything other than refrigerant and refrigerant oil in a refrigeration system; includes rust, dirt, moisture, and air.

continuity The uninterrupted flow of electricity through a circuit.

control arm A part of the suspension system designed to control wheel movement precisely.

controlled-combustion system An exhaust-emission control system used by General Motors; improves engine combustion through special settings of the carburetor, distributor, and vacuum advance; by heating the carburetor intake air; and by using a higher engine operating temperature. Also known as the "engine modification system," and used by other manufacturers under other names.

convection The transfer of heat by motion of the heated material. Moving currents of heated liquid or gas are called "convection currents."

coolant The liquid in the cooling system, which is a mixture of about 50 percent antifreeze and 50 percent water used to carry heat out of the engine.

cooling system The system that removes heat from the engine by the forced circulation of coolant, and thereby prevents engine overheating. It includes the water jackets, water pump, radiator, and thermostat.

cord The strands forming the plies in a tire.

core In a radiator, the coolant passages surrounded by fins through which air flows to carry away heat.

cornering wear A type of tire-tread wear caused by turning at excessive speeds.

corrosion Chemical action, usually by an acid, that eats away (decomposes) a metal.

cotter pin A type of fastener, made from soft steel in the form of a split pin, that can be inserted in a drilled hole. The split ends are spread to lock the pin in position.

counterbored ring A piston ring, used as a compression ring, which has a counterbore on its inside diameter to promote cylinder sealing.

countershaft In the transmission, a shaft which is driven by the clutch gear; gears on the countershaft drive gears on the main shaft when the latter are engaged.

counterweight A weight mounted on the crankshaft opposite each crankpin; reduces the vibration and bearing loads due to the inertia of moving parts.

crank Slang for **crankshaft.**

crankcase The part of the engine that surrounds the crankshaft; usually the lower section of the cylinder block.

crankcase breather The opening or tube that allows air to enter and leave the crankcase, thereby providing crankcase ventilation.

crankcase dilution Dilution of the lubricating oil in the oil pan by gasoline; caused by gasoline condensing from the blow-by in a cold engine and seeping down the cylinder walls.

crankcase emissions Pollutants emitted into the atmosphere from any portion of the engine crankcase ventilation or lubricating system.

crankcase ventilation The circulation of air through the crankcase of a running engine to remove water, blow-by, and other vapors; prevents oil dilution, contamination, sludge formation, and pressure buildup.

cranking motor See **starting motor.**

crankpin The part of a crankshaft to which a connecting rod is attached.

crankpin ridging A type of crankpin failure, typified by deep ridges worn into the crankpin bearing surfaces.

crankshaft The main rotating member or shaft of the engine, with cranks to which the connecting rods are attached; converts up-and-down, or reciprocating, motion into circular or rotary motion.

crankshaft gauge A special type of micrometer which can measure crankshaft wear while the crankshaft is in the cylinder block.

crankshaft gear A gear, or sprocket, mounted on the front of the crankshaft; used to drive the camshaft gear, chain, or toothed belt.

crank throw One crankpin with its two webs.

crank web The part of the crankshaft that lies between a crankpin and a main bearing of the crankshaft.

cross-firing Jumping of a high-voltage surge in the ignition secondary circuit to the wrong high-voltage wire, so that the wrong spark plug fires. Usually caused by improper routing of the spark-plug wires, faulty insulation, or a defective distributor cap or rotor.

crossflow radiator A radiator in which the coolant flows horizontally from the inlet tank on one side of the radiator, through the individual coolant passages, to the outlet tank on the opposite side of the radiator.

crowd An acceleration that maintains a constant manifold-vacuum reading. This requires a progressive opening of the throttle as the vehicle speed increases.

CRS Abbreviation for **coasting-richer system.**

cubic centimeter (cu cm or cc) A unit of volume in the metric system; equal to approximately 30 fluid ounces.

cubic-inch displacement The cylinder volume swept out by the pistons of an engine as they move from BDC to TDC, measured in cubic inches.

cu cm See **cubic centimeter.**

curb weight The weight of an empty vehicle without payload or driver but including fuel, coolant, oil, and all items of standard equipment.

current A flow of electrons, measured in amperes.

cut out In a running engine, the temporary complete loss of power, usually at irregular intervals, and worse during heavy acceleration.

cutout relay A device in the charging circuit between the generator and battery; closes when the generator charges the battery, and opens when the generator does not.

CVCC See **compound vortex-controlled combustion.**

cycle Any series of events which repeat continuously. In the engine, the four (or two) piston strokes that together produce power.

cycling-clutch system An air conditioner in which the conditioned-air temperature is controlled by starting and stopping the compressor.

cylinder A circular tubelike opening in an engine cylinder block or casting in which a piston moves up and down.

cylinder block The basic framework of the engine, in and on which the other engine parts are attached. It includes the engine cylinders and the upper part of the crankcase.

cylinder compression tester See **compression tester.**

cylinder head The part of the engine that covers and encloses the cylinders. It contains cooling fins or water jackets, the combustion chambers, and, on I-head engines, the valves.

cylinder hone An expandable rotating tool with abrasive stones turned by an electric motor; used to clean and smooth the inside surface of a cylinder.

cylinder leakage tester A testing device that forces compressed air into the cylinder through the spark-plug hole when the valves are closed and the piston is at TDC on the compression stroke. The percentage of compressed air that leaks out is measured, and the source of the leak accurately pinpoints the defective part.

cylinder liner See **cylinder sleeve.**

cylinder sleeve A replaceable sleeve, or liner, set into the cylinder block to form the cylinder bore.

D

dashpot A device on the carburetor that prevents the throttle valve from closing too suddenly.

DC or dc Abbreviation for **direct current.**

dead axle An axle that supports weight and attached parts but does not turn or deliver power to a wheel or other rotating member.

deceleration A decrease in velocity or speed. Also, allowing the car or engine to coast to idle speed from a higher speed with the accelerator at or near the idle position.

deceleration valve A device used in conjunction with the dual-diaphragm vacuum-advance unit to advance the timing under deceleration conditions.

de-energize The removal of the control from a device to allow it to return to its normal "at rest" position.

deflection rate For a spring, the weight required to compress the spring exactly 1 inch (25.4 mm).

defroster The part of the car heater system designed to melt frost or ice on the windshield; includes the required ducts.

degree Part of a circle; 1 degree is 1/360 of a complete circle.

dehumidify To remove water vapor from the air. In an air conditioner, the air is dehumidified as it passes through the evaporator, since water condenses from the air onto the cool evaporator coils.

dehydrator-filter In an air conditioner, a filter device in the refrigerant line between the condenser and evaporator; removes dirt and moisture from the liquid refrigerant.

Delco Eye A type of battery vent cap that shows a low electrolyte level in the cell without being removed from the battery.

desiccant A drying agent. In an air conditioner, desiccant is placed in the receiver-dehydrator to remove moisture from the refrigerant.

detent A small depression in a shaft, rail, or rod into which a pawl or ball drops when the shaft, rail, or rod is moved; this provides a locking effect.

detergent A chemical added to engine oil; helps keep internal parts of the engine clean by preventing the accumulation of deposits.

detonation Commonly called spark knock or ping. In the combustion chamber, an uncontrolled second explosion (after the spark occurs at the spark plug), with spontaneous combustion of the remaining compressed air-fuel mixture resulting in a pinging noise.

device A mechanism, tool, or other piece of equipment designed to serve a special purpose or perform a special function.

diagnosis A procedure followed in locating the cause of a malfunction. Also, to specifically identify and answer the question, What is wrong?

dial indicator A gauge that has a dial face and a needle to register movement; used to measure variations in dimensions and movements too small to be measured accurately by other means.

diaphragm A thin dividing sheet or partition which separates an area into compartments; used in fuel pumps, modulator valves, vacuum-advance units, and other control devices.

diaphragm spring A spring shaped like a disk with tapering fingers pointed inward, or like a wavy disk (crown type).

diaphragm-spring clutch A clutch in which a diaphragm spring, rather than a coil spring, applies pressure against the friction disk.

dichlorodifluoromethane Refrigerant-12, whose chemical formula is CCl_2F_2.

die A tool for cutting threads on a rod.

die out The condition in which an engine stalls without movement of the accelerator pedal.

diesel cycle An engine operating cycle in which air is compressed, and fuel oil is injected into the compressed air at the end of the compression stroke. The heat produced by the compression ignites the fuel oil, eliminating the need for spark plugs or a separate ignition system.

diesel engine An engine operating on the diesel cycle and burning oil instead of gasoline.

dieseling A condition in which a gasoline spark-ignition engine continues to run after the ignition is off. Caused by carbon deposits or hot spots in the combustion chamber glowing sufficiently to furnish heat for combustion.

differential A gear assembly between axle shafts that permits one wheel to turn at a different speed than the other, while transmitting power from the drive shaft to the wheel axles.

differential case The metal unit that encases the differential side gears and pinion gears, and to which the ring gear is attached.

differential side gears The gears inside the differential case which are internally splined to the axle shafts, and which are driven by the differential pinion gears.

dimmer switch A two-position switch, usually mounted on the car floor; operated by the driver to select the high or low headlight beam.

diode A solid-state electronic device that allows the passage of an electric current in one direction only, used in the alternator to convert alternating current to direct current for charging the battery.

dipstick See **oil-level indicator.**

direct-bonded bearing A bearing formed by pouring liquid babbitt (bearing metal) directly into the bearing housing, and machining the cooled metal to the desired bearing diameter.

direct current Electric current that always flows in the same direction.

directional signal A device on the car that flashes lights to indicate the direction in which the driver intends to turn.

disassemble To take apart.

disc brake See **disk brake.**

discharge In an air conditioner, to depressurize; to crack a valve to allow refrigerant to escape from an air conditioner; to bleed. In a battery, to draw an electric current from the battery.

discharge air Conditioned air leaving the evaporator of an air conditioner.

discharge line In an air conditioner, the hose that connects the compressor outlet and the condenser inlet. High-pressure refrigerant vapor flows through the hose.

discharge pressure In an air conditioner, the pressure of refrigerant being discharged from the compressor; also called the "high pressure."

discharge side In an air conditioner, the portion of the refrigerant system under high pressure; extends from the compressor outlet to the thermostatic expansion valve.

disk In a disk brake, the rotor, or revolving piece of metal, against which brake shoes are pressed to provide braking action.

disk brake A brake in which brake shoes, in a viselike caliper, grip a revolving disk to slow or stop it.

disk runout The amount by which a brake disk wobbles during rotation.

dispersant A chemical added to oil to prevent dirt and impurities from clinging together in lumps that could clog the engine lubricating system.

displacement In an engine, the total volume of air-fuel mixture an engine is theoretically capable of drawing into all cylinders during one operating cycle. Also, the volume swept out by the piston in moving from one end of a stroke to the other.

distributor Any device that distributes. The unit that makes and breaks the ignition primary circuit and distributes the resulting high-voltage surges to the proper spark plug at the correct time.

distributor advance See **centrifugal advance, ignition advance,** and **vacuum advance.**

distributor cam The cam on the top end of the distributor shaft which rotates to open and close the contact points.

distributor cap In the ignition system, an insulated cap for the distributor that has a center terminal (for the coil wire) and a series of terminals (one per cylinder) spaced around the cap in a circular pattern. High-voltage surges from the coil travel through the center terminal and are delivered to the outside terminals by the rotor.

distributorless ignition An electronic ignition system which does not use contact points to time or trigger the system, and does not use a distributor for distribution of the secondary voltage. One type is crankshaft-triggered.

distributor plate The plate in the ignition distributor that is fastened to the distributor housing and does not move.

distributor timing See **ignition timing.**

distributor vacuum-advance control valve See **deceleration valve.**

diverter valve In the air-injection system of exhaust-emission control, a valve that diverts air-pump output into the air cleaner or the atmosphere during deceleration; prevents backfiring and popping in the exhaust system.

DOHC See **double-overhead-camshaft engine.**

double-Cardan joint A near-constant-velocity universal joint which consists of two Cardan universal joints connected by a coupling yoke.

double-overhead-camshaft engine An engine with two camshafts in each cylinder head to actuate the valves; one camshaft operates the intake valves, and the other operates the exhaust valves.

double-reduction differential A differential containing an extra set of gears to provide a second gear reduction.

dowel A metal pin attached to one object which, when inserted into a hole in another object, ensures proper alignment.

downdraft carburetor A carburetor in which the air horn is so arranged that the air flows down through it on its way to the intake manifold.

downflow radiator A radiator in which the coolant enters the radiator at the top, and loses heat as it flows down through passages to the bottom of the radiator.

driveability The general operation of an automobile, usually rated from good to poor; based on characteristics of concern to the average driver, such as smoothness of idle, even acceleration, ease of starting, quick warmup, and tendency to overheat at idle.

drive line The driving connection between the transmission and the differential; made up of one or more drive shafts.

driven disk The friction disk in a clutch.

drive pinion A rotating shaft with a small gear on one end that transmits torque to another gear; used in the differential. Also called the **clutch shaft,** in the transmission.

drive shaft An assembly of one or two universal joints and slip joints connected to a heavy metal tube; used to transmit power from the transmission to the differential. Also called the "propeller shaft."

drop-center wheel The conventional passenger-car wheel, which has a well or drop, in the center for one tire bead to fit into while the other bead is being lifted over the rim flange.

drop light A portable light, with a long electric cord, used in the shop to illuminate the immediate work area.

drum brakes A brake in which curved brake shoes press against the inner circumference of a metal drum to produce the braking action.

drum lathe Special lathe for turning brake drums; some can be used to resurface disk-brake rotors.

dry-charged battery A new battery that has been charged and then stored with the electrolyte removed. Electrolyte must be added to activate the battery at the time of sale.

dry-disk clutch A clutch in which the friction faces of the friction disk are dry, as opposed to a wet-disk clutch, which runs submerged in oil. The conventional type of automobile clutch.

dry friction The friction between two dry solids.

drying agent See **desiccant.**

dry sump A type of engine-lubrication system in which the oil supply is carried in a separate oil tank instead of in the conventional oil pan.

dual-area diaphragm An automatic-transmission shift-control diaphragm which has sources of vacuum from the intake manifold and exhaust-gas recirculation port.

dual-brake system A brake system consisting of two separate hydraulic systems; usually, one operates the front brakes, and the other operates the rear brakes.

dual carburetors Two carburetors mounted on one engine.

dual-diaphragm vacuum advance A vacuum-advance mechanism with two diaphragms; attaches to the engine distributor to control spark timing. One diaphragm provides normal ignition timing advance for starting and acceleration; the other diaphragm retards the spark during the idling and part-throttle operation.

dual-displacement engine An engine that can run on either all its cylinders or, for fuel economy, half its cylinders. For example, a six-cylinder engine that can cut off the flow of air-fuel mixture to three cylinders during idle and part-throttle operation.

dual-point system A system that controls spark timing by electromechanical selection of separate advance and retard distributor points; used on Chevrolet LUV light trucks. Sometimes used to refer to any ignition system which has two sets of contact points in the distributor.

dual quad Performance term for a carburetion setup that uses two four-barrel carburetors.

duct A tube or channel used to convey air or liquid from one point to another. In emission systems, a tube on an air cleaner that has a vacuum motor mounted on it to help regulate the temperature of the carburetor intake air.

durability The quality of being useful for a long period of time and service. Used to indicate the useful life of a catalyst or emission-control system.

duration The length of time which something exists or lasts.

dwell The number of degrees the distributor cam rotates from the time the points close until they open again.

dwell meter A precision electric instrument used to measure the cam angle, or dwell, or the number of degrees the distributor points are closed while the engine is running.

Dyer drive A type of starting-motor drive, used on heavy-duty engines, which provides mechanical meshing of the drive pinion (as in an overrunning clutch) and automatic demeshing (as in a Bendix drive).

dynamic balance The balance of an object when it is in motion (for example, the dynamic balance of a rotating wheel).

dynamometer A device for measuring the power output, or brake horsepower, of an engine. An engine dynamometer measures the power output at the flywheel; a chassis dynamometer measures the power output at the drive wheels.

E

eccentric A disk or offset section (of a shaft, for example) used to convert rotary to reciprocating motion. Sometimes called a **cam.**

eccentric shaft In a Wankel rotary engine, the main shaft, or crankshaft.

ECU See **electronic control unit.**

efficiency The ratio between the power of an effect and the power expended to produce the effect; the ratio between an actual result and the theoretically possible result.

EGR system Abbreviation for **exhaust-gas recirculation system.**

electric-assist choke A choke in which a small electric heating element warms the choke spring, causing it to release more quickly. This reduces exhaust emissions during the start-up of a cold engine.

electric brakes A brake system with an armature-electromagnet combination at each wheel; when the electromagnet is energized, the magnetic attraction between the armature and the electromagnet causes the brake shoes to move against the brake drum.

electric current A movement of electrons through a conductor such as a copper wire; measured in amperes.

electric system In the automobile, the system that electrically cranks the engine for starting; furnishes high-voltage sparks to the engine cylinders to fire the compressed air-fuel charges, lights the lights, and powers the heater motor, radio, and other accessories. Consists, in part, of the starting motor, wiring, battery, alternator, regulator, ignition distributor, and ignition coil.

electrode In a spark plug, the spark jumps between two electrodes. The wire passing through the insulator is the center electrode. The small piece of metal welded to the spark-plug shell (and to which the spark jumps) is the side, or ground, electrode.

electrolyte The mixture of sulfuric acid and water used in lead-acid storage batteries. The acid enters into chemical reaction with active material in the plates to produce voltage and current.

electromagnet A coil of wire, usually wound around an iron core, which produces magnetism as long as an electric current (dc) flows through the coil.

electromagnetic induction The characteristic of a magnetic field that causes an electric current to be created in a conductor as it passes through the field, or when the field builds and collapses around the conductor.

electromechanical A device whose mechanical movement is dependent upon an electric current.

electron A negatively charged particle that circles the nucleus of an atom. The movement of electrons is an electric current.

electronic control unit A solid-state device that receives information from sensors and is programmed to operate various circuits and systems based on that information.

electronic fuel-injection system A system that injects gasoline into a spark-ignition engine, and that includes an electronic control unit to time and meter the fuel flow.

electronic ignition system A transistorized ignition system which does not have mechanical contact points in the distributor, but uses the distributor for distributing the secondary voltage to the spark plugs. Also called a "solid-state ignition system."

electronic spark control A system that controls the vacuum to the distributor, preventing vacuum advance below a selected vehicle speed; generally used by Ford on cars with automatic transmission.

electronics Electrical assemblies, circuits, and systems that use electronic devices such as diodes and transistors.

element A substance that cannot be further divided into a simpler substance. In a battery, the group of unlike positive and negative plates, separated by insulators, that make up each cell.

emission control Any device or modification added onto or designed into a motor vehicle for the purpose of reducing air-polluting emissions.

emission standards Allowable automobile emission levels, set by local, state, and federal legislation.

emitter An engine with measurable exhaust emissions; sometimes preceded by the word "high" or "low" to indicate the degree of emission.

end play As applied to a crankshaft, the distance that the crankshaft can move forward and backward in the cylinder block.

energize To activate; to cause movement or action.

energy The capacity or ability to do work. Usually measured in work units of pound-feet (kilogram-meters), but also expressed in heat-energy units [Btu's (joules)].

engine A machine that converts heat energy into mechanical energy. A device that burns fuel to produce mechanical power; sometimes referred to as a **power plant.**

engine fan See **fan.**

engine speed See **rpm.**

engine tuneup A procedure for inspecting, testing, and adjusting an engine, and replacing any work parts, to restore the engine to its best performance.

engine vacuum gauge See **vacuum gauge.**

Environmental Protection Agency The independent agency of the United States government that sets standards and coordinates activities related to automotive emissions and the environment.

EPA Abbreviation for **Environmental Protection Agency.**

epoxy A plastic compound that can be used to repair some types of cracks in metal.

equalizer line In an air conditioner, a line or connection used specifically for obtaining required operation from certain types of control valves. Very little (if any) refrigeration flows through this line.

ESC Abbreviation for **electronic spark control.**

ethyl See **tetraethyl lead.**

ethylene glycol Chemical name of a widely used type of permanent antifreeze.

evacuate To use a vacuum pump to remove any air and moisture from an air-conditioner refrigerant system; required whenever any component in the refrigerant system has been replaced.

evaporation The transforming of a liquid to its gaseous state.

evaporative control system A system which prevents the escape of gasoline vapors from the fuel tank or carburetor to the atmosphere while the engine is off. The vapors are stored in a charcoal canister or in the engine crankcase until the engine is started.

evaporator The heat exchanger in an air conditioner, in which refrigerant changes from a liquid to a gas (evaporates), taking heat from the surrounding air as it does so.

exhaust emissions Pollutants emitted into the atmosphere through any opening downstream of the exhaust ports of an engine.

exhaust gas The burned and unburned gases that remain (from the air-fuel mixture) after combustion.

exhaust-gas analyzer A device for sensing the amounts of air pollutants in the exhaust gas from an engine. The analyzers used in automotive shops check HC and CO; those used in testing laboratories can also check NO_x.

exhaust-gas recirculation (EGR) system An NO_x control system that recycles a small part of the inert exhaust gas back through the intake manifold at all throttle positions except idle and wide open in order to lower the combustion temperature.

exhaust manifold A device with several passages through which exhaust gases leave the engine combustion chambers and enter the exhaust piping system.

exhaust pipe The pipe connecting the exhaust manifold with the muffler.

exhaust stroke The piston stroke (from BDC to TDC) immediately following the power stroke, during which the exhaust valve opens so that the exhaust gases can escape from the cylinder to the exhaust manifold.

exhaust system The system through which exhaust gases leave the vehicle. Consists of the exhaust manifold, exhaust pipe, muffler, tail pipe, and resonator (if used).

exhaust valve The valve that opens during the exhaust stroke to allow burned gases to flow from the cylinder to the exhaust manifold.

expansion control See **cam-ground piston.**

expansion plug A slightly dished plug that is used to seal core passages in the cylinder block and cylinder head. When driven into place, it is flattened and expanded to fit tightly.

expansion tank A tank at the top of an automobile radiator which provides room for heated coolant to expand and to give off any air that may be trapped in the coolant. Also, a similar device used in some fuel tanks to prevent fuel from spilling out of the tank through expansion.

expansion valve A metering valve or device located between the condenser and evaporator in an air conditioner; controls the amount of refrigerant sprayed into the evaporator.

extreme-pressure lubricant A special lubricant for use in hypoid-gear differentials; needed because of the heavy wiping loads imposed on the gear teeth.

F

fan The bladed device on the front of the engine that rotates to draw cooling air through the radiator or around the engine cylinders; an air blower such as the heater fan or the air-conditioning blower.

fast flushing A method of cleaning the cooling system; uses a special machine to circulate the cleaning solution.

fast-idle cam A mechanism on the carburetor, connected to the automatic choke, that holds the throttle valve slightly open when the engine is cold; causes the engine to idle at a higher rpm as long as the choke is applied.

fatigue failure A type of metal failure resulting from repeated stress which finally alters the character of the metal so that it cracks. In engine bearings, frequently caused by excessive idling, or slow engine idling speed.

feeler gauge Strips of metal ground to an exact thickness, used to measure clearances between parts.

F-head engine An engine with some of the valves in the cylinder head and some in the cylinder block, giving the engine an F-shaped appearance.

field coil A coil, or winding, in a generator or starting motor which produces a magnetic field as current passes through it.

field-frame assembly The round, soft-iron frame in a generator or motor into which the field coils are assembled.

field relay A relay that is part of some alternator charging systems; connects the alternator field to the battery when the engine runs and disconnects it when the engine stops.

field winding See **field coil.**

fifth wheel A coupling device mounted on a tractor and used to connect a semitrailer. It acts as a hinge to allow the tractor and semitrailer to change direction independently.

file A cutting tool with a large number of cutting edges arranged along a surface.

filter A device through which air, gases, or liquids are passed to remove impurities.

fins On a radiator or heat exchanger, thin metal projections over which cooling air flows to remove heat from hot liquid flowing through internal passages. On an air-cooled engine, thin metal projections on the cylinder and head which greatly increase the area of the heat-dissipating surfaces and help cool the engine.

firing line The high-voltage vertical spike, or line, that appears on the oscilloscope pattern of the ignition-system secondary circuit. The firing line shows when the spark plug begins to fire, and the voltage required to fire it.

firing order The order in which the engine cylinders fire, or deliver their power strokes, beginning with No. 1 cylinder.

fixed-caliper disk brake Disk brake using a caliper which is fixed in position and cannot move; the caliper usually has four pistons, two on each side of the disk.

flasher An automatic-reset circuit breaker used in the directional-signal and hazard-warning circuits.

flat-head engine See **L-head engine.**

flat rate Method of determining pay for mechanics and technicians by use of a manual which indicates the time normally required to do each service job.

flat spot Lack of normal acceleration or response to throttle opening; implies no loss of power, but also no increase in power.

float bowl In a carburetor, the reservoir from which gasoline is metered into the passing air, and in which the float is located.

floating-caliper disk brake Disk brake using a caliper mounted through rubber bushings which permit the caliper to float, or move, when the brakes are applied; there is one large piston in the caliper.

float level The float position at which the needle valve closes the fuel inlet to the carburetor to prevent further delivery of fuel.

float system In the carburetor, the system that controls the entry of fuel and the fuel level in the float bowl.

flooded The condition in which the engine cylinders receive "raw" or liquid gasoline, or an air-fuel mixture too rich to burn.

floor jack A small, portable, hydraulically operated lifting device used to raise part of a vehicle from the floor for repair.

fluid Any liquid or gas.

fluid coupling A device in the power train consisting of two rotating members; transmits power from the engine, through a fluid, to the transmission.

flush In an air conditioner, to wash out the refrigerant passages with Refrigerant-12, to remove contaminants. In a brake system, to wash out the hydraulic system and the master and wheel cylinders, or calipers, with clean brake fluid to remove dirt or impurities that have gotten into the system.

flywheel A heavy metal wheel that is attached to the crankshaft and rotates with it; helps smooth out the power surges from the engine power strokes; also serves as part of the clutch and engine cranking system.

flywheel ring gear A gear, fitted around the flywheel, that is engaged by teeth on the starting-motor drive to crank the engine.

fog lamp A light which may be mounted to provide illumination forward of the vehicle; used with the lower-beam headlights to provide road illumination under conditions of rain, snow, dust, or fog.

Folo-Thru drive A type of inertia-starting-motor drive, similar to the Bendix drive, except that it has a locking pin to hold the pinion in mesh until the engine starts.

force Any push or pull exerted on an object; measured in units of weight, such as pounds, ounces, kilograms, or grams.

49 state Classification of engines for vehicles certified by the Environmental Protection Agency for sale in all states except California; see also **California.**

four-barrel carburetor A carburetor with four throttle valves. In effect, two two-barrel carburetors in a single assembly.

four-cycle See **four-stroke cycle.**

four on the floor Slang for a four-speed transmission with the shift lever mounted on the floor of the driving compartment, frequently as part of a center console.

four-speed A manual transmission having four forward gears.

four-stroke cycle The four piston strokes—intake, compression, power, and exhaust—that make up the complete cycle of events in the four-stroke-cycle engine. Also called "four-cycle" and "four-stroke."

421 tester A tester for batteries with a one-piece cover; applies timed discharge-charge cycles to the battery to determine its condition.

four-wheel drive On a vehicle, driving axles at both front and rear, so that all four wheels can be driven.

frame The assembly of metal structural parts and channel sections that supports the car engine and body and is supported by the wheels.

frame gauges Gauges that may be hung from the car frame to check its alignment.

Freon-12 Refrigerant used in automobile air conditioners. Also known as **Refrigerant-12** (R-12).

friction The resistance to motion between two bodies in contact with each other.

friction bearing Bearing in which there is sliding contact between the moving surfaces. Sleeve bearings, such as those used in connecting rods, are friction bearings.

friction disk In the clutch, a flat disk, faced on both sides with friction material and splined to the clutch shaft. It is positioned between the clutch pressure plate and the engine flywheel. Also called the **clutch disk** or **driven disk.**

friction horsepower The power used up by an engine in overcoming its own internal friction; usually increases as engine speed increases.

front-end drive A vehicle having its drive wheels located on the front axle.

front-end geometry The angular relationship between the front wheels, wheel-attaching parts, and car frame. Includes camber, caster, steering-axis inclination, toe, and turning radius.

fuel Any combustible substance. In an automobile engine, the fuel (gasoline) is burned, and the heat of combustion expands the resulting gases, which forces the piston downward and rotates the crankshaft.

fuel decel valve A device which supplies additional air-fuel mixture to the intake manifold during deceleration to control exhaust-gas hydrocarbon emissions.

fuel filter A device located in the fuel line, ahead of the float bowl; removes dirt and other contaminants from fuel passing through.

fuel gauge A gauge that indicates the amount of fuel in the fuel tank.

fuel-injection system A system which delivers fuel under pressure into the combustion chamber, or into the airflow just as it enters each individual cylinder. Replaces the conventional carburetor.

fuel line The pipe or tubes through which fuel flows from the fuel tank to the carburetor.

fuel mixture See **air-fuel mixture.**

fuel nozzle The tube in the carburetor through which gasoline feeds from the float bowl into the passing air. In a fuel-injection system, the tube that delivers the fuel into the compressed air or the passing airstream.

fuel pump The electric or mechanical device in the fuel system which draws gasoline from the fuel tank and forces it to the carburetor.

fuel system In an automobile, the system that delivers the fuel and air to the engine cylinders. Consists of the fuel tank and lines, gauge, fuel pump, and carburetor and intake manifold, or fuel-injection system.

fuel tank The storage tank for fuel on the vehicle.

fuel-vapor recovery system See **vapor recovery system.**

full coil suspension A vehicle suspension system in which each of the four wheels has its own coil spring.

full-floating piston pin A piston pin that is free to turn in the piston bosses and in the connecting rod.

full-floating rear axle An axle which only transmits driving forces to the rear wheels; the weight of the vehicle (including payload) is supported by the axle housing.

full-flow oil filter An oil filter designed so that all the oil from the oil pump flows through it before reaching the bearings.

full throttle Wide-open throttle position, with the accelerator pressed all the way down to the floorboard.

fuse A ribbon of fusible metal, used as a protective device, that burns through and opens an electric circuit to prevent damage when overheated by excess current flow. An open, or "blown," fuse must be replaced after the circuit problem is corrected.

fuse block A boxlike unit that holds the fuses for the various electric circuits in an automobile.

fusible link A type of fuse in which a special wire melts to open the circuit when the current is excessive. An open, or "blown," fusible link must be replaced after the circuit problem is corrected.

fusion Melting; conversion from the solid to the liquid state.

G

gallery A passageway inside a wall or casting. The main oil gallery within the block supplies lubrication to all parts of the engine.

gap The air space between two electrodes, as the spark-plug gap or the contact-point gap.

gas A state in which matter has neither a definite shape nor a definite volume; air is a mixture of several gases. In an automobile, the discharge from the tail pipe is called the **exhaust gas.** Also, gas is a slang expression for the liquid fuel gasoline.

gasifier section That part of a gas-turbine engine which draws in the air, compresses it, mixes it with fuel, and burns the mixture in the combustor.

gasket A layer of material, usually made of cork or metal, or both, placed between two parts to make a tight seal.

gasket cement A liquid adhesive material, or sealer, used to install gaskets; sometimes, a layer of gasket cement is used as the gasket.

gasoline A liquid blend of hydrocarbons obtained from crude oil; used as the fuel in most automobile engines.

gassing Hydrogen gas escaping from a battery; the gas is formed during battery charging.

gas-turbine engine A type of internal-combustion engine in which the shaft is spun by the pressure of combustion gases flowing against curved turbine blades located around the shaft.

gauge pressure A pressure reading on a scale which ignores atmospheric pressure. Thus, the atmospheric pressure of 14.7 psi absolute is equivalent to 0 psi gauge.

gauge set One or more instruments attached to a manifold (a pipe fitted with several outlets for connecting pipes) and used for measuring pressure.

GCW Abbreviation for "gross combination weight," the total weight of a tractor and semitrailer or trailer, including payload, fuel, driver, etc.

gear A toothed wheel that transmits power.

geared speed The theoretical vehicle speed, based on engine rpm, transmission-gear ratio, rear-axle ratio, and tire size.

gear lubricant A type of grease or oil designed especially to lubricate gears.

gear ratio The number of revolutions of a driving gear required to turn a driven gear through one complete revolution. For a pair of gears, the ratio is found by dividing the number of teeth on the driven gear by the number of teeth on the driving gear.

gear-type pump A pump in which a pair of rotating gears mesh to force oil (or some other liquid) from between the teeth to the pump outlet.

gears Mechanical devices that transmit torque from one shaft to another; gears contain teeth that mesh as the gears turn.

gearshift A linkage-type mechanism by which the gears in an automobile transmission are engaged.

generator A device that converts mechanical energy into electric energy; can produce either ac or dc electricity. In automotive usage, a dc generator (now seldom used).

glad hand The air-brake connector between a tractor and its trailer.

glaze The very smooth, mirrorlike finish that develops on engine-cylinder walls.

glaze breaker A tool, rotated by motor, used to remove the mirrorlike finish, or glaze, from engine-cylinder walls.

glow plug A plug-type heater containing a coil of resistance wire that is heated by a low-voltage current to ignite fuel sprayed into the intake manifold; used as a cold-starting aid.

goggles Special glasses worn over the eyes to protect them from flying chips, dirt, dust, and spraying refrigerant.

governor A device that controls, or governs, another device, usually on the basis of speed or load; for example, the governor used in certain automatic transmissions to control gearshifting in relation to car speed.

gradeability Ability of a truck to negotiate a given grade at a specified GCW or GVW.

gram A measurement of mass and weight in the metric system; 1 ounce equals 28.33 grams.

grams per mile Unit of measurement for the amount (weight) of pollutants emitted into the atmosphere with the vehicle exhaust gases. Antipollution laws set maximum limits for each exhaust pollutant in grams per mile.

grease Lubricating oil to which thickening agents have been added.

greasy friction The friction between two solids coated with a thin film of oil.

grinder A machine for removing metal by means of a rotating abrasive wheel or stone.

grinding wheel A wheel made of abrasive material; used for removing metal from objects held against it while it rotates.

grommet A device, usually made of hard rubber or a similar material, used to encircle or support a component. In emission systems, a grommet is located in the valve-cover assembly to support and help seal the PCV valve.

groove The space between two adjacent tread ribs of a tire.

gross torque The maximum turning effort developed by an engine with optimal ignition setting, without allowances for the power absorbed by the engine's fan, alternator, water pump, and exhaust system.

gross vehicle weight The total weight of a vehicle including the body, payload, fuel, driver, etc.

ground The terminal of the battery that is connected to the engine or metal frame of the car. In the United States, the negative terminal is grounded on 12-volt batteries in automotive electrical systems.

ground-return system Common system of electric wiring in which the chassis and frame of a vehicle are used as part of the electric return circuit to the battery or alternator; also known as the "single-wire system."

ground wire On electric tools and shop equipment, a wire that usually is green in color and that should be connected to a suitable ground, thereby protecting the operator or mechanic from electric shock.

growler An electric test instrument for checking starting motors and generator armatures.

Guide-Matic An electronic device that automatically controls the headlights, shifting between upper and lower beams as conditions require.

guide sleeve A tubular sleeve that is put on a connecting-rod bolt when the rod is removed to prevent scratching of the crankpin by the bolt threads.

gulp valve In the air-injection system, a type of antibackfire valve which allows a sudden intake of fresh air through the intake manifold during deceleration; prevents backfiring and popping in the exhaust system.

GVW Abbreviation for **gross vehicle weight**.

H

hacksaw A saw with a thin, removable blade; used to cut metals.

hand jack A small jack that can be carried by hand; usually hydraulically operated, and used to lift a corner of a vehicle.

hard start, cold Excessive cranking times or numerous "false" starts while starting a cold engine.

hard start, hot Excessive cranking times while starting a hot engine.

harmonic balancer See **vibration damper**.

hazard system Also called the "emergency signal system"; a driver-controlled system of flashing front and rear lights used to warn approaching motorists when a car has broken down.

HC Abbreviation for **hydrocarbon.**

head See **cylinder head.**

header Performance term for a special exhaust manifold or exhaust tubes.

head-land ring A compression ring with an L-shaped cross section; used as the top compression ring.

headlights Lights at the front of a vehicle; designed to illuminate the road ahead of the vehicle.

head pressure Pressure at the air-conditioner compressor outlet (the discharge pressure).

heat A form of energy, released by the burning of fuel, in an engine, heat energy is converted to mechanical energy.

heat-control valve In the engine, a thermostatically operated valve in the exhaust manifold; diverts heat to the intake manifold to warm it before the engine reaches normal operating temperature.

heat dam In a piston, a groove cut out to reduce the size of the path through which heat can travel; allows the piston skirt to run cooler.

heated-air system A system in which a thermostatically controlled air cleaner supplies hot air from a stove around the exhaust manifold to the carburetor during warmup; improves cold-engine operation.

heater core A small radiator, mounted under the dash, through which hot coolant circulates. When heat is needed in the passenger compartment, a fan is turned on to circulate air through the hot core. Also, any liquid-to-air heat exchanger.

heat exchanger A device in which heat is transferred from one fluid, across a tube or other solid surface, to another fluid.

heat of compression The temperature rise in a gas (such as air or an air-fuel mixture) as it is compressed.

heat range The operating temperature of a spark plug. Spark plugs are made which operate at different temperatures, depending on the thickness and length of the porcelain insulator.

heat sink A device for absorbing heat from electrical components and transferring it to the air, thereby preventing overheating of heat-sensitive devices, such as diodes and transistors.

HEI See **High-Energy Ignition System.**

helical gear A gear in which the teeth are cut at an angle to the center line of the gear.

Heli-Coil See **threaded insert.**

hemi Performance term for any engine with a hemispherical combustion chamber.

hemispherical combustion chamber A combustion chamber resembling a hemisphere, or one-half of a round ball.

hesitation A lack of response to initial throttle opening, occurring when driving from a standstill or accelerating from any speed.

high altitude Classification of engine certified by the Environmental Protection Agency to comply with federal emissions specifications for vehicles to be used above 4,000 feet (1219 m).

high compression Term used to refer to the increased compression ratios of modern automotive engines as compared to engines built in the past.

high-discharge test A battery test in which the battery is discharged at a high rate while the cell voltages are checked.

High-Energy Ignition System An electronic ignition system without contact points, and with all ignition-system components contained in the distributor. Capable of producing 35,000 volts.

high-load condition Situation in which an air conditioner must operate continuously at maximum capacity to provide the required cooling; for example, at high temperature and high humidity.

high-pressure lines The lines from the air-conditioner compressor outlet to the thermostatic-expansion-valve inlet that carry high-pressure refrigerant. The two longest high-pressure lines are the discharge and liquid lines.

high-pressure vapor line Same as **discharge line.**

high side Same as **discharge side.**

high-side pressure Same as **discharge pressure.**

high-speed system In the carburetor, the system that supplies fuel to the engine at speeds above about 25 mph (40 km/h). Also called the "main metering system."

high-voltage cables The secondary (or spark-plug) cables or wires that carry high voltage from the ignition coil to the spark plugs.

hone An abrasive stone that is rotated in a bore or bushing to remove material.

hood The part of the car body that fits over and protects the engine.

horn An electric noise-making device on a vehicle; used for signaling.

horn relay A relay connected between the battery and the horns. When the horn button is pressed, the relay is energized; it then connects the horns to the battery.

horsepower A measure of mechanical power, or the rate at which work is done. 1 horsepower equals 33,000 ft-lb (foot-pounds) of work per minute; it is the power necessary to raise 33,000 pounds a distance of 1 foot in 1 minute.

H_2O Chemical symbol for hydrogen oxide; commonly known as water.

Hotchkiss drive The type of rear suspension in which leaf springs absorb the rear-axle-housing torque.

hot-idle compensator A thermostatically controlled carburetor valve that opens whenever inlet air temperatures are high. Allows additional air to discharge below the throttle plates at engine idle to improve idle stability and prevent overly rich air-fuel mixtures.

hot patching A method of repairing a tire or tube by using heat to vulcanize a patch onto the damaged surface.

hot soak A condition that may arise when an engine is stopped for a prolonged period after a hard, hot run. Heat transferred from the engine evaporates fuel out of the carburetor, so that the carburetor needs priming before the engine will start and run smoothly. A longer cranking period is required.

hot tank See **boil tank.**

hub The center part of a wheel.

humidity A measure of the amount of water vapor in the air.

hydraulic brakes A brake system that uses hydraulic pressure to force the brake shoes against the brake drums, or rotors, as the brake pedal is depressed.

hydraulic clutch A clutch that is actuated by hydraulic pressure; used in heavy-duty equipment, and where the engine is some distance from the driver's compartment so that it would be difficult to use mechanical linkages.

hydraulic lifter A valve lifter that uses oil pressure from the engine lubricating system to keep it in constant contact with the cam lobe and with the valve stem, push rod, or rocker arm. As the hydraulic lifter automatically adjusts to any variation in valve stem length, valve noise is reduced.

hydraulic press A piece of shop equipment that develops a heavy force by use of a hydraulic piston-and-jack assembly.

hydraulic pressure Pressure exerted through the medium of a liquid.

hydraulics The use of a liquid under pressure to transfer force or motion, or to increase an applied force.

hydraulic valve A valve in a hydraulic system that operates on, or controls, the hydraulic pressure in the system. Also, any valve that is operated or controlled by hydraulic pressure.

hydraulic valve lifter See **hydraulic lifter.**

hydrocarbon (HC) A compound containing only carbon and hydrogen atoms, usually derived from fossil fuels such as petroleum, natural gas, and coal; an agent in the formation of photochemical smog. Gasoline is a blend of liquid hydrocarbons refined from crude oil.

hydrocarbon reactivity A measure of the smog-forming potential of a hydrocarbon.

hydrogen (H) A colorless, odorless, highly flammable gas whose combustion produces water; the simplest and lightest element.

hydrometer A float device used to measure specific gravity. In automotive servicing, a hydrometer is used to measure the specific gravity of battery electrolytes in order to determine the battery's state of charge, and to measure the specific gravity of coolant in order to determine its freezing temperature.

hypoid gear A type of gear used in the differential (drive pinion and ring gear); cut in a spiral form to allow the pinion to be set below the center line of the ring gear, so that the car floor can be designed lower.

I

IC See **internal combustion engine.**

idle Engine speed when the accelerator pedal is fully released, and there is no load on the engine.

idle limiter A device that controls the maximum richness of the idle air-fuel mixture in the carburetor; also aids in preventing overly rich idle adjustments. Limiters are of two types: the external plastic-cap type, installed on the head of the idle-mixture screw, and the internal-needle type, located in the idle passages of the carburetor.

idle limiter cap A plastic cap placed over the head of the idle-mixture adjustment screw to limit its travel and prevent the idle mixture from being set too rich.

idle mixture The air-fuel mixture supplied to the engine during idling.

idle-mixture screw The adjustment screw (on some carburetors) that can be moved in or out to lean or enrich the idle mixture.

idle port The opening into the throttle body through which the idle system in the carburetor discharges fuel.

idler arm In the steering system, a link that supports the tie rod and transmits steering motion to both wheels through the tie-rod ends.

idle speed The speed, or rpm, at which the engine runs without load when the accelerator pedal is released.

idle-stop solenoid An electrically operated two-position plunger used to provide a predetermined throttle setting at idle.

idle system In the carburetor, the passages through which fuel is fed when the engine is idling.

idle vent An opening from an enclosed chamber through which air can pass under idle conditions.

ignition The action of the spark in starting the burning of the compressed air-fuel mixture in the combustion chamber of a gasoline engine. In a diesel engine, the start of the burning of fuel after its temperature has been raised by the heat of compression.

ignition advance The moving forward, in time, of the ignition spark relative to the piston position. TDC or 1° ATDC is considered advanced as compared to 2° ATDC.

ignition coil The ignition-system component that acts as a transformer to step up (increase) the battery voltage to many thousands of volts; the high-voltage surge from the coil is transmitted to the spark plug to ignite the compressed air-fuel mixture.

ignition distributor The ignition-system component that closes and opens the primary circuit to the ignition coil at the proper times and distributes the resulting high-voltage surges from the ignition coil to the proper spark plugs.

ignition lag In a diesel engine, the delay in time between the injection of fuel and the start of combustion.

ignition reserve Difference between the minimum available and maximum required voltages. An adequate ignition reserve is important if an engine is to be reasonably free from troubles caused by moisture or dirt losses, leaky secondary leads, and fouled spark plugs.

ignition resistor A resistance connected into the ignition primary circuit to reduce the battery voltage to the coil during engine operation.

ignition retard The moving back, in time, of the ignition spark relative to the piston position. TDC or 1° BTDC is considered retarded as compared to 2° BTDC.

ignition switch The switch in the ignition system (usually operated with a key) that opens and closes the ignition-coil primary circuit. May also be used to open and close other vehicle electric circuits.

ignition system In the engine, the system that furnishes high-voltage sparks to the cylinders to fire the compressed air-fuel mixture. Consists of the battery, ignition coil, ignition distributor, ignition switch, wiring, and spark plugs.

ignition temperature The lowest temperature at which a fuel will begin to burn.

ignition timing The delivery of the spark from the coil to the spark plug at the proper time for the power stroke, relative to the piston position.

I-head engine An overhead-valve (OHV) engine; an engine with the valves in the cylinder head.

ihp Abbreviation for **indicated horsepower.**

IMCO Abbreviation for "Improved Combustion System."

impact wrench An air-powered or electrically driven hand-held tool that rapidly turns nuts and bolts using a series of sharp, fast blows, or impacts.

impeller A rotating finned disk; used in centrifugal pumps, such as water pumps, and in torque converters.

Improved Combustion System An exhaust-emission control system used by Ford and composed mainly of carburetor and distributor modifications. See also **controlled-combustion systems.**

impulse A wave of energy resulting in a physical activity.

included angle In the front-suspension system, camber angle plus steering-axis inclination angle.

independent front suspension The conventional front-suspension system in which each front wheel has its own spring.

indicated horsepower The power produced within the engine cylinders before any friction loss is deducted.

indicator A device used to make some condition known by use of a light or a dial and pointer; for example, the temperature indicator or oil-pressure indicator.

induction The action of producing a voltage in a conductor or coil by moving the conductor or coil through a magnetic field, or by moving the field past the conductor or coil.

inductive-type semiconductor ignition system An ignition system in which the primary energy is stored in an inductor or coil. This is the type now used in Chrysler, Ford, and General Motors HEI systems.

inertia Property of an object that causes it to resist any change in its speed or the direction of its travel.

infrared analyzer A nondispersive test instrument used to measure very small quantities of pollutants in exhaust gas. See **exhaust-gas analyzer.**

injector The tube or nozzle through which fuel is injected into the intake airstream or the combustion chamber. Also, a performance term used for an engine equipped with fuel injection.

in-line engine An engine in which all the cylinders are located in a single row or line.

in-line steering gear A type of integral power steering; uses a recirculating-ball steering gear to which are added a control valve and an actuating piston.

inner tube See **tire tube.**

inside micrometer A precision tool used to measure the inside diameter of a hole.

inspect To examine a part or system for surface condition or function to answer the question, "Is something wrong?"

install To set up for use on a vehicle any part, accessory, option, or kit.

insulated-return system System of vehicle electrical wiring in which a separate insulated wire is used to provide the electric return circuit to the battery or alternator; also known as the "two-wire system."

insulation Material that stops the travel of electricity (electric insulation) or heat (heat insulation).

insulator A poor conductor of electricity or heat.

intake manifold A device with several passages through which the air-fuel mixture flows from the carburetor to the ports in the cylinder head or cylinder block.

intake stroke The piston stroke from TDC to BDC immediately following the exhaust stroke, during which the intake valve opens, and the cylinder fills with air-fuel mixture from the intake manifold.

intake valve The valve that opens during the intake stroke to allow the air-fuel mixture to enter the cylinder from the intake manifold.

integral Built into, as part of the whole.

interaxle differential A two-position differential located between the two driving axles of a tandem axle. In the unlocked position it divides the power unevenly between two axles and permits one axle to turn faster than the other. In the locked position the power is divided approximately evenly between the two axles.

interchangeability The manufacture of similar parts to close tolerances so that any one of them can be substituted for another in a device, and the part will fit and operate properly; the basis of mass production.

internal-combustion engine An engine in which the fuel is burned inside the engine itself rather than in a separate device (as in a steam engine).

internal gear A gear with teeth pointing inward, toward the hollow center of the gear.

J

jack stand See **safety stand.**

jet A calibrated passage in the carburetor through which fuel flows.

journal The part of a rotating shaft which turns in a bearing.

K

Kettering ignition system An inductive ignition system commonly used for automobile engines; employs an induction coil, breaker contacts (points), a capacitor (condenser), and a power supply such as a battery. Also called the "breaker-point ignition system."

key A wedgelike metal piece, usually rectangular or semicircular, inserted in grooves to transmit torque while holding two parts in the same relative position. Also, the small strip of metal with coded peaks and grooves used to operate a lock, such as that for the ignition switch.

kg/cm² Abbreviation for kilograms per square centimeter, a metric engineering term for the measurement of pressure; 1 kilogram per square centimeter equals 4.22 pounds per square inch.

kickdown In automatic transmissions, a system that produces a downshift when the accelerator is pushed down to the floorboard.

kilogram (kg) In the metric system, a unit of weight and mass; approximately equal to 2.2 pounds.

kilometer (km) In the metric system, a unit of linear measure; equal to 0.621 miles.

kilowatt (kW) 1,000 watts; a unit of power, equal to about 1.34 horsepower.

kinetic energy The energy of motion; the energy stored in a moving body through its momentum; for example, the kinetic energy stored in a rotating flywheel.

kingpin In older cars and trucks, the steel pin on which the steering knuckle pivots; attaches the steering knuckle to the knuckle support or axle.

kingpin inclination Inward tilt of the kingpin from the vertical. See **steering-axis inclination.**

knock A heavy metallic engine sound which varies with engine speed; usually caused by a loose or worn bearing. Name also used for detonation, pinging, and spark knock. See **detonation.**

knuckle A steering knuckle; a front-suspension part that acts as a hinge to support a front wheel and permit it to be turned to steer the car. The knuckle pivots on ball joints, or, in earlier cars and trucks, on kingpins.

knurl A series of ridges formed on the outer surfaces of a piston or on the inner surface of a valve guide by a wheel which forces metal above the surface while making indentations below the surface.

kPa Abbreviation for kilopascals, the metric measurement of pressure; 1 kilopascal equals 0.145 pounds per square inch.

kW Abbreviation for **kilowatt.**

L

laminated Made up of several thin sheets or layers.

lamp A divisible assembly that provides light; contains a bulb or other light source and sometimes a lens and reflector.

landing gear Two small wheels at the forward end of a semitrailer; used to support the trailer when it is detached from the tractor.

lapping A method of seating engine valves in which the valve is turned back and forth on the seat; no longer recommended by car manufacturers.

lash The amount of free motion in a gear train, between gears, or in a mechanical assembly, such as the lash in a valve train.

latent heat "Hidden" heat required to change the state of a substance without changing its temperature. Latent heat cannot be felt or measured with a thermometer.

lead A cable or conductor to carry electric current (pronounced "leed"). A heavy metal; used in lead-acid storage batteries.

leaded gasoline Gasoline to which small amounts of tetraethyl lead are added to improve engine performance and reduce detonation.

lead sulfate A hard, insoluble layer that slowly forms on the plates of a discharging battery and which may be reduced only by slow charging.

leaf spring A spring made up of a single flat steel plate, or several plates of graduated lengths assembled one on top of another; used on vehicles to absorb road shocks by bending or flexing.

leak detector Any device used to locate an opening where refrigerant may escape. Common types are flame, electronic, dye, and soap bubbles.

lean mixture An air-fuel mixture that has a relatively high proportion of air and a relatively low proportion of fuel. An air-fuel ratio of 16:1 indicates a lean mixture, compared to an air-fuel ratio of 13:1.

L-head engine An engine with its valves located in the cylinder block.

lift See **car lift.**

lifter See **valve lifter.**

light A gas-filled bulb enclosing a wire that glows brightly when an electric current passes through it; a lamp. Also, any visible radiant energy.

light-duty vehicle Any motor vehicle manufactured primarily for transporting persons or property and having a gross vehicle weight of 6,000 pounds (2,727.6 kg) or less.

limited-slip differential A differential designed so that when one wheel is slipping, a major portion of the drive torque is supplied to the wheel with the better traction; also called a "nonslip differential."

linear measurement A measurement taken in a straight line; for example, the measurement of crankshaft end play.

line boring Using a special boring machine, centered on the original center of the cylinder-block main bearing bores, to rebore the crankcase into alignment.

lines of force See **magnetic lines of force.**

lining See **brake lining.**

linkage An assembly of rods, or links, used to transmit motion.

linkage-type power steering A type of power steering in which the power-steering units (power cylinder and valve) are part of the steering linkage; frequently a bolt-on type of system.

liquefied petroleum gas A hydrocarbon suitable for use as an engine fuel, obtained from petroleum and natural gas; it is a vapor at atmospheric pressure but becomes a liquid under sufficient pressure. Butane and propane are the liquefied gases most frequently used in automotive engines.

liquid-cooled engine An engine that is cooled by the circulation of liquid coolant around the cylinders.

liquid line In an air conditioner, a hose that connects the receiver-dehydrator outlet and the thermostatic-expansion-valve inlet. High-pressure liquid refrigerant flows through the line.

liter (L) In the metric system, a measure of volume; approximately equal to 0.26 gallons (U.S.), or about 61 cubic inches

(33.8 fluid ounces, or 1 quart 1.8 ounces). Used as a metric measure of engine-cylinder displacement.

live axle An axle that drives wheels which are rigidly attached to it.

loading An overrich air-fuel mixture that causes hard starting or rough engine operation and the emission of black smoke from the tail pipe.

load test A starting-motor test in which the current draw is measured under normal cranking load.

lobe A projecting part; for example, the rotor lobe or the cam lobe.

locknut A second nut turned down on a holding nut to prevent loosening.

lockwasher A type of washer which, when placed under the head of a bolt or nut, prevents the bolt or nut from working loose.

lower beam A headlight beam intended to illuminate the road ahead of a vehicle when it meets or follows another vehicle.

low-lead fuel Gasoline which is low in tetraethyl lead, containing not more than 0.5 g per gallon.

low-pressure line Same as **suction line.**

low-pressure vapor line Same as **suction line.**

low side Same as **suction side.**

low-speed system The system in the carburetor that supplies fuel to the air passing through during low-speed, part-throttle operation.

LPG Abbreviation for **liquefied petroleum gas.**

lubricant Any material, usually a petroleum product such as grease or oil, that is placed between two moving parts to reduce friction.

lubricating system The system in the engine that supplies engine parts with lubricating oil to prevent contact between any two moving metal surfaces.

lugging Low-speed, full-throttle engine operation in which the engine is heavily loaded and overworked; usually caused by failure of the driver to shift to a lower gear when necessary.

M

machining The process of using a machine to remove metal from a metal part.

Magna-Flux A process in which an electromagnet and a special magnetic powder are used to detect surface and subsurface cracks in iron and steel, which otherwise might not be seen.

magnetic Having the ability to attract iron. This ability may be permanent, or it may depend on a current flow, as in an electromagnet.

magnetic clutch A magnetically operated clutch used to engage and disengage the air-conditioner compressor.

magnetic field The area, or field, of influence of a magnet, within which it will exhibit magnetic properties; extends from the north pole of the magnet to its south pole. The strength of the field of an electromagnet increases with the number of turns of wire around the iron core and the current flow through the wire.

magnetic lines of force The imaginary lines by which a magnetic field may be visualized.

magnetic pole The point where magnetic lines of force enter or leave a magnet.

magnetic switch A switch with a winding (a coil of wire); when the winding is energized, the switch is moved to open or close a circuit.

magnetism The ability, either natural or produced by a flow of electric current, to attract iron.

magneto An engine-drive device that generates its own primary current, transforms that current into high-voltage surges, and delivers them to the proper spark plugs.

mag wheel A magnesium wheel assembly; also used to refer to any chromed, aluminum-offset, or wide-rim wheel of spoke design.

main bearings In the engine, the bearings that support the crankshaft.

main jet The fuel nozzle, or jet, in the carburetor that supplies fuel when the throttle is partially to fully open.

make A distinctive name applied to a group of vehicles produced by one manufacturer; may be further subdivided into carlines, body types, etc.

malfunction Improper or incorrect operation.

manifold A device with several inlet or outlet passageways through which a gas or liquid is gathered or distributed. See **exhaust manifold, intake manifold,** and **manifold gauge set.**

manifold gauge set A high-pressure and a low-pressure gauge mounted together as a set, used for checking pressures in the air-conditioning system.

manifold heat control See **heat-control valve.**

manifold vacuum The vacuum in the intake manifold that develops as a result of the vacuum in the cylinders during their intake strokes.

manual low Position of the units in an automatic transmission when the driver moves the shift lever to the low or first-gear position on the quadrant.

manufacturer Any person, firm, or corporation engaged in the production or assembly of motor vehicles or other products.

mass production The manufacture of interchangeable parts and similar products in large quantities.

master cylinder The liquid-filled cylinder in the hydraulic brake system or clutch, where hydraulic pressure is developed when the driver depresses a foot pedal.

matter Anything that has weight and occupies space.

measuring The act of determining the size, capacity, or quantity of an object.

mechanical efficiency In an engine, the ratio between brake horsepower and indicated horsepower.

mechanism A system of interrelated parts that make up a working assembly.

member Any essential part of a machine or assembly.

meshing The mating, or engaging, of the teeth of two gears.

meter (m) A unit of linear measure in the metric system, equal to 39.37 inches. Also, the name given to any test instrument that measures a property of a substance passing through it, as an ammeter measures electric current. Also, any device that measures and controls the flow of a substance passing through it, as a carburetor jet meters fuel flow.

metering rod and jet A device consisting of a small, movable, cone-shaped rod and a jet; increases or decreases fuel flow according to engine throttle opening, engine load, or a combination of both.

metering valve A valve in the disk-brake system which prevents hydraulic pressure to the front brakes until after the rear brakes are applied, and thereby helping to prevent rear-end skidding.

mica An insulating material used to separate the copper bars of commutators.

micrometer A precision measuring device used to measure small bores, diameters, and thicknesses. Also called a **mike.**

mike Slang term for **micrometer.**

millimeter (mm) In the metric system, a unit of linear measure, approximately equal to 0.039 inches.

millisecond One-thousandth of a second; 1,000 milliseconds equal 1 second.

MISAR Microprocessed Sensing and Automatic Regulation; a high-energy ignition system in which the centrifugal advance and vacuum advance units are replaced with sensors and an electronic control unit.

misfire In the engine, a failure to ignite the air-fuel mixture in one or more cylinders without stalling; may be intermittent or continuous.

miss See **misfire.**

mm See **millimeter.**

mode Term used to designate a particular set of operating characteristics.

model year The production period for new motor vehicles or new engines, designated by the calendar year in which the period ends.

modification An alteration; a change from the original.

modulator A pressure-regulated governing device; used, for example, in automatic transmissions.

moisture Humidity, dampness, wetness, or very small drops of water.

mold A hollow form into which molten metal is poured and allowed to harden.

molecule The smallest particle into which a substance can be divided and still retain the properties of that substance.

MON Abbreviation for **motor octane number.**

monolithic Made as a single unit. In catalytic-converter construction, a substrate or supporting structure for the catalyst, which is made as a single unit (usually in the shape of a honeycomb), is monolithic; however, the coated-bead or pellet-type catalytic converter is not.

monolithic timing Making accurate spark-timing adjustments with an electronic timing device which can be used while the engine is running.

motor A device that converts electric energy into mechanical energy; for example, the starting motor.

Motor Octane Number (MON) Laboratory octane rating of a fuel established on single-cylinder, variable-compression-ratio engines.

motor vehicle A vehicle propelled by a means other than muscle power, usually mounted on rubber tires, which does not run on rails or tracks.

mph Abbreviation for miles per hour, a measure of speed.

muffler In the engine exhaust system, a device through which the exhaust gases must pass and which reduces the exhaust noise. In an air-conditioning system, a device to minimize pumping sounds from the compressor.

multiple-disk clutch A clutch with more than one friction disk; usually there are several driving disks and several driven disks, alternately placed.

multiple-displacement engine An engine that can run either on all its cylinders or, for fuel economy, on various numbers of cylinders. For example, a six-cylinder engine that can cut off the flow of air-fuel mixture to three cylinders during idle, and then operate on four, five, or six cylinders as the load and power demands increase.

multiple-viscosity oil An engine oil which has a low viscosity when cold for easier cranking and a higher viscosity when hot to provide adequate engine lubrication.

mushroomed valve stem A valve stem that has worn so that the tip, or butt end, has spread (mushroomed), and metal is hanging over the valve guide. The valve cannot be removed from the valve guide until the mushroomed metal is removed.

mutual induction The condition in which a voltage is induced in one coil by a changing magnetic field caused by a changing current in another coil. The magnitude of the induced voltage depends on the number of turns in the two coils.

N

NASCAR Abbreviation for National Association for Stock Car Auto Racing.

neck A portion of a shaft that has a smaller diameter than the rest of the shaft.

needle bearing An antifriction bearing of the roller type, in which the rollers are very small in diameter (needle-sized).

needle valve A small, tapered, needle-pointed valve which can move into or out of a valve seat to close or open the passage through the seat. Used to control the carburetor float-bowl fuel level.

negative One of the two poles of a magnet, or one of the two terminals of an electric device.

negative terminal The terminal from which electrons flow in a complete electric circuit. On a battery, the negative terminal can be identified as the battery post with the smaller diameter; the minus sign (−) is also used to identify the negative terminal.

neoprene A synthetic rubber that is not affected by the various chemicals that are harmful to natural rubber.

net torque The turning effort developed by an engine with optimum ignition setting after allowances for the power absorbed by the engine's fan, alternator, water pump, and exhaust system.

neutral In a transmission, the setting in which all gears are disengaged, and the output shaft is disconnected from the drive wheels.

neutral-start switch A switch wired into the ignition switch to prevent engine cranking unless the transmission shift lever is in NEUTRAL, or the clutch pedal is depressed.

neutron A particle in the nucleus of an atom; weighs about the same as a proton, but has no electric charge.

NHTSA Abbreviation for National Highway Traffic Safety Administration.

nitro Performance term for nitromethane, a fuel additive used to obtain greater power from a racing engine.

nitrogen (N) A colorless, tasteless, odorless gas that constitutes 78 percent of the atmosphere by volume and is a part of all living things.

nitrogen oxides (NO_x) Any chemical compound of nitrogen and oxygen. Nitrogen oxides result from high temperature and pressure in the combustion chambers of automobile engines and other power plants during the combustion process. When combined with hydrocarbons in the presence of sunlight, nitrogen oxides form smog. A basic air pollutant; automotive exhaust-emission levels of nitrogen oxides are controlled by law.

no start Engine will not start.

noble metals Metals (such as gold, silver, platinum, and palladium) which do not readily oxidize or enter into other chemical reactions, but do promote reactions between other substances. Platinum and palladium are used as catalysts in catalytic converters.

no-load test A starting-motor test in which the starting motor is operated without load, and the current draw and armature speed at specified voltages are noted.

nonconductor Same as **insulator.**

nonleaded gasoline See **unleaded gasoline.**

nonslip differential See **limited-slip differential.**

north pole The pole from which the lines of force leave a magnet.

NO_x control system Any device or system used to reduce the amount of NO_x produced by an engine.

nozzle The opening, or jet, through which fuel passes when it is discharged into the carburetor venturi.

nucleus The central part of an atom; it has a positive charge (due to the protons).

nut A removable fastener used with a bolt to lock pieces together; made by threading a hole through the center of a piece of metal which has been shaped to a standard size.

O

octane number The number used to indicate the octane rating of a gasoline.

octane rating A measure of the antiknock properties of a gasoline. The higher the octane rating, the more resistant the gasoline is to spark knock or detonation.

octane requirement The minimum-octane-number fuel required to enable a vehicle to operate without knocking.

odometer The meter that indicates the total distance a vehicle has traveled, in miles or kilometers; usually located in the speedometer.

OEM Abbreviation for **original-equipment manufacturer.**

OHC See **overhead-camshaft engine.**

ohm A measurement for the resistance to flow of electricity in a circuit.

ohmmeter An instrument used to measure the resistance (in ohms) in an electrical device or circuit.

OHV See **overhead-valve engine.**

oil A liquid lubricant made from crude oil and used to provide lubrication between moving parts. In a diesel engine, oil is used for fuel.

oil bleed line In an air conditioner, a passageway that ensures positive oil return to the compressor at high compressor speeds and under low-charge conditions.

oil-control ring See **oil ring.**

oil cooler A small radiator that lowers the temperature of oil flowing through it.

oil dilution Thinning of oil in the crankcase; caused by liquid gasoline leaking past the piston rings from the combustion chamber.

oil filter A filter which removes impurities from the engine oil passing through it.

oil-injection cylinder A cylinder with which a measured quantity of refrigerant oil is added to an air-conditioning system or component.

oil-level indicator The indicator that is removed and inspected to check the level of oil in the crankcase of an engine or compressor. Usually called the **dipstick.**

oil pan The detachable thin steel cover bolted to the crankcase, which encloses the crankcase and acts as an oil reservoir.

oil-pressure indicator A gauge that indicates to the driver the oil pressure in the engine lubricating system.

oil pump In the lubricating system, the device that delivers oil from the oil pan to the moving engine parts.

oil pumping Leakage of oil past the piston rings and into the combustion chamber; usually the result of defective rings or worn cylinder walls.

oil ring The lower ring or rings on a piston. Designed to scrape oil from the cylinder wall, they allow the oil to pass through the ring and holes or slots in the piston groove and return to the oil pan. Also called an **oil-control ring.**

oil seal A seal placed around a rotating shaft or other moving part to prevent leakage of oil.

oil-seal-and-shield Two devices used to control oil leakage past the valve stem and guide, and into the ports or the combustion chamber of an engine.

oil separator A device for separating oil from air or from another liquid. Used with some engine-crankcase emission-control systems.

oil strainer A wire-mesh screen placed at the inlet end of the oil-pump pickup tube; prevents dirt and other large particles from entering the oil pump.

one-way clutch See **sprag clutch.**

one-wire system On automobiles, use of the car body, engine, and frame as a path for the grounded side of the electric circuits; eliminates the need for a second wire as a return path to the battery or alternator.

open circuit In an electric circuit, a break, or opening, which prevents the passage of current.

open system A crankcase emission-control system which draws air through the oil-filter cap, and does not include a tube from the crankcase to the air cleaner.

operational test Same as **performance test.**

orifice A small calibrated hole in a line carrying a liquid or gas.

orifice spark-advance control A system used on some engines to aid in the control of nitrogen oxides. Consists of a valve which delays the change in vacuum to the distributor vacuum-advance unit between idle and part-throttle.

O ring A type of sealing ring, made of a special rubberlike material; in use, the O ring is compressed into a groove to provide the sealing action.

OSAC Abbreviation for **orifice spark-advance control.**

oscillating Moving back and forth, as a swinging pendulum.

oscilloscope A high-speed voltmeter which visually displays voltage variations on a television-type picture tube. Widely used to check engine ignition systems; can also be used to check charging systems and electronic fuel-injection systems.

Otto cycle The cycle of events in a four-stroke-cycle engine. Named for the inventor, Dr. Nikolaus Otto.

output shaft The main shaft of the transmission, the shaft that delivers torque from the transmission to the drive shaft.

overcenter spring A spring used in some clutch linkages to reduce the foot pressure required to depress the clutch pedal.

overcharging Continued charging of a battery after it has reached the charged condition. This action damages the battery and shortens its life.

overdrive A device or transmission gear arrangement which causes the drive shaft to overdrive or rotate faster than the engine crankshaft.

overflow Spilling of the excess of a substance; also, to run or spill over the sides of a container, usually because of overfilling.

overflow tank See **expansion tank.**

overhaul To completely disassemble a unit, clean and inspect all parts, reassemble it with the original or new parts, and make all adjustments necessary for proper operation.

overhead-camshaft (OHC) engine An engine in which the camshaft is mounted over the cylinder head instead of inside the cylinder block.

overhead-valve (OHV) engine An engine in which the valves are mounted in the cylinder head above the combustion chamber, instead of in the cylinder block; in this type of engine, the camshaft is usually mounted in the cylinder block, and the valves are actuated by pushrods.

overheat To heat excessively; also, to become excessively hot.

overrunning clutch drive A type of clutch drive which transmits rotary motion in one direction only; when rotary motion attempts to pass through in the other direction, the driving member overruns and does not transmit the motion to the other member. Widely used as the drive mechanism for starting motors.

oversquare Term applied to an automotive engine in which the bore is larger than the stroke.

oversteer A built-in characteristic of certain types of rear-suspension systems; causes the rear wheels to turn toward the outside of a turn.

oxidation Burning or combustion; the combining of a material with oxygen; rusting is slow oxidation, and combustion is rapid oxidation.

oxidation catalyst In a catalytic converter, a substance that promotes the combustion of exhaust-gas hydrocarbons and carbon monoxide at a lower temperature.

oxides of nitrogen See **nitrogen oxides.**

oxygen (O) A colorless, tasteless, odorless, gaseous element which makes up about 21 percent of air. Capable of combining rapidly with all elements except the inert gases in the oxidation process called "burning." Combines very slowly with many metals in the oxidation process called "rusting."

P

pan See **oil pan.**

pancake engine An engine with two rows of cylinders which are opposed and on the same plane; usually set in a car horizontally. Examples are the Chevrolet Corvair and Volkswagen engines.

parade pattern An oscilloscope pattern showing the ignition voltages on one line, from left to right across the scope screen in engine firing order.

parallel The quality of two items being the same distance from each other at all points; usually applied to lines and, in automotive work, to machined surfaces.

parallel circuit The electric circuit formed when two or more electrical devices have their terminals connected together, positive to positive and negative to negative, so that each may operate independently of the others, from the same power source, as the current divides between them.

parallelogram linkage A steering system in which a short idler arm is mounted on the right side, so that it is parallel to the pitman arm.

parking brake Mechanically operated brake that is independent of the foot-operated service brakes on the vehicle; set when the vehicle is parked.

part A basic mechanical element or piece, which normally cannot be further disassembled, of an assembly, component, system, or unit. Also applied to any separate entry in a parts catalog, or one that has a "part number."

particle A very small piece of metal, dirt, or other impurity which may be contained in the air, fuel, or lubricating oil used in an engine.

particulates Small particles of lead occurring as solid matter in the exhaust gas.

passage A small hole or gallery in an assembly or casting, through which air, coolant, fuel, or oil flows.

passenger car Any four-wheeled motor vehicle manufactured primarily for use on streets and highways and carrying 10 or fewer passengers.

pawl An arm, pivoted so that its free end can fit into a detent, slot, or groove at certain times to hold a part stationary.

payload The weight of the cargo carried by a truck, not including the weight of the body.

PCV Abbreviation for **positive crankcase ventilation.**

PCV valve The valve that controls the flow of crankcase vapors in accordance with ventilation requirements for different engine speeds and loads.

pedal reserve The distance from the brake pedal to the floorboard after the brakes are applied.

peen To mushroom, or spread, the end of a pin or rivet.

percent of grade The quotient obtained by dividing the height of a hill by its length; used in computing the power requirements of trucks.

percolation The condition in which a bowl vent fails to open when the engine is turned off, and pressure in the fuel bowl forces raw fuel through the main jets into the manifold.

performance test The use of a manifold gauge set to measure the pressures in an air-conditioning system as a check of system performance.

permanent magnet A piece of steel that retains its magnetism without the use of an electric current to create a magnetic field.

petroleum The crude oil from which gasoline, lubricating oil, and other such products are refined.

photochemical smog Smog caused by hydrocarbons and nitrogen oxides reacting photochemically in the atmosphere. The reactions take place under low wind velocity, bright sunlight, and an inversion layer in which the air mass is trapped (as between the ocean and mountains in Los Angeles). Can cause eye and lung irritation.

pickup coil In an electronic ignition system, the coil in which voltage is induced by the reluctor.

pilot bearing A small bearing, in the center of the flywheel end of the crankshaft, which carries the forward end of the clutch shaft.

pilot shaft A shaft that is used to align parts, and which is removed before final installation of the parts; a dummy shaft.

ping Engine spark knock that occurs only during acceleration. Usually associated with medium to heavy throttle, acceleration, or lugging at relatively low speeds, especially with a manual transmission. However, it may occur in higher speed ranges under heavy-load conditions. Caused by too much advance of ignition timing or low-octane fuel.

pinion gear The smaller of two meshing gears.

pintle hook A hook mounted on a truck or trailer and used to couple a full trailer to a truck.

pintle valve An upright pivot pin on which another part moves.

piston A movable part, fitted in a cylinder, which can receive or transmit motion as a result of pressure changes in a fluid. In the engine, the round plug that slides up and down in the cylinder and, through the connecting rod, forces the crankshaft to rotate.

piston crown The top of the piston.

piston displacement The cylinder volume displaced by the piston as it moves from the bottom to the top of the cylinder during one complete stroke.

piston pin The round and hollow steel pin that passes through the piston, attaching the piston to the connecting rod. Also called the **wrist pin.**

piston-ring compressor A tool used in engine-overhaul work to compress the piston rings inside the piston grooves so the piston-and-ring assembly may be installed in the engine cylinder.

piston rings A split ring that is installed in a groove in the piston. There are two types: compression rings for sealing the compression in the combustion chamber, and oil rings to scrape excessive oil off the cylinder wall. See **compression ring** and **oil ring.**

piston skirt The lower part of the piston, below the piston-pin hole.

piston slap A hollow, muffled, bell-like sound made by an excessively loose piston slapping the cylinder wall.

pitch The number of threads per inch on any threaded part.

pitman arm In the steering system, the arm that is connected between the steering-gear sector shaft and the steering linkage, or tie rod; it swings back and forth for steering as the steering wheel is turned.

pivot A pin or shaft upon which another part rests or turns.

planet carrier In a planetary-gear system, the carrier or bracket that contains the shaft upon which the planet pinion turns.

planet pinions In a planetary-gear system, the gears that mesh with, and revolve about, the sun gear; they also mesh with the ring (or internal) gear.

planetary-gear system A gear set consisting of a central sun gear surrounded by two or more planet pinions which are, in turn, meshed with a ring (or internal) gear; used in overdrives and automatic transmissions.

plastic gasket compound A plastic paste which can be squeezed out of a tube to make a gasket in any shape.

Plastigage A plastic material available in strips of various sizes; used to measure crankshaft main-bearing and connecting-rod-bearing clearances.

plate In a battery, a rectangular sheet of spongy lead. Sulfuric acid in the electrolyte chemically reacts with the lead to produce an electric current.

plate group In a battery, all the positive plates or all the negative plates for one cell, connected together electrically.

plenum A chamber containing air under pressure.

plenum blower assembly In an air-conditioning system, the assembly through which air passes on its way to the evaporator or heater core. It is located on the engine side of the fire wall and contains a blower, air ducts, air valves, and doors that permit selection of air from outside or inside the car.

plies The layers of cord in a tire casing; each of these layers is a **ply.**

plug gapping Adjusting the side electrode of a spark plug to obtain the proper air gap between it and the center electrode.

plunger A sliding reciprocating piece driven by an auxillary power source, having the motion of a ram or piston.

ply rating A measure of the strength of a tire based on the strength of a single ply of designated construction.

pneumatic tool A tool powered by air, such as an air-powered impact wrench.

POA valve See **suction throttling valve.**

polarity The quality of an electric component or circuit that determines the direction of current flow.

polarizing a generator Correcting the generator field polarity so the generator will build up polarity in the proper direction to charge the battery.

pole See **magnetic pole.**

pole shoe The curved metal shoe around which a field coil is placed.

pollutant Any substance that adds to the pollution of the atmosphere. In a vehicle, any such substance in the exhaust gas from the engine or which has evaporated from the fuel tank or carburetor.

pollution Any gas or substance in the air which makes it less fit to breathe. Also, "noise pollution" is the name applied to excessive noise from machinery or vehicles.

polyurethane A synthetic substance used in filtration materials; normally associated with the filtering of carburetor inlet air.

poor gas mileage Excessive fuel consumption; may be caused by the driver, vehicle, or operating conditions.

pop-back Condition in which the air-fuel mixture is ignited in the intake manifold. Because combustion takes place outside the combustion chamber, the combustion may "pop back" through the carburetor.

poppet valve A mushroom-shaped valve, widely used in automotive engines.

porcelain The hard, heat-resistant material used to insulate the center electrode of the spark plug.

port In the engine, the opening in which the valve operates and through which air-fuel mixture or burned gases pass; the valve port.

ported vacuum switch A water-temperature-sensing vacuum control valve used in distributor and EGR vacuum systems. Sometimes called the "vacuum-control valve" or "coolant override valve."

positive One of the two poles of a magnet, or one of the two terminals of an electrical device.

positive crankcase ventilation (PCV) A crankcase ventilation system; uses intake-manifold vacuum to return the crankcase vapors and blow-by gases to the intake manifold to be burned, thereby preventing their escape into the atmosphere.

positive terminal The terminal to which electrons flow in a complete electric circuit. On a battery, the positive terminal can be identified as the battery post with the larger diameter; the plus sign (+) is used to identify the positive terminal.

post A point at which a cable is connected to the battery.

potential energy Energy stored in a body because of its position. A weight raised to a height has potential energy because it can do work coming down. Likewise, a tensed or compressed spring contains potential energy.

pounds per horsepower A measure of vehicle performance; the weight of the vehicle divided by the engine horsepower.

pour point The lowest temperature at which an oil will flow.

power The rate at which work is done. A common power unit is the horsepower, which is equal to 33,000 foot-pounds per minute.

power brakes A brake system that uses hydraulic or vacuum and atmospheric pressure to provide most of the effort required for braking.

power cylinder An operating cylinder which produces the power to actuate a mechanism. Both power brakes and power-steering units contain power cylinders.

power hop The loss of traction at the drive wheels caused by an excessive transfer of power resulting in wheel bounce.

power piston In some carburetors, a vacuum-operated piston that allows additional fuel to flow at wide-open throttle; permits delivery of a richer air-fuel mixture to the engine.

power plant The engine or power source of a vehicle.

power selection In a gas turbine engine, the section that contains the power-turbine rotors which, through reduction gears, turn the wheels of the vehicle.

power steering A steering system that uses hydraulic pressure from a pump to multiply the driver's steering effort.

power stroke The piston stroke from TDC to BDC immediately following the compression stroke, during which both valves are closed, and the air-fuel mixture burns, expands, and forces the piston down to transmit power to the crankshaft.

power take-off An attachment for connecting the engine to devices or other machinery when its use is required.

power team The combination of an engine, transmission, and specific axle ratio.

power tool A tool whose power source is not muscle power; a tool powered by air or electricity.

power train The mechanisms that carry the rotary motion developed in the engine to the car wheels; these include the clutch, transmission, drive shaft, differential, and axles.

ppm Abbreviation for "parts per million;" the unit used in measuring the level of hydrocarbons in exhaust gas with an exhaust-gas analyzer, 1 part per million is 1 drop in 16 gallons.

PR Abbreviation for **ply rating.**

precision-insert bearings Bearings that can be installed in an engine without reaming, honing, or grinding.

precombustion chamber In some diesel engines, a separate small combustion chamber into which the fuel is injected and where combustion begins.

preignition Ignition of the air-fuel mixture in the combustion chamber, by some unwanted means, before the ignition spark occurs at the spark plug.

preload In bearings, the amount of load placed on a bearing before actual operating loads are imposed. Proper preloading requires bearing adjustment and ensures alignment and minimum looseness in the system.

premium gasoline The best of highest-octane gas available to the motorist.

press fit A fit between two parts so tight that one part has to be pressed into the other, usually with an arbor press or hydraulic press.

pressure Force per unit area, or force divided by area. Usually measured in pounds per square inch (psi) and kilopascals (kPa).

pressure bleeder A piece of shop equipment that uses air pressure to force brake fluid into the brake system for bleeding.

pressure cap A radiator cap with valves which causes the cooling system to operate under pressure at a higher and more efficient temperature without boiling of the coolant.

pressure-differential valve The valve in a dual-brake system that turns on a warning light if the pressure drops in one part of the system.

pressure-feed oil system A type of lubricating system that makes use of an oil pump to force oil to various engine parts.

pressure line See **discharge line.** In an air conditioner, all refrigerant lines are under pressure.

pressure plate That part of the clutch which exerts pressure against the friction disk; it is mounted on and rotates with the flywheel.

pressure regulator A device that operates to prevent excessive pressure from developing. In the hydraulic system of automatic transmissions, a valve that opens to release oil from a line when the oil pressure reaches a specified maximum limit.

pressure-relief valve A valve in the oil line that opens to relieve excessive pressure.

pressure-sensing line In an air conditioner, prevents the compressor suction pressure from dropping below a predetermined level; opens the thermostatic expansion valve, allowing liquid refrigerant to flood the evaporator.

pressure tester An instrument that clamps in the radiator filler neck; used to pressure-test the cooling system for leaks.

pressurize To apply more-than-atmospheric pressure to a gas or liquid.

preventive maintenance The systematic inspection of a vehicle to detect and correct failures, either before they occur or before they develop into major defects. A procedure for economically maintaining a vehicle in a satisfactory and dependable operating condition.

primary The low-voltage circuit of the ignition system.

primary winding The low-voltage (6- or 12-volt) winding in the ignition coil, wound with heavy wire outside the secondary winding.

primary wires The wire carrying the low-voltage (6- or 12-volt) current in the ignition system, including the wiring from the battery to the ignition switch, resistor, coil, and distributor.

printed circuit An electrical circuit made by applying a conductive material to an insulating board in a pattern that provides current paths between components mounted on or connected to the board.

PROCO Short for **Programmed Combustion;** a type of stratified charge engine developed by Ford.

programmed combustion See **PROCO.**

programmed protection system A system employing bypass valves to protect the catalysts and their containers from destructive overtemperature conditions that might result from certain modes of operation, or from engine malfunctions.

progressive linkage A carburetor linkage used with multiple-carburetor installations to progressively open the secondary carburetors.

propane A type of LPG that is liquid below −44°F (−42°C) at atmospheric pressure and sometimes is used as an engine fuel.

propeller shaft See **drive shaft.**

proportioning valve A valve which admits more braking pressure to the front wheels when high fluid pressures develop during braking.

proton A particle in the nucleus of an atom; has a positive electric charge.

prussian blue A blue pigment; in solution, useful in determining the area of contact between two surfaces.

psi Abbreviation for "pounds per square inch," a measurement of pressure.

psig Abbreviation for "pounds per square inch of **gauge pressure.**"

pull The result of an unbalanced condition. For example, uneven braking at the front brakes or unequal front-wheel alignment will cause a car to swerve (pull) to one side when the brakes are applied.

puller Generally, a shop tool used to separate two closely fitted parts without damage. Often contains a screw, or several screws, which can be turned to apply gradual pressure.

pulley A metal wheel with a V-shaped groove around the rim; drives, or is driven by, a belt.

pulsation A surge felt in the brake pedal during low-pressure braking.

pump A device that transfers gas or liquid from one place to another.

puncture-sealing tires or tubes Tires or tubes coated on the inside with a plastic material. Air pressure in the tire or tube forces the material into a puncture; it hardens on contact with the air to seal the puncture.

purge To remove, evacuate, or empty trapped substances from a space. In an air conditioner, to remove moisture and air from the refrigerant system by flushing with nitrogen or Refrigerant-12.

purge valve A valve used on some charcoal canisters in evaporative emission-control systems; limits the flow of vapor and air to the carburetor during idling.

pushrod In an overhead-valve engine, the rod between the valve lifter and the rocker arm; transmits cam-lobe lift.

PVS Abbreviation for **ported vacuum switch.**

Q

quad Performance term for a four-barrel carburetor.

quad carburetor A four-barrel carburetor.

quadrant A term sometimes used to identify the shift-lever selector mounted on the steering column.

quench The removal of heat during combustion from the end gas or outside layers of air-fuel mixture by the cooler metallic surfaces of the combustion chamber; this reduces the tendency for detonation to occur.

quench area The area of the combustion chamber near the cylinder walls which tends to cool (quench) combustion through the effect of the nearby cool water jackets.

quick charger A battery charger that produces a high charging current which charges, or boosts, a battery in a short time.

R

races The metal rings on which ball or roller bearings rotate.

rack-and-pinion steering gear A steering gear in which a pinion on the end of the steering shaft meshes with a rack on the major cross member of the steering linkage.

radial tire A tire in which the plies are placed radially, or perpendicular to the rim, with a circumferential belt on top of them. The rubber tread is vulcanized on top of the belt and plies.

radiation One of the processes by which energy is transferred. For example, heat energy from the sun reaches the earth by radiation.

radiator In the cooling system, the device that removes heat from coolant passing through it; takes hot coolant from the engine and returns the coolant to the engine at a lower temperature.

radiator pressure cap See **pressure cap.**

radiator shutter system An engine-temperature control system, used mostly on trucks, that controls the amount of air flowing through the radiator by use of a shutter system.

radius ride Condition in which a crankshaft journal "rides" on the edge of the bearing. Caused by not cutting away enough of the radius of the journal, where it comes up to the crank cheek, when the crankshaft is reground.

rail job Performance term for a type of drag-racing car built on steel rails or tubes with very little body covering.

ram-air cleaner An air cleaner for high-performance cars that opens an air scoop on the hood to provide a ram effect when the throttle is wide open.

raster pattern An oscilloscope pattern showing the ignition voltages one above the other, from the bottom to the top of the screen, in the engine firing order.

ratio The relationship in size or quantity of two or more objects; a gear ratio is derived by dividing the number of teeth on the driven gear by the number of teeth on the drive gear.

RC engine Abbreviation for **rotary-combustion engine.** See **Wankel engine.**

reactor The stator in a torque converter; has reactive blades against which the fluid can change direction (under certain conditions) as it passes from the turbine to the pump.

reamer A round metal-cutting tool with a series of sharp cutting edges; enlarges a hole when turned inside it.

rear-end torque The reaction torque that acts on the rear-axle housing when torque is applied to the wheels; tends to turn the axle housing in a direction opposite to wheel rotation.

reassembly Putting back together the parts of a device.

rebore To increase the diameter of a cylinder.

recapping A form of tire repair in which a cap of new tread material is placed on the old casing and vulcanized into place.

receiver In a car air conditioner, a metal tank for holding excess refrigerant. Liquid refrigerant is delivered from the condenser to the receiver.

receiver-dehydrator In a car air conditioner, a container for storing liquid refrigerant from the condenser. A sack of desiccant in this container removes small traces of moisture that may be left in the system after purging and evacuating.

recharging The action of forcing electric current into a battery in the direction opposite that in which current normally flows during use. Reverses the chemical reaction between the plates and electrolyte.

reciprocating motion Motion of an object between two limiting positions; motion in a straight line either back and forth or up and down.

recirculating-ball-and-nut steering gear A type of steering gear in which a nut (meshing with a gear sector) is assembled on a worm gear; balls circulate between the nut and worm threads.

rectifier A device which changes alternating current to direct current.

reed valve A pressure-operated flap-type valve used in air-conditioning compressors and in the crankcases of some two-cycle engines.

refractometer An instrument used to measure the specific gravity of a liquid such as battery electrolyte or engine coolant; gives a reading that is already adjusted for the temperature of the liquid being tested.

refrigerant A substance used to transfer heat in an air conditioner through a cycle of evaporation and condensation.

Refrigerant-12 The refrigerant used in vehicle air-conditioning systems. It is sold under such trademarks as Freon-12.

refrigeration Cooling of an object or substance by removal of heat through mechanical means.

refrigeration cycle The complete sequence of changes (in temperature, pressure, and state) undergone by the refrigerant as it circulates through a refrigeration system.

regeneration system A system in a gas turbine that converts some of the heat that would otherwise be wasted into usable power.

regulator In the charging system, a device that controls alternator output to prevent excessive voltage.

relative humidity The actual moisture content of the air, as a percentage of the total moisture that the air can hold at a given temperature. For example, if the air contains three-fourths of the moisture it can hold at its existing temperature, then its relative humidity is 75 percent.

relay An electric device that opens or closes a circuit or circuits in response to a voltage signal.

release bearing See **throwout bearing.**

release fingers See **release levers.**

release levers In the clutch, levers that are moved by throwout-bearing movement, causing clutch-spring pressure to be relieved so the clutch is released, or uncoupled from the flywheel.

relief valve A valve that opens when a preset pressure is reached. This relieves or prevents excessive pressures.

reluctor In an electronic ignition system, the metal armature or rotor (with a series of tips) which replaces the cam in a contact-point distributor; used with a stator, it eliminates contact points.

remove and reinstall (R and R) To perform a series of servicing procedures on an original part or assembly; includes removal, inspection, lubrication, all necessary adjustments, and reinstallation.

replace To remove a used part or assembly and install a new part or assembly in its place; includes cleaning, lubricating, and adjusting as required.

required voltage The voltage required to fire a spark plug.

research octane number A number used to describe the octane rating of a marketed gasoline. See also **motor octane number.**

reserve capacity A battery rating; the number of minutes a battery can deliver a 25-amp current before the cell voltages drop to 1.75 volts per cell.

residual magnetism The magnetism that remains in a material after the electric current producing the magnetism has stopped flowiing.

resistance The opposition to a flow of current through a circuit or electrical device; measured in ohms. A voltage of 1 volt will cause 1 ampere to flow through a resistance of 1 ohm. This is known as Ohm's law, which can be written in three ways: amperes = volts/ohms; ohms = volts/amperes; and volts = amperes × ohms.

resistor An electric device placed in a circuit to lower voltage or decrease current flow.

resistor spark plug A spark plug containing a built-in resistor to suppress radio interference.

resonator A device in the exhaust system that reduces the exhaust noise.

retainer lock See **valve-spring-retainer lock.**

retard To make slower or hold back. To adjust ignition timing so the spark plug fires later or less degrees before TDC; the opposite of *advance*.

return spring A "pull-back" spring, often used in brake systems.

rev Performance term for "revolutions per minute" (rpm), or the speed of rotation of the engine crankshaft.

reverse flushing A method of cleaning a radiator or engine cooling system by flushing it in the direction opposite to normal coolant flow.

reverse idler gear In a transmission, an additional gear that must be meshed to obtain reverse gear; a gear used only in reverse that idles when the transmission is in any other position.

ribbon-cellular radiator core A type of radiator core consisting of ribbons of metal soldered together along their edges.

rich mixture An air-fuel mixture that has a relatively high proportion of fuel and a relatively low proportion of air. An air-fuel ratio of 13:1 indicates a rich mixture, compared to an air-fuel ratio of 16:1.

rim A metal support around the outside of a wheel for a tire, or a tire and tube assembly, and upon which the tire beads are seated.

ring See **compression ring** and **oil ring.**

ring expander A special tool used to expand piston rings for installation on the piston.

ring gap The gap between the ends of the piston ring when the ring is in place in the cylinder.

ring gear A large gear carried by the differential case; meshes with and is driven by the drive pinion.

ring grooves Grooves cut in a piston, into which the piston rings are assembled.

ring ridge The ridge formed at the top of a cylinder as the cylinder wall below is worn away by piston-ring movement.

ring-ridge remover A special tool used to remove the ring ridge from a cylinder.

rivet A semipermanent fastener used to hold two pieces together.

roadability The steering and handling qualities of a vehicle while it is being driven on the road.

road-draft tube A method of removing the fumes and pressure from the engine crankcase; used prior to crankcase emission-control systems. The tube, which was connected into the crankcase and suspended slightly above the ground, depended on venturi action to create a partial vacuum as the vehicle moved. The method was ineffective below about 20 mph (32 km/h).

road load A constant vehicle speed on a level road.

rocker arm In overhead-valve engines, an arm that rocks on a shaft (or pivots on a stud). As the camshaft rotates, the cam lobe raises one end of the rocker arm, which rocks, or pivots, in the center, forcing the other end down against the valve stem and opening the valve.

rod bearing In an engine, the bearing in the connecting rod in which a crankpin of the crankshaft rotates. Also called a **connecting-rod bearing.**

rod big end The end of the connecting rod that attaches around the crankpin.

rod bolts The bolts used to attach the cap to the connecting rod.

rod small end The end of the connecting rod through which a piston pin passes to connect the piston to the connecting rod.

roll bar A curved protective bar mounted over the driver's head in an off-road vehicle, high-performance car, or race car.

rolling radius The height of a tire, measured from the center of the rear axle to the ground.

RON Abbreviation for **research octane number.**

room temperature 68 to 72°F (20 to 22°C).

rotary Term describing the motion of a part that continually rotates or turns.

rotary-combustion engine See **Wankel engine.**

rotary-valve steering gear A type of power-steering gear.

rotor The rotating part of a machine, such as an alternator rotor, disk-brake rotor, or Wankel-engine rotor. In the ignition distributor, the rotor mounts onto the top end of the distributor shaft, and is in contact with the center terminal of the cap. As the rotor turns, it conducts the high-voltage surges to the outer terminals around the cap.

rotor oil pump A type of oil pump in which a pair of rotors, one inside the other, produce the pressure required to circulate oil to engine parts.

rough idle Unsteady, uneven, or erratic engine idle, which may make the car shake.

rpm Abbreviation for "revolutions per minute," a measure of rotational speed.

ruler A graduated straightedge used for measuring distances, usually up to 1 ft.

run-on See **dieseling.**

runout Wobble.

S

SA Designation for lubricating oil that is acceptable for use in engines operated under the mildest conditions.

SAE Abbreviation for Society of Automotive Engineers. Used to indicate a grade or weight of oil measured according to Society of Automotive Engineers standards.

safety Freedom from injury or danger.

safety rim A wheel rim with a hump on the inner edge of the ledge on which the tire bead rides. The hump helps hold the tire on the rim in case of a blowout.

safety

safety stand A pinned, or locked, type of stand placed under a car to support its weight after the car has been raised with a floor jack. Also called a **car stand** or **jack stand.**

sag The condition in which the engine responds initially, then flattens out or slows down, and then recovers; may cause engine stall if severe enough.

SB Designation for lubricating oil that is acceptable for minimum-duty engines operated under mild conditions.

SC Designation for lubricating oil that meets requirements for use in the gasoline engines in 1964-to-1967 passenger cars and trucks.

scale The accumulation of rust and minerals (from the water) within the cooling system. Also, a series of graduations used to designate specific values.

scavenging The displacement of exhaust gas from the combustion chamber by fresh air.

schematic A pictorial representation, most often in the form of a line drawing. A systematic positioning of components, showing their relationship to each other or to an overall function.

Schrader valve A spring-loaded valve through which a connection can be made to a refrigeration system; also used in tires.

scope Short for **oscilloscope.**

scored Scratched or grooved, as a cylinder wall may be scored by abrasive particles moved up and down by the piston rings.

SCR See **silicon controlled rectifier.**

scraper A device used in engine service to scrape carbon from the engine block, pistons, or other parts.

scraper ring On a piston, an oil-control ring designed to scrape excess oil back down the cylinder and into the crankcase.

screens Pieces of fine-mesh metal fabric; used to prevent solid particles from circulating through any liquid or vapor system and damaging vital moving parts. In an air conditioner, screens are located in the receiver-dehydrator, thermostatic expansion valve, and compressor.

screw A metal fastener with threads that can be turned into a threaded hole, usually with a screwdriver. There are many different types and sizes of screws.

screwdriver A hand tool used to loosen or tighten screws.

scuffing A type of wear in which there is a transfer of material between parts moving against each other; shows up as pits or grooves in the mating surfaces.

SD Designation for lubricating oil that meets requirements for use in the gasoline engines in 1968-to-1971 passenger cars and some trucks.

SDV Abbreviation for "spark delay valve;" a calibrated restrictor in the vacuum-advance hose which delays the vacuum spark advance.

SE Designation for lubricating oil that meets requirements for use in the gasoline engines in 1972-and-later cars, and in certain 1971 passenger cars and trucks.

seal A material, shaped around a shaft, used to close off the operating compartment of the shaft, preventing oil leakage.

sealed-beam headlight A headlight that contains the filament, reflector, and lens in a single sealed unit.

sealer A thick, tacky compound, usually spread with a brush, which may be used as a gasket or sealant, to seal small openings or surface irregularities.

seat The surface upon which another part rests, as a valve seat. Also, to wear into a good fit; for example, new piston rings seat after a few miles of driving.

seat adjuster A device that permits forward and backward (and sometimes upward and downward) movement of the front seat of a vehicle.

secondary air Air that is pumped to thermal reactors, catalytic converters, exhaust manifolds, or the cylinder-head exhaust ports, to promote the chemical reactions that reduce exhaust-gas pollutants.

secondary available voltage Voltage that is available for firing up the spark plug.

secondary circuit The high-voltage parts of the ignition system; consists of the coil, rotor, distributor cap, spark-plug cables, and spark plugs.

secondary wires The high-voltage wire (cable) from the ignition coil to the center tower of the distributor cap, and from the outer tower to the spark plugs.

section modulus A measure of the strength of the car-frame side rails; depends on the cross-sectional area and shape of the rails.

sector A gear that is not a complete circle. Specifically, the gear sector on the pitman shaft in many steering systems.

sediment The accumulation of matter which settles to the bottom of a liquid.

segments The copper bars of a commutator.

self-adjuster A mechanism used on drum brakes; compensates for shoe wear by automatically keeping the shoe adjusted close to the drum.

self-discharge Chemical activity in the battery which causes the battery to discharge even though it is furnishing no current.

self-induction The inducing of a voltage in a current-carrying coil of wire because the current in that wire is changing.

self-locking screw A screw that locks itself in place, without the use of a separate nut or lockwasher.

self-tapping screw A screw that cuts its own threads as it is turned into an unthreaded hole.

semiconductor A material that acts as an insulator under some conditions and as a conductor under other conditions.

semiconductor ignition system See **electronic ignition system.**

semifloating rear axle An axle that supports the weight of the vehicle on the axle shaft in addition to transmitting driving forces to the rear wheels.

sensible heat Heat which can be felt or measured with a thermometer. Sensible heat changes the temperature of a substance, but not its state.

sensor Any device that receives and reacts to a signal, such as a change in voltage, temperature, or pressure.

separator A thin sheet of wood, rubber, plastic, or fiberglass mat that is placed between each positive and negative plate in a battery cell to insulate the plates from each other.

series circuit An electric circuit in which the devices are connected end to end, positive terminal to negative terminal. The same current flows through all the devices in the circuit, because the current has only one path to take.

series-parallel system A starting system using two batteries, connected differently for different functions. For example, a system with a 24-volt starting motor, two 12-volt batteries, and a 12-volt alternator. For starting, the two batteries are connected in series to produce 24 volts; for charging, they are connected in parallel to produce 12 volts.

serviceable Parts or systems that can be repaired and maintained to continue in operation.

service manual A book published annually by each vehicle manufacturer, listing the specifications and service procedures for each make and model of vehicle. Also called a "shop manual."

service rating A designation that indicates the type of service for which an engine-lubricating oil is best suited. See **SA, SB, SC, SD,** and **SE.**

servo A device in a hydraulic system that converts hydraulic pressure to mechanical movement. Consists of a piston which moves in a cylinder as hydraulic pressure acts on it.

setscrew A type of metal fastener that holds a collar or gear on a shaft when its point is turned down into the shaft.

set up Performance term meaning to prepare a car for racing.

severe ring A piston ring which exerts relatively high pressure against the cylinder walls, sometimes by use of an expander spring located behind the ring; a ring that can be used in an engine with excessive cylinder wear.

shackle The swinging support by which one end of a leaf spring is attached to the car frame.

shaved A cylinder head that has been resurfaced to increase the cylinder compression ratio.

shift lever The lever used to change gears in a transmission. Also, the lever on the starting motor which moves the drive pinion into or out of mesh with the flywheel teeth.

shift valve In an automatic transmission, a valve that moves to produce the shifts from one gear ratio to another.

shim A slotted strip of metal used as a spacer to adjust the front-end alignment on many cars; also used to make small corrections in the position of body sheet metal and other parts.

shimmy Rapid oscillation. In wheel shimmy, for example, the front wheel turns in and out alternately and rapidly; this causes the front end of the car to oscillate, or shimmy.

shim stock Sheets of metal of accurately known thicknesses which can be cut into strips and used to measure or correct clearances.

shock absorber A device placed at each vehicle wheel to regulate spring rebound and compression.

shoe In the brake system, a metal plate that supports the brake lining and absorbs and transmits braking forces.

shop layout The locations of aisles, work areas, machine tools, etc., in a shop.

short-arm, long-arm (SALA) suspension Name given to the conventional front-suspension system, which uses a short upper control arm and a longer lower control arm.

short circuit A defect in an electric circuit which permits current to take a short path, or circuit, instead of following the desired path.

shrink fit A tight fit of one part into another, achieved by heating or cooling one part and then assembling it to the other part. A heated part will shrink on cooling to provide the tight fit; a cooled part will expand on warming to provide the tight fit.

shroud A hood placed around an engine fan to improve fan action.

shunt A parallel connection or circuit.

side clearance The clearance between the sides of moving parts when the sides do not serve as load-carrying surfaces.

sidewall That portion of the tire between the tread and the bead.

sight glass In a car air conditioner, a viewing glass or window set in the refrigerant line, usually in the top of the receiver-dehydrator; the sight glass allows a visual check of the refrigerant passing from the receiver to the evaporator.

silicon controlled rectifier (SCR) A type of three-element transistor that acts as an open circuit until a voltage is applied to the gate, which then opens to allow a large current to flow through from the cathode to the anode. Once conducting, the gate voltage can be removed without stopping the current, which is stopped by removing or reversing the cathode-to-anode voltage.

single-chamber capacity In a Wankel engine, a measurement of the displacement of maximum volume of the rotor chamber.

single-overhead-camshaft (SOHC) engine An engine in which a single camshaft is mounted over each cylinder head, instead of inside the cylinder block.

sintered bronze Tiny particles of bronze pressed tightly together so that they form a solid piece which is highly porous and which is often used as a filter for gasoline.

skid control See **antilock brake system.**

slant engine An in-line engine in which the cylinder block is tilted from the vertical plane.

slick Performance term for a smooth, treadless racing tire.

slip joint In the power train, a variable-length connection that permits the drive shaft to change its effective length.

slip rings In an alternator, the rings that form a rotating connection between the armature windings and the brushes.

sludge Black, soft deposits throughout the interior of the engine, caused by dirt, oil, and water being whipped together by moving parts; sludge is very viscous and tends to reduce lubrication.

sluggish The condition in which the engine delivers limited power under load or at high speed, and will not accelerate as fast as normal, loses too much speed on hills, or has a lower top speed than normal.

smog A term coined from the words "smoke" and "fog". First applied to the foglike layer that hangs in the air under certain atmospheric conditions; now generally used to describe any condition of dirty air and/or fumes or smoke. Smog is compounded from smoke, moisture, and numerous chemicals that are produced by combustion.

smoke Small gasborne or airborne particles, exclusive of water vapor, that result from combustion; such particles emitted by an engine into the atmosphere in sufficient quantity to be observable.

smoke in exhaust A visible blue or black substance often present in the automotive exhaust. A blue color indicates excessive oil in the combustion chamber; black indicates excessive fuel in the air-fuel mixture.

snap ring A metal fastener, available in two types: the external snap ring fits into a groove in a shaft; the internal snap ring fits into a groove in a housing. Snap rings must be installed and removed with special snap-ring pliers.

sodium-cooled valve A hollow valve partially filled with metallic sodium. The sodium transfers heat (by convection) from the hot head end of the valve to the stem, thereby reducing the valve temperature.

SOHC See **single-overhead-camshaft engine.**

soldering Joining pieces of metal with solder, flux, and heat.

solenoid An electrically operated magnetic device used to mechanically operate some other device through movement of an iron core placed inside a coil. When current flows through the coil, the core attempts to center itself in the coil, thereby exerting a strong force on anything connected to the core.

solenoid bypass valve In the air conditioner, a valve placed in a bypass line between the condenser and compressor, and operated by a solenoid. When the valve is open, refrigerant can bypass between the condenser and compressor, so no refrigeration takes place. When the valve is closed, the system cools normally.

solenoid relay A relay that connects a solenoid to a current source when its contacts close; for example, the starting-motor solenoid relay.

solid-state regulator An alternator regulator encapsulated in a plastic material and mounted in the alternator.

solvent A petroleum product of low volatility used in the cleaning of engine and vehicle parts.

solvent tank In the shop, a tank of cleaning fluid in which most parts are brushed and washed clean.

south pole The pole at which magnetic lines of force enter a magnet.

spark The bridging or jumping of a gap between two electrodes by an electric current.

spark advance See **advance.**

spark decel valve A vacuum-actuated valve, located between the carburetor and distributor, which advances the spark during deceleration to reduce emissions (should not be confused with the spark-delay valve.)

spark duration The length of time a spark is established across a spark gap, or the length of time current flows in a spark gap.

spark gap The space between the center and side electrode tips on a spark plug.

spark knock See **detonation.**

spark line Part of the oscilloscope pattern of the ignition secondary circuit; the spark line shows the voltage required to sustain the spark at the spark plug, and the number of distributor degrees through which the spark exists.

spark plug A device that screws into the cylinder head, containing two electrodes across which an electric spark jumps to produce the heat that ignites the air-fuel mixture in the combustion chamber.

spark-plug heat range The distance heat must travel from the center electrode to reach the outer shell of the spark plug and enter the cylinder head.

spark test A quick check of the ignition system; made by holding the metal spark-plug end of a spark-plug cable about 3/16 inch (5 mm) from the cylinder head, or block, cranking the engine, and checking for a spark.

specifications Information provided by the manufacturer that describes each automotive system and its components, operation, and clearances. The service procedures that must be followed for a system and its components, operation, and clearances. Also, the service procedures that must be followed for a system to operate properly.

specific gravity The relative weight of a given volume of a liquid compared to the weight of an equal volume of water.

specific heat The quantity of heat (in Btus) required to change the temperature of 1 lb. of a substance by 1°F.

specs Short for **specifications.**

speed The rate of motion; for vehicles, measured in miles per hour or kilometers per hour.

speedometer An instrument that indicates vehicle speed; usually driven from the transmission.

speed shift Performance term for a shift of gears in a manual transmission without releasing the accelerator.

splash-feed oil system A type of engine lubricating system in which oil is splashed onto moving engine parts.

splines Slots or grooves cut in a shaft or bore; splines on a shaft are matched to splines in a bore, to ensure that two parts turn together.

spongy pedal Term applied to the feel of a brake pedal when air is trapped in the hydraulic system.

spool valve A rod with indented sections; used to control oil flow in automatic transmissions.

sprag clutch A one-way clutch; it can transmit power in one direction, but not in the other.

spray cone A pattern formed when a material is atomized under pressure, narrow at the base and wider as it projects.

spring A device that changes shape under stress or pressure, but returns to its original shape when the stress or pressure is removed; the component of the automotive suspension system that absorbs road shocks by flexing and twisting.

spring rate The load required to move a spring or a suspended wheel a given distance; indicates the softness or firmness of a given spring or suspension.

spring retainer In the valve train, the piece of metal that holds the spring in place, and is itself locked in place by the valve-spring-retainer lock.

spring shackle See **shackle.**

sprung weight That part of the car which is supported on springs (includes the engine, frame, and body).

spur gear A gear in which the teeth are parallel to the center line of the gear.

square engine An engine in which the bore and stroke are equal.

squeak A high-pitched noise of short duration.

squeal A continuous, high pitched, low-volume noise.

squish The action in some combustion chambers in which the last part of the compressed air-fuel mixture is pushed, or squirted, out of a decreasing space between the piston and cylinder head.

stabilizer bar An interconnecting shaft between the two lower suspension arms; reduces body roll on turns.

stacked pattern See **raster pattern.**

stacks Performance term for short, tubular carburetor intake pipes; also, for short, individual exhaust pipes.

stall test A starting-motor test in which the current draw is measured with the motor stalled.

stalls The condition in which an engine quits running, at idle or while driving.

standpipe assembly See **vapor-liquid separator.**

starter See **starting motor.**

starting motor The electric motor that cranks the engine, or turns the crankshaft, for starting.

starting-motor drive The drive mechanism and gear on the end of the starting-motor armature shaft; used to couple the starting motor to, and disengage it from, the flywheel ring-gear teeth.

static balance The balance of an object while it is not moving.

static friction The friction between two bodies at rest.

stator The stationary member of a machine, such as an electric motor or generator, in or about which a rotor revolves; in an electronic ignition system, a small magnet imbedded in plastic (or a light-emitting diode) which when used with a reluctor replaces contact points. Also, the third member, in addition to the turbine and pump, in a torque converter.

steam cleaner A machine used for cleaning large parts with a spray of steam, often mixed with soap.

steam engine An external-combustion engine operated by steam generated in a boiler.

steering-and-ignition lock A device that locks the ignition switch in the OFF position and locks the steering wheel so that it cannot be turned.

steering arm The arm, attached to the steering knuckle, that turns the knuckle and wheel for steering.

steering axis The center line of the ball joints in a front-suspension system.

steering-axis inclination The inward tilt of the steering axis from the vertical.

steering-column shift An arrangement in which the transmission shift lever is mounted on the steering column.

steering gear That part of the steering system that is located at the lower end of the steering shaft; carries the rotary motion of the steering wheel to the car wheels for steering.

steering kickback Sharp and rapid movements of the steering wheel as the front wheels encounter obstructions in the road; the shocks of these encounters "kick back" to the steering wheel.

steering knuckle The front-wheel spindle, which is supported by upper and lower ball joints and by the wheel; the part on which a front wheel is mounted, and which is turned for steering.

steering shaft The shaft extending from the steering gear to the steering wheel.

steering system The mechanism that enables the driver to turn the wheels for changing the direction of vehicle movement.

steering wheel The wheel, at the top of the steering shaft, which is used by the driver to guide or steer the vehicle.

stepped feeler gauge A feeler gauge which has a thin tip of a known dimension, and is thicker along the rest of the gauge; a "go no-go" feeler gauge.

Stirling engine A type of internal-combustion engine in which the piston is moved by changes in the pressure of a working gas that is alternately heated and cooled.

stoplights Lights at the rear of a vehicle which indicate that the driver is applying the brakes to slow or stop the vehicle.

stoplight switch The switch that turns the stoplights on and off as the brakes are applied and released.

storage battery A device that changes chemical energy into electric energy; that part of the electric system which acts as a reservoir for electric energy, storing it in chemical form.

stratified charge In a gasoline-fueled spark-ignition engine, an air-fuel charge with a small layer of very rich air-fuel mixture; the rich layer is ignited first, after which ignition spreads to the leaner mixture filling the rest of the combustion chamber. The diesel engine is a stratified-charge engine.

streamlining The shaping of a car body or truck cab so that it minimizes air resistance and can be moved through the air with less energy.

stroke In an engine cylinder, the distance that the piston moves in traveling from BDC to TDC or from TDC to BDC.

stroker kit Performance term for a special crankshaft-and-connecting-rod kit designed to increase the displacement of an engine by lengthening the stroke of the piston.

strut A bar that connects the lower control arm to the car frame; used when the lower control arm is of the type that is attached to the frame at only one point. Also called a "brake reaction rod."

stud A headless bolt that is threaded on both ends.

stud extractor A special tool used to remove a broken stud or bolt.

stumble A severe sudden loss of engine power.

substance Any matter or material; may be a solid, a liquid, or a gas.

substrate In a catalytic converter, the supporting structure to which the catalyst is applied; usually made of ceramic. Two types of substrate used in catalytic converters are the monolithic, or one-piece, substrate and the bead- or pellet-type substrate.

suction line In an air conditioner, the tube that connects the evaporator outlet and the compressor inlet. Low-pressure refrigerant vapor flows through this line.

suction pressure The pressure at the air-conditioner compressor inlet; the compressor intake pressure, as indicated by a gauge set.

suction side That portion of the refrigeration system under low pressure; extends from the thermostatic expansion valve to the compressor inlet.

suction throttling valve In an air conditioner, a valve located between the evaporator and the compressor; controls the temperature of the air flowing from the evaporator to prevent freezing of moisture on the evaporator.

sulfation The lead sulfate that forms on battery plates as a result of the battery action that produces electric current.

sulfuric acid See **electrolyte.**

sulfur oxides (SO_x) Acids that can form in small amounts as the result of a reaction between hot exhaust gas and the catalyst in a catalytic converter.

sun gear In a planetary-gear system, the center gear that meshes with the planet pinions.

supercharger In the intake system of the engine, a device that pressurizes the in-going air-fuel mixture. This increases the amount of mixture delivered to the cylinders, which increases the engine output. If the supercharger is driven by the engine exhaust gas, it is called a **turbocharger.**

superheated vapor Refrigerant vapor at a temperature that is higher than its boiling point for a given pressure.

superimposed pattern On an oscilloscope, a pattern showing the ignition voltages one on top of the other, so that only a single trace, and variations from it, can be seen.

surface grinder A grinder used to resurface flat surfaces, such as cylinder heads.

surface ignition Ignition of the air-fuel mixture, in the combustion chamber, by hot metal surfaces or heated particles of carbon.

surge To occur suddenly to an excessive or abnormal value. The condition in which the engine speed increases and decreases slightly under constant throttle operation.

suspension system The springs and other parts which support the upper part of a vehicle on its axles and wheels.

suspension arm In the front suspension, one of the arms pivoted on the frame at one end, and on the steering-knuckle support at the other end.

S/V ratio The ratio of the surface area *S of the combustion chamber to its volume V,* with the piston at TDC. Often used as a comparative indicator of hydrocarbon emission levels from an engine.

sway bar See **stabilizer bar.**

switch A device that opens and closes an electric circuit.

synchro Performance term for synchromesh transmission.

synchromesh transmission A transmission with a built-in device that automatically matches the rotating speeds of the transmission gears, thereby eliminating the need for "double-clutching."

synchronize To make two or more events or operations occur at the same time or at the same speed.

synchronizer A device in the transmission that synchronizes gears about to be meshed, so that there will not be any gear clash.

synthetic oil An artificial oil that is manufactured; not a natural mineral oil made from petroleum.

system A combination or grouping of two or more parts or components into a whole which in operation performs some function that cannot be done by the separate parts.

T

tachometer A device for measuring the speed of an engine in revolutions per minute (rpm).

taillights Steady-burning low-intensity lights used on the rear of a vehicle.

tank unit The part of the fuel-indicating system that is mounted in the fuel tank.

tap A tool used for cutting threads in a hole.

taper A gradual reduction in the width of a shaft or hole; in an engine cylinder, uneven wear, more pronounced at the top than at the bottom.

tappet See **valve lifter.**

taxable horsepower The power of an engine, as calculated by a formula that provides a comparison of engines on a uniform basis. The formula is used in some localities for licensing vehicles.

TCS See **transmission-controlled spark system.**

TDC Abbreviation for **top dead center.**

technology The applications of science.

TEL Abbreviation for **tetraethyl lead.**

temperature The measure of heat intensity in degrees. Temperature is not a measure of heat quantity.

temperature gauge A gauge that indicates to the driver the temperature of the coolant in the engine cooling system.

temperature indicator See **temperature gauge.**

temperature-sending unit A device, in contact with the engine coolant, whose electric resistance changes as the coolant temperature increases or decreases; these changes control the movement of the indicator needle of the temperature gauge.

terminal A connecting point in an electric circuit.

tetraethyl lead A chemical which, when added to engine fuel, increases its octane rating, or reduces its tendency to detonate. Also called "ethyl."

thermactor See **air-injection system.**

thermal Of or pertaining to heat.

thermal-conductivity gas analyzer The conventional exhaust-gas analyzer, used in service shops for many years to check and adjust the carburetor air-fuel mixture at idle.

thermal efficiency Ratio of the energy output of an engine to the energy in the fuel required to produce that output.

thermal reactor A large exhaust manifold in which unburned exhaust-gas hydrocarbons and carbon monoxide react with oxygen so that the pollutants burn up almost completely. It is simple and durable, but must operate at very high temperatures. Used on the Mazda car with the Wankel engine.

thermistor A heat-sensing device with a negative temperature coefficient of resistance; as its temperature increases, its electric resistance decreases. Used as the sensing device for engine temperature–indicating devices.

thermometer An instrument which measures heat intensity (temperature) by the thermal expansion of a liquid.

thermostat A device for the automatic regulation of temperature; usually contains a temperature-sensitive element that expands or contracts to open or close off the flow of air, a gas, or a liquid.

thermostatically controlled air cleaner An air cleaner in which a thermostat controls the preheating of intake air.

thermostatic clutch A clutch operated by a **thermostatic switch.** Engages and disengages the compressor to prevent water from freezing on the evaporator core, thereby controlling the temperature of air flowing from the evaporator.

thermostatic expansion valve Component of a refrigeration system that controls the rate of refrigerant flow to the evaporator. Commonly called the "TE valve," "TXV," or the "expansion valve."

thermostatic gauge An indicating device (for fuel quantity, oil pressure, engine temperature) that contains a thermostatic blade or blades.

thermostatic switch An adjustable component used in a cycling-clutch air conditioner. Engages and disengages the compressor to prevent water from freezing on the evaporator core, and to control the temperature of air flowing from the evaporator.

thermostatic vacuum switch A temperature-sensing device extending into the coolant; connects full manifold vacuum to the distributor when the coolant overheats. The resultant spark advance causes an increase in engine rpm, which lowers the coolant temperature.

thread chaser A device, similar to a die, that is used to clean threads.

thread class A designation indicating the closeness of fit between a pair of threaded parts, such as a nut and bolt.

threaded insert A threaded coil that is used to restore the original thread size to a hole with damaged threads; the hole is drilled oversize and tapped, and the insert is threaded into the tapped hole.

thread series A designation indicating the pitch, or number of threads per inch, on a threaded part.

three-mode cycle A quick test procedure used to study the causes of high emissions and to compare different types of testers; consists of taking readings at idle speed and at 2,000 rpm, and maximum readings on deceleration. The test can be performed on a dynamometer under load, or in a service area without load.

three-phase Designating a combination of three interconnected ac circuits in which the alternations are one-third of a cycle apart.

throat Performance term for a carburetor venturi.

throttle A disk valve in the carburetor base that pivots in response to accelerator-pedal position; allows the driver to regulate the volume of air-fuel mixture entering the intake manifold, thereby controlling the engine speed. Also called the "throttle plate" or **throttle valve.**

throttle-return check See **dashpot.**

throttle solenoid positioner An electric solenoid which holds the throttle plate open (hot-idle position), but also permits the throttle plate to close completely when the ignition is turned off to prevent **dieseling.**

throttle valve A round disk valve in the throttle body of the carburetor; can be turned to admit more or less air, thereby controlling engine speed.

throw a rod In an engine, to have a loose, knocking connecting-rod bearing, or a broken connecting rod that has been forced through the cylinder block or oil pan.

throwout bearing In the clutch, the bearing that can be moved in to the release levers by clutch-pedal action to cause declutching, which disengages the engine crankshaft from the transmission.

thrust bearing In the engine, the main bearing that has thrust faces which prevent excessive end play, or forward and backward movement, of the crankshaft.

thyristor See silicon controlled rectifer.

tie-rod end A socket and ball stud in a housing. They rotate and tilt to transmit steering action under all conditions.

tie rods In the steering system, the rods that link the pitman arm to the steering-knuckle arms; small steel components that connect the front wheels to the steering mechanism.

tilt steering wheel A type of steering wheel that can be tilted at various angles, through a flex joint in the steering shaft.

timing In an engine, delivery of the ignition spark or operation of the valves (in relation to the piston) for the power stroke. See **ignition timing** and **valve timing.**

timing chain A chain that is driven by a sprocket on the crankshaft and that drives the sprocket on the camshaft.

timing gear A gear on the crankshaft; drives the camshaft by meshing with a gear on its end.

timing light A stroboscopic light that is connected to the secondary circuit of the ignition system and flashes each time the No. 1 spark plug fires; directing these flashes of light at the whirling timing marks makes the marks appear to stand still, thereby allowing timing to be set by aligning the moving and stationary marks.

timing marks The lines or numbers on the crankshaft vibration damper or on a fixed metal plate which are used to adjust the ignition system so that the spark plugs fire at the right time.

tire The casing-and-tread assembly (with or without a tube) that is mounted on a car wheel to provide pneumatically cushioned contact and traction with the road.

tire carcass The plies that constitute the underbody of the tire; the "skeleton" over which the rubber of the sidewalls and the thicker tread area are molded.

tire casing Layers of cord, called **plies,** shaped in a tire form and impregnated with rubber, to which the tread is applied.

tire rotation The interchanging of the running locations of the tires on a car, to minimize noise and to equalize tire wear.

tire tread See **tread.**

tire tube An inflatable rubber device mounted inside some tires to contain air at sufficient pressure to inflate the casing and support the vehicle weight.

tire-wear indicator Small strips of rubber molded into the bottom of the tire tread grooves; they appear as narrow strips of smooth rubber across the tire when the tread depth decreases to $1/16$ inch (1.6 mm).

toe-in The amount, in inches or millimeters, by which the front wheels point inward.

toe-out-on-turns See **turning radius.**

tolerance The range of variation in a given dimension.

top dead center (TDC) The piston position when the piston has reached the upper limit of its travel in the cylinder and the center line of the connecting rod is parallel to the cylinder walls.

torque Turning or twisting effort; usually measured in pound-feet or kilogram-meters. Also, a turning force such as that required to tighten a connection.

torque-converter In an automatic transmission, a fluid coupling which incorporates a stator to permit a torque increase.

Torqueflite An automatic transmission used on Chrysler-manufactured cars; it has three forward speeds and reverse.

torque test A starting-motor test in which both the torque developed and the current drawn are measured while the specified voltage is applied.

torque wrench A wrench that indicates the amount of torque or turning force being applied with the wrench.

torsional balancer See **vibration damper.**

torsional vibration Rotary vibration that causes a twist-untwist action on a rotating shaft, so that a part of the shaft repeatedly moves ahead of, or lags behind, the remainder of the shaft; for example, the action of a crankshaft responding to the cylinder firing impulses.

torsion-bar spring A long, straight bar that is fastened to the vehicle frame at one end and to a suspension part of the other. Spring action is produced by a twisting of the bar.

torsion-bar steering gear A rotary-valve power-steering gear.

tracking Rear wheels following directly behind (in the tracks of) the front wheels.

tractive effort The force available at the road surface in contact with the driving wheels of a truck. It is determined by engine torque, transmission ratio, axle ratio, tire size, and frictional losses in the drive line. "Rim pull" is also known as tractive effort.

tractor A truck or comparatively short-wheelbase vehicle used for pulling a semitrailer or trailer; a self-propelled vehicle having tracks or wheels, used for pulling agricultural implements or mounting construction implements.

tractor breakaway valve A valve that couples the tractor and trailer emergency-brake systems. Provides air to the trailer emergency-brake system for normal operating conditions. If the trailer brake system fails, the breakaway valve automatically seals off the tractor braking system and activates the trailer emergency brake.

tramp Up-and-down motion (hopping) of the front wheels at higher speeds, due to unbalanced wheels or excessive wheel runout. Also called "high-speed shimmy."

transaxle A power transmission device that combines the functions of the transmission and the drive axle (differential) into a single assembly; used in front-wheel-drive cars with front-mounted engines, and in rear-wheel-drive cars with rear-mounted engines.

transducer Any device which converts an input signal of one form into an output signal of a different form. For example, the automobile horn converts an electric signal to sound.

transformer An electrical device that transfers electric energy from one coil, or winding, to another by electromagnetic induction.

transistor A semiconductor device that can be used as an electronic (solid-state) switch, and can operate on low voltage. Used to replace the contact points in electronic ignition systems.

transmission An assembly that transmits power from the engine to the driving axle; it provides different forward-gear ratios, neutral, and reverse, through which engine power is transmitted to the differential.

transmission-controlled spark (TCS) system An NO_x exhaust-emission control system; makes use of the transmission-gear position to allow distributor vacuum advance in high gear only.

transmission-oil cooler A small finned tube, either mounted separately or as part of the engine radiator, which cools the transmission fluid.

transmission-regulated spark (TRS) system A Ford exhaust-emission control system, similar to the General Motors transmission-controlled spark system; allows distributor vacuum advance in high gear only.

tread That part of the tire that contacts the road. It is the thickest part of the tire, and is cut with grooves to provide traction for driving and stopping.

tread rib The tread section running circumferentially around the tire.

trouble diagnosis The detective work necessary to find the cause of a trouble.

TRS See **transmission-regulated spark system.**

truck Any motor vehicle primarily designed for the transportation of property which carries the load on its own wheels.

truck tractor Any motor vehicle designed primarily for pulling truck trailers and constructed so as to carry part of the weight and load of a semitrailer.

tube-and-fin radiator core A type of radiator core consisting of tubes to which cooling fins are attached; coolant flows through the tubes between the upper and lower radiator tanks.

tubeless tire A tire that holds air without the use of a tube.

tuned intake system An engine air-intake system in which the manifold has the proper length and volume to introduce a ramjet, or supercharging, effect.

tuneup A procedure for inspecting, testing, and adjusting an engine, and replacing any worn parts, to restore the engine to its best performance.

turbine A rotary machine that converts the kinetic energy in a stream of fluid (gas or liquid) into mechanical energy.

turbine engine An engine in which gas pressure created by combustion is used to spin a turbine and, through gears, move a vehicle.

turbocharger A supercharger driven by the engine exhaust gas.

Turbo Hydra-Matic An automatic transmission built by General Motors and used on many models of cars and light trucks; it has three forward speeds and reverse.

turbulence The state of being violently disturbed. In the engine, the rapid swirling motion imparted to the air-fuel mixture entering a cylinder.

turning radius The difference between the angles each of the front wheels makes with the car frame during turns, usually measured with the outside wheel turned 20°. On a turn, the inner wheel turns, or toes out, more. Also called **toe-out-on-turns.**

turn signal See **directional signal.**

TVS Abbreviation for **thermostatic vacuum switch.**

twenty-five-ampere rate A battery rating; the length of time a battery can deliver 25 amp before the cell voltage drops to 1.75 volts, starting with the electrolyte at 80°F (26.7°C).

twenty-hour rate A battery rating; the amount of current a battery can deliver for 20 hours before the cell voltage drops below 1.75 volts, starting with an electrolyte temperature of 80°F (26.7°C).

twin I-beam A type of front-suspension system used on some trucks.

twist drill A conventional drill bit.

two-barrel carburetor A carburetor with two throttle valves.

two cycle Short for **two-stroke cycle.**

two-disk clutch A clutch with two friction disks for additional holding power; used in heavy-duty equipment.

two-speed rear axle See **double-reduction differential.**

two-stroke cycle The two piston strokes during which fuel intake, compression, combustion, and exhaust take place in a two-stroke-cycle engine.

U

U bolt An iron rod with threads on both ends, bent into the shape of a U and fitted with a nut at each end.

under-dash unit The "hang-on" type of air-conditioning system installed under the dash after a vehicle leaves the factory. All air outlets are in the evaporator case, and the system normally uses only recirculated air. The discharge air temperature is controlled by a cycling thermostatic expansion switch or a suction throttling valve.

unit An assembly or device that can perform its function only if it is not further divided into its component parts.

unit distributor A General Motors ignition distributor that uses a magnetic pickup coil and timer core instead of points and a condenser. The ignition coil is assembled into the distributor as a unit.

unitized construction A type of automotive construction in which the frame and body parts are welded together to form a single unit.

universal joint In the power train, a jointed connection in the drive shaft that permits the driving angle to change.

unleaded gasoline Gasoline to which no lead compounds have been intentionally added. Gasoline that contains 0.05 g or less of lead per gallon; required by law to be used in 1975-and-later vehicles equipped with catalytic converters.

unloader A device linked to the throttle valve; opens the choke valve when the throttle is moved to the wide-open position.

unsprung weight The weight of that part of the car which is not supported on springs; for example, the wheels and tires.

upper beam A headlight beam intended primarily for distant illumination, not for use when meeting or following other vehicles.

upshift To shift a transmission into a higher gear.

USAC Abbreviation for United States Auto Club.

V

vacuum A pressure less than atmospheric pressure; a negative pressure. Vacuum can be measured in pounds per square inch, but is usually measured in inches or millimeters of mercury (Hg); a reading of 30 inches (762 mm) Hg would indicate a perfect vacuum.

vacuum advance The advancing or retarding of ignition timing by changes in intake-manifold vacuum. Also, the unit on the ignition distributor that uses intake-manifold vacuum working on a diaphragm to adjust ignition timing.

vacuum-advance control Any type of NO_x emission-control system designed to allow vacuum advance only during certain modes of engine and vehicle operation.

vacuum-advance solenoid An electrically operated two-position valve which allows or denies intake-manifold vacuum to the distributor vacuum-advance unit.

vacuum-control temperature-sensing valve A valve that connects manifold vacuum to the distributor advance mechanism under hot-idle conditions.

vacuum gauge In automotive-engine service, a device that measures intake-manifold vacuum and thereby indicates actions of engine components.

vacuum modulator In automatic transmissions, a device that modulates, or changes, the main-line hydraulic pressure to meet changing engine loads.

vacuum motor A small motor, powered by intake-manifold vacuum; used for jobs such as raising and lowering headlight doors.

vacuum power unit A device for operating accessory doors and valves using vacuum as a source of power.

vacuum pump A mechanical device used to evacuate, or pump out, a system.

vacuum-suspended power brake A type of power brake in which both sides of the piston are subjected to vacuum; therefore the piston is "suspended" in vacuum.

vacuum switch A switch that closes or opens its contacts in response to changing vacuum conditions.

valve Any device that can be opened or closed to allow or stop the flow of a liquid or gas. There are many different types.

valve clearance The clearance between the rocker arm and the valve-stem tip in an overhead-valve engine; the clearance in the valve train when the valve is closed.

valve float A condition in which the engine valves do not close completely, or fail to close at the proper time.

valve grinding Refacing a valve in a valve-refacing machine.

valve guide A cylindrical part in the cylinder block or head in which a valve is assembled and in which it moves up and down.

valve-in-head engine See **I-head engine.**

valve lash Same as **valve clearance.**

valve lifter A cylindrical part of the engine which rests on a cam of the camshaft and is lifted, by cam action, so that the valve is opened. Also called a "lifter," "tappet," "valve tappet," or "cam follower."

valve-lifter foot The bottom end of the valve lifter; the part that rides on the cam lobe.

valve overlap The number of degrees of crankshaft rotation during which the intake and exhaust valves are open together.

valve rack Any storage container or holder which identifies the valves and keeps them in order after they are removed from the engine.

valve refacer A machine for removing material from the seating face of a valve to true the face.

valve rotator A device which rotates the valve slightly each time it opens; this causes deposits to be wiped off the valve face and stem, ensuring good heat transfer from the face to the valve seat.

valve seat The surface against which a valve comes to rest to provide a seal against leakage.

valve-seat inserts Metal rings inserted in cylinder heads to act as valve seats (usually for exhaust valves); they are made of special metals able to withstand very high temperatures.

valve-seat recession The tendency for valves in some engines run on unleaded gasoline to contact the seat in such a way that the seat wears away, or recedes, into the cylinder head. Also known as "lash loss."

valve spool A spool-shaped valve, such as in the power-steering unit.

valve spring A coil spring used to close an intake or exhaust valve, and keep it closed.

valve-spring retainer The device on the valve stem that holds the valve spring in place.

valve-spring-retainer lock The device on the valve stem that locks the valve-spring retainer in place.

valve stem The long, thin section of the valve that fits in the valve guide.

valve-stem seal A device placed on or around the valve stem to reduce the amount of oil that can get on the stem and then work its way down into the combustion chamber.

valve tappet See **valve lifter.**

valve timing The timing of the opening and closing of the valves in relation to the piston position.

valve train The valve-operating mechanism of an engine; includes all components from the camshaft to the valve.

vane A flat, extended surface that is moved around an axis by or in a fluid. Part of the internal revolving portion of an air-supply pump.

vapor A gas; any substance in the gaseous state, as distinguished from the liquid or solid state.

vapor-fuel separator Same as **vapor-liquid separator.**

vaporization A change of state from liquid to vapor or gas by evaporation or boiling; a general term including both evaporation and boiling. In the carburetor, breaking gasoline into fine particles and mixing it with incoming air.

vapor lines Lines that carry refrigerant vapor. See **suction line, discharge line,** and **equalizer line.**

vapor-liquid separator A device in the evaporative emission-control system; prevents liquid gasoline from traveling to the engine through the charcoal-canister vapor line.

vapor lock A condition in the fuel system in which gasoline vaporizes in the fuel line or fuel pump; bubbles of gasoline vapor restrict or prevent fuel delivery to the carburetor, causing slow, hot starts, no starting, or reduced power.

vapor-recovery system An evaporative emission-control system that recovers gasoline vapor escaping from the fuel tank and carburetor float bowl. See **evaporative control system.**

vapor-return line A line from the fuel pump to the fuel tank; allows vapor that has formed in the fuel pump to return to the fuel tank.

vapor-saver system Same as **vapor-recovery system.**

vapor separator A device used on cars equipped with air conditioning to prevent vapor lock by sending gasoline vapors back to the fuel tank through a separate line.

variable-ratio power steering Power-steering system in which the response of the car wheels varies according to how much the steering wheel is turned.

variable-venturi carburetor A carburetor in which the size of the venturi changes according to engine speed and load.

V-block A metal block with an accurately machined V-shaped groove; used to support an armature or shaft while it is checked for roundness.

vehicle See **motor vehicle.**

vehicle identification number (VIN) The number assigned to each vehicle by its manufacturer, primarily for registration and identification purposes.

vehicle vapor recovery See **vapor-recovery system.**

V-8 engine An engine with two banks of four cylinders each, set at an angle to form a V.

V engine See **V-type engine.**

vent An opening through which air can leave an enclosed chamber.

ventilation The circulating of fresh air through any space, to replace impure air. The basis of crankcase ventilation systems.

venturi In the carburetor, a narrowed passageway or restriction which increases the velocity of air moving through it; produces the vacuum responsible for the discharge of gasoline from the fuel nozzle.

VI Abbreviation for **viscosity index.**

vibration A rapid back-and-forth motion; an oscillation.

vibration damper A device attached to the crankshaft of an engine to oppose crankshaft torsional vibration (the twist-untwist actions of the crankshaft caused by the cylinder firing impulses). Also called a **harmonic balancer.**

VIN Abbreviation for **vehicle identification number.**

viscosity The resistance to flow exhibited by a liquid. A thick oil has greater viscosity than a thin oil.

viscosity index A number indicating how much the viscosity of an oil changes with heat.

viscosity rating An indicator of the viscosity of engine oil. There are separate ratings for winter driving and for summer driving. The winter grades are SAE5W, SAE10W, and SAE20W. The summer grades are SAE20, SAE30, SAE40, and SAE50. Many oils have multiple-viscosity ratings, as, for example, SAE10W-30.

viscous Thick; tending to resist flowing.

viscous friction The friction between layers of a liquid.

vise A gripping device; used to hold a part steady while it is being worked on.

volatile Evaporating readily. For example, Refrigerant-12 is volatile (evaporates quickly) at room temperature.

volatility A measure of the ease with which a liquid vaporizes; has a direct relationship to the flammability of a fuel.

volt The unit of electrical pressure or force that will move a current of 1 ampere through a resistance of 1 ohm.

voltage The force which causes electrons to flow in a conductor. The difference in electrical pressure (or potential) between two points in a circuit.

voltage drop The reduction or lowering of voltage across an electric device or circuit; due to the resistance of the power-consuming device or circuit, excess wire length, undersize wire, or poor connections.

voltage potential The electrical pressure at a particular point.

voltage regulator A device that prevents excessive alternator or generator voltage by alternately inserting and removing a resistance in the field circuit.

voltmeter A device for measuring the potential difference (voltage) between two points, such as the terminals of a battery or alternator, or two points in an electric circuit.

volumetric efficiency The ratio of the amount of air-fuel mixture that actually enters an engine cylinder to the thoretical amount that could enter under ideal conditions.

V-type engine An engine with two banks, or rows, of cylinders, set at an angle to form a V.

vulcanizing A process of treating raw rubber with heat and pressure; the treatment forms the rubber and gives it toughness and flexibility.

VV carburetor See **variable-venturi carburetor.**

VVR Abbreviation for vehicle-vapor recovery. See **vapor-recovery system.**

W

Wankel engine A rotary engine in which a three-lobe rotor turns eccentrically in an oval chamber to produce power.

warning blinker See **hazard system.**

water jacket The space around cylinders and valves that is hollow so that coolant can flow through to provide cooling.

water pump In the cooling system, the device that circulates coolant between the engine water jackets and the radiator.

watt A unit of measurement of electrical power supplied to a circuit when 1 volt is forcing 1 ampere through a resistance of 1 ohm. Watts = voltage × current.

wedge combustion chamber A combustion chamber resembling a wedge in shape.

weight distribution The percentage of a vehicle's total weight that rests on each axle.

weight, sprung See **sprung weight.**

weight, unsprung See **unsprung weight.**

welding The process of joining pieces of metal by fusing them together with heat.

wet-disk clutch A clutch in which the friction disk (or disks) is operated in a bath of oil.

wheel A disk or spokes with a hub at the center which revolves around an axle, and a rim around the outside for mounting on the tire.

wheel alignment A series of tests and adjustments to ensure that wheels and tires are properly positioned on the vehicle.

wheel balancer A device that checks a wheel-and-tire assembly (statically, dynamically, or both) for balance.

wheelbase The distance between the center lines of the front and rear axles. For trucks with tandem rear axles, the rear center line is considered to be midway between the two rear axles.

wheel cylinders In a hydraulic brake system, hydraulic cylinders located in the brake mechanisms at the wheels. Hydraulic pressure from the master cylinder causes the wheel cylinders to move the brake shoes into contact with the brake drums for braking.

wheel tramp Tendency for a wheel to move up and down so that it repeatedly bears down hard, or "tramps," on the road. Sometimes called "high-speed shimmy."

winding Wire wound or coiled about an object such as an iron cone or armature that produces a magnetic field when current flows through it.

window regulator A device for opening and closing a window; usually operated by a crank.

windshield wiper A mechanism which moves a rubber blade back and forth to wipe the windshield; operated either by vacuum or electrically.

wire feeler gauge A set of round wires of known diameters; used to check clearances between electric contacts, such as distributor points and spark-plug electrodes.

wiring harness A group of two or more individually insulated wires, wrapped together to form a neat, easily installed bundle.

work The changing of the position of an object against an opposing force; measured in foot-pounds or meter-kilograms. The product of a force and the distance through which it acts.

worm Type of gear in which the teeth resemble threads; used on the lower end of the steering shaft.

WOT Abbreviation for "wide-open throttle."

wrist pin See **piston pin.**

Z

zener diode A type of diode used to control the direction of current flow and as a voltage regulator; also called a "breakdown diode."

zip gun An air-powered cutting tool often used for work on vehicle exhaust systems.

APPENDIX

Metric Conversion and Other Tables

S. I. METRIC–CUSTOMARY CONVERSION TABLES

HOW TO USE CONVERSION CHARTS

Left Column is units of 10, (0, 10, 20, 30 etc.);
Top Row is in units of one (0, 1, 2, 3, etc).

EXAMPLE: Feet to Inches Conversion Chart

feet	0	1	2	3	4	5	6	7	8	9	feet
	inches	inches	inches	inches	inches	inches	inches	inches	inches	inches	
--		12	24	36	48	60	72	84	96	108	--
10	120	132	144	156	168	180	192	204	216	228	10
20	240	252	264	276	288	300	312	324	336	348	20
30	360	372	384	396	408	420	432	444	456	468	30
40	480	492	504	516	528	540	552	564	576	588	40
50	600	612	624	636	648	660	672	684	696	708	50

12 feet equals 144 inches. Read across from 10 and down from 2.
6 feet equals 72 inches. Read down from 6.

FEET TO METERS

ft	0	1	2	3	4	5	6	7	8	9	ft
	m	m	m	m	m	m	m	m	m	m	
--		0.305	0.610	0.914	1.219	1.524	1.829	2.134	2.438	2.743	--
10	3.048	3.353	3.658	3.962	4.267	4.572	4.877	5.182	5.486	5.791	10
20	6.096	6.401	6.706	7.010	7.315	7.620	7.925	8.230	8.534	8.839	20
30	9.144	9.449	9.754	10.058	10.363	10.668	10.973	11.278	11.582	11.887	30
40	12.192	12.497	12.802	13.106	13.411	13.716	14.021	14.326	14.630	14.935	40
50	15.240	15.545	15.850	16.154	16.459	16.764	17.069	17.374	17.678	17,983	50
60	18.288	18.593	18.898	19.202	19.507	19.812	20.117	20.422	20.726	21.031	60
70	21.336	21.641	21.946	22.250	22.555	22.860	23.165	23.470	23.774	24.079	70
80	24.384	24.689	24.994	25.298	25.603	25.908	26.213	26.518	26.822	27.127	80
90	27.432	27.737	28.042	28.346	28.651	28.956	29.261	29.566	29.870	30.175	90
100	30.480	30.785	31.090	31.394	31.699	32.004	32.309	32.614	32.918	33.223	100

METERS TO FEET

m	0	1	2	3	4	5	6	7	8	9	m
	ft	ft	ft	ft	ft	ft	ft	ft	ft	ft	
--		3.2808	6.5617	9.8425	13.1234	16.4042	19.6850	22.9659	26.2467	29.5276	--
10	32.8084	36.0892	39.3701	42.6509	45.9318	49.2126	52.4934	55.7743	59.0551	62.3360	10
20	65.6168	68.8976	72.1785	75.4593	78.7402	82.0210	85.3018	88.5827	91.8635	95.1444	20
30	98.4252	101.7060	104.9869	108.2677	111.5486	114.8294	118.1102	121.3911	124.6719	127.9528	30
40	131.2336	134.5144	137.7953	141.0761	144.3570	147.6378	150.9186	154.1995	157.4803	160.7612	40
50	164.0420	167.3228	170.6037	173.8845	177.1654	180.4462	183.7270	187.0079	190.2887	193.5696	50
60	196.8504	200.1312	203.4121	206.6929	209.9738	213.2546	216.5354	219.8163	223.0971	226.3780	60
70	229.6588	232.9396	236.2205	239.5013	242.7822	246.0630	249.3438	252.6247	255.9055	259.1864	70
80	262.4672	265.7480	269.0289	272.3097	275.5906	278.8714	282.1522	285.4331	288.7139	291.9948	80
90	295.2756	298.5564	301.8373	305.1181	308.3990	311.6798	314.9606	318.2415	321.5223	324.8032	90
100	328.0840	331.3648	334.6457	337.9265	341.2074	344.4882	347.7690	351.0499	354.3307	357.6116	100

SOURCE: Cadillac Motor Car Division of General Motors Corporation.

S. I. METRIC–CUSTOMARY CONVERSION TABLES

MILES TO KILOMETERS

mile	0	1	2	3	4	5	6	7	8	9	mile
	km	km	km	km	km	km	km	km	km	km	
--		1.609	3.219	4.828	6.437	8.047	9.656	11.265	12.875	14.484	--
10	16.093	17.703	19.312	20.921	22.531	24.140	25.750	27.359	28.968	30.578	10
20	32.187	33.796	35.406	37.015	38.624	40.234	41.843	43.452	45.062	46.671	20
30	48.280	49.890	51.499	53.108	54.718	56.327	57.936	59.546	61.155	62.764	30
40	64.374	65.983	67.593	69.202	70.811	72.421	74.030	75.639	77.249	78.858	40
50	80.467	82.077	83.686	85.295	86.905	88.514	90.123	91.733	93.342	94.951	50
60	96.561	98.170	99.779	101.39	103.00	104.61	106.22	107.83	109.44	111.04	60
70	112.65	114.26	115.87	117.48	119.09	120.70	122.31	123.92	125.53	127.14	70
80	128.75	130.36	131.97	133.58	135.19	136.79	138.40	140.01	141.62	143.23	80
90	144.84	146.45	148.06	149.67	151.28	152.89	154.50	156.11	157.72	159.33	90
100	160.93	162.54	164.15	165.76	167.37	168.98	170.59	172.20	173.81	175.42	100

KILOMETERS TO MILES

km	0	1	2	3	4	5	6	7	8	9	km
	mil	mil	mil	mil	mil	mil	mil	mil	mil	mil	
--		0.621	1.243	1.864	2.486	3.107	3.728	4.350	4.971	5.592	--
10	6.214	6.835	7.457	8.078	8.699	9.321	9.942	10.562	11.185	11.805	10
20	12.427	13.049	13.670	14.292	14.913	15.534	16.156	16.776	17.399	18.019	20
30	18.641	19.263	19.884	20.506	21.127	21.748	22.370	22.990	23.613	24.233	30
40	24.855	25.477	26.098	26.720	27.341	27.962	28.584	29.204	29.827	30.447	40
50	31.069	31.690	32.311	32.933	33.554	34.175	34.797	35.417	36.040	36.660	50
60	37.282	37.904	38.525	39.147	39.768	40.389	41.011	41.631	42.254	42.874	60
70	43.497	44.118	44.739	45.361	45.982	46.603	47.225	47.845	48.468	49.088	70
80	49.711	50.332	50.953	51.575	52.196	52.817	53.439	54.059	54.682	55.302	80
90	55.924	56.545	57.166	57.788	58.409	59.030	59.652	60.272	60.895	61.515	90
100	62.138	62.759	63.380	64.002	64.623	65.244	65.866	66.486	67.109	67.729	100

GALLONS (U.S.) TO LITERS

U.S. gal	0	1	2	3	4	5	6	7	8	9	U.S. gal
	L	L	L	L	L	L	L	L	L	L	
--		3.7854	7.5709	11.3563	15.1417	18.9271	22.7126	26.4980	30.2834	34.0638	--
10	37.8543	41.6397	45.4251	49.2105	52.9960	56.7814	60.5668	64.3523	68.1377	71.9231	10
20	75.7085	79.4940	83.2794	87.0648	90.8502	94.6357	98.4211	102.2065	105.9920	109.7774	20
30	113.5528	117.3482	121.1337	124.9191	128.7045	132.4899	136.2754	140.0608	143.8462	147.6316	30
40	151.4171	155.2025	158.9879	162.7734	166.5588	170.3442	174.1296	177.9151	181.7005	185.4859	40
50	189.2713	193.0568	196.8422	200.6276	204.4131	208.1985	211.9839	215.7693	219.5548	223.3402	50
60	227.1256	230.9110	234.6965	238.4819	242.2673	246.0527	249.8382	253.6236	257.4090	261.1945	60
70	264.9799	268.7653	272.5507	276.3362	280.1216	283.9070	287.6924	291.4779	295.2633	299.0487	70
80	302.8342	306.6196	310.4050	314.1904	317.9759	321.7613	325.5467	329.3321	333.1176	336.9030	80
90	340.6884	344.4738	348.2593	352.0447	355.8301	359.6156	363.4010	367.1864	370.9718	374.7573	90
100	378.5427	382.3281	386.1135	389.8990	393.6844	397.4698	401.2553	405.0407	408.8261	412.6115	100

S. I. METRIC–CUSTOMARY CONVERSION TABLES

LITERS TO GALLONS (U.S.)

L	0	1	2	3	4	5	6	7	8	9	L
	gal	gal	gal	gal	gal	gal	gal	gal	gal	gal	
--		0.2642	0.5283	0.7925	1.0567	1.3209	1.5850	1.8492	2.1134	2.3775	--
10	2.6417	2.9059	3.1701	3.4342	3.6984	3.9626	4.2267	4.4909	4.7551	5.0192	10
20	5.2834	5.5476	5.8118	6.0759	6.3401	6.6043	6.8684	7.1326	7.3968	7.6610	20
30	7.9251	8.1893	8.4535	8.7176	8.9818	9.2460	9.5102	9.7743	10.0385	10.3027	30
40	10.5668	10.8310	11.0952	11.3594	11.6235	11.8877	12.1519	12.4160	12.6802	12.9444	40
50	13.2086	13.4727	13.7369	14.0011	14.2652	14.5294	14.7936	15.0577	15.3219	15.5861	50
60	15.8503	16.1144	16.3786	16.6428	16.9069	17.1711	17.4353	17.6995	17.9636	18.2278	60
70	18.4920	18.7561	19.0203	19.2845	19.5487	19.8128	20.0770	20.3412	20.6053	20.8695	70
80	21.1337	21.3979	21.6620	21.9262	22.1904	22.4545	22.7187	22.9829	23.2470	23.5112	80
90	23.7754	24.0396	24.3037	24.5679	24.8321	25.0962	25.3604	25.6246	25.8888	26.1529	90
100	26.4171	26.6813	26.9454	27.2096	27.4738	27.7380	28.0021	28.2663	28.5305	28.7946	100

GALLONS (IMP.) TO LITERS

IMP gal	0	1	2	3	4	5	6	7	8	9	IMP gal
	L	L	L	L	L	L	L	L	L	L	
--		4.5460	9.0919	13.6379	18.1838	22.7298	27.2758	31.8217	36.3677	40.9136	--
10	45.4596	50.0056	54.5515	59.0975	63.6434	68.1894	72.2354	77.2813	81.8275	86.3732	10
20	90.9192	95.4652	100.0111	104.5571	109.1030	113.6490	118.1950	122.7409	127.2869	131.8328	20
30	136.3788	140.9248	145.4707	150.0167	154.5626	159.1086	163.6546	168.0005	172.7465	177.2924	30
40	181.8384	186.3844	190.9303	195.4763	200.0222	204.5682	209.1142	213.6601	218.2061	222.7520	40
50	227.2980	231.8440	236.3899	240.9359	245.4818	250.0278	254.5738	259.1197	263.6657	268.2116	50
60	272.7576	277.3036	281.8495	286.3955	290.9414	295.4874	300.0334	304.5793	309.1253	313.6712	60
70	318.2172	322.7632	327.3091	331.8551	336.4010	340.9470	345.4930	350.0389	354.5849	359.1308	70
80	363.6768	368.2223	372.7687	377.3147	381.8606	386.4066	390.9526	395.4985	400.0445	404.5904	80
90	409.1364	413.6824	418.2283	422.7743	427.3202	431.8662	436.4122	440.9581	445.9041	450.0500	90
100	454.5960	459.1420	463.6879	468.2339	472.7798	477.3258	481.8718	486.4177	490.9637	495.5096	100

LITERS TO GALLONS (IMP.)

L	0	1	2	3	4	5	6	7	8	9	L
	gal	gal	gal	gal	gal	gal	gal	gal	gal	gal	
--		0.2200	0.4400	0.6599	0.8799	1.0999	1.3199	1.5398	1.7598	1.9798	--
10	2.1998	2.4197	2.6397	2.8597	3.0797	3.2996	3.5196	3.7396	3.9596	4.1795	10
20	4.3995	4.6195	4.8395	5.0594	5.2794	5.4994	5.7194	5.9394	6.1593	6.3793	20
30	6.5593	6.8193	7.0392	7.2592	7.4792	7.6992	7.9191	8.1391	8.3591	8.5791	30
40	8.7990	9.0190	9.2390	9.4590	9.6789	9.8989	10.9189	10.3389	10.5588	10.7788	40
50	10.9988	11.2188	11.4388	11.6587	11.8787	12.0987	12.3187	12.5386	12.7586	12.9786	50
60	13.1986	13.4185	13.6385	13.8585	14.0785	14.2984	14.5184	14.7384	14.9584	15.1783	60
70	15.3983	15.6183	15.8383	16.0582	16.2782	16.4982	16.7182	16.9382	17.1581	17.3781	70
80	17.5981	17.8181	18.0380	18.2580	18.4780	18.6980	18.9179	19.1379	19.3579	19.5779	80
90	19.7978	20.0178	20.2378	20.4578	20.6777	20.8977	21.1177	21.3377	21.5576	21.7776	90
100	21.9976	22.2176	22.4376	22.6575	22.8775	23.0975	23.3175	23.5374	23.7574	23.9774	100

S. I. METRIC–CUSTOMARY CONVERSION TABLES

POUNDS TO KILOGRAMS

lb	0	.1	2	3	4	5	6	7	8	9	lb
	kg	kg	kg	kg	kg	kg	kg	kg	kg	kg	
--		0.454	0.907	1.361	1.814	2.268	2.722	3.175	3.629	4.082	--
10	4.536	4.990	5.443	5.897	6.350	6.804	7.257	7.711	8.165	8.618	10
20	9.072	9.525	9.979	10.433	10.886	11.340	11.793	12.247	12.701	13.154	20
30	13.608	14.061	14.515	14.969	15.422	15.876	16.329	16.783	17.237	17.690	30
40	18.144	18.597	19.051	19.504	19.958	20.412	20.865	21.319	21.772	22.226	40
50	22.680	23.133	23.587	24.040	24.494	24.948	25.401	25.855	26.308	26.762	50
60	27.216	27.669	28.123	28.576	29.030	29.484	29.937	30.391	30.844	31.298	60
70	31.751	32.205	32.659	33.112	33.566	34.019	34.473	34.927	35.380	35.834	70
80	36.287	36.741	37.195	37.648	38.102	38.555	39.009	39.463	39.916	40.370	80
90	40.823	41.277	41.730	42.184	42.638	43.092	43.545	43.998	44.453	44.906	90
100	45.359	45.813	46.266	46.720	47.174	47.627	48.081	48.534	48.988	49.442	100

KILOGRAMS TO POUNDS

kg	0	1	2	3	4	5	6	7	8	9	kg
	lb	lb	lb	lb	lb	lb	lb	lb	lb	lb	
--		2.205	4.409	6.614	8.818	11.023	13.228	15.432	17.637	19.842	--
10	22.046	24.251	26.455	28.660	30.865	33.069	35.274	37.479	39.683	41.888	10
20	44.092	46.297	48.502	50.706	52.911	55.116	57.320	59.525	61.729	63.934	20
30	66.139	68.343	70.548	72.752	74.957	77.162	79.366	81.571	83.776	85.980	30
40	88.185	90.389	92.594	94.799	97.003	99.208	101.41	103.62	105.82	108.03	40
50	110.23	112.44	114.64	116.84	119.05	121.25	123.46	125.66	127.87	130.07	50
60	132.28	134.48	136.69	138.89	141.10	143.30	145.51	147.71	149.91	152.12	60
70	154.32	156.53	158.73	160.94	163.14	165.35	167.55	169.76	171.96	174.17	70
80	176.37	178.57	180.78	182.98	185.19	187.39	189.60	191.80	194.01	196.21	80
90	198.42	200.62	202.83	205.03	207.23	209.44	211.64	213.85	216.05	218.26	90
100	220.46	222.67	224.87	227.08	229.28	231.49	233.69	235.89	238.10	240.30	100

POUNDS PER SQUARE INCH TO KILOPASCALS

psi	0	1	2	3	4	5	6	7	8	9	psi
	kPa	kPa	kPa	kPa	kPa	kPa	kPa	kPa	kPa	kPa	
--	0.0000	6.8948	13.7895	20.6843	27.5790	34.4738	41.3685	48.2663	55.1581	62.0528	--
10	68.9476	75.8423	82.7371	89.6318	96.5266	103.4214	110.3161	117.2109	124.1056	131.0004	10
20	137.8951	144.7899	151.6847	158.5794	165.4742	172.3689	179.2637	186.1584	193.0532	199.9480	20
30	206.8427	213.7375	220.6322	227.5270	234.4217	241.3165	248.2113	255.1060	262.0008	268.8955	30
40	275.7903	282.6850	289.5798	296.4746	303.3693	310.2641	317.1588	324.0536	330.9483	337.8431	40
50	344.7379	351.6326	358.5274	365.4221	372.3169	379.2116	386.1064	393.0012	399.8959	406.7907	50
60	412.6854	420.5802	427.4749	434.3697	441.2645	448.1592	455.0540	461.9487	468.8435	475.7382	60
70	482.6330	489.5278	496.4225	503.3173	510.2120	517.1068	524.0015	530.8963	537.7911	544.6858	70
80	551.5806	558.4753	565.3701	572.2648	579.1596	586.0544	592.9491	599.8439	606.7386	613.6334	80
90	620.5281	627.4229	634.3177	641.2124	648.1072	655.0019	661.8967	668.7914	675.6862	682.5810	90
100	689.4757	696.3705	703.2653	710.1601	717.0549	723.9497	730.8445	737.7393	744.6341	751.5289	100

S. I. METRIC–CUSTOMARY CONVERSION TABLES

KILOPASCALS TO POUNDS PER SQUARE INCH

kPa	0	1	2	3	4	5	6	7	8	9	kPa
	Psi	Psi	Psi	Psi	Psi	Psi	Psi	Psi	Psi	Psi	
--		.1450	.2901	.4351	.5801	.7252	.8702	1.0153	1.1603	1.3053	--
10	1.4504	1.5954	1.7404	1.8855	2.0305	2.1556	2.3206	2.4656	2.6107	2.7557	10
20	2.9007	3.0458	3.1908	3.3359	3.4809	3.6259	3.7710	3.9160	4.0610	4.2061	20
30	4.3511	4.4961	4.6412	4.7862	4.9313	5.0763	5.2213	5.3664	5.5114	5.6564	30
40	5.8015	5.9465	6.0916	6.2366	6.3816	6.5267	6.6717	6.8167	6.9618	7.1068	40
50	7.2518	7.3969	7.5419	7.6870	7.8320	7.9770	8.1221	8.2671	8.4121	8.5572	50
60	8.7022	8.8473	8.9923	9.1373	9.1824	9.4274	9.5724	9.7175	9.8625	10.0076	60
70	10.1526	10.2976	10.4427	10.5877	10.7327	10.8778	11.0228	11.1678	11.3129	11.4579	70
80	11.6030	11.7480	11.8930	12.0381	12.1831	12.3281	12.4732	12.6182	12.7633	12.9083	80
90	13.0533	13.1984	13.3434	13.4884	13.6335	13.7785	13.9236	14.0686	14.2136	14.3587	90
100	14.5037	14.6487	14.7938	14.9388	15.0838	15.2289	15.3739	15.5190	15.6640	15.8090	100

POUND FEET TO NEWTON-METERS

ft-lb	0	1	2	3	4	5	6	7	8	9	ft-lb
	N-m	N-m	N-m	N-m	N-m	N-m	N-m	N-m	N-m	N-m	
--		1.3558	2.7116	4.0675	5.4233	6.7791	8.1349	9.4907	10.8465	12.2024	--
10	13.5582	14.9140	16.2698	17.6256	18.9815	20.3373	21.6931	23.0489	24.4047	25.7605	10
20	27.1164	28.4722	29.8280	31.1838	32.5396	33.8954	35.2513	36.6071	37.9629	39.3187	20
30	40.6745	42.0304	43.3862	44.7420	46.0978	47.4536	48.8094	50.1653	51.5211	52.8769	30
40	54.2327	55.5885	56.9444	58.3002	59.6560	61.0118	62.3676	63.7234	65.0793	66.4351	40
50	67.7909	69.1467	70.5025	71.8584	73.2142	74.5700	75.9258	77.2816	78.6374	79.9933	50
60	81.3491	82.7049	84.0607	85.4165	86.7724	88.1282	89.4840	90.3898	92.1956	93.5514	60
70	94.9073	96.2631	97.6189	98.9747	100.3305	101.6863	103.0422	104.3980	105.7538	107.1096	70
80	108.4654	109.8213	111.1771	112.5329	113.8887	115.2445	116.6003	117.9562	119.3120	120.6678	80
90	122.0236	123.3794	124.7353	126.0911	127.4469	128.8027	130.1585	131.5143	132.8702	134.2260	90
100	135.5818	136.9376	138.2934	139.6493	141.0051	142.3609	143.7167	145.0725	146.4283	147.7842	100

NEWTON-METERS TO POUND FEET

N-m	0	1	2	3	4	5	6	7	8	9	N-m
	ft-lb	ft-lb	ft-lb	ft-lb	ft-lb	ft-lb	ft-lb	ft-lb	ft-lb	ft-lb	
--		.7376	1.4751	2.2127	2.9502	3.6878	4.4254	5.1692	5.9005	6.6381	--
10	7.3756	8.1132	8.8507	9.5883	10.3258	11.0634	11.8010	12.5385	13.2761	14.0136	10
20	14.7512	15.4888	16.2264	16.9639	17.7015	18.4390	19.1766	19.9142	20.6517	21.3893	20
30	22.1269	22.8644	23.6020	24.3395	25.0771	25.8147	26.5522	27.2898	28.0274	28.7649	30
40	29.5025	30.2400	30.9776	31.7152	32.4527	33.1903	33.9279	34.6654	35.4030	36.1405	40
50	36.8781	37.6157	38.3532	39.0908	39.8283	40.5659	41.3035	42.0410	42.7786	43.5162	50
60	44.2537	44.9913	45.7288	46.4664	47.2040	47.9415	48.6791	49.4167	50.1542	50.8918	60
70	51.6293	52.3669	53.1045	53.8420	54.5796	55.3171	56.0547	56.7923	57.5298	58.2674	70
80	59.0050	59.7425	60.4801	61.2176	61.9552	62.6928	63.4303	64.1679	64.9055	65.6430	80
90	66.3806	67.1181	67.8557	68.5933	69.3308	70.0684	70.8060	71.5435	72.2811	73.0186	90
100	73.7562	74.4938	75.2313	75.9689	76.7064	77.4440	78.1816	78.9191	79.6567	80.3943	100

TABLE OF FREQUENTLY USED UNITS (U.S.)

SI (SYSTEME INTERNATIONAL d'UNITES)

Multiply	by	to get equivalent number of:
LENGTH		
Inch	25.4	millimetres (mm)
Foot	0.304 8	metres (m)
Yard	0.914 4	metres
Mile	1.609	kilometres (km)
AREA		
Inch²	645.2	millimetres² (mm²)
	6.45	centimetres² (cm²)
Foot²	0.092 9	metres² (m²)
Yard²	0.836 1	metres²
VOLUME		
Inch³	16 387.	mm³
	16.387	cm³
	0.016 4	litres (l)
Quart	0.946 4	litres
Gallon	3.785 4	litres
Yard³	0.764 6	metres³ (m³)
MASS		
Pound	0.453 6	kilograms (kg)
Ton	907.18	kilogram
Ton	0.907	tonne (t)
FORCE		
Kilogram (force)	9.807	newtons (N)
Ounce	0.278 0	newtons
Pound	4.448	newtons

Multiply	by	to get equivalent number of:
ACCELERATION		
Foot/sec²	0.304 8	metre/sec² (m/s²)
Inch/sec²	0.025 4	metre/sec²
TORQUE		
Pound-inch	0.112 98	newton-metres (N·m)
Pound-foot	1.355 8	newton-metres
POWER		
Horsepower	0.746	kilowatts (kW)
PRESSURE OR STRESS		
Inches of mercury	3.377	kilopascals (kPa)
Pounds/sq. in.	6.895	kilopascals
ENERGY OR WORK		
BTU	1 055.	joules (J)
Foot-pound	1.355 8	joules
Kilowatt-hour	3 600 000 or 3.6x10⁶	joules (J = W·s)
LIGHT		
Footcandle	10.764	lumens/metre² (lm/m²)
FUEL PERFORMANCE		
Miles/gal	0.425 1	kilometres/litre (km/l)
Gal/mile	2.352 7	litres/kilometre (l/km)
VELOCITY		
Miles/hour	1.609 3	kilometres/hr. (km/h)

TEMPERATURE

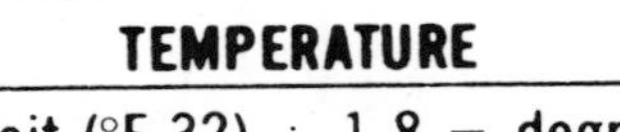

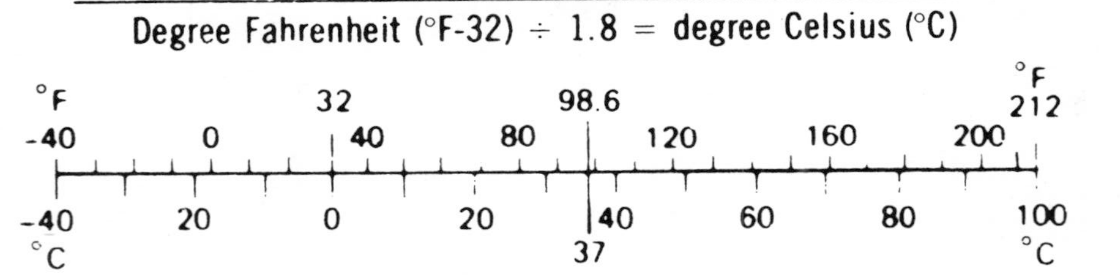

BOLT AND NUT IDENTIFICATION

THREADED FASTENERS

All of the vehicles covered in this service manual have some metric threaded fasteners and some customary or inch-system fasteners. It is most important that replacement fasteners be of the correct nominal diameter, thread pitch and strength. Original equipment metric fasteners (except beauty bolts such as exposed bumper bolts and cross recess head screws) are identified by a number marking indicating the strength of the material in the fastener as shown below. Metric cross recess screws are identified by a Posidriv or type 1-A cross recess. Either Phillips-head or type 1-A cross recess screw drivers can be used in Posidriv recess screw heads, but type 1-A cross recess screw drivers will perform better.

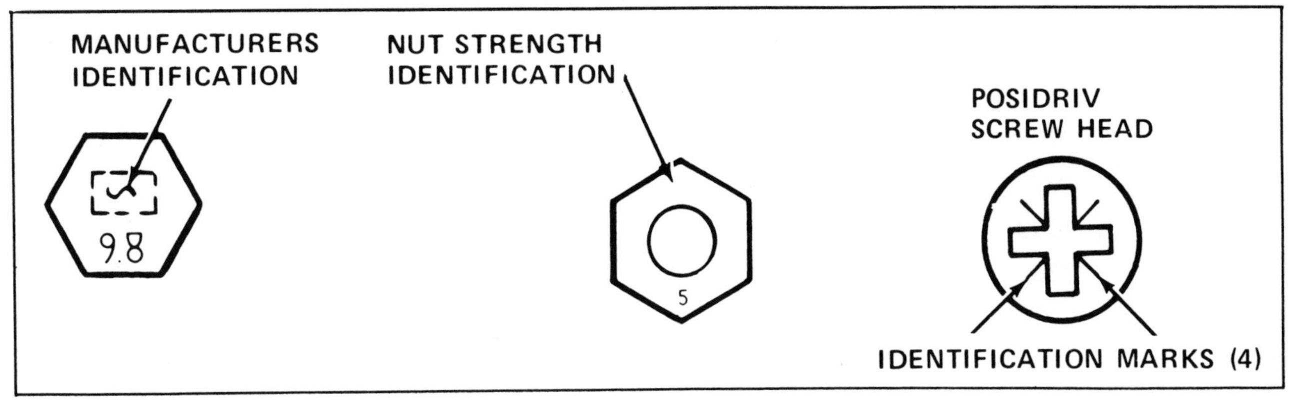

Metric Bolt and Nut Identification

FASTENER STRENGTH IDENTIFICATION

Common metric fastener strength property classes are 9.8 and 10.9 with the class identification embossed on the head of each bolt. Customary (inch) strength classes range from grade 2 to 8 with line identification embossed on each bolt head. Markings correspond to two lines less than the actual grade (i.e. grade 7 bolt will exhibit 5 embossed lines on the bolt head). Some metric nuts will be marked with single digit strength identification numbers on the nut face. The figure below illustrates the different strength markings.

When replacing metric fasteners, be careful to use bolts and nuts of the same strength or greater than the original fasteners (the same number marking or higher). It is likewise important to select replacement fasteners of the correct size. Correct replacement bolts and nuts are available from GMPD and other sources. However, many metric fasteners available in the after-market parts channels were designed to metric standards of countries other than the United States, and may be of lower strength, may not have the numbered head marking system, and may be of a different thread pitch. The metric fasteners used on Cadillac products are designed to new, international standards that may not yet be manufactured by some non-domestic bolt and nut suppliers. In general, except for special applications, the common sizes and pitches are:

M 6.3 X 1
M 8 X 1.25
M 10 X 1.5
M 12 X 1.75
M 14 X 2

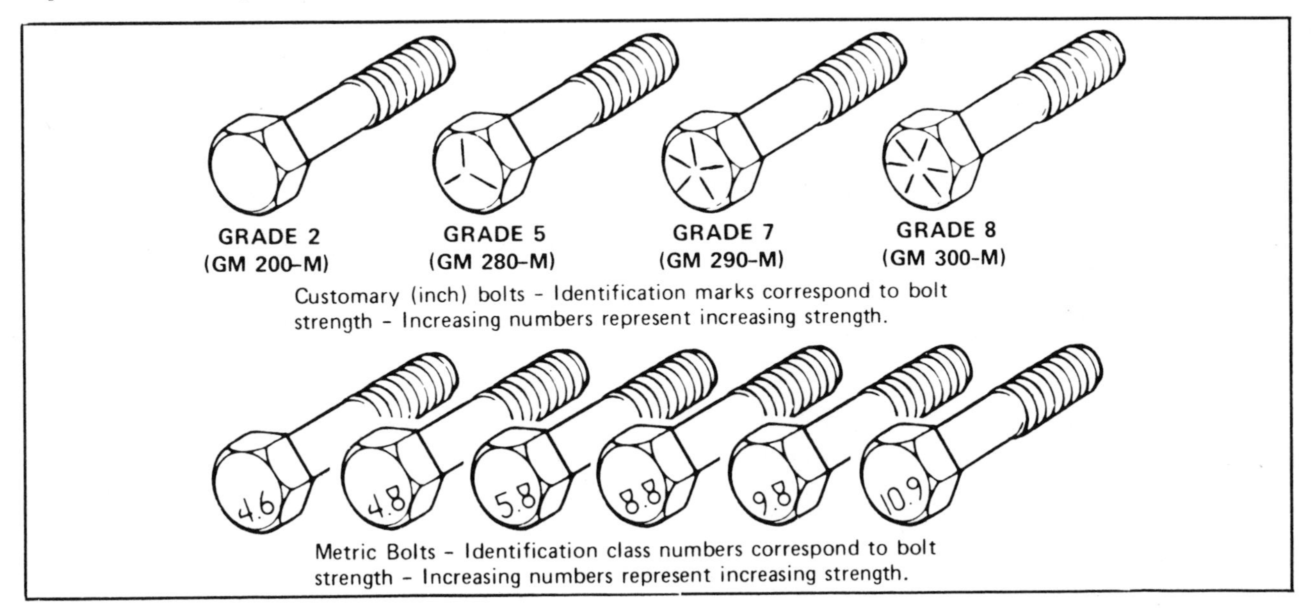

Bolt Strength Identification

SOURCE: Cadillac Motor Car Division of General Motors Corporation.

DECIMAL AND METRIC EQUIVALENTS

Fractions	Decimal In.	Metric mm.	Fractions	Decimal In.	Metric mm.
1/64	.015625	.39688	33/64	.515625	13.09687
1/32	.03125	.79375	17/32	.53125	13.49375
3/64	.046875	1.19062	35/64	.546875	13.89062
1/16	.0625	1.58750	9/16	.5625	14.28750
5/64	.078125	1.98437	37/64	.578125	14.68437
3/32	.09375	2.38125	19/32	.59375	15.08125
7/64	.109375	2.77812	39/64	.609375	15.47812
1/8	.125	3.1750	5/8	.625	15.87500
9/64	.140625	3.57187	41/64	.640625	16.27187
5/32	.15625	3.96875	21/32	.65625	16.66875
11/64	.171875	4.36562	43/64	.671875	17.06562
3/16	.1875	4.76250	11/16	.6875	17.46250
13/64	.203125	5.15937	45/64	.703125	17.85937
7/32	.21875	5.55625	23/32	.71875	18.25625
15/64	.234375	5.95312	47/64	.734375	18.65312
1/4	.250	6.35000	3/4	.750	19.05000
17/64	.265625	6.74687	49/64	.765625	19.44687
9/32	.28125	7.14375	25/32	.78125	19.84375
19/64	.296875	7.54062	51/64	.796875	20.24062
5/16	.3125	7.93750	13/16	.8125	20.63750
21/64	.328125	8.33437	53/64	.828125	21.03437
11/32	.34375	8.73125	27/32	.84375	21.43125
23/64	.359375	9.12812	55/64	.859375	21.82812
3/8	.375	9.52500	7/8	.875	22.22500
25/64	.390625	9.92187	57/64	.890625	22.62187
13/32	.40625	10.31875	29/32	.90625	23.01875
27/64	.421875	10.71562	59/64	.921875	23.41562
7/16	.4375	11.11250	15/16	.9375	23.81250
29/64	.453125	11.50937	61/64	.953125	24.20937
15/32	.46875	11.90625	31/32	.96875	24.60625
31/64	.484375	12.30312	63/64	.984375	25.00312
1/2	.500	12.70000	1	1.00	25.40000

DRILL SIZES

Letter Sizes	Drill Diam. Inches	Wire Gage Sizes	Drill Diam. Inches	Wire Gage Sizes	Drill Diam. Inches	Wire Gage Sizes	Drill Diam. Inches
Z	0.413	1	0.2280	28	0.1405	55	0.0520
Y	0.404	2	0.2210	29	0.1360	56	0.0465
X	0.397	3	0.2130	30	0.1285	57	0.0430
W	0.386	4	0.2090	31	0.1200	58	0.0420
V	0.377	5	0.2055	32	0.1160	59	0.0410
U	0.368	6	0.2040	33	0.1130	60	0.0400
T	0.358	7	0.2010	34	0.1110	61	0.0390
S	0.348	8	0.1990	35	0.1100	62	0.0380
R	0.339	9	0.1960	36	0.1065	63	0.0370
Q	0.332	10	0.1935	37	0.1040	64	0.0360
P	0.323	11	0.1910	38	0.1015	65	0.0350
O	0.316	12	0.1890	39	0.0995	66	0.0330
N	0.302	13	0.1850	40	0.0980	67	0.0320
M	0.295	14	0.1820	41	0.0960	68	0.0310
L	0.290	15	0.1800	42	0.0935	69	0.0292
K	0.281	16	0.1770	43	0.0890	70	0.0280
J	0.277	17	0.1730	44	0.0860	71	0.0260
I	0.272	18	0.1695	45	0.0820	72	0.0250
H	0.266	19	0.1660	46	0.0810	73	0.0240
G	0.261	20	0.1610	47	0.0785	74	0.0225
F	0.257	21	0.1590	48	0.0760	75	0.0210
E	0.250	22	0.1570	49	0.0730	76	0.0200
D	0.246	23	0.1540	50	0.0700	77	0.0180
C	0.242	24	0.1520	51	0.0670	78	0.0160
B	0.238	25	0.1495	52	0.0635	79	0.0145
A	0.234	26	0.1470	53	0.0595	80	0.0135
		27	0.1440	54	0.0550		

TAPS · DIES · GAGES · SCREW PLATES · SCREW EXTRACTORS

DECIMAL EQUIVALENTS AND TAP DRILL SIZES

DRILL SIZE	DECIMAL	TAP SIZE
1/64	.0156	
1/32	.0312	
60	.0400	
59	.0410	
58	.0420	
57	.0430	
56	.0465	
3/64	.0469	0-80
55	.0520	
54	.0550	1-56
53	.0595	1-64, 72
1/16	.0625	
52	.0635	
51	.0670	
50	.0700	2-56, 64
49	.0730	
48	.0760	
5/64	.0781	
47	.0785	3-48
46	.0810	
45	.0820	3-56,4-32
44	.0860	4-36
43	.0890	4-40
42	.0935	4-48
3/32	.0937	
41	.0960	
40	.0980	
39	.0995	
38	.1015	5-40
37	.1040	5-44
36	.1065	6-32
7/64	.1093	
35	.1100	
34	.1110	6-36
33	.1130	6-40
32	.1160	
31	.1200	
1/8	.1250	
30	.1285	
29	.1360	8-32, 36
28	.1405	8-40
9/64	.1406	
27	.1440	
26	.1470	
25	.1495	10-24
24	.1520	
23	.1540	
5/32	.1562	
22	.1570	10-30
21	.1590	10-32
20	.1610	
19	.1660	
18	.1695	
11/64	.1719	
17	.1730	
16	.1770	12-24
15	.1800	
14	.1820	12-28
13	.1850	12-32
3/16	.1875	
12	.1890	
11	.1910	
10	.1935	
9	.1960	
8	.1990	
7	.2010	1/4-20
13/64	.2031	
6	.2040	
5	.2055	
4	.2090	
3	.2130	1/4-28
7/32	.2187	
2	.2210	
1	.2280	
A	.2340	
15/64	.2344	
B	.2380	
C	.2420	
D	.2460	
E, 1/4	.2500	
F	.2570	5/16-18
G	.2610	
17/64	.2656	
H	.2660	
I	.2720	5/16-24
J	.2770	
K	.2810	
9/32	.2812	
L	.2900	
M	.2950	
19/64	.2968	
N	.3020	
5/16	.3125	3/8-16
O	.3160	
P	.3230	
21/64	.3281	
Q	.3320	3/8-24
R	.3390	
11/32	.3437	
S	.3480	
T	.3580	
23/64	.3594	
U	.3680	7/16-14
3/8	.3750	
V	.3770	
W	.3860	
25/64	.3906	7/16-20
X	.3970	
Y	.4040	
13/32	.4062	
Z	.4130	
27/64	.4219	1/2-13
7/16	.4375	
29/64	.4531	1/2-20
15/32	.4687	
31/64	.4844	9/16-12
1/2	.5000	
33/64	.5156	9/16-18
17/32	.5312	5/8-11
35/64	.5469	
9/16	.5625	
37/64	.5781	5/8-18
19/32	.5937	11/16-11
39/64	.6094	
5/8	.6250	11/16-16
41/64	.6406	
21/32	.6562	3/4-10
43/64	.6719	
11/16	.6875	3/4-16
45/64	.7031	
23/32	.7187	
47/64	.7344	
3/4	.7500	
49/64	.7656	7/8-9
25/32	.7812	
51/64	.7969	
13/16	.8125	7/8-14
53/64	.8281	
27/32	.8437	
55/64	.8594	
7/8	.8750	1-8
57/64	.8906	
29/32	.9062	
59/64	.9219	
15/16	.9375	1-12,14
61/64	.9531	
31/32	.9687	
63/64	.9844	
1	1.000	

PIPE THREAD SIZES

THREAD	DRILL	THREAD	DRILL
1/8-27	R	1 1/2-11 1/2	1 47/64
1/4-18	7/16	2-11 1/2	2 7/32
3/8-18	37/64	2 1/2-8	2 5/8
1/2-14	23/32	3-8	3 1/4
3/4-14	59/64	3 1/2-8	3 3/4
1-11 1/2	1 5/32	4-8	4 1/4
1 1/4-11 1/2	1 1/2		

Index